# The first person to invent a car that runs on water...

... may be sitting right in your classroom! Every one of your students has the potential to make a difference. And realizing that potential starts right here, in your course.

When students succeed in your course—when they stay on-task and make the breakthrough that turns confusion into confidence—they are empowered to realize the possibilities for greatness that lie within each of them. We know your goal is to create an environment where students reach their full potential and experience the exhilaration of academic success that will last them a lifetime. *WileyPLUS* can help you reach that goal.

Wiley**PLUS** is an online suite of resources—including the complete text—that will help your students:

- come to class better prepared for your lectures
- get immediate feedback and context-sensitive help on assignments and quizzes
- track their progress throughout the course

"I just wanted to say how much this program helped me in studying... I was able to actually see my mistakes and correct them. ... I really think that other students should have the chance to use *WileyPLUS*."

Ashlee Krisko, *Oakland University*

www.wiley.com/college/wileyplus

**80%** of students surveyed said it improved their understanding of the material. *

## FOR INSTRUCTORS

Wiley**PLUS** is built around the activities you perform in your class each day. With Wiley**PLUS** you can:

### Prepare & Present

Create outstanding class presentations using a wealth of resources such as PowerPoint™ slides, image galleries, interactive simulations, and more. You can even add materials you have created yourself.

### Create Assignments

Automate the assigning and grading of homework or quizzes by using the provided question banks, or by writing your own.

### Track Student Progress

Keep track of your students' progress and analyze individual and overall class results.

**Now Available with WebCT and Blackboard!**

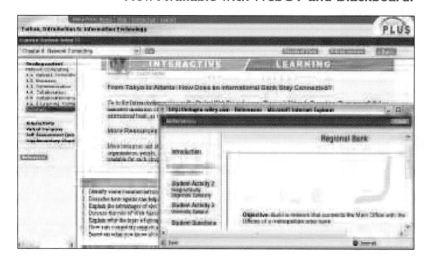

"It has been a great help, and I believe it has helped me to achieve a better grade."

Michael Morris,
*Columbia Basin College*

## FOR STUDENTS

### You have the potential to make a difference!

*WileyPLUS* is a powerful online system packed with features to help you make the most of your potential and get the best grade you can!

### With Wiley**PLUS** you get:

• A complete online version of your text and other study resources.

• Problem-solving help, instant grading, and feedback on your homework and quizzes.

• The ability to track your progress and grades throughout the term.

For more information on what *WileyPLUS* can do to help you and your students reach their potential, please visit www.wiley.com/college/*wileyplus*.

**76%** of students surveyed said it made them better prepared for tests. *

*Based on a survey of 972 student users of *WileyPLUS*

# 6th Edition

## Information Technology for Management

Transforming Organizations in the Digital Economy

## THE WILEY BICENTENNIAL—KNOWLEDGE FOR GENERATIONS

*Each* generation has its unique needs and aspirations. When Charles Wiley first opened his small printing shop in lower Manhattan in 1807, it was a generation of boundless potential searching for an identity. And we were there, helping to define a new American literary tradition. Over half a century later, in the midst of the Second Industrial Revolution, it was a generation focused on building the future. Once again, we were there, supplying the critical scientific, technical, and engineering knowledge that helped frame the world. Throughout the 20th Century, and into the new millennium, nations began to reach out beyond their own borders and a new international community was born. Wiley was there, expanding its operations around the world to enable a global exchange of ideas, opinions, and know-how.

For 200 years, Wiley has been an integral part of each generation's journey, enabling the flow of information and understanding necessary to meet their needs and fulfill their aspirations. Today, bold new technologies are changing the way we live and learn. Wiley will be there, providing you the must-have knowledge you need to imagine new worlds, new possibilities, and new opportunities.

Generations come and go, but you can always count on Wiley to provide you the knowledge you need, when and where you need it!

**WILLIAM J. PESCE**
PRESIDENT AND CHIEF EXECUTIVE OFFICER

**PETER BOOTH WILEY**
CHAIRMAN OF THE BOARD

# 6th Edition

# Information Technology for Management

## Transforming Organizations in the Digital Economy

**EFRAIM TURBAN,** University of Hawaii at Manoa

**DOROTHY LEIDNER,** Baylor University

**EPHRAIM MCLEAN,** Georgia State University

**JAMES WETHERBE,** Texas Tech University

with contributions by:

**LINDA VOLONINO,** Canisius College

**DONALD AMOROSO,** Appalachian State University

**LINDA LAI,** Macau Polytechnic University of China

**DANIEL TSE,** City University of Hong Kong

**MAGGIE LEW,** TSE Computer Ltd., Hong Kong

**CHRISTY CHEUNG,** Hong Kong Baptist University

BICENTENNIAL
1807
WILEY
2007
BICENTENNIAL

John Wiley & Sons, Inc.

EXECUTIVE EDITOR *Beth Golub*
SENIOR PRODUCTION EDITOR *Patricia McFadden*
ASSISTANT EDITOR *Jen Devine*
MARKETING MANAGER *Jillian Rice*
CREATIVE DIRECTOR *Harry Nolan*
SENIOR DESIGNER *Maddy Lesure*
SENIOR ILLUSTRATION EDITOR *Anna Melhorn*
SENIOR PHOTO EDITOR *Lisa Gee*
SENIOR EDITORIAL ASSISTANT *Maria Guarascio*
SENIOR MEDIA EDITOR *Louren Sapira*
PRODUCTION MANAGEMENT SERVICES *Ingrao Associates*
COVER PHOTO *Image Courtesy of Jennifer Golbeck. Second Life Avatars: Copyright 2007, Linden Research, Inc. All Rights Reserved*

This book was set in 10/12 Times Roman and printed and bound by Quebecor World. The cover was printed by Quebecor World.

This book is printed on acid free paper. ∞

To order books or for customer service, please call 1-800-CALL WILEY (225-5945).

ISBN-13 978-0-471-78712-9

Printed in the United States of America

10 9 8 7 6 5 4 3 2

# The Web Revolution

In the last decade, we have been witnessing one of the most important technological revolutions in the modern era—the Web revolution. The Web is not only changing the way that we work, study, play, and conduct our lives, but it is doing so much more quickly than any other revolution (such as the Industrial Revolution), with impacts that are more far-reaching. For example, four years ago, when we last revised this book, blogging was a novelty. Today more than four million bloggers are active on the Web and blogging is an instrument used in commerce, politics, and entertainment. In another developing technology, Apple sold over 100 million songs on iTunes during the first year of operation (July 2003 to July 2004.) Furthermore, we have seen only the tip of the iceberg. The Web revolution is facilitated by ever-changing information technologies.

**Managing Information Technology.** Companies such as Google, Apple, and Yahoo continuously are introducing innovations into our corporate and governmental operations as well as into our homes, offices, and almost any other aspect of life. The rate of innovation is constantly increasing and so are the capabilities of computers and information technologies. It is getting more and more difficult to keep up with all the new developments in most areas of business.

*Information Technology for Management,* 6th Edition, addresses the basic principles of MIS in light of these new developments. For example, one of the major changes occurring in IT is the ability to buy or lease computerized services similar to the way we buy electricity, to delivering applications over the Internet. This may be a strategic option for prudent managers of the digital economy. This is the beginning of the move toward utility, or "on-demand," computing which may change the need for software and hardware. But does utility computing fit all organizations? Such issues resulting from the Web revolution are discussed in this textbook. Its major objective is to prepare managers and staff in the modern enterprise to understand the role of information technology in the digital enterprise.

# Transforming Organizations to the Digital Economy

This book is based on the fundamental premise that the major role of information technology is to provide organizations with *strategic advantage by facilitating problem solving, increasing productivity and quality, increasing speed, improving customer service, enhancing communication and collaboration,* and *enabling business process restructuring.* By taking a practical, managerial-oriented approach, the book demonstrates that IT can be provided not only by information systems departments but also by end users and vendors as well. Managing information resources, new technologies, and communications networks is becoming a—or even *the*—critical success factor in the operations of many organizations, private and public, and will be essential to the survival of organizations in the future.

While recognizing the importance of the technology, system development, and functional transaction processing systems, we emphasize the *innovative* uses of information technology throughout the enterprise. The rapidly increased use of the Web, the Internet, intranets, extranets, e-business and e-commerce, and mobile computing changes the manner in which business is done in almost all organizations. This fact is reflected in our book: Every chapter and major topic point to the role of the Web in facilitating competitiveness, effectiveness, and profitability. Of special importance is the emergence of the second-generation e-commerce applications such as m-commerce, c-commerce, e-learning, and e-government. Also, the integration of ERP, CRM, and knowledge management with e-commerce is of great importance. Finally, there is a resurgence of intelligent systems, both for facilitating homeland security as well as for increasing productivity and competitive advantage. Of special interest are the automated decision systems that are described in Chapter 12 and several other chapters, computer forensics, which is of increasing importance in facilitating security (Chapter 16), and the role of IT in facilitating compliance management that is described throughout the book.

# Features of this Text

In developing the 6th Edition of *Information Technology for Management*, we have tried to craft a book that will serve the needs of tomorrow's managers. This book reflects our vision of where information systems are going and the direction of IS education in business and e-business programs. This vision is represented by the following features that we have integrated throughout the book.

- *Global Perspective and A Totally Revised Chapter on Global Information Systems.* The importance of global competition, partnerships, and trading is rapidly increasing; we've improved the chapter that focuses on global information systems (Chapter 9). International examples are highlighted with a special globe icon, a Global Index appears at the back of the book, and the book's Web site includes several international cases.

- *Agile and Responsive Enterprise.* The rapid and large fluctuations in the business environment require businesses to be able to respond quickly and properly to changes as well as to be leaders of innovation. Also, responses in real time are often required. IT is the facilitator of agility and flexibility. Furthermore, changing information systems or building new ones must be accomplished rapidly and efficiently. Thus, we are looking at the digital and agile enterprise that must be supported by information systems.

- *The On-Demand Revolution.* Demand-driven operations and on-demand enterprises refer to the changes brought on by e-business in which manufacturing starts only after an order (standard or customized) is received. To do this economically requires support of IT in many areas ranging from using RFID devices to collaborative technologies.

- *Focus on Security.* Computer and IT security issues are becoming more important, at the personal, organizational, and global levels. For example, spyware software is becoming more common, and the world's first mobile phone virus has been found. We show how IT is used to counter cyberterrorism on the personal and organizational levels, in addition to showing how governments use IT to strengthen homeland security. Finally, we introduce the topic of computer forensics.

- *Digital Economy Focus.* This book recognizes that organizations desire to transform themselves successfully to the digital economy. To do so companies need not only to use Web-based systems, but also to have an appropriate e-strategy and ability to implement click-and-mortar systems as well as new business models. Furthermore, they need to plan the transformation process, which is dependent on information technology and enabled by it.

- *Managerial Orientation.* Most IS textbooks identify themselves as either technology or socio-behavioral oriented. While we recognize the importance of both, our emphasis is on *managerial* orientation. To implement this orientation, we assembled all of the major technological topics in six Technology Guides, located on the book's Web site. Furthermore, we attempted not to duplicate detailed presentations of behavioral sciences topics, such as dealing with resistance to change or motivating employees. Instead, we concentrate on managerial decision making, cost-benefit justification, supply chain management, business process management, restructuring, and CRM as they relate to information technology.

- *Functional Relevance.* Frequently, non–IS major students wonder why they must learn technical details. In this text the relevance of information technology to the major functional areas is an important theme. We show, through the use of icons, the relevance of topics to accounting, finance, marketing, production/operations management, human resources management, and government. Finally, our examples also cover service industries, government, small businesses, as well as the international settings.

- *E-Business, E-Commerce, and the Use of the Web.* We strongly believe that e-business, e-commerce, and the use of the Internet, intranets, and extranets are changing the world of business. Not only is an entire chapter (Chapter 5) dedicated to e-business, but we also demonstrate the significance of e-business in every chapter and major topic. In this edition, we also have expanded coverage of m-commerce applications.

- *Real-World Orientation.* Extensive, vivid examples from large corporations, small businesses, government, and not-for-profit agencies make concepts come alive by showing students the capabilities of information technology, its cost and justification, and some of the innovative ways real corporations are using IT in their operations.

- *Failures and Lessons Learned.* We acknowledge the fact that many systems do fail. Many chapters include discussion or examples of failures, and the lessons learned from them. For example, Chapter 8 cites some ERP failures, and Chapter 14 discusses economic aspects of failures and runaway projects.

- ***Solid Theoretical Backing.*** Throughout the book we present the theoretical foundation necessary for understanding information technology, ranging from Moore's Law to Porter's competitiveness models, including his latest e-strategy adaptation.
- ***Up-to-Date Information.*** The book presents the most current topics of information technology, as evidenced by the many new cases and examples throughout the book and by 2005 and 2006 citations. Every topic in the book has been researched to find the most up-to-date information and features.
- ***Economic Justification.*** Information technology is mature enough to stand the difficult test of economic justification. It is our position that investment in information technology must be scrutinized like any other investment, despite the difficulties of measuring technology benefits. In addition to discussion throughout the text, we devote a complete chapter (Chapter 14, "IT Economics") to this subject. We emphasize enterprisewide, interorganizational, and global systems. We also present technologies that support this integration, including Web Services and XML.
- ***Ethics.*** The importance of ethics is growing rapidly in the digital economy. Topics relating to ethics are introduced in every chapter, and are highlighted by icons in the margin. A primer on ethics is provided in Online File W1.5; this resource poses 14 ethics scenarios and asks students to think about responses to these situations.

## What's New in this Edition?

In preparing the new, 6th Edition we made the following large-scale changes:

### Hands-On Experiences

- In this edition we introduce a large number of hands-on exercises in almost all chapters., These include: spreadsheet calculations of cost-benefits, creation of collaborative online groups who visit Web sites and conduct comparisons, view Web seminars, and answer questions about the topics covered, and view demos and summarize these experiences, and much more.
- We have completely revised and upgraded the IT security chapter including the introduction of computer forensics, expanded on the topic of computer fraud and crimes, as well as how to defend against them.
- We have expanded the topics of business intelligence and predictive analytics to a full chapter.

- The enterprise system chapter has been restructured to include business process management and product life cycle.
- A new chapter on data management has been created that includes the necessary technical material on files, data storage, and data warehousing.
- Chapter 1 has refocused on agility, flexibility, on-demand and real time strategy.
- The topic of networks (communication, collaboration, search), including more technical foundation in an Appendix to the chapter has been completely revised.
- We have introduced more applied topics to many chapters of the book (e.g., knowledge management, decision support, security).
- The chapter on interorganizational and global systems has been completely restructured, tying the topic to supply chain networks, virtual corporations, and collaboration. The technical material has been moved to an appendix.
- The coverage of strategic outsourcing has been expanded to include offshoring in several chapters.
- The topics of business (corporate) performance management (BPM) and automated decision systems (ADSs) have been introduced to supplement the coverage of decision support systems.
- Online Interactive Learning Sessions: The book's Student Web site contains engaging activities including interactive drag-and-drop exercises and simulations, as well as animations that help students to visualize IT processes.
- Most of the chapters have been completely revised to introduce new research, current examples and case studies, exercises, and updated reference materials.
- We have streamlined and smoothed the logical flow throughout the text, eliminating duplications, reducing the size of most chapters, as well as the number of topics covered in some cases.

## Organization of the Book

The book is divided into five major parts, composed of 17 regular chapters supplemented by six Technology Guides. Parts and chapters break down as follows.

*Part I: IT in the Organization.* Part I gives an overview of IT in the organization. Chapter 1 introduces the drivers of the use of information technology in the digital economy and gives an overview of information systems and IT trends. Chapter 2 presents the foundations of information systems and their strategic use. Special attention is given to cutting edge topics, such as "software-as-a service."

*Part II: IT Infrastructure.* This part introduces us to the two major building blocks of IT: data and networks (the other building blocks are covered in the Online Technology Guides). Both parts include basic infrastructure and most common applications.

*Part III: The Web Revolution.* The two chapters in Part III introduce the Web-based technologies and applications, starting with the topics of e-business and e-commerce (Chapter 5), and is followed by mobile and wireless computing in Chapter 6.

*Part IV: Organizational Applications.* Part IV begins with the basics: IT applications in transaction processing, functional applications, and integration of functional systems (Chapter 7). We then cover supply chain management, Web-based enterprise systems, customer relationship management (CRM), and business process management (BPM) (Chapter 8). Chapter 9 focuses on interorganizational and global systems.

*Part V: Managerial and Decision Support Systems.* Part V discusses the many ways information systems can be used to support the day-to-day operations of a company, with a strong emphasis on the use of IT in managerial decision making. The three chapters in this part address some of the ways businesses are using information technology to solve specific problems and to build strategic, innovative systems that enhance quality and productivity. Special attention is given to innovative applications of knowledge management (Chapter 10), business intelligence and predictive analysis (Chapter 11), and decision support and intelligent support systems (Chapter 12).

*Part VI: Implementing and Managing IT.* Part VI explores several topics related to the implementation, evaluation, construction, and maintenance of information systems. First we cover use of IT organizations and for strategic advantage including the topic of IT planning (Chapter 13). Then we consider several issues ranging from the economics of information technology (Chapter 14), to acquiring (building or outsourcing) information systems (Chapter 15), to the management of IT resources and IT security (Chapter 16). Finally, Chapter 17 (available online)assesses the impact of IT on individuals, organizations, and society.

The six **Technology Guides,** which are available online at the book's Web site, cover hardware, software, databases, telecommunications, and the essentials of the Internet, and  an introduction to systems analysis and design. They contain condensed, up-to-date presentations of all the material necessary for the understanding of these technologies. They can be used as a self-study refresher or as a basis for a class presentation. The Technology Guides are supplemented online by a glossary for the terms in the Tech Guides, questions for review and discussion, and case studies, all of which are available on our Web site (*wiley.com/college/ turban*).

## Pedagogical Features

We developed a number of pedagogical features to aid student learning and tie together the themes of the book.

• *Chapter Outline.* The chapter outline provides a quick indication of the major topics covered in the chapter.

• *Learning Objectives.* Learning objectives listed at the beginning of each chapter help students focus their efforts and alert them to the important concepts that will be discussed.

• *Opening Cases.* Each chapter opens with a *real-world* example that illustrates the use of information technology in modern organizations. These cases have been carefully chosen to demonstrate the relevance, for business students, of the topics introduced in the chapter. They are presented in a standard format (problem or opportunity, IT solution, and results) that helps model a way to think about business problems. The opening case is followed by a brief section called "Lessons Learned from This Case" that ties the key points of the opening case to the topic of the chapter.

• *"IT at Work" Boxes.* The IT at Work boxes spotlight some real-world innovations and new technologies that companies are using to solve organizational dilemmas or create new business opportunities. Each box concludes with "for further exploration" questions and issues. Some of these boxes are online.

• *"A Closer Look" Boxes.* These boxes contain detailed, in-depth discussions of specific concepts or procedures, often using real-world examples. Some boxes enhance the in-text discussion by offering an alternative approach to information technology. Some of these boxes are included in the online materials.

• **Highlighted Icons.** Icons appear throughout the text to relate the topics covered within each chapter to some major themes of the book. The icons alert students to the related functional areas, to IT failures, and to global and ethical issues. Icons also indicate where related enrichment resources can be found on the book's companion Web site. The following list summarizes these icons. (They also are summarized for students in a marginal annotation in Chapter 1.)

 Ethics-related topic

 Global organizations and issues

 Lessons to be learned from IT failures

 Accounting example

 Finance example

 Government example

 Human resources management example

 Marketing example

 Production/operations management example

 Service-company example (for example, health services, educational services, and other non-manufacturing examples)

 Material at the book's Web site: *wiley/com/college.turban*

• **Online Chapter Resources.** Each chapter is supported by many online files (up to 30 per chapter). These files are cited in the text, as they include in-depth discussions, technically oriented materials, examples, cases, and illustrations. The Online Chapter Resources can be accessed by going to the Student Website at *www.wiley.com/college/turban,* then clicking on Online Chapter Resources.

• **Managerial Issues.** The final text section of every chapter explores some of the special concerns managers face as they adapt to an increasingly technological environment. The issues highlighted in this section can serve as a springboard for class discussion and challenge business students to consider some of the actions they might take if placed in similar circumstances.

• **Key Terms.** The key terms and concepts are typeset in boldface blue when first introduced in a chapter, and are listed at the end of the chapter. All key terms are defined in the end-of-book glossary.

• **Chapter Highlights.** All the important concepts covered in the chapter are listed at the end of the chapter and are linked by number to the learning objectives introduced at the beginning of each chapter, to reinforce the important ideas discussed.

• **Virtual Company Assignment.** The Virtual Company Assignment centers around the ongoing situation at a simulated company, The Wireless Café. Students are "hired" by the restaurant as consultants and in each chapter are given assignments that require them to use the information presented in the chapter to develop solutions and produce deliverables to present to the owners of The Wireless Café. These assignments get the student into active, hands-on learning to complement the conceptual coverage of the text. The assignments are found on the Student Resources site at *www.wiley.com/college/turban.*

• **End-of-Chapter Questions and Exercises.** Different types of questions measure student comprehension and students' ability to apply knowledge. Questions for Review ask students to summarize the concepts introduced. Discussion Questions are intended to promote class discussion and develop critical thinking skills.

• **Exercises and Projects.** Exercises are challenging assignments that require the students to apply what they have learned in each chapter to a situation. This includes many hands-on exercises as described earlier, including the use of search engines and the Web.

• **Group Assignments.** Comprehensive group assignments, including Internet research, oral presentations to the class, and debates are available in each chapter.

- *Internet Exercises.* Close to 200 hands-on exercises send the students to interesting Web sites to explore those sites, find resources, investigate an application, compare, analyze, and summarize information, or learn about the state of the art of a topic.
- *Minicases.* Two real-world cases at the end of each chapter highlight some of the problems encountered by corporations as they develop and implement information systems. Discussion questions and assignments are included. A number of additional minicases are available online at the book's Web site.

## Supplementary Materials

An extensive package of instructional materials is available to support this 6th edition.

- *Instructor's Manual.* The Instructor's Manual presents objectives from the text with additional information to make them more appropriate and useful for the instructor. The manual also includes practical applications of concepts, case study elaboration, answers to end-of-chapter questions, questions for review, questions for discussion, and Internet exercises.
- *Test Bank.* The test bank contains over 1,000 questions and problems (about 70 per chapter) consisting of multiple-choice, short answer, fill-ins, and critical thinking/essay questions.
- *Computerized Test Bank.* This electronic version of the test bank allows instructors to customize tests and quizzes for their students.
- *PowerPoint Presentation.* A series of slides designed around the content of the text incorporates key points from the text and illustrations where appropriate.
- *Video Series.* A collection of video clips provides students and instructors with dynamic international business examples directly related to the concepts introduced in the text. The video clips illustrate the ways in which computer information systems are utilized in various companies and industries.
- *Business Extra Select.* (*www.wiley.com/college/bxs*) Business Extra Select enables you to add copyright-cleared articles, cases, and readings from such leading business resources as *INSEAD, Ivey and Harvard Business School Cases, Fortune, The Economist, The Wall Street Journal,* and more. You can create your own custom CoursePack, combining these resources along with content from Wiley's Business Textbooks, your own content such as lecture notes, and any other third-party content. Or you can use a ready-made CoursePack for Turban's *IT for Management,* 6th Edition.

- *The Turban Web Site.* (*wiley.com/college/turban*). The book's Web site greatly extends the content and themes of the text to provide extensive support for instructors and students. Organized by chapter, it includes Chapter Resources: tables, figures, cases, questions, exercises, and downloadable PowerPoint slides, self-testing material for students, working students' experiences with using IT, links to resources on the Web, and links to many of the companies discussed in the text and to the Virtual Company Web site.

## Acknowledgments

Several individuals helped us with the creation of the 6th Edition: Linda Volonino (Canisius College) played a major role in this edition, first as a contributor of several chapters and then as a "super reviewer" who read the entire manuscript making numerous improvements. Donald Amoroso (Appalachian State University) made a valuable contribution as a contributor to two chapters. Linda Lai (Macau Polytechnic University of China) revised a chapter, and Christy Cheung (Hong Kong Baptist University) helped with research issues assisted by Neil Rabjohn (York University) and Mei-Ting Cheung (City University of Hong Kong). Daniel Tse and Maggie Lew helped to update Technology Guides 1 through 6. Thanks to all for their contributions.

Faculty feedback was essential to the development of the book. Many individuals participated in focus groups and/or acted as reviewers. Several others created portions of chapters or cases, especially international cases, some of which are in the text and others on the Web site.

Thanks, too, to the following reviewers: Lawrence Andrew, Western Illinois University; Bay Arinze, Drexel University; Benli Asilani, University of Tennessee Chattanooga; Mary Astone, Troy State University; Cynthia Barnes, Lamar University; Andy Borchers, Kettering University; Sonny Butler, Georgia Southern University; Jason Chen, Gonzaga University; Roland Eichelberger, Baylor University; Jerry Flatto, University of Indianapolis; Marvin Golland, Polytechnic University of Brooklyn; Vipul Gupta, St. Joseph's University; Jeet Gupta, University of Alabama, Huntsville; David Harmann, University of Central Oklahoma; Shohreh Hashemi, University of Houston, Downtown; Richard Herschel, Saint Joseph's University; Phil Houle, Drake University; Jonathan Jelen, Mercy College; Tim Jenkins, ITT Institute of Technology, San Bernadino; Gerald Karush, Southern New Hampshire University; Joseph Kasten, Dowling College; Stephen

Klein, Ramapo College; Kapil Ladha, Drexel University; Albert Lederer, University of Kentucky; Chang-Yang Lin, Eastern Kentucky University; Liping Liu, The University of Akron; Steve Loy, Eastern Kentucky University; Dana Kristin McCann, Central Michigan University; Roberto Mejias, Purdue University; Luvai Motiwalla, University of Massachusetts, Lowell; Sean Neely, City University Bellevue; Luis Rabelo, University of Central Florida; W. Raghupathi, Fordham University; Mahesh Raisinghani, University of Dallas; Tom Schambach, Illinois State University; Werner Schenk, University of Rochester; Sheryl Schoenacher, SUNY Farmingdale; Richard Segall, Arkansas State University; Victor Smolensky, San Diego State University; Bruce White, Quinnipiac University; Geoffrey Willis, University of Central Oklahoma; Marie Wright, Western Connecticut State University.

Please see *wiley.com/college/turban* for a list of acknowledgements for past editions of this book.

Many individuals helped us with the administrative work. Of special mention is Judy Lang who devoted considerable time to typing and editing. Several other individuals helped with typing, figure drawing, and more. Among those are Kathy Sherman and Daphne Turban. Thanks to Rose Twardowski for help in graphic design and Rick Volonino for forensic accounting research. Hugh Watson of the University of Georgia, the Information Systems Advisor to Wiley, guided us through various stages of the project.

We would like to thank the dedicated staff of John Wiley & Sons: Jillian Rice, Jen Devine, Maria Guarascio, and Trish McFadden. We also appreciate the outside production management services of Suzanne Ingrao. A special thank you to Beth Lang Golub, whose considerable energy, time, expertise, and devotion have contributed significantly to the success of this project. Last, but not least, is the help provided by Judy Lang who has been with this book since its inception, helping with research, finding cases, and most importantly, trouble shooting.

Finally, we recognize the various organizations and corporations that provided us with material and permissions to use it.

*Efraim Turban*
*Dorothy Leidner*
*Ephraim McLean*
*James Wetherbe*

## DR. EFRAIM TURBAN

Dr. Efraim Turban obtained his M.B.A. and Ph.D. degrees from the University of California, Berkeley. His industry experience includes eight years as an industrial engineer, three of which were spent at General Electric Transformers Plant in Oakland, California. He also has extensive consulting experience to small and large corporations as well as to governments. In his over thirty years of teaching, Professor Turban has served as Chaired Professor at Eastern Illinois University, and as Visiting Professor at City University of Hong Kong, Nanyang Technological University in Singapore, and University of Science and Technology in Hong Kong. He has also taught at UCLA, USC, Simon Fraser University, Lehigh University, California State University, Long Beach, and Florida International University.

Dr. Turban was a co-recipient of the 1984/85 National Management Science Award (Artificial Intelligence in Management). In 1997 he received the Distinguished Faculty Scholarly and Creative Achievement Award at California State University, Long Beach.

Dr. Turban has published over 110 articles in leading journals, including the following: *Management Science, MIS Quarterly, Operations Research, Journal of MIS, Communications of the ACM, International Journal of Electronic Commerce, Information Systems Frontiers, Decision Support Systems, International Journal of Information Management, Heuristics, Expert Systems with Applications, International Journal of Applied Expert Systems, Journal of Investing, Accounting, Management and Information Systems, Computers and Operations Research, Computers and Industrial Engineering, IEEE Transactions on Engineering Management, Omega, International Journal of Electronic Commerce, Organizational Computing and Electronic Commerce,* and *Electronic Markets.* He has also published 23 books, including best sellers such as *Neural Networks: Applications in Investment and Financial Services* (2nd edition) (co-editor with R. Trippi), Richard D. Irwin, 1996; *Decision Support Systems and Business Intelligence* (Prentice Hall, 8th edition, 2007); *Expert Systems and Applied Artificial Intelligence,* (MacMillan Publishing Co., 1992), *Electronic Commerce: A Managerial Approach, 5th edition,* (Prentice Hall, 2008), *Introduction to Information Technology 4th edition* (Wiley, 2007), and *Introduction to Electronic Commerce* (Prentice Hall, 2003). His newest book, *Business Intelligence* (Prentice Hall) is coming in 2007.

Professor Turban is a Visiting Scholar with the Pacific Institute for Information Systems Management College of Business University of Hawaii at Manoa. His major research interests include electronic commerce, strategy, and implementation.

## DR. DOROTHY LEIDNER

Dr. Dorothy E. Leidner is the Randall W. and Sandra Ferguson Professor of Information Systems and Director of the Center for Knowledge Management at Baylor University. Prior to rejoining the Baylor faculty, she was associate professor at INSEAD and at Texas Christian University. She has also been visiting professor at Instituto Tecnologico y des Estudios Superiores de Monterrey, Mexico, at the Institut d'Administration Des Entreprises at the Universite de Caen, France, and at Southern Methodist University. Dr. Leidner received her Ph.D. in Information Systems from the University of Texas at Austin, where she also obtained her M.B.A. and her B.A. in Plan II.

Dr. Leidner's research has been published in a variety of journals, such as *MIS Quarterly, Information Systems, Decision Sciences, Decision Support Systems, and Organization Science.* She has received best-paper awards in 1993 from the Hawaii International Conference on Systems Sciences, in 1995 from *MIS Quarterly,* and in 1999 from the Academy of Management. She is currently serving as co-editor of the journal *Data Base for Advances in Information Systems.* She is also an associate editor for *MIS Quarterly* and a senior editor for the *Journal of Strategic Information Systems,* and is on the editorial board of *MISQ Executive.*

## DR. EPHRAIM R. McLEAN

Dr. Ephraim McLean earned his Bachelor of Mechanical Engineering degree from Cornell University in 1958. After brief service in the U.S. Army Ordinance Corps, he worked for the Procter & Gamble Co. for seven years, first in manufacturing management and later as a computer systems analyst. In 1965, he left P&G and entered the Sloan School of Management at the Massachusetts Institute of Technology, obtaining his master's degree in 1967 and his doctorate in 1970.

While at M.I.T., he began an interest in the application of computer technology to medicine, working on his dissertation at the Lahey Clinic in Boston. While there, he was instrumental in developing the Lahey Clinic Automated Medical History System. During the same period, he served as an instructor at M.I.T. and also assisted in the preparation of the books *The Impact of Computers on Management* (MIT Press, 1967), *The Impact of Computers on Collective Bargaining* (MIT Press, 1969), and *Computers in Knowledge-Based Fields* (MIT Press, 1970). While at M.I.T., he was elected to Sigma XI, the scientific research society.

Dr. McLean left M.I.T. and joined the faculty of the Anderson Graduate School of Management at The University of California, Los Angeles (UCLA) in winter 1970. He was the founding Director of the Information Systems Research Program and the first Chairman of the Information Systems area, both within the Anderson Graduate School of Management. In fall 1987, he was named to the George E. Smith Eminent Scholar's Chair in the Robinson College of Business at Georgia State University in Atlanta; in 2002, was appointed Regent's Professor in the University System of Georgia.

Dr. McLean has published over 125 articles in such publications as the *Harvard Business Review*, *Sloan Management Review*, *California Management Review*, *Communications of the ACM*, *MIS Quarterly*, *Information Systems Research*, *Management Science*, *Journal of MIS*, *Information & Management*, *DATABASE*, *InformationWEEK*, *DATAMATION*, *ComputerWorld,* and the *Proceedings of ICIS. HICSS,* and *AMCIS*. He is the co-author (with John Soden of Mckinsey & Co.) of *Strategic Planning for MIS* (Wiley Interscience, 1977), co-editor of a book of programs entitled *APL Applications in Management* (UCLA, 1981), and co-editor of *The Management of Information Systems* (Dryden Press, 2nd ed., 1994). He was a founding associate editor for Research of the *MIS Quarterly*, and for seven years the senior co-editor of *The DATA BASE for Advances in Information Systems.*

He has served four times on the national Executive Council of the Society for Information Management (SIM). In 1980, he co-chaired the organizing committee for the International Conference on Information Systems (ICIS) and was Conference Co-chairman in 1981 in Cambridge, MA; Conference Chairman in 1986 in San Diego, CA; and Conference Co-chairman in 1997 in Atlanta, CA. He is currently the Executive Director of the ICIS and of the Association for Information Systems (AIS) of which he was one of the founding members. In 1999, he was named a fellow of the AIS, one of the first in the world so honored. In 2003, he was named IS Educator of the Year by the Special Interest Group on Education of the Association for Information Technology Professionals (AITP).

## DR. JAMES C. WETHERBE

Dr. James C. Wetherbe is Stevenson Chair of Information Technology at Texas Tech University as well as Professor of MIS at the University of Minnesota where he directed the MIS Research Center for 20 years. He is internationally known as a dynamic and entertaining speaker, author, and leading authority on the use of computers and information systems to improve organizational performance and competitiveness. He is particularly appreciated for his ability to explain complex technology in straightforward, practical terms that can be strategically applied by both executives and general management.

Dr. Wetherbe is the author of 18 highly regarded books and is quoted often in leading business and information systems journals. He has also authored over 200 articles, was ranked by *InformationWEEK* as one of the top dozen information technology consultants, and is the first recipient of the MIS Quarterly Distinguished Scholar Award. He has also served on the faculties of the University of Memphis, where he was Fed Ex Professor and Director of the Center for Cycle Time Research, and the University of Houston.

Dr. Wetherbe received his Ph.D. from Texas Tech University.

# BRIEF CONTENTS

*This chapter can be accessed online at www.wiley.com/college/turban

# CONTENTS

*This chapter and the Technology Guides can be accessed online at www.wiley. com/college/turban.

## Chapter

# 1

# IT Support of Organizational Performance

## Learning Objectives

After studying this chapter, you will be able to:

❶ Describe the characteristics of the digital economy and digital enterprises.

❷ Recognize the relationships between performance, environmental pressures, organizational responses, and information technology.

❸ Identify the major pressures in the business environment and describe the major organizational responses to them.

❹ Define computer-based information systems and information technology.

❺ Describe the concept of the adaptive enterprise and why it is IT dependent.

❻ Describe the role of information technology in supporting the functional areas, public services, and specific industries.

❼ Understand the importance of learning about information technology.

## Integrating *IT*

 **ACC**  **FIN**  **MKT**  **POM**  **HRM**  **IS**  **SVC**

1

The competition in standard computer chip manufacturing is global and fierce. The profit margin is razor thin and even the industry leader Intel can be damaged. Here is what happened:

## The Problem

Intel is the world's largest chip maker of standard chips. With about 100,000 employees, revenue of $38.8 billion, and $8.7 billion profit (in 2005), Intel has been humbled by a small but scrappy rival, AMD, that has less than 10,000 employees. AMD's market share has been growing rapidly since 2003 when it introduced its Opteron chip. (AMD's revenue was $5.8 billion, profit $16.5 million in 2005).

Since the Opteron chip was introduced, Intel's revenue market share, profit, and stock price (see Figure 1.1) have been in trouble.

Opteron offered a low-energy-consumption, high-performance chip compared with Intel's old design, Pentium. With the rapid increase of energy costs starting in mid-2004, Intel customers of the high-end server business were not impressed with their electricity bills and switched to AMD. For example, VeriCenter is an outsourcer that runs software for 500 large customers on 8,000 servers that cost $500,000 per year in electricity. Switching to AMD saved the company over $150,000.

## The Solution

Intel realized that its good reputation was not sufficient to regain customers. So it started to design a new architecture for a family of chips, which would consume less energy than AMD's and increase performance. The first chip in the family (code named Sossaman) was released in April 2006 (when this case was written). It burns only one-fifth the energy consumed by an AMD chip, and was priced as low as $209 to target customers like VeriCenter and Google that run thousands of servers in tandem. VeriCenter's chief technology officer admitted that his company will return to Intel (Whelan, 2006). Intel is designing a set of chips with similar properties in all server categories.

In addition, Intel is expanding its manufacturing capacity, which enables it to be a low-cost manufacturer. Finally, Intel is adding innovative capabilities to the new chips for its corporate buyers, such as the ability to remotely access computers and run programs in isolation so that the system is less crash-prone.

Intel's problem now is time. The company is reducing prices to get rid of its inventory of old, unsold chips, sometimes at a loss. Also, as energy prices continue to climb, more customers move to AMD. To expedite the chip design, Intel is using several IT-based collaboration tools (see Chapter 4), as well as expediting systems testing and development (Chapter 15).

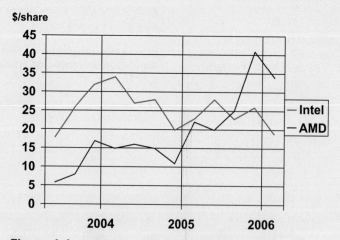

**Figure 1.1** Intel-AMD stock movement 2004–2006.

Each chapter opens with an example that illustrates the application of IT in a real-world organization and the relevance of the chapter topics. The format—problem, solution, results—helps model a way to think about business problems.

## The Results

Intel has a good chance to reclaim some and possibly all its old customers as well as to acquire new ones. How big the total damage will be and how effective the solution will be is difficult to assess. AMD, of course, is also developing a better line of products and some of the switched customers may not return to Intel.

*Sources:* Compiled from Whelan (2006), and from *money.CNN.com* news items (April 13 and 16, 2006).

## Lessons Learned from This Case

Organizational performance depends not only on how efficient they are, but also on what is going on in their *business environment.* AMD was able to produce a high-performance chip that uses less energy. Then the energy price escalation started giving AMD's chip a major competitive advantage. These are typical business environmental factors that, as described in this chapter, result in problems for some organizations and opportunities for others.

To counter the environmental and competitive pressures, Intel used traditional methods such as price cutting, but this was not enough. Intel had to redesign its products. In a rapidly changing environment, this must be done quickly, to shorten the *time-to-market.* And this is where Intel employed several information technologies. Intel has proven itself to be an *adaptive enterprise* thanks to information technology support. How all this comes together is the subject of Chapter 1.

This brief "Lessons Learned" section ties the key points of the opening case to the topics that will be covered in the chapter.

# 1.1 Doing Business in the Digital Economy

Various icons are used throughout the book to identify a particular perspective or functional area related to the nearby example. This icon, for example, indicates an international perspective. Refer to the preface for a listing of all of the icons.

**GLOBAL**

Conducting business in the digital economy means using Web-based systems on the Internet and other electronic networks to do transactions electronically. First we will describe digital organizations and the digital economy. Then we will consider the concepts of electronic commerce and networked computing and look at the impact they have made on how companies do business.

The opening case introduced us to a digital enterprise. And indeed, thousands of organizations are moving to become digital. What a digital enterprise is, and how it operates in the digital economy and society, is the subject of this section.

THE DIGITAL
ENTERPRISE

There are many definitions as to what is a **digital enterprise (organization).** For example, Davis (2005) believes that the digital enterprise is a new business model that uses IT in a fundamental way to accomplish one or more of three basic objectives: reach and engage customers more effectively, boost employee productivity, and improve operating efficiency. It uses converged communication and computing technology to improve business processes.

More specifically, the digital enterprise embraces a fundamentally different approach to the critical information infrastructure. This approach requires a modular, interoperable, cross-architecture environment that extends from the furthest edge of the network—where stationary and mobile employees, partners, and customers are located around the world—to the corporate data center and back again.

The digital enterprise shifts the focus from managing individual IT resources—devices, applications, and datasets—to *orchestrating the services and workflows* that define the business and ultimately deliver value to customers and end users.

A digital enterprise uses networks of computers to electronically connect:

- All its internal parts via an *intranet* (Chapter 4, TG 4)
- All its business partners via the *Internet,* or via a secured Internet, called an *extranet* (Chapter 4, TG4), or via value-added private communication lines

An example of how this is done is shown in Figure 1.2.

The term *digital enterprise* refers to an organization such as IHH (see Minicase 2), which uses computers and information system to perform all or most of its digitizable activities. Harrington (2006) describes why and how, as a CEO, he transformed the Thomson Corp. from a traditional $8 billion publishing business to an electronic information services provider and publisher for professionals in targeted markets. In five years, revenue increased over 20 percent and profit increased by more than 65 percent.

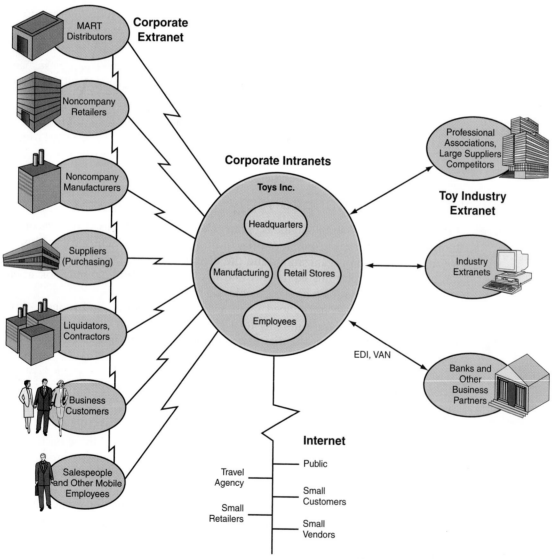

**Figure 1.2** Digital networked enterprise.

The following icon is used throughout the book to indicate that additional related resources are available at the book's Web site, www.wiley.com/college/turban.

The **digital economy** refers to an economy that is based on digital technologies. The digital economy is also sometimes called the *Internet economy,* the *new economy,* or the *Web economy* (see Brynolfsson et al., 2003 and Liebowitz, 2002).

In this new economy, digital networking (including wireless) and communication infrastructures provide a global platform over which people and organizations devise strategies, interact, communicate, collaborate, and search for information. This platform includes, for example, the following:

- A vast array of digitizable products—databases, news and information, books, magazines, electronic tags, TV and radio programming, movies, electronic games, musical CDs, and software—which are delivered over the digital infrastructure any time, anywhere in the world (see list in Online File W1.2)
- Consumers and firms conducting financial transactions digitally—through digital currencies or financial tokens carried via networked computers and mobile devices
- Physical goods such as home appliances and automobiles, which are equipped with microprocessors and networking capabilities

The term *digital economy* also refers to the convergence of computing and communication technologies on the Internet and other networks, and the resulting flow of information and technology that is stimulating electronic transactions and vast organizational change. This convergence enables all types of information (data, audio, video, etc.) to be stored, processed, and transmitted over networks to many destinations worldwide (see Brynjolfsson and Kahin, 2002). The digital economy has helped create an unprecedented economic performance (Lumpkin and Dess, 2004) and the longest period of uninterrupted economic expansion in history, from 1991 until 2000. After that there was a temporary collapse that was corrected four years later (Abramson, 2005). The major characteristics of the digital economy are shown in Table 1.1.

| TABLE 1.1 | Major IT Characteristics in the Digital Economy |
|---|---|
| **Area** | **Description** |
| Globalization | Global communication and collaboration; global electronic marketplaces. Global customers, suppliers, and partners. |
| Digital systems | From TV to telephones and instrumentation, analog systems are being converted to digital ones. |
| Speed | A move to real-time transactions, thanks to digitized documents, products, and services. Many business processes are expedited by 90 percent or more. |
| Information overload | Although the amount of information generated is accelerating, intelligent search tools can help users find what they need. |
| Markets | Markets are moving online. Physical marketplaces are being replaced by electronic markets; new markets are being created, increasing competition and market efficiency. |
| Digitization | Music, books, pictures, movies, and more are digitized for fast and inexpensive distribution. |
| Business models and processes | New and improved business models and processes provide opportunities to new companies and industries. Cyberintermediation and no intermediation are on the rise. |
| Innovation | Digital and Internet-based innovations continue at a rapid pace. More patents are being granted than ever before. |
| Obsolescence | The fast pace of innovations creates a high rate of obsolescence. |
| Opportunities | Opportunities abound in almost all aspects of life and business. |
| Fraud | Criminals employ a slew of innovative schemes on the Internet. Cybercons are everywhere. |
| Wars | Conventional wars are changing to cyberwars. |
| Organizations | Many companies are attempting to move to a full digital status. |

**Opportunities for Entrepreneurs.** The new digital economy is providing unparalleled opportunities for thousands of entrepreneurs, some of them in their teens, to create startup (or dot-com) companies and to apply EC business models to many business areas. These startup companies not only sell products (online music and movies), but also online services ranging from online dating to medical advice. Also provided are support services to EC and digital companies ranging from computer security to electronic payments. These companies saw an opportunity to do global business electronically. Some of these companies, notably Google, made their founders billionaires. An interesting example is entrepreneur Don Kogen and his Thaigem.com business, described in *IT at Work 1.1*.

"IT at Work" boxes spotlight innovations and technologies used by real organizations to solve business problems.
"Integrating IT" icons highlight examples of IT applications in major functional areas of business, in government, and in public services.
The codes used under these icons are:
**ACC**—accounting, **POM**—production/operations management, **MKT**—marketing, **HRM**—human resources management, **FIN**—finance,
**GOV**—government, **SVC**—other public services and service industries

## IT at Work 1.1

### Diamonds Forever—Online

ACC   POM   MKT   HRM   FIN   GOV   SVC   GLOBAL

The gems market is a global one with thousands of traders buying and selling about $45 billion worth of gems each year. This age-old business is very inefficient in terms of pricing: Seven-tier supply chain intermediaries can jack up the price of a gem 1,000 percent between the mine and final retail prices.

Chanthaburi, Thailand, is one of the world's leading centers for processing gems, and that is where Don Kogen landed, at the age of 15, to search for his fortune. And indeed, he found it there. After failing to become a gem cutter, Kogen moved into gem sorting, and soon he learned to speak Thai. After three years of observing how gem traders haggle over stones, he decided to try the business himself. Having only a small amount of "seed" money, Kogen started by purchasing low-grade gems from sellers who arrived early in the morning and selling them for a small profit to dealers from India and Pakistan who usually arrived late in the day. Using advertising, he reached the U.S. gem market and soon had 800 potential overseas customers. Using faxes, he shortened the order time, which resulted in decreasing the entire time from order to delivery. These various business methods enabled him to grow his mail-order business to $250,000 per year by 1997.

In 1998, Kogen decided to use the Internet. Within a month, he established a Web site, *thaigem.com*, and sold his first gem online. By 2001, the revenue reached $4.3 million, growing to $9.8 million in 2002. Online sales account for 85 percent of the company's revenue. The buyers are mostly jewelry dealers or retailers such as Wal-Mart or QVC. Kogen buys raw or refined gems from all over the world, some online, trying to cater to the demands of his customers. Then the site merged with NCS group, a large gem wholesaler.

Thaigem's competitive edge is low prices and profit margin. The proximity to gem-processing factories and the low labor cost there enable the company to offer prices significantly lower than his online competitors (such as Tiffany's at *tiffany.com*). Payments are made safely, securely, and conveniently using either PayPal or Escrow.com. Delivery to any place is made via Federal Express or the post office.

Dissatisfied customers can return merchandise within 30 days, no questions asked. No jewel is guaranteed, but Thaigem's name is trusted by over 68,000 potential customers worldwide. For example, the company uses eBay to auction gems as an additional selling channel. Customers' comments on eBay are 99 percent positive versus 1 percent negative.

Thaigem.com is the online marketing arm of Thaigem Global Marketing Ltd. (a sister company of NCS Group Ltd.), which operates traditional wholesale gem stores, as well as fulfilling orders generated by Thaigem.com, a profitable leader of EC. The company's strategy is to provide the least expensive gems, which they source from 60 countries, both by e-purchasing and traditional purchasing, with the best customer care.

The retail store is hosted by eBay.com, but sales are from e-catalogs (individual items in fixed prices). You can find the Thaigem.com story on eBay.com as well.

*Sources:* Compiled from *stores.ebay.com/www_thaigem_com/Thaigem_com_story.html* (no longer available online), Meredith (2002), and from *thaigem.com* (accessed April 2006).

*For Further Exploration:* Go to *blackstartrading.com* and compare them to *thaigem.com;* which site do you think is better? What kinds of business and revenue models were used? Were they effective? How is competitive advantage gained in this case? (See Group Assignment in Chapter 5.)

**ELECTRONIC COMMERCE AND NETWORKED COMPUTING**

As described in Online File W1.1, Siemens AG was an established "old-economy" company that has seen the need to transform itself into an *e-business*, a company that performs most of its business functions electronically, in order to enhance its operations and competitiveness. Its use of Web-based systems to support buying, selling, collaboration, and customer service exemplifies *electronic commerce* (*EC* or *e-commerce*). EC is becoming a very significant global economic element in the twenty-first century.

The infrastructure for digital organizations and EC is **networked computing** (also known as *distributed computing*), which connects computers and other electronic devices via telecommunication networks. Such connections allow users to access information stored in many places and to communicate and collaborate with others. While some people still use a standalone computer exclusively, or a network confined to one location, the vast majority of people use multiple-location networked computers. These may be connected to the *global networked environment,* known as the *Internet,* to private value-added networks (VANs), or to the Internet's counterpart within organizations, called an *intranet.* In addition, some companies link their intranets to those of their business partners over networks called *extranets.* The connection typically is done via wireline systems, but since 2000 more and more communication and collaboration is done via wireless systems.

Networked computing is helping some companies excel and is helping others simply to survive. Broadly, the collection of computing systems used by an organization is termed **information technology (IT)**; its use, strategy, and management are the focus of this book.

Information technology has become the major facilitator of business activities in the world today.* IT is also a catalyst of fundamental changes in the strategic structure, operations, and management of organizations, due to the capabilities shown in Table 1.2. These capabilities, according to Wreden (1997), support the

*Note that here and throughout the book, in using the term "business" we refer not only to for-profit organizations, but also to not-for-profit public organizations and government agencies, which need to be run like a business.

| TABLE 1.2 | Major Capabilities of Computerized Information Systems |
|---|---|

- Perform high-speed, high-volume, numerical computations.
- Provide fast, accurate, reliable, and inexpensive communication within and between organizations, any time, any place.
- Store huge amounts of information in an easy-to-access, yet small space.
- Allow quick and inexpensive access to vast amounts of information worldwide at any time.
- Enable collaboration anywhere, any time.
- Increase the effectiveness and efficiency of people working in groups in one place or in several locations.
- Vividly present information that challenges the human mind.
- Facilitate work in hazardous environments.
- Automate both semiautomatic business processes and manually done tasks.
- Facilitate interpretation of vast amounts of data.
- Facilitate global trade.
- Enable automation of routine decision making and facilitate complex decision making.
- Can be wireless, thus supporting unique applications anywhere.
- Accomplish all of the above much less expensively than when done manually.

following five business objectives: (1) improving productivity, (2) reducing costs, (3) improving decision making, (4) enhancing customer relationships, and (5) developing new strategic applications. Indeed, IT is creating a transformation in the way business is conducted, facilitating a transition to digital organizations and digital economy, and is comprised of many digital organizations.

<table>
<tr><td>THE NEW VS. THE OLD: ILLUSTRATIVE EXAMPLES</td></tr>
</table>

The changes brought by the digital economy are indeed significant. Computer-based information systems of all kinds have been enhancing business competitiveness and creating strategic advantage on their own or in conjunction with EC applications. In a study conducted by Lederer et al. (1998), companies ranked the number-one benefit of Web-based systems as "enhancing competitiveness or creating strategic advantage."

Let's look at a few examples that illustrate differences between doing business in the new economy and the old one.

**Example#1: Buying or Renting a Movie Online.** The cost of going to a movie is ever growing, and you can go only when there is a showing. But, when you rent or buy a movie, many can share the viewing, and you can do it any time and in the convenience of your home.

*Old Economy.* You go to a retail store, browse the selection, hopefully find what you want, pay, and take the movie home. Movies need to be returned, of course, usually within 2 days. Some stores are open 24 hours; others are not. In some areas you can buy or rent from unmanned kiosks, but the selection there is minimal. Even in a specialized store, such as Blockbuster, you will not find more than 10,000 different titles, with multiple copies available for only some titles.

*New Economy.* Netflix (*netflix.com*) rents out DVDs from a selection of about 60,000 titles. Ordering is done online. Rental is done by mail, and Netflix pays shipping to you and the return costs. A monthly subscription fee allows you to rent as many movies as you want each month (up to three at a time). This rental model increased the demand and motivated the company to create a recommendation intelligent agent (Cinematch) that recommends movies to each individual based on their personalities. For a general recommendation visit *movies.yahoo.com* (for further details see the Netflix case in Chapter 5).

Even more convenient is downloading films from Movielink, or CinemaNow, to your computer. Although currently the selection is very limited, the movie is yours forever, and you can stream a copy to a TV. You pay more for this pleasure than you pay at Netflix. You can also download TV episodes for $1.99 each using iTunes (there are no commercials in this service).

**Example #2: Paying for Goods: The Checkout Experience.** It sometimes takes more time to check out than to shop, which can be a really frustrating experience.

*Old Economy.* In the "old-old" economy, when you visited stores that sold any type of retail product (e.g., groceries, office supplies), you placed your items in a shopping cart and proceeded to checkout. At the checkout counter, you stood in line while a clerk punched in the price of each item on a manual adding machine. After the clerk added up all your items, you paid for them in cash. Note that in this situation no information was gathered about the item itself, other than the price.

Using the next generation of checkout technology, you take your items to a clerk, who swipes (sometimes twice or more) the *barcode* of each item over a "reader." The reader captures data on the price and description of each item and automatically enters that data into the organization's database. You receive an itemized printout of your purchases and the total price.

**New Economy.** In the new economy, you take your items to a self-service kiosk (e.g., visit the nearest Home Depot store), where you swipe the barcode of each item over a reader. After you have swiped all of your items, the kiosk gives you directions about how to pay (cash, credit card, or debit card). You still may have to wait if there are lines to get to the self-service kiosk; often, other shoppers need help to learn the technology. But, your checkout time could be much faster.

In the coming generation of checkout technology, all items will have wireless radio frequency identification (RFID) tags (see Chapters 2 and 6) either attached to or embedded in them. After you have finished shopping, you will simply walk your cart with all its items through a device similar to an airport security scanner. This device will "read" the wireless signals from each item, generate an itemized account of all your purchases, total up the price, and debit your debit card or credit card (after recognizing your face or fingerprint), all in a few seconds. You will not wait in line at all. (See Group Assignment #2.)

**Example #3: The Power of E-Commerce.** The power of e-commerce is demonstrated in the following three examples:

- Several banks in Japan issue smart cards that can be used only by their owners. When using the cards, the palm vein of the owner's hand is compared with a pre-stored template of the vein stored on the smart card. When the owner inserts the card into the ATM or vendor's card readers that are equipped with the system, it will dispense the person's money. The police are alerted if anyone other than the card's owner tries to use it.
- Jacobi Medical Center in New York tracks the whereabouts of patients in the hospital. Each patient has an RFID in a plastic band strapped to his or her wrist. Each time a patient passes an RFID reader, his or her location is transmitted in real-time to the responsible staff. The RFID is linked to the hospital's computer network, connecting the patient's records to labs, billing, and the pharmacy.
- CompUSA offers an ATM-like service that dispenses software like candy from a vending machine. A touch screen lets CompUSA consumers shop for software by choosing an operating system and selecting from categories such as business, education, and games. The consumer is presented with a list of titles and descriptions and prices. Once the consumer picks a title, an order ticket is dispensed. The consumer then presents the order ticket to a sales rep and pays for the software. The rep then enters information into a second machine, called an order-fulfillment station. This machine burns the software onto a CD. The sales rep then packages the CD and instructions in a box.

In each of the examples above, we can see the advantage of the new way of doing business over the old one in terms of at least one of the following: cost, quality, speed, strategic competitive advantage, and customer service. What is amazing is the *magnitude* of this advantage. In the past, business improvements were in the magnitude of 10 to 25 percent. Today, improvements can be hundreds or even thousands of times faster or cheaper. The new economy brings not only digitization but also the opportunity to use new business models, illustrated in the examples above and in the case of Don Kogen at Thaigem.com—selling and buying from the Internet.

A **business model** is a method of doing business by which a company can generate revenue to sustain itself. The model spells out how the company creates (or adds) value in terms of the goods and/or services the company produces in the course of its operations. Some models are very simple. For example, Nokia makes and sells cell phones and generates profit from these sales. On the other hand, a TV station provides free broadcasting. Its survival depends on a complex model involving factors such as advertisers and content providers. Internet portals, such as Yahoo, also use a similar complex business model. Further details of business models and examples of new business models brought about by the digital revolution are listed in *A Closer Look 1.1*. Further discussion of these models will be found throughout the book (especially in Chapter 5), Carrie (2004), and at *digitalenterprise.org*. In part, these new business models have sprung up because of the

# A Closer Look 1.1

"A Closer Look" boxes contain detailed, in-depth discussion of specific concepts, procedures, or approaches.

## Four Representative Business Models of the Digital Age

MKT

According to McKay and Marshall (2004), a comprehensive *business model* is composed of the following six elements:

1. A description of all *products* and *services* the business will offer
2. A description of the *business process* required to make and deliver the products and services
3. A description of the *customers* to be served and the company's relationships with these customers, including what constitutes value from the perspective of the customers (*customers' value proposition*)
4. A list of the *resources* required and the identification of which ones are available, which will be developed in-house, and which will need to be acquired
5. A description of the organization's *supply chain*, including *suppliers* and other *business partners*
6. A description of the revenues expected (*revenue model*), anticipated costs, sources of financing, and estimated profitability (*financial viability*)

Models also include a *value proposition*, which is an analysis of the benefits of using the specific model (tangible and intangible), including the customers' value proposition.

Four popular e-commerce models are listed below.

**Tendering via Reverse Auctions.** If you are a big buyer, private or public, you are probably using a *tendering* (bidding) system to make your major purchases. In what is called a *request for quote* (RFQ), the buyer indicates a desire to receive bids on a particular item, and would-be sellers bid on the job. The lowest bid wins (if price is the only consideration), hence the name *reverse auction*. Now tendering can be done online, saving time and money (see Chapter 5).

**Affiliate Marketing.** *Affiliate marketing* is an arrangement in which marketing partners place a banner ad for a company, such as Amazon.com, on their Web site. Every time a customer clicks on the banner, moves to the advertiser's Web site, and makes a purchase there, the advertiser pays a 3 to 15 percent commission to the host site. In this way, businesses can turn other businesses into their *virtual commissioned sales force*. Pioneered by CDNow (see Hoffman and Novak, 2000), the concept is now employed by thousands of retailers or direct sellers. For details see Chapter 5.

**Group Purchasing.** It is customary to pay less per unit when buying more units. Discounts are usually available for such quantity purchases. Using e-commerce and the concept of *group purchasing*, in which purchase orders of many buyers are aggregated, a small business or even an individual can participate and get a discount. EC brings in the concept of *electronic aggregation* for group purchasing, in which a third party finds the individuals or *SMEs* (small/medium enterprises) that want to buy the same product, aggregates their small orders, and then negotiates (or conducts a tender) for the best deal. The more that join the group, the larger the aggregated quantity, and the lower the price paid (see Chapter 5).

**E-Marketplaces and Exchanges.** Electronic marketplaces have existed in isolated applications for decades. An example is the stock exchanges, some of which have been fully computerized since the 1980s. But, since 1999, thousands of electronic marketplaces of different varieties have sprung up. E-marketplaces introduce operating efficiencies to trading, and if well organized and managed, they can provide benefits to both buyers and sellers. Of special interest are *vertical marketplaces*, which concentrate on one industry (e.g., *chemconnect.com* in the chemical industry). (Chapter 5 will explore e-marketplaces and exchanges in more detail.)

need to improve performance and in response or reaction to business pressures, which is the topic we turn to next.

**The Digital Society.** Having digital organizations and a digital economy revolutionizes the way we conduct business. But what about the rest of our life: the social, political, educational, and other aspects? Clearly, we have enough signs that what is going on in the business world is going on elsewhere. In other words, we are moving toward being a *digital society*. Mowshowitz and Turoff (2005) present views of a society changing under the influence of advanced IT (also see Wilhelm 2004). This transformation is accelerating and expanding to cover every facet of our life. IT is stimulating the transformation by altering the balance and roles in the market place, changing the way we train and educate, changing the way health and social services are delivered, introducing virtual communities, cities, and organizations providing online entertainments, altering the way we obtain information, process it, and deliver it, and much more. (See Chapter 17 for further discussion.) Although this book deals mainly with the business and economic aspects of the digital revolution, we cannot neglect the other aspects, which are frequently interrelated with the business aspects. Therefore, here we will cover some examples from social services, entertainment, education, and so on (e.g., see Minicase 1 at the end of this chapter).

## 1.2 Business Pressures, Organizational Performance and Responses, and IT Support

Organizations do not operate in isolation. They are part of a business environment that includes economic, legal, and other factors. They are usually part of an industry and are influenced by what is going on in that environment.

THE BUSINESS
ENVIRONMENT
AND ITS IMPACT

Most people, sports teams, and organizations are trying to improve their *performance* with time. For some, it is a challenge; for others it is a requirement for survival. Yet, for some it is the key to improved life, profitability, or reputation.

Most organizations measure their performance periodically, comparing it to some metrics and to the organization's mission, objectives, and plans. Unfortunately, frequently your performance level depends not only on what you do, but also on what others are doing, as well as on forces of nature. In the business world, we refer to such events, in totality, as the *business environment*. Such an environment may create significant pressures that may impact the performance in an uncontrollable, sometimes unpredictable way (recall the Intel case).

Companies need to react frequently and quickly to both the *problems* and the *opportunities* resulting from this new business environment. Because the pace of change and the degree of uncertainty in tomorrow's competitive environment are expected to accelerate, organizations are going to operate under increasing pressures to produce more, using fewer resources.

In order to succeed (or even merely to survive) in this dynamic world, companies must not only take traditional actions such as lowering costs, but also undertake innovative activities (such as changing structure or business processes) or devise a competitive strategy. We refer to these reactions, some of which are interrelated, as **critical response activities.** These activities can be performed in some or all of the processes of the organization, from the daily routines of preparing payroll and order entry, to strategic activities such as the acquisition of a company. A response can be

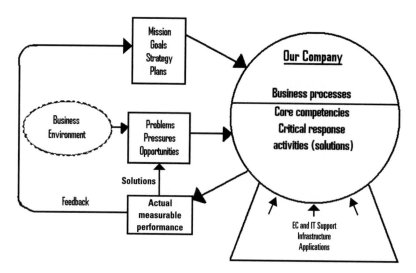

**Figure 1.3** The business environment impact model.

a reaction to a pressure already in existence, an initiative intended to defend an organization against future pressures, or an activity that *exploits an opportunity* created by changing conditions. Most response activities can be greatly facilitated by information technology.

We summarize the above discussion in a model titled the *business environment impact model.*

**The Business Environment Impact Model.**  The model shown in Figure 1.3 illustrates how the business environment (left) creates problems and opportunities that drive what organizations are doing in their business processes ("our company" circle). Other drivers are the organization's mission, goals, strategy, and plans. In addition to their *core activities,* organizations must respond to the environmental pressures that result in problems, constraints, and opportunities (what we earlier termed *critical response activities*). Organizational activities result in measurable performance that provides the solution to problems/opportunities, as well as feedback on the mission, strategy, and plans.

Notice that in Figure 1.3 IT provides support to organizations' activities and to actual performance to help in countering the business pressures. We will demonstrate it throughout the book.

In the remainder of this section, we will examine two components of our model—business environmental pressures and organizational responses—in more detail.

**BUSINESS ENVIRONMENTAL PRESSURES**

The business environment consists of a variety of factors—societal, legal, political, technological, and economic (market) (see Huber, 2004). Significant changes in any of these factors are likely to create business pressures on organizations. Figure 1.4 presents a schematic view of these major pressures, which may interrelate and affect each other. These pressures are described in Online File W1.4.

**Ethical Issues.**  Ethical issues may create pressures or at least constraints on the operations of an organization. **Ethics** relates to standards of right and wrong, and *information ethics* relates to standards of right and wrong in information processing practices. Organizations must deal with ethical issues relating to their employees, customers, and suppliers. Ethical issues are very important since they have the power to damage the image of an organization and to destroy the morale of the employees. Ethics is a difficult area because ethical issues are not cut-and-dried.

**ETHICS**

Use of this icon highlights IT-related ethics discussions.

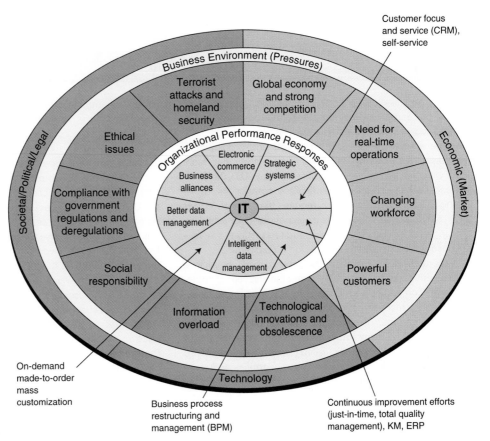

**Figure 1.4** Business pressures, organizational performance and responses, and IT support.

What is considered ethical by one person may seem unethical to another. Likewise, what is considered ethical in one country may be seen as unethical in another.

The use of information technology raises many ethical issues. These range from the monitoring of electronic mail to the potential invasion of privacy of millions of customers whose data are stored in private and public databases. At this chapter's Web site, in Online File W1.5, you will find resources that will help you develop and strengthen your understanding of ethical issues related to business, and to IT management in particular. The online file consists of two parts: (1) a general framework of ethics in business and society, and (2) an Ethics Primer that poses various ethical situations and asks you to think about responses to these situations. In addition to the materials in Online File W1.5, specific ethical issues are discussed in all chapters of the book (and are highlighted by an icon in the margin).

**The Impact of the Business Environment Factors.** The business environment factors presented in Figure 1.3 and Online File W1.4, can have major impacts on the performance of individuals, departments, and organizations. Some of these create severe constraints that limit the flexibility required for an agile organization. Others cost a great deal of money or create a considerable headache, such as the Sarbanes-Oxley Act (SOX) (see *A Closer Look 1.2*), especially when they are initiated.

In addition to compliance with SOX, companies need to comply with other legal requirements such as the USA PATRIOT Act, Gramm-Leach Blily Act, and HIPAA. For the results of a major survey on compliance conducted by *CIO Insight* editors, see *CIO Insight*, May 2005.

# A Closer Look 1.2

## Complying with SOX—A Major Challenge for Corporations

Passed in the wake of the Enron and WorldCom accounting scandals, the Sarbanes-Oxley Act (SOX) stipulates procedures for improving corporate reporting, such as requiring CEOs to certify the accuracy of financial statements and prohibiting a firm's outside auditors from engaging in any activity that might conflict with their auditing responsibilities. In May 2003, the Securities and Exchange Commission (SEC) adopted rules implementing SOX Section 404, which requires that annual reports contain a statement of management's responsibility for establishing financial controls and that outside auditors testify to the adequacy of a company's controls and reporting procedures.

According to D'Agostino (2005), the cost of compliance can spiral out of control especially during the first year of implementation. Companies had to invest heavily in software (security, document management, business process management, risk assessment, etc.). Therefore, special compliance modules were developed by many software vendors to "ease the pain." For example, one of these tools, called Horizon, is being offered by J.P. Morgan. This Web-based software identifies and manages operations risk, a catchall for the unpredictable calamities that can befall a company, from fraud to "acts of God" to computer glitches. Through a set of self-assessment tools, Horizon enables companies to gain a clearer picture of their operations risks and the steps needed to control them. Horizon also provides a practical solution to the challenges of complying with the requirements of SOX. The product helps companies establish sound practices in the area of financial reporting, conflicts of interests, corporate ethics, internal processes, and accounting oversight. (For other software, see Chapter 7.)

D'Agostino proposes approaches to reduce the cost. *Baseline* magazine offers (for a fee) a calculator to figure the cost, and Marchetti (2005) offers a methodology for effective risk management.

On the bright side, the effort to meet SOX requirements may produce substantial benefits to companies in the long run. For example, Rothfelder (2005) reports that in the case of Blue Rhino Corp., SOX lent urgency to a financial reengineering effort that the company had already begun. Faced with a growing retail network, Blue Rhino was drowning in inventory. This problem developed because distributors sent data on receivables and payables to headquarters piecemeal at the end of each month. Accounting staff members had to plug the data into spreadsheets manually and then integrate those spreadsheets into the centralized corporate network. Under this system, closing the books could take a week or more. During this interval, inventory levels in the field were not monitored with sufficient timeliness.

To solve this problem, Blue Rhino documented each process and its associated safeguards to ensure that information could not be changed without appropriate levels of permission.

Efforts to comply with SOX also helped Blue Rhino uncover processes that desperately needed to be fixed even though they were not directly related to financial systems. As one example, human resources traditionally had provided information about each new hire, such as start date and position, to the IT group via telephone or e-mail. This informal procedure slowed down the process of getting an employee into the flow of his or her job. To speed up this process, the company generated an automated human resources application that immediately sends details about a new hire to IT.

Blue Rhino has also changed its purchasing system from a manual process to online forms. Corporate buyers can enter their requests electronically and these are automatically sent to central purchasing. If the order is approved, based on spending limits and other criteria, it is filled instantly. In addition, the data pertaining to the order is shared with accounting, inventory, supply chain management, and the company's executives.

*Sources:* Compiled from Rothfelder (2004), D'Agostino (2005), and Marchetti (2005).

---

Note that some pressures can come from *business partners*. For example, in April 2004, Wal-Mart Stores, Inc. mandated that their top suppliers adopt the RFID technology (Chapters 6 and 9). Similar requirements are imposed by other large buyers including federal and state governments.

The environments that surrounded organizations are becoming more complex and turbulent. Advances in communications, transportation, and technology create many changes. Other changes are the result of political or economic activities. Thus, the pressures on organizations are mounting, and organizations must be ready to take responsive actions if they are to succeed. In addition, organizations may see opportunities in these pressures. (For a framework for change analysis, see Online File W1.6 at the book's Web site.) Organizational responses to the increasing business pressures are described next.

**ORGANIZATIONAL RESPONSES**

Traditional organizational responses may not be effective with new types of pressures and ever-increasing competition. Therefore many old solutions/responses need to be modified, supplemented, or eliminated. Organizations can also take *proactive* measures to create a change in the marketplace. Such activities also include exploiting opportunities created by the external pressures.

Organizations can respond in many different ways. As you recall, Intel innovated a new product and rushed it to the marketplace by using collaboration technologies. It also improved its customer service. We assembled a list of organizational responses and summarized them in Table 1.3. Some of these responses are discussed in Online File W1.7. Others are described in various chapters of the book.

| **TABLE 1.3** | Innovative Organizations' Responses to Pressures and Opportunities |
|---|---|
| **Response/Action** | **Description** |
| Develop strategic systems | Employ unique systems that provide strategic advantage (e.g., new features, low prices, super service) (Chapters 4–16). |
| Introduce customer-focused systems | Making the customer happy is a first priority (Chapters 5, 8). |
| Improve decision making and forecasting | Use analytical methods to optimize operations, reduce cost, expedite decision making, support collaboration, automate routine decisions (Chapters 11, 12). |
| Restructure business processes and organization structure | Restructure business processes to make them more efficient/effective. Use business process management methodology (Chapter 8) and business process reengineering (Chapter 15). |
| Use self-service approach | Have your customers, employees, or business partners use self-service whenever possible (e.g., tracking status, changing an address, or managing your inventory) (Chapters 5–9). |
| Continuous improvements should be everywhere | Sustain competitive edge by improving operations, asset management, quality, and performance (Chapters 7, 8, 10–12). |
| Use mass customization | Fulfill customized orders (like Dell Computer does; see Chapter 5) using efficient procedures and processes. Compete in price with standard products (Chapters 5–8). |
| Employ on-demand manufacturing/service | Meet the demands of your customers for standard or customized products/services efficiently and effectively (Chapters 5, 9). |
| Promote business alliances | Create business alliances, even with your competitors, to reduce risks and costs. Collaborate effectively; provide benefits to your partners (Chapters 4–9). |
| Innovation and creativity should be part of the culture | Encourage innovation and creativity via rewards and collaboration. Encourage learning (Chapters 4–6, 9, 10). |
| Use e-commerce and digital systems | Automate business processes, procedures, and routine operations. Use new business models (Chapters 2–17). |
| Share information and knowledge | Encourage information and knowledge creation, storage, and reuse (Chapters 3, 10, 12). |
| Go global—but do it carefully | Buy and/or sell globally, find business partners globally, and outsource offshore. Do it all with proper risk analysis (Chapters 9, 13–15). |
| Use leading-edge and emerging technologies, including digital ones | Keep yourself up on all technological developments, conduct competitive analysis, plan properly, and conduct cost/benefit/risk analyses (Chapters 6, 12–15). |
| Use enterprise and integrated systems | Integrated systems of internal information applications together with partners' systems facilitate collaboration, reduce costs and errors, and provide competitive advantage (Chapters 7–9, 15). |

While some critical response activities can be executed manually, the vast majority require the support of information systems. Before we relate the discussion of organizational responses to the adaptive enterprise, let us briefly explore the terms *information systems* and *information technology.*

## 1.3  Information Systems and Information Technology

An **information system (IS)** collects, processes, stores, analyzes, and disseminates information for a specific purpose. Like any other system, an information system includes *inputs* (data, instructions) and *outputs* (reports, calculations). It *processes* the inputs by using technology such as PCs and produces outputs that are sent to users or to other systems via electronic networks. A *feedback* mechanism that controls the operation may be included (see Figure 1.5). Like any other system, an information system also includes people, procedures, and physical facilities, and it operates within an *environment.* An information system is not necessarily computerized, although most of them are. (For a more general discussion of *systems,* see Online File W1.9 at the book's Web site.)

**Formal and Informal Information Systems.**  An information system can be formal or informal. *Formal* systems include agreed-upon procedures, standard inputs and outputs, and fixed definitions. A company's accounting system, for example, would be a formal information system that processes financial transactions. *Informal* systems take many shapes, ranging from an office gossip network to a group of friends exchanging letters electronically. Both types of information systems must be studied.

**What Is a Computer-based Information System?**  A **computer-based information system (CBIS)** is an information system that uses computer technology to perform some or all of its intended tasks. Such a system can include as little as a personal computer and software. Or it may include several thousand computers of various sizes with hundreds of printers, plotters, and other devices, as well as communication networks (wireline and wireless) and databases. In most cases

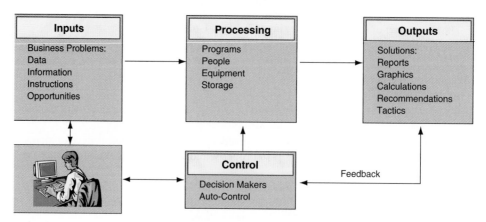

**Figure 1.5**  A schematic view of an information system.

an information system also includes people. The basic components of information systems are listed below. Note that not every system includes all these components.

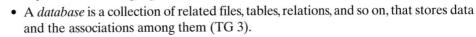

- *Hardware* is a set of devices such as processor, monitor, keyboard, and printer. Together, they accept data and information, process them, and display them (TG 1).
- *Software* is a set of programs that instruct the hardware to process data (TG 2).
- A *database* is a collection of related files, tables, relations, and so on, that stores data and the associations among them (TG 3).
- A *network* is a connecting system that permits the sharing of resources by different computers. It can be wireless (TG 4).
- *Procedures* are the set of instructions about how to combine the above components in order to process information and generate the desired output (TG 2, 6).
- *People* are those individuals who work with the system, interface with it, or use its output.

In addition, all information systems have a *purpose* and possibly a *social context*. A typical purpose is to provide a solution to a business problem. In the Siemens case (Online File W1.1), for example, the purpose of the system was to coordinate internal units, to collaborate with the many suppliers and customers, and to improve costs and customer service. The social context of the system consists of the values and beliefs that determine what is admissible and possible within the culture of the people and groups involved.

**The Difference Between Computers and Information Systems.** Computers provide effective and efficient ways of processing data, and they are a necessary part of an information system. An IS, however, involves much more than just computers. The successful application of an IS requires an understanding of the business and its environment that is supported by the IS. For example, to build an IS that supports transactions executed on the New York Stock Exchange, it is necessary to understand the procedures related to buying and selling stocks, bonds, options, and so on, including irregular demands made on the system, as well as all related government regulations.

In learning about information systems, it is therefore not sufficient just to learn about computers. Computers are only one part of a complex system that must be designed, operated, and maintained. A public transportation system in a city provides an analogy. Buses are a necessary ingredient of the system, but more is needed. Designing the bus routes, bus stops, different schedules, and so on requires considerable understanding of customer demand, traffic patterns, city regulations, safety requirements, and the like. Computers, like buses, are only one component in a complex system.

**What Is Information Technology?** Earlier in the chapter we broadly defined *information technology (IT)* as the collection of computing systems used by an organization. Information technology, in its narrow definition, refers to the technological side of an information system. It includes the hardware, software, databases, networks, and other electronic devices. It can be viewed as a subsystem of an information system. Sometimes, though, the term information technology is also used interchangeably with *information system*. In this book, we use the term *IT* in its broadest sense—to describe an organization's collection of information systems, their users, and the management that oversees them. The purpose of this book is to acquaint you with all aspects of information systems/information technology.

## 1.4 The Adaptive, Agile, Real-Time Enterprise

Charles Darwin, the renowned scientist of nature, said, "It's not the strongest of species that survives, nor the most intelligent; but the one most responsive to change." What is true in nature is true today in organizations that operate in a rapidly changing environment, which we described in Section 1.2. And, as we saw in the case of Intel, the adaptation needs to be done quickly.

The digital revolution and the rapid environmental changes bring myriad opportunities, as well as risks. Bill Gates is aware of this. Microsoft is continually developing new Internet and IT products and services. Yet Gates has stated that Microsoft is always two years away from failure—that somewhere out there is an unknown competitor who could render Microsoft's business model obsolete (Heller, 2005). Bill Gates knows that competition today is not only among products or services, but also among business models, customer service, and speed. What is true for Microsoft is true for just about every other company. The hottest and most dangerous new business models out there are on the Web, and the digital-related innovations.

This section deals with the **adaptive enterprise,** which can respond properly and in a timely manner to changes in the business environment. This section is divided into three parts. First, we deal with the process of becoming an adaptive, agile organization. Second, we provide an example of real-time systems using support IT which is provided using a methodology of a leading IT vendor. Finally, we describe some IT failures.

**THE PROCESS OF BECOMING AN ADAPTIVE ORGANIZATION**

In order to survive or succeed in the ever changing environment, organizations must become *adaptive* or *agile*. As such, they can deal properly, and in time, with changes that create problems and opportunities. To become adaptive, an organization should follow a process that:

- **Recognizes the environmental and organizational changes as quickly as they occur, or even before they occur.** Predictive analytical software, business intelligence software, and competitive intelligence software (Chapter 11) have proven to be extremely helpful. Systems such as Cisco's *virtual close* (Chapter 7) allow companies to know what's going on almost in real time. Early detection is critical.

- **Deals with changes properly and correctly.** For example, optimization software (Chapter 12) enables companies to determine prices of products (services) in real time. What-if analysis (Chapter 12) enables companies to evaluate possible courses of action and analyze risks in minutes.

- **Becomes a digital and agile enterprise.** This allows the previous two activities, as well as gaining competitive edge.

- **Does not wait for your competitor to introduce change.** Do it first if at all possible (*first-mover* strategy).

- **Changes your information systems quickly.** This can be done by using emerging technologies such as *service-as-an-architecture* (Chapter 2).

- **Follows as many as needed of the specific activities listed in Table 1.3.**

In order to follow the above process, one needs an appropriate IT infrastructure. One such infrastructure is offered by HP Development Company.

THE HP MODEL
OF BUILDING
ADAPTIVE
ENTERPRISE

Hewlett-Packard Development Company *hp.com,* a major IT company, envisioned a model of adaptive enterprise that helps organizations achieve business agility.

The basic idea is to synchronize IT with business processes to properly manage changes and facilitate the reach and innovation of the enterprise. In the 1980s and 1990s, IT helped organizations to increase internal efficiency, as will be described in Chapters 2, 7, and 8. Today organizations also need IT solutions that will increase business agility and performance, and improve competitive advantage.

**The Highlights of the Model.** The details of the model are described in two HP white papers (HP, July 2003 and HP, May 2004). The key points are:

- IT is the facilitator of the adaptive enterprise.
- It is necessary to measure, in very specific terms, how well the IT infrastructure will respond to business and environmental changes. This is done by a methodology developed with INSEAD (a leading international business school) that measures the *time* needed to adapt to a change, the *range* of implementation across the enterprise, and the degree of *relief* (the *breadth* and *scope* that the IT support can provide).
- Simplification of the IT support systems. They must be easy to adapt, use, connect, manage, and modify—all at a reasonable cost.
- Standardization of the supportive IT infrastructure.
- Modularity of the system, which will help change the existing IT systems quickly and inexpensively (e.g., see Web Services in Chapters 2 and 15).
- Integration of IT parts must be easy, rapid, and inexpensive.
- A collaborative approach of all people, including business partners.
- Improving the business processes with proper methodologies.

Some of these requirements utilize the emerging concepts of software-as-a-service, described in Chapters 2 and 15.

The anticipated benefits of the adaptive enterprise are:

- **Increased business agility.** With an adaptive IT infrastructure, organizations are able to identify and quickly respond to challenges and opportunities, and to adapt to changing business models, processes, and market demands, helping them to outperform and assert change on the competition quickly.
- **Reduced risk.** By simplifying and streamlining the technology environment, an adaptive infrastructure enables a more successful deployment of new solutions and supports business changes—more responsively, with less risk.
- **Improved quality of service.** An adaptive infrastructure enables organizations to establish and meet increasingly aggressive service requirements, assuring appropriate levels of availability, response time, and performance.
- **Improved total cost of ownership.** An adaptive infrastructure optimizes IT resources, reduces the cost of infrastructure management, and enables more choices that can lower cost of ownership.

To learn more about the adaptive enterprise, see large enterprise business solutions at *hp.com.* One of the major requirements of an adaptive enterprise is its ability to operate in a real-time, on-demand mode.

One of the major characteristics of the digital economy is that the speed of events is rapidly increasing. If you buy stocks or order airline tickets online, you get your confirmation in a second. Organizations need to know what is going on as close to real-time as possible. What companies need are *real-time systems*. A **real-time system** is an information system that provides real-time access to information or data. Such a system is a must in critical missions and tasks. In Minicase 2 we provide an example of a digital hospital. When a patient is admitted to the hospital, his or her medical records must be accessible in seconds. The longer the wait, the higher the risk. The same is true for the enterprise (see Hugos, 2004). According to Fingar and Bellini (2004), the real-time enterprise is a necessity since the basis of competition is often time (or speed). Web-based systems (such as tracking stocks online) provide us with these capabilities. Real-time systems allow us to accomplish things that were not possible before. Some examples are:

- Salespeople can check to see whether a product is in inventory by looking directly into the inventory system.
- Suppliers can ensure adequate supplies by looking directly into the forecasting and inventory systems.
- An online order payment by credit card is automatically checked for the balance and the amount of the purchase is debited all in one second.

To implement the real-time enterprise, companies must design information systems that can support all the relevant business processes, are tightly integrated are available at all times, and if necessary, function in multiple languages and currencies. Finally, business processes must be automated as much as possible.

The real-time enterprise is also referred to as on-demand enterprise. Such an enterprise must be able to fulfill orders as soon as they are needed (see Chapters 2 and 9). The proper use of IT infrastructure and applications is essential; otherwise failures are likely to occur.

So far we have introduced you to many success stories. You may wonder, though, is IT always successful? The answer is, "Absolutely not." There are many failures. We will show you some of these (marked with a "lessons from failures" icon) in this book, and in some cases we present them on our Web site. We can learn from failures as much as we can learn from successes, as illustrated in *IT at Work 1.2* (page 21).

One area of IT failure is that of the dot-coms. As will be seen in Chapter 5, hundreds of dot-coms folded in 2000 and 2001. It was a shakeout that resulted from a rush to capitalize on e-commerce (see Abramson, 2005). In addition there were many failures of Internet projects in established companies. (For example, the Go.com project of Walt Disney Company was supposed to manage all the Web sites owned by Disney and generate money from advertisers at the sites. Unfortunately, the income generated from advertising was not sufficient to keep the site going.) Like the gold rush and the rush to create companies when the automobile was invented, only a relatively few made it. The rest failed. According to Carrie (2004), the reason for EC failures is that many of the business models used were too narrow. In place of these models, he offers e-business value models.

Another reason for failure is that it is hard to predict the future. It is especially hard to predict the future in the field of information technology, which is evolving and continuously changing.

Use of this icon indicates a description of an IT failure, and discussion of the lessons that can be learned from it.

# IT at Work 1.2

## Failures at Nike and AT&T

In certain retail stores, fans of Nike's Air Terra Humara 2 running shoe hit the jackpot. Once selling for over $100 US, they were selling for less than $50 in fall 2001. The cheaper shoes were the aftermath of the breakdown in Nike's supply chain, a breakdown attributed to a software problem.

Nike had installed a $400 million supply chain system in early 2001. The system was supposed to forecast sales demand and plan supplies of raw materials and finished products accordingly. However, the newly deployed demand and supply planning application apparently overestimated the demand for certain shoes in some locations and underestimated demand in others. As a result, some raw materials were overpurchased, while inventory levels of other materials were insufficient. Some shoes were overmanufactured, while the most-demanded ones were undermanufactured. To speed the right shoes to market, Nike had to spend around $5 a pair in air freight cost, compared to the usual cost of 75 cents by ocean shipping. In all, Nike attributed some $100 million in lost sales in the third quarter of 2001 alone to this problem.

What went wrong? The system was developed with software from i2, a major supply chain management software producer. However, Nike insisted on modifying the i2 standard software, customizing it to its needs. Specifically, Nike wanted a forecast by style, by color, and by size in order to make thousands of forecasts, very rapidly, to quickly respond to changing market conditions and consumer preferences. To meet Nike's need it was necessary to customize the standard software, and to do so quickly because Nike wanted the system fast. The reprogramming was apparently done *too* fast. The

software had bugs in it when it was deployed. Almost any new software contains bugs that need to be fixed; appropriate testing is critical, and it is a time-consuming task.

Customizing standard software requires a step-by-step systematic process (see Technology Guide 6). It should be done only when it is absolutely necessary, and it must be planned for properly (see Chapter 15).

Nike fixed the problem after spending an undisclosed amount of time and money in 2002. Nike is not the only major corporation that suffered an IT failure. Hundreds of documented cases exist; the giant AT&T is an example.

A CRM system at AT&T Wireless that was upgraded in 2003 to improve customer care crashed during the upgrade. As a result, customer service representatives could not set up or access new accounts. The system breakdowns, which continued through February 2004, swamped other AT&T systems and gridlocked the customer service phone system. Thousands of furious customers moved to competitors, costing AT&T Wireless an estimated $100 million in lost revenue, and hastened its sale to Cingular for only $15/share—about half the value AT&T Wireless' shares were when it went public in April 2000 (see details at Koch, 2004).

*Sources:* Compiled from Sterlicchi and Wales (2001), from *nike.com* press releases (2002, 2003), and Koch (2004).

*For Further Exploration:* Why did Nike need the detailed forecasting? How can a company determine if it really needs to customize software? Whose responsibility is it to test and deploy the software: the software vendor's or the user's?

# 1.5 Information Technology Developments and Trends

In the previous sections, we described the role of IT in supporting business activities. We also pointed out (in Table 1.2, page 7) some of the capabilities that enable IT to play a support role. Next we will describe some of IT's developments and trends.

First imagine this scenario: It's a Monday morning in the year 2010. Executive Joanne Smith gets into her car, and her voice activates a wireless telecommunications-access workstation. She requests that all open and pending voice and mail messages, as well as her schedule for the day, be transmitted to her car. The office workstation consolidates these items from home and office databases. The message-ordering "knowbot" (knowledge robot), which is an enhanced e-mail messaging system, delivers the accumulated messages (in the order she prefers) to the voice and data wireless device in Joanne's car. By the time Joanne gets to the office, she has heard the necessary messages, sent some replies, revised her day's schedule, and completed a to-do list for the week, all of which have been filed in her virtual database by her personal organizer knowbot. She has also accessed the Internet by voice and checked the traffic conditions, stock prices, and top news stories.

The virtual organizer and the company intranet have made Joanne's use of IT much easier. No longer does she have to be concerned about the physical location of data. She is working on a large proposal for the Acme Corporation today; and although segments of the Acme file physically exist on several databases, she can access the data from her *wireless workstation* wherever she happens to be. To help manage this information resource, Joanne uses an *information visualizer* that enables her to create and manage dynamic relationships among data collections. This information visualizer has extended the graphical user interface to a three-dimensional graphic structure.

Joanne could do even more work if her car were able to drive itself and if it were able to find an empty parking space on its own. Although this kind of car is still in an experimental stage, it will probably be in commercial use before 2015 due to developments in pervasive computing (see Chapter 6).

It may be possible for parts of this year-2010 scenario to become a reality even sooner, owing to important trends in information technology. For example, voice access to the Internet is already becoming popular (e.g., see *tellme.com* and *bevocal.com*). These trends, which are listed in Table 1.4 (page 23), fall into two categories: general and networked computing. Others are described in Chapter 2 and in the Technology Guides on the book's Web site. A description of some of the trends is provided in Online File W1.10. Of the various topics in Table 1.4, we elect to discuss mobility here.

*Six Technology Guides at the book's Web site provide up-to-date presentations on hardware, software, databases, telecommunications, the Internet, and a technical view of systems analysis.*

## THE MOBILITY REVOLUTION

Around the world, enterprises are adopting mobile computing technologies at a tremendous rate. They are using wireless hardware and applications to compute anywhere. The productivity gains available with mobile technology continue to expand as the price of the technology drops. And in the case of mobility, the technology actually revolutionizes the way that people work.

Organizations are embracing mobile computing technologies for several reasons:

- Field service workers of all kinds need to be more productive.
- Wireless telecom support for mobility is growing quickly.
- More applications can run both online and offline.
- The prices of notebook computers, wireless handhelds, and smart phones continue to fall and their capabilities increase.

While mobility makes employees in all types of jobs more productive, one of the biggest areas of opportunity lies with field service personnel. There are an estimated 350 million field service workers around the world carrying clipboards and notepads. Only about 30 percent of these workers are computerized. Therefore, the potential for improvement is huge. (See Online File W1.11.)

**Example.** BNSF Railway Co., which operates one of the largest railroad networks in North America, gave key field maintenance workers notebooks with Intel Centrino mobile technology and equipped them with engineering applications to manage and track repairs, access electronic work orders and technical manuals, submit reports, and plan maintenance activities. In the past, engineers could handle these tasks only by driving back and forth to the regional office, which could be many miles away from the day's work site.

| TABLE 1.4 | Major Technological Developments and Trends |
|-----------|---------------------------------------------|

**General Developments and Trends**

- The cost-performance advantage of computers over manual labor will increase.
- Graphical and other user-friendly interfaces will dominate PCs.
- Storage capacity will increase dramatically.
- Data warehouses will store ever-increasing amounts of information.
- Multimedia use, including virtual reality, will increase significantly.
- Intelligent systems, especially artificial neural computing and expert systems, will increase in importance and be embedded in other systems.
- The use of intelligent agents will make computers "smarter."
- There is a push for open architecture (e.g., the use of Web Services and Linux).
- Object-oriented programming and document management will be widely accepted.
- Artificial intelligence systems are moving to learning-management systems.
- Computers will be increasingly compact and more portable.
- Limited capability computers are available for less than $100.
- There is proliferation of embedded technologies (especially intelligent ones).
- The use of plug-and-play software will increase (software-as-a-service, utility computing).

**Networked Computing Developments and Trends**

- Optical computing will increase network capacity and speed, facilitating the use of the home Internet.
- Storage networks will become popular.
- Mobile and wireless applications will become a major component of IT.
- Home computing will be integrated with the telephone, television, and other electronic services to create smart home appliances.
- The use of the Internet will grow, and it will change the way we live, work, and learn.
- Corporate portals will connect companies with their employees, business partners, and the public.
- Intranets will be the dominating network systems in most organizations.
- E-commerce over the Internet will grow rapidly, changing the manner in which business is conducted.
- Intelligent software agents will roam through databases and networks, conducting time-consuming tasks for their masters.
- Interpersonal transmission will grow (one-to-one, one-to-many, many-to-many).
- More transactions among organizations will be conducted electronically, in what is called business-to-business (B2B) commerce.
- Networks and intelligent systems will be major contributors toward improved national security and counterterrorism efforts.
- RFID (radio frequency identification) will change supply chains and retailing.

With the new mobile technology, field service workers can now access BNSF's maintenance and engineering systems from anywhere in their field territory. They can file reports, monitor maintenance activities, and better identify and resolve problems. All of this results in smoother, more efficient railroad operations.

**ILLUSTRATIVE EXAMPLES OF THE USEFULNESS OF EMERGING IT TECHNOLOGIES**

The following are examples of the potential usefulness of the emerging technologies:

1. Pervasive Computing at Royal Mile Pub (*IT at Work 1.3*)
2. The Digital University (Minicase #1)
3. The Digital Hospital (Minicase #2)

Five additional examples organized by functional areas are provided in Chapter 2.

# IT at Work 1.3

## Pervasive Computing at Royal Mile Pub

POM

All of us are familiar with the service at restaurants, and most of us have encountered inconvenient scenarios such as long waits, cold food, or even service of a wrong order. These inconveniences are the result of a conventional process that works like this: A server takes your drink order and then walks to the bar to place the order. She or he knows that after approximately five minutes your drink will be ready, so in the meantime the server takes an order from someone else and then heads back to the bar. If your order is not ready, the server comes to your table, apologizes for the delay, and takes your food order. That order is written on a piece of paper, which the server carries to the kitchen and places on a revolving wheel, which the chef rotates into view when he or she is ready to begin preparing the next order. At that point, the server may find that the kitchen is out of this selection, so he or she comes to your table and asks you to reorder. Sometimes, the server makes a mistake in writing your order, or the chef reads the handwritten order incorrectly. In such a case, after a long wait, the customer is frustrated at getting the wrong food.

The situation is different at Royal Mile Pub (Silver Springs, Maryland), thanks to pervasive computing. The Royal Mile is a medium-size restaurant (about 20 tables), with a bar that specializes in a wide selection of beverages. But what is really different about the Royal Mile is that the servers' green order pads have been replaced with iPaq PDAs connected to the kitchen using wireless networking.

The new system works as follows: The server uses a special PDA to take the orders. Most menu items are visible on the PDA, which also has handwriting capabilities for writing in special instructions. To take drink or food orders requires only one or two keystrokes. The server glances at the screen to verify that the correct item has appeared. Experienced servers can be trained in about 15 minutes on how to use the devices.

The Wi-Fi (wireless fidelity) system, which is a local area network, transmits the orders within the range of the restaurant (described further in Chapter 6). The orders appear immediately on screens in the kitchen and bar. After transmitting an order, the server can move to the next table rather than hurrying off to hand the orders to the cooks or bartenders.

The system is liked by all. Servers can spend more time with each customer and handle more tables because they make half as many trips out of the serving area. The PDA interface tells servers which menu items are unavailable; getting that information immediately to the customers reduces servers' trips to the kitchen, thus eliminating another source of customer and server dissatisfaction. Because the kitchen becomes aware of orders immediately, the food arrives more quickly. The system also totals each bill, eliminating arithmetic errors.

The owner is very positive about the system's effects on his business. The order system costs about $30,000 to install. Its benefits include fewer errors, better inventory control, and smaller payrolls. As orders transmit, they are processed against the inventory database, allowing kitchen managers to track raw material purchases

PPT 8800 from Symbol Technologies, another type of personal digital assistant, used for the same purpose as an iPaq PDA.

against the food orders and identify waste or other delivery and processing problems. Integration with the enterprise database and inventory control systems is fundamental to realizing cost reductions, improved workflow, and inventory and personnel management. The pervasive order system has reduced the error rate from several wrong meals per night to about one every two nights. Improvements occur not only in wasted (and replacement) meals, but also in customer satisfaction. In addition, now only three food servers are needed, meaning lasting cost reductions and lower overhead. Also, three data-entry stations on the serving floor for processing credit card charges were reduced to one, freeing up space on the serving floor.

*Sources:* Compiled from Stanford (2003), and *royalmilepub.com* (accessed April 2006).

*For Further Exploration:* Why would customers appreciate this pervasive computing system? What strategic advantage is generated? If such a system is beneficial to all, why have not all restaurants adopted it? Why it is classified as pervasive computing?

# 1.6 Why Should You Learn About Information Technology?

In this part of the chapter we describe some specific benefits you can derive from studying IT.

**BENEFITS FROM STUDYING IT**

A major role of IT is being an enabler and *facilitator* of organizational activities, processes, and change for increased performance and competitiveness. That role will become more important as time passes. Therefore, it is necessary that every manager and professional staff member learn about IT not only in his or her specialized field, but also in the entire organization and in interorganizational settings as well.

Obviously, you will be more effective in your chosen career if you understand how successful information systems are built, used, and managed. You also will be more effective if you know how to recognize and avoid unsuccessful systems and failures. Also, in many ways, having a comfort level with information technology will enable you, off the job and in your private life, to take advantage of new IT products and systems as they are developed. (Wouldn't you rather be the one explaining to friends how some new product works, than the one asking about it? For help in that role, by the way, see *howthingswork.com* and *wikipedia.org.*) Finally, you should learn about IT because being knowledgeable about IT can also increase employment opportunities. Even though computerization eliminates some jobs, it also creates many more (Wolff, 2005).

The demand for traditional staff—such as programmers, systems analysts, and designers—is substantial. In addition, many well-paid opportunities are appearing in emerging areas such as the Internet and e-commerce, m-commerce, network security, object-oriented programming, telecommunications, multimedia design, and document management. (See Online File W1.12 at the book's Web site for a listing of jobs in e-commerce.)

A study by Wolff (2005) found that the fastest growing sector in the U.S. economy over the last 50 years is *information workers,* who comprised 59 percent of the total U.S. workforce in 2000.

According to a study by the U.S. Bureau of Labor Statistics, each of the top seven fastest-growing occupations projected through 2010 fall within an IT- or computer-related field. These top seven occupations are (Pollock, 2003):

1. Computer software applications engineers
2. Computer support specialists
3. Computer software systems engineers
4. Network and computer systems administrators
5. Network systems and data communications analysts
6. Desktop publishers
7. Database administrators

Based on job available ads, Prabhakar et al. (2005) found that most available IT positions are in the areas of Web programming and related programming languages such as XML. *Business 2.0* (May 2006) predicted that five out of the 10 fastest growing jobs between 2006 and 2014 will be in IT.

At about $65,000 per year, workers in the software and information services industries were the highest-paid U.S. wage earners in 2006, about twice that of the average worker in the private sector. Furthermore, earnings of IT employees were growing twice as fast as those in the entire private sector. Thus, salaries for IT employees are generally high.

To exploit the high-paying opportunities in IT, a college degree in any of the following fields, or combination of them, is advisable: computer science, computer information systems (CIS), management information systems (MIS), electronic commerce, and e-business. Within the last few years, many universities have started e-commerce or e-business degrees (e.g., see *is.cityu.edu.hk* and *cgu.edu*). Many schools offer graduate degrees with specialization in information technology.

Majoring in an IT-related field can be very rewarding. For example, students graduating with baccalaureate degrees in MIS usually earn the highest starting salaries of all undergraduate business majors (more than $48,000 per year). MBAs with experience in Web technologies and e-commerce are getting starting salaries of over $100,000/year, plus bonuses. Many students prefer a double major, one of which is MIS. Similarly, MBAs with an undergraduate degree in computer science have little difficulty getting well-paying jobs, even during recessionary times. Many MBA students select IS as a major, a second major, or an area of specialization. In addition, nondegree programs are also available on hundreds of topics. For details about careers in IT, see *uniXL.com* and also "Career resources" and "Technology careers" at *wageweb.com*.

Finally, another benefit from studying IT is that it may contribute to future organizational leadership. In the past, most CEOs came from the areas of finance and marketing. Lately, however, we see a trend to appoint CEOs who have strong IT knowledge and who have emerged from the technology area.

## 1.7 Plan of the Book

A major objective of this book is to demonstrate how IT in general and Web systems in particular support different organizational activities. In addition, we will illustrate the role that networked computing plays in our society today and will play tomorrow. Furthermore, we describe how information systems should be developed, maintained, and managed.

The book is divided into seven parts. Figure 1.6 (page 27) shows how the chapters are positioned in each part and how the parts are connected. Notice that in the center of the figure are the six Technology Guides. These guides can be found on the book's Web site (*wiley.com/college/turban*).

## 1.8 Managerial Issues

At the end of every chapter, you will find a list of some of the special concerns managers face as they adapt technology to their organization's needs.

**1. Recognizing opportunities for using IT and Web-based systems for strategic advantage.** These opportunities are highlighted and discussed in most chapters of the book, but especially in Chapters 4–8 and 14.

**2. Who will build, operate, and maintain the information systems?** This is a critical issue because management wants to minimize the cost of IT while maximizing its benefits. Some alternatives are to outsource portions, or even all, of the IT activities, and to divide the remaining work between the IS department and the end users. Details are provided in Chapters 14 through 16 and in Technology Guide 6.

**3. How much IT?** This is a critical issue related to IT planning. IT does not come free, but *not* having it may be much costlier. Chapters 12 and 13 deal with this issue.

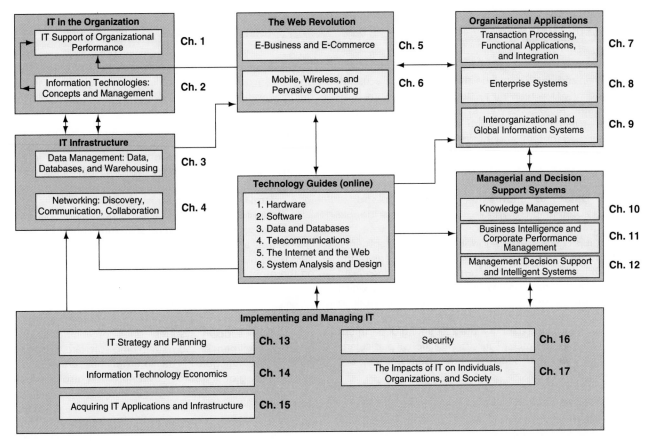

**Figure 1.6** Plan of the book.

**4. How important is IT?** In some cases, IT is the only approach that can help organizations. As time passes, the *comparative advantage* of IT increases.

**5. Is the situation going to change?** Yes, the pressures will be stronger as time passes. Therefore, the IT role will be even more important.

**GLOBAL**

**6. Globalization.** Global competition will have an impact on many companies. However, globalization opens many opportunities, ranging from selling and buying products and services online in foreign markets, to conducting joint ventures or investing in them. IT supports communications, collaboration, and discovery of information regarding all the above (Chapter 9).

**ETHICS**

**7. Ethics and social issues.** The implementation of IT involves many ethical and social issues that are constantly changing due to new developments in technologies and environments. These topics should be examined any time an IT project is undertaken. Online File W1.5 at the book's Web site presents an introduction to ethics. Ethical issues are highlighted in most chapters throughout the book.

**8. Transforming the organization to the digital economy.** The transformation can be done on several fronts, as Siemens AG (Online File W1.1) did. Management should study the opportunities, consider alternatives, and prioritize them. Large companies may consider proprietary services from companies such as HP.

# Integrating *IT*

Now that you have a sense of how this book is structured and organized, we'll conclude the chapter by discussing how and why IT is relevant to students with various business-related majors. As you review this section, keep in mind that technology is playing an increasingly vital role in every department and business process of modern organizations.

### For the Accounting Major

Data and information are the lifeblood of accounting. Therefore, many students double major in accounting/information systems. For those that do not, it is critical to keep up with new IT developments. Both groups, however, need to know the IT needs of the other functional areas. The Internet has vastly increased the number of transactions (especially global) in which modern businesses engage. Transactions such as billing customers, preparing payrolls, and purchasing and paying for materials provide data that the accounting department must record and track. These transactions, particularly with customers and suppliers, now usually take place online.

### For the Finance Major

The modern financial world turns on speed, volume, and accuracy of information flow. Information systems and networks make these things possible. You invest in stocks and get a confirmation in less than a second. Finance departments use information systems such as business intelligence to monitor world financial markets and to provide quantitative analyses (e.g., for cash flow projections and budgetary control). They use computerized analysis to support financial decision making (e.g., portfolio management). Financial managers use data mining software to analyze information in data warehouses. Finally, large-scale enterprise information systems (e.g., enterprise resource planning packages) tightly integrate finance with all other functional areas.

### For the Human Resources Management Major

Information systems provide valuable support for human resources management. For example, personnel record keeping has greatly improved in terms of speed, convenience, and accuracy as a result of technology. Further, disseminating HR information throughout the company via intranets enables employees to receive consistent information and handle much of their personal business (e.g., configuring their benefits) without help from HR personnel. The Internet revolutionized recruiting and training, moving them online; better selection can be made as well as personal development.

### For the IS Major

The Information Systems Department (ISD) directly supports all other functional areas in an organization. The overall objective of IS personnel is to help users increase performance and solve business problems using IT. The IS function is rapidly changing its role from computer programming to a major strategic player.

While some IS employees still write computer programs, they also act as analysts, interfacing between business users on one hand and the programmers or vendors on the other.

### For the Marketing Major

Marketing now uses customer databases, decision support systems, sales force automation, business intelligence, and data mining software to better perform its functions. The Internet has created an entirely new global trading environment. It also has dramatically increased the amount of information available to buyers and sellers, who can now compare prices quickly and thoroughly. As a result, shoppers' buying habits and strategies are changing. In turn, marketing managers must work harder to acquire and retain the well-informed customers. To accomplish this goal they now use customer relationship management software and special online promotions. The Internet helps here, because it provides for much closer contact between the customer and the supplier, as well as one-to-one seller/buyer relationship.

### For the Production/Operations Management Major

Organizations are competing on price, quality, time (speed), and customer service—all of which are concerns of productions and operations management. Every process in a company's operations that adds value to a product or service (e.g., purchasing inventory, quality control, receiving raw materials, and shipping products) can be enhanced by the use of Web-based information systems. Production is changing from mass production to on-demand mass customization. Further, information systems have enabled the POM function to link the organization to other organizations along the firm's supply chain. Performance in manufacturing can be significantly increased with IT support.

## Key Terms

Adaptive enterprise  *18*
Business model  *10*
Computer-based information system
 (CBIS)  *16*

Critical response activities  *11*
Digital economy  *4*
Digital enterprise (organization)  *3*
Ethics  *12*

Information system  *16*
Information technology (IT)  *7*
Networked computing  *7*
Real-time system  *20*

## Chapter Highlights

Numbers Refer to Learning Objectives

❶ The world is moving to a digital economy, which can be viewed as a major economic, societal, and organizational revolution. This revolution automates business processes by using the Internet, intranets, VANs, and extranets to connect organizations and people.

❶ The digital economy is characterized by extensive use of information technology in general and the Internet in particular. These drive new business models that dramatically reduce cost and increase quality, customer service, and speed.

❶ Companies are trying to transform themselves to e-businesses by converting their information systems to Web-based and by automating as many business processes as possible.

❷ Many market, technology, and societal pressures surround the modern organization, which is responding with critical response activities supported by information technology.

❸ An accelerated rate of technological change, complexity, and turbulence and a move toward a global economy today characterize the business environment. In addition, the competition faced by businesses is ever increasing.

❸ Organizational responses include strategic information systems, continuous improvements, business process restruc-

turing, electronic commerce, and business alliances. IT plays a major role in all of these.

❸ Organizations are adopting a customer-focused approach in order to succeed.

❸ Organizations are changing their mode of operation by using IT-supported innovative approaches such as e-commerce, mass customization, CRM, and business alliances.

❹ An information system collects, processes, stores, and disseminates information for a specific purpose. A computer-based information system uses computers to perform some or all of these activities.

❹ Information technology refers to the network of all information systems in an organization.

❺ To succeed or even survive, organizations must be able to adapt to quick and frequent changes. IT enables organizations to become adaptive.

❻ Information technology is a major agent of change, supporting critical response activities in all functional areas, in all industries, and in both the private and the public sectors.

❼ Learning about IT is essential because the role of IT is rapidly increasing in the support of organizations. We are getting more dependent on IT as time passes. Also, more IT-related jobs with high salaries are available.

## Virtual Company Assignment

### Starting Your Internship at The Wireless Café

Go to The Wireless Café's link on the Student Web Site. There you will find a description of your internship at this restaurant, as well some assignments that will help you learn more about how IT solutions could help the restaurant improve its business.

*Instructions for accessing The Wireless Café on the Student Web Site:*

1. Go to *wiley.com/college/turban*.
2. Select Turban/Leidner/McLean/Wetherbe's *Information Technology for Management*, Sixth Edition.
3. Click on Student Resources site, in the toolbar on the left.
4. Click on the link for Virtual Company Web site.
5. Click on Wireless Café.

## Online Resources

More resources and study tools are located on the Student Web Site and on WileyPLUS. You'll find additional chapter materials and useful Web links. In addition, self-quizzes that provide individualized feedback are available for each chapter.

## Questions for Review

1. Define an information system and list its major components.

2. Define digital economy and list its major characteristics.

3. Define a digital organization.

4. List the major components in the business environment impact model (Figure 1.3).

5. Define a business model by giving an example of one.

6. What are the major pressures in the business environment (by major categories)? See Figure 1.4.

7. List the major critical response activities used by organizations. (See Table 1.3.)

8. Define information technology (IT) and information systems.

9. Define an adaptive enterprise.

10. List the steps in the process of becoming an adaptive enterprise.

11. Explain the benefits of agility.

12. Define mobile computing and m-commerce.

13. List the major capabilities of IT.

14. List representative general technological developments.

15. List representative networked computing developments.

16. List some reasons for learning about IT.

17. Define the real-time enterprise and list its characteristics.

18. Describe mass customization (see Appendix 1A).

## Questions for Discussion

1. Discuss the motivation for becoming an e-business.

2. Review the examples of the new versus the old economy cases. In what way did IT make the difference?

3. Explain why IT is a business pressure and also an enabler of response activities that counter business pressures.

4. Why are there more opportunities for entrepreneurs in the digital economy?

5. Why is wireless mobility perceived as being able to increase EC applications?

6. It is said that networked computing and the Web change the way we live, work, and study. Why?

7. Explain the sequence of events in the business environment model (Figure 1.2).

8. Discuss the difference between computers and information systems.

9. Discuss the relationship between a digital enterprise and an e-business company.

10. Why is the Internet said to be the creator of new business models?

11. Discuss why some information systems fail.

12. Discuss the major concepts in HP's adaptive enterprise model.

13. Discuss why a digital enterprise is not necessarily an adaptive enterprise.

14. Explain why every adaptive enterprise is digital, but not every digital enterprise is adaptive.

15. Relate the real-time enterprise to the adaptive enterprise.

## Exercises and Projects

1. Review the examples of IT applications in Section 1.3, and identify the business pressures in each example. Also identify the business models used.

2. The market for optical copiers is shrinking rapidly. It is expected that by 2008 as much as 90 percent of all duplicated documents will be done on computer

printers. Can a company such as Xerox Corporation survive?

**a.** Read about the problems and solution of Xerox in 2000–2003 at *fortune.com, findarticles.com,* and *google.com.*

**b.** Identify all the business pressures on Xerox.

**c.** Find some of Xerox's response strategies (see *xerox.com, yahoo.com,* and *google.com*).

**d.** Identify the role of IT as a contributor to the business technology pressures (e.g., obsolescence).

**e.** Identify the role of IT as a facilitator of the critical response activities.

**3.** Reread the Intel case at the start of the chapter and prepare a presentation to the CEO of the competing company (AMD). Stress both the benefits and the cost and limitations of being an adaptive enterprise.

## Group Assignments and Projects

**1.** Create an online group for studying IT or a part of it you are interested in. Each member of the group must have a Yahoo e-mail account (free). Go to Yahoo: Groups (groups.yahoo.com) and at the bottom see a section titled "Create your own Group."

**Step 1:** Click on "Start a Group Now."

**Step 2:** Select a category that best describes your group (use the Search Group Categories, or use Browse Group Categories tool). You *must* find a category.

**Step 3:** Describe the purposes of the group and give it a name.

**Step 4:** Set up an e-mail address for sending messages to all group members.

**Step 5:** Each member must join the group (select a "profile"); click on "Join this Group."

**Step 6:** Go to Word Verification Section; follow instructions.

**Step 7:** Finish by clicking "Continue."

**Step 8:** Select a group moderator. Conduct a discussion online of at least two topics of the group's interest.

**Step 9:** Arrange for messages from the members to reach the moderator at least once a week.

**Step 10:** Find a similar group (use Yahoo's "find a group" and make a connection). Write a report for your instructor.

**2.** Conduct an investigation of how a barcode works when you pay for an item in a retail store. Enter a supermarket or a retail store and ask the manager what they do with the information collected by barcode readers. Prepare a diagram that shows the flow of information.

Which of the functional departments are involved? Find out the potential problems of using barcodes in the store as well as in the warehouses and factory environment.

**a.** It is suggested that customers will check themselves out at retail stores by using the barcode reader. Find stores (e.g., Home Depot, K-Mart) that already use the method. Observe how this is done. What problems can you envision? What are the benefits to the customer, and to the store owners?

**b.** One day stores will use RFID tags, both for self-checkout and for merchandise control. Find information about how this will work with self-checkout. List the benefits and limitations as compared with conventional checkout and to the self-service of part (a).

**c.** Compare the barcode against RFID.

**3.** Review the *Wall Street Journal, Fortune, Business Week,* and local newspapers of the last three months to find stories about the use of Web-based technologies in organizations. Each group will prepare a report describing five applications. The reports should emphasize the role of the Web and its benefit to the organizations. Cover issues discussed in this chapter, such as productivity, quality, cycle time, and globalization. One of the groups should concentrate on m-commerce and another on electronic marketplaces. Present and discuss your work.

**4.** Identify Web-related new business models in the areas of the group's interests. Identify radical changes in the operation of the functional areas (accounting, finance, marketing, etc.), and tell the others about them.

## Internet Exercises

**1.** Enter the Web site of UPS (*ups.com*).

**a.** Find out what information is available to customers before they send a package.

**b.** Find out about the "package tracking" system; be specific.

**c.** Compute the cost of delivering a $10'' \times 20'' \times 15''$ box, weighing 40 pounds, from your hometown to Long

Beach, California. Compare the fastest delivery against the least cost.

**d.** Prepare a spreadsheet for two different types of calculations available on the site. Enter data and solve for two different calculators.

**2.** Enter *digitalenterprise.org.* Prepare a report regarding the latest EC developments in the digital age.

3. Visit some Web sites that offer employment opportunities in IT (such as *execunet.com* and *monster.com*). Compare the IT salaries to salaries offered to accountants. For other information on IT salaries, check *Computerworld's* annual salary survey and *UniXL.com*.

4. Prepare a short report on the role of information technology in government. Start with *whitehouse.gov/ omb/egov/ctg.albany.edu*, *e-government.govt.nz*, and *worldbank.org/publicsector/egov*. Find e-government plans in Hong Kong and in Singapore (*cca.gov.sg*; check action plan).

5. Enter *hp.com/adapt* and find out what IT solutions are offered to enable the adaptive enterprise. Write a summary.

6. Enter *x-home.com* and find information about the easy life of the future.

7. Enter *tellme.com* and *bevocal.com*. Observe the demos. Write a report on the benefits of such technologies.

8. Enter *dell.com* and configure the computer of your dreams. (You do not have to buy it.) What are the advantages of such configuration? Any disadvantages?

## Minicase 1

### Dartmouth College Goes Wireless

**SVC**

Dartmouth College, one of the oldest in the United States (founded in 1769), was one of the first to embrace the wireless revolution. Operating and maintaining a campuswide information system with wires is very difficult, since there are 161 buildings with more than 1,000 rooms on campus. In 2000, the college introduced a campuswide wireless network that includes more than 500 Wi-Fi (wireless fidelity; see Chapter 6) systems. By the end of 2002, the entire campus became a fully wireless, always-connected community—a microcosm that provides a peek at what neighborhood and organizational life may look like for the general population in just a few years.

To transform a wired campus to a wireless one requires lots of money. A computer science professor who initiated the idea at Dartmouth in 1999 decided to solicit the help of alumni working at Cisco Systems. These alumni arranged for a donation of the initial system, and Cisco then provided more equipment at a discount. (Cisco and other companies now make similar donations to many colleges and universities, writing off the difference between the retail and the discount prices for an income tax benefit.)

As a pioneer in campuswide wireless, Dartmouth has made many innovative usages of the system, some of which are the following:

- Students are continuously developing new applications for the Wi-Fi. For example, one student has applied for a patent on a personal-security device that pinpoints the location of campus emergency services to one's mobile device.

- Students no longer have to remember campus phone numbers, as their mobile devices have all the numbers and can be accessed anywhere on campus.

- Students primarily use laptop computers on the network. However, an increasing number of Internet-enabled PDAs and cell phones are used as well. The use of regular cell phones is on the decline on campus.

- An extensive messaging system is used by the students, who send SMSs (Short Message Services) to each other. Messages reach the recipients in a split second, any time, anywhere, as long as they are sent and received within the network's coverage area.

- Usage of the Wi-Fi system is not confined just to messages. Students can submit their classwork by using the network, as well as by watching streaming video and listening to Internet radio.

- An analysis of wireless traffic on campus showed how the new network is changing and shaping campus behavior patterns. For example, students log on in short bursts, about 16 minutes at a time, probably checking their messages. They tend to plant themselves in a few favorite spots (dorms, TV room, student center, and on a shaded bench on the green) where they use their computers, and they rarely connect beyond those places.

- Some students invented special complex wireless games that they play online.

- One student has written a code that calculates how far away a networked PDA user is from his or her next appointment, and then automatically adjusts the PDA's reminder alarm schedule accordingly.

- Professors are using wireless-based teaching methods. For example, students can evaluate material presented in class and can vote online on a multiple-choice questionnaire relating to the presented material. Tabulated results are shown in seconds, promoting discussions. According to faculty, the system "makes students want to give answers," thus significantly increasing participation.

- Faculty and students developed a special voice-over-IP application for PDAs and iPAQs that uses live two-way voice-over-IP chat.

*Sources:* Compiled from McHugh (2002), Hafner (2003), and *dartmouth.edu* (April 2006).

## Questions for Minicase 1

1. In what ways is the Wi-Fi technology changing the life of Dartmouth students? Relate your answer to the concept of the digital society.

2. Some say that the wireless system will become part of the background of everybody's life—that the mobile devices are just an afterthought. Explain.

3. Is the system contributing to improved learning, or just adding entertainment that may reduce the time available for studying? Debate your point of view with students who hold a different opinion.

4. What are the major benefits of the wireless system over the previous wireline one? Do you think wireline systems will disappear from campuses one day? (Do some research on the topic.)

# Minicase 2

## A Digital Hospital Increases Performance and Saves Lives

SVC

America's largest industry, health care, is struggling to contain cost and improve quality. Thousands of facilities, private and public, attempt to do it. Not all are as successful as Indiana Heart.

### The Problem

Heart disease is the number-one killer in the United States, and in a cardiac crisis each minute matters. Indiana Heart Hospital (IHH) is a new cardiac digital hospital that wants to save lives by radically cutting the time it takes to treat a heart attack. In addition, this for-profit hospital must make sufficient profit for its investors. Decisions are being made constantly by physicians, nurses, administrators, and other employees. Some decisions must be made very quickly, so the necessary data and information must be available at the right time and place in seconds. Also, the hospital must be managed efficiently.

### The Solution

IHH is the first wholly *digital hospital* in the United States. At the heart of the hospital information system, there are 18 terabytes (in 2005; today more) of data stored in a network of IBM Shark storage servers. The Shark servers enable the storage of both historical and *real-time* data. When a patient arrives at the hospital, his or her medical records can be on a screen in 15 seconds, so a quick decision can be made on what treatment or tests the patient needs. The results of any new test are immediately added to the patient's medical record. Of the various software used for planning and analysis, especially in the financial area, IHH uses software solutions provided by *mezzia.com*. The software also enables improved collaboration as well as providing support for financial and operational decisions. The data and software tools are accessible to all

authorized staff. All doctors, for example, have pocket-size wireless tablet devices for data access, entry, and communication. The digital systems enable doctors to type in and send orders to the pharmacy or to testing laboratories using electronic templates. All records are digital, including X-ray films.

The hospital communications and collaboration systems (Centricity, from GE Healthcare) eliminate delays in the supply chain. Doctors and other employees can consult each other, make quicker joint decisions, and locate experts quickly when needed (even outside the hospital). Centricity runs across 60 Compaq servers with Window NT and 600 laptops and other devices. Some data can be accessed by touch screens to increase speed. In addition, there is a computer next to each patient room. Medications are tracked by more than 100 wireless barcode scanners.

New devices and technologies are added all the time (e.g., sensors for vital sign monitoring). The inputs from such devices go directly to the patient's electronic chart (near the bed) as well as to the medical records. The electronic chart enables nurses to enter patient status in real-time and also verify the output of the automatic vital signs monitoring. The doctors also enter data into the system when visiting the patients—no more scribbled notes in the hospital.

An example of digital applications is the use of digital pens that overcomes the problem of doctors with poor handwriting (see *logitech.com*).

### The Results

All this enables nurses to stay longer with patients, increasing their safety. The digitization contributes to a 40 percent reduction in stays at the hospital, 75 percent reduction in medical errors, and significant increase in the number of patients treated in the hospital (which helps profitability). Also, all computer transactions create an audit trail that increases accountability. In addition, having more consistent data to analyze promotes best practices that make the hospital more efficient and patients safer and healthier. Finally, the system helps the hospital to comply with government regulations.

*Sources:* Compiled from K. M. Nash, "Real-Time E.R.," *Baseline,* May 4, 2005, *baselinemag.com/article2/0,1397,1812777,00.asp,* (accessed April 2006), and from "Customer Success Story: The Indiana Heart Hospital," May 2005, *mezzia.com/tihh_case_ study.pdf* (accessed April 2006).

## Questions for Minicase 2

1. Why is IHH considered to be a digital enterprise?
2. A major environmental pressure in health care is the Health Insurance Portability and Accountability Act (HIPAA) of 1996 regulatory requirements. In what ways can a digital hospital help with compliance?
3. Relate this case to the concept of digital society.
4. Can you identify any ethical issues related to such a high level of automation? (Consult Online File W1.5 on ethics.)

# References

Abramson, B., *Digital Phoenix: Why the Information Economy Collapsed and It Will Rise Again.* Boston, MA: MIT Press, 2005.

Brynjolfsson, E., and B. Kahin, *Understanding the Digital Economy.* Boston, MA: MIT Press, 2002.

Currie, W., *Value Creation from E-Business Models.* Burlington, MA: Butterworth-Heinemann, 2004.

D'Agostino, D., "A Rock and Hard Place," *CIO Insight,* August 2005.

*Dartmouth.edu* (accessed March 2003).

Davenport, H. T., *Thinking for a Living.* Boston, MA: Harvard Business School Press, 2005.

Davis, J. E., "Toward the Digital Enterprise," white paper, Intel Corporation, 2005, *intel.com/it/digital-enterprise* (accessed April 2006).

Elrad, T., et al., "Aspect-Oriented Programming," Association for Computing Machinery; *Communications of the ACM,* October 2001.

Fingar, P., and J. Bellini, *The Real-Time Enterprise.* Tampa: FL: Meghan Kiffer Press, 2005.

Harrington, R., "The Transformer" (e-mail interview with *Baseline*'s editor-in-chief, J. McCormic), *Baseline,* April 2006.

Heller, R., "Strengths and Weaknesses: Assess the Strengths and Weaknesses of Your Business, as Well as the Opportunities and Threats, with SWOT Analysis," *Thinking Managers,* 2005, *thinkingmanagers. com/management/strengths-weaknesses.php* (accessed April 2006).

Hoffman, D. L., and T. P. Novak, "How to Acquire Customers on the Web," *Harvard Business Review,* May–June 2000.

HP, *Building an Adaptive Enterprise,* white paper, Hewlett Packard, May 2003, *fcw.com/solutions/hp/wp/HP_whitePaper_v19.pdf* (accessed April 2006).

HP, *The HP Vision of the Adaptive Enterprise: Achieving Business Agility,* white paper, Hewlett-Packard 5981-6177EN, July 2003, *h71028. www7.hp.com/enterprise/downloads/ae_business_white_paper_ final0703.pdf* (accessed June 2006).

Huber, G., *The Necessary Nature of Future Firms: Attributes of Survivors in a Changing World.* San Francisco: Sage Publications, 2004.

Hugos, M., *Building the Real-Time Enterprise.* New York: John Wiley & Sons, 2004.

Kirpatrick, D., "Intel Finally Fights Back," CNN.com, April 27, 2006, *money.cnn.com/2006/04/27/technology/fastforward_fortune0427intel/ index.htm* (accessed June 2006).

Koch, C., "Nike Rebounds," *CIO.com,* December 7, 2004, *cio.com. au/index.php/id;1800426724;fp;4;fpid;19* (accessed April 2006).

Lederer, A. L., et al., "Using Web-based Information Systems to Enhance Competitiveness," *Communications of the ACM,* July 1998.

Lumpkin, G. T., and G. G. Dess, "How the Internet Adds Value," *Organizational Dynamics,* April 2004.

Marchetti, A. M., *Beyond SOX Compliance: Effective Enterprise Risk Management.* Hoboken, NJ: John Wiley & Sons, 2005.

McHugh, J., "Unplugged U.," *Wired,* October 2002.

McKay, J., and P. Marshall, *Strategic Management of E-Business.* Milton Old, Australia: John Wiley & Sons, 2004.

Meredith, R., "From Rocks to Riches," *Forbes Global,* September 2, 2002.

*Mezzia.com,* "Customer Success Story: The Indiana Heart Hospital," May 2005, *mezzia.com/tihh_case_study.pdf* (accessed April 2006).

Mowshowitz, A., and M. Turoff, "The Digital Society," *Communications of the ACM,* October 2005, 48(10).

Nash, K. M., "Real-Time E.R.," *Baseline,* May 4, 2005, *baselinemag.com/ article2/0,1397,1812777,00.asp* (accessed April 2006).

*Nike.com* (accessed January 2003).

Pollock, J., "The 7 Fastest Growing Occupations," *encarta.msn.com/encnet/ departments/elearning/?article=7fastestgrowing* (accessed December 20, 2003).

Prabhakar, B., C. Litecky, and K. Arnett, "IT Skills in a Tough Job Market," *Communications of the ACM,* October 2005.

Rothfelder, J., "Better Safe than Sorry: Blue Rhino Corp.," *CIO Insight,* February 2004.

*RoyalMilePub.com* (accessed April 2006).

Stanford V., "Pervasive Computing Puts Food on the Table," *Pervasive Computing,* January 2003.

Sterlicchi, J., and E. Wales, "Custom Chaos: How Nike Just Did It Wrong," *Business Online* (*BolWeb.com*), June 2001.

*Thaigem.com* (accessed April 2006).

Whelan, D., "Only the Paranoid Resurge," *Forbes,* April 10, 2006.

Wilhelm, A. G., *Digital Nation.* Cambridge, MA: MIT Press. 2004.

Wolff, E. N., "The Growth of Information Workers in the U.S. Economy," *Communications of the ACM,* October 2005.

Wreden, N., "Business-Boosting Technologies," *Beyond Computing,* November–December 1997.

Zureik, E., and A. Mowshowitz, "Consumer Power in the Digital Society," *Communications of the ACM,* October 2005.

# Appendix 1A | Porter's Models

Researcher Michael Porter has proposed two models that have become classic ways to study and explain basic business activities—the *competitive forces model* and the *value chain model*. We present an overview of these two models in this appendix, and will refer to these models throughout the book.

## PORTER'S COMPETITIVE FORCES MODEL AND STRATEGIES

The most well-known framework for analyzing competitiveness is Porter's **competitive forces model** (Porter, 1985). It has been used to develop strategies for companies to increase their competitive edge. It also demonstrates how IT can enhance the competitiveness of corporations.

The model recognizes five major forces that could endanger a company's position *in a given industry*. (Other forces, such as those cited in Chapter 1, including the impact of government, affect all companies in the industry and therefore may have less impact on the relative success of a company within its industry.) Although the details of the model differ from one industry to another, its general structure is universal.

The five major forces in an industry can be generalized as follows:

1. The threat of entry of new competitors
2. The bargaining power of suppliers
3. The bargaining power of customers (buyers)
4. The threat of substitute products or services
5. The rivalry among existing firms in the industry

The strength of each force is determined by factors related to the industry's structure. Existing companies in an industry need to protect themselves against the forces, or they can use the forces to improve their position or to challenge the leaders in the industry.

Some have suggested semiradical changes in Porter's model. For example, Harmon et al. (2001) proposed adding a sixth force—bargaining power of employees—to the original five. Another major force is the Internet, which has changed the nature of doing business as well as the nature of competition in many industries.

Porter's model identifies the forces that influence competitive advantage in the marketplace. Of greater interest to most managers is the development of a *strategy* aimed at performing activities differently from a competitor. Porter (1985) proposed three such strategies—cost leadership, differentiation, and niche strategies. Other strategic-management authors have proposed additional strategies (e.g., see Neumann, 1994; Wiseman, 1988; and Frenzel, 1996).

In Table 1A.1 we cite 12 general strategies for competitive advantage. Each of these strategies (and some others) can be enhanced by IT, as will be shown throughout the book and especially in Chapter 12. Forthcoming chapters will show: (1) how different information technologies impact the five forces, and (2) how IT facilitates the 12 strategies.

## PORTER'S VALUE CHAIN MODEL

According to Porter's **value chain model** (Porter, 1985), the activities conducted in any manufacturing organization can be divided into two parts: *primary activities and support activities.*

The **primary activities** are those business activities through which a company produces goods, thus creating value for which customers are willing to pay. Primary activities involve the purchase of materials, the processing of materials into products, and delivery of products to customers. Typically, there are five primary activities:

1. Inbound logistics (inputs)
2. Operations (manufacturing and testing)
3. Outbound logistics (storage and distribution)
4. Marketing and sales
5. Services

The primary activities usually take place in a sequence from 1 to 5. As work progresses according to the sequence, value is added to the product in each activity. To be more specific, the incoming materials (1) are processed (in receiving, storage, etc.) in activities called *inbound logistics*. Next, the materials are used in *operations* (2), where significant value is added by the process of turning raw materials into products. The products need to be prepared for delivery (packaging, storing, and

| TABLE 1A.1 | Twelve Strategies for Competitive Advantage |
|---|---|
| **Strategy** | **Descritpion** |
| Cost leadership | Produce product/service at the lowest cost in the industry. |
| Differentiation | Offer different products, services, or product features. |
| Niche | Select a narrow-scope segment (*market niche*) and be the best in quality, speed, or cost in that segment. |
| Growth | Increase market share, acquire more customers, or sell more types of products. |
| Alliance | Work with business partners in partnerships, alliances, joint ventures, or virtual companies. |
| Innovation | Introduce new products/services; put new features in existing products/services; develop new ways to produce products/services. |
| Operational effectiveness | Improve the manner in which internal business processes are executed so that the firm performs similar activities better than rivals. |
| Customer orientation | Concentrate on customer satisfaction. |
| Time | Treat time as a resource, then manage it and use it to the firm's advantage. |
| Entry barriers | Create barriers to entry. By introducing innovative products or using IT to provide exceptional service, companies can create entry barriers to discourage new entrants. |
| Lock in customers or suppliers | Encourage customers or suppliers to stay with you rather than going to competitors. Locking in customers has the effect of reducing their bargaining power. |
| Increase switching costs | Discourage customers or suppliers from going to competitors for economic reasons. |

shipping) in the *outbound logistics* activities (3). Then *marketing and sales* (4) attempt to sell the products to customers, increasing product value by creating demand for the company's products. (The value of a sold item is much larger than that of an unsold one.) Finally, *after-sales service* (5) such as warranty service or upgrade notification is performed for the customer, further adding value. The goal of these value-adding, primary activities is to make a profit for the company.

Primary activities are sustained and furthered by the following **support activities:**

1. The firm's infrastructure (accounting, finance, management)
2. Human resources management
3. Technology development (R&D)
4. Procurement

Each support activity can be applied to any or all of the primary activities, and the support activities may also support each other (see Figure 1A.1). For an example of Porter's value chain model applied to the airline industry, see Online File W1.13.

A firm's value chain is part of a larger stream of activities, which Porter calls a value system. A **value system** (also called an *industry value chain*) includes the suppliers that provide the inputs necessary to the firm and their value chains. Once the firm creates products, these products pass through the value chains of distributors (which also have their own value chains), all the way to the buyers (customers). All parts of these chains are included in the value system. Gaining and sustaining a competitive advantage, and supporting that advantage by means of IT, requires an understanding of this entire value system.

In forthcoming chapters, we will show how different functional departments relate to Porter's value chain model and how IT impacts the addition of value (and hopefully profit) in companies. For in-depth discussion, see Chapter 13.

**Key Terms for Appendix 1A**

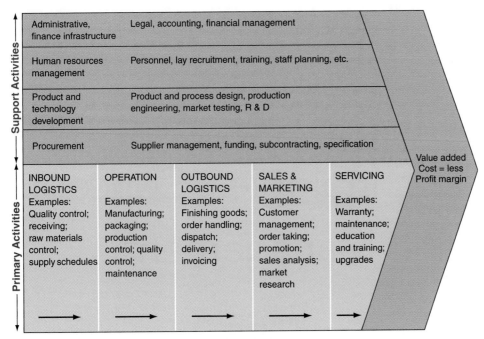

**Figure 1A.1** The firm's value chain. The arrows illustrate the flow of goods and services (the internal part of the supply chain). (*Source:* Drawn by E. Turban.)

### References for Appendix 1A

Frenzel, C. W., *Management of Information Technology,* 2nd ed. Cambridge, MA: Course Technology, 1996.

Harmon, P., et al., *Developing E-Business Systems and Architectures: A Manager's Guide.* San Francisco: Morgan Kaufmann Publishers, 2001.

Neumann, S., *Strategic Information Systems—Competition Through Information Technologies.* New York: Macmillan, 1994.

Porter, M. E., *Competitive Advantage: Creating and Sustaining Superior Performance.* New York: Free Press, 1985.

Wiseman, C., *Strategic Information Systems.* Burr Ridge, IL: Richard D. Irwin, 1988.

## Chapter

# 2

# Information Technologies: Concepts and Management

### Learning Objectives

After studying this chapter, you will be able to:

❶ Define information systems and describe various types of information systems and categorize specific systems you observe.

❷ Describe and contrast transaction processing and functional information systems.

❸ Identify the major enterprise internal support systems and relate them to managerial functions.

❹ Describe the support IT provides along the supply chain in using ERP and CRM.

❺ Discuss information infrastructure and architecture.

❻ Compare client/server architecture, mainframe-based legacy systems, and P2P architecture, and comment on their differences.

❼ Describe the major types of Web-based information systems and understand their functionalities.

❽ Describe software-as-a-service and service-oriented architecture environments.

❾ Describe how information resources are managed and what are the roles of the ISD and end users.

### Integrating *IT*

 **ACC**　 **FIN**　 **MKT**　 **POM**　 **HRM**　 **IS**　 **SVC**

FedEx Corporation was founded in 1973 by entrepreneur Fred Smith. Today, with a fully integrated physical and virtual infrastructure, FedEx's business model supports 24–48-hour package delivery to anywhere in the world. FedEx operates one of the world's busiest data-processing centers, handling over 100 million information requests per day from more than 3,000 databases and more than 500,000 archive files. It operates one of the largest real-time, online client/server networks in the world. The core competencies of FedEx are now in express transportation and in e-solutions.

## The Problem/Opportunity

Initially, FedEx grew out of pressures from mounting inflation and global competition. These pressures gave rise to greater demands on businesses to expedite deliveries at a low cost and to improve customer services. FedEx didn't have a business problem per se but, rather, has endeavored to stay ahead of the competition by looking ahead at every stage for opportunities to meet customers' needs for fast, reliable, and affordable overnight deliveries. Lately, the Internet has provided an inexpensive and accessible platform upon which FedEx has seen further opportunities to expand its business scope, both geographically and in terms of service offerings. For example, FedEx created an e-fulfillment system. Orders placed by customers to merchants are both managed and fulfilled by FedEx. FedEx is attempting to attain two of its major goals simultaneously: 100 percent customer service and 0 percent downtime.

## The IT Solution/Project

A prime software application used by FedEx is e-Shipping Tools, a Web-based shipping application that allows customers to check the status of shipments through the company's Web page. FedEx is also providing integrated solutions to address the entire selling and supply chain needs of its customers. Its e-Commerce Solutions provide a full suite of services that allow businesses to integrate FedEx's transportation and information systems seamlessly into their own operations. These solutions have taken FedEx well beyond a shipping company.

FedEx markets several e-commerce hardware/software solutions: FedEx PowerShipMC (a multicarrier hardware/software system), FedEx Ship Manager Server (a hardware/software system providing high-speed transactions and superior reliability, allowing an average of eight transactions per second), FedEx ShipAPI™ (an Internet-based application that allows customization, eliminating redundant programming), and FedEx Net-Return® (a Web-based item-return management system). This infrastructure is now known as FedEx Direct Link. It enables business-to-business electronic commerce through combinations of global virtual private network (VPN) connectivity, Internet connectivity, leased-line connectivity, and VAN (value-added network) connectivity.

Figure 2.1 (page 40) provides an example of one of FedEx's e-commerce solutions: ❶ Merchants place their catalogs online, and ❷ FedEx customers browse the catalog deciding what to buy. When a customer places a purchase order online, it is sent to a FedEx Web server ❸. Information about the order and the customer is then sent to the merchant's PC, and ❹ a message is sent to the customer to confirm receipt of the order. After the order is received and acknowledged, the FedEx Web server sends a message to the merchant's bank to obtain credit approval ❺. At the same time, the order is sent via electronic data interchange (EDI) to a FedEx mainframe ❻ that activates the *warehouse management system* ❼. The order is processed (goods are picked and packed), the warehouse inventory system is updated, and the shipping process is activated. Information regarding the processing of the order is accessible at the three remote electronic data centers (EDCs) located in the United States ❽ⓐ, the Europe/Mediterranean (EMEA) region ❽ⓑ, and the Asia Pacific (APAC) region. During the entire process the customer, the merchant, and FedEx employees ❽ⓒ can track at any time the status of the order and its fulfillment via the Web.

## The Results

The e-commerce-based FedEx business model creates value for customers in a number of ways: It facilitates better communication and collaboration between the various parties along the selling and supply chains. It promotes efficiency gains by reducing costs and speeding up the order cycle. It encourages customers not only to use FedEx as a shipper but also to outsource to FedEx all their logistics activities. It also provides FedEx a competitive edge and increased revenue and profits. Thus, FedEx has

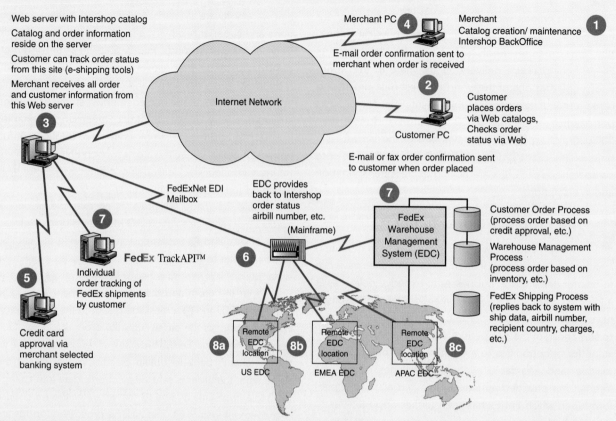

**Figure 2.1** An example of a FedEx e-commerce solution. (*Source:* Based on a SIM 2000 award-winning paper written by William L. Conley, Ali F. Farhoomand, and Pauline S.P. Ng, at *simnet.org/library/doc/2ndplace.doc,* no longer available online. Courtesy of William Conley.)

changed from an old-economy shipping company to an e-business logistics enterprise. In 2006, FedEx was delivering over 6 million packages a day in over 220 countries. It is considered the second most admired company in the United States and fourth in the world.

*Sources:* Based on a SIM 2000 award-winning paper written by William L. Conley, Ali F. Farhoomand, and Pauline S.P. Ng, *simnet.org/library/doc/2ndplace.doc* (no longer available online). Courtesy of William Conley. Updated with information from *fedex.com* (accessed May 2006), and Calvin (2006).

## Lessons Learned from This Case

In the digital economy, how well companies transform themselves from traditional modes of operation to e-business will depend on how well they can adapt their structure and processes to take advantage of emerging technologies and what architecture and infrastructure they use. FedEx has transformed itself into an e-business by integrating physical and virtual infrastructures across information systems, business processes, and organizational bounds. FedEx's experience in building an e-business shows how a company can

successfully apply its information technology expertise in order to pioneer "customercentric" innovations with sweeping structural and strategic impacts. It also shows the role of outsourcing, which frees companies to concentrate on their core business. Finally, we can see a variety of conformation systems applications in finance, operations, marketing, and customer service. In this chapter we describe how information systems of different kinds are structured, organized, and managed so that they can support businesses in the twenty-first century.

# 2.1 Information Systems: Concepts and Definitions

In Chapter 1 we defined an **information system (IS)** as one that collects, processes, stores, analyzes, and disseminates data and information for a specific purpose. The composition of information systems is usually the same: Each contains hardware, software, data, procedures, and people. Key elements of a simple desktop information system are shown in the nearby photo.

Another possible component of an information system is one or more smaller information systems. Information systems that contain smaller systems are typical of large companies. For example, FedEx's corporate information system contains hundreds of smaller information systems, which are referred to as "applications." An **application program** is a computer program designed to support a specific task or a business process (such as execute the payroll) or, in some cases, another application program.

There are dozens of applications in each functional area. For instance, in managing human resources, it is possible to find one application for screening job applicants and another for monitoring employee turnover. Some of the applications might be completely independent of each other, whereas others are interrelated. The collection of application programs in a single department is usually considered a *departmental information system,* even though it is made up of many applications. For example, the collection of application programs in the human resources area is called the *human resources information system (HRIS).*

Information systems are usually connected by means of *electronic networks.* The connecting networks can be *wireline* and/or *wireless.* Information systems can connect an entire organization, or even multiple organizations.

Before we focus on the details of IT and its management, it is necessary to describe the major concepts of information systems and organize the IT systems in some logical manner. That is the major purpose of this chapter.

## DATA, INFORMATION AND KNOWLEDGE

Information systems are built to attain one or several goals. One of the primary goals is to economically process data into information or knowledge. Let us define these concepts:

**Data items** refer to an elementary description of things, events, activities, and transactions that are recorded, classified, and stored, but not organized to convey any specific meeting. Data items can be numeric, alphanumeric, figures, sounds, or images. A student grade in a class is a data item, and so is the number of hours an employee worked in a certain week. A **database** consists of stored data items organized for retrieval.

**Information** is data that have been organized so that they have meaning and value to the recipient. For example, a student's grade point average is information. The recipient interprets the meaning and draws conclusions and implications from the information. Data items typically are processed into information by means of an application. Such processing represents a more specific use and a higher added value than simple retrieval and summarization from a database. The application might be a Web-based inventory management system, a university online registration system, or an Internet-based buying and selling system.

Finally, **knowledge** consists of data and/or information that have been organized and processed to convey understanding, experience, accumulated learning, and expertise as they apply to a current problem or activity. For example, the GPA of a student applying to a graduate school can provide an admissions officer with the knowledge of how good the student is only in comparison with the GPAs of other students and schools. Data that are processed to extract critical implications and to reflect past experiences and expertise provide the recipient with *organizational knowledge,* which has a very high potential value. Currently, *knowledge management* is one of the emerging topics in the IT field (see Chapter 10).

Data, information, and knowledge can be *inputs* to an information system, and they can also be *outputs*. For example, data about employees, their wages, and time worked are processed as inputs in order to produce an organization's payroll information (output). The payroll information itself can later be used as an input to another system that prepares a budget or advises management on salary scales or recruiting strategy.

**INFORMATION SYSTEMS CONFIGURATIONS**

Information systems are made out of components that can be assembled in many different configurations, resulting in a variety of information systems and applications, much as construction materials can be assembled to build different types and shapes of homes. The size and cost of a home depend on the purpose of the building, the availability of money, and constraints such as ecological, environmental, and legal requirements. Just as there are many different types of houses, so there are many different types of information systems. We classify houses as single-family homes, apartments (or flats), townhouses, and cottages. Similarly, it is useful to classify information systems into groups that share similar characteristics. Such a classification may help in identifying systems, analyzing them, planning new systems, planning integration of systems, and making decisions such as the possible outsourcing of systems. This classification can be done in several alternative ways, as shown next.

## 2.2 Classification and Types of Information Systems

Information systems are classified in this section by organizational levels and by the type of support provided. The section also looks at the evolution of support systems.

**CLASSIFICATION BY ORGANIZATIONAL LEVELS**

Organizations are made up of components such as divisions, departments, and work units, organized in hierarchical levels. For example, most organizations have functional departments, such as production and accounting, which report to plant management, which in turn reports to a division head. The divisions report to the corporate headquarters. Although some organizations have restructured themselves in innovative ways, such as those based on cross-functional teams, today the vast majority of organizations still have a traditional hierarchical structure. Thus, we can find information systems built according to this hierarchy. Such systems can stand alone, but usually they are interconnected.

The organizational levels that are supported by information systems are shown in Figure 2.2 as a triangle. The following are the specific levels recognized (from bottom up):

**Personal and Productivity Systems.**  These are small systems that are built to support many individuals. Known as **personal information management (PIM),** such a

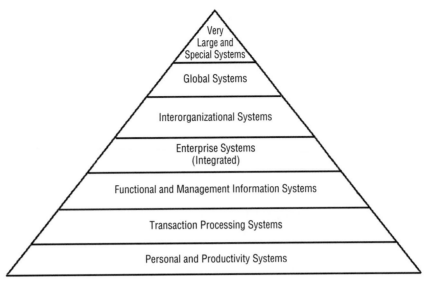

**Figure 2.2** Levels of information systems.

system intends to support the activities we, as individuals, perform to ease our work or life, through the acquisition, organization, maintenance, retrieval, and sharing of information. An example of such systems is the personal digital assistant (PDA), with functions such as calendars, calculators, schedulers, and computer memory. End-user decision support systems built with Excel is another example. Such systems are designed to increase our productivity and satisfaction. For issues and applications, see Teevan et al. (2006). Such systems are abundant in organizations, inexpensive, and have fairly standard capabilities.

**Transaction Processing Systems.** Any organization that performs periodic financial, accounting, and other routine business activities faces repetitive information processing tasks. For example, employees are paid at regular intervals, customers place purchase orders and are billed, and expenses are monitored and compared to the budget. Table 2.1 (page 44) presents a list of representative routine, repetitive business transactions in a manufacturing organization. The information system that supports such processes is called the *transaction processing system.*

A **transaction processing system (TPS)** supports the monitoring, collection, storage, processing, and dissemination of the organization's basic business transactions. It also provides the input data for other information systems. Sometimes several TPSs exist in one company. The transaction processing systems are considered critical to the success of any organization since they support core operations, such as purchasing of materials, billing customers, preparing a payroll, and shipping goods to customers.

The TPS collects data continuously, frequently on a daily basis, or even in *real time* (i.e., as soon as they are generated). Most of these data are stored in the corporate databases or data warehouse and are available for processing.

***Examples of TPS.*** In retail stores, data flow from POS (point-of-sale) terminals to a database where they are aggregated. When a sale is completed, an information transaction reduces the level of inventory on hand, and the collected revenue from the sale increases the company's cash position.

| TABLE 2.1 | Routine Business Transactions in a Manufacturing Company | |
|---|---|---|
| ***Payroll and Personnel*** | ***Sales*** | |
| Employee time cards | Sales records | |
| Employee pay and deductions | Invoices and billings | |
| Payroll checks | Accounts receivable | |
| Fringe benefits | Sales returns | |
| | Shipping | |
| ***Purchasing*** | | |
| Purchase orders | ***Production*** | |
| Deliveries | Production reports | |
| Payments (accounts payable) | Quality-control reports | |
| ***Finance and Accounting*** | ***Inventory Management*** | |
| Financial statements | Material usage | |
| Tax records | Inventory levels | |
| Expense accounts | | |

In banking, TPSs cover the area of deposits and withdrawals (which are similar to inventory levels). They also cover money transfers between accounts in the bank and among banks. Generating monthly statements for customers and setting fees charged for bank services are also typical transaction-processing activities for a bank. Further details on TPSs are provided in Chapter 7.

**Functional and Management Information Systems.** The transaction-processing system covers the core activities of an organization. The *functional areas,* however, cover many other activities; some of these are repetitive, while others are only occasional. For example, the human resources department hires, advises, and trains people. Each of these tasks can be divided into subtasks. Training may involve selecting topics to teach, selecting people to participate in the training, scheduling classes, finding teachers, and preparing class materials. These tasks and subtasks are frequently supported by information systems specifically designed to support functional activities.

The major functional information systems are organized around the traditional departments in a company. These are: *accounting, finance, production/operations, marketing and sales,* and *human resources management.* Functional information systems are put in place to ensure that business strategies come to fruition in an efficient manner. Typically, a functional system provides periodic reports about such topics as operational efficiency, effectiveness, and productivity by extracting information from databases and processing it according to the needs of the user.

Functional information systems are of two types: those that support managers, and those that support other employees in the functional areas (e.g., analysts, schedulers, staff). The systems that support managers are referred to as **management information systems (MISs).** MISs support functional managers by providing them with periodic reports that include summaries, comparisons, and other statistics. Examples are weekly sales volume and comparison of actual expenses to the budget.

Note that the term MIS is also used to describe the study of information systems in business. In many universities the name of the department that teaches the subject of IT was (and sometimes still is) the MIS Department. Also, in many organizations the title of the information systems department was (and sometimes still is) the Department of MIS.

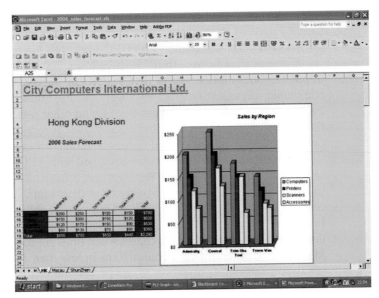

**Figure 2.3** Sales forecast by region, generated by marketing MIS.

Beginning here, and continuing throughout the book, icons positioned in the margins will call out the functional areas to which our real-world examples apply. In addition we will point to IT applications in government and in other public services such as health care and education by using icons. Finally, you've already seen that other icons will identify global examples—IT used by non-U.S.-based companies or by any company with significant business outside the country of its headquarters. For a key that identifies the icons, see the note in the Preface.

Management information systems are also used for planning, monitoring, and control. For example, a sales forecast by region is shown in Figure 2.3. Such a report can help the marketing manager make better decisions regarding advertising and pricing of products. Another example is that of a human resources information system (HRIS), which provides a manager with a daily report of the percentage of people who were on vacation or called in sick, as compared to forecasted figures.

Functional information systems that support analysts and other departmental employees can be fairly complex depending on the type of employees supported. Examples and descriptions are provided in Chapter 7.

**Examples of Functional/Enterprise Systems.** The following examples show the support IT provides to the five major functional areas. Some of the examples cover two functional areas. In each example, we explain the IT support to critical performance and response activities and agility described in Chapter 1.

**ACC**

**1. Computerized Analysis Helps Texas Collect $400 Million Additional Taxes.** Tax gaps exist between taxes owed and the amount collected in many public entities. The State of Texas is no exception. To overcome the problems, tax collectors use *audits*, which are expensive to conduct manually and time consuming. Also, many audits are unproductive—resulting in little or no tax recovery. In order to make better decisions on whom to audit (and thus increase the percentage of productive audits), the State of Texas uses *predictive analytics* (Chapter 11).

**FIN**

Millions of records are stored in the State data warehouse (Chapter 3). Using data mining–based software (Chapter 11) from *spss.com*, the agency can cross-match millions of records identifying promising leads. Specifically, the system helps identify thousands of businesses that were operating in the State without complying with the tax obligations. Also, it helps field auditors in adopting better audit target selections. Once the employees gained confidence in the program, they started to use it extensively, saving over $150 million a year. (*Sources:* Compiled from Gates, 2005, and from Staff, 2005.)

*Critical response activities supported*: analyzing large amounts of data, decision making, improved employee productivity, and increased revenue.

**POM    MKT**

**2. The Dallas Mavericks: Using IT for Successful Play and Business.** The Dallas Mavericks (of the National Basketball Association, NBA), expect to fill every seat at every game and to maximize sales from concessions and souvenir items.

In the 2002 season, the "Mavs" filled the 19,200-seat American Airlines Center to 103.7 percent capacity, bringing in folding chairs to handle the overflow demand for tickets. Dallas was named in 2003 the best NBA city by *The Sporting News*.

Filling seats is critical. To track attendance, the Mavs became the first NBA team to put barcodes on tickets and then scan them, in part to find out if group sales and community-organization giveaways were putting bodies in seats or just wasting tickets. The team's business managers have found other uses for the attendance information as well. By enabling improved attendance forecasting for particular games, for example, the system has helped reduce beverage inventories by 50 percent.

Each of the 144 luxury suites is equipped with a PC that handles orders for merchandise, food, and beverages. Wireless access from all seats in the arena is available so that fans can place orders directly from their seats. All 840 cash registers at concessions stands, restaurants, stores, and bars use a sophisticated point-of-sale system. In the big retail store on the ground floor, salespeople using handheld computing devices ring up credit-card purchases when lines get too long. The system allows the Mavs to process credit-card transactions in less than 3 seconds, because there is an always-on Internet connection to the processing facility. During a game, managers can see which concession stands are busy and which ones can be closed early to cut labor costs.

Technology also supports the Mavs on the court. The team has 10 assistant coaches, and each has a laptop computer and a handheld computing device. Game films can be streamed over the Web for coaches to view on the road or at home. A digital content management system developed in-house matches game footage with the precise, to-the-minute statistics provided for every play of every game by the NBA. The searchable database allows coaches to analyze the effectiveness of particular plays and combinations of players in different game situations. In 2006, the team was one of the NBA leaders.

In 2002, the Mavs started using handheld computers to track the performance of each referee in every one of their games. The coaches can look at patterns and trends—for example, to see which referee favors a given team or which one calls more 3-second violations—and they can tell the team's players. Another program logs different offensive and defensive schemes used against the Mavs. This system will let coaches make real-time adjustments using statistics from previous games. (*Source:* Compiled from Cone, 2003a and 2003b.)

*Critical response activities supported*: Decision making, increased sales, improved customer service, improved inventory management, better utilization of capacity.

**HRM**

**GLOBAL**

**3. State-of-the-Art Human Resources Management in China.** International Information Products Company LTD (IIPC) produces the PCs in Shenzhen, China. The company is one of China's top-10 exporters and one of the world's most efficient manufacturers of PCs. The company's success is attributed, in part, to its world-class Human Resources Information System (powered by PeopleSoft's HRMS now an Oracle company). In operation since October 2001, the system includes these basic elements: employee record management, recruitment, variable pay analysis, performance appraisal, payroll, and management of fringe benefits and absence records. In addition, employees can self-manage their personal data and report leaves and absences on the intranet. Using e-kiosks placed in several locations within the plant (e.g., the cafeteria), employees who do not have Internet access at work or home can use the system as well.

China's employee tax and benefits systems (e.g., health care and social insurance) are very complex, requiring many computations. Using HRMS and its Global Payroll component, IIPC was able to reduce the payroll cycle from 11 days to 4 days, and to reduce the computation run time from 6 hours to 2 hours, while eliminating errors. The system automates labor-intensive HR processes such as workforce administration, enabling HR staff to concentrate on staffing, training, career planning, rewards and promotions, and other nonclerical HR services. Furthermore, the data collected in the system are used by top management for supporting strategic decisions. (*Source*: Smith, 2002.)

*Critical response activities supported*: improved cycle time, improved dissemination of information, automated clerical tasks, use by employees for self-service.

GLOBAL

**4. Mobile Banking at Handelsbanken of Sweden.** Handelsbanken of Sweden is the largest bank in Scandinavia, where more than 80 percent of the population over 15 years old carry mobile phones. Operating in a very competitive banking environment, the bank is trying to meet customers' expectations of using their mobile phones to organize their personal and working lives while on the move. Mobile banking services, including stock trading, was an opportunity for the bank to gain a competitive edge, and so the bank became the world's first to have mobile banking applications.

An interactive service allows customers to access up-to-the-minute banking information, including the latest stock market and interest rate data, whenever and wherever they like. Handelsbanken's e-banking has become so popular that it is used by tens of thousands of customers. It opens up critical business and personal information to safe and easy access from mobile devices. Both the bank's financial advisors and its customers can access general and personalized stock market and account information, transfer money, request loans, buy and sell stocks and bonds, and pay bills. This move into mobile banking is a key first step in a strategy to exploit the potential of e-business, while also extending the bank's brand reach. (*Sources*: Compiled from IBM's case study: Handelsbanken at *www-3.ibm.com/e-business/doc/content/casestudy/35433.html,* accessed March 2003, and from press releases at *handelsbanken.com.*)

*Critical response activities supported*: improved customer service, innovative strategic marketing methods, competitive advantage.

**Enterprise Information Systems.** While functional systems support isolated activities within a department, enterprise systems support business processes that are performed by two or more departments. A **business process** is a collection of activities performed to accomplish a clearly defined goal. For example, evaluating a request for a loan is a business process, and so is purchasing a part, or conducting an advertising campaign. A business process has clearly defined starting and ending points. The activities in the process are frequently done in sequence, but some can be conducted simultaneously.

Figure 2.4 illustrates examples of four processes that cross not only departmental boundaries, but also organizational boundaries, such as extending activities to suppliers and/or customers. Process A describes a typical TPS, crossing three functional areas. Process B describes procurement and as such it is extended to a supplier. Process C involves customer service, reaching customers. Finally, Process D involves order taking (from customers) and fulfilling it after making some materials from a supplier.

Enterprise systems follow such processes, and they usually integrate tasks done in different departments. For examples and details, see Chapters 8 and 9. One of the most popular enterprise applications is *enterprise resources planning (ERP),* which enables companies to plan and manage the resources of an entire enterprise (see Chapter 8).

**Interorganizational Systems.** Some information systems connect two or more organizations. They are referred to as *interorganizational information systems* (IOSs). For example, the worldwide airline reservation system is composed of

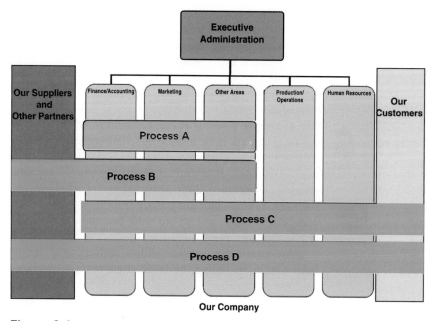

**Figure 2.4** Business processes across and beyond the enterprise.

several systems belonging to different airlines. Of these, American Airlines' SABRE system is the largest; thousands of travel agents and hundreds of airlines are connected to it.

Most common IOSs are systems that connect sellers and buyers. There one can order electronically, bill electronically, and pay electronically. Since such transactions are fairly standard, they can be supported by standardized computer languages such as XML and EDI (Chapter 9). Figure 2.5 shows IOSs connecting three organizations. The IOSs are connected with some internal systems, such as the functional systems shown for Corporate A, or to enterprise systems that were presented in Figure 2.4. Basically, IOSs enable computers to "talk" with other computers in different organizations.

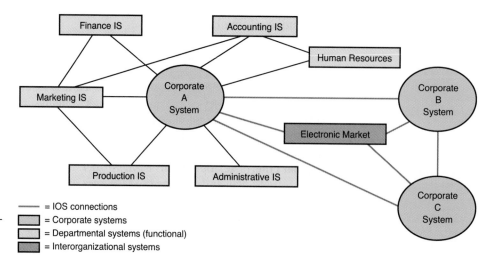

**Figure 2.5** Departmental, enterprise, and interorganizational information systems.

# *IT* at Work 2.1

## *Generating $62 Million per Employee at Western Petroleum*

Western Petroleum (*westernpetro.com*) buys petroleum products in bulk (e.g., 50,000 barrels) and sells them in smaller chunks (e.g., 5,000 barrels) to over 2,000 potential customers. The company operates on a razor-thin margin, so controlling purchasing costs determines profitability. The company grew rapidly, adding more employees, but by 2003, management capped the number of employees at 58. These few employees generate $3.6 billion (over $62 million per employee). How can they do it? The answer is: by using an industry-specific software platform that facilitates trading and helps schedule employees. The basic idea was to automate processes wherever possible, and outsource all noncritical functions. A key piece of the automation strategy is a software called PetroMan (see *sisugrp.com*). The industry-specific software includes a trading application (buying and selling triggers), contract management, risk management, accounting program, and pipeline scheduler. Basically, it is an integrated hybrid system. The software allows a company to place bids and automatically capture a contract for refined products. Then the system is used to schedule and confirm deliveries in

pipelines. It also handles the resale of fuels, including electronic invoicing and a credit module that checks and tracks a customer's credit risk. This is done by hedging large purchasing contracts by selling futures on the New York Mercantile (Commodities) Exchange. This way the company is protected against a large drop in oil price. The software is plugged directly into the primary commodity exchanges, thus automating the process.

Accounting/financial information flows automatically from PetroMan to the company's financial application, a package called Global Financials (from Global Software). Thus, the entire process of buying and selling fuels and moving the accounting/financial information is fully automated.

*Sources:* Compiled from Duvall (2005) and from *westernpetro.com* (accessed April, 2006).

*For Further Exploration:* What processes are being automated and why? How is risk being evaluated? It is probable that all major competitors use the same software. So, do you see any advantage for the company to use it too? Why?

---

**Global Information Systems.** IOSs that connect companies located in two or more countries are referred to as **global information systems.** Many e-commerce systems are now global. If you have customers from other countries who buy from you online, you may need the support of a global system. The same is true if your suppliers are overseas. For details see Chapter 9.

**Very Large and Special Systems.** Some systems are very large, and they are often global in nature. Such systems include many subsystems of the previous levels. Some information systems are designed for only one industry. For example, universities use administrative information systems as well as academic information systems. Banks, utilities, city governments, and retailers have their own specially tailored systems. In *IT at Work 2.1*, we provide an example of two systems in the petroleum industry: one system for finance/accounting and one system for operational decision making support.

In the next section, we will describe the classification of information systems by the type of support they provide.

**CLASSIFICATION BY THE TYPE OF SUPPORT PROVIDED**

Another way to classify information systems is according to the type of support they provide, regardless of the functional area. For example, an information system can support office workers in almost any functional area. Likewise, managers working from various geographical locations can be supported by a computerized decision-making system. The main types of support systems are listed and described in Table 2.2 (page 50) together with the types of employees they support. The evolution of these systems and a brief description of each is provided in Online File W2.2.

| TABLE 2.2 | Main Types of IT Support Systems |
|---|---|

| System | Employees Supported | Description | Detailed Description In: |
|---|---|---|---|
| Management information system (MIS) | Middle managers | Provides routine information for planning, organizing, and controlling operations in functional areas. | Chapter 7 |
| Office automation system (OAS) | Office workers | Increases productivity of office workers; includes word processing. | Chapters 4, 7 |
| CAD/CAM | Engineers, draftspeople | Allows engineers to design and test prototypes; transfers specifications to manufacturing facilities. | Chapter 7 |
| Communication and collaboration systems (e.g., e-mail, voice mail) | All employees | Enable employees partners, and customers to interact and work together more efficiently. | Chapter 4 |
| Desktop publishing system | Office workers | Combines text, photos, graphics to produce professional-quality documents. | Chapter 3 |
| Document management system (DMS) | Office workers | Automates flow of electronic documents. | Chapter 3 |
| Decision support system (DSS) | Decision makers, managers | Combines models and data to solve semistructured problems with extensive user involvement. | Chapter 12 |
| Group support system (GSS) | People working in groups | Supports working processes of groups of people (including those in different locations). | Chapter 12 |
| Expert system (ES) | Knowledge workers, nonexperts | Provides stored knowledge of experts to nonexperts and decision recommendations based on built-in expertise. | Chapters 10, 12 |
| Knowledge work system (KWS) | Managers, knowledge workers | Supports the gathering, organizing, and use of an organization's knowledge. | Chapters 10 |
| Neural networks, data mining | Knowledge workers, professionals | Learn from historical cases, even with vague or incomplete information. | Chapters 9, 11, 12 |
| Business intelligence | Decision makers, managers, knowledge workers | Gathers and uses large amounts of data for analysis by business analytics and intelligent systems. | Chapter 11, 12 |
| Mobile computing systems | Mobile employees | Support employees who work with customers or business partners outside the physical boundaries of the organization. | Chapter 6 |
| Automated Decision Support (ADS) | Frontline employees, middle managers | Support customer care employees and salespeople who need to make quick, real-time decisions involving small dollar amounts. | Chapter 12 |

**HOW DO DIFFERENT INFORMATION SYSTEMS RELATE TO EACH OTHER?**

The relationship among the different types of support systems can be described as follows: Each support system has sufficiently unique characteristics that it can be classified as a special entity. Moreover, there is information flow among these entities and systems. For example, an MIS extracts information from a TPS, and BI receives information from data warehouses and MIS (see Figure 2.6). In many cases, two or more support systems can be integrated to form a hybrid system, as is the case in business intelligence or CRM. Finally, as the technologies change, the

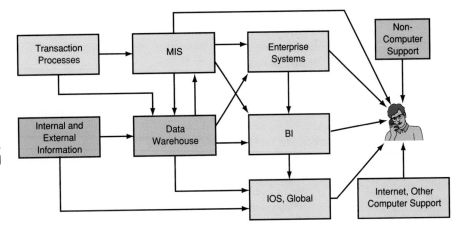

**Figure 2.6** Interrelated support systems. The TPS collects information that is used to build the DSS and ESS. The information in the data warehouse and DSS can be used as an input to the ESS.

interrelationships and coordination among the different types of systems continue to evolve.

**Integrated Support Systems.** From the time of their inception, support systems were used both as standalone systems and as integrated systems composed of two or more of the support systems. Notable were systems that include some intelligent components (e.g., a BI-ES combination). Such integration provides extended functionalities, making these systems more useful. As will be discussed in Chapters 7 and 9, there is an increasing trend to integrate the various support systems as well as to integrate support systems with other systems. Integrated support systems can provide solutions to complex problems, as shown in Online File W2.1.

Now that we have completed an overview of the different types of support systems, we will examine how they support people and whom they support.

## 2.3  How IT Supports People and Organizational Activities

Another important way to classify information systems is by the nature of activities they support. Such support can be for *operational, managerial,* or *strategic* activities, as well as for managers, knowledge workers, and other employees in an organization.

**OPERATIONAL ACTIVITIES**

*Operational activities* deal with the day-to-day operations of an organization, such as assigning employees to tasks and recording the number of hours they work, or placing a purchase order. Operational activities are short-term in nature. The information systems that support them are mainly TPSs, MISs, and mobile systems. Operational systems are used mostly by supervisors (first-line managers), operators, and clerical employees.

**MANAGERIAL ACTIVITIES**

*Managerial activities,* also called tactical activities or decisions, deal in general with middle-management activities such as short-term planning, organizing, and control. Computerized managerial systems are frequently *equated with MISs,* because MISs are designed to summarize data and prepare reports. Middle managers also can get quick answers to queries from such systems as the need for answers arises, using BI reporting and query capabilities.

| TABLE 2.3 | Support Provided by MISs and BI for Managerial Activities |
|---|---|
| **Task** | **MIS Support** |
| Statistical summaries | Summaries of new data (e.g., daily production by item, monthly electricity usage). |
| Exception reports | Comparison of actual performances to standards (or target). Highlight only deviations from a threshold (e.g., above or below 5%). |
| Periodic reports | Generated at predetermined intervals. |
| Ad-hoc reports | Generated as needed, on demand. These can be routine reports or special ones. |
| Comparative analysis and early detection of problems | Comparison of performance to metrics or standards. Includes analysis such as trends and early detection of changes. |
| Projections, forecasting | Projection of future sales, cash flows, market share, trend analysis, etc. |
| Automation of routine decisions | Standard modeling techniques applied to routine decisions such as when and how much to order or how to schedule work. |
| Connection and collaboration | Internal and external Web-based messaging systems, e-mail, voice mail, and groupware (see Chapter 4). |

Managerial information systems are broader in scope than operational information systems, but like operational systems, they use mainly internal sources of data. They provide the major, representative types of support shown in Table 2.3.

**STRATEGIC ACTIVITIES**

*Strategic activities* are activities or decisions that deal with situations that may significantly change the manner in which business is done. Traditionally, strategic activities involved only long-range planning. Introducing a new product line, expanding the business by acquiring supporting businesses, and moving operations to a foreign country, are prime examples of long-range activities. A long-range planning document traditionally outlines strategies and plans for the next five or even 10 years. From this plan, companies derive their shorter-range planning, budgeting, and resource allocation. In the digital economy, the planning period has been dramatically reduced to one to two years, or even months. Strategic activities help organizations in two other ways.

First, *strategic response* activities can react quickly to a major competitor's action or to any other significant change in the enterprise's environment. Although they can sometimes be planned for as a set of contingencies, strategic responses are frequently not included in the long-range plan because the situations they respond to are unpredictable. IT is often used to support the response or to provide the response itself. For instance, when Kodak Corporation learned that a Japanese company was developing a disposable camera, Kodak decided to develop one too. However, Kodak faced a time problem because the Japanese were already in the middle of the development process. By using computer-aided design and other information technologies, Kodak was able to cut its design time by half and beat the Japanese in the race to be the first to have the cameras in retail outlets.

*POM*

Second, instead of waiting for a competitor to introduce a major change or innovation, an organization can be the *initiator of change*. Such innovative strategic activities are frequently supported by IT, as shown by FedEx in the opening case and by many startup companies that exploit opportunities by using IT (e.g., see the Thaigem story in Chapter 1 and the Amazon.com story in Chapter 5).

| WHO PERFORMS WHAT ACTIVITIES IN ORGANIZATIONS, AND HOW ARE THEY SUPPORTED BY IT? |
| --- |

So far in this section, we have looked at operational, managerial, and strategic activities, and at how IT supports them. Here, we take a different look at these activities by looking at the people who typically perform them in an organization. For example, line managers and operators usually make operational decisions, and middle managers make most of the managerial decisions. Strategic decisions are made almost entirely by an organization's top managers. The relationships between the people supported in all functional areas and the decision types are shown in Figure 2.7. The triangular shape of the figure also illustrates the quantity of employees involved in the various types of activities and the decisions relating to those activities.

**Executives and Managers.**  At the top of the triangle are the executives. They are few in number and responsible for the strategic decisions. Their major support today is derived from business intelligence (BI) and corporate (business) performance management systems (Chapter 11).

Middle managers make tactical decisions, and are supported mainly by functional information systems and MIS in the areas where they work. Lately, they have started to enjoy the support of BI and intelligent systems available over intranets.

**Knowledge Workers, Clerical Staff, and Data Workers.**  As you can see in Figure 2.7, a level of *staff support* is introduced between top and middle management.

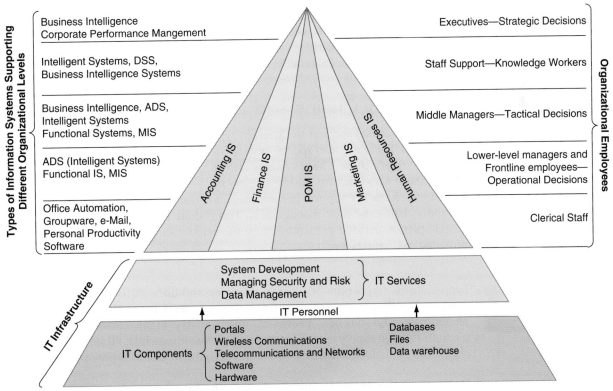

**Figure 2.7** The information systems support of people in organizations.

These are professional people, such as financial and marketing analysts. They act as advisors and assistants to both top and middle management. Many of these professional workers are classified as **knowledge workers,** people who create information and knowledge as part of their work and integrate it into the business. Knowledge workers are engineers, financial and marketing analysts, production planners, lawyers, and accountants, to mention just a few. They are responsible for finding or developing new knowledge for the organization and integrating it with existing knowledge. Therefore they must keep abreast of all developments and events related to their profession. They also act as change agents by introducing new procedures, technologies, or processes. In many developed countries, 60 to 80 percent of all workers are knowledge workers.

Information systems that support knowledge workers range from Internet search engines (which help knowledge workers find information) and expert systems (which provide advice and information interpretation), to Web-based computer-aided design (which shapes and speeds the design process) and sophisticated data management systems (which help increase productivity and quality of work). Knowledge workers are the major users of intranets and the Internet for business purposes.

Another large class of employees is *clerical workers,* who support managers at all levels. Among clerical workers, those who use, manipulate, or disseminate information are referred to as **data workers.** These include bookkeepers, secretaries who work with word processors, electronic file clerks, and insurance claim processors. Data workers are supported by office automation and communication systems including document management, workflow, e-mail, and coordination software.

**Infrastructure for the Support Systems.** All of the systems in the support (top) triangle are built on *information infrastructure.* Consequently, all of the employees who are supported work with infrastructure technologies such as the Internet, intranets, corporate portals, security systems, and corporate databases. Therefore, the information infrastructure is shown as the *foundation* of the triangle in Figure 2.7; it is described in more detail in Section 2.5.

## 2.4 How IT Supports Supply Chains and Enterprise Systems

So far, we described support to different types of employees at different organizational levels. There are also special systems designed to support business processes along the *supply chain.* These systems also support people in other organizations, such as those who work for business partners.

To understand IT support in such cases, it is worthwhile to review the essentials of supply chains and their management. This is done in Appendix 2B at the end of this chapter. A detailed presentation on the relationship of supply chain and IT is provided in Chapters 8 and 9.

**IT SUPPORT OF SUPPLY CHAINS**

Supply chains (Appendix 2B) can be complex and difficult to manage due to the need to coordinate several business partners, several internal corporate departments, numerous business processes, and possibly many customers. Managing medium to large supply chains manually is almost impossible. IT support of supply chains can be divided according to the three segments of the supply chain.

**Support of the Internal Supply Chain.** The IT support of the internal supply chain was described in the previous two sections. It involves the TPS and other corporatewide (enterprisewide) information systems, and it covers all of the functional information systems. Special software called supply chain management (SCM) software is available to support segments of the chain. For example, in manufacturing, there is software for production scheduling and inventory management. A description is provided in Chapter 7.

**Support of the Upstream Supply Chain.** The major IT support of the upstream supply chain is to improve procurement activities and relationships with suppliers. As will be seen in Chapters 5 and 8, using e-procurement is becoming very popular, resulting in major savings and improvements in buyer-seller relationships. E-procurement is done in private and public exchanges (Chapter 5). Relationships with suppliers can be improved by using a supplier portal (Chapter 4) and other supplier-relationship IT tools.

**Support of the Downstream Supply Chain.** IT support of the downstream segment of the supply chain is done in two areas. First, IT supports customer relationship management (CRM) activities such as providing a customer call center (Chapter 8). Second, IT supports order taking and shipments to customers (Chapters 7 and 8).

Many vendors provide IT support software to both the upstream and downstream segments of the supply chain, as described in the story about Best Buy in Online File W2.3.

**Managing Supply Chains.** IT provides two major types of software solutions for managing—planning, organizing, coordinating, and controlling—supply chain activities. First is *enterprise resource planning (ERP)* software, which helps in managing both the internal and the external relationships with the business partners. Second is *SCM* software, which helps in decision making related both to internal segments and to their relationships with external segments. Both types of software are described in Chapter 8.

Finally, the concepts of build-to-order production and e-commerce have put a new spin on supply chain management; for elaboration, see Appendix 2A at the end of this chapter.

---

**IT SUPPORT OF OTHER SYSTEMS**

So far we described IT support of internal parts of organizations and the different types of employees. We also described the support provided to business partners along the supply chain. But, IT supports other types of systems. Here are a few examples:

**Industry-Specific Systems.** These are systems that are designed to serve an industry such as banking, retail, transportation, oil, utilities, or universities. The systems can be specific for one or two applications, or they can be suites that cover multiple needs. An example of the petroleum industry was provided in *IT at Work 2.1* (page 49). Many software vendors specialize in industry-specific systems. One example is JDA Systems, which caters to the retail industry.

**Supporting E-Commerce Business Models.** The use of e-commerce implies using business models such as e-auctions, exchanges, e-procurement, or the use of electronic meetings. A large number of companies are developing IT software support for such business models. Many of these are IOSs; others are unique and do not fit any of our previous classifications. Of special interest are the many types of search engines and price comparison software.

# 2.5 Information Systems Infrastructure and Architecture

**INFRASTRUCTURE**

An **information infrastructure** consists of the physical facilities, services, and management that support all shared computing resources in an organization. There are five major components of the infrastructure: (1) computer hardware, (2) software, (3) networks and communication facilities (including the Internet and intranets), (4) databases and data workers, and (5) information management personnel. Infrastructures include these resources as well as their integration, operation, documentation, maintenance, and management. If you go back and examine Figure 2.1 (which describes the architecture of the FedExNet), and introduce specific names instead of general ones (e.g., instead of "Merchant PC," say "Dell server"), you will get a picture of the system's infrastructure. Infrastructures are further discussed in Chapters 14 and 15, and in Weill and Vitale (2001), and HP Company (2004). IT infrastructure is derived from the IT architecture.

**THE IT ARCHITECTURE**

Technology Guides are located at the book's Web site.

**Information technology architecture** is a high-level map or plan of the information assets in an organization including the physical design of the building that holds the hardware.* On the Web, IT architecture includes the content and organization of the site and the interface to support browsing and search capabilities. The IT architecture of an e-business (a travel agency) is shown in Technology Guide 6. IT architecture is a guide for current operations and a blueprint for future directions. It assures managers that the organization's IT structure will meet its strategic business needs. (See the *Journal of Information Architecture* for examples, tutorials, news, products, etc.)

Creating the IT architecture is a cyclical process, which is driven by the business architecture. This process is described in Technology Guide 6. It is based on **business architecture,** which describes organizational plans, visions, objectives and problems, and the information required to support them. The potential users of IT must play a critical role in the creation of business architecture, in order to ensure that business architectures are properly linked and meet the organization's long-term needs.

Once the business architecture is finished, the system developer can start a five-step process of building the IT architecture. The details and definitions of those steps are provided by Koontz (2000) and are shown in Technology Guide 6. Translating the business objectives into IT architecture can be a very complex undertaking (see Chapter 13).

The configurations of IT architecture are provided in Online File W2.4.

**WEB-BASED SYSTEMS**

Technically, the term **Web-based systems** refers to those applications or services that are resident on a server that is accessible using a Web browser and is therefore accessible from anywhere in the world via the Web. The only client-side software needed to access and execute Web-based applications is a Web browser environment, and of course the applications must conform to the Internet protocols. An example of such an application would be an online store. Additionally, two other very important features of Web-based functionalities are (1) that the generated content/data can be easily updated in real time, and (2) that Web-based systems are universally accessible via the Web to users.

---

*Information technology architecture* needs to be distinguished from *computer architecture* (see Technology Guide 1). For example, the architecture for a computer may involve several processors, or it may have special features to increase speed such as reduced instruction set computing (RISC). Our interest here is in information architecture only.

**Enterprise Web.** The **Enterprise Web** is an open environment for managing and delivering Web applications. It is the sum of a company's systems, information, and services that are available on the Web, working together as one entity. The Enterprise Web combines services from different vendors in a technology layer that spans rival platforms and business systems, creating a foundation for building applications at lower cost. This foundation consists of the services most commonly used by Web applications, including business integration, collaboration, content management, identity management, and search, which work together via integrating technologies such as middleware (see Technology Guide 2), component-based development (Technology Guide 6), and Web Services (Technology Guide 6).

The result is an environment that spans the entire enterprise, is open to all platforms for which adapters are available (or completely open with Web Services), and is available to all audiences. Enterprise Web environments are available from all major software vendors (e.g., Microsoft, IBM, SAP, Oracle, BEA Software, and more). For more on the Enterprise Web, see Online File W2.6 at the book's Web site.

**WEB 2.0**

The term *Web 2.0* refers to the second generation of the Web, meaning significant changes over the initial Web. The term was coined by O'Reilly Media. A comprehensive document titled "What Is Web 2.0" is available at *oreillynet.com/pub/a/ oreilly/tim/news/2005/09/03/what-is-Web 2.0 html.* According to this document, services, not software, are the basis of the Web 2.0 system. Other characteristics include: cost-effective scalability; control over unique, hard-to-re-create data sources that get richer as more people use them; users trusted as co-developers; harnessing collective intelligence; leveraging the "long tail" through customer self-service; software above the level of a single device; and lightweight user interfaces.

Several vendors are marketing their products as "Web 2.0-ready." Notable are RSS, blog development tools, and Web Services, which are described in Chapter 4. Generally speaking, there is no agreement on what is included in Web 2.0.

**WEB-BASED E-COMMERCE SYSTEMS**

Most e-commerce applications run on the Internet, intranet, and extranets, using Web-based features. Therefore, Web-based systems are the engines of e-commerce. They enable business transactions to be conducted seamlessly 24 hours a day, seven days a week. A central property of the Web and e-commerce is that you can instantly reach millions of people, anywhere, any time. The major components of Web-based EC are electronic storefronts and malls (Chapter 5), electronic markets (Chapter 5), and mobile commerce (Chapter 6).

**Electronic Markets.** Web-accessed electronic markets are rapidly emerging as a vehicle for conducting e-commerce. An **electronic market** is a network of interactions and relationships over which information, products, services, and payments are exchanged. (Details are provided in Chapter 5.) Electronic markets can reside in one company, where there is either one seller and many buyers, or one buyer and many sellers. These are referred to as *private marketplaces*. (See Online File W 2.7. for an example of a Web-based private marketplace.) Alternatively, electronic markets can have many buyers and many sellers. Then they are known as *public marketplaces* or *exchanges*.

**Electronic Exchanges.** A form of electronic markets is **electronic exchanges,** which are Web-based public marketplaces where many business buyers and many sellers interact dynamically. They were originally set as trading places for stocks and commodities. Since then a variety of exchanges have emerged for all kinds of products and services (see Chapter 5).

# 2.6 Emerging Computing Environments: SaaS, SOA, and More

During the last decade several new computing environments have emerged, some of which are based on Web technology. These systems are in the early stages of usage, and some are still under development, but they may reshape the IT field. In this section we provide several examples of these new initiatives. For a discussion of the requirements that new computing systems need to address, see Online File W2.8. The following are representative initiatives of emerging computing environments.

**THE SOFTWARE-AS-A-SERVICE BUSINESS MODEL**

An increasingly popular enterprise model in which computing resources are made available to the user when the resources are needed is the **Software-as-a-Service (SaaS)** model. Whether referred to as *SaaS, on-demand computing, utility computing,* or *hosted services,* the idea is basically the same: Instead of buying and installing expensive and pesky packaged enterprise applications, users can access applications over a network, with an Internet browser being the only absolute necessity. Thus, usually there is no hardware and software to buy since the applications are used over the Internet and paid for through a fixed subscription fee, or payable per an actual usage fee.

There are several variations of the concept. However, they all offer standardized, componentized, common, and lower cost software services sourced at will from some type of service provider.

The SaaS or on-demand model was developed to overcome the common challenge to an enterprise of being able to meet fluctuating demands efficiently, which is a requirement of the adaptive enterprise. Because an enterprise's demand on computing resources can vary drastically from one time to another, maintaining sufficient resources to meet peak requirements can be costly. Conversely, if the enterprise cuts costs by maintaining only minimal computing resources, there will not be sufficient resources to meet peak requirements. For details see Joshi and Namjoshi (2006).

A simple analogy is the use of an electrical appliance. The user does not directly negotiate with the electricity company to use power for a specific appliance. There are standards and controls, but they are broad enough that an electrical appliance can be plugged into the service without the user's notifying the electrical utility. On its side, the electrical utility company takes care of the complexity of power generation, including matching capacity to demand, and it can change which generators and circuits deliver the power—all without coordinating these events with the millions of users who rely on the service. This is why the concept is frequently referred to as *utility computing.*

A major issue in utility computing is who the provider should be. A natural provider can be a software developer/host such as IBM and Oracle. Another obvious choice is a third-party intermediary, such as an application services provider (ASP). For how this is done see Jakovljevic (2005a).

For more on the subject, see *utilitycomputing.itworld.com, utilitycomputing.com,* and *oracle.com/ondemand.*

**Suitability of SaaS.**  The growing success of Salesforce.com's on-demand service for *customer relationship management* (CRM) software begs the question whether the software-as-a-service model is suitable for other applications. According to Jakovljevic (2005b), the model is amendable to other applications that are frequently outsourced. This includes HR/payroll; financial and procurement management; and *business-to-customer* (B2C) e-commerce/product catalogs, including dynamic pricing models, customer loyalty groups, targeted sales promotions, and other sophisticated sales tactics. Integration with supply chain applications that do not necessarily require a large, internal team of sales support people may also find potential. The same can be said of businesses that rely on globalization and Web-based collaboration. For details see Joshi and Namjoshi (2006).

**SaaS and SOA.** An important factor in the shift to SaaS might be a change in the way the software itself is created nowadays. Rather than software components being developed and bundled together to form a monolithic, rigid solution, systems are increasingly being developed as a "federation," "mash-up" of services, or *composite applications,* which are tied together only at the point of execution. This will eventually enable alternative software components to be substituted between each use of a system, allowing much greater flexibility.

This is basically the idea of *service-oriented architecture.* Therefore, according to Jakovljevic (2006), SaaS, at its highest level, must be delivered as a service-oriented architecture (SOA) approach and must embody Web Services. These two topics are presented later in this section. Another topic related to utility computing delivery is grid computing. Some even equate the two concepts (e.g., Jakovljevic, 2005a), considering grid computing as a type of utility provider.

**Implementing SaaS: The Utility Computing Concept.** According to Bill Gates, **utility computing** is computing that is as available, reliable, and secure as electricity, water services, and telephony (reported by Ebringer, 2003). The vision behind utility computing is to have computing resources available on demand from virtual utilities around the globe—always on and highly available, secure, efficiently metered, priced on a pay-as-you-use basis, dynamically scaled, self-healing, and easy to manage. In this setting, enterprises would plug in, turn on the computer, and (it is hoped) save lots of money. IBM (*On-Demand* project), HP, Microsoft, Oracle, Sun Microsystems, SAP, and other major software companies are backing the idea (see Jakovljevic, 2005a).

If (or when) it becomes successful, utility computing will change the way software is sold, delivered, and used in the world. Some experts believe that all software will become a service and be sold as a utility one day. Preparing for this day, IBM is moving aggressively into the ASP area. The ASPs will operate the supply channels of utility computing (see Chapters 14 and 15).

An example of using utility computing is the case of the Mobil Travel Guide, which rates over 25,000 restaurants and hotels in the United States and publishes travel guides for various regions. To accommodate the ever-increasing traffic of Web servers that are looking for the ratings, the company is using IBM's on-demand hosting services. With this service, the company not only solved all capacity problems but also increased security—all at a 30 percent cost reduction compared to having its own servers (Greenmeier, 2003).

**Limitations of Utility Computing.** Despite the bright promises and the efforts of the major vendors, progress is slow. Key pieces of the technology are still missing. For example, utility computing is hard to do in heterogeneous data centers. Also, the utility concept works better for some applications than for others. Furthermore, utility computing needs extra security. Finally, distribution of software differs from distribution of utilities (see Wainewright, 2002).

According to a recent survey, 55.6 percent of the 310 respondents cited security and privacy as the number-one concern for failure to adopt utility computing (Dubie and Bednarz, 2004). Other concerns included vendor dependency and lock-in (50.8%), performance and reliability (45.9%), business data too critical to trust to outsiders (41.6%), and loss of control over key resources (38.3%).

These drawbacks need to be overcome by vendors in order to offer utility computing in a way that appeals to customers. However, it looks like utility computing will start inside companies, where the IT department can offer utility-style services to business units for internal use, and from there may eventually spread to the computing public (see Jakovljevic, 2005a, 2005b, 2006).

**GRID COMPUTING**

Conventional networks, including the Internet, are designed to provide communication among devices. The same networks can be used to support the concept of **grid computing,** in which the unused processing cycles of all computers in a given network can be harnessed to create powerful computing capabilities. Grid computing coordinates the use of a large number of servers and storage, acting as one computer. (See Online File W2.9.) Thus problems of spikes in demand are solved without the cost of maintaining reserve capacity (see *oracle.com/grid*).

Grid computing is already in limited use, and many of the current grid applications are in areas that formerly would have required supercomputers. Mason (2004) urged that companies doing multi-hour-long processing jobs, making complex scientific and mathematical calculations, and processing large data sets for business intelligence would be good candidates for taking advantage of the faster processing speed of grid computing.

A well-known grid-computing project is the SETI (Search for Extraterrestrial Intelligence) @ Home project. In this project, PC users worldwide donate unused processor cycle times to help the search for signs of extraterrestrial life by analyzing signals coming from outer space. The project relies on individual volunteers to allow the project to harness the unused processing power of the users' computers. This method saves the project both money and resources.

A major commercial application of grid computing in the consumer market is Sony's attempt to link online thousands of Sony video-game consoles. For details see Lohr (2003). Investment banks are embracing grid computing rapidly (Shread, 2006). An example of real-world use is provided in *IT at Work 2.2.*

**MOBILE COMPUTING AND MOBILE COMMERCE**

**Mobile computing** is a computing paradigm designed for mobile employees and others who wish to have a real-time connection from anywhere between a mobile device and other computing environments. **Mobile commerce** or **m-commerce** (see Chapter 6) is commerce (buying and selling of goods and services) in a *wireless environment,* such as through wireless devices like cellular telephones and PDAs. Also called "next-generation e-commerce," m-commerce enables users to access the Internet without needing to find a place to plug in. So-called *smart phones* offer Internet access, fax, e-mail, and phone capabilities all in one, paving the way for m-commerce to be accepted by an increasingly mobile workforce as well as millions of consumers. As *wireless computing*—content delivery over wireless devices— becomes faster, more secure, and scalable, there is wide speculation that m-commerce will surpass wireline e-commerce as the method of choice for digital commerce transactions (see *IT at Work 2.3,* page 61).

An emerging mobile technology is pervasive computing.

**Pervasive Computing.** As discussed in Chapter 1, with **pervasive computing** we envision a future in which computation becomes part of the environment. Computation will be embedded in *things,* not in computers. The use of pervasive computing does not just improve efficiency in work and living tasks but also enriches the quality of life through art, design, and entertainment (Benford et al., 2004). Relentless progress in semiconductor technology, low-power design, and wireless technology will make embedded computation less and less obtrusive. Pervasive computing is closely related with IT support systems, especially intelligent systems and BI.

# IT at Work 2.2

## Grid Computing at J.P. Morgan

J.P. Morgan Chase Investment Bank (*jpmorgan.com*) provides investment banking and commercial banking products and services. It also advises on corporate strategy and structure, risk management, and raising of capital. J.P. Morgan Chase, the largest financial institution in the United States, employs 11,000 IT professionals.

The company faced a problem of ever-increasing demand for computing resources. There were 2,000 PCs that run on 50 midsize servers. Some were overutilized, whereas others were underutilized, creating staffing inefficiencies and poor service to the company's securities traders. The PCs were designed to help traders assess and manage financial exposures, such as interest rates, equities, foreign exchange, and credit derivatives.

In 2003, the company began use of grid computing, at a cost of $4.5 million. The system saved $1 million in computing costs in 2003 and $5 million in 2004. The savings come from lower costs for hardware, reduced development and operation costs, and a more effective system management. For example, when an isolated server fails, the system can still provide the real-time information required by the traders.

The system also provides scalability: New applications are now being built in 10 weeks instead of 20. Also, any increase in new business volume is handled quickly and efficiently. The system was considered the world's largest-known grid computing commercial application in 2004.

The introduction of grid computing was an impressive project because of the huge mindshift away from the old system. It was necessary to make an organizational shift, overcoming skepticism from internal users who for years had run applications on their own dedicated servers. It was necessary to take away the perceived flexibility that the business units thought they had, and there was lots of resistance to the change. A major success factor was the emphasis on problem-solving rather than on pushing a new technology.

Other banks and financial institutions are experimenting with or already using grid computing. For the application at Capital One see Schneider (2004). For other applications see *egenera.com* and Shread (2006).

*Sources:* Compiled from Hamblen (2004), *jpmorgan.com* (accessed May 2006), and from Schneider (2004).

*For Further Exploration:* Why is grid computing so popular with investment banking? Is this a functional, enterprise, or global system?

# IT at Work 2.3

## Wireless Pepsi Increases Productivity

Pepsi Bottling Group (PBG), the largest manufacturer, seller, and distributor of Pepsi-Cola, has a mountainous job stocking and maintaining their Pepsi vending machines—including a huge amount of paperwork and frustrating searches for parts and equipment necessary to fix the machines. Any time a machine is out of stock or not functioning, the company loses revenue and profits. There are tens of thousands of machines to serve.

In 2002, the company began to equip its service technicians with handheld devices, hooked into a wireless wide area network (WWAN). A mobile database application allows wireless communications around the United States in real time. The database includes the repair parts inventory that is available on each service truck, so dispatchers know where and who to send for maintenance at any given moment. It also has a back-office system that maintains the overall inventory. In the near future the company will also be able to locate the whereabouts of each truck in real time, using global positioning systems (GPSs). The aim is to make scheduling and dispatching more effective.

In the summer of 2002 only about 700 technicians used the wireless system, but already the company was saving $7 million per year. Each technician has been able to handle one more service call each day than previously. PBG provided the wireless capability to about 300 more technicians in 20 more locations in late 2002, and to most corporate technicians by 2006.

*Sources:* Compiled from Rhey (2002) and from *pepsi.com* (accessed January 2006).

*For Further Exploration:* What are the capabilities of the handheld devices? Relate the handheld devices to the mobile database. The case deals with the maintenance issue. In what ways, if any, can wireless help with stocking issues? How is Pepsi's competitive advantage increased?

Recall from our discussion in Chapter 1 that enterprises face significant IT-related challenges that, if left unaddressed, could have a major negative impact on how well organizations perform.

For one thing, IT resources and budgets can't keep pace with the changes required to meet new business demands. Enterprises increasingly are expected to be adaptive and respond more quickly to customer demands, and at the same time ensure security, data integrity, and regulatory compliance.

Many companies are also constrained by their current IT architectures and infrastructures, which don't support the level of *flexibility* needed in rapidly changing business environments. Furthermore, many enterprises have a great deal of intellectual capital and other resources tied up in older, legacy systems. Much of the IT expertise today is focused on these older systems rather than on newer Web-based technologies. An attempted solution is SOA.

**Concepts and Benefits of SOA.** A growing number of enterprises are addressing these and other challenges by moving to the **service-oriented architecture (SOA).** SOA is an architectural concept that defines the use of services to support a variety of business needs. The basic idea of SOA is to *reuse* and *reconnect* existing IT assets (called services) rather than more time consuming and costly development of new systems.

In a service-oriented environment, organizations make resources available to participants via a network (in distributed computing), as independent services that can be accessed in a standardized way using Web Services.

Research firm Gartner, Inc., predicted in a June 2005 special report that 80 percent of software development projects will be based on SOA by 2008, naming it as one of the five hottest technology topics of 2005 (Clearly et al., 2005). D'Agostino (2006) provides an example of successful application at Starwood Hotels, and cited an IDC prediction that spending on SOA will increase from $3.6 billion in 2006 to $33 billion in 2010.

SOA is emerging as a way for organizations to bring business objectives and IT together. Organizations that are introducing SOA are achieving significant real-time results. Indeed, many experts agree that adoption of SOA can lead to significant benefits. The major benefits are:

• Reduced integration cost
• Improved business/IT alignment
• Extension and leveraging of existing IT investments
• Faster time to assemble new applications
• Lower IT maintenance cost

For additional information on SOA, see Erl (2005) and Bieberstein et al. (2006), *en.wikipedia.org/wiki/Service-oriented_architecture*, Joshi and Namjoshi (2006), and *service-architecture.com*. Also see the *SOA Web Services Journal*. For a comprehensive discussion on the usability of SOA see *blogs.ittoolbox.com/emergingtech/soa/archives/005834.asp*.

Most SOAs are implemented in Web Services.

**Web Services.** **Web Services** are self-contained, self-describing business and consumer modular applications, delivered over the Internet, that users can select and combine through almost any device, ranging from personal computers to mobile phones. By using a set of shared protocols and standards, these applications permit disparate systems to "talk" with one another—that is, to share data and services—without requiring human beings to translate the conversation. The result promises

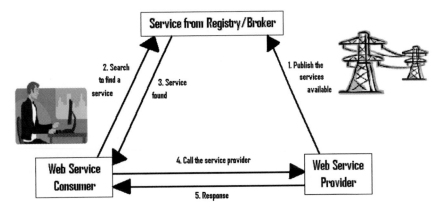

**Figure 2.8** Using Web Services in software-oriented architecture.

to be on-the-fly and in-real-time links among the online processes of different systems and companies. These links could shrink corporate IT departments, foster new interactions among businesses, and create a more user-friendly Web for consumers. Web Services provide for inexpensive and rapid solutions for application integration, access to information, and application development. In September 2003, Microsoft and IBM demonstrated how Web Services technology can allow their software to interact, and they pledged to cooperate in establishing standards. Such cooperation is expected to help speed up the adoption of Web Services (*The Economist*, 2004). For more, see Technology Guide 6 and also the special section on Web Services in *Communications of the ACM* (October 2003).

The basic idea of Web Services is shown in Figure 2.8. The figure illustrates four components:

**1.** A *service* is the means by which the needs of a consumer are fulfilled with the capabilities of the software provided. Examples of business services are "updating a loan application" or "checking an inventory level."

**2.** A *consumer* is the function that consumes the result of a service supplied by a provider.

**3.** A *provider* is the function that performs a service in response to a request by a consumer.

**4.** A *registry* (or directory) contains all the information regarding registered services, including detailed descriptions.

The consumer tries to find an existing programmed service in a registry of services maintained either inside a company (private registry) or outside the company (public registry). Providers of services publish (register) them (Step 1) in the registry. The consumer conducts a search (Step 2) in the registry. Once the consumer finds a match (Step 3), he sends a request to the service holder to get (for fee or free) the specific programmed service (Step 4). The provider then provides the services to the customer (Step 5). Details are provided in Chapter 15 and in TG 6.

**Open Source.** Implementing SOA and Web Services requires a set of standards for the flow of information among the participants. These are related to the concept of *open source* (see Chapter 15). Open source enables easy flow of information and integration in different computing systems. According to Fanini (2005), open source is entering the mainstream of IT and it is growing very rapidly.

**VIRTUALIZATION**

*Virtualization or virtualization computing* is a new concept that has several meanings in information technology and therefore several definitions. The major type of virtualization is *hardware virtualization* (usually referred to just as *virtualization*). In general, **virtualization** separates business applications and data from hardware resources. This allows companies to pool hardware resources—rather than to dedicate servers to applications—and assign those resources to applications as needed.

The major types of virtualization are:

- *Storage virtualization* is the pooling of physical storage from multiple network storage devices into what appears to be a single storage device that is managed from a central console.

- *Network virtualization* combines the available resources in a network by splitting the network load into manageable parts, each of which can be assigned (or reassigned) to a particular server on the network (Chapter 4).

- *Hardware virtualization* is the use of software to emulate hardware or a total computer environment other than the one the software is actually running in. It allows a piece of hardware to run multiple operating system images at once. This kind of software is sometimes known as a *virtual machine*.

Virtualization can increase the flexibility of IT assets, allowing companies to consolidate IT infrastructure, reduce maintenance and administration costs, and prepare for strategic IT initiatives such as grid computing, utility computing, and service-oriented architecture.

Virtualization helps to bring new products and services to the market quicker, and also enables business continuity (Chapter 16) in the event of a system failure. Finally, it enables sharing computing resources with other organizations. For more information see *virtualization.info, roughtype.com*, Wolf and Halter (2005), and Carr (2006).

**COMMERCIAL EFFORTS IN NEW COMPUTING ENVIRONMENTS**

Three software companies currently are developing major products in the emerging computer environments. All will incorporate utility computing, pervasive computing, and Web Services sometime in the future. Microsoft launched a major research effort, known as *Microsoft.Net* (*www.microsoft.com/net/default.asp*). IBM is developing its WebSphere platform (*ibm.com/software/websphere*). And Sun Microsystems is building a new system architecture in its N1 Project. For more about these commercial ventures, see Online File W2.10.

Whether an organization uses mainframe-based legacy systems or cutting-edge Web-based ones, its information resources are extremely important organizational assets that need to be protected and managed. This topic is presented in Section 2.7 and Chapters 14 through 16.

# 2.7 Managerial Issues

A modern organization possesses many information resources. In addition to the infrastructures, numerous applications exist, and new ones are continuously being developed. Applications have enormous strategic value. Firms rely on them so heavily that, in some cases, when they are not working even for a short time, an organization cannot function. Furthermore, the acquisition, operation, security, and maintenance of these systems may cost a considerable amount of money. The resources are scattered throughout the organization, and some of them change frequently. Therefore, it may be rather difficult to manage IS resources. It is essential to manage these information systems properly.

1. **Which IT resources are managed by whom?** The responsibility for the management of information resources is usually divided between two organizational entities: the *information systems department (ISD),* which is a corporate entity,

and the *end users,* who are scattered throughout the organization. This division of responsibility raises important questions such as: Which resources are managed by whom? What is the role of the ISD, its structure, and its place in the organization? What are the relationships between the ISD and the end users? Brief answers to these questions are provided in this section.

There is no standard menu for the division of responsibility for the development and maintenance of IS resources between the ISD and end users. In some organizations, the ISD manages most of these resources, regardless of where they are located and how they are used. In others, the ISD manages only a few. The division depends on many things: the size and nature of the organization, the amount and type of IT resources, the organization's attitudes toward computing, the attitudes of top management toward computing, the maturity level of the technology, the amount and nature of outsourced IT work, and even the country in which the company operates.

Generally speaking, the ISD is responsible for corporate-level and *shared resources,* while the end users are responsible for departmental IT resources. Sometimes the division between the ISD and the end users is based on other approaches. For example, the ISD may acquire or build systems and the end users operate and maintain them.

Because of interdependencies of information resources, it is important that the ISD and the end users work closely together and cooperate regardless of who is doing what. See Chapter 13.

2. **The role of the IS department.** The role of the ISD is changing from purely technical to more managerial and strategic (see Online File W2.11). As a result of this changing role, the position of the ISD within the organization is tending to be elevated from a unit reporting to a functional department (such as accounting) to a unit reporting to a senior vice president of administration or even to the CEO. In this new role, the ISD must be able to work closely with external organizations such as vendors, business partners, consultants, research institutions, and universities. In addition, the ISD and the end-user units must be close partners. The mechanisms that build the required cooperation are described in Chapter 13.

The role of the director of the ISD is also changing, from a technical manager to a senior executive, sometimes referred to as the **chief information officer (CIO),** or the *chief technology officer (CTO).* Details are provided in *cio.com/summaries/roledescription* and in Chapter 13.

3. **The transition to a digital enterprise.** Converting an organization to a networked-computing-based digital enterprise may be a complicated process. The digital enterprise requires a client/server architecture, an intranet, an Internet connection, and e-commerce policy and strategy, all in the face of many unknowns and risks. However, in many organizations this potentially painful conversion may be the only way to succeed or even to survive. When to do it, how to do it, what will be the role of the enabling information technologies, and what will be the impacts of such a conversion are major issues for organizations to consider.

The transition process may involve a move from the legacy systems to a Web-based client/server enterprisewide architecture. While the general trend is toward Web-based client/server, there have been several unsuccessful transformations and many unresolved issues regarding the implementation of these systems. The introduction of intranets seems to be much easier than that of other client/server applications. Yet, moving to any new architecture requires new infrastructure and a decision about what to do with the legacy systems, which may have a considerable impact on people, quality of work, and budget. A major aspect is the introduction of wireless infrastructure. These important issues are discussed in detail in Chapters 13 and 15 and in Technology Guide 6.

It should be noted that many companies need high-speed computing of high-volume data. Here the client/server concept may not be effective. In such cases, management should consider transformation of the legacy systems to new types of mainframes that use innovations that make the systems smaller and cheaper. Other options such as grid computing are available.

4. **How to deal with the outsourcing and utility computing trends.** As opportunities for outsourcing are becoming cheaper, available, and viable, the concept becomes more attractive. In the not-so-distant future, we will see outsourcing in the form of software-as-a-service. How much to outsource is a major managerial issue (see Chapters 14 and 15). Another issue is the offshore outsourcing to countries such as India and China.

**ETHICS**

5. **Ethical issues.** Systems developed by the ISD and maintained by end users may introduce some ethical issues. The ISD's major objective should be to build efficient and effective systems. But, such systems may invade the privacy of the users or create advantages for certain individuals at the expense of others. See Ethics in IT Management, including the Ethics Primer (Online File W1.5), and Online Chapter 17 for details.

# Integrating *IT*

### For the Accounting Major

Accountants must understand the types of information systems that exist in organizations and the way they support users to better design and audit systems. Furthermore, they must understand how TPSs work since most TPSs are accounting-related information flows. Finally, the accountants must be familiar with various compliance requirements and the flow of data and information to comply with the requirements.

### For the Finance Major

Financial analysts and managers are often involved in cost/benefit and justification of IT applications and, therefore, they must understand the various configurations of information systems, the options available, and the ways systems support users in other departments. Financial issues are critical both in assessing information systems (Chapter 14) and in managing the health of organizations (Chapter 11). Finally, understanding emerging systems and their capabilities and benefits will help finance people to better review the budgets requested from users for their acquisition and operations.

### For the Human Resources Management Major

Information systems are designed to support people in various job positions and functional areas. Understanding how this is done can help HRM people in assessing human performance and in improving recruiting and training programs. Furthermore, some of the emerging technologies provide the HRM function with opportunities to improve its own performance.

### For the IS Major

The Information Systems Department (ISD) is a support service to other departments and an extremely important and growing field. The ISD must understand the use of IT by end users and the interdependency among systems. Furthermore, the ISD may be involved in IT training as well as problem resolution in the functional areas. The IS people must understand all the options to acquire and build both traditional and emerging types of systems. Finally, IS people are responsible for shared information resources and their protection a and appropriate use in the functional areas.

### For the Marketing Major

Understanding the internal flow of information in organizations is vital for improving order fulfillment and status tracking so marketing and salespeople can be responsive to customer inquiries. Furthermore, knowledge of emerging systems allows the marketing department to improve its own operations. Several enterprise systems are crucial for marketing (e.g., CRM, ERP) so knowledge about their architecture can be very useful.

### For the Production/Operations Management Major

Changing production/operations to on-demand, real time, and mass customization requires changes in the supporting information systems. Therefore, knowledge about types of systems available and the support they render is critical. Furthermore, POM interact with partners along the supply chain so collaborative systems and their operations must be understood.

## Key Terms

Application program  *41*
Business architecture  *56*
Business process  *47*
Chief information officer
  (CIO)  *65*
Data item  *41*
Data workers  *54*
Database  *41*
Electronic exchanges  *57*
Electronic markets  *57*
Enterprise Web  *57*
Global IS  *49*
Grid computing  *60*

Information  *41*
Information infrastructure  *56*
Information system (IS)  *41*
Information technology
  architecture  *56*
Knowledge  *41*
Knowledge workers  *54*
Management information system
  (MIS)  *44*
Mobile commerce
  (m-commerce)  *60*
Mobile computing  *60*

Personal information management
  (PIM)  *42*
Pervasive computing  *60*
Service-oriented architecture
  (SOA)  *62*
Software-as-a-service (SaaS)  *58*
Transaction processing system
  (TPS)  *43*
Utility computing  *59*
Virtualization  *64*
Web-based systems  *56*
Web Services  *62*

## Chapter Highlights                                       Numbers Refer to Learning Objectives

**❶** Information systems collect, process, store, analyze, and disseminate data and information for a specific purpose. They do it primarily in application programs.

**❶** Information systems can be organized according to organizational hierarchy (e.g., departmental, enterprisewide, and interorganizational) or by the nature of supported task (e.g., operational, managerial, and strategic).

**❶** Interorganizational information systems (IOSs) connect two or more organizations and play a major role in e-commerce.

**❷** The transaction processing system (TPS) covers the core repetitive organizational transactions such as purchasing, billing, or payroll.

**❷** The data collected in a TPS are used to build other support systems.

**❷** The major functional information systems in an organization are accounting, finance, manufacturing (operations), human resources, and marketing.

**❷**, **❸** The term *management information system (MIS)* refers to the department that manages information systems in organizations. The acronym MIS is also used more generally to describe the field of IT as well as systems that support routine tasks of middle-level managers.

**❸** The main IT support systems are TPS, MIS, office automation systems, decision support systems, business intelligence systems, group support systems, knowledge management systems, enterprise information systems, expert systems, and artificial neural networks.

**❸** Managerial activities and decisions can be classified as operational, managerial (tactical), and strategic.

**❹** Three of the major IT-supported managerial activities are (1) improving supply chain operations, (2) integrating departmental systems with ERP, and (3) introducing a variety of customer relationship management (CRM) activities. IT is a major enabler of all of these.

**❺** Information architecture provides the conceptual foundation for building the information infrastructure and specific applications. It maps the information requirements as they relate to information resources.

**❺** There are three major configurations of information architecture: the mainframe environment, the PC environment, and the distributed (networked) environment. An emerging architecture is peer-to-peer.

**❺** The information infrastructure refers to the shared information resources (such as corporate networks, databases) and their linkages, operation, maintenance, and management. These support an array of applications.

**❻** In client/server architecture, several PCs (the clients) are networked among themselves and are connected to databases and other devices (the servers) that provide services to the client computers.

**❻** An enterprisewide information system is a system that provides computing capabilities to all of the organization's employees. It also provides accessibility to any data or information needed by any employee at any location.

**❻** Legacy systems are typically older systems in which the mainframe is or was at the core of the system.

**❼** Web-based systems refer to those applications or services that reside on a server that is accessible using a Web browser and work with Internet protocols. Examples are e-procurement, corporate portals, electronic markets and exchanges, and mobile commerce.

**8** There is a trend for renting application software as needed rather than buying it. This way, there is no need to build systems or own software. This approach, called software-as-a-service (*utility computing*) is similar to buying water or electricity when needed.

**8** Service-oriented architecture refers to architecture that assembles small information systems, one for each business service, to create new applications, usually by using Web Services technology.

**9** Information resources are extremely important, and they must be managed properly by both the ISD and end users. In general, the ISD manages shared enterprise information resources such as networks, while end users are responsible for departmental information resources, such as PCs and functional applications.

**9** The role of the ISD is becoming more managerial, and its importance is rapidly increasing.

## Virtual Company Assignment

### Information Architecture at The Wireless Café

Go to The Wireless Café's link on the Student Web Site. There you will be asked to study the restaurant's existing information technologies and document its information architecture.

#### Instructions for accessing The Wireless Café on the Student Web Site:

1. Go to *wiley.com/college/turban*.
2. Select Turban/Leidner/McLean/Wetherbe's *Information Technology for Management*, Sixth Edition.
3. Click on Student Resources site, in the toolbar on the left.
4. Click on the link for Virtual Company Web Site.
5. Click on Wireless Café.

## Online Resources

More resources and study tools are located on the Student Web Site and on WileyPLUS. You'll find additional chapter materials and useful Web links. In addition, self-quizzes that provide individualized feedback are available for each chapter.

## Questions for Review

1. Define data, information, and knowledge.
2. Describe a TPS.
3. What is an MIS?
4. How does a KMS work?
5. Describe operational, managerial, and strategic activities.
6. What information systems support the work of groups?
7. What is an enterprisewide system?
8. What is information architecture?
9. Define information infrastructure.
10. What is a Web-based system?
11. Define SOA.
12. What is mobile commerce?
13. Define software-as-a-service (SaaS).
14. Define virtualization.
15. List the information resources that are usually managed by end users.
16. Distinguish between a mainframe and a distributed environment.
17. Define a legacy system.
18. What is a client/server system?
19. Define utility computing.
20. What/who are knowledge workers?
21. Define grid computing.
22. Define Web Services.
23. What are the major characteristics of enterprise systems?

## Questions for Discussion

1. Discuss the logic of building information systems in accordance with the organizational hierarchical structure.
2. Distinguish between interorganizational information systems (IOS) and electronic markets.
3. Describe how business architecture, IT architecture, and information infrastructure are interrelated.
4. Explain how operational, managerial, and strategic activities are related to various IT support systems.
5. Relate the following concepts: client/server, distributed processing, and enterprisewide computing.
6. Discuss the capabilities of P2P architecture.
7. Web-based applications such as e-commerce and e-government exemplify the platform shift from legacy systems to Web-based computing. Discuss the advantages of a Web-based computing environment.
8. Is the Internet an infrastructure, architecture, or application program? Why? If none of the above, then what is it?
9. Discuss why SOA is considered the key to business agility.
10. Some speculate that utility computing will be the dominating option of the future. Do you agree? Discuss why or why not.
11. Compare and contrast grid computing and utility computing.
12. Discuss the relationship between SOA and on-demand computing.

## Exercises and Projects

1. Classify each of the following systems as one (or more) of the IT support systems:
   a. A student registration system in a university.
   b. A system that advises farmers about which fertilizers to use.
   c. A hospital patient-admission system.
   d. A system that provides a marketing manager with demand reports regarding the sales volume of specific products.
   e. A robotic system that paints cars in a factory.
2. Select two companies you are familiar with and find their mission statement and current goals (plans). Explain how these goals are related to operational, managerial, and strategic activities on a one-to-one basis. Then explain how information systems (by type) can support the activities (be specific).
3. Review the list of key IT management issues (see the item titled, "The Role of the IS Department," page 65).
   a. Present these issues to IT managers in a company you can access. (You may want to develop a questionnaire.)
   b. Have the managers vote on the importance of these items. Also ask them to add any items that are important to them but don't appear on the list. Report the results.
4. Review the following systems in this chapter and identify the support provided by IT:
   • Maybelline (Minicase 1)
   • J.P. Morgan (IT at Work 2.2)
   • Bomb detection by the FAA (see Online File W2.3)
   • Best Buy online (see Online File W2.4)

## Group Assignments and Projects

1. Observe a checkout counter in a supermarket that uses a scanner. Find some material that describes how the scanned code is translated into the price that the customers pay.
   a. Identify the following components of the system: inputs, processes, and outputs.
   b. What kind of a system is the scanner (TPS, DSS, ESS, ES, etc.)? Why did you classify it as you did?
   c. Having the information electronically in the system may provide opportunities for additional managerial uses of that information. Identify such uses.
   d. Checkout systems are now being replaced by self-service checkout kiosks and scanners. Compare the two.
2. Divide the class into teams. Each team will select a small business to start (a restaurant, dry cleaning business, small travel agency, etc.). Assume the business wants to become an e-business. Each team will plan the architecture for the business's information systems, possibly in consultation with Microsoft or another vendor. Make a class presentation.
3. Enter *oracle.com* and find material on SOA. Also see Joch (2005) and Online File W2.11. Identify the components of the SOA life cycle and describe them briefly. Explain why it is a cyclical process. Then search for Oracle Fusion Middleware and learn how it intends to implement the entire SOA life cycle. What are the benefits of using such middleware? Finally, describe why it is necessary to follow the six steps in the SOA life cycle to succeed with SOA.

# Internet Exercises

1. Enter the site of Federal Express (*fedex.com*) and find the current information systems used by the company or offered to FedEx's customers. Explain how the systems' innovations contribute to the success of FedEx.

2. Surf the Internet for information about airport security regarding bomb- and weapon-detecting devices. Examine the available products, and comment on the IT techniques used.

3. Enter the Web site of Hershey Foods (*hersheys.com*). Examine the information about the company and its products and markets. Explain how an intranet can help such a company compete in the global market.

4. Investigate the status of utility computing by visiting *utilitycomputing.com/forum*, *aspnews.com* (discussion forum), *google.com*, *ibm.com*, *oracle.com*, and *cio.com*. Prepare a report that will highlight the progress today and the current inhibitors.

5. Enter *argus-acia.com* and learn about new developments in the field of information architecture. Also, view the tutorials at *webmonkey.com* on this topic. Summarize major new trends.

6. Investigate the status of pervasive computing by looking at *ibm.com/software/pervasive*, *computer.org/pervasive*, and *percom.org*. Prepare a report.

7. Enter *cio.com* and find recent information on the changing role of the CIO and the ISD. Prepare a report.

8. Enter *oracle.com* and *sap.com* and identify material related to supply chain and enterprisewide systems. Prepare a report.

9. Enter *oracle.com* and read about grid computing. View the demo. Write a summary on business applications of grid computing.

10. Enter *vmware.com*, *xensource.com*, and *virtuozzo.com*. Identify their visualization products. List the major capabilities by vendor.

11. Enter *truecredit.com* and obtain your credit report. Then learn there about credit rating (provide a summary). Finally, download advice on how to improve your credit score (if necessary).

12. Enter *savvis.com* and identify their products related to virtualization and utility computing. Prepare a list of related capabilities.

13. Experience customizations by designing your own shoes at *nike.com*, your car at *jaguar.com*, your CD at *saregama.com*, and your business at *iprint.com*. Summarize your experiences (see Appendix 1A).

## Minicase 1

# E-Commerce Supports Field Employees at Maybelline

MKT

### The Business Problem

Maybelline is a leader in color cosmetics products (eye shadow, mascara, etc.), selling them in more than 70 countries worldwide (*maybelline.com*). The company uses hundreds of salespeople (field merchandising representatives, or "reps"), who visit drugstores, discount stores, supermarkets, and cosmetics specialty stores, in an attempt to close deals. This method of selling has proved to be fairly effective, and it is used by hundreds of other manufacturers such as Kodak, Nabisco, and Procter & Gamble. Sales managers from any company need to know, as quickly as possible, when a deal is closed or if there is any problem with the customer.

Information technology has been used extensively to support sales reps and their managers. Until 2000, Maybelline, as well as many other large consumer product manufacturers, equipped reps with an interactive voice response (IVR) system, by means of which they were to enter, every evening, information about their daily activities. This solution required that the reps collect data with

paper-based surveys completed for every store they visited each day. For example, the reps noted how each product was displayed, how much stock was available, how items were promoted, etc. In addition to the company's products the reps surveyed the competitors' products as well. In the evening, the reps translated the data collected into answers to the voice response system, which asked them routine questions. The reps answered by pressing the appropriate telephone keys.

The IVR system was not the perfect way to transmit sales data. For one thing, the IVR system consolidated information, delivering it to top management as a hard copy. However, unfortunately, these reports sometimes reached top management days or weeks too late, missing important changes in trends and the opportunities to act on them in time. Frequently, the reps themselves were late in reporting, thus further delaying the needed information.

Even if the reps did report on time, information was inflexible, since all reports were menu-driven. With the voice system the reps answered only the specific questions that applied to a situation. To do so, they had to wade through over 50 questions, skipping the irrelevant ones. This was a waste of time. In addition, some of the material that needed to be reported had no matching menu questions. Considered a success in the 1990s, the system was unable to meet the needs of the twenty-first century. It was cumbersome to set up and operate and was also prone to input errors.

### The Mobile Solution

Maybelline replaced the IVR system by equipping its reps with a mobile system, called Merchandising Sales Portfolio (MSP), from Thinque Corp. (*thinque.com*, now part of *meicpg.com*). It runs on handheld, pen-based PDAs, which have hand-writing recognition capability (from NEC), powered by Microsoft's CE operating system. The system enables reps to enter their information by handwriting their reports directly at the clients' sites. From the handheld device, data can be uploaded to a Microsoft SQL Server database at headquarters every evening. A secured Internet connection links the PDA to the corporate intranet (a synchronization process). The new system also enables district managers to electronically send daily schedules and other important information to each rep.

The system also replaced some of the functions of the EDI (electronic data interchange) system, the pride of the 1990s. For example, the reps' reports include inventory-scanned data from retail stores. These are processed quickly by an *order management system,* and passed whenever needed to the shipping department for inventory replenishment.

In addition to routine information, the new system is used for decision support. It is not enough to speed information along the supply chain; managers need to know the *reasons why* certain products are selling well, or not so well, in every location. They need to know what the conditions are at retail stores affecting the sales of each product, and they need to know it in a timely manner. The new system offers those capabilities.

### The Results

The system provided managers at Maybelline headquarters with an interactive link with the mobile field force.

Corporate planners and decision makers can now respond much more quickly to situations that need attention. The solution is helping the company forge stronger ties with its retailers, and it considerably reduces the amount of after-hours time that the reps spend on data transfer to headquarters (from 30–50 minutes per day to seconds).

The new system also performs market analysis that enables managers to optimize merchandising and customer service efforts. It also enables Maybelline to use a more sophisticated interactive voice response unit—to capture data for special situations. Moreover, it provides browser-based reporting tools that enable managers, regardless of where they are, to view retail information within hours of its capture. Using the error-checking and validation feature in the MSP system, reps make significantly fewer data entry errors.

Finally, the quality of life of Maybelline reps has been greatly improved. Not only do they save 30 to 40 minutes per day, but also their stress level has been significantly reduced. As a result, employee turnover has declined appreciably, saving money for the company.

*Sources:* Compiled from "Industry Solutions—Maybelline," at *thinque.com* (accessed May 2002), and from Seeley (2002).

### Questions for Minicase 1

1. IVR systems are still popular. What advantages do they have over even older systems in which the reps mailed or faxed reports?
2. Summarize the advantages of the new system over the IVR one.
3. Draw the flow of information in the system.
4. The existing technology enables transmission of data any time an employee can access the Internet with a wireline. Technically, the system can be enhanced so that the data can be sent *wirelessly* from any location as soon as they are entered. Would you recommend a wireless system to Maybelline? Why or why not?
5. Identify all information systems applications in this case and classify them per the text's classifications.

# Minicase 2

## How TrueCredit Utilizes SOA to Build Fast, Reliable Applications

### The Business Problem

TrueCredit is a subsidiary of TransUnion, a national U.S. credit bureau. It develops and markets credit-based products and services. The company needs to quickly develop

applications to maintain its competitive advantage. An example is an application that can support 50,000 simultaneous users (in 2006 vs. 25,000 in 2005). Another application is to improve application response time to less than a second (down from 3 seconds). Furthermore, software application development used to take 180 days or more per application. Management needed new applications in 90 days or less.

## The Business Solution

To meet its challenge, the company adopted SOA, coupled with changes in IT infrastructure, business practices, and software development methods. The company started by organizing the discrete functions in its application into standards-based interoperable software units, called services. Each service represents a chunk of data or instructions on how to perform an activity. Using the SOA approach, TrueCredit was able to combine and reuse the "services" to create new applications to meet other business needs, negating the need to build these from scratch, thus speeding up software development.

## The Results

A big advantage was the ability to quickly and easily collect and analyze data from multiple sources. For example, when you want to find your credit rating, data are accumulated from different credit agencies. These data are passed in SOA in little pieces across a number of different servers, permitting up to 50,000 simultaneous users to work at TrueCredit's Web site.

TrueCredit offers consumers credit reporting, credit scoring, and related financial services on both its own and its partners' Web sites. Thus, a customer of a credit card company (e.g., Providian or Citicorp) can go to his or her company Web site and see offers for credit products and services. TrueCredit is the engine behind many of these products.

Being a pioneer in applying SOA, the company encountered many SOA implementation challenges. For example, an underpowered hardware platform had to be replaced, and integration difficulties occurred with some of the partners' applications. Nevertheless, the company accomplished the implementation even though it was not an easy project. At the end, all objectives were achieved, and TrueCredit became a true adaptive, agile enterprise.

*Sources:* Compiled from McCormick (2006), and from *truecredit. com* (accessed April 2006).

## Questions for Minicase 2

1. What were the major reasons the company had to use SOA?
2. In what ways did they gain competitive advantage by using SOA?
3. What specific "services" can you identify in a business like this?
4. Why is it so important to serve 50,000 simultaneous users?
5. Classify this application using the material in Section 2.2.

# References

Agre, P. E., "P2P and the Promise of Internet Equality," *Communications of the ACM*, 46(2), February 2003.

Amato-McCoy, D. M., "Thin-Client Technology Trims IT Maintenance Costs, Adds Flexibility and Growth," *Stores*, November 2002.

Benford, S., et al., "Guest Editors' Introduction: Art, Design, and Entertainment in Pervasive Environments," *Pervasive Computing,IEEE*, 3(1), January–March 2004, pp. 12–13.

Bieberstein, N., et al., *Service-Oriented Architecture Compass-Business Value, Planning and Enterprise Roadmap*. Indianapolis, IN: Pearson Education, IBM Press, 2006.

Bills, S., "In Brief: Aurum to Do Imaging for JPM Chase Unit," *American Banker*, 167(210), October 22, 2002.

Carr, D. F., "Out of a Jam," *Baseline*, April 2006.

Clearly, D. W., J. Fenn, and D. C. Plummer, "Gartner's Position on the Five Hottest IT Topics and Trends in 2005," Gartner special report, May 12, 2005.

Colvin, G., "The FedEx Edge," *Fortune*, April 3, 2006.

Cone, E., "Customer Management," *eWeek*, October 2003a, *findarticles.com/p/articles/mi_zdewk/is_200310/ai_ziff109716* (accessed May 2006).

Cone, E., "Dallas Mavericks: Small Companies, Big Returns," *Baseline Magazine*, October 1, 2003b, *baselinemag.com/article2/0,1540, 1313703,00.asp* (accessed May 2006).

Conley, W. L., A. F. Farhoomand, and P. S. P. Ng, "Building an E-Business at FedEx Corporation," *Society for Information Management Annual Awards Paper Competition*, 2000, *simnet.org/library/doc/2ndplace. doc* (no longer available online).

Cortese, A., "The Power of Optimal Pricing," *Business 2.0*, September 2002.

D'Agostino, D., "Starwood Hotels Uses SOA to Improve Guest Services and Cut Costs," *CIO Insight*, April 27, 2006.

Dubie, D., and A. Bednarz, "Utility Computing Services Catching On," *Network World*, 21(15), April 12, 2004, p. 10.

Ebringer, T., "Microsoft Aims to be 'Trustworthy,'" *The Age*, April 8, 2003, *theage.com.au/articles/2003/04/07/1049567604820.html* (accessed May 2006).

Erl, T., *Service-Oriented Architecture*. Upper Saddle River, NJ: Prentice Hall PTR, 2005.

Erlikh, L., "Leveraging Legacy Systems in Modern Architecture," *Journal of Information Technology Cases and Applications*, July–September 2002.

Fanin, B., "Open Source Poised to Transform IT Management," *Linux Insider,* Marcy 7, 2006.

*FedEx.com* (accessed May 2006).

Duvall, M., "Supercharged," *Baseline,* October, 2005.

Gates, L., "State of Texas Recovers $400 Million through Predictive Analytics," *ADTmag.com,* May 26, 2005, *adtmag.com/article.asp?id=11214* (accessed May 2006).

Greenemeier, L., "IBM Expands On-Demand Services," *Information Week,* September 30, 2003.

Hamblen, M., "J.P. Morgan Harnesses Power with Grid Computing System," *ComputerWorld,* March 15, 2004.

"Handelsbanken," IBM Case Study, *www-3.ibm.com/e-business/doc/content/casestudy/35433.html* (no longer available online).

*Handelsbanken.com* (accessed May 2006).

Hewlett-Packard Company, "IT Consolidation: Journey to an Adaptive Enterprise—An Overview," *hp.com,* February 1, 2004, *wp.bitpipe.com/resource/org_1000733242_857/IT_Consolidation_Journey_WP4_In_Network.pdf?site_cd=gtech* (accessed May 2006).

"Industry Solutions—Maybelline," *Thinque.com,* May 15, 2002, *google.com/search?hl=en&lr=&q=industry+solutions+Maybelline+thinque.com* (accessed May 2006).

Jakovljevic, P. J., "Get on the Grid: Utility Computing," *Technology Evaluation Centers,* March 31, 2005a.

Jakovljevic, P. J., "Software as a Service Business Model," *Technology Evaluation Centers,* April 2, 2005b.

Jakovljevic, P. J., "What is Software as a Service," *Technology Evaluation Centers,* March 15, 2006.

Joch, A., "Modern Design," *Oracle Magazine,* May–June 2005, *oracle.com/technology/oramag/oracle/05-may/o35design.html* (accessed May 2006).

Joshi, M., and J. Namjoshi, "Evolving an Agile Enterprise: A Business Case for SOA Adoption," Patni white paper. India: Patni Computer Systems Ltd., February 2006.

Kawahara, Y., et al., "A Peer-to-Peer Message Exchange Scheme for Large-Scale Networked Virtual," *Telecommunications Systems,* 25(3–4), March–April 2004.

Koontz, C., "Develop a Solid Architecture," *e-Business Advisor,* January 2000.

Kumar, R., "Do Not Expect Utility Computing to Deliver Until 2006; Beware Utility Promises," *Computer Weekly,* October 28, 2003.

Lohr, S., "Sony to Supercharge Online Gaming," *International Herald Tribune,* February 28, 2003.

Margulius, D., "The Realities of Utility Computing," *Infoworld.com,* April 15, 2002, *infoworld.com/article/02/04/12/020415feutilitytci_1.html?UTILITY%20COMPUTING* (accessed May 2006).

Mason, B., "Grid Computing: More Questions than Answers," *CIO.com, www2.cio.com/analyst/report2153.html* (accessed May 2006).

McCormick, J., "Charging Ahead," *Baseline,* March 2006.

*Pepsi.com* (accessed January 2006).

Rhey, E., "Pepsi Refreshes, Wirelessly," *PC,* September 17, 2002, pp. 4–5.

Schneider, I., "Balance of Power: Capital One's Split-Focus IT Team," *Bank Systems & Technology,* May 25, 2004.

Schwartz, J., "Banking on Outsourcing: Jumbo Deals with Outsourcers Are Enabling Major Banks to Save on Costs," *VARbusiness,* February 24, 2003.

Seeley, R., "Wireless Storm Brewing?" *Atmag.com,* February 1, 2002, *adtmag.com/article.aspx?id=6011&amp;page=* (accessed May 2006).

Shread, P., "Banking on Grids," *Gridcomputingplant.com,* April 25, 2006, *gridcomputingplanet.com/news/article.php/3601451* (accessed May 2006).

Smith K., "IIPC: Vision to See, Faith to Believe, Courage to Do," *People Talk,* September–December 2002.

Staff, "SPSS Predictive Analytics Helps Texas Recover $400 Million in Unpaid Taxes," *B-eye-network.com,* May 16, 2005, *b-eye-network.com/view/868* (accessed May 2006).

Teevan, J., W. Jones, and B. B. Bederson, "Personal Information Management," *Communications of the ACM,* January 2006.

Wainewright, P., "The Power of Utility Computing," *ASPnews.com,* September 30, 2002.

Weill, P., and M. R. Vitale, *Place to Space: Migrating to eBusiness Models.* Boston: Harvard Business Press, 2001.

Wolf, C., and E. Halter, *Virtualization: From the Desktop to the Enterprise.* Berkeley, CA: Apress, 2005.

# Appendix 2A | Build-to-Order Production

The concept of build-to-order means that you start to make a product (service) only *after* an order for it is placed. This concept is as old as commerce itself, and was the only method of production until the Industrial Revolution began. According to this concept, if you need a pair of shoes, you go to a shoemaker who takes the measurement. You negotiate quality, design, and price, and you make a down payment. The shoemaker buys the materials and makes a customized product for you. Customized products were expensive, and it took a long time to finish them. This changed with the coming of the Industrial Revolution.

The Industrial Revolution started with the concept of dividing work into small parts. Such *division of labor* makes the work simpler, requiring less training for employees. It also allows for *specialization*. Different employees become experts in executing certain tasks. Because the work segments are simpler, it is easier to *automate* them. All this reduces the prices to consumers, and demand increases. So the concept of *build-to-market* developed. To build to market, it was necessary to design standard products, produce them, store them, and then sell them. The creation of standard products by automation drove prices down still further and demand accelerated. To meet the ever-increasing demand, the solution of mass production was created.

According to the concept of *mass production,* a manufacturer produces large amounts of standard products at a very low cost, and then "pushes" (markets) them to consumers. With increased competition and the desire to sell in remote markets, it was necessary to create special marketing organizations to do the sales. This new model also required the creation of large factories, and finance, accounting, personnel, and other departments to keep track of the many new and specialized business activities. In mass production, the workers do not know who the customers are, and frequently do not care about customers' needs or product quality. But the products are inexpensive, and their price fueled demand, so the concept became a dominant one. Mass production also required inventory systems at various places in the supply chain, which were based on forecasted demand. If the forecasted demand was wrong, the inventories were incorrect: Either the inventories were insufficient to meet demand, or there was too much inventory at hand.

As society became more affluent, the demand for customized products, especially cars, increased. To make sales, manufacturers had to meet this kind of demand. As long as the demand for customized product was small, there was no problem of meeting it. In purchasing a new car, for example, customers were asked to pay a premium and wait for a long time, and they were willing to do so. Slowly, the demand for customized products and services increased. In the 1970s, Burger King introduced the concept of "having it your way," and manufacturers began looking for solutions for providing customized products in large quantities. This idea is the essence of *mass customization.* Such solutions were usually enhanced by some kind of information technologies (Pine and Gilmore, 1999). Later, Dell Computer introduced the idea of customized PCs. This customization strategy was so successful that many other industries also wanted to try mass customization. However, they found that it is not so easy to do so (Zipkin, 2001 and Agrawal et al., 2001).

Using e-commerce can facilitate the use of customization and even the use of mass customization (Holweg and Pil, 2001). To understand this strategy, let's look first at a comparison of mass production, also known as a *push system,* with mass customization, also known as a *pull system,* as shown in Figure 2A.1.

One important area in the supply chain is ordering. Using EC a customer can self-configure the desired product online. The order is received in seconds, and once it is verified and payment arranged, the order is sent electronically to the production floor. This saves processing time and money. For complex products, customers may collaborate in real time with the manufacturer's designers, as is done at Cisco Systems. Again, time and money are saved, and errors are reduced due to better communication and collaboration.

Other contributions of EC to mass customization are the following: The customers' needs are visible to all partners in the order-fulfillment chain (fewer delays, faster response time); inventories are reduced due to rapid communication; and digitizable products and services can be delivered electronically, at almost no additional cost.

Another key area in mass customization is understanding what the customers want, and EC is also very helpful here (see Chapter 5 and Holweg and Pil, 2001). E-commerce can help in expediting the production changeover from one item to another. Also, since most mass production is based on assembly of standard components, EC can help make the

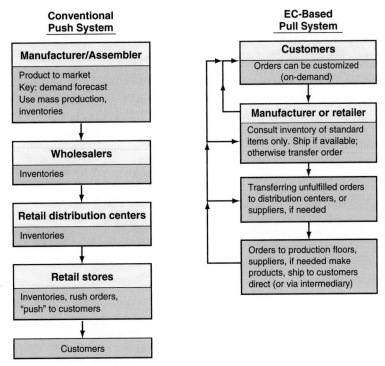

**Figure 2A.1** Comparison of a push-based supply chain and a pull-based supply chain.

production configuration in minutes, including the identification of the needed components and their location. Furthermore, a production schedule can be automatically generated, detailing deployment of all needed resources, including money. This is why many industries, and particularly the auto manufacturers, are planning to move to build-to-order using EC. As a result of this change in production methods, they are expecting huge cost reductions, shorter order-to-delivery time, and lower inventory costs. (See Exhibit 1 in Agrawal et al., 2001, and Holweg and Pil, 2001.)

Mass customization on a large scale is not easy to attain (Zipkin, 2001 and Agrawal et al., 2001), but if properly performed, it may become the dominant model in many industries.

**References for Appendix 2A**

Agrawal, M. T. V. et al., "The False Promise of Mass Customization," *McKinsey Quarterly,* No. 3, 2001.

Holweg, M., and F. Pil, "Successful Build-to-Order Strategies Start with the Customer," *MIT Sloan Management Journal,* 43(1), Fall 2001, pp. 74–83.

Pine, B. J., and J. Gilmore, "The Four Faces of Mass Customization," *Harvard Business Review,* January–February 1997.

Zipkin, P., "The Limits of Mass Customization," *MIT Sloan Management Review,* Spring 2001.

# Appendix 2B | Basics of Supply Chains

A **supply chain** is a concept describing the flow of *materials, information, money,* and *services* from raw material suppliers through factories and warehouses to the end customers. A supply chain also includes the *organizations* and *processes* that create and deliver these products, information, and services to the end customers. The term *supply chain* comes from a picture of how the partnering organizations are linked together. As shown in Figure 2B.1, a simple linear supply chain links a company that processes milk

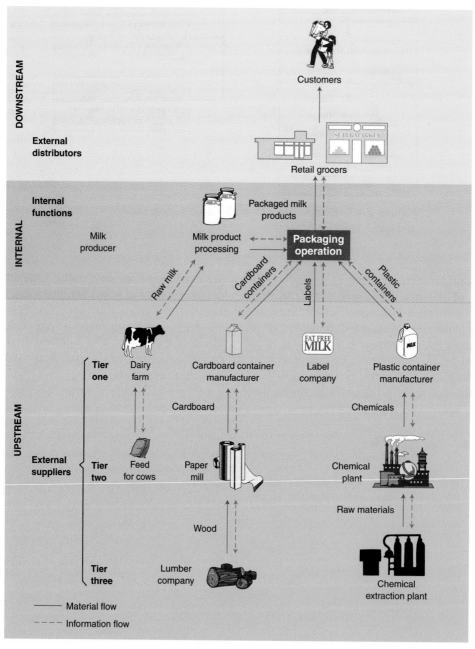

**Figure 2B.1** A simple supply chain for a manufacturer. Note: Only representative processes are shown. (*Source:* Modified from Reid and Sanders, 2002.)

(middle of the chain) with its suppliers (on the bottom) and its distributors and customers (on the top). The supply chain shown in Figure 2B.1 is fairly simple. As will be shown in Chapter 9, supply chains can be much more complex. Note that the supply chain shows both physical flows and the flow of information. Not shown is the flow of money, which usually goes in the direction opposite to the flow of the physical materials.

## SUPPLY CHAIN PARTS

A supply chain can be broken into three major parts: upstream, internal, and downstream as shown in Figure 2B.1.

- **The upstream supply chain.** The *upstream* part of the supply chain includes the activities of a company (a milk producer, in our case), with its first-tier suppliers and their connection to their suppliers (referred to as second-tier and third-tier suppliers). The supplier relationship can be extended several tiers, all the way to the origin of the material (e.g., mining ores, growing crops). In the upstream supply chain, the major activity is *procurement*.

- **The internal supply chain.** The *internal* part of the supply chain includes all of the *in-house* processes used in transforming the inputs received from the suppliers into the organization's outputs. It extends from the time the inputs enter an organization to the time that the products go to distribution outside of the organization. The internal supply chain is mainly concerned with production management, manufacturing, and inventory control (e.g., processing and packaging in Figure 2B.1).

- **The downstream supply chain.** The *downstream* part of the supply chain includes all the activities involved in delivering the products to the final customers. The downstream supply chain is directed at distribution, warehousing, transportation, and after-sale services (e.g., retail grocers in Figure 2B.1).

A company's supply chain involves an array of business processes that not only effectively transform raw items to finished goods or services but that also make those goods or services attractive to customers. The activities that add value to the company's goods or services are part of what is called the *value chain,* which we discuss in Chapter 13.

**Key Term for Appendix 2B**
Supply chain  *76*

## Reference for Appendix 2B

Reid, D., and N. Sanders, *Operations Management*. New York: John Wiley & Sons, 2002.

## Chapter 3

# Data Management: Data, Databases, and Warehousing

## Learning Objectives

After studying this chapter, you will be able to:

❶ Recognize the importance of data, their managerial issues, and their life cycle.

❷ Describe the sources of data, their collection, and quality issues.

❸ Describe document management systems.

❹ Explain the operation of data warehousing.

❺ Describe analytical processing.

❻ Discuss databases and database management systems.

❼ Describe the benefits of database management systems.

❽ Understand the difference between conceptual, logical, and physical data models.

❾ Understand how to use entity-relationship diagrams to model data.

❿ Discuss the role of marketing databases and provide examples.

⓫ Recognize the role of the Internet in data management.

## Integrating IT

 **ACC**
 **FIN**
 **MKT**
 **POM**
 **HRM**
 **IS**
 **SVC**

# FINDING DIAMONDS BY DATA MINING AT HARRAH'S

## The Problem

Harrah's Entertainment (*harrahs.com*) is a very profitable casino chain. With 40 casinos worldwide, it had $6.2 billion sales in 2005 and net income of $442 million. One of Harrah's casinos, located on the Las Vegas strip, typifies the marketing issues that casino owners face. The problem is very simple: how to attract visitors to come and spend money in your casino, and to do it again and again. There is no other place like the Las Vegas strip, where dozens of megacasinos and hundreds of small ones lure visitors by operating attractions ranging from fiery volcanoes to pirate ships.

Most casino operators use intuition to plan inducements for customers. Almost all have loyalty cards, provide free rooms to customers who visit frequently, give tickets for free shows, and more. The problem is that there is little differentiation among the casinos. Casinos believe they must give those incentives to survive, but do they help casinos to excel? Sandeep Khera, director of operational customer relationship management (CRM), has been using data warehousing technologies to provide analytical data for the company's CRM in order to market to the customers.

## The Solution

Harrah's strategy is based on technology-based CRM and the use of customer database marketing to test promotions. This combination enables the company to fine-tune marketing efforts and service-delivery strategies that keep customers coming back. Noting that 82.7 percent of its revenue comes from slot machines, Harrah's started by giving each player a loyalty smart card. A smart-card reader on each slot machine in all 40 of its casinos records each customer's activities. (Readers are also available in Harrah's restaurants, gift shops, etc., to record any spending.)

Logging your activities, you earn credit, as in other loyalty programs, for which you get free hotel rooms, dinners, etc. Such programs are run by most competitors, but Harrah's goes a step further: It uses a transactional database, known as a *data warehouse*, to analyze the data recorded by the card readers. By tracking millions of individual transactions, the IT systems assemble a vast amount of data on customer habits and preferences.

These data are fed into the enterprise data warehouse, which contains not only millions of transactional data points about customers (such as names, addresses, ages, genders) but also details about their gambling, spending, and preferences. This database has become a very rich repository of customer information, and it is mined for decision support.

**MKT**

The information found in Harrah's database indicated that a loyalty strategy based on same-store (same casino, in this case) sales growth could be very beneficial. The goal is to get a customer to visit your establishment regularly. For example, analysis discovered that the company's best customers were middle-aged and senior adults with discretionary time and income, who enjoyed playing slot machines. These customers did not typically stay in a hotel, but visited a casino on the way home from work or on a weekend night out. They responded better to an offer of $60 of casino chips than to a free room, two steak dinners, and $30 worth of chips, because they enjoyed the anticipation and excitement of gambling itself (rather than seeing the trip as a vacation get-away).

This strategy offered a way to differentiate Harrah's brand. Understanding the lifetime value of the customers became critical to the company's marketing strategy. Instead of focusing on how much people spend in the casinos during a single visit, the company began to focus on their total spending over a long time. By gathering more and more specific information about customer preferences, running experiments and analyses on the newly collected data, and determining ways of appealing to players' interests, the company was able to increase the amount of money customers spent there by appealing to their individual preferences.

As in other casinos with loyalty programs, players are segregated into three tiers, and the biggest spenders get priorities in waiting lines and in awards. There is a visible differentiation in customer service based on the three-tier hierarchy, and every experience in Harrah's casinos was redesigned to drive customers to want to earn a higher-level card. Customers have responded by doing what they can to earn the higher-tiered cards.

However, Harrah's transactional database is doing much more than just calculating gambling spending. For example, the casino knows which specific customers were playing at particular slot machines and at what time. Using data mining techniques, Harrah's can discover what specific machines appealed to specific customers. This knowledge enabled Harrah's to configure the casino floor with a mix of slot machines that benefited both the customers and the company.

In addition, by measuring all employee performance on the matrices of speed and friendliness and analyzing these results with data mining, the company is able to provide its customers with better experiences as well as earn more money for the employees. Harrah's implemented a bonus plan to reward hourly workers with extra cash for achieving improved customer satisfaction scores. The bonus program worked because the reward depends on everyone's performance. The general manager of a lower-scoring property might visit a colleague at a higher-scoring casino to find out what he could do to improve his casino's scores.

Harrah's realized many benefits from the upgrade in data warehousing applications, including being able to grab real-time information flowing off the casino floor (e.g., customer machine transactions, length of time the customer was playing, and the historical relationship with the casino). Using Teradata for the backend data warehouse, Harrah's has been able to provide more personalized floor service for its customers. They recognize first-time customers and customers who have been away from the casino for an extended period of time and need additional services. Another important program possible because of the active data warehousing components is

Harrah's player contact system (PCS). This program manages high-volume players who will be most profitable to the casino by assigning VIP hosts to them to maintain a long-term relationship.

## The Results

Harrah's experience has shown that the better the experience a guest has and the more attentive you are to him or her, the more money will be made. For Harrah's, good customer service is not a matter of an isolated incident or two but of daily routine. So, while somewhere along the Las Vegas strip a "Vesuvian" volcano erupts loudly every 15 minutes, a fake British frigate battles a pirate ship at regular intervals, and sparkling fountains dance in a lake, Harrah's continues to enhance benefits to its Total Rewards program, improves customer loyalty through customer service supported by the *data mining*, and of course makes lots of money.

The success of the active data warehouse project allowed Harrah's to initiate over 14,000 proactive customer interactions. It has seen a huge increase in customer service scores, enhancing customer loyalty. From 2004 to 2006, using the PCS, the growth in the VIP program has exceeded 20 percent. Harrah's has been able to maximize revenues while enhancing casino experiences.

*Sources:* Compiled from Loveman (2003), Levinson (2001), and Evans (2006).

## Lessons Learned from This Case

The opening case about Harrah's illustrates the importance of data analysis to a large entertainment company. It shows that it is necessary to collect vast amounts of data, organize and store them properly in one place, and then analyze the data and use the results to make better marketing and other corporate decisions. The case shows us that new data go through a process and stages: Data are collected, processed, and stored in a data warehouse. Then, data are processed by analytical tools such as data mining and decision modeling. The findings of the data analysis direct promotional and other decisions. Finally, continuous collection and analysis of fresh data provide management

with feedback regarding the success of management strategies.

This case also illustrates the importance of using active data warehouse solutions to enhance customer experiences with products and services. Organizations are better able to personalize customer interactions because of the data they have collected on the behavior of their customers.

In this chapter we explain how this process is executed with the help of IT. We will also deal with some additional topics that typically supplement the data management process. Data warehouse technology is important to the overall data management process.

# 3.1 Data Management: A Critical Success Factor

**DATA MANAGEMENT CONCERNS**

Corporate data are key strategic assets and so managing data quality is vital to organizations. Dirty data can result in poor business decisions, poor customer service, and inadequate product design.

The goal of data management is to provide the infrastructure to transform raw data into corporate information of the highest quality. The foundation of data management has four building blocks:

1. Data profiling—understanding the data
2. Data quality management—improving the quality of data
3. Data integration—combining similar data from multiple sources
4. Data augmentation—improving the value of the data

Consider the complexity of data management.

Data management at the National Security Archive is extremely difficult since only 22 staff manage over 2 million documents from 80 government agencies, and that volume is growing by 50,000 documents annually. It is an incredible task to manage, search, and retrieve data located throughout the organization. Fortunately, they have the methodology, models, software, and infrastructure available in order to manage large blocks of data.

**DATA MANAGEMENT**

Since data are processed in several stages and possibly places, they may be subject to some problems and difficulties.

**Data Problems and Difficulties.** Managing data in organizations is difficult for various reasons:

- The amount of data increases exponentially with time. Much past data must be kept for a long time, and new data are added rapidly. However, only small portions of an organization's data are relevant for any specific application, and that relevant data must be identified and found in order to be useful.
- Data are scattered throughout organizations and are collected by many individuals using several methods and devices. Data are frequently stored in several servers and locations, and in *different* computing systems, databases, formats, and human and computer languages. This may create problems, as demonstrated in the case of data needed for homeland security (see Minicase 1, which also discusses a solution).
- An ever-increasing amount of external data needs to be considered in making organizational decisions.
- Data security, quality, and integrity are critical, yet are easily jeopardized. In addition, legal requirements relating to data differ among countries and change frequently.
- Data management tool selection can be a major problem because of the huge number of products available.
- Data are being created and used offline without going through quality control checks; hence the validity of the data is questionable.
- Data throughout an organization are redundant and often out-of-date, creating a huge maintenance problem for data managers.

These difficulties, and the critical need for timely and accurate information, have prompted organizations to search for effective and efficient data management solutions.

**Solutions to Managing Data.** Historically, data management has been geared to supporting transaction processing by organizing the data in a *hierarchical format* in one location. This format supports secured and efficient high-volume processing. With more data on end-user computers, it may be inefficient for queries and other ad-hoc applications to use traditional data management methods. Therefore, *relational databases*, based on organization of data in rows and columns, were added to facilitate end-user computing and decision support. (Data organization is described further in Section 3.3.)

With the introduction of client/server environments and Web technologies, databases became distributed throughout organizations, creating problems in managing data. This was the major reason that Harrah's sought the creation of a *data warehouse*. As we will see later, the intranet, extranets, and Web technologies can also be used to improve data management.

It is now well recognized that data are an asset, although they can be a burden to maintain. The purpose of appropriate data management is to ease the burden of maintaining data and to enhance the power from their use. To see how this is done, let's begin by examining how data are processed during their life cycle.

**DATA LIFE CYCLE PROCESS**

Businesses do not run on raw data. They run on data that have been processed to information and knowledge, which managers apply to business problems and opportunities. As seen in the Harrah's case, *knowledge* fuels solutions. Everything from innovative product designs to brilliant competitive moves relies on knowledge (see Markus et al., 2002). However, because of the difficulties of managing data, cited earlier, deriving knowledge from accumulated data may not be simple or easy.

Transformation of data into knowledge and solutions is accomplished in several ways. In general, it resembles the process shown in Figure 3.1. It starts with new data collection from various sources. These data are stored in a database(s). Then the data are preprocessed to fit the format of a data warehouse or data marts, where they are stored. Users then access the warehouse or data mart and take a copy of the needed data for analysis. The analysis is done with data analysis and mining tools, which look for patterns, and with intelligent systems, which support data interpretation.

Note that not all data processing follows this process. Small and medium companies do not need data warehouses, and even many large companies do not need them. (We will see later who needs them.) In such cases data go directly from data sources or databases to an analysis (broken line in Figure 3.1). An example of direct processing is an application that uses real-time data. These can be processed as they are collected and immediately analyzed. Many Web data are of this type. In such a case, as we will see later, we use Web mining instead of data mining.

The result of these activities is the generating of information and knowledge. Both the data (at various times during the process) and the knowledge (derived at the end of the process) may need to be presented to users. The presentation can be accomplished by using different visualization tools. The created knowledge may be stored in an organizational knowledge base (as shown in Chapter 10) and used, together with decision support tools, to provide solutions to organizational problems. The elements and the process shown in Figure 3.1 are discussed in the remaining sections of this chapter and in Chapters 11 and 12.

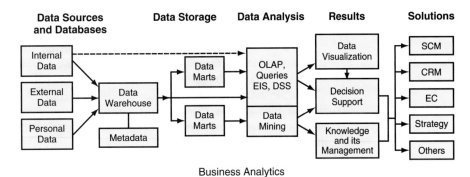

**Figure 3.1** Data life cycle.

The data life cycle begins with the acquisition of data from data sources. Data sources can be classified as internal, personal, and external.

**Organizational Data.**  An organization's internal data are about people, products, services, and processes. Such data may be found in one or more places. For example, data about employees and their pay are usually stored in the corporate database. Data about equipment and machinery may be stored in the maintenance department database. Sales data can be stored in several places—aggregate sales data in the corporate database, and details at each regional database. Internal data are usually accessible via an organization's intranet.

**End User Data.**  IS users or other corporate employees may create data that are not centralized. These data are not necessarily just facts, but may include concepts, thoughts, and opinions. They include, for example, subjective estimates of sales, opinions about what competitors are likely to do, or certain rules and formulas developed by end users. These data can reside on the user's PC or be placed on departmental or business units' databases or on the corporate knowledge bases.

**External Data.**  There are many sources for external data, ranging from commercial databases to sensors and satellites. Government reports constitute a major source for external data. Data are available on CD-ROMs and memory chips, on Internet servers, as films, and as sound or voices. Pictures, diagrams, atlases, and television are other sources of external data. Hundreds of thousands of organizations worldwide place publicly accessible data on their Web servers, flooding us with data. Most external data are irrelevant to any single application. Yet, much external data must be monitored and captured to ensure that important data are not overlooked. Many thousands of databases all over the world are accessible through the Internet. Much of the database access is free. Some external data flow to an organization on a regular basis through EDI or through other company-to-company channels.

The diversity of data and the multiplicity of sources make the task of data collection fairly complex. Raw data can be collected manually or electronically. Some examples of manual data collection methods are surveys, observations, and contributions from experts. Electronic data collection includes using a wide variety of hardware and software for data storage, communication, transmission, and presentation. **Clickstream data** are those that can be collected automatically using special software from the company's Web site. Other types of external data collection include online surveys, online polls, data warehousing data, Web site profiling, and transmitted or scanned data.

The collection of data from multiple external sources may be an even more complicated task. One way to improve it is to use a *data flow manager* (*DFM*), which takes information from external sources and puts it where it is needed, when it is needed, in a usable form (e.g., see *smartdraw.com*). A DFM consists of (1) a decision support system, (2) a central data request processor, (3) a data integrity component, (4) links to external data suppliers, and (5) the processes used by the external data suppliers.

The complexity of data collection can create data-quality problems. Therefore, regardless of how they are collected, data need to be validated. A classic expression that sums up the situation is "garbage in, garbage out" (GIGO). Safeguards for data quality are designed to prevent data problems.

**DATA QUALITY AND INTEGRITY**

**Data quality (DQ)** is an extremely important issue since quality determines the data's usefulness as well as the quality of the decisions based on the data. It has the following dimensions: *accuracy, accessibility, relevance, timeliness,* and *completeness.* Data are frequently found to be inaccurate, incomplete, or ambiguous, particularly in large, centralized databases. The economical and social damage from poor-quality data has actually been calculated to have cost organizations billions of dollars (see Chapter 17). Data quality is the cornerstone of effective business intelligence.

An example of typical data problems, their causes, and possible solutions is provided in Table 3.1. For a discussion of data auditing and controls, see Chapter 16.

Although business executives recognize the importance of having high-quality data, they discover that numerous organizational and technical issues make it difficult to reach this objective. For example, data ownership issues arise from the lack of policies defining responsibility and accountability in managing data. Inconsistent data-quality requirements of various standalone applications create an additional set of problems as organizations try to combine individual applications into integrated enterprise systems. Interorganizational information systems add a new level of complexity to managing data quality. Companies must resolve the issues of administrative authority to ensure that each partner complies with the data-quality standards. The tendency to delegate data-quality responsibilities to the technical teams, as opposed to business users, is another common pitfall that stands in the way of high-quality data (Loshin, 2004).

The different categories of data quality are *standardization* (for consistency), *matching* (of data if stored in different places), *verification* (against the source), and *enhancement* (adding of data to increase its usefulness). Whichever system is used, once the major variables and relationships in each category are identified, an attempt can be made to find out how to better manage the data.

One approach to data management is a three-step method that begins with analyzing the actual organizational processes, moves on to analyzing the entities that these elements comprise, and finishes by analyzing the relationship between the data in the business processes that the data must support. Before beginning, make sure you understand the business process data flows. Questions to ask are: What information is input to the process? What information is changed or created during the process? What happens to the information once the process is complete? What value-added information does the process produce?

A critical component in the data quality equation is having subject matter experts on hand. The subject matter expert is the person who knows whether the actual data are correct, or could be correct based on the company's business processes.

| TABLE 3.1 | Data Problems and Possible Solutions | |
|---|---|---|
| **Problem** | **Typical Cause** | **Possible Solutions** |
| Incorrect data | Bad data entry | Automated data entry, scanning systems for data entry, Web forms for individuals entering data with drop-down menus and radio buttons. |
| Redundant data | Poor database design | Redesign the data model, normalize the relational database. |
| Stolen data | Poor security | Take appropriate security measures. |
| Irrelevant data | Wrong data collected | Collect data that are appropriate for the task and avoid related data that are not relevant. |
| Missing data | Required data never existed | Generate and enter data needed for use. |

*Sources:* Compiled and modified from Alter (1980) and Kroenke (2006).

An area of increasing importance is the quality of data that are processed very fast in *real time*. Many decisions are being made today in such an environment.

Another major data quality issue is data integrity. Many definitions of data integrity in the context of managing data have been proposed. In general, the concept of integrity means that data must be accurate, correct, and valid.

Organizational members need to realize the value of their data and treat their data as valuable assets. This can be achieved with processes that support and reward data quality. Often the true stewards of data quality are the employees who enter the data at their source, and functional area managers who are responsible for the integrity and reliability of the organization's data.

**DATA PRIVACY, COST, AND ETHICS**

Collecting data about employees, customers, or any other people raises the concern about privacy protection. Data need to be accessible only to authorized people. Keeping data secure costs money during collection, storage, and use. Furthermore, providing information required by the government means even more cost to organizations. An example is the situation of homeland security described in *A Closer Look 3.1.*

**DOCUMENT MANAGEMENT**

There are several major problems with paper documents. For example, in maintaining paper documents, we can pose the following questions: (1) Does everyone have the current version? (2) How often does it need to be updated? (3) How secure are the documents? (4) How can the distribution of documents to the appropriate individuals be managed in a timely manner? and (5) How can a company reduce the paper usage from the viewpoints of protecting the environment and saving natural resources? The answers to these and similar questions may be difficult, as described in *A Closer Look 3.2.*

Electronic data processing overcomes some of these problems. One of the earliest IT-enabled tools of data management is called *document management*. When documents are provided in electronic form from a single repository (typically a Web server), only the current version is provided.

# A Closer Look 3.1

## National Security Depends on Intelligence and Data Mining

Those driven by ideological or political motives and the intent to do harm use the Internet to plan and coordinate their activities, as had been done to plan operations for the September 11, 2001 attacks. Terrorists use every tactic and technology to carry out their destructive plans—hacking, spamming, phishing, identity theft, and Web site propaganda and recruitment. Computers seized in Afghanistan reportedly revealed that al Qaeda was collecting intelligence on targets and sending encrypted messages via the Internet.

Given these threats and tactics, national security depends on timely intelligence efforts for early detection and deterrence of these activities. Intelligence agencies, such as the FBI (*fbi.gov*) and CIA (*cia.gov*) in the United States and MI6 (*intelligence.gov.uk/agencies/mi6.asp*) and Defence Intelligence Staff (DIS) (intelligence.gov.uk/agencies/dis.asp) in the United Kingdom, mine enormous amounts of data to monitor potential threats to national security. Some data collection might infringe on privacy. The DIS, for example, conducts all-source intelligence analysis from both overt and covert sources.

Data mining for intelligence purposes combines statistical models, powerful processors, and artificial intelligence to find and retrieve valuable information. There are two types of data mining systems: *subject-based systems* that retrieve data to follow a lead, and *pattern-based systems* that look for suspicious behaviors. An example of a subject-based data mining technique is *link analysis,* which uses data to make connections between seemingly unconnected people or events. With link analysis software, other people with whom a suspect may be interacting can be uncovered. For example, a suspicious link could be a spike in the number of e-mail exchanges between two parties (one of which is a suspect), checks written by different people to the same third party, or plane tickets bought to the same destination on the same departing date. Many experts believe that the U.S. National Security Agency project analyzing millions of domestic phone records is a link analysis system.

These efforts are considered crucial to global security. Some military experts believe that war between major nations is becoming obsolete and that our future defense will rely far more on intelligence officers with databases than upon battle tanks and artillery. A key lesson of September 11 is that America's intelligence agencies must work together as a single unified intelligence enterprise.

*Sources:* Compiled from *Whitehouse.gov* (2004); Volonino et al. (2007), and Worthen (2006).

**Document management** is the automated control of electronic documents, page images, spreadsheets, voice word processing documents, and other complex documents through their entire life cycle within an organization, from initial creation to final archiving. Document management offers various benefits: It allows organizations to exert greater control over production, storage, and distribution of documents, yielding greater efficiency in the reuse of information, the control of a document through a workflow process, and the reduction of product cycle times. Document management deals with knowledge in addition to data and information.

The major tools of document management are workflow software, authoring tools, scanners, and databases (known as object-relational database management systems). **Document management systems (DMSs)** provide decision makers with information in an electronic format and usually include computerized imaging systems that can result in substantial savings.

One of the major vendors of document management is Lotus Development Corporation. Its document databases and their replication property provide many advantages for group work and information sharing (see *lotus.com*).

Organic Information Abstraction (OIA) is a new layer in the technology infrastructure that connects separate environments of data, content, and text. This integrated architecture will allow organizations to deal with problems across structured and unstructured information sources and result in improved information access, recall, and accuracy.

# A Closer Look 3.2

## How Companies Use Document Management Systems

Here are some examples of how companies use document management systems to manage data and documents:

The Surgery Center of Baltimore stores all of its medical records electronically, providing instant patient information to doctors and nurses anywhere and any time. The system also routes charts to the billing department, whose employees can scan and e-mail any related information to insurance providers and patients. The DMS also helps maintain an audit trail, including providing records for legal purposes or action. Business processes have been expedited by more than 50 percent, the cost of such processes is significantly lower, and morale of office employees in the center is up (see *laserfiche.com/newsroom/ baltimore.html*).

American Express is using a DMS to collect and process over one million customer satisfaction surveys each year. The data are collected in templates of over 600 different survey forms, in 12 languages, in 11 countries. The system (TELEform from Alchemy and Cardiff Software) is integrated with AMEX's legacy system and is capable of distributing processed results to many managers. Staff who process these forms have been reduced from 17 to 1, saving AMEX over $500,000 each year (see case studies at *captaris.com*).

LifeStar, an ambulance service in Tulare, California, is keeping all historical paper documents on optical disks. Hundreds of boxes with documents were digitized, and so are all new documents. Furthermore, all optical disks are backed up and are kept in different locations for security purposes (see *laserfiche.com/newsroom/tulare.html*).

In Toronto, Canada, the Works and Emergency Services Department uses a Web-based record document-retrieval solution. With it, employees have immediate access to drawings and the documents related to roads, buildings, utility lines, and more. Quick access to these documents enables emergency crews to solve problems, and even save

lives, much faster. Laptop computers are installed in each departmental vehicle, loaded with maps, drawings, and historical repair data (see *laserfiche.com/newsroom/ torantoworks.html*).

The University of Cincinnati, a state university in Ohio, is required to provide authorized access to the personnel files of 12,000 active employees and tens of thousands of retirees. There are over 75,000 queries about the personnel records every year, and answers need to be found among 2.5 million records. Using an antiquated microfilm system to find answers took days. The solution was a DMS that digitized all paper and microfilm documents, making them available via the Internet and the intranet. An authorized employee can now use a browser and access a document in seconds (see *captaris.com/alchemy*).

The European Court of Human Rights (44 countries in Europe) created a Web-based document and KM system which was originally stored on an intranet and now is stored in a separate organizational knowledge base. The DMS has had over 20 million hits in 2002 (Canada NewsWire, 2003). Millions of euros are saved each year just on printing and mailing documents.

McDonnell-Douglas (now part of the Boeing Company) distributed aircraft service bulletins to its customers around the world using the Internet. The company used to distribute a staggering volume of bulletins to over 200 airlines, using over 4 million pages of documentation every year. Now it is all on the Web, saving money and time both for the company and for its customers.

Motorola uses a DMS not only for document storage and retrieval, but also for small-group collaboration and company-wide knowledge sharing. It develops virtual communities where people can discuss and publish information, all with the Web-enabled DMS.

## 3.2  File Management

A computer system organizes data in a hierarchy that begins with bits, and proceeds to bytes, fields, records, files, and databases (see Figure 3.2). A *bit* represents the smallest unit of data a computer can process (i.e., a 0 or a 1). A group of eight bits, called a *byte*, represents a single character, which can be a letter, a number, or symbol. A logical grouping of characters into a word, a group of words, or a complete number is called a *field*. For example, a student's name would appear in the name field.

A logical group of related fields, such as customer's name, product sold, and hours worked, are examples of a *record*. A logical group of related records is called a *file*. For example, the student records in a single course would constitute a data file for that course. A logical group of related files would constitute a **database.** All stu-

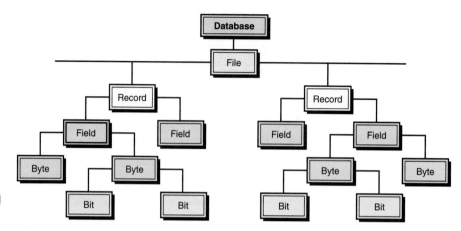

**Figure 3.2** Hierarchy of data for a computer-based file.

dents' course files could be grouped with files on students' personal histories and financial backgrounds to create a students' database.

Another way of thinking about database components is that a record is a physical description of an *entity*. An entity is a person, place, thing, or event on which we maintain data. Each characteristic or quality describing a particular entity is called an **attribute** (corresponds to a field on a record). Examples of attributes are customer name, invoice number, and order date.

Every record in a file should contain at least one field that uniquely identifies that record so that the record can be retrieved, updated, and sorted. This identifier field is called the **primary key.** For example, a student record in a U.S. college could use the Social Security number as its primary key. In addition, locating a particular record may require the use of secondary keys. **Secondary keys** are other fields that have some identifying information, but typically do not identify the file with complete accuracy. For example, the student's last name might be a secondary key. It should not be the primary key, as more than one student can have the same last name. **Foreign keys** are keys that provide relationships between two tables.

**ACCESSING RECORDS FROM COMPUTER FILES**

Records can be arranged in several ways on a storage medium, and the arrangement determines the manner in which individual records can be accessed. In **sequential file organization,** data records must be retrieved in the same physical sequence in which they are stored. (The operation is like a tape recorder.) In **direct** or **random file organization,** users can retrieve records in any sequence, without regard to actual physical order on the storage medium. (The operation is like a CD drive.) Magnetic tape utilizes sequential file organization, whereas magnetic disks use direct file organization.

The **indexed sequential access method (ISAM)** uses an index of key fields to locate individual records (see Figure 3.3). An *index* to a file lists the key field of each record and where that record is physically located in storage. Records are stored on disks in their key sequence. A *track index* shows the highest value of the key field that can be found on a specific track. To locate a specific record, the track index is searched to locate the cylinder and the track containing the record. The track is then sequentially read to find the record.

The **direct file access method** uses the key field to locate the physical address of a record. This process employs a mathematical formula called a *transform algorithm*

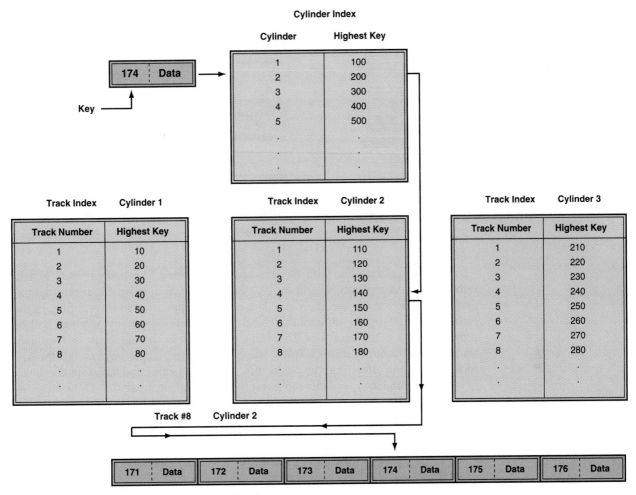

**Figure 3.3** Indexed sequential access method.

to translate the key field directly into the record's storage location on disk. The algorithm performs a mathematical calculation on the record key, and the result of that calculation is the record's address. The direct access method is most appropriate when individual records must be located directly and rapidly for immediate processing, when a few records in the file need to be retrieved at one time, and when the required records are found in no particular sequence.

PROBLEMS ARISING FROM THE FILE ENVIRONMENT

Organizations typically began automating one application at a time. These systems grew independently, without overall planning. Each application required its own data, which were organized into a data file. This approach led to redundancy, inconsistency, data isolation, and other problems. Figure 3.4 uses a university file environment as an example.

The applications (e.g., marketing, accounting, or finance) would share some common core functions, such as input, report generation, querying, and data browsing. However, these common functions would typically be designed, coded, documented, and tested, at great expense, for each application. Moreover, users must be trained to use each application. File environments often waste valuable resources creating and maintaining similar applications, as well as in training users how to use them.

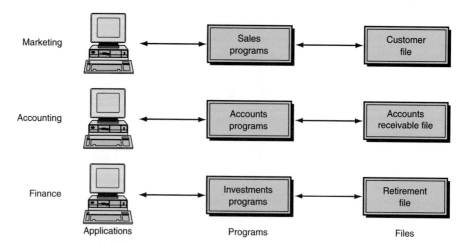

**Figure 3.4** Computer-based files of this type cause problems such as redundancy, inconsistency, and data isolation.

Other problems arise with file management systems. The first problem is **data redundancy:** As applications and their data files were created by different programmers over a period of time, the same data could be duplicated in several files. In the example, each data file will contain records about customers many of whom will be represented in other data files. Therefore, customers in the aggregate will contain some amount of duplicate data. This wastes physical computer storage media, the customer's time and effort, and the clerks' time needed to enter and maintain the data.

Data redundancy leads to the potential for data inconsistency. **Data inconsistency** means that the actual values across various copies of the data no longer agree or are not synchronized. For example, if a student changes his or her address, the new address must be changed across all applications in the university that require the address.

File organization also leads to difficulty in accessing data from different applications, a problem called **data isolation.** With applications uniquely designed and implemented, data files are likely to be organized differently, stored in different formats (e.g., height in inches versus height in centimeters), and often physically inaccessible to other applications. In the example, a manager who wanted to know which products customers were buying and which customers also owed in the accounts receivable system would most likely not be able to get the answer from the computer-based file system. He or she would probably have to manually compare printed output data from two data files. This process would take a great deal of time and effort and would ignore the greatest strengths of computers—fast and accurate processing.

Additionally, *security* is difficult to enforce in the file environment, because new applications may be added to the system on an ad-hoc basis; with more applications, more people have access to data.

The file environment may also cause **data integrity** problems. Data values must often meet integrity constraints. For example, the students' Social Security data field should contain no alphabetic characters, and the students' grade-point-average field should not be negative. It is difficult to place data integrity constraints across multiple data files.

Moreover, the shared file environment may have concurrency problems. While one application is updating a record, another application may access that record. As a result, the second application may not get the desired information.

Finally, applications should not have to be developed with regard to how the data are stored. That is, applications and data in computer systems should have *application/data independence*—that is, they should be independent. In the file environment, the applications and their associated data files are dependent on each other.

Storing data in data files that are tightly linked to their applications eventually led to organizations having hundreds of applications and data files, with no one knowing what the applications did or what data they required. There was no central listing of data files, data elements, or definitions of the data. The numerous problems arising from the file environment approach led to the development of *databases*.

# 3.3 Databases and Database Management Systems

The amount of data the average business collects and stores is doubling each year. Businesses collect data from multiple sources, including customer-relationship management and enterprise resource planning applications, online e-commerce systems, and suppliers and business partners. The steadily falling price of storage also fuels the data deluge, with the cost of storing 1 Mbyte of data now about 1 percent of what it was 10 years ago. Organizations have found databases to be the optimal way to store and access such huge amounts of data.

**DATABASES**

A *database* is an organized logical grouping of related files. In a database, data are integrated and related so that one set of software programs provides access to all the data, alleviating many of the problems associated with data file environments. Therefore, data redundancy, data isolation, and data inconsistency are minimized, and data can be shared among all users of the data. In addition security and data integrity are increased, and applications and data are independent of one another.

A *centralized database* has all the related files in one physical location. See Figure 3.5. Centralized database files on large, mainframe computers were the main data-base platform for decades, primarily because of the enormous capital and operating costs of other alternatives. Not only do centralized databases save the expenses associated with multiple computers, but they also provide database administrators with the ability to work on a database as a whole at one location. Files can generally be made more consistent with each other when they are physically kept in one location because file changes can be made in a supervised and orderly fashion. Files are not accessible except via the centralized host computer, where they can be protected more easily from unauthorized access or modification. Also, recovery from disasters can be more easily accomplished at a central location.

Like all centralized systems, however, centralized databases are vulnerable to a single point of failure. When the centralized database computer fails to function properly, all users suffer. Additionally, access speed is often a problem when users are widely dispersed and must do all of their data manipulations from great distances, thereby incurring transmission delays.

A *distributed database* has complete copies of a database, or portions of a database, in more than one location, which is usually close to the user (see Figure 3.5). There are two types of distributed databases: replicated and partitioned.

A *replicated database* has complete copies of the entire database in many locations, primarily to alleviate the single-point-of-failure problems of a centralized database as well as to increase user access responsiveness. There is significant overhead, however, in maintaining consistency among replicated databases, as records are added, modified, and deleted.

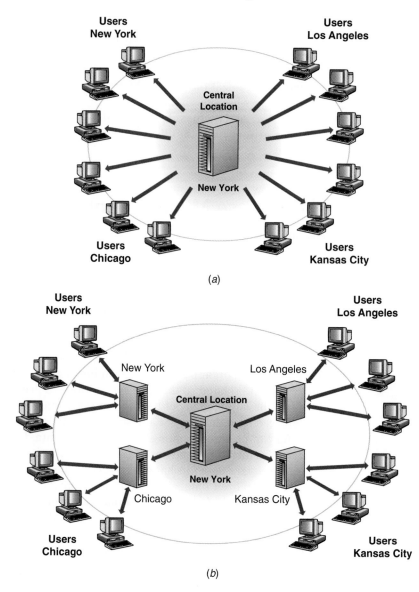

**Figure 3.5** (a) Centralized database. (b) Distributed database with complete or partial copies of the central database in more than one location.

A *partitioned database* is subdivided, so that each location has a portion of the entire database (usually the portion that meets users' local needs). This type of database provides the response speed of localized files without the need to replicate all changes in multiple locations. One significant advantage of a partitioned database is that data in the files can be entered more quickly and kept more accurate by the users immediately responsible for the data. On the other hand, widespread access to potentially sensitive company data can significantly increase corporate security problems. Telecommunications costs and associated time delays can also be major factors.

**DATABASE MANAGEMENT SYSTEMS**

The program (or group of programs) that provides access to a database is known as a **database management system (DBMS).** The DBMS permits an organization to centralize data, manage them efficiently, and provide access to the stored data by application programs. (For a list of capabilities and advantages of the DBMS, see Table 3.2.) The DBMS acts as an interface between application programs and physical data files

| TABLE 3.2 | Advantages and Capabilities of a DBMS |
|---|---|

- **Persistence.** Attributes are permanently stored on a hard drive or other fast, reliable medium until explicitly removed or changed.
- **Query ability.** Querying is the process of requesting attribute information from various perspectives. Example: "How many 2-door cars in Texas are green?"
- **Concurrency.** Many people may want to change or read the same attributes at the same time. Without organized, predetermined rules for sharing changes, the attributes may become inconsistent or misleading. For example, if you change the color attribute of car 7 to be "blue" at the very same time somebody is changing it to "red," results are unpredictable. DBMSs provide various tools and techniques to deal with such issues. "Transactions" and "locking" are two common techniques for concurrency management.
- **Backup and replication.** Backup copies of attributes need to be made in case primary disks or other equipment fail. A periodic copy of attributes may also be created for a distant organization that cannot readily access the original. DBMSs usually provide utilities for backups and duplicate copies.
- **Rule enforcement.** Often one wants to apply rules to attributes so that the attributes are clean and reliable. For example, we may have a rule that says each car can have only one engine associated with it (identified by Engine Number). If somebody tries to associate a second engine with a given car, we want the DBMS to deny such a request and display an error message. However, with new technology such as hybrid gas-electric cars, such rules may need to be relaxed. Ideally such rules should be able to be added and removed as needed without significant data layout redesign.
- **Security.** Limits on who can see or change attributes are necessary.
- **Computation.** Common computations requested on attributes are counting, summing, averaging, sorting, grouping, cross-referencing, etc. Rather than have each computer application implement these from scratch, they can rely on the DBMS to supply such calculations.
- **Change and access logging.** Often one wants to know who accessed what attributes, what was changed, and when it was changed. Logging services allow this by keeping a record of access occurrences and changes.
- **Automated optimization.** If there are frequently occurring usage patterns or requests, many DBMSs can adjust themselves to improve the speed of those interactions. In some cases the DBMS will merely provide tools to monitor performance, allowing a human expert to make the necessary adjustments after reviewing the statistics collected.

*Source: Wikipedia* (2005).

(see Figure 3.6) and provides users with tools to add, delete, maintain, display, print, search, select, sort, and update data. These tools range from easy-to-use natural language interfaces to complex programming languages used for developing sophisticated database applications.

DBMSs are used in a broad range of information systems. Some are loaded on a single user's personal computer and used in an ad-hoc manner to support individual decision making (for example, Microsoft's Access). Others (such as IBM's DB2) are located on several interconnected mainframe computers and are used to support large-scale transaction processing systems, such as order entry and inventory control systems. Still others (such as Oracle's 13) are interconnected throughout an organization's local area networks, giving individual departments access to corporate data.

A database management system provides the ability for many different users to share data and process resources. But as there can be many different users, there are many different database needs. How can a single, unified database meet the differing requirements of so many users? For example, how can a single database be structured

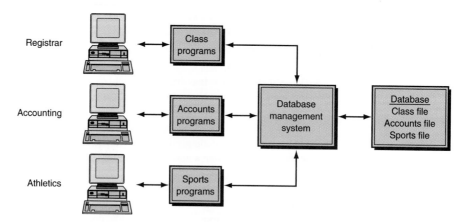

**Figure 3.6** Database management system provides access to all data in the database.

so that sales personnel can see customer, inventory, and production maintenance data while the human resources department maintains restricted access to private personnel data?

A DBMS minimizes these problems by providing two views of the database data: a physical view and a logical view. The **physical view** deals with the actual, physical arrangement and location of data in the *direct access storage devices (DASDs).* Database specialists use the physical view to make efficient use of storage and processing resources.

Users, however, may wish to see data differently from how they are stored, and they do not want to know all the technical details of physical storage. After all, a business user is primarily interested in using the information, not in how it is stored. The **logical view,** or user's view, of a database program represents data in a format that is meaningful to a user and to the software programs that process those data. That is, the logical view tells the user, in user terms, what is in the database.

One strength of a DBMS is that while there is only one physical view of the data, there can be an endless number of different logical views—one specifically tailored to each individual user, if necessary. This feature allows users to see database information in a more business-related way rather than from a technical, processing viewpoint. Clearly, users must adapt to the technical requirements of database information systems to some degree, but DBMS logical views allow the system to adapt to the business needs of the users.

Database management systems are designed to be relatively invisible to the user. To interact with them, however, one needs to understand the procedures for interacting, even though much of their work is done behind the scenes and is therefore invisible or "transparent" to the end user. Most of this interaction occurs by using DBMS languages.

**DBMS Languages.** A DBMS contains four major components: the data model, the data definition language, the data manipulation language, and the data dictionary. The **data model** defines the way data are conceptually structured. Examples of model forms include the hierarchical, network, relational, object-oriented, object-relational, hypermedia, and multidimensional models. The **data definition language (DDL)** is the language used by programmers to specify the types of information and structure of the database. It is essentially the link between the logical and physical views of the database. ("Logical" refers to the way the user views data, and "physical" to the way the data are physically stored and processed.)

A DBMS user defines logical views or schema using the DDL. The **schema** is the logical description of the entire database and the listing of all the data items and the relationships among them. A *subschema* is the specific set of data from the database that is required by each application. The DDL is used to define the physical characteristics of each record, the fields within a record, and each field's logical name, data type, and character length.

The **data manipulation language (DML)** is used with a third- or fourth-generation language to manipulate the data in the database. This language contains commands that permit end users and programming specialists to extract data from the database to satisfy information requests and develop applications. The DML provides users with the ability to retrieve, sort, display, and delete the contents of a database. The DML generally includes a variety of manipulation verbs (e.g., SELECT, MODIFY, DELETE) and operands for each verb.

Requesting information from a database is the most commonly performed operation. Because users cannot generally request information in a natural language form, query languages form an important component of a DBMS. **Structured query language (SQL)** is the most popular relational database language, combining both DML and DDL features. SQL offers the ability to perform complicated searches with relatively simple statements. Keywords such as SELECT (to specify desired attribute(s)), FROM (to specify the table(s) to be used), and WHERE (to specify conditions to apply in the query) are typically used for the purpose of data manipulation. For example, a state legislator wants to send congratulatory letters to all students from her district graduating with honors from a state university. End users often use an approach called *query-by-example (QBE)* instead of SQL. The user selects a table and chooses the fields to be included in the answer. Then the user enters an example of the data he or she wants. The QBE provides an answer based on the example. QBE hides much of the complexity involved with SQL.

The **data dictionary** stores definitions of data elements and data characteristics such as usage, physical representation, ownership (who in the organization is responsible for maintaining the data), authorization, and security. A *data element* represents a field. Besides listing the standard data name, the dictionary lists the names that reference this element in specific systems and identifies the individuals, business functions, applications, and reports that use this data element.

Data dictionaries provide many advantages to the organization. Because the data dictionary provides standard definitions for all data elements, the potential for data inconsistency is reduced. That is, the probability that the same data element will be used in different applications, but with a different name, is reduced. In addition, data dictionaries provide for faster program development because programmers do not have to create new data names. Data dictionaries also make it easier to modify data and information because programmers do not need to know where the data element is stored or what applications use the data element in order to make use of it in a program.

Data dictionaries are a form of metadata. **Metadata** is information about information. Metadata matters in the business-to-business world as well. As more corporate transactions are conducted over the Net, each needs metadata so that companies can track the transaction and analyze its success.

Database environments ensure that data in the database are defined once and consistently, and that they are used for all applications whose data reside in the database. Applications request data elements from the database and are found and delivered by the DBMS. The programmer and end user do not have to specify in detail how or where the data are to be found.

**DBMS Benefits.** Database management systems provide many advantages to the organization:

- Improved strategic use of corporate data
- Reduced complexity of the organization's information systems environment
- Reduced data redundancy and inconsistency
- Enhanced data integrity
- Application-data independence
- Improved security
- Reduced application development and maintenance costs
- Improved flexibility of information systems
- Increased access and availability of data and information

# 3.4  Creating Databases

Before building a database, the builder has to develop the blueprints for data used in the organization. In building a house, (1) the artist draws a conceptual model, (2) the architect draws the blueprints, and (3) the construction company builds the house. A three-stage approach to building a database is also extremely effective, as shown in Figure 3.7. The data model represents the conceptual view of the organization's data; **entity-relationship diagrams (ERDs)** represent the logical view of how the data are organized, and **data tables** represent the physical view of the data.

**BUILDING THE DATA MODEL (LEVEL 1: CONCEPTUAL)**

The first step in creating a database is to develop a conceptual design for the data. The conceptual design is a high-level model of the data in an organization. The conceptual model uses entity-relationship (E-R) diagramming techniques. The design team identifies what data an organization needs to capture and use. For example, most organizations have data about employees, customers, products, vendors, and other entities. The conceptual data model identifies what the business needs to know about data objects that are essential to its operation. Objects may represent people (employees, customers), places (buildings, facilities), things (orders, products, equipment), events (projects, jobs), and intellectual property (new product designs, chart of accounts).

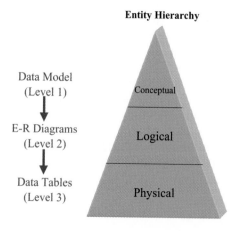

**Figure 3.7** Data modeling.
(*Source:* Drawn by Donald Amoroso.)

**Data Model**

Figure 3.8 shows a data model for the typical organization. *Attributes* detail the type of data that we want to collect. For example, the attributes for customer data include product preferences, customer contact, shop locations, and product sales. Attributes for entities in the data model answer the business question of what type of data we want to collect about that entity.

Entities are associated with one another in relationships. The number of entities in a relationship represents the "degree" of the relationship. Relationships of "degree two" are common and are called binary relationships. E-R symbols are used at the end of each line indicating the relationship. See Figure 3.9. For example, a product *is made by* many vendors and a vendor *makes* one or many products.

**BUILDING THE ENTITY-RELATIONSHIP MODEL SET (LEVEL 2: LOGICAL)**

A completed logical model for the new system defines all the rules for data used in the business operation. The diagrams force people to define and document systematically the information that they will use in the business. The logical data model set of E-R diagrams at Level 2 more fully defines attributes from Level 1. See Figure 3.10. The attributes at Level 1 become the data entities at Level 2. For example, the customer entity in the conceptual data model has four attributes: product preferences, customer contact, shop locations, and product sales. If there were 10 entities in the data model, and each had four attributes, there would be 10 Level 2 logical models and 40 new entities.

**Possible Symbols for Reference**

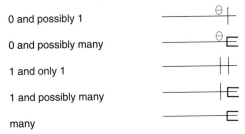

**Figure 3.9** Entity relationship symbols. (*Source:* Drawn by Donald Amoroso.)

**Level 2 Customer Diagram**

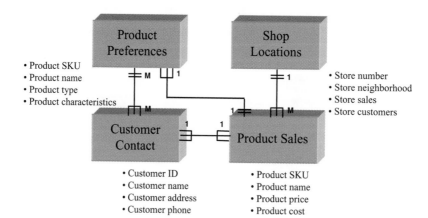

**Figure 3.10** Entity relationship diagrams. (*Source:* Drawn by Donald Amoroso.)

## BUILDING THE DATABASE TABLES (LEVEL 3: PHYSICAL)

The third level is the physical model level, composed of the database tables. Here we convert the E-R diagrams to database tables. Each of the entities at Level 2 becomes tables at Level 3. In the example, the four entities have become four database tables at the physical level. The set of attributes for an entity becomes a field in the table. For example, the product preferences entity (Level 2) has four attributes that define a field in the product preferences table (Level 3). The unique field (Product SKU, for example) is the primary key for the table. The relationships from the E-R diagrams link the tables through primary and foreign keys. See examples of primary and foreign (secondary) keys in Figure 3.11.

## FINAL SET OF DATA MODELS

The hierarchy of data models is important. Database tables should be built from the top down as diagrammed in Figure 3.12.

**Level 3 Customer Data Tables**

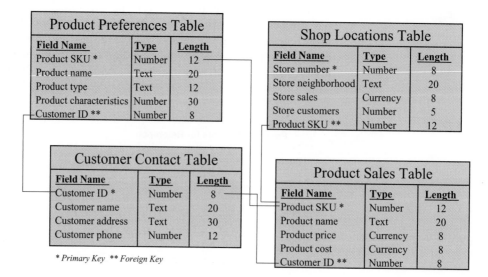

**Figure 3.11** Entity relationship diagrams. (*Source:* Drawn by Donald Amoroso.)

**Entity Hierarchy**

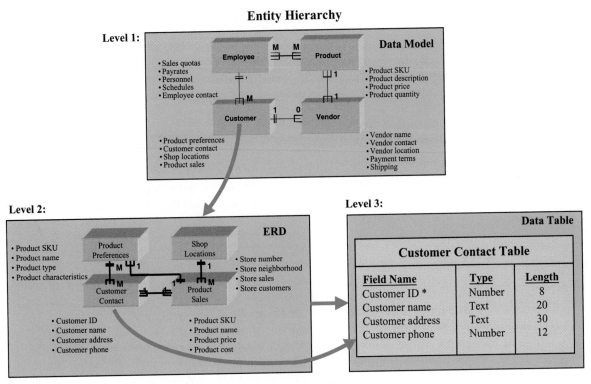

**Figure 3.12** Data modeling. (*Source:* Drawn by Donald Amoroso.)

# 3.5 Data Warehousing

Many large and medium-size companies are using data warehousing to make it easier and faster to process, analyze, and query data.

**THE NEED FOR DATA WAREHOUSING**

The most successful companies are those that can respond quickly and flexibly to market changes and opportunities, and the key to this response is the effective and efficient use of data and information, as shown in the Harrah's case. This is done not only via transaction processing, but also through **analytical processing,** which involves analysis of accumulated data, frequently by end users. Analytical processing, also referred to as *business intelligence*, includes data mining, decision support systems (DSSs), enterprise information systems (EISs), Web applications, querying, and other end-user activities. Placing strategic information in the hands of decision makers aids productivity and empowers users to make better decisions, leading to greater competitive advantage. A good data delivery system should be able to support easy data access by the end users themselves, as well as quick, accurate, flexible and effective decision making.

There are basically two options for conducting analytical processing. One is to work directly with the operational systems (the "let's use what we have" approach), using software tools and components known as front-end tools and *middleware* (see Technology Guide 2). The other is to use a data warehouse.

The first option can be optimal for companies that do not have a large number of end users running queries and conducting analyses against the operating systems. It is also an option for departments that consist mainly of users who have the necessary technical skills for an extensive use of tools such as spreadsheets and graphics.

Although it is possible for those with fewer technical skills to use query and reporting tools, they may not be effective, flexible, or easy enough to use in many cases.

The problem with this approach, however, is that the tools are only effective with end users who have a medium to high degree of knowledge about databases. This situation improved drastically with the use of Web-based tools. Yet, when data are in several sources and in different formats, it is difficult to bring them together to conduct an analysis.

The second option, a data warehouse, overcomes these limitations and provides for improved analytical processing. It involves three concepts:

**1.** A business representation of data for end users

**2.** A Web-based environment that gives the users query and reporting capabilities

**3.** A server-based repository (the data warehouse) that allows centralized security and control over the data

**THE DATA WAREHOUSE**

A **data warehouse** is a repository of data that are organized to be readily acceptable for analytical processing activities (such as data mining, decision support, querying, and other applications). Examples are revenue management, customer-relationship management, fraud detection, and payroll-management applications.

According to Teradata, benefits of an enterprise data warehouse (EDW) are both business and IT-related. Better business decisions can be made due to better information. Information is delivered more effectively and efficiently. Numerous areas of an organization benefit from an EDW (*teradata.com, 2006*):

- **Marketing and Sales** uses an EDW for product introductions, product information access, marketing program effectiveness, and product line profitability.
- **Customer and Channel Partner** gains customer profitability, customer and market penetration, and channel partner performance.
- **Pricing and Contracts** can better understand pricing to optimize gross margin and monitoring price differentials among subsidiaries.
- **Forecasting** is assisted in the timely visibility of end customer demand.
- **Sales Performance** determines sales profitability and productivity for all territories and regions; results by geography, product, sales group, or individual.
- **Financial** receives daily, weekly, or monthly results quickly; enhances financial management throughout the organization.
- **Supply Chain** gains fast, thorough analysis of purchase quantities and prices.
- **Customer Service Improvements and Order Enhancement** delivers consistent customer service metrics for all facilities.
- **Information Systems and Processes,** through portal capabilities, provide each user with fast and easy access to regularly used queries, reports, or analyses.

The process of building and using a data warehouse is shown in Figure 3.13. The organization's data are stored in operational systems (left side of the figure). Using special software called ETL (extraction, transformation, load), data are processed and then stored in a data warehouse. Not all data are necessarily transferred to the data warehouse. Frequently only a summary of the data is transferred. The data that are transferred are organized within the warehouse in a form that is easy for end users to access and locate. The data are also standardized. Then, the data are organized by subject, such as by functional area, vendor, or product. In contrast, operational data are organized according to a business process, such as shipping, purchasing, or inventory control and/or functional department. (Note that ERP data can be input to a

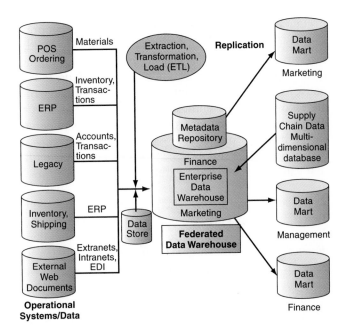

**Figure 3.13** Data warehouse framework and views. (*Source:* Drawn by E. Turban.)

data warehouse, and ERP and SCM decisions use the output from the data warehouse. See Grant, 2003.)

Data warehouses provide for the storage of *metadata*. Metadata include software programs about data, rules for organizing data, and data summaries that are easier to index and search, especially with Web tools. The design and use of metadata may involve ethical issues such as organizing the metadata so that it will influence users one way or another.

**Characteristics of a Data Warehouse.** Nine major characteristics of data warehousing are:

1.  **Organization.** Data are organized by subject (e.g., by customer, vendor, product, price level, and region), and contain information relevant for decision support only.
2.  **Consistency.** Data in different operational databases may be encoded differently. For example, gender data may be encoded 0 and 1 in one operational system and "m" and "f" in another. In the warehouse they will be coded in a consistent manner.
3.  **Time variant.** The data are kept for many years so they can be used for trends, forecasting, and comparisons over time.
4.  **Nonvolatile.** Once entered into the warehouse, data are not updated.
5.  **Relational.** Typically the data warehouse uses a relational structure.
6.  **Client/server.** The data warehouse uses the client/server architecture mainly to provide the end user an easy access to its data.
7.  **Web-based.** Today's data warehouses are designed to provide an efficient computing environment for Web-based applications.
8.  **Integration.** Data from various sources are integrated. Web Services is used to support integration.
9.  **Real time.** Although most applications of data warehousing are not in real time, it is possible to arrange for real-time capabilities.

Some of the benefits of using a data warehouse are illustrated in Online File W3.1.

**BUILDING A DATA WAREHOUSE**

Building and implementing a data warehouse can present problems. Since the data warehouse project is very large and expensive to build, it is important to understand the key success factors in implementing a data warehouse. First, does top management support the data warehouse? Second, do the users support the data warehouse? Third, do users want access to a broad range of data? And if they do, is a single repository to be built or a set of standalone data marts? Fourth, do users want data access and analysis tools? Fifth, do users understand how the data warehouse solves business problems? Sixth, do users perceive the information technology department to be supportive? Seventh, does the unit have one or more power users that can understand data warehouse technologies?

**Architecture and Tools.** There are several basic architectures for data warehousing. Two common ones are two-tier and three-tier architectures. In three-tier architecture, data from the warehouse are processed twice and deposited in an additional *multidimensional database,* organized for easy multidimensional analysis and presentation or replicated in data marts. The architecture of the data warehouse determines the tools needed for its construction (see Kimball and Ross, 2002).

There are two main reasons for creating a data warehouse as a separate data store. First, the performance of operational queries degrades when competing with intensive queries. It's difficult to model a database that can be used for both operational and analytical purposes. Figure 3.14 represents an EDW developed by Teradata Corp. This centralized approach reduces the amount of data the technical team has to transfer, simplifying data management and administration; users are also provided with access to all data in the data warehouse instead of being limited to data marts.

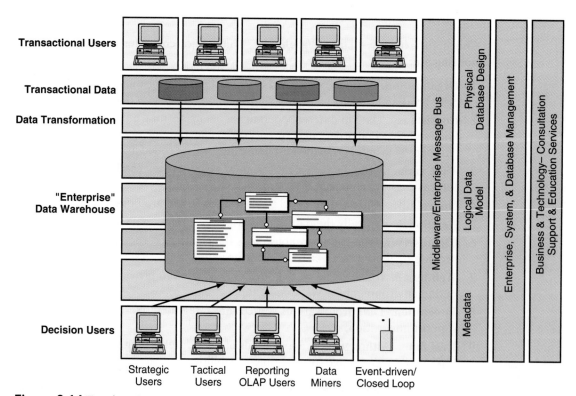

**Figure 3.14** Teradata Corp.'s enterprise data warehouse. (*Source:* Teradata Corporation [*teradata.com*], with permission.)

**Putting the Warehouse on the Intranet.**  Delivery of data warehouse content to decision makers throughout the enterprise can be done via an intranet. Users can view, query, and analyze the data and produce reports using Web browsers. This is an extremely economical and effective method of delivering data.

**Suitability.**  Data warehousing is most appropriate for organizations in which some of the following apply:

- Large amounts of data need to be accessed by end users (see the Harrah's case).
- The operational data are stored in different systems.
- An information-based approach to management is in use.
- There is a large, diverse customer base (such as in a utility company or a bank; for example, AT&T's 26-terabyte data warehouse is used by 3,000 employees for doing marketing analysis).
- The same data are represented differently in different systems.
- Data are stored in highly technical formats that are difficult to decipher.
- Extensive end-user computing is performed (many end users performing many activities).

Some of the successful applications are summarized in Table 3.3. Hundreds of other successful applications are reported (e.g., see client success stories and case studies at Web sites of vendors such as Hyperion Inc., Business Objects, Cognos Corp., Information Builders, NCR Corp., Oracle, Computer Associates, and Software A&G). For further discussion visit the Data Warehouse Institute (*tdwi.org*).

Many organizations, seeing the success of their data warehouse efforts, are taking data warehouse public. One organization taking their data warehouse public is Wells Fargo. The development effort uses the resources of a Teradata warehouse to provide an online tool that collects and summarizes transactions for consumers—credit card, debit card, online bill payments, checking account—and generates an analysis of online banking sessions. Consumers are better able to understand their spending patterns and have reported a higher level of customer satisfaction.

Travelocity continues to grow its enterprise using a public data warehouse. Part of the company's success lies in its innovative use of its EDW for marketing and CRM.

**DATA MARTS, OPERATIONAL DATA STORES, AND MULTIDIMENSIONAL DATABASES**

Data warehouses are frequently supplemented with or substituted by the following: data marts, operational data stores, and multidimensional databases.

**Data Marts.**  The high cost of data warehouses confines their use to large companies. An alternative used by many other firms is creation of a lower cost, scaled-down version of a data warehouse called a data mart. A **data mart** is a small warehouse designed for a strategic business unit (SBU) or a department.

The advantages of data marts include: low cost (prices under $100,000 versus $1 million or more for data warehouses); significantly shorter lead time for implementation, often less than 90 days; local rather than central control, conferring power on the using group. They also contain less information than the data warehouse. Hence, they have more rapid response and are more easily understood and navigated than an enterprisewide data warehouse. Finally, they allow a business unit to build its own decision support systems without relying on a centralized IS department.

| TABLE 3.3 | Strategic Uses of Data Warehousing | |
|---|---|---|
| **Industry** | **Functional Areas of Use** | **Strategic Use** |
| Airline | Operations and Marketing | Crew assignment, aircraft deployment, mix of fares, analysis of route profitability, frequent-flyer program promotions |
| Apparel | Distribution and Marketing | Merchandising, and inventory replenishment |
| Banking | Product Development, Operations, and Marketing | Customer service, trend analysis, product and service promotions, reduction of IS expenses |
| Credit card | Product Development and Marketing | Customer service, new information service for a fee, fraud detection |
| Defense contracting | Product Development | Technology transfer, production of military applications |
| E-Business | Distribution and Marketing | Data warehouses with personalization capabilities, marketing/shopping preferences allowing for up-selling and cross-selling |
| Government | Operations | Reporting on crime areas, homeland security |
| Health care | Operations | Reduction of operational expenses |
| Investment and insurance | Product Development, Operations, and Marketing | Risk management, market movements analysis, customer tendencies analysis, portfolio management |
| Personal care products | Distribution and Marketing | Distribution decisions, product promotions, sales decisions, pricing policy |
| Retail chain | Distribution and Marketing | Trend analysis, buying pattern analysis, pricing policy, inventory control, sales promotions, optimal distribution channel decisions |
| Steel | Manufacturing | Pattern analysis (quality control) |
| Telecommunications | Product Development, Operations, and Marketing | New product and service promotions, reduction of IS budget, profitability analysis |

*Sources:* Park (1997), p. 19, Table 2, and Chenoweth et al. (2006).

There are two major types of data marts:

1. **Replicated (dependent) data marts.** Sometimes it is easier to work with a small subset of the data warehouse. In such cases one can replicate some subsets of the data warehouse in smaller data marts, each of which is dedicated to a certain area, as was shown in Figure 3.14 (page 102). In such a case the data mart is an *addition* to the data warehouse.

2. **Standalone data marts.** A company can have one or more independent data marts without having a data warehouse. Typical data marts are for marketing, finance, and engineering applications.

**Operational Data Stores.** An **operational data store** is a database for transaction processing systems that uses data warehouse concepts to provide clean data. It brings the concepts and benefits of the data warehouse to the operational portions of the business, at a lower cost. It is used for short-term decisions involving mission-critical applications rather than for the medium- and long-term decisions associated with the regular data warehouse. These decisions depend on much more current information. For example, a bank needs to know about all the accounts for a given customer who is calling on the phone. The operational data store can be viewed as situated between the operational data (in legacy systems) and the data warehouse.

| TABLE 3.4 | Reasons Data Warehouses Fail |
|---|---|

**Data Warehousing Design:**

- Unrealistic expectations
- Inappropriate architecture
- Vendors overselling capabilities
- Insufficient logical design
- Lack of development expertise
- Unclear business objectives
- Lack of effective project sponsorship

**Data Warehousing Implementation:**

- Poor user training
- Failure to align data warehouses and data marts
- Lack of attention to cultural issues
- Corporate policies not updated

**Data Warehousing Operation:**

- Poor upkeep of technology
- Failure to upgrade modules
- Lack of integration
- Poor data quality
- Inappropriate format of information

*Sources:* Carbone (1999) and Jekic (2006).

**Multidimensional Databases. Multidimensional databases** are specialized data stores that organize facts by dimensions, such as geographical region, product line, salesperson, or time (see Online File W3.2). The data in multidimensional databases are usually preprocessed and stored in what is called a (multidimensional) *data cube*. A data cube is shown on the left side of the figure in Online File W3.2. Each cell in the cube represents some attribute of a specific mix of dimensions. (There are three dimensions in the figure.) Facts, such as quantities sold, are placed at the intersection of the dimensions. One such intersection might be the quantities of washers sold in the Central Division of the company in July 2007.

Dimensions often have a hierarchy. Sales figures, for example, might be presented by day, by month, or by year. They might also roll up an organizational dimension from store to region to company. Multidimensional databases can be incorporated in a data warehouse, sometimes as its core, or they can be used as an additional layer of storage.

Carbone provided examples and identified a number of reasons for failures (which are typical for many other large information systems): These are summarized in Table 3.4. Suggestions on how to avoid data warehouse failure are provided at *datawarehouse.com,* at *bitpipe.com,* and at *teradatauniversitynetwork.com.*

# 3.6 Marketing Databases in Action

**MKT**

Data warehouses and data marts serve end users in all functional areas. However, the most dramatic applications of data warehousing and mining are in marketing, as seen in the Harrah's case, in what is referred to as *marketing databases* (also referred to as *database marketing*).

In this section we examine how data warehouses, their extensions, and data mining are used, and what role they play in new marketing strategies, such as the use of Web-based marketing transaction databases in interactive marketing.

**THE MARKETING TRANSACTION DATABASE**

Many databases are static: They simply gather and store information about customers. They appear in the following categories: operations databases, data warehouses, and marketing databases. Success in marketing today requires a new kind of database, oriented toward targeting the personalizing marketing messages in real time. Such a database provides the most effective means of capturing information on customer preferences and needs. In turn, enterprises can use this knowledge to create new and/or personalized products and services. Such a database is called a **marketing transaction database (MTD).** The MTD combines many of the characteristics of the current databases and marketing data sources into a new database that allows marketers to engage in real-time personalization and target every interaction with customers.

**MTD's Capabilities.** The MTD provides dynamic, or interactive, functions not available with traditional types of marketing databases. In marketing terms, a transaction occurs with the exchange of information. With interactive media, each exposure to the customer becomes an opportunity to conduct a marketing "transaction." Exchanging information (whether gathered actively through registration or user requests, or passively by monitoring customer behavior) allows marketers to refine their understanding of each customer continuously and to use that information to target him or her specifically with personalized marketing messages. This is done most frequently on the Web.

**IMPLEMENTATION EXAMPLES**

Few companies can afford traditional marketing approaches, which include big-picture strategies and expensive marketing campaigns. Marketing departments are being scaled down (and so are the traditional marketing approaches), and new approaches such as one-to-one marketing, speed marketing, interactive marketing, and relationship marketing are being employed (see Strauss et al., 2003).

The following examples illustrate how companies use data mining and warehousing to support the new marketing approaches. For other examples, see Online File W3.3.

*MKT*

- Through its online registry for expectant parents, Burlington Coat Factory tracks families as they grow. The company then matches direct-mail material to the different stages of a family's development over time. Burlington also identifies, on a daily basis, top-selling styles and brands. By digging into reams of demographic data, historical buying patterns, and sales trends in existing stores, Burlington determines where to open its next store and what to stock in each store.

*FIN*

- Bank of America gets more than 100,000 telephone calls from customers every day. Analyzing customers' banking activities, the bank determines what may be of interest to them. So when a customer calls to check on a balance, the bank tries to sell the customer something in which he or she might be interested.

*SVC*

- In its data warehouse, the *Chicago Tribune* stores information about customer behavior as customers move through the various newspaper Web sites. Data mining helps to analyze volumes of data ranging from what browsers are used to what hyperlinks are clicked on most frequently.

The data warehouses in many companies include several terabytes or more of data. They need to use supercomputing to sift quickly through the data. Wal-Mart, the world's largest discount retailer, has a gigantic database.

# 3.7 Web-Based Data Management Systems

Data management and business intelligence activities—from data acquisition (e.g., Atzeni et al., 2002), through warehousing, to mining—are often performed with Web tools, or are interrelated with Web technologies and e-business (see Liautaud, 2001). Users with browsers can log onto a system, make inquiries, and get reports in a real-time setting. This is done through intranets and, for outsiders, via extranets (see *remedy.com*).

The challenge these days for data management and business intelligence activities is information integration. The reason this is a challenging task is that today's enterprise systems extend beyond the walls of the corporate data center to include customers, suppliers, partners, and electronic marketplaces. Information integration is a technology approach that combines core elements from data management systems, content management systems, data warehouses, and other enterprise applications into a common platform (Roth et al., 2002). Web Services are a commonly used programming interface in information integration.

E-commerce software vendors are providing Web tools that connect the data warehouse with EC ordering and cataloging systems. Hitachi's EC tool suite, Tradelink (at *hitachi.com*), combines EC activities such as catalog management, payment applications, mass customization, and order management with data warehouses and marts and ERP systems. Oracle (see Winter, 2001) and SAP offer similar products.

Web-based data management systems have multiple components consisting of structured and unstructured data (see Figure 3.15) leading to the ability to manage online content and check inventory levels of suppliers.

**INTELLIGENT DATA WAREHOUSE WEB-BASED SYSTEMS**

The amount of data in the data warehouse can be very large. While the organization of data is done in a way that permits easy search, it still may be useful to have a search engine for specific applications. An intelligent agent can improve the operation of a data warehouse. This application supplements the monitoring and scanning of external strategic data. The intelligent agent application can serve both managers' ad-hoc query/reporting information needs and the external data needs of a strategic management support system for forest companies in Finland.

**CLICKSTREAM DATA WAREHOUSE**

Large and ever-increasing amounts of B2C data about consumers, products, an so on can be collected. Such data come from several sources: internal data (e.g., sales data, payroll data, etc.), external data (e.g., government and industry reports), and clickstream data. *Clickstream data* (also known as *Web logs*) occur inside the Web environment, when customers visit a Web site. They provide a trail of the users' activities in the Web site, including user behavior and browsing patterns. By looking at clickstream data, an e-tailer can find out such things as which promotions are effective and which population segments are interested in specific products.

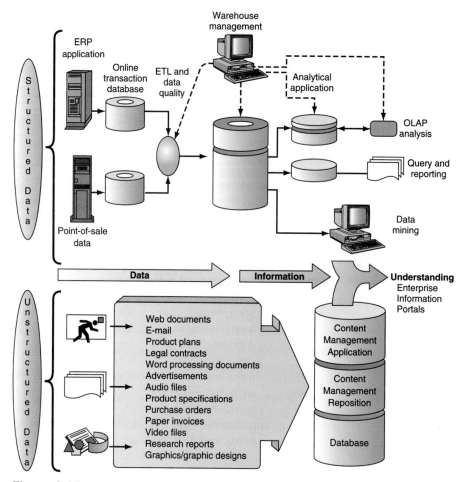

**Figure 3.15** Sources of content for an enterprise information portal. (*Source:* Merrill Lynch, 1998.)

Analyzing Web logs quickly can be very useful. For example, quick analysis allows management to gauge the effectiveness of a Web-based sales promotion. Popular tools are Web Trends (from NetIQ) and Mach5 Analyzer (from Mach5.com).

Clickstream data can reveal information to answer questions such as the following: What goods has the customer looked at or purchased? What items did the customer buy in conjunction with other items? What ads and promotions were effective? Which were ineffective? Are certain products too hard to find? Are certain products too expensive? Is there a substitute product that the customer finds first?

The Web is an incredibly rich source of *business intelligence,* and many enterprises are scrambling to build data warehouses that capture the knowledge contained in the clickstream data from their Web sites. By analyzing the user behavior patterns contained in these clickstream data warehouses, savvy businesses can expand their markets, improve customer relationships, reduce costs, streamline operations, strengthen their Web sites, and hone their business strategies. One has two options: Incorporate Web-based data into preexisting data warehouses, or build new **clickstream data warehouses** that are capable of showing both e-business

# IT at Work 3.1

## Victoria's Secret's Data Warehouse

For direct-to-consumer merchants, the "death of an order" can occur at any time during the transaction. The "death of an order" means that customers change their minds at some point during the ordering process. By using an enterprise data warehouse to capture customer information and decision-support tools to analyze shopping patterns, however, Victoria's Secret (*victoriassecret.com*) is keeping orders alive and working to provide a better shopping experience.

Unlike a bricks-and-mortar purchase, the direct sale of products through electronic storefronts provides vast amounts of unique and diverse data elements at all stages of an order's life. To turn collected data into actionable information, the company uses a data warehouse solution from Teradata (a division of NCR Corp.). The retailer monitors all customer touches and shopping patterns.

The data warehouse holds data collected from several data streams:

- The first data source is the customer. Besides having access to all customer names, addresses, and purchase history, the company also differentiates orderers from product recipients, based on storing each different shipping address.
- The company also stores customer payment information. Victoria's Secret uses the payment data to monitor the purchasing habits of the company's shoppers.
- The third data stream comes from direct customer contacts via the firm's direct-mail operations. For example, the company has more than 50 domestic and international catalog mailings (300 million catalogs per year).
- The retailer's call center provides another data stream. Each day hundreds of fashion consultants examine thousands of calls ranging from orders and "up-sell"

opportunities (opportunities to sell customers more expensive items) to complaints and resolutions about merchandise.

- The company's online channel produces a huge amount of customer data, as it accepts thousands of orders daily for both online and catalog merchandise. Each customer's activities on the Web site are stored in the data warehouse.

Victoria's Secret puts all of these data into action in many ways. The company creates targeted e-mail messages, adding up to 150 million outbound e-mail messages each year. These messages include offers, merchandise specials, invitations, announcements, and other calls to action.

The company analyzes the status of every individual product by customer, by day, for each order. The data warehouse is enabling Victoria's Secret to improve predictions of customer behavior. The data warehouse also enables the company to stay abreast of each order's profit equation. To measure the revenue of each order, Victoria's Secret starts with the merchandise price and subtracts shipping, handling, and related taxes, as well as special service charges, such as shipping upgrades and gift wrapping. This process means that the retailer can measure the profitability of every customer, order, catalog, and product.

*Source:* Compiled from Amato-McCoy (2003) and Jekic (2006).

*For Further Exploration:* What does Victoria's Secret mean by "keeping an order alive?" Would this phrase apply to other businesses? Why or why not? Give examples. Finally, describe the various data streams that feed Victoria's Secret's data warehouse.

---

activities and the non-Web aspects of the business in an integrated fashion (see Sweiger at el., 2002). For an application used by Victoria's Secret, see *IT at Work 3.1.*

# 3.8 Managerial Issues

**1. Cost-benefit issues and justification.** Some of the data management solutions discussed in this chapter are very expensive and are justifiable only in large corporations. Smaller organizations can make the solutions cost effective if they leverage existing databases rather than create new ones. A careful cost-benefit analysis must be undertaken before any commitment to the new technologies is made.

**2. Where to store data physically.** Should data be distributed close to their users? This could potentially speed up data entry and updating, but adds replication and security risks. Or should data be centralized for easier control, security, and disaster recovery? This alternative offers fewer communications and single-point-of-failure risks.

**3. Legal issues.** Data mining may suggest that a company send electronic or printed catalogs or promotions to only one age group or one gender. A man sued Victoria's Secret Corp. because his female neighbor received a mail order catalog with deeply discounted items and he received only the regular catalog (the discount was actually given for volume purchasing). Settling discrimination charges can be very expensive.

**4. Internal or external?** Should a firm invest in internally collecting, storing, maintaining, and purging its own databases of information? Or should it subscribe to external databases, where providers are responsible for all data management and data access?

**5. Disaster recovery.** Can an organization's business processes, which have become dependent on databases, recover and sustain operations after a natural or other type of information systems disaster? (See Chapter 16.) How can a data warehouse be protected? At what cost?

**6. Data security and ethics.** Are the company's competitive data safe from external snooping or sabotage? Are confidential data, such as personnel details, safe from improper or illegal access and alteration? A related question is, Who owns such personal data?

ETHICS

**7. Ethics: Paying for use of data.** Compilers of public-domain information, such as Lexis-Nexis, face a problem of people lifting large sections of their work without first paying royalties. The Collection of Information Antipiracy Act (Bills HR 2652 and HR 354 in the U.S. Congress) may provide greater protection from online piracy. This, and other intellectual property issues are being debated in Congress and adjudicated in the courts. (See Chapter 17.)

ETHICS

**8. Privacy.** Storing data in a warehouse and conducting data mining may result in the invasion of individual privacy. What will companies do to protect individuals? What can individuals do to protect their privacy? (See Chapter 17.)

**9. The legacy data problem.** One very real issue, often known as the legacy data acquisition problem, is what to do with the mass of information already stored in a variety of systems and formats. Data in older, perhaps obsolete, databases still need to be available to newer database management systems. Many of the legacy application programs used to access the older data simply cannot be converted into new computing environments without considerable expense. Basically, there are three approaches to solving this problem. One is to create a database front end that can act as a translator from the old system to the new. The second is to cause applications to be integrated with the new system, so that data can be seamlessly accessed in the original format. The third is to cause the data to migrate into the new system by reformatting it. A new promising approach is the use of Web Services (see Technology Guide 6).

**10. Data delivery.** Moving data efficiently around an enterprise is often a major problem. The inability to communicate effectively and efficiently among different groups, in different geographical locations, is a serious roadblock to implementing distributed applications properly, especially given the many remote sites and mobility of today's workers. Mobile and wireless computing are addressing some of these difficulties.

## Integrating *IT*

### For the Accounting Major

Transaction data are crucial for financial statements, cost control, inventory control, accounts payable, and accounts receivable. Determining financial performance with accurate transaction data can be very costly to organizations, as we have seen in the past decade. In accounting, data must be reliable and accurate.

### For the Finance Major

Financial systems rely on database management systems for their successful operation. Financial analysts use historical data residing in data warehouses to create forecasts and analytical reports for investors.

### For the Human Resources Management Major

Human resources managers use database management systems to manage employee data (e.g., health benefits, retirement, and insurance).

### For the IS Major

Managing information systems means managing data. Data administrators manage all aspects of how data are entered into the system as well as how data are accessed from the system.

### For the Marketing Major

Web-based systems allow personalization of direct marketing approaches that in turn attract new customers and build customer loyalty.

### For the Production/Operations Management Major

By employing data available about inventory, production, distribution, logistics, and shipping, managers can make better decisions faster.

## Key Terms

Analytical processing  *99*
Attributes  *88*
Clickstream data  *83*
Clickstream data warehouses  *108*
Database  *87*
Database management system (DBMS)  *92*
Data definition language (DDL)  *94*
Data dictionary  *95*
Data inconsistency  *90*
Data integrity  *90*
Data isolation  *90*
Data manipulation language (DML)  *95*
Data mart  *103*

Data models  *94*
Data quality (DQ)  *84*
Data redundancy  *90*
Data tables  *96*
Data warehouse  *100*
Direct file access method  *88*
Document management  *86*
Document management system (DMS)  *86*
Entity-relationship diagram (ERD)  *96*
Foreign key  *88*
Indexed sequential access method (ISAM)  *88*
Logical view  *94*

Marketing transaction database (MTD)  *106*
Metadata  *95*
Multidimensional database  *105*
Operational data store  *104*
Physical view  *94*
Primary key  *88*
Schema  *95*
Secondary key  *88*
Sequential, direct, or random file organization  *88*
Structured query language (SQL)  *95*

## Chapter Highlights

(Numbers Refer to Learning Objectives)

❶ Data are the foundation of any information system and need to be managed throughout their useful life cycle, which converts data to useful information, knowledge, and a basis for decision support.

❷ Data exist in internal and external computerized and other sources. Personal data and knowledge are often stored in people's minds.

❷ The Internet is a major source of data and knowledge. Other sources are databases, paper documents, videos, maps, pictures, and more.

❷ Many factors that impact the quality of data must be recognized and controlled.

❸ Today data and documents are managed electronically. They are digitized, stored, and used in electronic management systems.

❸ Electronic document management, the automated control of documents, is a key to greater efficiency in handling documents in order to gain an edge on the competition.

**❹** Data warehouses and data marts are necessary to support effective information discovery and support of decision making. Relevant data are indexed and organized for easy access by end users.

**❺** Online analytical processing is a data discovery method that uses analytical approaches.

**❻** The program that manages the data and provides access to the database is called the database management system.

**❼** The benefits of using a DBMS include: improved strategic use of corporate data, reduced complexity of the data environment, reduced data redundancy and enhanced data integrity, improved security, reduced data maintenance costs, and better access to data.

**❽** The conceptual data model is the highest level for modeling organizational data.

**❽** The logical model is a detailed view of the data, breaking down high-level entities into manageable data entities (e.g., customer data into product preferences, customer contact, shop locations, and product sales).

**❽** The physical model is the database tables with relationships and primary keys. Each detailed entity in the logical view becomes a database table in the physical model.

**❾** Entity-relationship diagrams are diagramming tools that help the database designer draw a blueprint of the data in the organization.

---

## Virtual Company Assignment

### Data Management at The Wireless Café
Go to The Wireless Café's link on the Student Web Site. There you will be asked to think about how to better manage the various types of data that the restaurant uses in its activities.

**Instructions for accessing The Wireless Café on the Student Web Site:**

1. Go to *wiley.com/college/turban*.
2. Select Turban/Leidner/ McLean/Wetherbe's *Information Technology for Management, Sixth Edition*.
3. Click on Student Resources site, in the toolbar on the left.
4. Click on the link for Virtual Company Web site.
5. Click on Wireless Café.

---

## Online Resources

More resources and study tools are located on the Student Web Site and on WileyPlus. You'll find additional chapter materials and useful Web links. In addition, self-quizzes that provide individualized feedback are available for each chapter.

---

## Questions for Review

1. List the major sources of data.
2. List some of the major data problems.
3. What is a terabyte? (Write the number.)
4. Review the steps of the data life cycle and explain them.
5. List some of the categories of data available on the Internet.
6. Define data quality.
7. Define document management.
8. Describe the hierarchy of a file management system.
9. What are the problems that arise from the file environment?
10. Discuss a relational database and how it differs from other databases.
11. What are the components of a database management system (DBMS)?
12. What is the difference between the conceptual, logical, and physical views of data?

13. How can you get data out of a database?
14. What are the benefits of using a DBMS?
15. What is the difference between entities and attributes?

16. Describe a data warehouse.
17. Describe a data mart.
18. Define a marketing transaction database.

## Questions for Discussion

1. Compare data quality to data integrity. How are they related?

2. Discuss business intelligence and distinguish between decision support and information and knowledge discovery.

3. Discuss the factors that make document management so valuable. What capabilities are particularly valuable?

4. Relate document management to imaging systems.

5. Discuss the major drivers and benefits of data warehousing to end users.

6. A data mart can substitute for a data warehouse or supplement it. Compare and discuss these options.

7. Discuss the steps in building a high-level, conceptual data model.

8. How do you move from the data model to the logical E-R diagrams?

9. What is the difference between the conceptual, logical, and physical views of data?

10. How are organizations using their data warehouses to gain consumer satisfaction?

11. Discuss the advantages of terabyte marketing databases to a large corporation. Does a small company need a marketing database? Under what circumstances will it make sense to have one?

12. What is the logic of targeted marketing, and how can data management be used in such marketing?

13. Distinguish between operational databases, data warehouses, and marketing data marts.

14. Discuss the interaction between marketing and management theories and IT support in the Harrah's case.

## Exercises and Projects

1. Review the list of data management difficulties in Section 3.1. Explain how a combination of data warehousing and data mining can solve or reduce these difficulties. Be specific.

2. Interview a knowledge worker in a company you work for or to which you have access. Find the data problems they have encountered and the measures they have taken to solve them. Relate the problems to Strong's four categories.

3. Create a typical breakdown of attributes for employee data in a for-profit organization.

4. Draw a picture of how a database management system is put together including all of its components.

5. Draw three database tables given entity-relationship diagram (ERD) entities and attributes:

**Product Availability Data**

Product SKU
Product name
Number of items
Location of items
Warehouse number
Date of Availability

**Product Description Data**

Product SKU
Product name

Product features
Product price

**Product Vendor Data**

Product SKU
Product name
Product type
Vendor name
Vendor shipping terms

6. For the exercise above, determine which tables are related to which others, determine primary keys and foreign keys (as needed), field type (text, number, date), and field length.

7. At *teradatastudentnetwork.com*, read and answer the questions to the case: "Harrah's High Payoff from Customer Information." Relate results from Harrah's to how other casinos utilize their customer data.

8. Go to *Teradata Magazine* Volume 6, Number 2 and read "The Big Payoff." Then go to *teradatastudentnetwork.com*, and read the case study "Harrah's High Payoff from Customer Information." What kind of payoff are they having from this investment in data warehousing?

9. At *teradatastudentnetwork.com*, read and answer the questions of the assignment entitled: "Data Warehouse Failures." Since there are eight cases described, choose one case and discuss the failure and the potential remedy.

# Group Assignments and Projects

1. In groups, create a data model for a pet store to include:
   - Customer data
   - Product data
   - Employee data
   - Financial data
   - Vendor data
   - Sales data
   - Inventory data
   - Building data
   - Other data (specify)

   Create attributes (4+ per entity) for each data entity. Create relationships between the entities, and name the relationships.

2. Prepare a report on the topic of "data management and the intranet." Specifically, pay attention to the role of the data warehouse, the use of browsers for query, and data mining. Each group will visit one or two vendors' sites, read the white papers, and examine products (Oracle, Red Bricks, Brio, Siemens Mixdorf IS, NCR, SAS, and Information Advantage). Also, visit the Web site of the Data Warehouse Institute (*tdwi.org*).

3. Using data mining, it is possible not only to capture information that has been buried in distant courthouses, but also to manipulate and cross-index it. This can benefit law enforcement but invade privacy. In 1996, Lexis-Nexis, the online information service, was accused of permitting access to sensitive information on individuals. The company argued that the firm was targeted unfairly, since it provided only basic residential data for lawyers and law enforcement personnel. Should Lexis-Nexis be prohibited from allowing access to such information or not? Debate the issue.

4. Ocean Spray Cranberries is a large cooperative of fruit growers and processors. Ocean Spray needed data to determine the effectiveness of its promotions and its advertising and to make itself able to respond strategically to its competitors' promotions. The company also wanted to identify trends in consumer preferences for new products and to pinpoint marketing factors that might be causing changes in the selling levels of certain brands and markets.

   Ocean Spray buys marketing data from InfoScan (*infores.com*), a company that collects data using barcode scanners in a sample of 2,500 stores nationwide and from A.C. Nielsen. The data for each product include sales volume, market share, distribution, price information, and information about promotions (sales, advertisements).

   The amount of data provided to Ocean Spray on a daily basis is overwhelming (about 100 to 1,000 times more data items than Ocean Spray used to collect on its own). All the data are deposited in the corporate marketing data mart. To analyze this vast amount of data, the company developed a DSS. To give end users easy access to the data, the company uses an expert system–based data-mining process called CoverStory, which summarizes information in accordance with user preferences. CoverStory interprets data processed by the DSS, identifies trends, discovers cause-and-effect relationships, presents hundreds of displays, and provides any information required by the decision makers. This system alerts managers to key problems and opportunities.

   a. Find information about Ocean Spray by entering Ocean Spray's Web site (*oceanspray.com*).
   b. Ocean Spray has said that it cannot run the business without the system. Why?
   c. What data from the data mart are used by the DSS?
   d. Enter *infores.com* or *scanmar.nl* and review the marketing decision support information. How is the company related to a data warehouse?
   e. How does InfoScan collect data? (Check the Data Wrench product.)

# Internet Exercises

1. Conduct a survey on document management tools and applications by visiting *dataware.com*, *documentum.com*, *mobius.com*, and *aiim.org/aim/publications*.

2. Access the Web sites of one or two of the major data management vendors, such as Oracle, IBM, and Sybase, and trace the capabilities of their latest BI products.

3. Access the Web sites of one or two of the major data warehouse vendors, such as NCR or SAS; find how their products are related to the Web.

4. Access the Web site of the GartnerGroup (*gartnergroup.com*). Examine some of their research notes pertaining to marketing databases, data warehousing, and data management. Prepare a report regarding the state of the art.

5. Explore a Web site for multimedia database applications. Visit such sites as *leisureplan.com*, *illustra.com*, or *adb.fr*. Review some of the demonstrations, and prepare a concluding report.

6. Enter *microsoft.com/solutions/BI/customer/biwithinreach_demo.asp* and see how BI is supported by Microsoft's tools. Write a report.

7. Enter *teradatauniversitynetwork.com*. Prepare a summary on resources available there. Is it valuable to a student? To practicing managers?

8. Enter *websurvey.com*, *clearlearning.com*, and *tucows.com/webforms*, and prepare a report about data collection via the Web.

9. Enter *infoscan.com*. Find all the services related to dynamic warehouse and explain what it does.

# Minicase 1

## Homeland Security Data Integration

*GOV*

The CIO of the U.S. Department of Homeland Security (DHS) is responsible for determining which existing applications and types of data can help the organization meet its goal, migrating the data into a secure, usable, state-of-the-art framework, and integrating the disparate networks and data standards of 22 federal agencies, with 170,000 employees, that merged to form the DHS. The real problem is that federal agencies have historically operated autonomously, and their IT systems were not designed to interoperate with one another. Essentially, the DHS needs to link large and complex silos of data together.

The challenge of moving data from legacy systems, within or across agencies, is the first challenge DHS must address. Complicating the issue is the plethora of rapidly aging applications and databases throughout government. Data integration improvement is underway at the federal, local, and state levels. The government is utilizing tools from the corporate world.

Major problems have occurred because each agency has its own set of business rules that dictate how data are described, collected, and accessed. Some of the data are unstructured and not organized in relational databases, and they cannot be easily manipulated and analyzed. Commercial applications are used for the major integration, mostly data warehouse and data-mart technologies. Informatica, among other software vendors, has developed data integration solutions that enable organizations to combine disparate systems to make information more widely accessible throughout an organization. Such software may be suitable for such a large-scale project (see *informatica.com*).

The idea is to decide on and create an enterprise architecture for federal and state agencies involved in homeland security. The architecture will help determine the success of homeland defense. The first step in migrating data is to identify all the applications and data in use. After identifying applications and databases, the next step is to determine which to use and which to discard. Once an organization knows which data and applications it wants to keep, the difficult process of moving the data starts. First, it is necessary to identify and build on a com-

mon thread in the data. Another major challenge in the data-migration arena is data security, especially when dealing with data and applications that are decades old.

Homeland Security will also have information-analysis and infrastructure-protection components. Developing these components may be the single most difficult challenge for the DHS. Not only will Homeland Security have to make sense of a huge mountain of intelligence gathered from disparate sources, but then it will have to get that information to the people who can most effectively act on it. Many of them are outside the federal government. Data analysis, including data mining, OLAP, and more, will help in early detection of planned attacks, as well as in finding terrorists.

Even the central government recognizes that data deficiencies may plague the DHS. Moving information to where it is needed, and doing so when it is needed, is critical and exceedingly difficult. Some 650,000 state and local law enforcement officials "operate in a virtual intelligence vacuum, without proper access to terrorist watch lists provided by the State Department to immigration and consular officials," according to the October 2002 Hart-Rudman report, titled "America Still Unprepared—America Still in Danger."

*Sources:* Compiled from Datz (2002), Foley (2003), Nazarov (2003), Thibodeau (2003), and Peters (2003).

### Questions for Minicase 1

1. List the data problems and difficulties (see Section 3.1).
2. Why is the data warehouse beneficial?
3. What kind of analysis can the government perform with the IT support? What tools do you suggest be used?
4. How can Informatica.com products help? (Visit the company's site, *informatica.com*.)
5. Would you suggest a document management system (DMS)? For what purpose?

# Minicase 2

## Precision Buying, Merchandising, and Marketing at Sears

*SVC*

### The Problem

Sears, Roebuck and Company, the largest department store chain and the third-largest retailer in the United States, was caught by surprise in the 1980s as shoppers

defected to specialty stores and discount mass merchandisers, causing the firm to lose market share rapidly. In an attempt to change the situation, Sears used several response strategies, ranging from introducing its own specialty stores (such as Sears Hardware) to restructuring its mall-based stores. Recently, Sears has moved to selling on the Web. It discontinued its over 100-year-old paper catalog. Accomplishing the transformation and restructuring required the retooling of its information systems.

Sears had 18 data centers, one in each of 10 geographical regions as well as one each for marketing, finance, and other departments. The first problem was created when the reorganization effort produced only seven geographical regions. Frequent mismatches between accounting and sales figures and information scattered among numerous databases forced users to query multiple systems, even when they needed an answer to a simple query. Furthermore, users found that data that were already summarized made it difficult to conduct analysis at the desired level of detail. Finally, errors were virtually inevitable when calculations were based on data from several sources.

## The Solution

To solve these problems, Sears constructed a single sales information data warehouse. This replaced the 18 old databases which were packed with redundant, conflicting, and sometimes obsolete data. The new data warehouse is a simple repository of relevant decision-making data such as authoritative data for key performance indicators, sales inventories, and profit margins. Sears, known for embracing IT on a dramatic scale, completed the data warehouse and its IT reengineering efforts in under one year—a perfect IT turnaround story.

Using an NCR enterprise server, the initial 1.7 terabyte (1.7 trillion bytes) data warehouse is part of a project dubbed the Strategic Performance Reporting System (SPRS). By 2003, the data warehouse had grown to over 70 terabytes. SPRS includes comprehensive sales data; information on inventory in stores, in transit, and at distribution centers; and cost per item. This has enabled Sears to track sales by individual items (skus) in each of its 1,950 stores (including 810 mall-based stores) in the United States and 1,600 international stores and catalog outlets. Thus, daily margin by item per store can be easily computed, for example. Furthermore, Sears now fine-tunes its buying, merchandising, and marketing strategies with previously unattainable precision.

SPRS is open to all authorized employees, who now can view each day's sales from a multidimensional perspective (by region, district, store, product line, and individual item). Users can specify any starting and ending dates for special sales reports, and all data can be accessed via a highly user-friendly graphical interface. Sears managers can now monitor the precise impact of advertising, weather, and other factors on sales of specific items. This means that Sears merchandise buyers and other specialists can examine and adjust, if needed, inventory quantities, merchandising, and order placement, along with myriad other variables, almost immediately, so they can respond quickly to environmental changes. SPRS users

can also group together widely divergent kinds of products, for example, tracking sales of items marked as "gifts under $25." Advertising staffers can follow so-called "great items," drawn from vastly different departments, that are splashed on the covers of promotional circulars. SPRS enables extensive data mining, but only on sku- and location-related analysis.

In 1998 Sears created a large customer database, dubbed LCI (Leveraging Customer Information), which contained customer-related sale information (which was not available on SPRS). The LCI enables hourly records of transactions, for example, guiding hourly promotion (such as 15% discounts for early-bird shoppers).

In the holiday season of 2001, Sears decided to replace its regular 10% discount promotion by offering deep discount during early shopping hours. This new promotion, which was based on SPRS, failed, and only when LCI was used was the problem corrected. This motivated Sears to combine LCI and SPRS in a single platform, which enables sophisticated analysis (in 2002).

By 2001, Sears also had the following Web initiatives: an e-commerce home improvement center, a B2B supply exchange for the retail industry, a toy catalog (*wishbook .com*), an e-procurement system, and much more. All of these Web-marketing initiatives feed data into the data warehouse, and their planning and control are based on accessing the data in the data warehouse.

## The Results

The ability to monitor sales by item per store enables Sears to create a sharp local market focus. For example, Sears keeps different shades of paint colors in different cities to meet local demands. Therefore, sales and market share have improved. Also, Web-based data monitoring of sales at LCI helps Sears to plan marketing and Web advertising.

At its inception, the data warehouse had been used daily by over 3,000 buyers, replenishers, marketers, strategic planners, logistics and finance analysts, and store managers. By 2004, there were over 6,000 users, since users found the system very beneficial. Response time to queries has dropped from days to minutes for typical requests. Overall, the strategic impact of the SPRS-LCI data warehouse is that it offers Sears employees a tool for making better decisions, and Sears retailing profits have climbed more than 20 percent annually since SPRS was implemented.

*Sources:* Compiled from Amato-McCoy (2002), Beitler and Leary (1997), and press releases of Sears (2001–2004).

### Questions for Minicase 2

1. What were the drivers of SPRS?
2. How did the data warehouse solve Sears's problems?
3. Why was it beneficial to integrate the customers' database with SPRS?
4. How could RFID change Sears's operations?

# References

Alter, S. L., *Decision Support Systems*. Reading, MA: Addison Wesley, 1980.

Amato-McCoy, D. M., "Victoria's Secret Works to Keep Orders Alive," *Stores*, January 2003.

Beitler, S. S., and R. Leary, "Sears' Epic Transformation: Converting from Mainframe Legacy Systems to OLAP," *Journal of Data Warehousing*, April 1997.

Canada NewsWire, "European Court of Human Rights Saves Time and Money for a News Wire," April 29, 2003, NAICS#922110.

Carbone, P. L., "Data Warehousing: Many of the Common Failures," presentation, *mitre.org/support/papers/tech...9_00/d-warehoulse_presentation.htm* (May 3, 1999).

Chenoweth, T., Corral, K., and Demirkan, H., "The Seven Key Interventions for Data Warehouse Success," *Communications of the ACM*, 49(1), January 2006.

D'Agostino, D., "Applications: Data Management at Work at the National Security Archive," *CIO Insight*, April 21, 2006.

Datz, T., "Integrating America," *CIO, December 2002.*

Delcambre, L., et al., "Harvesting Information to Sustain Forests," *Communications of the ACM*, January 2003.

*DM Review*, "Deploy SQL Server 2005 with Confidence,"

*DM Review*, "Data Quality," May 23, 2006.

*DM Review*, "Review," April 17, 2004

*DM Review*, "Reality IT: Data Quality—It Is All About Not Being Worse Than Anyone Else," May 5, 2005.

Evans, G., "The Big Payoff: Harrahs," *Teradata*, March 2006.

Ferrell, K., "Getting a Handle on Data," *Teradata*, March 2006.

Foley, J., "Data Debate," *Information Week*, May 19, 2003.

Helmaan, P., "Beyond Internet Banking: Wells Fargo Is Taking the Data Warehouse Public," March 2006.

Herlein, S., "A Business Approach to Data Quality: Achieving and Maintaining First-Class Organizational Data," *Journal of Data Warehousing*, 7(2), Spring 2002.

Jekic, N., "Modeling Strategies and Alternatives for Data Warehousing Projects," *Communications of the ACM*, 49(4), April 2006.

Kroenke, D. M., *Database Processing Fundamentals*, 10th ed. Upper Saddle River, NJ: Prentice Hall, 2006.

Levinson, M., "Jackpot! Harrah's Entertainment," *CIO Magazine*, February 1, 2001.

Liautaud, B., *E-Business Intelligence*. New York: McGraw-Hill, 2001.

Loshin, D., "Issues and Opportunities in Data Quality Management Coordination," *DM Review*, April 2004.

Loveman, G., "Diamonds in the Data," *Harvard Business Review*, May 2003.

Marinos, G., "How Executives Around the World are Addressing Data Management," *DMReview*, January 2005.

Markus, M. L., et al., "A Design Theory for Systems that Support Emergent Knowledge Processes," *MIS Quarterly*, September 2002.

Merrill Lynch, 1998.

Moad, J., "Mining a New Vein," *PC Week*, January 5, 1998.

Nazarov, A. R., "Information Seeks Partners to Gain Traction in Fed Market," *CRN*, June 9, 2003.

Orlov, L., and Ramos, L., "Organic Information Abstraction," *Forrester Big Idea*, May 12, 2004.

Park, Y. T., "Strategic Uses of Data Warehouses," *Journal of Data Warehousing*, April 1997.

Peters, K. M., "5 Homeland Security Hurdles," *Government Executive*, 35(2), February 2003.

Roth, M. A., et al., "Information Integration: A New Generation of Information Technology," *IBM Systems Journal*, December 2002.

Sears (2001–2003).

Solomon, M., "It's All About the Data," *Information Systems Management*, Summer 2005.

Strauss, J. et al., *E-Marketing*. Upper Saddle River, NJ: Prentice Hall, 2003.

Tannenbaum, A., "Identifying Meta Data Requirements," *Journal of Data Warehousing*, 7(2), Spring 2002.

Teradata, "Overview: Benefits of an Enterprise Data Warehouse for Manufacturers," *Teradata.com*, 2006. *teradata.com/t/page/85158/index.html* (accessed September 2006).

Thibodeau, P., "DHS Sets Timeline for IT Integration," *Computer World*, June 16, 2003.

Volonino, L., R. Anzaldua, and J. Godwin, *Computer Forensics: Principles and Practice*, Chapter 10. Upper Saddle River. NJ: Prentice-Hall, 2007.

Weiss, T. R., "Online Retail Sales On the Rise," *PC World*, January 2003.

Whitehouse.gov, "President Signs Intelligence Reform and Terrorism Prevention Act," December 17, 2004. *whitehouse.gov/news/releases/2004/12/20041217-1.html* (accessed September 2006).

Wikipedia.org, "Database Management Systems," October 2005. *en.wikipedia.org/wiki/Relational_database_management_system* (accessed September 2006).

Winter, R., *Large Scale Data Warehousing with Oracle 9i Database*, Special Report. Waltham MA: Winter Corp., 2001.

Worthen, B., "IT versus Terror," *CIO*, August 1, 2006.

Chapter

# 4

# Networking: Discovery, Communication, Collaboration

## Learning Objectives

After studying this chapter, you will be able to:

❶ Discuss the characteristics and standards of network computing.

❷ Explain the business benefits of interoperability and converged networks.

❸ Describe the role of intranet and extranet portals and how they support supply chain management.

❹ Understand the role of discovery, communication, and collaboration capabilities for organizations.

❺ Describe how new communication technologies are replacing or filling the gaps left by conventional technologies.

❻ Describe how IT-based collaboration and communication support group work and decision making.

❼ Describe the fundamental principles and capabilities of group work technologies.

❽ Evaluate the managerial, social, and ethical issues related to the use of network computing, messaging, and collaboration.

## Integrating *IT*

 **ACC**
 **FIN**
 **MKT**
 **POM**
 **HRM**
 **IS**
 **SVC**

# SUPER BOWL XXXIX COLLABORATION PORTAL

The National Football League (NFL, *nfl.com*) designated Florida's Jacksonville Sheriff's office (JSO) as the lead agency for coordinating and protecting local operations for Super Bowl XXXIX. Planning for the February 6, 2005 game began 18 months in advance.

When Jacksonville had hosted Super Bowl XXXIV in 2000, the key security concerns were traffic and crowd control. But the September 11 attacks changed that scope. The U.S. federal government mandated new processes and practices, such as *in-synch command* for terrorist prevention and intervention. Higher levels of security required collaboration with federal and national security agencies.

## The Problem/Opportunity

Providing security and logistic support for Super Bowl XXXIV was a challenge of unprecedented scope and scale for the JSO. The JSO had to manage an influx of 150,000 spectators into their community, provide security at 6,000 related events, and coordinate 53 separate agencies at the local, county, state, and federal levels. Those agencies included the Jacksonville Fire and Rescue Department, Florida Highway Patrol, FBI, FEMA (Federal Emergency Management Agency), U.S. Secret Service, and Department of Homeland Security.

JSO's mission was to provide a safe and nondisrupted Super Bowl experience for the teams, fans, two former Presidents, and superstar Paul McCartney. To do so, JSO's Sheriff John Rutherford had to ensure collaboration of over 4,000 personnel to plan, build, and execute comprehensive land, sea, and air initiatives of both traditional and nontraditional activities. To provide security in the water and air, cruise ships had to be checked before entering the harbor and flights had to be restricted on game day for a 10-mile radius around Alltel Stadium.

Security and continuity plans (i.e., incident response) had to be coordinated at 35 venues for 10 days leading up to and including the game. For example, an Event Operations Center would be the top-level command post, but in the event of a terrorist act, the Joint Operations Center would mobilize immediately to become the lead command post. In addition, Bomb Management Centers were needed at strategic locations. Practices and movements of the New England Patriots and Philadelphia Eagles staying at the Renaissance Resort at the World Golf Village and the Marriott at Sawgrass, respectively, had to be monitored by mobile units.

## The Solution

Sheriff Rutherford deployed *E-Sponder,* a real-time Web-based communication and collaboration portal from Convergence Communications (*convergencecom.com*). E-Sponder is accessed through the Internet Explorer 6 (IE6) browser. Being able to train users on the E-Sponder system in less than an hour, which was possible because of its familiar Office interface, was a major factor. All users were able to view everything that was going on, alleviating the need to coordinate personnel moves using radio frequencies (RF).

All the various agencies created what was called an *incident action plan*. Preparation of incident response plans was facilitated by Microsoft Project, Word, Excel, Powerpoint, and InfoPath, which were all rolled up into a Microsoft SharePoint Portal Server. See the demo at *microsoft.com/office/sharepoint/prodinfo/demo.mspx.*

Critical communications were integrated into the E-Sponder incident management system. E-Sponder's role in Super Bowl XXXIX was to provide critical information and enhanced situational awareness to both the command staff and the professionals in the field who were in charge of protecting the public during the event. (For a video of the role of E-Sponder for Super Bowl XXXIX collaboration efforts, download *e-sponder.com/downloads/Superbowl-large.wmv.*)

## The Results

Key benefits of the collaboration tool were:

- Centralized command functions
- Real-time communication and collaboration
- Optimized situational awareness
- Deployment with minimal training in a compressed time frame

The communications and collaboration tools gave the JSO the ability to prevent and respond to acts that could jeopardize public safety, thereby enhancing the security and enjoyment of Super Bowl XXXIX.

*Sources:* Compiled from Microsoft Case Study (2005), Careless (2006), and E-Sponder Case Study (2005).

Integrating IT in logistics and sports

# 4.1 Network Computing—Overview and Drivers

Various information services—data and documents, voice, and video—have functioned independently of each other. Traditionally, they were transmitted using different protocols and carried on different networks as shown in Table 4.1. Multiple networks were needed because of the lack of **interoperability** or connectivity between devices. Problems stemming from the lack of interoperability (the ability to provide services to and accept services from other systems or devices) include limited access to information and computing and communications resources. For more information on interoperability and networking protocols, see Technology Guide 4.

To prepare data and documents for transmission, they are converted into digital packets based on the **Internet Protocol (IP)** and sent via computer (i.e., packet-switched) networks or LANs. As shown in Table 4.1, packets are transmitted using the **Transmission Control Protocol (TCP),** which provides a reliable, connection-oriented method of packet delivery. This combination of protocols is referred to as the TCP/IP model. Voice is sent as analog signals over circuits on telephone (circuit-switched) networks. Video streams are compressed and sent as IP packets using the **User Datagram Protocol (UDP).** This combination of protocols is referred to as the UDP/IP model. UDP provides no error recovery services, but also does not have the overhead that a connection-oriented protocol like TCP has. Perfection is sacrificed for efficiency. Compared to TCP, UDP sends packets much faster and more efficiently, but is less reliable because it does not check packets for errors. See Technology Guide 4 for details.

As of 2006, 75 percent of Internet traffic was sent using TCP and 20 percent was sent using UDP (Pessach, 2006). UDP is used by many common applications such as Voice Over IP (VoIP), streaming media, and online games. VoIP will be discussed as a technology for competitive advantage later in the chapter. Until networking technology had advanced to enable all (or most) information services to be transmitted the same way, convergence was not possible.

Today, data, voice, and video networks are converging into a single network based on packet (such as IP and VoIP) technology. The convergence is at various

| TABLE 4.1 | Networks, Protocols, and Transfer Methods of Information Services | | | |
|---|---|---|---|---|
| Information Service | Network | Format | Protocol | Transfer Method |
| Data and documents | Packet | Converted to (broken into) packets based on Internet Protocol (IP). | TCP (Transmission Control Protocol) | Each packet can take a different route to the destination where the packets are recompiled. If a packet does not arrive, the entire transmission is resent. |
| Voice | Circuit | Sent as analog signals between the telephone and the telco's central office (called *local loop*). Traffic between telephone offices is digital. | | Whether analog or digital, each call creates a circuit that reserves a channel between two parties for the entire session. The entire message follows the same path in order. |
| Video streams | Packet | Compressed and converted to IP packets. | UDP (User Datagram Protocol) | No checking for missing packets. Malformed packets are simply dropped (i.e., discarded). |

stages of maturity and far from complete. For example, watching streamed TV on mobile phones has been a frustrating experience. The viewing experience is compromised by the small size of the phone's screen, the jerky nature of the images due to transmission problems, and the draining impact of streaming video on a phone's battery life. Quality improves as the technology matures.

**PACKET TECHNOLOGIES: AN ENABLER**

**Packet technologies** convert voice, video, and data into packets that can be transmitted together over a single, high-speed network—eliminating the need for separate networks. High-speed networks can be wireline, wireless, or both. These networks are more commonly called **broadband,** which comes from the words *broad bandwidth.*

When all information services are handled the same way by one high-speed packet network using either wireline or wireless, the technical barriers to collaborative work are eliminated. Then it is no longer difficult (or prohibitively expensive) to use multimedia applications simultaneously because the network would not restrict the kinds of computing devices that could be used. For example, users would access the company network from home through a desktop computer and wireline connection or be on the move with a laptop or PDA via a wireless connection. With secure access through converged networks, exciting new forms of business communication and collaboration using multimedia applications and digital devices become possible. See Online File W4.1 for a list of wireless computing and mobile commerce security challenges. This chapter will focus on the applications and technology, while security defenses will be discussed in Chapter 16.

**CONVERGED NETWORKS: A POWERFUL ARCHITECTURE**

The Internet revolution was characterized by two opposing forces: chaos and convergence. Chaos stemmed from existing and emerging technologies that were not interoperable. The same was true in the business communications industry, which is still fragmented. Although business collaboration tools have been around for many years, commonly accepted industry standards were not. As a result, collaboration tools have relied heavily on proprietary protocols and standalone products that

# IT at Work 4.1

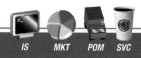

## The Future and Force of Convergent Solutions

IS    MKT    POM    SVC

At the *2006 3GSM World Congress* in Barcelona, there were products and services from 962 companies, a 40 percent increase over the number who participated in the *2005 Congress* in Cannes. At the pace technology is developing, users will soon be able to watch TV and make mobile phone calls while simultaneously transferring files or videos over a wireless network. The Siemens Communications Group showed how mobile communication technology was going to change leisure and work. There was a live demonstration of mobile TV over DVB-H (digital video broadcast-handheld) and new IP-based mobile applications.

Special DVB-H devices enabled attendees to receive 16 different TV programs live, including music channel MTV, news networks CNN and BBC World, and coverage of the Winter Olympic Games in Turin. Mobile TV and mobile e-mail access were the favorites among mobile users. A survey of 5,300 mobile users in eight countries—Brazil, Canada, China, Germany, Italy, Korea, Russia, and the United States—showed 74 percent wanted mobile e-mail access.

Siemens third-generation wireless turbo-service based on 3G allows better user experience of existing wireless applications such as video calls and Internet downloads. In areas where mobility is not required, WiMax deploys wireless high-speed broadband services to the public over a larger coverage area than is possible with existing Wi-Fi hotspots. The 450 MHz FLASH-OFDM (Fast Low-latency Access with Seamless Handoff—Orthogonal Frequency Division Multiplexing) allows usage in moving vehicles such as cars, buses, and trains.

Siemens' convergent solution for VoIP allows users to make cheaper calls over GSM-based and UMA (Unlicensed Mobile Access, e.g., Wi-Fi) technologies. For example, when a mobile user makes a VoIP call in a hotspot and moves out of the Wi-Fi coverage area, the call is uninterrupted as the device then switches over to a GSM-based wireless broadband technology such as 3G.

*Sources:* Compiled from Cruez (2006) and *3gsmworldcongress.com* (accessed June 2006).

*For Further Exploration:* What collaborative efforts are possible with these networking advancements? How might business processes change as a result of convergence?

---

severely limited interoperability with other systems and tools. Convergent solutions were needed to make great opportunities for productivity possible.

A converged network is a powerful new architecture that enables the enterprisewide convergence and integration of voice, data, video, and other communication applications. Improved collaboration along the entire supply chain—partners, suppliers, and customers—is possible. With a single converged network, companies can improve their business-to-business (B2B) and business-to-customer (B2C) processes. A look at the future of convergence and wireless technologies, including **Global System for Mobile Communications Services (GSM),** and applications is presented in *IT at Work 4.1.* GSM is an internationally accepted standard for digital cellular communication originating in Europe. It is the most popular standard for mobile phones in the world. See Appendix 4A for details on GSM and the problems caused by competing network standards.

**SIP (Session Initiation Protocol).** With converged networks, management of their interface becomes a key factor. Users need easy and intuitive access to the network from any device, anywhere, any time, seamlessly. The protocol and industry standard for doing this is **Session Initiation Protocol (SIP).** SIP standardizes the signaling of calls or communications between different types of devices/end-points from different vendors such as IP phones, instant messaging (IM) clients, soft phones, smart phones, and so on. In effect, SIP integrates voice, video, and data to make management of communications possible. A benefit of SIP is that multiple users can join an online meeting with simultaneous voice and data interaction and be talking, sharing a spreadsheet or slide presentation, or browsing Web sites together regardless of the users' locations. These innovations can revolutionize the management of inventory,

# A Closer Look 4.1

## *Tech-Fueled Productivity Gains*

Information technology has been a vital part of Alan Greenspan's era. During his 18 years as Federal Reserve chairman, Greenspan highlighted IT's role in shaping the U.S. economy. He noted its role in providing the kind of economic flexibility that has allowed the economy to withstand shocks, such as Hurricane Katrina and terrorist attacks, and to keep growing. In his speech, Greenspan stated: "Beyond deregulation, innovative technologies, especially information technologies, have contributed critically to enhanced flexibility. A quarter-century ago, for example, companies often required weeks to discover the emergence of inventory imbalances, allowing production to continue to exacerbate the excess."

Tech-fueled productivity gains powered the economy, as financial, retail, and manufacturing industries automated transactions, cut inventory, and increased employee output. For IT to keep delivering impressive business-productivity gains, it needs a new source. The gains of 1995 to 2005 were mostly around transactions (e.g., orders taking, inventory replenishing, and accounts payable). The next wave will come from improving the way people and companies collaborate. With wireless and wireline technologies, there can be real-time collaboration that taps into a greater breadth of expertise and resources.

Other economists have also recognized that it is how IT gets implemented—not just that the investment was made—that determines productivity gains. According to Catherine Guillemineau, a Conference Board economist, even though the U.S. productivity pace slowed in 2005, it still outperformed the 15-nation European Union (EU). The EU's productivity growth was only 0.5 percent. IT provided U.S. companies and managers flexibility and ability to adapt quickly to innovation, which Guillemineau credited for the higher productivity rate.

*Sources:* Federal News Service (2005) and Chabrow and McGee (2006).

---

global supply chains, and offshore operations—as well as group decision making, order fulfillment, and database marketing (topics covered throughout the book). Online meetings will be discussed in detail in Section 4.4.

**Benefits of Converged Networks.** Having fewer networks to maintain and support can decrease networking costs significantly. The costs of integrating applications and bandwidth are lower because traffic is consolidated over one network. Converged networks can save travel costs associated with intra- and interorganizational meetings. On a national level, by improving the speed at which companies collaborate and respond to opportunities and threats, the convergence of wireline and wireless networks can support productivity growth. See *A Closer Look 4.1* for an explanation of how networks can lead to productivity and economic growth.

IP telephony has enabled convergence of LAN/WAN corporate infrastructures to the desktops. Network carriers are converging, too, by offering voice, data, video, and signaling on one pipe, and with the addition of security services, the pipe should be clean, free of spam and viruses.

Despite advances in converged networks and SIP—and vendors' forecasted products discussed in *IT at Work 4.1*—there are still barriers to full integration. At this time, globally accepted standards and protocols do not exist. We will discuss several issues hindering convergence in this chapter and Appendix 4A.

**THE INTERNET AND WWW**

Many people believe that the Web is synonymous with the Internet, but that is not the case. The Internet functions as the *transport mechanism,* and the Web (WWW, or W3) is an *application* that *uses* those transport functions. Other applications also run on the Internet, with e-mail being the most widely used.

The Web is a system with universally accepted standards for storing, retrieving, formatting, and displaying information via client/server architecture. The Web handles all types of digital information, including text, hypermedia, graphics, and sound. It uses graphical user interfaces, so it is very easy to use. See Technology Guide 5 for details.

**The Evolution of Commercial Applications on the Internet.** With the commercialization of the Internet in the early 1990s, we have seen an explosion of commercial applications. Specific applications are demonstrated throughout this book.

**Internet Application Categories.** The Internet supports applications in the following major categories:

- **Discovery.** Discovery involves browsing and information retrieval. As shown in Online Minicase W4.1, it provides customers the ability to view information in databases, download it, and/or process it. Discovery is automated by software agents since the amount of information on the Internet and intranets is growing rapidly. Discovery methods and issues are described in Section 4.2.
- **Communication.** New and exciting developments in Internet-based and wireless communication such as podcasting, RSS, and BitTorrents will alter business communications, marketing channels, and supply chain management—to name a few. They will be discussed in Section 4.4.
- **Collaboration.** As you have read, electronic collaboration between individuals, groups, and organizations is becoming common. Numerous tools and technologies are available ranging from online meetings with screen sharing to videoconferencing and group support systems. Collaboration software products, called groupware and workflow, can be used on the Internet or other networks.

**THE NETWORK COMPUTING INFRASTRUCTURE: INTRANETS AND EXTRANETS**

In addition to the Internet and the Web there are a few other major infrastructures of network computing: value-added networks (VANs) (see Technology Guide 4), intranets, and extranets.

**Intranets.** As discussed in Chapter 2, an **intranet** is a network designed to serve the internal informational needs of a company, using Internet concepts and tools. It is a network confined to an organization for its internal use. It provides easy and inexpensive browsing and search capabilities.

Intranets also support communication and collaboration. They are frequently connected to the Internet, enabling a company to conduct e-commerce activities. (Such activities are facilitated by *extranets,* as described later in this chapter and in Chapter 8.) Using screen sharing and other groupware tools, intranets can be used to facilitate the work of groups. Companies also publish newsletters and deliver news to their employers via their intranets. For extensive information about intranets, see *intranetjournal.com.*

Intranets have the power to change organizational structures and cultures as well as procedures, and to help restructure corporations. Intranets can be implemented using different types of local area network (LAN) technologies including wireless LANs (see Technology Guide 4 and Chapter 5).

Intranets are used in all types of organizations, from manufacturers to health care providers to government agencies to educational institutions. Examples of several intranet applications and portals are available in Online File W4.2.

EXTRANETS

An **extranet** is a private (company-owned) network that uses Internet technology and the public telecommunication system to securely share part of a business's information or operations with suppliers, vendors, partners, customers, or other businesses. Extranets may use virtual private networks (VPNs). VPNs are, in effect, private tunnels within a public network (typically, the Internet) created by encryption. (VPNs are covered in Chapter 16.)

Basically, an extranet is a means of networking two or more companies so they can securely share information. In some cases, an extranet is an extension of the company's intranet—to connect to a customer or trading partner for B2B commerce. Or an extranet makes use of the public Internet to create a restricted portal that, for example, gives account customers instant access to their account details. In this way, customers can manage their own accounts quickly and easily. United Rentals, the largest equipment rental company in the world, has more than 750 rental locations throughout the United States, Canada, and Mexico with a diverse customer base of construction and industrial companies, utilities, municipalities, and homeowners. United Rentals' extranet portal at *URdata.UR.com* makes it convenient for account customers worldwide to request equipment, manage rental equipment by project, view invoices, calculate job costs, and so on—and at lower cost. Figure 4.1 illustrates the familiar Internet-interface of an extranet, the use of usernames and passwords for access control and authentication, and self-help features.

Extranets usually have a central server storing data, documents, and applications. Authorized users can remotely access them from any Internet-enabled device, which can drastically reduce storage space on individual hard drives. To protect the privacy of the information that is being transmitted, extranets need secure communication lines, encryption technologies, and access and authentication control. These security topics are covered in detail in Chapter 16. The National Semiconductor Corporation (NSC) case study in Online Minicase W4.2 explains

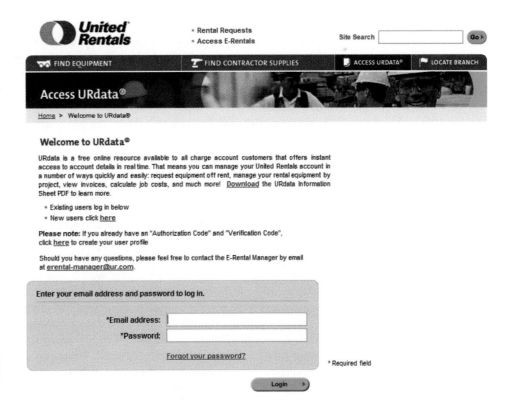

**Figure 4.1** United Rentals' extranet portal. (Copyright © 2005 United Rentals, Inc. Photo courtesy of United Rentals, Inc. Used with permission.)

how NSC's customers save time and effort in design by using design support available via extranets.

Extranets improve communication throughout the entire supply chain (for details see Technology Guide 4 and *cio.com/enterprise/scm*). An example of how a hypothetical company, Toy Inc., uses digital network portals was shown in Figure 1.2.

**INFORMATION PORTALS**

A challenge facing organizations is information overload because of the growing use of intranets. Information is scattered across numerous documents, e-mail messages, and databases at different locations and systems. Accessing relevant, accurate, and complete information can be time consuming and require access to multiple systems.

To avoid losing a lot of productive employee time, companies use portals. A **portal** (or information portal) is a Web-based personalized gateway to information and knowledge in network computing. It attempts to minimize information overload through an intranet-based environment to search and access information from disparate IT systems and the Internet using advanced search and indexing techniques.

The portal was introduced in 1997 when several Internet search engines and directories began offering free e-mail accounts, stock quotes, news, and other Web Services to their sites to become jumping-off points for Web surfers. Since then portals have grown immensely.

People within an organization can work with Internet tools and procedures through enterprise information portals. Specific applications can include important internal documents and procedures, corporate address lists, e-mail, tool access, and software distribution. Seven types of portals are described below.

1. **Corporate (enterprise) portals** are gateways to corporate Web sites that enable communication, collaboration, and access to company information. A corporate portal is a personalized, single point of access through a Web browser to critical business information located inside and outside of an organization. Corporate portals provide a single point of access to information and applications available on the Internet, intranets, and extranets of a specific organization. Many large organizations have already implemented corporate portals to cut costs, free up time for busy executives and managers, and improve profitability.

2. **Commercial portals** such as Yahoo! and MSN are gateways to general information on the Internet.

3. **Decision portals** provide team members with models they can use to evaluate decision criteria, objectives, and alternatives from their desktops.

4. **Publishing portals** are intended for communities with specific interests. These portals involve relatively little customization of content, but they provide extensive online search in a specific area and some interactive capabilities. Examples are *techweb.com* and *zdnet.com*.

5. **Mobile portals** are those accessible from mobile devices. One example is NTT DoCoMo's i-mode portal in Japan, which has over 42 million subscribers in Japan and has been the mobile Internet phenomenon that Western network operators have sought to match. *Time Out* has expanded its portfolio of mobile services with the launch of a branded dating service on O2's i-mode mobile portal. *Time Out Dating* enables O2 i-mode users to chat with each other for a monthly fee. They can search for dates based on age, location, or interests. In addition, I-mode launched *iChannel,* which is all about pushing content that refreshes itself automatically overnight.

6. **Voice portals** are Web portals with audio interfaces that make them accessible via a standard cell phone. Using *advanced speech recognition* and *text-to-speech* techniques, voice portals allow users to retrieve e-mail, credit card data, airline flight information, and so on.

7. **Vertical portals,** also called **vortals,** target specific markets. Vortals usually offer relevant news headlines, industry event calendars, links to related sites, and lists of vendors and businesses that offer pertinent products and services. Examples are Pharmaceutical Online at *pharmaceuticalonline.com* and Bakery Online at *bakeryonline.com.*

**Integration of Portals.**  Many organizations are creating several corporate portals. While in some cases these portals are completely independent of each other, in other cases they are interrelated. For example, they may share content, and they may draw from the same applications and databases.

Tool-building software, such as WebSphere Portal (from IBM), allows companies to create multiple portals as one unit. It enables three different portals to be used by a single company—a portal for business partners (B2B), a portal for employees (B2E), and a portal for customers (B2C).

Discovery, communication, and collaboration capabilities available at low cost on the Internet as well as intranet and extranet portals can offer many useful and time-saving applications. Online File W4.3 lists examples of potential competitive advantages from intranets and extranets.

*IT at Work 4.2* describes how Kaiser Permanente used a Google tool for its corporate portal. The degree of usefulness of these nets depends on the design and users' knowledge of search techniques. It is estimated that Internet searchers are successful at finding what they seek only 50 percent of the time or less. Not surprisingly, the same problem applies to intranets. According to IDC's 2004 report, *The High Cost of Not Finding Information,* 40 percent of corporate users cannot find on their intranets the information they need to do their jobs (reported by Feldman,

# *IT* at Work 4.2

## *Kaiser Permanente Uses Google to Build a Portal*

**SVC**

Kaiser Permanente (*kaiserpermanente.org*), America's largest not-for-profit health maintenance organization (HMO), has almost 9 million members. The amount of available medical knowledge doubles about every 7 years, so keeping up with new knowledge is an important aspect of good caregiving by HMOs.

When Kaiser Permanente developed a clinical-knowledge corporate portal for its 50,000 doctors, nurses, and other caregivers, search was a part of the plan. The Permanente Knowledge Connection, available from anywhere in the Kaiser wide area network, gives medical staff access to diagnostic information, best practices, publications, educational material, and other clinical resources. The portal's resources are distributed across the entire United States. Putting the right information quickly and easily into caregivers' hands is essential to the clinical portal's success.

Kaiser turned to the Google Search Appliance, which enabled the HMO to index 150,000 documents across the Kaiser network. Clinicians now search the site in situations that range from leisurely research to urgent care, from the exam room to the emergency room. Doctors and nurses use the search engine to help them reach diagnoses and specify treatments, check the side-effects of new medications, and consult clinical research studies and other medical publications. Google's spell checking capability is especially useful in the medical profession: Doctors' handwriting can be problematic, and pharmaceutical product names are difficult.

*Sources:* Compiled from Google.com (2005) and Kantzer (2003).

*For Further Exploration:* Why did Kaiser Permanente need Google's Serach Appliance? What benefits did Kaiser gain from implementing Google's Search Appliance?

2004). Consequently, companies incur the costs of time wasted searching for information that could not be found and then re-creating it—and costs arising from the inability to use existing information at the time it was needed.

FACTORS
DETERMINING
THE USES OF
INFORMATION
TECHNOLOGIES FOR
COMMUNICATION

*Communication* is an interpersonal process of sending and receiving symbols with messages attached to them. Through communication, people exchange and share information as well as understand and influence each other. Most managers spend as much as 90 percent of their time communicating. Managers serve as "nerve centers" in the information-processing networks called organizations, where they collect, distribute, and process information continuously. Since poor communication can mean poor management, managers must communicate effectively among themselves and with others, both inside and outside of organizations. Information technologies have come to play a major role in providing communication support for organizations.

On the Web we distinguish three communication modes:

1. **People-to-people.** This was the earliest mode of network communication, when people used e-mail and newsgroups. They also discovered information on bulletin boards and communicated there.
2. **People-to-machine.** This was the next step, when people conducted discovery on the Web, searching and finding information.
3. **People and machine-to-machine.** This mode occurs when applications need to "talk" to applications, either in complete automation or in automation but including people.

Several factors determine the IT technologies that could be used to provide communication support to a specific organization or group of users. The major ones are the following:

- **Participants.** The number of people sending and receiving information can range from two to many thousands.
- **Nature of sources and destinations.** Sources and destinations of information can include people, databases, sensors, and so on.
- **Media.** Communication can involve one or several IT-supported media, such as text, voice, graphics, video, pictures, and animation. Using different media for communicating can increase the effectiveness of a message, expedite learning, and enhance problem solving. Working with multiple media may, however, reduce the efficiency and effectiveness of the system (its speed, capacity, quality) and may significantly increase its cost.
- **Place (location).** The sender(s) and receiver(s) can be in the same room (face-to-face) or at different locations.
- **Time.** Messages can be sent at a certain time and received almost simultaneously. Such *synchronous (real-time) communication* is provided by telephones, instant messaging online, teleconferencing, and face-to-face meetings. *Asynchronous communication,* on the other hand, refers to communication in which the receiver gets an answer sometime after a request was sent. E-mail and electronic bulletin boards are examples.

**A Time/Place Framework.** The last two factors in the preceding list—place and time—were used by DeSanctis and Gallupe (1987) to create a framework for classifying IT communication and collaboration support technologies. According to this framework, IT communication can be divided into four cells, as shown in

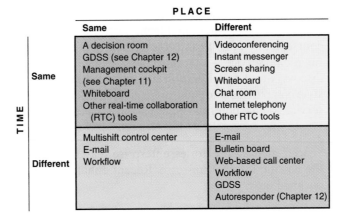

PLACE

|  | | Same | Different |
|---|---|---|---|
| **TIME** | **Same** | A decision room<br>GDSS (see Chapter 12)<br>Management cockpit<br>(see Chapter 11)<br>Whiteboard<br>Other real-time collaboration<br>(RTC) tools | Videoconferencing<br>Instant messenger<br>Screen sharing<br>Whiteboard<br>Chat room<br>Internet telephony<br>Other RTC tools |
|  | **Different** | Multishift control center<br>E-mail<br>Workflow | E-mail<br>Bulletin board<br>Web-based call center<br>Workflow<br>GDSS<br>Autoresponder (Chapter 12) |

**Figure 4.2** A framework for IT communication support.

Figure 4.2, with representative technologies in each cell. The time/place cells are as follows:

1. **Same-time/same-place.** In this setting, participants meet face-to-face in one place and at the same time. An example is communication in a meeting room, which can be electronically supported by group support system software (see *groupsystems.com*).

2. **Same-time/different-place.** This setting refers to a meeting whose participants are in different places but communicate at the same time. A telephone conference call, desktop videoconferencing, chat rooms, and instant messaging are examples of such situations.

3. **Different-time/same-place.** This setting can materialize when people work in shifts. The first shift leaves electronic or voice messages for the second shift.

4. **Different-time/different-place.** In this setting, participants are in different places, and sending and/or receiving messages at different times (e.g., e-mail). This setting is known as *virtual meetings*.

In the next section, we discuss capabilities and features of discovery and collaboration, which are also presented throughout the book. These capabilities are feasible because collaboration and productivity improvements may not require major IT spending. Companies have made huge investments in data warehouses, BI (business intelligence), ERP (enterprise resource planning) systems, Internet connectivity, and handheld devices for over a decade and those technologies now serve as platforms for newer technologies. Employees get more productive when they can quickly and easily tap into back-office systems using powerful wireless handhelds.

## 4.2 Discovery, Search, and Customized Delivery

Trying to describe information on the Internet is like trying to describe the universe—*it's everything*. The sheer endlessness of the information available through the Internet, which seems like its major strength, is also its greatest weakness. As you have read and experienced, often it is too hard to find the right data or answers. The amounts of information at your disposal are too vast.

Since you are familiar with the Internet and Web searches, this section will focus on business solutions being made possible by new technologies and innovative ideas. Topics include advanced search tools and Internet technologies that deliver customized information to users, often as soon as it becomes available, such as robust search engines, intelligent software agents, podcasting, XML, and RSS. Of course, many tools fit into more than one category. For example, wikis are cross-functional services—that continue to expand in scope. A **wiki** is a software program, discovery tool, collaboration site, and a leading *social network*. In June 2006, a wiki-style comparison-shopping engine, ShopWiki (*shopwiki.com)*, added a video review service to give potential buyers a virtual hands-on experience.

**SEARCH ENGINES, DIRECTORIES, AND ENTERPRISE SEARCH**

Search engines, directories, enterprise search engines, and wikis help bring order to the chaotic Internet universe. Recent enhancements to improve search results are outlined next.

**Search Engines, Directories, and Intelligent Agents.** **Search engines** are Web sites designed to help people find information stored on other sites. They index billions of pages, and respond to tens of millions of queries per day. There are differences in the ways various search engines work, but they all perform three basic tasks:

1. They search the Internet based on key words.
2. They keep an index (database) of the words they find, and where they find them.
3. They allow users to search for words or combinations of words found in that index.

There are three types of search engines: (1) those powered by **intelligent agents** (also called software agents, robots, or bots); (2) those powered by human submissions; and (3) hybrids of the two. Intelligent agent technology provides a mechanism for information systems to act on behalf of their users. Specifically, intelligent agents are computer programs that carry out a set of routine computer tasks. Every Internet task seems to have an agent (e.g., shopping bots, tracking bots, pop-up killer bots, newsgroup search bots, personal assistant bots, etc.). They are also used by search engine companies such as Yahoo!, Google, Excite, and AltaVista.

Spider-based search engines, also called **spiders** or **crawlers,** use automated software agents that scour the Web every few minutes searching for information on Web pages. Bots read the information on the actual site, read the sites' **meta-tags** (information that influences the description of a Web page in crawlers), and follow the sites' hyperlinks. The crawler returns the information to a central database where the data is indexed. Crawlers periodically return to Web sites to check for any changes. The index is used to find pages that match a set of user-specified keywords.

Human-powered search engines rely on humans to submit information that is subsequently indexed and catalogued. Only information that is submitted is put into the index. As the name implies, a directory organizes topics into categories. Directories need some human support. Popular directories are *Yahoo.com* and *google.com/dirhp.*

Ask, Google, del.icio.us, flikr, and other search engines compete fiercely for Web visitors, although Google is by far the most popular search engine. *IT at Work 4.3* describes competitive changes among the browsers and search engines to attract business customers by better serving their information needs.

**Enterprise Search Technology.** **Enterprise search** offers the potential of cutting much of the complexity accumulated in applications and intranet sites throughout an organization. An example of enterprise search architecture is shown in Figure 4.3. These engines can crawl through various types of content—external Web sites, network shares and local file servers, Microsoft Exchange and Lotus Notes folders, and databases. Tools are available to help users create queries and do custom

# *IT* at Work 4.3

## *Browsers Compete for Business*

ACC    MKT    IS

Major Web browsers are upgrading to become the focal point for handling business transactions and running programs over the Internet rather than simply displaying Web sites. E-mail, maps, word processing, and other traditionally standalone applications are migrating online. Major Internet companies such as Google, Yahoo!, and Microsoft are devoting tremendous resources to developing these Web applications.

The upgrades are part of the browser war that began in the mid-1990s and led to Microsoft's triumph over Netscape. The next battle occurred in 2004 when Mozilla's Firefox offered user-attracting features. In late-June 2006, Opera Software ASA released its Opera 9 browser, while Microsoft's Internet Explorer (IE) and Firefox are undergoing major upgrades. Microsoft's IE6 browser had slowly lost market

share to Firefox because people drastically changed the way they used the Web and there was a lot more malicious intent on the Web. IE7 added features to defend against phishing scams and make browsing more secure.

Opera 9 offers *widgets*, which are Web-based applications that run off its browser, but appear detached as standalone tools. Opera 9 also formally supports the file-sharing mechanism, BitTorrent, and lets users customize preferences, such as whether to allow JavaScript, on a site-by-site basis.

*For Further Exploration:* How have people changed the way they use the Web since 2001? What changes are occurring at this time?

---

searches. Content is indexed for faster results. Enterprise search takes advantage of available metadata and provides access control, simple and advanced search, and browser-based administration. They also can support HTML, PDF, and the usual office file formats, and European, Arabic, and Asian languages.

**Google.**  Google has made a bigger move on the corporate market with the release of two hardware search appliances that index content on a corporate network. *Google Search Appliance* is aimed at big business. It has a range of tools for searching corporate

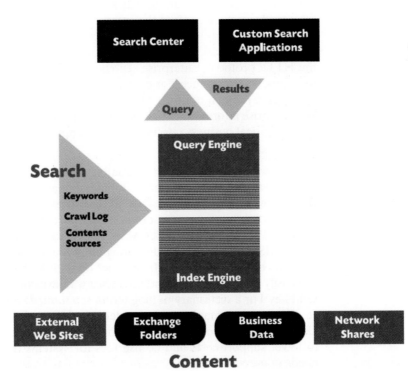

**Figure 4.3** Enterprise search architecture.

# A Closer Look 4.2

ACC    FIN    MKT    IS

## Web Search Leader Google Simplifies Data Sharing

Google planned to reinvent the spreadsheet as a Web-based application that makes it simple for users to input and share data. *Google Spreadsheet* is a free Web-based application that can be shared with up to 10 users simultaneously, overcoming a key limitation of Microsoft's Excel. Google chose spreadsheets because that is what most people use to organize information—instead of databases. Google Spreadsheet, which can import or export data from Excel's .xls format or the open *Comma Separated Value* (.csv) format, is aimed at small work teams in social life or small business, but not big enterprises.

The program is designed to help people organize their own information and make it more easily accessible to others via the Web. Data in the spreadsheets are saved automatically with each user action over the Web onto Google computer

servers. Users can sort data and take advantage of 200 functions and common spreadsheet formulas for doing basic calculations. Several user productivity applications are *Google Spreadsheet, Writely* (a word processing application), and *Google Calendar. Google Base* is an online database service that allows Google users to post various types of information online. Google Base is viewed by analysts as a steppingstone into the classified advertising or e-commerce markets in that it helps users feature relevant information on Google's main search index, its *Froogle* shopping site (*froogle.google.com*), and Google Local search (*local.google.com*).

*Sources:* Compiled from *google.com* (accessed September 2006), and Carr (2006).

---

databases and enterprise resource planning systems. *Google Mini* is a Web search appliance aimed at small businesses that want to index content. Google says the index the appliances create is encrypted and secure. The companies Google is working with have existing security standards, which are maintained in Google Search Appliance. Google's other business applications are described in *A Closer Look 4.2*.

Google partnered with BearingPoint, an IT consulting firm, to supply enterprise search. BearingPoint has experience in extending Google to provide search services to specific industries. A crucial enterprise search issue is programming the search engines to crawl through all the various data sources at a company and index their contents.

Oracle also entered into the enterprise search arena by offering a search engine that can crawl through and index information from e-mail, corporate documents, Web servers, portals, mainframe applications, and sources that can be reached via the HTTP protocol. Enterprise searches can be integrated with other applications to improve performance. For example, *Cognos Go! Search Service* is a BI (business intelligence) search utility. It offers a familiar search interface for accessing strategic enterprise information such as reports, metrics, analyses, and business events that answer critical business questions with a simple keyword search.

**BLOGS AND WEBLOGGING (BLOGGING)**

**Blogs** started out as Internet journaling and personal publishing tools, but enterprises now use these systems to replace e-mail and support collaborative work. Blogs are simple to build due to user-friendly programs from blogger.com, blogspot.com, pitas.com, and others. Some portals offer blog services. For example, in December 2004, Microsoft's MSN Internet division debuted a preliminary version of MSN Spaces, designed to bring blogs to the masses. Bloggers who create and maintain blogs are handed a fresh space on their Web site to write in each day. They can easily edit, add entries, and broadcast whatever they want by simply clicking the send key. For a dictionary of blog terms, see *samizdata.net*.

Blog servers require far fewer dedicated resources than an enterprise intranet. Using blog platforms can free up IT hardware and support resources for other uses to lower support costs and license fees for systems that may no longer serve the needs of users.

Blogs have become one of the fastest growing enterprise solutions as businesses recognize that the ability to easily find information contained within enterprise blogs is critical to improving worker productivity. The combination of enterprise blogging technology with searching capabilities helps organizations improve the quality and efficiency of collaboration internally and externally. Blogging provides the ability to supplement corporate public relations, press releases, and brochures with more personal, "from the heart" talk and offer convenient links to related sources.

## WIKIS

Wikis are a user-driven response to the shortcomings of search engines. Technically, a wiki is server software that allows users to freely create and edit Web page content. This is possible because wikis support hyperlinks and have simple text syntax for creating new pages and crosslinks between internal pages.

The wiki is unusual among group communication mechanisms in that it allows the organization of contributions to be edited in addition to the content itself. The immensely content-rich, multilingual **Wikipedia** (*wikipedia.org*) collects knowledge by consensus. Wiki Web pages are created through the collaboration efforts of numerous contributors. The relevance of these efforts—the wiki—is often better than that of algorithmically ranked lists of search results. These collaborations fill the gaps left by conventional search tools.

A single page in a wiki is referred to as a "wiki page," while the entire body of pages, which are usually highly interconnected via hyperlinks, is "the wiki"—in effect, a very simple, easy-to-use database.

**Wikilog.** Wiki comes in many shapes and formats, one of which is **wikilog.** A wikilog (or wikiblog) is an extension of a blog. A blog usually is created by an individual (or maybe a small group) and may have a discussion board; a wikilog is essentially a blog that allows everyone to participate as a peer (a combination of wikis and blogs, also known as *bliki*). Anyone may add, delete, or change content. It is like a looseleaf notebook with a pencil and eraser left in a public place. Anyone can read it, scrawl notes, tear out a page, and so on. Unlike protected Web pages, articles added to a wiki are at the editorial mercy of the wiki's other participants. For further details see *usemod.com/cgi-bin/mb.pl?WikiLog.*

**Commercial Aspects of Wikis and Their Derivatives.** Being a relatively new technology, it is difficult to assess the commercial potential of wikis. However, research firm Gartner Group predicts that wikis will become mainstream collaboration tools in at least 50 percent of companies by 2009 (reported by *WikiThat.com* 2005). In addition to collaboration, wikis can replace e-mail, since using wikis is an open source, spam-free communication tool. For a list of vendors of enterprise wikis, see Online File W4.4.

Angel.com, a subsidiary of MicroStrategy Inc., develops integrated voice response (IVR) and call center automation software. The company uses wikis as a central communications tool for its sales teams. They use a wiki to log daily lead counts, post partnership information, and read documents posted by product management and marketing. The wiki is used to publish position papers, marketing material, messaging, and scripts for customer inquiries. It is shared with customers and helps the team cope with a 14-hour time difference with an Australian client.

## PODCASTING

**Podcasting** is a way to distribute or receive audio and, more recently, video files called **pods** or **podcasts** over the Internet. The term *pod* came about from Apple's iPod digital player, although an iPod is not needed to hear or view a podcast. Pods can be downloaded or streamed from a Web site. Authors called **podcasters** create a pod by making a file such as an MP3 audio file available on the Internet. This can be done by posting the file on a Web server or **BitTorrent tracker,** which is a server used in the communication between peers using the BitTorrent protocol. BitTorrents will be discussed later. For more on podcasting see Ahrens (2006). For a directory of podcasts, see *ipodder.org,* and *podcast.net* or *podcastdirectory.com.*

Many content providers offer podcast feeds at no cost. These feeds deliver audio broadcasts to a computer, which can be listened to using iTunes; or they can be loaded onto an MP3 player or iPod. To automate notice and delivery of new content, iTunes uses RSS to auto-download new podcasts as they become available.

**RSS**

**RSS** refers to various standards of Web feed formats, usually Really Simple Syndication, but also Rich Site Summary or RDF Site Summary. RSSs automate the delivery of Internet content. They are an easy way to receive newly released information customized to a person's interests and needs. Web feeds provided through RSS offer headlines, summaries, and links from sites in an XML file that can be viewed using software called a *reader* (newsreader) or *aggregator* that brings the information directly to a computer or iPod.

RSS readers are software that monitors blogs or sites for new content. With RSS and a newsreader, whenever there is new content, it is delivered and shows up automatically on the newsreader. RSS feeds dramatically cut down on the time it takes to search for information online and you can then go back for greater detail after finding out first what is available. See Figure 4.4 for an example of how an RSS can be searched and RSS feeds located.

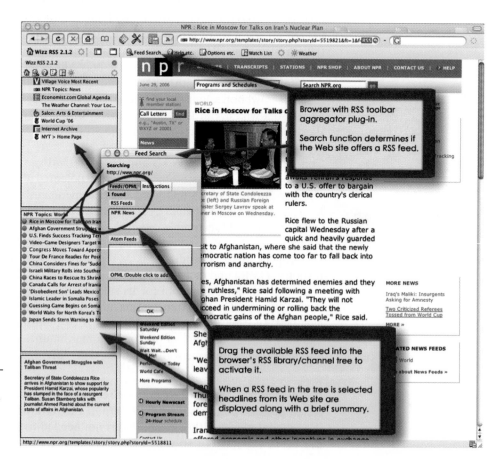

**Figure 4.4** National Public Radio's (NPR) Web site with RSS toolbar aggregator and search function. (Courtesy of NPR. Used with permission.)

Mainstream media such as NPR are using RSS. News organizations are setting up their own RSS feeds as are operators of traditional informational Web sites and government agencies. Companies are using RSS feeds to get their messages out to anyone who wants them—a key goal of marketing. RSS technology could be a valuable marketing tool and is becoming a greater part of firms' overall marketing mix. RSS technology is simple, and RSS content is easily produced by the conversion of existing content. Content can be sent using a subscription plan, replacing the current e-mail delivery process.

All of these tools and technologies help deal with Internet information overload. They can minimize time and effort wasted looking for information that exists, but cannot be found or accessed. Clearly, the future is in highly customized information that gets pulled through podcasts, videos on demand, RSS feeds, mobile devices, blogs, interactive wizards, and other yet-unknown vehicles for experiencing services in ways and at times of users' choosing.

**XML AND XBRL**

Another valuable format for locating and sharing information is **eXtensible Markup Language (XML).** (XML is discussed more fully in Appendix 9B.) XML is a meta-language for describing markup languages for documents containing structured information. XML-based systems facilitate data sharing across different systems and particularly systems connected via the Internet. Actually, RSS is a form of XML. RSS files must conform to the XML 1.0 specification (see *w3.org/TR/REC-xml*), as published on the World Wide Web Consortium (W3C) Web site.

The **eXtensible Business Reporting Language (XBRL)** is a version of XML for capturing financial information throughout a business's information processes. XBRL makes it possible to format reports that need to be distributed to shareholders, SOX regulators, banks, and other parties. The goal of XBRL is to make the analysis and exchange of corporate information more reliable (trustworthy) and easier to facilitate.

In the next section, we examine communication technologies focusing on the latest developments in Web-based, cellular, and wireless. Appendix 4A also explains communication protocols and development in more technical detail.

# 4.3 Communication

According to *NetworkWorld* (*networkworld.com*), 90 percent of employees work away from their company's headquarters and 40 percent work at a remote location, away from their supervisors. In this section, the latest exciting developments in telecommunications (telecom), mobile computing hardware, software, and networks are described.

The primary business benefit of mobile communications is keeping workers connected. In a *Baseline* survey of 143 IT executives, 81 percent of respondents cited better communication and collaboration among employees as the key advantage of providing mobile hardware and software, followed by 69 percent who said increased responsiveness to customers was the core benefit. These and other factors are driving enterprises to budget more for mobile computing projects, which encompass everything from wireless e-mail devices to special-purpose software for salespeople using laptops. The average business expected to increase mobile computing spending from 1 to 4 percent in 2006, according to *Baseline*'s survey, which was conducted in March 2006. And for larger companies with over 1,000 employees, the median expected increase was 5 to 14 percent over the $250,000 to $500,000 that was spent in 2005 (Gler, 2006).

By 2009, 90 percent of mobile devices will have features for sending and receiving e-mail, according to Gartner Inc. Increasingly mobile work forces, falling prices, and more advanced wireless networks are driving adoption of mobile e-mail. The cost of smart phones is expected to drop from the $500 range to less than $120 by 2009 (Bunkley, 2006).

Mobile phones are turning into ubiquitous media devices. Technological advances on a wide range of fronts such as faster wireless networks, longer battery life, and more powerful processors and memory chips are transforming phones into powerful computing devices, capable of processing, storing, and displaying all types of media.

The convergence of voice and data networking is ongoing. As high-bandwidth networks become increasingly common, converged networking solutions are available for companies of any size. These converged networks are referred to as *IP networks* or *IP telephony* because all content (including voice) is digitized into packets and then transmitted using the Internet Protocol (IP) over the Internet or other type of network. For details about basic elements of telecom networks, see Appendix 4A. Descriptions of four wireless networks and their protocols—*CDMA, GSM, EDGE,* and Wi-Fi—are next.

## CDMA NETWORKS

**CDMA (Code Division Multiple Access)** is a spread-spectrum (wide-band) technology created by the U.S. company Qualcomm. Spread-spectrum radio communication has been used by the military because it resists jamming and is hard to intercept. For details on spread spectrum, see *sss-mag.com/ss.html.*

CDMA allows many users to occupy the same time and frequency allocations in a given band. The CDMA air interface is used in both 2G (second-generation) and 3G (third-generation) networks. For details on the generations, see Online File W4.5. CDMA is the foundation for 3G services. Visit the TIA Web site at *tiaonline.org* for more information on CDMA standards. The competing network to CDMA is GSM.

## GSM AND 3GSM NETWORKS

**3GSM (Third-generation Global System for Mobile Communications Services)** enables the delivery of mobile multimedia services such as music, TV and video, and Internet access. GSM is an internationally accepted standard for digital cellular communication originating in Europe. It is the most popular standard for mobile phones in the world. GSM signaling and speech channels are digital call quality. For a tutorial on GSM concepts, specifications, networks, and services, see *iec.org/online/tutorials/gsm.* Popular GSM features include SMS and SIM cards, described next.

**SMS.** **Short Message Service (SMS)** is a low-bandwidth messaging service for short text (up to 160 bytes) messages. Messages are transported using store-and-forward in one of two modes. In **point-to-point SMS** mode, a message is sent to another subscriber. In **cell-broadcast SMS** mode, messages such as traffic updates or news updates are sent to multiple recipients. SMS text messages are used throughout companies, for example, by those in sales who want prices for procurement managers closing purchases.

**SIM Card.** Messages can also be stored in a SIM (Subscriber Identity Module) card for later retrieval. The SIM is a smart card (i.e., has a portable memory chip) used with carriers that operate on the GSM network. It acts like a tiny hard drive that activates the phone into which it is inserted. The SIM holds personal identifying information, cell phone number, phone book, text messages, and other data. A SIM card makes it easy to switch to a new phone since it can be removed and inserted into a different phone. For international travel, a local SIM card can be bought and inserted into the phone, which saves international roaming charges from the home carrier.

**EDGE NETWORKS**

**EDGE (Enhanced Data rates for GSM Evolution)** technology significantly increased the capacity of GSM networks to enable data speeds of up to 384 kilobits per second (Kbps). See *gsmworld.com/index.shtml*. EDGE allows the delivery of advanced mobile services such as the downloading of video and music clips, full multimedia messaging, high-speed color Internet access, and e-mail on the move.

**TDMA (Time-Division Multiple Access)** is a technology for delivering digital wireless service using time-division multiplexing. TDMA is used by the GSM digital cellular system.

**WI-FI NETWORKS**

Wi-Fi (wireless fidelity) is used to connect laptops, PCs, and handhelds to the Internet. Wi-Fi hotspots are found in restaurants, coffee shops, and hotels. The technology also is used in hospital, university, and corporate settings to connect cabled networks in different buildings.

Wi-Fi had not been used extensively with mobile phones. Cellular service providers initially saw Wi-Fi as a threat to sales of cellular data services such as weather reports and stock quotes. But this perception changed when service providers recognized the marketability of phones capable of handling both cellular and Wi-Fi signals. Wi-Fi research is leading to longer ranges and interoperability for the popular protocol as described in *IT at Work 4.4*. Wi-Fi networks are cheap and easy to set up, but their inherently short range had been a severe limitation.

# *IT* at Work 4.4

## *Wi-Fi Mesh Networks, Google Talk, and Interoperability*

Researchers in India have developed a protocol that will enable wide area coverage of Wi-Fi networks—called Wi-Fi **mesh networks.** In conventional Wi-Fi networks that are common in Internet cafés and airports, radio signals are exchanged between portable devices and the base station that has a wired connection to the Internet. Their range is only 100 meters or less. With a Wi-Fi mesh network, several nodes can exchange radio signals with each other as well as with the devices. The Wi-Fi mesh range is up to 40 kilometers and at speeds up to 20 percent faster. This arrangement provides wider geographical Wi-Fi coverage at lower cost than a series of conventional Wi-Fi networks because not all of the nodes have to be wired to the Internet.

Another development is Google's Google Talk service, which allows for voice connections and IM. In May 2006, Google and Nokia launched a handheld Internet browsing device that contained Google Talk, which relies on Wi-Fi instead of cell phone networks. As many as 300 municipalities, including San Francisco, Philadelphia, and Suffolk County on Long Island, New York, and the entire state of Connecticut

plan to offer the Wi-Fi service free of charge. Initially, because of the different protocols, the device cannot call regular phones. However, cell phone equipment manufacturers, including Avaya, Cisco Systems, and Motorola, are testing devices that have both Wi-Fi and cell phone network capabilities. For example, Motorola partnered with eBay's VoIP provider Skype. Customers with Wi-Fi-enabled mobile phones will have the option of using Skype's service in place of a landline service as long as they are within range of a Wi-Fi signal. Once out of Wi-Fi range, the phone switches to cellular technology. Sales of mobile phones with both cellular and Wi-Fi capability will be booming by 2010, according to a study by market research company In-Stat.

*Sources:* Compiled from Fleetwood (2006) and *Technology Review* (2005).

*For Further Exploration:* What cell phone providers offer interoperability between cell phone and Wi-Fi networks? What new developments are occurring in the cellular and Wi-Fi markets?

**MOBILE AND WIRELESS INFRASTRUCTURE**

Mobile multimedia technologies make it possible for businesses to reinvent the traditional workplace from an office-based activity to a virtual one. Employees can collaborate closely in real time with other employees, customers, or partners regardless of anyone's location.

Mobile or wireless infrastructure consists of the integration of technology, software, support, security measures, and devices for the management and delivery of wireless communications. Figure 4.5 illustrates the components of a WiMax communication network. WiMax is essentially an 802.16-based broadband wireless metropolitan-area network (MAN) access standard that can deliver voice and data services at distances of up to 30 miles, without the expense of cable or the distance limitations of DSL. WiMax does not require a clear line of sight to function. Mobile WiMax enables multi-Mb/s network access for mobile users because it facilitates real-time applications such as Voice Over IP (VoIP). Also see Appendix 4A.

**Cell (Mobile) Phones and Smart Phones.** Cell phones (cells) are mobile multimedia business tools. Cells continue to morph into all-purpose messaging devices. Internet-enabled phones, or **smart phones,** are optimized for use on high-speed EDGE networks. Some cells can be customized with applications that make mobile users more productive. Business and personal productivity features include:

- Support for business-focused applications, including word processing, expense reporting, document management, and travel-related software packages.

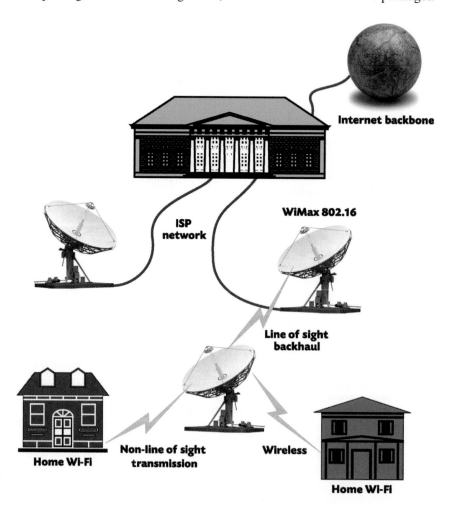

**Figure 4.5** Components of a WiMax communication network.

- PDA functionality that can be synchronized over the air or directly to a PC using cable, infrared, or **Bluetooth** connectivity. Bluetooth is how mobile phones, mobile and fixed computers, and PDAs can be easily interconnected using a short-range RF wireless connection.
- E-mail and instant messaging clients for text communication, and **presence functionality** that allows users to communicate their current availability to associates.
- Support for VPN clients for access behind corporate firewalls, improving access to corporate online information sources such as intranet sites.

For example, the Samsung SCH-i730 offers five-way wireless support: IrDA (Infrared Data Association), Bluetooth, Wi-Fi, CDMA, and **EV-DO (Evolution Data Optimized).** EV-DO is fast wireless broadband access (3G) that does not need a Wi-Fi hotspot. See *evdoinfo.co*m. The Nokia N90 offers a digital camera with digital zoom; MPEG-4 video-capture capabilities; EDGE capable; external memory slot; MP3 player; Bluetooth; USB connectivity; and e-mail. See *reviews.cnet.com* for current detailed features of cell phones. LG and Samsung offer models with keyboards for faster and easier text messaging.

**Personal Digital Assistants (PDAs).** Like cells, Internet-enabled PDAs are widely available. PDAs for *corporate mobile users* include e-mail synchronization, data exchange, and file backups with corporate servers. Examples of PDAs for corporate users are BlackBerry from RIM, iPAQ from HP, CLIE from Sony, and MobilePro from NEC. Despite possible signal interference (e.g., extremely overcast weather conditions), PDAs also can be used as a redundant network for business continuity as described in *A Closer Look 4.3*.

A key BlackBerry feature is e-mail that lets users compose, send, and receive e-mail messages from their regular e-mail accounts. E-mail is automatically pushed to the BlackBerry device. Other features are a phone, organizer, SMS, IM, corporate

## A Closer Look 4.3

### PDA as a Business Continuity Tool

ACC    HRM    FIN    IS    MKT    POM    SVC

Two-thirds of U.K. companies are planning to use a work-from-home method to maintain business continuity in the event of workplace disruption. Information from an investigation commissioned by Citrix, an on-demand access provider (*citrix.com*), showed that 90 percent of those surveyed had some form of contingency to keep employees working in the event of a terrorist strike or a bird-flu pandemic. If such an event happened, companies plan to use server-based computing to keep staff working, and three-quarters of those questioned would use Web mail.

The popularity of tools such as PDAs and BlackBerries and other mobile working tools has also made the possibility of working from home more realistic as 60 percent cited them as being good ways to work away from the office.

Business continuity is also at risk in most small offices and home offices (SOHOs). Unlike corporate networks, redundant access lines from multiple providers are not standard practice at SOHOs. If DSL or cable service access is interrupted, so is the ability to do work or business. While redundant broadband lines can provide a high level of reliability, a cheaper alternative may be a wireless-enabled PDA service. Unlimited e-mail and Web access cost about $45 a month. By adding a portable keyboard, productivity is maintained.

Nearly 80 percent of organizations support PDAs, such as BlackBerries or Treos, according to Nemertes' research. Although that may sound high, the penetration within the average organization is relatively low at less than 3 percent. Provided that the cellular network and broadband access do not go dark at the same time (a possibility), PDAs can provide backup and business continuity for SOHOs.

*Sources:* Compiled from *citrix.com*, *Financial Adviser* (2006), and Gareiss (2006).

data access, and paging Internet access to HTML and **WAP (Wireless Application Protocol)** Web pages. WAP is an Internet protocol developed for transferring information on the Internet to and from wireless clients. Wireless clients can run on cellular phones, palm computing devices, and other small, portable terminals. A key WAP issue is the display limitations, since wth a WAP device the screen real estate is greatly reduced. For protocol details, visit the WAP Forum at *wapforum.org.*

For details about BlackBerry Business Solutions or interactive product demos, see *blackberry.com/solutions/index.shtml* or *blackberry.com/products/handhelds/demos/index.shtml.* These keyboard devices are integrated so there is no need to dial into an ISP for access. A national law firm deployed BlackBerry handhelds to its 900 lawyers, who receive their e-mail in real time and can enter billing information remotely. Furthermore, they are alerted whenever they have a voice mail or fax waiting. A third of the company's lawyers have returned their laptops, saving the company $260,000 each year.

**Tablet PCs.** **Tablet PCs,** also called **pen-based computing,** are fast becoming a popular device for professionals. They have a stylus to write handwritten notes on the screen, usually about 12 inches. Tablet PCs typically work with Wi-Fi, Bluetooth, and EDGE. Options include a biometric fingerprint swipe sensor for extra security. Fujitsu's LifeBook B6210 notebook offers the most security. The Portege M400 Tablet PC, positioned as the industry's first tablet PC with Intel Centrino Duo Mobile Technology, can run robust business applications.

**Instant Messaging and ICQ.** Instant messaging (IM) has become a mission-critical collaboration tool for an estimated 135 million workers in businesses of all sizes. Analysts estimate that this number will grow to more than 477 million by 2009 (Delaney, 2005). As with other communication tools and technologies, the mobility boom has increased the rate of IM usage. Having these mobile extensions means the network is no longer tied to the desktop, but to the person, enabling huge productivity enhancements. ICQ (pronounced "I seek you") is an IM computer program that America Online had bought from Mirabilis in 1998.

**Converged Devices.** Many other wireless support devices are on the market. For example, the Seiko SmartPad for Pocket PC expedites text entry. With the pen included, you write or draw on a regular pad of paper. As you write, an infrared transceiver sends your notes and drawings directly to your Pocket PC using its infrared port. It also allows you to hand-write from a notepad instantly to a cell phone or PDA screen, overcoming the small screen size of these devices. Most cell phones have built-in cameras that can take and e-mail pictures immediately from any location. Finally there is a wireless mouse, which works up to 15 feet, so it can be used for presentations.

There is a significant trend toward the *convergence* of PDAs and cell phones. PDA manufacturers are providing PDAs with cellular or wireless capabilities. And cellular phone manufacturers and systems providers are offering phones with PDA capabilities. TV broadcasts to mobile devices became a reality at the 2006 World Cup as described in *IT at Work 4.5.*

In addition to the hardware described previously, mobile computing and mobile commerce (m-commerce) also require the following infrastructure hardware, most of which the user does not see or know about, but which is essential for wireless connectivity:

- A suitably configured wireline or wireless *WAN modem, wireless LAN adapter,* or *wireless MAN* (metro-area network) adapter.

# IT at Work 4.5

## Mobile TV Broadcast to Mobile Devices Became a Reality at 2006 World Cup

The U.K. was the world's test-bed for *TV broadcast to mobile devices*—or simply *mobile TV*. It became the testing-ground for engineering trials of digital television broadcast to mobile devices. However, it was World Cup football in Germany (*fifaworldcup.yahoo.com*) in 2006 that brought the technology out of the laboratory and into commercial use. Broadcast technology, backed by Nokia, is essentially a pared-down version of the existing TV signal called DVB-H.

Broadcasting television programs to mobile devices is already a reality in South Korea, where 600,000 receivers had been sold between December 2005 and June 2006. The technology had gone live in Germany because of the World Cup.

Industry analysts agree that mobile TV is a growth technology. David McQueen, an analyst with the consultancy Informa Telecoms and Media, predicted that: "By the 2008 Olympics (in China) we will all be prepared to watch TV on our phones and by the 2010 World Cup, the infrastructure will be mature and one-in-13 mobile phone users worldwide will own a mobile TV handset" (Cane, 2006). China will be well prepared for digital video broadcasting by the time it hosts the Olympics.

The research arm of the Canadian bank CIBC has little doubt that mobile TV is about to come into its own: "We believe the mobile food chain has reached critical mass," it says, concluding that all the necessary pieces are now in place. "We expect commercial activity to move from Korea where it started in 2005 to the U.S. in 2006 and Europe and other regions in 2007 and thereafter."

Questions of broadcasting standards and spectrum allocation will need to be resolved, however. There are at least four standards in play that are accepted in some markets. Just as with mobile phones, there seems little chance of a world standard, despite the efforts of the International Telecommunication Union.

*Sources:* Compiled from Cane (2006) and Wray (2006).

*For Further Exploration:* What are possible marketing uses of broadcast video to handheld devices? How might the technology be used to improve supply chain management processes?

---

- A *Web server* with wireless support, a WAP gateway, a communications server, and/or a mobile communications server switch (MCSS). Such a Web server provides communications functionality that enables the handheld device to communicate with the Internet or intranet infrastructure (see *mobileinfo.com*).
- An *application* or *database server* with application logic and a business application database.
- A large enterprise application server.
- A GPS locator to determine the location of the mobile device.

**VOICE OVER INTERNET PROTOCOL (VoIP)**

**Internet telephony,** or **VoIP (Voice Over Internet Protocol),** is rapidly replacing conventional telephony. In 2005, U.S. companies bought more new IP phone connections than conventional phone lines for the first time. Demand for VoIP connections is high because businesses can create their own customized voice communication to give them a competitive edge. The competitive advantage of VoIP stems from its use as a unifying platform for business applications that require flexible or intelligent voice communications. As several innovative firms have proven, flexibility allows companies to set up and conduct business in ways that could not have been done before because they were technically or economically infeasible.

With VoIP, voice and data transmissions go over telephone wires, but the information is sent as packets. In general, telephony service via VoIP costs less than equivalent service from traditional telecommunications companies. Figure 4.6 illustrates the common components of a VoIP network.

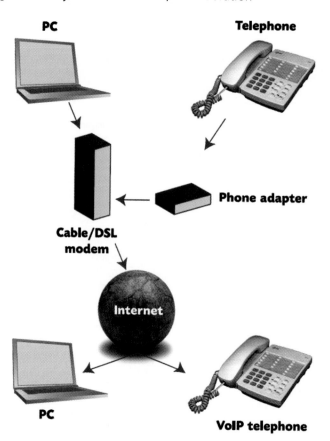

**Figure 4.6** Components of a VoIP network.

With non-IP phones, calls originate from a hardware device (e.g., phone on your desk), travel as analog signals along a dedicated circuit-switched telephone network, and then arrive at the destination hardware devices at specific locations (phones on the recipients' desks). In contrast, with VoIP calls, calls originate from a VoIP phone or PC, are digitized, and then sent via a packet-switched network such as a WAN or the Internet. Calls are tied neither to physical locations nor to specific devices. Since VoIP uses common IP standards, it can talk to any device that uses IP.

As shown in Figure 4.6, making VoIP calls is simple. Callers can use an ordinary telephone connected to a VoIP adapter (converter) box, which plugs into an Internet connection. Or callers can use an IP phone that looks like a traditional telephone, but connects directly to the Internet instead of a phone jack. A third option is to use softphone software on a PC or PDA with a headset. With VoIP service, a businessperson could take a VoIP adapter to Europe or Asia, plug it into a broadband connection at a hotel, and seamlessly receive calls at the home office phone number. With a VoIP softphone, the adapter is not needed.

Considerable cost savings are possible by using a single network to carry voice and data, especially when companies have underutilized network capacity. VoIP is used by companies to eliminate call charges between offices by using their data network to carry interoffice calls. VoIP is attractive for international calls because it eliminates international long-distance fees. VoIP is not just a new technology for making cheaper calls. It is fundamentally changing how companies use voice communications. What makes VoIP powerful is that by turning voice into digital data packets, they can be stored, copied, combined with other data, and distributed to other devices that connect to the Internet. All the functionality of a corporate phone

# A Closer Look 4.4

## VoIP for Competitive Advantage

With a VoIP infrastructure, the phone system is an environment for developing and managing communications. VoIP will be able to support new communications functions that do not yet exist. Just as the first generation of static corporate Web sites evolved into multimedia, interactive, business-enhancing uses of the Internet, VoIP will serve as a platform for more strategic converged voice-and-data communications.

According to Werbach (2005), VoIP's potential as a strategic tool comes from three types of capability: virtualization, customization, and intelligence.

**Virtualization.** Virtualization makes it easy for users to operate in a seamless and consistent fashion across a geographically diverse network environment. A virtual version of one's phone can exist anywhere at any time without the time and expense of setting up a traditional phone system. This gives teleworkers, customer service representatives, and mobile workers access to communication and information systems to perform their jobs from anywhere. The government of Marin County, California, uses VoIP to give its employees and officials location-independent access to resources. Using an IP system that integrates voice recognition, voice synthesis, and e-mail, they can listen to and compose e-mails by phone, check and schedule appointments, create task lists, and launch calls from a contact list as well as customize preferences for notification based on priority level or sender.

**Customization.** Voice applications can be deployed that reinforce branding, enhance customer service, and improve internal communications. Developer Steve Wynn installed VoIP as part of a competitive strategy to address changing demand and differentiate service at his Las Vegas Wynn hotel and casino. In the early 2000s, the primary revenue source for Las Vegas resorts shifted from gambling to guest services such as entertainment, dining, and recreation. Using VoIP phones in every room, guests can call the concierge to arrange dinner reservations while browsing menus and pictures of dining rooms on the phone's color display.

**Intelligence.** Business processes are dependent on communication for coordination. Recall the Super Bowl case at the beginning of the chapter. With VoIP, communication can be precisely targeted according to business rules to define who needs to be contacted, when, and how. Avaya Labs, the research arm of a VoIP vendor, has a demo of how VoIP can enhance supply chain management (SCM). A simulated supply chain disruption automatically launched a multicompany VoIP conference call. The VoIP system reached participants through whatever device they were closest to and then automatically linked their computers to IM, streaming video, and a secure Web site with key documents. VoIP platforms have the intelligence to know whom to contact and how, because they are linked into corporate directories, databases, and SCM applications. In a real application, at Rhode Island Hospital, nurses wear small wireless clip-on badges made by Vocera (vocera.com). Instead of having to leave a patient's bedside for help or information, a nurse just pushes a button on the badge. The system uses speech recognition, connected to the hospital's directory system, to route the request to the right person or to broadcast it to team members.

*Sources:* Compiled from Resende (2005), Werbach (2005), and vocera.com (accessed July 2006).

---

can be provided to anyone, anywhere there is broadband access. VoIP can be used to achieve business objectives and competitive advantage as explained in *A Closer Look 4.4.*

**WLAN (WIRELESS LOCAL AREA NETWORK)**

A WLAN is a type of local-area network that uses high-frequency radio waves rather than wires to communicate between computers or devices such as printers, which are referred to as nodes on the network. According to research firm IDC, the number of wireless LANs in the United States tripled between 2001 and 2004, to 12 million installed (reported by Bury, 2005). A WLAN typically extends an existing wired LAN. WLANs are built by attaching an AP to the edge of the wired network.

**WIMAX**

Making WiMax available in portable devices is the goal for companies such as Intel. The technology already is being deployed in developing countries in the Middle East, Asia, and Africa that have unreliable or no fixed-line broadband networks. PeterStar, a St. Petersburg–based fixed-line operator, plans to launch a WiMax network in the city of Kaliningrad in early 2007, while regional provider Sibirtelecom will roll out WiMax and Wi-Fi in various cities. In the future, the company plans to launch the network in other Russian cities.

Next we will discuss messaging and collaboration capabilities that are possible and practical given the huge strides in communication networks and devices.

# 4.4 Messaging and Collaboration

Several factors are driving the need for messaging and collaboration. People need to work together and share documents. Groups make most of the complex decisions in organizations. And organizational decision making is difficult when team members are geographically spread out and working at different times.

Messaging and collaboration tools include older communications media like e-mail, videoconferencing, fax, and IM—and new media like blogs, podcasts, RSS, wikis, VoIP, Web meetings, and torrents (for sharing very large files). As media move to IP, there will not be much left that is not converged onto data networks. As you have learned, interoperability between incompatible network protocols (e.g., cellular and Wi-Fi) is becoming a reality.

The Telecommunications Industry Association (TIA) (*tiaonline.org*) indicates that global revenues from collaboration will show a 66.5 percent compound annual growth rate, reaching $11.4 billion in 2007 (Telecommunications Industry Association, 2004). The reason for its amazing growth is that nearly 87 percent of employees around the world work in remote offices. The trend in convergence, virtualization, and service-oriented architecture (SOA) tools is toward standards-based, multichannel, fully integrated collaboration. (SOA is discussed in Chapter 9.) These technologies offer opportunities for greater group productivity improvements and operational efficiencies.

The results of the *April 2006 "CIO Role" Survey* showed that IT investments are driven by their ability to support "achievement" and not simply "survival" (Alter, 2006). CIOs (chief information officers) are focusing more on new infrastructure and tools than on new applications. Table 4.2 presents some of the survey results.

| TABLE 4.2 | Technologies Considered Most Likely to Provide Business Value | | | |
|---|---|---|---|---|
| **Networking, Mobile, and Collaboration Technology** | **Deployed** | **Testing or Piloting** | **Evaluating** | **Total** |
| Smart cards | 18% | 14% | 29% | *61%* |
| 3G wide-area services | 13% | 12% | 28% | *53%* |
| Location-based services and GPS | 13% | 10% | 24% | *47%* |
| RFID/wireless sensors | 11% | 11% | 31% | *53%* |
| WiMax | 9% | 14% | 34% | *57%* |
| Team collaboration tools | 47% | 27% | 17% | *91%* |
| Web mapping | 27% | 23% | 24% | *84%* |
| RSS | 18% | 15% | 30% | *63%* |
| Podcasts | 14% | 14% | 23% | *51%* |
| Social networks | 14% | 12% | 23% | *49%* |
| Wikis | 13% | 14% | 26% | *53%* |

*Source:* Alter (2006)

Survey results showed that companies are deploying technologies (architecture, infrastructure, and data quality tools) to achieve the business goals of improving processes and making better use of information. By a wide margin (over 47%), the most deployed IT was *team collaboration tools* to improve productivity and help users work with data.

One of the biggest components of many Web 2.0 sites and technologies is collaboration. Much of Web 2.0 is about harnessing the knowledge and work of many people to create value. McAfee (2006) described Web 2.0 "as the point in the history of the Internet where technologists finally got out of the way and built tools to let users collaborate without a lot of up-front structure." See his blog at *blog.hbs/edu/faculty/amcafee*. Salesforce.com, which uses Web 2.0 principles in its online customer management service, did $105 million in sales in 2005, an increase of 63 percent from the previous year (Wyatt, 2005). Wikipedia, MySpace, Del.icio.us, Flickr, and many other popular resources are the result. The core mission of Web 2.0 is also the core mission of business—open collaboration. Even though Microsoft's SharePoint is a good Web collaboration platform, a limitation is that everyone who needs to collaborate on a project must have the latest version of the Microsoft productivity suite. This can be very frustrating for businesses that do not have it (Rapoza, 2006).

**VIRTUAL COLLABORATION**

Leading businesses are moving quickly to realize the benefits of e-collaboration. For example, the real estate franchiser RE/MAX uses an e-collaboration platform to improve communications and collaboration among its nationwide network of independently owned real estate franchises, sales associates, and suppliers. Similarly, Marriott International, the world's largest hospitality company, started with an online brochure and then developed a c-commerce system that links corporations, franchisees, partners, and suppliers, as well as customers, around the world.

There are many examples of e-collaboration. Here we present some additional representative ones.

*POM*

**Information Sharing Between Retailers and Their Suppliers: P&G and Wal-Mart.** One of the most publicized examples of information sharing is between Procter & Gamble (P&G) and Wal-Mart. Wal-Mart provides P&G access to sales information on every item Wal-Mart buys from P&G. The information is collected by P&G on a daily basis from every Wal-Mart store, and P&G uses the information to manage the inventory replenishment for Wal-Mart.

*MKT*

**Retailer–Supplier Collaboration: Asda Corporation.** Supermarket chain Asda (*asda.com*) has begun rolling out Web-based electronic data interchange (EDI) technology to 650 suppliers. Web-EDI technology is based on the AS2 standard, an internationally accepted HTTP-based protocol used to send real-time data in multiple formats securely over the Internet. It promises to improve the efficiency and speed of traditional EDI communications, which route data over third-party value-added networks (VANs).

*POM*

**Lower Transportation and Inventory Costs and Reduced Stockouts: Unilever.** Unilever's 30 contract carriers deliver 250,000 truckloads of shipments annually. Unilever's Web-based database, the Transportation Business Center (TBC), provides these carriers with site specification requirements when they pick up a shipment at a manufacturing or distribution center or when they deliver goods to retailers. TBC gives carriers all the vital information they need: contact names and phone numbers, operating hours, the number of dock doors at a location, the height of the dock doors, how to make an appointment to deliver or pick up shipments, pallet configuration, and other special requirements. All mission-critical information that Unilever's carriers need to make pickups, shipments, and deliveries is now available electronically 24/7.

**POM**

**Reduction of Product Development Time: Caterpillar, Inc.** Caterpillar, Inc. (*caterpillar.com*) is a multinational heavy-machinery manufacturer. In the traditional mode of operation, cycle time along the supply chain was long because the process involved paper-document transfers among managers, salespeople, and technical staff. To solve the problem, Caterpillar connected its engineering and manufacturing divisions with its active suppliers, distributors, overseas factories, and customers, through an extranet-based global collaboration system. By means of the collaboration system, a request for a customized tractor component, for example, can be transmitted from a customer to a Caterpillar dealer and on to designers and suppliers, all in a very short time. Customers also can use the extranet to retrieve and modify detailed order information while the vehicle is still on the assembly line.

Next we will discuss group decision processes and ways to improve them. Then developments in messaging and collaboration technologies are covered.

**THE NATURE OF GROUP WORK**

Managers and staff continuously make decisions: They design and manufacture products, develop policies and strategies, prepare financial statements, determine how to meet compliance mandates, design software, and so on. By design or default, group processes emerge with varying degrees of functionality.

**Group Decision Processes.** When people work in groups, they perform **group work,** which simply refers to work done together by two or more people. While the definition is simple, the process can be quite complex depending on the task, human factors, and available decision support. Some characteristics of group work are listed below:

- Group members may be located in different places or work at different times.
- Group members may work for the same or for different organizations.
- A group can be at a single managerial level or span several levels.
- There can be synergy (process and task gains) or conflict in group work.
- There can be gains and/or losses in productivity from group work.
- Some of the needed data, information, or knowledge may be located in many sources, several of which are external to the organization.
- The expertise of non-team members may be needed.
- Groups perform many tasks; however, groups of managers and analysts concentrate frequently on decision making.

Despite the long history and benefits of collaborative work, groups are not always successful. A key reason is that collaborative work processes can be plagued by dysfunctions, as listed in Tables 4. 3 and 4.4 (from Turban, 2006).

**Improving Meeting Processes and Small Group Dynamics.** Meetings are the most universal—and universally despised—part of business life. More and more companies are team-based (e.g., project management teams) in which most work gets done in meetings. Meetings can be more effective if one understands what can go wrong and intelligently manages decision processes and group dynamics to avoid

| TABLE 4.3 | Benefits of Working in Groups (Process Gains) |
| --- | --- |

- It provides learning. Groups are better than individuals at understanding problems.
- People readily take ownership and responsibility of problems and their solutions.
- Group members have their egos embedded in the decision, and so they will be committed to the solution.
- Groups are better than individuals at catching errors.
- A group has more information (knowledge) than any one member. Groups can leverage this knowledge to create new knowledge. More creative alternatives for problem solving can be generated, and better solutions can be derived (e.g., through stimulation).
- A group may produce synergy during problem solving. The effectiveness or quality of group work can be greater than the sum of what is produced by independent individuals.
- Working in a group may stimulate the creativity of the participants and process.
- A group may have better and more precise communication working together.

problems. For example, newly formed groups whose members do not know each other have much different dynamics than groups with an established history and routine and need more socialization time before they become productive. Researchers have developed methods for improving the processes of group work, namely, increase the benefits of meetings and minimize the detriments. Some of these methods are known as *group dynamics.* (See *en.wikipedia.org/wiki/Group_dynamics.*)

Two group dynamic methods are the **nominal group technique (NGT),** which is a simple brainstorming process for nonelectronic meetings, and the **Delphi method,** which is a qualitative forecasting method using anonymous questionnaires. The questionnaires are effective for technological forecasting and forecasts involving sensitive issues. These two methods were initially manual approaches to supporting group work. See Online File W4.6 for explanations of these two group work methods. Also see *Technography.com* for information, surveys, and tips about how to run meetings more effectively.

The challenges of group work processes are more intense for virtual group work as described in *IT at Work 4.6.*

| TABLE 4.4 | Dysfunctions of the Group Process (Process Losses) |
| --- | --- |

- Social pressures of conformity may result in **groupthink** (people begin to think alike and do not tolerate new ideas—yielding to conformance pressure).
- It is a time-consuming, slow process (only one member can speak at a time).
- Lack of coordination of the meeting and poor meeting planning.
- Inappropriate influences (domination of time, topic, opinion by one or few individuals; fear of contributing because of the possibility of flaming, and so on).
- Tendency of group members to either dominate the agenda or rely on others to do most of the work (free-riding).
- Some members may be afraid to speak up.
- Tendency to produce compromised solutions of poor quality.
- Nonproductive time (socializing, preparing, waiting for latecomers—air-time fragmentation).
- Tendency to repeat what was already said (because of failure to remember or process).
- High cost of meeting (travel, participation, etc.).

# IT at Work 4.6

## Virtual Teams at Sabre, Inc.

Sabre, Inc. is one of the leading firms providing travel reservation services worldwide. The company's roots go back to 1960, when American Airlines developed a proprietary computerized travel reservation system. This unique system made American Airlines the originator of electronic commerce in the travel industry. In March 2000, AMR (the parent company of American Airlines) spun off Sabre as a separate company headquartered in Texas. Today, Sabre, Inc. employs over 6,000 people in 45 countries and generates over $2 billion in annual revenues. Sixty thousand travel agents in 114 countries rely on Sabre to make travel arrangements for their clients. The total volume of reservations processed by the system each year exceeds 400 million, which represents 40 percent of all travel reservations worldwide. Consumers may be familiar with Travelocity.com, which is Sabre's business-to-consumer travel site; corporate travel agents would recognize Get-There—the world's leading supplier of business-to-business online travel reservation systems operated by Sabre.

With employees working both in headquarters and field offices scattered around the globe, Sabre made a decision to use *virtual teams*, whose overall purpose was to improve customer focus, enhance productivity, and grow market share and profitability. The company discovered that cross-functional teams were better suited for the marketplace demands than the single-function teams it had used in the past. Now, a typical virtual team at Sabre includes representatives from several areas of the company: Account executives sell reservation systems, technicians install and service the systems, trainers teach travel agents how to use the systems, account management specialists handle billing and collections, and customer service representatives respond to miscellaneous inquiries.

Following the introduction of virtual teams, Sabre encountered several challenges related to managing and working in the teams. One of the primary challenges was building trust among team members. Managers and employees soon recognized that building trust requires a high level of responsiveness to electronic communications from other team members, dependable performance, and a proactive approach to completing team tasks. The second challenge involved generating synergy in virtual teams—making the team greater than the sum of its parts. To resolve this challenge, Sabre offered team-building activities, as well as extensive classroom and computer-based training that preceded the launch of new virtual teams.

A third challenge was that team members had to cope with the feeling of isolation and detachment that characterizes virtual teamwork. The company discovered that certain employees preferred independent work and operated well without much social interaction. Thus, Sabre conducted interviews with potential team members to determine their suitability for virtual teamwork. Furthermore, the company's teams are only partially virtual—the relationships may occasionally involve face-to-face interactions during certain meetings and teambuilding exercises. In addition, employees have the option to work either from home or from an office where they can interact with other employees, who may or may not be their teammates.

The fourth challenge involved balancing technical and interpersonal skills among team members. Sabre was surprised to find that despite the infrequent face-to-face communications, interpersonal abilities were extremely valuable and important to virtual teams. As a result, the company made a change in its hiring and team-member selection practices, to shift the emphasis from technical to interpersonal skills.

A fifth major challenge was related to employee evaluation and performance measurement. Over time, the company implemented a system of team-level and individual metrics that were intended to measure objective, quantifiable contributions of each team member and the performance of the virtual team as a whole. Nevertheless, the company admits that striking the right balance between the measures of individual contributions and group performance continues to be difficult.

The results of creating virtual teams at Sabre have been quite positive. Most managers and employees of the company agree that the shift from functional face-to-face teams to cross-functional virtual teams improved customer service. Customers themselves support these assertions: Sabre's customer satisfaction ratings have increased from 68 percent in 1997 to 85 percent in 2000. Besides, the company increased its market share in North America from 43 percent in 1997 to 50 percent in 2000. While virtual teams are not the only factor contributing to these positive changes, they seem to indicate that the use of virtual teams may be a rewarding choice for a global organization.

*Sources:* Compiled from Kirkman et al. (2002) and *sabre-holdings.com* (2006).

*For Further Exploration:* Are the challenges faced by virtual teams at Sabre unique to this company? What additional challenges with virtual teams might Sabre encounter in the future? If you were an employee at Sabre, would you prefer to work in a physical face-to-face environment or in a virtual team?

IP technology allows enterprises to choose new architectures to support their voice applications. As organizations switch their voice and other data to IP networks, the use of collaborative technologies from the desktop becomes feasible. It is fostering the evolution of the PC from mere data processing and communication toward a tool for collaboration. For an example of how Internet-based collaboration tools improved SCM at Fila, see Online File W4.7.

**Vendors' Collaborative Products.** Numerous vendors offer collaborative technologies. Here are several vendors and their products:

- IBM has enhanced its collaborative platform software, Lotus Sametime, with new features and functionalities designed to increase productivity among end users. The new Lotus Sametime 7.5 offers a new Web-conferencing interface that makes it easier for end users to connect and manage online meetings efficiently. This allows anyone to join the meeting, whether he is inside or outside the firewall.
- WebEx, a provider of on-demand collaborative business applications, has teamed with Sony to market Web collaboration services to all Sony VAIO Pro users. The agreement gives customers immediate access to collaborative services.
- Microsoft's Groove Networks offers decentralized collaboration tools that are IT-infrastructure agnostic. It offers offline and cross-organizational capabilities. It features automated synchronization to ensure that all newly changed content is replicated and distributed.
- Oracle Collaboration Services 10*g* (OCS 10*g*) offers features such as Workspaces, which provide a team environment for carrying out collaborative tasks and for managing content and activities. IM functions include chat conferencing, Web conferencing, and voice chat, as well as presence facilities for individuals and groups.

The key features for supporting group work, and which are typically bundled with vendors' product lines, are described next.

**Real-Time Collaboration.** Collaborative IM, online meetings (also called Web conferencing), and presence are becoming critical components of communication and collaboration strategies.

*Collaborative Instant Messaging.* As companies become comfortable with telecommuting and at-home workers, it is IM, more so than e-mail, that ties their staffs together and supports distributed project teams. There are several reasons for the growth in corporate IM use. Workers are more mobile and harder to track down. The next generation of IM is not just about text chats, but offers integration with voice and video. IM's real-time features and the ability to track someone down no matter where they are located have proven attractive to customers, partners, and suppliers who need a guaranteed method of communication. For more details see Strom (2006) and McAdams (2006).

*Web or Online Conferencing.* Web or online conferencing is evolving into platforms that support real-time collaboration among ad-hoc groups and task teams. A number of companies have improved Web conferencing software, making it more of a viable option for business applications. The proliferation of broadband has helped push the trend, allowing senders and receivers to stream rich media right to the desktop.

Web conferencing can refer to a simple online setup (e.g., an IM program that allows for group discussion) or a sophisticated solution. In most cases, each participant in a Web conference has a Web cam to capture video, a microphone to capture audio, speakers, and a software program to bundle everything together and help broadcast it on the Web. Overall, participants can view video, see slide shows, participate in posting to an interactive whiteboard, view information on a computer desktop, share files, or answer questions through audio chat. Unlike videoconferencing, Web conferencing typically services many users at once.

With online conferencing, everyone sees the same thing at the same time, with easy-to-use redline and markup tools that create a robust environment for working with all types of information. As an example, the e-commerce site offered by Accredited Home Lenders offers IM features to its potential customers looking for mortgages. For Accredited Home Lenders, mortgage brokers can work with loan specialists in real time to resolve issues with loan applications and provide up-to-the-minute application status.

**Unified Messaging (UM).** Unified messaging (UM) is the concept of bringing together all messaging media such as e-mail, voice, mobile text, SMS, and fax into a combined communications medium. Minimally, UM can involve a unified mailbox with alert service. Or it can give users the ability to retrieve and send voice, fax, and e-mail messages from a single interface, including mobile phone, fixed network phone, or personal computer. The market need for UM consists of customers who need more control over communications.

<table>
<tr><td>

**FILE-SHARING BITTORRENT**

</td><td>

There are basically two ways users can get files from one computer to another over the Internet. The first is to connect directly to the server that holds the files and download from there. This is fine for files that are neither huge nor in high-demand. But when there are very large files (e.g., online video) or numerous people downloading at once, the process slows significantly. For situations where thousands of people request the file (e.g., during a Webinar), the server will crash.

</td></tr>
</table>

The second way is to use **BitTorrents.** BitTorrent is a protocol designed for transferring or sharing files. The most distinctive feature of BitTorrents is that they were designed to handle huge files. It is similar to peer-to-peer (P2P) with users connecting to each other directly to send and receive portions of the file. However, unlike P2P, it has a central server called a *tracker* that coordinates the action of all the peers. The tracker only manages connections and does not have any knowledge of the contents of the files being distributed. With this architecture, BitTorrent can distribute large files to a wide audience without the high costs of servers and bandwidth resources. The distribution process is typically started with a *torrent,* which is a pointer file that contains all the information needed to start downloading the needed file.

BitTorrent clients are programs that implement the BitTorrent protocol. (To get started with BitTorrent, users visit *bittorrent.com* to download the appropriate client—Mac, Windows, or Linux.) Each BitTorrent client is capable of preparing, requesting, and transmitting any type of computer file over a network using the BitTorrent protocol. This includes text, audio, video, encrypted content, and other types of digital information.

For businesses trying to share information among many workers, BitTorrents offer significant savings in bandwidth costs by distributing the load across many users. BitTorrent greatly reduces network load because client computers (peers) are used to download fragments of files from each other, instead of from one central repository. BitTorrent's structure is remarkably efficient at providing access to any large file at minimum cost. While BitTorrents have been criticized for illegal file sharing, they represent another tool for collaborative work that growing numbers of people (several millions) worldwide are comfortable using. The tools are also social forces that will change the way businesses design their processes, manage employees, and reach customers. In the next section, social and ethical issues of collaborative tools are discussed.

# 4.5 Social and Ethical Issues

**ETHICS**

Two topics of importance to managers in our highly networked world with a global workforce are social networking and ethics.

A **social network** is a place where people create their own space, or homepage, on which they write blogs (Web logs), post pictures, videos, or music, share ideas, and link to other Web locations they find interesting. Social networkers *tag* the content they post with keywords they choose themselves, which makes their content searchable. In effect, they create online communities of people with similar interests.

The Association to Advance Collegiate Schools of Business (AACSB International, *aacsb.edu*) has defined Assurance of Learning Requirements for ethics at both the undergraduate and graduate levels. In *Standard 15: Management of Curricula* (AACSB Accreditation Standards, 2006), AACSB identifies general knowledge and skill learning experiences that include "ethical understanding and reasoning abilities" at the undergraduate level. At the graduate level, *Standard 15* requires learning experiences in management-specific knowledge and skill areas to include "ethical and legal responsibilities in organizations and society." Ethical issues are discussed after social networks (AACSB International Ethics Education Resource Center, 2006).

**SOCIAL NETWORKS AND WIKIS**

Social networks, or social networking services, are Web sites that allow anyone to build a homepage for free. People can list personal information, communicate with others, upload files, communicate via IM, or blog. Social networks can contain links to user-generated content. Although blogs and wikis are influential social tools, social software also includes IM, RSS, Internet forums, and social network services such as MySpace and Bebo.

**Social Networks.** Social networks are redefining the way people communicate. **MySpace** is a social network that started as a site for fans of independent rock music in Los Angeles. MySpace was bought by Rupert Murdoch for $580 million in 2005 (Lush, 2006). By July 2006, MySpace (*myspace.com*) had about 90 million users—and was estimated to be the world's fourth most popular English-language Web site. Competition in the social networking arena is fierce. Bebo (*bebo.com*) attracts a majority of U.K. visitors and had over 22 million registered members by March 2006 (Wikipedia, 2006). Buzznet, Facebook, Xanga, TagWorld, and Friendsorenemies are competitors. A list of all notable social networks is available at *en.wikipedia.org/wiki/List_of_social_networking_websites*.

**LIFE OUT OF CONTROL**

The technologies covered in this chapter blur work, social, and personal time. IT keeps people connected with no real off-switch. Tools that are meant to improve the productivity and quality of life in general can also intrude on personal time. Managers need to be aware of the huge potential for abuse by expecting 24/7 response from workers. See *IT at Work 4.7* for a look at life in a connected world.

# IT at Work 4.7

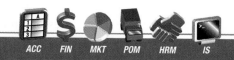

## Internet 2007—Life in the Connected World

ACC   FIN   MKT   POM   HRM   IS

Changes brought about by the Internet are as profound as previous historic milestones such as the Renaissance or Industrial Revolution. Every person can be a creative artist and freely distribute work to millions—characteristics of both the Renaissance and Industrial Revolution. Google's existence is a testament to the power of the individual in the connected age—a better research tool than major corporations had in the 1990s. Other empowering tools such as VoIP and wikis enable anyone to call or share files for free.

Communication technologies—writing, printing, cable, telephone, radio, and TV—have always played a central role in human history. The marginal cost of collecting, storing, accessing, and transmitting information is approaching zero. Over a billion people have Internet access and over 1.5 billion use mobile phones. The potential for the spread of wireless access to the Internet is enormous.

Major companies face small but powerful challenges and competitors that are undermining traditional business models.

Consumers and employees can counteract marketing strategies by posting harsh criticisms in blogs. Ebay shops can underprice. Intranets, extranets, and social networks are diminishing perimeters between companies and individuals' lives—and making them more transparent. People check Internet resources for ratings and prices before they buy books, vacations, cars, and so on. Amazingly, in places like Tanzania, political activists worked on a new constitution using a wiki. Communication and collaboration tools can collectively create a compelling force whose impacts are not yet known.

Businesses have to learn to cope with a world that is far more competitive, dynamic, and connected.

*Sources:* Compiled from Kirkpatrick (2006) and Wolf (2006).

*For Further Exploration:* How has the use of communication tools impacted your ability to get your work done? How has it impacted your personal life? Has IT been liberating or overwhelming? What ethical issues does this raise for managers?

# 4.6 Managerial Issues

1. **Organizational impacts.** Technology-supported communications are having various organizational impacts. The primary business benefit of networks and mobile communications is keeping workers connected. Mobile and collaboration technologies need to be in place to ensure that employees can be productive.

2. **Future of technology support.** From a technology perspective the second half of this decade will be seen as a period in which technology moved to support collaboration. Whereas for the past five years the computer industry has been focused on providing computing for the individual (PC + laptop + notebook + PDA), the emphasis is now firmly on connectivity, communication, and collaboration.

3. **Extending organizational boundaries.** Extranets connect businesses to their customers and supply chain partners. As high-bandwidth networks become increasingly common, collaborative networking solutions are available for companies of any size.

4. **Virtual work.** Mobile multimedia technologies make it possible for businesses to reinvent the traditional workplace from an office-based activity to a virtual one. Employees can collaborate closely in real time with other employees, customers, or partners regardless of anyone's location.

5. **Single view of the truth.** Information silos are the bane of most organizations as they try to integrate and share data to get a clearer understanding of customers, products, and other objects of interest. Regulatory compliance, performance management, and collaborative business relationships demand a single view of relevant information.

6. **Social and ethical issues.** Social networks are redefining the way people communicate. Tools that are meant to improve the productivity and quality of life in general can also intrude on the personal lives of managers and employees.

## Integrating IT

### For the Accounting Major

Accounting information systems are dependent on networks. Payment functions such as accounts payable and receivable are done over networks. To meet regulatory compliance requirements, accountants need to compile data from various remote databases, consolidate financial statements, and distribute financial performance reports to shareholders and regulators on a quarterly and annual basis. Significant cost-savings result when financial statements are distributed via networks instead of conventional paper methods. Federal agencies, such as the SEC, require that reports be submitted electronically.

### For the Finance Major

Financial systems rely on speed and accuracy. Investment and quantitative analyses demand real-time data delivered via computing networks. Transactional and operational data may reside in countries without a reliable wireline communications infrastructure—making wireless networks a necessity. Financial analysts rely on networks for the delivery of real-time data. Financial planning and budgeting meetings can be held via Web conferencing or collaboration portals instead of in-person.

### For the Human Resources Management Major

Intranets can be used as efficient HR portals. Intranets more cheaply and reliably distribute government forms, policies, handbooks, and other materials to employees. HR portals can be used to keep employees informed of the status of performance evaluations, vacations, medical plans, and so on. These self-help capabilities reduce costs and better support employees' information needs. Training employees in local or remote locations can be done via streamed video to PCs or handheld devices.

### For the IS Major

Business operations are fully dependent on the capabilities of their information networks—wireline and wireless. Networks and collaboration tools are strategic assets. Senior executives look to the ISD for help in managing those assets. Other departments look to the ISD to help them meet their communication and collaboration requirements. Information systems professionals must keep up-to-date with rapid changes in wireless protocols that enable convergence of various technologies.

### For the Marketing Major

Wireless networks, podcasts, RSS, wikis, social networks, and streaming technologies provide new ways to reach customers—anywhere and any time. Customer relationship management and customer retention programs can be improved through creative uses of these technologies. Marketers will need to design and develop programs designed for delivery to portable devices over various types of network protocols. Voice applications can be deployed that reinforce branding, enhance customer service, and improve internal communications.

### For the Production/Operations Management Major

The performance, efficiency, and cost of a company's supply chain operations—inventory purchasing, receiving, quality control, production, and shipping—are fully dependent on communication networks. Production managers can be kept informed in real time of potential disruptions in logistics and are able to take action directly from handheld devices that connect them to databases and suppliers. By integrating collaboration tools, mobile computing networks, wireless devices, and instant communication such as text messaging, production and operations departments can replace inefficient paper-based processes and reduce required personnel for operations and administration.

## Key Terms

# Chapter Highlights

(Numbers Refer to Learning Objectives)

❶ To prepare data and documents for transmission, they are converted into digital packets based on the Internet Protocol (IP) and sent via computer (i.e., packet-switched) networks or LANs.

❶ Data, voice, and video networks are converging into a single network based on packet technology, such as IP and VoIP.

❶ The major drivers of mobile computing are large numbers of users of mobile devices, especially cell phones; widespread use of cell phones throughout the world; new vendor products; declining prices; increasing bandwidth; and the explosion of collaboration tools.

❷ Transparency, or real-time awareness, provided by Web-based collaboration solutions can significantly improve the outcome of complex operations involving numerous remote or mobile workers.

❷ Convergence eliminates the need for separate networks. When all information services are handled the same way by one high-speed packet network, the technical barriers to collaborative work are eliminated. Multimedia applications become possible because the network does not restrict the kinds of computing devices that could be used.

❸ Intranets distribute frequently needed employee handbooks, government forms, policies, and other materials to employees over the company network.

❸ An extranet connects the company with its customers or trading partners for B2B commerce and real-time supply chain management. Extranets give account customers instant access to their account details.

❹ Search engines, directories, enterprise search engines, and wikis help bring order to the chaotic Internet universe.

❹ Mobile portals provide multimedia broadcasts and other content (e.g., news and sports) to billions.

❹ Wireless technology can give a company a competitive advantage through increased productivity, better customer care, and more timely communication and information exchange.

❺ Many B2B and B2C applications in the service and retail industries can be conducted with wireless devices. SMS and IM provide employees with relatively low-cost connectivity.

❺ VoIP can be customized as a strategic tool because of its virtualization, customization, and intelligence capabilities. Location-based advertising and advertising via SMSs on a very large scale is expected.

❻ Broadband wireless computing allows users to collaborate via the Internet at any time, share files, or perform other group work functions that previously required a PC and wireline infrastructure.

❼ Messaging and collaboration tools include older media like e-mail, videoconferencing, fax, and IM—and new media like podcasts, RSS newsfeeds, wikis, VoIP, Web meetings, and torrents (for sharing very large files). As media move to IP, there will not be much left that is not converged onto data networks.

❼ Managers and staff continuously make decisions: They design and manufacture products, develop policies and strategies, prepare financial statements, determine how to meet compliance mandates, design software, and so on.

❽ Collaboration and communication technologies covered in this chapter blur work, social, and personal time. IT keeps people connected with no real off-switch. Tools that are meant to improve the productivity and quality of life in general can also intrude on personal time. Managers need to be aware of the huge potential for abuse by expecting 24/7 response from workers.

## Virtual Company Assignment

### Network Computing at The Wireless Café

Go to The Wireless Café's link on the Student Web Site. There you will find a description of some communications problems the restaurant is having as a result of its 24/7 operations. You will be asked to identify ways network computing can facilitate better staff communications.

***Instructions for accessing The Wireless Café on the Student Web Site:***

1. Go to *wiley.com/college/turban*.
2. Select Turban/Leidner/ McLean/Wetherbe's *Information Technology for Management*, Sixth Edition.
3. Click on Student Resources site, in the toolbar on the left.
4. Click on the link for Virtual Company Web site.
5. Click on Wireless Café.

## Online Resources

More resources and study tools are located on the Student Web Site and on WileyPLUS. You'll find additional chapter materials and useful Web links. In addition, self-quizzes that provide individualized feedback are available for each chapter.

## Questions for Review

1. Describe why various information services have functioned independently of each other.
2. Define interoperability.
3. Describe the difference between TCP and UDP.
4. Describe packet technology, broadband, and proprietary protocols.
5. Define GSM and SIP.
6. Explain the various uses of intranets, extranets, wikis, podcasts, RSS feeds, XML, and XBRL.
7. List the major standards used by mobile phone systems (e.g., GSM).
8. Explain SMS, SIM, Wi-Fi, Wi-Fi mesh, and Google Talk.
9. Explain intelligent agents, spiders, crawlers, meta-tags, and enterprise search.
10. Define the following terms: smart phone, personal digital assistant, tablet PC, and converged devices.
11. Describe the major components of a mobile communication network.
12. Define VoIP, WLAN, and WiMax.
13. Define social networks, BitTorrent, and MySpace.

## Questions for Discussion

1. Nobody thought in the early 1990s that the Internet would be carrying a significant amount of the telephone traffic. List at least three factors enabling or driving this change in the Internet.
2. There is growing demand for video to handheld devices. Explain at least three factors enabling or driving this demand.
3. Why attend class if you can view or listen to the podcast?
4. Discuss some of the potential applications of collaborative technologies in the service sector and manufacturing sector.
5. Discuss some of the potential applications of wireless technologies in the financial sector.
6. Discuss the components of a mobile communication network.
7. Explain the role of protocols in mobile computing and their limitations.

8. Discuss the impact of wireless computing on emergency response services.

9. Describe the ways in which WiMax is affecting the use of cellular phones for m-commerce.

10. Which of the current mobile computing limitations do you think will be minimized within five years? Which ones will not?

11. It is said that Wi-Fi is winning a battle against 3G. In what sense is this true? In what sense is this false?

12. Discuss the ethical issues of social networks and anytime-anywhere accessibility.

## Exercises and Projects

1. CALEA is the Communications Assistance for Law Enforcement Act, a federal requirement to allow law enforcement agencies to conduct electronic surveillance of phone calls or other communications. What dilemmas are caused by the convergence of voice, video, and data and the requirements of CALEA?

2. Compare the various features of broadband wireless networks (e.g., 3G, Wi-Fi, and WiMax). Visit at least three broadband wireless network vendors.
   a. Prepare a list of capabilities of each network.
   b. Prepare a list of actual applications that each network can support.
   c. Comment on the value of such applications to users. How can the benefits be assessed?

3. Compare the advanced features of three search engines.
   a. Prepare a table listing five advanced features of each search engine.
   b. Perform a search for "VoIP vendors" on each of those search engines.
   c. Compare the results.
   d. In your opinion, which search engine provided the best results. Why?

4. Read *IT at Work 4.4* on Wi-Fi mesh networks, Google Talk, and interoperability and answer the discussion questions.

5. Read *IT at Work 4.5* on mobile TV broadcast to mobile devices and answer the discussion questions.

## Group Assignments and Projects

1. Visit *podcasting-tools.com*. Read how to record a podcast. Each team will design and develop content from this course for a podcast. Then create a podcast and make it available online.

2. Each team should examine a major vendor of mobile devices (Nokia, Kyocera, Motorola, Palm, BlackBerry, etc.). Each team will research the capabilities and prices of the devices offered by each company and then make a class presentation, the objective of which is to convince the rest of the class why one should buy that company's products.

3. Each team should explore the commercial applications of mobile communication in one of the following areas: financial services, including banking, stocks, and insur-

ance; marketing and advertising; manufacturing; travel and transportation; human resources management; public services; or health care. Each team will present a report to the class based on their findings.

4. Each team will investigate an online (Web) meeting software suite, such as GoToMeeting. Download the free trial or demonstration. The teams will investigate the features and business purposes of the software, and then present a report to the class based on their findings.

5. Each team will investigate a standards-setting organization and report on its procedures and progress in developing wireless standards. Start with the following: *atis.org, etsi.org,* and *tiaonline.org.*

## Internet Exercises

1. Enter *e-sponder.com* and describe its Collaboration Portal.

2. Enter *podcasting-tools.com* Explain how to record a podcast and make it available.

3. Enter *searchenginewatch.com/.* The site claims to "want marketers to understand how to reach an audience through search engines." Does the Web site achieve its mission? Explain.

4. Learn about PDAs by visiting vendors' sites such as Palm, SONY, Hewlett-Packard, IBM, Philips, NEC,

Hitachi, Casio, Brother, Texas Instruments, and others. List some m-commerce devices manufactured by these companies.

5. Access *progessive.com,* an insurance company, from your cell phone (use the "Go to..." feature). If you have a Sprint PCS wireless phone, do it via the Finance menu. If you have a Palm i705 (or newer), you can download the Web-clipping application from Progressive. Report on these capabilities.

6. Research the status of 3G and the future of 4G by visiting *itu.int*, *4g.newstrove.com*, and *3gnewsroom.com*. Prepare a report on the status of 3G and 4G based on your findings.

7. Explore *nokia.com*. Prepare a summary of the types of mobile services and applications Nokia currently supports and plans to support in the future.

8. Enter *kyocera-wireless.com*. Take the smart tour and view the demos. What is a smart phone? What are its capabilities? How does it differ from a regular cell phone?

9. Enter *mobile.commerce.net* and find information about car navigation systems. Write a report.

10. Enter *ibm.com*. Search for *wireless e-business*. Research the resulting stories to determine the types of wireless capabilities and applications IBM's software and hardware supports. Describe some of the ways these applications have helped specific businesses and industries.

11. Using a search engine, try to determine whether there are any commercial Wi-Fi hotspots in your area. Enter *wardriving.com*. Based on information provided at this site, what sorts of equipment and procedures could you use to locate hotspots in your area?

12. Enter *mapinfo.com* and look for the location-based services demos. Try all the demos. Find all of the wireless services. Summarize your findings.

13. Enter *packetvideo.com* and *microsoft.com/mobile/pocketpc*. Examine their demos and products and list their capabilities.

14. Enter *internethomealliance.com* and review their white papers. Based on these papers, what are the major appliances that are currently in most U.S. homes? Which of these appliances would most homeowners be likely to connect to a centrally controlled network?

15. Enter *onstar.com*. What types of *fleet* services does OnStar provide? Are these any different from the services OnStar provides to individual car owners?

16. Enter *autoidcenter.org*. Read about the Internet of Things. What is it? What types of technologies are needed to support it? Why is it important?

17. Enter *mdsi-advantex.com* and review the wireless products for the enterprise. Summarize the advantages of the different products.

18. Enter *attwireless.com/mlife* and prepare a list of the services available there.

19. Enter *wirelesscar.com*. Examine all the services provided and relate them to telemetry.

20. Enter the site of a wireless e-mail provider (BlackBerry, T-mobile, Handspring); collect information about the capabilities of the products and compare them.

## Minicase 1

# Dresdner Kleinwort Wasserstein Uses Wiki for Collaboration

Dresdner Kleinwort Wasserstein (DrKW) is the international investment banking arm of Dresdner Bank. Based in Europe, DrKW provides a range of capital markets and advisory services employing approximately 6,000 people worldwide.

Because of the large number employees, their geographic distribution, and the diversity of cultures, it became necessary to provide a range of collaborative tools, from blogs and wikis to instant messenger, chat, and audio/videoconferencing, in order to allow people to move between modes, depending on which was most appropriate at the time. DrKW installed a primitive open source wiki in 1997. The company reviewed Socialtext products in March 2004 and ran a small pilot on the hosted service in July 2004. Based on the pilot, DrKW decided to upgrade to Socialtext Enterprise, which was installed in the third quarter of 2004.

DrKW chose Socialtext because the company was willing to work with DrKW on better authentication, permissioning, and sharing of information and communication among silos, as well as the vendor, and understood the necessity for information to flow across multiple forms of communications. Because DrKW is highly regulated, everything must be recordable, archivable, searchable, and retrievable.

## Usage and Benefits

The Information Strategy team was the first group to use Socialtext on a hosted service. Because its work needed structure, skills were geographically dispersed, and publication and collaboration at individual levels gained many capabilities through the Socialtext workspace. The team uses it as a communications tool, a collective discussion tool, and as a storehouse for documents and information.

The User-Centered Design (UCD) team incorporates usability into external-facing applications used across all business lines. The wiki allows all team members to upload information more easily, which encourages collaboration and transparency through making the sharing of e-mail conversations and other ideas uncomplicated. UCD also uses the wiki to help explain what "user-centered design" is and why it is important to a wider DrKW community as well as to share presentations, documents, and reports.

One of the most important roles of the wiki is to track project development so that the team and management know what progress is being made regardless of individual geographical locations and raising the awareness of the team about what each person is doing, the status of each project, and what actions should follow.

In 2004, the Equity Delta1 equity financing team was one of the largest users of the wiki. This unit deals with loans, equity swaps, and so on. They use the wiki workspace to eliminate the cumbersome number of e-mails, to view the development of business plans, and to store commonly used information. The team also creates an open forum where anyone can post views, comments, and questions on given subjects, publish and share whitepapers and bulletins, coordinate sales and marketing activities, and organize important team tasks.

The E-Capital London Team develops back-end applications for the Digital Markets business line and supports a number of legacy systems. They use Socialtext to share and develop new system specifications and product overviews, and help with documentation. The wiki provides an instantly editable collaboration platform that simplifies the publication process. The version his-tory function is useful for product specs where it is important to retain a complete audit trail.

Socialtext also enables individuals to edit the intranet quickly and easily. For example, it will also help build an internal glossary that will define company "jargon" through employees doing similar jobs. The Wikipedia-style usage cuts down the training time and costs of new hires as it will help them to understand internal and external jargon and terms with less difficulty. It also simplifies the roles of people writing in other locations and languages. Eventually, the wiki will be used for informal training, which will encourage its use.

*Sources:* Compiled from SocialText (2004) and BusinessWeek Online (2005).

## Questions for Minicase 1

1. What are the capabilities of the wiki not available in a regular e-mail?
2. Describe the applications in finance and operations.
3. How does the wiki increase employee productivity?
4. Relate wiki to foreign languages and training.
5. What are some social, cultural, and ethical issues involved in the use of wikis for business collaboration?

# Minicase 2

## Converged Networks Support Complex and Global Business Relationships

What a business can do depends on what its networks can do. And those effects are cumulative; there tend to be increasing returns from deploying several new networking technologies. Network convergence, based upon the Internet Protocol (IP) and SIP (Session Initiation Protocol), makes it possible to economically develop and offer a wide range of complex, multifunction services. Those services merge voice, data, video, and mobile in the same application. Given the flexibility of the new technologies, innovative personalized services and specialized applications can be developed.

To illustrate, consider IP, SIP, and SOA (service-oriented applications). An SOA architecture is essentially a collection of services. These services communicate with each other. The communication can involve either simple data passing or it could involve two or more services coordinating some activity. SIP is critical because some means of connecting services to each other is needed. With SIP, signaling of communications is standardized between various types of devices and end-points, such as IP phones and IM clients, from different vendors.

From a business value perspective, this enables remote and instant collaboration among employees, supply chain partners, and customers—regardless of the hardware devices they have. Recall that different devices could not communicate because of incompatible protocols.

From an IT development perspective, SIM has made it easier to develop communication applications. This is important because business applications that incorporate communications can lead to greatly improved organizational efficiency.

### IP Telephony Offers Significant Strategic and Operational Value

Enormous value can be achieved in procurement and supply chain management through the use of converged networks. Supply-chain capabilities are the set of processes, technology, and people that enable acquisition, inventory management, and distribution of a company's products. Factors such as globalization, outsourcing, and competition have contributed to more complicated business relationships—and the need for robust and efficient communication.

Global businesses need ways of collaborating more effectively with third-party suppliers and partners. To do so, they need to standardize on their information systems and communication processes.

One of the biggest challenges for managers is to get decision-making information—to know what is happening and where things are not being done—and to be able to communicate with those responsible for getting the work done regardless of time and location. Without transparency to see bottlenecks and the ability to work around them, costs cannot be minimized.

According to a World Bank study, global trade volume of merchandise is approximately $8 trillion a year. Of that, 7 percent, or more than $500 billion, goes to administrative costs. Automated processes would cut those costs. It is estimated that one working day of capital could be saved by automating collaboration on purchase orders, two or three more days could be saved on letters of credit, and another two to three days saved on customs filings.

For example, New York–based Liz Claiborne uses technology to monitor movements of goods from overseas factories and notify the U.S. Customs Service prior to goods' arrival at the borders. As a result, the company improved operational efficiency and has better visibility into import operations. It also avoided regulatory noncompliance, maintained its "low-risk" rating with U.S. Customs, reduced duties paid, and cut cycle times by a week.

*Sources:* Compiled from Bartels (2006), Beasley (2004), *servicearchitecture.com* (accessed July 2, 2006).

## Questions for Minicase 2

1. List three business processes that depend on networks. How do the network's capabilities limit the function or reach of those processes?
2. Explain the importance of standardization of network protocols.
3. Why it is difficult for managers to get the decision-making information they need?
4. How could automated processes reduce administrative costs?
5. How can the ability to monitor operations provide a company with competitive advantage?

# References

AACSB Accreditation Standards, Management of Curricula, *aacsb.edu/eerc/std-15.asp* (accessed July 3, 2006).

AACSB International, Ethics Education Resource Center, Accreditation Standards, *aacsb.edu/resource_centers/EthicsEdu/standards.asp* (accessed July 3, 2006).

Ahrens, F., "Peer-to-Peer Networking For Podcasts and People," *Washington Post,* May 14, 2006.

Alter, A. E., "Emerging Computing and Software Technologies," *CIO Insight,* May 4, 2006, *cioinsight.com/article2/0,1540,1957596,00.asp* (accessed July 3, 2006).

Bartels, N., "Twenty-one-Century Logistics," *Manufacturing Business Technology,* March 1, 2006.

Beasley, J. S., *Networking.* Upper Saddle River, NJ: Prentice-Hall, 2004.

Bunkley, N., "Smartphones Now Essential Business Tool," *The Detroit News,* March 28, 2006.

Bury, S., "From Wireless to Wi-Fi," *Manufacturing Business Technology,* April 1, 2005.

*BusinessWeek Online,* "E-mail Is So Five Minutes Ago." November 28, 2005, *businessweek.com/magazine/content/05_48/b3961120.htm* (accessed February 2006).

Cane, A., World Cup Football Forces Mobile Television Out of the Lab," *Financial Times,* June 21, 2006.

Careless, J., "Convergence Communications E-SPONDER," *Law and Order,* March 2006, *hendonpub.com/publications/lawandorder/otherarticles.asp?ID=545* (accessed June 20, 2006).

Carr, D., "How Google Works (In Mysterious Ways)," *ExtremeTech.com,* July 7, 2006.

Chabrow, E., and M.K. McGee, "Productivity's Second Act," *InformationWeek,* January 23, 2006.

Cruez, A. F., "Small Screen, Big Picture," *New Straits Times,* March 5, 2006.

Delaney, K. J., "Microsoft, Yahoo Ink Instant-Message Pact," *Wall Street Journal,* October 12, 2005.

DeSanctis, G., and B. Gallupe, "A Foundation for the Study of Group Decision Support Systems," *Management Science,* 33(5), 1987.

E-Sponder Case Study, "Embracing Technology At Super Bowl XXXIX," *Convergence Communications,* March 1, 2005, *convergencecom.com/casestudy_techatsuperbowl.shtml* (accessed June 21, 2006).

Federal News Service, "Remarks by Federal Reserve Board Chairman Alan Greenspan to the National Italian American Foundation," October 12, 2005.

Feldman, S., "The High Cost of Not Finding Information," KMWorld.com, May 1, 2004. *kmworld.com/Articles/ReadArticle.aspx?ArticleID=9534* (accessed September 2006).

*Financial Adviser,* "Technology Trumps Terror to Keep Up Work, Claims Citrix," May 11, 2006.

Fleetwood, C., "New Nokia, Google Partnership Highlights WiFi Trend," *CNNMoney.com,* May 12, 2006.

Gareiss, R., "Hail to the PDA: The Business Continuity Factor," *NetworkWorld,* May 2, 2006, *networkworld.com/newsletters/net/2006/0501networker1.html* (accessed June 19, 2006).

Gler, T., "Baseline Survey: The Mobile Motive," *Baseline.com,* May 6, 2006.

Google.com, "Kaiser Permanente and the Google Search Appliance," 2005, *google.com/enterprise/gsa/kaiser.html* (accessed September 2006).

Johnson, R., "A Smaller World with Cup Blogs," *Los Angeles Times,* June 27, 2006.

Kirkman, B., et al., "Five Challenges to Virtual Team Success: Lessons from Sabre, Inc.," *Academy of Management Executive,* 16(3), August 2002.

Kirkpatrick, D., "Life in a Connected World," *Fortune,* July 10, 2006.

Kontzer, T., "Search On," *InformationWeek.com,* January 20, 2003, *informationweek.com/shared/printableArticleSrc.jhtml?articleID= 6500054* (accessed September 2006).

Lush, E. G., "Rupert Murdoch's Cool New Thing," *The Spectator,* June 24, 2006.

McAdams, J., "Telecommuters: These Stay-at-Home Workers Want Collaboration with Colleagues," *Computerworld,* May 11, 2006.

McAfee, A., "It's Ready or Not for Enterprise 2.0," *Optimize,* July 1, 2006.

Microsoft Case Study, "Communications Solution Helps Ensure Public Safety for Milestone Event," March 2005.

Pessach, Y., "Take Total Control of Your Networking with .NET and UDP," *MSDN,* February 2006, *msdn.microsoft.com/msdnmag/issues/ 06/02/UDP* (accessed September 2006).

Rapoza, J., "All Together Now. Microsoft Must Change If It's to Wend Its Way to Web 2.0," *eWeek,* July 10, 2006.

Resende, P., "R.I. Hospital Keeps Nurses Connected with Wi-Fi Badges," *Journal of New England Technology,* February 12, 2005, *vocera.com/downloads/Vocera_20Communications.pdf* (accessed July 2, 2006).

Sabre, Inc., *sabre-holdings.com* (accessed September 2006).

SocialText, "Dresdner Kleinwort Wasserstein (DrKW)," *Customer Success Story at SocialText.com,* 2004, *socialtext.com/customers/customerdrkw* (accessed February 2006).

Strom, D., "Managing Your Instant Messaging Frontier," *Business Communications Review,* April 1, 2006.

*Technology Review,* "Long-Distance Wi-Fi," October 2005.

Telecommunications Industry Association, "IP Market Expected to Reach $15.2 Billion in 2005, Growing 17.2 Percent from 2003," February 10, 2004, *tiaonline.org/business/media/press_releases/legacy. cfm?parelease=04-09* (accessed September 2006).

Turban, E. et al., *Electronic Commerce,* 4th ed. Upper Saddle River, NJ: Prentice-Hall, 2006.

Werbach, K., "Using VoIP to Compete," *Harvard Business Review,* September 2005.

Wikipedia, "MySpace," 2006, *en.wikipedia.org/wiki/MySpace* (accessed September 2006).

Wikithat.com, "*BusinessWeek* Highlights Wiki Use (Again)," November 18, 2005, *wikithat.com/wiki_that/case_studies/index.html* (accessed September 2006).

"Wired Workers," *Business Times Singapore,* June 27, 2005.

Wolf, M., "The World Must Get to Grips with Seismic Economic Shifts," *Financial Times,* February 1, 2006.

Wray, R., "Mobile TV Watch Beckham Bend It on the Bendy Bus," *The Guardian* (London), June 26, 2006.

Wyatt, I., "Not Software, Salesforce," *Bigideainvestor.com,* 2005. *bigideainvestor.com/index.cfm?D=827* (accessed September 2006).

| Appendix 4A | **The Future of Networking Infrastructure** |
|---|---|

Worldwide growth in wireline and wireless telecommunications (telecom) is forecasted to be steady, but the growth rate of wireless is eight times greater than the growth rate of wireline. In 2005, the wireless services market increased by 16.6 percent while wireline services (also referred to as *landline services*) grew at 2 percent. The availability of high-speed wireless bandwidth and the mobile services it can support, as discussed in *A Closer Look 4A.1,* has increased demand for wireless services.

Total telecom revenues in five regions—Canada, Europe, the Middle East/Africa, Latin America, and Asia/Pacific—increased 11.4 percent in 2005 to reach $1.8 trillion, according to TIA's (*tiaonline.org*) 2006 Telecom Market Review and Forecast (Telecommunications Industry Association, 2006). Those revenues are expected to grow at a 10.4 percent compound annual growth rate reaching $2.7 trillion by 2009—at which time wireless will have 58 percent of the market.

Wireline usage will still be widely used because Voice Over IP (VoIP) will lessen the migration to wireless. VoIP had been primarily for residential use because, until now, it was too unreliable for business use.

The world of voice communications is undergoing dramatic changes, as we describe in this appendix. The telecommunications industry is transitioning from a circuit-based network to a packet-based (IP) network to meet companies' needs for converged networks that integrate multiple services: voice (including cellular), video, and data communications.

### MOBILE COMPUTING SOFTWARE

Developing software for wireless devices is challenging because (as of late 2006) there is no widely accepted standard for wireless devices. Therefore, software applications need to be customized for each type of device with which the application communicates. Major software products needed for mobile computing are presented in Table 4A.1.

To keep down the cost of wireless services, software engineers have had to develop code that optimizes resource usage. Supporting different displays can force painstaking changes to multiple software modules and applications. Different CPUs, operating systems, storage media, and mobile platform environments create time-consuming porting and testing issues. Yet, despite these many challenges, development timelines are shrinking and wireless service operators and consumers demand a reliable device with a high-quality user experience.

#### Wireless Wide Area Networks (WWANs)

There are three general types of mobile networks: *wide area networks* (WANs), *WiMax* (Worldwide Interoperability for Microwave Access), and *local*

## A Closer Look 4A.1

### *Mobile Services for Corporate Customers Launched in Taiwan and Japan*

In summer 2006, RIM (Research In Motion) and Taiwan Mobile Co., the area's second-largest mobile phone company, launched the BlackBerry wireless e-mail device and service in Taiwan. Taiwan Mobile began offering RIM's BlackBerry Enterprise Server and BlackBerry Internet Service with BlackBerry handsets for both corporate and individual customers. Over 85 percent of Taiwan's 23 million residents are estimated to have mobile subscriptions. The market is huge because of the massive corporate presence of both foreign multinationals in Japan and Japanese multinationals that operate abroad.

In the last quarter of 2006, NTT DoCoMo, Japan's largest mobile phone company, started selling BlackBerry wireless e-mail devices—and target marketed them to corporate customers. To make the devices attractive to business users, the BlackBerries sold in Japan will operate on both **CDMA (***Code Division for Multiple Access***)** and **GSM (***Global System for Mobile Communications***)** networks. With dual-network functionality, the devices can be used around the world for voice and data communications.

*Sources:* Compiled from CNET (2006) and Reuters (2006).

| TABLE 4A.1 | Software for Mobile Computing |
|---|---|
| **Software** | **Description** |
| Microbrowser | A browser with limited bandwidth and memory requirements. Provides wireless access to the Internet. |
| Operating system (OS) for mobile client | An OS for mobile devices. |
| Bluetooth (named for a Viking king) | Chip technology for short-range communication among wireless devices. Uses digital two-way radio frequency (RF). It is an almost universal standard for Wireless Personal Area Network (WPAN) for data and voice. See *bluetooth.com*. |
| User interface | Application logic for handheld devices. It is often controlled by the microbrowser. |
| Legacy application software | Residing on the mainframe, it is a major source of data to wireless systems. |
| Application middleware | Provides connection among applications, databases, and Web-based servers. |
| Wireless middleware | Links wireless networks to application servers. |
| Wireless Application Protocol (WAP) | A set of communication protocols that enables wireless devices to "talk" to a server on a mobile network, so users can access the Internet. Specially designed for small screen. A competing standard is the J2ME platform that offers better security and graphics (see *wapforum.org*). |
| Wireless Markup Language (WML) | An XML-based scripting language for creating content for wireless systems. |
| Voice XML | An extension of XML designed to accommodate voice. |

*area networks* (LANs). WANs for mobile computing are known as **wireless wide area networks (WWANs).** The breadth of coverage of a WWAN depends on the transmission media and the wireless generation, which directly affects the availability of services.

A simple mobile system is shown in Figure 4A.1. At the edge of the system are the mobile handsets. A **mobile handset** consists of two parts: terminal equipment that hosts the applications (e.g., a PDA) and a mobile terminal (e.g., a cell phone) that connects to the mobile network.

### WiMax

The WiMax Forum (*wimaxforum.org*) describes **WiMax** as "a standards-based technology enabling the delivery of last mile wireless broadband access as an alternative to cable and DSL." WiMax is essentially an 802.16-based broadband wireless metropolitan-area network (MAN) access standard that promises to deliver voice and data services at distances of up to 30 miles, without the expense of cable or the distance limitations of DSL.

WiMax does not require a clear line of sight to function like satellite. Mobile WiMax enables 3 megabit

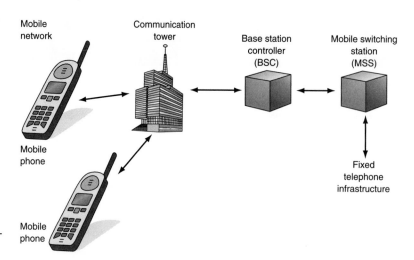

**Figure 4A.1** Mobile system architecture.

per second (Mbps) network access for mobile users because it facilitates real-time applications such as VoIP. Frost & Sullivan (*frost.com*) analysts say that WiMax is responsible for reinvigorating the stagnant broadband wireless access market in the Asia Pacific region. They estimate revenues to increase from $65.3 million at the end of 2006 to $5.4 billion in 2010. The lack of infrastructure in the area helps the WiMax growth potential.

### Transmission Media

Several transmission media can be used for wireless transmission. These media differ in both capabilities and cost. The major ones are shown in Technology Guide 4. For more detail on transmission media, see *ictglobal.com/trans_types.html*.

### Communication Generations of Wireless Wide Area Networks

The success of mobile computing depends on the capabilities of the WWAN communication systems. Four generations of communications technology are discussed in Online File W4.5.

### MUNICIPAL Wi-Fi

**Wi-Fi** is a technology that allows computers to share a network or internet connection wirelessly without the need to connect to a commercial network. Wi-Fi networks beam large chunks of data over short distances using part of the radio spectrum. Municipal Wi-Fi networks are not cheap. The city of Philadelphia debated whether to go forward with its plans to install a wireless network, which would cost the 135-square-mile city $10 million to install, or about $75,000 per square mile. The cost for running the network the first two years would be $5 million.

Wi-Fi networks usually consist of a router, which transmits the signal, and one or more adapters, which receive the signal and are usually attached to computers. More powerful transmitters, which cover a wider area, are known as base stations. See the Wi-Fi Alliance at *wi-fi.org*. Wi-Fi networking standards are:

- **802.11b.** This standard shares spectrum with 2.4 GHz cordless phones, microwave ovens, and many Bluetooth products. Data are transferred at up to 11 megabits per second per channel, at distances up to 300 feet.

- **802.11a.** This standard runs on 12 channels in the 5 GHz spectrum in North America, which reduces interference issues. Data are transferred about five times faster than 802.11b, improving the quality of streaming media. It has extra bandwidth for large files. Since the 802.11a and b standards are not interoperable, data sent from an 802.11b network cannot be accessed by 802.11a networks.

- **802.11g.** This standard runs on three channels in 2.4 GHz spectrum, but at the speed of 802.11a. It is compatible with the 802.11b standard.

### Key Terms for Appendix 4A

802.11a *163*
802.11b *163*
802.11g *163*
Mobile handset *162*
Wi-Fi *163*
WiMax *162*
Wireless wide area networks (WWANs) *162*

### References for Appendix 4A

CNET, "RIM to Launch BlackBerry in Japan," June 8, 2006, *news.com.com/RIM+to+launch+BlackBerry+in+Japan/2100-1039_3-6081480.html* (accessed June 2006).

*Reuters*, "RIM, Taiwan Mobile to Launch BlackBerry This Summer," June 22, 2006.

Telecommunications Industry Association, *2006 Market Review and Forecast*, 2006.

Chapter

# 5

# E-Business and E-Commerce

## Learning Objectives

After studying this chapter, you will be able to:

❶ Describe electronic commerce, its scope, benefits, limitations, and types.

❷ Understand the basics of how online auctions and bartering work.

❸ Describe the major applications of business-to-consumer commerce, including service industries and the major issues faced by e-tailers.

❹ Describe business-to-business applications.

❺ Describe intrabusiness and B2E e-commerce.

❻ Describe e-government activities and consumer-to-consumer e-commerce.

❼ Describe the e-commerce support services, specifically payments and logistics.

❽ Discuss the importance and activities of online advertising.

❾ Discuss some ethical and legal issues relating to e-commerce.

❿ Describe EC failures and strategies for success.

## Integrating *IT*

| ACC | FIN | MKT | POM | HRM | IS | SVC |

# DELL IS USING E-COMMERCE FOR SUCCESS

## The Business Problem/Opportunity

Founded in 1984 by Michael Dell, Dell Computer Corp. (now known as Dell) was the first company to offer personal computers (PCs) via mail order. Dell designed its own PC system and allowed customers to configure their own customized systems using the build-to-order concept (see Appendix 2A) and shipped to them by direct mail. These concepts were, and are, Dell's cornerstone *business models*. By 1993, Dell had become one of the top-five computer makers worldwide, threatening Compaq, which started a price war. At that time, Dell was taking orders by fax and snail mail and losing money. Losses reached over $100 million by 1994. The company was in trouble.

## The Solution: Direct Marketing Online

The commercialization of the Internet in the early 1990s and the introduction of the Web in 1993 provided Dell with an *opportunity* to expand rapidly by selling online. Dell implemented aggressive online order-taking and opened subsidiaries in Europe and Asia. Dell also started to offer additional products on its Web site. This enabled Dell to batter Compaq, and in 1999 Dell became number one in worldwide PC shipments. Today, Dell (*dell.com*) sells about $60 billion a year in computer-related products online, from network switches to printers, employing over 63,000 people.

Dell sells to: individuals for their homes and home offices; small businesses (up to 200 employees); medium and large businesses (over 200 employees); government, education, and health-care organizations.

Sales to the first group are classified as *business-to-consumer* (B2C). Sales to the other three groups are classified as *business-to-business* (B2B). Consumers shop at *dell.com* using online electronic catalogs. The sales are completed using mechanisms described later in this chapter.

In addition, Dell sells refurbished Dell computers and other products in electronic auctions at *dellauction.com*.

Here are Dell's major EC initiatives:

**Business-to-Business.** Most of Dell's sales are to businesses. These sales are facilitated by standard shopping aids (e.g., catalogs, shopping carts, comparison engine, and credit card payments). B2B customers obtain additional help from Dell. Dell provides each of its nearly 100,000 business customers with Premier Dell service.

For example, British Airways (BA) considers Dell to be a strategic supplier. Dell provides notebook and desktop computers to 25,000 BA users. Dell offers two e-procurement services to BA purchasing agents. The more basic service, Premier Dell, allows BA (and other businesses) to browse, buy, and track orders on a Dell Web site customized for the user's requirements. The site enables authorized users to select preconfigured PCs for their business unit or department. This provides automatic requisition and order fulfillment once an authorized user has chosen to buy a PC from Dell. BA has placed the e-procurement tools on their E-Working intranet. This allows authorized staff to purchase PCs through a portal that connects directly into Dell's systems.

**Business-to-Consumer (B2C).** Dell sells direct to individuals from its private marketplace (store). Using fairly standard mechanisms such as electronic catalog, shopping carts, and payment gateway and shipping, any customer can configure and price a desktop, laptop, or other product sold by Dell. Payment must be arranged in advance.

Customers can also participate in auctions of refurbished computers, which are periodically conducted online.

In addition to supporting its business customers with *e-procurement* tools, such as in the case of BA, Dell is using EC in its own procurement. Actually, Dell developed an e-procurement model that it shares with its business partners, such as BA. One aspect of this model is the use of electronic tendering to conduct bids, known as *reverse auctions*. Dell uses electronic tendering when it buys the components for its products.

**E-Collaboration.** Dell has many business partners with which communication and collaboration is necessary. For example, Dell uses shippers such as UPS and FedEx to deliver its computers to individuals. It also uses third-party logistics companies to collect, maintain, and deliver components from its suppliers, and it has many other partners. Dell is using leading-edge technologies such as Web Services to facilitate communication and reduce inventories. Web Services facilitate B2B integration that links customers' existing ERP or procurement systems directly with Dell and other trading partners.

Finally, Dell has a superb communication system with its over 15,000 service providers around the globe.

**E-Customer Service.** Dell uses a number of different tools to provide superb customer service around the clock. To leverage customer relationship management (CRM), a customer service approach that is customer centered is implemented for lasting relationships. Dell provides a virtual help desk for self-diagnosis and service as well as direct access to technical support data. In addition, a phone-based help desk is open 24/7. Product support includes troubleshooting, user guides, upgrades, downloads, news and press releases, FAQs, order status information, a "my account" page, a community forum (to exchange online ideas, information, and experiences), bulletin boards and other customer-to-customer interaction features, training books (at a discount), and much more. Dell keeps a large database of its customers. Using data mining tools, it learns a great deal about its customers and attempts to make them happy. The database is used to improve marketing as well.

**Intrabusiness EC.** To support its build-to-order capabilities, significantly improve its demand-planning and factory-execution accuracy, reduce order-to-delivery time, and enhance customer service, Dell partnered with Accenture to create a high-performance supply chain management solution. Now in place in Dell's plants around the world, the program, which paid for itself five times during the first 12 months of operation, enables Dell to adapt more quickly to rapidly changing technologies and the business environment and maintain its position as a high-performance business.

Dell also has automated its factory scheduling, demand-planning capabilities, and inventory management using information technology and e–supply chain models.

Dell is using many other EC initiatives. For example, you can join Dell's *affiliate program* by placing Dell's banner and logo on your Web site. If a customer comes to your site and clicks on Dell's banner and then purchases an item at Dell, you get 1–4 percent commission for the referral. Another example is EducateU at LearnDell.com, which allows online self-learning about Dell products as well as about many IT and management topics. Finally, using an intranet (*inside.dell.com*), Dell serves its own employees with information they need to do their job better, providing them with customer data, financial reports, product information, training, and much more.

## The Results

Dell has been one of *Fortune*'s top five "Most Admired" companies since 1999, and it continuously advances in the rankings of the Fortune 500 and the Fortune Global 500. Dell has over 100 country-oriented Web sites in many languages, and profits are nearing $4 billion a year. If you had invested $10,000 in Dell's initial public offering (IPO) in 1987, you would be a millionaire just from that investment. Dell actively supports EC research at the University of Texas in Austin (Dell's headquarters are in Austin).

Dell is expanding its business not only in the computer industry, but also in consumer electronics.

*Sources:* Compiled from *dell.com* and *dellauction.com* (accessed October 2006), and from Kraemer and Dedrick (2001) and Rappa (2006).

## Lesson Learned from This Case

Dell exemplifies the major EC business models. First, it pioneered the *direct-marketing model* for PCs, and then it moved online. Furthermore, Dell supplemented its direct marketing with the build-to-order or custom-built model on a large scale (mass customization). In doing so, Dell benefited from the elimination of intermediation by selling direct, from extremely low inventories, and from superb cash flow by getting paid in advance. To meet the large demand for its quality products, Dell is using other EC models, notably e-procurement for improving the purchasing of components, collaborative commerce with its partners, and intrabusiness EC for improving its internal

operations. Finally, Dell uses e-CRM (CRM done online; see Chapter 8 for details) with its customers. Dell believes that the most efficient path to customers is through a direct relationship that minimizes confusion and cost. By successfully using e-commerce models, Dell became a world-class company, winning over all of its competitors. Dell's EC business models have become classic examples of best practices, and they are followed today by many other manufacturers, notably car makers.

This chapter defines EC and lists the types of transactions that are executed in it. Various EC models and the benefits and limitations of EC are also examined.

# 5.1 Overview of E-Business and E-Commerce

**DEFINITIONS AND CONCEPTS**

**Electronic commerce** (EC or e-commerce) describes the process of buying, selling, transferring, serving, or exchanging products, services, or information via computer networks, including the Internet. Some people view the term *commerce* as describing only *transactions* conducted between business partners. When this definition is used, some people find the term *electronic commerce* to be fairly narrow. Thus, many use the term *e-business* instead. **E-business** refers to a broader definition of EC, not just the buying and selling of goods and services, but also servicing customers, collaborating with business partners, conducting e-learning, and conducting electronic transactions within an organization. Others view e-business as the "other than buying and selling" activities on the Internet, such as collaboration and intrabusiness activities.

In this book we use the broadest meaning of electronic commerce, which is basically equivalent to e-business. The two terms *will be used interchangeably* throughout the chapter and the remainder of the text.

**Pure versus Partial EC.** EC can take several forms depending on the *degree of digitization*—the transformation from physical to digital—involved. The degree of digitization can relate to: (1) the product (service) sold, (2) the process, or (3) the delivery agent (or intermediary).

Choi et al. (1997) created a framework that explains the possible configurations of these three dimensions. A product can be physical or digital, the process can be physical or digital, and the delivery agent can be physical or digital. In traditional commerce all three dimensions are physical. Purely physical organizations are referred to as **brick-and-mortar organizations.** In *pure EC* all dimensions are digital. All other combinations that include a mix of digital and physical dimensions are considered EC (but not pure EC).

If there is at least one digital dimension, we consider the situation *partial EC*. For example, buying a shirt at Wal-Mart Online or a book from Amazon.com is partial EC, because the merchandise is physically delivered by a shipper. However, buying an e-book from Amazon.com or a software product from Buy.com is *pure EC*, because the product, its delivery, payment, and transfer agent are all done online. In this book we use the term EC to denote either pure or partial EC.

Note that some pure EC companies add some physical facilities. For example, Expedia.com opened sales offices, and Amazon.com has physical warehouses and allows customers to pick up merchandise at physical locations.

**EC Organizations.** Companies that are engaged only in EC are considered **virtual** (or pure-play) **organizations. Click-and-mortar** (or click-and-brick) **organizations** are those that conduct some e-commerce activities, yet their primary business is done in the physical world, such as Godiva (see Online File W5.1). Gradually, many brick-and-mortar companies are expanding to click-and-mortar ones (e.g., Wal-Mart Online). So, many people expect traditional companies to offer some form of e-commerce, as your bank, airline, or Godiva and Wal-Mart do.

**THE EC LANDSCAPE**

To better understand how EC works, let's look at Figure 5.1. As can be seen in the figure, a company like Dell (labeled "our company") provides products and/or services to customers (individuals or organizations), shown on the right side. To do so, our company buys inputs such as material, parts, and/or services

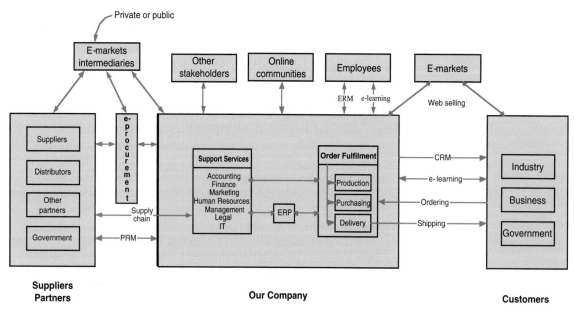

**Figure 5.1** E-Commerce in our company. (*Source:* Drawn by E. Turban.)

from suppliers and other business partners in a procurement process. Processing the inputs is done in its production/operations department. Other departments (e.g., finance, marketing) support the conversion of inputs to outputs and the sale to customers.

The basic idea of EC is to *automate* as many business processes as possible. A process can be order initiation, order fulfillment, procurement of material, manufacturing parts (production), delivery, or providing CRM.

EC activities support selling, buying, and providing relationships, as well as the internal and external transactions involved. This is done by EC mechanisms such as e-markets, e-procurement, and e-CRM as shown in Figure 5.1. Note that the processes in the figure involve several types of transactions.

## TYPES OF E-COMMERCE TRANSACTIONS

E-commerce transactions can be done between various parties. The common types of e-commerce transactions are described below.

- **Business-to-business (B2B).** In B2B transactions, both the sellers and the buyers are business organizations. The vast majority of EC volume is of this type.

- **Collaborative commerce (c-commerce).** In c-commerce, business partners collaborate (rather than buy or sell) electronically. Such collaboration frequently occurs between and among business partners along the supply chain (see Chapter 9).

- **Business-to-consumers (B2C).** In B2C, the sellers are organizations, and the buyers are individuals. B2C is also known as *e-tailing*.

- **Consumer-to-consumer (C2C).** In C2C, an individual sells products or services to other individuals. You also will see the term C2C used as "customer-to-customer." The terms are interchangeable, and both will be used in this book.

- **Business-to-business-to-consumers (B2B2C).** In this case a business sells to a business but delivers the product or service to an individual consumer, such as in Godiva's case (online File W5.1).

- **Consumers-to-businesses (C2B).** In C2B, consumers make known a particular need for a product or service, and suppliers compete to provide the product or service to consumers. An example is Priceline.com, where the customer names a product or service and the desired price, and Priceline tries to find a supplier to fulfill the stated need.
- **Intrabusiness (intraorganizational) commerce.** In this case an organization uses EC internally to improve its operations. A special case of this is known as **B2E (business-to-its-employees) EC,** in which an organization delivers products or services to its employees.
- **Government-to-citizens (G2C) and to others.** In this case a government entity (unit) provides services to its citizens via EC technologies. Government units can do business with other government units **(G2G)** or with businesses **(G2B).**

**EC BUSINESS MODELS**

Each of the above types of transaction is executed in one or more *business models,* the method by which a company generates revenue to sustain itself. For example, in B2B one can sell from catalogs or in auctions. The major business models of EC are summarized in Table 5.1. A complete list is available at *digitalenterprise.org/models/models.html.*

**BRIEF HISTORY AND SCOPE OF EC**

EC applications began in the early 1970s with such innovations as electronic transfer of funds (EFT). However, the applications were limited to large corporations and a few daring small businesses. Then came electronic data interchange (EDI), which automated routine transaction processing and extended EC to all industries. (See Chapter 9 for details about EDI.)

In the early 1990s, EC applications expanded rapidly, following the commercialization of the Internet and the introduction of the Web. A major shakeout in EC activities began in 2000 and lasted about three years; hundreds of dot-com companies went out of business. Since 2003, EC has continued to show steady progress. Today, most organizations are practicing some type of EC transaction.

Over the last 12 years, EC has continuously added products and services. According to Forrester (June 2006), EC retail sales in the United States grew from about $75 billion in 2002 to over $176 billion in 2005 and $211 billion in 2006. In the same period, high-speed Internet connection in the United States grew from 5 million to over 75 million. Also, in addition to buying and selling on the Internet, new services are booming.

### EC Newcomers: Representative Examples

- *Bloggers*—There are millions of them.
- *Chemistry* will find you a perfect match if Match.com will not.
- *Craigslist* is a popular classifieds meeting place.
- *Flickr*—This is a place for sharing photos and putting together a photo album (a Yahoo! company).
- *Grouper* allows users to share photos, videos, and music on their PCs.
- *Intrade*—You can invest in current events—try it!
- *MySpace* is a hip online hangout for over 50 million visitors.
- *Pandora*—Customize and share your own radio station.
- *Wikipedia* provides a free online encyclopedia and answers to "what is?"

| TABLE 5.1 | E-Commerce Business Models |
|---|---|
| **EC Model** | **Description** |
| **Online direct marketing** | Manufacturers or retailers sell directly online to customers. Very efficient for digital products and services. Can allow for product or service customization. |
| **Electronic tendering system** | Businesses conduct online tendering, requesting quotes from suppliers. Used in B2B with a *reverse auction* mechanism (see Section 5.2). |
| **Online auctions** | Companies or individuals run auctions of various types on the Internet. Fast and inexpensive way to sell or liquidate items. |
| **Name-your-own-price** | Customers decide how much they are willing to pay. An intermediary (e.g., Priceline.com) tries to match a provider. |
| **Find-the-best-price** | Customers specify a need; an intermediary (e.g., Hotwire.com) compares providers and shows the lowest price. Customers must accept the offer in a short time or may lose the deal. |
| **Affiliate marketing** | Vendors ask partners to place logos (or banners) on partner's site. If customers click on logo, go to vendor's site, and buy, then vendor pays commissions to partners. (See *performics.com*.) |
| **Viral marketing** | Receivers of e-mails send the received or related information about your product to their friends (word-of-mouth). (Be on the watch for viruses.) |
| **Group purchasing (e-co-ops)** | Small buyers aggregate several demands to get a large volume; then the buying group conducts tendering or negotiates a low price (see *njnonprofits.org/groupbuy.html*). |
| **Product customization** | Customers use the Internet to self-configure products or services. Sellers then price them and fulfill them quickly (*build-to-order*). |
| **Electronic marketplaces and exchanges** | Transactions are conducted efficiently (more information to buyers and sellers, less transaction cost) in virtual marketplaces (private or public). |
| **Value-chain integrators** | Integrators aggregate information and package it for customers, vendors, or others in the supply chain. |
| **Value-chain service providers** | Service provider offers specialized services in supply chain operations such as providing logistics or payment services. |
| **Information brokers and matching services** | Brokers provide services related to EC information such as trust, content, matching buyers and sellers, evaluating vendors and products. |
| **Bartering online** | Intermediary administers online exchange of surplus products and/or company receives "points" for its contribution, and the points can be used to purchase other needed items. |
| **Deep discounters** | Company (e.g., Half.com) offers deep price discounts. Appeals to customers who consider only price in their purchasing decisions. |
| **Membership** | Only members can use the services provided, including access to certain information, conducting trades, etc. (e.g., Egreetings.com). |
| **Supply-chain improvers** | Organizations restructure supply chains to hubs or other configurations. Increases collaboration, reduces delays, and smoothes supply chain flows. |
| **E-Classifieds** | Presentation of items for sale at fixed prices. Popular sites are *craigslist.com* and *classifieds2000.com*. |

Many of these sites target certain groups such as teenagers, senior citizens, women, or students (see *A Closer Look 5.1*). Because many of these Web sites offer social networking, they do not sell (or sell minimally) and need a sponsor to pay their expenses. For example, MySpace is owned by News Corporation, Match.com by Yahoo!, and eBay owns 25 percent of Craigslist.com.

CarnivalConnections is an example of how a socially oriented site is sponsored by a company.

# A Closer Look 5.1

## Interesting Student-Targeted Web Sites

Including high schools and universities, there are millions of students in the United States and every year new students join schools while others join the workforce. No wonder that many Web sites were developed for such a large population. Note that college students spend more than $200 billion a year (*harrisinteractive.com*), making students' sites attractive to online advertisers and marketers. Here are a few examples:

- *Facebook* is a popular place for students to socialize (available to nonstudents as of summer 2006).
- *Swook* is one of several sites that enables students to exchange textbooks.
- *Collegerecruiting.com* matches students with universities for best admission and helps you write your resume.

- *RateMyProfessor.com* provides a free message board where students can post opinions about college professors. The site attracts 2 million new visitors each month.
- *Finaid.com* is a comprehensive site about getting financial aid with all related information, dozens of calculators, and information about college admissions and jobs.
- *Powerstudents.com* combines information from over 20 leading student-oriented Web sites from searchable scholarships to file sharing.
- *Collegerecruiter.com* helps you find an internship or a job once you have graduated.

**Example: CarnivalConnections in Action.** Carnival Cruise Line is sponsoring a social networking site (*carnivalconnections.com*) that attracts cruise fans to the site to exchange opinions, get organized in groups for a trip, and much more. It cost the company $300,000 to set up the site, but the company anticipates covering the cost through increased business. For details see Fass (2006).

**The Scope of EC.** Figure 5.2 describes the broad field of e-commerce. As can be seen in the figure, there are many *EC applications* (top of the figure); most of these are shown throughout the book. Figure 5.2 shows that the EC applications are supported by an *infrastructure* (bottom part), which includes hardware, software, and networks, ranging from browsers to multimedia, and also by the following five support areas (shown as pillars in the middle):

1. **People.** They are the sellers, buyers, intermediaries, information systems specialists and other employees, and any external participants.
2. **Public policy.** There are legal and other policy and regulating issues, such as privacy protection and taxation, that are determined by the government and by international agreements.
3. **Marketing and advertising.** EC usually requires the support of marketing and advertising, like any other business. This is especially important in online transactions where the buyers and sellers usually do not know each other.
4. **Support services.** Many services, ranging from payments to order fulfillment and content creation, are needed to support EC.
5. **Business partnerships.** Joint ventures, e-marketplaces, and business partnerships are common in EC. These occur especially throughout the supply chain (i.e., the collaboration between a company and its suppliers, customers, and other partners).

All of these EC components require good coordination and *management practices* to unify the applications, infrastructure, and support. This means that companies

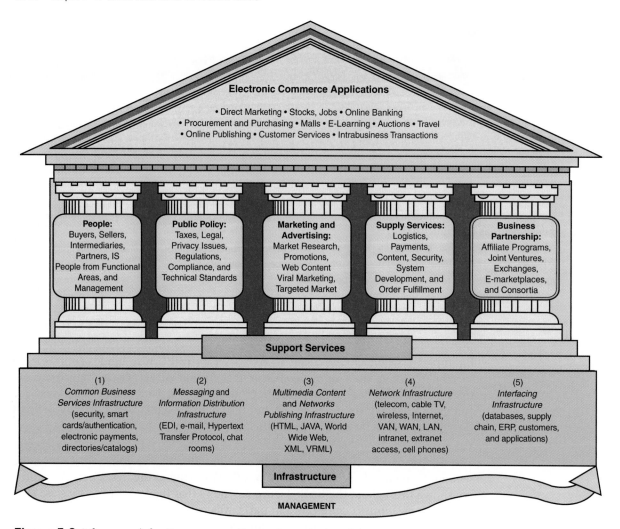

**Figure 5.2** A framework for E-commerce. (*Source:* Drawn by E. Turban.)

need to plan, coordinate, organize, motivate, devise strategy, and restructure processes as needed, that is, to manage the EC.

**BENEFITS AND LIMITATIONS OF E-COMMERCE**

Few innovations in human history encompass as many benefits to organizations, individuals, and society as does e-commerce. These benefits will increase significantly as EC expands. The major benefits are listed in Table 5.2 (page 173).

Counterbalancing its many benefits, EC has some limitations, both technological and nontechnological, which have slowed its growth and acceptance. The major limitations are listed in Table 5.3 (page 173). As time passes, the limitations, especially the technological ones, will lessen or be overcome. In addition, appropriate planning can minimize the negative impact of some of them.

Despite its limitations, e-commerce has made very rapid progress. Also, various B2B activities, e-auctions, e-government, e-learning, and some B2C activities are ballooning. As experience accumulates and technology improves, the ratio of EC benefits to cost will increase, resulting in an even greater rate of EC adoption.

| TABLE 5.2 | Benefits of E-Commerce |
|---|---|

**To Organizations**

- Expands a company's selling and buying opportunities to national and international markets. With minimal capital outlay, a company can quickly locate more customers, the best suppliers, and the most suitable business partners worldwide.
- Enables companies to procure material and services from other countries, rapidly and at less cost.
- Shortens or even eliminates marketing distribution channels, making products cheaper and vendors' profits higher.
- Decreases (by as much as 90 percent) the cost of creating, processing, distributing, storing, and retrieving digitizable products and services (e.g., music, software).
- Allows lower inventories by facilitating "pull"-type supply chain management (see Online Appendix 2A). This allows product customization and reduces inventory costs.
- Lowers telecommunications costs because the Internet is much cheaper than value-added networks (VANs).
- Helps some small businesses compete against large companies.
- Enables a very specialized niche market (e.g., *cattoys.com*).

**To Customers**

- Frequently provides less expensive products and services by allowing consumers to conduct quick online searches and comparisons (e.g., *Froogle.com*).
- Gives consumers more choices in selecting products and vendors.
- Enables customers to shop or make other transactions 24 hours a day, from almost any location.
- Retrieves relevant and detailed information in seconds.
- Enables consumers to get customized products or services, from PCs to cars, at competitive prices.
- Makes it possible for people to work and study at home.
- Makes possible electronic auctions that benefit buyers and sellers.
- Allows consumers to interact in electronic communities and to exchange ideas and compare experiences.

**To Society**

- Enables individuals to work at home and to do less traveling, resulting in less road traffic, less energy use, and less air pollution.
- Allows some merchandise to be sold at lower prices, thereby increasing people's standard of living.
- Enables people in developing countries and rural areas to enjoy products and services that otherwise are not available. This includes opportunities to learn professions and even earn college degrees, or to receive better medical care.
- Facilitates delivery of public services, such as government entitlements, reducing the cost of distribution and chance of fraud, and increasing the quality of social services, police work, health care, and education.

| TABLE 5.3 | Limitations of E-Commerce |
|---|---|

| Technological Limitations | Nontechnological Limitations |
|---|---|
| • Lack of universally accepted standards for quality, security, and reliability. | • Some unresolved legal issues (see Section 5.7). |
| • Insufficient telecommunications bandwidth. | • Lack of national and international government regulations and industry standards. |
| • Still-evolving software development tools. | • Lack of mature methodologies for measuring benefits of and justifying EC. |
| • Difficulties in integrating the Internet and EC applications and software with some existing (especially legacy) applications and databases. | • Many sellers and buyers waiting for EC to stabilize before they take part. |
| • Need for special Web servers in addition to the network servers. | • Customer resistance to changing from a real to a virtual store. Many people do not yet sufficiently trust paperless, faceless transactions. |
| • Expensive and/or inconvenient Internet accessibility for many would-be users. | • Perception that EC is expensive and unsecured. |
| | • An insufficient number (critical mass) of sellers and buyers exists for many EC products and services. |

## 5.2 Major EC Mechanisms

The major mechanisms for buying and selling on the Internet are electronic markets, electronic catalogs, electronic auctions, and online bartering. (Other mechanisms— e-storefronts, e-malls, and exchanges—are described later; see Sections 5.3 and 5.5.)

**ELECTRONIC MARKETS**

The major place for conducting EC transactions is the electronic market (e-market). An **e-market** is a virtual marketplace in which sellers and buyers meet and conduct different types of transactions. The functions of e-market are the same as those of a physical marketplace; however, computerized systems tend to make markets much more efficient by providing more updated information to buyers and sellers. The functions of e-markets are provided in Online File W5.2. The major types of such markets are described in Section 5.4.

**ELECTRONIC CATALOGS AND CLASSIFIEDS**

Catalogs have been printed on paper for generations. Electronic catalogs on CD-ROM and the Internet have gained popularity. Electronic catalogs consist of a product database, directory and search capabilities, and a presentation function. They are the backbone of most e-commerce sites. For merchants, the objective of electronic catalogs is to advertise and promote products and services. For the customer, the purpose of such catalogs is to provide a source of information on products and services.

For types of catalogs and a comparison of paper and online catalogs, see Online File W5.3.

**ELECTRONIC AUCTIONS (E-AUCTIONS)**

An **auction** is a competitive process in which either a seller solicits bids from buyers or a buyer solicits bids from sellers. The primary characteristic of auctions, whether offline or online, is that prices are determined dynamically by competitive bidding. Auctions have been an established method of commerce for generations, and they are well-suited to deal with products and services for which conventional marketing channels are ineffective or inefficient. Electronic auctions generally increase revenues for sellers by broadening the customer base and shortening the cycle time of the auction. Buyers generally benefit from e-auctions by the opportunity to bargain for lower prices and the convenience of not having to travel to an auction site to "attend" the auction. They can also find rare and collector's items online. Additional benefits of electronic auctions are shown in Online File W5.4.

The Internet provides an efficient infrastructure for executing auctions at lower administrative cost and with many more involved sellers and buyers. Individual consumers and corporations can participate in this growing form of e-commerce. There are several types of electronic auctions, each with its motives and procedures. Auctions are divided here into two major types: *forward* auctions and *reverse* auctions.

**Forward Auctions.** **Forward auctions** are auctions that *sellers* use as a selling channel to many potential buyers. Usually, items are placed at a special site for auction, and buyers will bid continuously for the items. The highest bidder wins the items. Sellers and buyers can be individuals or businesses. The popular auction site eBay.com conducts mostly forward auctions.

There are two types of forward e-auctions. One is to *liquidate* existing inventory, the other one is to *increase marketing outreach and efficiency*. Customers in the first type seek the lowest price on widely available goods or services; customers in the second type seek access to unique products or services. Online File W5.5 graphically demonstrates these two types of forward auctions.

**Reverse Auctions.** In **reverse auctions,** there is one buyer, usually an organization, that wants to buy a product or a service. Suppliers are invited to submit bids. Online bidding is much faster than conventional bidding, and it usually attracts many more bidders. The reverse auction is the most common auction model for large purchases (in terms of either quantities or price). Everything else being equal, the lowest-price bidder wins the auction. Governments and large corporations frequently mandate this approach for procurements (known as request for quotes.), which may provide considerable savings.

Auctions are used in B2C, B2B, C2B, e-government, and C2C commerce, and they are becoming popular in many countries. The Internet opens many opportunities for e-auctions. Auctions can be conducted from the seller's site, the buyer's site, or from a third party's site. For example, as described in *IT at Work 5.1*, eBay, the

# IT at Work 5.1

## EBay—World's Largest Auction Site

EBay (*ebay.com*) is the world's largest auction site, and one of the most profitable e-businesses. The successful online auction house has its roots in a 50-year-old novelty item—Pez candy dispensers. Pamela Kerr, an avid collector of Pez dispensers, came up with the idea of trading them over the Internet. When she shared this idea with her boyfriend (now her husband), Pierre Omidyar, he was instantly struck with the soon-to-be-famous e-business auction concept.

In 1995, the Omidyars started the company, later renamed eBay, that has since become the premier online auction house. The business model of eBay was to provide an electronic infrastructure for conducting mostly C2C auctions, although it caters to businesses (sellers and buyers) as well. Technology replaces the traditional auctioneer as the intermediary between buyers and sellers.

On eBay, people can buy and sell just about anything. It has millions of unique auctions in progress and over 500,000 new items are added each day. The company collects a submission fee upfront, plus a commission as a percentage of the sale amount. The submission fee is based on the amount of exposure you want your item to receive. For example, a higher fee is required if you would like to be among the "featured auctions" in your specific product category, and an even higher fee if you want your item to be listed on the eBay home page under Featured Items.

The seller must specify a minimum opening bid. Sellers might set the opening bid lower than the *reserve price*, a minimum acceptable bid price, in order to generate bidding activity. If a successful bid is made, the seller and the buyer negotiate the payment method, shipping details, warranty, and other particulars. EBay serves as a liaison between the parties; it is the interface through which sellers and buyers can conduct business.

After a few years of successful operations and tens of millions of loyal users, eBay started to do B2C (e-tailing), mostly in fixed prices (known as classifieds). By 2003, eBay operated several specialty sites, such as eBay Motors. eBay also operates a *business exchange* in which small- and medium-sized

enterprises can buy and sell new and used merchandise, in B2B or B2C modes. In addition, *half.com*, the famous discount e-tailer, is now part of eBay and so is PayPal.com, the person-to-person payment company. EBay has become so popular that it has led to academic recognition with the creation of a new course at the University of Birmingham (U.K.). The course, "Buying and Selling on eBay.co.uk," offers a step-by-step guide to trading online (Lyons, 2004).

A special feature is eBay Stores. These stores are rented to individuals and companies. The renting companies can use these stores to sell from catalogs or conduct auctions. In 2002, eBay introduced the Business Marketplace, located at *ebay.com/businessmarketplace*. This site brings together all business-related listings on eBay to one destination, making it easier for small businesses to find the equipment and supplies they need.

Many individuals are using eBay Stores and Marketplace to make a living. Some of them are very successful. Holden (2006) describes how 10 different entrepreneurs tapped into the power of eBay and are making millions.

EBay operates *globally*, permitting international trades to take place. Country-specific sites are located in over 25 countries. Buyers from more than 160 other countries also participate. Finally, eBay operates locally: It has over 60 local sites in the United States that enable users to easily find items located near them, to browse through items of local interest, and to meet face-to-face to conclude transactions. As of winter 2005, eBay had over 180 million registered users. According to company financial statements, eBay reports $44 billion in sales in 2005, and it expects net revenue of $5.9 billion in 2006.

For more on eBay, see *digitalenterprise.org/cases/ebay.html*.

*Sources:* Compiled from press releases and descriptions at *eBay.com* (2002–2006); Staff (2005) and Schonfield (2005), and from Holden (2006).

*For Further Exploration:* Does eBay's 2003 change of business model, from pure auctions to adding classifieds and e-tailing, make sense? Why are wireless auctions promoted?

best-known third-party site, offers hundreds of thousands of different items in several types of auctions. Over 300 other major companies, including Amazon.com and Dellauction.com, offer online auctions as well.

**BARTERING AND NEGOTIATIONS**

Related to auctions is **electronic bartering,** the electronically supported exchange of goods or services *without a monetary transaction.* Electronic bartering is done through means of individual-to-individual bartering ads that appear in some newsgroups, bulletin boards, and chat rooms. There also are several intermediaries that arrange for corporate e-bartering (e.g., *barterbrokers.com*). These intermediaries try to match online partners to a barter transaction. Online negotiation can be done via sites like *offer.com*.

Until recently, e-bartering matched only two individuals at a time who basically exchanged products or services (e.g., see Peerflix, Bookins, and La La). A new company, Swaptree (*swaptree.com*), developed a mechanism that allows up to four traders to exchange products/services in one transaction (initially CDs, videogames, books, and DVDs). Each trade lists what they have to give and what they need. Swaptree does the matching, assuming all items have the same value. Swaptree.com provides the service for free and plans to make money from advertising. For details see Copeland (2006).

# 5.3 Business-to-Consumer Applications

B2C E-commerce began when companies like Amazon.com and Godiva.com (Online File W5.1) started selling directly to consumers using the Internet. Here we will look at some of the major categories of B2C applications, which are expected to exceed $1 trillion by 2007.

**ELECTRONIC RETAILING MECHANISMS: STOREFRONTS AND MALLS**

For generations home shopping from catalogs has flourished, and television shopping channels have been attracting millions of shoppers for more than two decades. Shopping online offers an alternative to catalog and television shopping. **Electronic retailing (e-tailing)** is the direct sale of products and services through electronic storefronts or electronic malls, usually designed around an electronic catalog format and/or auctions. For the difference between retailing and e-tailing, see Online File W5.6 and also Lee and Brandyberry (2003).

Like any mail-order shopping experience, e-commerce enables you to buy from anywhere, and to do so 24 hours a day, 7 days a week. However, EC offers a wider variety of products and services, including the most unique items, often at lower prices. Furthermore, within seconds, shoppers can get very detailed supplementary information on products and can easily search for and compare competitors' products and prices. Finally, using the Internet, buyers can find hundreds of thousands of products and sellers.

Both goods and services are sold online. Goods that are bought most often online are computers and computer-related items, office supplies, books and magazines, CDs, cassettes, movies and videos, office supplies, clothing and shoes, and toys. Services that are bought most often online include entertainment, travel services, stocks and bonds trading, electronic banking, insurance, and job matching. (Services will be presented as a separate topic later in this section.) Directories and hyperlinks from other Web sites and intelligent search agents help buyers find the best stores and products to match their needs.

Two popular B2C shopping mechanisms online are electronic storefronts and electronic malls.

**Electronic Storefronts.**  Hundreds of thousands of solo storefronts can be found on the Internet, each with its own Internet address (URL), at which orders can be placed. Called **electronic storefronts,** they may be an *extension* of physical stores such as Home Depot, The Sharper Image, Godiva.com, or Wal-Mart. Or they may be new businesses started by entrepreneurs who saw a niche on the Web, such as CDNow.com, Uvine.com, Restaurant.com, and Alloy.com. Besides being used by retailers (e.g., Officedepot.com), storefronts also are used by manufacturers (e.g., Dell.com). Retailers' and manufacturers' storefronts may sell to individuals (B2C) and/or to organizations (B2B).

**Electronic Malls.**  An **electronic mall,** also known as a cybermall or e-mall, is a collection of individual shops under one Internet address. The basic idea of an electronic mall is the same as that of a regular shopping mall—to provide a one-stop shopping place that offers many products and services. Each cybermall may include thousands of vendors. For example, *shopping.msn.com* include tens of thousands of products from thousands of vendors. A special mall that provides discounts and cash back is *cashbackstores.net.*

Two types of malls exist. First, there are *referral malls* (e.g., *hawaii.com/market place*). You cannot buy in such a mall, but instead you are automatically transferred from the mall to a participating storefront. In the second type of mall (e.g., *shopping.yahoo.com*), you can actually make a purchase. At this type of mall, you might shop from several stores but you make only one purchase transaction at the end; an *electronic shopping cart* enables you to gather items from various vendors and pay for them all together in one transaction. (The mall organizer, such as Yahoo, takes a commission from the sellers for this service.)

As is true for vendors that locate in a physical shopping mall, a vendor that locates in an e-mall gives up a certain amount of independence. Its success depends on the popularity of the mall, as well as on its own marketing efforts. On the other hand, malls generate streams of prospective customers who otherwise might never have stopped by the individual store. For interesting malls, see *shopping-headquarters.com* and *choicemall.com.*

**E-TAILING: THE ESSENTIALS**

The concept of *retailing* implies sales of goods and/or services from many manufacturers to many individual customers. When it is done online, it is referred to as e-tailing. One of the most interesting properties of e-tailing is the ability to offer *customized* products and services to individual customers at a reasonable price and fairly fast (as done by Dell Computer). Many sites (e.g., *nike.com* and *lego.com*) offer product *self-configuration* from their B2C portals. The most well known B2C site is *Amazon.com,* whose story is presented in *IT at Work 5.2.* A potential major competitor is *Wal-Mart.com* (see Online File W5.7).

**ONLINE SERVICE INDUSTRIES**

Selling books, toys, computers, and most other products on the Internet may reduce vendors' selling costs by 20 to 40 percent. Further reduction is difficult to achieve because the products must be delivered physically. Only a few products (such as software or music) can be digitized to be delivered online for additional savings. On the other hand, delivery of *services,* such as buying an airline ticket or buying stocks or insurance online, can be done 100 percent electronically, with considerable cost reduction potential. This is why the airlines are pushing self-service e-tickets and your stock broker wants you to get your confirmations electronically. Therefore, online delivery of services is growing very rapidly.

We will take a quick look here at the leading online service industries: banking, trading of securities (stocks, bonds), job matching, travel services, and real estate.

# *IT* at Work 5.2

## Amazon.Com: The King of E-Tailing

MKT    GLOBAL

Entrepreneur and e-tailing pioneer Jeff Bezos, envisioning the huge potential for retail sales over the Internet, selected books as the most logical product for e-tailing. In July 1995, Bezos started Amazon.com, offering books via an electronic catalog from its Web site. Key features offered by the Amazon.com "superstore" were broad selection, low prices, easy searching and ordering, useful product information and personalization, secure payment systems, and efficient order fulfillment. Early on, recognizing the importance of order fulfillment, Amazon.com invested hundreds of millions of dollars in building physical warehouses designed for shipping small packages to hundreds of thousands of customers.

Over the years since its founding, Amazon.com has continually enhanced its business model by improving the customer's experience. For example, customers can personalize their Amazon accounts and manage orders online with the patented "One-Click" order feature. This personalized service includes an *electronic wallet,* which enables shoppers to place an order in a secure manner without the need to enter their address, credit card number, and so forth, each time they shop. One-Click also allows customers to view their order status and make changes on orders that have not yet entered the shipping process.

In addition, Amazon has been adding services and alliances to attract customers to make more purchases. For example, the company now offers specialty stores, such as its professional and technical store. It also is expanding its offerings beyond books. For example, in June 2002 it became an authorized dealer of Sony Corp. for selling Sony products online. Today you can find almost any product that sells well on the Internet, ranging from beauty aids to sporting goods to cars.

Amazon has more than 500,000 affiliate partners that refer customers to Amazon.com. Amazon pays a 3 to 5 percent commission on any resulting sale. In yet another extension of its services, in September 2001 Amazon signed an agreement with Borders Group Inc., providing Amazon's users with the option of picking up books, CDs, and so on at Borders' physical bookstores. Amazon.com also is becoming a Web-fulfillment contractor for national chains such as Target and Circuit City.

In January 2002, Amazon.com declared its first-ever profit—for the 2001 fourth quarter; 2003 was the first year with profit in each quarter. For more on Amazon, see *digitalenterprise.org/cases/amazon.html.*

*Sources:* Compiled from C. Bayers (2002), and from Daisey (2002).

*For Further Exploration:* What are the critical success factors for Amazon.com? What advantages does it have over other e-tailers (e.g., *Wal-Mart.com* or see *barnesandnoble.com*)? What is the purpose of the alliances Amazon.com has made?

**Cyberbanking.** Electronic banking, also known as **cyberbanking,** includes various banking activities conducted from home, a business, or on the road instead of at a physical bank location. Electronic banking has capabilities ranging from paying bills to applying for a loan. It saves time and is convenient for customers. For banks, it offers an inexpensive alternative to branch banking (for example, about 2 cents' cost per transaction versus $1.07 at a physical branch) and a chance to enlist remote customers. Many conventional banks now offer online banking, and some use EC as a major competitive strategy. In addition to regular banks with added online services, we are seeing the emergence of *virtual banks,* dedicated solely to Internet transactions, such as *netbank.com.*

**International and Multiple-Currency Banking.** International banking and the ability to handle trading in multiple currencies are critical for international trade. Transfers of electronic funds and electronic letters of credit are important services in international banking. An example of support for EC global trade is provided by TradeCard (*tradecard.com*) in conjunction with MasterCard. Banks and companies such as Oanda also provide currency conversion of over 160 currencies. Although some international retail purchasing can be done by giving a credit card number, other transactions may require cross-border banking support. For example, Hong Kong and Shanghai Bank (*hsbc.com.hk*) has developed a special system (called Hexagon) to provide electronic banking in 60 countries. Using this system, the bank has leveraged its reputation and infrastructure in the developing economies of Asia, to rapidly become a major international bank without developing an extensive new branch network.

**Online Securities Trading.** In Korea, more than half of stock traders are using the Internet for their trades. Why? Because it makes a lot of dollars and "sense": An online trade typically costs the trader between $5 and $15, compared to an average fee of $100 from a full-service broker and $25 from a discount broker. Orders can be placed from anywhere, any time, even from your cell phone, and there is no waiting on busy telephone lines. Furthermore, the chance of making mistakes is small because online trading does away with oral communication of orders. Investors can find on the Web a considerable amount of information regarding specific companies or mutual funds in which to invest (e.g., *money.cnn.com, bloomberg.com*).

**FIN**

*Example.* Let's say that you have an account with Charles Schwab. You access Schwab's Web site (*schwab.com*) from your PC or your Internet-enabled mobile device, enter your account number and password to access your personalized Web page, and then click on "stock trading." Using a menu, you enter the details of your order (buy or sell, margin or cash, price limit, market order, etc.). The computer tells you the current "ask" and "bid" prices, much as a broker would do on the telephone, and you can approve or reject the transaction. Some well-known companies that offer only online trading are E*Trade, and Ameritrade.

However, both online banking and securities trading require tight security. Otherwise, your money could be at risk. (See Online File W5.8 for an example.) Most online banks and stock traders protect you with ID numbers and passwords. Yet even this may not be secure enough. See Section 5.6 on how to improve online security.

**The Online Job Market.** The Internet offers a promising environment for job seekers and for companies searching for hard-to-find employees. Thousands of companies and government agencies advertise available positions, accept résumés, and take applications via the Internet. The online job market is especially effective and active for technology-oriented jobs (e.g., *dice.com*).

The online job market is used by job seekers to reply online to employment ads, to place résumés on various sites, and to use recruiting firms (e.g., *monster.com, jobdirect.com, jobcenter.com*). Companies who have jobs to offer advertise openings on their Web sites or search the bulletin boards of recruiting firms. In many countries governments must advertise job openings on the Internet. In addition, hundreds of job-placement brokers and related services are active on the Web. (You can get help from *jobweb.com* or *brassring.com* to write your résumé.)

**Travel Services.** The Internet is an ideal place to plan, explore, and economically arrange almost any trip. Online travel services allow you to purchase airline tickets, reserve hotel rooms, and rent cars. Most sites also offer a fare-tracker feature that sends you e-mail messages about low-cost flights to your favorite destinations or from your home city. Examples of comprehensive online travel services are Expedia.com, Travelocity.com, and Orbitz.com. Services are also provided online by all major airline vacation services, large conventional travel agencies, car rental agencies, hotels (e.g., *hotels.com*), and tour companies. Priceline.com allows you to set a price you are willing to pay for an airline ticket or hotel accommodations and then attempts to find a vendor that will match your price. A similar service offered by Hotwire.com tries to find the lowest available price for you.

**Real Estate.** Real estate transactions are ideal for e-commerce. You can view many properties on the screen, and sort and organize properties according to your preferences and decision criteria. In some locations, brokers allow the use of real estate databases only from inside their offices, but considerable information is now available on the Internet. For example, Realtor.com allows you to search a database of over 2.5 million homes across the United States. The database is composed of local "multiple listings" of all available properties, in hundreds of locations. Those who are looking for an apartment can try Apartments.com or Rents.com. Housevalues.com offers many services at several URLs (see Internet Exercise #9).

## CUSTOMER SERVICE

Whether an organization is selling to organizations or to individuals, in many cases a competitive edge is gained by providing superb customer service, which is part of CRM (Chapter 9). In e-commerce, customer service becomes even more critical, since customers and merchants do not meet face-to-face.

**Phases in the Customer Service Life Cycle.** Customer service should be approached as a business life cycle process, with the following four phases:

**Phase 1: Requirements.** Assist the customer to determine needs by providing photographs of a product, video presentations, textual descriptions, articles or reviews, sound bites on a CD, or downloadable demonstration files. Also use intelligent agents to make requirements suggestions and help in comparing other product/vendor attributes (e.g., see *froogle.google.com*).

**Phase 2: Acquisition.** Help the customer acquire a product or service (online order entry, negotiations, closing of sale, and delivery).

**Phase 3: Ownership.** Support the customer on an ongoing basis (interactive online user groups, online technical support, FAQs (frequently asked questions) and answers, resource libraries, newsletters, and online renewal of subscriptions).

**Phase 4: Retirement.** Help the client dispose of a service or product (online resale, classified ads).

Many activities can be conducted in each of these phases. For example, when an airline offers information such as flight schedules and fare quotes on its Web site, it is supporting phases 1 and 2. Similarly, when computer vendors provide electronic help desks for their customers, they are supporting phase 3. Dell will help you to auction your obsolete computer, and Amazon.com will help you to sell used books. These are activities that support phase 4.

*Example:* Fidelity Investments provides investors with "the right tools to make their own best investment decisions." The site (*fidelity.com*) has several sections, which include daily updates of financial news, information about Fidelity's mutual funds, material for interactive investment and retirement planning, and brokerage services. This is an example of support given to phase 1 in the online selling of services. The site also helps customers buy Fidelity's products (phase 2), handle their accounts (phase 3), and sell their securities (phase 4).

**E-Entertainment.** During the last few years, we saw an explosion of e-entertainment on the Web. Some is free and some for fee. Some of the entertainment is pure EC and some enhances a click-and-mortar business such as that of Netflix (*IT at Work 5.3*).

**Customization and Personalization.** A major benefit of EC is its ability to offer product and service customization or personalization at an affordable cost. Using the build-to-order concept, a manufacturer can offer you a product of your choice, as Dell is doing. Of course, the product/service is made of standard components in most cases. This is why it can be offered at a low price.

# *IT* at Work 5.3

## Netflix Gains High Customer Satisfaction from DVD Recommendations

**The Problem.** Netflix (*netflix.com*) is an online DVD rental company with more than 4.9 million subscribers in 2006. It has an inventory of over 60,000 titles. (A typical neighborhood video store generally has less than 3,000 titles, with multiple copies available only for a fraction of these titles.) Netflix distributes a million DVDs each day. (See *digitalenterprise.org/cases/netflix.html*.)

Netflix introduced a monthly subscription model to video rentals. The model is extremely successful. EC is used not only to provide the online catalog and take orders, but also to help customers select videos that they did not even know about.

A problem with the rapid increase of DVD rental was that there were so many titles that customers often had difficulty sorting out the ones that they like. In most cases, they picked up the popular ones, which increased the need to maintain more and more copies of the same title; and some less popular titles were not selling well, even though they matched certain customers' preference very well. Finding the right titles for customers and managing the right level of inventory became critical.

**The Solution.** Netflix reacted successfully to the problem by taking advantage of a recommendation intelligent agent (Chapter 12) called CineMatch, a combination of 29,000 unique lines of code and a database of 180 million film ratings. With the recommendation system, Netflix tells subscribers which titles they'll probably like. The utilization of the recommender is based on the assumption that movie viewers watch the same narrow range of big-budget films only because they don't know any better. The service is free.

CineMatch doesn't focus on the mass market; it caters to the individual. Netflix encourages subscribers to rate the movies they've viewed (each viewer rates about 200 movies in a five-year period), and CineMatch recommends titles similar to those well liked—regardless of a film's popularity at the box office. Netflix subscribers also can invite one another to become "friends" and make movie recommendations, peek

at one another's rental lists, and see how other subscribers have rated other movies. All these personalized functions make the online rental store very customer friendly.

**The Benefits.** The major benefits are:

- **The company has seen a very fast growth in sales and membership.**
- **Increased customer satisfaction and loyalty.**
- **Broaden title coverage.** Sixty percent of the movies Netflix customers rent are recommended to them on the site. This decreases demand for popular new releases whose revenue-sharing agreements require larger payouts for such films by Netflix.
- **Better understanding of customer preference.** Netflix's recommendation system collected more than two million ratings forms from subscribers to add to its huge database of users' likes and dislikes. This valuable information helps the company make much more accurate predictions of customer interests.
- **Fast membership growth.** The recommendation is based on the premise that the most reliable prediction for how much a customer will like a movie is what he or she thought of other movies. The company credits the system's ability to make automated yet accurate recommendations as a major factor in its growth from 600,000 subscribers in 2002 to nearly five million today.

*Sources:* Compiled from Flynn (2006); Null (2003); and from *netflix.com* (accessed June 2006).

*For Further Exploration:* Do you like a Web site to make recommendations for when you visit a physical video store such as Blockbuster, or do you prefer to listen to a person? How about recommendations from an online rental store such as Netflix? Why do you like or dislike them? What about downloading the movies from Movielink and CinemaNow? You pay much more, but you download the movie in an hour and it is yours to keep!

For example, Motorola gathers customer needs for a pager or a cellular phone, transmits the customer's specifications electronically to the manufacturing plant where the device is manufactured, and then sends the finished product to the customer within a day. General Motors and other car manufacturers use the same approach in building their products. Customers can use the Web to design or configure products for themselves. For example, customers can use the Web to design T-shirts, furniture, cars, jewelry, and even a Swatch watch. With the use of mass-customization methods, the cost of customized products is at or slightly above the comparable retail price of standard products. Figure 5.3 shows how customers can order customized Nike shoes.

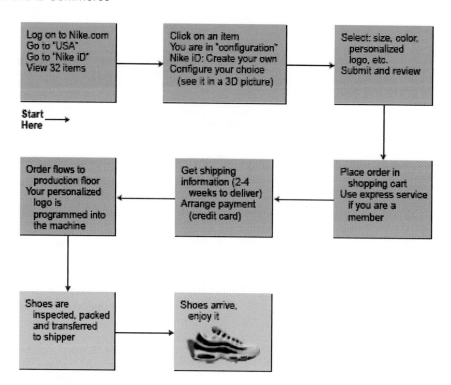

**Figure 5.3** How customization is done online: The case of Nike shoes.

According to *Business 2.0*, Timberland Boot Studio gets three times as many hits on their customized boots (allowing different leathers and colors), and Lands' End is enjoying more repeat customers and higher sales on their customized product online (reported by Esfahani, 2005).

**ISSUES IN E-TAILING**

Despite e-tailing's ongoing growth, many e-tailers continue to face some major issues related to e-tailing. If not solved, they can slow the growth of an organization's e-tailing efforts. Major representative issues are described below.

1. **Resolving channel conflict.** If a seller is a click-and-mortar company, such as Levi's or GM, it may face a conflict with its regular distributors when it sells directly online. Known as **channel conflict,** this situation can alienate the regular distributors. Channel conflict has forced some companies (e.g., Lego.com, see Chapter 9) to limit their B2C efforts; others (e.g., some automotive companies) have decided not to sell direct online. An alternative approach is to try to collaborate in some way with the existing distributors whose services may be restructured. For example, an auto company could allow customers to configure a car online, but require that the car be picked up from a dealer, where customers could also arrange financing, warranties, and service.

2. **Resolving conflicts within click-and-mortar organizations.** When an established company decides to sell direct online on a large scale, it may create a conflict within its offline operations. Conflicts may arise in areas such as pricing of products and services, allocation of resources (e.g., advertising budget), and logistics services provided by the offline activities to the online activities (e.g., handling of returns of items bought online). As a result of these conflicts, some companies have completely separated the "clicks" (the online portion of the organization) from the "mortar" or "bricks" (the traditional brick-and-mortar part of the organization). Such separation may increase expenses and reduce the synergy between the two organizational parts.

3. **Organizing order fulfillment and logistics.** E-tailers face a difficult problem of how to ship very small quantities to a large number of buyers. This can be a difficult undertaking, especially when returned items need to be handled.

4. **Determining viability and risk of online e-tailers.** Many purely online e-tailers folded in 2000–2002 (see Kaplan, 2002), the result of problems with cash flow, customer acquisition, order fulfillment, and demand forecasting. Online competition, especially in commodity-type products such as CDs, toys, books, or groceries, became very fierce due to the ease of entry to the marketplace. So a problem most young e-tailers face is to determine how long to operate while you are still losing money and how to finance the losses.

5. **Identifying appropriate revenue models.** One early dot-com model was to generate enough revenue from advertising to keep the business afloat until the customer base reached critical mass. This model did not work. Too many dot-coms were competing for too few advertising dollars, which went mainly to a small number of well-known sites such as AOL, MSN, Google, and Yahoo. Advertising is the primary source of income of such portals (Luo and Najdaw, 2004). In addition, there was a "chicken-and-egg" problem: Sites could not get advertisers to come if they did not have enough visitors. To succeed in EC, it is necessary to identify appropriate revenue models. (For further discussion of EC revenue models, see Turban et al., 2008).

To successfully implement e-tailing and solve the five issues just discussed (and others), it is frequently necessary to conduct *market research*. Market research is needed for product design, marketing, and advertising decisions, pricing, and strategy. For a discussion of market research in e-commerce, see Online File W5.9.

# 5.4 B2B Applications

In *business-to-business (B2B) applications,* the buyers, sellers, and transactions involve only organizations. Business-to-business comprises about 85 percent of EC volume. It covers applications that enable an enterprise to form electronic relationships with its distributors, resellers, suppliers, customers, and other partners. By using B2B, organizations can restructure their supply chains and partner relationships.

There are several business models for B2B applications. The major ones are sell-side marketplaces, buy-side marketplaces, and electronic exchanges. Other B2B systems are described in Chapter 9.

**SELL-SIDE CORPORATE MARKETPLACES**

In the **sell-side marketplace** model, organizations attempt to sell their products or services to other organizations electronically from their own private e-marketplace and/or from a third-party site. This model is similar to the B2C model in which the buyer is expected to come to the seller's site, view catalogs, and place an order. In the B2B sell-side marketplace, however, the buyer is an organization.

The key mechanisms in the sell-side model are: (1) electronic catalogs that can be customized for each large buyer and (2) forward auctions. Sellers such as Dell Computer (*dellauction.com*) use auctions extensively. In addition to auctions from their own Web sites, organizations can use third-party auction sites, such as eBay, to liquidate items. Companies such as Overstock.com (see *liquidation.com*) are helping organizations to auction obsolete and old assets and inventories.

The sell-side model is used by hundreds of thousands of companies and is especially powerful for companies with superb reputations. The seller can be either a manufacturer (e.g., Dell, IBM), a distributor (e.g., *avnet.com*), or a retailer (e.g., *bigboxx.com*). The seller uses EC to increase sales, reduce selling and advertising expenditures, increase delivery speed, and reduce administrative costs. The sell-side model is especially suitable to customization. For example, organizational customers can configure their orders online at *cisco.com,* and others. Self-configuration of orders results in fewer misunderstandings about what customers want and much faster order fulfillment.

**BUY-SIDE CORPORATE MARKETPLACES**

The **buy-side marketplace** is a model in which organizations attempt to buy needed products or services from other organizations electronically. A major method of buying goods and services in the buy-side model is a *reverse auction.* Here, a company that wants to buy items places a *request for quotation* (RFQ) on its Web site or in a third-party bidding marketplace. Once RFQs are posted, sellers (usually preapproved suppliers) submit bids electronically. Such auctions attract large pools of willing sellers, who can be either manufacturers, distributors, or retailers. The bids are routed via the buyer's intranet to the engineering and finance departments for evaluation. Clarifications are made via e-mail, and the winner is notified electronically.

The buy-side model uses EC technology to streamline the purchasing process in order to reduce the cost of items purchased, the administrative cost of procurement, and the purchasing cycle time. Procurements using a third-party buy-side marketplace model are especially popular for medium and small organizations.

**E-Procurement.** Purchasing by using electronic support is referred to as **e-procurement.** E-procurement uses *reverse auctions* (as discussed) as well as two other popular mechanisms: group purchasing and desktop purchasing.

*Group Purchasing.* In **group purchasing,** the orders of many buyers are aggregated so that they total to a large volume, in order to merit more seller attention and discounts. The aggregated order can then be placed on a reverse auction, and a volume discount can be negotiated. Typically, the orders of small buyers are aggregated by a third-party vendor, such as United Sourcing Alliance *(usa-llc.com).* Group purchasing is especially popular in the health-care industry (see *all-health.com*), and in education (*tepo.org*).

*Desktop Purchasing.* In a special case of e-procurement known as **desktop purchasing,** suppliers' catalogs are aggregated into an internal master catalog on the buyer's server, so that the company's purchasing agents (or even end users) can shop more conveniently. Desktop purchasing is most suitable for *indirect maintenance, replacement, and operations (MRO) items,* such as office supplies. (The term *indirect* refers to the fact that these items are not inputs to manufacturing.) In the desktop purchasing model, a company has many suppliers, but the quantities purchased from each are relatively small. This model is most appropriate for government entities and for large companies, such as Defra in the U.K., as described in *IT at Work 5.4.*

**PUBLIC EXCHANGES**

E-marketplaces in which there are many sellers and many buyers (usually both businesses), and where entry is open to all, are called **public exchanges** (in short, **exchanges**). They frequently are owned and operated by a third party. According to Kaplan and Sawhney (2000), there are four basic types of exchanges:

1. **Vertical distributors for direct materials.** These are B2B marketplaces where direct materials (materials that are inputs to manufacturing) are traded, usually in large quantities in an environment of long-term relationship known as *systematic sourcing.* Examples are Plasticsnet.com and Papersite.com.

2. **Vertical exchanges for indirect materials.** Here indirect materials in *one industry* are purchased usually on an as-needed basis (called *spot sourcing*). Buyers and

# IT at Work 5.4

## E-Procurement at Defra

The U.K. Government Department for Environment, Food, and Rural Affairs (Defra) spends about £.5 billion each year on prepurchasing from a pool of thousands of suppliers. The agency uses over 16,500 purchasing orders, 120,000 supplier invoices, and over 100,000 other payments.

**The Problem.** Defra set challenging e-procurement goals to provide systems that would offer electronic solutions for all procurement processes, which included:

1. Reduce maverick (last-minute, unplanned) spending.
2. Capture all expenditures.
3. Enable full automation of month-end accrual processes.
4. Eliminate unmatched invoices and improve immediate invoice registration.
5. Reduce the number of vendors supplying Defra.
6. Provide for better value for money.
7. Align corporate services and systems to business needs.

**The Process.** The following e-procurement applications were implemented in Defra:

1. The desktop purchasing method "buy4defra" for initiating all maverick buying with many standard products and services being included in the online catalogs.
2. An e-contract management system.
3. An e-tendering system (reverse auction).
4. E-auction4defra (regular auctions).
5. E-billing4defra.

**Implementation Steps.** The system was implemented with Oracle e-Business Suite (11i). Defra remodeled its processes to match the software using practical suggestions from Oracle User Group members.

- By the end of 2004, 1,000 users registered, processing well over 2,500 requisitions per month.
- Twenty supplier catalogs were online.
- Electronic transmission of purchase orders went live.

**The Benefits.**

- Smarter use of e-procurement was generating a savings of £600,000 each year.
- Removal of many unnecessary paper and manual processes.
- Reduction in maverick buying.
- Ninety percent of supplier invoicing matched by mid-2005.
- By March 2006, over 60 percent of Defra's £1.4 billion expenditures had been processed through the e-procurement solution.

*Sources: defra.gov.uk* (accessed June 2006), and Office of Government Commerce (2005).

*For Further Exploration:* Why did the government concentrate on procurement costs? Is there any e-procurement activity not covered here? Can Defra do even better? How?

---

sellers may not even know each other. ChemConnect.com and Isteelasia.com are examples. In such vertical exchanges, prices are continually changing, based on the matching of supply and demand. Auctions are typically used in this kind of B2B marketplace, sometimes done in private trading rooms, which are available in exchanges like ChemConnect.com (see *IT at Work 5.5* on page 186). Companies may trade the same commodity or parts in both types of markets.

3. **Horizontal distributors.** These are many-to-many e-marketplaces for indirect (MRO) materials, such as office supplies, used by *any industry*. Prices are fixed or negotiated in this systematic sourcing-type exchange. Examples are EcEurope.com, Globalsources.com, and Alibaba.com.

4. **Functional exchanges.** Here, needed services such as temporary help or extra space are traded on an as-needed basis (spot sourcing). For example, Employease.com can find temporary labor using employers in its Employease Network. Prices are dynamic, and vary depending on supply and demand.

All four types of exchanges offer support services, ranging from payments to logistics. Vertical exchanges are frequently owned and managed by a group of big players in an industry (referred to as a *consortium*). For example, Marriott and Hyatt own a procurement consortium for the hotel industry, and ChevronTexaco

# *IT* at Work 5.5

## *Chemical Companies "Bond" at ChemConnect*

Buyers and sellers of chemicals and plastics today can meet electronically in a large vertical commodity exchange called ChemConnect (*chemconnect.com*). Using this exchange, global chemical-industry leaders such as British Petroleum, Dow Chemical, BASF, Hyundai, and Sumitomo can reduce trading cycle time and cost and can find new markets and trading partners around the globe.

ChemConnect provides a public trading marketplace and an information portal to more than 9,000 members in 150 countries. In 2003, over 60,000 products were traded in this public, third-party-managed e-marketplace. ChemConnect provides three marketplaces: a commodity markets platform, a marketplace for sellers, and a marketplace for buyers, as described below.

At the *commodity markets platform*, prequalified producers, customers, and distributors come together in real time to sell and buy chemical-related commodities like natural-gas liquids, oxygenates, olefins, and polymers. They can even simultaneously execute multiple deals. Transactions are done through regional trading hubs.

The *marketplace for sellers* has many tools ranging from electronic catalogs to forward auctions. It enables companies to find buyers all over the world. ChemConnect provides all the necessary tools to expedite selling and achieving the best prices. It also allows for negotiations.

The *marketplace for buyers* is a place where thousands of buyers shop for chemical-related indirect materials (and a few direct materials). The market provides for automated request for proposal (RFP) tools as well as a complete online reverse auction. The sellers' market is connected to the buyers' market, so that sellers can connect to the RFPs posted on the marketplace for buyers. (Note that RFP and RFQ are interchangeable terms; RFP is used more in government bidding.)

In the three marketplaces, ChemConnect provides logistics and payment options. In all of its trading mechanisms, up-to-the-minute market information is available and can be translated into 30 different languages. Members pay transaction fees only for successfully completed transactions. Business partners provide several support services, such as financial services for the market members. The marketplaces work with certain rules and guidelines that ensure an unbiased approach to the trades. There is full disclosure of all legal requirements, payments, trading rules, and so on. (Click on "Legal info and privacy issues" at the ChemConnect Web site.) ChemConnect is growing rapidly, adding members and trading volume.

In 2006, ChemConnect expanded its offerings in the petroleum coke marketplace, enabling better price visibility, more efficient inventory management, broader sales channels, more efficient procurement, and effective risk management. Also, the exchange offers real-time dynamic auctions, real-time market intelligence, trade in real time, and detailed reporting and analytics.

*Sources:* Compiled from *chemconnect.com* (accessed June 2006), and Case Study: ChemConnect (2006).

*For Further Exploration:* What are the advantages of the ChemConnect exchange? Why are there three trading places? Why does the exchange provide information portal services?

owns an energy e-marketplace. The vertical e-marketplaces offer services particularly suited to the community they serve.

Since B2B activities involve many companies, specialized network infrastructure is needed. Such infrastructure works either as an Internet/EDI or as extranets (see Chapter 9).

# 5.5 Major Models of E-Business: From E-Government to C2C

In addition to pure e-commerce activities of buying and selling, one can find many other models online, mostly of the nontrading nature.

**BUSINESS-TO-EMPLOYEES (B2E) COMMERCE**

Companies are finding many ways to do business electronically with their own employees. They disseminate information to employees over the company intranet, for example, as part of their employee relationship management (see Chapter 8). Employees can manage their fringe benefits and take training classes electronically. In addition, employees can buy on the corporate intranet discounted insurance, travel packages, and tickets to events, and they can electronically order supplies and material needed for their work.

**E-COMMERCE BETWEEN AND AMONG UNITS WITHIN THE BUSINESS**

Large corporations frequently consist of independent units, or *strategic business units* (SBUs), which "sell" or "buy" materials, products, and services from each other. Transactions of this type can be easily automated and performed over the intranet. An SBU can be either a seller or a buyer. An example would be company-owned dealerships, which buy goods from the main company. This type of EC helps improve the internal supply chain operations.

The major benefits of such e-commerce are smoothing the supply chain, reducing inventories along the supply chain, reducing operating costs, increasing customer satisfaction, and increasing a company's competitive edge. The challenges faced by the collaborators are software integration issues, technology selection, trust and security, and overcoming resistance to change.

**E-COMMERCE BETWEEN AND AMONG CORPORATE EMPLOYEES**

Many large organizations allow employees to post classified ads on the company intranet, through which employees can buy and sell products and services from each other. This service is especially popular in universities, where it has been conducted since even before the commercialization of the Internet.

**COLLABORATIVE COMMERCE**

*Collaborative commerce (c-commerce)* refers to the use of digital technologies that enable companies to collaboratively plan, design, develop, manage, and research products, services, and innovative EC applications. These activities differ from selling and buying. An example would be a company that is collaborating electronically with a vendor that designs a product or a part for the company. C-commerce implies communication, information sharing, and collaborative planning done electronically using tools such as groupware and specially designed EC collaboration tools.

Numerous studies (e.g., *line56.com,* 2002) suggest that collaborative relationships may result in significant improvement in organizations' performance. Major benefits cited are cost reduction, increased revenues, and better customer retention. These benefits are the results of fewer stockouts, less exception processing, reduced inventory throughout the supply chain, lower materials costs, increased sales volume, and increased competitive advantage. For examples, see Brook (2004).

C-commerce activities usually are conducted between and among supply chain partners as shown in Online File W5.10.

There are several varieties of c-commerce, ranging from joint design efforts to forecasting. Collaboration can be done both between and within organizations.

**E-GOVERNMENT**

As e-commerce tools and applications improve, greater attention is being given to its use to improve the business of public institutions and governments (country, state, county, city, etc). **E-government** is the use of Internet technology and e-commerce to deliver information and public services to citizens, business partners and suppliers of government entities, and those working in the public sector.

E-government offers a number of benefits: It improves the efficiency and effectiveness of the functions of government, including the delivery of public services. It enables governments to be more transparent to citizens and businesses by giving access to more of the information generated by government. E-government also offers greater opportunities for citizens to provide feedback to government agencies and to participate in democratic institutions and processes. As a result, e-government may facilitate fundamental changes in the relationships between citizens and governments.

E-government applications can be divided into three major categories: *government-to-citizens* (G2C), *government-to-business* (G2B), and *government-to-government* (G2G). In the G2C category, government agencies increasingly are using the Internet to provide services to citizens. An example is *electronic benefits transfer* (EBT), in which governments (usually state or national) transfer benefits, such as Social Security and pension payments, directly to recipients' bank accounts or to smart cards. In G2B, governments use the Internet to sell to or buy from businesses. For example, *electronic tendering systems* using reverse auctions are becoming mandatory, to ensure the best price for government procurement of goods and services. G2G includes intragovernment EC (transactions between different governments) as well as services among different governmental agencies. For an overview, *see egov.gov.*

## CONSUMER-TO-CONSUMER E-COMMERCE

*Consumer-to-consumer* (C2C) e-commerce refers to e-commerce in which both the buyer and the seller are individuals (not businesses). C2C is conducted in several ways on the Internet, where the best-known C2C activities are auctions.

**C2C Auctions.** In dozens of countries, C2C selling and buying on auction sites is exploding. Most auctions are conducted by intermediaries, like eBay.com. Consumers can select general sites such as *auctionanything.com;* they also can use specialized sites such as *bid2bid.com.* In addition, many individuals are conducting their own auctions. For example, *greatshop.com* provides software to create online C2C reverse auction communities.

**Classified Ads.** People sell to other people every day through classified ads in newspapers and magazines. Internet-based classified ads have one big advantage over these more traditional types of classified ads: They offer a national, rather than a local, audience (e.g., see *craigslist.com* or *traderonline.com*). This wider audience greatly increases the supply of goods and services available and the number of potential buyers. Internet-based classifieds often can be edited or changed easily, and in many cases they display photos of the product offered for sale.

The major categories of online classified ads are similar to those found in the newspaper: vehicles, real estate, employment, pets, tickets, and travel. Classified ads are available through most Internet service providers (AOL, MSN, etc.), at some portals (Yahoo, etc.), and from Internet directories, online newspapers, and more. To help narrow the search for a particular item on several sites, shoppers can use search engines. Once users find an ad and get the details, they can e-mail or call the other party for additional information or to make a purchase. Classified sites generate revenue from affiliate sites.

**Personal Services.** Numerous personal services (lawyers, handy helpers, tax preparers, investment advisors, dating services) are available on the Internet. Some are in the classified ads, but others are listed in specialized Web sites and directories. Some are for free, some for a fee. *Be very careful before you purchase any personal services online.* Fraud or crime could be involved. For example, an online lawyer may not be an expert in the area he or she professes, or may not deliver the service at all.

**Support Services to C2C.** When individuals buy products or services from individuals, they usually buy from strangers. The issues of ensuring quality, receiving payments, and preventing fraud are critical to the success of C2C. One service that helps C2C is payments by companies such as PayPal.com (see Section 5.6). Another one is *escrow services*, intermediaries that take the buyer's money and the purchased goods, and only after making sure that the seller delivers what was agreed upon, deliver the goods to the buyer and the money to the seller (for a fee).

## 5.6 E-Commerce Support Services: Advertising, Payment, and Order Fulfillment

The implementation of EC may require several support services. B2B and B2C applications require payments and order fulfillment; portals require content. Figure 5.4 portrays the collection of the major EC services. They include: e-infrastructure (mostly technology consultants, system developers and integrators, hosting, security, wireless, and networks), e-process (mainly payments and logistics), e-markets (mostly marketing and advertising), e-communities (different audiences and business partners), e-services (CRM, PRM, and directory services), and e-content (supplied by content providers). All of these services support the EC applications in the center of the figure, and all of the services need to be managed.

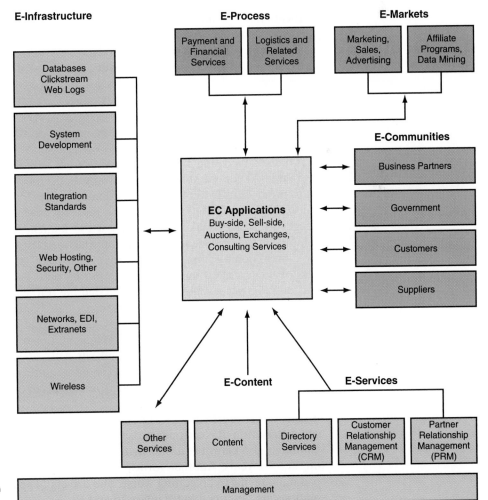

**Figure 5.4** E-commerce support services. (*Source:* Drawn by E. Turban. Based on S. Y. Choi et al. 1997, p. 18.)

Here we will focus on two of the above topics—payments and order fulfillment. For details on the other services, see Turban et al. (2006).

Advertising is an attempt to disseminate information to influence a buyer–seller transaction. Traditional advertising on TV or in newspapers is impersonal, one-way mass communication. Direct-response marketing (telemarketing) contacts individuals by direct mail or telephone and requires them to respond to make a purchase. The direct-response approach personalizes advertising and marketing, but it can be expensive, slow, and ineffective (and from the consumer's point of view, annoying).

Internet advertising redefines the advertising process, making it media-rich, dynamic, targeted, and interactive. It improves on traditional forms of advertising in a number of ways: Internet ads can be updated any time at minimal cost and therefore can be always timely. Internet ads can reach very large numbers of potential buyers all over the world, and they are sometimes cheaper in comparison to print (newspaper and magazine), radio, or television ads. Internet ads can be interactive and targeted to specific interest groups and/or to individuals. Finally, it makes sense to move advertising to the Internet, where the number of viewers is rapidly growing. Internet ads are used mainly in B2C, but some methods (e.g., catalogs) are used in B2B and other types of EC.

Nevertheless, the Internet as an advertising medium does have some shortcomings, most of which relate to the difficulty in measuring the effectiveness and cost-justification of the ads. For example, it is difficult to measure the actual results of placing a banner ad or sending a marketing e-mail.

Despite the limitations, Internet ads are growing rapidly, reaching more than 6 percent of all advertising in 2005 (over $12 billion), and growing by about 20 percent per year (Delaney, 2006). Also, the availability and power of online advertising methods are increasing.

There are over a dozen online advertising methods. They are summarized in Table 5.4 with details provided in Online File W5.11.

Online advertising can be similar to TV ads with rich media. Here is an example: In mid-2005, Ford Motor Company unveiled a *roadblock* approach on the Internet to promote its F-150 truck. A "roadblock" refers to running a commercial on all major TV channels at exactly the same time, so viewers switching channels cannot escape the commercial. On the day of the launch, Ford placed banner ads for 24 hours on the three leading Internet portals—AOL, MSN, and Yahoo!—introducing a three-month campaign. Some 50 million Web surfers saw Ford's banner. Millions of them clicked on the banner, pouring onto Ford's Web site at a rate that reached 3,000 per second. Ford claimed that the traffic led to a 6 percent increase in sales over the first three months of the campaign. For details, see Baker (2004).

There are many issues related to the implementation of Internet advertising: how to design ads for the Internet, where and when to advertise, and how to integrate online and offline ads. Most such decisions require the input of marketing and advertising experts. Here, we illustrate some issues in online advertising.

**Unsolicited Advertising.** As discussed in Chapter 4, *spamming* is the indiscriminate distribution of electronic messages without permission of the receiver. E-mail spamming, also known as *unsolicited commercial e-mail* (UCE), has been part of the Internet for years. Another form of spamming is the pop-up ad. Unfortunately, spamming seems to be getting worse. The drivers of spamming and some potential solutions are described in Chapters 16 and 17.

| TABLE 5.4 | Internet Advertising Methods |
| --- | --- |
| **Method** | **Description** |
| Banners and buttons | Brief ads that can be targeted or customized; you can click on them to go to the advertiser's site. |
| Pop up, pop under | Automatically launched, unsolicited, when you wait, enter, or exit Web sites. |
| Automated targeted advertising (search-related ads) | Google's AdSense and Microsoft's AdCenter are leading examples. These are targeted text hints that appear when you conduct a search. |
| Sponsored links in search engine results | Appear on top or right side of a page; bring you search results of Google, Yahoo, MSN, or other search engine. Paid by sponsors to be on first page. |
| E-mail | Relatively inexpensive. Can be targeted to a group of recipients or individuals; frequently unsolicited. |
| Electronic catalogs and rich media ads | Advertise products/services; some with price comparisons. |
| Spyware banners | Advertiser-sponsored unsolicited ads; can be in different formats. |
| Classified ads | Similar to newspaper classifieds. Search them to find what you need. |
| Wireless localization | Knowing where you are, an ad is sent to your cell phone or PDA regarding a business close to your location (see Chapter 6). |
| Online chat | Customers are invited to text chat with sales representatives. |
| Affiliated marketing | Advertisers pay Web sites ("partners") to place a banner on partners' sites. Partners are paid commission if their visitors go to the advertisers' sites and make a purchase there. |
| Blog advertising | Advertisers pay blog owners commission if visitors click (and buy) on banners displayed in the blogs. |
| Viral marketing | Online "word-of-mouth," "forward our information to others." |
| Online promotions | Several innovations that provide entertainment or incentives to be exposed to ads. |

On October 22, 2003, the U.S. Senate passed an antispam bill requiring spammers to clearly identify themselves and the products they are selling. Since the bill became law, several companies were fined in court (e.g., *craigslist.com*).

Permission marketing is one answer to e-mail and pop-up spamming.

**Permission Marketing. Permission marketing** asks consumers to give their permission to voluntarily accept online advertising and e-mail. Typically, consumers are asked to complete an electronic form that asks what they are interested in and requests permission to send related marketing information. Sometimes consumers are offered incentives to receive advertising; at the least, marketers try to send information in an entertaining, educational, or other interesting manner.

Permission marketing is the basis of many Internet marketing strategies. For example, millions of users receive e-mails periodically from airlines such as American and Southwest. Users of this marketing service can ask for notification of low fares from their hometown or to their favorite destinations. Users can easily unsubscribe at any time. Permission marketing is also extremely important for market research (e.g., see Media Metrix at *comscore.com*).

In one particularly interesting form of permission marketing, companies such as *paidsurveysonline.com* and CashSurfers.com have built customer lists of millions of people who are happy to receive advertising messages whenever they are on the Web. These customers are paid $0.25 to $0.50 an hour to view messages while they do their normal surfing. They may also be paid $0.10 an hour for the surfing time of any friends they refer to the site.

**Interactive and Targeted Advertising.** All advertisers, whether online or not, attempt to target their ads to the desired market and, if possible, even to individuals. A good salesperson is trained to interact with sales prospects, asking questions about the features they are looking for and handling possible objections as they come up. Online advertising comes closer to supporting this one-to-one selling process than more traditional advertising media possibly can.

Ideally, in interactive marketing, advertisers present customized, one-on-one ads. The term *interactive* points to the ability to address an individual, to gather and remember that person's responses, and to serve that customer based on his or her previous, unique responses. When the Internet is combined with databases, interactive marketing becomes a very effective and affordable competitive strategy.

**Targeted Advertising.** Since EC began in the mid-1990s, many attempts have been made to target advertising to groups (called segmentation) or even to individuals. Using groups as targets is fairly simple: You go to a student site or a women's site, and you place appropriate ads there. It is clearly more effective than nontargeted advertising. Companies also tried to simply ask individuals what they like, and also to observe what they do or order online. This was not very successful, since few people answered the questionnaires and some did not tell the truth. Amazon.com, for example, recommends books on the same topic that you buy or explore. Companies such as DoubleClick developed proprietary formulas to decide what people like and created an advertising network of participating advertisers (e.g., see Turban et al., 2008). However, nothing worked as well as Google's AdSense and AdWords models (see *A Closer Look 5.2*).

**ELECTRONIC PAYMENTS**

Payments are an integral part of doing business, whether in the traditional way or online. Unfortunately, in several cases traditional payment systems are not effective for EC, especially for B2B. Cash cannot be used because there is no face-to-face contact. Not everyone accepts credit cards or checks, and some buyers do not have credit cards or checking accounts. Finally, contrary to what many people believe, it may be less secure for the buyer to use the telephone or mail to arrange or send payment, especially from another country, than to complete a secured transaction on a computer. For all of these reasons, a better way is needed to pay for goods and services in cyberspace. This better way is *electronic payment systems.*

**Electronic Payment Systems.** There exist several alternatives for paying for goods and services on the Internet. The major ones are summarized in Table 5.5. The details of these are provided in Online File W5.12.

The most common methods, paying with credit cards and electronic bill payments, are discussed briefly here.

**Electronic Credit Cards.** *Electronic credit cards* make it possible to charge online payments to one's credit card account. For security, only encrypted credit cards should be used. Credit card details can be encrypted by using the SSL protocol in the buyer's computer (available in standard browsers). (Payment protocols are described in Online File W5.12.1)

Here is how electronic credit cards work: When you buy a book from Amazon, your credit card information and purchase amount are encrypted in your browser, so the information is safe while "traveling" on the Internet. Furthermore, when this information arrives at Amazon, it is not opened but is transferred automatically (in encrypted form) to a clearinghouse, where the information is decrypted for verification and authorization. The complete process of how e-credit cards work is shown

# A Closer Look 5.2

## Google's AdSense and AdWords

Google's *AdSense* is an affiliates program in which Google offers Web site owners ("publishers") a chance to earn commissions. Here is how it works:

AdSense will automatically deliver advertiser's text and image ads that are precisely targeted to each site. This is a major improvement over matching individuals based on their preferences (which is less accurate in many cases and much more expensive). The matching (contextual matching) is done based on a proprietary algorithm (Google filed for over 60 patents on these and other innovations). Google helps you customize the appearance of the ad and your Web pages—to attract more visitors (see attached figure). The key is the quality and appearance of both the pages and the ads. Google even provides you with analytics that help convert visitors into customers.

Each time a visitor clicks on an ad (which takes her or him to the advertiser's site), the site owner shares the commission paid by the advertiser with Google (or shares fees based on the number of impressions).

If Google knows any of the characteristics and demographics of the visitors, those factors are also considered in the match. Competitors, such as MSN, with their AdCenter methodology, do the same. The closer the match, and the less intrusive the ad is to the visitor, the better the chance of the visitor clicking on the ad.

Google's *AdWords* is the complementary program for advertisers. Google helps them to design the ads. Another companion is *AdSense for Search,* which lets Web site owners place Google *search boxes* on their pages. When a user searches the Web or the site with the search box, Google shares any ad revenue it makes from those searches with the site owner. For an example of a site with AdSense, see *rtcmagazine.com.*

Google's success is attributed to the quality of the matches, the large number of advertisers in its network, its ability to use ads in many languages, and its ability to understand the content of Web sites.

*Sources:* Compiled from *google.com/adsense* and from *en.wikipedia.org/wiki/AdSense* (sites accessed June 2006).

Google's AdSense. (*Source: google.com/services/adsense_tour/.*)

in Figure 5.5. Electronic credit cards are used mainly in B2C and in shopping by SMEs (small-to-medium enterprises).

***Electronic Bill Payments.*** There are three major ways to pay bills over the Internet:

1. **Online banking.** The consumer signs up for a bank's online bill-pay service and makes all of his or her payments from a single Web site. Some banks offer the service for free with a checking account, or if the account holder maintains a minimum balance.

| TABLE 5.5 | Electronic Payments Methods |
|---|---|
| **Method** | **Description** |
| Electronic funds transfer | Popular for paying bills online. Money is transferred electronically from payer's account to the recipient's. |
| Electronic checks | Digitally signed e-check that is encrypted and moved from the buying customer to the merchant. |
| Electronic credit cards | Paying with regular credit cards (encrypted numbers). Example: eCharge.com. |
| Purchasing e-cards | Corporate credit cards with limits. Work like regular credit cards, but must be paid quicker (e.g., in one week). |
| e-cash—stored-value money cards | Prepaid card that can be used for transportation, making copies in the library, parking (in some cities), telephone calls, etc. |
| e-cash—smart cards | Cards that contain considerable information and can be manipulated as needed. Used for several purposes including transfer of money. |
| e-cash—person-to-person | Creation of special online account from which funds can be sent to others. PayPal is the best-known company (an eBay company). You can pay businesses as well. Another example is Yahoo Pay Direct. |
| Electronic bill presentment and payments | Bills are presented for payer's approval. Payment is made online (e.g., funds transfer). Examples: CheckFree.com, Yahoo Bill Pay. |
| Pay at ATMs | ATM allows you to pay monthly bills (e.g., to utility companies) by transferring money from your account to the biller. |
| Micropayments | Payments are too small to be paid with credit cards. Can be paid with stored-value money cards, or with special payment methods, including payments from cell phones. |
| B2B special methods | Enterprise invoice presentment and payment, wire transfer, and electronic letter of credit are popular methods. |

2. **Biller direct.** The consumer makes payments at each biller's Web site either with a credit card or by giving the biller enough information to complete an electronic withdrawal directly from the consumer's bank account. The biller makes the billing information available to the customer (presentment) on its Web site or the site of a billing hosting service. Once the customer views the bill, he or she authorizes and initiates payment at the site. The payment can be made with a credit/debit card or an ACH debit. The biller then initiates a payment transaction that moves

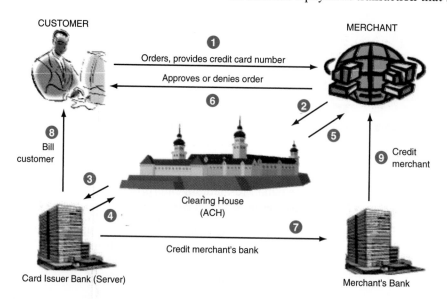

**Figure 5.5** How e-credit cards work. (The numbers 1–9 indicate the sequence of activities.) (*Source:* Drawn by E. Turban.)

funds through the payment system, crediting the biller and debiting the customer. This method is known as electronic bill presentment and payments (EBPP).

3. **Bill consolidator.** The customer enrolls to receive and pay bills for multiple billers with a third-party bill consolidator. The customer's enrollment information is forwarded to every biller that the customer wishes to activate (service initiation). For each billing cycle, the biller sends a bill summary or bill detail directly to the consolidator. The bill summary, which links to the bill detail stored with the biller or the consolidator, is made available to the customer (presentment). The customer views the bill and initiates payment instructions. The consolidator initiates a credit payment transaction that moves funds through the payment system to the biller.

**Security in Electronic Payments.** Two main issues need to be considered under the topic of payment security: what is required in order to make EC payments safe, and the methods that can be used to do so.

*Security Requirements.* Security requirements for conducting EC are the following:

- **Authentication.** The buyer, the seller, and the paying institutions must be assured of the identity of the parties with whom they are dealing.
- **Integrity.** It is necessary to ensure that data and information transmitted in EC, such as orders, replies to queries, and payment authorizations, are not accidentally or maliciously altered or destroyed during transmission.
- **Nonrepudiation.** Merchants need protection against the customer's unjustified denial of placing an order. On the other hand, customers need protection against merchants' unjustified denial of payments made. (Such denials, of both types, are called *repudiation*.)
- **Privacy.** Many customers want their identity to be secured. They want to make sure others do not know what they buy. Some prefer complete anonymity, as is possible with cash payments.
- **Safety.** Customers want to be sure that it is safe to provide a credit card number on the Internet. They also want protection against fraud by sellers or by criminals posing as sellers.

*Security Protection.* Several methods and mechanisms can be used to fulfill the above requirements. One of the primary mechanisms is *encryption* (making messages indecipherable by using a key), which is often part of the most useful security schemes. For more detailed explanation of encryption, see Online File W5.13 and Chapter 16. Other representative methods are discussed below.

*E-Wallets.* **E-wallets** (or **digital wallets**) are software mechanisms that provide security measures and convenience to EC purchasing. The wallet stores the financial information of the buyer, such as credit card number, shipping information, and more. Thus, sensitive information does not need to be reentered for each purchase. If the wallet is stored at the vendor's site, it does not have to travel on the Net for each purchase, making the information more secure.

The problem is that you need an e-wallet with each merchant. One solution is to have a wallet installed on your computer (e.g., MasterCard Wallet or AOL Wallet). In that case, though, you cannot use the e-wallet to make a purchase from another computer, nor is it a totally secured system.

*Virtual Credit Cards.* A **virtual credit card** allows you to shop with an ID number and a password instead of with a credit card number. Such cards are used primarily by people who do not trust browser encryption sufficiently to use their credit card numbers on the Internet. The virtual credit card gives an extra layer of security. The bank that supports your traditional credit card, for example, can provide you with a transaction number valid for online use for a short period. For example, if you want to make a $200 purchase, you would contact your credit card company to charge that amount to your regular credit card account. You would be given a transaction number that is good for charges up to $200. This transaction number is encrypted for security, but even in the worst possible case (that some unauthorized entity obtained the transaction number), your loss would be limited, in this case to $200.

*Payment Using Fingerprints.* An increasing number of supermarkets allow their regular customers to pay by merely using their fingerprint for identification. A computer template of your fingerprint is kept in the store's computer system. Each time you shop, your fingerprint is matched with the template at the payment counter. You approve the amount, which is then charged either to your credit card or bank account.

**ORDER FULFILLMENT**

We now turn our attention to another important EC support service—*order fulfillment.* Any time a company sells direct to customers a product delivered physically, it is involved in various order-fulfillment activities. It must perform the following activities: Quickly find the products to be shipped; pack them; arrange for the packages to be delivered speedily to the customer's door; collect the money from every customer, either in advance, by COD, or by individual bill; and handle the return of unwanted or defective products.

It is very difficult to accomplish these activities both effectively and efficiently in B2C, since a company may need to ship small packages to many customers, and do it quickly. For this reason, both online companies and click-and-mortar companies often have difficulties in their B2C supply chain and they outsource deliveries and sometimes packaging (see the FedEx case in Chapter 2). Here, we provide a brief overview of order fulfillment. For a more detailed discussion, see Bayles (2001), Croxton (2003), and Turban et al. (2006).

Order fulfillment includes not only providing customers with what they ordered and doing it on time, but also providing all related customer service. For example, the customer must receive assembly and operation instructions to a new appliance. (A nice example is available at *livemanuals.com.*) In addition, if the customer is not happy with a product, an exchange or return must be arranged. (See *fedex.com* for how returns are handled via FedEx.) Order fulfillment is basically a part of what are called a company's *back-office operations* (activities such as inventory control, shipment, and billing).

# 5.7 Ethical and Legal Issues in E-Business

**ETHICS**

Ethical standards and laws frequently lag technological innovation. E-commerce is taking new forms and enabling new business practices that may bring numerous risks—particularly for individual consumers—along with their advantages. We begin by considering ethical issues relating to e-business.

**ETHICAL ISSUES**

Many of the ethical and global issues related to IT in general apply also to e-business. These are discussed in the Ethics Primer at our Web site (Online File W1.5). In this section we touch on issues particularly related to e-commerce.

**Privacy.** Most electronic payment systems know who the buyers are; therefore, it may be necessary to protect the buyers' identities. A privacy issue related to employees also involves tracking: Many companies monitor employees' e-mail and have installed software that performs in-house monitoring of Web activities to discover employees who extensively use company time for non-business-related activities, including harassing other employees. Many employees don't like being watched, but companies may be obligated to monitor.

**Web Tracking.** Log files are the principal resources from which e-businesses draw information about how visitors use a site. Applying analytics to log files means either turning log data over to an application service provider (ASP) or installing software that can pluck relevant information from files in-house. By using tracking software, companies can track individuals' movements on the Internet. Programs such as cookies raise privacy concerns. The tracking history is stored on your PC's hard drive, and any time you revisit a certain Web site, the computer knows it (see NetTracker at *sane.com*). In response, some users install programs such as Cookie Cutter, CookieCrusher, and Spam Butcher, which are designed to allow users to have some control over cookies. Or they delete their cookie files.

However, the battle between computer end users and Web trackers has just begun. There are more and more "pesticides" for killing these "parasites." For example, Privacy Guardian, MyPrivacy, and Tracks Eraser Pro are examples of software that can protect users' online privacy by erasing a browser's cache, surfing histories, and cookies. Programs like Ad-Aware are specially designed to detect and remove spyware and data miners such as SahAgent, an application that collects and combines users' Internet browsing behavior and sends it to ShopAtHomeSelect servers. (For more information about anti-spy software, see Chapter 16.)

**Loss of Jobs.** The use of EC may result in the elimination of some company employees as well as brokers and agents. The manner in which these unneeded workers are treated may raise ethical issues, such as how to handle the displacement and whether to offer retraining programs.

**Disintermediation and Reintermediation.** One of the most interesting EC issues relating to loss of jobs is that of *intermediation*. Intermediaries provide two types of services: (1) matching and providing information and (2) value-added services such as consulting. The first type of services (matching and providing information) can be fully automated, and therefore these services are likely to be assumed by e-marketplaces and portals that provide free services. The second type of services (value-added services) requires expertise, and these can be only partially automated. Intermediaries who provide only (or mainly) the first type of service may be eliminated, a phenomenon called **disintermediation** (elimination of the intermediaries). On the other hand, brokers who provide the second type of service or who manage electronic intermediation, also known as *infomediation,* are not only surviving, but may actually prosper. This phenomenon is called **reintermediation.**

Disintermediation may cause channel conflicts. Intermediaries therefore fight back against manufacturers in fear that the traditional sales channel will be negatively affected by disintermediation (Lee et al., 2003). For instance, Wal-Mart and Home Depot warned Black & Decker that they would take its products off their shelves if Black & Decker began to sell its products through the Internet. Also, confronted with dealer complaints, Ford executives recently agreed to discontinue plans for future direct online car sales.

The Web offers new opportunities for reintermediation by providing services (manual or computerized) required to support or complement EC. First, services are especially valuable when the number of participants is enormous, as with job finding, or when complex information products are exchanged. Second, many brokering services require extensive information processing; electronic versions of these services can offer more sophisticated features at a lower cost than is possible with human labor. Finally, for delicate negotiations, a computer mediator may be more predictable, and hence more trustworthy, than a human. For example, suppose a mediator's role is to inform a buyer and a seller whether a deal can be made, without revealing either side's initial price to the other. An independent auditor can verify that a software-based mediator will reveal only the information it is supposed to; a human mediator's fairness is less easily verified. For reintermediation in the travel industry, see Gilden (2004).

**LEGAL ISSUES SPECIFIC TO E-COMMERCE**

Many legal issues are related to e-commerce. When buyers and sellers do not know each other and cannot even see each other (they may even be in different countries), there is a chance of fraud and other crimes over the Internet. During the first few years of EC, the public witnessed many of these, ranging from the creation of a virtual bank that disappeared along with the investors' deposits, to manipulation of stock prices on the Internet. Unfortunately, fraud on the Internet is increasing. Representative examples of legal issues specific to e-commerce are discussed below and in Online File W5.14.

**PROTECTION OF EC BUYERS AND SELLERS**

There are several ways buyers can be better protected against fraud in e-commerce. Representative methods are described next.

**Buyer Protection.** Some tips for safe electronic shopping are shown in Table 5.6. In short, do not forget that you have shopper's rights. Consult your local or state consumer protection agency for general information on your consumer rights.

**Seller Protection.** Online sellers, too, need protection. They must be protected against consumers who refuse to pay or who pay with bad checks and from buyers' claims that the merchandise did not arrive. They also have the right to protect

| TABLE 5.6 | Tips for Safe Electronic Shopping |
|---|---|

- Look for reliable brand names at sites like Wal-Mart Online, Disney Online, and Amazon.com. Before purchasing, make sure that the site is authentic by entering the site directly and not from an unverified link.
- Search any unfamiliar selling site for the company's address and phone and fax numbers. Call up and quiz the employees about the seller.
- Check out the vendor with the local Chamber of Commerce or Better Business Bureau (*bbbonline.org*). Look for seals of authenticity such as TRUSTe.
- Investigate how secure the seller's site is by examining the security procedures and by reading the posted privacy policy.
- Examine the money-back guarantees, warranties, and service agreements.
- Compare prices to those in regular stores. Too-low prices could prove too good to be true, and some "catch" is probably involved.
- Ask friends what they know. Find testimonials and endorsements in community sites and well-known bulletin boards.
- Find out what your rights are in case of a dispute. Consult consumer protection agencies and the National Fraud Information Center (*fraud.org*).
- Check *consumerworld.org* for a listing of useful resources.
- Check *cfenet.com* and *isaca.org*.

against the use of their name by others as well as to protect the use of their unique words and phrases, slogans, and Web address (trademark protection). Security features such as authentication, nonrepudiation, and escrow services provide some needed protections. Another seller protection applies particularly to electronic media: Sellers have legal recourse against customers who download without permission copyrighted software and/or knowledge and use it or sell it to others, as the music industry has proved.

## 5.8 Managerial Issues

**1. E-commerce failures.** Failures of EC initiatives are fairly common. Furthermore, during 2000–2002, large numbers of dot-com companies failed.

    **a. Dot-com failures.** Pioneering organizations saw the potential for e-commerce, but expertise and EC business models were just developing. Failures of EC projects started as early as 1996. However, the major wave of Internet-based EC failures started in 2000, as second-round funding (funding subsequent to a firm's original funding but before it goes to the stock market with a stock offering) began to dry up. For some examples see Online File W5.15.

        According to Useem (2000), the major reasons for EC failure are: incorrect revenue model, lack of strategy and contingency planning, inability to attract enough customers, lack of funding, channel conflict with distributors, too much online competition in standard (commodity) products (e.g., CDs, toys), poor order-fulfillment infrastructure, and lack of qualified management. To learn more about EC failures, visit *whytheyfailed.com* and *techdirt.com*.

    **b. Failed EC initiatives within organizations.** Whereas failed companies, especially publicly listed ones, are well advertised, failed EC initiatives within companies, especially within private companies, are less known. However, news about some failed EC initiatives has been publicized. For example, Levi Strauss stopped online direct sales of its apparel (jeans and its popular Levi's and Dockers brands) on its Web site (*levistrauss.com*) after its major distributors and retailers put pressure on the company not to compete with their brick-and-mortar outlets (channel conflict). Another EC initiative that failed was a joint venture between Intel and SAP, two world-class companies, which was designed to develop low-cost solutions for SMEs. It collapsed in August 2000 due to low demand and too few customers. Large companies such as Citicorp, Disney, and Merrill Lynch also closed EC initiatives after losing millions of dollars in them.

**2. Success stories and lessons learned.** Offsetting the failures are hundreds of EC success stories, primarily in specialty and niche markets (see Athitakis, 2003). Some of the reasons for EC success and some suggestions from EC experts on how to succeed are provided in Online File W5.16.

**3. Strategy-related Issues.**

    **a. Managing resistance to change.** Electronic commerce can result in a fundamental change in how business is done, and resistance to change from employees, vendors, and customers may develop. Education, training, and publicity over an extended time period offer possible solutions to the problem.

    **b. Integration of e-commerce into the business environment.** E-commerce needs to be integrated with the rest of the business. Integration issues involve planning, competition for corporate resources with other projects, and interfacing EC with databases, existing IT applications, and infrastructure.

4. **Implementation-related issues.**
   a. **Lack of qualified personnel and outsourcing.** Very few people have expertise in e-commerce. There are many implementation issues that require expertise, such as when to offer special promotions on the Internet, how to integrate an e-market with the information systems of buyers and sellers, and what kind of customer incentives are appropriate under what circumstances. For this reason, it may be worthwhile to outsource some e-commerce activities. Yet, as shown in Chapter 14, outsourcing decisions are not simple.
   b. **Implementation plan.** Because of the complexity and multifaceted nature of EC, it makes sense to prepare an implementation plan. Such a plan should include goals, budgets, timetables, and contingency plans. It should address the many legal, financial, technological, organizational, and ethical issues that can surface during implementation.
   c. **Managing the impacts.** The impacts of e-commerce on organizational structure, people, marketing procedures, and profitability may be dramatic. Therefore, establishing a committee or organizational unit to develop strategy and to manage e-commerce is necessary.

5. **Deployment-related issues.**
   a. **Alliances.** It is not a bad idea to join an alliance or consortium of companies to explore e-commerce. Alliances can be created at any time. Some EC companies (e.g., Amazon.com) have thousands of alliances. The problem is which alliance to join, or what kind of alliance to form and with whom.
   b. **Choosing the company's strategy toward e-commerce.** Generally speaking there are three major options: (1) *Lead:* Conduct large-scale innovative e-commerce activities. (2) *Watch and wait:* Do nothing, but carefully watch what is going on in the field in order to determine when EC is mature enough to enter it. (3) *Experiment:* Start some e-commerce experimental projects (learn by doing). Each of these options has its advantages and risks.
   c. **Justifying e-commerce by conducting a cost-benefit analysis is very difficult.** Many intangible benefits and lack of experience may produce grossly inaccurate estimates of costs and benefits. Nevertheless, a feasibility study must be done, and estimates of costs and benefits must be made. For example, see the proposal for assessing EDI investment presented by Hoogeweegen and Wagenaar (1995).

**CONCLUSION**

Analyzing successful companies, researchers have suggested that if they do careful planning to reach profitability quickly, many click-and-mortar companies are likely to succeed. Joint ventures and partnerships are very valuable, and planning for satisfactory infrastructure and logistics to meet high demand is needed. In short, do not forget that e-business has a "business" side!

Finally, let's not forget that history repeats itself. When the automobile was invented, there were 240 startup companies between 1904 and 1908. In 1910 there was a shakeout, and today there are only three U.S. automakers. However, the auto industry has grown by a hundredfold. The same is happening in EC: Despite the 2000–2003 failures, the total volume of EC activities continued to grow exponentially. For example, *emarketer.com* reported on May 19, 2003, that B2C revenues in 2002 reached $76 billion—a 48 percent increase over 2001. The figure for 2003 was over $96 billion—close to a 30 percent increase over 2002. For recent data see Lashinsky (2006).

## Integrating *IT*

### For the Accounting Major

Accounting personnel are involved in several IT/EC activities. For example, designing an e-ordering system and its relationship with inventory management requires accounting attention. Billing and payments are also accounting activities, as are determining cost and profit allocation. Replacing paper documents by electronic means will affect many of the accountant's tasks, especially the auditing of EC activities and systems. Taxing online transactions requires accountants' attention as do some compliance and security issues. Finally, building a cost-benefit and cost-justification system of which products/services to take online, and creating a chargeback system, are critical to the success of EC.

### For the Finance Major

The worlds of banking, securities and commodities markets, and other financial services are being reengineered due to EC. Online securities trading and its supporting infrastructure are growing more rapidly than any other EC activity. Many innovations already in place are changing the rules of economic and financial incentives for financial analysts and managers. Online banking, for example, does not recognize state boundaries, and it may create a new framework for financing global trades. Public financial information is now accessible in seconds. Compliance with regulations, and especially with SOX, can be facilitated by EC software as can pricing optimization and investment decisions.

### For the Human Resources Management Major

HR majors need to understand both the new labor markets and the impacts of EC on old labor markets. Also, the HRM department may use EC tools for such functions as procuring office supplies. Becoming knowledgeable about new government online initiatives and online training is critical. Finally, HR personnel must be familiar with the major legal issues related to EC and employment.

### For the IS Major

The information systems department (ISD) is responsible for providing the IT infrastructure necessary for EC to function. In particular, this infrastructure includes the company's networks, intranets, extranets, EC portals, and EC mechanisms. The ISD is also responsible for training in the use of EC initiatives, in deploying applications, in collaborating with EC vendors and users, and in ensuring that EC transactions are secure.

### For the Marketing Major

EC changed marketing and sales with online direct sales, CRM, one-on-one advertising and sales, and customized and interactive marketing. Also, marketing channels are being combined, eliminated, or recreated. The EC revolution is creating more new products and markets and significantly altering others. The direct producer-to-consumer channel is expanding rapidly and is fundamentally changing the nature of customer service. As the battle for customers intensifies, marketing and sales personnel are becoming the most critical success factor in many organizations. The major changes may introduce conflicts internally and with distributors and must be clearly understood. Finally, many opportunities for sales and marketing, including going global, are being created by EC.

### For the Production/Operations Management Major

EC is changing the manufacturing system from product-push mass production to order-pull mass customization. This change requires a robust supply chain, information support, and redesign of internal and external business processes. Using extranets, suppliers can monitor and replenish inventories without the need for manual reorders. In addition, EC initiatives help reduce cycle times and increase quality. Many production/operations problems that have persisted for years, such as complex scheduling and excess inventories, are being solved with the use of Web technologies. Also, the Web is enabling e-procurement by helping companies conduct electronic bids for parts and subassemblies, thus reducing cost.

## Key Terms

Auction *174*

B2E (business-to-employees) EC *169*

Brick-and-mortar organizations *167*

Business-to-business (B2B) *168*

Business-to-business-to-consumers (B2B2C) *168*

Business-to-consumers (B2C) *168*

Buy-side marketplace *184*

Channel conflict *182*

Click-and-mortar organizations *167*

## Chapter Highlights

(Numbers Refer to Learning Objectives)

**❶** E-commerce can be conducted on the Web and on other networks. It is divided into the following major types: business-to-business, collaborative commerce, business-to-consumers, consumer-to-consumer, business-to-business-to consumer, consumers-to-business, intrabusiness, e-government, and mobile commerce. In each type you can find several business models.

**❶** E-commerce offers many benefits to organizations, consumers, and society, but it also has limitations (technological and nontechnological). The current technological limitations are expected to lessen with time.

**❷** A major mechanism in EC is auctions. The Internet provides an infrastructure for executing auctions at lower cost, and with many more involved sellers and buyers, including both individual consumers and corporations. Two major types of auctions exist: forward auctions and reverse auctions. Forward auctions are used in the traditional process of *selling* to the highest bidder. Reverse auctions are used for *buying,* using a tendering system to buy at the lowest bid.

**❷** A minor mechanism is online bartering, in which companies or individuals arrange for *exchange* of physical items and/or services.

**❸** B2C e-tailing can be pure (such as Amazon.com), or part of a click-and-mortar organization. Direct marketing is done via solo storefronts or in malls. It can be done via electronic catalogs or by using electronic auctions. The leading online B2C service industries are banking, securities trading, job markets, travel, and real estate.

**❸** The major issues faced by e-tailers are channel conflict, conflict within click-and-mortar organizations, order fulfillment, determining viability and risk, and identifying appropriate revenue models.

**❹** The major B2B applications are selling from catalogs and by forward auctions (the sell-side marketplace), buying

in reverse auctions and in group and desktop purchasing (the buy-side marketplace), and trading in electronic exchanges.

**❺** EC activities can be conducted inside organizations. Three types are recognized: between a business and its employees, between units of the business, and among employees of the same organization.

**❻** E-government commerce can take place between government and citizens, between businesses and governments, or among government units. It makes government operations more effective and efficient.

**❻** EC also can be done between consumers (C2C), but should be undertaken with caution. Auctions are the most popular C2C mechanism. C2C also can be done by use of online classified ads.

**❼** New electronic payment systems are needed to complete transactions on the Internet. Electronic payments can be made by e-checks, e-credit cards, purchasing cards, e-cash, stored-value money cards, smart cards, person-to-person payments via services like PayPal, electronic bill presentment and payment, and e-wallets.

**❼** Order fulfillment is especially difficult and expensive in B2C, because of the need to ship relatively small orders to many customers.

**❽** As with any type of commerce, e-commerce requires advertising support. In EC, though, much of the advertising can be done online by methods such as banners, pop-ups, e-mail, electronic catalogs, and customized ads. Permission marketing, interactive and viral marketing, making it to the top of search-engine listings, and online promotions offer additional ways for vendors to reach more customers.

**❾** There is increasing fraud and unethical behavior on the Internet, including invasion of privacy by sellers and misuse of domain names.

⑨ The value of domain names, taxation of online business, and how to handle legal issues in a multicountry environment are major legal concerns.

⑨ Protection of customers, sellers, and intellectual property is also important.

⑩ Periods of innovation produce both successes and failures. There have been many of both in e-commerce. Major reasons for failure are insufficient cash flow, too much competition, conflicts with existing systems, wrong revenue models, and lack of planning. Despite the failures, overall EC volume is growing exponentially.

⑩ Five key strategies for EC success are: an appropriate revenue model, sufficient funding for the initial period, selection of the right products to sell online, entry into an area with not too many competitors, and proper planning.

## Virtual Company Assignment

### E-Commerce at The Wireless Café

Go to The Wireless Café's link on the Student Web Site. There you will find a description of the e-commerce activities that have been taking place at the restaurant. You will be asked to identify ways to use both B2C and B2B e-commerce at The Wireless Café.

*Instructions for accessing The Wireless Café on the Student Web Site:*

1. Go to *wiley.com/college/turban*.
2. Select Turban/Leidner/McLean/Wetherbe's *Information Technology for Management, Sixth Edition*.
3. Click on Student Resources site, in the toolbar on the left.
4. Click on the link for Virtual Company Web Site.
5. Click on Wireless Café.

## Online Resources

More resources and study tools are located on the Student Web Site and on WileyPLUS. You'll find additional chapter materials and useful Web links. In addition, self-quizzes that provide individualized feedback are available for each chapter.

## Questions for Review

1. Define e-commerce and distinguish it from e-business.
2. List the major types of EC (by transaction).
3. Distinguish between business-to-consumer, business-to-business, and intrabusiness EC.
4. Describe forward and reverse auctions.
5. How are forward auctions used as a selling channel?
6. Describe the process of using reverse auctions for purchasing.
7. Define electronic bartering.
8. Describe electronic storefronts and malls.
9. What are some general features (critical success factors) that make the delivery of online services (e.g., cyberbanking, securities trading, job hunting, travel services) successful for both sellers and buyers?
10. Describe how customer service is provided online and list its four phases.
11. List the major issues relating to e-tailing.
12. Describe online advertising, its methods, and benefits.
13. Describe permission marketing.
14. What is viral marketing?
15. List popular online promotion methods.
16. Briefly differentiate between the sell-side marketplace and the buy-side marketplace.
17. Describe how forward and reverse auctions are used in B2B commerce.
18. Describe the various methods of e-procurement.
19. Describe the role of exchanges in B2B.
20. Describe intrabusiness EC and list its major types.
21. Define B2E.
22. Define e-government and list its various types.
23. Describe typical G2B activities.

24. Describe customization and define mass customization.
25. Define C2C EC and list some types of C2C activities.
26. List the various electronic payment mechanisms. Which of these are most often used for B2B payments?
27. List the security requirements for EC.
28. Describe the issues in EC order fulfillment.
29. List some ethical issues in EC.
30. List the major legal issues of EC.
31. Describe buyer protection in EC.
32. Describe seller protection in EC.
33. List five reasons for EC failures.
34. List five suggestions for EC success.
35. Describe collaborative commerce.

## Questions for Discussion

1. Discuss the major limitations of e-commerce. Which of them are likely to disappear? Why?
2. Discuss the reasons for having multiple EC business models in one company.
3. Distinguish between business-to-business forward auctions and buyers' bids for RFQs.
4. Discuss the benefits to sellers and buyers of a B2B exchange.
5. What are the major benefits of e-government?
6. Discuss the various ways to pay online in B2C. Which one(s) would you prefer and why?
7. Why is order fulfillment in B2C considered difficult?
8. Discuss the reasons for EC failures.
9. Discuss the benefits of AdSense and AdWords to Web page owners (publishers) and to advertisers.
10. Discuss the role of recommendation agents in EC.

## Exercises and Projects

1. Assume you're interested in buying a car. You can find information about cars at *autos.msn.com*. Go to *autoweb. com* or *autobytel.com* for information about financing and insurance. Decide what car you want to buy. Configure your car by going to the car manufacturer's Web site. Finally, try to find the car from *autobytel.com*. What information is most supportive of your decision-making process? Write a report about your experience.
2. Consider Minicase 2 about Hi-Life.
   a. How was the corporate decision making improved?
   b. Summarize the benefits to the customers, suppliers, store management, and employees.

c. The data collected at Activesys can be uploaded to a PC and transmitted to the corporate intranet via the Internet. It is suggested that transmission be done using a wireless system. Comment on the proposal.
3. Compare the various electronic payment methods. Specifically, collect information from the vendors cited in the chapter and find more with *google.com*. Pay attention to security level, speed, cost, and convenience.
4. Go to *nacha.org*. What is NACHA? What is its role? What is the ACH? Who are the key participants in an ACH e-payment? Describe the "pilot" projects currently underway at ACH.
5. Enter *espn.com*. Identify at least five different ways it makes revenue.

## Group Assignments and Projects

1. Have each team study a major bank with extensive EC offerings. For example, Wells Fargo Bank is well on its way to being a cyberbank. Hundreds of brick-and-mortar branch offices are being closed. In Spring 2003, the bank served more than 1.2 million cyberaccounts (see *wellsfargo.com*). Other banks to look at are Citicorp, Netbank, and HSBC (Hong Kong). Each team should attempt to convince the class that its e-bank activities are the best.
2. Assign each team to one industry. Each team will find five real-world applications of the major business-to-business models listed in the chapter. (Try success stories of vendors and EC-related magazines.) Examine the problems the applications solve or the opportunities they exploit.
3. Have teams investigate how B2B payments are made in global trade. Consider instruments such as electronic letters of credit and e-checks. Visit *tradecard.com* and examine their services to SMEs. Also, investigate what Visa and MasterCard are offering. Finally, check Citicorp and some German and Japanese banks.
4. Conduct a study on selling diamonds and gems online. Each group member investigates one company such as *bluenile.com*, *diamond.com*, *thaigem.com*, *tiffany.com*, or *jewelryexchange.com*.
   a. What features are used in these sites to educate buyers about gemstones?
   b. How do the sites attract buyers?

c. How do the sites increase trust for online purchasing?

d. What customer service features are provided?

e. Would you buy a $5,000 diamond ring online? Why, or why not?

5. Enter *dell.com* and read Rappa (2006) and find information on the EC direct model, affiliate programs, and Enterprise Command Center (*dell.com/ecc*). Write a report.

6. Conduct a study on social networking sites. Each group will check a specific type. For example, one group can check company-sponsored sites, such as *MyCoke.com*, *CarnivalConnections.com* or *Nissanclub.com*. Each group prepares a report on the objectives of the sites, on their members, content, and mode of operation. Find how they are sponsored or generate ad revenue.

## Internet Exercises

1. Use the Internet to plan a trip to Paris. Visit *lonelyplanet.com, yahoo.com,* and *expedia.com.*
   a. Find the lowest airfare.
   b. Examine a few hotels by class.
   c. Get suggestions of what to see.
   d. Find out about local currency, and convert $1,000 to that currency with an online currency converter.
   e. Compile travel tips.
   f. Prepare a report.

2. Access *realtor.com*. Prepare a list of services available on this site. Then prepare a list of advantages derived by the users and advantages to realtors. Are there any disadvantages? To whom?

3. Enter *alibaba.com*. Identify the site's capabilities. Look at the site's private trading room. Write a report. How can such a site help a person who is making a purchase?

4. Enter *campusfood.com*. Explore the site. Why is the site so successful? Could you start a competing one? Why or why not?

5. Enter *dell.com,* go to "desktops" and configure a system. Register to "my cart" (no obligation). What calculators are used there? What are the advantages of this process as compared to buying a computer in a physical store? What are the disadvantages?

6. Enter *checkfree.com* and *lmlpayment.com* and find their services. Prepare a comparison.

7. Enter *resumix.yahoo.com* and summarize the services they provide.

8. Read the Amazon.com case 52 and WalMart.com (Online File W5.7). Visit both sites and search for the same products. Compare the sites' functionalities and ease of use. Prepare a report.

9. Enter *housevalues.com* and find the various services it provides under several URLs. What is its revenue model?

10. Enter *queendom.com* and examine its offerings. Try some. What type of EC is this? How does the site make money?

11. Enter *ediets.com*. Prepare a list of all services the company provides. Identify its revenue model. Check the company's stock (NASDAQ: DIET).

12. Enter *tradecard.com*. Run the procure-to-pay demo. Summarize the processes and benefits of the service to a small exporter.

13. Enter *cybersource.com*. Identify the services available for B2B payments. Write a report.

14. Enter *knot.com* and identify its revenue sources.

## Minicase 1

### From Paper to E-Payments: The Story of Wells Fargo Home Mortgage

The largest home mortgage originator in the United States is Wells Fargo Home Mortgage. It has a portfolio of more than 4.6 million loans. For most of its history, Wells Fargo's loan customers have made their payments the old-fashioned way—mailing their checks on a monthly basis to Wells Fargo's network of external lockboxes. A sizeable portion of its customers even drop off payments at local Wells Fargo Bank branches. For some time, it has provided a telephone payment program enabling customers, who have forgotten to mail their checks, to make payments at the last minute in order to avoid late fees.

With this large of a portfolio, the costs of handling paper collections can have a substantial impact on the bottom line. The cost to Wells Fargo of just clearing checks was more than US$1 million annually. To address this problem, in 2000, Wells Fargo embarked on a program to increase collections efficiency and reduce the costs of processing payments.

In the first quarter of 2000, the ratio of paper to e-payments was four to one. At that time, three e-payment options were available to customers: direct payment, equity payments, and third-party processors. Of those using e-payment options, 350,000 were using direct payment, 100,000 were using equity payments, and 133,000 were utilizing third parties. By 2002, Wells Fargo Home Mortgage was offering a full suite of e-payments methods, including:

- Automatic mortgage payments—ACH direct payments.
- Online payments—Internet-initiated ACH debits.
- Just in time—telephone-initiated ACH debits.
- EBPP. Statements are presented and bills can be paid online at a Wells Fargo–hosted Web site.
- Wells Fargo Equity Enhancement Program (EEP). Payments are debited from a customer's bank account every two weeks.

With the addition of these methods, customer acceptance and use of e-payments methods began to grow. In the first quarter of 2002, Wells Fargo processed 3.4 million e-payments. By the third quarter of 2003, the number was 4.3 million e-payments, an increase of 26 percent. In that quarter, the ratio of paper to e-payments was 1.9 to 1. Even with the growth in e-payments, however, in 2003, lockbox payments still accounted for close to 60 percent of all payments.

For Wells Fargo, the lockboxes were by far the most expensive payment method. The cost was US$3 per loan annually. At the other end, ACH direct payments produced US$11 in cost reduction and float annually.

In 2002, the NACHA rules governing accounts receivable (check) conversion (ARC) went into effect. ARC is a service that allows consumer checks sent to a lockbox or drop box location to be converted to an ACH electronic debit. Under these rules, consumers authorize the conversion of the check payments to electronic payments when they mail their remittance and check to the biller. Before the conversion can take place, the biller must communicate its conversion intentions to the customer in the billing documentation. In essence, the conversion takes place unless the customer objects. ARC is well suited for repetitive payments, such as mortgages, utility bills, insurance payments, and the like. The challenge for the biller rests with streamlining and automating the process of

converting checks to ACH debits to achieve a high acceptance rate by consumers.

In 2003, Wells Fargo Home Mortgage became the first mortgage company to implement ARC. By November 2004, four out of five of its lockbox locations were converted. Few customers opted to remain with paper check payments. Overall, the ACR program succeeded in turning the tide toward e-payments. By the end of the first quarter of 2004, e-payments comprised 88 percent of Well Fargo's loan portfolio, up from 35 percent in the pre-ARC era. At the end of the fourth quarter of 2004, the ratio of paper payments to electronic payments was one to seven.

The financial impact of the ARC program has been twofold. First, there has been close to a US$2 million savings from decreased bank fees and increased float. Second, the collection rate for checks returned due to NSF (insufficient funds) has increased significantly.

Wells Fargo Home Mortgage's experiences with ARC are not unique, although the shift from paper to e-payments is groundbreaking. According to the NACHA, ARC entries went from 5.3 million in 2002 to 43.7 million in 2003 to 208 million in the second quarter of 2004. In 2004, ARC payments totaled US$60.8 billion. ARC is now the largest e-check ACH application.

*Sources:* Compiled from Banwart (2004) and PRNewsWire (2004).

### Questions for Minicase 1

1. As with many other financial institutions, Wells Fargo Home Mortgage (WFHM) has offered a number of e-payment options to its customers. Describe the options WFHM offered before ARC. Why weren't these options sufficient to move WFHM's customers from paper to e-payment?

2. Using information from the NACHA Web site, describe the basic rules underlying ARC. Why did this result in the shift from paper to e-payment for WFHM's loan customers?

3. Based on WFHM's experience, if a company wanted to convince its customers to adopt online payment, what advice would you offer?

## Minicase 2

POM  GLOBAL

# E-Commerce Improves Inventory Control at Hi-Life Corporation

### The Business Problem

Hi-Life Corporation owns and operates 720 convenience retail stores in Taiwan, where the company sells over 3,000 different products. A major problem is keeping a proper level of inventory of each product in each store. Over-

stocking is expensive due to storage costs and tying up space and money to buy and maintain the inventory. Understocking reduces potential sales and could result in unhappy customers who may go to a competitor.

To calculate the appropriate level of inventory, it is necessary to know exactly how many units of each product are in stock at specific times. This is done by what is known as *stock count*. Periodic stock count is needed since the actual amount in stock frequently differs from the computed one (inventory = previous inventory − sales + new arrivals). The difference is due to "shrinkage" (e.g., theft, misplaced items, spoilage, etc.). Until 2002, stock counts at Hi-Life were done manually. Employees counted the quantity of each product and recorded it on data collection sheets on which the products' names were preprinted. Then, the data were painstakingly keyed into each store's PC. The process took over 21 person-hours, in each store, each time a count was needed, sometimes once a week. This process was expensive and frequently was delayed, causing problems along the entire supply chain due to delays in count and mismatches of computed and actual inventories.

### The IT Solution

The first phase of improvement was introduced in spring 2002. Management introduced a Pocket PC (a handheld device) from Hewlett-Packard. The Pocket PC (called Jornada) enables employees to enter the inventory tallies directly into electronic forms using Chinese characters for additional notes. Once the Pocket PC is placed in its synchronized cradle (see Chapter 6), inventory information can be relayed instantly to Hi-Life's headquarters.

In the second phase of improvement, in summer 2003, a compact barcode scanner was added on in the Pocket PC's expansion slot. Employees can now scan the products' barcodes and then enter the quantity found on the shelf. This new feature expedites data entry and minimizes errors in product identification. The up-to-the second information enables headquarters to compute appropriate inventory levels in minutes, to better schedule shipments, and to plan purchasing strategies using decision-support system formulas. The stores use the Internet (with a secured feature known as VPN; see Technology Guide 4) to upload data to the intranet at headquarters.

### The Results

The results have been astonishing. Inventory taking has been reduced from 21 to less than 4 hours per store, per count. Errors are down by more than 90 percent, order placing is simple and quick, and administrative paperwork has been eliminated. Furthermore, quicker and more precise inventory counts have resulted in lower inventory levels and in quicker response times for changes in demand. The entire product-management process has become more efficient, including stocking, price checks, and reticketing.

For the employees, the new system is very user friendly, both to learn and to operate. Hi-Life's employees now have more time to plan, manage, and chat with customers. More important, faster and better inventory and purchasing decisions are enabled at headquarters, contributing to greater competitiveness and profitability for Hi-Life.

*Sources:* Compiled from *hp.com/jornada* (accessed May 2003) and from *microsoft.com/asia/mobile* (accessed May 2003).

### Questions for Minicase 2

1. Explain why this is B2E.
2. How is corporate decision making improved?
3. Summarize the benefits to customers, employees, and the company.

# References

Athitakis, M., "How to Make Money on the Net," *Business 2.0*, May 2003.

Baker, S., "The Online Ad Surge," *Business Week*, November 22, 2004.

Banwart, J., "From 81 Percent Paper to 88 Percent E-Payments in Four Years," NACHA, 2004, *nacha.org/otherresources/buyers2004/BuyersGuide2004_81=88_ePay.pdf* (accessed December 2004).

Bayers, C., "The Last Laugh (of Amazon's CEO)," *Business 2.0*, September 2002.

Bayles, D. L., *E-Commerce Logistics and Fulfillment.* Upper Saddle River, NJ: Prentice Hall, 2001.

Brook, O., "Auto-Tech Display Shows Promis for Future of Collaborative Commerce," *MSI*, 22(11), 2004.

"Case Study: ChemConnect," *digitalenterprise.org/cases/chemconnect.html* (accessed September 2006).

Chase, L., "Top Ten Success of Secrets of Email Marketing," *rightnow.com/resource/RN_EmailSuccess.html?look=p* (accessed March 2006).

Choi, S. Y., et al., *The Economics of Electronic Commerce.* Indianapolis: Macmillan Technical Publications, 1997.

Cohen, P., "iTunes Music Store Tops 250 Million Songs Sold," *MacWorld*, January 24, 2005, *macorld.com/news/2005/01/24/itunes/index.php* (accessed June 2006).

Copeland, M. V., "The eBay of Swap," *Business 2.0*, May 2006.

Copeland, M. V., et al., "How to Succeed in 2005" (eBay, Amazon and more), *Business 2.0*, December 2004.

Croxton, K. L., "The Order Fulfillment Process," *International Journal of Logistics Management*, 14(1), 2003, pp. 19–32.

Daisey, M., *21 Dog Years: Doing Time @ amazon.com.* New York: Free Press, 2002.

Delaney, K. J., "Once-Wary Industry Giants Embrace Internet Advertising," *Wall Street Journal*, April 17, 2006.

Esfahani, E., "Why 'Buy' Buttons Are Booming," *CNNMoney.com*, July 1, 2006, *money.cnn.com/magazines/business2/business2_archive/2005/07/01/8265513/index.htm* (accessed June 2006).

Fass, A., "TheirSpace.com," *Forbes*, May 8, 2006.

Ferguson, R. B., "Microsoft, GXS Announce Partnership," *eWeek*, May 8, 2006.

Flynn, L. J., "Like This? You'll Hate That. (Not All Web Recommendations Are Welcome.)," *New York Times*, January 23, 2006.

Freedman, L., "Merchant Secret for Driving Conversion," *Ecommerceguide.com*, November 14, 2005.

Gilden, J., "Popularity of Web Forces Travel Agents to Adjust," *Chicago Tribune*, March 14, 2004.

Gross, D., "Birth of a Salesman," *Fortune*, August 8, 2005.

Gross, D., et al., "The Future of Advertising," *Fortune*, August 8, 2005.

Hines, M., "Digital Content Spurs Micropayment Resurgence," *ZDNet-News*, September 7, 2004, *news.zdnet.com/2100-3513_22-5347513.html* (accessed June 2006).

Holden, G., "Fast Forward," *Entrepreneur*, May 2006.

Hoogeweegen, M. R., and R. W. Wagenaar. "Assessing Costs and Benefits of EDI." *The Eighth International Conference in EDI-IOS,* Bled, Slovenia, Moderna Organizadija, Kranj, Slovenia, June 5-8, 1995.

Ignatius, A., "In Search of the Real Google," *Time*, February 20, 2006.

Jiang, Z., W. Wang, and I. Benbasat, "Online Consumer Decision Support," *Communications of the ACM*, September 2005.

Kambil, A., and E. van Heck, *Making Markets*. Boston: Harvard Business School Press, 2002.

Kaplan, P. J., *The F'd Companies: Spectacular Dot.Com Flameouts*. New York: Simon & Schuster, 2002.

Kaplan, S., and M. Sawhney, "E-Hubs: The New B2B Marketplaces," *Harvard Business Review,* May 1, 2000.

Kraemer, K., and J. Dedrick, *"Dell Computer: Using E-Commerce to Support a Virtual Company,"* special report, June 2001. Available in Rappa (2006).

Lashinsky, A., "The Boom is Back," *Fortune*, May 1, 2006.

Lee, S. C., and A. A. Brandyberry, "The E-Tailer's Dilemma," *Data Base*, Spring 2003.

Lee, Y., et al., "Coping with Internet Channel Conflict," *Communications of the ACM,* 46(7), 2003, pp. 137–142.

Luo, W., and M. Najdawi, "Trust-Building Measures: A Review of Consumer Health Portals," *Communications of the ACM,* 47(1), 2004, pp. 108–113.

Lyons, R., "eBay Course for Beginners at University," *Birmingham Post*, Birmingham, UK, April 23, 2004, p. 4.

Null, C. "How Netflix Is Fixing Hollywood by Finding a Market for Niche Titles," *CNNMoney.com,* July 1, 2003.

Office of Government Commerce, "eProcurement in Action: A Guide to eProcurement for the Public Sector," *Ocg.gov.uk*, Spring 2005, *ogc.gov.uk/embedded_object.asp?docid=1003723* (accessed June 2006).

Papazoglou, M. P., and P. M. A. Ribbers, *e-Business*. West Sussex, England: John Wiley & Sons Ltd., 2006.

Parks, L., "Music Retailer Tunes Up Marketing Programs," *Stores*, February 2006.

Patrick, A. O., "Commercials by Cellphone," *Wall Street Journal*, August 22, 2005.

Peppercoin, "Quantifying the Small Payments Potential," 2005, *peppercoin.com/marketvision/pov.shtml* (accessed June 2006).

PRNewsWire, "Wells Fargo Home Mortgage Receives NACHA's 2004 Payments System Award," *PRNewsWire.com*, February 2, 2004, *prnewswire.com/cgibin/stories.pl?ACCT=104&STORY=/www/story/02-02-2004/0002100786&EDATE=* (accessed June 2006).

Rappa, M., "Case Study: Dell Computer," *digitalenterprise.org/cases/dell.html* (accessed May 2006).

Savitz, E., "Look Who's Storming the Net," *SmartMoney*, June 2005.

Schonfield, E., "The World According to eBay," *Business 2.0*, January 19, 2005.

Smith, S., "Sharing the Wealth" (contextual advertising), *EContent*, April 2004.

Staff, "The Complete Guide to Using e Bay," Reference Series, *Smart Computing*, 9(2), 2005.

Stafford, M. R., and R. J. Faber, *Advertising, Promotion and New Media*. Armonk, NY: M. E. Sharpe, 2004.

Turban, E., et. al., *Electronic Commerce: A Managerial Perspective 2008*. Upper Saddle River, NJ: Prentice Hall, 2008.

Useem, J., "Dot-Coms: What Have We Learned?" *Fortune*, October 2000.

Vogelstein, F., "Yahoo's Brilliant Solution," *Fortune*, August 8, 2005.

# Chapter

# 6

# Mobile, Wireless, and Pervasive Computing

Food Lion Excels with Wireless Innovations

**6.1** Mobile Computing and Commerce: Overview, Benefits, and Drivers

**6.2** Mobile Applications in Financial Services

**6.3** Mobile Shopping, Advertising, and Content-Providing

**6.4** Mobile Enterprise and Interbusiness Applications

**6.5** Mobile Consumer Services and Entertainment

**6.6** Location-Based Services and Commerce

**6.7** Pervasive Computing

**6.8** Managerial Issues

## Minicases:

1. *Hertz*
2. *Washington Township (OH)*

## Learning Objectives

After studying this chapter, you will be able to:

❶ Discuss the characteristics and attributes of mobile computing and m-commerce.

❷ Describe the drivers of mobile computing.

❸ Understand the technologies that support mobile computing.

❹ Describe wireless standards and transmission networks.

❺ Discuss m-commerce applications in financial and other services, advertising, and providing of content.

❻ Describe the applications of m-commerce within organizations (mobile enterprise).

❼ Understand B2B and supply chain applications (interorganizational) of m-commerce.

❽ Describe consumer and personal applications of m-commerce.

❾ Describe some non-Internet m-commerce applications.

❿ Describe location-based commerce (l-commerce).

⓫ Discuss the key characteristics and current uses of pervasive computing.

⓬ Describe the major inhibitors and barriers of mobile computing and m-commerce.

## Integrating *IT*

**ACC**

**FIN**

**MKT**

**POM**

**HRM**

**IS**

**SVC**

# FOOD LION EXCELS WITH WIRELESS INNOVATIONS

## The Problem

Food Lion grocer is a supermarket chain (1,200 stores) that decided to distinguish itself from the competition, which is extremely fierce among grocers. (A major competitor is Wal-Mart.) The company created *Bloom*, an upscale brand of grocery store that provides a sensible, uncomplicated, hassle-free shopping experience that leaves shoppers feeling smart, relaxed, and confident. The problem was to find the appropriate technology to achieve it.

## The Solution

The company decided to use wireless technology. Here are some of the projects:

- **Mobile checkstand.** This is a mobile check-out POS terminal equipped with wheels that can be moved to any location in the store or outside (e.g., front for special sales). This brings flexibility and ability to expedite checkout time. These devices can be added whenever checkout lines are getting long.
- **Personal scanner.** This is a handheld device that is a POS terminal emulating the IBM checkout system. The device is given to the customers. When a shopper picks up an item off the shelf, he or she scans that item before putting it into the cart. The device shows the price of the item and the running $ subtotal of all items bagged. The Personal Scanner (from Symbol Technology) also enables sending messages to the customers while shopping, including special marketing offers. The final bill is downloaded to the cash register.
- **Employee handheld devices.** These devices enable employees to execute inventory counts, enter orders for depleted items, do shelf-tag printing, and conduct price management, anywhere in the store.
- **Cart-mounted tablet PC.** This device enables customers to check prices and get product location and information while pushing their carts. Currently, this is done on an experimental basis due to the high cost.
- **Tablet PCs for employees.** The device is docked in the office and carried around wherever the manager goes while maintaining a wireless connection to the store system. Employees may prefer it over PDAs and smart cell phones due to the large screen (but it is heavy, so not all employees like it).
- **Mobile manager.** This is a cell-phone-sized portable device used to improve communication and supervision.

- **Wi-Fi access.** This is an in-store wireless network (WLAN) that supports the above devices.

To deter cheating in the self-scanning, a random audit is done, but this may alienate a customer, especially if the customer is in a hurry. In the future, the company will install an RFID system that will improve the existing system and reduce the possibility of cheating.

## The Results

Speedier checkout is the main benefit since all the customer has to do is to pay. Also, in the future, the purchase can be debited directly from the customers' bank account to make checkout even faster. The customers are also happy since they can compare the running total against their budget while shopping. The use of the personal scanner enables the company to reduce prices and increase revenue. Other devices helped increase employee productivity and satisfaction.

*Note:* Food Lion is a Delhaige Group Company. Separate financial results are not available. The Bloom concept is still under experimentation in several stores. If successful, it will be installed in many stores.

*Sources:* Compiled from Clark (2005) and McGuire (2004).

*Note:* Food Lion is not the only retailer experimenting with wireless devices. Metro Group in Germany (2,400 stores) is experimenting with future stores with all the devices cited earlier plus some more. For example, a tablet PC helps shoppers navigate their way to any product, using the store map (see photo). For details, see Heinrich (2005).

METRO Shopping cart with display screen. (*Source:* C. Heinrich, *RFID and Beyond,* Indianapolis, Wiley Publishing, 2005, Figure 3.1, p. 59.)

## Lessons Learned from This Case

The opening case illustrates several applications of different wireless devices. We can see that the technology improved the operation of the business in what is known as *mobile enterprise*. Benefits are observed for the customers, employees, and management. Using wireless technologies, one can create applications that are not available with wireline systems. However, some may be expensive (e.g., the cart-mounted tablet PCs). The case's applications are based on a local area infrastructure, called Wi-Fi. All this is part of the *mobile computing* field.

This opening case is an example of mobile computing, in which EC services are provided to customers located at specific places at the time they need services. This capability, which is not available in regular EC, may change many things in our lives. Mobile computing is a computing paradigm designed for workers who travel outside the boundaries of their organizations or for people on the move.

Mobile computing and commerce are spreading rapidly, replacing or supplementing wired computing. Mobile computing involves mostly wireless infrastructure. Mobile computing may reshape the entire IT field (see Deans, 2004; D'Agostino, 2005; and Longino, 2006). The technologies, applications, and limitations of mobile computing and mobile commerce are the main focus of this chapter. Later in the chapter, we will look briefly at futuristic applications of *pervasive computing*.

# 6.1 Mobile Computing and Commerce: Overview, Benefits, and Drivers

**THE MOBILE COMPUTING LANDSCAPE**

In the traditional computing environment it was necessary to come to the computer to do some work on it. All computers were connected to each other, to networks, servers, and so on via *wires*. This situation limited the use of computers and created hardship for people and workers on the move. In particular, salespeople, repair people, service employees, law enforcement agents, and utility workers can be more effective if they can use information technology while at their jobs in the field or in transit. There are also mobile vacationers, people on holiday who wish to be connected with the Internet from any place, at any time.

The first solution was to make computers small enough so they can be easily carried around. First, the laptop computer was invented, and later on smaller and smaller computers, such as the PDAs and other handhelds, appeared. These *mobile devices* have become lighter and more powerful as far as processing speed and storage. At the end of the day, mobile workers could download (or upload) information from (or to) a regular desktop computer in a process known as *synchronization*. To speed up the "sync," special connecting cradles (docking stations) were created (see Minicase 2 at the end of this chapter and the Maybelline Minicase in Chapter 2).

Salespeople can make proposals at customers' offices; a traveler could read and answer all of the day's e-mails while on the road.

**POM**

For example, National Distributing Company (NDC), one of the three top alcoholic beverage distributors in the United States, needed a point-of-service (POS) tool for its 1,000-person sales team to perform order entry and CRM applications while at the customer location. The company chose Fujitsu's pen tablet PCs and a cellular phone. NDC's sales representatives now dial up the company's mainframe computer directly and access its CRM applications and Web-enabled order entry. The pen tablet PCs provide NDC's sales representatives with real-time data on order status, product availability, customer account status, and other information, while they meet face-to-face with the customer (Fujitsu Computer Systems, 2006).

The second solution to the need for mobile computing was to replace wires with *wireless communication media.* Wireless systems have been in use in radio, TV, and telephones for a long time, so it was natural to adapt them to the computing environment (for more, see *Wired,* 2003).

The third solution was a combination of the first two, namely to use mobile devices in a wireless environment. Referred to as **wireless mobile computing,** this combination enables a real-time connection between a mobile device and other computing environments, such as the Internet or an intranet. This innovation changed the way people use computers. It is used in education, health care, entertainment, security, and much more. This computing model is basically leading to *ubiquity*—meaning that computing is available anywhere, at any time. (Note: Since many mobile applications now go wireless, the term *mobile computing* today is often used generally to describe wireless mobile computing.)

Due to some current technical limitations, we cannot (yet) do with mobile computing all the things that we do with regular computing. On the other hand, we can do things in mobile computing that we cannot do in the regular computing environment. A major boost to mobile computing was provided in 2003 by Intel with its Centrino chip. This chip, which became a standard feature in most laptops by 2005, includes three important capabilities: (1) a connection device to a wireless local area network, (2) low usage of electricity, enabling users to do more work on a single battery charge, and (3) a high level of security. The Centrino is expected to make mobile computing the common computing environment.

A second driving development of mobile computing is the introduction of the third- and fourth-generation wireless environments known as 3G and 4G, and the adoption of Wi-Fi as a wireless local area network (LAN). They were described in Chapter 4.

## MOBILE COMMERCE

While the impact of mobile computing on our lives will be very significant, a similar impact is already occurring in the way we conduct business. This impact is described as *mobile commerce* (also known as *m-commerce*), which is basically any e-commerce or e-business done in a wireless environment, especially via the Internet. Like regular EC applications, m-commerce can be done via the Internet, private communication lines, smart cards, or other infrastructures (e.g., see Mennecke and Strader, 2003; Shi, 2004; and Frolick and Chen, 2004).

M-commerce is not merely a variation on existing Internet services; it is a natural extension of e-business. Mobile devices create an opportunity to deliver new services to existing customers and to attract new ones. Varshney and Vetter (2000) classified the applications of m-commerce into 12 categories, as shown in Online File W6.1. (A classification by industry is provided at *mobile.commerce.net.* Also see *mobiforum.org.*)

Many of these applications, as well as some additional ones, will be discussed in this chapter. For an overview see Urbazewaski et al. (2003).

## MOBILE COMPUTING BASIC TERMINOLOGY

Let's build a foundation for further discussion by defining some common mobile computing terms (Table 6.1).

With these terms in mind, we can now look more deeply at the attributes and drivers of mobile computing.

| TABLE 6.1 | Mobile Computing Basic Terminology |
|---|---|

**Global positioning system (GPS).** A satellite-based tracking system that enables the determination of a GPS device's location. (See Section 6.7 for more on GPS.)

**Personal digital assistant (PDA).** A small portable computer, such as Palm handhelds and the Pocket PC devices from companies like H-P.

**Short Messaging Service (SMS).** A technology for sending short text messages (up to 160 characters in 2006) on cell phones. SMS messages can be sent or received concurrently, even during a voice or data call. Used by hundreds of millions of users, SMS is known as "the e-mail of m-commerce." Some companies offer multilanguage text creation.

**Enhanced Messaging Service (EMS).** An extension of SMS that is capable of simple animation, tiny pictures, and short melodies.

**Multimedia Messaging Service (MMS).** The next generation of wireless messaging, this technology will be able to deliver rich media.

**Bluetooth.** A chip technology wireless standard designed for temporary, short-range connection (data and voice) among mobile devices and/or other devices (see *bluetooth.org*).

**Wireless Application Protocol (WAP).** A technology that offers Internet browsing from wireless devices.

**Smart phones.** Internet-enabled cell phones that can support mobile applications. These "phones with a brain" are becoming standard devices. They include WAP microprocessors for Internet access and the capabilities of PDAs as well.

**Wi-Fi (**short for **Wireless Fidelity).** Refers to the standard 802.11b on which most of the wireless local area networks (WLANs) run.

**(Wireless Local Area Network (WLAN)).** A broad term for all 802.11 standards. Basically, it is a wireless version of the Ethernet networking standard. (For discussion of the Ethernet standard, see Technology Guide 4.)

**WiMax.** A wireless technology based on the IEEE 802.16-2004 standard, designed to provide Internet access across metro areas to fixed (not moving) users. It is considered wireless broadband technology. For details see Chapter 4 and Technology Guide 4.

---

**ATTRIBUTES AND DRIVERS OF MOBILE COMPUTING**

Generally speaking, many of the EC applications described in Chapter 5 can be done in m-commerce. For example, e-shopping, e-banking, and e-stock trading are gaining popularity in wireless B2C. Auctioning is just beginning to take place on cell phones, and wireless collaborative commerce in B2B is emerging. However, there are several *new* applications that are possible *only* in the mobile environment. To understand why this is so, first let's examine the major attributes of mobile computing and m-commerce.

**Specific Attributes of Mobile Computing and M-Commerce.** Mobile computing has two major characteristics that differentiate it from other forms of computing: *mobility* and *broad reach*.

1. **Mobility.** Mobile computing and m-commerce are based on the fact that users carry a mobile device anywhere they go. Mobility implies portability. Therefore, users can initiate a *real-time* contact with other systems from wherever they happen to be if they can connect to a wireless network.

2. **Broad reach.** In mobile computing, people can be reached at any time. Of course, users can block certain hours or certain messages, but when users carry an open mobile device, they can be reached instantly.

These two characteristics break the barriers of geography and time. They create the following five value-added attributes that drive the development of m-commerce: ubiquity, convenience, instant connectivity, personalization, and localization of products and services.

**Ubiquity.** *Ubiquity* refers to the attribute of being available at *any location* at *any given time.* A smart phone or a PDA offers ubiquity—that is, it can fulfill the need both for real-time information and for communication, independent of the user's location.

**Convenience.** It is very convenient for users to operate in the wireless environment. All they need is an Internet-enabled mobile device such as a smart phone. By using *GPRS* (General Packet Radio Service, a cell phone standard), it is easier and faster to access the Web without booting up a PC or placing a call via a modem. Also, more and more places are equipped with Wi-Fi, enabling users to get online from portable laptops any time (as was shown in the Dartmouth College case in Chapter 1). You can even watch an entire movie on a PDA (see *pocketpcfilms.com*).

**Instant Connectivity.** Mobile devices enable users to connect easily and quickly to the Internet, intranets, other mobile devices, and databases. Thus, wireless devices could become the preferred way to access information.

**Personalization.** *Personalization* refers to the preparation of customized information for individual consumers. For example, a user who is identified as someone who likes to travel might be sent travel-related information and advertising. Product personalization is still limited on mobile devices. However, the need for conducting transactions electronically, availability of personalized information, and transaction feasibility via mobile portals will move personalization to new levels, leading ultimately to the mobile device becoming a major EC tool. The process of personalization is described by Dogac and Turner (2002).

**Localization of Products and Services.** Knowing where the user is physically located at any particular moment is key to offering relevant products and services. E-commerce applications based on localization of products and services are known as **location-based e-commerce** or **l-commerce.** Precise location information is known when a GPS is attached to a user's wireless device. For example, you might use your mobile device to find the nearest ATM or FedEx drop box. In addition, the GPS can tell others where you are. Localization can be general, such as to anyone in a certain location (e.g., all shoppers at a shopping mall). Or, even better, it can be targeted so that users get messages that depend both on where they are and what *their preferences* are, thus combining localization and personalization. For instance, if it is known that you like Italian food and you are strolling in a mall that has an Italian restaurant, you might receive an SMS that tells you that restaurant's "special of the day" and gives you a 10 percent discount. GPS may be a standard feature in many mobile devices by 2008.

**Drivers of Mobile Computing and M-Commerce.** In addition to the value-added attributes just discussed, the development of mobile computing and m-commerce is driven by the following factors.

**Widespread Availability of Mobile Devices.** The number of cell phones throughout the world exceeded 1.8 billion in 2006 (Maier, 2006). It is estimated that within a few years, about 70 percent of cell phones will have Internet access. Thus, a potential mass market is available for conducting discovery, communication, collaboration, and m-commerce. Cell phones are spreading quickly even in developing countries.

**No Need for a PC.** Today's cell phones have as much processing power as personal computers did just a few years ago, and possess the range of software available to PC users. This suggests that the cell phone—not the PC—may soon become the foremost tool that connects people to the Internet (Maier, 2006). Smart phones and other wireless devices obviate the need for a PC.

**The Handset Culture.** Another driver of m-commerce is the widespread use of cell phones, which is a social phenomenon, especially among the 15-to-25-year-old age group. These users will constitute a major force of online buyers once they begin to make and spend larger amounts of money. The use of SMS has been spreading like wildfire in several European and Asian countries. In the Philippines, for example, SMS is a national phenomenon in the youth market. As another example, Japanese send many more messages through mobile phones than do Americans, who prefer the desktop or laptop for e-mail.

**Declining Prices and Increased Functionalities.** The price of wireless devices is declining, and the per-minute pricing of mobile services declined by 50 percent before 2006 (U.S. 2003 prices). At the same time, functionalities are increasing. For ROI studies, see Chapter 14.

**Improvement of Bandwidth.** To properly conduct m-commerce, it is necessary to have sufficient bandwidth for transmitting text; however, bandwidth is also required for voice, video, and multimedia. The 3G (third-generation) technology (described in Chapter 4) provides the necessary bandwidth.

| M-COMMERCE VALUE CHAIN AND REVENUE MODELS | Like EC, m-commerce is a complex process involving a number of operations and a number of players (customers, merchants, mobile operators, service providers, and the like). Several types of vendors provide value-added services to m-commerce. These include: mobile portals, advertisers, software vendors, content providers, mobile portal, mobile network operators, and more. (See Sadeh, 2002, p. 34.) |

The revenue models of m-commerce are the following: access fees, subscription fees, pay-per-use, advertising, transaction fees, hosting, payment clearing, and point-of-traffic (Coursaris and Hassanein, 2002).

The capabilities and attributes of mobile computing presented earlier provide for many applications, as shown in Figure 6.1. These attributes are supported by infrastructure. According to Alter (2005) and to Nokia's advertising, mobility moves from productivity improvement to a strategic part of the enterprise's IT portfolio.

| WIRELESS LOCAL AREA NETWORKS AND WI-FI | As you read in Chapter 4 and Appendix 4a, wireless local area networks have been making their way to the wireless forefront. A *wireless LAN (WLAN)* is like a wired LAN without the cables. WLANs transmit and receive data over the airwaves from a short distance in what is known as Wi-Fi. |

**The Wi-Fi Revolution.** In a typical configuration, a transmitter with an antenna, called a *wireless access point* (WAP) connects to a wired LAN from a fixed location or to satellite dishes that provide an Internet connection. A WAP provides service to a number of users within a couple hundred feet, known as a "hotspot zone," or *hotspot.* Several WAPs are needed to support larger numbers of users across a larger geographical area. End users can access a WLAN with their laptops, desktops,

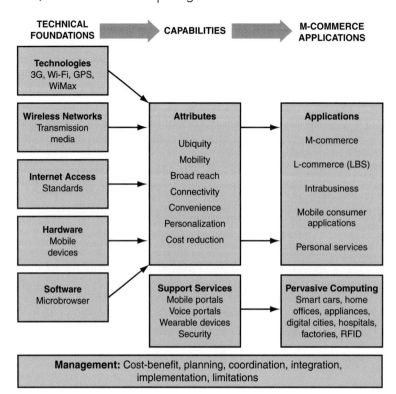

**Figure 6.1** The landscape of mobile computing and commerce. (*Source:* Drawn by E. Turban.)

or PDAs by adding a wireless network card. Figure 6.2 shows how Wi-Fi works. Null et al. (2004) provide a step-by-step guide for building Wi-Fi at home or in small-business settings.

WLANs provide fast and easy Internet or intranet broadband access from public hotspots like airports, hotels, Internet cafes, and conference centers. WLANs are also being used in universities (recall the Dartmouth case in Chapter 1), offices, and homes in place of the traditional wired LANs (see *weca.net*).

Most WLANs run on the *802.11b* standard that was developed by the IEEE (Institute of Electrical and Electronics Engineers). That standard is also called *Wi-Fi (wireless fidelity)*. WLANs employing this standard have communication speeds of 11 Mbps. While most wired networks run at 100 Mbps, 11 Mbps is actually sufficient for many applications. While PCs can take advantage of 54 Mbps, today's (2006) PDAs cannot, because their expansion (network) cards are limited to the 11 Mbps speed. As of 2004 there was hardware and software that supports voice over Wi-Fi *(telephony)*.

The major benefits of Wi-Fi are its lower cost and ability to provide simple Internet access. As a matter of fact it is the greatest facilitator of the *wireless Internet* (see Anderson, 2003).

**Wireless Personal Area Networks (WPANs).** A *wireless personal area network* (WPAN) is a kind of WLAN that people have at their home or small offices. With such a network, one can connect PCs, PDAs, mobile phones, and digital music players that detect each other and can interact. Also, one can add a digital payment system and personal security technologies. The network maintains constant connectivity among devices, which is useful for users in office settings, including those who use wearable devices.

**Figure 6.2** How Wi-Fi works.

1    **Radio-equipped access point connected to the internet (or via a router). It generates and receives radio waves (up to 400 feet).**
2    **Several client devices, equipped with PC cards, generate and receive radio waves.**
3    **Router is connected to the internet via a cable or DSL modem, or is connected via a satellite.**

**Illustrative Applications of Wi-Fi.** The years 2004 through 2006 were a breakthrough era for wireless networking in offices, airports, hotels, and campuses around the United States. Since then, each month brings new examples of businesses that have added Wi-Fi, RFID, or other wireless services for their employees, business partners, or customers. Several examples are presented in Table 6.2. Many more examples of Wi-Fi are included in this chapter and throughout the book.

Despite all of the development, progress is still slow, as shown next.

**Barriers to Commercial Wi-Fi Growth.** Two factors are standing in the way of Wi-Fi market growth: cost and security. First, some analysts question why anyone would pay $30 a month, $7.95 a day, or any other fee for Wi-Fi access when it is readily available in many locations for free. Because it's relatively inexpensive to set up a wireless access point that is connected to the Internet, a number of businesses offer their customers Wi-Fi access without charging them for the service. In fact, there is an organization, Freenetworks.org, aimed at supporting the creation of free community wireless network projects around the globe. In areas like San Francisco, where there is a solid core of high-tech professionals, many "gear heads" have set up

| **TABLE 6.2** | Examples of Wi-Fi Applications |
|---|---|

- Like other airports in the United States, the Minneapolis–St. Paul International airport is served by Wi-Fi. The fee is $7.95 for unlimited daily access. Northwest Airlines has 570 hotspots in the United States (*JiWire.com,* accessed May 2006).
- Lufthansa offers in-flight Wi-Fi service on its long-haul fleet. The hotspots on the planes are connected to the Internet via satellites (ITVibe, 2004).
- Since 2002, T-Mobile has installed Wi-Fi networks in several thousand Starbucks stores in the United States. T-Mobile is also installing Wi-Fi in hundreds of Borders Books & Music stores. T-Mobile charges annually, monthly, daily, or pay as you go (see *hotspot.t-mobile.com/services_plans.htm*).
- McDonald's now offers Wi-Fi hotspots in more than 7,000 restaurants around the world, and the number is increasing daily. Local service providers provide high-quality wireless service through online credit card payment, subscriptions, prepaid cards, and sometimes promotional coupons (see *mcdonalds.com/wireless.html*).
- Using a wireless ticketing system, Universal Studios in Hollywood is shortening the waiting lines for tickets at its front gate. The ticket sellers, armed with Wi-Fi–enabled devices and belt-mounted printers, not only sell tickets but also provide information. For details, see Scanlon (2003).
- CVS Corp., the largest retail pharmacy in the United States, uses Wi-Fi–based devices throughout its 4,100 stores. The handheld computers support a variety of in-store applications, including direct store delivery, price management, inventory control, and receiving. Benefits include faster transfer rates, increasing productivity and performance, reduced cost, and improved customer service. For details see *symbol.com* (1998, 2003).
- Several mining companies in Europe installed hundreds of Wi-Fi hotspots in their coal mines. Information from drills and trucks, such as their positions and the weight of their loads, is transmitted wirelessly to the control center. It increases both productivity and safety.

their own wireless hotspots that give passersby free Internet connections. This is a part of a new culture known as *war chalking* and *war driving* (see *A Closer Look 16.6* in Chapter 16).

One of the primary aims of people engaged in war driving is to highlight the lax security of Wi-Fi hotspots. This is the second barrier to widespread acceptance of Wi-Fi. Using radio waves, Wi-Fi can be interrupted by walls (resulting in poor quality at times), and it is difficult to protect. Wi-Fi does have a built-in security system, known as **Wireless Encryption Protocol (WEP),** which encrypts the communications between a client machine (laptop or PDA) and a wireless access point. However, WEP provides weak encryption, meaning that it is secured against casual hacking as long as the person setting up the network remembers to turn on the encryption. Unfortunately, many small business owners and homeowners with wireless LANs fail to do just that. For more on WEP, see Chapter 15. For more on Wi-Fi security, see Judge (2004).

**INFRASTRUCTURE AND WI-FI APPLICATIONS**

Mobile computing requires hardware, software, and networks. The major infrastructure components of mobile computing are described in Chapter 4. For details regarding Wi-Fi applications see Technology Guide 4.

# 6.2 Mobile Applications in Financial Services

**FIN**

Mobile financial applications include banking, wireless payments and micropayments, wireless wallets, bill payment services, brokerage services, and money transfers. While many of these services are simply a subset of their wireline counterparts, they have the potential to turn a mobile device into a business tool, replacing banks,

ATMs, and credit cards by letting a user conduct financial transactions with a mobile device, any time and from anywhere. In this section we will look at some of the most popular mobile applications in banking (Mallat et al., 2004) and in financial services.

**MOBILE BANKING AND STOCK TRADING**

Mobile banking is generally defined as carrying out banking transactions and other related activities via mobile (handheld) devices. The services offered include bill payments and money transfers; access administration and check book requests; balance inquiries and statements of account; interest and exchange rates, and so on; and sale/purchase of stocks (Tiwari, 2006).

Throughout Europe, the United States, and Asia, an increasing percentage of banks offer mobile access to financial and account information. For instance, Merita Bank in Sweden pioneered many services (Sadeh, 2002), and Citibank in the United States has a diversified mobile banking service. Consumers in such banks can use their mobile handsets to access account balances, pay bills, and transfer funds using SMS. The Royal Bank of Scotland, for example, uses a mobile payment service, and Banamex, one of Mexico's largest banks, is a strong provider of wireless services to customers. Many banks in Japan allow for all banking transactions to be done via cell phone. A study of banks in Germany, Switzerland, and Austria found that over 60 percent offered some form of mobile financial services (Hornberger and Kehlenbeck, 2002).

As the wireless technology and transmission speeds improve the rate of mobile financial service increases. The same picture holds true for other mobile financial applications like mobile brokering, insurance, and stock market trades.

**WIRELESS ELECTRONIC PAYMENT SYSTEMS**

Wireless payment systems transform mobile phones into secure, self-contained purchasing tools capable of instantly authorizing payments over the cellular network. The city of Montreal, Canada installed smart payment terminals that process *Pay & Go mode* wireless secure e-payments powered by solar panels. The parking terminals ensure totally secure transactions and provide information on parking space utilization to a central system (*8d.com*, 2006). In Europe and Japan, wireless purchase of tickets to movies and other events is popular (Sadeh, 2002).

**Micropayments.** If you were in Frankfurt, Germany, for example, and took a taxi ride, you could pay the taxi driver using your cell phone. As discussed in Chapter 5, electronic payments for small-purchase amounts (generally $3 or less) are called *micropayments*. The demand for wireless micropayments systems is fairly high. An A.T. Kearney study (*clickz.com/stats*, 2002) found that more than 40 percent of mobile phone users surveyed would like to use their mobile phone for small cash transactions such as transit fares or vending machines. The percentage of mobile phone users who had actually used their phones for this purpose (in 2002) was only 2 percent, reflecting the fact that very few vendors participate in micropayments systems. (The author estimates about 5 percent in 2006.) A 2004 TowerGroup study showed that the $2 billion micropayment market in 2003 will reach $11.5 billion by 2009 (reported by Hines, 2004).

**SVC**

An Israeli firm, TeleVend, Inc. (*televend.com*), has pioneered a secure platform that allows subscribers to make payments using mobile phones of any type on any cellular infrastructure. A customer places a mobile phone call to a number stipulated by the merchant, to authorize a vending device to dispense the service. Connecting to a TeleVend server, the user selects the appropriate transaction option to authorize payment. Billing can be made to the customer's bank or credit card account or to the mobile phone bill. Micropayment technology has wide-ranging applications, such as making payments to parking garages, restaurants, grocery stores, and public transportation.

**Mobile (Wireless) Wallets.** An *e-wallet* (see Chapter 5) is a piece of software that stores an online shopper's credit card numbers and other personal information so that the shopper does not have to reenter that information for every online purchase. In the recent past, companies like SNAZ offered **m-wallet** (*mobile wallet*, also known as *wireless wallet*) technologies that enabled cardholders to make purchases with a single click from their mobile devices. While most of these companies are now defunct, some cell phone providers have incorporated m-wallets in their offerings. NTT DoCoMo has been selling phones with chips in them in Japan that can be scanned by a short-range wireless reader at tens of thousands of stores since 2004. Similar capabilities using Near Field Communications (NFC) are forecast to grow in the United States beginning in 2007 and reach more than half all handsets sold by 2010 (Smith, 2006).

In the near future, Motorola plans to roll out the first cell phone m-wallet service to go national in the United States. The service would be compatible with other manufacturers' devices (Perton, 2006).

**Wireless Bill Payments.** In addition to paying bills through wireline banking or from ATMs, a number of companies are now providing their customers with the option of paying their bills directly from a cell phone (Lipset, 2003). HDFC Bank of India *(hdfcbank.com),* for example, allows customers to pay their utility bills using SMS. An example of how bill payments can be made using a mobile device is shown in Online File W6.2. This service is offered by Nordea, a pioneering provider of wireless banking services in Scandinavia.

## 6.3 Mobile Shopping, Advertising, and Content-Providing

M-commerce B2C applications are concentrated in three major areas—retail shopping (for products and services), advertising, and providing content (e.g., music, news, games) for a fee via portals. Let's examine these areas.

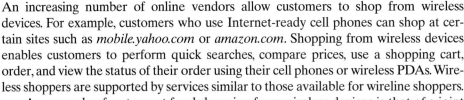

**SHOPPING FROM WIRELESS DEVICES**

An increasing number of online vendors allow customers to shop from wireless devices. For example, customers who use Internet-ready cell phones can shop at certain sites such as *mobile.yahoo.com* or *amazon.com*. Shopping from wireless devices enables customers to perform quick searches, compare prices, use a shopping cart, order, and view the status of their order using their cell phones or wireless PDAs. Wireless shoppers are supported by services similar to those available for wireline shoppers.

MKT

An example of restaurant food shopping from wireless devices is that of a joint venture between Motorola and Food.com. The companies offer restaurant chains an infrastructure that enables consumers to place an order for pickup or delivery virtually any time, anywhere. Donatos Pizzeria was the first chain to implement the system in 2002.

Cell phone users can also participate in online auctions. For example, eBay offers "anywhere wireless" services. Vendio and gNumber partnered to provide mobile eBay applications and PayPal introduced its pay-by-phone service. The ShopWiki Mobile Search engine is accessible from a PDA or cell phone browser. It allows you to comparison shop instantly and see pricing from online stores from any physical location. ShopWiki serves 60 million products from more than 120,000 stores (Comiskey, 2006).

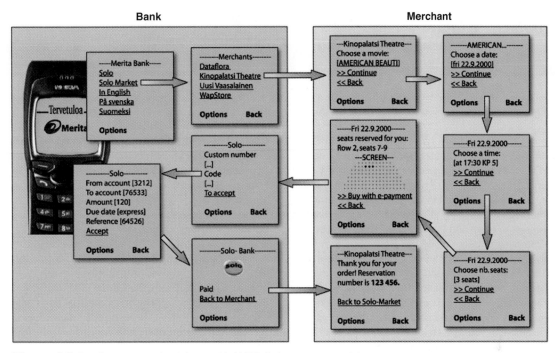

**Figure 6.3** Purchasing movie tickets with WAP Solo. (*Source:* Sadeh, 2002, Fig. 1.5.)

An example of purchasing movie tickets by wireless device is illustrated in Figure 6.3. Notice that the reservation is made directly with the merchant. Then money is transferred from the customer's account to the merchant's account.

**TARGETED
ADVERTISING**

Knowing the current location of mobile users (e.g., when a GPS is attached to the cell phone) and their preferences or surfing habits, marketers can send user-specific advertising messages to wireless devices. Advertising can also be location-sensitive, informing about shops, malls, and restaurants close to a potential buyer. (Section 6.7). SMS messages and short paging messages can be used to deliver this type of advertising to cell phones and pagers, respectively. Many companies are capitalizing on targeted advertising, as shown in *A Closer Look 6.1.*

As more wireless bandwidth becomes available, content-rich advertising involving audio, pictures, and video clips will be generated for individual users with specific needs, interests, and inclinations.

**Getting Paid to Listen to Advertising.** Would you be willing to listen to a 10-second ad when you dial your cell phone if you were paid 2 minutes of free long-distance time? As in the wireline world, some consumers are willing to be paid for exposure to advertising. It depends on which country you are in. In most places where it was offered in the United States, this service was a flop and was discontinued.

*MKT*

In Singapore, though, getting paid to listen to advertising works very well. Within a few months of offering the ads, more than 100,000 people subscribed to the free minutes in exchange for listening to the ads offered by SingTel Mobile (Eklund, 2001). Subscribers to SingTel's service fill out a personal questionnaire when they sign up. This information is fed into the Spotcast database *(spotcastnetwork.com)* and encrypted to shield subscribers' identities—Spotcast cannot match phone numbers to names, for example. To collect their free minutes—one minute per call, up to

# A Closer Look 6.1

## *Wireless Advertising in Action*

The following are a few examples of wireless advertising in action.

Vindigo.com (*vindigo.com*) has a large database of customers (over a million in May 2004) willing to accept promotional materials on their wireless devices. This is known as *permission marketing*. The users download special software on their PDAs that allows Vindigo.com to deliver timely, accurate information about places to go and things to do in their area. Along with every listing, the company can deliver a customized message to the users at a time and place where it is of most interest to them and they are most likely to act on it.

The company targets ads by city (New York, San Francisco, Los Angeles, etc.) and channel (Eat, Shop, or Play). Vindigo.com tracks which ads a user sees and selects, and even allows a user to request information from an advertiser via e-mail. Vindigo.com determines a user's location through GPS or by asking which neighborhoods they want to be matched with. For example, if you own an Italian restaurant chain, you can use Vindigo.com to send a message to anyone looking for Italian food within a few blocks of one of your locations. You can give them directions to that restaurant and even offer them the list of specials on the menu and discounts.

MyAvantGo.Com (*avantgo.com*) has several thousand content channels and over 7 million registered users (AvantGo, 2004). The content is delivered to PDAs and handsets running Palm or PocketPC operating systems. MyAvantGo offers an m-business channel and direct promotions to deliver advertising from some of the world's top brands including American Airlines, Chevy Trucks, the Golf Channel, CNN, the *New York Times*, and Yahoo. For details see Stanford (2002).

Hoping to become the king of location-based Web domains, Go2Online (*go2online.com*) helps mobile travelers find everything from lodging (choose *go2hotels*) to Jiffy Lube stations. Partnering with Sprint, NexTel, Verizon, and Boost, Go2 makes its services available on every Web-enabled phone, Palm i705, and BlackBerry RIM pager in America. Entering "JiffyLube" or any of hundreds of other brand names into the Go2 system will bring up the nearest location where one can find that product or service.

*Sources:* Compiled from the Web sites of Vindigo.com, AvantGo.com, and Go2Online.com (accessed June 2006).

100 minutes a month—subscribers dial a four-digit code, then the phone number of the person they want to talk to. The code prompts SingTel to forward the call to Spotcast and, in an instant, Spotcast's software finds the best ad to send to the subscriber based on the subscriber's profile.

**MOBILE PORTALS**

A **mobile portal** is a customer channel, optimized for mobility, that aggregates and provides content and services for mobile users. These portals offer services similar to desktop portals such as AOL, Yahoo, and MSN. (See Chapter 4 for additional discussion of portals). An example of the best "pure" mobile portal (whose only business is to be a mobile portal) is *zed.com* from Sonera in Finland. The world's best-known mobile portal, with over 45 million members, mostly in Japan, is i-mode from DoCoMo.

The services provided by mobile portals include news, sports, e-mail, entertainment and travel information; restaurants and event information; leisure-related services (e.g., games, TV and movie listings); community services; and stock trading. A sizeable percentage of the portals also provide downloads and messaging, music-related services, and health, dating, and job information. Mobile portals frequently charge for their services. For example, you may be asked to pay 50 cents to get a weather report over your mobile phone. Alternatively, you may pay a monthly fee for the portal service and get the report free any time you want it. In Japan, for example, i-mode generates revenue mainly from subscription fees. A special service for travelers is offered at Avantgo (from iAnywhere).

Increasingly, the field of mobile portals is being dominated by a few big companies (Global Mobile Suppliers Association, 2002). The big players in Europe, for instance, are companies like Vodafone, Orange, O2, and T-Mobile; in the United

States the big players are Cingular, Verizon, and Sprint PCS. Also, mobile-device manufacturers offer their own portals (e.g., Club Nokia portal, My Palm portal). And, finally, the traditional portals (such as Yahoo, AOL, and MSN) have mobile portals as well. For example, Google Mobile provides news, e-mail, and more to cell phones.

Sina Corporation, a major portal network in China (*Sina.com*), in its Sina Mobile, offers mobile value-added services including news and information, community services such as dating and friendship, and multimedia downloads of ring tones, pictures, and screensavers. Users can order these services through the Sina Web site or through their mobile phones on either a monthly subscription or per-message basis.

**VOICE PORTALS**

A **voice portal** is a Web site with an audio interface. Voice portals are not really Web sites in the normal sense because they are accessed through a standard phone or a cell telephone. A certain phone number connects you to a participating Web site where you can request information by speaking. The system finds the information on the Internet or intranet, translates it into a computer-generated voice reply, and tells you what you want to know. Several of these new sites are in operation. An example of this application is the voice-activated 511 traveler information line developed by Tellme.com. *Tellme.com* and *bevocal.com* allow callers to request information about weather, local restaurants, current traffic, and other handy information (see Kumagai, 2002).

In addition to retrieving information, some sites provide true interaction. *iPing.com* is a reminder and notification service that allows users to enter information via the Web and receive reminder calls. In addition, iPing.com can call a group of people to notify them of a meeting or conference call.

The real value for Internet marketers is that these voice portals can help businesses find new customers. Several of these sites are supported by ads; thus, the customer profile data they have available can deliver targeted advertising very precisely. For instance, a department-store chain with an existing brand image can use short audio commercials on these sites to deliver a message related to the topic of the call.

With the development of technical standards and continuing improvement of wireless infrastructure, the number of m-commerce applications is growing rapidly. Applications are derived from providing wireless access to existing B2C, intrabusiness, and CRM applications and from creating new location-based and SMS-based applications. In Sections 6.2 through 6.6 of this chapter, we will study m-commerce applications in a number of diverse categories.

## 6.4  Mobile Enterprise and Interbusiness Applications

Although B2C m-commerce is getting considerable publicity, most of today's applications are used within organizations. This section looks at how mobile devices and technologies can be used *within, outside,* and *between* organizations.

**MOBILE ENTERPRISE APPLICATIONS**

Many companies offer innovative mobile and wireless applications in the enterprise. Examples of three applications are provided in Online File W6.3. Wireless applications fall into the following categories:

- Supporting salespeople while they are visiting customers (see Online File W6.4 for examples)
- Supporting field employees doing repairs or maintenance on corporate premises or for clients

- Supporting traveling (or off-corporate-site) executives, managers, or other employees
- Supporting employees while they do work inside the enterprise, but where there is no easy access to desktop computers (e.g., in a warehouse, outdoor facilities, or as in the case of Food Lion, when employees check inventory in the store)
- Employees driving trucks, while they are on the road

The basic objective is to provide employees with communication and collaboration tools, and access to data, information, and people inside the organization.
   Two types of support are:

1. Using portable devices that are connected to wireline networks using docking stations or other connecting devices, usually at the end of the day. In this category, we can use tablet PCs, PDAs, laptop computers, etc. These are portable, but not necessarily wireless.

2. Using wireless devices that enable real-time connection to corporate data or the Internet.

   There are myriad smaller, simple wireless devices—the smart phones and handheld companions carried by mobile workers and the in-vehicle information systems installed in cars.

**MOBILE ENTERPRISE APPLICATIONS: EXAMPLES**

In this section we will provide illustrative examples of popular applications ranging from wearable devices for field/service employees to salesforce automation.

**In Retailing.** The Food Lion example is only one of many applications. Symbol Technology (*symbol.com*) provides small, rugged handheld computers that enable data capture applications, collaboration, and price markdowns. The Symbol MC series, for example, can facilitate inventory taking and management. Warehouse management systems are greatly improved with software that is combined with the device (e.g., from M-Netics). Wild Oats employees use handheld computers to reorder. When an employee scans the barcode of a product, the handheld recommends how much to order.

**Sales Force Automation (SFA).** Sales representatives need to check inventory availability, special pricing, order status, and so on, during their visits with customers. For example, a customer may want to know how soon the order will arrive. Devices such as Palm OS and BlackBerry products offer such capabilities. (For details check (*wireless.eweek.com.*)
   The use of tablet PCs by salespeople is widespread. For example, most Market-Source employees work outside their company. They need to capture sales information, competitive data, and inventories; and they need to report sales. According to Microsoft, 650 corporate and remote workers use the device successfully. (See *tech.msn.com/guides/itdecision/article.aspx?cp-documentid=103131.*) For SFA cases, see *symbol.com* and *Sybase.com*.

**Hospitals.** Many hospitals introduce wireless applications ranging from wearable push-button communication devices (badge clips from Vocera Communications) to wireless laptops for bedside registration (Walsh and Yamarick, 2005).

**In Operations.** Many devices can facilitate different tasks of mobile employees. For example, Driscoll Strawberry Associates use wireless data collection devices, mobile printers, and handheld devices to accelerate transactions, increase accuracy, and enable real-time receiving and inventory management. The companies arrange the delivery of berries to market. The company achieved a 25 percent reduction in transaction processing time, 30 percent reduction in account reconciliation errors, and improved employee feedback on ease of use. For details, see the Driscoll's Berries case study at *symbol.com* (accessed June 2006).

Home Depot equipped close to 12,000 service agents with the EnfoTrust system (Wi-Fi based). The system can take photos as well. See Nobel (2005) for details.

**Tracking Employees.**  Using PDAs, Todd Pacific Shipyards knows that accurately tracking employees, including the hours and projects they've worked, and assessing daily staffing needs is a key to profitability (see Schuman, 2004).

**Wearable Devices.**  Employees who work on buildings, electrical poles, or other difficult-to-climb places may be equipped with a special form of mobile wireless computing devices called **wearable devices.** People wear these devices on their bodies (e.g., arms, clothes, or helmets). Examples of wearable devices include:

- **Screen.** A computer screen is mounted on a safety hat, in front of the wearer's eyes, displaying information to the worker.
- **Camera.** A camera is mounted on a safety hat. Workers can take digital photos and videos and transmit them instantly to a portable computer nearby. (Photo transmission is made possible via Bluetooth technology.)
- **Touch-panel display.** In addition to the wrist-mounted keyboard, mobile employees can use a flat-panel screen, attached to the hand, which responds to the tap of a finger or stylus.
- **Keyboard.** A wrist-mounted keyboard enables typing by the other hand. (Wearable keyboards are an alternative to voice recognition systems, which are also wireless.)
- **Speech translator.** For those mobile employees who do not have their hands free to use a keyboard, a wearable speech translator is handy.
- **Watch-like device.** Such a device is carried on the arm like a watch and can display information or be used as a cell phone. Swatch and Microsoft offer such watches. You can get news, weather, and so forth from Microsoft's MSN broadcasts.

For examples of wearable devices used to support mobile employees, see *IT at Work 6.1, xybernaut.com* and *essworld.net.*

**Job Dispatch.** Mobile devices are becoming an integral part of groupware and workflow applications. For example, nonvoice mobile services can be used to assist in dispatch functions—to assign jobs to mobile employees, along with detailed information about the task. The target areas for mobile delivery and dispatch services include the following: transportation (delivery of food, oil, newspapers, cargo, courier services, tow trucks, and taxis); utilities (gas, electricity, phone, water); field service (computer, office equipment, home repair); health care (visiting nurses, doctors, social services); and security (patrols, alarm installation).

**POM**

A dispatching application for wireless devices allows improved response with reduced resources, real-time tracking of work orders, increased dispatcher efficiency, and a reduction in administrative work. AirIQ (*airiq.com*), for example, offers an interesting solution. AirIQ's OnLine system combines Internet, wireless, GPS, digital mapping, and intelligent information technologies. The system tracks vital information about a vehicle's direction, speed, and location, which is provided by a device housed in each of the vehicles being tracked. Managers can view and access information about

# IT at Work 6.1

## Wearable Devices for Bell Canada Workers

POM GLOBAL

For years mobile employees, especially those who had to climb trees, electric poles, or tall buildings, were unable to enjoy the computerized technologies designed to make employees work or feel better. Thus, their productivity and comfort were inferior. That is all beginning to change.

On a cold, damp November day in Toronto, Chris Holm-Laursen, a field technician with Bell Canada (*bell. ca*), is out and

about as usual, but this time with a difference: A small but powerful computer sits in a pocket of his vest, a keyboard is attached to the vest's upper-left side, and a flat-panel display screen hangs by his waist. A video camera attached to his safety hat enables him to take pictures without using his hands and send them immediately to the office. A cell phone is attached as well, connected to the computer. A battery pack to keep everything going sits against his back. (See nearby photo.)

Holm-Laursen and 18 other technicians on this pilot project were equipped like this for 10 weeks during fall 2000.

By summer 2003 an increasing number of Bell Canada's employees had been equipped with similar devices. The wearable devices enabled the workers to access work orders and repair manuals wherever they were. These workers are not typical of the group usually most wired up, that is, white-collar workers. The hands-free aspect and the ability to communicate any time, from anywhere, represent major steps forward for these utility workers. A wide variety of employees—technicians, medical practitioners, aircraft mechanics, and contractors—are using or testing such devices. By 2006, many more employees were equipped with wearable devices.

So far, only a few companies make and sell wearables for mobile workers. Bell Canada's system was developed by Xybernaut, a U.S. company that in 2002 had more than a thousand of its units in use around the world, some in operation and others in pilot programs (see *xybernaut.com*, 2003).

Of course, a practical problem of wearable devices in many countries is the weather: What happens when the temperature is minus 50 degrees or the humidity is 99 percent? Other potential problems also exist: If you are wearing thick gloves, how can you use a keyboard? If it is pouring rain, will the battery short circuit? Various solutions are being developed, such as voice input, tapping on a screen instead of typing, and rainproof electrical systems.

*Sources:* Compiled from XyberFlash (2000), and *xybernaut.com* (2003).

*For Further Exploration:* What are some other industrial applications of similar wearable devices? How do you think wearable devices could be used in entertainment?

---

the fleet on digital maps, monitor vehicles on the Internet, and maintain top operating condition of their fleet. AirIQ promises savings of about 30 percent in communication costs and increases in workforce efficiency of about 25 percent (*edispatch.com*).

**Supporting Other Types of Work.** Wireless devices may support a wide variety of mobile workers. The applications will surely grow as the technology matures and as workers think up new ways to apply the functions of wireless devices to their jobs. Here are four examples.

POM

1. Tractors equipped with sensors, onboard computers, and a GPS help farmers save time, effort, and money. GPS determines the precise location of the tractor and can direct its automatic steering. Because the rows of planting resulting from GPS-guiding are more exact, the farmers save both on seeds and on fertilizers, due to minimized overlapping and spillage. Farmers can also work longer hours with the satellite-controlled steering, taking advantage of good weather, for example. Another saving is due to instant notification to the maintenance department about any machine that breaks down.

POM

2. Like e-mail, SMS can be used to bolster collaboration. According to Kontzer (2003), the following are 10 applications of SMS for mobile workers: (1) alerting mobile technicians to system errors, (2) alerting mobile execs to urgent voice messages, (3) confirming with mobile sales personnel that a faxed order was received, (4) informing travelers of delays and changes, (5) enabling contract workers to receive and accept project offers, (6) keeping stock traders up to date on urgent stock activity, (7) reminding data services subscribers about daily updates, (8) alerting doctors to urgent patient situations, (9) enabling mobile sales teams to input daily sales figures into corporate database, and (10) sending mobile sales reps reminders of appointments and other schedule details.

GOV

3. To increase national security and safeguard national borders, countries are using facial-recognition and iris-scanning biometrics (Chapter 16), both of which are supported by wireless systems (see Morpho.com, 2006).

**CUSTOMER SUPPORT AND CRM**

Mobile access extends the reach of CRM—both inside and outside the company—to both employees and business partners on a 24/7 basis, to any place where recipients are located. A 2006 Visiongain study predicts that mobile CRM will grow from 2006 portion of 10 percent of total CRM revenues to 20 percent by 2010 (Lyman, 2006).

MKT

In the large software suites like Siebel's CRM (an Oracle company) the two CRM functions that have attracted the most interest are *sales force automation* and *field service.* For instance, a salesperson might be on a sales call and need to know recent billing history for a particular customer. Or, a field service representative on a service call might need to know current availability of various parts in order to fix a piece of machinery. It is these sorts of situations where mobile access to customer and partner data is invaluable. Two of the more recent offerings in this arena are Salesforce.com's App Exchange Mobile and CRMondemand's Alerts (*crmondemand.com*). See *A Closer Look 6.2* (page 228) for descriptions of the use of mobile applications for customer support.

Voice portal technology can also be used to provide enhanced customer service or to improve access to data for employees. For example, customers who are away from the office could use a vendor's voice portal to check on the status of deliveries to a job site. Salespeople could check on inventory status during a meeting to help close a sale. There are a wide variety of CRM applications for voice portal technology. The challenge is in learning how to create the navigation and other aspects of interaction that makes customers feel comfortable with voice-access technology.

**WIRELESS INTRABUSINESS APPLICATIONS**

Wireless applications in the non-Internet environment have been around since the early 1990s. Examples include such applications as: wireless networking, used to pick items out of storage in warehouses via PCs mounted on forklifts; delivery-status updates, entered on PCs inside distribution trucks; and collection of data such as competitors' inventories in stores and customer orders, using a handheld (but not networked) device, from which data were transferred to company headquarters each evening. (See the Maybelline minicase in Chapter 2, and the Hi-Life minicase in Chapter 5.)

Since then, a large number of Internet-based wireless applications have been implemented inside enterprises. Some examples follow:

POM

- Kemper Insurance Company has piloted an application that lets property adjusters report from the scene of an accident. Kemper attached a wireless digital imaging system to a camera that lets property adjusters take pictures in the field and transmit them to a processing center (Henning, 2002; Nelson, 2000). The cameras are linked to Motorola's Private Data File data-enabled cellular phone service, which sends the information to a database. These applications

# A Closer Look 6.2

## Mobile Application for Sports

MKT

- In May 2006, Nike and Apple introduced an iPod shoe called Nano that can provide real-time feedback on distance, time, and calories burned during a workout. A sensor and receiver embedded in the shoe provide a wireless connection to the iPod, with workout information stored on the device and displayed on the screen. Runners can get audible feedback through the headphones, and data stored on the Nano can be downloaded to a Mac or PC after a run. In addition to these functions, the Nike+iPod system delivers music and commentary to help joggers make it through their workouts. Nike is offering workout-related podcasts that include advice from marathon runner Alberto Salazar and inspiration from bicycling champion Lance Armstrong. In fall 2006, Nike delivered six additional footwear styles designed to hold the iPod sensor. The company also is planning to unveil a collection of jackets, tops, shorts, and armbands designed for the Nike+iPod Sport Kit. A similar service is offered by BonesinMotion.com together with Sprint. It uses a GPS to turn mobile phones into exercise-tracking devices.

- In winter 2006, Levi Strauss introduced a new line of jeans specifically geared toward iPod users. The $200 trousers come complete with headphones, a joystick, and even a docking cradle.

- ESPN's Sport Center with Sanyo offers a cell phone dedicated to sports. You can get quick access to news and your favorite teams. Video clips of up to 30 seconds are available and so is a built-in camera. To alleviate waiting time, sports trivia are offered. Alerts are sent by request. The service is relatively expensive.

- Several stadiums, golf courses, and other sports facilities are equipped with Wi-Fi networks. For example, in Round Rock, Texas, fans, sport reporters, coaches, players, vendors, and management can use various handheld devices in the stadium (Ellison, 2005).

- *Invisible* is a term that characterizes a device manufactured and sold by Fitsense Technology (*fitsense.com*), a Massachusetts developer of Internet sports and fitness monitors. With this one-ounce device that is clipped to a shoelace, runners are able to capture their speed and the distance they have run. The device transmits the data via a radio signal to a wrist device that can capture and transmit the data wirelessly to a desktop computer for analysis. Along the same lines, Champion Chip (*championchip.com*), headquartered in the Netherlands, has developed a system that keeps track of the tens of thousands of participants in very popular long-distance races. The tracking system includes miniature transponders attached to the runners' shoelaces or ankle bracelets and antenna mats at the finish line that use radio frequencies to capture start times, splits, and finish times as the runners cross them.

SVC

eliminate delays in obtaining information and in film processing that exist with conventional methods.

MKT

- A medical care organization developed a mobile enterprise application that allows sales representatives to check order status and inventory levels during their visits with physicians and instantly report on what they can deliver to the physician's office and when (Ellison, 2004).

As these two examples indicate, a variety of intrabusiness workflow applications are possible. Online File W6.5 shows typical intrabusiness workflow applications before and after the introduction of wireless services. Some of these can be delivered on a wireless intranet; some are offered on the Internet. (For details on intrabusiness applications, see *mdsi-advantex.com* and *symbol.com*. The advantages offered by intrabusiness wireless solutions can be seen through an examination of workflow applications at *mdsi-advantex.com*.) Finally, RFID is gaining popularity in both intrabusiness and interbusiness applications.

Mobile intrabusiness applications are very popular and are typically easier to implement than nonmobile interbusiness applications. Now let's examine B2B and supply chain applications.

**MOBILE B2B AND SUPPLY CHAIN APPLICATIONS**

Mobile computing solutions are also being applied to B2B and supply chain relationships. Such solutions enable organizations to respond faster to supply chain disruptions by proactively adjusting plans or by shifting resources related to critical supply chain events as they occur. With the increased interest in collaborative commerce comes the opportunity to use wireless communication to collaborate along the supply chain. For this to take place, interorganizational systems integration is needed.

An integrated messaging system is at the center of B2B communications. By integrating the mobile terminal into the supply chain, it is possible to check availability of a particular item in the warehouse, order a particular product from the manufacturing department, or provide security access to obtain confidential financial data from a management information system.

One example of an integrated messaging system is wireless *telemetry,* which combines wireless communications, vehicle monitoring systems, and vehicle location devices. (Telemetry is described further in Section 6.6.) Mobile intrabusiness technology makes possible large-scale automation of data capture, improved billing timeliness and accuracy, less overhead than with the manual alternative, and increased customer satisfaction through service responsiveness. For example, vending machines can be kept replenished and in reliable operation by wirelessly polling inventory and service status continually to avert costly machine downtime.

Mobile devices can also facilitate collaboration among members of the supply chain. There is no longer any need to call a partner company and ask someone to find certain employees who work with your company. Instead, you can contact these employees directly, on their mobile devices.

By enabling sales force employees to type orders straight into the ERP while at a client's site, companies can reduce clerical mistakes and improve supply chain operations. By allowing them to check production schedules and inventory levels, and to access product configuration and *available-to-promise/capacity-to-promise* (ATP/CTP) functionality to obtain real-time delivery quotes, they empower their sales force to make more competitive and realistic offers to customers. Today's ERP systems tie into broader supply chain management solutions that extend visibility across multiple tiers in the supply chain. Mobile supply chain management (mSCM) empowers the workforce to leverage these broader systems through inventory management and ATP/CTP functionality that extend across multiple supply chain partners and take into account logistics considerations. Finally, RFIDs will automate many activities of supply chain management (e.g., see Caton, 2004).

## 6.5 Mobile Consumer Services and Entertainment

A large number of applications exist that support consumers and provide personal services (see Kou and Yesha, 2006, and Roush, 2005). As an example, consider the situation of a person going to an international airport. Tasks such as finding the right check-in desk, checking for delayed flights, waiting for lost luggage, and even finding a place to eat or the nearest washroom can be assisted by mobile devices.

Other consumer and personal service areas in which wireless devices can be used are described in the following sections. (See also *attws.com.*)

**MOBILE ENTERTAINMENT**

Mobile entertainment is expanding on wireless devices. Notable are music, videos, games, adult entertainment, sports, gambling, and more. See Online File W6.6. As an illustration, we provided several examples of what is offered in sports in *A Closer Look 6.2* (p. 228).

**MOBILE GAMES**

In the handheld segment of the gaming market, Nintendo has been the longtime leader. In contrast, Nintendo has shown minimal interest in online or mobile games. By 2005, Sonic the Hegdgehog (from Sega) and his friends were among the most familiar icons in video games. Since 1991, he has appeared in over 30 games that have sold more than 38 million units of software and is consistently a top-selling franchise (Business Wire, 2005). In Japan, where millions of commuters kill time during long train rides, cell phone games have become a cultural phenomenon. Now mobile games are very popular in China and other countries.

With more than 1.8 billion cell phones in use by 2003 (Maier, 2006), the potential audience for mobile games is substantially larger than the market for other platforms, PlayStation and Gameboy included. Because of the market potential, Nokia has decided to enter the mobile gaming world, producing not only the phone/console but also the games that will be delivered on memory cards. It also develops and markets near-distance multiplayer gaming (over Bluetooth) and wide area gaming (using cellular networks) (Nokia, 2002).

In July 2001, Ericsson, Motorola, Nokia, and Siemens established the Mobile Games Interoperability Forum (MGIF) (*openmobilealliance.org*) to define a range of technical standards that will make it possible to deploy mobile games across multigame servers, wireless networks, and over different mobile devices. Microsoft is moving into this field as well.

A topic related to games is *mobile entertainment,* discussed in Online File W6.6. Mobile gambling, another related topic, is extremely popular in some countries (e.g., horse racing in Hong Kong and racing and other events in Australia). (For more on mobile gambling, see *sportodds.com*.)

**HOTEL SERVICES AND TRAVEL GO WIRELESS**

A number of hotels now offer their guests in-room, high-speed Internet connection. Some of these same hotels offer Wi-Fi Internet access in public areas and meeting rooms. One of these is Marriott, which manages 2,500 hotels worldwide. Marriott has partnered with STSN (*stsn.com*), an Internet service provider specializing in hotels, to provide Wi-Fi services in many Marriott hotels. In the same vein, AT&T has partnered with Wayport Inc. to offer Wi-Fi in 475 hotels throughout the United States. In India the Taj Group is offering Wi-Fi access in its hotels (Taj Hotel, 2002), and Megabeam (a wireless provider in England) offers the same service in many Holiday Inn and Crowne Plaza hotels in London.

While Wi-Fi provides guests with Internet access, to date it has had minimal impact on other sorts of hotel services (e.g., check-in). However, a small number of hotels are testing use of the Bluetooth technology. Guests are provided with Bluetooth-enabled phones that can communicate with access points located throughout the hotel. This technology can be used for check-in and checkout, for making purchases from hotel vending machines and stores, for tracking loyalty points (see *tesalocks.com*), and for opening room doors in place of keys.

**OTHER MOBILE-COMPUTING SERVICES FOR CONSUMERS**

Many other mobile computer services exist for consumers, in a variety of service categories. Examples include services providing news, weather, and sports reports; online language translations; information about tourist attractions (hours, prices); and emergency services. Many applications are in the area of telemedicine (see Online File W6.7). For more examples, see the case studies at *mobileinfo.com*.

**NON-INTERNET MOBILE-COMPUTING APPLICATIONS FOR CONSUMERS**

Non-Internet mobile applications for consumers, mainly those using smart cards, have existed since the early 1990s. Active use of the cards is reported in transportation, where millions of "contactless" cards (also called *proximity cards*) are used to pay bus and subway fares and road tolls. Amplified remote-sensing cards that have an RF (radio frequency) of up to 30 meters are used in several countries for toll collection. *IT at Work 6.2* describes one use of proximity cards for toll collection. Other non-Internet applications are embedded in cell phones, especially payments.

# IT at Work 6.2

## The Highway 91 Project

SVC

Route 91 is a major eight-lane, east-west highway near Los Angeles. Traffic is especially heavy during rush hours. California Private Transportation Company (CPT) built six express toll lanes along a 10-mile stretch in the median of the existing Highway 91. The express lane system has only one entrance and one exit, and it is totally operated with EC technologies. The system works as follows.

Only prepaid subscribers can drive on the road. Subscribers receive an automatic vehicle identification (AVI) device that is placed on the rearview mirror of the car. The device, about the size of a thick credit card, includes a microchip, an antenna, and a battery. A large sign over the tollway tells drivers the current fee for cruising the express lanes. In a recent year it varied from $0.50 in slow traffic hours to $3.25 during rush hours.

Sensors in the pavement let the tollway computer know that a car has entered; the car does not need to slow or stop. The AVI makes radio contact with a transceiver installed above the lane. The transceiver relays the car's identity through fiber-optic lines to the control center, where a computer calculates the fee for that day's trip. The system accesses the driver's account and the fare is automatically deducted from the driver's prepaid account. A monthly statement is sent to the subscriber's home.

Surveillance cameras record the license numbers of cars without AVIs. These cars can be stopped by police at the exit or fined by mail. Video cameras along the tollway also enable managers to keep tabs on traffic, for example, sending a tow truck to help a stranded car. Also, through knowledge of the traffic volume, pricing decisions can be made. Raising the price as traffic increases ensures that the tollway will not be jammed. In similar systems, nonsubscribers are allowed to enter via special gates where they pay cash.

The system saves commuters between 40 and 90 minutes each day, so it is in high demand. An interesting extension of the system is the use of the same AVIs for other purposes. For example, they can be used in paid parking lots. Someday you may be even recognized when you enter the drive-through lane of McDonald's and a voice asks you, "Mr. Smart, do you want your usual meal today?"

*Sources:* 91expresslanes.com (accessed June 2006) and en.wikipedia.org/wiki/91_Expresslanes (accessed June 2006).

*For Further Exploration:* What is the role of the wireless component of this system? What are the advantages of the system to commuters? (Take the virtual "test drive.")

# 6.6 Location-Based Services and Commerce

**Location-based commerce (l-commerce)** refers to the delivery of advertisements, products, or services to customers whose location is known at a given time (also known as location-based services [LBSs]). Location-based services are beneficial to both consumers and businesses alike. From a consumer's viewpoint, l-commerce offers safety (you can connect to an emergency service with a mobile device and have the service pinpoint your exact location), convenience (you can locate what is near you without having to consult a directory, pay phone, or map), and productivity (you can optimize your travel and time by determining points of interest within close proximity). From a business supplier's point of view, l-commerce offers an opportunity to sell more.

The basic l-commerce services revolve around five key areas:

1. **Location:** determining the basic position of a person or a thing (e.g., bus, car, or boat), at any given time
2. **Navigation:** plotting a route from one location to another
3. **Tracking:** monitoring the movement of a person or a thing (e.g., a vehicle or package) along the route
4. **Mapping:** creating digital maps of specific geographical locations
5. **Timing:** determining the precise time at a specific location

Providing location-based services requires the following location-based and network technologies:

- **Position Determining Equipment (PDE).** This equipment identifies the location of the mobile device (either through GPS or by locating the nearest base station). The position information is sent to the mobile positioning center.

- **Mobile Positioning Center (MPC).** The MPC is a server that manages the location information sent from the PDE.

- **Location-based technology.** This technology consists of groups of servers that combine the position information with geographic- and location-specific content to provide an l-commerce service. For instance, location-based technology could present a list of addresses of nearby restaurants based on the position of the caller, local street maps, and a directory of businesses.

- **Geographic content.** Geographic content consists of digitized streets, road maps, addresses, routes, landmarks, land usage, Zip codes, and the like. This information must be delivered in compressed form for fast distribution over wireless networks (e.g., as digital maps).

- **Location-specific content.** Location-specific content is used in conjunction with the geographic content to provide the location of particular services. Yellow-pages directories showing the location of specific business and services exemplify this type of content.

Figure 6.4 shows how these technologies are used in conjunction with one another to deliver location-based services. Underlying these technologies are global positioning and geographical information systems.

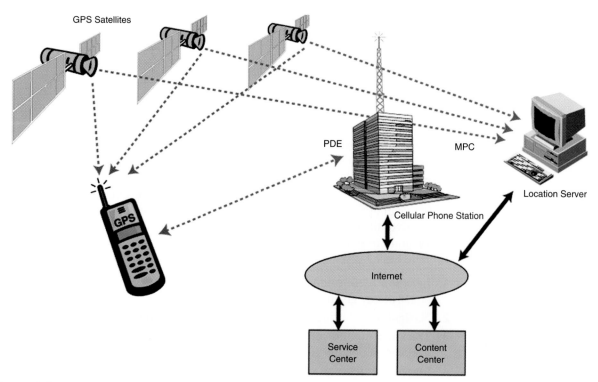

**Figure 6.4** A smart phone with GPS system in l-commerce.

**Global Positioning System (GPS).** As indicated at the start of the chapter, a *global positioning system (GPS)* is a wireless system that uses satellites to enable users to determine their position anywhere on the earth. GPS equipment has been used extensively for navigation by commercial airlines and ships and for locating trucks and buses (as in the opening case study).

GPS is supported by 24 U.S. government satellites that are shared worldwide. Each satellite orbits the earth once every 12 hours on a precise path, at an altitude of 10,900 miles. At any point in time, the exact position of each satellite is known, because the satellite broadcasts its position and a time signal from its onboard atomic clock, which is accurate to one-billionth of a second. Receivers also have accurate clocks that are synchronized with those of the satellites.

GPS handsets can be standalone units or can be plugged into or embedded in a mobile device. They calculate the position (location) of the handsets (or send the information to be calculated centrally). Knowing the speed of the satellite signals (186,272 miles per second), engineers can find the location of any receiving station (latitude and longitude) to within 50 feet by *triangulation,* using the distance from a GPS to *three* satellites to make the computation. GPS software then computes the latitude and longitude of the receiver. For an online tutorial on GPS, see *trimble.com/gps.*

**Geographical Information System (GIS).** The location provided by GPS is expressed in terms of latitude and longitude. To make that information useful to businesses and consumers it is necessary in many cases to relate those measures to a certain place or address. This is done by inserting the latitude and longitude onto a digital map, which is known as a **geographical information system (GIS).** The GIS data visualization technology integrates GPS data onto digitized map displays. (See the description in Chapter 11.) Companies such as *mapinfo.com* provide the GIS core spatial technology, maps, and other data content needed in order to power location-based GIS/GPS services (see Figure 6.5).

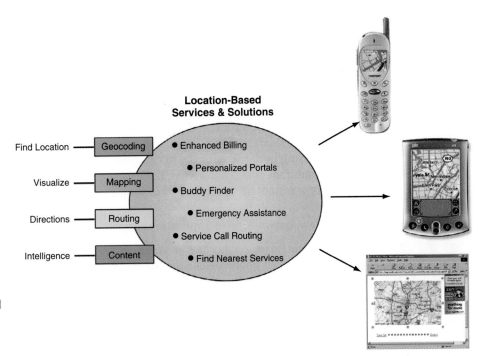

**Figure 6.5** Location-based services involving maps. (*Source: Mapinfo.com,* 2001.)

**LOCATION-BASED
APPLICATIONS**

**SVC**

An increasing number of applications is evidenced in several industries, particularly in transportation. These applications mainly relate to customer service, advertising/marketing, and operations. One example of customer information about public transportation is Nextbus. NextBus.com provides information about bus/shuttle arrivals in real time. The system is based on GPS, and it is described in *IT at Work 6.3*.

An interesting application of GPS/GIS is now available from several car manufacturers (e.g., Toyota, Cadillac) and car rental companies (e.g., Hertz; see Minicase 1). Some cars have a navigation system that indicates how far away the driver is from gas stations, restaurants, and other locations of interest. The GPS can map the route for the driver to a particular destination.

**CAR NAVIGATION
SYSTEMS MAY BE
HAZARDOUS FOR
YOUR HEALTH**

According to *Ananova News* (October 14, 2003), a U.S. tourist's trip through Germany ended with an unexpected visit to a supermarket when his car's navigation system led him straight through the store's doors. The car only came to a stop when the driver crashed into a row of shelves. The driver, who has not been named, but was celebrating his birthday the same day, told police that he had relied entirely on the automatic navigation system as he did not know the area. He added that he did not notice the doors of the supermarket looming before him until he had crashed through them. The driver, luckily, was unhurt, but he has been told he will have to foot the bill for the damage caused.

**Location-Based Advertising.** Imagine that you are walking near a Starbucks store, but you do not even know that one is there. Suddenly your cell phone beeps with a message: "Come inside for a latte." The location of your wireless device was detected, and similar to the pop-up ads on your PC, advertising was directed your way (Needleman, 2002). You could use permission marketing to shield yourself from location-based advertising; if the system knows that you do not drink coffee, for example, you would not be sent a message from Starbucks.

Another (experimental) use of wireless devices for advertising is described by Raskin (2003). In this case, a dynamic billboard ad could be personalized specifically for you when your car approaches a certain billboard and the system knows what your likes and preferences are. Your car will be tracked by a GPS, every 20 seconds. A computer scans the areas in which billboards are visible, and by cross-referencing information about your location and your likes, a *personalized ad* could be placed on the billboard so you would see it as you pass.

Yet another method of location-based advertising involves putting ads on the top of taxicabs. The ad is changed based on the taxi location. For example, a taxi cruising in the theater district in New York City might show an ad for a play or a restaurant in that area; when the cab goes to another neighborhood, the ad might be for a restaurant or a business in that area of the city.

**APPLICATIONS OF
LOCATION-BASED
SERVICES (LBSs)**

New and innovative applications appear almost daily. Here are some examples:

- The Luxor casino in Las Vegas preregisters guests when they land and turn on their cell phones. Also, the hotel can determine when guests leave the hotel, luring them back with mobile incentives and pitches.
- GlobalPetFinder (*globalpetfinder.com*) is an under-5-ounce, $290 (on sale) device that snaps onto your pet's collar. If Fido wanders outside the "virtual fence" you set up, you'll receive a text alert and the pet's whereabouts on your phone. Monthly monitoring fees start at $17, plus there's a one-time $35 activation charge.

# *IT* at Work 6.3

SVC

## NextBus: A Superb Customer Service

**The Problem.** Buses in certain parts of San Francisco have difficulty keeping up with the posted schedule, especially in rush hours. Generally, buses are scheduled to arrive every 20 minutes, but at times, passengers may have to wait 30 to 40 minutes. The schedules become meaningless, and passengers are unhappy because they waste time.

**The Solution.** San Francisco bus riders carrying an Internet-enabled wireless device, such as a cell phone or PDA, can quickly find out when a bus is likely to arrive at a particular bus stop. The system tracks public transportation buses in *real time*. Knowing where each bus is and factoring in traffic patterns and weather reports, NextBus (*nextbus.com*) dynamically calculates the estimated arrival time of the bus to each bus stop on the route. The arrival times are also displayed on the Internet and on a public screen at each bus stop.

The NextBus system has been used successfully in several other cities around the United States (e.g., Fairfax Virginia), in Finland, and in several other countries. The figure shows how the NextBus system works. The core of the NextBus system is a GPS satellite that can tell the NextBus information center where a bus is at any given time. Based on a bus's location, the scheduled arrival time at each stop can be calculated in real time. Users can access the information from their cell phones or PCs, any time, anywhere. NextBus schedules are also posted in real time on passengers' shelters at bus stops and public displays.

Currently, NextBus is an ad-free customer service, but in the near future advertising may be added. As the system knows exactly where you are when you request information and how much time you have until your next bus, it could send you to the nearest Starbucks for a cup of coffee, giving you an electronic discount coupon for a cup of coffee as you wait.

*Sources:* Compiled from ITS America 2001, and *nextbus.com* (accessed June 2006).

*For Further Exploration:* Can NextBus make money? How? Who should sponsor the service? How can marketing/advertising work?

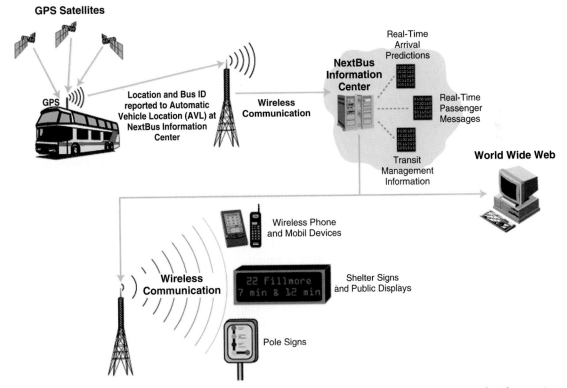

NextBus operational model. (*Source: NextBus.com/corporate/works/index.htm, 2002.* Used with permission of NextBus Information Systems.)

- KnowledgeWhere's Mobile Pooch (*knowledgewhere.ca*), Kamida's Socialight (*socialight.com*), and Proxpro (*proxpro.com*) are applying LBSs to social networking. Socialight, now in beta, lets people publish pictures, words, sound, and video tagged to specific locales; you might offer your take on a tourist spot.

E-911 EMERGENCY
CELL PHONE CALLS

If someone dials 911 from a regular wired phone, it is easy for the emergency 911 service to pinpoint the location of the phone. But, what happens if someone places a 911 call from a mobile phone? How can the emergency service locate the caller? A few years ago, the U.S. Federal Communications Commission (FCC) issued a directive to wireless carriers, requiring that they establish services to handle **wireless 911 (e-911)** calls. To give you an idea of the magnitude of this requirement, more than 156,000 wireless 911 calls are made every day, representing more than half the 911 calls made daily in the United States (Sarkar, 2003).

The e-911 directive is to take effect in two phases, although the specifics of the phases vary from one wireless carrier (e.g., T-Mobile, Cingular, Sprint, etc.) to another. Phase I requires carriers, upon appropriate request by a local *Public Safety Answering Point* (PSAP), to report the telephone number of a wireless 911 caller and the location of the cellular antenna that received the call. Phase II, which was rolled out over a four-year period from October 2002 to December 2005, requires wireless carriers to provide information that will enable the PSAP to locate a caller within 50 meters 67 percent of the time and within 150 meters 95 percent of the time. By the end of Phase II, 100 percent of the new cell phones and 95 percent of all cell phones will have these location capabilities. It is expected that many other countries will follow the example of the United States in providing e-911 service.

Some expect that in the future cars will have a device for **automatic crash notification (ACN).** This still-experimental device will automatically notify the police of an accident involving an ACN-equipped car and its location. Also, following a school bus hijacking in Pennsylvania, the state legislature is considering a bill to mandate satellite tracking in all school buses. Another up-coming device is GPS-based from Motorola. Cars equipped with this device will be able to avoid accidents at intersections (see Dizikes, 2006).

TELEMATICS
AND TELEMETRY
APPLICATIONS

**Telematics** refers to the integration of computers and wireless communications in order to improve information flow (see Chatterjee et al., 2002, and Zhao, 2002). It uses the principles of *telemetry,* the science that measures physical remoteness by means of wireless transmission from a remote source (such as a vehicle) to a receiving station. MobileAria (*mobilearia.com*) is a proposed standards-based telematics platform designed to bring multimedia services and m-commerce to automobiles.

Using *mobile telemetry,* technicians can diagnose from a distance maintenance problems in equipment. Car manufacturers use the technology for remote vehicle diagnosis and preventive maintenance. Finally, doctors can monitor patients and control medical equipment from a distance.

General Motors Corporation popularized automotive telematics with its OnStar (*onstar.com*) system. Nokia has set up a business unit, called Smart Traffic Products, that is focusing solely on telematics. Nokia believes that every vehicle will be equipped with at least one Internet Protocol (IP) address by the year 2010. Smart cars and traffic products are discussed in more detail in Section 6.7.

*SVC*

BARRIERS TO
L-COMMERCE

What is holding back the widespread use of location-based commerce? Several factors come into play:

- **Accuracy.** Some of the location-finding devices are not as accurate as people expect them to be. However, a good GPS provides a location that is accurate up to 15 meters. Less expensive, but less accurate, technologies can be used instead to find an approximate location (within about 500 meters).

- **The cost-benefit justification.** For many potential users, the benefits of l-commerce do not justify the cost of the hardware or the inconvenience and time required to utilize the service (e.g., Hamblen, 2001). After all, they seem to feel, they can just as easily obtain information the old-fashioned way.
- **The bandwidth of GSM networks.** GSM bandwidth is currently limited; it is improving as 3G technology spreads. As bandwidth improves, applications will improve, which will attract more customers.
- **Invasion of privacy.** When "always-on" cell phones are a reality, many people will be hesitant to have their whereabouts and movements tracked throughout the day, even if they have nothing to hide. This issue will be heightened when our cars, homes, appliances, and all sorts of other consumer goods are connected to the Internet, as discussed in the next section.

# 6.7 Pervasive Computing

Steven Spielberg's sci-fi thriller *Minority Report* depicts the world of 2054. Based on a 1956 short story by Philip K. Dick, the film immerses the viewer in the consumer-driven world of pervasive computing 50 years from now. Spielberg put together a three-day think tank, headed by Peter Schwartz, president of Global Business Network (*gbn.com*), to produce a realistic view of the future (Mathieson, 2002). The think tank projected out from today's marketing and media technologies—Web cookies, GPS, Bluetooth, personal video recorders, RFID scanners, and the like—to create a society where billboards beckon you by name, newspapers are delivered instantly over broadband wireless networks, holographic hosts greet you at retail stores, and cereal boxes broadcast live commercials. While the technologies in the film were beyond the leading edge, none was beyond the realm of the plausible.

A world in which virtually every object has processing power with wireless or wired connections to a global network is the world of **pervasive computing**. (The term *pervasive computing* also goes by the names *ubiquitous computing, embedded computing, ambient computing,* or *augmented computing.*) The idea of pervasive computing has been around for years. However, the current version was articulated by Mark Weiser in 1988 at the computer science lab of Xerox PARC. From Weiser's perspective, pervasive computing was the opposite of virtual reality. In virtual reality, the user is immersed in a computer-generated environment. In contrast, pervasive computing is invisible "everywhere computing" that is embedded in the objects around us—the floor, the lights, our cars, the washing machine, our cell phones, our clothes, and so on (Weiser, 1991, 2002).

INVISIBLE
COMPUTING
EVERYWHERE

By "invisible," Weiser did not mean to imply that pervasive computing devices would not be seen. He meant, rather, that unlike a desktop computer, these embedded computers would not intrude on our consciousness. Think of a pair of eyeglasses. The wearer does not have to think about using them. He or she simply puts them on and they augment the wearer's ability to see. This is Weiser's vision for pervasive computing. The user does not have to think about how to use the processing power in the object; rather, the processing power automatically helps the user perform a task (see Streitz and Nixon, 2005).

Invisible is how you would describe some of the new embedded technology already in use at Prada's "epicenter" stores in New York, San Francisco, and Los Angeles (Duan, 2002). Prada is a high-end fashion retailer. In the company's epicenters, the items for sale have an **RFID (radio frequency identification)** tag attached. The tag contains a processor and an antenna. If a customer wants information about a particular item, she or he can move with the item toward one of the many electronic screen displays around the store. The display automatically detects the item and provides sketches, video clips of models wearing the item, and other information about the item (color, cut, fabric, materials, and availability). If a customer takes a garment into one of the dressing rooms, the tags are automatically scanned and detected via an antenna embedded in the dressing room. Information about the item will be automatically displayed on an interactive touch screen in the dressing room. The dressing rooms also have a video-based "Magic Mirror." When the customer tries on the garment and turns around in front of the mirror, the images will be captured and played back in slow motion. (See Section 6.8 and Lohlou et al., 2005 for a related privacy issue.)

*Active badges* can be worn as ID cards by employees who wish to stay in touch at all times while moving around the corporate premises. The clip-on badge contains a microprocessor that transmits its (and its wearer's) location to the building's sensors, which send it to a computer. When someone wants to contact the badge wearer, the phone closest to the person is identified automatically. When badge wearers enter their offices, their badge identifies them and logs them on to their personal computers.

Similarly, *memory buttons* are nickel-sized devices that store a small database relating to whatever it is attached to. These devices are analogous to a barcode, but with far greater informational content and a content that is subject to change. For example, the U.S. Postal Service is placing memory buttons in some mailboxes to track and improve collection and delivery schedules.

For a short list of the technical foundations of pervasive computing, see Online File W6.8 at the book's Web site.

---

**CONTEXTUAL COMPUTING AND CONTEXT AWARENESS**

Location can be a significant differentiator when it comes to advertising services. However, knowing that the user is at the corner of the street will not tell you what he or she is looking for. For this, we might need to know the time of day, or access our user's calendar or other relevant *contextual attributes*. **Context awareness** refers to capturing a broad range of contextual attributes to better understand what the consumer needs, and what products or services he or she might possibly be interested in (Banavar et al., 2005).

Context awareness is part of **contextual computing,** which refers to the enhancement of a user's interactions by understanding the user, the context, and the applications and information being used, typically across a wide set of user goals (see Schmidt et al., 2004 for details). Contextual computing is about actively adapting the computational environment for each user, at each point of computing.

Contextual computing and context awareness are viewed by many as the Holy Grail of m-commerce. They feel that contextual computing ultimately offers the prospect of applications that could anticipate our every wish and provide us with the exact information and services we are looking for—and also help us filter all those annoying promotional messages that we really do not care for. Such applications are futuristic at the present time, but as shown in *IT at Work 6.4* they already exist in a research university.

# IT at Work 6.4

## Context-Aware Environment at Carnegie Mellon University

*SVC*

Carnegie Mellon University (CMU) is known for its advanced science projects including robotics and artificial intelligence. Students participate in a context-awareness experiment in the following manner: Each participating student is equipped with a PDA from which he or she can access Internet services via the campus Wi-Fi network. The students operate in a context-aware environment whose architecture is shown in the attached figure.

A user's context (left of figure) includes his or her:

- Calendar information
- Current location (position), which is regularly updated using location-tracking technology
- Weather information, indicating whzether it is sunny, raining, or snowing, and the current outside temperature (environment)
- Social context information, including the student's friends and his or her teachers, classmates, and so forth

The preferences of each student are solicited and entered into system, to create a personal profile, shown as "Preferences and Permissions" in the figure. All of the above information helps the system to filter incoming messages, and determine what to show to the students, and when. For example, while attending classes the student may block all messages. That is, certain messages will be shown only if the student is in a certain place and/or time; others will not be shown at all.

A user's context information can be accessed by a collection of *personal agents,* each in charge of assisting with different tasks, while locating and invoking relevant Internet services identified through services registries (see the figure). An example of a simple agent is a restaurant concierge that gives suggestions to students about places to have lunch, depending on their food preferences, the time they have available before their next class, their location on campus, and the weather. For example, when it is raining, the agent attempts to find a place that does not require going outside of the building where the student is located. The recommendation (usually several choices) appears on the PDA, with an overall rating and a "click for details" possibility.

*Source:* Compiled from Sadeh (2002) and Gardon and Sadeh (2004).

***For Further Exploration:*** Does the usefulness of such a service justify the need to disclose private preferences? Can such a system be developed for consumers who are not members of a defined community such as a university?

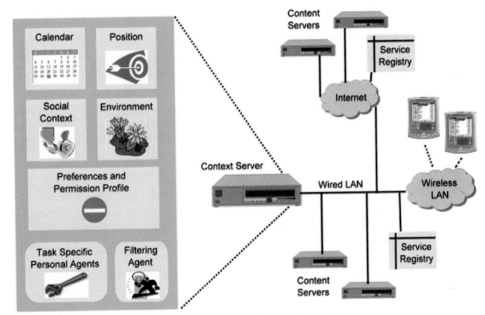

Carnegie Mellon's context-awareness system. (*Source:* Sadeh, 2002.)

**APPLICATIONS OF PERVASIVE COMPUTING**

According to Estrin et al. (2000), 98 percent of all processors on the planet are not in traditional desktop computer systems, nor even in laptops. They are in household appliances, vehicles, and machines. Such existing and future applications of pervasive computing are illustrated in Online File W6.9. Notice that all 14 devices can be connected to the Internet. Some of these applications are described in the remainder of this section. Here we will look at smart homes and smart cars. Smart appliances and other smart items are described in Online File W6.10.

**SMART HOMES**

In a *smart home,* your home computer, television, lighting and heating controls, home security system, and many appliances within the home can "talk" to each other via the Internet or a home intranet. These linked systems can be controlled through various devices.

In the United States, tens of thousands of homes are already equipped with home-automation devices, and there are signs that Europe—which has much lower home Internet penetration levels—is also warming to the idea. For instance, a 2001 study by the U.K.'s Consumers' Association found that almost half those surveyed were interested in having the functions a "smart home" could offer, if they were affordable (Bertoluccl, 2006).

Some of the tasks supported today by home automation systems are:

- **Lighting.** You can program your lights to go on, off, or dim to match your moods and needs for comfort and security.

- **Energy management.** A home's HVAC (heat, ventilation, and air conditioning) system can be programmed for maximum energy efficiency, controlled with a touch panel, and can be accessed via your telephone or PDA.

- **Water control.** Watercop (*watercop.com*) is a device that relies on a series of strategically placed moisture-detection sensors. When the moisture level rises in one of these sensors, it sends a wireless signal to the Watercop control unit, which turns off the main water supply.

- **Home security and communications.** The window blinds, garage doors, front door, smoke detectors, and home security systems can all be automated from a network control panel. These can all be programmed to respond to scheduled events (e.g., when you go on vacation).

- **Home theater.** You can create a multisource audio and video center around your house that you can control with a touch pad or remote. For example, if you have a DVD player in your bedroom but want to see the same movie in your child's room, you can just click a remote to switch rooms.

Do-it-yourself components of a smart home are available at Home Depot, Lowe's, and online at *smarthome.com* and *bestbuy.com.* Look for ZigBee and Z-Wave products. For entertainment in the smart home, see Malik (2004).

Analysts generally agree that the market opportunities for smart homes will take shape over the next 3 to 5 years. These opportunities are being driven by the increasing adoption of broadband services and the proliferation of wireless local area networks (Wi-Fi) within the home and by the trend to integrate currently independent devices. Online File W6.11 shows a wireless connected house.

**SMART CARS**

Every car today has at least one computer on board to operate the engine, regulate fuel consumption, and control exhaust emissions. The average automobile on the road today has actually 20 or more microprocessors, which are truly invisible. They are under the hood, behind the dash, in the door panels, and on the undercarriage.

Microprocessors control the radio, decide when your transmission should shift gears, remember your seat position, and adjust the temperature in the passenger cabin. They can make the suspension work better, help you see in the dark, and warn when a tire is low. In the shop, the onboard microprocessors are used to diagnose problems. Car computers often operate independently, but some swap data among themselves—a growing trend. The microprocessors in a car require little maintenance, continuing to operate through extreme temperature, vibration, and humidity.

In 1998, the U.S. Department of Transportation (DOT) identified eight areas where microprocessors and intelligent systems could improve or impact auto safety (*its.dot.gov/ivi/ivi.htm*). The list included four kinds of collision avoidance (see Jones, 2001), computer "vision" for cars, vehicle stability, and two kinds of driver monitoring. The automotive industry is in the process of testing a variety of experimental systems addressing the areas identified by the DOT. For example, GM in partnership with Delphi Automotive Systems has developed an Automotive Collision Avoidance System that employs radar, video cameras, special sensors, and GPS to monitor traffic and driver actions in an effort to reduce collisions with other vehicles and pedestrians (Sharke, 2003).

There is also a growing trend to connect car microprocessors to mobile networks and to the Internet (see Moore, 2000). Emergency assistance, driving directions, and e-mail are some of the services these connections can support. To increase safety, drivers can use voice-activated controls, even to access the Web (Bretz, 2001). GM's OnStar system (*onstar.com*) already supports many of these services (see Online File W6.12).

*SVC*

OnStar is the forerunner of smart cars of the future. The next generation of smart cars is likely to provide even more automated services, especially in emergency situations. For instance, although OnStar will automatically signal the service center when the air bags are deployed and will immediately contact emergency services if the driver and passengers are incapacitated, what OnStar cannot provide yet is detailed information about a crash. Newer systems can automatically determine the speed upon impact, whether the car has rolled over, and whether the driver and passengers were wearing seat belts. Information of this sort might be used by emergency personnel to determine the severity of the accident and what types of services will be needed.

Ideally smart cars eventually will be able to drive themselves. Known as *autonomous land vehicles* (ALVs), these cars follow GIS maps and use sensors in a wireless environment to identify obstacles. These vehicles are already on the roads in California, Pennsylvania, and Germany (on an experimental basis, of course).

**RFID: A POTENTIAL REVOLUTION—BUT CONSIDER THE RISKS**

One of the major objectives of IT is the ability to sense information in real time from various sources and interpret it. The data collection is done by devices ranging from GPS to wireless sensor networks (to be discussed later). This ability is referred to as *real-world awareness* (Heinrich, 2005), and the most promising device is RFID.

*Radio frequency identification* (RFID) technology uses radio waves to identify items. An RFID system consists of (1) an RFID tag that includes an antenna and a chip with information about the item and (2) an RFID reader that contains a radio transmitter and receiver. An RFID tag remains inactive until radio frequency energy from the radio transmitter hits its antenna, giving the chip enough power to emit a string of information that is read by the radio receiver. This is several times the amount of information a barcode can hold, and the tag can be read through cardboard, wood, and plastic at a range of up to 30 feet. The reader passes this

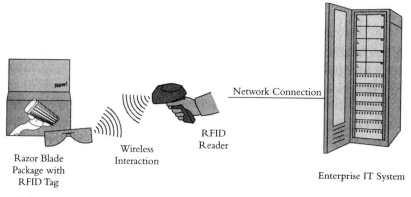

**Figure 6.6** How RFID works. (*Source:* C. Heinrich, *RFID and Beyond,* Indianapolis, Wiley Publishing, 2005, Figure 3.5, p.65.)

information to a computer for processing, either wirelessly or through a wireline. Incidentally, RFID tags attached to clothes can be washed, ironed, and pressed (news item, *itworld.com,* May 2006).

Figure 6.6 shows the RFID tag attached to a product (razor blade). The RFID reader collects the information from the tag, wirelessly transporting it to the corporate network. For details on how RFID works, see Heinrich (2005). Other advantages of RFID over a barcode are that it is much faster and the margin or error of barcode usage is higher.

**Potential Applications.** There are hundreds of potential applications of RFID (e.g., see *symbol.com*) with many potential benefits. (See the list in Online File W6.14.) We provide a sampler in *IT at Work 6.5.*

**Implementing RFID.** Until now the problem with RFID implementation has been the expense. Tags have cost at least 50 cents, which makes them unusable for low-priced items. A California company called Alien Technology (*alientechnology.com*) has invented a way to mass-produce RFID tags for less than 10 cents apiece for large production runs. In January 2003, Gillette placed an order with Alien Technology for 500 million RFID tags (*RFID Journal,* 2002). Gillette is using the tags in a number of trial programs. In one of the early trials, Gillette attached the tags to the Mach 3 razors they ship to Wal-Mart, whose store shelves are equipped with special RFID readers. The overall success of RFID tags in the marketplace will depend on the outcome of trials such as this.

Several factors will determine the speed with which RFID will take off. The first of these is how many companies will mandate that business partners use RFID. So far, only Wal-Mart and the U.S. Department of Defense and a small number of other companies have required such use. The second factor is the success of attempted legislation to limit the amount of information on the tag (pending in the state of California) or to force removal of the tags when customers pay for the items (state of Massachusetts). More legislation will be attempted to protect the privacy of consumers. In the interim, some companies maintain a wait-and-see attitude. Finally, the cost of the tags and the needed information systems support is still high and is likely to remain so at least in the short-run (Spivey-Overby, 2004). However, Ryan (2004) suggests that in order to be winners, manufacturers must embrace the technology. For an overview of the implementation issues and

# IT at Work 6.5

## Illustrative Examples of RFID Use

MKT    GOV    SVC    POM

- **Circuit City stores are embedding RFID into loyalty cards.** When customers enter the store, their card is scanned by a reader. A coupon dispenser at the door then dispenses specific coupons based on their past buying habits. Going further, when the customer's card is read, the store automatically knows that he or she was on the Circuit City Web site recently evaluating plasma TVs. So, when the customer's card is read in the plasma TV section, Circuit City could offer the customer a $500 coupon right on the spot. For further details see Schuman (2005) and Ulanoff (2005).

- **RFID in Federal Government/U.S. Department of Defense (DoD).** Inventory tracking is a logistical challenge throughout the armed services and federal agencies. At the same time, there is an urgent need to ensure the safety of military personnel and improve security worldwide. The end result is that RFID-based applications in the federal government and defense sectors are growing exponentially. RFID technology offers a viable solution with reliable, secure identification and tracking that integrates into existing enterprise mobility systems. For example, the U.S. Marine Corp. uses RFID to improve flows in their supply chains (Ferguson, 2004).

- **Tracking moving vehicles.** The E-Z Pass prepay toll system uses RFID, as does Singapore's Electronic Road Pricing system, which charges different prices to drive on different roads at different times. *IT at Work 6.2* provides an example of the use of RFID technology for toll collection.

- **Tracking people.** In some Japanese schools, tags in backpacks or clothes track students' entry and departure from school buildings. In Denmark, the Legoland amusement park offers parents a child-tracking system that combines RFID and Wi-Fi. Beginning in 2006, all new U.S. passports will contain an RFID tag, scanned upon entry and departure from the United States (see attached photo).

- **Protecting secure areas.** FedEx uses RFID-tagged wristbands to give drivers access to their vehicles, reducing theft and speeding delivery time. The New York Police Department uses RFID tags embedded in ID tags to track visitors.

- **Improving supply chains.** This is probably one of the most promising uses of RFID, as will be illustrated in Chapters 7 through 9.

**Other Uses**

- An RFID chip with patient information (called SurgiChip) approved by the FDA goes with the patient into surgery to help prevent errors. RFIDs are also used for patient identification in hospitals.

- RFID embedded in cell phones will soon replace credit cards, cash, train passes, keys to your car and home, business cards, and more (see Kharif, 2006). DoCoMo of Japan introduced such a cell phone in 2004 (see Mann, 2004).

U.S. passport with RFID chip. (*Source:* "U.S. Issues First RFID Passports," *Engadget.com*, March 13, 2006, *engadget.com/ 2006/03/13/us-issues-first-rfid-passports/*, accessed July 2006.)

attempted solutions, see Kharif (2004). The potential risks of RFID are summarized *A Closer Look 6.3.*

**LARGE-SCALE PERVASIVE SYSTEMS**

Smart appliances, cars, and barcodes can certainly make our lives more comfortable, but pervasive computing can make an even larger contribution when large numbers of computing devices are put together, creating massive intelligent systems. These systems include factories, airports, schools, and even entire cities. At the moment

# A Closer Look 6.3

## RFID and Privacy and Other Risks

**ETHICS**

Since its introduction in the late 1990s, several advocacy groups raised objections to the use of RFID, citing privacy concerns. Several states started legislation that aims to protect privacy.

Privacy concerns are frequently addressed by controlling access to the database that links the tag to individual information, and more narrowly restricting the uses of RFID to those areas of concern.

A major privacy concern is that when individual items are tagged, and they are taken by customers out of stores, it might be possible to track the movements of the customer (remote surveillance). Therefore, some recommend that the tags be removed before a sale is recorded. This increases the cost to the store. Tracking customers is currently very difficult since the readers have a very limited range from which they can be read. In contrast, if a person carries a GPS device, he or she can be tracked anywhere.

Neumann and Weinstein (2006) review certain concerns regarding data integrity, personal well-being, and privacy. They claim, for example, that tags may be counterfeited, duplicated, swapped, damaged, intentionally disabled, or otherwise misused. The encryption protocols may be weak. In addition to the tags themselves, their supporting databases can be misused, providing an opportunity for identity theft,

fraud, harassment, and blackmail. All of these must be considered prior to implementation.

Other risks are possible interferences of metals and fluids with the radio signals, tag quality may be uneven, cost of attaching the tags can be too high, and the cost of the tags is too high. For an RFID failure story, see Reda (2004).

RFID vendors already include a number of security features designed to address privacy issues by protecting consumer information. For example:

- In most applications, RFID safety tags placed on cargo pallets or ID cards contain nothing more than a unique identifying number, much like a license plate on a car. Sensitive information is maintained in a separate database and protected by firewalls and other security features.
- To guard against unauthorized access, transmissions between RFID readers and safety tags can be protected by encryption and authentication protocols. Generally, transmissions between an RFID reader and a back-end database also are encrypted to protect confidential and personal information.

*Sources:* Compiled from Neumann and Weinstein (2006) and Reda (2004).

---

such applications are experimental and on a relatively small scale. Let's look at some examples.

**SVC**

**Smart Schools.** The University of California at Los Angeles is experimenting with a smart kindergarten (Chen et al., 2002). Exploring communication between students, teachers, and the environment, the project aims to create a smart learning environment.

**SVC**

**Intelligent Elder Care.** The increased age of the population in many countries brings a problem of caring for more elderly for longer times. Long-term care facilities, where different patients require different levels of care, bring the problem of how to provide such care efficiently and effectively. The experimental project titled Elite Care has demonstrated the benefits of using pervasive computing in such settings, as described in *IT at Work 6.6*.

**Smart Offices.** The original work of Weiser (1991) centered around an intelligent office. And indeed several projects are experimenting with such an environment, which can interact with users through voice, gesture, or movements and can anticipate their activities. By monitoring office employees, the SmartOffice (*Indiatimes*, 2006) even anticipates user intentions and augments the environment to communicate useful information.

**Digital Cities.** According to Ishida (2002a) the concept of *digital cities* is to build an area in which people in regional communities can interact and share knowledge, experiences, and mutual interests. Digital cities integrate urban information (both real

# IT at Work 6.6

## Using Pervasive Computing to Deliver Elder Care

Delivering health services to the elderly is becoming a major societal problem in many countries, especially in countries where there are relatively fewer and fewer young people to take care of more and more elderly. The problem is already acute in Japan, and it is expected to be very serious in 10 to 15 years in several European countries and in China. Managing and delivering health care involves large numbers of diversified decisions, ranging from allocation of resources to determining what treatment to provide to each patient at each given time.

Elderly residents in assisted-living facilities require differing levels of care. Some residents need minimal assistance, others have short-term memory problems, and yet others have more severe problems like Alzheimer's disease so they require more supervision and help. At Elite Care's Estates Cluster Residential Care Facility in Milwaukie, Oregon, pervasive computing is being used to increase the autonomy and care level of all of its residents, regardless of their individual needs.

Elite Care, a family-owned business (*elite-care.com*), has been built from the ground up to provide "high-tech, high-touch" programs. Its advisory committee, which includes, among others, representatives from the Mayo Clinic, Harvard University, the University of Michigan, the University of Wisconsin, and Sandia National Laboratory, has contributed a number of ideas that have been put into practice.

The entire facility is designed with a 30-mile network (wireline and wireless) of unobtrusive sensors and other devices including: biosensors (e.g., weight sensors) attached to each resident's bed; movement sensors embedded in badges worn by the residents and staff; panic buttons used to call for help; Internet access via touch screens in each room; videoconferencing using Webcams; and climate control, lights, and other regulated appliances.

These devices and others allow the staff to monitor various patient activity. For example, staff can determine the location of any patient, to tell whether he or she is in an expected area of the facility. Devices that monitor length of absence from bed might alert personnel that the patient has fallen or is incapacitated in other ways. Medical personnel can watch for weight loss (possibly indicating conditions like impending congestive heart failure), restlessness at night (indicating conditions like insufficient pain medication), and frequency of trips to the bathroom (indicating medical problems like infection). Also, close monitoring of conditions enables staff to give medicine and/or other treatments as needed, rather than at predetermined periods. All of these capabilities enable true one-to-one care, which is both more effective and less expensive.

One of the initial concerns with these monitors is that the privacy of the residents would be unnecessarily invaded. To alleviate these concerns, residents and their families are given the choice of participating or not. Most choose to participate because the families believe that these monitors provide better tracking and care. The monitors also increase the autonomy of all the patients because their use reduces the need for staff to constantly monitor residents in person, especially those with more acute care needs.

All of these sensors and systems are connected through a high-speed Ethernet (see Technology Guide 4). The data produced by the sensors and systems are stored in a database and can be used to alert the staff in real time if necessary. These data are used for analytical purposes and for developing individualized care programs. The same database is also used for administrative purposes such as monitoring staff performance in timely delivery.

A similar concept is used in Swan Village of Care in Bentley, Australia. At the present time such projects are experimental and expensive, but some day they will be affordable to many.

*Sources:* Compiled from Stanford (2002), *elite-care.com*, and *ECC. online.wa.gov.au/news* (January 14, 2003).

*For Further Exploration:* What types of data do these devices provide? How can pervasive computing increase the quality of elder care? What about the privacy issue?

---

time and stored) and create public spaces for people living in or visiting the cities. Digital cities are being developed all over the world (see Wireless Internet Institute, 2006). In Europe alone there are over 100 projects (e.g., Amsterdam, Helsinki).

In the city of Kyoto, Japan, for example, the digital city complements and corresponds to the physical city (Ishida, 2002a). Three layers are constructed: The first is an information layer, where Web archives and real-time sensory data are integrated to provide information anywhere, any time. The second layer is 2-D and 3-D interfaces, which provide views of cars, buses, and pictures that illustrate city services (for attractive and natural presentation). Finally, there is an interactive layer.

Extensive use of GIS supports the project. One area of emphasis is a digital tour guide for visitors. Also, the system uses avatars (animated computer characters) that appear on a handheld device and "walk" with visitors around the city in real time.

*GOV*

Another digital-city experiment is the city of Lancaster (UK), where wireless devices are being used to improve services to both visitors and residents (Davies et al., 2002). The experimental Lancaster City Guide is based on a network of Wi-Fi context-sensitive and location-aware applications. One area that was developed first is services to tourists. By knowing where the tourist is (using a GPS) and his or her preferences, the system can recommend tourist sites in the same general area. (This application is similar to the Carnegie Mellon application described in *IT at Work 6.4*, page 239.)

For other digital-city experiments, see Mankins (2002). For information on other large-scale pervasive computing projects, see Weise (2002), and Stanford (2002).

**Wireless Sensor Networks (WSNs).** **Wireless sensor networks (WSNs)** are networks of interconnected, battery-powered, wireless sensors called *motes* (analogous to nodes) that are placed into specific physical environments. Each mote collects data and contains processing, storage, and radio frequency sensors and antennas. The motes provide information that enables a central computer to integrate reports of the same activity from different angles within the network. Therefore, the network can determine information such as the direction a person is moving, the weight of a vehicle, or the amount of rainfall over a field of crops with great accuracy.

A new type of wireless sensor network is mesh networking. A **mesh network** is composed of motes, where each mote "wakes up" or activates for a fraction of a second when it has data to transmit and then relays that data to its nearest neighbor. So, instead of every mote transmitting its information to a remote computer at a base station, an "electronic bucket brigade" moves the data mote by mote until it reaches a central computer where it can be stored and analyzed. An advantage of a mesh network is that, if one mote fails, another one can pick up the data. This process makes a mesh network very efficient and reliable. Also, if more bandwidth is needed, it is easy to boost performance by placing new motes when and where they are required. There are many diverse uses for WSNs (e.g., see Online File W6.15 for a vineyard), as the following example indicates:

**WSN Enhances Homeland Security.** Science Applications International Corporation (*saic.com*) is using motes from Dust Networks (*dust-inc.com*) to help secure border crossings and other sensitive areas. This application combines the networked motes, which can detect people, vehicles, voices, and motion, with a tiny camera for capturing images. SAIC is also working on applications to use motes on ships or in shipping containers to detect radiation from a nuclear weapon emitted during transit. See Ricadela (2005), *saic.com*, and *dust-inc.com* (accessed March 2006).

# 6.8 Managerial Issues

**1. Inhibitors and barriers of mobile computing.** Several limitations either are slowing down the spread of mobile computing or are leaving many m-commerce customers disappointed or dissatisfied (e.g., see Islam and Fayad, 2003). Representative inhibitors and barriers of mobile computing are covered in Online File W6.16.

*ETHICS*

**2. Ethical and legal issues.** Several ethical and legal issues are unique to mobile computing. For example, fashion retailer Benetton Group SpA was considering attaching RFID "smart tags" to its Sisley line of clothing to help track shipping, inventory, and sales in the company's 5,000 stores worldwide. (Also, the tags could help prevent shoplifting.) The idea was to integrate the RFID tag into the clothing labels. Using the tags, the store would know where each piece of clothing is, at any given time. However, privacy groups expressed concern that the tags could also be used to track buyers, and some groups even urged that the company's clothing be boycotted. As a result, Benetton backed away from the plan, at least until an impact study is done (Rosencrance, 2003).

Numerous states have pending legislation regarding privacy issues about RFID tags in retail goods. Most legislation is "RFID right to know," requiring disclosure of the use of RFID devices and personal information that is gathered; labeling of retail products or packages containing an RFID tag; point-of-sale removal of RFID tags; restricting of aggregation and disclosure of personal information; and provision for enforcement by a legal agency (RFID Public Information Center, 2006).

According to Hunter (2002), privacy is in great danger in the world of ubiquitous computing because of the proliferation of networked devices used by individuals, businesses, and government. The Elite Care project described in *IT at Work 6.6* (page 245), for example, raised the issue of protecting information collected by sensors. Also, privacy is difficult to control in other types of context-aware systems. As indicated earlier, security is especially difficult in Wi-Fi systems.

**3. Failures in mobile computing and m-commerce.** As with any other technology, especially a new one, there have been many failures of applications as well as entire companies in mobile computing and m-commerce. It is important to anticipate and plan for possible failures as well as to learn from them.

*SVC*

The case of Northeast Utilities provides some important insights. According to Hamblen (2001), Northeast Utilities (located in Berlin, Connecticut), which supplies energy products and services to 1.2 million customers from Maine to Maryland, embarked on a wireless project in 1995 in which its field inspectors used wireless devices to track spills of hazardous material and report them to headquarters in real time. After spending a year and a half and $1 million, the project failed. Some of the lessons learned were:

- Do not start without appropriate infrastructure.
- Do not start a full-scale implementation; use a small pilot for experimentation.
- Pick up an appropriate architecture. Some users don't need to be persistently connected, for example.
- Talk with a range of users, some experienced and some not, about usability issues.
- Users must be involved; hold biweekly meetings if possible.
- Employ wireless experts if you are not one.
- Wireless is a different medium from other forms of communication. Remember that people are not used to the wireless paradigm.

Having learned from the failure, Northeast made its next wireless endeavor a success. Today, all field inspectors carry rugged wireless laptops that are connected to the enterprise intranet and databases. The wireless laptops are used to conduct measurements related to electricity transformers, for example. Then the laptops transmit the results, in real time, to chemists and people who prepare government reports about hazardous materials spills. In addition, time is saved, because all the information is entered directly into proper fields of electronic forms without having to be transcribed. The new system is so successful that it has given IT workers the confidence to launch other applications such as sending power-outage reports to managers via smart phones and wireless information to crews repairing street lights.

**4. Other implementation issues.** Three representative implementation issues are:

    **a. Timetable.** Although there has been much hype about m-commerce in the last few years, only a small number of large-scale mobile computing applications have been deployed to date. The most numerous applications are in e-banking, stock trading, emergency services, and some B2B tasks. Companies still have time to carefully craft an m-commerce strategy. This will reduce the number of failed initiatives and bankrupted companies. For calculating the total cost of wireless computing ownership and how to justify it, see Intel (2002).

**b. Setting applications priorities.** Finding and prioritizing applications is a part of an organization's e-strategy. Although location-based advertising is logically attractive, its effectiveness may not be known for several years. Therefore, companies should be very careful in committing resources to m-commerce. For the near term, applications that enhance the efficiency and effectiveness of mobile workers are likely to have the highest payoff.

**c. Choosing a system.** The multiplicity of standards, devices, and supporting hardware and software can confuse a company planning to implement mobile computing. An unbiased consultant can be of great help. Checking the vendors and products carefully, as well as who is using them, is also critical. This issue is related to the issue of whether to use an application service provider (ASP) for m-commerce. For additional implementation issues, see Urbaczewski et al. (2003).

# Integrating *IT*

### For the Accounting Major

Wireless applications help with inventory counting and auditing. They also assist in expediting the flow of information for cost control. Price management (recall the Food Lion case), inventory control, and other accounting-related activities can be improved by use of wireless technologies.

### For the Finance Major

Wireless services can provide banks and other financial institutions with a competitive advantage. For example, wireless electronic payments, including micropayments, are more convenient (any place, any time) than traditional means of payments, and they are also less expensive. Electronic bill payment via mobile devices is becoming more popular, increasing security and accuracy, expediting cycle time, and reducing processing costs.

### For the Human Resources Management Major

Mobile computing can improve HR training and extend it to any place at any time. Payroll notices can be delivered as SMSs. Self-service selection of benefits and updating of personal data can be extended to wireless devices, making these functions even more convenient for employees to handle their own benefits management.

### For the IS Major

IS personnel provide the wireless infrastructure that enables employees to compute and communicate any time, anywhere. This convenience provides exciting, creative new applications for organizations to cut costs and improve the efficiency and effectiveness of operations (for example, to gain transparency in supply chains). Unfortunately, as we discussed earlier, wireless applications might not be secure. Lack of security is a serious problem for which IS personnel are responsible.

### For the Marketing Major

Imagine a whole new world of marketing, advertising, and selling with the potential to increase sales dramatically. This is the promise of mobile computing. Of special interest for marketing are location-based advertising as well as the new opportunities resulting from pervasive computing and RFIDs. Finally, wireless technology also provides new opportunities in sales force automation (SFA), enabling faster and better communications with both customers (CRM) and corporate partners.

### For the Production/Operations Management Major

Wireless technologies offer many opportunities to support mobile employees of all kinds. Wearable computers enable repair personnel working in the field and off-site employees to service customers faster, better, and at lower cost. Wireless devices can also increase productivity within factories by enhancing communication and collaboration as well as managerial planning and control. In addition, mobile computing technologies can increase safety by providing quicker warning signs and instant messaging to isolated employees.

## Key Terms

Automatic crash notification
  (ACN) *236*
Bluetooth *213*
Context awareness *238*
Contextual computing *238*
Enhanced Messaging Service
  (EMS) *213*
Geographical information system
  (GIS) *233*
Global positioning system (GPS) *213*
Location-based e-commerce
  (l-commerce) *214*
M-wallet (mobile wallet) *220*

Mesh network *246*
Mobile portals *222*
Multimedia Messaging Service
  (MMS) *213*
Personal digital assistant
  (PDA) *213*
Pervasive computing *237*
Radio frequency identification
  (RFID) *238*
Short Messaging Service (SMS) *213*
Smart phone *213*
Telematics *236*
Voice portal *223*

Wearable devices *225*
WiMax *213*
Wireless Application Protocol
  (WAP) *213*
Wireless Encryption Protocol
  (WEP) *218*
Wireless fidelity (Wi-Fi) *213*
Wireless local area network
  (WLAN) *213*
Wireless 911 (e-911) *236*
Wireless mobile computing *212*
Wireless sensor network
  (WSN) *246*

## Chapter Highlights

(Numbers Refer to Learning Objectives)

**1** Mobile computing is based on mobility and reach. These characteristics provide ubiquity, convenience, instant connectivity, personalization, and product and service localization.

**2** The major drivers of mobile computing are: large numbers of users of mobile devices, especially cell phones; no need for a PC; a developing "cell phone culture" in some areas; vendor marketing; declining prices; increasing bandwidth; and the explosion of EC in general.

**3** Mobile computing and m-commerce require mobile devices (e.g., PDAs, cell phones) and other hardware, software, and wireless technologies. Commercial services and applications are still emerging. These technologies allow users to access the Internet any time, anywhere.

**3** For l-commerce, a GPS receiver is also needed.

**4** Standards are being developed by several organizations in different countries, resulting in competing systems. It is expected that with time some of these will converge.

**5** Many EC applications in the service industries (e.g., banking, travel, and stocks) can be conducted with wireless devices. Also, shopping can be done from mobile devices.

**5** Location-based advertising and advertising via SMSs on a very large scale is expected.

**5** Mobile portals provide content (e.g., news) to millions.

**6** Large numbers of intrabusiness applications, including inventory management, sales force automation, wireless voice, job dispatching, wireless office, and more are already evident inside organizations.

**7** Emerging mobile B2B applications are being integrated with the supply chain and are facilitating cooperation between business partners.

**8** M-commerce is being used to provide applications in travel, gaming, entertainment, and delivery of medical services. Many other applications for individual consumers are planned for, especially targeted advertising.

**9** Most non-Internet applications involve various types of smart cards. They are used mainly in transportation, security, and shopping from vending machines and gas pumps.

**10** Location-based commerce, or l-commerce, is emerging in applications such as calculating arrival time of buses (using GPS) and emergency services (wireless 911). In the future, it will be used to target advertising to individuals based on their location. Other innovative applications also are expected.

**11** In the world of invisible computing virtually every object has an embedded microprocessor that is connected in a wired and/or wireless fashion to the Internet. This Internet of things—homes, appliances, cars, and any manufactured items—will provide a number of life-enhancing, consumer-centric, and B2B applications.

**11** In context-aware computing, the computer captures the contextual variables of the user and the environment and then provides, in real time, various services to users.

**12** The major limitations of mobile computing are: small screens on mobile devices, limited bandwidth, high cost, lack of (or small) keyboards, transmission interferences, unproven security, and possible health hazards. Many of these limitations are expected to diminish over time. The primary legal/ethical limitations of m-commerce relate to privacy issues.

## Virtual Company Assignment

### Mobile Computing at The Wireless Café

Go to The Wireless Café's link on the Student Web Site. You will be asked to consider mobile and wireless applications that can be implemented at the restaurant.

**Instructions for accessing The Wireless Café on the Student Web site:**

1. Go to *wiley.com/college/turban*.
2. Select Turban/Leidner/McLean/Wetherbe's *Information Technology for Management, Sixth Edition*.
3. Click on Student Resources site, in the toolbar on the left.
4. Click on the link for Virtual Company Web site.
5. Click on Wireless Café.

## Online Resources

More resources and study tools are located on the Student Web Site and on WileyPLUS. You'll find additional chapter materials and useful Web links. In addition, self-quizzes that provide individualized feedback are available for each chapter.

## Questions for Review

1. Define mobile computing and m-commerce.
2. Define the following terms: PDA, WAP, SMS, GPS, Wi-Fi, WiMax, and smart phone.
3. List the value-added attributes of mobile computing.
4. List at least five major drivers of mobile computing.
5. List some of the uses of voice portals.
6. Discuss mobile micropayments.
7. Describe the m-wallet and wireless bill payments.
8. Describe how mobile devices can be used to shop.
9. Explain targeted advertising in the wireless environment and in pervasive computing.
10. Describe mobile portals and what kind of information they provide.
11. Describe wireless job dispatch.
12. Discuss how wireless applications can be used to provide customer support.
13. List some of the major intrabusiness wireless applications (mobile enterprise).
14. Describe wireless support along the supply chain.
15. How can telemetry improve supply chain operations?
16. Describe the application of wireless and mobile technologies to games and entertainment.
17. Discuss some of the potential applications of Wi-Fi and Bluetooth technologies in hotels.
18. Describe some potential uses of mobile and wireless technologies in providing medical care.
19. Describe some of the potential uses of l-commerce.
20. Discuss the technologies used in providing l-commerce services.
21. Describe GPS and GIS.
22. List some of the barriers to l-commerce.
23. Define pervasive computing.
24. List some of the major properties of pervasive computing.
25. Discuss some of the ways that pervasive computing can be used in the home.
26. Describe a smart car.
27. What is contextual computing?
28. List the technical limitations of m-commerce.

## Questions for Discussion

1. Discuss how mobile computing can solve some of the problems of the *digital divide* (the gap within a country or between countries with respect to people's ability to access the Internet). (See International Communications Union 1999 and Chapter 16).

2. Discuss how m-commerce can expand the reach of e-business.

3. Explain the role of protocols in mobile computing.

4. Discuss the impact of wireless computing on emergency medical services.

5. How do smart phones and screenphones differ? What characteristics do they share?

6. How are GIS and GPS related?

7. List three to four major advantages of wireless commerce to consumers, presented in this chapter, and explain what benefits they provide to consumers.

8. You can use location-based tools to help you find your car or the closest gas station. However, some people see location-based tools as an invasion of privacy. Discuss the pros and cons of location-based tools.

9. Discuss how wireless devices can help people with disabilities.

10. Discuss the benefits of telemetry-based systems.

11. Discuss the ways in which Wi-Fi is being used to support mobile computing and m-commerce. Describe the ways in which Wi-Fi is affecting the use of cellular phones for m-commerce.

12. Which of the applications of pervasive computing—smart cars, homes, appliances, and things—do you think are likely to gain the greatest market acceptance in the next few years? Why?

13. Which of the current mobile computing and m-commerce limitations do you think will be minimized within 5 years? Which ones will not?

14. Describe some m-commerce B2B applications along the supply chain.

15. It is said that Wi-Fi is winning a battle against 3G. In what sense is this true? In what sense is this false?

## Exercises and Projects

1. Enter *kyocera-wireless.com* and view the demos. What is a smart phone? What are its capabilities? How does it differ from a regular cell phone?

2. Investigate commercial applications of voice portals. Visit several vendors (e.g., *tellme.com, bevocal.com*, etc.). What capabilities and applications are offered by the various vendors?

3. Using a search engine, try to determine whether there are any free or for-fee Wi-Fi hotspots in your area. (*Hint:* Access *wifinder.com* or *techworld.com/hotspot-locator.*) Enter *wardriving.com*. Based on information provided at this site, what sorts of equipment and procedures could you use to locate hotspots in your area?

4. Examine how new data capture devices such as RFID tags help organizations to accurately identify and segment their customers for activities such as targeted marketing. Browse the literature and the Web, and develop five potential new applications of RFID technology (not listed in this text). What issues could arise if a country's

laws required such devices to be embedded in everyone's body as a national identification system?

5. Conduct a study on wearable computers. Find five vendors. Start with *nexttag.com, mobileinfo.com, xybernaut.com*, and *eg3.com,* and look for others as well.

   a. Identify 5 to 10 consumer-oriented wearable devices. What are the capabilities of these products? What advantages do they offer users?

   b. Identify 5 to 10 industry-oriented wearable devices. What are the capabilities of these products? What advantages do they offer users?

   c. See if you can find "What's cooking" in the research labs. For example, visit MIT's wearable computing lab.

6. Investigate commercial uses of GPS. Start with *gpshome.ssc.nasa.gov;* then go to *gpsstore.com*. Can some of the consumer-oriented products be used in industry? Prepare a report on your finding.

7. Enter *google.com* and find all their mobile activities. Prepare a summary.

## Group Assignments and Projects

1. Each team should examine a major vendor of mobile devices (Nokia, Kyocera, Motorola, Palm, BlackBerry, etc.). Each team will research the capabilities and prices of the devices offered by each company and then make a class presentation, the objective of which is to convince the rest of the class why one should buy that company's products.

2. Each team should explore the commercial applications of m-commerce in one of the following areas: financial services, including banking, stocks, and insurance; marketing

and advertising; manufacturing; travel and transportation; human resources management; public services; and health care. Each team will present a report to the class based on their findings. (Start at *mobiforum.org*.)

3. One group studies *blackberry.com/go/fieldforce* also including enterprise solutions from the company. Make a list of all the services offered. A second group studies the services offered by Sony Ericsson for mobile workers. A third group investigates Nokia's Enterprise Solutions. Finally, a group checks Symbol

Technology Inc's. offerings. Prepare a list of capabilities and present them to the calss.

4. Each team should take one of the following areas—homes, cars, appliances, or other consumer goods like clothing—and investigate how embedded microprocessors are currently being used and will be used in the future to support consumer-centric services. Each team will present a report to the class based on their findings.

5. Assign teams to vendors of mobile enterprise devices (e.g., Symbol and Sybase). Find their major products and list their capabilities.

## Internet Exercises

1. Learn about PDAs by visiting vendors' sites such as Palm, Sony, Hewlett-Packard, IBM, Philips, NEC, Hitachi, Casio, Brother, Texas Instruments, and others. List some m-commerce devices manufactured by these companies.

2. Access *progressive.com,* an insurance company, from your cell phone (use the "Go to . . ." feature). If you have a Sprint PCS wireless phone, do it via the Finance menu. If you have a Palm i705 (or newer), you can download the Web-clipping application from Progressive. Report on these capabilities.

3. Research the status of 3G and the future of 4G by visiting *itu.int, 4g.newstrove.com,* and *3gnewsroom.com.* Prepare a report on the status of 3G and 4G based on your findings.

4. Explore *nokia.com.* Prepare a summary of the types of mobile services and applications Nokia currently supports and plans to support in the future.

5. Enter *mobile.commerce.net* and find information about car navigation systems. Write a report.

6. Enter *ibm.com.* Search for *wireless e-business.* Research the resulting stories to determine the types of wireless capabilities and applications IBM's software and hardware supports. Describe some of the ways these applications have helped specific businesses and industries.

7. Using a search engine, try to determine whether there are any commercial Wi-Fi hotspots in your area. Enter *wardriving.com.* Based on information provided at this site, what sorts of equipment and procedures could you use to locate hotspots in your area?

8. Enter *mapinfo.com* and look for the location-based services demos. Try all the demos. Find all of the wireless services. Summarize your findings.

9. Visit *ordersup.com, astrology.com,* and similar sites that capitalize on l-commerce. What features do these sites share?

10. Enter *packetvideo.com* and *microsoft.com/mobile/pocketpc.* Examine their demos and products and list their capabilities.

11. Enter *internethomealliance.com* and review their whitepapers. Based on these papers, what are the major appliances that are currently in most U.S. homes? Which of these appliances would most homeowners be likely to connect to a centrally controlled network?

12. Enter *onstar.com.* What types of *fleet* services does OnStar provide? Are these any different from the services OnStar provides to individual car owners? Look for the demo and video.

13. Enter *autoidcenter.org.* Read about the Internet of Things. What is it? What types of technologies are needed to support it? Why is it important?

14. Enter *mdsi-advantex.com* and review the wireless products for the enterprise. Summarize the advantages of the different products.

15. Enter *wirelesscar.com.* Examine all the services provided and relate them to telemetry.

16. Enter the site of a wireless e-mail provider (BlackBerry, T-mobile, Handspring); collect information about the capabilities of the products and compare them.

17. Enter *zilog.com/about/partners/011600.html* and find information about smart appliances.

18. Enter *media.mit.edu/wearables* and prepare a report about new developments (most recent 12 months).

19. Enter *med-i-nets.com* and find information about Pharm-i-net. Trace the supply chain and the support of wireless. Make a diagram of the supply chain.

20. Enter *rfgonline.com* and *mobilecommerce.net* and find information about RFID benefits and risks. Write a summary.

## Minicase 1

### Hertz Goes Wireless

**MKT**

The car rental industry is very competitive, and Hertz (*hertz.com*), the world's largest car rental company, competes against hundreds of companies in thousands of locations. The competition focuses on customer acquisition and loyalty. In the last few years, competition has intensified, and profits in the industry have been drifting downward. Hertz has been a "first mover" to information technologies since the 1970s, so it has pioneered some mobile commerce applications:

- **Quick rentals.** Upon arrival at the airport, Hertz's curbside attendant greets you and transmits your name wirelessly to the renting booth. The renting-booth employee advises the curbside attendant about the location of your car. All you need to do is go to the slot where the car is parked and drive away. This system, which once operated over a WLAN, is now part of a national wireless network that can check credit cards, examine your rental history, determine which airline to credit your loyalty mileage to, and more.

- **Instant returns.** A handheld device connected to a database via a wireless system expedites the car return transaction. Right in the parking lot, the lot attendant uses a handheld device that automatically calculates the cost of the rental and prints a receipt for the renter. You check out in less than a minute, and you do not have to enter the renting booth at all.

- **In-car cellular phones.** Starting in 1988, Hertz began renting cell phones with its cars. Today, of course, this is not as big a deal as it was in 1988, when it was a major innovation.

- **NeverLost Onboard.** Some Hertz cars come equipped with an onboard GPS system, which provides route guidance in the form of turn-by-turn directions to many destinations. The information is displayed on a screen with computer-generated voice prompts. An electronic mapping system (GIS) is combined with the GPS, enabling you to see on the map where you are and where you are going. Also, consumer information about the locations of the nearest hospitals, gas stations, restaurants, and tourist areas is provided.

- **Additional customer services.** Hertz's customers can download city guides, Hertz's location guide, emergency telephone numbers, city maps, shopping guides, and even reviews of restaurants, hotels, and entertainment into their PDAs and other wireless devices. Of course, driving directions are provided.

- **Car locations.** Hertz is experimenting with a GPS-based car-locating system. This will enable the company to know where a rental car is at any given time, and even how fast it is being driven. Although the company promises to provide discounts based on your usage pattern, this capability is seen by many as an invasion of *privacy*. On the other hand, some may feel safer knowing that Hertz knows where they are at all times.

*Sources: hertz.com (2003) and Martin (2003).*

## Questions for Minicase 1

1. Which of these applications are intrabusiness in nature?

2. Identify any finance- and marketing-oriented applications.

3. What are the benefits to Hertz of knowing exactly where each of its cars is? As a renter, how do you feel about this capability?

---

# Minicase 2

## Washington Township Fire Department Goes Wireless

**SVC**

The Washington Township Fire Department (WTFD) is located just north of Columbus, Ohio. WTFD responds to more than 4,500 emergency medical services (EMS) calls every year. Time is critical when WTFD is responding to emergencies, which range from heart attacks to fire injuries to highway accidents. The service is run by emergency medical technicians (EMTs).

Rushing victims to the hospital is only one part of the service offered by these dedicated technicians. Providing first aid at the accident scene and while transporting the injured in the ambulances is the other part. When a patient is transferred to the hospital, the EMTs must also provide information on what treatments and medications were administered, and what health-related signs they observed in the patient. Such patient care reports are critical to the continuance of the treatment in the hospital, and they become a permanent part of the medical record. The information is also used to keep EMS records for planning, budgeting, training, and reporting to the state of Ohio.

In the past, the department had problems using 8" × 14," multipart, multicopy paper forms. Using paper forms caused several problems. First, not everyone's handwriting is legible, so it was often difficult for hospital personnel as well as the WTFD office people to decipher the information. Second, on many occasions, the information was incomplete, or even inaccurate. To restore the information took considerable valuable time. Office employees at WTFD had to spend close to 1,800 hours a year processing information after the completion of the patient care report. In fact, 85 percent of one full-time office employee's time was required just to reenter data that were already entered on the paper reports. But the major problem was the time spent by EMTs filling out forms, since this prevented them from returning quickly to the station, to respond to other emergency calls.

A solution to the paperwork problems was a mobile data collection device (MobilEMS of Clayton I.D.S. Corp. powered by SQL Anywhere Studio from Sybase Corp.). The device allows EMTs to collect patient information quickly, easily, and accurately at the scene and to deliver that information to the hospital in a printout. This is done by using a series of data entry screens with drop-down menus containing vital information such as diagnoses, treatment rendered, drug administered, and even street names. It also includes a signature-capture feature that allows EMTs to document a patient's refusal of treatment as well as transfer of care to the hospital.

Once the incident data are entered into the system's embedded SQL database, printing reports is simple. The technician beams the information from MobilEMS to the hospital printer's infrared port and a clear document is produced. Back at the station, the EMTs synchronize the data in their handhelds with the department computer systems by placing MobilEMS in a docking station.

It now takes about 15 seconds to move the data into the system. This is a significant improvement over manual rekeying; using MobilEMS has reduced costs by more than 90 percent. Also by eliminating handwriting and mandating the completion of required data fields that previously could have been skipped, the accuracy increased significantly.

Finally, the system is customizable. Fields can be added and additional information can be stored. Thus, additional applications are leading to a completely paperless environment.

*Sources:* Compiled from Sybase.com (2003) and Walsh (2003).

## Questions for Minicase 2

1. The system uses a mobile device with a docking station for data synchronization, but no wireless is used. Would you recommend adding wireless? What for? Why or why not?

2. What are the potential legal and pricing issues in this case?

3. The system is based on electronic forms with checkmarks. Why not use a similar set of paper forms?

4. What are the benefits of the mobile system to the patient, to the hospital, and to the employees?

5. What are the benefits to WTFD?

# References

8d.com, "Cale Uses 8D Technologies' 8D ECO to Deliver World-Leading Parking System that Features Wireless, Secure Online Payment—From Solar-Powered Terminals—and Advanced Management Functions, to Large North American City," *8d.com,* 2006, *8d.com/content.php?section=products&subsection=eco&subsubsection=eco_case&id=1* (accessed May 2006).

*91expresslanes.com* (accessed June 2006).

Baard, M., "After the Fall: Help for Climbers," *Wired News,* December 24, 2002, *wired.com/news/technology/0,1282,56146,00.html* (accessed June 2006).

Banavar, G., et al., "Driving Long-Term Value from Context-Aware Computing," *Information Systems Management,* Fall 2005.

Becker, D., "Sega Forms Mobile Games Division," *CNET News.com,* April 2002, *news.com.com/Sega+forms+mobile+games+division/2100-1040_3-885668.html* (accessed June 2006).

Bertolucci, J., "Make Your Home a Smart Home," *Kiplinger's,* May 2006.

Bretz, E., "The Car, Just a Web Browser with Tires," *IEEE Spectrum,* 38(1), January 2001, pp. 92–94.

Bughin, J., et al., "Mobile Portals Mobilize for Scale," *McKinsey Quarterly,* April–June 2001.

Business Wire, "SEGA Reinvents Sonic The Hedgehog Experience for Next-Generation Video Game Platforms; Gaming Icon to Celebrate 15th Year on PS3 and Xbox 360," *BusinessWire.com,* September 9, 2005, *tmcnet.com/usubmit/2005/sep/1180490.htm* (accessed May 2006).

Caton, M., "RFID Reshapes Supply Chain Management," *e-Week,* April 19, 2004.

Chatterjee, A., et al., "A Road Map for Telematics," *McKinsey Quarterly,* April–June 2002.

Chen, A., et al., "A Support Infrastructure for Smart Kindergarten," *Pervasive Computing,* 1(2), April–June 2002, pp. 49–57.

Clark, K., "Food Lion's High Wireless Act," *Retail Technology Quarterly,* July 2005.

Cohen, A., "Off-Site, Online," *PC Magazine,* September 17, 2002.

Comiskey, D., "ShopWiki Launches Mobile Shopping Search Engine," *Ecommerce-guide.com,* May 17, 2006, *ecommerce-guide.com/news/article.php/3606926* (accessed June 2006).

Coursaris, C., and H. Hassanein, "Understanding M-Commerce: A Consumer-Centric Model," *Quarterly Journal of Electronic Commerce,* 3(3), July–September 2002, pp. 247–271.

D'Agostino, D., "Mobile MyoPia," *CIO Insight,* November 2005.

Davies, N., and H. W. Gellersen, "Beyond Prototyping: Challenges in Deploying Ubiquitous Systems," *Pervasive Computing,* January–March 2002.

Davies, N., et al., "Future Wireless Applications for a Networked City," *IEEE Wireless Communications,* February 2002.

Deans, P. C., *E-Commerce and M-Commerce Technologies.* Hershey, PA: IRM Press, 2004.

Dizikes, P., "Wireless Highway," *Technology Review,* March–April 2006.

Dogac, A., and A. Tumer, "Issues in Mobile Electronic Commerce," *Journal of Database Management,* January–February 2002.

Duan, M., "Enhancing the Shopping Experience, One $2,000 Suit at a Time," *Mpulse Magazine,* November 2002, *cooltown.hp.com/mpulse/1102-prada.asp* (accessed June 2003); *redherring.com/Article.aspx?a=1294* (accessed May 2004).

Eklund, R., "Mobile CRM Comes of Age," *CRM,* July 15, 2002, *destinationcrm.com/articles/default.asp?ArticleID_2352* (accessed May 2004).

*elite-care.com* (accessed May 2004).

Ellison, C., "Opening Day in Texas Opens Up to Wi-Fi," *eWeek,* March 31, 2005, *eweek.com/article2/0,1895,1781233,00.asp* (accessed June 2006).

Ellison, C., "Palm Sees Uptick in Development of Mobile Enterprise Applications," *e-Week*, May 18, 2004.

Engadget, "U.S. Issues First RFID Passports," *Engadget.com*, March 13, 2006, *engadget.com/2006/03/13/us-issues-first-rfid-passports/* (accessed June 2006).

Estrin, D., et al., "Embedding the Internet," *Communications of the ACM*, 43(5), May 2000, pp. 38–42.

Ferguson, R. B., "Marines Deploy RFID," *eWeek*, November 15, 2004), *eweek.com/article2/0,1759,1723353,00.asp* (accessed June 2006).

Frolick, M. N., and L. D. Chen, "Assessing M-Commerce Opportunities," *Information Systems Management*, Spring 2004.

Fujitsu Computer Systems, "Fujitsu Computer Systems National Distributing Company Case Study," *fujitsupc.com/www/about.shtml? aboutus/casestudies/ndc* (accessed June 2006).

Gandon, F. L., and N. M. Sadeh, "Context-Awareness, Privacy and Mobile Access: A Web Semantic and Multiagent Approach," *ACM International Conference Proceeding Series;* Vol. 64, 2004.

Gershman, A., and A. Fano, "Examples of Commercial Applications of Ubiquitous Computing," *Communications of the ACM,* March 2005.

Global Mobile Suppliers Association (GSA), "Survey of Mobile Portal Services," Quarter 4, 2002, *gsacom.com/downloads/MPSQ4_2002.pdf* (no longer available online).

Hamblen, M., "Get Payback on Wireless," *Computer World*, January 1, 2001, *computerworld.com/printthis/2001/0,4814,54798,00.html* (accessed June 2006).

Heinrich, C., *RFID and Beyond*. Indianapolis: Wiley Publishing, 2005. *hertz.com* (accessed June 2006).

Henning, T., "Wireless Imaging," *The Future Image Report*, 2002.

Hines, M., "Digital Content Spurs Micropayment Resurgence," *CNetnews.com*, September 4, 2004, *news.com.com/2100-1030_3-5347513.html* (accessed June 2006).

Hornberger, M., and C. Kehlenbeck, "Mobile Financial Services on the rise in Europe," September 19, 2002, *banktech.com/story/wireless/ BNK20020919S0005* (no longer available online).

Hunter, R., *World Without Secrets: Business, Crime, and Privacy in the Age of Ubiquitous Computing*. New York: Wiley, 2002.

*Indiatimes*, "Offices, They Are A-Changing," *Indiatimes.com*, May 12, 2006, *infotech.indiatimes.com/articleshow/1527370.cms* (accessed June 2006).

Intel, "Building the Foundation for Anytime Anywhere Computing," White Paper 25 1290–002, Intel Corporation, June 13, 2002, *intel.com/ pressroom/kits/events/ idffall_2002/wireless_mobility_whitepaper.pdf* (accessed June 2006).

International Telecommunications Union, "Challenges to the Network: Internet for Development," October 1999, *itu.int/ITU-D/ict/publications/inet/1999/ExeSum.html* (accessed June 2006).

Ishida, T., "Digital City Kyoto," *Communications of the ACM*, 45(7), July 2002a, pp. 76–81.

Ishida, T. (ed.), *Understanding Digital Cities: Cross Cultural Perspective*. Cambridge MA: MIT Press, 2002b.

Islam, N., and M. Fayad, "Toward Ubiquitous Acceptance of Ubiquitous Computing," *Communications of the ACM*, February 2003.

ITS America, "NextBus Expands Real-Time Transit Information in the Bay Area with AC Transit," August 9, 2001, *nextbus.com/corporate/ press/* (accessed June 2006).

ITVib, "Wi-Fi Internet Installed on Lufthansa," *ITVibe.com*, May 18, 2004. *itvibe.com/news/2530/* (accessed June 2006).

Jones, W. D., "Keeping Cars from Crashing," *IEEE Spectrum*, 38(9), September 2001, pp. 40–45.

Juniper Research, "Mobile Payments to Rise from $155m in 2005 to $10bn Total Revenue by 2010, with Increasing Consumer Adoption of m-Payment Schemes," *Juniper Research press release*, May 2006, *juniperresearch.com/reports/17_MCommerce/press_release.htm* (accessed May 2006).

Judge, P., "Wi-Fi Switch Security Nothing but a White Elephant," *Computerworld.com*, May 14, 2004, *computerworld.co.nz/news.nsf/ default/659A221342614499CC256E940069D6ED* (accessed June 2006).

Kharif, O., "Like It or Not, RFID Is Coming," *Business Week Online*, March 18, 2004.

Kharif, O., "What's Lurking in That RFID Tag?" *BusinessWeekOnline*, March 16, 2006, *businessweek.com/technology/content/mar2006/ tc20060316_117677.htm* (accessed June 2006).

Kontzer, T., "Top Ten Uses for SMS," *Information Week*, June 11, 2003, *informationweek.com/story/showArticle.jhtml;jsessionid=1M2IE0XV SIDMMQSNDBCSKHSCJUMEIJVN?articleID=10300804* (accessed June 2006).

Kou, W., and Y. Yesha (eds.), *Enabling Technologies for Wireless E-Business*. Heidelberg, Germany: Springer, 2006.

Kumagai, J., "Talk to the Machine," *IEEE Spectrum*, 39(9), September 2002.

Lahlou, S., M. Langheinrich, and C. Rocker, "Privacy and Trust Issues with Invisible Computers," *Communications of the ACM*, March 2005.

Lipset, V., "Bluefish and Zaryba Enable Mobile Bill Payment," *MCommerce Times*, January 21, 2003.

Longino, C., "Your Wireless Future," *Business 2.0*, May 2006.

Lyman, J., "Will Mobile CRM Finally Break Through in 2006?" *CRMBuyer.com*, January 3, 2006, *crmbuyer.com/story/48054.html* (accessed June 2006).

Maier, M., "Is that a PC in Your Pocket? *Business 2.0*, February 6, 2006, *money.cnn.com/2006/02/06/technology/b2_thirdscreen0206* (accessed May 2006).

Malik, O., "Home Entertainment to Go," *Business 2.0*, December 2004.

Mallat, N., et al., "Mobile Banking Services," *Communications of the ACM*, May 2004.

Mankins, M., "The Digital Sign in the Wired City," *IEEE Wireless Communication*, February 2002.

Mann, C. C., "A Remote Control for Your Life," *Technology Review*, July–August 2004.

Mathieson, R., "The Future According to Spielberg: Minority Report and the World of Ubiquitous Computing," *MPulse*, August 2002, *rickmathieson.com/articles/0802-minorityreport.html* (accessed June 2006).

McGuire, C., "Food Lion Checking Out with Wi-Fi," *Wi-Fi Plant News*, May 27, 2004, *wi-fiplant.com/news/article.php/3360601* (accessed June 2006).

Mennecke, B. E., and T. J. Strader, *Mobile Commerce: Technology, Theory and Applications*. Hershey, PA: Idea Group Publishing, 2003.

Moore, J. F., "The Race to Put the Web into Cars," *Business 2.0*, Dec. 6, 2000.

Needleman, R., "Targeted Wi-Fi," *Business 2.0*, December 2002.

Neumann, P. G., and L. Weinstein, "Risks of RFID," *Communications of the ACM*, May 2006.

Nobel, C., "Home Depot Tackles Network Challenge," *eWeek*, November 21, 2005.

Nokia, "Nokia Brings Mobility to the Games Industry by Making Rich Games Mobile," November 4, 2002, *press.nokia.com/PR/200211/ 880085_5.html* (accessed June 2006).

Payment News, "Mobile Banking Stages a Remarkable Comeback," *Paymentnews.com*, February 6, 2006, *paymentsnews.com/2006/02/ mobile_banking_.html* (accessed June 2006).

Perton, M., "Motorola M-Wallet Cellphone Payment Sysetm Coming to U.S.," *Engadget.com*, February 8, 2006, *engadget.com/2006/02/08/*

motorola-m-wallet-cellphone-payment-system-coming-to-us/ (accessed June 2006).

Poropudas, T., "ATM Connection to Boost Mobile Payments," *Mobile CommerceNet,* February 15, 2003.

Raskin, A., "Your Ad Could Be Here! (And Now We Can Tell You Who Will See It)," *Business 2.0,* May 2003, money.cnn.com/magazines/business2/ business2_archive/2003/05/01/341929/index. htm (accessed June 2006).

Reda, S., "Prada's Pratfall," *Stores,* June 2004.

Republica IT, "Busta Paga in Pensione Lo Stipendio Arriva Via Sms," March 20, 2001, repubblica.it/online/tecnologie_internet/tim/tim/tim.html (accessed May 2004).

*RFID Journal,* "Gillette to Buy 500 Million EPC Tags," November 15, 2002.

RFID Public Information Center, "RFID and Privacy," rfidprivacy. mit.edu/access/happening_legislation.html (accessed June 2006).

Ricadela, A., "Sensors Everywhere," *Information Week,* January 24, 2005.

Rosencrance, L., "Update: Benetton Backs Away from 'Smart Tags' in Clothing Line," *Computer World,* April 4, 2003.

Rothfeder, J., "What's Wrong with RFID," *CIO Insight,* August 2004.

Roush, W., "Social Machines," *Technology Review,* August 2005.

Ryan, T., "RFID in the Consumer Industries," Research Report, Aberdeen Group, March 2004.

Sadeh, N., *M-Commerce.* New York: Wiley, 2002.

morpho.com (accessed June 2006).

Sarkar, D., "Lawmakers Form 911 Caucus," *Federal Computer Week,* February 25, 2003, fcw.com/article78901 (accessed June 2006).

Sarshar, A., "How Do 'Dot-Net,' Mobile Computing and PDAs Contribute to Your Bottom Line?" *Knowledgestorm: The Upshot,* February 2003, knowledgestorm.com/info/user_newsletter/022003/geneva.jsp (accessed June 2006).

Scanlon, J., "The Way We Work," special Wired Report, *Wired,* May 2003, wired.com/wired/archive/11.05/unwired/work.html (accessed June 2006).

Schmidt, A., T. Gross, and M. Billing-Hurst, "Introduction to Special Issue on Context-Aware Computing in CSCW," *Computer Supported Cooperative Work,* August 2004.

Schuman, E., "Circuit City's New Approach to Customer Service," *eWeek,* January 17, 2005.

Schuman, E., "A Tight Ship," *Baseline,* March 2004.

Sharke, P., "Smart Cars," *MEmagazine.org,* May 2003, memagazine.org/backissues/mar03/features/smartcar/smartcar.html (accessed June 2006).

Shi, N., *Wireless Communications and Mobile Commerce.* Hershey, PA: Idea Group Publishing, 2004.

Smith, B., "Goodbye Wallet, Hello Phone," *Wireless Week,* April 1, 2006, wirelessweek.com/article/CA6321122.html?spacedesc=Features (accessed June 2006).

Spivey-Overby, C., "RFID at What Cost? What Wal-Mart Compliance Really Means," ForrTel (Webcast plus telephone), *Forrester Research,* May 25, 2004.

Spice, B., "At CMU, Scientists Are Building Sense into Cell Phones," *Post-gazette.com,* September 2, 2003, post-gazette.com/pg/03245/217276.stm (accessed June 2006).

Staff, "Electronic Payment Volumes Predicted to Double by 2010," *Computer Business Review Online,* May 5, 2006, cbronline.com/

article_news.asp?guid=91D4193B-75C8-4C28-8DB9-B02F05A2A25B (accessed May 2006).

Stanford, V., "Pervasive Computing Goes to Work: Interfacing to the Enterprise," *Pervasive Computing,* 1(3), July–September 2002.

Streitz, N., and P. Nixon (eds.), "The Disappearing Computer," *Communications of the ACM,* March 2005.

Sybase.com, "Clayton I.D.S and Washington/Norwich Township Fire Departments," Sybase Inc., ianywhere.com/success_stories/clayton_ids.html (accessed June 2006).

Symbol.com, "CVS Selects Symbol's Wireless Network System, Hand-Held Computers, June 3, 1998, symbol.com/news/pressreleases/cvs.html (no longer available online).

Symbol.com, "Driscoll's Berries Picks Perfect Mobile Solution for Distribution, Account Reconciliation," *Symbol.com case study,* symbol.com/products/oem/driscoll_case.html (accessed June 2006).

Taj Hotel, "Taj Hotels Introduce Wi-Fi Facilities," *The Hindu,* July 31, 2002, hinduonnet.com/2002/07/31/stories/2002073102321600.htm (accessed June 2006).

Tech Live Staff, "Future of Mobile Commerce Murky," techtv.com, November 2, 2001, g4tv.com/**tech**tvvault/features/34355/Future_of_Mobile_Commerce_Murky.html?detectflash=false& (accessed June 2006).

Tiwari, R., "Mobile Commerce: Mobile Banking, a Strategic Analysis of Opportunities in the Banking Sector," *University of Hamberg Research Project,* January 2006, uni-hamburg.de/m-commerce/banking/index_e.html (accessed May 2006).

Ulanoff, L., "Bargain Hunting Online," *PC Magazine,* November 17, 2004.

Urbaczewski, A., et al. (eds.), "Mobile Commerce: Opportunities and Challenges," *Communications of the ACM,* special issue, December 2003.

Varshney, U., and R. Vetter, "Recent Advances in Wireless Networking," *IEEE Computer,* 33(6), June 2000, pp. 107–109.

Walsh, B., and W. K. Yamarick, "Beam Me Up, Scotty," *Health Management Technology,* July 2005.

Walsh, T., "Wireless Gets EMS Crews Between Scenes Faster," *GNC.com,* March 28, 2003, gcn.com/online/vol1_no1/21516-1.html?topic=mobile-wireless (accessed June 2006).

Wang, F. Y., et al., "Toward Intelligent Transportation System for the 2008 Olympics," *IEEE Intelligent Systems,* November–December 2003.

Weise, E., "Laundry Spins on the High Tech Cycle," *USA Today,* September 3, 2002.

Weiser, M., "The Computer for the Twenty-First Century," *Scientific American,* September 1991. Reprinted in *Pervasive Computing,* January–March 2002.

Wired, "Get Wireless," special *Wired* report. Supplement to *Wired,* May 2003 (11 articles).

Wireless Internet Institute, "Digital Cities Convention," w2i, 2006, w2idigitalcitiesconvention.com/ (accessed June 2006).

XyberFlash, "Wearable Computers for the Working Class," *New York Times,* December 14, 2000.

*Xybernaut.com,* "Xybernaut Mobile Assistant: Productivity Gains in the Telecommunication Field," *ABCUS.com,* abcusinc.com/XybernautCaseStudy-BellCanada.html (accessed June 2006).

Zhao, Y., "Telematics: Safe and Fun Driving," *IEEE Intelligent Systems,* 17(1), January–February 2002, pp. 10–14.

Part IV | **Organizational Applications**

▶ 7. Transaction Processing, Functional Applications, and Integration
8. Enterprise Systems
9. Interorganizational and Global Information Systems

Chapter

# 7

# Transaction Processing, Functional Applications, and Integration

## Learning Objectives

After studying this chapter, you will be able to:

❶ Relate functional areas and business processes to the value chain model.

❷ Identify functional management information systems.

❸ Describe the transaction processing system and demonstrate how it is supported by IT.

❹ Describe the support provided by IT and the Web to production/operations management, including logistics.

❺ Describe the support provided by IT and the Web to marketing and sales.

❻ Describe the support provided by IT and the Web to accounting and finance.

❼ Describe the support provided by IT and the Web to human resources management.

❽ Describe the benefits and issues of integrating functional information systems.

❾ Describe how IT supports compliance, especially that of SOX.

## Integrating *IT*

ACC     FIN     MKT     POM     HRM     IS     SVC

# WIRELESS INVENTORY MANAGEMENT SYSTEM AT DARTMOUTH-HITCHCOCK MEDICAL CENTER

## The Problem

Dartmouth-Hitchcock Medical Center (DHMC) is a large medical complex in New Hampshire with hospitals, a medical school, and over 600 practicing physicians in its many clinics. DHMC was growing rapidly and was encountering a major problem in the distribution of medical supplies. These supplies used to be ordered by nurses. But nurses are usually in short supply, so having nurses spending valuable time ordering supplies left them less time for their core competency—nursing. Furthermore, having nurses handling supply orders led to inventory management problems: Busy nurses tended to overorder in an effort to spend less time in managing inventory. On the other hand, they frequently waited until the last minute to order supplies, which led to costly rush orders.

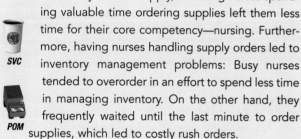

One solution would have been to transfer the task of inventory ordering and management to other staff, but doing so would have required hiring additional personnel and the DHMC was short on budget. Also, the coordination with the nurses to find what was needed and when, as well as maintaining the stock, would have been cumbersome.

What the medical center needed was a solution that would reduce the burden on the nurses, but also reduce the inventory levels and the last-minute, expensive ordering. Given the size of the medical center, and the fact that there are over 27,000 different inventory items, this was not a simple task.

## The Solution

DHMC realized that their problem was related to the supply chain, and so it looked to IT for solutions. The idea the DHMC chose was to connect wireless handheld devices with a purchasing and inventory management information system. Here is how the new system works (as of the summer of 2002): The medical center has a wireless LAN (Wi-Fi) into which handhelds are connected. Information about supplies then can be uploaded and downloaded from the devices to the network from anywhere within the range of the Wi-Fi. In remote clinics without Wi-Fi, the handhelds are docked into wireline network PCs.

For each item in stock a "par level" (the level at which supplies must be reordered) was established, based on actual usage reports and in collaboration between the nurses and the materials management staff. Now nurses simply scan an item when it is consumed, and the software automatically adjusts the recorded inventory level. When a par level is reached for any inventory item, an order to the supplier is generated automatically. Similarly, when the inventory level at each nursing station dips below the station's par level, a shipment is arranged from the central supply room to that nursing station. The system also allows for nurses to make restocking requests, which can be triggered by scanning an item. The system works for the supplies of all non-nursing departments as well (e.g., human resources or accounting). Overall, the Wi-Fi system includes over 27,000 line items.

The system is integrated with other applications from the same vendor (PeopleSoft Inc., now an Oracle company). One such application is Express PO, which enables purchasing managers to review standing purchase orders, e-procurement, and contract management.

## The Results

Inventory levels were reduced by 50 percent, paying for the system in just a few months. Materials purchasing and management now are consistent across the enterprise, the last-minute, sometimes expensive ordering, has been eliminated, the time spent by nurses on ordering and tracking materials has been drastically reduced, and access to current information has been improved. All of this contributed to reduced costs and improved patient care.

*Sources:* Compiled from Grimes (2003), and *peoplesoft.com* (now at *Oracle.com;* material no longer available online).

## Lessons Learned from This Case

The DHMC case provides some interesting observations about implementing IT: First, IT can support the routine processes of inventory management, enabling greater efficiency, more focus on core competencies, and greater satisfaction for employees and management. The new system also helped to modernize and redesign some of the center's business processes (e.g., distribution, procurement), and was able to support several business processes (e.g., operations, finance, and accounting), not just one. Although the system's major application is in inventory management, the same software vendor provided ready-made modules, which were *integrated* with the inventory module and with each other (for example, with purchasing and contract management). The integration also included connection to suppliers, using the Internet. This IT solution has proven useful for an organization whose business processes cross the traditional functional departmental lines. (In this case nursing is considered operations/production, and so is inventory control; purchasing and contract management are in the finance/accounting area.)

Functional information systems get much of their data from the systems that process routine transactions (*transaction processing systems, TPSs*). Also, many applications in business intelligence, e-commerce, CRM, and other areas use data and information from two or more functional information systems. Therefore, there is a need to integrate the functional systems applications among themselves, with the TPS, and with other applications. These relationships are shown in Figure 7.1, which provides a pictorial view of the topics discussed in this chapter. (Not shown in the figure are related applications discussed in other chapters, such as e-commerce and knowledge management.)

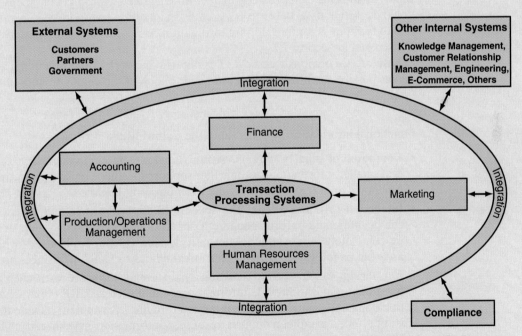

**Figure 7.1** The functional areas, TPS, and integration connection. Note the flow of information from the TPS to the functional systems. Flow of information between and among functional systems is done via the integration component.

# 7.1 Functional Information Systems

The major functional areas in many companies are the production/operations, marketing, human resources, accounting, and finance departments. (See the value chain model in Chapter 13 for their role.) Traditionally, information systems were designed within each functional area, to support the area by increasing its internal effectiveness and efficiency. However, as we will discuss in Chapters 8 and 9, the traditional functional hierarchical structure may not be the best structure for some organizations, because certain business processes involve activities that are performed in several functional areas. Suppose a customer wants to buy a particular product. When the customer's order arrives at the marketing department, the customer's credit needs to be approved by Finance. Someone (usually in the production/operations area) checks to find if the product is in the warehouse. If it is there, then someone needs to pack the product and forward it to Shipping, which arranges for delivery. Accounting prepares a bill for the customer, and Finance may arrange for shipping insurance. The flow of work and information between the different departments may not work well, creating delays or poor customer service.

One possible solution is to restructure the organization. For example, the company can create cross-functional teams, each responsible for performing a complete business process. Then, it is necessary to create appropriate information systems applications for the restructured processes. In other cases, the company can use IT to create minor changes in the business processes and organizational structure, but this solution may not solve problems such as lack of coordination or an ineffective supply chain. One other remedy may be an *integrated approach* that keeps the functional departments as they are, but creates an integrated supportive information system to facilitate communication, coordination, and control. The integrated approach is discussed in Section 7.7.

Before we demonstrate how IT facilitates the work of the functional areas, and makes possible their integration, we need to look at the characteristics of the functional areas.

**MAJOR CHARACTERISTICS OF FUNCTIONAL INFORMATION SYSTEMS**

Functional information systems share the following characteristics:

- **Composed of smaller systems.** A functional information system consists of several smaller information systems that support specific activities performed in the functional area (e.g., recruiting and promotions in HRM).
- **Integrated or independent.** The specific IS applications in any functional area can be integrated to form a coherent departmental functional system, or they can be completely independent. Alternatively, some of the applications within each area can be integrated across departmental lines to match a business process.
- **Interfacing.** Functional information systems may interface with each other to form the organization-wide information system such as ERP (Chapter 8). Some functional information systems interface with the environment outside the organization. For example, a human resources information system can collect data about the labor market.
- **Supportive of different levels.** Information systems applications support the three levels of an organization's activities: *operational, managerial,* and *strategic* (see Chapter 2).

An illustration of the IS applications in the production/operations area is provided in Online File W7.1. Other functional information systems have a similar basic structure.

In this chapter we describe some representative functional IT applications. However, since information systems applications receive much of the data that they process from the corporate *transaction processing system* or are integrated with it, we deal with this system first.

# 7.2 Transaction Processing Information Systems

The core operations of organizations are enabled by transaction processing systems.

**COMPUTERIZATION OF ROUTINE TRANSACTION PROCESSES**

In every organization there are business transactions that provide its mission-critical activities. Such transactions occur when a company produces a product or provides a service. For example, to produce toys, a manufacturer needs to order materials and parts, pay for labor and electricity, create a shipment order, and bill customers. A bank that maintains the toy company's checking account must keep the account balance up-to-date, disperse funds to back up the checks written, accept deposits, and mail a monthly statement.

Every transaction may generate additional transactions. For example, purchasing materials will change the inventory level, and paying an employee reduces the corporate cash on hand. Because the computations involved in most transactions are simple and the transaction volume is large and repetitive, such transactions are fairly easy to computerize.

The *transaction processing system* (TPS) monitors, collects, stores, processes, and disseminates information for all routine core business transactions. These data are input to functional information systems applications, as well as to data warehouse, customer relationship management (CRM), and other systems. The TPS also provides critical data to e-commerce, especially data on customers and their purchasing history.

Transaction processing occurs in all functional areas. Some TPSs occur within one area, others cross several areas (such as payroll). Online File W7.2 provides a list of TPS activities by the major functional areas. The information systems that automate transaction processing can be part of the departmental systems, and/or part of the enterprisewide information systems. For a comprehensive coverage of TPSs, see Wikipedia (2006) and Subrahmanyam (2002).

**OBJECTIVES AND EXAMPLES OF TPS**

The primary goal of a TPS is to provide all the information needed by law and/or by organizational policies to keep the business running properly and efficiently. Specifically, a TPS has to efficiently handle high volume, avoid errors, be able to handle large variations in volume (e.g., during peak times), avoid downtime, never lose results, and maintain privacy and security. To meet these goals, a TPS is usually automated and is constructed with the major characteristics listed in Table 7.1

**Examples of Computerized TPSs.** Here are some examples of TPSs:

- American Airlines (AA) and American Express partnered to offer passengers the convenience of in-flight card payments. A pilot program in 2005 led to AA customers' use of their credit and charge cards to purchase sandwiches, drinks, or headsets. Wireless, handheld devices process the transactions. The new system, which accepts most major credit and debit cards, became available across the entire fleet in June 2006 (*Cheapflights.com,* 2006). Other airlines use a similar device. These systems are so successful that cash is not accepted any more.

- To process companies' tax returns faster and with fewer errors, the U.S. government (and other governments) mandate electronic filing. Furthermore, a preliminary analysis by smart programs identifies potential cheaters.

| **TABLE 7.1** | The Major Characteristics of a TPS |
| --- | --- |

- Typically, *large amounts of data* are processed.
- The *sources of data are mostly internal,* and the output is intended mainly for an *internal audience.* This characteristic is changing somewhat, since trading partners may contribute data and may be permitted to use TPS output directly.
- The TPS processes information on a *regular basis:* daily, weekly, biweekly, and so on.
- *High processing speed* is needed due to the high volume.
- The TPS basically *monitors and collects current or past data.*
- Input and output *data are structured.* Since the processed data are fairly stable, they are formatted in a standard fashion.
- A *high level of detail* (raw data, not summarized) is usually observable, especially in input data but often in output as well.
- *Low computation complexity* (simple mathematical and statistical operations) is usually evident in a TPS.
- A high level of *accuracy, data integrity, and security* is needed. Sensitive issues such as privacy of personal data are strongly related to TPSs.
- *High reliability* is required. The TPS can be viewed as the lifeblood of the organization. Interruptions in the flow of TPS data can be fatal to the organization.
- *Inquiry processing* capacity is a must. The TPS enables users to query files and databases (sometimes in real time).

- Many organizations allow their employees to electronically enter changes in their personnel files (e.g., change of address, having a new baby). Furthermore, many companies allow employees to electronically select fringe benefits packages.

Specific objectives of a TPS may include one or more of the following: to allow for efficient and effective operation of the organization, to provide timely documents and reports, to increase the competitive advantage of the corporation, to provide the necessary data for tactical and strategic systems, to ensure accuracy and integrity of data and information, and to safeguard assets and security of information. It is also important to remember that TPSs must closely interface with many IT initiatives, especially with e-payment, e-procurement, and e-marketing.

**ACTIVITIES AND METHODS OF TPS**

Regardless of the specific data processed by a TPS, a fairly standard process occurs, whether in a manufacturer, in a service firm, or in a government organization. First, raw data are collected by people or sensors (or data are already in files), and then the data are entered into the computer via any input device. Generally speaking, organizations try to automate the TPS data entry as much as possible because of the large volume involved.

Next, the system processes data in one of two basic ways: *batch* or *online processing.* In **batch processing,** the firm collects data from transactions as they occur, and stores them. The system then prepares and processes the collected data periodically (say, once every night). Batch processing is particularly useful for operations that require processing for an extended period of time. Once a batch job begins, it continues until it is completed. In **online processing,** data are processed as soon as a transaction occurs, possibly even in *real time* (instantly).

To implement online transaction processing, *master transaction files* containing key information about important business entities are placed on hard drives, as an operational database (see Figure 7.2) where they are directly accessible.

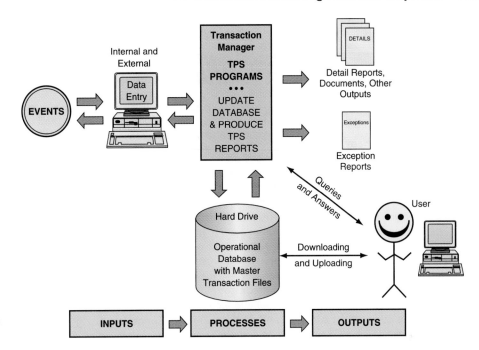

**Figure 7.2** The flow of information in transaction processing.

The *transaction files* containing information about business activities, such as orders placed by customers, are also held in online files until they are no longer needed for everyday transaction processing activity. This ensures that the transaction data are available to all applications, and that all data are kept up-to-the-minute. These data can also be processed and stored in a data warehouse. The entire process is managed by a *transaction manager* (see Subrahmanyam, 2002, for details).

The flow of information in a typical TPS is shown in Figure 7.2. An event, such as a customer purchase, is recorded by the TPS program (e.g., by a barcode reader). The processed information (output) can be either a report or an activity in the database. In addition to a scheduled report, users can query the TPS for nonscheduled information (such as, "What was the impact of our price cut on sales during the first five days, by day?"). The system will provide the appropriate answer by accessing a database containing transaction data (see bidirectional arrows in Figure 7.2).

**WEB-BASED AND ONLINE TRANSACTION PROCESSING SYSTEMS**

Transaction processing systems may be fairly complex, involving customers, vendors, telecommunications, and different types of hardware and software. Traditional TPSs are centralized and run on a mainframe. In **online transaction processing (OLTP),** transactions are processed as soon as they occur. For example, when you pay for an item at a POS at a store, the system records the effects of the sale by instantly reducing the inventory on hand by a unit, increasing the store's cash position by the amount you paid, and increasing sales figures for the item by one unit. For more on OLTP see Chapter 11.

With OLTP and Web technologies such as a portal and an extranet, suppliers can look at the firm's inventory level or production schedule in *real time*. The suppliers themselves, in partnership with their customers, can then assume responsibility for inventory management and ordering in what is known as vendor-managed inventory (VMI); see Chapter 9. Customers too can enter data into the TPS to track orders and even query it directly, as described in *IT at Work 7.1*.

# *IT* at Work 7.1

## Modernizing the TPS Cuts Delivery Time and Saves Money

Here are some examples of how modernizing transaction processing systems has saved time and/or money:

**Kinko's (a FedEx company).** Each time you make a copy at Kinko's, a copying transaction and a payment transaction occur. In the past you received a device (a card, the size of a credit card) and inserted it into a control device attached to the copy machine, and it recorded the number of copies that you made. Then you stood in line to pay: The cashier placed the device in a reader to see how many copies were made. Your bill was computed, with tax added. Kinko's cost was high in this system, and some customers were unhappy about standing in line to pay for only a few copies. Today, using Kinko's new system, you insert your credit card (or a stored-value card purchased from a machine) into a control device, make the copies, print a receipt, and go home. You no longer need to see a Kinko's employee to complete your purchase.

**Carnival Line.** Carnival Line, the operator of cruise ships, needs to rapidly process sometimes over 2,500 people leaving the ship at the ports of call, and later returning to the ship. The company used to use printed name lists with room for checkmarks. Today, passengers place a smart card into a reader. This way the company knows who left the ship and when, and who returns. Each smart-card reader can process over 1,000 people in 30 minutes. In the past it was necessary to use 10–15 employees to process the people leaving and returning to the ship, and it took almost an hour. Today, one person supervises two card readers for less than 30 minutes.

**California Department of Motor Vehicles.** The California DMV processes 15 million vehicle registration fees each year. To smooth the process, the DMV is using a rule-based expert system that calculates the fees (see *blazesoft.com* for details).

**UPS Store.** Seconds after you enter an address and a Zip code into a terminal at UPS delivery outlets at a UPS Store, a shipping label and a receipt are generated. Your shipping record stays in the database, so if you send another package to the same person, you do not need to repeat the address again.

**Sprint Inc.** Using an object-oriented approach, Sprint Inc. has improved its order processing for new telephones. In the past it took a few days for a customer to get a new telephone line; with its new system, Sprint can process an order in only a few hours. The order application itself takes less than 10 minutes, experiences fewer errors, and can be executed on electronic forms on a salesperson's desktop or laptop computer.

*For Further Exploration:* Could Kinko's operate completely without employees at their outlets? What effect does Carnival's smart-card reader have on security? Whose time is being saved at UPS and Sprint?

---

**TYPICAL TASKS IN TRANSACTION PROCESSING**

Transaction processing exists in all functional areas. Here we describe in some detail one application that crosses several functional areas—order processing.

**Order Processing.** Orders for goods and/or services may flow from customers to a company by phone, on paper, or electronically. Fast and effective order processing is recognized as a key to customer satisfaction. Orders can also be internal—from one department to another. Once orders arrive, an order processing system needs to receive, document, route, summarize, and store the orders. A computerized system can also track sales by product, by zone, by customer, or by salesperson, providing sales or marketing information that may be useful to the organization. As described in Chapter 6, more and more companies are providing systems for their salespeople that enable them to enter orders from a business customer's site using wireless notebook computers, PDAs, or Internet-enabled smart phones (see Minicase 2). Some companies spend millions of dollars reengineering their order processing as part of their transformation to e-business. IBM, for example, restructured its procurement system so its own purchasing orders are generated quickly and inexpensively in its e-procurement system.

Orders can be for services as well as for products. Otis Elevator Company, for example, tracks orders for elevator repair. The processing of repair orders is done

# *IT* at Work 7.2

## Automatic Vehicle Location and Dispatch System in Singapore

*SVC   POM   GLOBAL*

Taxis in Singapore are tracked by a *global positioning system* (GPS), which is based on the 24 satellites originally set up by the U.S. government. The system allows its users to get an instant fix on the geographical position of each taxi equipped with GPS (see the figure).

Here's how the system works: Customer orders are usually received via cell phone, regular telephone, fax, or e-mail. Customers can also dispatch taxis from special kiosks (called CabLink) located in shopping centers and hotels. Other booking options include portable taxi-order terminals placed in exhibition halls. Frequent users enter orders from their offices or homes by keying in a PIN number over the telephone. That number identifies the user automatically, together with his or her pickup point. Infrequent customers use an operator-assisted system.

Once an order has been received, the system finds a vacant cab nearest the caller, and a display panel in the taxi alerts the driver to the pickup address. The driver has 10 seconds to push a button to accept the order. If he does not, the system automatically searches out the next-nearest taxi for the job.

The system completely reengineered taxi order processing. First, the transaction time for processing an order for a frequent user is much shorter, even during peak demand, since they are immediately identified. Second, taxi drivers are not able to pick and choose which trips they want to take, since the system will not provide the commuter's destination. This reduces the customer's average waiting time significantly, while minimizing the travel distance of empty taxis. The system increases the capacity for taking incoming calls by 1,000 percent, providing a competitive edge to those cab companies that use the system. It also reduces misunderstanding between drivers and dispatchers, and driver productivity increased since they utilize their time more efficiently. Finally, customers who use terminals do not have to wait a long time just to get a telephone operator (a situation that exists during rush hours, rain, or any other time of high demand for taxis). Three major taxi companies with about 50,000 taxis are connected to the system.

*Sources:* Compiled from Liao (2003) and *entersingapore.com* (2006).

*For Further Exploration:* What TPS tasks do computers execute in this order processing system? What kinds of priorities can be offered to frequent taxi customers?

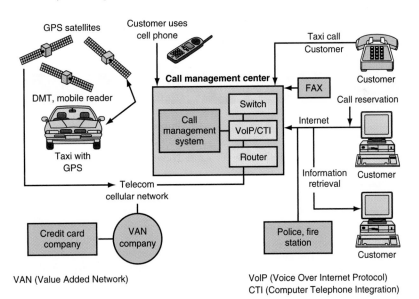

Location tracking of taxicabs in Singapore.

via wireless devices that allow effective communication between repair crews and Otis physical facilities. Orders also can be processed by using innovative IT technologies such as global positioning systems; see *IT at Work 7.2.*

**Other TPS Activities.** Other typical TPS activities are summarized in Table 7.2 (page 266). Most of these routine tasks are computerized.

| TABLE 7.2 | Typical TPS Activities |
|---|---|
| **Activities** | **Description** |
| The ledger | The entire group of an organization's financial accounts. Contains all of the assets, liabilities, and owner's (stockholders') equity accounts. |
| Accounts payable and receivable | Records of all accounts to be paid and those owed by customers. Automated system can send reminder notes about overdue accounts. |
| Receiving and shipping records | Transaction records of all items sent or received, including returns. |
| Inventory-on-hand records | Records of inventory levels as required for inventory control and taxation. Use of barcodes improves ability to count inventory periodically. |
| Fixed-assets management | Records of the value of an organization's fixed assets (e.g., buildings, cars, machines), including depreciation rate and major improvements made in assets, for taxation purposes. |
| Payroll | All raw and summary payroll records. |
| Personnel files and skills inventory | Files of employees' history, evaluations, and record of training and performance. |
| Reports to government | Reports on compliance with government regulations, taxes, etc. |
| Other periodic reports and statements | Financial, tax, production, sales, and other routine reports. |

**WHAT IF TPS FAILS?** TPSs deal with the core activities of the organization. Their failure can cause a disaster. Several years ago, the U.S. Social Security Administration had some major TPS failures, as did insurance companies, hospitals, and banks. One might think that a large financial institution should be immune from IT failure, but this was not the case with TIAA/CREF, as illustrated in *IT at Work 7.3*.

# IT at Work 7.3

## The TIAA-CREF Computerized Reporting Failed

TIAA-CREF is a huge company serving the retirement, insurance, investment, and other needs of teachers and professors. It is one of the largest financial institutions of its kind.

In September 2005, thousands of TIAA-CREF members were unable to access funds from their own accounts. Clients were unable to withdraw funds or receive under- or overpayments in their pensions. The company assured clients that this was just a small delay due to the IT platform upgrade. However, according to Boucher-Fergusen (2006a), the problems lingered for months and expanded to inflow of money as well. The problem resulted from an attempt to introduce a powerful new platform, called Open Plan Solutions, whose objectives were to bring together fixed annuities, variable annuities, mutual funds, and homegrown platforms onto a single, connected platform with:

- **Flexible,** state-of-the-art record keeping
- **Streamlined** enrollment process
- **Comprehensive** remittance services

- **Improved** Web-based institutional reporting on accumulations, transactions, and salary reduction agreements
- **New** and improved participant quarterly statements

The problems included synchronization issues between the company's Web-access software and the record-keeping system during the batch transaction processing. In other words, the new system was not in sync with the old one. By April 2006, the problem became a disaster (Boucher-Ferguson, 2006b) because of the inability to solve all the integration problems fast enough. At that time, the company set up a new cross-functional team to catch issues before they escalated. By the time this book was written (July 2006), major progress had been made, but some problems still persist.

*Sources:* Compiled from Boucher-Ferguson (2006a, 2006b) and from *tiaa-cref.org* (2006).

*For Further Exploration:* If such a giant finance company had such problems, what about small companies? Could proper IT planning (Chapter 13) have prevented the problem? What are the damages to TIAA/CREF?

**TRANSACTION PROCESSING SOFTWARE**

There are dozens of commercial TPS software products on the market. Many are designed to support Internet transactions. (See a sampler of TPS software products and vendors in Online File W7.3).

The problem, then, is how to evaluate so many software packages. In Chapter 15, there is a discussion on software selection that applies to TPS as well. But the selection of a TPS software product has some unique features. Therefore, one organization, the Transaction Processing Performance Council (*tpc.org*), has been trying to assist in this task. This organization is conducting *benchmarking* for TPS. It checks hardware vendors, database vendors, middleware vendors, and so forth. Recently it started to evaluate e-commerce transactions (*tpc.org/tpcw;* there, see "transactional Web e-commerce benchmark"). Also, the organization has several decision support benchmarks (e.g., TPC-App, TPC-H, and TPC-R).

## 7.3 Managing Production/Operations and Logistics

**POM**

The *production and operations management* (POM) function in an organization is responsible for the processes that transform inputs into useful outputs (see Figure 7.3). In comparison to the other functional areas, the POM area is very diversified and so are its supporting information systems. It also differs considerably among organizations. For example, manufacturing companies use completely different processes than do service organizations, and a hospital operates much differently from a university. (Look again at Online File W7.1 for an example of the complexity of the POM field. Note that the internal interfaces are on the left and the external ones on the right.)

Because of the breadth and variety of POM functions, here we present three IT-supported POM topics: in-house logistics and materials management, planning production/operations, and computer-integrated manufacturing (CIM).

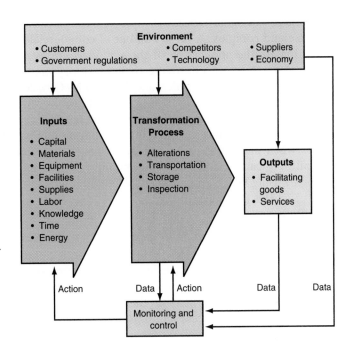

**Figure 7.3** The production/operations management functions transform inputs into useful outputs. (*Source:* J. R. Meredith and S. M. Shafer, *Operations Management.* New York: Wiley, 2002. Reprinted by permission of John Wiley & Sons, Inc.)

**IN-HOUSE
LOGISTICS AND
MATERIALS
MANAGEMENT**

Logistics management deals with ordering, purchasing, inbound logistics (receiving), and outbound logistics (shipping) activities. In-house logistics activities are a good example of processes that cross several functional departments. Both conventional purchasing and e-procurement result in incoming materials and parts. The materials received are inspected for quality and then stored. While the materials are in storage, they need to be maintained until distributed to those who need them. Some materials are disposed of when they become obsolete or their quality becomes unacceptable.

All of these activities can be supported by information systems (Robb, 2003 and Ho, 2004). For example, many companies today are moving to some type of e-procurement (Chapter 5). Scanners, RFID, and voice technologies, including wireless ones, can support inspection, and robots can perform distribution and materials handling. Large warehouses use robots to bring materials and parts from storage, whenever needed. The parts are stored in bins, and the bins are stacked one above the other (similar to the way safe deposit boxes are organized in banks). Whenever a part is needed, the storekeeper keys in the part number. The mobile robot travels to the part's "address," takes the bin out of its location (e.g., using magnetic force), and brings the bin to the storekeeper. Once a part is taken out of the bin, the robot is instructed to return the bin to its permanent location. In intelligent buildings in Japan, robots bring files to employees and return them for storage. In some hospitals, robots even dispense medicines. An example of a parts-tracking system is provided by Carr (2005).

**Inventory Management.** *Inventory management* determines how much inventory to keep. Overstocking can be expensive; so is keeping insufficient inventory. Three types of costs play important roles in inventory decisions: the cost of maintaining inventories, the cost of ordering (a fixed cost per order), and the cost of not having inventory when needed (the shortage or opportunity cost). The objective is to minimize the total of these costs.

Two basic decisions are made by operations: when to order, and how much to order. Inventory models, such as the economic order quantity (EOQ) model, support these decisions. Dozens of models exist, because inventory scenarios can be diverse and complex. A large number of commercial inventory software packages to automate the application of these models are available at low cost. More and more companies are improving their inventory management and replenishment, better meeting customers' demand (Amato-McCoy, 2002c).

Many large companies (such as Wal-Mart) allow their suppliers to monitor the inventory level and ship when needed, eliminating the need for sending purchasing orders. Such a strategy, in which the supplier monitors inventory levels and replenishes when needed, is called **vendor-managed inventory (VMI)** (Chapter 8). The monitoring can be done by using mobile agents over the Internet. It also can be done by using Web Services, as Dell Computer is doing. An emerging solution is the use of RFIDs (Chapter 9).

Reducing inventories and managing them properly is a major objective of supply chain management (Chapter 8).

**Quality Control.** Manufacturing quality-control systems can be standalone systems or can be part of an enterprisewide total quality management (TQM) effort. They provide information about the quality of incoming materials and parts, as well as the quality of in-process semifinished and finished products. Such systems record the results of all inspections. They also compare actual results to metrics. One such matrix is the Six Sigma (Chapter 8).

Quality-control data may be collected by Web-based sensors and interpreted in real time, or they can be stored in a database for future analysis. Also, RFIDs can be used to collect data. Periodic reports are generated (such as percentage of defects, percentage of rework needed), and management can compare performance among departments on a regular basis or as needed.

Web-based quality control information systems are available from several vendors (e.g., HP and IBM) for executing standard computations such as preparing quality control charts. First, manufacturing data are collected for quality-control purposes by sensors and other instruments. After the data have been recorded, it is possible to use Web-based expert systems to make interpretations and recommend actions (e.g., to replace equipment).

| PLANNING PRODUCTION/ OPERATIONS | The POM planning in many firms is supported by IT. Some major areas of planning and their computerized support are described here. An automatic defect-reporting system is described by Duvall (2005). |

**Just-in-Time Systems.** In mass customization and build-to-order production, the just-in-time concept is frequently used. **Just-in-time (JIT)** is an approach that attempts to minimize waste of all kinds (of space, labor, materials, energy, and so on) and to continuously improve processes and systems. For example, if materials and parts arrive at a workstation *exactly when needed,* there is no need for inventory, there are no delays in production, and there are no idle production facilities or underutilized workers. Many JIT systems are supported by software from vendors such as HP, IBM, CA, and Cincom Systems. For how IT works with JIT, see Gillium et al. (2005).

As of 2001, car manufacturers were rapidly adopting a make-to-order process. To deliver customized cars quickly and with cost efficiency, manufacturers need a JIT system. Oracle, PeopleSoft, and other vendors offer a demand-driven *lean manufacturing,* which is a derivative of JIT (see Gillium et al., 2005).

**Project Management.** A *project* is usually a one-time effort composed of many interrelated activities, costing a substantial amount of money, and lasting for weeks or years. The management of a project is complicated by the following characteristics.

- Most projects are unique undertakings, and participants have little prior experience in the area.
- Uncertainty exists due to the generally long completion times.
- There can be significant participation of outsiders, which is difficult to control.
- Extensive interaction may occur among participants.
- The many interrelated activities make changes in planning and scheduling difficult.
- Projects often carry high risk but also high profit potential.

The management of projects is enhanced by computerized project management tools such as the *program evaluation and review technique* (PERT) and the *critical path method* (CPM). For example, developing Web applications is a major project, and several IT tools are available to support and help manage these activities (see Project Net from *citadon.com*). Merrill-Lynch uses such computerized tools to plan and manage its main projects, significantly improving resource allocation and decision making. For project cost estimation using special software, see Vijayakumar (2002). Project management can be streamlined through online solutions, as demonstrated by Perkins-Munn and Chen (2004). Microsoft offers several project management tools (e.g., Project and Enterprise Project Management).

**Other areas.** Many other areas of planning production and operations are improved by IT. For example, Lee and Chen (2002) developed a Web-based production planning optimization tool. Factory layout planning and design also have been greatly improved due to IT tools (Benjaafar et al., 2002).

Korolishin (2003) describes a Web-based system at Office Depot that matches employee scheduling with store traffic patterns to increase customer satisfaction and reduce costs. Parks (2004b) describes how Schurman Fine Papers (a retailer and manufacturer of greeting cards and specialty products) uses special *warehouse management software* to improve forecasting and inventory processes. Its two warehouses distribute products to over 30,000 retail stores.

**COMPUTER-INTEGRATED MANUFACTURING**

**Computer-integrated manufacturing (CIM)** is a concept or philosophy that promotes the integration of various computerized factory systems. CIM has three basic goals: (1) the *simplification* of all manufacturing technologies and techniques, (2) *automation* of as many of the manufacturing processes as possible, and (3) *integration and coordination* of all aspects of design, manufacturing, and related functions via computer hardware and software. Typical technologies to be integrated are flexible-manufacturing systems (FMSs), JIT, MRP, CAD, CAE, and group technology (GT). For details see Online File W7.4.

The major advantages of CIM are its comprehensiveness and flexibility. These are especially important in business processes that are being completely restructured or eliminated. Without CIM, it may be necessary to invest large amounts of money to change existing information systems to fit the new processes. For an example of how a furniture company uses CIM, see *kimball.com* (click on Kimball Electronics). For more on a unified framework for integrated manufacturing see Zaremba and Morel (2003).

## 7.4 Managing Marketing and Sales Systems

*MKT*

In Chapters 1 through 6 we emphasized the increasing importance of a customer-focused approach and the trend toward customization. How can IT help? First we need to understand how products reach customers, which takes place through a series of marketing entities known as *channels*.

**Channel systems** (in marketing) are all the systems involved in the process of getting a product or service to customers and dealing with all customers' needs. The complexity of channel systems can be observed in Figure 7.4 (page 272), where six major marketing systems are interrelated.

Channel systems can link and transform marketing, sales, procurement, logistics and delivery, and other activities. Added market power comes from the integration of channel systems with the corporate functional areas. The problem is that a change in any of the channels may affect the other channels. Therefore, the supporting information systems must be coordinated or even integrated.

Channel-driven advantages are (1) transaction speed (real-time response) because of the interactive nature of the process, (2) global reach, (3) reduced costs, (4) multimedia content, and (5) reliability.

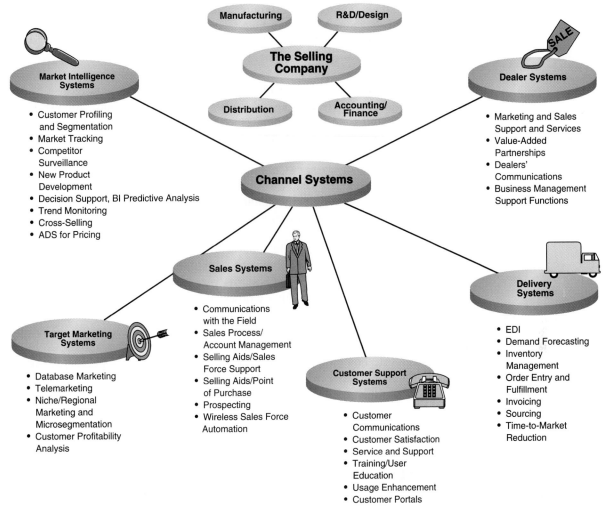

**Figure 7.4** Marketing channel systems.

We describe only a few of the many channel-system activities here, organizing them into three groups: customer relations, distribution channels and in-store innovations, and marketing management. A fourth topic, telemarketing and online shopping, is presented in Online File W7.5.

**"THE CUSTOMER IS KING/QUEEN"**

It is essential for companies today to know who their customers are and to treat them like royalty. New and innovative products and services, successful promotions, customization, and world-class customer service are becoming a necessity for many organizations. In this section we will briefly describe a few activities related to *customer-centric* organizations. More are described in Chapter 8, where customer relationship management (CRM) is presented.

**Customer Profiles and Preference Analysis.** Information about existing and potential customers is critical for success. Sophisticated information systems have been developed to collect data on customers, their demographics (age, gender, income level), and preferences. For example, shoppers' in-store activities can be monitored and then analyzed to better arrange the layouts and employees' scheduling. Analysis of shopping habits can help in organizing layouts of stores and carts (see Nishi, 2005).

**Prospective Customer Lists and Marketing Databases.** All firms need to know who their customers are, and IT can help create customer databases of both existing and potential customers. It is possible today to purchase computerized lists from several sources and then merge them electronically. These prospective-customer lists then can be analyzed and sorted by any desired classification for direct mailing, e-mailing, or telemarketing. Customer data can be stored in a corporate database or in special marketing databases (Chapter 3) for future analysis and use. For how Sears uses a marketing database, see Amato-McCoy (2002b). For example, Staples, Inc. uses software to identify its profitable customers as well as those who try to get refunds for shoplifted items or other kinds of refund fraud.

**Mass Customization.** Increasingly, today's customers want customized products. Some manufacturers offer different product configurations, and in some products dozens of options are available. The result is *mass customization,* as practiced successfully by Dell Computer and many other companies (see Appendix 2A). Customization is possible both in manufactured goods and in services.

Wind (2001) analyzed the impact of customization on marketing and the resultant changes (see Online File W 7.6). As shown throughout this book, these changes are being supported by IT. For example, the Web can be used to expedite the ordering and fulfillment of customized products, as demonstrated in *IT at Work 7.4,* about building a Jaguar.

# *IT* at Work 7.4

## *Build Your Jaguar Online*

MKT   GLOBAL

Prospective Jaguar car buyers can build, see, and price the car of their dreams online. As of October 2000, you can configure the car at *jaguar.com* in real time. Cars have been configured online since 1997, but Jaguar was the industry's first to offer comprehensive services, delivered in many languages.

Using a virtual car, users can view more than 1,250 possible exterior combinations, rotating the car through 360 degrees, by moving directional arrows. As you select the model, color, trim, wheels, and accessories, both image and price information automatically update. The design choices are limited to current models. Up to 10 personalized car selections per customer can be stored in a "virtual garage." Customers can "test" virtual cars and conduct comparisons of different models. Once the buyer makes a decision, the order is forwarded to a dealer of his or her choice.

Like most other car manufacturers, Jaguar will not let you consummate the purchase online. To negotiate price, customers can go to a Jaguar dealer or use Auto By Tel (*autobytel.com*), which connects nearby dealers to the customer. However, Jaguar's system helps get customers to the point of purchase. It helps them *research* the purchase and

explore, price, and visualize options. Customers thus familiarize themselves with the Jaguar before even visiting a showroom. The ability to see a 3-D photo of the car is an extremely important customer service. Finally, the order for the customer-configured car can be transmitted electronically to the production floor, reducing the time-to-delivery cycle.

The IT support for this innovation includes a powerful configuration database integrated with Jaguar's production system (developed by Ford Motor Company and Trilogy Corp.) and the "virtual car" (developed by Global Beach Corp.).

As of mid-2000, most car manufacturers had introduced Web-based make-to-order systems. In order to avoid channel conflicts, these systems typically involve the dealers in the actual purchase. All major car manufacturers are attempting to move some part of car ordering to the Web.

*Sources:* Compiled from *jaguar.com* press releases (October–November 2000); *ford.com* (2006) (go to Services); and *autobytel.com* (2006).

*For Further Exploration:* Why would manufacturers be interested in the Web if the actual purchase is done at the dealers' site?

Mass customization is not for everyone, and it does have several limitations (Butcher, 2006). The major limitations are that it requires a highly flexible production technology, an elaborate system for eliciting customers' wants and needs, and strong direct-to-customer logistics system. Another limitation is cost: Some people are unable or unwilling to pay even the slightly higher prices that customization often entails. Butcher (2006) provides some guidelines for how to overcome these limitations.

**Personalization.** Using cameras, retailers can find what people are doing while they visit physical stores. Similarly, tracking software can find what people are doing in a virtual store. This technology provides information for real-time marketing and is also used in m-commerce (see Chapter 6). Personalized product offers then are made, based on where the customer spent the most time and on what he or she purchased. A similar approach is used in Web-based *cross-selling* (or *up-selling*) efforts, in which advertising of related products is provided. For example, if you are buying a car, car insurance is automatically offered (see Johnson, 2006).

**Advertising and Promotions.** The Internet opens the door to a new advertising medium. As was shown in Chapter 5, online advertising, mainly via e-mail and targeted banners, is growing rapidly. Innovative methods such as viral marketing (Reda, 2002) are possible only on the Internet. Wireless and pervasive computing applications also are changing the face of advertising (Chapter 6). For example, in order to measure attention to advertising, a mobile-computing device from Arbitron (see Portable People Meter at *arbitron.com*) is carried by customers. Whoever is wearing the device automatically logs advertising seen or heard any time, anywhere in their daily movements.

**DISTRIBUTION CHANNELS AND IN-STORE INNOVATIONS**

Organizations can distribute their products and services through several delivery channels. For instance, a company may use its own outlets or distributors. Digitizable products can be distributed online, or can be delivered on CD-ROMs. Other products can be delivered by trucks or trains, with the movement of goods monitored by IT applications. The Web is revolutionizing distribution channels. Here we look at some representative topics relating to distribution channels.

**Improving Shopping and Checkout at Retail Stores.** The modern shopper is often pressed for time, and most are unhappy about waiting in long lines. Using information technology, it is possible to reengineer the shopping and the checkout process, as illustrated in Chapter 6. Additional examples are:

- An information kiosk enables customers to view catalogs in stores, conduct product searches, and even compare prices with those of competitors. Kiosks at some stores (e.g., 7-Eleven stores in some countries) can be used to place orders on the Internet. (For details about use of in-store kiosks, see Online File W7.7.) In Macy's you can check the current price on computerized screens with barcode readers.

- Some stores that have many customers who pay by check (e.g., large grocery stores, Costco, Wal-Mart stores) have installed check-writers. All you have to do is submit the blank check to the cashier, who runs it through a machine attached to the cash register. The machine prints the name of the store as the payee and the amount, you sign the check, and in seconds the check is validated, your bank account is debited, and you are out of the store with your merchandise.

U-Scan kiosk.

- The Exxon Mobil Speedpass allows customers to fill their tanks by waving a token, embedded with an RFID device, at a gas-pump sensor. Then the RFID starts an authorization process, and the purchase is charged to your credit card. Customers no longer need to carry their Mobil credit cards (See *mobil.com/speedpass.*)
- An increasing number of retailers are installing self-checkout machines. For example, Home Depot in 2003 added self-checkouts in their stores. Not only does the retailer save the cost of employees' salaries, but customers are happier for saving time. (And some enjoy "playing cashier" briefly.) A major vendor is U-Scan, which is used in many supermarkets (see photo). Soon, RFIDs will improve the process even further.

## MARKETING MANAGEMENT

Many marketing management decision applications are supported by computerized information systems. (Online File W7.8 shows the marketing management decision framework.) Here are some representative examples of how marketing management is being done.

**Pricing of Products or Services.** Sales volumes are largely determined by the prices of products or services. Price is also a major determinant of profit. Pricing is a difficult decision, and prices may need to be changed frequently. For example, in response to price changes made by competitors, a company may need to adjust its prices or take other actions. Checking competitors' prices is commonly done by retailers. But instead of carrying paper and pen, one can use wireless price checkers (e.g., PriceMaster Plus, from SoftwarePlus). These devices make data collection easy.

Pricing decisions are supported by a number of computerized systems. Many companies are using business analytical processing to support pricing and other marketing decisions (see Chapters 11 and 12). In Chapter 2 we discussed the optimization models used to support prices at Longs Drug Stores and others (see Online File W2.1). Web-based comparison engines enable customers to select a vendor at the price they want, and they also enable vendors to see how their prices compare with others. For an example of price optimization, see Rapt (2006) and Chapter 12. For more on price optimization, see Parks (2004a).

**Salesperson Productivity.** Salespeople differ from each other; some excel in selling certain products, while others excel in selling to a certain type of customer or in a certain geographical zone. This information, which is usually collected in the sales and marketing TPS, can be analyzed, using a comparative performance system in which sales data by salesperson, product, region, and even the time of day are evaluated. Actual current sales can be compared to historical data and to standards. Multidimensional spreadsheet software facilitates this type of analysis. Assignment of salespeople to regions and/or products and the calculation of bonuses can also be supported by this system.

In addition, sales productivity can be boosted by Web-based systems. For example, in a Web-based call center, when a customer calls a sales rep, the rep can look at the customer's history of purchases, demographics, services available where the customer lives, and more. This information enables reps to work faster, while providing better customer service (see Minicase 2).

***Productivity Software.*** **Sales automation software** is especially helpful to small businesses, enabling them to rapidly increase sales and growth. Such Web-based software (e.g., from *salesforce.com*) can manage the flow of messages and assist in writing contracts, scheduling, and making appointments. Of course it also provides word processing and e-mail, and it helps with mailings and follow-up letters. Electronic stamps (e.g., *stamps.com*) can assist with mass mailings.

**Profitability Analysis.** In deciding on advertising and other marketing efforts, managers often need to know the profit contribution of certain products and services. Profitability information for products and services can be derived from the cost-accounting system. For example, profit performance analysis software available from IBM, Oracle, SAS, and Microstrategy, Inc. is designed to help managers assess and improve the profit performance of their line of business, products, distribution channels, sales regions, and other dimensions critical to managing the enterprise. Northwest Airlines, for example, uses expert systems to set prices based on profitability. They also use a similar system to audit tickets and for calculating commissions to travel agents.

**New Products, Services, and Market Planning.** The introduction of new or improved products and services can be expensive and risky. An important question to ask about a new product or service is, "Will it sell?" An appropriate answer calls for careful analysis, planning, and forecasting. These can best be executed with the aid of IT because of the large number of determining factors and the uncertainties that may be involved (e.g., using predictive analysis, Chapter 11). Market research also can be conducted on the Internet. A related issue is the speed with which products are brought to market. An example of how Procter & Gamble expedites the time-to-market by using the Internet is provided in *IT at Work 7.5*.

# IT at Work 7.5

## Internet Market Research Expedites Time-to-Market at Procter & Gamble

MKT

For decades, Procter & Gamble (P&G) and Colgate-Palmolive have been competitors in the market for personal care products. Developing a major new product, from concept to market launch, used to take over 5 years. First, a concept test was done; the companies sent product photos and descriptions to potential customers, asking whether they might buy it. If the feedback was negative, they tried to improve the product concept and then repeated the concept testing. Once positive response was achieved, sample products were mailed out, and customers were asked to fill out detailed questionnaires. When customers' responses met the companies' internal hurdles, the company would start with mass advertising on television and in magazines.

However, thanks to the Internet, it took P&G only three-and-a-half years to get Whitestrips, the teeth-brightening product, onto the market and to a sales level of $200 million a year—considerably quicker than other oral care products. In September 2000, P&G threw out the old marketing test model and instead introduced Whitestrips on the Internet, offering the product for sale on P&G's Web site. The company spent several months studying who was coming to the site and buying the product; it collected responses to online questionnaires, which was much faster than the old mail-outs.

The online research, which was facilitated by data mining conducted on P&G's huge historical data (stored in a data warehouse) and the new Internet data, revealed the most enthusiastic groups. These included teenage girls, brides-to-be, and young Hispanic Americans. Immediately, the company started to target these segments with appropriate advertising. The Internet created a product awareness of 35 percent, even before any shipments were made to stores. This "buzz" created a huge demand for the product by the time it hit the shelves.

From this experience, P&G learned important lessons about flexible and creative ways to approach product innovation and marketing. The whole process of studying the product concept, segmenting the market, and expediting product development has been revolutionized.

*Sources:* Compiled from Buckley (2002), and from *pg.com* (accessed July 2006).

*For Further Exploration:* How did the Internet decrease time-to-market in this situation? What is the role of data mining? Why is so much testing needed?

**Web-Based Systems in Marketing.** The use of Web-based systems in support of marketing and sales has grown rapidly, as demonstrated by the P&G case. A summary of some Web-based impacts is provided in Online File W7.8.

**Other Applications.** Many other applications exist. For example, Howarth (2004) describes the use of IT to reduce theft in stores.

Marketing activities conclude the *primary* activities of the value chain. Next we look at the functional systems that are *secondary* (support) activities in the value chain: accounting/finance and human resources management.

# 7.5 Managing the Accounting and Finance Systems

*ACC*

*FIN*

A primary mission of the accounting/finance functional area is to manage money flows into, within, and out of organizations. This is a very broad mission since money is involved in all functions of an organization. Some repetitive accounting/financing activities such as payroll, billing, and cash management were computerized as early as the 1950s. Today, accounting/finance information systems are very diverse and comprehensive. Note that while in universities accounting and finance are separate departments, in the real world they are frequently united in one department.

The general structure of an accounting/finance system is presented in Online File W7.9. It is divided into three levels: strategic, tactical, and operational. Information technology can support almost all the activities listed, as well as the communication and collaboration of accounting/finance with internal and external environments. We describe selected activities in the rest of this section.

**FINANCIAL PLANNING AND BUDGETING**

Appropriate management of financial assets is a major task in financial planning and budgeting. Managers must plan for both the acquisition of financial resources and their use. Financial planning, like any other functional planning, is tied to the overall organizational planning and to other functional areas. It is divided into short-, medium-, and long-term horizons, much like activities planning. Financial analysts use Web resources and computerized analytics (Chapters 11 and 12) to accomplish the organization's financial planning and budgeting activities.

**Financial and Economic Forecasting and Budgeting.** Knowledge about the availability and cost of money is a key ingredient for successful financial planning. Especially important is the projection of cash flow, which tells organizations what funds they need and when, and how they will acquire them. This function is important for all firms, but is especially so for small companies, which tend to have little financial cushion. Inaccurate cash flow projection is the number-one reason why many small businesses go bankrupt. Availability and cost of money depend on corporate financial health and the willingness of lenders and investors to infuse money into the company.

Financial and economic analysis can be facilitated by intelligent systems such as neural computing (Chapter 12). Many software packages are available for conducting economic and financial forecasting, which are frequently available for a fee, over the Internet.

**Budgeting.** The best-known part of financial planning is the annual budget, which allocates the financial resources of an organization among participants and activities. The budget is the financial expression of the organization's plans. It allows management to allocate resources in the way that best supports the organization's mission and goals. IT enables the introduction of financial logic and efficiency into the budgeting process.

*Software Support.* Several software packages, many of which are Web-based, are available to support budget preparation and control (e.g., Budget 2000 from PROPHIX Software, and budgeting modules from Oracle and Capterra.com) and to facilitate communication among all participants in the budget preparation.

*Example:* Software support for budgeting is available from PROPHIX. The key benefits of the package are: a familiar Windows Explorer interface, customizable flexibility that supports a variety of budgeting templates, a controlled database that secures data and allows for multiple user accessibility, and various data manipulation tools for complicated budgeting.

PROPHIX's New Model Wizard creates a new budgeting model in seconds. Using the Account Manager, the Dimension Manager, and the Import Data modules, individual companies' distinctive account and organization structures are populated with data at the beginning of the budgeting process. PROPHIX has multicurrency budgeting capabilities ensuring precision to budgets by adjusting exchange rates based on business exposure and risk. More accurate reporting is achieved through the conversion and consolidation of multiple currencies into the company's home currency (*Prophix.com,* 2006).

Since budget preparation may involve both top-down and bottom-up processes, modeling capabilities in some packages allow the budget coordinator to take the top-down numbers, compare them with the bottom-up data from the users, and reconcile the two.

The major benefits of using budgeting software are that it can: reduce the time and effort involved in the budget process, explore and analyze the implications of organizational and environmental changes, facilitate the integration of the corporate strategic objectives with operational plans, make planning an ongoing, continuous process, and automatically monitor exceptions for patterns and trends.

**Capital Budgeting.** *Capital budgeting* is the financing of asset acquisitions, including the disposal of major organizational assets. It usually includes a comparison of options, such as keep the asset, replace it with an identical new asset, replace it with a different one, or discard it. The capital budgeting process also evaluates buy-versus-lease options.

Capital budgeting analysis uses standard financial models, such as net present value (NPV), internal rate of return (IRR), and payback period (all presented in Chapter 14), to evaluate alternative investment decisions. Most spreadsheet packages include built-in functions of these models.

**MANAGING FINANCIAL TRANSACTIONS**

An accounting/finance information system is also responsible for gathering the raw data necessary for the accounting/finance TPS, transforming the data into information, and making the information available to users, whether aggregate information about payroll, the organization's internal reports, or external reports to stockholders or government agencies.

Many packages exist to execute routine accounting transaction processing activities. Several are available free on the Internet (try *tucows.com*). Many software packages are integrated. In these integrated systems, the accounting/finance activities are combined with other TPSs such as those of marketing and production and operations management. The data collected and managed for the accounting/finance transaction processing system are also inputs for the various functional information systems.

One such integrated system is MAS 90 ERP, MAS 200 ERP, and Sage MAS 500 ERP (from *bestsoftware.com*). It is a collection of standard accounting modules, as

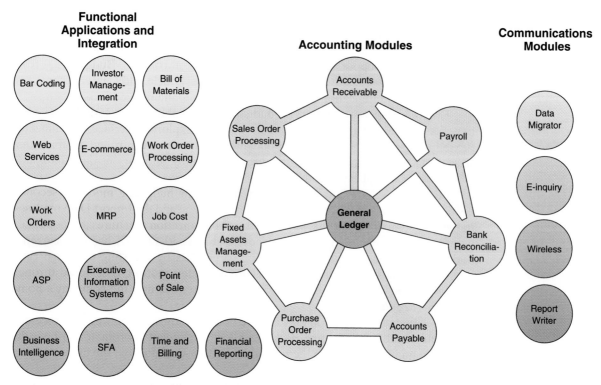

**Figure 7.5** Integrated accounting/business software.

shown in Figure 7.5 (the "wheel" in the diagram). Communication and inquiry modules (right side) support the accounting modules. The user can integrate as many of the modules as needed for the business. On the left side is a list of other business processes and functional applications that can interface with accounting applications. Note that the software includes an e-commerce module, which provides dynamic Web access to MAS 90. This module includes account and order inquiry capabilities as well as a shopping cart for order entry. The 2006 version of MAS 90 includes modules for business intelligence, e-commerce, CRM, sales force automation (SFA), and financial reporting.

Another integrated accounting software package is *peachtree.com,* which offers a sales ledger, purchase ledger, cash book, sales order processing, invoicing, stock control, job casting, fixed-assets register, and more. Other accounting packages can be found at *2020software.com* and *findaccountingsoftware.com.*

The accounting/finance TPS also provides a complete, reliable audit trail of all transactions transmitted through the network. This feature is vital to accountants and auditors. (For more, see the "Control and Auditing" section below.)

**XBRL: Extensible Business Reporting Language. XBRL** is a programming language and an international standard for electronic transmission of business and financial information. As of September 2005, it can be used to file financial reports electronically with the SEC and FDIC. With XBRL all the company's financial data are collected, consolidated, published, and consumed without the need to use Excel spreadsheets. Figure 7.6 illustrates how XBRL works. Such submission allows government analysts to validate information submitted in hours instead of two to three weeks.

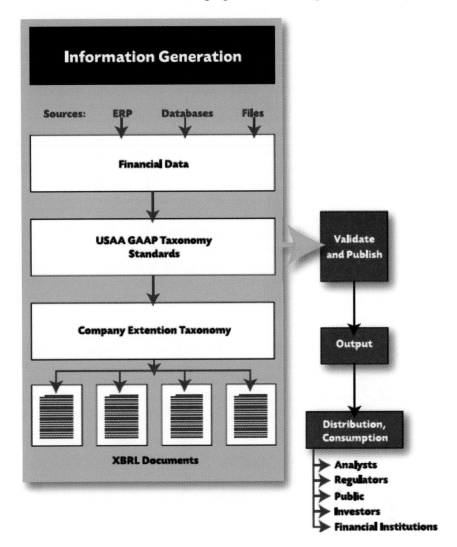

**Figure 7.6** How XBRL works.

The U.S. government agencies plan to mandate the use of XBRL. According to Malykhina (2006), the Federal Financial Institutions Examination Council found that XBRL helps banks:

- Generate cleaner data, including written explanations and supporting notes.
- Produce more accurate data with fewer errors that require follow-up by regulators.
- Transmit data faster to regulators and meet deadlines.
- Increase the number of cases and amount of information that staffers can handle.
- Make information available faster to regulators and the public.
- Address issues and concerns in their filings rather than after the fact.

For additional applications in financial transactions, see Online File W7.10.

**INVESTMENT MANAGEMENT**

Effective investment management is a difficult task, both for individuals and for corporations. For one thing, there are thousands of investment alternatives. On the New York Stock Exchange alone, there are more than 2,000 stocks, and millions of possible combinations for creating portfolios. Investment decisions are based on economic and financial forecasts and on various multiple and conflicting objectives (such as high yield, safety, and liquidity). The investment environment also includes opportunities in other countries. Another factor that contributes to the complexity of investment management is that investments made by many organizations are subject to complex regulations and tax laws. Finally, investment decisions need to be made quickly and frequently. Decision makers can be in different locations, and they need to cooperate and collaborate. Therefore, computerization is especially popular in financial institutions that are involved in investments. Many other banks and financial institutions have similar systems, especially for portfolio management. An example is Opti-Money, which is successfully used in Israel (see Avriel et al., 2004). Companies today conduct shareholders' votes online and send reports to shareholders. Brokers attempt to replace all paper reports with electronic ones.

In addition, data-mining tools and neural networks (Chapter 12) are used by many institutional investment managers to analyze historical databases, so they can make better predictions. For a data-mining tool, see *wizsoft.com*. Some typical financial applications of neural computing are provided in Online File W7.11.

The following are the major areas of support that IT can provide to investment management.

**Access to Financial and Economic Reports.** Investment decisions require managers to evaluate financial and economic reports and news provided by federal and state agencies, universities, research institutions, financial services, and corporations. There are hundreds of Web sources, many of which are free; a sampling is listed in Online File W7.12. Most of these services are useful both for professional investment managers and for individual investors.

**Financial Analysis.** Financial analysis can be executed with a spreadsheet program, or with commercially available ready-made decision support software (e.g., see *tradeportal.com/matrixsuite.asp*). Or it can be more sophisticated, involving intelligent systems. Other information technologies can be used as well. For example, Morgan Stanley and Company uses virtual reality on its intranet to display the results of risk analysis in three dimensions. Seeing data in 3-D makes it easier to make comparisons and intuitive connections than would seeing a two-dimensional chart or spreadsheet data.

One area of analysis that is becoming popular is referred to as **financial value chain management (FVCM).** According to this approach, financial analysis is combined with operations analysis. All financial functions are analyzed (including international trades). Combining financial and operations analysis provides better financial control. For example, if the organization runs its operations at a lower-than-planned level, it is likely to need less money; if it exceeds the operational plan, it may well be all right to exceed the budgeted amounts for that plan. For details see *Aberdeen.com* (2002).

**CONTROL AND AUDITING**

A major reason organizations go out of business is their inability to forecast and/or secure sufficient *cash flow*. Underestimated expenses, overspending, financial mismanagement, and fraud can lead to disaster. Good planning is necessary, but not sufficient, and must be supplemented by skillful control. Control activities in organizations take many forms, including control and auditing of the information systems themselves (see Chapter 16). Information systems play an extremely important role in supporting organizational control, as we show throughout the text. Specific forms of financial control are presented next.

**Risk Analysis.** Companies need to analyze the risk of doing business with partners or in other countries. Giving credit to customers can be risky, so one can use products such as FICO (from *fairisaac.com*) for calculating risk. Also see @RISK for Excel from *palisade.com.*

**Budgetary Control.** Once the annual budget has been decided upon, it is divided into monthly allocations. Managers at various levels then monitor departmental expenditures and compare them against the budget and operational progress of the corporate plans. Simple reporting systems summarize the expenditures and provide *exception reports* by flagging any expenditure that exceeds the budget by a certain percent or that falls significantly below the budget. More sophisticated software attempts to tie expenditures to program accomplishment. Numerous software programs can be used to support budgetary control; most of them are combined with budget preparation packages from vendors such as *outlooksoft.com, clarifysystems. com,* and *capterra.com.*

**Auditing.** The major purpose of auditing is to ensure the accuracy and condition of the financial health of an organization. Internal auditing is done by the organization's accounting/finance personnel, who also prepare for external auditing by CPA companies.

IT can facilitate auditing. For example, intelligent systems can uncover fraud by finding financial transactions that significantly deviate from previous payment profiles. Also, IT provides real-time data whenever needed (see *oracle.com*).

**Financial Ratio Analysis.** A major task of the accounting/finance department is to watch the financial health of the company by monitoring and assessing a set of financial ratios. These ratios are mostly the same as those used by external parties when they are deciding whether to invest in an organization, loan money to it, or buy it. But internal parties have access to much more detailed data for use in calculating financial ratios.

The collection of data for ratio analysis is done by the transaction processing system, and computation of the ratios is done by financial analysis models. The *interpretation* of the ratios, and especially the prediction of their future behavior, requires expertise and is sometimes supported by expert systems.

**Profitability Analysis and Cost Control.** Many companies are concerned with the profitability of individual products or services as well as with the financial health of the entire organization. Profitability analysis DSS software (see Chapter 12) allows accurate computation of profitability. It also allows allocation of overheads. One way to control cost is by properly estimating it. This is done by special software; see Vijayakumar (2002).

Profitability Management from Hyperion provides potent multidimensional and predictive analysis, and proven query, reporting, and dashboard functionality with ease-of-use and deployment. See Chapter 11, Figure 11.2 for illustrations of Hyperion's dashboards. The solution delivers powerful, insightful activity-based cost analysis and what-if modeling capabilities to help create and test new business strategies. Sophisticated business rules are stored in one place, enabling

# A Closer Look 7.1

## Expense and Spend Management Automation

Companies are interested in controlling all types of expenses, not just for travel. For these purposes there are several specialized IT programs. Most notable are those from Ariba.com. Ariba Spend Management software provides tools to analyze spending, buy products and services from suppliers via the Web, host online auctions (to reduce purchasing prices), and manage the bid process for prospective suppliers. Ariba even provides software tools to save money on SOX compliance as well as allocating resources for online sourcing.

Another company that provides tools for **spend management** and analysis is Ketera Technologies (*ketera.com*). They

also provide procurement and sourcing services (e.g., automating interactions with suppliers). Finally, they provide a repository for contracts and manage approval workflow.

Frictionless Commerce (*frictionless.com*) provides software to analyze spending transactions to see whether purchases are being made with suppliers that have negotiated contracts (SRM Explorer). Online auctions and RFP are managed by Enterprise Sourcing.

About a dozen other companies provide tools for expense and spend management. Some relate it to compliance software.

---

analyses and strategies to be shared easily across an entire enterprise (*Hyperion. com*, 2006).

**Expense Management Automation.** **Expense management automation (EMA)** refers to systems that automate data entry and processing of travel and entertainment expenses. These expenses can account for 20 percent of the operating expenses of large corporations (Degnan, 2003). EMA systems (by companies such as Captura, Concur, Extensity, and Necho) are Web-based applications that replace the paper forms and rudimentary spreadsheet. These systems let companies quickly and consistently collect expense information, enforce company policies and contracts, and reduce unplanned purchases of airline and hotel services. The software forces travelers to be organized before a trip starts. In addition to benefits to the companies, employees also benefit from quick reimbursement (since expense approvals are not held up by sloppy or incomplete documentation). (For details, see "What EMA systems now offer...," 2002.)

For more on expense and spend management automation, see *A Closer Look 7.1.*

Several more applications in the financial/accounting area are described in Online File W7.13. Many more can be found at Reed et al. (2001).

## 7.6 Managing Human Resources Systems

HRM

Developments in Web-based systems increased the popularity of human resources information systems (HRISs) as of the late 1990s. Initial HRIS applications were mainly related to transaction processing systems. (For examples, see Thomas and Ray, 2000; and Bussler and Davis, 2001–2002.) In recent years, as systems generally have been moved to intranets and the Web, so have HRIS applications, many of which can be delivered via an HR portal. Many organizations use their Web portals to advertise job openings and conduct online hiring and training. Gomez-Mejia et al. (2007) describe the impact of the Internet on acquiring, rewarding, developing, protecting, and retaining human resources. Their findings are summarized in Online File W7.14. Perhaps the biggest benefit to companies of human relations IT services is the release of HR staff from intermediary roles (e.g., by self-services, such as self-entry of an address change), so they can focus on strategic planning and human resources organization and development. In the following sections we describe in more detail how IT facilitates the management of human resources (HRM).

**RECRUITMENT**

*Recruitment* is finding employees, testing them, and deciding which ones to hire. Some companies are flooded with viable applicants, while others have difficulty finding the right people. Information systems can be helpful in both cases. Here we present some examples.

**Using the Web for Recruitment.** With millions of resumes available online, it is not surprising that companies are trying to find appropriate candidates on the Web, usually with the help of specialized search engines. Also, hundreds of thousands of jobs are advertised on the Web (see Field, 2006). Many matching services exist (see Internet Exercise 3). Online recruiting is able to "cast a wide net" to reach more candidates faster (Field, 2006), which may bring in better applicants. In addition, the costs of online recruitment are lower. Other benefits of online recruitment for employers, plus some disadvantages, are shown in Online File W7.15.

Recruitment online is beneficial for candidates as well. They are exposed to a larger number of job offerings, can get details of the positions quickly, and can begin to evaluate the prospective employer. To check the competitiveness of salary offerings, or to see how much one can make elsewhere in several countries, job candidates can go to *monster.com*.

As more companies expand operations overseas, global recruiting is becoming a vexing problem. Companies simply have problems finding qualified people, especially engineers and salespeople. Using the Internet to recruit from other countries is becoming popular, yet it requires expertise (see Shah, 2006).

*Example:* Field (2006) provides an example of recruiting by Finish Line Corp. In a 12-month period, more than 330,000 candidates applied for employment with the company; more than 75 percent of them applied online. Using screening software (by Unicru), 112,154 candidates were eliminated immediately. More than 60,000 hours of store managers' time were saved because of the reduction in the number of interviews conducted.

For a complete analysis of and guidelines for e-recruitment, see Field (2006).

**HRM Portals and Salary Surveys.** One advantage of the Web is the large amount of information related to job matching. There are also many private and public HR-related portals. The portal is a search engine, an index of jobs, posted on corporate-member sites. For example, several large companies (e.g., IBM, Xerox, GE) created jointly with 120 companies a career portal called DirectEmployer.com. Commercial, public online recruiters, such as Monster.com, help corporate recruiters find candidates for difficult-to-fill positions. For details see *JobCentral.com*.

Another area for HR portals is salary surveys. Salary surveys help companies determine how much to pay their employees. Companies used to pay consultants up to $10,000 for a one-time survey (Bussler and Davis, 2001–2002). Now they can conduct such surveys themselves by utilizing free data from vendors such as Salary.com (check "What you are worth"). Salary Wizard Pro covers pay scales in small businesses.

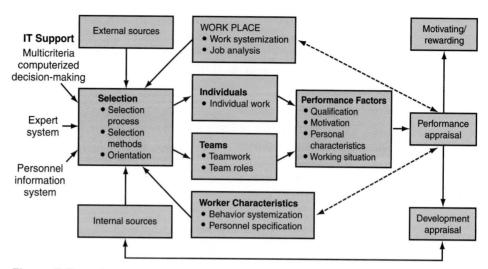

**Figure 7.7** Intelligent personnel selection model. (*Source:* Jareb and Rajkoric, 2001.)

**Employee Selection.** The human resources department is responsible for screening job applicants, evaluating, testing, and selecting them in compliance with state and federal regulations. The process of employee selection can be very complex since it may involve many external and internal candidates and multiple criteria. To expedite the testing and evaluation process and ensure consistency in selection, companies use information technologies such as Web-based expert systems. Figure 7.7 shows the multiple criteria involved in employee selection and illustrates the role of an expert system in this process and in related tasks such as performance appraisal.

**HUMAN RESOURCES MAINTENANCE AND DEVELOPMENT**

Once recruited, employees become part of the corporate human resources pool, which needs to be maintained and developed. Some activities supported by IT are the following.

**Performance Evaluation.** Most employees are periodically evaluated by their immediate supervisors. Peers or subordinates may also evaluate others. Evaluations are usually recorded on paper or electronic forms. Using such information manually is a tedious and error-prone job. Once digitized, evaluations can be used to support many decisions, ranging from rewards to transfers to layoffs. For example, Cisco Systems is known for developing an IT-based human capital strategy (Chatman et al., 2005). Many universities evaluate professors online. The evaluation form appears on the screen, and the students fill it in. Results can be tabulated in minutes. Corporate managers can analyze employees' performances with the help of expert systems, which provide systematic interpretation of performance over time.

Wage review is related to performance evaluation. For example, Hewlett-Packard's Atlanta-based U.S. Field Services Operations (USFO) Group has developed a paperless wage review (PWR) system. The Web-based system uses intelligent agents to deal with quarterly reviews of HP's 15,000 employees. (A similar system is used by most other groups, covering a total of 150,000 employees.) The agent software lets USFO managers and personnel access employee data from both the personnel and functional databases. The PWR system tracks employee review dates and automatically initiates the wage review process. It sends wage review forms to first-level managers by e-mail every quarter.

**Training and Human Resources Development.** Employee training and retraining is an important activity of the human resources department. Major issues are planning of classes and tailoring specific training programs to meet the needs of the organization and employees. Sophisticated human resources departments build a career development plan for each employee. IT can support the planning, monitoring, and control of these activities by using workflow applications.

IT also plays an important role in training (see discussion on e-learning in Chapter 17, and Harris, 2005). Some of the most innovative developments are in the areas of *intelligent computer-aided instruction* (ICAI) and application of multimedia support for instructional activities. Instruction is provided online at 38 percent of all Fortune 1,000 corporations, according to OmniTech Consulting ("Web Breathes Life," 1988). Training salespeople is an expensive and lengthy proposition. To save money on training costs, companies are providing sales-skills training over the Internet or intranet. Online File W7.16 provides examples of the variety of employee training available on the Internet and intranets. Interesting implementations of computer-based training at Shoney's are reported by McKinley (2003) and at Sheetz convenience stores by Korolishin (2004b).

Training can be improved using Web-based video clips. For example, using a digital video-editing system, Dairy Queen's in-house video production department produced a higher-quality training video at 50 percent lower cost than by outsourcing it. The affordability of the videos encourages more Dairy Queen franchisees to participate in the training program. This improves customer service as well as employee skill. For tools for online training, see *Softsim.com* and Camtasia from *Techsmith.com*.

Mobile devices are increasingly being used for training as well as for performance improvement (Gayeski, 2004). Finally, training can be enhanced by virtual reality. Intel, Motorola, Samsung Electronic, and IBM are using virtual reality (Chapter 11) to simulate different scenarios and configurations. The training is especially effective in complex environments where mistakes can be very costly (see Boisvert, 2000).

**HUMAN RESOURCES PLANNING AND MANAGEMENT**

Managing human resources in large organizations requires extensive planning and detailed strategy (Gomez-Mejia, 2007). In some industries, labor negotiation is a particularly important aspect of human resources planning and it may be facilitated by IT. For most companies, administering employee benefits is also a significant part of the human resources function. Here are some examples of how IT can help.

**Personnel Planning and HR strategies.** The human resources department forecasts requirements for people and skills. In some geographical areas and for overseas assignments it may be difficult to find particular types of employees. In such cases the HR department plans how to find (or develop from within) sufficient human resources. Also, compliance with regulations regarding safety and privacy is facilitated by IT (Section 7.8).

Large companies develop qualitative and quantitative workforce planning models. Such models can be enhanced if IT is used to collect, update, and process the information. Radio Shack uses special software to develop HR strategies (see Reda, 2004, for details).

**Benefits Administration.** Employees' contributions to their organizations are rewarded by salary/wage, bonuses, and other benefits. Benefits include those for health and dental care as well as contributions for pensions. Managing the benefits system can be a complex task, due to its many components and the tendency of organizations to allow employees to choose and trade off benefits ("cafeteria style"). In large companies, using computers for self-benefits selection can save a tremendous amount of labor and time for HR staff (see *iemployee.com*).

Providing flexibility in selecting benefits is viewed as a competitive advantage in large organizations. It can be successfully implemented when supported by computers. Some companies have automated benefits enrollments. Employees can self-register for specific benefits using the corporate portal or voice technology. Employees self-select desired benefits from a menu. Payroll pay cards are now in use in numerous companies, such as Payless Shoes, which has 30,000 employees in 5,000 stores (see Korolishin, 2004a). The system specifies the value of each benefit and the available benefits balance of each employee. Some companies use intelligent agents to assist the employees and monitor their actions. Expert systems can answer employees' questions and offer advice online. Simpler systems allow for self-updating of personal information such as changes in address, family status, and so on. Self-entry saves money for the company and is usually more accurate.

For a comprehensive resource of HRM on the Web, see *shrm.org/hrlinks*.

**Employee Relationship Management.** In their effort to better manage employees, companies are developing *human capital management* (HCM), facilitated by the Web, to streamline the HR process. These Web applications are more commonly referred to as **employee relationship management (ERM).** For example, self-services such as tracking personal information and online training are very popular in ERM. Improved relationships with employees results in better retention and higher productivity. ERM technologies and applications are very similar to those of customer relationship management (CRM), which we discuss in Chapter 8. For an example in the U.S. Navy, see Online File W7.17.

# 7.7 Integrating Functional Information Systems

Functional information systems can be built in-house, they can be purchased from large vendors (such as Computer Associates, Best Software Inc., Microsoft, Oracle, or IBM), or they can be leased from application service providers (ASPs). In any of these cases, there is a need for their integration with other information systems, including databases.

**REASONS FOR INTEGRATION**

For many years most IT applications were developed in the functional areas, independent of each other. Many companies developed their own customized systems that dealt with standard procedures to execute transaction processing/operational activities. These procedures are fairly similar, regardless of what company is performing them. Therefore, the trend today is to buy commercial, off-the-shelf functional applications or to lease them from ASPs. The smaller the organization, the more attractive such options are. Indeed, several hundred commercial products are available to support each of the major functional areas.

Development tools are also available to build custom-made applications in a specific functional area. For example, there are software packages for building financial applications, a hospital pharmacy management system, and a university student registration system. Some software vendors specialize in one or a few areas. For example, Lawson Software concentrates on retailing (see Minicase 1), and Oracle's strength is in HRM.

However, to build information systems along business processes (which cross functional lines) requires a different approach. Matching business processes with a combination of several functional off-the-shelf packages may be a solution in some areas. For example, it may be possible to integrate manu-facturing, sales, and accounting software if they all come from the same software vendor (as shown in the opening case). However, combining existing packages from several vendors may not be practical or effective. To build applications that will easily cross functional lines and reach separate databases often requires new approaches such as Web Services and integrated suites, such as Oracle 9i (McCullough, 2002).

Information systems integration tears down barriers between and among departments and corporate headquarters and reduces duplication of effort. For example, Palaniswamy and Frank (2000) studied five ERP systems and found in all cases that better cross-functional integration was a critical success factor.

One of the key factors for integration, especially with business partners, is agree-ment on appropriate standards (see *openapplications.org*). Integration can be done by middleware (Technology Guide 2) and by Web Services (Technology Guide 6).

Integrated information systems can be built easily in a small company. In large organizations, and even in multinational corporations, integration may require more effort, as shown in *IT at Work 7.6* (page 288).

Another approach to integration of information systems is to use ERP software (Chapter 8). However, ERP requires a company to fit its business processes to the software. As an alternative to ERP, companies can choose the *best-of-breed systems* on the market, or use some of their own home-grown systems and integrate them. The latter approach may not be simple, but it may be more effective.

By whatever method it is accomplished, integrating information systems helps to reduce cost, increase employees' productivity, and facilitate information sharing and collaboration, which are necessary for improving customer service.

## INTEGRATION OF FRONT-OFFICE WITH BACK-OFFICE OPERATIONS

In Chapters 2 and 5 we discussed the need to integrate front-office with back-office operations. This is a difficult task. It is easier to integrate the front-office operations among themselves and the back-office operations among themselves (which is basi-cally what systems such as MAS 90 are doing).

Software from various vendors offers some front-office and back-office integra-tion solutions. Oracle Corp., for example, is continuously expanding its front-office software, which offers a capability of connecting back-office operations with it. To do so, the software uses new integration approaches, such as process-centric inte-gration. **Process-centric integration** refers to integration solutions designed, developed, and managed from a business-process perspective, instead of from a technical or middleware perspective. The Oracle 9i product, for example, offers not only internal integration of the back office and front office, but also integra-tion with business partners (see McCullough, 2002). Among its capabilities are:

- **Online field sales:** a Web-based customer management application.

# IT at Work 7.6

## Software Helps Cirque du Soleil

Cirque du Soleil is a Canada-based traveling circus. Using IT, the circus is able to entertain more people each year than the Red Sox and Yankees combined (over seven million in 2005, in four continents). How do they do it? First, this is no ordinary circus. It features astonishing acrobatics and Broadway-caliber music and dance in 11 different shows (in addition to traditional circus and opera). All this is done by 20,000 performers and 3,500 management employees who are constantly on the move using 250 tractor-trailers. Twenty thousand performers are scheduled and transported with all the stage equipment and costumes that are constantly changing. The company grew very rapidly between 2000 and 2005, and several problems were created as a result of the rapid growth.

The logistics of people, transportation, accommodations, food, supplies, and so on, in hundreds of different cities each year, for several traveling groups is fairly difficult. And there are 200 different applications in all functional areas, from finance to POM, accounting, marketing, and human resources management. These applications were unable to share data, threatening the productivity of people and causing delays, problems, and unnecessary expenses. For example, if an employee gets sick, how quickly can a replacement be found? What is done if equipment is lost, or a tractor-trailer is delayed?

The problem was compounded by the rapid growth of the business and the frequent changes in programs and plans.

Because of the unique nature of the business, most of the applications were done in-house. For example, special software was needed to make or buy costumes and to assign artists to the "make" job. In addition, the company installed ERP, for human resources management, production scheduling, logistics, and finance. Even the medical records of the performers were tracked. To enable the various applications communicating with each other, the company implemented IBM WebSphere Business Integration software to connect all of its disparate systems and applications. The integrated system replaced the manual work of the production managers, who do an inventory whenever a group arrives at a destination. If something was missing, several people were engaged in finding a replacement. Now due to data sharing, there are very few cases of missing items. Furthermore, IBM WebSphere helped cut the development time for new applications, as well as the modification time of existing applications, by about 25 percent. Also, time to connect new business software to the intranet has been reduced by 20 percent. All this helped increase productivity. In 2001, there were 65 tickets sold per employee, but by 2005 the total was about 200.

*Sources:* Compiled from Barrett (2005b) and from IBM (2005).

*For Further Exploration:* Why was it necessary to integrate the functional applications? Could the company grow so rapidly otherwise?

- **Service contracts:** contract management and service options.
- **Mobile sales and marketing:** wireless groupware for connecting different management groups.
- **Call center and telephony suite:** a Web-based call center.
- **Internet commerce:** an order-taking and payment unit interconnected with ERP back-office applications. It is also tightly connected to the call center for order taking.
- **Business intelligence:** identification of most-valuable customers, analysis of why customers leave, and evaluation of sales forecast accuracy.

Another integration software product is IBM's WebSphere architecture, which includes front office (WebSphere Portal), back office, and supportive infrastructure. Special software for integrating front- and back-office applications is provided by Best Software.

Many other vendors offer complete enterprise packages. For example, SAP-AG, in its ERP R/3 product, offers more than 70 integrated modules, as will be shown in Chapter 8.

# 7.8 How IT Supports Compliance

*Regulatory compliance* refers to an organization's activities conducted to meet federal, state, and other regulatory requirements, and relevant laws. As of 2002, the issue of compliance occupies the mind of management and is listed as one of the top five topics of concern both for CEOs and CIOs.

According to D'Agostino (2005), U.S. companies are spending an average of $4 million per company each year on their SOX compliance alone (see Chapter 1). Gartner Inc. estimated that in 2006 about 80 percent of all large and medium U.S. corporations employed a *chief compliance officer.*

**THE MAJOR TOPIC: SOX**

The SOX Act of 2002, Title III, Section 302, states:

> (4) The signing officers (A) are responsible for establishing and maintaining internal (financial) controls, (B) have designed such internal controls to ensure that material information relating to the issuer. . . is made known, (C) have evaluated the effectiveness of the internal controls . . . , and (D) have presented their conclusions about the effectiveness of the internal controls. (*Openpages.com,* 2006)

To many, this statement is confusing, intimidating, and overwhelming. Several vendors and management consultants developed software and guidelines for how to comply with SOX. For more on SOX, see Marchetti (2005). For an example of implementation, see Online File W7.18.

**THE COMPLIANCE PROCESS**

Several vendors and consultants recommended appropriate compliance processes. For example, Symantec Corp., in special advertising sections in *eWeek,* and *Baseline* (several times during 2005 and 2006), recommends the following eight steps (*Baseline,* December 15, 2005):

1. Establish compliance leadership and hire a compliance officer.
2. Know the compliance mandates, including international regulations.
3. Document and measure policy compliance, using such tools as Symantec Enterprise Security Manager.
4. Master information retention and retrieval. Leverage tools such as VERITAS Enterprise Vault to ensure data are properly archived and can be easily discovered.
5. Develop and review your business continuity plan.
6. Identify all critical applications, and don't overlook mobile CRM applications—which are prone to system theft and data loss.
7. Test the contingency plan at least quarterly.
8. Partner wisely with IT vendors that provide access to senior compliance experts.

For details see *information-integrity.com. CIO Advisor Searchcio.com* (Executive Guide section) offers several guides on how to handle compliance (e.g., budgeting for compliance). D'Agostino (2005) cited a Gartner Inc. recommendation that cost-effective compliance requires:

- **Organizational support.** Compliance officers, compliance committees, and internal auditor functions will be essential to doing business. Without the assignment of responsibility, there can be no real compliance.
- **Process control methodology.** Using open, accessible, and peer-reviewed frameworks for risk management and different kinds of control—whether inside or outside the IT organization—will make compliance regimes more transparent to outsiders.

- **Content control.** The only indisputable trail of evidence—of right practice or wrongdoing—comes through the electronic and paper records that companies keep and 99.9 percent of companies need to work on this area of compliance management.

The following seven steps are suggested by Gartner Inc.:

1. **Establish** the scope of the compliance effort. (*Pitfall: Not adequately delineating lines of responsibility.*)
2. **Assign** employees to specific compliance-related tasks. (*Pitfall: "But I already have a day job!"*)
3. **Screen** personnel to ensure job functions don't overlap. (*Pitfall: Personnel screening not connected to program goals.*)
4. **Communicate and train** employees on good compliance practices. (*Pitfall: Lack of an auditable training record.*)
5. **Monitor** ongoing compliance efforts and consider improvements. (*Pitfall: Risk assessment disconnected from business goals.*)
6. **Enforce** corporate policies and rules around compliance. (*Pitfall: Belief that reporting and oversight is enough.*)
7. **Prevent** policy breaches through monitoring and enforcement. (*Pitfall: Lack of attention to prevention and anticipation.*)

In its performance management suite, Geac Computer Corp. (a Golden Gate Capital company) offers a detailed technology checklist for effective performance management and regulatory compliance.

To execute these and similar steps in the compliance process, supportive software is needed.

**SOFTWARE FOR COMPLIANCE**

The following three types of technologies are suggested by D'Agostino (2005):

1. Management tools such as automated control testing and workflow.
2. Identity and authentication tools for change management and segregation of duties.
3. Content management software for records and e-mail archiving.

These are usually supported by software and computerized process.

Almost all major software vendors (e.g. IBM, HP, SAP Ag, Microsoft, AXentis, Symantec) offer compliance solutions, especially for SOX (see Armour, 2005). The basic purpose of the software is to automate compliance activities.

*Example:* According to Spangler (2006), compliance tracking was one of the top-10 IT projects in 2006. For example, in order to comply with SOX, BMO Financial Group (a Canadian financial services company whose subsidiaries include Chicago-based banking firm Harris) must confirm that users have appropriate access privileges to minimize "segregation of duties" conflicts that create opportunities for fraud (e.g., if an employee somehow had the ability to cut himself a check without authorization). Fraud is discussed in greater detail in Chapter 16.

In fall 2005, Harris installed software from Logical Apps to automate checks for such conflicts, based on rules about which job functions are allowed to have certain change privileges. The software also records changes to the accounts-payable system, such as if the amount of an invoice were altered, and lets support staffers configure the system, but prevents unauthorized changes. The software cut the time to monitor conflicts and system security from two months to about a week.

To cope with changing regulations or internal policies, Ilog.com also offers rule-based compliance software in its business solutions. Cybersource.com offers software called Export Compliance that automatically checks all the details involved when a request for export is made to ensure compliance with U.S. government regulations (e.g., restrictions). Finally, according to Popkin (2002), *business process modeling* (Chapter 8) can be used to improve regulatory compliance.

Also see Group Assignment #4 at the end of this chapter.

## 7.9 Managerial Issues

**1. Integration of functional information systems.** Integration of existing stand-alone functional information systems is a major problem for many organizations. Although client/server architecture is more amenable to integration than legacy systems, there are still problems of integrating different types of data and procedures used by functional areas. Also, there is an issue of willingness to share information, which may challenge existing practices and cultures.

**2. Priority of transaction processing.** Transaction processing may not be an exotic application, but it deals with the core processes of organizations. It must receive top priority in resource allocation, balanced against innovative applications needed to sustain competitive advantage and profitability, because the TPS collects the information needed for most other applications.

**3. Finding innovative applications.** Tools such as Lotus Notes, corporate portals, and Web-based business intelligence enable the construction of many applications that can increase productivity and quality. Finding opportunities for such applications can be best accomplished cooperatively by end users and the IS department.

**4. Using the Web.** Web-based systems should be considered in all functional areas. They are effective, cost relatively little, and are user friendly. In addition to new applications, companies should consider conversion of existing applications to Web-based ones.

**5. Systems integration.** Although functional systems are necessary, they may not be sufficient if they work independently. It is difficult to integrate functional information systems, but there are several approaches to doing so. In the future, Web Services could solve many integration problems, including connecting to a legacy system.

**ETHICS**

**6. Ethical issues.** Many ethical issues are associated with the various topics of this chapter. Professional organizations, relating to the functional areas (e.g., marketing associations), have their own codes of ethics. These codes should be taken into account in developing functional systems. Likewise, organizations must consider privacy policies. Several organizations provide comparisons of privacy policies and other ethics-related topics. For an example, see *socap.org*.

HRM applications are especially prone to ethical and legal considerations. For example, training activities that are part of HRM may involve ethical issues in recruiting and selecting employees and in evaluating performance. Likewise, TPS data processing and storage deal with private information about people, their performance, etc. Care should be taken to protect this information and the privacy of employees and customers.

For more on business ethics as it applies to topics in this chapter, see *ethics.ubc.ca/resources/business*.

## Integrating *IT*

### For the Accounting Major

Executing TPSs effectively is a major concern of any accountant. It is also necessary to understand the various activities of all functional areas and how they are interconnected and supported by IT. Also, many supply chain management issues, ranging from inventory management to risk analysis, fall within the realm of accounting.

Other accounting tasks are taxation, auditing, and government reports. They all can be improved with appropriate accounting software. Appropriate controls and auditing can eliminate fraud and are executed with software.

### For the Finance Major

IT helps financial analysts and managers perform their tasks better. Of particular importance is analyzing cash flows and securing the financing required for smooth operations. In addition, financial applications can support such activities as risk analysis, investment management, and global transactions involving different currencies and fiscal regulations.

A major area of concern for the finance department is compliance with SOX. Many innovative software packages can help here. Also, financial performance, budgeting and its analysis, and many more finance activities can be facilitated with IT.

### For the Human Resources Management Major

Human resources managers can increase their efficiency and effectiveness by using IT for some of their routine functions. Using the Web for recruiting, for example, has revolutionized the HRM area. Human resources personnel need to understand how information flows between the HR department and the other functional areas.

Preparing and training employees to work with business partners (frequently in foreign countries) requires knowledge about how IT collaboration software operates. Finally, compliance with government safety regulations and other human resources–related requirements can be facilitated by IT software.

### For the IS Major

The IS function is responsible for the shared enterprise information systems infrastructure, and the transaction processing systems. TPSs provide the data for the databases. In turn, all other information systems use these data. IS personnel develop applications that support all levels of the organization (from clerical to executive) and in all functional areas (or they work with vendors that develop them). The applications also enable the firm to work better with its partners.

### For the Marketing Major

Due to increased competition, marketing decisions about advertising, promotions, and pricing become critical, and in many cases require software support. E-CRM is frequently a critical success factor. In addition, marketing and sales expenses are usually targets in a cost-reduction program. Also, sales force automation not only improves salespeople's productivity (and thus reduces costs), but also improves customer service.

As competition intensifies globally, finding new global markets and global partners becomes critical. Use of electronic directories, for example, provides an opportunity to improve marketing and sales. Understanding the capabilities of marketing and sales support technologies and their implementation issues will enable the marketing department to excel.

### For the Production/Operations Management Major

Managing production tasks, materials handling, and inventories in short time intervals, at a low cost, and with high quality is critical for competitiveness. These activities can be achieved only if they are properly supported by IT. Because they are in charge of procurement, production/operations managers must understand how their supporting information systems interface with those of their business partners. In addition, collaboration in design, manufacturing, and logistics requires knowledge of how modern information systems can be connected. Finally, on-demand manufacturing must be done at a competitive cost. Optimization with appropriate computerized analysis is very helpful.

## Key Terms

Batch processing  *262*

Channel systems  *270*

Computer-integrated manufacturing (CIM)  *270*

Employee relationship management (ERM)  *286*

Expense management automation (EMA)  *282*

Financial value chain management (FVCM)  *280*

Just-in-time (JIT)  *269*

Online processing  *262*

## Chapter Highlights

(Numbers Refer to Learning Objectives)

❶ Information systems applications can support many functional activities. Considerable software is readily available on the market for much of this support (for lease or to buy).

❷ The major business functional areas are production/operations management, marketing, accounting/finance, and human resources management.

❸ The backbone of most information systems applications is the transaction processing system (TPS), which keeps track of the routine, mission-central operations of the organization.

❹ The major area of IT support to production/operations management is in logistics and inventory management: JIT, mass customization, and CIM.

❺ Marketing and sales information systems deal with all activities related to customer orders, sales, advertising and promotion, market research, customer service, and product and service pricing. Using IT can increase sales, customers' satisfaction, and profitability.

❻ Financial information systems deal with topics such as investment management, financing operations, raising capital, risk analysis, and credit approval.

❻ Accounting information systems also cover many non-TPS applications in areas such as cost control, taxation, and auditing.

❼ Most tasks related to human resources development can be supported by human resources information systems. These tasks include employee recruitment and selection, hiring, performance evaluation, salary and benefits administration, training and development, labor negotiations, and work planning.

❼ Web-based HR systems are extremely useful for recruiting and training.

❽ Integrated functional information systems are necessary to ensure effective and efficient execution of activities that cross functional lines or that require functional cooperation.

❽ Integrating applications is difficult; it can be done in different ways, such as buying off-the-shelf applications from one vendor or using special connecting software known as middleware. A promising new approach is that of Web Services.

❾ Compliance can be very time consuming and expensive, especially SOX. Using software makes it possible to expedite the process and eliminate errors.

## Virtual Company Assignment

### Transaction Processing at The Wireless Café

Go to The Wireless Café's link on the Student Web Site. There you will be asked to think about the business activities and transactions, other than cooking, that the restaurant engages in. You will be asked to consider types of transaction processing applications that could be implemented at The Wireless Café.

*Instructions for accessing The Wireless Café on the Student Web Site:*

1. Go to *wiley.com/college/turban*.
2. Select Turban/Leidner/McLean/Wetherbe's *Information Technology for Management, Sixth Edition*.
3. Click on Student Resources site, in the toolbar on the left.
4. Click on the link for Virtual Company Web site.
5. Click on Wireless Café.

## Online Resources

More resources and study tools are located on the Student Web Site and on WileyPLUS. You'll find additional chapter materials and useful Web links. In addition, self-quizzes that provide individualized feedback are available for each chapter.

## Questions For Review

1. What is a functional information system?
2. List the major characteristics of a functional information system.
3. What are the objectives of a TPS?
4. List the major characteristics of a TPS.
5. Distinguish between batch and online TPS.
6. Explain how the Web enables mass customization.
7. Describe spend management.
8. Define XBRL.
9. Describe VMI.
10. Define CIM, and list its major benefits.
11. Define channel systems.
12. Define JIT, and list some of its benefits.
13. What is product/customer profitability?
14. Describe some tactical and strategic accounting/finance applications.
15. List some budgeting-related activities.
16. List some EC activities in finance.
17. List IT-supported recruitment activities.
18. How can training go online?
19. Explain human resources information systems.
20. Describe the need for application integration.
21. Describe regulatory compliance.

## Questions for Discussion

1. Why is it logical to organize IT applications by functional areas?
2. Describe the role of a TPS in a service organization.
3. Why are transaction processing systems a major target for restructuring?
4. Which functional areas are related to payroll, and how does the relevant information flow?
5. Discuss the benefits of Web-based TPS.
6. It is said that in order to be used successfully, MRP must be computerized. Why?
7. The Japanese implemented JIT for many years without computers. Discuss some elements of JIT, and comment on the potential benefits of computerization.
8. Describe the role of computers in CIM.
9. Explain how Web applications can make the customer king/queen.
10. Why are information systems critical to sales-order processing?
11. Describe how IT can enhance mass customization.
12. Describe how XBRL can help banks.
13. Describe cost-effective compliance.
14. Discuss how IT facilitates the budgeting process.
15. Why is risk management important, and how can it be enhanced by IT?
16. Compare bill presentment to check re-presentment. How are they facilitated by IT?
17. How can the Internet support investment decisions?
18. Describe the benefits of an accounting integrated software such as MAS 90; compare it to MAS 200.
19. Discuss the role IT plays in support of auditing.
20. Investigate the role of the Web in human resources management.
21. Geographical information systems are playing an important role in supporting marketing and sales. Provide some examples not discussed in the text. (See Chapter 11.)
22. Discuss the need for application integration and the difficulty of doing it.
23. Discuss the approaches and reasons for integrating front-office with back-office operations.
24. Discuss why some of the services provided by *iEmployee.com* are considered support to on-demand workforce management solutions.

## Exercises and Projects

1. Review the Dartmouth-Hitchcock Medical center case. Assume that RFID tags cost 5 cents each. How might use of RFID tags change the supply chain management? Would the new system at the medical center still be needed? Write a report on your conclusions.
2. The chart shown in Figure 7.3 portrays the flow of routine activities in a typical manufacturing organization. Explain in what areas IT can be most valuable.
3. Argot International (a fictitious name) is a medium-sized company in Peoria, Illinois, with about 2,000 employees.

The company manufactures special machines for farms and food-processing plants, buying materials and components from about 150 vendors in six different countries. It also buys special machines and tools from Japan. Products are sold either to wholesalers (about 70) or directly to clients (from a mailing list of about 2,000). The business is very competitive.

The company has the following information systems in place: financial/accounting, marketing (primarily information about sales), engineering, research and development, and inventory management. These systems are independent of each other although they are all connected to the corporate intranet.

Argot is having profitability problems. Cash is in high demand and short supply, due to strong business competition from Germany and Japan. The company wants to investigate the possibility of using information technology to improve the situation. However, the vice president of finance objects to the idea, claiming that most of the tangible benefits of information technology are already being realized.

You are hired as a consultant to the president. Respond to the following:

**a.** Prepare a list of 10 potential applications of information technologies that you think could help the company.

**b.** From the description of the case, would you recommend any portals? Be very specific. Remember, the company is in financial trouble.

**c.** How can Web Services help Argot?

**4.** Enter *extensity.com*. Take the demo. Prepare a list of all the product's capabilities.

## Group Assignments and Projects

**1.** Each group should visit (or investigate) a large company in a different industry and identify its channel systems. Prepare a diagram that shows the components shown in Online File W7.8. Then find how IT supports each of those components. Finally, suggest improvements in the existing channel system that can be supported by IT technologies and that are not in use by the company today. Each group presents its findings.

**2.** The class is divided into groups of four. Each group member represents a major functional area: production/operations management, sales/marketing, accounting/finance, and human resources. Find and describe several examples of processes that require the integration of functional information systems in a company of your choice. Each group will also show the interfaces to the other functional areas.

**3.** Each group investigates an HRM software vendor (Oracle, SAP, Lawson Software). The group prepares a list of all HRM functionalities supported by the software. Then the groups make a presentation to convince the class that its vendor is the best.

**4.** Each group is assigned to a compliance vendor(s). Document the regulation they are dealing with and the capabilities of the software offered.

## Internet Exercises

**1.** Surf the Net and find free accounting software (try *shareware.com, rkom.com, tucows.com, passtheshareware.com,* and *freeware-guide.com*). Download the software and try it. Write a report on your findings.

**2.** Enter the site of Federal Express (*fedex.com*) and learn how to ship a package, track the status of a package, and calculate its cost. Comment on your experience.

**3.** Finding a job on the Internet is challenging; there are almost too many places to look. Visit the following sites: *careerbuilder.com, careermag.com, hotjobs.yahoo.com, jobcenter.com,* and *monster.com.* What do these sites provide you as a job seeker?

**4.** Enter the Web site *tps.com* and some of those listed in Online File W7.3, and find information about software products available from those sites. Identify the software that allows Internet transaction processing. Prepare a report about the benefits of the products identified.

**5.** Enter *sas.com* and access revenue optimization there. Explain how the software helps in optimizing prices.

**6.** Enter *hyperion.com/downloads/profitability_management.pdf,* and download the brochure on profitability management. Prepare a summary.

**7.** Enter *iemployee.com* and find the support they provide to human resources management activities by IT. View the demos and read the white paper by Shah (2006). Prepare a report.

**8.** Enter *softsim.com* and view the demo of the product. Do you think it is a valuable tool?

**9.** Enter *authorial.com* and *successfactors.com*. Examine their software products and make a comparison.

**10.** Examine the capabilities of the following financial software packages: TekPortal (from *teknowledge.com*), Financial Analyzer (from Oracle), and CFO Vision (from SAS Institute). Prepare a report comparing the capabilities of the software packages.

**11.** Surf the Internet and find information from three vendors on sales force automation (try *sybase.com* first). Prepare a report on the state of the art.

**12.** Enter *teknowledge.com* and review the products that help with online training (training systems). What are the most attractive features of these products?

**13.** Enter *microsoft.com/dynamics/sl/default.mspx*. View three of the demos in different functional areas of your choice. Prepare a report on the capabilities.

**14.** Enter *sagesoftware.com*. Identify functional software, CRM software, and e-business software products. Are these standalone or integrated? Explain.

## Minicase 1

## Dollar General Uses Integrated Software

ACC HRM

Dollar General (*dollargeneral.com*) operates more than 6,000 general stores in the United States, fiercely competing with Wal-Mart, Target, and thousands of other stores in the sale of food, apparel, home-cleaning products, health and beauty aids, and more. The chain doubled in size between 1996 and 2002 and has had some problems in addition to the stiff competition, due to its rapid expansion. For example, moving into new states means different sales taxes, and these need to be closely monitored for changes. Personnel management also became more difficult with the organization's growth. An increased number of purchasing orders exacerbated problems in the accounts payable department, which was using manual matching of purchasing orders, invoices, and what was actually received in the "receiving" department before bills were paid.

The IT department was flooded with requests to generate long reports on topics ranging from asset management to general ledgers. It became clear that a better information system was needed. Dollar General started by evaluating information requirements that would be able to solve the above and other problems that cut into the company's profit.

A major factor in deciding which software to buy was the integration requirement among the existing information systems of the various functional areas, especially the financial applications. This led to the selection of the Financials suite (from Lawson Software). The company started to implement applications one at a time. Before 1998, the company installed the suite's asset management, payroll, and some HR applications which allow the tens of thousands of employees to monitor and self-update their benefits, 401k contributions, and personal data (resulting in big savings to the HR department). After 1998, the accounts payable and general ledger modules of Lawson Software were activated. The accounting modules allow employees to route, extract, and analyze data in the accounting/finance area with little reliance on IT personnel. During 2001–2003, Dollar General moved into the sales and procurement areas, thus adding the marketing and operation activities to the integrated system.

Here are a few examples of how various parts of the new system work: All sales data from the point-of-sale scanners of some 6,000 stores are pulled each night, together with financial data, discounts, etc., into the business intelligence application for financial and marketing analysis. Employee payroll data, from each store, are pulled once a week. This provides synergy with the sales audit system (from STS Software). All sales data are processed nightly by the STS System, broken into hourly journal entries, processed and summarized, and then entered into the Lawson's general ledger module.

The original infrastructure was mainframe based (IBM AS 400). By 2002, the 800 largest suppliers of Dollar General were submitting their bills on the EDI. This allowed instantaneous processing in the accounts payable module. By 2003, service providers, such as utilities, were added to the system. To do all this the system was migrated in 2001 from the old legacy system to the Unix operating system, and then to a Web-based infrastructure, mainly in order to add Web-based functionalities and tools.

A development tool embedded in Lawson's Financials allowed users to customize applications without touching the computer programming code. This included applications that are not contained in the Lawson system. For example, an employee-bonus application was not available at Lawson, but was added to Financial's payroll module to accommodate Dollar General's bonus system. A customized application that allowed additions and changes in dozens of geographical areas also solved the organization's state sales-tax collection and reporting problem.

The system is very scalable, so there is no problem in adding stores, vendors, applications, or functionalities. In 2003, the system was completely converted to Web-based, enabling authorized vendors, for example, to log on the Internet and view the status of their invoices by themselves. Also, the Internet/EDI enables small vendors to use the system. (An EDI is too expensive for small vendors, but the EDI/Internet is affordable.) Also, the employees can update personal data from any Web-enabled desktop in the store or at home. Future plans call for adding an e-purchasing (procurement) module using a desktop purchasing model (see Chapter 5).

*Sources:* Compiled from Amato-McCoy (2002a) and *lawson.com* (accessed May 2004).

### Questions for Minicase 1

1. Explain why the old, nonintegrated functional system created problems for the company. Be specific.

2. The new system cost several million dollars. Why, in your opinion, was it necessary to install it?

3. Lawson Software Smart Notification Software (*lawson.com*) is being considered by Dollar General. Find information about the software and write an opinion for adoption or rejection.

4. Another new product of Lawson is Services Automation. Would you recommend it to Dollar General? Why or why not?

---

## Minicase 2

## Musco Food Uses IT to Improve Sales and Operations

Musco Food Corp. (*muscofood.com*) is a distributor of food products (meats, cheese, olive oil, and other deli-need products) in Queens, New York. It has only an eight-man sales force who visit customers and, until recently, showed them a paper catalog and took orders orally ("Just give us the same as last time," or "I need fourteen cases of Italian cheese"). The salesman then went to his car and called a customer service employee, who then typed the information into the company's computerized order processing system that generated the order to the warehouse for preparation and delivery, and an invoice for the customer.

The system was in place for about 10 years; however, mistakes occurred about five times a week. The quantity ordered differed from that delivered. Either the customer service employee made a mistake or the salesman forgot the exact number while walking to his car. In either case, customers were unhappy, inventories were incorrect, and expensive rush orders (order corrections) had to be made.

Salesman productivity was low and other expenses were too high. In addition, price changes and promotions that might be of interest to specific customers were not communicated in time. Finally, inventory availability was not known in real time.

Using Treo smart phones (from *Palm.com*) that display product images and order entry e-forms, the salesmen struggled at the beginning to pull up the products and enter orders. However, after a few weeks, the salesmen became experts in locating a product out of more than 1,000 in the e-catalog. Now, an order is punched in the minute it is expressed by the customer. An electronic invoice is generated in seconds and shown to the deli owner for verification on the spot. Also, the customer service representatives who used to enter the orders in the computers are not needed. Instead, they have been retrained to help locate new customers. The wireless Treo enters the order information directly to the corporate computer system. In addition, the Treo provides instant access to pricing changes and promotions. The salesmen can check, in real time, any customer accounts receivable balance. Finally, real-time inventory availability can be checked at the customer's site.

Each salesman now visits six instead of five customers on an average day. Orders get instant attention from the warehouse employees. Most important, errors, correcting trips, and expenses have been reduced by over 50 percent for an annual savings of $25,000. Finally, the process fulfillment time takes one to two instead of three days. The system paid for itself in just a few months.

*Sources:* Compiled from Barrett (2005a) and from *Palm.com* (2006).

### Questions for Minicase 2

1. Identify the real-time activities.

2. How is customer service improved?

3. Which functional information systems need to be integrated to support the new system?

4. Which types of errors were eliminated?

5. Enter *sco.com/products/meinc* and identify the software on the back end (order fulfillment).

---

# References

*Aberdeen.com,* "Best Practices in Streamlining the Financial Value Chain: Top Seven FVCM Implementations," Aberdeen Group, 2002, *aberdeen.com/summary/report/other/FVCMBestPracticesReport10. asp* (accessed July 2006).

Amato-McCoy, D. M., "Dollar General Rings Up Back-Office Efficiencies with Financial Suite," *Stores,* October 2002a.

Amato-McCoy, D. M., "Sears Combines Retail Reporting and Customer Databases on a Single Platform," *Stores,* November 2002b.

Amato-McCoy, D. M., "Linens 'n Things Protects Inventory Investment with Supply Planning Suite," *Stores,* November 2002c.

*autobytel.com* (accessed July 2006).

Avriel, M., et al., "Opti-Money at Bank Hapoalim," *Interfaces,* January–February 2004.

Barrett, L., "Dial-a-Deli," *Baseline,* November 2005a.

Barrett, L., "Juggling Act," *Baseline,* June 2005b.

Benjaafar, S. et al., "Next Generation Factory Layouts," *Interfaces,* November–December 2002.

Buckley, N., "E-Route to Whiter Smile," *Financial Times,* August 26, 2002.

Bussler, L., and E. Davis, "Information Systems: The Quiet Revolution in Human Resource Management," *Journal of Computer Information Systems,* Winter 2001–2002.

Butcher, D. R., "Mass Customization: A Leading Paradigm in Future Manufacturing," February 14, 2006.

Carr, D. F., "Leaner Machine," *Baseline,* June 2005.

Chatman, J., C. O'Rielly, and V. Chang, "Cisco Systems: Developing a Human Cupid Strategy," *California Management Review,* Winter 2005.

*Cheapflights.com,* "Plastic Purchases Onboard American Airlines," May 4, 2006, *news.cheapflights.com/airlines/2006/05/plastic_purchas.html#more* (accessed July 2006).

D'Agostino, D., "A Rock and a Hard Place," *Baseline,* August 2005.

Degnan, C., "Best Practices in Expense Management Automation," Special Report. Boston: Aberdeen Group, January 2003, *ofm.wa.gov/roadmap/modeling/expense/Aberdeen_BestPractices_Spend_Management.pdf* (accessed July 2006).

Duvall, M., "Lemon Aid," *Baseline,* June 2005.

*Entersingapore.com,* "Public Transport," *entersingapore.info/sginfo/public-transport.php* (accessed July 2006).

Field, K., "High Speed Hiring," *Chain Store Age,* June 2006.

*ford.com* (accessed July 2006).

Fujitsu Corp. (sponsor), "Smart Stores," advertising supplement, *Stores,* January 2004.

Gayeski, D., "Going Mobile," *TD,* November 2004.

Gibson, S., "Tech Behind the Trophy," *e-Week,* November 29, 2004.

Gillium, D., et al., *The Quantum Leap: Next Generation—The Manufacturing Strategy for Business.* Fort Lauderdale, FL: J. Ross Publishers, 2005.

Gomez-Mejia, L., et al., *Managing Human Resources,* 5th ed. Upper Saddle River: NJ, Prentice Hall, 2007.

Grimes, S., "Declaration Support: The B.P.M. Drumbeat," *Intelligent Enterprise,* April 23, 2003.

Harris, P., "Training's New Wave," *TD,* August 2005.

Ho, G. T. S., et al., "An Intelligent Information Infrastructure to Support the Streamlining of Integrated Logistics Workflow," *Expert Systems,* July 2004.

Howarth, B., "To Catch a Thief," *BRW,* January 15–21, 2004.

*Hyperion.com,* "Profitability Management from Hyperion," *hyperion.com/solutions/project/profitability_management/index.cfm* (accessed July 2006).

IBM, "Increasing Cirque du Soleil's Agility," *IBM.com,* July 1, 2005, *www-1.ibm.com/businesscenter/smb/us/en/contenttemplate/gcl_xmlid/33893/nav_id/resources* (accessed July 2006).

*jaguar.com* (accessed July 2006).

Jareb, E., and V. Rajkovic, "Use of an Expert System in Personnel Selection," *Information Management,* July–December 2001.

Johnson, S., "Five Components of Personalization," *iMediaConnection,* April 6, 2006, *imediaconnection.com/content/8952.asp* (accessed July 2006).

Korolishin, J., "Meeting the Employee Scheduling Challenge," *Stores,* September 2003.

Korolishin, J., "Payroll Pay Cards Pay Off at Payless," *Stores,* February 2004a.

Korolishin, J., "Sheetz Keeps Tab on Training Compliance via Web Portal," *Stores,* February 2004b.

Kroll, K. M., "Video-Based Systems Seek Cleaner Focus on Store Traffic," *Stores,* April 2002.

*Lawson.com* (accessed July 2006).

Lee, Y. M., and E. J. Chen, "BASF Uses a Framework for Developing Web-Based Production-Planning Optimization Tools," *Interfaces,* November–December 2002.

Liao, Z., "Real Time Tax: Dispatching Using GPS," *Communications of the ACM,* May 2003.

Malykhina, E., "XBRL: More Than a Must-Do," *Information Week,* May 29, 2006.

Marchetti, A. M., *Beyond Sarbanes-Oxley Compliance.* Hoboken NJ: Wiley, 2005.

Maxemchuk, N. F., and D. H. Shur, "An Internet Multicast System for the Stock Market," *ACM Transactions on Computer Systems,* August 2001.

McCullough, D. C., *Oracle 9i.* New York: Hungry Minds, 2002.

McKinley, E., "Multicasting Solution Ushers in New Era of Computer-Based Training," *Stores,* April 2003.

Meredith, J. R., and S. M. Shafer, *Operations Management.* New York: Wiley, 2002.

Nishi, D., "Market-Basket Mystery," *Retail Technology Quarterly,* May 2005.

*Openpages.com,* "Sarbanes-Oxley Act of 2002: Title III, Section 302—Corporate Responsibility for Financial Reports," *openpages.com/solutions/sarbanes-oxley/sarbanes-oxley-sec302.asp* (accessed July 2006).

*Palm.com,* "Musco Food Corp. Expand Customer Base with Treo Smartphones," *solutions.palm.com/regac/success_stories* (accessed July 2006).

Palaniswamy, R., and T. Frank, "Enhancing Manufacturing Performance with ERP Systems," *Information Management Journal,* Summer 2000.

Parks, L., "Making Sure the Price Is Right" (price optimization), *Stores,* August 2004a.

Parks, L., "Schurman Fine Papers Racks Up Labor Savings," *Stores,* February 2004b.

Perkins-Munn, T. S., and Y. T. Chen, "Streamlining Project Management Through Online Solutions," *Journal of Business Strategy,* January 2004.

*pg.com* (accessed July 2006).

Popin, J., "Improving Regulatory Compliance with Business Process Modeling," *Business Integration Journal,* June 2005.

*Prophix.com,* "Features: Budgeting," *prophix.com/solutions/prophix_features.php#Budgeting* (accessed July 2006).

*Rapt.com,* "Case Study: Delivering Profit-Optimal Prices for Configured Products," 2006, *rapt.com/cases/high_tech-hp.htm* (accessed July 2006).

Reda, S., "Digital Signage Helps Tesco Inform, Entertain and Boost Sales," *Stores,* March 2005.

Reda, S., "Evelyn Follit Fuses Technology, Business, and HR Strategies," *Stores,* March 2004.

Reda, S., "Word-of Mouth Marketing Enjoys New Life as Potent Online Advertising Strategy," *Stores,* October 2002.

Reed, C. et al., *eCFO: Sustaining Value in New Corporations.* Chichester, U.K.: Wiley, 2001.

Shah, S., *The Five Foundations of Next Generation HRO Technology,* a white paper from *iemployee.com* (downloaded July 2006).

Spangler, T., "The Top Ten Projects in 2006," *Innovations,* Issue 2, 2006 (supplement to *Baseline* and *eWeek*).

Subrahmanyam, A., "Nuts and Bolts of Transaction Processing: A Comprehensive Tutorial," *subrahmanyam.com...articles/transactions/NutsAndBoltsOfTP.html* (no longer available online).

TIAA CREF, *Annual Report 2005*. tiaa-cref.org, July 2006. Available for download at *tiaacref.org/about/governance/corporate/topics/annual_ reports.html* (accessed October 2006).

Thomas, S. L., and K. Ray, "Recruiting and the Web: High-Tech Hiring," *Business Horizons*, May–June 2000.

Turban, E. et al., *Electronic Commerce 2008*. Upper Saddle River, NJ: Prentice Hall, 2008.

Vijayakumar, S., "Improving Software Cost Estimation," *Project Management Today,* May 2002.

Virzi, A. M., "Cleaning Up" *Baseline*, September 2005.

"Web Breathes Life into Medical Firm's Training Program," *Internet Week,* July 27, 1988, *internetwk.com/search/results.jhtml?queryText_Omnitech&site_id_3* (no longer available online).

"What EMA Systems Now Offer Accounting Departments" *Accounting Department Management & Administration Report,* February 2002.

*Wikipedia.org,* "Transaction Processing Systems," *en.wikipedia.org/wiki/Transaction_Processing_System* (accessed July 2006).

Zaremba, M. B., and G. Morel, "Integration and Control of Intelligence in Distributed Manufacturing," *Journal of Intelligent Manufacturing,* February 2003.

## Part IV | Organizational Applications

7. Transaction Processing, Functional Applications, and Integration
▶ 8. Enterprise Systems
9. Interorganizational and Global Information Systems

Chapter

# 8

# Enterprise Systems

ChevronTexaco Modernized Its Supply Chain with IT

## 8.1 Essentials of Enterprise Systems and Supply Chains

## 8.2 Supply Chain Challenges

## 8.3 Supply Chain Opportunities

## 8.4 Business Value of Enterprise Systems

## 8.5 Enterprise Resource Planning Systems

## 8.6 Business Process Management

## 8.7 Product Lifecycle Management

## 8.8 Customer Relationship Management

## 8.9 Managerial Issues

## Minicases:
1. *Northern Digital*
2. *QVC*

## Learning Objectives

After studying this chapter, you will be able to:

❶ Understand the essentials of enterprise systems and computerized supply chain management.

❷ Describe the various types of supply chains.

❸ Describe some major problems of implementing supply chains and some innovative solutions.

❹ Describe the need for integrated software and how ERP does it.

❺ Understand business process management and how to enhance effectiveness.

❻ Describe the product life cycle management stages.

❼ Describe CRM and its support by IT.

## Integrating *IT*

 **ACC**  **FIN**  **MKT**  **POM**  **HRM**  **IS**  **SVC**

# CHEVRONTEXACO MODERNIZED ITS SUPPLY CHAIN WITH IT

## The Problem

ChevronTexaco, the largest U.S. oil company, is multinational in nature. Its main business is drilling, refining, transporting, and selling gasoline (oil). In this competitive business, a saving of even a quarter of a penny per gallon totals up to millions of dollars. Two problems have plagued the oil industry: running out of gasoline at individual pumps, and a delivery that is aborted because a tank at the gas station is too full (called "retain"). Run-outs and retains, known as the industry's "twin evils," have been a target for improvements for years, with little success.

The causes of the twin evils have to do with the supply chain: Gasoline flows in the supply chain start with oil hunting, drilling, and extraction. After the oil is taken from the ground, it is delivered to and then processed in refineries, and finally it goes to storage **POM** and eventually to the retail pump and to the customer. The difficulty is to match the three parts of the supply chain: oil acquisition, processing, and distribution.

ChevronTexaco owns oil fields and refineries, but it also buys both crude and refined oil to meet peak demand. Purchases are of two types: those that are made through long-term contracts, and those that are purchased "as needed," in what is called the *spot market*, at prevailing prices (usually higher than contract purchases).

In the past, ChevronTexaco acted like a mass-production manufacturing company, just trying to make lots of oil products and then sell them (a supply-driven strategy). The problem with this strategy is that each time you make too much, you are introducing extra inventory or storage costs. If you make too little, you lose sales.

## The Solution

The company decided to change its business model from *supply driven* to *demand driven*. Namely, instead of focusing on how much oil it would process and "push" to customers, the company started thinking about how much oil its customers wanted and then about how to get it. This change necessitated a major transformation in the business and extensive support by information technologies.

To implement the IT support, the company installed in each tank in each gas station an electronic monitor. The monitor transmits real-time information about the oil level, through a cable, to the station's IT-based management system. That system then transmits the information via a satellite to the main inventory system at the company's main office. There, an advanced DSS-based planning system processes the data to help refining, marketing, and logistics decisions. This DSS also includes information collected at trucking and airline companies, which are major customers. Using an enterprise resource planning (ERP) and business planning system (BPS), ChevronTexaco determines how much to refine, how much to buy in spot markets, and when and how much to ship to each retail station.

To combine all of these data, it is necessary to integrate the supply and demand information systems, and this is where the ERP software is useful. These data are used by planners at various points across the supply chain (e.g., refinery, terminal management, station management, transportation, and production) who process and share data constantly. This data processing and data sharing are provided by the various information systems.

Recent IT projects support the supply chain and extend it to a global reach. These projects include the NetReady initiative that enables the operations of 150 e-business projects, the Global Information Link (GIL2) that enables connectivity throughout the company, the e-Guest project that enables sharing of information with business partners, and a global human resources information system.

## The Results

The integrated system that allows data to be shared across the company has improved decision making at every point in the customer-facing and processing parts of the supply chain. It resulted in an increase in the company's profit by more than $300 million in 1999 and by more than an additional $100 million each year after.

According to Worthen (2002), studies indicate that companies in the top 20 percent of the oil industry operate their supply chains twice as efficiently as average companies. These successful companies also carry half as much inventory, can respond to a significant rise in demand

(20% or higher) twice as fast, and know how to minimize the number of deliveries to the gas stations. ChevronTexaco is in this category.

*Sources:* Compiled from Worthen (2002); and from *chevrontexaco.com,* see "Technology Ventures" (accessed October 2006).

### Lessons Learned from This Case

The ChevronTexaco case illustrates the need to drastically improve the management of the supply chain. All decision makers along the supply chain need to share information and collaborate. Doing so is not a simple task, as will be seen in this chapter, but IT solutions enable even a large multinational company to manage its supply chain.

ChevronTexaco successfully implemented the concepts of *supply chain management* and *enterprise resource planning.* Figure 8.1 shows how these two topics are interrelated. Such a system is an enterprise system. In addition, the figure shows other enterprise systems. Enterprise systems such as supply chains, ERP, and CRM are the subjects of this chapter.

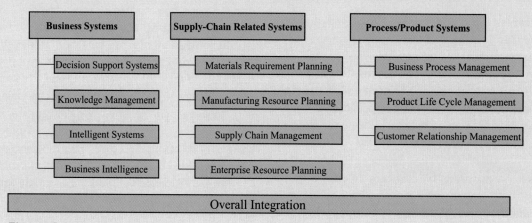

**Figure 8.1** Overview of enterprise systems. (*Source:* Prepared by E. Turban and D. Amoroso.)

## 8.1 Essentials of Enterprise Systems and Supply Chains

**Enterprise systems** (also called **enterprisewide systems**) are systems or processes that involve the entire enterprise or major portions of it. This is in contrast to functional systems, which are confined to one department (functional area) each.

Several enterprise systems can be found in organizations. Typical examples are:

- Enterprise resource planning (ERP), which supports the internal supply chain.
- Extended ERP, which supports business partners as well. Most ERP systems today are extended.
- Customer relationship management (CRM), which provides customer care.
- Partner relationship management (PRM), which is designed to provide care to business partners.
- Business process management (BPM), which involves the understanding and realignment of processes in the organization, including reengineering and managing the flow of activities and tasks.

- Product life cycle management (PLM), which involves conceptualization, design, building, and support of products and services. The management of PLM seeks to reduce cycle times, streamline production costs, and get more products to market.
- Decision support systems (DSSs), whose purpose is to support decision making throughout the enterprise, frequently with the help of a data warehouse. This category includes executive information systems.
- Knowledge management (KM) systems, whose objective is to support knowledge creation, storage, maintenance, and distribution throughout the enterprise.
- Intelligent systems, which include a knowledge component, such as an expert system or neural network.
- Business intelligence, which is computer-based decision analysis usually done online by managers and staff. It includes forecasting, analyzing alternatives, and evaluating risk and performance.

The first three systems are described in this chapter; PRM is described in Chapter 9, KM in Chapter 10, business intelligence in Chapter 11, and decision support and intelligent systems in Chapter 12.

**WHAT IS A SUPPLY CHAIN?**

A *supply chain* is defined as a set of relationships among suppliers, manufacturers, distributors, and retailers that facilitate the transformation of raw materials into final products. The supply chain includes all of the interactions between suppliers, manufacturers, distributors, warehouses, and customers. Supply chains involve the flow of materials, information, money, and services from raw materials suppliers, through factories and warehouses, to the end-consumers. Although the supply chain is comprised of several businesses, the chain itself is viewed as a single entity.

The supply chain also includes the organization processes for developing and delivering products, information, and services to end-customers. Notice in Figure 8.2 that inventory moves from supplier to supplier until it reaches the manufacturer. Market research data, scheduling information, design data, and order and cash flow data move from the customer to the suppliers. Material flow, design ideas, and credit flow move from the supplier-side to the customer-side of the supply chain.

Information technology must support the basic infrastructure and coordination needed for the supply chain to function. Configuration-level issues include the following:

- Procurement and supplier decisions
- Production decisions

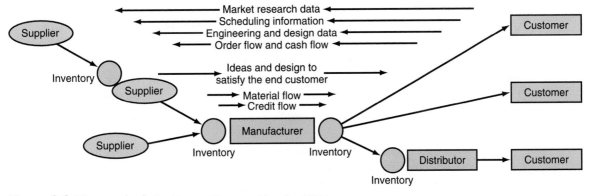

**Figure 8.2** The supply chain. (*Source:* Heizer and Render, 2004.)

- Distribution decisions
- Information support decisions
- Material flow decisions
- Cash flow decisions

**Supply chain management (SCM)** is the efficient management of the end-to-end processes that start with the design of the product or service and end when it is sold, consumed, or used by the end-consumer. Some activities include inventory management, materials acquisition, transformation of raw materials into finished goods, shipping, and transportation. As shown in Figure 8.2, supply chain management involves vendors, financial accounting transfers, warehousing and inventory levels, order fulfillment, distributors, and the information needed to manage it.

Effective management of the supply chain provides a major opportunity for an organization to reduce costs while increasing operating efficiencies. Organizations need to know how much, and in what sequence, they will be investing in various supply chain efforts to leverage the benefits of the technology. SCM models need to focus on more than one variable. The optimal strategy will look at multiple variables including inventory, forecasting, lead time, capacity, and price.

**Internal Supply Chain.** These are the processes in an organization that are devoted to managing its supply chain, including inventory management, accounting processes, warehousing, logistics, and shipping.

**Supply Chain Management Software.** **SCM software** refers to software needed to support specific segments of the supply chain, such as in manufacturing, inventory control, scheduling, and transportation. This software concentrates on improving decision making, optimization, and analysis.

**E-Supply Chain.** When a supply chain is managed electronically, usually with Web-based software, it is referred to as an **e-supply chain.** As will be shown in this chapter, improvements in supply chains frequently involve attempts to convert a traditional supply chain to an e-supply chain, namely to automate the information flow in the chain.

There are typically three types of flows in the supply chain: materials, information, and financial. In managing the supply chain, it is necessary to coordinate all the flows among all the parties involved in the chain.

1. **Material flows.** These are all physical products, raw materials, supplies, and so forth, that flow along the chain. The concept of material flows also includes *reverse* flows—returned products, recycled products, and disposal of materials or products. A supply chain thus involves a *product life cycle* approach, from "dirt to dust."
2. **Information flows.** This includes all data related to demand, shipments, orders, returns, and schedules, and changes in the data.
3. **Financial flows.** The financial flows are all transfers of money, payments, credit card information and authorization, payment schedules, e-payments, and credit-related data.

The flow of goods, services, information, and financial resources is usually designed not only to effectively transform raw items to finished products and services, but also to do so in an *efficient manner* (e.g., by using proper planning). IT makes a major contribution to both efficiency and effectiveness of information flows.

The goals of SCM are to reduce uncertainty and risks along the supply chain, thereby decreasing inventory levels and cycle time, and improving business processes and customer service. All of these benefits contribute to increased profitability and competitiveness, as demonstrated in the opening case. The benefits of supply chain management have long been recognized both in business and in the military. To enjoy the above benefits it is necessary to overcome the limitations and problems described in the next section of the chapter.

## 8.2 Supply Chain Challenges

Supply chain challenges have been recognized in business, services, government, and the military for generations. The problems are most evident in complex or long supply chains and in cases where many business partners are involved. There are numerous examples of supply chain problems, such as companies that were unable to meet demand. Some of these companies paid substantial penalties, and others even went out of business. On the other hand, some world-class companies such as Wal-Mart, Federal Express, and Dell have supply chains with innovative IT-enhanced applications.

Problems along the supply chain can occur between business units within a single enterprise; they also can occur between (and among) enterprises. A major symptom of ineffective supply chains is poor customer service, which hinders people or businesses from getting products or services when and where needed or gives them poor-quality products. Other symptoms are high inventory costs, loss of revenues, and extra cost of expediting shipments.

**REASONS FOR SUPPLY CHAIN PROBLEMS**

The problems along the supply chain stem mainly from two sources: (1) from uncertainties and (2) from the need to coordinate several activities, internal units, and business partners. Here we will address several of the uncertainties that contribute to supply chain problems. Throughout the chapter, we will consider how IT can help enterprises improve supply chain coordination and reduce uncertainties.

Actual demand for a product is influenced by several factors such as competition, prices, weather conditions, technological developments, and customers' general confidence. These are external, usually uncontrollable, factors. ChevronTexaco overcame this uncertainty by measuring demand in real time and using a demand-driven production strategy. Other supply chain uncertainties include delivery times, which depend on many factors, ranging from production machine failures to road conditions and traffic jams that may interfere with shipments. Quality problems in materials and parts may also create production delays, which lead to supply chain problems. One of the major difficulties in properly setting inventory levels in various parts of the supply chain is known as the bullwhip effect. The **bullwhip effect** refers to erratic changes in orders (along the) supply chain and is discussed later in the chapter.

**TRUST AND COLLABORATION**

**Trust** is vitally important in a collaboration relationship between suppliers and buyers in the supply chain. Trust involves a calculated process wherein an organization estimates the costs and/or the rewards of another party cheating or staying in the relationship. Because of the increase in the Internet-enabled supply chain, organizations are collaborating to a greater extent. For example, in the operation of e-marketplaces, trust between organizations could be an obstacle for the effective management of the supply chain. Trust has been linked not only to successful implementation of supply chain systems, but also to the ongoing operation of these systems.

What are the factors leading to a trusting behavior in a supplier–buyer relationship? One of the factors is information sharing because it lets all the firms in the supply chain know enough to be assured about other firms' capabilities and intentions. Another factor that leads to trust in the supply chain is the prediction process, which is one party's ability to forecast the other party's behavior. Repeated interaction enables one party to interpret projected outcomes better for another party. A third factor that leads to trust is the perception of mutually sharing both the risks and the benefits of the collaboration. The fourth factor involves determining the party's ability to meet its obligations. This factor is important as the two organizations will assess each other's propensity to perform on the mutually agreed contract. Trust, risk perception, and relationship commitment all ultimately affect whether an organization continues in a cooperative electronic relationship.

## GLOBAL SUPPLY CHAIN MANAGEMENT ISSUES

Managing a supply chain with international concerns adds many layers of complexity. The development of a supply chain strategy must include political concerns, currency risk, governmental concerns, production quality, and infrastructure issues. An excellent source of information on economic and political stability is the CIA's World Factbook at *cia.gov/cia/publications/factbook/index.html.*

## OUTSOURCING: MAKE-OR-BUY DECISIONS

Make-or-buy decisions can be extremely complex. Make decisions involve manufacturing or developing a product internally, whereas buy decisions involve externally built products and services. Choosing between producing a product or service in-house or purchasing it from an outside source involves looking at the core competencies of the organization, analyzing the costs of producing or acquiring, assessing the suitability of suppliers, examining the expertise within the organization, and examining the ability to inventory products. Activities that are outsourced are usually not part of the core competencies of the organization. Resources that are transferred to the outsourced company often include facilities, people, equipment, and finances. Because **outsourcing** transfers some of the organization's internal processes and resources to outside vendors, outsourcing decisions involve complex legal contracts, payment schedules, and service-level agreements.

General Motors (GM) has spent two years planning for changes in its supply chain network. CIO and Vice President Ralph Szygenda stated that major supply chain redesign was needed because the whole process had to better accomodate globalization (Bacheldor, 2005). GM is truly a global company and therefore puts a lot of effort into outsourcing contracts on a global level. Outsourcing management involves the forecasting and prediction of cost trends, labor availability, expertise, and the ability to meet schedules (Gibson, 2005).

## MANY-SUPPLIER STRATEGY

In an environment where there are many suppliers, organizations need a strategy to evaluate supplier products, services, and the approach they will use to decide which supplier is most appropriate. When supplies or products are commodities, organizations can play one supplier against another based on price. Long-term partnering relationships are usually not entered into for commodity products using a many-supplier strategy. However, when the product is not a commodity and there is clear differentiation, this strategy will depend on the uniqueness of the product and the proprietariness of the product or process used to manufacture the product. Having many suppliers tends to decrease risk and increase costs.

| VENDOR SELECTION | Another challenge in managing the supply chain is the selection of vendors. A decision needs to be made regarding from whom to buy goods and services. There are three stages to the vendor selection process: (1) vender evaluation, (2) vendor development, and (3) vendor negotiation. Vendor evaluation involves finding potential vendors and determining the likelihood of their being good suppliers in the future. Vendor development assumes you will be working with a particular vendor and includes training, engineering and production help, infrastructure development, and procedures for information transfer. Negotiations focus on vendor quality, delivery, payment, and cost. Vendor selection must consider factors such as strategic fit, vendor competence, delivery capability, production process capability, financial strength, facilities and location, product selection, vendor quality, and product pricing. |

| DIFFICULTY IN FORECASTING DEMAND | Because it is often difficult to forecast demand for products and services, it then becomes equally difficult to predict supply. Demand and supply mismatches are receiving increased visibility and coverage as businesses look for solutions. Demand and supply mismatches can lead to both short- and long-term loss in sales and market share, or to lower sales price due to markdowns of excess inventories, or prevent the firm from capitalizing on strong market demand due to the unavailability of products. Mismatches can negatively impact the productivity and utilization of organizational assets, such as equipment over- or underutilization. Companies can end up with costly inventory balances and carrying costs. |

| COST OF REVERSE LOGISTICS | **Reverse logistics** is the process of continuously taking back products and/or packaging materials to avoid waste. Reverse logistics affects many components of the logistics process as well as the supply chain because companies are responsible for products after they've been sold and after customers have disposed of them. Another aspect of reverse logistics is handling and disposition of damaged goods returned by the consumer. Reverse logistics programs can be costly for many organizations and can create difficulties when managing the supply chain life cycle. |

# 8.3 Supply Chain Opportunities

| MANAGING INFORMATION | A common way to solve supply chain problems, and especially to improve demand forecasts, is *sharing information* along the supply chain. Such information sharing is frequently referred to as the collaborative supply chain. |

Many companies are now looking at **master data management (MDM)** for one version of data. The purpose of master data management is to integrate all data in an organization at the highest level, both internally and externally. SAP, Oracle Corp., and IBM are all focusing on MDM by looking at customer data jobs and buying functionality, and offering vertically oriented repositories for MDM. Figure 8.3 shows the complexity in managing data. Data management at the high level is very complex. This figure illustrates the processes of managing data at the "master data" (or the metadata) level. To manage the intricacy of data, the MDM system manages the flow of data from all of the repositories, internal and external sources, and applications that use the data. Also shown in Figure 8.3 is a set of business rules that must be updated as well.

One of the most notable examples of information sharing is between large manufacturers and retailers. For example, Wal-Mart provides Procter & Gamble (P&G) access to daily sales information from every store for every item P&G makes for Wal-Mart. Then P&G is able to manage the *inventory replenishment* for Wal-Mart's

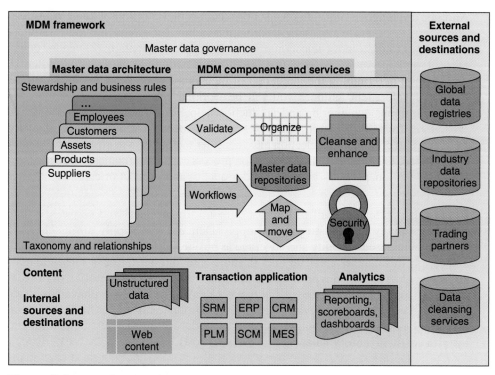

**Figure 8.3** MDM framework. (*Source:* Ferguson, 2005b.)

stores. By monitoring inventory levels, P&G knows when inventories fall below the reorder threshold for each product at any Wal-Mart store. These data trigger an immediate shipment.

Such information sharing between Wal-Mart and P&G is done automatically. It is part of a *vendor-managed inventory* (VMI) strategy, which is discussed later in this chapter. P&G has similar agreements with other major retailers. The benefit for P&G is accurate and timely demand information. Thus, P&G can plan production more accurately, minimizing the bullwhip effect. To do so, in 2000, P&G deployed a Web-based "Ultimate-Supply System," which replaced 4,000 different EDI links to suppliers and retailers in a more cost-effective way and is reaping huge cost savings in 2006. Information sharing can be facilitated by RFID.

**MANAGING E-BUSINESS**

The increase in e-commerce has resulted in new opportunities to improve the performance of the supply chain. Primary advantages of Internet utilization in SCM are speed, decreased costs, flexibility, and the potential to shorten the supply chain. Alternatively, using the Internet to deploy SCM processes can improve customer satisfaction, reduce costs, smooth production flows, and shorten cycle times. **E-business** systems can show significant improvements in SCM in the following areas:

- Cost performance from improved productivity and lower input pricing
- Enhanced customer service from improved quality of service
- Improved process capabilities from online business quality consistency
- Higher productivity and dependability from increased control of material flows along the supply chain

*Electronic marketplaces* (using business-to-business Internet-based technologies) allow organizations, often competitors in the supply chain, to identify upstream suppliers. Electronic marketplaces provide for more efficient resource allocation within the organization and between organizations, better information flow and dissemination on products and services in the supply chain, and the ability to better manage risk in the organization.

*Electronic ordering and funds transfer* (EOFT) is an important component in e-business transactions. Transactions between organizations often use electronic data interchange (EDI), which is a standardized data-transmittal format for electronic commerce transactions. The expanded version of EDI is called *advanced shipping notice* (ASN), which is a shipping notice delivered directly from the vendor to the purchaser.

The **s**upply chain integration hub allows for the electronic connection of trading partners with the organization's e-business systems. It transmits information while simultaneously populating the customer's systems on demand. One option is to change a linear supply chain into a hub. In linear supply chains, information is processed in a sequence, which slows down its flow.

## MANAGING LOGISTICS

Logistics is composed of materials acquisition, movement, and storage activities. Shipping, warehousing, and inventory management are activities that are all part of a logistics system. Inventory management and procurement will be discussed separately. Distribution of goods to and from factories, distribution centers, and warehouses, and to the retailer can represent as much as 25 percent of the cost of some products. Fixed management systems are those technology-based systems that manage all of the processes in an integrated way, simultaneously managing scheduling, shipping, and product movement.

E-logistics tools are important to minimize transportation and shipping costs in managing e-marketplace processes. *Drop shipping* is a term that connotes that the supplier will ship directly to the end-consumer, rather than to the seller, both saving time and lowering costs. This means the shipment of products must be direct from the supplier to the consumer. E-business component modules that address shipping often include drop shipping and special packaging, linked directly from the e-business shopping site to the vendor's enterprise resource management (ERP) system.

*Channel assembly* allows the aggregation of individual components and modules to the distributor for final assembly. In essence, distributors become manufacturers or aggregators of products. For example, Coca-cola has always used distributors to produce the final product using a formula.

## MANAGING INVENTORY

Undoubtedly, the most common solution used by companies to solve supply chain problems is *building inventories* as "insurance" against supply chain uncertainties. The main problem with this approach is that it is very difficult to correctly determine inventory levels for each product and part. If inventory levels are set too high, the cost of keeping the inventory will be very large. (And, as we have seen, high inventories at multiple points in the supply chain can result in the bullwhip effect.) If the inventory is too low, there is no insurance against high demand or slow delivery times, and revenues (and customers) may be lost. In either event, the total cost— including the cost of holding inventories, the cost of lost sales opportunities, and bad reputation—can be very high. Thus, companies make major attempts to optimize and control inventories.

*Collaborative fulfillment networks (CFNs)* require coordination among the multiple participating firms at different stages of the supply chain. Supply chain coordination is a challenge facing many organizations and collaborative fulfillment networks can help alleviate some of those concerns. Supply chain partners can benefit from the coordination approach to managing inventory replenishment, especially when order quantities vary from period to period. It has been found that if organizations use a coordinated inventory approach with a replenishment policy that does order smoothing to reduce order size variability, then overall system costs will be reduced (both inventory and transportation costs).

**Vendor managed inventory (VMI)** indicates that the vendor, usually a distributor, maintains the inventories for the manufacturer or buyer. This reduces warehousing costs for suppliers. These systems make automated decisions based on inventory levels.

*Lot size reduction* techniques reduce lot sizes by developing financially feasible shipments of less than full truckload lots. This may be possible by providing discounts based on total annual volume rather than the size of individual shipments. Electronic purchasing, with standing orders based on optimization methods, helps make this possible.

*Single-stage control of replenishment* refers to designating a party in the supply chain for monitoring and matching inventories based on consumer pull. Control of inventory replenishment may be in the hands of the retailer (such as Amazon.com), a distributor (such as Coca Cola Bottling), or a manufacturer that has a well-managed distribution system (such as Procter & Gamble).

### MANAGING E-PROCUREMENT

**E-procurement** is the use of Internet technologies to purchase or provide goods and services. E-procurement systems require the use of integrated database systems, WAN communication systems, Web-based systems, inventory systems, and interaction with accounting systems.

Cost efficiencies in the purchasing process have been a major catalyst for the adoption of e-procurement. E-procurement reduces purchase prices through greater transparency of market pricing and lower search costs. E-procurement allows organizations that purchase similar products to form a cooperative in the supply chain to get significantly lower pricing through volume discounts. Organizations can use e-procurement systems to standardize purchasing processes within the organization, thereby improving internal employee satisfaction. Procurement auctions allow firms that participate in the supply chain to have access to raw materials at very reduced costs. In e-procurement, requesters directly search for and select products in electronic catalogs. Part of this strategy is a shift from managing transactions to managing suppliers.

### MANAGING COLLABORATION

Proper SCM and inventory management require coordination of all the different activities and links in the supply chain. Successful coordination enables goods to move smoothly and on time from suppliers to manufacturers to distributors to customers to keep inventories low and costs down. Collaboration of supply chain partners is needed since companies depend on each other, but do not always work together toward the same goal. Both suppliers and buyers must participate together in the design or redesign of the supply chain to achieve their shared goals. As part of the collaboration effort, business partners must *trust* each other and each other's information systems.

To help control the uncertainties associated with supply chain problems, it is necessary to identify and understand their causes, determine how uncertainties in some activities will affect other activities up and down the supply chain, and then formulate specific ways to minimize the uncertainties. An effective and efficient communication environment among all business partners is also needed (see Chapter 9). A rapid flow of information along a supply chain tends to improve efficiency. For example, computerized point-of-sale (POS) information can be transmitted in real time to distribution centers, suppliers, and shippers. Having real-time information enables firms to achieve optimal inventory levels. Another example of supply chain collaboration that requires system integration is product-development systems. These allow suppliers to dial into a client's intranet, pull product specifications, and view illustrations and videos of a manufacturing process.

<table>
<tr><td>

**MANAGING OTHER IT-ASSISTED SOLUTIONS**

</td><td>

Large companies employ multiple methods to achieve supply chain superiority. Wal-Mart, for example, is well-known for its ability to collaborate with companies across its supply chain. It is able to combine information from its suppliers with demand and inventory data from its stores to minimize operating costs and reduce prices. Nestlé USA even created a vice-president-level position exclusively to manage business with Wal-Mart. Several other mechanisms, such as supply chain teams and virtual factories, heavily utilize IT to generate information, share it among the suppliers, and update it as needed.

</td></tr>
</table>

**Supply Chain Teams.** The change from the linear supply chain to a hub model points to the need to create **supply chain teams.** A supply chain team is a group of tightly coordinated employees who work together to serve the customer. Each task is done by the member of the team who is best positioned, trained, and capable of doing that specific task, regardless of which company the member works for. For example, in a supply chain team, the team member who deals with the delivery will handle a delivery problem, even if he or she works for the delivery company rather than for the retailer whose product is being delivered. This way, redundancies will be minimized. The delivery company will deal with the customer about a delivery problem, rather than passing the problem along to the retailer, who would end up having to contact the delivery company. Thus, the retailer will not have to spend valuable resources following up on the delivery.

**Virtual Factories.** A **virtual factory** is a collaborative enterprise application that provides a computerized model of a factory. In the virtual factory, proposed designs can be tested, relationships with suppliers can be simulated, and manufacturing processes and how they are connected can be modeled. If potential problems in these areas are spotted in the digital model of the factory, simulated solutions can be worked out in the virtual model before they are implemented in the real-world factory. Usually, the virtual factory application would connect suppliers to the B2B system and clearly present the needed demand to suppliers. This "demand visibility" can help the company focus on two important key performance indicators, lead times and transaction cost. Uniting the entire supply chain and creating visibility between suppliers and buyers can help the companies forecast and plan demand more effectively. Virtual factories also enable all companies involved to work together collaboratively using common tools, and they provide greater flexibility and responsiveness by getting information and goods flowing much more quickly.

**Wireless Solutions.** In the last few years we have seen an increased number of wireless solutions to supply chain problems. In addition to RFID, one can use mobile devices, as illustrated in *IT at Work 8.1.*

<table>
<tr><td>

**ETHICAL ISSUES RELATED TO SUPPLY CHAIN SOLUTIONS**

</td><td>

Conducting an SCM project may result in the need to lay off, retrain, or transfer employees. Should management notify the employees in advance regarding such possibilities? And what about older employees who may have been loyal employees? Other ethical issues may involve sharing of personal information, which may

</td></tr>
</table>

# *IT* at Work 8.1

## Peacocks Retails Uses Wireless to Smooth Its Supply Chain

POM    GLOBAL

Peacocks Retails of Wales operates about 250 retail stores, selling clothes and home furniture in Wales and the south of England. The company had a problem in its internal supply chain: Its paper-based system of managing the distribution of products was prone to problems such as incorrectly completed pick-lists, wrongly picked items, transcription errors, delays in generating and receiving data, and much more. These interfered with the company's growth strategy and reduced its profit.

In 1997, Peacocks Retails consolidated its six warehouses to a single distribution center (100,000 square feet). Stores were ordering more than 4,000 SKUs (stock-keeping units) each day. These needed to be picked and shipped to stores effectively and efficiently. Using one warehouse instead of six solved some problems, but the paper-based communication system was as bad as before. With a paper-based pick system, it is easy to run out of product in a specific location. Then the picker has to either wait for more product to arrive or return to the location. There is always a built-in delay, and the company has no idea about potential stock problems until they happen.

In 1998, Peacocks Retails started to replace the paper-based system with a wireless system (from Symbol.com). Specifically, the fully automated distribution center is equipped with a hands-free and real-time putaway and picking system. It is based on a combination of 28 wearable computers and 6 truck-mounted terminals supported by wireless LAN.

The wireless system provides real-time control. Whether an item is moved by hand or by truck, Peacocks knows precisely where it is. If at any point in the process someone is at the wrong location, handling the wrong product, or trying to send it to the wrong place, the system simply sends out an alert and prevents the action. When Peacocks receives a delivery from a manufacturer, the consignment is checked, and the individual cartons from each delivery are given an identifying barcode label and scanned to report receipt. In this way, every item can be tracked through the distribution center from the minute it arrives. Immediately, the system will know if there is a requirement at a pick location. Once individual cartons are labeled, Peacocks uses an automated conveyor system to send cartons to the desired location, as directed by the wireless warehouse management system.

Each member of the picking team wears a wrist-mounted terminal that receives picking instructions via the wireless LAN from Peacocks' host system. As empty trolleys arrive in the pick area, a picker scans its barcode, and the terminal's LCD screen tells the picker which aisle to go to, which location to pick from, and which items to pick. When a picker arrives at the pick face, she first scans the barcode mounted at the end of the aisle. This verifies that she is in the correct aisle. She then scans another barcode at the product location to verify she is at the correct place. Finally, she scans each item as it is picked into the trolley. Once each pick is complete, the conveyor system takes each trolley to the dispatch area to be loaded into crates for delivery to a Peacocks store.

Because data are sent to the host in real time, as the picking operation proceeds, the system knows when pick "face stocks" are approaching the replenishment level set by Peacocks. Once this happens, the system sends an alert to a truck-mounted terminal in the pallet store. As with the wrist-mounted terminals, an LCD screen on the truck terminal directs the driver to a precise location in the pallet racking. On arrival at the location, the driver uses a handheld scanner to scan the location barcode. This confirms that he is at the right location and selecting the right product.

Some other benefits: The hands-free arrangement saves time; it is not necessary to keep putting down the terminals when hands are needed. Also, wearable computers are not dropped, so they are not damaged. The system is user-friendly, so training is minimal. Another benefit is the positive impact on team morale. Everyone likes the wearables because they are comfortable to wear and easy to use, making the job easier and leading to efficiency improvements.

*Source:* Compiled from Peacocks Case Study (2004, accessed May 2004) and *gmb.org.uk* (2005).

*For Further Exploration:* Identify all segments of the supply chain that are improved by the system and describe the improvement. Also, investigate how RFID may impact this system.

---

be required for a collaborative organizational culture, but which some employees may resist. Finally, individuals may have to share computer programs that they designed for their personal use on the job. Such programs may be considered the intellectual property of the individuals. (Should the employees be compensated for the programs' use by others?) To provide the solutions discussed in this section, IT utilizes a number of software packages. These are described in the next two sections.

# 8.4 Business Value of Enterprise Systems

The flows of goods, services, information, and financial resources are usually designed to effectively transform raw items to finished products and services, and to do so *efficiently*. The goals of SCM are to reduce uncertainty and risks along the supply chain, thereby decreasing inventory levels and cycle time, and improving business processes and customer service. All of these benefits contribute to increased profitability and competitiveness, as demonstrated in the opening case. The benefits of SCM have long been recognized both in business and in the military. To enjoy these benefits, it is necessary to overcome the limitations and problems described in Section 8.2.

Coca-Cola Enterprises (CCE) will save millions in distribution costs by implementing new technologies to manage the supply chain network. SAP-based direct-store-delivery systems allow CCE to react to rivals' sales and promotions as soon as delivery representatives send competitive data back from the retail stores.

Sears, Roebuck and Co. and Kmart Holding Company have to integrate 40 different supply chain systems between the two organizations operating 3,500 stores. There will be a large IT integration effort needed to manage supply chain operations. Sears Holding, the new company, must determine how to merge two different businesses and consolidate supply chain operations (Croom, 2005).

Oracle is rolling out new enterprise applications to enable manufacturers to have better control over their supply chain, especially partners and suppliers. The Oracle business suite upgrade includes RFID support for SCM processes.

Corning Inc., a glass manufacturer headquartered in upstate New York, is looking for solutions to enable the optimization of its global supply chain network. The supply chain technology strategy group and the process owners in the organization conducted a wide-ranging analysis of each business unit. Because of planned improvements in the supply chain process, Corning is able to integrate the relevant activities of manufacturers, suppliers, customer service organizations, sales organizations, and technology innovators.

A PVC (polyvinyl chloride) manufacturer had a fragmented management strategy for its supply chain due primarily to multiple acquisitions. With fragmented spare capacity around North America, a falling stock price, and a need to rationalize its supply chain data acquisition, strategic supply chain planning was conducted. The areas that were examined included whether to open or close plants and distribution centers, how to modify capacity, whether to manufacture in-house or outside, and the degree to which outsourcing was feasible.

**INTEGRATION**

Twentieth-century computer technology was *functionally* oriented. Functional systems may not let different departments communicate with each other in the same language. Worse yet, crucial sales, inventory, and production data often have to be painstakingly entered manually into separate computer systems every time a person who is not a member of a specific department needs ad-hoc information related to the specific department. In many cases, employees using functionally oriented technology simply do not get the information they need, or they get it too late (e.g., see Minicase 1). Thus, managing the twenty-first-century enterprise cannot be done effectively with such technology.

**Internal versus External Integration.** There are two basic types of systems integration—internal and external. *Internal integration* refers to integration within a company between (or among) applications, and/or between applications and databases. For example, an organization may integrate inventory control with an ordering system, or a CRM suite with the database of customers. Large companies that have hundreds of applications may find it extremely difficult to integrate the newer Web-based applications with the older legacy systems.

*External integration* refers to integration of applications and/or databases among business partners—for example, the suppliers' catalogs with the buyers' e-procurement system. Another example of external supply chain integration is product-development systems that allow suppliers to dial into a client's intranet, pull product specifications, and view illustrations and videos of a manufacturing process. External integration is especially needed for B2B and for partner relationship management (PRM) systems, as will be discussed in Chapter 9. For more on integration, see Jinyoul et al. (2003) and Siau and Tian (2004).

# 8.5 Enterprise Resource Planning Systems

One of the most successful tools for managing supply chains, especially internal ones, is enterprise resource planning (ERP).

**WHAT IS ERP?**

With the advance of enterprisewide client/server computing comes a new challenge: how to control all major business processes in *real time* with a single software architecture. The most common *integrated software* solution of this kind is known as **enterprise resource planning (ERP)** or just *enterprise systems*. This software integrates the planning, management, and use of all resources in the entire enterprise. It is comprised of *sets of applications* that automate routine back-end operations (such as financial, inventory management, and scheduling) to help enterprises handle jobs such as order fulfillment. For example, there is a module for cost control, for accounts payable and receivable, and for fixed assets and treasury management. ERP promises benefits ranging from increased efficiency to improved quality, productivity, and profitability. (See Ragowsky and Somers, 2002, for details.)

ERP's major objective is to *integrate all departments and functional information flows across a company* onto a single computer system that can serve all of the enterprise's needs. For example, improved order entry allows immediate access to inventory, product data, customer credit history, and prior order information. Such availability of information raises productivity and increases customer satisfaction (Gattiker and Goodhue, 2004). ERP systems are in use in thousands of large and medium companies worldwide, and some ERP systems are producing dramatic results (see *erp.ittoolbox.com*). ERP integrates all routine transactions within a company, including internal suppliers and customers. Later it was expanded, in what is known as *extended ERP software,* to incorporate external suppliers and customers.

*Example: Rolls-Royce.* The implementation of ERP enables Rolls-Royce not only to lower its IT costs but also to deliver to the customer on time. Timely delivery improves customer satisfaction and confidence in the company and, it is hoped, will lead to an increase of orders in the future (Yusuf et al., 2004).

*Example: Comark Corp.* Using ERP, Comark Corp (*comarkcorp.com*) reduced inventories and eliminated voluminous reports. It also is used to track information more accurately.

*Example: Consolidation Applications via ERP.* Exxon Mobil consolidated 300 different information systems by implementing SAP R/3 (see below) in its U.S. petrochemical operations alone.

For businesses that want to use ERP, one option is to self-develop an integrated system, either by linking together existing functional packages or by programming a new, custom-built system. Another option, which is often quicker and/or less expensive, is to use commercially available integrated ERP software (see Minicase 1). The leading ERP software is **SAP R/3** (from SAP AG Corp.). This highly integrated software package contains more than 115 business activities modules. Oracle, Computer Associates, and PeopleSoft also make similar products. All of these products include Web modules.

Yet another way for a business to implement ERP is to lease ERP systems from *application service providers* (ASPs). A major advantage of the leasing approach is that even a small company can enjoy ERP: A small company can lease only relevant modules, rather than buy an entire ERP package. Some companies, such as Starbucks, have chosen a *best-of-breed* approach—building their own customized ERP with ready-made components leased or purchased from several vendors.

Because application service providers (ASPs) can provide ERP leasing and/or development services at a much lower cost, there is a growing use of ERP in midsized companies. ERP investments are much more affordable for smaller enterprises today than they were 10 years ago. Smaller companies can even rent ERP solutions from ASPs. ERP application modules are shown in Figure 8.4.

ERP also can be used to manage resources, including employees. MySAP ERP Human Capital Management is one example of an ERP module that optimizes HR activities by aligning employees' skills, activities, and incentives with business objectives and strategies. The module provides tools for managing, measuring, and rewarding individual contributions. Human capital management modules are fully integrated with payroll functions, regulatory requirements for hiring, employee development, and best practices across the world.

Corporate services is another module within an ERP system that gives functionality for travel management; managing real estate and facilities; environment, health, and safety concerns; and an incentive and commission management. In an ERP system, financial management and accounting are managed and integrated into the supply chain and internal control processes. Financial modules provide transaction accounting, management of internal controls, and financial analysis.

An ERP system is composed of modules for managing all the routine activities performed by a business. For example, an ERP suite for a manufacturing company would include modules that cover activities such as production scheduling, inventory management, entering sales orders, coordinating shipping, and providing after-sales

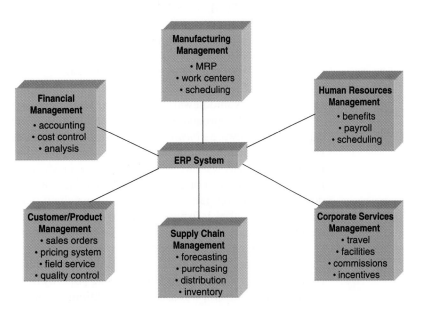

**Figure 8.4** ERP application modules. (*Source:* Prepared by D. Amoroso.)

customer service. The modules in an ERP suite are accessed through a single interface. Lately, however, there has been a trend to have the ERP functionally oriented. For example, SAP offers the following products: mySAP financial, ERP human capital management, ERP operations, and ERP service.

**Integration of ERP Software.** Use of ERP and SCM software is not necessarily an either–or decision. Rather, the two can be combined and used together. To illustrate how ERP and SCM may work together, consider the task of order processing. There is a fundamental difference between SCM and ERP in order processing: The ERP approach is, "How can I best take or fulfill your order?" In contrast, the question that SCM software asks is, "Should I take your order?" The answer might be "no" if taking the order would lose money for the company or interfere with production. Thus, SCM software focuses on planning, optimization, and decision making in segments of the supply chain.

Thus, the *analytical* SCM information systems have emerged as a *complement* to ERP systems, to provide intelligent decision support or business intelligence (Chapters 11 and 12) capabilities. An SCM system is designed to overlay existing systems and to pull data from every step of the supply chain. It is therefore able to provide a clear, organizational-level picture of where the enterprise is heading.

*Example: How IBM Is Using SCM.* An example of a successful SCM effort is IBM's restructuring of its *global supply chain.* The goal of the restructuring was to achieve quick responsiveness to customers and to do it with minimal inventory. To support this effort, IBM developed a supply chain analysis tool, called the Asset Management Tool (AMT), for use by a number of IBM business units and their channel partners. IBM is using AMT to analyze and improve such issues as inventory budgets and turnover, customer-service targets, and new-product introductions. AMT integrates graphical process modeling, analytical performance optimization, simulation, activity-based costing, and enterprise database connectivity into a system that allows quantitative analysis of interenterprise supply chains. The system was also a prerequisite to a major e-procurement initiative at IBM.

Creating a plan from an SCM system allows companies to quickly assess the impact of their actions on the entire supply chain, including customer demand. But this can be done only if ERP software is added. Therefore, it makes sense to integrate ERP and SCM.

How is integration of ERP and SCM done? One approach is to work with different software products from different vendors. For example, a business might use SAP as an ERP and add to it Manugistics' manufacturing-oriented SCM software, as shown in the Warner-Lambert case (*IT at Work 8. 2*). Such an approach requires fitting together different software, which may be a complex task unless special connectors provided by middleware vendors exist. (See also Kovács and Paganelli, 2003.)

The second approach is for ERP vendors to add decision support and analysis capabilities, known as *business intelligence,* to their major product. Business intelligence (as defined in Chapter 11) refers to analysis performed by DSS, ESS, data mining, and intelligent systems. Using a combined product from a single vendor solves the integration problem. For example, Gayialis and Tatsiopoulos (2004) describe how a downstream oil company combined a supply chain management (SCM) application with a geographical information system (GIS), integrated with ERP software. The result was an innovative decision support system for routing and scheduling purposes.

However, most ERP vendors offer a combined product for another reason: It is cheaper for the customers. The added business intelligence functionalities, which create the *second-generation ERP,* include not only decision support, but also CRM, e-commerce, and data warehousing and mining. Some systems include a *knowledge*

# IT at Work 8.2

## How Warner-Lambert Applies an Integrated Supply Chain

Warner-Lambert is a major U.S. pharmaceutical company that is now owned by Pfizer (*pfizer.com*). One of its major products is Listerine antiseptic mouthwash. The materials for making Listerine come mainly from eucalyptus trees in Australia and are shipped to the Warner-Lambert (WL) manufacturing plant in New Jersey. The major problem there is to *forecast* the *overall demand* to determine how much Listerine to produce. Then one can figure how much raw materials are needed and when. A wrong forecast will result either in high inventories of raw materials and/or of finished products, or in shortages. Inventories are expensive to keep; shortages may result in loss of business (to competitors).

WL forecasts demand with the help of Manugistics Inc.'s Demand Planning Information System (an SCM product). Used with other software in Manugistics' Supply Chain Planning suite, the system analyzes manufacturing, distribution, and sales data against expected demand and business cli-

mate information. Its goal is to help WL decide how much Listerine (and other products) to make and how much of each raw ingredient is needed, and when. For example, the model can anticipate the impact of seasonal promotion or a production line being down.

WL's supply chain excellence stems from the Collaborative Planning, Forecasting, and Replenishment (CPFR) program. This is a retailing industry project for which piloting was done at WL.

Overall, WL can determine the right quantity of raw materials to buy from its suppliers with its demand planning system. The system analyzes manufacturing, distribution, and sales data against expected demand and business climate information to help WL decide how much product to make and distribute. Because WL can smooth seasonality forecasts, it has dramatically cut costs in the manufacturing and raw materials inventory areas.

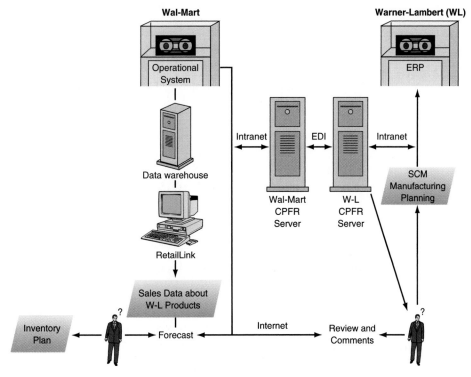

With its supply chain systems and ERP modules, WL increased its products' shelf-fill rate—the extent to which a store's shelves are fully stocked—from 87 percent to 98 percent, earning the company about $8 million a year in additional sales. This was the equivalent of a new product launch, but for much less investment. WL is now using the Internet to expand the CPFR program to all its major suppliers and retail partners.

*Sources:* Compiled from *Wikipedia* (2006b); *Pfizer.com* (2006); Institute of Business Forecasting (2004); and Bresnahan (1998).

*For Further Exploration:* Why would Listerine have been a target for the pilot CPFR collaboration? For what industries, besides retailing, would such collaboration be beneficial?

# IT at Work 8.3

## Colgate-Palmolive Uses ERP to Smooth Its Supply Chain

Colgate-Palmolive is the world leader in oral-care products (toothpaste, toothbrushes, and mouthwashes) and a major supplier of personal-care products (baby care, deodorants, shampoos, and soaps). In addition, the company's Hill's Health Science Diet is a leading pet-food brand worldwide. International sales account for about 70 percent of Colgate's total revenues.

To stay competitive, Colgate continuously seeks to streamline its supply chain, through which thousands of suppliers and customers interact with the company. At the same time, Colgate faces the challenges of accelerating new-product development, which has been a factor in driving faster sales growth and improved market share. Also, Colgate is devising ways to offer consumers a greater choice of better products at a lower cost to the company. To better manage the complexities of its manufacturing and the supply chains, Colgate embarked on an ERP implementation. The new system allows the company to access more timely and accurate data and reduce costs. The structure of the ERP is pictured below.

In 2005, Colgate started to see return on investment with the successful implementation of the Advanced Planning and Optimization module, a SAP R/3 module that includes demand and production planning for the integration of raw materials in regional procurement decisions. More than 100 business processes were standardized worldwide to enable SAP process definitions to be widely accepted.

An important factor for Colgate was whether it could use the ERP software across the entire spectrum of the business. Colgate needed to coordinate globally and act locally. Colgate's U.S. division installed SAP R/3 for this purpose. The new initiative for 2007 was the full integration of the business warehouse, supply chain, and CRM systems into the core functionality of SAP R/3 functions.

*Sources:* Compiled from Sullivan (2005), and Kalakota and Robinson (2001).

*For Further Exploration:* What is the role of the ERP for Colgate-Palmolive? Who are the major beneficiaries of the new system? How is the SCM being improved?

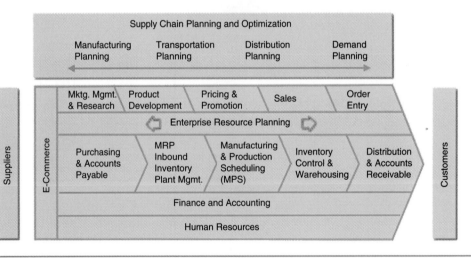

Colgate-Palmolive ERP implementation. (*Source:* R. Kalakota and M. Robinson, *E-Business 2.0*, Boston, MA, Addison Wesley, 2001.)

*management* component as well. In 2003, vendors started to add PLM in an attempt to optimize the supply chain. An example of an ERP application that includes an SCM module is provided in *IT at Work 8.3*.

**Capabilities of ERP.** ERP projects are focused on specific business process areas, such as:

- Combining logistics across business units with neighboring facilities
- Combining distribution centers and *less than truckloads* (LTLs) in order to fill trucks, reduce pickup/delivery lanes, and eliminate unneeded facilities
- Dynamically sourcing products from different manufacturing and distribution facilities based on inventory and capacity

# *IT* at Work 8.4

## *Integrating EC and ERP at Cybex*

POM    GLOBAL

Cybex International (*cybexintl.com*), a global maker of fitness machines, was unable to meet the demand for its popular fitness machines, which increased dramatically in the late 1990s. To maintain its market share, the company had to work with rush orders from its nearly 1,000 suppliers. The cost of responding to rush orders was extremely high. This problem was a result of a poor demand forecast for the machine's components. The demand forecast was produced using three different legacy systems that Cybex had inherited from merger partners.

After examining existing vendors' supply chain software, Cybex decided to install an ERP system (from PeopleSoft Inc.) for its supply chain planning and manufacturing applications. In conjunction with the software installation, the company analyzed and redesigned some of its business processes. It also reduced the number of suppliers from 1,000 to 550.

In the new system, customers' orders are accepted at the corporate Web site. Each order is electronically forwarded to one of the company's two specialized manufacturing plants. The ERP uses its *planning module* to calculate which parts are needed for each model. Then, the ERP's *product configurator* constructs, in just a few seconds, a component list and a bill-of-materials needed for each order.

The ERP system helps with other processes as well. For example, Cybex can e-mail to a vendor a detailed purchase order with engineering changes clearly outlined. These changes are visible to everyone; if one engineer is not at work, his or her knowledge remains in the system and is easy to find. Furthermore, dealers now know that they will get deliveries in less than two weeks. They can also track the status of each

order (see *peopletalkonline.com*, July–September 2003), which allows Cybex to provide superb customer care.

The system also helps Cybex to better manage its 550 suppliers. For example, the planning engine looks at price variations across product lines, detecting opportunities to negotiate price reductions by showing suppliers that their competitors offer the same products at lower prices. Also, by giving suppliers projected long- and short-term production schedules, Cybex helps ensure that all parts and materials are available when needed. This also reduces the inventory level at Cybex. Furthermore, suppliers that cannot meet the required dates are replaced after quarterly reviews.

Despite intense industry price-cutting in 2002, Cybex remained profitable, mainly due to its improved supply chain. Some of the most impressive results were the following: Cybex cut its bill-of-material count from thousands to hundreds; reduced the number of vendors from 1,000 to 550; cut paperwork by two-thirds; and reduced build-to-order time from four to two weeks.

Implementing the system cost money, of course. In addition to the cost of the software, the technology staff increased from three to 12. Yet the company feels that the investment was worthwhile, especially because it provided for much greater harmony between Cybex and its customers and suppliers.

*Sources:* Compiled from Extreme Networks (2005), Sullivan et al. (2002), and from press releases at *cybex.com*.

*For Further Exploration:* What are the relationships between the EC applications and ERP? What are the critical success factors for implementation?

---

- Shared services for manufacturing (like having one's own internal contract manufacturer)
- Global order management, showing a single face to global customers across business lines
- Consolidating country-based sales, marketing, and distribution operations in geographic areas, such as Europe, that have high density and falling barriers to trade
- Coordinating procurement of key commodities across business units and geographies
- Creating supplier portals that consolidate the needs of each business unit and provide a way of deepening the partnership with the supplier

Projects can be run in parallel, potentially generating benefits more quickly. In addition, fewer people are affected by each project, reducing retraining issues. Also, the ERP work is often to turn on or reconfigure functionality already owned, reducing the pressure to upgrade ERP and lowering IT costs. Note that using this new generation of ERP requires business units to give up total control and cooperate with their peers.

In addition to integrating ERP with SCM systems, ERP can be integrated with other enterprise systems, most notably with e-commerce. *IT at Work 8.4* describes the integration of ERP and EC at Cybex International.

**ERP SYSTEM SELECTION**

**The Problem.** ERP is such a complex, fully reaching technology that it is daunting to executives. How can they assess the needs of numerous people and processes within their organization? These technologies that link together various processes in the organization are also very expensive. How does an executive understand the differences between ERP vendors?

**The Solution.** It is important to understand how much of the ERP solution is required in the timeframe for rolling out the new technology. What is the specific business value for each module in the ERP system? Determine business priorities, identifying high-priority business requirements within a process and across the organization. What ERP components will be implemented over what time period? We will talk about the need for process matching later in this chapter.

Organizations need to understand that the objective of ERP selection is the support of the business goals and strategies of the enterprise. This also includes the standardization of business processes across the organization, while at the same time cutting costs in the area of transaction processing.

**ERP AND PROCESSES**

ERP systems force organizations to adopt standardized processes. Many organizations operating in the same industry or within the same supply chain have similar processes. Why is that?

**The Problem.** After the ERP system is selected, ERP system processes need to be mapped against organizational processes. This is difficult because organizations that have unique processes will want to retain those processes after the ERP development effort. ERP vendors, who have standardized processes based on best practices, will try to convince organizational leaders to use their processes. The organization will resist if it does not want to have exactly the same processes as its competitors. The more ERP customization required, the more expensive the implementation and the longer it will take. In future upgrades, the organization will have to do a great deal more customization than if it had adopted the ERP system standard processes.

**The Solution.** Organizations should conduct a business process management effort *before* selecting an ERP vendor. Business process management (BPM) will be discussed in more depth in Section 8.6. Organizations should have detailed process maps reflecting what is called the "as-is" business system. Then when they are in the selection process, they can search for the vendor most closely aligned with the way they want to do business, as reflected in their business processes. Several steps can be taken to overcome the challenges of business process mismatch:

1. Understand the business strategy related to each process in the organization.
2. Understand the current business capability of each process and the effectiveness of the process.
3. Understand what automated solutions are currently implemented.

**ERP DEVELOPMENT AND IMPLEMENTATION**

**The Problem.** ERP packages are difficult to install because they are so large in scope. The top reasons why ERP installations fail are: (1) unrealistic expectations, (2) inability to map business processes, (3) inaccurate data, and (4) failure to factor in hidden costs. The implementation of an ERP system can take up to 24 months depending on the number of modules that are implemented. Project management activities are extremely complex with multiple layers of resource concerns. Change management processes are extremely important in ERP systems development and implementation, yet this is often overlooked by many organizations. Postimplementation issues that are of concern include the quality of training manuals, hands-on training provided, help-desk and user navigation, and productivity using the new system.

**The Solution.** Two factors were found to predict implementation success of ERP systems: (1) the consultant–client relationship, with a shared understanding of what needs to get done, and (2) a problem-solving approach to get ERP modules implemented. There are a number of things that must be done when implementing an ERP program:

1. Create a steering group with a strong executive champion.
2. Get help from a consulting team.
3. Set expectations and manage the project effectively.
4. Manage the change in the organization.
5. Enable the infrastructure to support the change.
6. Communicate to all interested parties.

Top management must be engaged in the ERP project for it to be successful. Brown and Vessey (2003) found that given the complexity of enterprise system projects, the organization's project managers and leaders need to buy into a satisficing mindset, where 80 percent of the solutions, in terms of functionality, are deemed good enough.

In order to avoid failures and ensure success, it is necessary for the partners involved in ERP implementation (the software vendor, the management consultant, the implementing company, and the support-service vendors) to hold open and honest dialogue at the start of each project. Included in this initial dialogue should be consideration of the following factors: the company's expectations; the ERP product capabilities and limitations; the level of change the company has to go through to make the system fit; the level of commitment within the organization to see the project through to completion; the risks presented by politics within the organization, and (if applicable) the capabilities, responsibilities, and role of the implementing IT consultants. In addition, the organization and the IT consultants should nail down the critical success factors (CSFs) of the implementation. Failures can also be minimized if appropriate cost-benefit and cost justification is done in advance.

**OPEN SOURCE ERP5**

ERP5 combines an object-oriented database and innovative open-source ERP components targeted at small and medium-sized companies. Open-source ERP has five basic modules: (1) planning, (2) CRM, (3) content management, (4) e-business, and (5) groupware. ERP5 offers common ERP functions like production planning and control, materials management, finances, accounting, billing, budgeting, human resources, and other business process functions (Smets-Solanes, 2003). ERP5 tracks customer relations and provides a reporting engine to classify customers into categories. ERP5 can act as a content management system, storing, indexing, and classifying all documents. ERP5 implements B2C and B2B systems. ERP5 integrates with groupware products, including e-mail, directories, shared workspaces, IP conferencing, and instant messaging.

**SWITCHING ERP SYSTEMS**

Is it worth it for an organization to switch ERP systems? The original ERP system may have originally cost as much as $3,000 per user for organizations that have 4,000 users or more. Switching costs could be millions of dollars, depending on the size of the company and scope of the implementation. Add to the project costs consultant fees, migration of data, project team time, annual ERP operating costs, and software training costs—on top of the annual software maintenance and ERP operating costs. It is not cheap, despite the potential benefits of changing ERP systems. This means it is crucial to plan correctly for the implementation of the ERP system from the beginning to avoid costly switching costs.

## VALUE FROM ERP SYSTEMS

There are a number of key issues for ensuring that an organization receives business value from an ERP that must be examined in advance of undertaking an ERP implementation project. First, you have to look at different ERP vendors and select the vendor that meets the company needs most effectively. Second, organizations need process redesign to optimize their business processes prior to, or in conjunction with, the ERP system development processes. Business process management will be discussed in the next section; however it deals with the reengineering of processes and the realignment of processes to improve process efficiencies and effectiveness (King, 2005).

The business case for funding an ERP project should not be made solely on cost savings, but rather predominantly on the business benefits to be gained from added functionality. Infrastructure costs can be high given the need for data integration across the organization. Customizations that must be carried over from one version of ERP software to another can create large technology headaches and increase downstream implementation costs (Beatty, 2006).

# 8.6 Business Process Management

## WHAT IS BUSINESS PROCESS MANAGEMENT?

**Business process management (BPM)** refers to activities performed by businesses to optimize and adapt their processes. A *business process* is a collection of related activities that produce something of value to the organization, its stakeholders, or its customers. A process has both inputs and outputs, with activities and tasks that can be measured. A process cuts across functional areas of the enterprise (see Figure 8.5). A business process, such as product development, cuts across departments of the business including marketing, development, and production. (See Chapter 2 for more details regarding process management.)

A process can be broken down into lower-level processes, has goals, and needs feedback. A *strategic value stream* has high-level processes that contribute to value-added products and/or services (see Figure 8.6). Strategic value-stream processes enhance the core competencies of the organization.

## THE NEED TO REENGINEER BUSINESS PROCESSES

Reengineering business processes has been a constant activity in businesses over the past 20 years. Organizations have implemented quality programs, and efficiency measures for cutting labor, reducing inventories, and managing logistics. With the increase in collaboration due to the Internet-enabled supply chain, organizations need to improve their internal business processes, and match their processes with those of other organizations that would link to them in the supply chain.

**Figure 8.5** Processes cut across functional areas. (*Source: Prepared by D. Amoroso.*)

Product development: from requirements to product

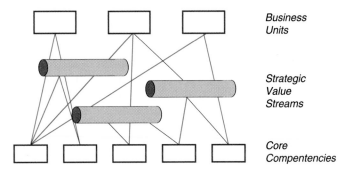

**Figure 8.6** Strategic value streams. (*Source:* Prepared by D. Amoroso.)

A strategic value stream of high-level processes that add value to products and/or services.

A number of process improvement initiatives have emerged as crucial to improving the supply chain, including space management, inventory management, dynamic forecasting, quick manufacturing response, vendor-managed inventories, efficient consumer response, and product life cycle management. Product life cycle management will be discussed later in this chapter.

**WHY USE BPM?**

The Business Project Management Institute (IDS Scheer AG, 2005) has reported that an effective BPM strategy can:

- Reduce product design time by 50 percent.
- Result in faster time-to-market of competitive products.
- Reduce order fulfillment time by 80 percent.
- Improve customer satisfaction with the ordering process.
- Help organizations achieve efficiency gains of 60 percent in call centers.

**THE DIFFERENCE IN PROCESS THINKING**

Process thinking is a different mental paradigm because it focuses only on activities, not on the people who accomplish those activities. Process thinking is independent of people and departments and is defined in context by higher-level processes in the organization. A *function* is considered a group or cluster of processes at the high level of the organization (not to be confused with functional area); an *activity* is considered to be a lower-level process that is more procedure oriented; whereas a *task* is the lowest-level activity in the organization, usually sequential and part of a series of steps for getting something done. Processes at any level (functions, processes, activities, or tasks) all are named with active verbs, such as "manage finances" at the high level and "pay employees" at the lower level.

When thinking in terms of processes, here is a set of "don'ts" to consider:

- Don't think in terms of people.
- Don't think sequentially at the high level.
- Don't forget to interconnect the processes.
- Don't name processes the same as departments.
- Don't forget that all processes have value-added.
- Don't forget to measure the input and output of all processes.
- Don't think physically when modeling process (it's *what* you do, not *how* you do it).

Business **process modeling** includes techniques and activities used as part of the larger business process management discipline. Business process modeling is an activity similar to drafting a blueprint for a house. The purpose of modeling business processes is to create a blueprint of how the company works, much like the blueprint created by architects prior to building a house. No house can have any type of reasonable structure without having extensive time put into building a set of agreed-upon blueprints. Likewise the set of business process models are blueprints for how the system will work after it is built: by developing new processes, redesigning existing processes, or eliminating processes and redirecting data flows.

A process model is similar to an income statement in accounting in that it looks at the entire organization over a long period of time (e.g., a year). It is not a "snapshot" of specific time periods. Therefore time is not a fundamental driver in creating business process models. To create a process model for a set of high-level processes, one must address the question, "what do we do here in this organization?" We might find that we get a very similar set of high-level processes for many organizations, regardless of their size or industry. For example, a set of processes for a local pet store at the high level might be:

- Sell products to customers.
- Manage finances.
- Order and supply products.
- Manage employees.
- Maintain facilities.

Processes can be represented pictorially by circles, data flows by lines between the processes, while external entities are represented by squares (see Figure 8.7). Notice that processes are connected to each other within the organization. The open-ended rectangle represents a *data store,* which is used by the processes to store data and for processes to use data that are already stored. A *data flow* is a link between two entities transferring information or communication.

The heart of BPM is **reengineering**—the radical redesign of an organization's business. Reengineering takes the current process model and makes changes to processes to increase efficiency and create new process models. What makes reengineering so valuable is that the organization can save a tremendous amount

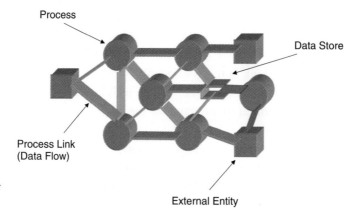

**Figure 8.7** Components of a process model. (*Source:* Prepared by D. Amoroso.)

of money by reengineering processes before automating them with expensive ERP software.

Reengineering initiatives, often conducted by IT specialists, require cross-functional teams. All enterprise systems, including ERP, SCM, KM systems, collaborative systems, GroupWare, human resources management systems, and CRM systems, use reengineering techniques.

**Measuring Processes.** Before reengineering efforts can proceed and designers can know which processes are effective and which are inefficient, they must be measured. Six Sigma, total quality management, and ISO 9000 are quality programs that seek to measure and improve an organization's processes. *Six Sigma* is a methodology to manage process variations that cause defects, defined as unacceptable deviation from the mean or target, and to systematically work toward managing variation to prevent those defects. *Total quality management* (TQM) is a management strategy aimed at embedding awareness of quality in all organizational processes. *ISO 9000* is a family of ISO (International Organization for Standardization) standards for quality management systems.

TQM comprises four process steps:

1. *Kaizen* focuses on continuous process improvement, to make processes visible, repeatable, and measurable.
2. *Atarimae Hinshitsu* focuses on intangible effects on processes and ways to optimize and reduce their effects.
3. *Kansei* examines the way the user applies the product, which leads to improvement in the product itself.
4. *Miryokuteki Hinshitsu* broadens management concern beyond the immediate product.

Six Sigma has as its basic methodology the following five phases:

1. **Define.** Formally define the goals of the design activity that are consistent with customer demands and enterprise strategy.
2. **Measure.** Identify product capabilities, production process capability, risk assessment, etc.
3. **Analyze.** Develop and design alternatives, create high-level design, and evaluate design capability to select the best design.
4. **Design.** Develop detailed design specifications, optimize design, and plan for design verification. This phase may require simulations.
5. **Verify.** Check designs, set up pilot runs, implement production process, and hand over to process owners.

**Reengineering Principles.** There are six actions (see Table 8.1) that you can take to reengineer processes: (1) add a new process, (2) delete a process, (3) expand a process, (4) reduce a process, (5) combine a process, and (6) split a process. It is important to understand the designer must keep up with changes in process when the organization changes. Each of these process actions requires updates in the repository (see the section on CASE tools) where every data flow in and out of the changed process must be updated as well. Given that some organizations have process models that include over 10,000 processes with 60 to 80 percent interconnectivity of unique data flows (6,000–8,000 data flows), and many data stores to manage, the repository will be quite full of objects to manage (Coffee, 2005).

| **TABLE 8.1** | Reengineering Actions |
| --- | --- |

***Adding a New Process***
Create an entirely new process.
Understand the functionality.
Add the new flows by deciding which processes are most affected/impacted by the new process.

***Deleting a Process***
Analyze the value added of each process by setting up metrics, collecting data, and analyzing the results.
Identify little- or no-value-added processes targeted for deletion.
Redirect, move, or delete the data flows first before deleting the process.

***Expanding a Process***
Decide which activities should be added to a process.
Add new process bubbles and related data flows at the exploded level.
Add the appropriate data flows (minimum of one additional outflow).
Decide where the data flows are to go.

***Reducing a Process***
Decide which activities should be deleted from a process.
Delete process bubbles and related data flows at the exploded level.
Delete the appropriate data flows (minimum of one additional outflow).
Refocus disconnected but needed data flows.

***Combining Processes***
Decide which process activities should be combined.
Move the activities and related data flows in the exploded diagram to the new processes.
Redirect data flows and/or deleted data flows.
Add at least one new data flow to the new system.

***Splitting a Process***
Decide which process activities should be split off into a new process.
Move the activities and related data flows in the exploded diagram.
Redirect data flows and provide some interrelationship between the new processes.

*Source:* Amoroso (2006).

**HOW INFORMATION TECHNOLOGY SUPPORTS BPM**

There are a number of technologies that can support the development of process models in the organization: notably CASE tools and BPM software.

**CASE Tools.** **Computer-aided software engineering (CASE)** is the use of software tools to assist in the development and maintenance of software. Tools used to assist in this way are known as CASE tools. All aspects of the software development life cycle can be supported by CASE tools (from project management software through tools for business and functional analysis, system design, code storage, programming tools, translation tools, and test software). CASE tools keep each object in a repository so that BPM managers can keep process models current and active as the business changes. Oracle Designer and Visible Analyst are examples of CASE tools that integrate the design of process through the generation of code (Jakovijevic, 2005).

**BPM Software.** BPM software tools (business process management systems or BPMS) allow for the direct execution of the business processes without a costly and time-intensive development of the required software. In addition, these tools can also monitor the execution of business processes, providing managers with the means to analyze their performance and make changes to the original processes in real time. Using a BPMS, the modified process can then be merged into the current business process environment (Wikipedia, 2006a).

BPR Designer packages by Bluespring Software (*bluespringsoftware.com*) allow for the design, deployment, and management of business processes, ranging from $75,000 to $100,000 for total enterprise process modeling. Fujitsu's Interstage BPM 7 allows for Web modeling of business processes with process rules updates and management tools, starting at $60,000 per workstation. TIBCO Software Inc. (*tibco.com*) has released software that spans BPM, workflow, and enterprise application integration (EAI) areas. Mendocino is a workflow product developed by Microsoft, integrating Microsoft operating systems with desktop management tools for enterprise control systems. Gartner predicts that the BPM software market will grow from $1.2 billion in 2005 to over $2.7 billion by 2009 (Vollmer and Moore, 2006).

**BUSINESS VALUE OF BPM**

The value of BPM can be seen in a number of organizations that are using IT tools to manage their business processes. Hasbro Inc. has deployed Team Works software to streamline the toy maker's ordering process (Chen, 2004). Hasbro reengineered not only the toy order process, but also the inquiry process. Hospitals have reported combining process management and information technology to redesign patient flow for maximum efficiency. From the arrival at the emergency room, the initial evaluation, test results, physician confirming diagnosis, and consultation, to specialization—BPM can improve patient flow and minimize long waiting times. Park University in Missouri used BP tools to change University processes, manage documents, and create literally close to a paperless environment. Automotive firms are using BPM to change processes to create scheduling stability and manage production in transit batch sizes.

Just gaining a better understanding of the current state of organizational processes is valuable in itself. However, eliminating non-value-added processes can have major positive effects in the organization.

# 8.7 Product Life Cycle Management

**WHAT IS PRODUCT LIFE CYCLE MANAGEMENT?**

**Product life cycle management (PLM)** is a business strategy that enables manufacturers to control and share product-related data as part of product design and development efforts and to support supply chain operations. In PLM, Web-based and other new technologies are applied to *product development* to automate its *collaborative aspects,* which even within a given organization can prove tedious and time consuming. By overlapping formerly disparate functions, such as a manufacturing process and the logistics that support it, a dynamic collaboration takes place among the functions, forming a single large product team from the product's inception. The core of PLM is the central management of all product data and the technology used to access this information (see Figure 8.8).

**PHASES OF THE PRODUCT LIFE CYCLE**

There are four phases of the product life cycle (PLC), each phase having different technologies that must be implemented and integrated with other technologies in other phases (see Figure 8.9). PLC processes cut across the entire organization from marketing, cost accounting, and estimating to manufacturing and shipping. The four phases of the PLC are:

1. *Conceive* (imagine, specify, plan, innovate).
2. *Design* (describe, define, develop, test, analyze, validate).
3. *Realize* (manufacture, make, build, procure, produce, sell, deliver).
4. *Service* (use, operate, maintain, support, sustain, phase-out, retire, recycle, dispose).

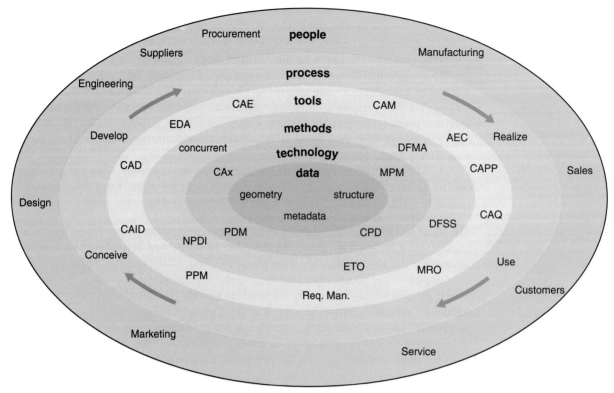

**Figure 8.8** Product life cycle management. (*Source:* Wikipedia, 2006b).

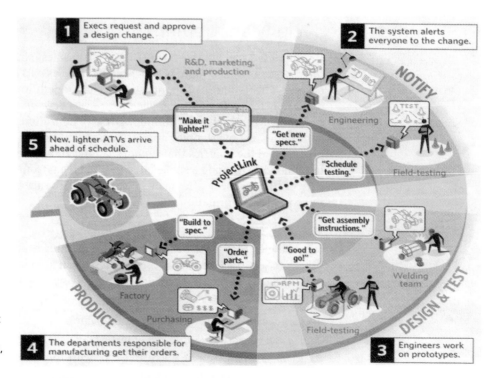

**Figure 8.9** How product life cycle management works. (*Sources:* Raskin, 2002, p. 50; Brown, 2005, p. 3.)

Phase 1 is the development of the product idea, the requirements for the product, the value-added of the product to the organization, the customer, and other constituencies. In the second phase, the detailed blueprint is designed, and development of the product and/or service starts, is prototyped, and is tested as it readies for production. The method of manufacturing is defined in phase 3 and the product and/or service is delivered. Finally, in phase 4 the focus is on managing customer service processes.

**HOW INFORMATION TECHNOLOGY SUPPORTS PLM**

PLM tools are offered by SAP (mySAP PLM), Matrix One, EDS, PTC, Dassault Systems, and IBM (IBM PLM). An example of a Web-based PLM product (from PTC Corp.) for designing popular ATV bikes is shown at *ptc.com*. The collaboration is achieved via "ProjectLink" (at the center of Figure 8.9). Using this PLM, bike-maker Cannondale was able to design its 2003 model significantly faster. Microsoft and Dassault created a product that shares information across multiple platforms (*Technoclicks.com*, 2005). Arena Solutions Inc. (*arenasolutions.com*) is giving away a free version of their PLS and tool for manufacturing and design teams in the medical manufacturing field. The workgroup module provides users with the ability to manage a complete product record, bill of material management, automated item number eight, vendor-managed method, and document tracking. IBM has released products that work with customers to design business processes and implement third-party PLM software using their process modeling tools. SAP has a product called mySAP PLM that creates an integrated solution for collaborative engineering, product development, management of projects, product structures, quality concerns, and documents. Agile Software Corp. (*agile.com*) leads the industry with a number of PLM software solutions, with new focus on small- and medium-sized businesses with a pay-as-you-go, on-demand PLM application.

**BUSINESS VALUE OF PLM**

PLM can have a significant beneficial impact on engineering change, cycle time, design reuse, and engineering productivity. Studies have shown that electronic-based collaboration can reduce product cost and travel expenses, as well as significantly reduce costs associated with product-change management. Moreover, an explosion of new products that have short life cycles, as well as increasing complexity in supply chain management, are driving the need for PLM. PLM is a big step for an organization, requiring it to integrate a number of different processes and systems. Ultimately, its overall goal is to move information through an organization as quickly as possible to reduce the time it takes to get a product to market and increase profitability.

Dell used PLM technology to more rapidly launch new products and provide the customers the capability to configure computers to order, resulting in $125 million in bottom-line production savings (Agile, 2006a).

ZF Group, a leading worldwide automotive supplier for driveline and chassis technology, used PLM for managing over 1 million parts and documents, and integrating design and manufacturing communication. This resulted in a 97 percent reduction in time to communicate changes from development to manufacturing (Agile, 2006b).

Roche Diagnostics of Switzerland and Aesculap of Germany have developed a set of product development process tools using mySAP that are now integrated and transparent, yielding a 75 percent increase in efficiency (SAP, 2004).

# 8.8 Customer Relationship Management

**Customer relationship management (CRM)** is an enterprisewide effort to acquire and retain profitable customers. CRM focuses on building long-term and sustainable customer relationships that add value for both the customer and the company. (See *crm-forum.com* and *crmassist.com.*) There are many definitions of CRM. The reason is that CRM is new and still evolving. Also, it is an interdisciplinary field, so each discipline (e.g., marketing, management) defines CRM differently.

In general, CRM is an approach that recognizes that customers are the core of the business and that the company's success depends on effectively managing relationships with them (see Figure 8.10). In other words: "CRM is a business strategy to select and manage customers to optimize long-term value. CRM requires a customer-centric business philosophy and culture to support effective marketing, sales, and services processes" (Thompson, 2003). It overlaps somewhat with the concept of *relationship marketing,* but not everything that could be called relationship marketing is in fact CRM (see Peppers and Rogers, 2004).

CRM is much broader in that it includes a *one-to-one* relationship between a customer and a seller. To be a genuine one-to-one marketer, a company must be willing and able to change its behavior toward a specific customer, based on what it knows about that customer. So, CRM is basically a simple idea: *Treat different customers differently,* because their needs differ and their value to the company may be different. CRM involves much more than just sales and marketing because a firm must be able to change how its products are configured or its service is delivered,

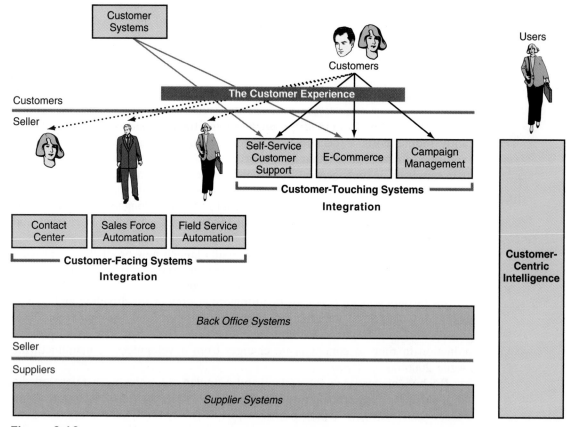

**Figure 8.10** CRM applications. (*Source:* Patricia Seybold Group, *An Executive's Guide to CRM,* March 21, 2002.)

based on the needs of individual customers. Smart companies have always encouraged the active participation of customers in the development of products, services, and solutions.

For the most part, however, being customer oriented has traditionally meant being oriented to the needs of the *typical* customer in the market—the average customer. To build enduring one-to-one relationships in a CRM initiative, a company must continuously interact with customers *individually*. One reason so many firms are beginning to focus on CRM is that this kind of service can create high customer loyalty and, additionally, help the firm's profitability. Involvement of almost all other departments, and especially engineering (design), accounting, and operations, is critical in CRM.

We distinguish among three major types of CRM *activities* involved: operational, analytical, and collaborative. *Operational CRM* is related to typical business functions involving customer services, order management, invoice/billing, and sales/marketing automation and management. *Analytical CRM* involves activities that capture, store, extract, process, interpret, and report customer data to a corporate user, who then analyzes them as needed. *Collaborative CRM* deals with all the necessary communication, coordination, and collaboration between vendors and customers.

**CLASSIFICATION OF CRM APPLICATIONS**

Another way of looking at CRM is to focus on the tools used by the CRM applications. The Patricia Seybold Group (2002) distinguishes among *customer-facing*, *customer-touching*, and *customer-centric intelligence* CRM applications. These three categories of applications are described below and are shown in Figure 8.10. The exhibit also shows how customers interact with these applications.

1. **Customer-facing applications.** These include all the areas where customers interact with the company: call centers, including help desks; sales force automation; and field service automation. Such CRM applications basically automate the information flow or support employees in these areas.
2. **Customer-touching applications.** In this category, customers interact directly with the applications. Notable are self-service, campaign management, and general-purpose e-commerce applications.
3. **Customer-centric intelligence applications.** These are applications that are intended to analyze the results of operational processing and use the results of the analysis to improve CRM applications. Data reporting and warehousing and data mining are the prime topics here.

To this classification of CRM applications we add a fourth category:

4. **Online networking applications.** Online networking refers to methods that provide the opportunity to build personal relationships with a wide range of people in business. These include chat rooms and discussion lists.

(Further details on the first three categories can be found at *psgroup.com*, in the free download of *An Executive's Guide to CRM*.)

**E-CRM**

CRM has been practiced manually by corporations for generations. However, since the mid-1990s various types of information technologies have enhanced CRM. CRM technology is an evolutionary response to changes in the business environment, making use of new IT devices and tools. The term **e-CRM** (electronic CRM) was coined in the mid-1990s, when businesses started using Web browsers, the Internet, and other electronic touchpoints (e-mail, POS terminals, call centers, and direct sales) to manage customer relationships. E-CRM covers a broad range of topics, tools, and methods, ranging from the proper design of digital products and services to pricing and to loyalty programs (e.g., see *e-sj.org*, *Journal of Service Research*, and *ecrmguide.com*). The use of e-CRM technologies has made customer service, as well as service to partners, much more effective and efficient.

Through Internet technologies, data generated about customers can be easily fed into marketing, sales, and customer service applications for analysis. E-CRM also includes online applications that lead to segmentation and personalization. The success of these efforts can be measured and modified in real time, further elevating customer expectations. In a world connected by the Internet, e-CRM has become a requirement for survival, not just a competitive advantage.

**The Scope of E-CRM.**  We can differentiate three levels of e-CRM:

1. **Foundational service.** This includes the *minimum necessary* services such as Web site responsiveness (e.g., how quickly and accurately the service is provided), site effectiveness, and order fulfillment.
2. **Customer-centered services.** These services include order tracking, product configuration and customization, and security/trust. These are the services that *matter the most* to customers.
3. **Value-added services.** These are *extra services* such as online auctions and online training and education.

**Customer Service on the Web.**  A primary activity of e-CRM is customer service on the Web, which can take many forms. We describe some of these different kinds of Web-based customer service below. (For fuller details, see Greenberg, 2004.)

*Search and Comparison Capabilities.*  With the hundreds of thousands of online stores, it is difficult for customers to find what they want, even inside a single electronic mall. Search and comparison capabilities are provided internally in large malls (e.g., *smartmall.biz*) or by independent comparison sites (*mysimon.com*).

*Free Products and Services.*  One approach companies use to differentiate themselves is to give away some product or service. For example, Compubank.com once offered free bill payments and ATM services. Companies can offer free samples over the Internet, as well as free entertainment, customer education, and more.

*Technical and Other Information and Services.*  Interactive experiences can be personalized to induce the consumer to commit to a purchase or to remain a loyal customer. For example, General Electric's Web site provides detailed technical and maintenance information and sells replacement parts for discontinued models for those who need to fix outdated home appliances. Such information and parts are quite difficult to find offline. Another example is Goodyear, which provides information about tires and their use at *goodyear.com*. The ability to download manuals and problem solutions at any time is another innovation of electronic customer service.

*Customized Products and Services.*  Dell Computer revolutionized the purchasing of computers by letting customers configure their own systems. This mass customization process is now used extensively by online vendors. Consumers are shown prepackaged "specials" and are given the option to "custom-build" products using online product configurators.

Other companies have found ways that are unique to their industries to offer customized products and services online. Web sites such as *gap.com* allow you to "mix and match" your entire wardrobe. Web sites such as *hitsquad.com*, *musicalgreeting.com*, or *surprise.com* allow consumers to handpick individual music titles from a library and customize a CD, a feature that is not offered in traditional music stores. Instant delivery of any digitized entertainment is a major advantage of EC.

***Account or Order Status Tracking.*** Customers can view their account balances or check merchandise shipping status at any time from their computers or cell phones. If you ordered books from Amazon, for example, you can find the anticipated arrival date. Many companies follow this model and provide similar services.

All of these examples of customer service on the Web demonstrate an important aspect of CRM: a focus on the individual customer.

**Other Tools for Customer Service.** There are many innovative Web-related tools to enhance customer service and CRM. Here are the major ones.

***Personalized Web Pages.*** Many companies allow customers to create their own individual Web pages. These pages can be used to record purchases and preferences, as well as problems and requests. For example, using intelligent agent techniques, American Airlines generates personalized Web pages for each of about 800,000 registered travel-planning customers.

Also, customized information (such as product and warranty information) can be efficiently delivered when the customer logs on to the vendor's Web site. Not only can the customer pull information as needed, but the vendor also can push information to the customer. Transaction information stored in the vendor's database can be used to support marketing of more products, for example.

***FAQs.*** Frequently asked questions (FAQs) are the simplest and least expensive tool for dealing with repetitive customer questions. Customers use this tool by themselves, which makes the delivery cost minimal. However, any nonstandard question requires an e-mail.

***E-Mail and Automated Response.*** The most popular tool of customer service is e-mail. Inexpensive and fast, e-mail is used mostly to answer inquiries from customers but also to disseminate information (e.g., confirmations), to send alerts, to send product information, and to conduct correspondence regarding any topic.

***Chat Rooms.*** Another tool that provides customer service, attracts new customers, and increases customers' loyalty is a chat room. For example, retailer QVC offers a chat room where customers can discuss their QVC shopping experiences (see Minicase 2 at the end of this chapter).

***Call Centers.*** One of the most important tools of customer service is the *call center*. Call centers are typically the "face" of the organization to its customers. For example, investment company Charles Schwab's call center effectively handles over 1 million calls from investment customers every day.

New technologies are extending the functionality of the conventional call center to e-mail and to Web interaction. For example, *epicor.com* combines Web channels, such as automated e-mail reply, Web knowledge bases, and portal-like self-service, with call center agents or field service personnel. Such centers are sometimes called *telewebs*.

***Troubleshooting Tools.*** Large amounts of time can be saved by customers if they can solve problems by themselves. Many vendors provide Web-based troubleshooting software to assist customers in this task. The vendors dramatically reduce their expenses for customer support when customers are able to solve problems without further intervention of customer service specialists.

**Wireless CRM.** Many CRM tools and applications are going wireless. As shown in Chapter 6, mobile sales force automation is becoming popular. In addition, use of wireless devices by mobile service employees is enabling these employees to provide better service while they are at the customer's site. Also, using SMS and e-mail from handheld devices is becoming popular as a means of improving CRM. Overall, we will see many CRM services going wireless fairly soon. For example, the Expedia case in Chapter 13 illustrates a wireless CRM application.

## CRM FAILURES

As with many IT innovations, there have been initially a large number of CRM failures, which have been reported in the media. Numerous failures have been reported by *thinkanalytics.com*, *cio.com*, *CRM-forum.com*, and many more. However, according to *itgreycells.com*, CRM failures are declining, from a failure rate of up to 80 percent in 1998 to about 40 percent in 2003.

Some of the major issues relating to CRM failures are the following:

- Difficulty in measuring and valuing intangible benefits. There are only a few tangible benefits to CRM.
- Failure to identify and focus on specific business problems.
- Lack of active senior management (non-IT) sponsorship.
- Poor user acceptance. This issue can occur for a variety of reasons such as unclear benefits (i.e., CRM is a tool for management, but it may not help a rep sell more effectively) and usability problems.
- Trying to automate a poorly defined process.

Strategies to deal with these and other problems are offered by many. (For example, see *cio.com* for CRM implementation, Kotorov, 2003, and Newell and Godin, 2003. Also see *conspectus.com* for "10 steps for CRM success.") Finally, the use of metrics to compare results is highly recommended.

CRM failures can create substantial problems. Some companies are falling behind in their ability to handle the volume of site visitors and the volume of buyers. Managerial guidelines for implementing CRM and avoiding CRM failure are provided in Table 8.2.

| **TABLE 8.2** | **How to Implement CRM to Avoid Its Failure** |
|---|---|

- Conduct a survey to determine how the organization responds to customers.
- Carefully consider the four components of CRM: sales, service, marketing, and channel/partner management.
- Survey how CRM accomplishments are measured; use defined metrics. Make sure quality, not just quantity, is addressed.
- Consider how CRM software can help vis-à-vis the organization's objectives.
- Decide on a strategy: refining existing CRM processes, or reengineering the CRM.
- Evaluate all levels in the organization but particularly frontline agents, field service, and salespeople.
- Prioritize the organization's requirements as one of the following: *must, desired,* or *not so important.*
- Select appropriate CRM software. There are more than 60 vendors. Some (like Siebel) provide comprehensive packages; others provide only certain functions. Decide whether to use the best-of-breed approach or to go with one vendor. ERP vendors (e.g., PeopleSoft and SAP) also offer CRM products.

*Source:* Compiled from DeFazio (2002).

**CRM DEVELOPMENT AND IMPLEMENTATION**

CRM software packages support a number of cross-functional business processes. To effectively implement CRM, you need to consider the following success factors:

- Create a customer-based culture in the organization.
- Adopt customer-based managers to assess satisfaction.
- Develop an end-to-end process to serve customers.
- Recommend questions to be asked to help a customer solve a problem.
- Track all aspects of selling to customers, as well as prospects.

**BUSINESS VALUE OF CRM**

Many organizations are adopting CRM systems, with software to help acquire, manage, and retain loyal customers. DePaul University manages students and information using the CRM module of PeopleSoft Enterprise technology. Bell Canada, one of North America's largest communications providers, has adopted the CRM package from SSA that focuses on inbound marketing. There are three areas of CRM that should be given priority to realize the total business value of CRM: (1) marketing, (2) sales, and (3) service. The rise of Internet technologies has made obsolete many traditional concepts of CRM. Most of the benefits are realized in conjunction with Internet-based applications. The State of Florida Department of Revenue implemented a CRM initiative that provided the customer service where Florida residents can access account information online (Sayer and Cowley, 2005). First Union lagged at customer service, but using Wachovia's CRM system they were able to provide a higher level of service to customers. Boston Medical Center is a 547-bed hospital using CRM to attract physicians with special expertise and give access to information to enhance customer satisfaction (Chen, 2005).

# 8.9  Managerial Issues

**ETHICS**

**1. Ethical issues.** Conducting a supply chain management project may result in the need to lay off, retrain, or transfer employees. Should management notify the employees in advance regarding such possibilities? And what about those older employees who are difficult to retrain? Other ethical issues may involve sharing of personal information, which may be required for a collaborative organizational culture.

**2. How much to integrate?** While companies should consider extreme integration projects, including ERP, SCM, and e-commerce, they should recognize that integrating long and complex supply chain segments may result in failure. Therefore, many times companies tightly integrate the upstream, inside-company, and downstream activities, each part by itself, and loosely connect the three.

**3. Role of IT.** Almost all major SCM projects use IT. However, it is important to remember that in most cases the technology plays a supportive role, and the primary role is organizational and managerial in nature. On the other hand, without IT, most SCM efforts do not succeed.

**4. Organizational adaptability.** To adopt ERP, organization processes must, unfortunately, conform to the software, not the other way around. When the software is changed, in a later version for example, the organizational processes must change also. Some organizations are able and willing to do so; others are not.

**GLOBAL**

**5. Going global.** EC provides an opportunity to expand markets globally. However, it may create long and complex supply chains. Therefore, it is necessary to first check the logistics along the supply chain as well as regulations and payment issues.

**6. The customer is king/queen.** In implementing IT applications, management must remember the importance of the customer/end-user, whether external or internal. Some innovative applications intended to increase customers' satisfaction are difficult to justify in a traditional cost-benefit analysis. Empowering customers to enter into a corporate database can make customers happy since they can conduct self-service activities such as configuration and tracking and get quick answers to their queries. Self-services can save money for a company as well, but it may raise security and privacy concerns. Corporate culture is important here, too. Everyone in the organization must be concerned about customers. Management should consider installing a formal CRM program for this purpose.

**7. Set CRM policies with care.** In practicing CRM, companies may give priority to more valuable customers (e.g., frequent buyers). This may lead to perceived discrimination. For example, in one case, when a male catalog customer found that Victoria's Secret charged him more than it did female buyers, he sued. In court it was shown that he was buying less frequently than the specific female he cited; the company was found not guilty of discrimination. Companies need to be very careful with CRM policies.

# Integrating IT

### For the Accounting Major

Accounting systems are totally dependent on enterprise resource planning systems and many modules are available for organizations to implement, including accounts payable, accounts receivable, inventory control, and general ledger. Accounting personnel need to be trained in the use of these complex organizational systems.

### For the Finance Major

Financial systems are critical in the enterprise resource planning modules as they are needed to generate payment of invoices and supplies. Automated payment systems are standard in e-business for customers ordering products and services from the organization and are also important for suppliers.

### For the Human Resources Management Major

Human resources managers use enterprise systems to enable employees to be more effective in their work. Supply chain systems enable staff to more closely align with suppliers and build key relationships. Training in the use of CRM and ERP systems is vital as most areas of the organization are using these systems for their work.

### For the IS Major

There are a lot of system pieces to enterprise systems. Information systems personnel are key in the customization of enterprise resource planning systems and have to provide the interface between organizations as well as get current modules upgraded and running within the organization. Business process management systems are vital for IS personnel to cross-functionally redesign corporate processes to be more effective and efficient. Processes then have to be matched to ERP industry processes to provide the best value to the organization.

### For the Marketing Major

The entire supply chain is crucial when marketing and selling online products to consumers. For the consumer to know that a product or service usually ships within 24 hours, the e-commerce systems have to check the inventory levels of all suppliers via the enterprise resource planning systems. Customer relationship management systems help marketing and sales staff to more effectively meet the needs of their customers.

### For the Production/Operations Management Major

Enterprise resource planning systems are crucial for organizations that are managing their supply chains. ERP systems require the production person to understand logistics, shipping and product distribution, and even tailor product design to meet customer needs in reverse supply chain systems.

## Key Terms

Bullwhip effect *305*

Business process management (BPM) *322*

CASE tools *326*

Customer relationship management (CRM) *330*

E-business *308*

E-CRM *331*

E-procurement *310*

E-supply chain *304*

Enterprise resource planning (ERP) *314*

Enterprise systems (enterprisewide systems) *302*

Master data management (MDM) *307*

Outsourcing *306*

Process modeling *324*

Product life cycle management (PLM) *327*

Reengineering *324*

Reverse logistics *307*

SAP R/3 *315*

SCM software *304*

Supply chain management (SCM) *304*

Supply chain team *311*

Trust *305*

Vendor-managed inventory (VMI) *310*

Virtual factory *311*

## Chapter Highlights                    (Numbers Refer to Learning Objectives)

❶ Enterprise systems are information systems that support several departments and/or the entire enterprise. The most notable are ERP, which supports supply chains, and CRM.

❶ Supply chains connect suppliers to a manufacturing company, departments inside a company, and a company to its customers. The supply chain must be completely managed, from the raw material to the end customers. Typical supply chains involve three segments: upstream, internal, and downstream. Most supply chains are supported by a variety of IT application programs.

❷ The major types of supply chains are integrated make-to-stock (manufacture to inventory), continuous replenishment, build-to-order, and channel assembly. Each type can be global or local.

❸ It is difficult to manage the supply chain due to the uncertainties in demand and supply and the need to coordinate several (sometimes many) business partners' activities. One of the major problems is known as the bullwhip effect, in which lack of coordination and/or communication results in large, unnecessary inventories.

❸ A number of solutions to supply chain problems are supported by IT, such as appropriate inventory management, vertical integration, information sharing, VMI, supply chain hubs, supply chain collaboration, RFID, supply chain teams, virtual factories, and wireless solutions.

❹ During the last 50 years, software support for supply chain management (SCM) has increased both in coverage and scope. SCM supports mostly decision making in short segments, such as resource optimization and inventory management. MRP pulled together production, purchasing, and inventory management of interrelated products. MRP II software added labor requirements and financial planning to the MRP model.

❹ The next step in SCM was to integrate routine transactions, including internal suppliers/customers and external suppliers/customers, in ERP and extended ERP software. The latest step in the evolution of integrated supply chain software is the addition of business intelligence and CRM applications.

❹ ERP software, which is designed to improve standard business transactions from all of the functional departments, is enhanced with decision-support capabilities as well as Web interfaces, and it provides an integrated framework of all routine activities in the enterprise. ERP enables different functional applications to work seamlessly so that data can flow automatically (from production to marketing, for example). ERP also provides easy interfaces to legacy systems as well as to partners' systems.

❺ Business process management (BPM) is a strategy for creating processes, modeling processes, monitoring processes, and reengineering them.

❺ BPM utilizes IT tools and quality control methods to track and improve process efficiency and effectiveness.

❻ Product life cycle management is a business strategy and process flow that cuts across all areas of the enterprise (from marketing to manufacturing) in order to enhance product design efforts.

❼ CRM is an enterprisewide activity through which an organization takes care of its customers and their needs. It is based on the idea of one-to-one relationships with customers. CRM is done by providing many communication and collaboration services, most of which are IT-supported and many of which are delivered on the Web.

## Virtual Company Assignment

### Enterprise Systems at The Wireless Café

Go to The Wireless Café's link on the Student Web Site. There you will be asked to apply some ERP principles to The Wireless Café and to propose some enterprisewide applications that could benefit the restaurant's operations.

**Instructions for accessing The Wireless Café on the Student Web Site:**

1. Go to *wiley.com/college/turban*.
2. Select Turban/Leidner/McLean/Wetherbe's *Information Technology for Management, Sixth Edition.*
3. Click on Student Resources site, in the toolbar on the left.
4. Click on the link for Virtual Company Web site.
5. Click on Wireless Café.

## Online Resources

More resources and study tools are located on the Student Web Site and on WileyPLUS. You'll find additional chapter materials and useful Web links. In addition, self-quizzes that provide individualized feedback are available for each chapter.

## Questions for Review

1. Define and list enterprise systems.
2. Define a supply chain and supply chain management (SCM).
3. List the major components of supply chains.
4. List the benefits of effective SCM.
5. Describe typical supply chain problems and the reasons for such problems.
6. Describe solutions to supply chain problems.
7. How does collaboration solve supply chain problems?
8. How do trust and collaboration play a major role in selecting and managing suppliers?
9. What are the issues in demand forecasting?
10. List the benefits of collaborative fulfillment networks.
11. Describe the need for, and types of, systems integration.
12. Define ERP and describe its functionalities.
13. List the additions provided by second-generation ERP.
14. Describe the logic of integrating ERP and SCM software.
15. Why should organizations analyze their processes before implementing an ERP solution?
16. List the capabilities of ERP systems.
17. What is open source ERP?
18. List some reasons for ERP failures.
19. Discuss business process management (BPM) and the benefits of developing a BPM strategy.
20. What is a process model and how can it be used to map business processes?
21. State the modeling guidelines for developing process models.
22. Define CRM.
23. List the major types of CRM.
24. What is e-CRM?
25. List some customer-facing, customer-touching, and customer-intelligent CRM tools.

## Questions for Discussion

1. Distinguish between ERP and SCM software. In what ways do they complement each other? Relate them to system integration.
2. Discuss how cooperation between a company that you are familiar with and its suppliers can reduce inventory cost.

3. Find examples of how organizations improve their supply chains in two of the following: manufacturing, hospitals, retailing, education, construction, agribusiness, and shipping. Discuss the benefits to the organizations.

4. It is said that supply chains are essentially "a series of linked suppliers and customers; every customer is in turn a supplier to the next downstream organization, until the ultimate end-user." Explain. Use of a diagram is recommended.

5. Discuss how outsourcing is used when considering make-or-buy decisions.

6. Discuss why Web-based call centers are critical for a successful CRM.

7. Find examples of how organizations use master data management in the supply chain to exploit opportunities.

8. Discuss why it is difficult to justify CRM and how metrics can help.

9. A supply chain is much more powerful in the Internet marketplace. Discuss how Internet technologies can be used to manage the supply chain.

10. Explain how vendor-managed inventory can save costs in the supply chain.

11. Discuss technology-assisted solutions and how they help alleviate supply chain problems.

12. State the business value of enterprise systems and how they can be used to make management of the supply chain more effective.

13. Discuss each of the steps in the ERP selection process.

14. What are the problems in implementing ERP systems? State solutions that make implementations more successful.

15. Why should a company change ERP solutions? List the pros and cons of switching.

16. Discuss the rationale behind reengineering and why organizations need to reengineer their business processes.

17. Discuss the rationale for using CASE tools to support BPM.

## Exercises and Projects

1. Identify the supply chain(s) and the flow of information described in the opening case. Draw it. Also, answer the following.
   a. "The company's business is not to make the product, but to sell the product." Explain this statement.
   b. Why was it necessary to use IT to support the change?
   c. Identify all the segments of the supply chain.
   d. Identify all supporting information systems in this case.

2. Enter *aberdeen.com* and observe its "online supply chain community" (go to *supply chain access*). Most of the information there is free. Prepare an outline of the major resources available in the site.

3. Go to a bank and find out the process and steps of obtaining a mortgage for a house. Draw the supply chain. Now assume that some of the needed information, such as the value of the house and the financial status of the applicant, is found in a publicly available database (such a database exists in Hong Kong, for example). Draw the supply chain in this case. Explain how such a database can shorten the loan approval time.

4. Go to a small local video store. Using Visio or Word, draw a high-level process map of the major functions (high-level processes) and connect them to each other using data flows and to external entities. Assume the external entities are: Customers, Vendors, Bank, and Employees. You should have between 5 and 10 processes in your process map and at least 10 data flows within processes. Be sure to name your processes with active verbs and your data flows with nouns.

5. Go to *amazon.com* and go through the ordering process for a book. Explain how the software is able to say "This item usually ships within 24 hours." Draw a picture of how the ERP works to gather that information from the supply chain and send it back to the customer.

6. Take the process model created earlier for the local video store. Apply the six reengineering techniques to change processes by streamlining the flow between and among the business processes.

## Group Assignments and Projects

1. Each group in the class will be assigned to a major ERP/SCM vendor such as SAP, PeopleSoft, Oracle, etc. Members of the groups will investigate topics such as: (a) Web connections, (b) use of business intelligence tools, (c) relationship to CRM and to EC, (d) major capabilities, and (e) availability of ASP services by the specific vendor.

   Each group will prepare a presentation for the class, trying to convince the class why the group's software is best for a local company known to the students (e.g., a supermarket chain).

2. Assign each team to one type of supply chain, such as build-to-order or continuous replenishment. The team

should find two examples of the assigned type, draw the supply chains, and explain the IT and EC solutions used.

3. Create groups to investigate the major CRM software vendors, their products, and the capabilities of those products in the following categories. (Each group represents a topical area of several companies.)

- Sales force automation (Oracle, Onyx, Salesforce, Siebel, Saleslogix, Pivotal)
- Call centers (Clarify, LivePerson, NetEffect, Inference, Peoplesoft)

- Marketing automation (Annuncio, Exchange Applications, MarketFirst, Nestor)
- Customer service (Brightware, Broadvision, Primus, Silknet)
- Sales configuration (Exactium, Newtonian)

Start with *searchcrm.com* and *crmguru.com* (to ask questions about CRM solutions). Each group must present arguments to the class to convince class members to use the product(s) the group investigated.

## Internet Exercises

1. Enter *ups.com*. Examine some of the IT-supported customer services and tools provided by the company. Write a report on how UPS contributes to supply chain improvements.

2. Enter *supply-chain.org, cio.com, findarticles.com,* and *google.com* and search for recent information on supply chain management integration.

3. Enter *mySap.com*. Identify its major components. Also review the Advanced Planning and Optimization tool. How can each benefit the management of a supply chain?

4. Enter *i2.com* and review its SCM products that go beyond ERP. Examine the OCN Network and Rhythm. Write a report.

5. Enter *siebel.com*. View the demo on e-business. Identify all e-business–related initiatives. Why is the company considered as the leader of CRM software?

6. Enter *anntaylor.com* and identify the customer service activities offered there.

7. Enter *oracle.com*. Find the ERP modules offered by Oracle and identify their connection to CRM and customer services.

8. Enter *salesforce.com* and take the tour. What enterprisewide system does the company support? How?

9. Enter *2020software.com*. Find information about the top 10 ERP applications. View the demo; write a report on your findings.

## Minicase 1

POM    GLOBAL

# ERP Helps Productivity at Northern Digital Inc.

Northern Digital Inc. (*ndigital.com*) in Ontario, Canada, is a supplier of 3D/6D measurement products. The relatively small company employs 90 people and generates over $20 million in annual revenue.

### The Problem

Northern Digital Inc. (NDI) faced a challenge when rapid growth and aging technology threatened to stand in the way of company goals. Instead of enabling operational improvements, NDI's existing systems were impeding progress. Existing technology was causing missed deliveries and creating a high number of back orders. Inventory control was poor, and the planning was inaccurate. With some customers expecting shipment in as long as 9 months and others expecting shipment in as little as 9 days or even less, more sophisticated and accurate planning was critical.

Customer satisfaction was at risk, and internal morale was slipping. With almost 20 years in business, NDI's well-established reputation for high-quality, high-performance products was at risk.

### The Solution

NDI selected an ERP system (from Intuitive Manufacturing Systems) based on factors that directly supported corporate objectives. Intuitive's ERP provided a level of system functionality that could immediately improve inventory management and the expandability and flexibility to support NDI's growth. The software includes a complete planning system, automated inventory management, and enhanced technology infrastructure. Equally important was the system's level of ease of implementation and ease of use.

## The Results

After implementing Intuitive ERP, Northern Digital experienced continued success in improving inventory management and increasing revenue. Prior to implementation, the company struggled to achieve even two inventory "turns" (turnovers) per year. Inventory turns have now more than doubled, and expectations are that the company will better that in the near future. Since implementation, Northern Digital's revenue has increased from $10 million to over $20 million with little increase in inventory value. In addition, the company has reduced order cycle time for its flagship product from 4 months to 4 weeks, an improvement of almost 80 percent. This was a result of improved planning capabilities due to the ERP.

Improvements in production control and inventory management have had a direct impact on customer delivery. The Material Requirements Planning and Forecasting capabilities of Intuitive ERP have allowed Northern Digital to better service its customers. The addition of better planning capabilities had an immediate positive impact on labor and materials. "We were able to better understand what was in stock, what we were buying, and what was needed," said Tom Kane, production manager. "Improved planning has made a huge difference in improving delivery."

Ease of use and system scalability have been important in utilizing Intuitive ERP to improve operations. When the system was first implemented, NDI needed only five user seats (user licenses). As NDI grew, that number increased to 25. Significantly increasing the number of users, and doing so without a lot of training, allowed the company to expand without worrying about putting constraints on its business infrastructure, supporting the growth strategy.

For Northern Digital, improving operations is more than just a way to reduce expenses. With the implementation of Intuitive ERP, the NDI has found a way to increase the value it provides to customers while also improving financial performance.

*Sources:* Compiled from *managingautomation.com* (May 2004), and from *ndigital.com* (accessed June 2004).

## Questions for Minicase 1

1. For a small company like NDI, why is an ERP better than SCM applications?
2. Identify the supply chain segments that the ERP supports; be specific.
3. Relate this case to Porter's value chain and to its competitive model (Appendix 1A). Show the ERP's contribution.
4. Enter *intuitivemfg.com* and report on the capabilities of the company's ERP product.
5. Relate this case to business planning and strategy.

# Minicase 2

## QVC Provides Superb CRM

MKT

QVC (*qvc.com*) is known for its TV shopping channels, and it is selling on the Web, too. It is a very competitive business, since retail selling is done in several marketing channels. In 2000, QVC served more than 6 million customers, answered 125 million phone calls, shipped about 80 million packages, and handled more than a billion page views on its Web site. In February 2006, QVC topped the $800 million online domestic sales mark. QVC's business strategy is to provide top-notch customer service in order to keep its customers loyal. QVC also appointed a senior vice president for customer service. The problem was how to provide top-notch customer care and do it economically.

To manage its huge business (about $5 billion a year), QVC must use the latest IT support. For example, QVC operates four state-of-the-art call centers, one of these for overseas operations. However, before using technology to boost loyalty and sales, QVC had to develop a strategy to put its customers at the core of corporate decision making. "Exceeding the expectations of every customer" is a sign you can see all over QVC's premises. As a matter of fact, the acronym QVC stands for Quality, Value, and Convenience—all from the customers' perspective.

In pursuit of this goal, QVC created a truly excellent service organization. Among other things, QVC provides education (demonstrating product features and functions), entertainment, and companionship. Viewers build a *social* relationship with show hosts, upon which the *commercial* relationship is built. Now QVC is also attempting to build a social relationship with its customers on the Web (see *qvc.com*).

QVC knows that building trust on the TV screen is necessary, but not sufficient to draw customers. So everyone in the company contributes to the customer service goals. QVC's president randomly checks customers' letters, including e-mail. All problems are fixed quickly. Everything is geared toward the long run. In addition, to make CRM work, QVC aligns senior executives, IT executives, and functional managers so that they work toward the same goals, collaborate, have plans that do not interfere with others' plans, and so forth. Also, the company adopts the latest IT applications and continuously offers training to its customer service reps in the new CRM applications.

QVC is using metrics to measure customer service. These include: friendliness of the call center reps; how knowledgeable the reps are about the products; clarity of the instructions about how to order and how to use the products purchased; the number of people a customer has to speak with to get a satisfactory answer; and how often a customer has to call a second time to get a problem resolved.

Data on customer service are collected in several ways, including tracking of telephone calls and Web-site movements. Cross-functional teams staff the call centers, so complete knowledge is available in one place. Corrective actions are taken quickly, to prevent repeat problems in the future.

To get the most out of the call center's employees, QVC strives to keep them very satisfied. They must enjoy the work in order to provide excellent customer service. The employees are called "customer advocates," and they are handsomely rewarded for innovative ideas.

In addition to call centers, QVC uses computer-telephony integration technology (CTI), which identifies the caller's phone number and matches it to customer information in the database. This information pops up on the rep's screen when a customer calls. The rep can greet the customer by saying, "Nice to have you at QVC again, David. I see that you have been with us twice this year, and we want you to know that you are important to us. Have you enjoyed the jacket you purchased last June?"

To know all about the customer history, QVC maintains a large data warehouse. Customers' buying history is correlated by Zip code with psychodemographic data from Experian (*experian.com*), a company that analyzes consumer information. This way, QVC can know instantly, for example, whether a new product is a hit with wealthy retirees or with young adults. The information is used for e-procurement, advertising strategy, and more. QVC also uses viral marketing (word-of-mouth of its loyal customers). In order not to bother its customers, QVC does not send any mail advertisements.

*Sources:* Compiled from "Nice Guys Finish First . . ." (2000), and from *qvc.com* (accessed October 2006).

## Questions for Minicase 2

1. Enter *qvc.com* and identify actions that the company takes to increase trust in its e-business. Also, look at all customer-service activities. List as many as you can find.

2. List the advantages of buying online versus buying over the phone after watching QVC. What are the disadvantages? Is this a CRM service?

3. Enter the chat room of *qvc.com* and the bulletin board. What is the general mood of the participants? Are they happy with QVC? Why or why not? What is the advantage of having customers chat live online?

4. QVC is using a data warehouse to provide customer service (e.g., find what customers purchased in the past). Explain how this is done. The data warehouse now operates in real time. Why?

# References

Agile, "Customer Results: Dell," 2006a, *agile.com/customers/results/dell.asp* (accessed October 2006).

Agile, "Customer Results: ZF Group," 2006, *agile.com.customers/results/zf.asp* (accessed October 2006).

Bacheldor, B., "General Motors Takes Design Up a Notch," *Information Week,* February 23, 2004.

Beatty, R., and C. Williams, "ERP II: Best Practices for Successfully Implementing an ERP Upgrade, "*Communications of the ACM,* 49(3), 2006.

Bresnahan, J., "The Incredible Journey," *CIO.com,* August 15, 1998, *cio.com/archive/enterprise/081598_jour.html* (accessed June 2003).

Brown, C., and I. Vessey, "Managing the Next Wave of Enterprise Systems: Leveraging Lessons from ERP," *MIS Quarterly Executive,* 2(1), 2003.

Brown, T., "Singularity Integrates the Process Lifecycle," *Business Integration Journal,* June 2005.

Chen, A., "Hasbro Plays to Win with BPM," *Eweek,* August 2, 2004.

Chen, A., "CRM Pays Off For," *Eweek,* May 23, 2005.

Coffee, P., "Measuring Up-and Up," *Eweek,* June 6, 2005.

Croom, S., "The Impact of E-Business on Supply Chain Management," *International Journal of Operations and Production Management,* 25(1), 2005.

Extreme Networks, "Cybex International Gets Its Network In Shape with Extreme Networks," 2005, *extremenetworks.com/libraries/casestudies/Cybex_CS.asp* (accessed October 2006).

Ferguson, R., "A Community in the Making," *Eweek,* March 28, 2005a.

Ferguson, R., "SAP Speeds MDM Development," *Eweek,* December 2005b.

Gattiker, T., Huang, X., and Schwarz, J., "Negotiation, Email, and Internet Reverse Auctions: How Souring Mechanisms Deployed by Buyers Affect Suppliers "Trust," *Journal of Operations Management,* 2006.

Gayialis, S. P., and I.P Tatsiopoulos, "Design of an IT-Driven Decision Support System for Vehicle Routing and Scheduling," *European Journal of Operational Research,* 152(2), January 16, 2004.

Gibson, S., "GM Pushes Outsourcing Envelop," *Eweek,* December 2005.

*gmb.org.uk,* "Regional Distribution Centres," June 3, 2005, *gmb.org.uk/.../uploadedfiles/95420EED-6333-4746-9BC0-432145FDD379_RegionalDistributionCentres.doc* (accessed October 2006).

Greenberg, P., *CRM at the Speed of Light: Capturing and Keeping Customers in Internal Real Time,* 3rd ed. New York: McGraw-Hill, 2004.

Heizer, L., and B. Render, *Operations Management,* 7th ed. Upper Saddle River, NJ: Pearson Education, 2004.

IDS Scheer AG, "Business Process Management," Whitepaper, May–June 2005.

Jakovijevic, P.J., "Business Process Management: A Crash Course on What It Entails and Why to Use It," *Technology Evaluation Centers,* December 8, 2005.

Jinyoul, L., et al., "Enterprise Integration with ERP and EAI," *Communications of the ACM,* February 2003.

Kalakota, R., and M. Robinson, *E-Business 2.2 Roadmap for Success.* Boston, MA: Addison Wesley, 2001.

King. W., "Ensuring ERP Implementation Success," *Information Systems Management,* Summer 2005.

Kotorov, R., "Customer Relationship Management Strategic Lessons and Future Directions," *Business Process Management Journal,* 9(5), 2003.

Kovacs, G. L., and P. Paganelli, "A Planning and Management Infrastructure for Large, Complex, Distributed Products—Beyond ERP and SCM," *Computers in Industry,* 51(2), June 2003.

Patricia Seybold Group, *An Executive's Guide to CRM.* Boston, MA: Patricia Seybold Group, 2002, *psgroup.com/freereport/imedia/resport/asp* (accessed April 15, 2003).

Peacocks Case Study, *symbol.com/uk/solutions/case_study_peacocks.html,* 2004 (accessed May 2004).

Peppers, D., and M. Rogers, *Managing Customer Relationships: A Strategic Framework.* New York: Wiley, 2004.

Picarille, L., "The BPM Market Is Expected to Grow 15 Percent," DestinationCRM.com, February 8, 2004, *destinationcrm.com/articles/default.asp?ArticleID=3845* (accessed October 2006).

Ragowsky, A., and T. M. Somers (eds.), "Enterprise Resource Planning.," special issue, *Journal of Management Information Systems,* Summer 2002.

Raskin, A., "A Faster Ride to Market," *Business 2.0,* October 2002.

Sayer, P., and S. Cowley, "Microsoft Reveals Details of CRM 3.0," *Tech World,* July 06, 2005.

SAP, "Customer Success Story: Roche Diagnostics," 2004, *sap.com/solutions/busniess-suite/plm/pdf/CS_Roche_Diagnostics.pdf* (accessed October 2006).

Siau, K., and Y. Tian, "Supply Chains Integration: Architecture and Enabling Technologies," *Journal of Computer Information Systems,* Spring 2004.

Smets-Solanes, J., and R. Atem de Carvalho, "ERP5: A Next-Generation, Open Source ERP Architecture," *IT Pro* July–August, 2003.

Sullivan, L., "Global Smarts: Colgate-Palmolive Finesses Procurement," *InformationWeek,* July 11, 2005.

Sullivan, M., et al., "Case Studies: Digital Do-Overs," *Forbes.com,* October 7, 2002.

Technoclicks.com, "Dassault Systemes and Microsoft Announce V5 PLM Solutions Availability on Windows XP Professional x64 Edition," October 5, 2005, *technoclicks.com/article-40.php* (accessed October 2006).

Thompson, B., "What Is CRM?" *CRMguru,* 2003.

Vollmer, K., and C. Moore. "Demand for Business Process Management Suites Will Accelerate through 2009," Forester Research, January 26, 2006, *forrester.com/Research/Document/Excerpt/0,7211,38560,00.html* (accessed October 2006).

Wikipedia, "Business Process Management," 2006a, *en.wikipedia.org/wiki/Business_Process_Management* (accessed October 2006).

Wikipedia, "Product Life Cycle Management," 2006b, *en.wikipedia.org/wiki/Product_Lifecycle_Management* (accessed October 2006).

Worthen, B., "Drilling for Every Drop of Value," *CIO Management,* June 1, 2002.

Yusuf, Y., A. Gunasekaran, and M. Abthorpe, "Enterprise Information Systems Project Implementation: A Case Study of ERP in Rolls-Royce," *International Journal of Production Economics,* 87(3), February 2004.

Part IV | Organizational Applications

7. Transaction Processing, Functional Applications, and Integration
8. Enterprise Systems
▶ 9. Interorganizational and Global Information Systems

# Chapter

# 9

# Interorganizational and Global Information Systems

## Learning Objectives

After studying this chapter, you will be able to:

❶ Describe interorganizational activities, particularly order fulfillment.

❷ Define and classify interorganizational information systems and virtual corporations.

❸ Define and classify global information systems.

❹ Present the major issues surrounding global information systems.

❺ Describe demand-driven networks and RFID as supply chain facilitators.

❻ Describe B2B exchanges, hubs, and directories.

❼ Describe interorganizational integration issues and solutions.

❽ Describe EDI and EDI/Internet and their benefits and limitations.

❾ Describe extranets, XML, and Web Services.

## Integrating IT

ACC    FIN    MKT    POM    HRM    IS    SVC

# LIMITED BRANDS CREATES A SUPERB SUPPLY CHAIN

Limited Brands is a large retailer (over $10 billion in 2005) comprised of many well-known brands (Victoria's Secret, Express, The Limited, White Barn Candle, Bath & Body Works) and about 4,000 retail stores.

## The Problem

As a result of rapid growth by acquisitions, Limited ended up with a complex hodgepodge of IT systems and applications, many of which did not "talk" to each other. Due to strong competition beginning in 2001 from discount retailers (recall the changing business environment, Chapter 1), Limited had to shift to a high-end product line (less competition, fatter margins). Limited needed new supply chain technologies and processes to drive the speed-to-market requirements of this new growth strategy. Specifically, they needed to integrate and leverage the supply chain and logistics supporting all brands for maximum brand value.

Their old technology was inadequate. For example, in one day about 400 trailers with merchandise turned up in the parking lot of a distribution center that had a capacity of 150 trailers. This happened just before the sales period and many stores did not get merchandise on time. Planners did not have the necessary information, nobody knew where supplies had come from, or where they were going; the supply chain was not synchronized! Finally, inventories were too large sometimes and insufficient at other times.

## The Solution

Limited embarked on a consolidation project to move its legacy systems into an integrated, high-visibility supply chain platform. The objective was to stay on top of both the supply side and the demand side. This was a difficult and long undertaking, given that Limited also sells via catalog, the Internet, and third-party retailers.

The new system is based on TIBCO's EAI (Enterprise Application Integration) IT product, which was modified to deal with Limited's special needs. The result was a global application integration platform. This is critical since many of Limited's 1,000 suppliers are in several different countries. A special feature during the implementation was to get the cooperation of the various brand managers. This happened especially after they saw positive results, and after encouragement from top management.

The major vendor was TIBCO (for information integration efforts, see Section 9.5). Several other IT vendors were involved (e.g., Manugistics, a supplier of demand-driven supply chain management solutions). In addition, the company installed an ERP from SAP (Chapter 8) that includes not only financial modules, but also business intelligence (Chapter 11) to facilitate decision making. The supporting technology of an *extranet* was used to provide efficient and secure communication.

## The Results

By 2004, Limited was able to increase its sales per square foot to $530 (from $468 in 2001, and around $300 for the competition). Earnings increased by about 10 percent in 2006. Business processes were improved and real-time reporting and communication was implemented with about 50 delivery agents (third-party shippers). Limited's outbound supply chain reporting and accountability is now integrated with logistics applications. Changes can be made quickly and easily (e.g., adding a delivery agent). The new system also enables real-time communication with suppliers. The business partners are happy since they can share shipment tracking and order visibility with Limited. The company's 100,000 sales associates can now do what they do best—sell. Finally, the time needed to get products to market has been reduced by 10 days, and the system provides a secure environment for business documents.

*Sources*: Compiled from McCartney (2006) and *Tibco.com* (accessed July 2006).

## Lessons Learned from This Case

Limited's information system along its supply chain had to be modified to accommodate changing strategy. Problems occurred both upstream and downstream of the supply chain. The solution was *integration* of both the internal and external information systems. Integration is a difficult process and, therefore, a third-party expert vendor was involved. We also see the importance of collaborating with business partners (suppliers and logistic companies in this case), and the need for effective communication channels. Finally, there was a need to conduct business process management (BPM) prior to the IT planning. The topics described in the case are the subjects of this chapter.

# 9.1 Interorganizational Activities and Order Fulfillment

**ON-DEMAND ENTERPRISE AND REAL-TIME OPERATIONS**

The new business environment described in Chapters 1 and 2 contains the elements of *on-demand enterprise* and *real-time* operations. These two concepts have a great impact on the topics discussed in this chapter. So, before we start our presentation, we review them:

- **On-demand enterprise.** The concept of on-demand enterprise is based on the premise that manufacturing (or service fulfillment) will start only after an order is received (Dell case, Chapter 1). We referred to this as build-to-order and mass customization as well. As time passes, more and more enterprises are converting to this concept (or adding it to the traditional "produce-to-stock" manufacturing).
- **On-demand and real-time.** An on-demand process implies that no production step would be ahead or behind because the entire fulfillment cycle would be primed to respond to real-time conditions. There will be no backorders, safety stock, lag time, or excess inventory. We discuss the topic of real-time response in Chapter 11.

These two concepts have revolutionized the supply chain. For on-demand and real-time processes, companies must reengineer their entire supply chain. This is referred to as demand-driven supply networks, which is discussed in Section 9.4.

**INTERORGANIZA-TIONAL ACTIVITIES**

Before we delve into the topic of information systems that support two or more organizations, let's briefly describe some of the common activities conducted between and among business partners. They are:

**Buying and Selling.** Probably the most common activity that is going on between organizations is buying and selling. This activity includes finding a partner, viewing catalogs, negotiating, order taking, order fulfillment, billing, payments, after-sale service, and more. To show why IT support is needed, we use order fulfillment as an example (see the overview section below).

**Joint Ventures.** Business partners conduct large numbers of joint ventures, sometimes as virtual corporations (see Section 9.2). Such activities require collaboration.

**Collaboration.** This topic was presented in Chapters 4 and 8. Later in this chapter, we will discuss the topic of collaborative commerce. For an interesting example, see Cone (2006) and the Boeing case at the beginning of Chapter 13.

**Other Activities.** Several other activities can take place between companies. For example, they may work jointly on standards, conduct research, appeal to the government, and refer business they cannot do.

In all the above, communication, collaboration, and search using the support of IT are involved (Chapter 4).

The major objective of this chapter is to show how to improve interorganizational activities, most of which are related to the supply chain, using IT. We begin by presenting the major activity of the order fulfillment process.

**Order fulfillment** refers not only to providing customers with what they have ordered and doing so on time, but also to providing all related customer services. For example, a customer must receive assembly and operation instructions with a new appliance. This can be done by including a paper document with the product or by providing the instructions on the Web. (A nice example of this is available at *livemanuals.com*.) In addition, if the customer is not happy with a product, an exchange or return must be arranged.

Order fulfillment is basically a part of **back-office operations,** which are the activities that support the fulfillment of orders, such as accounting, inventory management, and shipping. It also is strongly related to **front-office operations,** or *customer-facing activities,* which are activities, such as sales and advertising, that are visible to customers.

**Overview of Logistics. Logistics** is defined by the Council of Logistics Management as "the process of planning, implementing, and controlling the efficient and effective flow and storage of goods, services, and related information from point of origin to point of consumption for the purpose of conforming to customer requirements" (*Logisticsworld.com,* 2006). Note that this definition includes inbound, outbound, internal, and external movement and the return of materials and goods. It also includes *order fulfillment.* However, the distinction between logistics and order fulfillment is not always clear, and the terms are sometimes used interchangeably, as we do in this text.

Obviously, the key aspects of order fulfillment are delivery of materials or services at the right time, to the right place, and at the right cost.

**The EC Order Fulfillment Process.** To understand why there are problems in order fulfillment, it is beneficial to look at a typical order fulfillment process, as shown in Figure 9.1. The process starts on the left, when an order is received (by e-mail, fax, phone, etc.). Several activities take place, some of which can be done simultaneously; others must be done in sequence. These activities include the following steps:

**Step 1: Make sure the customer will pay.** Depending on the payment method and prior arrangements, the validity of each payment must be determined. This activity may be done in B2B by the company's finance department or financial institution (i.e., a bank or a credit card issuer such as Visa). Any holdup may cause a shipment to be delayed, resulting in a loss of goodwill or a customer. In B2C, the customers usually prepay by credit card.

**Step 2: Check for in-stock availability.** Regardless of whether the vendor is a manufacturer or a retailer, as soon as an order is received, an inquiry needs to be made regarding stock availability. Several scenarios are possible here that may involve the material management and production departments, as well as outside suppliers and warehouse facilities. For small orders, an automatic search by an intelligent software agent may be done. In this step, the order information needs to be connected to the information about in-stock inventory availability. Sometimes buyers can check availability by themselves using IT.

**Step 3: Arrange shipments.** If the product is available, it can be shipped to the customer (otherwise, go to step 5). Products can be digital or physical. If the item is physical and it is readily available, packaging and shipment arrangements need to be made. Both the packaging/shipping department and internal

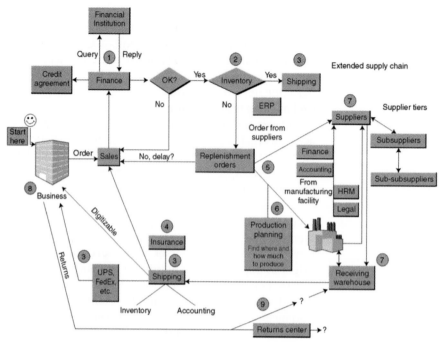

**Figure 9.1** Order fulfillment and the logistics system.

Note: Demand forecasts and accounting are conducted at various points throughout the process.

shippers or outside transporters may be involved. Digital items are usually available because their "inventory" is not depleted. However, a digital product, such as software, may be under revision, and thus unavailable for delivery at certain times. In either case, information needs to flow among several partners.

**Step 4: Insurance.** Sometimes the contents of a shipment need to be insured. Both the finance department and an insurance company could be involved, and again, information needs to flow, not only inside the company, but also to and from the customer and insurance agent.

**Step 5: Replenishment.** Customized (build-to-order) orders will always trigger a need for some manufacturing or assembly operation. Similarly, if standard items are out of stock, they need to be produced or procured. Production can be done in-house or by contractors. The suppliers involved may have their own suppliers.

**Step 6: In-house production.** In-house production needs to be planned. Production planning involves people, materials, components, machines, financial resources, and possibly suppliers and subcontractors. In the case of assembly and/or manufacturing, several plant services may be needed, including possible collaboration with business partners. Services may include scheduling of people and equipment, shifting other products' plans, working with engineering on modifications, getting equipment, and preparing content. The actual production facilities may be in a different country than the company's headquarters or retailers. This may further complicate the flow of information and communication.

**Step 7: Use suppliers.** A manufacturer may opt to buy products or subassemblies from suppliers. Similarly, if the seller is a retailer, such as in the case of *Amazon.com* or *Walmart.com,* the retailer must purchase products from its manufacturers. In this case, appropriate receiving and quality assurance of incoming materials and products must take place.

Once production (step 6) or purchasing from suppliers (step 7) is completed, shipments to the customers (step 3) are arranged.

**Step 8: Contacts with customers.** Sales representatives need to keep in constant contact with customers, especially in B2B, starting with notification of orders received and ending with notification of a shipment or a change in delivery date. These contacts are usually done via e-mail and are frequently generated automatically.

**Step 9: Returns.** In some cases, customers want to exchange or return items. Such returns can be a major problem, as more than $100 billion in North American goods are returned each year (Kuzeljevich, 2004). Returns cost U.K. retailers EU$720 million a year (Boles, 2004). The movement of returns from customers back to vendors is called **reverse logistics.**

Order fulfillment processes may vary, depending on the product and the vendor. The order fulfillment process also differs between B2B and B2C activities, between the delivery of goods and of services, and between small and large products. Furthermore, additional steps may be required in certain circumstances, such as in the case of perishable materials or foods. Finally, there are differences in fulfilling regular orders with a long lead time or on-demand orders that must be fulfilled quickly.

***Order Fulfillment and the Supply Chain.*** The nine-step order fulfillment process just described, as well as order taking, are integral parts of the *supply chain*. The flows of orders, payments, information, materials, and parts need to be coordinated among all the company's internal participants, as well as with and among external partners.

**Problems and Solutions: An Overview.** The process presented in Figure 9.1 can be lengthy. Since it involves material, information, money, and possibly many people located in different places (even different countries), it is very likely that one or more of the following will occur:

- Delays in transportation/shipments
- Human errors in information sending
- Misunderstanding of orders
- Over- or understocked inventories
- Shipments to wrong places or wrong quantities
- Late or wrong reporting on delivery
- Slow or incorrect billing
- Difficult product/part configuration
- Inability of IT systems of two organizations to "talk" to each other
- High cost of expedited shipments

If a foreign country is involved, additional problems may develop (see Section 9.3).

While many solutions have been developed over the years in an attempt to solve these problems, some of which were very successful, the most successful and promising approach is to *automate* as many of the activities as possible. ERP, for example, has been extended to include suppliers and customers. Automation is done by using IT, and due to its capabilities (Chapters 1 and 2) it is possible to increase speed, reduce (or eliminate) errors, reduce cost of administering the process, minimize delays, reduce inventories, and so forth.

We will describe in Sections 9.4 through 9.6 and Appendices 9A and 9B how IT helps. But first, let's look at interorganizational and global systems in more detail.

# 9.2 Interorganizational Information Systems and Virtual Corporations

An **interorganizational information system (IOS)** involves information flow among two or more organizations. Its major objectives are efficient processing of transactions, such as transmitting orders, bills, and payments, and to support collaboration and communication. As we will show in this chapter, an IOS can be local or global, dedicated to only one activity (e.g., transfer of funds) or intended to support several activities (e.g., to facilitate trade, research, communication, and collaboration).

Interorganizational systems have developed in direct response to two business pressures: the desire to reduce costs, and the need to improve the effectiveness and timeliness of business processes. More specifically, by connecting the information systems of business partners, IOSs enable both partners to: reduce the costs of routine business transactions; improve the quality of the information flow by reducing or eliminating errors; compress cycle time in the fulfillment of business transactions; eliminate paper processing and its associated inefficiencies and costs; and make the transfer and processing of information easy for users.

A major characteristic of an IOS is that the customer–supplier relationship frequently is determined in advance (as in the case of Dell), with the expectation that it will be ongoing. Advance arrangements result in agreements between organizations on the nature and format of the business documents and payments that will be exchanged. Both parties also know which communication networks will be integral to the system. Interorganizational systems may be built around privately or publicly accessible networks.

When IOSs use telecommunications companies for communication, they may employ *value-added networks* (VANs). These are *private,* third-party networks that can be tailored to specific business needs. However, use of *publicly accessible* networks (Internet, extranet) is growing with the increased use of the Internet.

**VIRTUAL CORPORATIONS AND IT SUPPORT**

One category of IOS is virtual corporations.

A **virtual corporation (VC)** is an organization composed of two or more business partners, in different locations, sharing costs and resources for the purpose of producing a product or service. The VC can be temporary, with a one-time mission such as launching a satellite, or it can be permanent. Permanent virtual corporations are designed to create or assemble a broad range of productive resources rapidly, frequently, and concurrently. Each partner in a VC creates a portion of a product or service, in an area in which they have special advantage (such as expertise or low cost). The major characteristics of VCs are listed in Online File W9.1.

The concept of VCs is not new, but recent developments in IT allow new implementations. The modern VC can be viewed as a *network* of creative people, resources, and ideas connected via online services and/or the Internet, who band together to produce products or services. In a VC the resources of the business partners remain in their original locations but are integrated for the VC's use. Because the partners are in different locations, they need IOSs to support communication and collaboration. (Note: Some people use the term *virtual corporation* more narrowly, to describe a pure online company.)

*Example: Virtual Corporation Works with IT Support.* Sundia Corp. is a micro-multinational startup that produces and sells fruit juices (currently watermelon). The headquarters, which consists of two people, is in San Francisco. Here is how this virtual corporation works:

1. Growers in Mexico and California ship fruits to a plant near Seattle.
2. The plant makes watermelon concentrate and ships it to bottlers in California.
3. The bottlers make juice from concentrate, bottle the drink, and ship it to warehouses in California and in Wisconsin.
4. Marketing, payment verification, and arrangement is done in San Francisco, London, and Singapore.
5. Orders go to marketing, and if approved are forwarded to customer service in the Philippines.
6. Orders are generated in the Philippines and transferred to the warehouses nearest to each customer. A copy of the order goes to the accounting/finance office in India.
7. The warehouse sends fulfilled orders to customers and notifies India to bill the customer, which is completed via headquarters in San Francisco.
8. The customer pays the bill.

IT support facilitates the process using VoIP, e-mail, a wiki, instant messaging (IM), and collaborative services. For more details, see Coopland (2006).

*POM*

*Example: No Need to Buy Office Furniture for Turnstone.* Steelcase Inc. (*steelcase. com*) is a major U.S. maker of office furniture. It formed a virtual corporation subsidiary called Turnstone that sells its products through catalogs designed and printed by a third-party company (and now also available on the Web; e.g., see *shopping.com*). Turnstone's customers e-mail or phone in credit card–based orders to a telemarketing company based in Denver, Colorado, which transmits the order data to computers at warehouses operated by Excel Logistics, Inc. in Westerville, Ohio. From there, subcontracted carriers ship the products to manufacturing plants. Excel's computer systems handle all order processing, shipment tracking, and inventory control applications. Marketing, financial management, and coordinating the virtual company's business partners are the only major functions left to Turnstone's managers. A comprehensive IOS provides seamless communication and effective collaboration among all partners.

Steelcase is using several other technologies. For example, to facilitate collaboration (including its own virtual teams; see Chapter 4) the company uses Groove Virtual Office software. For details see Groove.net (2006).

**TYPES OF INTER-ORGANIZATIONAL INFORMATION SYSTEMS**

Interorganizational information systems include a variety of business activities, from data interchange to messaging services to funds transfers. The most prominent types of interorganizational systems are the following.

- **B2B trading systems.** These systems are designed to facilitate trading between (among) business partners. The partners can be in the same or in different countries. B2B trading systems were covered in Chapter 5, where we described both company-centric (private) e-marketplaces and many-to-many public exchanges.
- **B2B support systems.** These are nontrading systems such as hubs, directories, and other services.
- **Global systems.** Global information systems connect two or more companies in two or more countries. The airline reservations system SABRE is an example of a huge global system.

- **Electronic funds transfer (EFT).** In EFT, telecommunications networks transfer money among financial institutions.
- **Groupware.** Groupware technologies (Chapter 4) facilitate communication and collaboration between and among organizations. These include a transmission system that can be used to deliver electronic mail and fax documents between organizations.
- **Shared databases.** Trading partners sometimes share databases and other information in order to reduce time in communicating information between parties and to arrange cooperative activities.
- **Systems that support virtual companies.** These IOSs provide support to *virtual companies*—two or more business partners, in different locations, sharing costs and resources to provide a product or service.

Four major IOS infrastructure technologies are described in this chapter:

**IOS INFRASTRUCTURE TECHNOLOGIES**

Technology Guides are located at the book's Web site.

1. **Electronic data interchange (EDI).** The electronic movement of business documents between business partners. EDI runs on VANs (see Chapter 4 and Technology Guide 4), but it can be Internet-based, in which case it is known as EDI/Internet.
2. **Extranets.** Extended intranets that link business partners.
3. **XML.** An emerging B2B standard, promoted as a companion or even a replacement for EDI systems.
4. **Web Services.** The emerging technology for integrating B2B and intrabusiness applications (see Technology Guide 6).

In addition, there are specialized technologies such as BRL in finance (Chapter 7). The above IOS infrastructure technologies are the subject of Appendices 9A and 9B.

## 9.3 Global Information Systems

Interorganizational systems that connect companies (or parts of one company) located in two or more countries are referred to as **global information systems.** Multinational companies, international companies, and virtual global companies typically need global information for their B2B operations. Companies that have global B2C operations usually use the Internet.

*Multinational companies* are those that operate in several countries. Examples are Coca-Cola, McDonald's, IBM, and Siemens (a German company). Multinational organizations may have sales offices and/or production facilities in several countries (e.g., see Minicase 1). They may conduct operations in locations where factory workers are plentiful and inexpensive, or where highly skilled employees are available at low salaries, or where there is a need to be close to the market. SAP/AP, for example, has a large research and development division in Silicon Valley, California, and distribution and sales offices in dozens of countries. Microsoft has a research center in China.

*International companies* are those that do business with other companies in different countries. For example, Boeing Corporation solicits bids from and does contract work with manufacturers in over 40 countries.

*Virtual global companies* are joint ventures whose business partners are located in different countries. The partners form a company for the specific purpose of producing a product or service. Such companies can be temporary, with a one-time mission (such as building an oil pipeline), or they can be permanent.

All of the above companies use some global information systems. Examples include airline reservation systems such as SABRE (*sabre.com*), police and immigration systems, electronic funds transfer (EFT) systems (including networks of ATMs), and many commercial and educational systems for international organizations such as the United Nations.

**BENEFITS OF GLOBAL INFORMATION SYSTEMS**

Regardless of its structure, a company with global operations relies heavily on IT (see Lucas, 2005, and Chapter 5). The major benefits of global information systems for such organizations, made possible by IT, are:

- **Effective communication at a reasonable cost.** The partners are far from each other, yet they are able to work together, make decisions, monitor transactions, and provide controls. Business partners communicate through e-mail, EDI, Web Services (see Online File W9.2), and extranets. Communication is even more critical if the partners speak different languages. Intelligent IT systems can provide automatic language and Web page translation (to be described later).
- **Effective collaboration to overcome differences in distance, time, language, and culture.** Collaboration can be enhanced with groupware software (Chapter 4), group decision support systems (see Chapter 12), extranets, and teleconferencing devices (Chapter 4). For an interesting case, see the Boeing 787 case in Online File W4.4 (Chapter 4).
- **Access to databases of business partners and ability to work on the same projects while their members are in different locations.** Information technologies such as video teleconferencing and screen sharing (Chapter 4) are useful for this purpose.

**ISSUES IN GLOBAL IS DESIGN AND IMPLEMENTATION**

The task of designing any effective interorganizational information system is complicated. It is even more complex when the IOS is a *global system,* because of differences in cultures, regulations, economics, and politics among parties in different countries.

Although the potential for a global economy certainly exists, some countries are erecting artificial borders through local language preference, local regulation, and access limitations. In addition, barriers of various sorts must be dealt with before global information systems can achieve their potential. Some issues to consider in designing global IOSs are cultural differences, localization, economic and political differences, and legal and ethical issues (see Porter, 2006).

**Cultural Differences.** *Culture* consists of the objects, values, and other characteristics of a particular society. It includes many different aspects ranging from tradition, to legal and ethical issues, to what information is considered offensive. When companies plan to do business in countries other than their own, they must consider the cultural environment. A well-known example is GM's car Nova. *No va* means "no go" in Spanish. GM did not pay attention to this issue, and the model's sales in Spanish-speaking countries suffered as a result. For details see Burgess and Hunter (2005).

**Localization.** Many companies use different names, colors, sizes, and packaging for their overseas products and services. This practice is referred to as *localization*. In order to maximize the benefits of global information systems, the localization approach should also be used in the design and operation of the supporting information system. For example, many Web sites offer different language and/or currency options, as well as special content. Europcar (*europcar.com*), for example, offers portals in 118 countries, each with an option for one of 10 languages (see Chapter 7). For more on localization see *A Closer Look 9.1.*

# A Closer Look 9.1

When companies bring their products and services to foreign markets, they may need to move away from standardization. The problem is how to do it in an efficient way. Rigby and Vishwanath (2006) provide a list of items that demand attention. Details are available in the original article.

**Variables Considered in Localization**

- Branding (names, language)
- Store formats (size, layout)
- Merchandise spaces and assortment (size, color, style, flavor, package design)
- Pricing (range, changes, financing)
- Promotions (types, duration, discount level)

- Vendor policies
- Management programs
- Store service levels
- Vendor services
- Operating policies

**Location Variables**

- Consumer characteristics
- Special demand drivers
- Competitor characteristics
- Company's own stores' characteristics versus others

*Sources:* Rigby and Vishwanath (2006) and SDL International (2005).

**Economic and Political Differences.** Countries also differ considerably in their economic and political environments. One result of such variations is that the information infrastructures may differ from country to country. For example, many countries own the telephone services; others control communications very tightly. France, for example, insisted for years that French should be the sole language on French Web sites. Additional languages are now allowed, but French must also appear in every site with a URL address ending with .fr. China controls the content of the Internet, blocking some Web sites from being viewed in China.

**Legal Issues.** Legal systems differ considerably among countries. Examples are copyrights, patents, computer crimes, file sharing, privacy, and data transfer. All of these issues have the potential to affect what is transmitted via global information systems, and so they must be considered. The impact of legal, economic, and political differences on the design and use of global information systems can be clearly seen in the issue of cross-border data transfer.

*Transfer of Data Across International Borders.* Several countries, such as Canada and Brazil, impose strict laws to control **cross-border data transfer,** the flow of corporate data across nations' borders. These countries usually justify their laws as protecting the privacy of their citizens, since corporate data frequently contain personal data. Other justifications are intellectual property protection and keeping jobs within the country by requiring that data processing be done there.

The transfer of information in and out of a nation raises an interesting legal issue: Whose laws have jurisdiction when records are in a different country for reprocessing or retransmission purposes? For example, if data are transmitted by a Polish company through a U.S. satellite to a British corporation, whose laws control the data, and when? In order to solve some of these issues, governments are developing laws and standards to cope with the rapid increase of information technology, and international efforts to standardize these laws and standards are underway (e.g., see *oecd.org*). Some issues of cross-border data transfer are shown in Online File W9.3. Legal issues can be complicated when regulations and compliance are involved. They are similar to the compliance issues described in Chapter 7.

**Designing Web Sites for a Global Audience.** Designing Web sites for a global audience is important. Web sites need to address cultural, legal, language, and other factors. These factors are summarized by Dubie (2003), who points out that 60 percent of all Internet users are non-English–speaking. Thus, doing business on the Internet must include *localization*, which includes translating languages, adapting content to meet cultural standards, and more. Dubie suggests how to customize Web sites and evaluates the power of machine translation (only 60% accurate).

**Globalization and Offshoring of Software and Other IT Activities.** One of the key issues related to IT and globalization is that of offshore outsourcing. Initially, there was only outsourcing of programming. However, since 2000 there is outsourcing of many other IT activities ranging from call centers to software research and development. A comprehensive report on the topic was published by *Communications of the ACM*, as it related to the migration of jobs worldwide (see details in Aspray et al., 2006). We return to this topic in Chapters 14 and 15 where we explore the issue in greater detail.

**Globalization and Personnel Issues.** A major issue in globalization is the orientation and, if needed, training of personnel. Companies may need to send their employees to other countries and also hire local personnel. IT programs can help in finding people and hiring them, and in training. For details, see the HRM section in Chapter 7. Large organizations may have a major undertaking in this area, as the case of Hewlett-Packard (HP) demonstrates.

*Example: HP Consulting.* HP has over 6,000 consultants who live and work all across the globe, speak scores of different languages, and operate in a multitude of business cultures. HP created a special Global People Development unit whose mission is to make sure the consultants stay on top of technical issues from e-intelligence to IT infrastructure, and then help them tailor their consulting and client-relationship skills to their particular business environment.

To organize and plan the training session, HP is using a special software from Mindjet Corp. (*mindjet.com*). The company uses the MindManager tool that allows them to map the activities involved in various tasks of the planning. The maps enable the HRM managers to convey complex ideas in a very simple, visually appealing format. The presentation is not an outline that uses line after line of text, or a slide-based presentation that asks viewers to remember previous screens. MindManager maps use a system of text, graphics, and icons to present complex ideas on a one-page map.

**CHARACTERISTICS AND PROBLEMS ALONG GLOBAL SUPPLY CHAINS**

A special issue for global companies and their global information systems is how to optimize their supply chains. Supply chains that involve suppliers and/or customers in other countries are referred to as *global supply chains* (e.g., see Robinson et al., 2005). E-commerce has made it much easier to find suppliers in other countries (e.g., by using e-directories and electronic bidding) as well as to find customers in other countries (see Handfield et al., 2002, and Turban et al., 2008).

Global supply chains are usually longer than domestic ones, and they may be complex. Therefore, interruptions and uncertainties are likely. Some of the issues that may create difficulties in global supply chains are legal issues, customs fees and taxes, language and cultural differences, fast changes in currency exchange rates, and political instabilities. An example of difficulties in a global supply chain can be seen in *IT at Work 9.1*.

Information technologies have proven to be extremely useful in supporting global supply chains, but one needs to carefully design global information systems. For

# IT at Work 9.1

## Lego Struggles with Global Issues

*MKT     GLOBAL*

Lego Company of Denmark (*lego.com*) is a major producer of toys, including electronic ones. It is the world's best-known toy manufacturer (voted as "the toy of the 20th century") and has thousands of Web sites and blogs created by fans all over the world.

In 1999 the company decided to market its Lego Mindstorms on the Internet (now MindStorm NXT). This product is a unique innovation. Its users can build a Lego robot using more than 700 traditional Lego elements, program it on a PC, and transfer the program to the robot. Lego sells its products in many countries using several regional distribution centers.

When the decision to do global electronic commerce was made, the company had the following concerns. (Note that although this is a B2C example, many of the concerns are common to B2B as well.)

- It did not make sense to go online to all countries, since sales are very low in some countries and some countries offer no logistical support services. In which countries should Lego sell the product?

- A supportive distribution and service system would be needed for e-commerce sales, including returns and software support.

- There was an issue of merging the offline and online operations versus creating a new centralized unit, which seemed to be a complex undertaking.

- Existing warehouses were optimized to handle distribution to commercial buyers (retailers), not to individual customers. E-commerce sales to individual customers would need to be accommodated.

- It would be necessary to handle returns around the globe.

- Lego products were selling in different countries in different currencies and at different prices. Should the product be sold on the Net at a single price? In which currency? How would this price be related to the offline prices?

- How should the company handle the direct mail and track individual shipments?

- Invoicing must comply with the regulations of many countries.

- Should Lego create a separate Web site for Mindstorms? What languages should be used there?

- Some countries have strict regulations regarding advertising and sales to children. Also laws on consumer protection vary among countries. Lego needed to understand and deal with these differences.

- How should the company handle restrictions on electronic transfer of individuals' personal data?

- How should the company handle the tax and import duty payments in different countries?

In the rush to get its innovative product to the online market, Lego did not solve all of these issues before it introduced the direct Internet marketing. The resulting problems forced Lego to close the Web site for business in 1998. It took about a year to solve all global trade-related issues and eventually reopen the site. By 2001 Lego was selling online many of its products, priced in U.S. dollars, but the online service was available in only 19 countries (2006).

As of 2003, *Lego.com* has been operating as an independent unit, allowing online design of many products (e.g., see "Make and Create"). Lego also offers electronic games at *club.lego.com/eng/games/default.asp?bhcp=1*. The site offers many Web-only deals, and it is visited by over 5 million unique visitors each day.

*Sources:* Compiled from *lego.com* (2006), Damsgaard and Horluck (2000), Stoll (2006), and from *mindstorm.lego.com*.

*For Further Exploration:* Is the Web the proper way to go global? Why does it make sense to sell the Lego products on the Internet? Some companies sell certain products only online. Does it make sense for Lego to do this, too?

---

example, TradeNet in Singapore connects sellers, buyers, and government agencies via electronic data interchange (EDI). (TradeNet's case is described in detail in Online File W9.4.) A similar network, TradeLink, is operating in Hong Kong, using both EDI and EDI/Internet and attempting to connect about 70,000 potential trading partners.

IT provides not only EDI and other communication infrastructure options, but also online expertise in sometimes difficult and fast-changing regulations. IT also can be instrumental in helping businesses find trading partners (via electronic directories and search engines, as in the case of *alibaba.com*). In addition, IT can help solve language problems through use of automatic Web page translation (see *A Closer Look 9.2*).

**Machine Translation of Languages.** A major application of natural language processing (NLP; Chapter12), is *automatic translation* of documents from one language

# A Closer Look 9.2

**Automatic Translation of Web Pages**

Here are some major vendors and their automatic translations products:

- WorldPoint (*worldpoint.com*) offers a WorldPoint Passport multilingual software tool that allows Web developers to create a Web site in one language and deploy it in several other languages.
- Altavista offers the free Babel Fish Translation (*world.altavista. com*) that translates Web pages, e-mail, and text. Babel Fish supports 19 language pairs. It is linked to *Newstran.com*, which translates online newspapers to English.
- Alis Technologies and Netscape developed *AutoTranslate* offered in Netscape browser. Available in the "View" menu (click on "translate"), users can see a translation to a desired language (out of 10 available languages).
- The U.S. Air Force Research Lab (*rl.af.mil/div/IFB/techtrans/ datasheets/ASLT.html*) developed an automatic spoken language translation. The project has been expanded so that it now includes Web translation as well.
- *Google.com/language-tools* offers a service called "BETA" that translates automatically to English the content of

Web pages published in French, German, Italian, Spanish, Portuguese, and more. All you have to do is click on the "Translate This Page" button that appears after a title in a foreign language.

- *Uniscape.com* (now *trados.com*) offers software that does multilingual translation for companies that want to provide translated Web pages from their URLs. Product documentation, Web sites, marketing materials, and software interfaces can be localized in many languages quickly and cost-effectively. The company's site, *Translationzone.com*, also is a portal for translation professionals worldwide and offers resources to help translators expand their customer bases. Professional translators can purchase the latest releases of Trados software (*trados.com*) as well as create online professional profiles, through which they can market themselves to potential clients. The portal currently has more than 12,000 registered users.
- *Rikai.com* is an online character translator that allows users to translate Japanese Web pages.

to another. Such translation is important for creating Web pages for a multinational audience, understanding large volumes of documents in foreign languages (e.g., for security reasons), learning foreign languages, collaboration in teams whose members speak different languages, and conducting global e-business. Let's see how such translation works.

**Translation of Content to Other Languages.** In the global marketplace, content created in one language often needs to be translated to another to reach collaborative business partners in other countries. This is true both for paper and electronic documents. For example, in some cases, an effective Web site may need to be specifically designed and targeted to the market that it is trying to reach. Language translation is especially important in countries such as China, Japan, and Korea, where relatively few people understand English well enough to use it online. The language barrier between countries and regions presents an interesting and complicated challenge (see *worldlingo.com*).

For example, travelers may not be able to read signs in other countries, or they prefer information to be in their native, or a selected language. A device called Info-Scope (from IBM) can read signs, restaurant menus, and other text written in one language and translate them into several other languages. Currently, these translators are available only for short messages.

The primary problems with language translation, especially for the Web sites, are cost and speed. It currently takes a human translator about a week to translate a medium-size Web site into just one language. For larger sites, the cost ranges from $30,000 to $500,000, depending on the complexity of the site and languages of translation.

WorldPoint (*worldpoint.com*) presents a creative solution to these translation issues with its WorldPoint Passport multilingual software tool. The WorldPoint Passport solution allows Web developers to create a Web site in one language and deploy it in several other languages. However, automatic translation may be inaccurate. Therefore, many experts advocate manual translation with the help of the computer as a productivity booster. As time passes, though, automatic translation is improving.

According to Sullivan (2001), the best way to assess machine translation is to use the following criteria: (1) intelligibility (i.e., How well can a reader get the gist of a translated document?); (2) accuracy (i.e., How many errors occur during a translation?); and (3) speed (i.e., How many words per second are translated?).

For more on automatic language translation for Web pages including some translation tools, see Online File W9.5.

In order to overcome logistics problems along the supply chain, especially global ones, companies are outsourcing logistics services to logistics vendors. Global information systems help enable tight communication and collaboration among supply chain members, as shown in *IT at Work 9.2* (page 359).

As IT technologies advance and global trade expands, more organizations will find the need to implement global information systems.

**Financial Global Supply Chains.** As explained in Chapter 8, supply chains involve flows of money as well as products. This may be a problem in some companies or countries.

The flow of money in global trade is usually facilitated by IT systems starting with an electronic letter of credit and ending with solutions provided by companies such as TradeCard. A major topic is how to pay suppliers in other countries. For how it is done by RITE Aid, see Robbins-Gentry (2006). Electronic funds transfer (EFT), which has been in place for decades, is more sophisticated so payments can be transferred faster.

One crucial issue is dynamic currency conversion. Some currencies fluctuate very fast, so an exact exchange rate must be known to sellers and buyers all the time. Currency conversion sites may provide inaccurate information such as the closing exchange rate the previous day. Currency conversion may be subject to government regulations and restrictions. These regulations may be important to trade partners.

With increased emphasis on real-time demand and fast order fulfillment, e-payments have become a critical element in financial global supply chains. For more on the topic, see Gustin (2005).

Several organizations and individuals have developed guides for properly managing IT in a global organization. A summary of principles for managing IT in global organizations proposed by Spatz is available in Online File W9.6.

# 9.4 Facilitating IOS and Global Systems: From Demand-Driven Networks to RFID

A large number of IT solutions are available to facilitate information flow and processing in IOS and global systems. Some of these solutions are presented next.

**DEMAND-DRIVEN SUPPLY NETWORKS (DDSNs)**

Traditionally, the supply chain has been driven from the back, by producers and manufacturers "driving products to market." The dominant action in a traditional supply chain was to forecast demand, make-to-stock, and push products downstream toward end customers. Businesses in the supply chain were merely accepting of demand based on the orders received from businesses in front of them in the supply chain. They rarely had any view into the true market demand for a product. To maintain downstream momentum to reduce inventory investments, upstream businesses constantly had to exert pressure on the downstream businesses to place

# *IT* at Work 9.2

## *How BikeWorld Uses Global Information Systems to Fulfill Orders*

POM    GLOBAL

BikeWorld (San Antonio, Texas) is a small company (16 employees) known for its high-quality bicycles and components, expert advice, and personalized service. The company opened its Web site (*bikeworld.com*) in February 1996, using it as a way to expand its reach to customers outside of Texas, including other countries.

BikeWorld encountered two of Internet retailing's biggest problems: fulfillment and after-sale customer service. Sales of its high-value bike accessories over the Internet steadily increased, including global markets. But the time BikeWorld spent processing orders manually, shipping packages, and responding to customers' order status inquiries was overwhelming for the company.

In order to focus on its core competency (making bicycles and their components), BikeWorld decided to outsource its order fulfillment. FedEx offered reasonably priced, quality express delivery, exceeding customer expectations while automating the fulfillment process. Whit Snell, BikeWorld's founder, knew that his company needed the help that FedEx's global systems could provide: "To go from a complete unknown to a reputable worldwide retailer was going to require more than a fair price. We set out to absolutely amaze our customers with unprecedented customer service. FedEx gave us the blinding speed we needed," Snell said. The ship-ping is free for a normal delivery. You pay extra for expedited delivery on some items.

The nearby figure shows the five steps in the fulfillment process. (Explanations are provided in the figure.) Notice that the logistics vendor (FedEx), with its sophisticated information system, provides services to the customers (such as order tracking).

Four years after BikeWorld ventured online, its sales volume more than quadrupled and is consistently profitable. Thanks to its outsourcing of order fulfillment, and to FedEx's world-class information systems, BikeWorld has a fully automated and scalable fulfillment system; has access to real-time order status data, which enhances customer service and leads to greater customer retention; and has the capacity to service global customers. The site offers free topographical maps (take the tour), order tracking, customer support, employment opportunities, and more.

*Sources:* Compiled from FedEx (2000), and from *bikeworld.com* (accessed June 2006).

*For Further Exploration:* Identify the necessary IOSs between FedEx and the customers, and between BikeWorld and FedEx. Visit *fedex.com* and find out how FedEx can help any company in global trade.

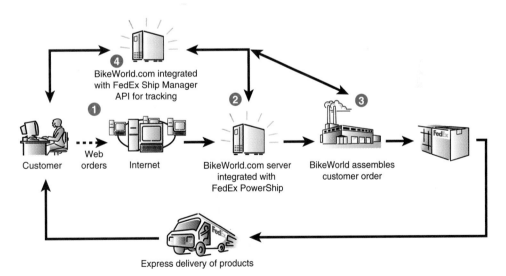

BikeWorld's order fulfillment process. (*Source:* FedEx, 2000.)

orders. In this environment, demand could often be erratic and therefore hard to predict. Items could go from a situation of understock to overstock in a very short time, resulting in large safety overstocks (a situation known as the bullwhip effect (see *A Closer Look 9.3*), and businesses across the supply chain did not have timely and accurate information to balance the turbulence.

# A Closer Look 9.3

## The Bullwhip Effect

POM

The **bullwhip effect** (as described in Chapter 8) refers to erratic shifts in orders up and down the supply chain. This effect was initially observed by Procter & Gamble (P&G) with its disposable diapers product (Pampers). While actual sales in retail stores were fairly stable and predictable, orders from distributors to the manufacturer, P&G, had wild swings, creating production and inventory problems. An investigation revealed that distributors' orders were fluctuating because of poor demand forecast, price fluctuation, order batching, and rationing within the supply chain. These dysfunctions resulted in unnecessary and costly inventories in various locations along the supply chain, fluctuations in P&G production levels as well as in orders to P&G's suppliers, and flow of inaccurate information. Distorted information can lead to tremendous inefficiencies, excessive inventories, poor customer service, lost revenues, ineffective shipments, and missed production schedules (Donovan, 2002/2003).

The bullwhip effect is not unique to P&G, however. Firms ranging from Hewlett-Packard in the computer industry to Bristol-Myers Squibb in pharmaceuticals have experienced a similar phenomenon. Basically, demand variables can become magnified when viewed through the eyes of managers at each link in the supply chain. If each distinct entity makes ordering and inventory decisions with an eye to its own interest above those of the chain, stockpiling may be simultaneously occurring at as many as seven or eight locations along the supply chain. Study has shown that such hoarding has led in some cases to as many as 100 days of inventory that is waiting, "just in case" (versus 10–20 days in the normal case).

A 1998 industry study projected that $30 billion in savings could materialize in grocery industry supply chains alone, by sharing information and collaborating. Thus, companies are trying to avoid the "sting of the bullwhip" as well as to solve other SCM problems.

*Sources: Donovan (2002/2003) and Logic Tools (2006)*

In contrast, **demand-driven supply networks (DDSNs)** are driven from the front by customer demand. Instead of products being pushed to market, they are pulled to market by customers. Is the once-dominant force of pushing merely being replaced by a dominant force of pulling? Not entirely; DDSN does not remove the ability of a company to push product to market. It merely defines that companies in a supply chain will work more closely to shape market demand *sharing* and *collaborating* information. In doing so, they will have a greater and more timely view of demand. The aim of this collaboration is to better position everyone in the supply chain with the ability to more closely follow market demand and produce, in tandem, what the market wants. The methodology behind DDSN is to bring the supply chain ecosystem into balance.

The benefits of DDSN according to Swift (2005), Wheller (2005), and Lee et al. (2004) are:

- More accurate and detailed demand forecasting (often to SKU-level detail or location/store-level detail).
- Lower supply chain costs (with reduced inventories, expediting, and write-offs).
- Improved perfect-order performance (an order that is delivered complete, accurate, on time, and in perfect condition).
- Reduced days of inventory (average days of inventory on hand, including raw materials, components, work in process, and finished goods).
- Improved cash-to-cash performance (the length of time between when a company spends cash to buy raw materials and the time the cash flows back into the company from its customers).
- It provides a customer-centric approach, as opposed to a factory-centric approach.
- All participants in the supply chain are able to take part in shaping demand, minimizing the bullwhip effect.
- Probabilistic optimization is used to better deal with uncertainties (e.g., simulation and "what-if"; see Chapter 12).

According to Lee et al. (2004), DDSN capabilities provide for agility, adaptability, and alignment, which are defined as follows:

**Agility**—the ability to respond quickly to short-term change in the demand and supply equation and manage external disruptions more effectively

**Adaptability**—the ability to adjust the design of the supply chain to meet structural shifts in markets and modify supply network strategies, products, and technologies

**Alignment**—the ability to create shared incentives that align the interests of businesses across the supply chain

Demand-driven supply network software is available from Oracle, Teradata, IBM, SAP, Sypro, Microsoft, and many other vendors. For details, see *amrresearch.com/content/* (click on resource center).

One component of DDSN is real-time demand-driven manufacturing.

**Real-Time Demand-Driven Manufacturing.** Successful manufacturing organizations must respond quickly and efficiently to demand. Strategies and techniques of the past no longer work, and it's a challenge to transform from the traditional, inventory-centric model to a more profitable and flexible demand-driven enterprise. *Demand-driven manufacturing* (DDM) provides customers with exactly what they want, when and where they want it. Effective communication between the supply chain and the factory floor is needed to make it happen. Partnerships must be focused on reducing costs through shared quality goals, shared design responsibility, on-time deliveries, and continuous performance reviews. The DDM process is shown in Figure 9.2. An explanation of the headings in the figure is provided in Online File W9.7.

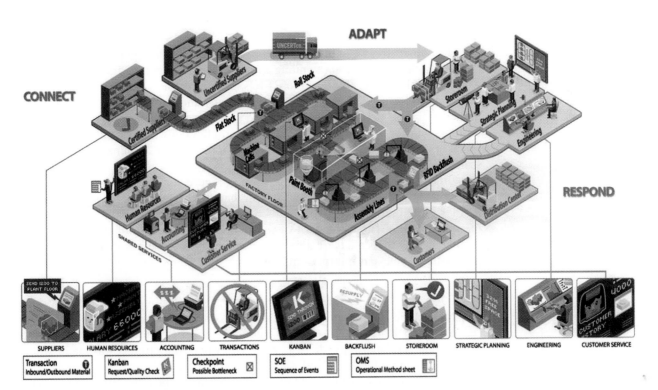

**Figure 9.2** Real-time demand-driven manufacturing. (*Source:* PeopleTalk, "Real Time Demand Driven Manufacturing," 15(3), July–Sept. 2004, pp. 14–15. XXPLANATIONS© by XPLANE©, 2005, *XXPLANE.com*, courtesy of Oracle.)

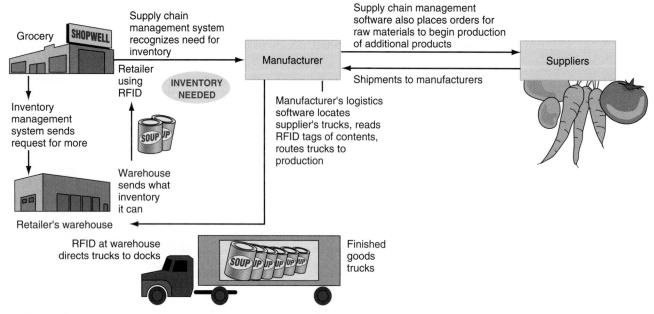

**Figure 9.3**  How radio frequency ID tags smooth supply chains.

**USING RFID TO IMPROVE SUPPLY CHAINS**

One of the newest (and possibly most revolutionary) solutions to supply chain problems is RFID. We introduced the concept of RFID in Chapters 6 and 7. We said that large companies and governments require that their largest suppliers attach RFID tags to every pallet or box they ship to them. Eventually, RFIDs will be attached to every item. This can be done due to their tiny size (a grain of sand) and the low cost (less than 5 cents apiece).

How might RFIDs improve the supply chain? Look at Figure 9.3, which shows the supply chain relationships among a retailer, a manufacturer, and suppliers, all of whom use RFID tags. Because the RFIDs are used by all companies in the figure, automatic alerts can be sent within each company and between companies. There is no longer a need to count inventories, and visibility of inventories is provided to all business partners. These benefits can go several tiers down the supply chain. Additional applications, such as rapid checkout in a retail store, eliminating the need to scan each item, will be available in the future.

Other applications of RFID are shown in Figure 9.4. The upper part of the figure shows how the tags are used when merchandise travels from the supplier to the retailer. Note that the RFID transmits real-time information about the location of the merchandise. The lower part of the figure shows the use of the RFID at the retailer, mainly to locate merchandise, control inventory, prevent theft, and expedite processing of relevant information.

**More About RFID.**  The RFID tag is about the size of a pinhead or grain of sand. The tag includes an antenna and a chip that contains an electronic product code (EPC; see discussion of Auto-ID in Chapter 6). The EPC stores much more information than a regular barcode (e.g., when and where the product was made, where the components come from, and when they might perish).

Unlike barcodes, which need line-of-sight contact to be read, RFID tags also act as passive tracking devices, signaling their presence over a radio frequency when they pass within yards of a special scanner. The tags have long been used in high-cost

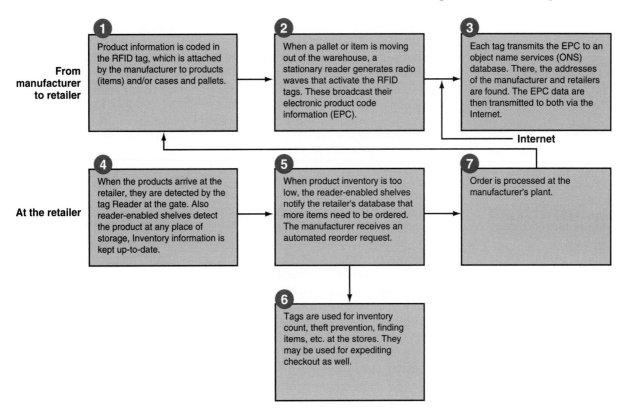

**1** Product information is coded in the RFID tag, which is attached by the manufacturer to products (items) and/or cases and pallets.

**2** When a pallet or item is moving out of the warehouse, a stationary reader generates radio waves that activate the RFID tags. These broadcast their electronic product code information (EPC).

**3** Each tag transmits the EPC to an object name services (ONS) database. There, the addresses of the manufacturer and retailers are found. The EPC data are then transmitted to both via the Internet.

**From manufacturer to retailer**

**Internet**

**4** When the products arrive at the retailer, they are detected by the tag Reader at the gate. Also reader-enabled shelves detect the product at any place of storage, Inventory information is kept up-to-date.

**5** When product inventory is too low, the reader-enabled shelves notify the retailer's database that more items need to be ordered. The manufacturer receives an automated reorder request.

**7** Order is processed at the manufacturer's plant.

**At the retailer**

**6** Tags are used for inventory count, theft prevention, finding items, etc. at the stores. They may be used for expediting checkout as well.

**Figure 9.4** How RFID works in a manufacturer–retailer supply chain. (*Source:* Drawn by E. Turban.)

applications such as automated tolling systems and security-ID badges. Recent innovations have caused the price of the tags to plummet and their performance to improve, enabling them to be used more widely.

The prospect of affordable RFID tags has retailers drooling. If every item in a shop were tagged, RFID technology could be used to locate mislaid products, to deter theft, and even to offer customers personalized sales pitches through displays mounted in dressing rooms. Ultimately, tags and readers could replace barcodes and checkout labor altogether. For more about RFID, see Kinsella (2003) and Reda (2003).

**Limitations of RFID.** For small companies, the cost of an RFID system may be too high (at least for some time). Also, there may be atmospheric interference (expected to be minimized in the future), as well as limited range (only 30–50 feet at this time). The fear of violating customers' privacy is another issue. Agreeing on universal standards, as well as connecting the RFIDs with existing IT systems, are technical issues to be solved. For other limitations, see Kinsella (2003).

**Where Does RFID Go?** In Chapter 6, we presented the benefits and limitations of RFID and pointed to its potential use in supply chains. Here we provide an illustration of how RFID can work. The question is, given its potential benefits and limitations, where does RFID go?

By 2006, several large retailers (e.g., Sears, Target) were using the technology at least on containers and trucks (e.g., Scheraga, 2006; Angeles, 2005; and Barrett and Carr, 2005). Placing tags on individual items has proven to be expensive, and was resisted by privacy advocates (e.g., in the case of Levi Strauss). Applications started to spread to nonretailing, such as in airports to improve baggage handling and security (e.g., the Hong Kong airport, see Robinson, 2005). The military is using RFID extensively in its global supply chain (Boucher Ferguson, 2006). Philip Morris is using tags to track the flow of illegal movement of cigarettes (Barrett and Carr, 2005). Pharmaceutical companies use RFID tags to track their products, and the list of applications is increasing rapidly.

Despite the limitations and privacy advocates' objections to the use of RFID (Chapter 6, and Angeles, 2005), it seems that the benefits, especially in the supply chain area, have the upper hand over the negatives. Tags and system cost are still a major issue (*Baseline* provides a calculator; and see Nolan, 2005).

## B2B EXCHANGES

Considerable support to B2B supply chains can be provided by electronic exchanges (see Ranganatan, 2003). *B2B exchanges,* as discussed in Chapter 5, can be either *private* (one buyer and many sellers, or one seller and many buyers) or *public* (many sellers and buyers). In either case, the communications and transactions are done on IOSs. The IOS in a private exchange is usually controlled by the sole seller or buyer; it usually uses an extranet or EDI. In a public exchange, the IOS can be an extranet or the Internet, usually with a virtual private network (VPN) for increased security.

A system of several interconnected public exchanges is shown in Figure 9.5. Notice that in this example there are three interconnected exchanges (designated by the ovals in the center of the figure). In other cases there may be only one exchange for an entire industry.

B2B public exchanges provide an alternative to private exchanges. As described in Chapter 5, the public exchange manager provides all the necessary information systems to the participants. Thus, buyers and sellers merely have to "plug in" in order to trade. The technology used by the B2B exchange depends on its size and the nature of transactions.

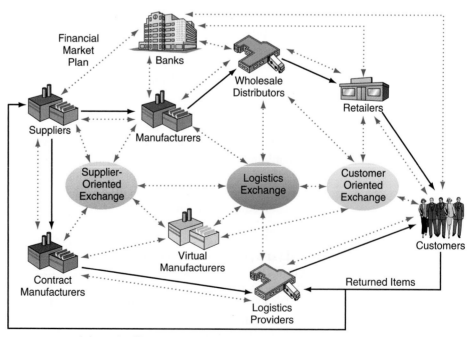

**Figure 9.5** Web-based supply chain involving public exchanges.

B2B public exchanges are sometimes the initial point for contacts between business partners. Once such contact is made, the partners may move to a private exchange or to the private trading rooms provided by many public exchanges to do their subsequent trading activities. Also, partners may continue to work directly with each other, avoiding the public exchange.

**ELECTRONIC HUBS**

B2B exchanges are used mainly to facilitate trading among companies. In contrast, a *hub* is used to facilitate communication and coordination among business partners, frequently *along the supply chain.* Hubs are structured in such a way that each partner can access a Web site, usually a portal, which is used for an exchange of information. Furthermore, each partner can deposit new information, make changes, and receive or leave messages. In some hubs it is possible to conduct trade as well. A structure of an electronic hub is shown in Figure 9.6. An example of a company that provides an electronic hub as well as some public exchange capabilities is Asite, as described in *IT at Work 9.3* (page 366).

A variation of a hub is *supplier networks,* which can be used for purposes such as ordering and even for training (Dyer and Hatch, 2004).

B2B hubs are popular in global trading. Hubs are related to or even combined with directories.

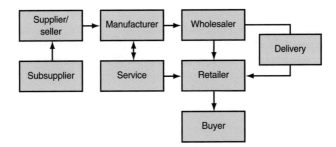

**Traditional Intermediaries**

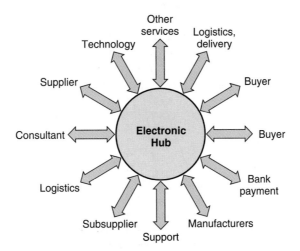

**Figure 9.6** Electronic hub (bottom) compared to traditional intermediaries (top). (*Source:* Drawn by J. Lee and E. Turban.)

**Electronic Hub**

# *IT* at Work 9.3

## Asite's B2B Exchange and E-Hub for the Construction Industry

Asite Network (*asite.com/network.shtml*) is a B2B exchange for the construction industry in the United Kingdom. The construction industry is typified by a high degree of physical separation and fragmentation, and communication among the members of the supply chain (e.g., contractors, subcontractors, architects, supply stores, and building inspectors) has long been a primary problem. Founded in February 2000 by leading players in the construction industry, Asite understands two of the major advantages of the Internet: the ability it provides to communicate more effectively, and the increase in processing power that Internet technologies make possible. Taking advantage of the functions of an online portal as information broker, Asite developed a comprehensive portal for the construction industry. The company's goal is to be the leading information and transaction hub in the European construction industry.

Asite drew on partner organizations with profound industry knowledge and expertise. It made the decision not to build its own technology, but to establish partnerships with technology vendors that have highly specialized products (see *asite.com/partners.shtml*).

Within its portal, Asite set up several interconnected marketplaces (e.g., logistics, insurance, etc.; see the oval area in the figure). These marketplaces serve the needs of the participants in the construction industry—building owners, developers, trade contractors, general contractors, engineers, architects, and materials suppliers—from design through procurement to materials delivery. Participating firms need nothing more sophisticated than a browser to connect to Asite's portal. This ease of access makes it particularly well suited to an industry such as construction, which is distinguished by a high proportion of small, and even single-person, firms.

Asite's partnerships allow it to seamlessly interact with other e-marketplaces. The open standards espoused by vendors in these e-marketplaces enable Asite's technology to be easily incorporated with participating firms' back-end technologies. Such linkages allow full visibility of the supply and demand chains.

The combination of strong backing from industry participants, experienced management from the construction industry, and the commitment to working with best-of-breed technology infrastructure providers is helping construction firms streamline their supply chains.

*Sources:* Compiled from Aberdeen Group (2001) and *asite.com* (accessed July 2006).

*For Further Exploration:* What type of IOS is this (per Section 4.2)? What are the advantages to the participating companies? Why is the exchange connected to the seven marketplaces?

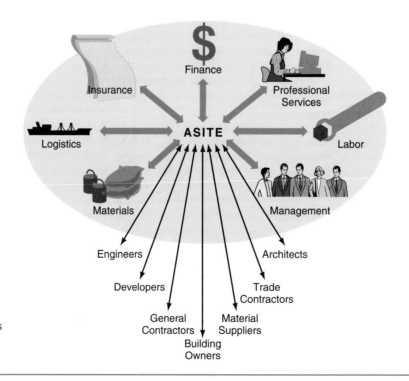

The participants in Asite's E-Marketplace. (*Source:* Aberdeen Group, Inc.)

DIRECTORY
SERVICES

The B2B landscape is huge, with thousands of companies online. Directory services can help buyers and sellers manage the task of finding potential partners. Directories appear as B2B information portals, which usually include catalogues of products offered by each seller, lists of buyers and what they want, and other industry or general information. Buyers can then hyperlink to sellers' sites to complete trades. (Note that the last three entries in the table are search engines, which can be used to discover information about B2B. Some of these search engines are embedded in the directories.)

However, B2B information portals may have a difficult time generating revenue, and so they are starting to offer, for a fee, additional services that support trading. An example of a B2B portal is MyBoeingFleet.com (*myboeingfleet.com*), which is a Web portal for airplane owners, operators, and MRO (maintenance, repair, and operations) vendors (who supply indirect items such as light bulbs and cleaning materials), who have limited access. Developed by Boeing Commercial Aviation Services, MyBoeingFleet.com provides customers (primarily businesses) direct and personalized access to information that is essential to the operation of Boeing aircraft.

Like exchanges, information portals can be horizontal (e.g., Alibaba.com), offering a wide range of products to different industries. Or, they can be vertical, focusing on a single industry or industry segment. Vertical portals are often referred to as *vortals*.

## 9.5 Interorganizational Information Integration

Only a few organizations have an open source infrastructure and applications. In many cases, companies' technologies are proprietary. Therefore, there are difficulties in connecting information systems of different organizations and transfering data in IOSs and global information systems. Furthermore, integrating new technologies, such as RFID, becomes a challenge to organizations (Coffee, 2004).

In this section, we'll cover a few representative issues that are related to IOS and global systems.

INTEGRATING THE
INFORMATION
SYSTEMS OF
MERGING
COMPANIES

When Sears and Kmart united in 2005, their comprehensive and complex systems had to be integrated as well. A similar situation exists with many other companies (e.g., Verizon and MCI, Wells Fargo and First Interstate). According to Chabrow et al. (2006), the ability to integrate an acquired company's IT systems can determine whether a merger is a hit or miss. They provide three examples with lessons learned. Brown et al. (2003) provide an analysis of the successful IT integration of USA Group into Sallie Mae. Among the lessons learned are:

- Establish an IT leadership team to direct the integration.
- For customer-facing applications, select the option with the lowest business integration risks.
- Customer-facing applications must have priority over back-office applications.
- Offer generous retention packages for top-talent IT personnel to ensure they do not leave.
- Maintain high morale among IT personnel.
- Increase the company's normal level of project risk to achieve aggressive business integration goals.
- Use rich communication media to read emotions and recognize successes because a merger is an emotional event.

Chabrow et al. (2006) provide a case study in which proper steps were taken in integrating the IT departments of two large companies.

According to Duvall (2004), Bank of America spent tens of millions of dollars to convert the 1,500 branches of FleetBoston after its acquisition. Duvall also looks at the many difficulties other companies have had in similar cases.

**FACILITATING INTEGRATION**

The first step in conducting a large-scale integration is to check the business processes, understand them, and make improvements if necessary (e.g., Limited Brands case). Here IT plays a major role (see BPM, Chapter 8).

Once processes are improved, the necessary IT infrastructure needs to be planned for (Umar, 2005).

**INTEGRATING IT TECHNOLOGIES**

Several IT technologies assist in IOS and global integration (as well as in internal integration). Note that several types of integration exist. Most applicable to our chapter are *data integration* and *application integration*.

- The most recognized integration technologies are EDI and EDI/Internet. They are covered in detail in Appendix 9A. Modern systems are offered by GXS Inc. (*gxs.com*), Sterling Commerce (*sterlingcommerce.com*), and Inovis, Inc. (*inovis.com*).
- Extranets are emerging that provide a less expensive and more flexible option than VANs (Appendix 9B and Chapter 4).
- XML and similar standards and the related Web Services provide for an open source environment that facilitates integration (Appendix 9B and Chapter 15).
- Portals can piece together services from multiple applications where data sharing is supported by SOAs (Chapters 2 and 15).
- Converters that have the capability to change EDI to SML, for example, are useful.
- Enterprise application integration (EAI) platforms include tools such as FTP, MOM, and CORBA for transporting messages. For further details see Umar (2005).
- Other integrated suites include Oracle's 9i, 10i, 11i, and Fusion Project (see Online File W9.8).

## 9.6 Partner Relationship Management and Collaborative Commerce

Due to their complexity and the involvement of two or more organizations, IOSs and global systems face issues relating to partner relationship management and collaborative commerce.

**PARTNER RELATIONSHIP MANAGEMENT**

Every company that has business partners has to manage the relationships with them. Partners need to be identified, recruited, and maintained. Communication needs to flow between the organizations. Information needs to be updated and shared. **Partner relationship management (PRM)** is a business strategy that recognizes the need to develop long-term relationships with business partners, by providing each partner with the services that are most beneficial to that partner. This strategy is similar to that of CRM, and it is supported by similar IT tools.

Before the spread of Internet technology, there were few automated processes to electronically support business partnerships. Organizations were limited to manual methods of phone, fax, and mail. EDI was used by large corporations, but usually only with their largest partners. Also, there was no systematic way of conducting PRM. Internet technology changed the situation by offering a way to connect different organizations easily, quickly, and affordably.

**What PRM Does.** PRM solutions connect companies with their business partners (suppliers, customers, services) using Web technology to securely distribute and manage information. At its core, a PRM application facilitates partner relationships. Specific functions include: partner profiles, partner communications, management of customer leads, targeted information distribution, connecting the extended enterprise, partner planning, centralized forecasting, group planning, e-mail and Web-based alerts, messaging, price lists, and community bulletin boards. Many large companies offer suppliers or partners portals for improved communication and collaboration. (For more on PRM, see *blueroads.com,* and Murtaza and Shah, 2004.)

**POM**

*Example: Supporting PRM at SkyMall.* *SkyMall.com* (now a subsidiary of Gem-Star TV Guide International) is a retailer that sells from catalogs on board airplanes, over the Internet, and by mail order. It relies on its catalog partners to fill the orders. For small vendors that do not handle their own shipments and for international shipments, SkyMall contracts with distribution centers owned by fulfillment outsourcer Sykes Enterprise.

To coordinate the logistics of sending orders to thousands of customers, Sky-Mall uses integrated EC order-management software called Order Trust. SkyMall leases this software and pays transaction fees for its use. As orders come in, SkyMall conveys the data to Order Trust, which disseminates the information to the appropriate partners (either a vendor or a Sykes distribution center). A report about the shipment is then sent to SkyMall, and SkyMall pays Order Trust the transaction fees. This arrangement has allowed SkyMall to increase its online business by more than 3 percent annually without worrying about order fulfillment. The partners (the makers of the products) also benefit by receiving the electronically transmitted orders quickly.

A Gartner Group survey about CRM, conducted in December 2002, showed that of all sales-related applications, PRM programs had the highest return on investment (*Business Wire,* 2003). For this reason, companies are interested in finding ways to use PRM extensively, as shown in *IT at Work 9.4* (page 370).

**Supplier Relationship Management.** One of the major categories of PRM is **supplier relationship management (SRM),** where the partners are the suppliers. For many companies (e.g., retailers and manufacturers), the ability to work properly with suppliers is a major critical success factor. PeopleSoft, Inc. (*peoplesoft.com*) developed a model for managing relationships with suppliers.

*PeopleSoft's (now an Oracle company) SRM Model.* PeopleSoft's (*oracle.com/ applications/peoplesoft/srm/ent/index.html*) SRM model is generic and could be considered by any large company. It includes 12 steps, illustrated in Figure 9.7 (page 371). The details of the steps are shown in Online File W9.9. The core idea of this model is that an e-supply chain is based on integration and collaboration. The supply chain processes are connected, decisions are made collectively, performance metrics are based on common understanding, information flows in real time (whenever possible), and the only thing a new partner needs in order to join the SRM system is just a Web browser.

# IT at Work 9.4

## CRM/PRM Initiatives at New Piper Aircraft

MKT   POM

Today, New Piper Aircraft is the only general-aviation manufacturer offering a complete line of business and pleasure aircraft (from trainers and high-performance aircraft for personal and business use to turbine-powered business aircraft). In 1992, the company (then Piper Aircraft) was making fewer than 50 planes per year and had $15 million in bank debt and only $1,000 in cash. However, by 2001, the company delivered 441 planes and took in $243 million in revenue. How was this possible?

The fundamental reason for the company's success was its new ownership and management that realized that its ability to provide assistance to customers and partners needed to be completely overhauled. The company purchased Siebel Systems' MidMarket, a CRM software tool, and customized it for PRM. The result was the PULSE Center. PULSE stands for Piper Unlimited Liaison via Standards of Excellence. The system tracks all contacts and communications between New Piper and its dealers and customers. It also helps meet the growing needs of its partner- and customer-care programs.

In less than one year after implementation, the Web-based call center's productivity increased 50 percent, the number of lost sales leads was reduced 25 percent, and sales representatives handled 45 percent more sales. Before the system was instituted, an 11-person call center used spiral notebooks crammed into numerous cabinets to store the data and contacts; it took 30 minutes to locate a contact. Today, the call center tracks 70,000 customers among 17 dealers, and contact information is available in less than a minute.

Development of the PULSE Center took place in stages. The first three phases had been completed by October 2002: Phase 1—loading current aircraft owners, dealers, fleet customers' aircraft, and new customer service employees into the system to develop the organization infrastructure; Phase 2—enabling the Customer Service Center to process activities; and Phase 3—enabling dealers to access sales opportunities pertinent to their territory.

The company is in Phases 4 and 5. Phase 4 is the opening of the Dealer Web Portal, which allows partners (aircraft dealers) access to particular areas of PULSE and provides the technology to make online service requests. Phase 5 streamlines entry of warranty claims. Phase 6, the Partner Web Portal, will allow key suppliers access to areas of the PULSE system and assist in communication with those suppliers. Phase 7 will provide for ordering parts online, and Phase 8 will be the Customer Web Portal giving customers access to open service requests, online logbooks, and product and survey information.

Piper's Vice President for Customers, Dan Snell, says, "New Piper's goal is to lead the industry with respect to quality, excellence, and customer care. It is a challenging mission, but certainly not daunting, and will be achieved through initiatives such as PULSE."

*Sources:* Compiled from Galante (2002); and *New Piper* news releases (2002, 2004).

*For Further Exploration:* Describe the major features of the CRM/PRM program. Why does the company need such an elaborate program? How would you justify it?

---

**COLLABORATIVE COMMERCE**

*Collaborative commerce (c-commerce)* refers to non–selling/buying electronic transactions within, between, and among organizations. An example would be a company collaborating electronically with a vendor that is designing a product or part for this company. C-commerce implies communication, information sharing, and collaboration done electronically by means of tools such as groupware and specially designed collaboration tools. That means that IOSs and c-commerce coexist. Use of c-commerce requires some IOS technology, such as an extranet, EDI, or groupware. Let's look at some areas of collaboration using IOSs.

**Retailer-Suppliers.** As discussed in Chapter 8, large retailers like Wal-Mart collaborate with their major suppliers to conduct production and inventory planning and forecasting of demand. Such forms of collaboration enable the suppliers to improve their production planning as well.

**Product Design.** All the parties that are involved in a specific product design may use software tools that enable them to share data and collaborate in product design.

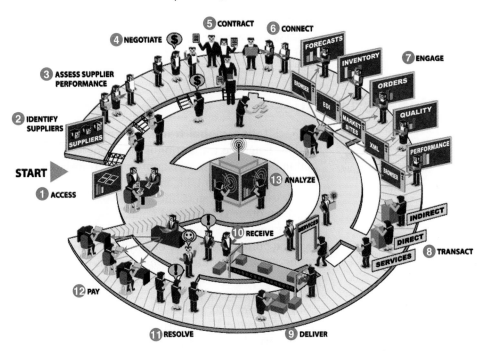

**Figure 9.7** Supplier relationship management (SRM). (*Source:* B. Schecterle, "Managing and Extending Supplier Relationships," *People Talk*, April–June 2003, courtesy of Oracle Corp.)

One such tool is screen sharing (see Chapter 4), in which several people can work on the same document on a computer screen while in different locations. Changes made in one place are visible to others instantly. Documents that can be processed through a collaborative product design IOS include blueprints, bills of material, accounting and billing documents, and joint reports and statements.

**Collaborative Manufacturing.** Manufacturers can create dynamic collaborative production networks by means of IOSs. For example, original equipment manufacturers (OEMs) outsource components and subassemblies to suppliers. (For example, if you buy a Kenmore product from Sears, Sears does not make the product; it just buys and resells it. Some other manufacturer, such as Maytag, is the OEM.) In the past, these relationships often created problems in coordination, workflows, and communication. Web-based collaborative IOSs have improved the outsourcing process and are especially useful in tracking changes that may be initiated by any partner along the supply chain.

**OTHER IOS INFRASTRUCTURES**

Information systems of two or more organizations can be connected in less structured ways than by EDI or extranets. As a matter of fact, most large software vendors, such as Microsoft, Oracle, SAP, and IBM, offer several solutions that can be customized to include existing systems, such as ERPs. An example can be seen in Online File W9.10, where the construction of a global system connecting 40 sites in eight countries is demonstrated. In Europe, Pierre Lang Corp. of Austria, a large jewelry company, gained control over 60 million customers throughout Western European countries by using mySAP ERP (see SAP AG, 2004). Oracle 9i is used extensively to provide infrastructure support to IOSs. Finally, one should remember that VANs, while more expensive, provide more functionalities to IOSs and are used not only for EDI but also for other types of systems (e.g., EFT).

# 9.7 Managerial Issues

**GLOBAL**

**1. Facilitating global trade.** As countries' borders begin to disappear in global trading, language translation is becoming very important. This topic is very important in e-commerce, where appropriate translation of Web pages is a critical success factor. The use of intelligent systems in automatic language translation has been progressing rapidly since the mid-1990s.

Many other systems and applications are used to facilitate international trade. An example is the use of intelligent systems to fight money laundering across international borders, or the use of a hybrid intelligent system for developing global marketing strategy. As international trade is expanding, mainly due to the Internet and trading blocks like the European Union and NAFTA, expertise will be needed in many areas, ranging from legal issues to export and import licenses. Such expertise can be provided to a global audience online. Also, expert systems can provide to users in developing countries the advice of top experts in the fields of medicine, safety, agriculture, and crime fighting. These various systems and applications work with different types of IOSs and technologies.

**2. Selecting a system.** Companies have an option to select an IOS infrastructure from several types and vendors. Selection could follow the guidelines suggested in Chapter 15.

**3. Partners' collaboration.** An IOS has at least two participating organizations, so collaboration is critical. Many failures of EDI adoption, for example, result from lack of partners' cooperation. If you are Wal-Mart, you may be able to mandate that your partner cooperate (or be excluded from doing business with you). But most other companies need to *persuade* partners, showing them mutual benefits, or provide them with incentives.

**4. New infrastructures.** XML, Web Services, and other tools are gaining converts but are not universally accepted. Companies like Dell can lead in using such new infrastructures, but smaller companies might be better off to wait and see. However, management must assess the risk of waiting while competitors are moving.

**GLOBAL**

**5. Globalization.** The issue of going global or not, or to what extent, depends on what information systems are needed for supporting the globalization. Issues such as multiple languages, different currencies, tax requirements, legal aspects, and cultural considerations need to be reflected in the supporting IT. Globalization may not be simple or inexpensive.

**6. Using exchanges, hubs, and other services.** These are viable options since the service providers provide the IOS infrastructure. Also, frequently the Internet can be used. Using third-party providers can be cheaper, but you may lose some control over the system. Again, selecting the appropriate system(s) is critical.

**7. Partner and supplier relationship management.** Modern business is increasingly using partners, as we have seen in several examples throughout the book. The trend for outsourcing, for example, means more partners. (Even Microsoft has used a partner to implement its business solutions.) Cultivating PRM and especially SRM is not a simple task and needs to be planned for and organized properly (look again at Figure 9.7).

## Integrating *IT*

### For the Accounting Major

Organizations may have different accounting systems, especially if they are in different countries. These need to be considered when IT applications are planned. Also, integration and flow of information to and from organizations may impact the accountant's work, especially in auditing.

### For the Finance Major

Financial supply chains and global flows of information are of utmost importance for the finance staff, and so is currency conversion, electronic letters of credit, and other IT-support payment mechanisms. Also, standards such as EDI and XBRL play an increasing role in financial transactions.

### For the Human Resources Management Major

E-training for preparing personnel for foreign countries is just one reason why HRM should be interested in this chapter. Recruitment for a global mission using the Internet is another one. Also, overcoming resistance to change during integration can be critical.

### For the IS Major

Interorganizational and global systems have several characteristics that must be considered during IT design and implementation. Understanding the issues and the impacting factors is of high importance as well. Finally, working with the IT vendors that usually build these systems is of paramount importance.

### For the Marketing Major

An effective supply chain starts and ends with customers. Salespeople and marketing must, therefore, understand supply chain problems, impacting factors, and solutions. Furthermore, localization is key for selling in certain markets, especially foreign ones. Also, integration issues with customers' systems are vital. Finally, relating advertising campaigns to logistics and synchronizing interorganizational processes impact the marketer's success.

### For the Production/Operations Management Major

Manufacturers are usually in the middle of the supply chain and must interact with both customers and suppliers. Inventory problems in IOS, such as the bullwhip effect, need to be understood and addressed.

## Key Terms

Adaptability *361*
Agility *361*
Alignment *361*
Back-office operations *347*
Bullwhip effect *360*
Cross-border data
  transfer *354*

Demand-driven supply networks
  (DDSNs) *360*
Front-office operations *347*
Global information systems *352*
Interorganizational information
  system (IOS) *350*
Logistics *347*

Order fulfillment *347*
Partner relationship management
  (PRM) *368*
Reverse logistics *349*
Supplier relationship management
  (SRM) *369*
Virtual corporation (VC) *350*

## Chapter Highlights                                   (Numbers Refer to Learning Objectives)

❶ The major interorganizational activities are buying and selling, collaborating with business partners, conducting joint ventures, and communicating. IT enables smoother interaction between organizations, usually at a reasonable cost.

❶ A major IOS activity is order taking and fulfillment. This is a process that requires a considerable amount of interaction among business partners. There are many potential problems in this process ranging from fulfilling wrong orders to late deliveries and the inability to deliver on time (backlogging).

❷ Information systems that involve two or more organizations are referred to as interorganizational information systems (IOSs). They can be local or global, dedicated to only one activity (e.g., transfer funds), or intended to support several activities (e.g., to facilitate trade, communication, or collaboration).

❷ IOSs are classified into the following types: B2B trading, global systems, EFT, integrated messaging, shared databases, and systems that support virtual corporations. Technologies that support IOSs are EDI, extranets, groupware, XML, and Web Services.

➋ Virtual corporations are joint ventures involving several companies that create one entity for a special purpose. Since working groups of the VC are in different locations, IT is needed to facilitate coordination and collaboration.

➌ Global information systems exist when at least two parties of an information system are in different countries.

➌ Three types of companies that use global information systems exist: multinational (one company operates in two or more countries), international (at least one business partner is in a different country), and virtual global (partners in at least two countries form one company jointly).

➍ Some of the major issues that affect global information systems are cultural issues, political and economic issues (including currency conversion), legal issues such as cross-border data transfer, different languages, and logistics. Global supply chains are usually longer, requiring complex supporting information systems.

➎ Demand-driven supply networks support on-demand systems where the cycle starts with customer orders. Their major mission is to provide the agility and flexibility needed to be successful. Such networks may work in real time and frequently are connected to enterprise systems such as ERP.

➎ RFID may create a revolution in supply chains by allowing much quicker and easier identification of tagged items. It may replace a barcode in many cases. While today companies use it mainly for identifying merchandise in containers and pallets, it may one day be on every single item if the cost of tags continues to decrease.

➎ RFID can be beneficial for suppliers, buyers, logistics companies, and manufacturers for a number of interesting applications.

➏ Communication and collaboration among companies can be done via IOSs that are organized as either public or private B2B exchanges (usually designed for trading) or hubs (designed to improve the supply chain). Directories provide listings of B2B products, vendors, and services.

➐ Integrating IOS and global systems' components is necessary to assure frictionless flows of goods, material, and money along the supply chain.

➑ EDI provides a systematic framework for information exchange between business partners. It both translates routine business documents to national or international standard formats and provides a secure transmission over VANs.

➑ The major benefits of EDI and EDI/Internet include minimization of errors and cycle time, increased understanding and collaboration among business partners, reduced cost of processing information, better customer service, and improved employee productivity.

➑ The major limitations of EDI and EDI/Internet are high cost and complexity, long training periods required, high investment and operating costs, and inflexibility. EDI/Internet overcomes most of the above limitations by using the Internet and its tools to reduce cost and to increase flexibility and ease of use.

➒ Extranets connect the intranets of business partners by using the Internet (over secure VPNs). This connection enables partners to conveniently enter portions of their partners' intranets.

➒ XML is a standard, used mainly for B2B transactions, that enables communication among business partners, regardless of the software they use.

➒ Web Services support IOSs and facilitate integration of B2B applications by enabling disparate systems to share data and services.

➒ Some representative IOS implementation issues are appropriate partner relationship management, c-commerce, and the use of automatic language translation and other methods to facilitate global trade.

---

## Virtual Company Assignment

### Interorganizational Systems at The Wireless Café

Go to The Wireless Café's link on the Student Web Site. There you will be asked to propose some interorganizational systems that could benefit the restaurant's operations.

*Instructions for accessing The Wireless Café on the Student Web site:*

1. Go to *wiley.com/college/turban*.
2. Select Turban/Leidner/McLean/Wetherbe's *Information Technology for Management, Sixth Edition*.
3. Click on Student Resources site, in the toolbar on the left.
4. Click on the link for Virtual Company Web site.
5. Click on Wireless Café.

## Online Resources

More resources and study tools are located on the Student Web Site and on WileyPLUS. You'll find additional chapter materials and useful Web links. In addition, self-quizzes that provide individualized feedback are available for each chapter.

## Questions for Review

1. Define order fulfillment and logistics.
2. List the nine steps of the order fulfillment process.
3. Compare logistics with reverse logistics.
4. Define an interorganizational information system (IOS).
5. List the major types of IOSs.
6. What is the bullwhip effect?
7. List the IT technologies that can support IOSs.
8. Define a global information system.
9. Describe how RFID improves supply chain operations.
10. List some of the difficulties in managing global supply chains.
11. How can global information systems facilitate global trade?
12. What is a B2B exchange?
13. Why is a B2B exchange considered an IOS?
14. Define a B2B hub and contrast it with an exchange.
15. List the major benefits of a hub to the participating companies. (*Hint:* See *IT at Work 9.3.*)
16. Describe B2B directories.
17. Define virtual corporations (VCs).
18. Describe the support IT provides to VCs.
19. Define EDI.
20. List the major benefits of EDI.
21. List the limitations of traditional EDI.
22. Explain the benefits of Internet-based EDI.
23. Define an extranet and explain its infrastructure.
24. List and briefly define the major types of extranets.
25. Describe XML and explain how it facilitates IOSs.
26. Describe how Web Services can enhance IOSs.
27. Describe PRM and SRM.
28. Describe the major SRM activities (refer to Figure 9.7).
29. What is collaborative commerce? What are some of its areas?
30. How can global trade be facilitated by IT?

## Questions for Discussion

1. Discuss some reasons for the complexity of global trade and the potential assistance of IT.
2. In what way is a B2B exchange related to a global supply chain? To a global information system?
3. Compare an EDI to an extranet and discuss the major differences.
4. When a company opens a private marketplace (for selling and/or buying), it may use EDI, an extranet, EDI/Internet, or just the Internet with regular encryption. Discuss the *criteria* a company needs to consider when making this decision.
5. Explain the bullwhip effect. In what type of business is it most likely to occur? How can the effect be controlled?
6. Discuss why RFID may completely revolutionize the management of supply chains. Can it solve the bullwhip problem? If so, how?
7. Discuss the relationships between RFID and DDSN.
8. Discuss the relationships between the global supply chain and the global financial supply chain.

## Exercises and Projects

1. Enter *oracle.com* and find material on the different IOSs discussed in this chapter. Prepare a report.
2. General Electric Information Systems is the largest provider of EDI services. Investigate what services GEIS and other EDI vendors provide. If you were to evaluate their services for your company, how would you plan to approach the evaluation? Prepare a report.
3. Examine the Lego case and *lego.com*. Design the conceptual architecture of the relevant IOSs you think Lego needs. Concentrate on the marketing portion of

the supply chain, but point out some of the suppliers of plastic, paper, electronics, and wood that Lego uses, as well as the payment flow and inventory management.

4. Enter *bluenile.com*, *bluenile.ca*, and *bluenile.co.uk*. Identify all the features of localization. Does the company really need three Web sites?

## Group Assignments and Projects

1. Have each team locate several organizations that use IOSs, including one with a global reach. Students should contact the companies to find what IOS technology support they use (e.g., an EDI, extranet, etc.). Then find out what issues they faced in implementation. Prepare a report. (*Hint:* Use customer success stories of EDI vendors.)

2. Team members will work on the EDI-XML connection. Start with *XML-EDI.org* and *xmlglobal.com* (see the tutorials at those sites) and find more resources. Prepare a report to convince management of a hypothetical company to use XML/EDI.

## Internet Exercises

1. Enter *i2.com* and review the products presented there. Explain how some of the products facilitate collaboration.

2. Enter *collaborate.com* and read about recent issues related to collaboration. Prepare a report.

3. Enter *smarterwork.com*. Find out how collaboration is done. Summarize the benefits of this site to the participants. Then enter *vignette.com;* look at the products listed under Collaboration. Compare the two sites.

4. Enter *1edisource.com* and see the demo of WebSource. What are the benefits of this product?

5. Visit *xenos.com* and *google.com* and find recent applications of XML related to interorganizational transactions. Prepare a report.

6. Enter *amresearch.com* and find their resource center. Find information about DDSN. Determine where the ERP backbone fits into the networks. Write a report.

## Minicase 1

# How Volkswagen Runs Its Supply Chain in Brazil

*POM*   *GLOBAL*

### The Problem

Like many other companies, Volkswagen (VW) works with many vendors in its assembly plants. However, there were problems in coordination and communication with some vendors. Vendors' materials were shipped to VW factories, where VW employees assembled trucks. But the supply chain was long, and problems with materials often developed. Each time there was a problem, VW had to wait for a partner to come to the plant to solve the problem. Also, materials arrived late, and so VW held large inventories to have safety stock of materials on hand to deal with problems such as a delayed shipment. Finally, quality was frequently compromised. There was a need for a computer-based collaborative system.

### The Solution

In its Brazilian plant truck 100 miles northwest of Rio de Janeiro, Volkswagen (VW) radically altered its supply

chain in 2002. The Rio plant is relatively small: Its 1,000 workers are scheduled to produce 100 trucks per day. Only 200 of the 1,000 workers are Volkswagen employees; they are responsible for overall quality, marketing, research, and design. The other 800 workers, who are employees of suppliers such as Rockwell International and Cummins Engines, do the specific assembly work. The objective of the lean supply chain was to reduce the number of defective parts, cut labor costs, and improve efficiency.

Volkswagen's major suppliers are assigned space in the VW plant, but they supply and manage their own components, supplies, and workers. Workers from various suppliers build the truck as it moves down the assembly line. The system is illustrated in the nearby figure. At the first stop in the assembly process, workers from Iochepe-Maxion mount the gas tank, transmission lines, and steering blocks. As the chassis moves down the line, employees from Rockwell mount axles and brakes. Then workers from Remon put on wheels and adjust tire pressure. The MWM/Cummins team installs the engine and

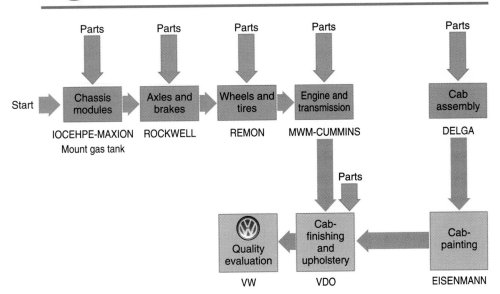

**Truck Assembly Plant in Brazil**
800 assembly-line workers of other companies
200 VW employees research design, quality, markets

transmission. Truck cabs, produced by the Brazilian firm Delga Automotivea, are painted by Eisenmann, and then finished and upholstered by VDO, both of Germany. Volkswagen employees do an evaluation of the final truck. The various national groups still need to communicate with their headquarters, but only infrequently (mostly by e-mail).

### The Results

Volkswagen's innovative supply chain has already improved quality and driven down costs, as a result of each supplier having accepted responsibility for its units and workers' compensation. Encouraged by these results, VW is trying a similar approach in plants in Buenos Aires, Argentina, and with Skoda, in the Czech Republic. Volks-

wagen's new level of integration in supply chain management may be the wave of the future.

*Sources:* Compiled from Heizer and Render (2006), and from *vw.com.*

### Questions for Minicase 1

1. Draw the supply chain of VW's manufacturing plant.

2. What IOSs might be necessary to support such an arrangement? Distinguish between upstream, internal, and downstream supply chain activities. (See Chapter 8 for review of these terms.)

3. Which of the following is most appropriate for the old process: extranet, EDI, EDI/Internet, or Web Services?

4. What IT support is needed in the new arrangement?

## Minicase 2

### How UNICEF Manages Its Global IT

*POM*

UNICEF is a not-for-profit organization established, but not funded, by the U.N. General Assembly to advocate for children's rights and health (specifically childhood diseases), work to prevent the spread of HIV/AIDS, and promote children's education. UNICEF assists civilians in the wake of natural disasters, droughts, wars, and famine. They operate on about $2 billion annual budget, competing for

funding with other humanitarian organizations such as CARE. UNICEF has about 10,000 paid staff and volunteers working from 250 centers in about 160 countries. This minicase describes how the organization manages its IT.

Until 1999, the organization worked with old Wang computers with a few LANs and no WANs. Internet connection to the New York headquarters was a slow dial-up connection and it was easier to send diskettes and paper printouts with the diplomatic mail than to send them electronically. In 1999, Andre Spatz, the new Swiss CIO, changed it all. Today, UNICEF has one of the most progressive global IT systems. Such a transformation was not easy since Spatz had to convince top management that every dollar spent on IT would do more, in the long run, than a dollar spent on medicines (e.g., for vaccines intended for poor countries). Spatz received the funds and today's system includes:

- Standardized desktop programs and server architecture (Technology Guides 1 and 2)
- Fully deployed ERP (from SAP/AG) for managing all back-office operations in many different languages and subject to different regulations (Chapter 8)
- Global wide area communication networks (Chapter 4)
- A virtual private network (VPN) accessible from 126 field offices that provides secure and inexpensive communication over the Internet (Technology Guide 5)
- Voice-Over-IP phones in close to 100 countries (Chapter 4)
- Internet access at a minimum of 128 K in every country and office
- "Fly Away Emergency IP VAST," a satellite-based wireless system with all the basic programs packaged in rugged metal boxes that can be landed by plane and up-and-running in less than four hours (e.g., operating in Iraq)
- Enterprise global help desk and operations
- Global intranets deployed in most regions
- Very effective communications lines with UNICEF's partners, donors, governments, and communities

The IT system was so successful that it is being used for fund raising. With shrinking funds for humanitarian initiatives and increasing natural disasters, IT has become a "competitive differentiator" for UNICEF. Donors can see the effectiveness of UNICEF versus other relief agencies.

Spatz used a unique strategy to deploy the new IT. The new IT strategy was taken around the world as a "management road show" to teach managers and users the strategy and potential benefits. Valuable feedback was collected and adjustments were made accordingly. This helped to reconcile the centralized IT with the decentralized operations and chain-of-command management. The IT strategy was presented as a "hypothesis," which needed to be tested and validated; this enhanced credibility. In addition, specific plans, projects, and milestones followed the global strategy. Users were impressed by the global, flexible, adoptive, and responsive IT system and networks.

The success of the IT was so great that the organizational climate changed. Before the new system, it was necessary to push technology to people. Now users come to the IT centers with requests, suggestions, and so on. This also changed the role of the CIO. One of the most important issues was how to deal with people of different cultures. It was necessary to adopt a single framework for local environments. Finally, it was difficult to integrate so many diverse pieces of the IT system into a single, unified system.

*Sources:* Compiled from Spatz (2004) and from *sap.com* (2004).

## Questions for Minicase 2

1. What IOS and global activities were supported by the new system?
2. Relate the IT global system to multicultures.
3. Why is Spatz's (2004) *CIO Insight* article called "Think Locally, Act Globally?"
4. Why was it necessary to have an ERP in the system?
5. VoIP is considered the cornerstone of the system. Based on what you learned in Chapter 4, explain why.
6. What are some of the lessons you learned about successful implementation of such a global system?

# References

Aberdeen Group Inc., "Asite Builds E-Marketplace Using Combined Strength of Commerce One, Microsoft, and Attenda," *Aberdeen Group Profile*, 2001.

Angeles, R., "RFID Technologies: Supply-Chain Applications and Implementation Issues," *Information Systems Management*, Winter 2005.

Aspray, W., et al., *Globalization and Offshoring of Software*, special report #001-0782/06/0200. New York: Association for Computing Machinery, 2006.

Barrett, L., and D. F. Carr, "Smoke Screen," *Baseline*, February 2005.

Boles, T. "Returned Goods Clog British Roads," *Knight Ridder Tribune Business News*, October 24, 2004.

Boucher-Ferguson, R., "RFID: Locked and Loaded," February 20, 2006.

Brown, C. V., et al., "A Post Merger IT Integration Success Story: Sallie Mae," *MIS Quarterly Executive*, March 2003.

Burgess, S., and M. G. Hunter, "Studies in IT and Small Business Involving International and/or Cross Cultural Aspects," *Journal of Global Information Systems*, July–Sept. 2005.

*Business Wire* (2003).

Chabrow, E., et al., "No One Size Fits All," *Information Week*, June 20, 2006.

Coffee, P., "Data Integration Is IT's Frontier," *eWeek*, February 23, 2004.

Cone, E., "Flyin' in Formation," *CIO Insight*, March 2006.

Coopland, M. V., "The Mighty Micro-Multinational," *Business 2.0*, July 2006.

Damsgaard, L., and J. Horluck, "Designing *www.LEGO.com/shop:* Business Issues and Concerns," case 500-0061, *European Clearing House*, 2000.

Donovan, R. M., "Supply Chain Management: Cracking the Bullwhip Effect," *Material Handling Management,* Director Issue, 2002/2003.

Dubie, D., "Going Global," *ebusinessiq.com,* News Features, March 13, 2003, *findarticles.com/p/articles/mi_zd4149/is_200410/ai_n9476589* (accessed July 2006).

Duvall, M., "Aiming Higher," *Baseline,* November 2004.

Dyer, J. H., and N. W. Hatch, "Using Supplier Networks to Learn Faster," *MIT Sloan Management Review,* Spring 2004.

FedEx, "BikeWorld Goes Global Using FedEx Technologies and Shipping," *FedEx.com,* 2000, *fedex.com/us/ebusiness/ecommerce/bikeworld.pdf?link=4* (accessed July 2006).

Finger, P., and J. Bellini, *The Real Time Enterprise.* Tampa FL: Meghan-Kiffer, 2004.

Galante, D., "Case Studies: Digital Do-Overs," *Forbes,* October 7, 2002.

Groove.net, "Customer Case Studies: Steelcase," *Groove.net,* 2006. *groove.net/index.cfm?pagename=CaseStudy_Steelcase* (accessed July 2006).

Gustin, D., "New Data Triggers for International Supply Chain Finance," *TechnologyEvaluation.com,* July 8, 2005.

Handfield, R. B., et al., *Supply Chain Redesign: Transforming Supply Chains into Integrated Value Systems.* Upper Saddle River, NJ: Financial Times/Prentice Hall, 2002.

Heizer, L., and B. Render, *Principles of Operations Management,* 6th ed. Upper Saddle River, NJ: Prentice Hall, 2006.

Infographic, 5W, "How RFID Will Help Retailer. From Supply Chains to Store Shelves," *MIT Enterprise Technology*, March 2004 (slide demonstration).

Lee, H. L., et al., "The 21st Century Supply Chain," *Harvard Business Review*, December 2004.

*Logisticsworld.com,* "What Is Logistics," 2006, *logisticsworld.com/logistics.htm* (accessed July 2006).

*Logictools.* "Is Better Forecasting a Solution to the Bullwhip Effect?" 2006. *logic-tools.com/resources/articles/bullwhip./html* (accessed October 2006).

Lucas, H. C., Jr., *Information Technology: Strategic Decision Making for Managers.* Hoboken, NJ: Wiley, 2005.

Kinsella, B., "Wal-Mart Factor," *Industrial Engineer*, November 2003.

Kuzeljevich, J., "Targeting Reverse Logistics," *Canadian Transportation Logistics,* 107(9), 2004.

McCartney, L., "A Clothes Call," *Baseline*, April 2006.

Murtaza, M. B., and J. R. Shah, "Managing Information for Effective Business Partner Relationships," *Information Systems Management,* Spring 2004.

New Piper, "New Piper Rolls Out Further Customer Relations Initiatives," news release, *newpiper.com,* 2002, 2004.

Nolan, S., "Planner: Calculating the Cost of Tracking Individual Items with RFID," *Baseline*, February 20, 2005.

Porter, K., "Guide to Globalization Issues," *About.com, globalization.about.com/od/whatisit/.*

Ranganatan, C., "Evaluating the Options for B2B E-Exchanges," *Information Systems Management,* Summer 2003.

Reda, S., "The Path to RFID," *Stores,* June 2003.

Rigby, D. K., and V. Vishwanath, "Localization: The Revolution in Consumer Markets," *Harvard Business Review,* April 2006.

Robbins-Gentry, C., "Moving Money," *Chain Store Age,* February 2006.

Robinson, B., "Hong Kong Airport Tunes," *FCWCOM,* August 29, 2005.

SAP AG, Customer Success Story #50868084, *sap.com,* March 2004.

Sap.com, "SAP Success Story: Public Sector—UNICEF," *sap.com,* 2004.

Schecterle, B., "Managing and Extending Supplier Relationships," *People Talk,* April–June 2003, *sap.com/industries/publicsector/pdf/CS_UNICEF.pdf* (accessed July 2006).

Scheraga, D., "Wal-Smart: The World's Largest Retailer is Building a Better Supply Chain and RFID Is Only Part of It," *Retail Technology Quarterly,* January 2006.

SDL International, "Creating, Managing, and Maintaining a Global Web Site," *SDL.com,* March 2005, *sdl.com/files/pdfs/white-paper-creating-managing-maintaining-global-website.pdf* (accessed July 2006).

Spatz, A., "Think Locally, Act Globally," *CIO Insight,* August, 1, 2004.

Stoll, R., "How We Built Lego.com," *Practical Internet,* March 2003.

Sullivan, D., "Machine Translation: It Can't Match the Human Touch," *E-Business Advisor,* June 2001.

Swift, R. S., "Building a Better Supply Chain," *Teradata Magazine,* 5(3), September 2005.

Thomas, D., "Ford Rolls out Dealer Portal Over 18 Countries," *ComputerWeekly.com,* October 14, 2003, *computerweekly.com/Articles/2003/10/14/197901/Ford+rolls+out+dealer+portal+across+18+countries.htm* (accessed July 2006).

*Tibco.com,* "Customer Success Story: Limited Brands," *tibco.com/resources/international/japan/The-Limited-Brands_J.pdf* (accessed July 2006).

Turban, E., et al., *Electronic Commerce 2008.* Upper Saddle River, NJ: Prentice Hall, 2008.

Umar, A., "IT Infrastructure to Enable Next Generation Enterprise," *Information Systems Frontiers,* 7(3), 2005.

Wheller, S., "Demand-Driven Supply Networks for SMEs," *Technology Evaluation.com,* March 4, 2005.

## Appendix 9A | Electronic Data Interchange (EDI)

One of the early contributions of IT to facilitate B2B e-commerce and other IOSs is electronic data interchange (EDI).

### TRADITIONAL EDI

*Electronic data interchange (EDI)* is a communication standard that enables the electronic transfer of routine documents, such as purchase orders, between business partners. It formats these documents according to agreed-upon standards. EDI has been around for about 30 years in the non-Internet environment (usually VANs). EDI often serves as a catalyst and a stimulus to improve the standard of information that flows between organizations. It reduces costs, delays, and errors inherent in a manual document-delivery system.

**Major Components of EDI.** The following are the major components of EDI:

- *EDI translators.* An EDI translator converts data into a standard format before it is transmitted; then the standard form is converted to the original data.
- *Business transactions messages.* These include purchase orders, invoices, credit approvals, shipping notices, confirmations, and so on.
- *Data formatting standards.* Because EDI messages are repetitive, it makes sense to use formatting (coding) standards. In the United States and Canada, EDI data are formatted according to the ANSI X.12 standard. An international standard developed by the United Nations is called EDIFACT.

**The Process and Benefits of EDI.** The process of EDI (as compared with a non-EDI process) is shown in Figure 9A.1. The figure shows that in EDI, computers talk to computers. Messages are coded using the standards before they are transmitted using a converter. Then, the message travels over a value-added network (VAN) or the Internet (secured). When received, the message is automatically translated into a business language.

The benefits of this process are that data entry errors are minimized (only one entry, and an automatic check by the computer), the length of the message can be shorter, the messages are secured, and EDI fosters collaborative relationships and strategic partnerships. Other benefits are: reduced cycle time, better inventory management, increased productivity, enhanced customer service, minimized paper usage and storage, and increased cash flow (per *1edisource.com*).

### APPLICATIONS OF TRADITIONAL EDI

Traditional EDI has changed the business landscape of many industries and large corporations. It is used extensively by large corporations, sometimes in a global network such as the one operated by General Electric Information System (which has over 100,000 corporate users). Well-known retailers such as Home Depot, ToysRUs, and Wal-Mart would operate very differently without EDI, because it is an integral and essential element of their business strategies. Thousands of global manufacturers, including Procter & Gamble, Levi Strauss, Toyota, and Unilever, have been using EDI to redefine relationships with their customers through such practices as quick-response retailing and just-in-time (JIT) manufacturing. These highly visible, high-impact applications of EDI by large companies have been extremely successful.

### LIMITATIONS OF TRADITIONAL EDI

However, despite the tremendous impact of traditional EDI among industry leaders, the set of adopters represented only a small fraction of potential EDI users. In the United States, where several million businesses participate in commerce every day, only about 100,000 companies have adopted traditional EDI. Furthermore, most of these companies have had only a small number of their business partners on EDI, mainly due to its high cost. Therefore, in reality, few businesses have benefited from traditional EDI.

Various factors held back more universal implementation of traditional EDI. For example: Significant initial investment is needed, and ongoing operating costs are high (due to use of expensive, private VANs). Another cost is the purchase of a converter, which is required to translate business transactions to EDI code. Other major issues for some companies relate to the fact that the traditional EDI system is inflexible. For example, it is difficult to make quick changes, such as adding business partners, and a long startup period is needed. Further, business processes must sometimes be restructured to fit EDI requirements. Finally,

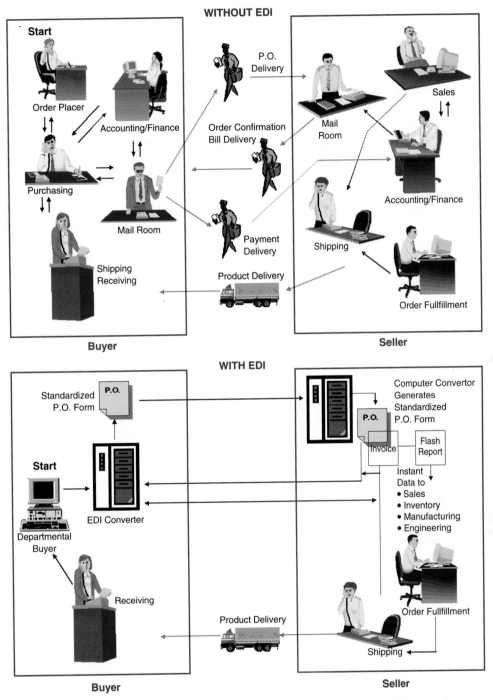

**Figure 9A.1** Comparing purchasing order (P.O.) fulfillment with and without EDI. (*Source:* Drawn by E. Turban.)

multiple EDI standards exist, so one company may have to use several standards in order to communicate with different business partners. However, as some functions are automated into digital format, EDI is becoming simplified and easier to implement.

These factors suggest that traditional EDI—relying on formal transaction sets, translation software, and VANs—is not suitable as a long-term solution for most corporations. Therefore, a better infrastructure was needed; *Internet-based EDI* is such an infrastructure.

## INTERNET-BASED EDI

Internet-based (or Web-based) EDI is becoming very popular (e.g., see Witte et al., 2003). Let's see why this is the case.

**Why Internet-Based EDI?** When considered as a channel for EDI, the Internet appears to be a most feasible alternative to VANs for putting online B2B trading within reach of virtually any organization, large or small. There are a number of reasons for firms to create EDI ability over the Internet.

- *Accessibility.* The Internet is a publicly accessible network with few geographical constraints. Its largest attribute, large-scale connectivity (without the need for any special company networking architecture), is a seedbed for growth of a vast range of business applications.
- *Reach.* The Internet's global network connections offer the potential to reach the widest possible number of trading partners of any viable alternative currently available.
- *Cost.* The Internet's communication cost can be 40 to 70 percent lower than that of VANs. Transmission of sensitive data can be made secure with VPN (see Technology Guide 4).
- *Use of Web technology.* Using the Internet to exchange EDI transactions is consistent with the growing interest of business in delivering an ever-increasing variety of products and services via the Web. Internet-based EDI can complement or replace many current EDI applications.
- *Ease of use.* Internet tools such as browsers and search engines are very user-friendly, and most employees today know how to use them.
- *Added functionalities.* Internet-based EDI has several functionalities not provided by traditional EDI, which include collaboration, workflow, and search engine capabilities (see Boucher-Ferguson, 2002). A comparison between EDI and EDI/Internet is provided in Figure 9A.2.

**Types of Internet-Based EDI.** The Internet can support EDI in a variety of ways. For example, Internet e-mail can be used to transport EDI messages in place of a VAN. To this end, standards for encapsulating the messages within Secure Internet Mail Extension (S/MIME) exist and need to be used. Another way to use the Internet for EDI is to create an extranet that enables a company's trading partners to enter information into a Web form, the fields of which correspond to the fields in an EDI message or document.

Alternatively, companies can use a Web-based EDI hosting service, in much the same way that companies rely on third parties to host their EC sites. Harbinger

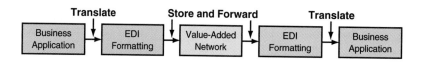

**TRADITIONAL ELECTRONIC DATA INTERCHANGE (EDI)**

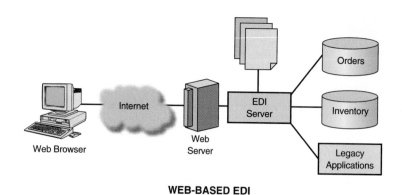

**WEB-BASED EDI**

**Figure 9A.2** Traditional and Web-based EDI. (*Source:* Drawn by E. Turban.)

Commerce (*inovis.com*) is an example of those companies that provide third-party hosting services.

## THE PROSPECTS OF INTERNET-BASED EDI

Many companies that used traditional EDI in the past have had a positive experience when they moved to Internet-based EDI. With traditional EDI, companies have to pay for network transport, translation, and routing of EDI messages into their legacy processing systems. The Internet serves as a cheaper alternative transport mechanism. The combination of the Web, XML, and Java makes EDI affordable even for small, infrequent transactions. Whereas EDI is not interactive, the Web and Java were designed specifically for interactivity as well as ease of use.

The following examples demonstrate the application range and benefits of Internet-based EDI.

*Example: Rapid Growth at CompuCom.* CompuCom Systems, a leading IT services provider, was averaging 5,000 transactions per month with traditional EDI. In just a short time after the transition to Web-based EDI, the company was able to average 35,000 transactions. The system helped the company to grow rapidly.

*Example: Recruitment at Tradelink.* Tradelink of Hong Kong had a traditional EDI that communicated with government agencies regarding export/import transactions, but was successful in recruiting only several hundred of the potential 70,000 companies to the traditional system. After switching to an Internet-based system, Tradelink registered thousands of new companies to the system; hundreds were being added monthly, reaching about 18,000 by 2004.

*Example: Better Collaboration at Atkins Carlyle.* Atkins Carlyle Corp. a wholesaler of industrial, electrical, and automotive parts, buys from 6,000 suppliers and has 12,000 customers in Australia. The large suppliers were using three different traditional-EDI platforms. By moving to an Internet-based EDI, the company was able to collaborate with many more business partners, reducing the transaction cost by about $2 per message.

Note that many companies no longer refer to their IOSs as EDI. However, some *properties* of EDI are embedded in new e-business initiatives such as collaborative commerce, extranets, PRM, and electronic exchanges. The new generation of EDI/Internet is built around XML (see Appendix 9B.)

### References for Appendix 9A

Boucher-Ferguson, R., "A New Shipping Route (Web-EDI)," *eWeek,* September 23, 2002.

Witte, C. L., et al., "The Integration of EDI and the Internet," *Information Systems Management,* Fall 2003.

## Appendix 9B | Extranets, XML, and Web Services

Companies involved in an IOS need to be connected in a secure and effective manner and their applications must be integrated with each other. This can be done by using extranets, XML, and Web Services.

### EXTRANETS

In building IOSs, it is necessary to connect the internal systems of different business partners, which are usually connected to the partners' corporate intranets. A common solution is to use an extranet. Extranets are generally understood to be networks that link business partners over the Internet by providing access to certain areas of each other's corporate intranets. This arrangement is shown in Figure 9B.1. (An exception to this definition is an extranet that offers individual customers or suppliers one-way access to a company's intranet.) The term *extranet* comes from "extended intranet."

The main goal of extranets is to foster collaboration between business partners. An extranet is open to selected B2B suppliers, customers, and other business partners, who access it through the Internet. Extranets enable people who are located outside a company to work together with the company's internally located employees. An extranet enables external business partners and telecommuting employees to enter the corporate intranet, via the Internet, to access data, place orders, check status, communicate, and collaborate.

**The Components, Structure, and Benefits of Extranets.** An extranet uses the same basic infrastructure components as the Internet, including servers, TCP/IP protocols, e-mail, and Web browsers. In addition, extranets use virtual private network (VPN) technology to make communication over the Internet more secure. The Internet-based extranet is far less costly than proprietary networks (VANs). It is a nonproprietary technical tool that can support the rapid evolution of electronic communication and commerce.

Why would a company allow a business partner access to its intranet? To answer this question, let's look at Dr. Pepper in the following example.

*Example: Dr. Pepper Notifies Bottlers of Price Changes.* Dr. Pepper/Seven Up, the $2 billion division of Cadbury Schweppes, uses an extranet to improve efficiency for its diverse community of 1,400 independent and franchise bottlers. The Bottler Hub/Extranet is made available to Dr. Pepper's entire group of registered bottlers and retailers. The extranet has helped automate the process of communicating price changes to retailers in real time.

Such automation was necessary for Dr. Pepper because the company depends on contract bottlers, who

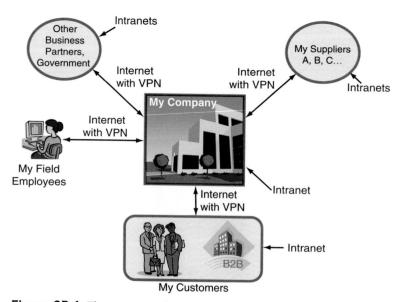

**Figure 9B.1** The structure of an extranet.

set the pricing of Dr. Pepper products in stores. Customer retailers such as Wal-Mart had complained about the bottlers' practice of faxing weekly price changes. Because many bottlers were mom-and-pop organizations and did not have the resources to modernize the process, Dr. Pepper decided to put in an extranet-based centralized system that would make the pricing information available online, in real time, to retail outlets.

Dr. Pepper also uses its extranet for other purposes. In addition, the company collects sales data online, enabling merchants to report how many cases of soda they sell. The data are used to measure sales growth and to analyze brands and packages that are sold by a bottler within a territory to the major retail chains. The information is also used to help the national accounts department find opportunities to sell more Dr. Pepper/Seven Up brands within a particular account.

As seen in the example, the extranet enables effective and efficient real-time collaboration. It also enables partners to perform self-service activities such as checking the status of orders or inventory levels.

**Types of Extranets.** Depending on the business partners involved and the purpose, there are three major types of extranets, as described here.

***A Company and Its Dealers, Customers, or Suppliers.*** Such an extranet is centered around one company. An example would be the FedEx extranet that allows customers to track the status of a package. To do so, customers use the Internet to access a database on the FedEx intranet. By enabling a customer to check the location of a package, FedEx saves the cost of having a human operator do that task over the phone. Ford Motor is using an extranet-based portal with its dealers in Europe, as described in *IT at Work 9B.1*. Similarly, Toshiba uses an extranet with its dealers, as shown in Online File W9.11.

***An Industry's Extranet.*** The major players in an industry may team up to create an extranet that will benefit all. The world's largest industry-based, collaborative extranet is used by General Motors, Ford, and DaimlerChrysler. That extranet, called the Automotive Network Exchange (ANX), links the carmakers with more than 10,000 suppliers. The suppliers can then use a B2B marketplace, Covisint (*covisint.com,* now a division of Compuware) located on ANX, to sell directly and efficiently to the carmakers, cutting communications costs by as much as 70 percent.

***Joint Ventures and Other Business Partnerships.*** In this type of extranet, the partners in a joint venture use the extranet as a vehicle for communications and

# *IT* at Work 9B.1

## Dealer Connection Portal at Ford

Ford Motor Co. in Europe serves 7,500 dealers, speaking 15 different languages, in 18 countries. In order to connect them all, Ford created a portal, called DealerConnection. The portal provides dealers with a single point of real-time access to all the information and tools they need to manage daily tasks efficiently, such as warranty checks and parts ordering. It also frees dealers from having to access separate systems. In addition, all information on pricing, products, servicing, customer services, and marketing is now available to the dealers online. Prior to the portal, updating dealers on new information often took five days for preparation, printing, and distribution of material; thus, the portal is achieving real efficiencies for Ford in its distribution of company information.

DealerConnection provides local dealers and Ford representatives in each country with control of their own Enterprise Web application. Unlike traditional applications, Enterprise Web applications, built on Plumtree (*plumtree.com*) portal software, combine existing data and processes from enterprise systems with new shared services. These applications are managed within one administrative framework at the corporate level, allowing the company to create real, working online communities. DealerConnection also facilitates self-service among dealers, allowing Ford to implement a more streamlined and centralized back office.

Instead of creating 18 different portals for the countries in which Ford operates, the company has developed one pan-European portal with applications for each respective country and each line of business. By adopting this approach, Ford is empowering each country to create its own environment under the European umbrella of DealerConnection, even though Ford still has central control over its brand, image, and communications. The vendor believes that the portal has delivered a positive return of investment for both Ford and its network of dealers.

*Source:* Compiled from Plumtree Software Inc. (2003) (acquired by BEA Systems in October 2005), and Thomas (2003).

*For Further Exploration:* Why only one portal? What about the multilanguage, multicultural aspects?

collaboration. An example is Bank of America's extranet for commercial loans. The partners involved in making such loans are a lender, loan broker, escrow company, title company, and others. The extranet connects lenders, loan applicants, and the loan organizer, Bank of America. A similar case is Lending Tree (*lendingtree.com*), a company that provides mortgage quotes for your home and also sells mortgages online, which uses an extranet for its business partners (e.g., the lenders).

**Benefits of Extranets.** As extended versions of intranets, extranets offer benefits similar to those of intranets, as well as other benefits. The major benefits of extranets include faster processes and information flow, improved order entry and customer service, lower costs (e.g., for communications, travel, and administrative overhead), and overall improvement in business effectiveness.

Extranets are fairly permanent in nature, where all partners are known in advance. For on-demand relationships and one-time trades, companies can instead use B2B exchanges and hubs (Chapter 4) and directory services.

Two emerging technologies that are extremely important for IOSs are XML and Web Services.

### XML

An emerging technology that can be used effectively to integrate internal systems as well as systems of business partners is a language (and its variants) known as XML (see Raisinghani, 2002; *XML (eXtensible Markup Language)* is a simplified version of a general data description language known as SGML (Standard Generalized Markup Language). XML is used to improve compatibility between the disparate systems of business partners by defining the meaning of data in business documents. XML is considered "extensible" because the markup symbols are unlimited and self-defining. This new standard is promoted as a new platform for B2B and as a companion or even a replacement for EDI systems. It has been formally recommended by the World Wide Web Consortium (*W3C.org*).

**XML Differs from HTML.** People sometimes wonder if XML and HTML are the same. The answer is, they are not. The purpose of HTML is to help build Web pages and display data on Web pages. The purpose of XML is to describe data and information. It does not say *how* the data will be displayed (which

HTML does). XML can be used to send complex messages that include different files (and HTML cannot). See Technology Guide 2 for details.

**Benefits of XML.** XML was created in an attempt to overcome limitations of EDI implementation. XML can overcome EDI barriers for three reasons:

1. *Flexibility.* XML is a flexible language. Its flexibility allows new requirements and changes to be incorporated into messages, thus expanding the rigid ranges of EDI.

2. *Understandability.* XML message content can be easily read and understood by people using standard browsers. Thus, message recipients do not need EDI translators. This feature enables SMEs to receive, understand, and act on XML-based messages.

3. *Less specialized.* In order to implement EDI, it is necessary to have highly specialized knowledge of EDI methodology. Implementation of XML-based technologies requires less-specialized skills.

XML supports IOSs and makes B2B e-commerce a reality for many companies that were unable to use the traditional EDI. These and other benefits of XML are demonstrated in *IT at Work 9B.2* and in Korolishin (2004). For more information see *xml.com*.

Despite its many potential benefits, XML has, according to McKinsey Research (Current Research Note, 2003), several serious limitations, especially when compared to EDI. These include lack of universal XML standards, lack of experience in XML implementation, and sometimes less security than EDI. However, this is rapidly changing and XML is being used more frequently.

Another technology that supports IOSs and uses XML in its core is Web Services.

### WEB SERVICES

As described in Chapter 2, *Web Services* are universal, prefabricated business process software modules, delivered over the Internet, that users can select and combine through almost any device, enabling disparate systems to share data and services. Web Services can support IOSs by providing easy integration for different internal and external systems. (Also see Technology Guide 6.) Such integration enables companies to develop new applications, as the following example demonstrates.

# IT at Work 9B.2

## Fidelity Uses XML to Standardize Corporate Data

FIN   ACC

Fidelity Investments has made all its corporate data XML-compatible. The effort helped the world's largest mutual fund company and online brokerage eliminate up to 75 percent of the hardware and software devoted to middle-tier processing and speeded the delivery of new applications.

The decision to go to XML began when Fidelity developed its Powerstreet Web trading service. At the time, Fidelity determined it would need to offer its most active traders much faster response times than its existing brokerage systems allowed. The move to XML brought other benefits as well. For example, the company was able to link customers who have 401(k) pension plans, brokerage accounts, and IRAs under a common log-in. In the past, they required separate passwords.

Today, two-thirds of the hundreds of thousands of hourly online transactions at *fidelity.com* use XML to link the Web to back-end systems. Before XML, comparable transactions took many seconds longer because they had to go through a different proprietary data translation scheme for each back-end system from which they retrieved data.

Fidelity's XML strategy is critical to bringing new applications and services to customers faster than rivals. By using XML as a common language into which all corporate data—from Web, database, transactional, and legacy systems—are translated, Fidelity is saving millions of dollars on infrastructure and development costs. Fidelity no longer has to develop translation methods for communications between the company's many systems. XML also has made it possible for Fidelity's different databases—including Oracle for its customer account information and IBM's DB2 for trading records—to respond to a single XML query.

*Source:* Compiled from "Fidelity Retrofits All Data . . ." (2001); and from *fidelity.com*.

*For Further Exploration:* Why did Fidelity decide to use XML? Why is it possible to develop applications faster with XML?

---

***Example: Web Services Facilitate Communication at Allstate.*** The Allstate Financial Group, with 41,000 employees and $29 billion in annual sales, used Microsoft.NET (a Web Services implementation) to create AccessAllstate.com (*accessallstate.com*). This Web portal allows its 350,000 sales representatives to access information about Allstate investment, retirement, and insurance products.

Before the portal was developed, independent agents had to call Allstate customer service representatives for information, and transactions were done via mail, fax, or phone. The necessary information resided on five policy-management information systems running on mainframe computers—substantial technology investments that Allstate was not willing to lose. But because Web Services enables easy communications between applications and systems, Allstate did not have to lose its mainframe investment. The agents use the Web portal to access the policy-management systems residing on the mainframe. Web Services make this connection seamless and transparent to the agents.

AccessAllstate.com has about 13,000 registered users and receives 500,000 hits per day. By unlocking the information on Allstate's proprietary mainframes, the company increases revenues and reduces costs. The Web portal eliminates the need to call the service center to perform common account service tasks. Allstate estimates that the portal will pay for itself through lower call center and mailing costs. The company is also making all printed correspondence available online via the portal. (*Sources:* Compiled from Grimes, 2003; and *allstate.com*, accessed June 2006.)

## References for Appendix 9B

Current Research Note, "The Truth about XML," *McKinsey Quarterly*, 3, 2003.

"Fidelity Retrofits All Data for XML," *InternetWeek*, August 6, 2001.

Grimes, B., "Microsoft.NET Case Study: Allstate Financial Group," *PC Magazine*, March 25, 2003.

Korolishin, J., "Industry-Specific XML Reduces Paperwork for C-store Chain," *Stores*, February 2004.

Plumtree Software Inc., "Food Connects European Dealer Network," *plumtree.com*, October 14, 2003.

Raisinghani, M. (ed.), *Cases on Worldwide E-Commerce.* Hershey, PA: The Idea Group, 2002.

# Chapter
# 10
# Knowledge Management

## Learning Objectives

After studying this chapter, you will be able to:

❶ Define knowledge and describe the different types of knowledge.

❷ Understand the concepts of organizational learning, memory, and the impact of organizational culture.

❸ Describe the activities involved in knowledge management.

❹ Describe different approaches to knowledge management.

❺ Describe the technologies that can be utilized in a knowledge management system.

❻ Describe the activities of the chief knowledge officer and others involved in knowledge management.

❼ Describe benefits and drawbacks to knowledge management initiatives.

❽ Understand the valuation approaches to KMS, as well as its successes and potential failure.

## Integrating *IT*

**ACC**

**FIN**

**MKT**

**POM**

**HRM**

**IS**

**SVC**

# KNOWLEDGE MANAGEMENT AT INFOSYS TECHNOLOGIES

## The Problem

A global software services company based in India, Infosys Technologies, is a worldwide leader in outsourcing. With over 23,000 employees and globally distributed operations, Infosys develops IT solutions for some of the largest corporations in the world. During the past 10 years, Infosys has experienced 30 percent annual growth rates. Infosys faced a challenge of keeping its large employee base up-to-date and ahead of both its competitors and clients, and ensuring that the lessons learned in one part of the organization were available to other parts. Said a member of the knowledge management (KM) group: "An IT company like ours cannot survive if we don't have mechanisms to reuse the knowledge that we create. . . . 'Learn once, use anywhere' is our motto." The vision is that every instance of learning within Infosys should be available to every employee. But how does an organization turn such a vision into a reality?

## The Solution

Infosys Technologies' effort to convert each employee's knowledge into an organizational resource began in the early 1990s and extended well into the first decade of 2000. In the early 1990s, Infosys launched its bodies of knowledge (BOK) initiative. This involved encouraging employees to provide written accounts of their experiences across various topics, such as technologies, software development, and living abroad. These were shared in hard-copy form with all other employees. This early effort ballooned into a full-fledged KM effort supported by e-mail, bulletin boards, and various knowledge repositories. In 1996, a corporate intranet was developed to make BOKs, in HTML format, easily accessible to all, and in 1999, Infosys began an organizationwide program to integrate the various knowledge initiatives. A central knowledge portal was created, called KShop, and while the KM group developed the technology infrastructure, local groups were encouraged to maintain their own content on KShop.

The content of KShop consisted of different content types—BOKs, case studies, reusable artifacts, and downloadable software—each with its own homepage. Content was carefully categorized by the KM group to ensure that as the amount of content increased, it would still be possible for people to quickly find what they needed.

In early 2000, Infosys appeared to have a very functional KM system, and yet patronage by employees remained low. The KM group therefore initiated a reward scheme to increase participation. The scheme gave employees who contributed to KShop knowledge currency units (KCUs) that could be accumulated and exchanged for monetary rewards or prizes.

## The Results

Within a year of the introduction of the KCU scheme, 2,400 new knowledge assets had been contributed to KShop by some 20 percent of Infosys' employees. However, as the volume of content increased, so too did problems relating to finding useful information. Moreover, the heavy growth in contributions taxed the limited number of volunteer reviewers, who served an important quality control function. The KM group therefore modified the KCU incentive scheme. It developed a new KCU scheme that rated the usefulness of knowledge from the perspective of the users of the knowledge, rather than the reviewers. And, to increase accountability, the KM group requested tangible proof to justify any high ratings. Finally, the KM group raised the bar for cashing in KCU points for monetary awards.

*Sources:* Compiled from *Infosys.com* (accessed Jun 2006), and from Garud and Kumaraswamy (2005).

## Lessons Learned from This Case

This case illustrates that knowledge management initiatives are much more than the implementation of technology tools to allow employees to post knowledge. Such initiatives involve processes to organize knowledge, to categorize knowledge, and to rate knowledge usefulness as well as processes to encourage knowledge sharing and reuse.

In this chapter we describe the characteristics and concepts of knowledge management. In addition, we will explain how firms are using information technology to implement knowledge management systems and how these systems are transforming modern organizations.

# 10.1 Introduction to Knowledge Management

With roots in expert systems, organizational learning, and innovation, the idea of knowledge management is itself not new. Successful managers have always used intellectual assets and recognized their value. But these efforts were not systematic, nor did they ensure that knowledge gained was shared and dispersed appropriately for maximum organizational benefit. Moreover, sources such as Forrester Research, IBM, and Merrill Lynch estimate that 85 percent of a company's knowledge assets are not housed in relational databases, but are dispersed in e-mail, Word documents, spreadsheets, and presentations on individual computers. The application of information technology tools to facilitate the creation, storage, transfer, and application of previously uncodifiable organizational knowledge is a new and major initiative in organizations.

**Knowledge management (KM)** is a process that helps organizations identify, select, organize, disseminate, and transfer important information and expertise that are part of the organization's memory and that typically reside within the organization in an unstructured manner. This structuring of knowledge enables effective and efficient problem solving, dynamic learning, strategic planning, and decision making. Knowledge management initiatives focus on identifying knowledge, explicating it in such a way that it can be shared in a formal manner, and leveraging its value through reuse. For an overview, see *brint.com/KM*.

Through a supportive organizational climate and modern information technology, an organization can bring its entire organizational memory and knowledge to bear upon any problem anywhere in the world and at any time. For organizational success, *knowledge, as a form of capital, must be exchangeable among persons, and it must be able to grow*. Knowledge about how problems are solved can be captured, so that knowledge management can promote organizational learning, leading to further knowledge creation. See Schwartz (2006) and *wikipedia.org/wiki/knowledge_management*.

**Knowledge.** In the information technology context, knowledge is very distinct from data and information (see Figure 10.1 and Online File W10.1). Whereas *data* are a collection of facts, measurements, and statistics, *information* is organized or processed data that are timely (i.e., inferences from the data are drawn within the time frame of applicability) and accurate (i.e., with regard to the original data) (Holsapple, 2003). **Knowledge** is information that is *contextual, relevant,* and *actionable*.

For example, a map giving detailed driving directions from one location to another could be considered data. An up-to-the-minute traffic bulletin along the freeway that indicates a traffic slowdown due to construction could be considered information. Awareness of an alternative, back-roads route could be considered knowledge. In this case, the map is considered data because it does not contain current relevant information that affects the driving time and conditions from one location to the other. However, having the current conditions as information is useful only if the individual has knowledge that will enable him or her to avoid the

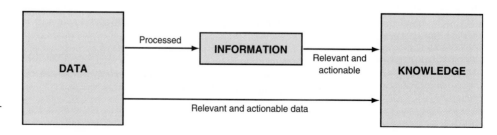

**Figure 10.1** Data, information, and knowledge.

construction zone. Having knowledge implies that it can be used to solve a problem, whereas having information does not carry the same connotation.

An *ability to act* is an integral part of being knowledgeable. For example, two people in the same context with the same information may not have the same ability to use the information to the same degree of success. Hence there is a difference in the human capability to add value. The differences in ability may be due to differences in experiences, training, perspectives, and so on. While data, information, and knowledge may all be viewed as assets of an organization, knowledge provides a higher level of meaning about data and information. It conveys *meaning,* and hence tends to be much more valuable, yet more ephemeral.

Knowledge has the following characteristics that differentiate it from an organization's other assets (Holsapple, 2003):

- **Extraordinary leverage and increasing returns.** Knowledge is not subject to diminishing returns. When it is used, it is not consumed. Its consumers can add to it, thus increasing its value.
- **Fragmentation, leakage, and the need to refresh.** As knowledge grows, it branches and fragments. Knowledge is dynamic; it is information in action. Thus, an organization must continually refresh its knowledge base to maintain it as a source of competitive advantage.
- **Uncertain value.** It is difficult to estimate the impact of an investment in knowledge. There are too many intangible aspects.
- **Uncertain value of sharing.** Similarly, it is difficult to estimate the value of sharing the knowledge, or even who will benefit most.
- **Rooted in time.** The utility and validity of knowledge may vary with time; hence, the immediacy, age, perishability, and volatility of knowledge are important attributes.

There is a vast amount of literature about what knowledge and knowing means in epistemology (study of the nature of knowledge), the social sciences, philosophy, and psychology (Polanyi, 1958, 1966). Though there is no single definition of what knowledge and knowledge management specifically mean, the business perspective on them is fairly pragmatic. Information as a resource is not always valuable (i.e., information overload can distract from the important); knowledge is a resource when it is clear, relevant, and important to an individual processing the knowledge (Holsapple, 2003). Knowledge implies an implicit understanding and experience that can discriminate between its use and misuse. Over time, information accumulates and decays, while knowledge evolves. The word *knowledge* tends to carry positive connotations (Schultze and Leidner, 2002). However, because *knowledge is dynamic in nature,* today's knowledge may well become tomorrow's ignorance if an individual or organization fails to update knowledge as environmental conditions change. For more on the potential drawbacks of managing and reusing knowledge, see Section 10.7.

**Intellectual capital** (or **intellectual assets**) is another term often used for knowledge, and it implies that there is a financial value to knowledge (Tseng and Goo, 2005). Though intellectual capital is difficult to measure, some industries have tried. For example, the value of the intellectual capital of the property-casualty insurance industry has been estimated to be between $270 billion to $330 billion (Mooney, 2000). The Organization for Economic Co-operation and Development (OECD) has scored its 30 member nations according to their investments in intellectual capital such as R&D, education, and patents. According to OECD, those countries with the most intellectual capital activities will be the winners of future wealth (Tseng and Goo, 2005).

Knowledge evolves over time with experience, which puts connections among new situations and events in context. Given the breadth of the types and applications of knowledge, we adopt the simple and elegant definition that knowledge is *information in action*.

**Tacit and Explicit Knowledge. Explicit knowledge** deals with more objective, rational, and technical knowledge (data, policies, procedures, software, documents, etc.). **Tacit knowledge** is usually in the domain of subjective, cognitive, and experiential learning; it is highly personal and difficult to formalize (Nonaka and Takeuchi, 1995). Other types of knowledge are displayed in Online File W10.2.

*Explicit knowledge* is the policies, procedural guides, white papers, reports, designs, products, strategies, goals, mission, and core competencies of the enterprise and the information technology infrastructure. It is the knowledge that has been codified (documented) in a form that can be distributed to others or transformed into a process or strategy without requiring interpersonal interaction. Explicit knowledge has also been called **leaky knowledge** because of the ease with which it can leave an individual, document, or the organization, after it has been documented.

*Tacit knowledge* is the cumulative store of the experiences, mental maps, insights, acumen, expertise, know-how, trade secrets, skill sets, and learning that an organization has, as well as the organizational culture that has embedded in it the past and present experiences of the organization's people, processes, and values. Tacit knowledge, also referred to as *embedded knowledge* (Tuggle and Goldfinger, 2004), is usually either localized within the brain of an individual or embedded in the group interactions within a department or a branch office. Tacit knowledge typically involves expertise or high skill levels. It is generally slow and costly to transfer and can be plagued by ambiguity (Teece, 2003).

Sometimes tacit knowledge is easily documentable but has remained tacit simply because the individual housing the knowledge does not recognize its potential value to other individuals. Other times, tacit knowledge is unstructured, without tangible form, and therefore difficult to codify. It is frequently difficult to put some tacit knowledge into words. For example, an explanation of how to ride a bicycle would be difficult to document explicitly, and thus is tacit. Tacit knowledge also has been called **sticky knowledge** because it may be relatively difficult to pull it away from its source.

Successful transfer or sharing of tacit knowledge usually takes place through associations, internships, apprenticeships, conversations, other means of social and interpersonal interactions, or even through simulations (e.g., see Marwick, 2007). Nonaka and Takeuchi (1995) claim that intangibles like insights, intuitions, hunches, gut feelings, values, images, metaphors, and analogies are the often-overlooked assets of organizations. Harvesting this intangible asset can be critical to a firm's bottom line and its ability to meet its goals (Shariq and Vendelo, 2006).

**THE NEED FOR KNOWLEDGE MANAGEMENT SYSTEMS**

The goal of knowledge management is for an organization to be aware of individual and collective knowledge so that it may make the most effective use of the knowledge it has (Bennet and Bennet, 2003a). Historically, MIS has focused on capturing, storing, managing, and reporting explicit knowledge. Organizations now recognize the need to integrate both explicit and tacit knowledge in formal information systems. **Knowledge management systems (KMSs)** refers to the use of modern information technologies (e.g., the Internet, intranets, extranets, LotusNotes, software filters, agents, data warehouses) to systematize, enhance, and expedite intra- and interfirm knowledge management (Alawat, 2006). KMSs are intended to help an organization cope with turnover, rapid change, and downsizing by making the expertise of the organization's human capital widely accessible. They are being built in part from increased pressure to maintain a well-informed, productive workforce. Moreover, they are built to help large organizations provide a consistent level of customer service. They also help organizations retain the knowledge of departing employees, as described in *IT at Work 10.1*. Many organizations have been building KM systems in order to capitalize on the knowledge and experience of employees worldwide. Online File W10.3 describes Siemens's experience with knowledge management. Online File W10.4 describes how ChevronTexaco was able to reduce operating expenses by implementing a KMS, and Online File W10.5 describes how Frito-Lay uses knowledge management to support its dispersed sales team.

## *IT* at Work 10.1

### Northrop Grumman Uses Knowledge Management to Prevent "Brain Drain"

As Northrop Grumman (*northropgrumman.com*), manufacturers of the B-2 bomber, faced the unpleasant task of firing nearly 12,000 workers in 1997, the company dealt with the disturbing fact that these employees took with them years of experience and in-depth knowledge about what was then considered to be the most complex aircraft ever built. In an attempt to retain the valuable knowledge these workers possessed, Northrop Grumman formed a knowledge management team, which identified top experts and videotaped interviews with them before they left. However, capturing this knowledge in a single interview proved difficult. Northrop Grumman's director of knowledge management (KM) for the Western region of the integrated systems sector, Scott Shaffar, said of this, "We did lose some of that knowledge. In an exit interview, you can capture certain things, but not a lifetime of experience." After frantically attempting to identify experts in key areas related to the program and to create a central repository for project documents, the aerospace giant managed to keep enough knowledge to maintain and move forward with B-2-related upgrade projects.

Eight years later, it is apparent that Northrop Grumman learned some important lessons about preventing a colossal "brain drain" in the future. After researching the issues it faced, the company implemented a variety of tools to retain and transfer knowledge from its engineers—well in advance of retirement. Such tools include document management systems and common work spaces that record, for future reference, how an engineer did his job. Shaffar and his team have also started programs that bring together older and younger engineers across the country to exchange information about technical problems, in addition to using software that helps people find experts within the company.

The atmosphere has changed at Northrop Grumman since 1997's massive downsizing. Although a large percentage

of its workforce is approaching retirement, the company has started hiring more college graduates over the past four years, thereby lowering the average age of employees from the upper forties to the mid-forties. Shaffar is currently working on balancing the more gradual transfer of knowledge from older to younger workers with the need to capture some vital expertise quickly before it's too late. For example, Northrop Grumman engineers are competing on a proposal for a "crew exploration vehicle," which is being designed to replace the space shuttle and travel to the moon (and eventually to Mars). These engineers met in August 2005 with a group of retirees who worked on the Apollo program that sent men to the moon more than 35 years ago. Using Quindi, a computer program, and a camera attached to a laptop, a facilitator recorded retirees telling stories about how they handled the technical problems of sending a man to the moon. Engineers working on this project will be able to view these tales as Web pages. Shaffar admits that employees would rather go to another person than a system for advice, but he says the exercise helped capture knowledge that would otherwise fade away.

Above all, Shaffar acknowledges that the problem surpasses looking at what skills you presently have. "There have always been new generations, and we're not any different in that way," he says. "Mentoring, training and passing on knowledge is not something you can do at the last minute. You have to plan ahead."

*Sources:* Compiled from Patton (2006) and *CIO.com* (accessed June 2006).

*For Further Exploration:* Is there any way to improve knowledge acquisition in such a case? What role does document management play? What is the impact of corporate culture in this case?

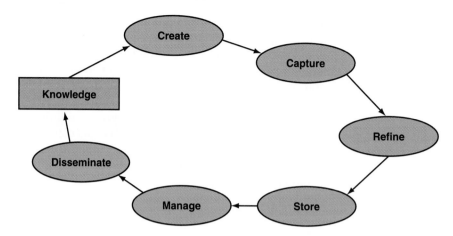

**Figure 10.2** The knowledge management cycle.

A functioning knowledge management system follows six steps in a cycle (see Figure 10.2). The reason the system is cyclical is that knowledge is dynamically refined over time. The knowledge in a good KM system is never finished because, over time, the environment changes, and the knowledge must be updated to reflect the changes. The cycle works as follows:

1. **Create knowledge.** Knowledge is created as people determine new ways of doing things or develop know-how. Sometimes external knowledge is brought in.
2. **Capture knowledge.** New knowledge must be identified as valuable and be represented in a reasonable way.
3. **Refine knowledge.** New knowledge must be placed in context so that it is actionable. This is where human insights (tacit qualities) must be captured along with explicit facts.
4. **Store knowledge.** Useful knowledge must then be stored in a reasonable format in a knowledge repository so that others in the organization can access it.
5. **Manage knowledge.** Like a library, the knowledge must be kept current. It must be reviewed to verify that it is relevant and accurate.
6. **Disseminate knowledge.** Knowledge must be made available in a useful format to anyone in the organization who needs it, anywhere and any time.

As knowledge is disseminated, individuals develop, create, and identify new knowledge or update old knowledge, with which they replenish the system. Knowledge is a resource that is not consumed when used, though it can age. (For example, driving a car in 1900 was different from driving one now, but many of the basic principles still apply.) Knowledge must be updated. Thus, the amount of knowledge grows over time.

For the essentials of KM see Levinson (2005) and *brint.com/KM*.

## 10.2 Organizational Learning and Memory

Knowledge management is rooted in the concepts of organizational learning and organizational memory. When members of an organization collaborate and communicate ideas, teach, and learn, knowledge is transformed and transferred from individual to individual (see Bennet and Bennet, 2003b; Jasimuddin et al., 2006).

| THE LEARNING ORGANIZATION | The term **learning organization** refers to an organization's capability of learning from its past experience. Before a company can improve, it must first learn. Learning involves an interaction between experience and competence. In communities of practice, these are tightly related. Communities of practice provide not only a context for newcomers to learn, but also a context for new insights to be transformed into knowledge. (We discuss communities of practice later in this chapter.) To build a learning organization, three critical issues must be tackled: (1) meaning (determining a vision of what the learning organization is to be), (2) management (determining how the firm is to work), and (3) measurement (assessing the rate and level of learning). A learning organization is one that performs five main activities well: systematic problem solving, creative experimentation, learning from past experience, learning from the best practices of others, and transferring knowledge quickly and efficiently throughout the organization (Vat, 2006). Best Buy deliberately and successfully structured its knowledge management efforts around creating a learning organization where it captured best practices as discussed above. |

| ORGANIZATIONAL MEMORY | A learning organization must have an **organizational memory** and a means to save, represent, and share its organizational knowledge. Estimates vary, but it is generally believed that only 10 to 20 percent of business data are actually used. Organizations "remember" the past in their policies and procedures. Individuals ideally tap into this memory for both explicit and tacit knowledge when faced with issues or problems to be solved. Human intelligence draws from the organizational memory and adds value by creating new knowledge. A knowledge management system can capture the new knowledge and make it available in its enhanced form. See Nevo and Wand (2005) and Jennex and Olfman (2003). |

| ORGANIZATIONAL LEARNING | **Organizational learning** is the development of new knowledge and insights that have the potential to influence an organization's behavior. It occurs when associations, cognitive systems, and memories are shared by members of an organization. Learning skills include (per Garvin, 2000): |

- Openness to new perspectives
- Awareness of personal biases
- Exposure to unfiltered data
- A sense of humility

Establishing a corporate memory is critical for success (Hinds and Aronson, 2002). Information technology plays a critical role in organizational learning, and management must place emphasis on this area to foster it (see Ali et al., 2006; Craig, 2005).

Since organizations are becoming more virtual in nature they must develop methods for effective organizational learning. Modern collaborative technologies can help in knowledge management initiatives. Organizational learning and memory depend less on technology than on the people issues, as we describe next.

| ORGANIZATIONAL CULTURE | The ability of an organization to learn, develop memory, and share knowledge is dependent on its culture. Culture is a pattern of shared basic assumptions (Kayworth and Leidner, 2003). Over time, organizations learn what works and what doesn't work. As the lessons become second nature, they become part of the *organizational culture*. New employees learn the culture from their mentors along with know-how. |

The impact of corporate culture on an organization is difficult to measure. However, strong culture generally produces strong, measurable bottom-line results: net income, return on invested capital, and yearly increases in stock price. For example, Buckman Laboratories, a pharmaceutical firm, measures culture impact by sales of new products. Buckman undertook to change its organizational culture by making knowledge sharing part of the company's core values (see Minicase 2). After instituting a knowledge-sharing initiative, sales of products less than five years old rose to 33 percent of total sales, up from 22 percent (see Martin, 2000). Sharing initiatives and proper motivation are critical for knowledge management success. This is even trickier in the public sector. On the other hand, an organizational culture that does not foster sharing can severely cripple a KM effort (Alavi et al., 2005/06; Jones et al., 2006; Riege, 2005).

Encouraging employees to use a knowledge management system, both for contributing knowledge and for seeking knowledge, can be difficult. Riege (2005) reviewed past studies and identified a number of possible reasons that *people do not like to share knowledge:*

- General lack of time to share knowledge and to identify colleagues in need of specific knowledge
- Apprehension or fear that sharing may reduce or jeopardize people's job security
- Low awareness and realization of the value and benefit of possessed knowledge to others
- Dominance in sharing explicit over tacit knowledge such as know-how and experience that requires hands-on learning, observation, dialogue, and interactive problem solving
- Use of strong hierarchy, position-based status, and formal power
- Insufficient capture, evaluation, feedback, communication, and tolerance of past mistakes that would enhance individual and organizational learning effects
- Differences in experience and educational levels
- Poor verbal/written communication and interpersonal skills
- Age and gender differences
- Lack of social network
- Taking ownership of intellectual property due to fear of not receiving just recognition and accreditation from managers and colleagues
- Lack of trust in people because they may misuse knowledge or take unjust credit for it
- Differences in national culture or ethnic background, and values and beliefs associated with it

Sometimes a technology project fails because the technology does not match the organization's culture. (This is a much deeper issue than having a low fit between the technology and the task and hand; see McCarthy et al., 2001.) This is especially true for knowledge management systems, because they rely so heavily on individuals contributing their knowledge. Most KM systems that fail in practice do so because of organizational culture issues (see Zyngier, 2006).

# 10.3 Knowledge Management Activities

When asked why the organization was building a worldwide knowledge management system, the chief knowledge officer (CKO) of a large multinational consulting firm replied, "We have 80,000 people scattered around the world that need information to do their jobs effectively. The information they needed was too difficult to find and, even if they did find it, often inaccurate. Our intranet is meant to solve this problem" (Leidner, 2003). A survey of European firms by KPMG Peat Marwick in 1998 found that almost half of the companies reported having suffered a significant setback from losing key staff (KPMG, 1998). Similarly, a survey conducted in the same year by Cranfield University found that the majority of responding firms believed that much of the knowledge they needed existed inside the organization, but that finding and leveraging it were ongoing challenges. It is precisely these types of difficulties that have led to the systematic attempt to manage knowledge.

Most knowledge management initiatives have one of three aims: (1) to make knowledge visible mainly through maps, yellow pages, and hypertext, (2) to develop a knowledge-intensive culture, or to (3) build a knowledge infrastructure. These aims are not mutually exclusive, and indeed, firms may attempt all three as part of a knowledge management initiative.

There are several activities or processes that surround the management of knowledge. These include the creation of knowledge, the sharing of knowledge, and the seeking and use of knowledge. Various terms have been used to describe these processes. What is important is an understanding of how knowledge flows through an organization, rather than any particular label assigned to a knowledge activity.

**KNOWLEDGE CREATION**

*Knowledge creation* is the generation of new insights, ideas, or routines. It may also be referred to as *knowledge acquisition* (Holsapple and Joshi, 2003). It is helpful to distinguish between the creation of fundamentally new knowledge versus the acquisition of existing knowledge (Ford, 2003). Some people view knowledge creation as interplay between tacit and explicit knowledge and as a growing spiral as knowledge moves among the individual, group, and organizational levels. For further discussion see Wickramasinghe et al. (2006).

There are four modes of knowledge creation: socialization, combination, externalization, and internalization. The *socialization* mode refers to the conversion of tacit knowledge to new tacit knowledge through social interactions and shared experience among organizational members (e.g., mentoring). The *combination* mode refers to the creation of new explicit knowledge by merging, categorizing, reclassifying, and synthesizing existing explicit knowledge (e.g., statistical analyses of market data). The other two modes involve interactions and conversion between tacit and explicit knowledge. *Externalization* refers to converting tacit knowledge to new explicit knowledge (e.g., producing a written document describing the procedures used in solving a particular client's problem). *Internalization* refers to the creation of new tacit knowledge from explicit knowledge (e.g., obtaining a novel insight through reading a document). These final two modes of knowledge creation deal less with the creation of new knowledge than with the conversion of existing knowledge to a new mode. Figure 10.3 depicts these modes of knowledge creation.

**KNOWLEDGE SHARING**

Knowledge sharing is the willful explication of one's ideas, insights, solutions, and experiences (i.e., knowledge) to another individual either via an intermediary, such as a computer-based system, or directly. However, in many organizations, information and knowledge are not considered organizational resources to be shared, but individual competitive weapons to be kept private. Organization members may share personal knowledge with a certain trepidation—the perceived threat that they are of less value if their knowledge is part of the organizational public domain. Research in organizational learning and knowledge management suggests that some facilitating conditions include trust, interest, and shared language (Ford,

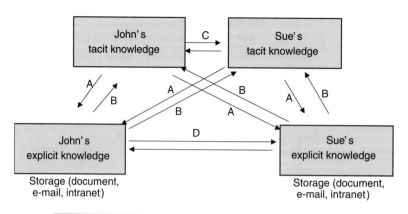

**Figure 10.3** Forms of knowledge creation. (*Source:* Adapted from Alavi and Leidner, 2001.)

Legend: Each arrow represents a form of knowledge creation
A–Externalization; B–Internalization; C – Socialization;
D–Combination

2003), fostering access to knowledgeable members, and a culture marked by autonomy, redundancy, requisite variety, intention, and fluctuation (King, 2006).

The World Bank includes such factors as openness to new ideas, continual learning, and sharing of knowledge as part of their annual performance evaluation of employees (Liebowitz and Chen, 2003).

## KNOWLEDGE SEEKING

*Knowledge seeking,* also referred to as *knowledge sourcing* (Gray and Meister, 2003), is the search for and use of internal organizational knowledge. While the lack of time or the lack of reward may hinder the sharing of knowledge, the same can be said of knowledge seeking. Individuals may sometimes feel compelled to come up with new ideas, rather than use tried-and-true knowledge, if they feel that their own performance review is based on the originality or creativity of their ideas. Such was the case for marketing employees in a global consumer goods organization described in Alavi et al. (2003).

An important objective of KM efforts is to enable individuals to learn from other individuals as well as to allow the various organizational units to learn from one another. Take the example of a Managing Director of Asia for a U.S.-based global chemical company who oversees accounts in Asia and prepares bids for new accounts. Suppose this managing director needs information on the proper chemicals required for a pulp mill and suppose this is his first time working with a pulp mill. Where does he go to find information that will help him secure the bid? Perhaps he is fortunate enough to have co-workers with the relevant experience, but more likely he will need some expertise that the firm has in other offices. Without some systems and processes in place to help this managing director tap into the firm's extensive knowledge base, the managing director would be on his own. This example comes from Buckman Labs. Indeed Buckman had implemented a global knowledge management system. The rep posted a query to the KM system and, within a couple of hours, had received 11 replies from 6 different countries (Pan and Leidner, 2003). For information on how to deal with such situations see Online File W10.6.

Individuals may engage in knowledge creation, sharing, and seeking with or without the use of information technology tools. We next describe two common approaches to knowledge management.

# 10.4 Approaches to Knowledge Management

There are three fundamental approaches to knowledge management: the process, the practice, and the best practices approaches.

**THE PROCESS APPROACH**

The **process approach** attempts to codify organizational knowledge through formalized controls, processes, and technologies. Organizations adopting the process approach may implement explicit policies governing how knowledge is to be collected, stored, and disseminated throughout the organization. The process approach frequently involves the use of information technologies to enhance the quality and speed of knowledge creation and distribution in the organizations. These technologies may include intranets, data warehousing, knowledge repositories, decision support tools, and groupware (Kiaraka and Manning, 2005). For further details see Online File W10.7.

**THE PRACTICE APPROACH**

In contrast, the **practice approach** to knowledge management assumes that a great deal of organizational knowledge is tacit in nature and that formal controls, processes, and technologies are not suitable for transmitting this type of understanding. Rather than building formal systems to manage knowledge, the focus of this approach is to build the social environments or communities of practice necessary to facilitate the sharing of tacit understanding (Brown and Duguid, 2000; Leidner, et al., 2006). **Communities of practice (COPs)** are groups of individuals with a common professional interest who work together informally. Within such a community, individuals collaborate directly, teach each other, and share experiences. See Section 10.7.

The practice approach is typically adopted by companies that provide highly customized solutions to unique problems. The valuable knowledge for these firms is tacit in nature, which is difficult to express, capture, and manage. In this case, the environment and the nature of the problems being encountered are extremely dynamic. For these firms, knowledge is shared mostly through person-to-person contacts. Collaborative computing methods (for example, Lotus Notes/Domino Server or e-mail) help people communicate. Because tacit knowledge is difficult to extract, store, and manage, the explicit knowledge that points to *how* to find the appropriate tacit knowledge (people contacts, consulting reports) is made available to an appropriate set of individuals who might need it.

To make their practice approach work, firms like Bain and Co. (*bain.com*) invest heavily in building networks of people and communications technology such as telephone, e-mail, and videoconferencing. Also they commonly have face-to-face meetings.

Online File W10.8 summarizes the process and practice approaches.

**BEST PRACTICES**

**Best practices** are the activities and methods that the most effective organizations use to operate and manage various functions. Chevron, for example, recognizes four levels of best practices (O'Dell et al., 1998). They include:

1. A good idea that is not yet proven, but makes intuitive sense.
2. A good practice, an implemented technique, methodology, procedure, or process that has improved business results.
3. A local best practice, a best approach for all or a large part of the organization based on analyzing hard data. In other words, the scope within the organization

of the best practice is identified: Can it be used only in a single department or geographical region, or can it be used across the organization, or anywhere in between?

4. An industry best practice, similar to the third level, but using hard data from industry.

Historically, the first knowledge repositories simply listed best practices and made them available within the firm. Now that knowledge repositories are electronic and Web-accessible, they can have wide-ranging impact on the use of knowledge throughout a firm. Raytheon successfully uses best practices to merge three distinct corporate cultures. See O'Dell et al. (2003) for more on best practices.

**Hybrid Approaches.** In reality, a knowledge management initiative can, and probably will, involve both process and practice approaches. The two are not mutually exclusive. Alavi et al. (2003) describe the case of an organization that began its KM effort with a large repository but evolved the knowledge management initiative into a community-of-practice approach that existed side-by-side with the repository. In fact, community members would pass information from the community forum to the organizational repository when they felt that the knowledge was valuable outside their community. *IT at Work 10.2* illustrates how Monsanto successfully manages its knowledge using a combination of the two approaches.

# 10.5 Information Technology in Knowledge Management

Knowledge management is more a methodology applied to business practices than a technology or product. Nevertheless, information technology is *crucial* to the success of every knowledge management system. Information technology enables KM by providing the enterprise architecture on which it is built.

**COMPONENTS OF KNOWLEDGE MANAGEMENT SYSTEMS**

Knowledge management systems are developed using three sets of technologies: *communication, collaboration,* and *storage and retrieval.*

*Communication technologies* allow users to access needed knowledge, and to communicate with each other—especially with experts (see Chapter 4 and Van de Van, 2005).

*Storage and retrieval technologies* originally meant using a database management system to store and manage knowledge. This worked reasonably well in the early days for storing and managing most explicit knowledge, and even explicit knowledge about tacit knowledge. However, capturing, storing, and managing tacit knowledge usually requires a different set of tools. Electronic document management systems and specialized storage systems that are part of collaborative computing systems fill this void.

**TECHNOLOGIES SUPPORTING KNOWLEDGE MANAGEMENT**

Several technologies have contributed to significant advances in knowledge management tools. Artificial intelligence, intelligent agents, knowledge discovery in databases, and Extensible Markup Language (XML) are examples of technologies that enable advanced functionality of modern knowledge management systems and form the base for future innovations in the KM field.

**Artificial Intelligence.** In the definition of knowledge management, *artificial intelligence* is rarely mentioned. However, practically speaking, AI methods and tools are embedded in a number of knowledge management systems, either by vendors

# *IT* at Work 10.2

*POM   GLOBAL*

## Cultivating Knowledge at Monsanto

Following a series of mergers and divestitures in the late 1990s and early 2000s, Monsanto transformed itself from a chemical company into a leading life sciences and biotechnology firm. Today, along with a number of other products, Monsanto develops and produces seeds with impressive genetic traits, such as herbicide tolerance and insect protection. Not surprisingly, succeeding in this knowledge-intensive field requires Monsanto to focus on knowledge management.

Monsanto's board of directors realized the need for knowledge management quite early and readily approved a substantial investment in KM. In fact, one of the company's business units was specifically created to focus on growth opportunities by creating and enabling "a learning and sharing environment where knowledge and information are effectively used across the enterprise."

The objectives of knowledge management initiatives at Monsanto included connecting people with other knowledgeable people, connecting people with information, enabling the conversion of information to knowledge, encapsulating knowledge to make it easier to transfer, and distributing knowledge around the company.

Information technology played a crucial role in achieving these objectives. Data warehousing, full-text search engines, Internet/intranet capabilities, collaborative workgroup software, and other systems contributed to creating connections among knowledgeable people, as well as between people and sources of information. Information technology also helped the company create an enterprisewide infrastructure, which enabled end-user applications to tap into the struc-tured and unstructured knowledge available throughout the organization. In addition to technology, Monsanto used dedicated "knowledge teams" that created and maintained the guide to the company's knowledge and served as points of contact for employees seeking information.

The wealth of tacit knowledge possessed by Monsanto's highly educated scientists and researchers was colossal. However, the prevailing culture in some parts of the organization rewarded employees for their individual, specialized expertise. As a result, employees guarded their knowledge carefully. Internal KM initiatives, supported by external consultants, managed to convince employees that it is their collective knowledge that brings power, rather than the knowledge of any particular individual.

The quality of Monsanto's knowledge management programs earned the company a place on the prestigious list of Most Admired Knowledge Enterprises. More importantly, active management of knowledge contributes to the company's performance, such as increasing the speed of obtaining regulatory approvals for its innovative products.

*Sources:* Sharp (2003), "Most Admired Knowledge Companies Recognized" (1999), and *monsanto.com* (accessed June 2006).

*For Further Exploration:* Monsanto employs a variety of KM initiatives related to its people, processes, and technology. Is this multifaceted method more effective than relying on a narrower, more focused program? Review the five objectives of knowledge management at Monsanto. Discuss which of them can be accomplished best with the practice approach to KM.

---

or by system developers. AI methods can assist in identifying expertise, eliciting knowledge automatically and semiautomatically, interfacing through natural language processing, and in intelligent search through intelligent agents. AI methods, most notably expert systems, neural networks, fuzzy logic, and intelligent agents, are used in knowledge management systems to do the following:

- Assist in and enhance searching knowledge (e.g., intelligent agents in Web searches).
- Help establish knowledge profiles of individuals and groups.
- Help determine the relative importance of knowledge when it is contributed to and accessed from the knowledge repository.
- Scan e-mail, documents, and databases to perform knowledge discovery, determine meaningful relationships, glean knowledge, or induce rules for expert systems.
- Identify patterns in data (usually through neural networks).
- Forecast future results using existing knowledge.
- Provide advice directly from knowledge by using neural networks or expert systems.
- Provide a natural language or voice command–driven user interface for a knowledge management system.

**Intelligent Agents.** *Intelligent agents* are software systems that learn how users work and provide assistance in their daily tasks. For example, when these software programs are told what the user wants to retrieve, passive agents can monitor incoming information for matches with user interests, and active agents can seek out information relevant to user preferences (Gray and Tehrani, 2003). Intelligent agents of various kinds are discussed in Chapter 12.

There are a number of ways that intelligent agents can help in knowledge management systems. Typically they are used to elicit and identify knowledge. Examples are:

- IBM (*ibm.com*) offers an intelligent data mining family, including Intelligent Decision Server (IDS), for finding and analyzing massive amounts of enterprise data.
- Gentia (Planning Sciences International, *gentia.com*) uses intelligent agents to facilitate data mining with Web access and data warehouse facilities.

Combining intelligent agents with enterprise knowledge portals is a powerful technique that can deliver to a user exactly what he or she needs to perform his or her tasks. The intelligent agent learns what the user prefers to see, and how he or she organizes it. Then, the intelligent agent takes over to provide it at the desktop like a good administrative assistant would.

**Knowledge Discovery in Databases.** **Knowledge discovery in databases (KDD)** is a process used to search for and extract useful information from volumes of documents and data. It includes tasks known as knowledge extraction, data archaeology, data exploration, data pattern processing, data dredging, and information harvesting. All of these activities are conducted automatically and allow quick discovery, even by nonprogrammers. Data are often buried deep within very large databases, data warehouses, text documents, or knowledge repositories, all of which may contain data, information, and knowledge gathered over many years. *Data mining,* the process of searching for previously unknown information or relationships in large databases, is ideal for eliciting knowledge from databases, documents, e-mail, and so on. (For more on data mining, see Chapter 11.)

# 10.6 Knowledge Management Systems Implementation

The KMS challenge is to identify and integrate the three essential components—communication technologies, collaboration technologies, and storage and retrieval technologies—to meet the knowledge management needs of an organization. The earliest knowledge management systems were developed with networked technology (intranets), collaborative computing tools (groupware), and databases (for the knowledge repository). They were constructed from a variety of off-the-shelf IT components. Many organizations, especially large management consulting firms like Accenture, developed their knowledge architecture with a set of tools that provided the three technology types. Collaborative computing suites such as Lotus Notes/Domino Server provide many KMS capabilities. Other systems were developed by integrating a set of tools from a single or multiple vendors.

In the early 2000s, KMS technology has evolved to integrate the three components into a single package. These include enterprise knowledge portals and knowledge management suites. In addition, there were some innovative applications such as expert locating systems.

**Finding Experts Electronically and Using Expert Location Systems.** Companies know that information technology can be used to find experts. People who need help may post their problem on the corporate intranet and ask for help. Similarly, companies may ask for advice on how to exploit an opportunity. IBM frequently uses this method. Sometimes it obtains hundreds of useful ideas within a few days. It is a kind of brainstorming. The problem with this approach is that it may take days to get an answer, if an answer is even provided, and the answer may not be from the top experts. Therefore, companies employ expert location systems. **Expert location systems (ELSs)** are interactive computerized systems that help employees find and connect with colleagues with expertise required for specific problems—whether they are across the country or across the room—in order to solve specific, critical business problems in seconds (see Totty, 2006, for details and examples). Such software is made by companies such as AskMe (*askmecorp.com*). They work similarly, exploring knowledge bases either for an answer to the problem (if it exists there) or to locate qualified experts. The process includes the following steps (see Figure 10.4):

**Step 1:** An employee submits a question into the expertise location management system.

**Step 2:** The software searches its database to see if an answer to the question already exists. If it does, the information (research reports, spreadsheets, etc.) is returned to the employee. If not, the software searches documents and archived communications for an "expert."

**Step 3:** Once a qualified candidate is located, the system asks if he is able to answer a question from a colleague. If so, he submits a response. If the

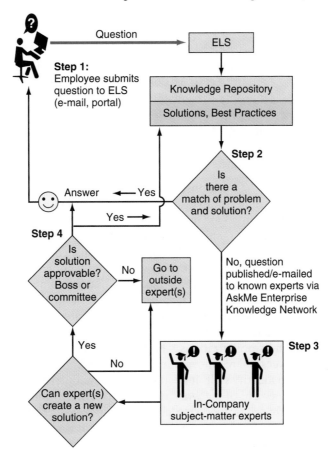

**Figure 10.4** Expert location system of AskMe Corp. (*Source:* Drawn by E. Turban.)

# IT at Work 10.3

## How the U.S. Department of Commerce Uses an Expert Location System    GOV    SVC

The U.S. Commercial Service Division at the Department of Commerce (DOC) conducts approximately 200,000 counseling sessions a year involving close to $40 billion in trade. The division employs many specialists who frequently need to do research or call on experts to answer a question posed by a U.S. corporation.

For example, in May 2004, a U.S.-based software company called Brad Anderson, a DOC specialist, for advice. The software company wanted to close a deal with a customer in Poland, but the buyer wanted to charge the U.S. company a 20 percent withholding tax, a tax it attributed to Poland's recent admission into the European Union. Was the tax legitimate?

To find out, Anderson turned to the DOC Insider, an *expertise location system* (from AskMe). After typing in his question, Anderson first found some documents that were related to his query, but they did not explain the EU tax code completely. Anderson next asked the system to search the 1,700-expert-strong Commercial Service for a real live expert, and within seconds he was given a list of 80 people in the DOC who might be able to help him. Of those, he chose the six people he felt were most qualified and then forwarded his query.

Before the DOC Insider was in place, Anderson says, it would have taken him about three days to get the answer to the question. "You have to make many phone calls and deal with time zones," he says. Thanks to the expertise location system, however, he had three responses within minutes, a complete answer within an hour, and the sale went through the following morning. Anderson estimates that he now uses the system for roughly 40 percent of the work he does.

The DOC Insider is an invaluable tool. Anderson thinks the tool is vital enough to provide it to other units at the agency. In the first nine months the system has been in place, it has saved more than 1,000 hours of work. For more applications at DOC, see Totty (2006).

*Sources:* Compiled from D. D'Agostino (2004). Fox (2004).

*For Further Exploration:* What are the benefits of such a system? Will the system impact privacy? Can it be integrated with wireless devices? For what?

---

candidate is unable (perhaps he is in a meeting or otherwise indisposed), he can elect to pass on the question. The question is then routed to the next appropriate candidate until one responds.

**Step 4:** After the response is sent, it is reviewed for accuracy and sent back to the querist. At the same time, it is added to the knowledge database. This way, if the question comes up again, it will not be necessary to seek real-time assistance.

*IT at Work 10.3* demonstrates how such a system works for the U.S. government.

According to Levinson (2005), companies that have been frustrated by traditional KM efforts are increasingly looking for ways to find out how knowledge flows through their organization, and *social network analysis (SNA)* can show them just that. SNA is a process of mapping a group's contacts (whether personal or professional) to identify who knows whom and who works with whom. In enterprises, it provides a clear picture of the ways that far-flung employees and divisions work together and can help identify key experts in the organization who possess the knowledge needed to, say, solve a complicated programming problem or launch a new product. M&Ms maker Mars used SNA to identify how knowledge flows through its organizations, who holds influence, who gives the best advice, and how employees share information. The Canadian government's central IT unit used SNA to identify skills it needed to retain and develop, and to determine who among the 40 percent of the workforce due to retire within five years had the most important knowledge and experience to begin transferring to others.

SNA isn't a replacement for traditional KM tools such as knowledge databases or portals, but it can provide companies with a starting point for how best to proceed with KM initiatives. As a component of a larger KM strategy, SNA can help companies identify key leaders and then set up mechanisms—such as communities of practice—so that those leaders can pass on their knowledge to colleagues. To identify experts in their organizations, companies can use software programs that track e-mail and other kinds of electronic communication.

KNOWLEDGE MANAGEMENT PRODUCTS AND VENDORS

Technology tools that support knowledge management are called **knowware.** Most knowledge management software packages include one or more of the following seven tools: collaborative computing tools, knowledge servers, enterprise knowledge portals, electronic document management systems, knowledge harvesting tools, search engines, and knowledge management suites. Many packages provide several tools because several are necessary in an effective knowledge management system. For example, most electronic document management systems also include collaborative computing capabilities. A directory of about 40 KM software companies is available at *capterra.com.*

Knowledge management systems can be purchased in whole or in part from one of numerous software development companies and enterprise information systems vendors, they can be acquired through major consulting firms, or they can be outsourced to the application service providers (ASPs). All three alternatives will be discussed in the latter part of this chapter. (See *KMWorld* for a Buyer's Guide in every April issue.)

**Software Development Companies and Enterprise Information Systems Vendors.** Software development companies and enterprise information systems vendors offer numerous knowledge management packages, from individual tools to comprehensive knowledge management suites. The variety of knowware that is readily available on the market allows companies to find the tools that will meet their unique knowledge management needs. Following is a review of some software packages and their vendors in each of the seven knowware categories cited earlier.

**Collaborative Computing Tools.** Collaboration tools, or groupware, were the first used to enhance tacit knowledge transfer within an organization. See Chapters 4 and 12 for details.

**Knowledge Servers.** A knowledge server contains the main knowledge management software, including the knowledge repository, and provides access to other knowledge, information, and data. Examples of knowledge servers include the Hummingbird Knowledge Server, the Intraspect Software Knowledge Server, the Hyperwave Information Server, the Sequoia Software XML Portal Server, and Autonomy's Intelligent Data Operating Layer (IDOL) Server. Autonomy's IDOL Server connects people to content, content to content, and people to people through modules that enable organizations to integrate various personalization, collaboration, and retrieval features. The server provides a **knowledge repository,** a central location for searching and accessing information from many sources, such as the Internet, corporate intranets, databases, and file systems, thereby enabling the efficient distribution of time-sensitive information. The server seamlessly extends and integrates with the company's e-business suite, allowing rapid deployment applications that span the enterprise and leverage AI-assisted technology to harvest knowledge assets.

**Enterprise Knowledge Portals.** *Enterprise knowledge portals* (EKPs) are the doorways into many knowledge management systems. They have evolved from the concepts underlying executive information systems, group support systems, Web-browsers, and database management systems. According to an IDC report, individuals may spend as much as 30 percent of their time looking for information (Ziff-Davis, 2002). An enterprise knowledge portal presents a single access point for a vast body of explicit information, such as project plans, functional requirements, technical specifications, white papers, training materials, and customer feedback survey data (Kesner, 2003).

Enterprise knowledge portals are a means of organizing the many sources of unstructured information in an organization (see the example in Online File W10.9). Most combine data integration, reporting mechanisms, and collaboration, while document and knowledge management is handled by a server. The portal aggregates each user's total information needs: data and documents, e-mail, Web links and queries, dynamic feeds from the network, and shared calendars and task lists. The personal information portal has evolved into an enterprise knowledge portal (Silver, 2000).

**HRM**

One highly successful portal is Cisco's Employee Connection. The portal provides any time, anywhere access to the company's intranet; it has been credited with helping save the company $551 million, thanks primarily to improved self-service (Anderson, 2002). The intent of the system is to connect as many systems and applications as possible so that the user has a single entree into all of Cisco's information systems (Anderson, 2002).

When enterprise information portals first entered the market, they did not contain knowledge management features. Now, most do. Leading portal vendors include Autonomy, Brio, Corechange, Dataware, Intraspect, Hummingbird, InXight, IBM/Lotus, Knowmadic, OpenText, Plumtree, Verity, Viador, and Vignette. Database vendors such as Microsoft, Oracle, and Sybase are also selling knowledge portals. Portals can range in cost from less than $500,000 to $8 million (Steinberg, 2002).

Hyperwave's Hyperwave Information Portal (HIP) aggregates information from disparate sources and features dynamic link management, which verifies the quality of the link and hides links to unauthorized content. HIP manages connections between information sources and makes structured and unstructured corporate information searchable via a standard browser. For more on such portals, see Baalen et al. (2005) and Chapter 4.

**Electronic Document Management.** Electronic document management (EDM) systems focus on the document in electronic form as the collaborative focus of work. For details see Chapter 3.

A new approach to electronic document management, called **content management systems (CMSs),** is changing the way documents and their content are managed. A content management system produces dynamic versions of documents, and automatically maintains the "current" set for use at the enterprise level. With the explosion of Web-based materials, organizations need a mechanism to provide content that is consistent and accurate across the enterprise. EDM systems, enterprise information portals, and other CMSs fill that need. The goal is to provide large numbers of knowledge workers with access to large amounts of unstructured text. An IDC survey of attendees at the KMWorld 2001 Conference and Exposition indicated that 63 percent of all respondents had or planned to implement a CMS, while 59 percent rated CMS as very to critically important (Feldman, 2002).

See *IT at Work 10.4* for how HealthPartners Medical Group and Clinics (HPMG) uses electronic medical records to implement evidence-based best practices.

**Knowledge Harvesting Tools.** Tools for capturing knowledge unobtrusively are helpful since they allow a knowledge contributor to be minimally (or not at all) involved in the knowledge-harvesting efforts. Embedding this type of tool in a KMS is an ideal approach to knowledge capture.

# IT at Work 10.4

## Using Electronic Medical Records to Enable Evidence-Based Medicine

SVC   HRM

Evidence-based medicine involves the judicious application of new scientific knowledge by clinicians; yet many physicians, as many as 45 percent, rely on outdated treatments even when clinical trials and other studies have provided strong support for newer, more effective treatments. Several knowledge challenges are responsible for this tendency to rely on the old rather than new knowledge. First, clinicians are faced with an overwhelming volume of information on clinical trials of various new treatments. Second, payment programs often do not reimburse for the new treatments until they become standard. Third, and perhaps most significantly, lack of understanding and clarity about the new best practices often impedes the flow of information from clinical trials, making it unrealistic for physicians to use best practices in a timely fashion.

HealthPartners Medical Group & Clinics (HPMG) is a group of more than 600 physicians who practice in 35 medical

and surgical specialties. HPMG has embarked on a program to support best-science cases. Using medical records, and based on a patient's symptoms and signs, the system will provide a best-practice alert. The alert will provide a checklist summary of the guidelines and recommended case steps. Relevant educational material is available at the click of a mouse. To keep the information up-to-date, HPMG relies on the Institute for Clinical Systems Improvement (ICSI). ICSI includes expert panels of physicians who collaborate and review the clinical research and decide when to update the guidelines in the system.

Ultimately, HPMG hopes to provide the best quality of care available to patients while keeping the entire medical team informed of the latest medical best-practice treatments.

*Sources:* Patton (2005), and Evidence-Based Medicine Online at *ebm.bmjjournals.com* (accessed June 2006).

---

For example, Tacit Knowledge Systems' KnowledgeMail is an expertise-location software package that analyzes users' outgoing e-mail to parse subject expertise. It maintains a directory of expertise and offers ways to contact experts, while maintaining privacy controls for those experts. Autonomy's ActiveKnowledge performs a similar analysis on e-mail and other standard document types. Intraspect Software's Intraspect platform monitors an organization's group memory, captures the context of its use (such as who used it, when, for what, how it was combined with other information, and what people said about it), and then makes the information available for sharing and reuse.

**Search Engines.** Search engines perform one of the essential functions of knowledge management—locating and retrieving necessary documents from vast collections accumulated in corporate repositories. Companies like Google, Verity, Inktomi, and Nervana (see *A Closer Look 10.1*) are offering a wide selection of search engines that are capable of indexing and cataloging files in various formats as well as retrieving and prioritizing relevant documents in response to user queries.

**Knowledge Management Suites.** Knowledge management suites are complete knowledge management solutions out-of-the-box. They integrate the communications, collaboration, and storage technologies into a single convenient package. A knowledge management suite must still access internal databases and other external knowledge sources, so some integration is required to make the software truly functional. Knowledge management suites are powerful approaches to developing a KMS because they offer one user interface, one data repository, and one vendor.

IBM/Lotus offers an extensive range of knowledge management products including the Domino platform and the WebSphere portal. Several vendors also provide fairly comprehensive sets of tools for KM initiatives, which include Dataware Knowledge Management Suite, KnowledgeX by KnowledgeX, Inc., and many others. Autonomy Knowledge Management Suite offers document categorization and workflow integration. Microsoft provides central components of

# A Closer Look 10.1

## Nervana's Knowledge Discovery Solution

MKT SVC IS

Knowledge discovery companies are continually seeking to provide the most accurate and useful real-time information for product users. Nervana (*nervana.com*) is one such company that is dedicated to increasing the efficiency of knowledge-based workers through their Nervana Discovery Solution, a natural language query system that enables these workers to ask questions naturally, within the context of their meanings.

The Nervana Discovery Solution leads the industry in knowledge discovery technology, with the ability to understand and translate the true semantic meaning of a query and give immediate access to significant data. Based on content semantics, and not page-to-page hyperlinks, Nervana's search technology far surpasses a typical Web search and integrates with enterprise software applications such as Microsoft SQL Server, Outlook, Lotus Notes, Documentum, and Oracle DBA. This is made possible through the combination of multiple powerful technologies and services (i.e., true semantic technology, federated ontologies, and online content services that cross multiple domains) and allows

researchers and knowledge workers in life sciences and related markets to quickly perform data queries across a broad range of available resources. Users of the Nervana Discovery Solution receive relevant, timely results that benefit everyone who relies on the information.

Nervana's most recent version, Nervana Discovery Solution 3.0, includes new features such as drag-and-drop, Live Mode, and collaboration, all of which aid in inputting, retrieving, sorting, and sharing information. While digital information has grown exponentially, typical search engines have not been able to keep up with this information growth, mostly because they lack the ability to intelligently understand, process, and interpret information to transform it into knowledge. With their innovative Nervana Discovery Solution, Nervana is seeking to change that by providing the strongest and most intelligent knowledge discovery solution to date.

*Sources:* Compiled from "Livelier Life Sciences" (2006) and *nervana.com* (accessed July 2006).

knowledge management solutions, and is working on developing an encompassing KM framework. Some EIS vendors, such as SAP and Oracle, are developing knowledge management–related technologies as a platform for business applications. Siebel Systems is repositioning itself as a business-to-employee knowledge management platform. Knowledge management suites are powerful approaches to developing a KMS because they offer one user interface, one data repository, and one vendor.

**Consulting Firms.** All of the major consulting firms (Accenture, Ernst & Young, and so on) have massive internal knowledge management initiatives. Usually these become products after they succeed internally and provide assistance in establishing knowledge management systems and measuring their effectiveness. Consulting firms also provide some direct, out-of-the-box proprietary systems for vertical markets. Most of the major consulting firms define their knowledge management offerings as a *service*. For more on consulting firm activities and products, see McDonald and Shand (2000).

**Knowledge Management Application Service Providers.** Application service providers (ASPs) have evolved as a form of KMS outsourcing on the Web. There are many ASPs for e-commerce on the market.

For example, Communispace (*communispace.com*) is a high-level ASP collaboration system that focuses on connecting people to people (not just people to documents) to achieve specific objectives, regardless of geographic, time, and organizational barriers. As a hosted ASP solution, it is easy to rapidly deploy within organizations. Unlike conventional KM systems that organize data and documents, or chat rooms where people simply swap information,

Communispace contains a rich assortment of interactions, activities, and tools that connect people to the colleagues who can best help them make decisions, solve problems, and learn quickly. Communispace is designed to build trust online. It attempts to make a community self-conscious about taking responsibility for its actions and knowledge. Its Climate component helps participants to measure and understand how people are feeling about the community. The Virtual Café gives dispersed employees a way to meet and learn about each other through pictures and profiles.

**INTEGRATION OF KM SYSTEMS WITH OTHER BUSINESS INFORMATION SYSTEMS**

Since a knowledge management system is an enterprise system, it must be integrated with other enterprise and other information systems in an organization. Obviously, when it is designed and developed, it cannot be perceived as an add-on application. It must be truly integrated into other systems. Through the structure of the organizational culture (changed if necessary), a knowledge management system and its activities can be directly integrated into a firm's business processes. For example, a group involved in customer support can capture its knowledge to provide help on customers' difficult problems. In this case, help-desk software would be one type of package to integrate into a KMS, especially into the knowledge repository. A major challenge is to integrate data that reside in a variety of systems and formats (see *IT at Work 10.5*).

In the remainder of this section, we look at how KM systems can be integrated with other types of business information systems.

# *IT* at Work 10.5

## *X1 Provides Governmental Knowledge Management Solution*

**GOV**

With all of the challenges facing government agencies and organizations, knowledge management is an essential function for capturing data that reside in myriad formats, systems, and locations. Although today's $12 billion knowledge management market offers a variety of solutions for such obstacles, successful implementation of these solutions is highly dependent on organizations' willingness and ability to pledge considerable resources as well as adaptation of employees. The inability to supply or control those factors often interferes with knowledge management efforts to provide desired effects.

A new user-centric approach to managing structured and unstructured organizational documents and data is seeking to eliminate the shortcomings that exist with so many knowledge management systems. One such system that implements this approach is X1™ (*x1.com*). X1's knowledge management model is based on the intelligent indexing and searching of a company's data, no matter where they are stored and regardless of whether they are organized. This solution acknowledges the fundamental truth that traditional knowledge management solutions do not: People have various organizational skills and work in different ways. All knowledge workers have too much information and not enough

time to find it, so they generally seek the shortest path between A and B.

X1 provides a state-of-the-art, customizable search interface that returns an entire data set of matching items, allows access to any element in the results, presents high-quality previews of each data item, allows real-time modification of multiple search parameters, and frees the IT department from management tasks required by other knowledge management systems. X1 Government Edition has been established for use and positioned at secure installations in both military and agency accounts. This is certainly a positive step, as a user-centric approach in knowledge management will support faster response times, especially in times of crisis. Since the actions of the government affect us all, we should be concerned about the knowledge management issues that government agencies face. Through user-centric technologies such as X1, the government will be better equipped to meet the needs of the people.

*Sources:* Nenov (2005) and *kmworld.com* (accessed June 2006).

*For Further Exploration:* How does X1 solve governmental KM problems? Why is this tool important for the government? Could it be a risk to security? Why is it a user-centric tool?

**Integration with Decision Support Systems.** Knowledge management systems typically do not involve running models to solve problems, which is an activity typically done in decision support systems (DSSs). However, since a knowledge management system provides help in solving problems by applying knowledge, part of the solution may involve running models. A KMS could integrate into an appropriate set of models and data and activate them, when a specific problem may call for it. For details, see intelligent DSS in Chapter 12.

**Integration with Artificial Intelligence.** Knowledge management has a natural relationship with artificial intelligence (AI) methods and software, though knowledge management, strictly speaking, is not an artificial intelligence method. There are a number of ways in which KM and artificial intelligence can integrate. For example, if the knowledge stored in a KMS is to be represented and used as a sequence of if-then-else rules, then an expert system becomes part of the KMS. An expert system could also assist a user in identifying how to apply a chunk of knowledge in the KMS.

A common use of this integration is in identifying and classifying expertise by examining e-mail messages and documents. These include artificial intelligence–based tools, such as Tacit Knowledge Systems Inc. (*tacit.com*) ActiveNet and Knowledge-mail, and Inxight Software Categorizer (*inxight.com*).

**Integration with Customer Relationship Management Systems.** Customer relationship management (CRM) systems help users in dealing with customers. One aspect is the help-desk notion described earlier. But CRM goes much deeper. It can develop usable profiles of customers and predict their needs, so that an organization can increase sales and better serve its clients. A KMS can certainly provide tacit knowledge to people who use CRM directly in working with customers.

**Integration with Supply Chain Management Systems.** The supply chain is often considered to be the logistics end of the business. If products do not move through the organization and go out the door, the firm will fail. So it is important to optimize the supply chain and manage it properly. As discussed in Chapter 8, supply chain management (SCM) systems attempt to do so. SCM can benefit through integration with KMS because there are many issues and problems in the supply chain that require the company to combine both tacit and explicit knowledge. Accessing such knowledge will directly improve supply chain performance.

# 10.7 Roles of People in Knowledge Management

Managing the knowledge repository typically requires a full-time staff, similar to a reference-library staff. This staff examines, structures, filters, catalogues, and stores knowledge so that it is meaningful and can be accessed by the people who need it. The staff assists individuals in searching for knowledge and performs "environmental scanning": If they identify specific knowledge that an employee or client might need, they send it directly to them, thus adding value to the organization. (This is standard procedure for Accenture knowledge management personnel.) Finally, the knowledge repository staff may create communities of practice to gather individuals with common knowledge areas to identify, filter, extract, and contribute knowledge to a knowledge repository.

Most of the issues concerning the success, implementation, and effective use of a knowledge management system are people issues. And since a knowledge management system is an enterprisewide effort, many people need to be involved in it (Robb, 2003). They include the chief knowledge officer (CKO), the CEO, the other officers and managers of the organization, members and leaders of communities of practice, KMS developers, and KMS staff. Each person or group has an important role in either the development, management, or use of a KMS. By far, the CKO has the most visible role in a KMS effort, but the system cannot succeed unless the roles of all the players are established and understood. Ensuring that a KM team is properly constituted is therefore an essential factor in the success of any KM initiative (Robb, 2003).

**THE CHIEF KNOWLEDGE OFFICER**

Knowledge management projects that involve establishing a knowledge environment conducive to the transfer, creation, or use of knowledge attempt to build *cultural receptivity*. These attempts are centered on changing the behavior of the firm to embrace the use of knowledge management. Behavioral-centric projects require a high degree of support and participation from the senior management of the organization to facilitate their implementation. Most firms developing knowledge management systems have created a knowledge management officer, a **chief knowledge officer (CKO),** at the senior level. The objectives of the CKO's role are to maximize the firm's knowledge assets, design and implement knowledge management strategies, effectively exchange knowledge assets internally and externally, and promote system use.

A chief knowledge officer must do the following (adapted from Duffy, 1998):

- Set strategic priorities for knowledge management.
- Establish a knowledge repository of best practices.
- Gain a commitment from senior executives to support a learning environment.
- Teach information seekers how to ask better and smarter questions.
- Establish a process for managing intellectual assets.
- Obtain customer satisfaction information in near real time.
- Globalize knowledge management.

The CKO is responsible for creating an infrastructure and cultural environment for knowledge sharing. He or she must assign or identify the *knowledge champions* within the business units. The CKO's job is to manage the content their group produces, continually add to the knowledge base, and encourage their colleagues to do the same. Successful CKOs should have the full and enthusiastic support of their managers and of top management. Ultimately, the CKO is responsible for the entire knowledge management project while it is under development, and then for management of the system and the knowledge once it is deployed.

**CEO, OFFICERS, AND MANAGERS OF THE ORGANIZATION**

Vis-à-vis knowledge management, the CEO is responsible for championing the KM effort. He or she must ensure that a competent and capable CKO is found and that the CKO can obtain all the resources (including access to people with knowledge sources) needed to make the project a success. The CEO must also gain organization-wide support for the contribution to and use of the KMS. The CEO must also prepare the organization for the cultural changes that are expected to occur when the KMS is implemented. Support for the KMS and the CKO is the critical responsibility of the CEO.

Managers must also support the KM effort and provide access to sources of knowledge. In many KMSs, managers are an integral part of the communities of practice.

**COMMUNITIES OF PRACTICE**

The success of many KM systems has been attributed to the active involvement of the people who contribute to and benefit from using the knowledge. Consequently, communities of practice have appeared within organizations that are serious about their knowledge management efforts. As discussed earlier, a *community of practice* (COP) is a group of people in an organization with a common professional interest. Ideally, all the KMS users should each be in at least one COP. Creating and nurturing COPs properly is one key to KMS success.

In a sense, a community of practice "owns" the knowledge that it contributes, because it manages the knowledge on its way into the system, and as owner, must approve modifications to it. The community is responsible for the accuracy and timeliness of the knowledge it contributes and for identifying its potential use. For further discussion, see Online File W10.10.

**KMS STAFF**

Enterprisewide KM systems may require a full-time staff to catalogue and manage the knowledge. This staff is either located at the firm's headquarters or dispersed throughout the organization in the knowledge centers. Most large consulting firms have more than one knowledge center.

# 10.8 Ensuring Success of KM Efforts

Organizations can gain several benefits from implementing a knowledge management strategy. Tactically, they can accomplish some or all of the following: reduce loss of intellectual capital due to people leaving the company; reduce costs by decreasing the number of times the company must repeatedly solve the same problem, and by achieving economies of scale in obtaining information from external providers; reduce redundancy of knowledge-based activities; increase productivity by making knowledge available more quickly and easily; and increase employee satisfaction by enabling greater personal development and empowerment. The best reason of all may be a strategic need to gain a *competitive advantage* in the marketplace (Levinson, 2005).

**KNOWLEDGE MANAGEMENT VALUATION**

In general, companies take either an asset-based approach to knowledge management valuation or one that links knowledge to its applications and business benefits. The former approach starts with the identification of intellectual assets and then focuses management's attention on increasing their value. The second uses variants of a *balanced scorecard,* where financial measures are balanced against customer, process, and innovation measures. Among the best-developed financial measurement methods in use are the balanced-scorecard approach, Skandia's Navigator, Stern Stewart's economic value added (EVA®), M'Pherson's inclusive valuation methodology, the return on management ratio, and Levin's knowledge capital measure. See *brint.com/KM* for details on how these measures work in practice.

Success indicators with respect to knowledge management are similar to those for assessing the effectiveness of other business-change projects. They include growth in the resources attached to the project, growth in the volume of knowledge content and usage, the likelihood that the project will survive without the support of a particular individual or individuals, and some evidence of financial return either for the knowledge management activity itself or for the entire organization.

There are in general two types of measures that can be used to assess the effectiveness of a KM initiative: results-oriented and activity-oriented (O'Dell et al., 2003). The results-oriented measures are financial in nature and might include such things as increase in goods sold. The activities-based measures consider how frequently users are accessing knowledge or contributing to knowledge (O'Dell et al., 2003).

**Financial Metrics.** Even though traditional accounting measures are incomplete for measuring KM, they are often used as a quick justification for a knowledge management initiative. Returns on investment (ROIs) are reported to range from 20:1 for chemical firms to 4:1 for transportation firms, with an average of 12:1, based on the knowledge management projects assisted on by one consulting firm (Abramson, 1998). In order to measure the impact of knowledge management, experts recommend focusing KM projects on specific business problems that can be easily quantified. When the problems are solved, the value and benefits of the system become apparent and often can be measured (MacSweeney, 2002).

At Royal Dutch/Shell Group, the return on investment was explicitly documented: The company had invested $6 million in a knowledge management system in 1999 and within two years obtained $235 million in reduced costs and new revenues (King, 2001). Hewlett-Packard offers another example of documented financial returns: Within six months of launching its @HP companywide portal in October 2000, Hewlett-Packard realized a $50 million return on its initial investment of $20 million. This was largely due to a reduction in volume of calls to internal call centers and to the new paperless processes (Roberts-Witt, 2002). For an interesting approach, see *A Closer Look 10.2*.

The financial benefit might be perceptual, rather than absolute, but it need not be documented in order for the KM system to be considered a success.

**Nonfinancial Metrics.** Traditional ways of financial measurement may fall short when measuring the value of a KMS, because *they do not consider intellectual capital an asset.* Therefore there is a need to develop procedures for valuing the *intangible* assets of an organization, as well as to incorporate models of intellectual capital that in some way quantify innovation and the development and implementation of core competencies.

When evaluating intangibles, there are a number of new ways to view capital. In the past, only customer goodwill was valued as an asset. Now the following are also included (adapted from Allee, 1999):

- **External relationship capital:** how an organization links with its partners, suppliers, customers, regulators, and so on

# A Closer Look 10.2

## How Much Is the Knowledge in Your Company Worth?

Paul Strassmann, an IT consultant and writer (*strassman.com*), devised several ways to measure KM (visit his Web site as well as *baselinemag.com*). One of his measures postulates that in the case of public companies, it is possible to assess the know-how of employees by following this simple calculation:

1. Find the market capitalization of a company. This is done by multiplying the number of shares by the price of the share, on any given date (capitalization is also provided by *money.cnn.com*, *bloomberg.com*, and others).
2. Take the shareholder equity from the balance sheet for the same date (also available at the above URLs).
3. Subtract item 2 from item 1. If it is negative, stop—there is no value to your KM.

4. The difference is the knowledge value.
5. Divide the knowledge value by the shareholder equity. You get a percentage. The higher the percentage, the higher the value of the KM.
6. Find the number of employees (use the same sources).
7. Divide the total knowledge value (item 5) by the number of employees. This will give you the knowledge value per employee.

Now you can compare companies for their KM value. See Exercise #7.

*Sources:* Compiled from Strassmann (2005a and 2005b).

- **Structural capital:** systems and work processes that leverage competitiveness, such as information systems, and so on
- **Human capital:** the individual capabilities, knowledge, skills, and so on, that people have
- **Social capital:** the quality and value of relationships with the larger society
- **Environmental capital:** the value of relationships with the environment

SVC

For example, a knowledge management initiative undertaken by Partners HealthCare System, Inc. has not resulted in quantifiable financial benefits, but has greatly increased the social capital of the company. The knowledge management system for physicians implemented by Partners reduced the number of serious medication errors by 55 percent at some of Boston's most prestigious teaching hospitals. Calculating return on investment for such a system turns out to be an extremely difficult proposition, which is why only a small fraction of hospitals use similar systems. While the company is unable to determine how the system affects its bottom line, it is willing to justify the costs based on the system's benefits to society (Melymuka, 2002). For more on KM valuation and metrics, see Kankanhalli et al. (2005) and Chen (2005).

**CAUSES OF KM FAILURE**

No system is infallible. There are many cases of knowledge management failure. Estimates of KM failure rates range from 50 percent to 70 percent, where a failure is interpreted to mean that all of the major objectives were not met by the effort (e.g., see Online File W10.11).

Some reasons for failure include having too much information that is not easily searchable (Steinberg, 2002) and having inadequate or incomplete information in the system so that identifying the real expertise in an organization becomes foggy (Desouza, 2003). Failure may also result from an inability to capture and categorize knowledge as well as from the overmanagement of the KM process such that creativity and communities of practice are stifled (Desouza, 2003). Other issues include lack of commitment (this occurred at a large Washington, D.C., constituent lobbying organization), not providing incentive for people to use the system (as occurred at Pillsbury Co.; see Barth, 2000, and Silver, 2000), and an overemphasis on technology at the expense of larger knowledge and people issues (Hislop, 2002). *IT at Work 10.6* illustrates how Frito-Lay narrowly avoided failure of its KMS.

A recent study of KM in organizations found that the factors contributing to a perception of KM failure include the lack of management involvement, lack of a clear understanding of KM benefits, lack of adequate staff and resources, and an overambitious scope for the KM effort (Leidner et al., 2006). The same data suggested that the most important success factors were management involvement and priorities, adequate technical infrastructure, user education and training, adequate nontechnical infrastructure, and adequate deployment of the KM system (Wiig, 2006).

A common overarching reason behind KM failure, or for KM failing to achieve the benefits desired, occurs when an organization implements KM in an effort to imitate the competition without really grasping all the cultural changes that a KM system will introduce. The mere introduction of KM tools and the existence of a KM vision will not guarantee KM success. Incentive schemes often backfire, and in spite of advanced IT tools to facilitate knowledge capture, codification, and distribution, employees often prefer face-to face conversation over technology (Chan and Chau, 2005).

# IT at Work 10.6

## Escaping a Knowledge Management Failure

MKT

Online File W9.5 describes the successful KM portal to assist Frito-Lay's sales teams. Here we describe the near brush with failure that preceded the successful implementation of Frito-Lay's knowledge portal.

Frito-Lay selected a pilot sales team to describe the kinds of knowledge they needed. The requests ranged from simple information, such as why Frito-Lay merchandises Lays and Ruffles products in one part of a store and Doritos in another, to more complex questions on what motivates shoppers as they move through a store. To collect the required knowledge, developers searched Frito-Lay's databases in departments such as marketing, sales, and operations. They also referenced external sources such as trade publications and industry organizations, and identified in-house subject matter experts.

In October 1999, a working prototype of the system was presented to the pilot sales team. Only then did Frito-Lay discover that in the quest for speed, a classic and crippling mistake had been made: The development team had failed to obtain sufficient input from the sales team and did not involve users in the design process. The prototype had the potential to be marginally useful to any sales team, but it was not specific enough to offer fundamental benefits for the pilot team. Therefore, the pilot team was reluctant to accept the system. "Conceptually, it was a great idea," said Frito-Lay sales team leader Joe Ackerman. "But when folks are not on the front line, their view of what is valuable is different from those running 100 miles an hour in the field."

Frito-Lay learned valuable lessons from that mistake and chose to redesign the system. However, at this stage, it not only needed to add the missing features, but also had to win back the sales force and convince them that the redesigned system would indeed streamline their work by facilitating knowledge exchange. The team of developers spent the following four months working with salespeople to transform the prototype into a system they would embrace.

The redesigned portal has been a big success. Better collaboration has helped to significantly reduce turnover, while improved access to knowledge-base resources has enabled salespeople to present themselves as consultants with important knowledge to share. Today, the knowledge management portal is used for daily communication, call reporting, weekly cross-country meetings, training, document sharing, and access to data and industry news. The pilot team exceeded its sales plan for 2000 and grew its business at a rate almost twice that of Frito-Lay's other customer teams. The KMS concept is now being tailored to three other Frito-Lay sales teams and departments, and other divisions of PepsiCo have expressed interest in it as well.

*Source:* Adapted from Melymuka (2001) and from Shein (2001).

*For Further Exploration:* Why did Frito-Lay find it difficult to correct the mistake identified in a late stage of the development cycle? If you were responsible for the development of a knowledge management system, what specific actions would you take to ensure that it satisfies the needs of end users?

---

**FACTORS LEADING TO KM SUCCESS**

To increase the probability of success of knowledge management projects, companies must assess whether there is a strategic need for knowledge management in the first place. The next step is to determine whether the current process of dealing with organizational knowledge is adequate and whether the organization's culture is ready for procedural changes. Only when these issues are resolved should the company consider technology infrastructure and decide if a new system is needed. When the right technological solution is chosen, it becomes necessary to properly introduce the system to the entire organization and to gain participation of every employee (Kaplan, 2002).

A case study of Nortel Network's KM initiative indicated that there were three major issues that influenced the success of KM: (1) having effective managerial influence in terms of coordination, control and measurement, project management, and leadership; (2) having key resources such as financial resources and cross-functional expertise, and (3) taking advantage of technological opportunities. Together, these enabled a well-defined process, the understanding of people issues, and the successful incorporation of technology (Massey et al., 2002). Other factors that may lead to knowledge management project success are shown in Table 10.1.

Effective knowledge sharing and learning requires cultural change within the organization, new management practices, senior management commitment, and

| **TABLE 10.1** | Major Factors that Lead to KM Project Success |
|---|---|

- A link to a firm's economic value, to demonstrate financial viability and maintain executive sponsorship.
- A technical and organizational infrastructure on which to build.
- A standard, flexible knowledge structure to match the way the organization performs work and uses knowledge. Usually, the organizational culture must change to effectively create a knowledge-sharing environment.
- A knowledge-friendly culture leading directly to user support.
- A clear purpose and language, to encourage users to buy into the system. Sometimes simple, useful knowledge applications need to be implemented first.
- A change in motivational practices, to create a culture of sharing.
- Multiple channels for knowledge transfer—because individuals have different ways of working and expressing themselves. The multiple channels should reinforce one another. Knowledge transfer should be easily accomplished and be as unobtrusive as possible.
- A level of process orientation to make a knowledge management effort worthwhile. In other words, new, improved work methods can be developed.
- Nontrivial motivational methods, such as rewards and recognition, to encourage users to contribute and use knowledge.
- Senior management support. This is critical to initiate the project, to provide resources, to help identify important knowledge on which the success of the organization relies, and to market the project.

*Source:* Adapted from Davenport et al. (1998).

technological support. We recognize that organizational culture must shift to a culture of sharing. This should be handled through strong leadership at the top, and by providing knowledge management tools that truly make people's jobs better. As far as encouraging system use and knowledge sharing goes, people must be *properly* motivated to contribute knowledge. The mechanism for doing so should be part of their jobs, and their salaries should reflect this. People must also be motivated to utilize the knowledge that is in the KMS. Again, this should be part of their jobs and their reward structures.

**POTENTIAL DRAWBACKS TO KNOWLEDGE MANAGEMENT SYSTEMS**

While there are many positive outcomes of managing knowledge, as discussed in examples throughout this chapter, it would be short-sighted not to consider the potential negative outcomes associated with reusing knowledge. As an example, Henfridsson and Söderholm (2000) analyzed the situation that faced Mrs. Fields cookies, as described in *A Closer Look 10.3*.

The case of Mrs. Fields illustrates that while organizations might achieve significant short-term gains through knowledge management systems, they must not neglect to allow for the creative process of new knowledge creation, lest they eventually find themselves applying yesterday's solutions to tomorrow's problems.

## 10.9 Managerial Issues

**1. Organizational culture change.** This issue is how we can change organizational culture so that people are willing both to contribute knowledge to and use knowledge from a KMS. There must be strong executive leadership, clearly expressed goals, user involvement in the system, and deployment of an easy-to-use

# A Closer Look 10.3

## *Adaptability—a Missing Ingredient*

Mrs. Fields Cookies, a national chain of cookie stores, grew remarkably fast and successfully during the early 1980s. A key aspect of the company's strategy was to provide expertise directly from the headquarters to every store. As the number of stores increased, the only feasible way to achieve such direct control was through the use of information systems that were designed to mimic the decision making of Mrs. Fields herself. Decision-making systems were placed in each store. The system would take input (such as the temperature, the day of the week, the date, and so forth), would process the data, and would provide, as output, information to each store manager about how many cookies of each type to bake each hour. In essence, the software provided each store manager with explicit directions for planning each day's production, sales, and labor scheduling, along with inventory control and ordering. Because of

the well-functioning computer systems, which in principle were systems designed to make Mrs. Fields' tacit knowledge available to all stores, the company was able to successfully function with few managerial levels.

However, as the market began to change and consumers became more health conscious, Mrs. Fields was very slow to respond. In a sense, by embedding so much knowledge into systems that were incapable of adaptation, the organization tied itself to a certain way of doing things and failed to engage in knowledge creation. That is, it failed to pick up the signals in the environment, which might have suggested a change in strategy or product focus. By the early 1990s, the company had fallen into bankruptcy.

*Source:* Adapted from Henfridsson and Söderholm (2000) and Park City Group (2003).

system that provides real value to employees. A viable reward structure for contributing and using knowledge must also be developed.

**2. How to store tacit knowledge.** This is extremely difficult. Most KMSs (based on the network storage model) store explicit knowledge about the tacit knowledge that people possess. When the knowledgeable people leave an organization, they take their knowledge with them. Since knowledge requires active use by the recipient, it is important for the person generating knowledge to articulate it in a way that another, appropriately educated person can understand it.

**3. How to measure the tangible and intangible benefits of KMS.** Organizations need to identify ways to measure the value of intellectual assets and the value of providing them to the organization, as discussed in Section 9.7.

**4. Determining the roles of the various personnel in a KM effort.** A knowledge management staff, led by a chief knowledge officer (CKO), can provide structure to an organization's ongoing KM efforts.

**5. The lasting importance of knowledge management.** Knowledge management is extremely important. It is not another management fad. If it is correctly done, it can have massive impact by leveraging know-how throughout the organization. If it is not done, or is not correctly done, the company will not be able to effectively compete against another major player in the industry that does KM correctly.

**6. Implementation in the face of quickly changing technology.** This is an important issue to address regarding the development of many IT systems. Technology has to be carefully examined, and experiments done, to determine what makes sense. By starting now, an organization can get past the managerial and behavioral issues, which have greater impact on the eventual success (or not) of a KMS. As better and cheaper technology is developed, the KMS can be migrated over to it, just as legacy systems have migrated to the PC.

## Integrating IT

### For the Accounting Major

Major CPA and management service companies (e.g., Accenture) pioneered KM applications and the creation of organizational knowledge bases. This way they can provide better consultation to their customers and continuously improve their best practices. Understanding KM, its structure, benefits, and IT support is necessary for those accountants working with KM systems and their derivatives.

### For the Finance Major

One of the tasks that finance people are involved with is the valuation and justification of investments in KM systems. These systems may stand alone or be modules in enterprise systems software. Understanding how these systems work and why they are important is therefore critical for any financial analyst.

### For the Human Resources Management Major

Implementing KM involves several HRM issues. First is the motivation (and perhaps compensation) of employees who contribute and document their expertise. Second, job descriptions and requirements for those working with KMS must be rewritten. Finally, there is a need to recruit the right CKO. In all the above and other situations, HRM must understand how these systems operate, interface, and impact people and their work.

### For the IS Major

KM systems are constantly evolving, interfacing, and integrating with other IT systems (e.g., CRM, portals, collaboration, e-training, intelligent systems). Understanding the objectives, processes, and methods of KM is essential for acquiring, deploying, and using KMSs in organizations. Also, working with vendors and their products is a critical necessity.

### For the Marketing Major

An integral part of KMSs is their interface with customer service and CRM. Understanding the potential benefits to customers and how these are accomplished is clearly important. Furthermore, KMSs can help employees in call centers and assist salespeople in the field by providing them with real-time knowledge of how to handle different situations and scenarios.

### For the Production/Operations Management Major

POM systems are complex and require expertise and knowledge for their implementation (e.g., production scheduling and sequencing, multi-item inventory systems, logistics, maintenance, and new technology purchasing). The accumulation, updating, and use of knowledge can assist many POM people in their strategies, tactics, and operations.

## Key Terms

Best practice  *399*
Chief knowledge officer (CKO)  *411*
Communities of practice (COPs)  *399*
Content Management Systems (CMSs)  *406*
Expert location systems  *403*
Explicit knowledge  *392*
Intellectual capital (intellectual assets)  *391*

Knowledge  *390*
Knowledge discovery in databases (KDD)  *402*
Knowledge management (KM)  *390*
Knowledge management systems (KMSs)  *392*
Knowledge repository  *405*
Knowware  *405*

Leaky knowledge  *392*
Learning organization  *395*
Organizational learning  *395*
Organizational memory  *395*
Practice approach  *399*
Process approach  *399*
Sticky knowledge  *392*
Tacit knowledge  *392*

## Chapter Highlights                                    (Numbers Refer to Learning Objectives)

❶ Knowledge is different from information and data. Knowledge is information that is contextual, relevant, and actionable. It is dynamic in nature.

❶ Explicit (structured, leaky) knowledge deals with more objective, rational, and technical knowledge. Tacit (unstructured, sticky) knowledge is usually in the domain of subjective, cognitive, and experiential learning. Tacit knowledge is highly personal and hard to formalize.

❶ Knowledge management is a process that helps organizations identify, select, organize, disseminate, and transfer important information and expertise that typically reside within the organization in an unstructured way.

❶ The knowledge management model involves the following cyclical steps: create, capture, refine, store, manage, and disseminate knowledge.

❷ Knowledge management requires a major transformation in organizational culture to create a desire to share (give and receive) knowledge, plus a commitment to KM at all levels of a firm.

❷ Learning from past experiences of the organization or others needs to be formalized. Documented best practices is one way to achieve this.

❸ Standard knowledge management initiatives involve the creation of knowledge bases, active process management, knowledge centers, and collaborative technologies.

❹ Knowledge management is an effective way for an organization to leverage its intellectual assets.

❹ The three strategies used for KM initiatives are the process approach, the practice approach, and the best practices approach.

❺ A knowledge management system is generally developed using three sets of technologies: communication, collaboration, and storage.

❺ A variety of technologies can make up a knowledge management system: the Internet, intranets, data warehousing, decision-support tools, groupware, and so on. Intranets are the primary means of displaying and distributing knowledge in organizations.

❺ Knowledge management systems can be purchased in whole or in part from one of numerous software development companies and enterprise information systems vendors, can be acquired through major consulting firms, or can be outsourced to application service providers (ASPs).

❺ Knowledge portals can be used to provide a central location from which various KM applications are searched.

❻ The chief knowledge office (CKO) is primarily responsible for changing the behavior of the firm to embrace the use of knowledge management and then managing the development operation of a knowledge management system.

❻ Knowledge management typically involves the cooperation of managers, developers, KM staff, and users.

❻ Communities of practice (COPs) provide pressure to break down the cultural barriers that hinder knowledge management efforts.

❼ KM has many potential benefits resulting from reuse of expertise. The problem is how to collect, store, update, and properly reuse the knowledge.

❽ It is difficult to measure the success of a KMS. Traditional methods of financial measurement fall short, as they do not consider intellectual capital an asset. Nonfinancial metrics are typically used to measure the success of a KM, yet some firms have been able to determine financial payoffs.

## Virtual Company Assignment

### Knowledge Management at The Wireless Café

Go to The Wireless Café's link on the Student Web Site. There you will be asked to think about the problems of retaining knowledge in an organization, such as a restaurant, that experiences high turnover. You will also be asked to identify types of knowledge at the restaurant and to propose how that knowledge could be captured in information systems.

**Instructions for accessing The Wireless Café on the Student Web Site:**

1. Go to *wiley.com/college/turban*.
2. Select Turban/Leidner/ McLean/Wetherbe's *Information Technology for Management, Sixth Edition.*
3. Click on Student Resources site, in the toolbar on the left.
4. Click on the link for Virtual Company Web site.
5. Click on Wireless Café.

## Online Resources

More resources and study tools are located on the Student Web Site and on WileyPLUS. You'll find additional chapter materials and useful Web links. In addition, self-quizzes that provide individualized feedback are available for each chapter.

## Questions for Review

1. Discuss what is meant by an intellectual asset.
2. Define knowledge and knowledge management.
3. Define explicit knowledge. Why is it also called leaky?
4. Define tacit knowledge. Why is it also called sticky?
5. How can tacit knowledge be transferred or shared?
6. List some ways in which organizational culture can impact a knowledge management effort.
7. What is the primary goal of knowledge management?
8. Define learning organizations and their characteristics.
9. Define organizational memory.
10. Define organizational culture and relate it to KM.
11. Describe the process approach to knowledge management.
12. Describe the practice approach to knowledge management.
13. Describe the roles and responsibilities of the people involved in a knowledge management system, especially the CKO.
14. What is a community of practice?
15. List the steps in the cyclical model of knowledge management. Why is it a cycle?
16. Define an expert location system.
17. List the major knowledge management success factors.
18. Describe the role of IT in knowledge management.

## Questions for Discussion

1. Why is the term *knowledge* so hard to define?
2. Describe and relate the different characteristics of knowledge.
3. Explain why it is important to capture and manage knowledge.
4. Compare and contrast tacit knowledge and explicit knowledge.
5. Explain why organizational culture must sometimes change before knowledge management is introduced.
6. How does knowledge management attain its primary objective?
7. How can employees be motivated to contribute to and use knowledge management systems?
8. What is the role of a knowledge repository in knowledge management?
9. Explain the importance of communication and collaboration technologies to the processes of knowledge management.
10. Explain why firms adopt knowledge management initiatives.
11. Explain the role of the CKO in developing a knowledge management system. What major responsibilities does he or she have?
12. Discuss some knowledge management success factors.
13. Why is it hard to evaluate the impacts of knowledge management?
14. Explain how the Internet and its related technologies (Web browsers, intranets, and so on) enable knowledge management.
15. Explain the roles of a community of practice.
16. Describe an enterprise knowledge portal and explain its significance.
17. Distinguish between organizational learning and learning organizations.
18. Discuss the need for expert locating systems.

## Exercises and Projects

1. Make a list of all the knowledge management methods you use during your day (work and personal). Which are the most effective? Which are the least effective? What kinds of work or activities does each knowledge management method enable?
2. Investigate the literature for information on the position of CKO. Find out what percentage of firms with KM initiatives have CKOs and what their responsibilities are.
3. Investigate the literature for new measures of success (metrics) for knowledge management and intellectual capital. Write a report on your findings.
4. Describe how each of the key elements of a knowledge management infrastructure can contribute to its success.
5. Based on your own experience or on the vendor's information, list the major capabilities of a particular knowledge management product, and explain how it can be used in practice.
6. Describe how to ride a bicycle, drive a car, or make a peanut butter and jelly sandwich. Now, have someone else try to do it based solely on your explanation. How can you best convert this knowledge from tacit to explicit (or can't you)?

**7.** Using the calculations in *A Closer Look 10.2,* compare the knowledge value per employees in Google, GM, and Microsoft.

**8.** Enter *askmecorp.com* and review their AskMe Enterprise and Employee Knowledge Networks concepts and products. Prepare a report.

## Group Assignments and Projects

**1.** Compare and contrast the capabilities and features of electronic document management with those of collaborative computing and those of knowledge management systems. Each team represents one type of system. Present the ways in which these capabilities and features can create improvements for an organization.

**2.** Search the Internet for knowledge management products and systems and create categories for them. Assign one vendor to each team. Describe the categories you created and justify them.

**3.** If you are working on a decision-making project in industry for this course (or if not, use one from another class or from work), examine some typical decisions in

the related project. How would you extract the knowledge you need? Can you use that knowledge in practice? Why or why not?

**4.** Read the article by A. Genusa titled "Rx for Learning," available at *cio.com* (February 1, 2001), which describes Tufts University Medical School's experience with knowledge management. Determine how these concepts and such a system could be implemented and used at your college or university. Explain how each aspect would work, or if not, explain why not.

**5.** Enter expertise-providing sites such as *guru.com, knowledgebase.net, askmehelpdesk.com* and *rightanswers.com.* Each team member presents the capabilities of one company.

## Internet Exercises

**1.** How does knowledge management support decision making? Identify products or systems on the Web that help organizations accomplish knowledge management. Start with *brint.com, decisionsupport.net,* and *knowledge management.ittoolbox.com.* Try one out and report your findings to the class.

**2.** Try the KPMG Knowledge Management Framework Assessment Exercise at *kmsurvey.londonweb.net* and assess how well your organization (company or university) is doing with knowledge management. Are the results accurate? Why or why not?

**3.** Search the Internet to identify sites dealing with knowledge management. Start with *google.com, kmworld.com,* and *km-forum.org.* How many did you find? Categorize the sites based on whether they are academic, consulting firms, vendors, and so on. Sample one of each and describe the main focus of the site.

**4.** Identify five real-world knowledge management success stories by searching vendor Web sites (use at least three different vendors). Describe them. How did knowledge management systems and methods contribute to their success? What features do they share? What different features do individual successes have?

**5.** Search the Internet for vendors of knowledge management suites, enterprise knowledge portals, and out-of-the-box knowledge management solutions. Identify the major features of each product (use three from each), and compare and contrast their capabilities.

**6.** Enter *askmecorp.com.* View the three demos and examine their products. Write a report about their capabilities.

**7.** Enter *internetdashboard.com.* View their products and relate them to KM.

## Minicase 1

SVC  POM

### Data Sharing That's Saving Lives

When Dr. John T. Finnell, an attending physician in the ER of Wishard Memorial Hospital (*wishard.edu*) in Indianapolis, needed medical records for a 40-year-old woman who was rushed to the emergency room suffering from an unknown condition, he used information from her driver's license to pull up an electronic record detailing recent hospital visits. Within 30 seconds, he discovered that she had a seizure disorder and had not been taking her medication. Without immediate access to the patient's medical record, Finnell would have had to administer drugs to temporarily stop her breathing, insert a breathing tube, and order a battery of blood work. Her paper file, he says, could have taken hours (or even days) to locate, and the procedures would have put her at risk for brain damage and other complications. "When you're in an emergency and you can't find information about a patient, everybody suffers," Finnell says.

The patient was saved in that situation because Wishard Memorial and the city of Indianapolis are at the head of a national effort to link medical records electronically, and to allow doctors and other health-care providers to share medical data that had been virtually hidden from view. In Indianapolis, the five major hospitals' emergency rooms share patient data using an electronic medical network. The area also has an electronic messaging service, which more than 1,300 doctors use to share patients' laboratory results and other clinical information.

Hospitals, clinics, and doctors' offices around the country are trying desperately to implement such systems to connect patient medical records electronically between health-care organizations. All across the country, efforts are being made to create such regional health information networks. Not only can linking medical data improve patient safety, it can lower health-care costs as well. After linking up to a pilot electronic medical network, three of the hospitals in Indianapolis began to save $26 per ER visit. As health-care organizations increasingly adapt the medical data-sharing system, the central Indiana region could save $562 million per year in health-care costs, says Dr. Marc Overhage, CEO of the nonprofit Indiana Health Information Exchange (IHIE). Overall, an estimated $78 billion a year could be saved by moving to electronic medical records (EMRs), reported a recent article in the journal *Health Affairs*.

The effort to share data between hospitals in Indianapolis began in 1997, when the city's five major hospital groups transferred all the information from their computers to a citywide medical database that would enable emergency rooms to share patient data. That initial collaborative effort, the Indianapolis Network for Patient Care, allowed emergency room doctors to easily locate information on patients who had visited any one of the area hospitals. Last year, the IHIE implemented a system that allows data from 13 specific-care hospitals and dozens of medical practices to be shared, so the scope is reaching beyond emergency rooms.

Dr. Overhage and others involved with the IHIE say they gained support for the system by involving doctors in the effort and moving slowly. EMRs are used by only 20 percent of the doctors, so the IHIE developed a process enabling delivery of the information over the Internet or by fax for those who do not yet use the Internet.

Dr. Finnell has been using EMRs in the emergency room for nearly three years, ever since he came to Indianapolis and says the system has completely changed the way he performs his job. For example, if Finnell sees a new patient who has diabetes, he can find out from the EMRs about recent tests, blood sugar levels, and hospitalization. Before EMRs, hours would have been spent quizzing the patient about information that may have been forgotten and trying to obtain patient files from a variety of locations. The added time would have caused treatment to be slower, potentially less effective, and more costly.

One way to advance EMRs, says Dr. Marc Pierson, a vice president on the executive team at PeaceHealth St. Joseph Hospital in Bellingham, Washington, is for medical information exchanges to prove their value before asking for money. Pierson took this approach in Whatcom County, Washington, where he oversees a health information network that links 300 doctors, by allowing caregivers to use the system for three years without any cost. After the three years, doctors began paying $71 per month for the service that allows them to share medical data and receive lab information online. Pierson reports that the system worked so well that only three of the 300 doctors who tried the system for free dropped out once they were charged.

Over the next several years, Dr. Overhage predicts a continued push toward a national health network that will allow patient data sharing for hospitals and physicians across the country. This year, he is looking to expand the current clinical messaging system in Indianapolis to a greater number of doctors throughout the state of Indiana. He is also expecting expansion of the system itself to include more types of needed data and information. For example, when patients are in need of flu shots or routine checkups, doctors could start receiving electronic "clinical reminders" to inform them of this.

"People are seeing that with the continuing crisis in health-care costs, we have to do something," Overhage says. "Sharing our data looks like the best bet."

*Sources*: Adapted from Patton (2005) and *CIO.com* (accessed June 2006).

## Questions for Minicase 1

1. In what ways is an electronic medical records system a KM system?

2. What are some of the challenges in creating a national health network system?

3. How effective are electronic medical records systems if they are shared within only a single health-care network, and not nationally?

4. What are the major issues in terms of the KM processes of knowledge creating, sharing, storing, and transferring that you think would be challenging for a national health network system?

# Minicase 2

## Buckman Labs Improves Global Knowledge Sharing

*GLOBAL*

Buckman Labs (*buckman.com*), a US$300 million chemical company with operations in 21 different countries, sells more than 1,000 different specialty chemicals. Sales in 2003 increased 10% from 2002, in spite of economic and political instability in the world. Gross profits rose by 5.7%. Buckman's 2003 annual report states, "Our ability to share knowledge within our company and use that knowledge for the benefit of our customers distinguishes Buckman Laboratories from our competitors." In the 1990s, Buckman began a global knowledge management initiative that has continued to yield positive results a decade later.

The first project was to design and implement a global forum, based on intranet technology. The resulting TechForum created a taxonomy of knowledge areas based upon business functions across all of the different systems and repositories with a common interface. By the mid-90s, TechForum had become the central pivot of Buckman's global KMS. TechForum had 20 sections, each with its own message board, conference rooms to facilitate debate, and library section, where the communication threads and other pertinent knowledge were stored. Thirteen of the 20 sections were devoted to the business areas within Buckman Labs (e.g., Pulp and Paper, and Leather). These forums were expected to help improve client companies' productivity. Six of the 20 sections were primarily internal and designed to improve the operational efficiency and effectiveness of Buckman Labs (e.g., human resources, plant operations, safety/environment, KT topics/help). The Bulab News and Breakroom sections were general discussion sections in TechForum, where Buckman employees were free to discuss topics of their choice.

In terms of content design, the majority of Tech-Forum was devoted to business-related activities designed to provide employees access to relevant knowledge needed for their tasks. Other sections, such as Breakroom, provided a social environment. Topics discussed in Breakroom ranged from support for sports teams, to requests sent to employees in foreign countries for vacation recommendations in their area, and other non-business-related activities.

Setting up the technology and forums was an important part of Buckman's KM initiative, but so too was putting in place a management structure that would ensure that the knowledge was kept valuable, current, and easy to locate. Buckman's management combined Information Services, Telecommunications, and the Technical Information Center (which included a full-fledged corporate library) to form the Knowledge Transfer Department (KTD). Forty-five KTD employees were responsible for the design, development, implementation, and maintenance of the software and hardware of the ICT-based KM system. Another five KTD employees were responsible for the monitoring and processing of the knowledge generated within the various sections of Buckman forums.

A knowledge-processing team was assembled to reduce the need for each associate to retrieve and store the accumulated knowledge that each section captured as a result of discussions within the sections. Members of the specialist knowledge-processing team included a number of forum specialists and section leaders (two or more per section from various departments). Section leaders were recruited to help manage knowledge activities. These were highly trained chemists or microbiologists with specialized industry knowledge and experience. The section leaders wrote weekly abstracts for a central database accessible to most employees. They were responsible not only for facilitating the knowledge-sharing process but also for assisting in "processing" knowledge—for example, by writing abstracts for storage and facilitating the re-use of the obtained knowledge. Members of the specialist team assumed the additional responsibility of preparing a summary of the discussion points that occurred in each section and posting the information at the end of each week.

Forums specialists facilitated the process of responding to online requests. If an online request went unattended for a few hours, two scenarios could emerge. First, one of the forum specialists would pick up the request and then identify the potential experts based on their previous industrial experience and reputation of their willingness to share knowledge. Alternatively, a team of experts with related industrial experience who had volunteered as "section leaders" would also help answer any requests and prepare weekly summaries to be stored in the knowledge repositories for later use. When an information search was completed, responses were then formulated and presented to customers for problem solving. The request was kept on the forum for as long as there was an active discussion.

Together, Buckman's KM technology, structure, and processes enabled front-line employees to continue serving customers while a specialized knowledge-processing team devoted time to capturing company knowledge into a reusable form.

*Sources:* Buckman Annual Report 2003 (*buckman.com*); Pan and Leidner (2003).

## Questions for Minicase 2

1. What are the advantages to an organization of having a global knowledge management system, as opposed to having multiple systems dispersed around the world?

2. What are the key roles played by the KM staff?

3. How can management continue to show support for the volunteer section leaders?

4. How would you measure the success of Buckman Labs' KM initiative?

# References

Abramson, G., "Measuring Up," *CIO*, June 15, 1998.

Alavi, M., and D. Leidner, "Knowledge Management," *MIS Quarterly*, 25(1), March 2001.

Alavi, M., T. Kayworth, and D. Leidner, "An Empirical Examination of the Influence of Knowledge Management on Organizational Culture," working paper, Baylor University, 2003.

Alavi, M., T. Kayworth, and D. Leidner, "An Empirical Examination of the Influence of Organizational Culture on Knowledge Management Practice," *Journal of Management Information Systems*, 22(3), 2005/06.

Ahlawat, S. S., and S. Ahlawat, "Competing in the Global Knowledge Economy: Implications for Business Education," *Journal of American Academy of Business*, 8(1), March 2006.

Ali, Irena, L. Warne, and C. Pascoe, "Learning in Organizations," in *Encyclopedia of Knowledge Management*, D. G. Schwartz (ed.). Hershey, PA: Idea Group Reference, 2006.

Allee, V., "Are You Getting Big Value from Knowledge?" *KMWorld*, September 1999.

Anderson, L., "Cisco Employee Connection: Saving Money, Keeping Employees," *Smartbusinessmag.com*, June 2002.

Averbeck, B., "Bringing Evidence-based Best Practices into Practice," *Health Management Technology*, November 2005.

Baalen, P. V., J. Bloemhof-Ruwaard, and E. V. Heck, "Knowledge Sharing in an Emerging Network of Practice: The Role of Knowledge Portal," *European Management Journal*, 23(3), June 2005.

Barth, S., "KM Horror Stories," *Knowledge Management*, October 2000.

Bennet, A., and D. Bennet, "The Partnership-between Organizational Learning and Knowledge Management," in *Handbook on Knowledge Management*, Volume 1k, C. W. Holsapple (ed.). New York: Springer-Verlag, 2003a.

Bennet, D., and A. Bennet, "The Rise of the Knowledge Organization." Chapter 1 in *Handbook of Knowledge Management: Knowledge Matters*, Vol. 1, C. W. Holsapple (ed.). Heidelberg: Springer Verlag, 2003b.

Brown, S. J., and P. Duguid, "Balancing Act: How to Capture Knowledge Without Killing It," *Harvard Business Review*, May–June 2000.

Chan, I; and P. Chau, "Why Knowledge Management Fails: Lessons from a Case Study," in *Case Studies in Knowledge Management*, Murray Jennex (ed.). Hershey, PA: Idea Group Inc., 2005.

Chen, A. N. K., "Assessing Value in Organizational Knowledge Creation: Consideration for Knowledge Workers," *MIS Quarterly*, 29(2), June 2005.

Craig, C. R., "Purchasing Social Responsibility and Firm Performance: The Key Mediating Roles of Organizational Learning and Supplier Performance," *International Journal of Physical Distribution & Logistics Management*, 35(3). Emerald Group Publishing Ltd., 2005.

D'Agostino, D. "Expertise Management: Who Knows about This?" *CIO Insight*, July 1, 2004.

Davenport, T. H., and L. Prusak, *Working Knowledge: How Organizations Manage What They Know*. Boston: Harvard Business School Press, 1998.

Desouza, K. C., "Knowledge Management Barriers: Why the Technology Imperative Seldom Works," *Business Horizons*, January–February 2003, pp. 25–29.

Duffy, D., "Knowledge Champions," *CIO* (Enterprise-Section 2), November 1998.

Feldman, S., "What Technologies Are KM Professionals Buying?" *KMWorld*, June 2002.

Ford, D. P., "Trust and Knowledge Management: The Seeds of Success," in *Handbook on Knowledge Management*, Volume 1k, C. W. Holsapple (ed.). New York: Springer-Verlag, 2003, pp. 553–576.

Fox, P. "Using IT to Tap Experts' Know-How," *Computerworld*, March 15, 2004.

Garud, R., and A. Kumaraswamy, "Vicious and Virtuous Circles in the Management of Knowledge: The Case of Infosys Technologies," *MIS Quarterly*, 29(1), March 2005.

Garvin, D. A., *Learning in Action*. Boston: Harvard Business School Press, 2000.

Genusa, A., "Rx for Learning," *cio.com*, February 1, 2001, *cio.com/archive/020101/tufts.html* (accessed July 2006).

Gray, P., and D. Meister, "Knowledge Sourcing Effectiveness," working paper, University of Pittsburgh, 2003.

Gray, P., and S. Tehrani, "Technologies for Disseminating Knowledge," in *Handbook on Knowledge Management*, Volume 1k, C. W. Holsapple (ed.). New York: Springer-Verlag, 2003.

Hargadon, A. B., "Firms as Knowledge Brokers: Lessons in Pursuing Continuous Innovation," *California Management Review*, 40(3), Spring 1998.

Henfridsson, O., and A. Söderholm, "Barriers to Learning: On Organizational Defenses and Vicious Circles in Technological Adoption," *Accounting, Management and Information Technologies*, 10(1), 2000.

Hislop, D., "Mission Impossible? Communicating and Sharing Knowledge via Information Technology," *Journal of Information Technology*, September 2002.

Hinds, R. S., and J. E. Aronson, "Developing the Requisite Organizational, Attitudinal, and Behavioral Conditions for Effective Knowledge Management." *Proceedings of the Americas Conference for Information Systems*, Dallas, August 2002.

Holsapple, C. W., "Knowledge and its Attributes," in *Handbook on Knowledge Management*, Volume 1k, C. W. Holsapple (ed.). New York: Springer-Verlag, 2003.

Holsapple, C. W., and K. D. Joshi, "A Knowledge Management Ontology," in *Handbook on Knowledge Management*, Volume 1k, C. W. Holsapple (ed.). New York: Springer-Verlag, 2003.

IBM, "IBM Launches Software to Help Hospitals and Government Healthcare Agencies Identify and Manage Medical Challenges," *IBM.com*, February 3, 2005, *306.ibm.com/software/swnews/swnews.nsf/n/rdhn693m2e* (accessed July 2006).

Jasimuddin, Sajjad M., N. A. D. Connell, and J. H. Klein, "Understanding Organizational Memory," in *Encyclopedia of Knowledge Management*, D. G. Schwartz (ed.). Hershey, PA: Idea Group Reference, 2006.

Jennex, M., and L. Olfman, "Organizational Memory and Its Management," Chapter 11 in *Handbook of Knowledge Management: Knowledge Matters,* Vol. 1, C. W. Holsapple (ed.). Heidelberg: Springer-Verlag, 2003.

Jones, M. C., M.Cline, S. Ryan, "Exploring Knowledge Sharing in ERP Implementation: An Organizational Culture Framework," *Decision Support Systems,* 41(2), January 2006.

Kankanhalli, A., B. C. Y. Tan, and K. K.Wei, "Contributing Knowledge to Electronic Knowledge Repositories: An Empirical Investigation," *MIS Quarterly,* 29(1), March 2005.

Kayworth, T., and D. Leidner, "Organizational Culture as a Knowledge Resource," Chapter 12 in *Handbook of Knowledge Management: Knowledge Matters,* Vol. 1, C. W. Holsapple (ed.). Heidelberg: Springer Verlag, 2003.

Kaplan, S., "KM the Right Way," *CIO,* July 15, 2002.

Kesner, R. M., "Building a Knowledge Portal: A Case Study in Web-Enabled Collaboration," *Information Strategy: The Executive's Journal,* Winter 2003.

Kiaraka, R. N., and K. Manning, "Managing Organizations through a Process-Based Perspective: Its Challenges and Rewards," *Knowledge and Process Management,* 12(4), JohnWiley and Sons Ltd., 2005.

King, W. R., "Knowledge Sharing," in *Encyclopedia of Knowledge Management,* D. G. Schwartz (ed.). Hershey, PA: Idea Group Reference, 2006.

King, J., "Shell Strikes Knowledge Gold," *Computerworld,* July–August 2001.

*Knowledge Management,* Volume 1k (ed. C. W. Holsapple). New York: Springer-Verlag, 2003.

KPMG Management Consulting, *Knowledge Management: Research Report,* 1998.

Leidner, D. E., "The Ongoing Challenges of Knowledge Management Initiatives," *Cutter Benchmark Review,* 6(3), March 2006.

Leidner, D. E., "Understanding Information Culture: Integrating Knowledge Management Systems into Organizations," in *Strategic Information Management,* R. D. Galliers and D. E. Leidner (eds.). Oxford: Butterworth Heinemann, 2003.

Leidner, D., M. Alavi, and T. Kayworth, "The Role of Culture in Knowledge Management: A Case Study of Two Global Firms," *International Journal of e-Collaboration,* 2(1), 2006.

Levinson, M., "The ABCs of KM," *CIO.com,* December 27, 2005, *cio.com/research/knowledge/edit/kmabcs.html* (accessed July 2006).

Liebowitz, J., and Y. Chen, "Knowledge Sharing Proficiencies: The Key to Knowledge Management," in *Handbook on Knowledge Management,* Volume 1k, C. W. Holsapple (ed.). New York: Springer-Verlag, 2003.

"Livelier Life Sciences," *KMWorld,* June 7, 2006, *kmworld.com/Articles/ReadArticle.aspx?CategoryID=59&ArticleID=15897* (accessed July 2006).

MacSweeney, G., "The Knowledge Management Payback," *Insurance & Technology,* June 2002.

Martin, B., "Knowledge Management Within the Context of Management: An Evolving Relationship," *Singapore Management Review,* 22(2), 2000.

Marwick, A. D., "Knowledge Management Technology," *IBM Systems Journal,* 40(4), 2001.

Massey, A. P., M. Montoya-Weiss, and T. O'Driscoll, "Knowledge Management in Pursuit of Performance: Insights from Nortel Networks," MIS *Quarterly,* 26(3), September 2002.

McCarthy, R. V., K. Mazouz, and J. E. Aronson, "Measuring the Validity of Task-Technology Fit for Knowledge Management Systems," *Proceedings of the Americas Conference on Information Systems (AMCIS 2001),* Boston, MA, August 2001.

Melymuka, K., "Profiting from Mistakes," *Computerworld,* April 2001.

Melymuka, K., "Knowledge Management Helps Cut Errors by Half," *Computerworld,* July 8, 2002, *computerworld.com/databasetopics/data/story/0,10801,72513,00.html* (accessed July 2006).

"Monsanto at a Glance," *monsanto.com* (accessed July 2006).

Mooney, S. F., "P-C 'Knowledge Capital' Can Be Measured," *National Underwriter,* 104(51–52), December 25, 2000.

"Most Admired Knowledge Companies Recognized," *Knowledge Management Review,* January–February 1999.

Nenov, D., "New Approaches to KM in Government User-Centric Enterprise Information Retrieval," *KMWorld* June 2005, *kmworld.com/PDF/KMWhitePaper.aspx?IssueID=357* (accessed July 2006).

Nevo, D., and Y. Wand, "Organizational Memory Information Systems: A Transactive Memory Approach," *Decision Support Systems,* 39(4). Elsevier Science Publishers B.V., 2005.

Nonaka, I., and H. Takeuchi, *The Knowledge-Creating Company: How Japanese Companies Create the Dynamics of Innovation.* New York: Oxford University Press, 1995.

O'Dell, C. S., S. Elliot, and C. Hubert, "Achieving Knowledge Management Outcomes," in *Handbook on Knowledge Management,* Volume 1k, C. W. Holsapple (ed.). New York: Springer-Verlag, 2003.

O'Dell, C., F. Hasanali, C. Hubert, K. Lopez, P. Odem, C. Raybourn, "Successful KM Implementations: A Study of Best Practice Organizations," Chapter 51 in *Handbook of Knowledge Management: Knowledge Directions,* Vol. 2, C. W. Holsapple (ed.). Heidelberg: Springer-Verlag, 2003.

Pan, S. L., and D. E. Leidner, "Bridging Communities of Practice with Information Technology in Pursuit of Global Knowledge Sharing," *Journal of Strategic Information Systems,* 12, 2003.

Park City Group, "Meet Our CEO," *ParkCityGroup.com,* 2003, *parkcitygroup.com/meet_ceo.htm* (accessed July 2006).

Patton, S., "Beating the Boomer Brain Drain Blues," *CIO Magazine,* January 15, 2006, *cio.com/archive/011506/boomer.html* (accessed July 2006).

Patton, S., "Sharing Data, Saving Lives," *CIO Magazine,* March 1, 2005, *cio.com/archive/030105/healthcare.html* (accessed July 2006).

Riege, A., "Three-Dozen Knowledge-Sharing Barriers Managers Must Consider," *Journal of Knowledge Management,* 9(3), 2005.

Robb, D., "Assembling Knowledge Management Teams," *Information Strategy Executive Journal,* Winter 2003.

Roberts-Witt, S. L., "The @HP Way," *Portals Magazine,* November 2002.

Schwartz, D. G. (ed.), *Encyclopedia of Knowledge Management.* Hershey, PA: Idea Group Reference, 2006.

Shariq, S. G., and M. T. Vendelø, "Tacit Knowledge Sharing" in *Encyclopedia of Knowledge Management,* D. G. Schwartz. (ed.). Hershey, PA: Idea Group Reference, 2006.

Sharp, D., "Knowledge Management Today: Challenges and Opportunities," *Information Systems Management,* Spring 2003.

Shein, E., "The Knowledge Crunch," *CIO Magazine,* May 1, 2001.

Silver, C. A., "Where Technology and Knowledge Meet," *Journal of Business Strategy,* 21(6), November–December 2000.

Strassmann, P., "How Much Is Know-How Worth?" *Baseline,* November 8, 2005a.

Strassamann, P., "Putting a Price on Brainpower," *Baseline,* November 8, 2005b.

Steinberg, D., "Bringing Order to the Information Explosion," *Smartbusinessmag.com,* June 2002.

Totty, M., "A New Way to Keep Track of Talent," *Wall Street Journal,* May 15, 2006.

Tseng, C., and J. Goo, "Intellectual Capital and Corporate Value in an Emerging Economy: Empirical Study of Taiwanese Manufacturers," *R&D Management,* 35(2), 2005.

Van de Van, A. H., "Running in Packs to Develop Knowledge-Intensive Technologies," *MIS Quarterly,* 29(2), June 2005.

Vat, K. H., "Developing a Learning Organization Model for Problem-Based Learning: The Emergent Lesson of Education from the IT Trenches," *Journal of Cases on Information Technology*, 8(2), April–June 2006.

Wickramasinghe, N., "Knowledge Creation," in *Encyclopedia of Knowledge Management,* D. G. Schwartz (ed.). Hershey, PA: Idea Group Reference, 2006.

Wiig, K. M. "A 2005 Perspective on Knowledge Management Practices," *Cutter Benchmark Review*, 6(3), March 2006.

Ziff Davis Smart Business, "Inside Information," *Smartbusinessmag. com,* June 2002.

Zyngier, S., "Knowledge Management Governance," in *Encyclopedia of Knowledge Management,* D.G. Schwartz (ed.). Hershey, PA: Idea Group Reference, 2006.

## Part V | Managerial and Decision Support Systems

10. Knowledge Management
▶ 11. Business Intelligence and Corporate Performance Management
12. Management Decision Support and Intelligent Systems

Chapter

# 11

# Business Intelligence and Corporate Performance Management

## Learning Objectives

After studying this chapter, you will be able to:

❶ Understand the drivers for business intelligence (BI) initiatives in modern organizations and BI benefits.

❷ Understand the structure, components, and process of BI.

❸ Learn about OLAP, reports and querying databases, and multidimensional analysis.

❹ Learn about different models of business analytics.

❺ Learn about data, text, Web mining, and predictive analysis—and their current and potential uses.

❻ Gain familiarity with data visualization in BI and with GIS systems.

❼ Understand the importance of real-time BI and competitive intelligence.

❽ Learn about business (corporate) performance management.

## Integrating *IT*

**ACC**   **FIN**   **MKT**   **POM**   **HRM**   **IS**   **SVC**

# TOYOTA USES BUSINESS INTELLIGENCE TO EXCEL

## The Problem

Toyota Motor Sales USA (*toyota.com*) is the U.S. distributor of cars and trucks built by Toyota. The company buys the cars at the Toyota factories in Japan and elsewhere, takes ownership of the vehicles, and then sells them to Toyota dealers across the United States. An average vehicle costs $8/day to keep, while in transit. Since it used to take 9 to 10 days in transit, the financial charge was $72–$80 per car. For two million cars a year the cost to the company was $144–$160 million a year. This was too much.

In the late 1990s, the company faced increased problems in its supply chain and its operations, and its "car keeping" costs mounted. Also, the inability to deliver cars to the dealers on time resulted in unhappy customers who purchased cars from competitors, such as Honda. This became extremely important in 2003 and 2004, when hybrid cars were introduced and the competition with Honda intensified.

In the past, management used computers that generated tons of directionless reports and data. Management was unable to use such data and reports strategically. Furthermore, internal departments regularly failed to share information, or did it too slowly. Actionable reports were being produced too late. In addition, overlapping reporting systems provided data that were not always accurate. Management was unable to make timely decisions since they were not certain what portion of the data was still valid. The data quality situation was especially dire in the Toyota Logistic Services (TLS) division, which manages the transport of the vehicles.

The management of TLS requires precision inventory of cars, tracking, and supply chain management in order to assure that the right cars go to the right dealers in a timely manner. Manual scheduling and other related business processes, which were conducted with incorrect information, caused additional problems. For example, if one individual made a data entry mistake when a ship docked, the mistake would endure throughout the entire supply chain. (For example, some data indicated to management that ships never made it to a port weeks after the ships had safely docked.) The IT organization was unable to respond to the growing needs of the business. Finally, a new CIO was hired in 1997 to fix the problems.

## The Solution

Barbara Cooper, the new CIO, started by trying to identify the real problems. One thing became clear: A data warehouse (Chapter 3) was needed. It also became clear that software tools to process, mine, and manipulate the data were needed. Namely, a *business intelligence* (BI) solution was needed. After an unsuccessful experiment with BI (the right concept with wrong vendors and software), in 2000 Toyota switched to a better technology. Using Oracle's data warehouse and Hyperion's business intelligence platform, a new system was created. The system also includes Hyperion's *dashboard* feature (Section 11.6) that allows executives to visually examine hot spots in their business units and investigate further to identify the exact problems and their causes.

Using different colors (e.g., red for danger) a business manager can see in real time, for example, when delivery times are slowing, and immediately find the sources of the problems and even evaluate what-if potential solutions.

## The Results

Within a few days, the system started to provide eye-popping results. For example, the system helped discover that Toyota was getting billed twice for a specific rail shipment (an $800,000 error). Overall, Toyota USA has managed to increase the volume of cars it handled by 40 percent between 2001 and 2005, while increasing head count by just 3 percent. In addition, in-transit time has been reduced by more than 5 percent. Word of the success of TLS with its BI quickly spread throughout Toyota USA and then all over the company, and many started to adopt BI. For example, the former manager of TLS, who now runs the Toyota Customer Services Division, uses dashboards in his office, as do CFOs and other top executives throughout Toyota (e.g., to better manage expenses, purchasing, etc). It is clear now that the more people who use data analysis tools, the more profit Toyota can earn. The system was upgraded between 2003 and 2005; tools are continuously added as needed. These and many other benefits of the system helped the parent, Toyota Motor Corp., reach the highest profit margins in the automotive industry as of 2003. Also, market share is increasing consistently. Incidentally, Toyota, being an adaptive enterprise, will start to produce consumer-helping robots (e.g., service robots for the elderly) in the year 2010, believing a great opportunity is there.

Finally, an independent study by IDC Inc. about the justification of business performance management (see Section 11.6) and BI systems indicates that Toyota achieved a 506 percent return on the BI investment. (The median ROI for the 43 other Fortune 500 companies that participated in the study was 112 percent.)

*Sources:* Compiled from Briody (2005), Hyperion (2006), and *toyota.com* (accessed May 2006).

## Lessons Learned from This Case

This case illustrates a typical situation where information flow cannot meet the needs of managers. Information is late, sometimes inaccurate, and is not shared by all. The old systems do not meet the need to make speedy or good decisions, evaluate large amounts of data stored in different locations, and collaborate. The solution is a technology called *business intelligence*, which is based on data warehouse technology and provides strategic advantage. The major objective of this chapter is to show how this is accomplished.

# 11.1 A Framework for Business Intelligence: Concepts and Benefits

BI concepts have been implemented under different names by many vendors who created tools and methodologies over a period of three decades. Let's see some of the capabilities of BI by looking at some points observed in the Toyota case.

**CHARACTERISTICS OF TOYOTA'S SYSTEM**

As you may recall, Toyota's system was driven by:

- Too much directionless data that were full of errors and could not be trusted
- Strong competition in the automotive industry, mostly from Honda
- Problems of communication and coordination along the supply chain
- Departments' inability to share data in a timely manner
- Management's inability to get information they needed for decision making

Toyota's systems included:

- A data warehouse with historical data
- Tools for conducting analysis and data manipulation
- A visualized user interface (a dashboard), mainly for top managers

As the case indicates, the use of BI solved the company's problems and was an overwhelming success. Let's explore BI and see why it is such a successful technology.

**DEFINITIONS OF BI**

**Business intelligence (BI)** is an umbrella term that combines architectures, tools, databases, applications, and methodologies (see Raisinghani, 2004). It is, like IT and MIS, a content-free expression, so it means different things to different people. Part of the confusion about BI lies in the flurry of acronyms and buzzwords that are associated with BI (such as *business performance management*, BPM). BI's major objective is to enable interactive access to data, enable manipulation of these data, and to provide business managers and analysts the ability to conduct appropriate analysis. By analyzing historical and current data, situations, and performances, decision makers get valuable insights so they can make more informed and better decisions (see Zaman, 2005). The process of BI is based on the *transformation* of data to information, then into decisions, and finally into actions.

BI, as in the Toyota case, has four major components: *data warehouse* (with its source data), *business analytics* (a collection of tools for manipulating, mining, and analyzing the data in the data warehouse), *business performance management* (BPM) for monitoring and analysis of performance, and *user interface* (such as the dashboard). The relationship among these components can be seen in Figure 11.1.

Notice that the data warehousing environment is mainly the responsibility of technical staff, while the analytical environment (known also as *business analytics*) is in the realm of business users. Any user can connect to the system via a user interface, such as a browser, and top managers may use the BPM component and dashboard.

Some tools of business analytics and user interface will be introduced briefly in Sections 11.3 and 11.4. However, one set of tools, *intelligent systems* (Chapter 12), can be viewed as a futuristic component of BI. According to Zaman (2005), this may cause the field's name to be changed to *artificial business intelligence*.

**Data Warehousing.** Starting from the left of Figure 11.1, we see data flow from operational systems (e.g., CRM, ERP, etc.) to a *data warehouse* (DW), which is a special database, or repository of data, that has been prepared to support decision-making applications, ranging from simple reporting and querying to complex optimization. The DW is constructed with methodologies, mainly metadata and ELT, as described in Chapter 3. Also described there are *data marts*, which are data repositories for departments (e.g., marketing) or specific functions. The data warehouse and its variants are the cornerstone of any medium-to-large BI system. Originally, it included only historical data that were organized and summarized so end-users could easily view or manipulate data. Today, some data warehouses include current data as well, so they are capable of providing real-time decision support.

**Business Analytics.** There are many software tools for users to create on-demand reports and queries and analyze data. They appeared originally under the name *online analytical processing* (OLAP). For example, users could analyze different dimensions of data and trends. Business users can quickly and easily identify performance trends by using trend analysis and graphing tools. These products support more sophisticated

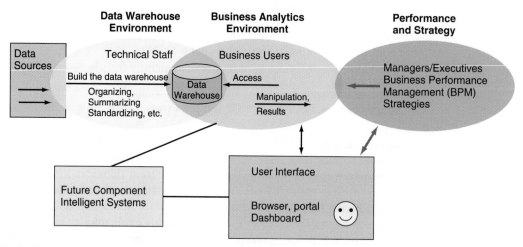

**Figure 11.1** The major components of business intelligence. (*Source:* Drawn by E. Turban.)

data analysis and reports. For instance, users can quickly isolate and identify products, customers, regions, or other areas that are trending significantly up or down. Some solutions also include a fully integrated, powerful data graphing function to create detailed data visualizations. These capabilities plus more sophisticated ones are presented in Section 11.4. To conduct business analytics, the user needs interactivity software called *middleware* (to access the data warehouse).

End-users can work with a variety of BI tools and techniques. We divided them in this chapter into three categories:

***Reporting and Queries.*** Here we deal with both static and dynamic reporting, and with all types of queries, discovery of information, multidimensional view, drill-down to details, and so on. These are presented in Section 11.2.

***Advanced Analytics.*** These include many statistical, financial, mathematical, and other models that are used in analyzing data and information (Section 11.2).

***Data, Text, and Web Mining.*** *Data mining* (DM) (Section 11.3) is the process of searching for unknown or nonobvious relationships or information in large databases or data warehouses, using intelligent tools such as *neural computing* or advanced statistical methods. Mining can be done on quantitative data, text, or Web data.

**Business Performance Management.** The final component of the BI process is *business (or corporate) performance management* (BPM). This component is based on the *balanced scorecard* methodology, which is a framework for defining, implementing, and managing and enterprise's business strategy by linking objectives with factual measures. In other words, it is a way to link top-level metrics, like the financial information created by the *chief financial officer* (CFO), with actual performance all the way down the corporate pecking order. BPM uses BI analysis reporting and queries. The objective of BPM is to optimize the overall performance of an organization. The details of BPM are presented in Section 11.6.

**User Interface: Dashboards and Other Information Broadcasting Tools. Dashboards** (like the dashboard of a car) organize and present information in a way that is easy to read. They present corporate performance measures (*Key Performance Indicators*), trends, and exceptions. For example see *businessobjects.com*. They present graphs, charts, and tables that show actual performance vs. desired metrics for at-a-glance views of the health of the organization (see details in Section 11.6). Other tools that "broadcast" information are corporate portals (Chapter 4), digital cockpits, and visualization tools. Dashboards are interactive user interfaces.

***Visualization Tools.*** Many visualization tools ranging from multidimensional cube presentations to virtual reality are integral parts of BI systems. Technologies such as geographical information systems (GISs) are used in visualization (Section 11.4).

In this chapter, we describe these components and their role in creating the field of business intelligence. For details see Thompson and Jakovljeric (2005), Loschin (2003), and Baum (2006).

| THE BENEFITS OF BI | Managers need the *right information* at the *right time* and in the *right place* to work smart. This is the mantra for modern approaches to business intelligence. It is no surprise that organizations are relying on BI to monitor and understand business activities. Examples of typical applications are provided in Table 11.1. |

As seen in the Toyota case, the major benefit of BI was its ability of provide accurate information when needed, including a real-time view of the details of corporate performance. Such information is a must for all types of decisions, strategic planning, and even survival.

| TABLE 11.1 | Business Value of BI Analytical Applications | |
|---|---|---|
| **Analytical Application** | **Business Question** | **Business Value** |
| Customer segmentation | What market segments do my customers fall into and what are their characteristics? | Personalize customer relationships for higher customer satisfaction and retention. |
| Propensity to buy | Which customers are most likely to respond to my promotion? | Target customers based on their need to increase their loyalty to your product line. Also, increase campaign profitability by focusing on the most likely to buy. |
| Customer profitability | What is the lifetime profitability of my customers? | Make business interaction decisions based on the overall profitability of customers or customer segments. |
| Fraud detection | How can I detect which transactions are likely to be fraudulent? | Quickly detect fraud and take immediate action to minimize cost. |
| Customer attrition | Which customers are at risk of leaving? | Prevent loss of high-value customers and let go of lower-value customers. |
| Channel optimization | What is the best channel to reach my customers in each segment? | Interact with customers based on their preference and your need to manage cost. |

*Source:* Ziama and Kasher (2004). Courtesy of Teradata, divison of NCR Corp.

Eckerson (2003) reports the results of a survey of 510 corporations that indicates the benefits as viewed by the participants. The major benefits reported were:

- Time savings (60 percent)
- Single version of the truth (59 percent )
- Improved strategies and plans (57 percent )
- Improved tactical decisions (56 percent )
- More efficient processes (55 percent )
- Cost savings (37 percent )
- Improved customers and partners relationships (36 percent )

Thompson (2004) reported the following to be the major benefits of BI, found in a survey:

- Faster, more accurate reporting (81 percent )
- Improved decision making (78 percent )
- Improved customer service (56 percent )
- Increased revenue (49 percent )

Notice that many of the benefits are *intangible;* this is why according to Eckerson (2003) so many executives *do not* insist on a rigorous cost-justification for BI projects. For example, BI helps companies to comply with SOX (see Online File W11.1).

Thompson (2004) also noticed that the most common application areas of BI are: general reporting, sales and marketing analysis, planning and forecasting, financial consolidation, statutory reporting, budgeting, and profitability analysis.

**THE MAJOR CHARACTERISTICS OF BUSINESS INTELLIGENCE**

The major characteristics of BI can be illustrated in different ways (e.g., a factory and warehouse).

**A Factory and Warehouse.** The term *warehouse* is associated with the concept of factory. Factories have their own warehouses, receive supplies from warehouses, and deliver finished products to them. Some use the term *enterprise information factory*

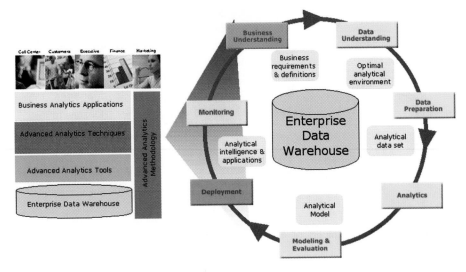

**Figure 11.2** Teradata Advanced Analytics Methodology. (*Source:* Courtesy of Teradata, division of NCR Corp.)

as a way to describe how companies conduct and organize BI efforts. A cornerstone of that factory concept is the data warehouse (Inmon, 2005).

**Teradata Advanced Analytics Methodology.** Teradata, a division of NCR, created a methodology for BI that is shown in Figure 11.2. As can be seen in the figure, BI applications (upper-left side) are supported by advanced analytics techniques and tools (left side). The methodology is shown on the right side as a cyclical process that circles the enterprise data warehouse. The process includes steps such as business understanding and data understanding (right side of figure). Some of the advanced analytical tools are described in Section 11.2. The Teradata methodology provides a business-focused approach comprising all techniques that help build models, enable new views of data, assist in simulations to test different scenarios, and predict future states and results (details are available in different issues of the free online magazine: *Teradata, teradatamagazine.com*).

The characteristics of BI enable the benefits that provide competitive intelligence and advantage as described in Online File W11.2.

**THE TYPICAL DATA WAREHOUSE AND BI USER COMMUNITY**

Which personnel in the organization would be the most likely to make use of BI? One of the most important aspects of a successful DW/BI is that it must benefit the enterprise as a whole. This implies that there are likely to be a host of users in the enterprise, many of whom should be involved from the outset of a DW investment decision. Not surprisingly, there are likely to be users who focus at the strategic level and those who are more oriented to the tactical level. An appropriate framework for describing user communities is to discuss the following categories: *farmers, tourists, operators, explorers,* and *miners* (suggested by Imhoff and Pettit, 2004). The details are provided in Online File W11.3.

Gartner Inc. (2004) distinguishes six types of users. Table 11.2 shows these different users, their numbers, the BI tools they use, and the strategic value of their usage.

The various classes of DW and BI users (HR, Accounting, Marketing, etc.) that exist in an organization help guide how the DW is to be structured and the types of BI tools and supporting software that are needed. Members of each group are an excellent source of information for assessing the costs and benefits of specific BI projects once a DW is in place.

| TABLE 11.2 | Match User Types and Functionality of Maximum Value | | | | | |
|---|---|---|---|---|---|---|
| | **Types of Users** | | | | | |
| | **IT** | **Power Users** | **Executives** | **Functional Manager** | **Occasional Information Consumers** | **Extranet: Partners, Customers** |
| **Number of Users** | Few | Dozens | Dozens | Dozens to Hundreds | Hundreds to Thousands | Hundreds to Thousands |
| **BI Tools and Functions** | Developer Administration of: Metadata Security Data management | Ad-hoc query OLAP Reports Data mining Advanced analysis | Dashboard Scorecard Reports CPM (corporate performance management) | Reports Spreadsheet OLAP view BAM (business activity monitoring) CPM | Reports Spreadsheet | Reports |
| **Strategic Value** | | High | High | Medium | Low | High |

*Source:* Gartner Inc. (2004).

**How Business Intelligence Works.** Operational raw data are usually kept in corporate databases (Figure 11.3). For example, a national retail chain that sells everything from grills and patio furniture to plastic utensils has data about inventory, customer information, data about past promotions, and sales numbers in various databases. Though all this information may be scattered across multiple

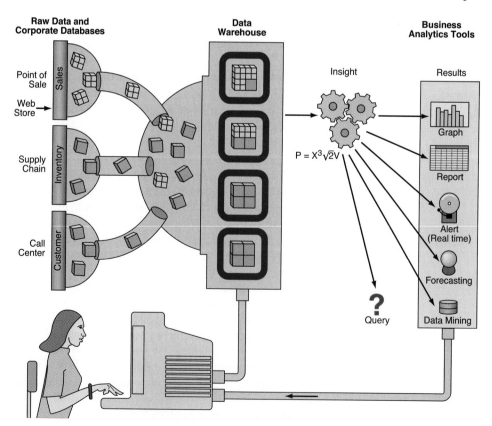

**Figure 11.3** How business intelligence works.

systems—and may seem unrelated—using special software can bring it together to the data warehouse. In the DW, tables can be linked, and *data cubes* (another term for multidimensional databases) are formed. For instance, inventory information is linked to sales numbers and customer databases, allowing for extensive analysis of information. Some DWs have a dynamic link to the databases; others are static.

# 11.2 Business Analytics, Online Analytical Processing, Reporting, and Querying

In a recent article in *Harvard Business Review,* Davenport (2006) argues that the latest strategic weapon for companies is analytical decision making. He gives examples of companies such as Amazon, Capital One, Marriott International, and others that have employed analytics to better understand their customers and optimize their extended supply chains to maximize the return on investments (ROI) while providing the best customer service. This level of success is highly dependent on a company clearly understanding its customers, vendors, supply chain, and so forth. This understanding comes from analyzing the data that a company collects. The cost of storing and processing data has decreased dramatically and, as a result, the amount of data stored in electronic form has grown at an explosive rate. With the creation of large databases came the possibility of analyzing the data stored in them.

*Business analytics* provides the models and procedures to BI. It also involves tracking data and then analyzing them for competitive advantage. Let's see the essentials of business analytics. In an article on business intelligence ROI, Gessner and Volonino (2005) provided examples of several models that illustrate how business analytics improve performance (see Online File W11.4)

**THE ESSENTIALS OF BUSINESS ANALYTICS**

**Analytics** is the science of analysis. In this book it refers to analysis of data and information. There are many methods and hundreds of software tools to conduct the analysis.

**Business analytics (BA)** is a broad category of applications and techniques for gathering, storing, analyzing, and providing access to data to help enterprise users make better business and strategic decisions. Business analytics is also known as *analytical processing, business intelligence tools, business intelligence applications,* or just *business intelligence.* BA is becoming a major tool of most medium and large corporations. Pizza Hut, for example, has significantly boosted its sales revenue by using BA tools (Langnau, 2003). Based on 20 years' worth of data on consumers, Pizza Hut knows what kind of pizzas customers order, what kind of coupons they usually use, and how much customers spend in a given time period. Marketing managers can take this information and run it through a BA analysis that forecasts, for example, the probability of a customer's next order. The company then uses this information to determine marketing strategies to influence the customer to buy more pizzas without spending more on that marketing strategy than it has to.

An analytical application is a step upward in sophistication from merely providing analytical techniques or tools. It allows for activities such as:

- Automating the thinking and, in most cases, a portion of the decision making of a human being
- Typically using complex quantitative techniques, such as multivariate regression analysis, data mining, artificial intelligence, or nonlinear programming

# IT at Work 11.1

## Ben & Jerry's Keeps Track of Its Pints

At the Ben & Jerry's (*benjerry.com*) factory in Waterbury, Vermont, huge pipes pump out more than 200,000 pints of ice cream each day. Throughout the day, refrigerated tractor trailers pull up, pick up the pints, and deliver them to depots. From there, the ice cream is shipped out to about 60,000 grocery stores in the United States and 14 other countries. There, the ice cream is placed on the freezer shelves for sale.

At the company's headquarters, the life of each pint of ice cream—from ingredients to sale—is tracked. Once the pint is stamped and sent out, Ben & Jerry's stores its tracking number in an Oracle data warehouse and later analyzes the data. Using business analytics software, the sales team can check to see if Chocolate Chip Cookie Dough is gaining ground on Cherry Garcia for the coveted Number 1 sales position. The marketing department checks to see whether company promotions

and advertising are leading to increased sales. The finance people use the tracking number in their analyses to show the profit generated from each type of ice cream. Since the company started using the software, the accounting department has sharply reduced the amount of time it takes to close the monthly books. And probably most important to a company focused on customer loyalty, the consumer affairs staff matches up each pint with the 225 calls and e-mails received each week, checking to see if there were any complaints.

*Sources:* Compiled from Schlosser (2003) and from *essaypage.com* (2006).

*For Further Exploration:* What other analyses can Ben & Jerry's do with its business intelligence software? What is the role of Ben & Jerry's information technology department?

---

*Example.* An analytical application used for credit scoring for a loan applicant might:

- Calculate a creditworthiness score.
- Automatically accept or deny the loan application.
- Select the loan limit.
- Select which credit card product (interest rate, payment terms, etc.) to issue this applicant, or which other type of loan to approve.

Using BA software, the user can make queries, request ad-hoc reports, or conduct analyses. For example, because all the databases are linked, you can search for which products are overstocked in a particular store. You can then determine which of these products commonly sell with popular items, based on previous sales. After planning a promotion to move the excess stock along with the popular products (e.g., bundling them together), you can dig deeper into the data to see where this promotion would be most popular (and most profitable). The results of your request can be reports, predictions, alerts, and/or graphical presentations. These can be disseminated to decision makers. For an example of an application at Ben & Jerry's, see *IT at Work 11.1*.

More advanced applications of BA include activities such as financial modeling, budgeting, resource allocation, and competitive intelligence. Advanced BA systems include components such as decision models, business performance analysis, metrics, data profiling, reengineering tools, and much more. (For details see *dmreview.com.*) Finally BA can be conducted in real time (see Bonde and Kuckuk 2004; Davenport 2006; and Microsoft's IT business Intelligence at *microsoft.com*).

**THE TOOLS AND TECHNIQUES OF BUSINESS ANALYTICS**

BA employs large numbers of analytical tools and techniques. We divided these into three major categories as shown in Figure 11.4. As seen in the figure, the first category is that of *information and knowledge discovery*. Some of its activities are discussed in this chapter. The second category is that of *decision support and intelligent systems*, which is described in Chapter 12. Finally, visualization is discussed here.

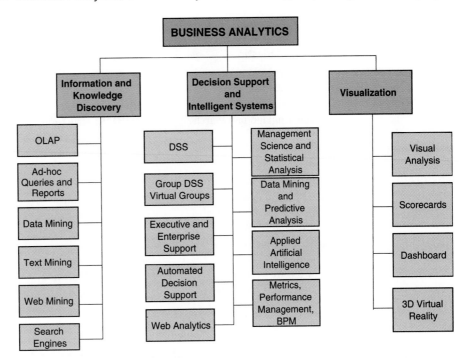

**Figure 11.4** Categories of business analytics.

Vendors classify BA tools in several different ways. (See Online File W11.5.)

We divided this chapter into sections that follow the major tools of Figure 11.4. They are presented next.

**THE TOOLS AND TECHNIQUES OF INFORMATION AND KNOWLEDGE DISCOVERY**

Information and knowledge discovery differs from decision support in its main objective: discovery. Once discovery is done, the results can be used for decision support. Let's distinguish first between information and knowledge discovery.

**The Evolution of Information and Knowledge Discovery.** *Information discovery* started in the late 1960s and early 1970s with data collection techniques. It was basically simple data collection and answered queries that involved one set of historical data. This analysis was extended to answer questions that involved several sets of data with tools such as SQL and relational database management systems (see Table 11.3, page 438, for the evolution). During the 1990s, a recognition of the need for better tools to deal with the ever-increasing amount of data was initiated. This resulted in the creation of the data warehouse and the appearance of OLAP and multidimensional databases and presentation. When the amount of data to be analyzed exploded in the mid-1990s, *knowledge discovery* emerged as an important analytical tool.

The process of extracting useful knowledge from volumes of data is known as *knowledge discovery in databases* (KDD), or *just knowledge discovery*. KDD's major objective is to identify valid, novel, potentially useful, and ultimately understandable patterns in data. KDD is useful because it is supported by three technologies that are now sufficiently mature: massive data collection, powerful multiprocessor computers, and data mining and other algorithms. KDD processes have appeared under various names and have shown different characteristics. As time has passed, KDD has become able to answer more complex business questions. In this section we will describe three tools of information discovery: OLAP, reports, and ad-hoc queries. Data mining as a KDD tool is described in Section 11.3. We discuss multidimensionality in Section 11.2.

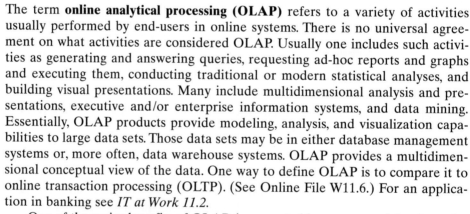

| TABLE 11.3 | Stages in the Evolution of Knowledge Discovery | | |
|---|---|---|---|
| **Evolutionary Stage** | **Business Question** | **Enabling Technologies** | **Characteristics** |
| Data collection (1960s) | What was my total revenue in the last five years? | Computers, tapes, disks | Retrospective, static data delivery |
| Data access (1980s) | What were unit sales in New England last March? | Relational databases (RDBMS), structured query language (SQL) | Retrospective, dynamic data delivery at record level |
| Data warehousing and decision support (early 1990s) | What were the sales in region A, by product, by salesperson? | OLAP, multidimensional databases, data warehouses | Retrospective, dynamic data delivery at multiple levels |
| Intelligent data mining (late 1990s) | What's likely to happen to the Boston unit's sales next month? Why? | Advanced algorithms, multiprocessor computers, massive databases | Prospective, proactive information delivery |
| Advanced intelligent system Complete integration (2000–2004) | What is the best plan to follow? How did we perform compared to metrics? | Neural computing, advanced AI models, complex optimization, Web Services | Proactive, integrative; multiple business partners |

**ONLINE ANALYTICAL PROCESSING (OLAP)**

The term **online analytical processing (OLAP)** refers to a variety of activities usually performed by end-users in online systems. There is no universal agreement on what activities are considered OLAP. Usually one includes such activities as generating and answering queries, requesting ad-hoc reports and graphs and executing them, conducting traditional or modern statistical analyses, and building visual presentations. Many include multidimensional analysis and presentations, executive and/or enterprise information systems, and data mining. Essentially, OLAP products provide modeling, analysis, and visualization capabilities to large data sets. Those data sets may be in either database management systems or, more often, data warehouse systems. OLAP provides a multidimensional conceptual view of the data. One way to define OLAP is to compare it to online transaction processing (OLTP). (See Online File W11.6.) For an application in banking see *IT at Work 11.2.*

One of the major benefits of OLAP (as reported by *temtec.com*) has been the elimination of the need for manually (or semiannually) writing reports and abstracting data for end-users. The major activities of OLAP are *reporting, querying,* and *analysis,* which are described next in more detail.

OLAP appears in different shapes and formats and has special characteristics and tools as shown in Online File W11.7.

**REPORTS**

Two types of reports are distinguished: routine and ad-hoc.

**Routine Reports.** Routine reports are generated automatically and distributed periodically to internal and external subscribers on mailing lists. Examples are weekly sales figures, units produced each day and each week, and monthly hours worked. Here is an example of how a report is used in BI: A store manager receives Store Performance reports generated weekly by the BI software. After a review of one weekly report on store sales, the manager notices that sales for computer peripherals have dropped off significantly from previous weeks. She clicks on her report and immediately drills down to another enterprise report for details, which shows her that the three best-selling hard drives are surprisingly underselling. Now

# *IT* at Work 11.2

## *TCF Bank's Conducting OLAP, Reporting, and Data Mining*

One of the largest regional banks in the midwestern region of the United States, TCF Bank (*tcfbank.com*), has more than 400 branches in six states and serves customers from all income groups. TCF Bank also operates the fourth-largest supermarket branch-banking system in the United States. TCF focuses on being a convenient one-stop shop for customers; it is one of the few banks in the United States that is open 12 hours per day, seven days a week, including holidays.

Users in the bank's major groups (retail banking, consumer loans, mortgage banking, and brokerage) found that the IT reports were not meeting their decision support needs. Instead, they have had to develop custom processes to download files from operational raw data and then load the data into spreadsheets for further analysis. The time required to create a standard graph report was up to a month. It took up to six weeks to generate a customer marketing list.

The information management department needed to come up with a better process to enable users to gain customer insight so as to uncover opportunities and effectively offer new services to customers. TCF adopted Informatica's PowerCenter and PowerAnalyzer in mid-2002.

PowerAnalyzer's report-creating wizard, metrics-based reporting, and analysis-path drilldown features were important due to their ease-of-use functions in the adoption decision. A number of key-indicator starter reports for user dashboards were also developed. In a week, 550 loan officers and executives were using these and other reports on a daily basis.

With the new OLAP system, which includes a cross-sell application, TCF is able to identify classes of customers to approach with specific matching services and products. This is especially critical in identifying the needs of new customers. In addition, reports are generated and OLAP provided for easy further analysis.

*Sources:* Adapted from Ledman (2003), *securityindustry.com*'s breaking news, June 20, 2005, and *informatica.com* (accessed February 2006).

---

the manager needs to investigate why. Further drilldown by individual day may reveal that bad weather caused the drop in sales.

Reports can be generated directly from operational data (e.g., ERP, payroll, etc.) and/or from the data warehouse.

**Ad-hoc (On-Demand) Reports.** These reports are customized for a specific user when needed. These reports can be similar to routine reports, but for different time intervals or for only a subset of the data. An example would be "to provide a list of all customers who purchased products for more than $5,000 each during January of 2006."

**Multilingual Support.** Several vendors offer report translation into several languages (e.g., Microsoft into 12 languages). The support includes all interface help (e.g., menu bars, character sets, currency conversion and formats, and business attributes).

**Representative Types of Reports.** BI software can be used to produce dozens of reports in all functional areas. For representative examples of vendors and products, see Online File W11.8.

**Scorecards and Dashboards.** Scorecards and dashboards are considered extended reporting since they provide tabular and graphical views of various reports including comparisons to metrics. These are presented in Section 11.6. Similarly, data visualization (Section 11.4) includes visual presentation of reports.

**Report Delivery and Alerting.** All major vendors of BI software offer *report delivery and alerting* designed to proactively distribute a large number of reports and alerts to a potentially very large number of users (both internal and external to the enterprise). For example, software products can centrally distribute e-mails to a large user population, with enclosures, and on a scheduled basis. For details, see MicroStrategy (2005).

**AD-HOC QUERIES**

Any query that cannot be determined prior to the moment the query is issued is considered an **ad-hoc query.** The user may decide to place such a query after she gets a report. Ad-hoc queries allow users to request information that is not available in periodic reports, as well as to generate new queries or modify old ones with significant flexibility over content, layout, and calculations. These answers are needed to expedite or facilitate decision making. The system must be intelligent enough to understand what the user wants. Simple ad-hoc query systems are often based on menus. More intelligent systems use structured query language (SQL; see Chapter 3) and query-by-example approaches. The most intelligent systems are based on natural language understanding (Chapter 12), and some can communicate with users using voice recognition. Queries can be done on static data or on dynamic data (real time). Later on we will describe the use of Web tools to facilitate queries. Finally, BusinessObjects provides an "Intelligent Questions" tool that guides users to ask the right questions.

**ANALYSIS OF REPORTS' RESULTS**

In many cases the data provided by reports require further investigation. Such investigation needs to be done fairly quickly, sometimes immediately after data are viewed, and frequently it must be done by the end-users at a low cost. For this reason, BI vendors provide tools that enable further investigation. Many of these tools, typical to executive information systems (EISs), are described in Chapter 12. These tools provide a set of capabilities that are illustrated in Online File W11.9. For example, a quick drilldown may provide an explanation for lost sales. A trend analysis may set up an alert.

**MULTIDIMEN-SIONALITY**

Raw and summary data can be organized in different ways for analysis and presentation. An efficient way to do this is called **multidimensionality.** The major advantage of *multidimensionality* is that data can be organized the way individual managers, rather than system analysts, like to see them.

**Multidimensional Presentation.**  Spreadsheet tables have two dimensions. Information with three or more dimensions can be presented by using a *set* of two-dimensional tables or one fairly complex table. In decision support, an attempt is made to simplify information presentation and allow the user easily and quickly to change the structure of tables to make them more meaningful (e.g., by flipping columns and rows, aggregating several rows and columns-rollup, or disaggregating a set of rows of columns).

Three factors are considered in multidimensionality: *dimensions, measures,* and *time.* Here are some examples:

- **Dimensions:** products, salespeople, market segments, business units, geographic locations, distribution channels, countries, industries
- **Measures:** money, sales volume, head count, inventory, actual vs. forecasted profit
- **Time:** daily, weekly, monthly, quarterly, yearly

A manager may want to know the sales of a product (by units or dollars) in a certain geographic area, by a specific salesperson, during a specified month. The answer to such a question can be provided faster by the user herself, if the data are organized in *multidimensional databases* or if the query or related software products are designed for multidimensionality. In either case, users can navigate through the many dimensions and levels of data via tables or graphs and are able to make quick interpretations, such as uncovering significant deviations or important trends.

**ADVANCED BUSINESS ANALYTICS**

While OLAP concentrated on reporting and queries, other analytics were developed to analyze data and information in more sophisticated ways. As a matter of fact, hundreds of mathematical, financial, statistical, and other models are used today by companies worldwide for problem solving, opportunity exploring, productivity improvements, and gaining strategic advantage (Davenport, 2006).

An example of the power of BA can be seen in the case of KeySpan, a distributor of natural gas in the northeastern United States. KeySpan's business customers, the "marketers" that sell gas to end-users, can log into the KeySpan extranet, view gas-usage projections, and make informed decisions about how much gas should be brought through the pipelines on any given day. KeySpan uses MicroStrategy technology to analyze such factors as historical data and weather conditions to project how much gas should be distributed. Four times a day, MicroStrategy Narrowcast Server compares the actual flow of gas to the projection made earlier in the day and then sends an exception report via e-mail or pager to the marketer and the gas operations department controlling the valves. The alerts notify marketers when they have under- or over-projected gas usage so that they can make appropriate adjustments. For additional examples, see customer success stories at vendor sites such as SAS.com and SPSS.com.

Users can perform sophisticated statistical and mathematical analyses such as hypothesis testing, multiple regression and correlation, churn predictions, and customer scoring models. For representative tools, see Online File W11.10. Such investigations cannot be done with basic OLAP and require special tools, including data mining and predictive analysis.

# 11.3 Data, Text, Web Mining, and Predictive Analytics

*Data mining* derives its name from the similarities between searching for valuable business information in a large database, and mining a mountain for a vein of valuable ore. Both processes require either sifting through an immense amount of material or intelligently probing it to find exactly where the value resides. For multiple definitions of data mining, see Miller (2005) and Hormozi and Giles (2004).

IBM has identified six factors behind the recent rise in popularity of data mining (IBM, 2006):

1. General recognition of the untapped value in large databases
2. Consolidation of database records tending toward a single customer view
3. Consolidation of databases, including the concept of a data (information) warehouse
4. Reduction in the cost of data storage and processing, providing for the ability to collect and accumulate data
5. Intense competition for a customer's attention in an increasingly saturated marketplace
6. The movement toward the demassification of business practices

The most common usage of data mining has been in finance, retail, and health-care sectors. Data mining is used to reduce fraudulent behavior, especially in insurance claims and credit card use; to identify buying patterns of customers; to reclaim profitable customers; to identify trading rules from historical data; and to aid in market basket analysis.

*Data mining* is a term used to describe knowledge discovery in databases. **Data mining (DM)** is a process that uses statistical, mathematical, artificial intelligence, and machine-learning techniques to extract and identify useful information and subsequent knowledge from large databases, including data warehouses. This information includes patterns usually extracted from large sets of data. These patterns can be rules, affinities, correlations, trends, or prediction models. The following are the major characteristics and objectives of data mining:

- Data are often buried deep within very large databases, which sometimes contain data from several years. In many cases, the data are cleaned and consolidated in a data warehouse.
- Sophisticated new tools, including advanced visualization tools, help to remove the information buried in corporate files or archival public records. Finding it involves massaging and synchronizing these data to get the right results. Cutting-edge data miners are also exploring the usefulness of soft data (unstructured text stored in such places as Lotus Notes databases, text files on the Internet, or an enterprisewide intranet).
- The miner is often an end-user, empowered by data drills and other power query tools to ask ad-hoc questions and obtain answers quickly with little or no programming skill.
- Striking it rich often involves finding an unexpected result and requires end-users to think creatively.
- Data mining tools are readily combined with spreadsheets and other software development tools. Thus, the mined data can be analyzed and processed quickly and easily.
- Because of the large amounts of data and massive search efforts, it is sometimes necessary to use parallel processing or supercomputers to execute data mining.
- The data mining environment is usually a client/server architecture or a Web-based architecture.

Data mining offers organizations an indispensable decision-enhancing environment to exploit new opportunities by transforming data into a strategic weapon.

According to Dunham (2003), data mining discovers intelligence from data warehouses that queries and reports cannot discover. Data mining tools find patterns and relationships in data. For example, convenience stores discovered that beer and baby diapers were very often bought at the same time—and moved those products nearby. Three methods are used to identify patterns in data.

1. Simple models (SQL-based query, OLAP, human judgment)
2. Intermediate models (regression, decision trees, clustering)
3. Complex models (neural networks, other rule induction)

These patterns and rules can be used to guide decision making and forecast the effect of decisions. Data mining can speed analysis by focusing attention on the most important variables. The dramatic drop in the cost/performance ratio of computer systems has enabled many organizations to start applying the complex algorithms of data mining techniques.

**CAPABILITIES OF DATA MINING**

Given databases or data warehouses of sufficient size and quality, data mining technology can generate new business opportunities by providing these capabilities:

- **Automated prediction of trends and behaviors.** Data mining automates the process of finding predictive information in data warehouses or large databases. Questions that traditionally required extensive hands-on analysis can now be answered directly and quickly from the data. A typical example of a predictive problem is *targeted marketing*. Data mining can use data from past promotional mailings to identify the targets most likely to respond favorably to future mailings. Other predictive examples include forecasting bankruptcy and other forms of default and fraud, and identifying segments of a population likely to respond similarly to given events.
- **Automated discovery of previously unknown patterns and relationships.** Data mining tools identify previously hidden patterns among data variables. An example of pattern discovery is the analysis of retail sales data to identify seemingly unrelated products that are often purchased together, such as baby diapers and beer. Other pattern discovery problems include detecting fraudulent credit card transactions and identifying invalid (anomalous) data.

When data mining tools are implemented on powerful computers, they can analyze massive databases in minutes. Larger databases, in turn, yield improved predictions (see IBM, 2006). Often, these databases will contain data stored for several years. Faster analysis means that users can experiment with more models to understand complex data and examine hypothetical or simulated scenarios (e.g., to assess potential solutions to problems).

Data mining also can be conducted by nonprogrammers. The "miner" is often an end user, empowered by "data drills" and other power query tools to ask ad-hoc questions and get answers quickly, with little or no programming skill. Data mining tools can be combined with spreadsheets and other end-user software development tools, making it relatively easy to analyze and process the mined data.

**THE TOOLS OF DATA MINING**

For an example of data mining techniques and information types, see Online File W11.11. Among different data-mining software, Oracle's Darwin, SAS's Enterprise Miner, and IBM's Intelligent Miner are some dominant players, with SPSS's Clementine being used by a smaller number of Fortune 500 companies (Calderon et al., 2003).

**DATA MINING APPLICATIONS**

Large numbers of data mining applications exist, both in business (see Miller, 2005) and other fields. According to a GartnerGroup report (*gartnergroup.com*), more than half of all the Fortune 1000 companies worldwide are using data mining technology. Also, a large number of commercial products is available (e.g., *dataminers.com, dbminer.com*).

**A Sampler of Data Mining Applications.** The following are typical application examples whose intent is to identify a business opportunity in order to create a sustainable competitive advantage.

- **Retailing and sales.** Predicting sales; determining correct inventory levels and distribution schedules among outlets and loss prevention. For example, retailers such as AAFES (store in military bases) use data mining to combat fraud done by employees in their 1,400 stores, using the Fraud Watch solution from a Canadian company, Triversity (see Amato-McCoy, 2003c). Eddie Bauer (see Online File W11.12) uses data mining for several applications.

- **Banking.** Forecasting levels of bad loans and fraudulent credit card use, credit card spending by new customers, and which kinds of customers will best respond to (and qualify for) new loan offers (see Hormozi and Giles, 2004).

- **Manufacturing and production.** Predicting machinery failures; finding key factors that control optimization of manufacturing capacity.

- **Policework.** Tracking crime patterns, locations, and criminal behavior; identifying attributes to assist in solving criminal cases (Zdanowicz, 2004).

- **Airlines.** Capturing data on where customers are flying and the ultimate destination of passengers who change carriers in hub cities; thus, airlines can identify popular locations that they do not service and can check the feasibility of adding routes to capture lost business.

- **Health care.** Correlating demographics of patients with critical illnesses; developing better insights on symptoms and their causes and how to provide proper treatments.

- **Broadcasting.** Predicting what is best to air during prime time and how to maximize returns by interjecting advertisements.

- **Marketing.** Classifying customer demographics that can be used to predict which customers will respond to a mailing or Internet banners, or buy a particular product, as well as to predict other consumer behavior.

- **Fighting terrorist activities and financing.** Governments are fighting terrorism by using data mining to cut the financial support to terrorist groups. The same is true for money-laundering (see Zdanowicz, 2004). For a discussion of use of data mining in homeland security, see Online File W11.13.

| TEXT MINING AND WEB MINING |
|---|

**Text Mining.** **Text mining** is the application of mining methods to nonstructured or less-structured text files (see Miller, 2005). Data mining takes advantage of the infrastructure of stored data to extract predictive or associative information. For example, by data mining a customer database, an analyst might discover that everyone who buys product A also buys products B and C, but does so six months later. Text mining, however, operates with less structured information such as advertising content, legal documents, purchasing orders, and research reports. Documents rarely have strong internal infrastructure, and when they do, it is frequently focused on document format rather than document content. Text mining helps organizations to do the following: (1) find the "hidden" content of document (e.g., in metadata), including additional useful relationships; (2) relate documents across previous unnoticed divisions; for example, discover that customers in two different product divisions have the same characteristics; and (3) group documents by common themes; for example, find all the customers of an insurance company who have similar complaints.

Text mining is not the same thing as a search engine on the Web. In a search, we are trying to find what others have prepared. With text mining, we want to discover new patterns that may not be obvious or known.

Organizations are now recognizing that a major source of competitive advantage is the firm's unstructured knowledge in the form of documents, memos, e-mails, policies and procedures, minutes of meetings, and so forth. All of this textual information needs to be codified (e.g., with XML) and extracted so that predictive data mining tools can be used to generate real value (see Miller, 2005). Given that perhaps 80 percent of all information we collect and store is in text (at least *nonnumeric* data) format, it is natural that text mining is a major growth area. Though we do not have full natural language processing capabilities yet, much progress has been made in this area in the last few years. It is one area where significant potential for the next generation of useful applications exists. For application of text mining, see Online File W11.14.

**WEB MINING**

It is trite to say that the Web is perhaps the world's biggest data/text repository and the amount of information on the Web is growing every day. There is interesting information in which home page is linked to which other pages, how many people have hyperlinks to a specific Web page on their own site, and how a particular site is organized. In addition, each visitor to a Web site, each search on a search engine, each click on a link, and each transaction on an e-commerce site leads to creation of additional data. Analysis of this information can help us make better use of the Web sites, and also helps provide a better relationship and value to visitors of our own Web sites. For different areas of Web mining, see Online File W11.15.

**Web mining** is the application of data mining techniques to discover actionable and meaningful patterns, profiles, and trends from Web resources (see Linoff and Berry, 2002). The term Web mining is used to refer to both Web-content mining and Web-usage mining. *Web-content mining* is the process of mining Web sites for information. *Web-usage mining* involves analyzing Web access logs and other information connected to user browsing and access patterns on one or more Web localities.

Web mining is used in the following areas: information filtering (e-mails, magazines, and newspapers); surveillance (of competitors, patents, technological development); mining of Web-access logs for analyzing usage (clickstream analysis); assisted browsing; and services that fight crime on the Internet.

In e-commerce, Web-content mining is especially critical, due to the large number of visitors to e-commerce sites. For example, when you look for a certain book on Amazon.com, the site will use mining tools to also provide you with a list of books purchased by the customers who have bought the specific book you are looking for. By providing such mined information, the Amazon.com site minimizes the need for additional search by customers, providing them with a valuable service.

**PREDICTIVE ANALYSIS**

Managers need to predict and forecast. The simplest predictive methods involve only two variables, say *sales* over *time,* or *price* over *time*. Many statistical formulas conduct such an analysis (e.g., crosstabs, regression and correlation, trend analysis). The formulas for such methods appear as Excel or MicroStrategy "functions."

Complex predictions involve more than two variables. Complex statistical methods include multiple regression analysis or special forecasting and prediction methods. Predictive analysis is explained next.

The importance of predictive analysis is explored by Ranadive (2006), who stresses that it could be used to make supply chains more reliable and efficient. Whiting (2006) describes the benefits of predictive analysis to companies in health care, law enforcement, and aviation.

**Definition and Capabilities.** **Predictive analytics** are tools that help determine the probable future outcome for an event or the likelihood of an occurring situation. In effect, gamblers may use predictive analytics to calculate outcomes of Blackjack and craps. They also identify relationships and patterns. According to Whiting (2006), BI is shifting its emphasis from data analysis to forecasting what might happen. An example is provided in *IT at Work 11.3.*

# *IT* at Work 11.3

## *Predictive Analysis Can Help You Avoid Traffic Jams*

SVC  POM

Computerized analysis now can be used to predict traffic congestion levels hours or even days in advance with almost 90 percent accuracy. Inrix *inRix.com* is a start-up company that provides such predictions. The prediction is done with a mass of data obtained from government and private sources and from sensors, including:

- Real-time traffic flow and incident information collected by gadgets installed on highways (such as closed circuit TV, cameras, radar units, and magnetic sensors embedded in the pavement)
- Speed and location data collected by GPS units of vehicles owned by participating trucking and delivery companies (customers of InRix)
- Freeway access ramps traffic flow in real and historical times (of those ramps controlled by access lights)
- Two years of historical traffic flow and accident data
- Weather forecasts and real-time conditions
- Other events (e.g., road construction schedules, school calendars, sports, concerts, and other special events schedules)

The proprietary predictive algorithms use the above data, yielding a snapshot of current traffic flows and *expected* congestion and road conditions over the next hours and even days. Obviously, each city requires its own unique model and database (.2–2 terabytes per city). The predictions were offered in 30 cities in 2006. The service is combined with digital maps (see *navteg.com*), as well as InRix partners with cell phone operators and traditional satellite broadcasters, and with in-car navigation services. Traffic information is broadcast via smart phones and electronic boards on sections of highways, using color codes for signals (currently in the Seattle area where InRix is located). The boards and cell phones also display estimated time for the roads either to be clear or to become jammed.

The analysis is used by both individuals and organizations who pay $20–$120 a year, depending on the service they want.

Here are some examples of information suggested by the system:

- Best route for a delivery van or a truck at any given time
- Estimated time before a traffic jam is cleared
- Ideal time to go to or leave from work (if you are on a flex schedule)
- How to reroute a trip to avoid a potential traffic jam or an accident

The systems' architecture is shown in the attached figure.

*Sources:* Compiled from Jonietz (2005/2006), Barke (2005), and *inrix.com* (accessed April 2006).

*For Further Exploration:* Which individuals may use this service? Which companies? What are the societal benefits?

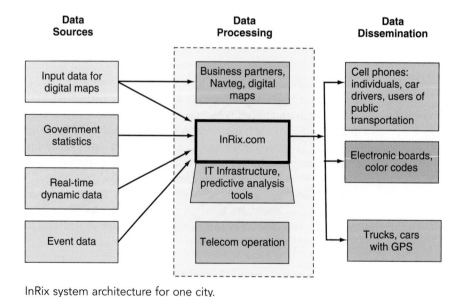

InRix system architecture for one city.

According to Fogarty (2004), *predictive analysis* uses sophisticated algorithms designed to sift through a data warehouse and identify patterns of behavior that suggest, for example, what offers customers might respond to in the future, or which customers you may be in danger of losing. For instance, when sifting through a bank's data warehouse, predictive analytics might *recognize* that customers that cancel an automatic bill payment or automatic deposit often move to another bank within a certain period of time.

Predictive analysis appears in many different formats as illustrated in the following example:

*Example: Recognizing What Customers Want Even Before They Enter a Restaurant.* HyperActive Technologies (*hyperactivetechnologies.com*) developed a system in which cameras mounted on the roof of a fast-food restaurant track vehicles pulling into the parking lot (or drive-through). Other cameras track the progress of customers moving through the ordering queue. Using predictive analysis, the system predicts what arriving customers may order. A database includes historical car-ordering data, such as "20 percent of cars entering the lot will usually order at least one cheeseburger at lunch time." Based on the camera's real-time input and the database, the system predicts what customers will order 1.5–5 minutes before they actually order. This gives the cooks a chance to prepare the food, so customers' waiting time is minimized. Also, the food does not have a chance to get cold (reheating takes time, expense, and makes the food less tasty). For details, see McKinley (2004).

The *core element* of predictive analytics is the *predictor,* a variable that can be measured for an individual or entity to predict future behavior. For example, a credit card company could consider age, income, credit history, other demographics as predictors determining an applicant's risk factor. For more on predictive analysis, see Zaman (2005).

# 11.4 Data Visualization, Geographical Information Systems, and Virtual Reality

Visual technologies can condense a thousand numbers into one picture, and make IT applications more attractive and understandable to users.

**CONCEPTS AND BENEFITS**

**Data visualization** refers to technologies that support visualizing and sometimes interpretating data. It includes digital images, geographical information systems, GUI, graphs, virtual reality, dimensional presentations, videos, and animation. Visual tools can help identify relationships such as trends. The ability to quickly identify important trends in corporate and market data can provide competitive advantage. Once we visually recognize trends, we can check their magnitude with statistical predictive models to determine their potential business advantages.

Data visualization also enables business analytics utilizing Web-based tools. Rather than wait for reports or compare sterile columns of numbers, a manager can use a browser interface to look at vital performance data. By using visual analysis technologies, managers, engineers, and other professionals may spot problems that went undetected by standard analysis methods for years.

Data visualization is easier to implement when the necessary data are in a data warehouse, or better yet in a multidimensional special database or server (Chapter 3). An example is Harrah's Entertainment (see Exercise #3), which installed Compudigm International's visualization technology at its Las Vegas headquarters and other casinos. Harrah's decision makers now can view the flow of traffic across the casino floor in real time. They can identify which slot machines are popular with the

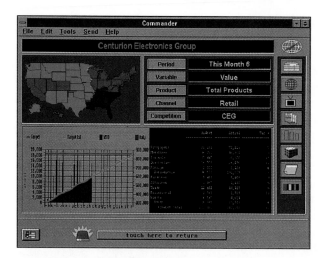

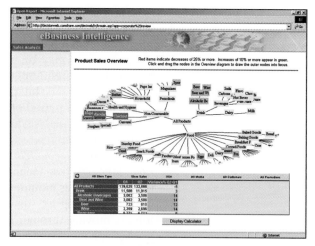

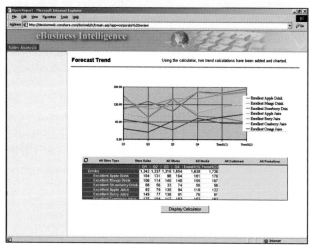

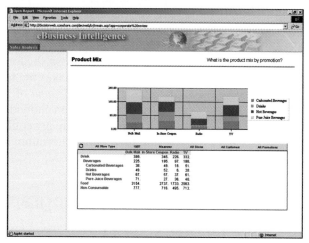

**Figure 11.5** Sample screens from Comshare Decision (now a subsidiary of Geac Computer Corp.)—a modular system for generating a business intelligence report.

customers and which are most profitable by the minute. They can install more of the more profitable ones when needed. The data-visualization software also enables managers to determine casino layout on-the-fly. They can also examine their CRM Rewards program visually.

A typical BI visualization is shown in Figure 11.5. The screens show different BI outputs designed for management viewing.

Visualization is becoming more and more popular on the Web not only for entertainment, but also for decision support (see *spss.com, microstrategy.com*). *IT at Work 11.4* describes use of visualization by Danskin. Visualization software packages offer users capabilities for self-guided exploration and visual analysis of large amounts of data. By using visual analysis technologies, people may spot problems that have existed for years, undetected by standard analysis methods. Data visualization can be supported in a dynamic way (e.g., by video clips). It can also be done in real time. Visualization technologies can also be integrated among themselves to create a variety of presentations, as demonstrated in Online File W11.16.

# IT at Work 11.4

## Danskin's Virtual Showroom

MKT    POM

Danskin (*danskin.com*), a manufacturer of women's activewear and dancewear, needed an easier way to communicate with the company's more than 3,000 specialty store partners that buy from Danskin. Danskin has an external sales force of 15 people for the specialty store market, but at most, the company's reps can meet or deal extensively with a total of only 150 to 250 partners during each selling season. The remaining stores primarily receive a Danskin catalog and are asked to communicate via phone and fax with a special team of customer service reps.

Traditionally, store buyers travel to New York City four to six times a year to preview upcoming collections of apparel, accessories, and shoes. Faxes and phone calls were (and sometimes still are) the main communications channel between retailers (e.g., the specialty stores) and suppliers like Danskin. This process is very inefficient for both the retailers and suppliers. To improve the process, Danskin established a virtual online showroom where specialty store buyers can view products, read descriptions, check inventory availability, place orders, and keep abreast of changes in Danskin's product lines.

To create this visual business-to-business Web presence, Danskin formed a partnership with 7thOnline (*7thonline.com*), a company that provides visual merchandising and assortment planning technology to the global fashion industry. The 7thOnline platform streamlines the merchandising and communications process between manufacturers and retailers by offering a visual, online product catalog. 7thOnline also provides electronic data interchange (EDI) integration, which enables retailers to transmit product purchase orders over the Internet.

While some "touch and feel" elements cannot be replaced by the virtual showroom, it can help decrease potential human errors and the high travel and operating costs associated with the manual buying routine. Buyers from the specialty stores now have earlier and more convenient access to product information, giving them time to plan, so that they come to market better equipped to make final purchasing decisions. Essentially, the 7thOnline system provides for much closer collaboration between Danskin and specialty stores.

And the external Danskin reps? They can now concentrate on the company's biggest, most profitable accounts as well as developing new accounts.

*Sources:* Compiled from Buss (2003) and from *danskin.com/bzb.html* (accessed June 2006).

*For Further Exploration:* Why is a visual B2B solution so important for the fashion industry? Would a visual solution be as important in other industries? Provide some examples.

---

**VISUALIZING MULTIDIMEN-SIONALITY**

The use of multidimensional tables described in Section 11.2 is usually supplemented by what is known as *views*. Figure 11.6 shows three views of the same data, organized in different ways, using multidimensional software, usually available with spreadsheets. Part a shows travel hours of a company's employees by means of transportation and by country. The "next year" column gives projections automatically generated by an embedded formula. In part b the data are reorganized, and in part c they are reorganized again and manipulated as well. All this is easily done by the end user with one or two clicks of the mouse.

**GEOGRAPHICAL INFORMATION SYSTEMS**

A **geographical information system (GIS)** is a computer-based system for capturing, storing, modeling, retrieving, checking, integrating, manipulating, analyzing, and displaying geographically referenced data with digitized maps. For more on digitized maps, see *gpsy.com/maps*. Its most distinguishing characteristic is that every record or digital object has an identified geographic location. By integrating maps with spatially oriented (geographic location) databases (called *geocoding*) and other databases, users can generate information for planning, problem solving, and decision making, thereby increasing their productivity and the quality of their decisions, as many banks and large retailers have done. Areas as diverse as retailing, banking, transportation, agriculture, natural resource management, public administration, NASA, the military, emergency preparedness, and urban planning

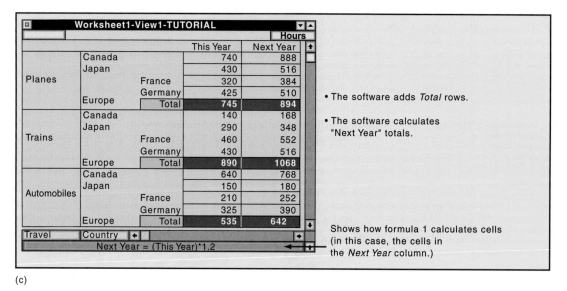

(a)

(b)

(c)

**Figure 11.6** Multidimensionality views.

have all successfully used GIS since the beginning of the 1970s (Ursery, 2004). For typical sources of geographic data, see Saarenvirta (2004).

The field of GIS can be divided into two major categories: *functions* and *applications*. There are four major functions: design and planning, decision modeling, database management, and spatial imaging. These functions support six areas of applications as shown in Figure 11.7. Note that the functions (shown as pillars) can support all the applications. The applications they support the most are shown closest to each pillar.

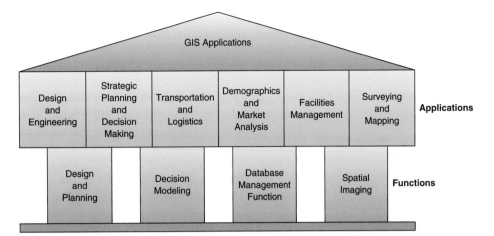

**Figure 11.7** GIS functions and applications.

As GIS tools become increasingly sophisticated and affordable, they help more companies and governments understand precisely where their trucks, workers, and resources are, where they need to go to service a customer, and the best way to get from here to there. The areas of targeted marketing are growing rapidly, and organizations can easily segment a population using GIS. For example, the Credit Union of Texas (*cuoftexas.org*) utilizes a GIS to help decide where to place billboards and ATMs, and to help identify the areas most responsive to direct mailing. The typical response rate for this credit union is from 5 to 10 percent, much better than the traditional average of 1 to 2 percent. Customers also enjoy receiving less mail from the credit union; they receive only targeted mailings. See Franklin (2002) and Ursery (2004) for details. Another example is the state of Louisiana, which is using WebFocus from Information Builders (*informationbuilders.com/products/webfocus/index.html*) to identify individuals who were trafficking in food stamps. They also use GIS in their police departments to find geographic patterns in crimes as well as to deploy officers. It is also used in physical asset management. For details, see Schwartz (2005).

For many companies, the intelligent organization of data within a GIS can provide a framework to support decision making and designing alternative strategies. Some examples of successful GIS applications are summarized in Online File 11.17. Leading companies incorporate geographical information systems into their business intelligence systems. GISs *ideally* incorporate census data (see *census.gov*) as a source of demographic data for effective decision making. For many organizations, GIS and related spatial analysis are a top priority. For example, Sears invested several million dollars in GIS technology for logistics, leading to a savings of $52 million per year (see Gonzales, 2003).

**GIS Software.** GIS software varies in its capabilities, from simple computerized mapping systems to enterprisewide tools for decision support data analysis (see Online File W11.17). Because a high-quality graphics display and high computation and search speeds are necessary, most early GIS implementations were developed for mainframes. Initially, the high cost of GISs prevented their use outside experimental facilities and government agencies. Since the 1990s, however, the cost of GIS software and its required hardware has dropped dramatically. Now relatively inexpensive, fully functional PC-based packages are readily available. Representative GIS software vendors are ESRI, Intergraph, and Mapinfo.

**GIS Data.** GIS data are available from a wide variety of sources. Government sources (via the Internet and CD-ROM) provide some data, while vendors provide diversified commercial data as well. Some are free (see CD-ROMs from MapInfo, and downloadable material from *esri.com* and *gisdatadepot.com*).

**GIS and the Web.** A number of firms are deploying GISs on the Internet for internal use or for use by their customers. A common application on the Internet is a store locator. For example, Visa Plus, which operates a network of automated teller machines, has developed a GIS application that lets Internet users call up a locator map for any of the company's 300,000 ATM machines worldwide. Not only do you get an address near you, but you are also told how to get there in the shortest way (e.g., try *frys.com*). Maps, GIS data, and information about GISs are available over the Web through a number of vendors and public agencies. An example is *maptech.com,* a major vendor of digitized maps.

**GIS COMBINED WITH GPS**

The U.S. Defense Department has invested $21 billion in the satellite system that feeds **geographical positioning systems (GPSs).** GPS devices are wireless and use satellites to enable users to detect the position on earth of items (e.g., cars or people) the devices are attached to, within a reasonable precision (see *trimble.com/gps*). GPS in conjunction with GIS is making major inroads in business intelligence applications. Commercial and government uses are endless, since detection devices are relatively inexpensive. See *IT at Work 11.5* for examples of how these technologies are being used.

**VIRTUAL REALITY AND OTHER VISUALIZATION TECHNIQUES**

Several other visualization techniques exist. Notable are virtual realty, which is described briefly next, and visual interactive models and simulation, which are described in Online File W11.18.

# *IT* at Work 11.5

## GIS and GPS Track Where You Are and Help You with What You Do     GOV   POM

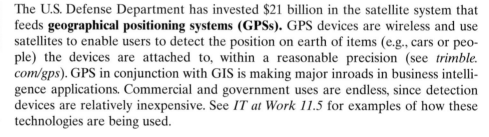

Here are some examples of how GIS in conjunction with GPS help firms differentiate their products and delivery services and improve performance.

- UltraEx, a West Coast company that specializes in same-day deliveries of items like emergency blood supplies and computer parts, equips all of its vehicles with @Road's GPS receivers and wireless modems. In addition to giving dispatchers a big-picture view of the entire fleet, @Road helps UltraEx keep clients happy by letting *them* track the location and speed of their shipments on the Web in real time. This service shows customers a map of the last place the satellite detected the delivery vehicle and how fast it was traveling.

- New York City pioneered CompStat, which uses GIS to map criminal activity and police deployment by data, time, and location. By making precinct commanders accountable for their own policing strategies, it has been a major

factor in reducing the city's violent crime rate by nearly 70 percent in the past decade.

- CSX Transportation Inc. has equipped 3,700 locomotives with a GPS. The Union Pacific Railroad has installed satellite-based monitoring devices on thousands of its freight cars for car tracking. By combining GIS with a GPS, a freight company can identify the position of a railroad car or truck within 100 meters at any time. For example, it can identify locomotives that have left their route, and the specific cars that have been left behind or sent with the wrong locomotive. Further benefits include the ability to minimize accidents.

- In location commerce (L-commerce), advertising is targeted to an individual whose location is known (via a GPS and GIS combination). Similarly, emergency medical systems identify the location of a car accident in seconds, and the attached GIS helps in directing ambulances to the scene.

*Sources:* Adapted partly from Dragoon (2003) and Rosencrance (2000).

**VIRTUAL REALITY**

There is no standard definition of virtual reality. The most common definitions usually imply that **virtual reality (VR)** is interactive, computer-generated, three-dimensional graphics delivered to the user through a head-mounted display. Defined technically, virtual reality is an environment and/or technology that provides artificially generated sensory cues sufficient to engender in the user some willing suspension of disbelief. So in VR, a person "believes" that what he or she is doing is real even though it is artificially created.

More than one person and even a large group can share and interact in the same artificial environment. VR thus can be a powerful medium for communication, entertainment, and learning. Instead of looking at a flat computer screen, the VR user interacts with a three-dimensional computer-generated environment. To see and hear the environment, the user wears stereo goggles and a headset. To interact with the environment, control objects in it, or move around within it, the user wears a computerized display and hand position sensors ("gloves"). Virtual reality displays achieve the illusion of a surrounding medium by updating the display in real time. The user can grasp and move virtual objects.

For example, virtual videoconferencing, facemail, and "virtual humans" are three recent examples of applied VR.

**Virtual Reality Applications.** Most VR applications to date have been used to support decision making indirectly. For example, Boeing has developed a virtual aircraft mockup to test designs. Several other VR applications for assisting in manufacturing and for converting military technology to civilian technology are being utilized at Boeing. At Volvo, VR is used to test virtual cars in virtual accidents; Volvo also uses VR in its new model-designing process. British Airways offers the pleasure of experiencing first-class flying to its Web site visitors.

*FIN*

Another VR application area is data visualization. VR helps financial decision makers make better sense of data by using visual, spatial, and aural immersion virtual systems. For example, some stock brokerages have a VR application in which users surf over a landscape of stock futures, with color, hue, and intensity indicating deviations from current share prices. Sound is used to convey other information, such as current trends or the debt/equity ratio. VR allows side-by-side comparisons with a large assortment of financial data. It is easier to make intuitive connections with three-dimensional support. Morgan Stanley & Co. uses VR to display the results of risk analyses.

Extensive use is expected in e-commerce marketing. For example, Tower Records offers a virtual music store on the Internet where customers can "meet" each other in front of the store, go inside, and preview CDs and videos. They select and purchase their choices electronically and interactively from a sales associate. Applications of virtual reality in other areas are shown in Online File W11.19.

Virtual supermarkets could spark greater interest in home grocery shopping. In the future, shoppers will enter a virtual supermarket, walk through the virtual aisles, select virtual products, and put them in their virtual carts. This could help remove some of the resistance to virtual shopping. Virtual malls, which can be delivered even on a PC, are designed to give the user a feeling of walking into a shopping mall. In another recent virtual reality project, the National Science Foundation (NSF), a U.S. research and education organization, has revealed its plans to develop a virtual tour (Telecomworldwire, 2003). The tour will let visitors see a 3-D view of the various rooms at Thomas Jefferson's home Monticello, by "looking in" through the windows of the virtual house.

Virtual reality is just beginning to move into many business applications. An interactive, three-dimensional world on the Internet should prove popular because it is a metaphor to which everyone can relate.

# 11.5 Real-Time Business Intelligence and Competitive Intelligence

Two emerging technologies are closely related to business analytics: real-time BI and competitive intelligence, which are described here.

Business users demand access to real-time data that are integrated with the contents of their data warehouse (see Devlin, 2003). For example, the buses in Houston, Texas, have been more reliable and efficient ever since they were equipped with instantaneous data-gathering devices, giving the traffic controllers access to information so they can modify traffic light intervals. In many cases, real-time data updates and access are critical for the organization's success or even survival. For example, according to Baer (2002), the City of Richmond, British Columbia, Canada, uses real-time data collection and analysis. Richmond is on a coastal island and has an average elevation of only three feet (one meter) above sea level. It is important for city officials to know instantly whether its network of flood-control pumps is operating, how well it is working, and if there are any problems. Clearly, this is important in other parts of the world, as in New Orleans and the Netherlands.

Data warehousing and BI tools traditionally focused on assisting managers in making strategic and tactical decisions using *historical data.* In 2003, with the advent of real-time data warehousing, there was the start of a shift toward utilizing these technologies for operational decisions. This "active" use of data warehouses is changing the focus of these tools (see Coffee, 2003 and Gessner and Volonino, 2005), and so are IBM, Oracle, Microsoft, and many other IT vendors. Hewlett-Packard moved toward an adaptive enterprise strategy (Chapter 1) for delivering on-demand computing.

The trend to BI software producing real-time data updates for real-time analysis and real-time decision making is growing rapidly (see *CIO Insight,* 2003; Patel, 2005; and White, 2004). Part of this push involves getting the right information to operational and tactical personnel so that they can utilize new business analytics tools and up-to-the-minute results on which to base their decisions, since these employees generally deal with the short-term aspects of running an organization. Figure 11.8 shows an example of the real-time analysis that might occur when a customer makes a bank deposit.

Today, many customers demand very current data. Therefore, IT managers are facing the question of how to conduct the analytical systems in real time. More *real-time* data warehousing/analytics projects are under development and being deployed. The demand for real-time applications continues to grow. The proliferation of ADSs and business rules management, for example, creates pressure to implement more automated business processes that can best be implemented in a real-time data warehouse environment. When processes that require instantaneous updates (as Figure 11.8 demonstrates) are needed for answering analytical questions, a real-time response is necessary; therefore, query, OLAP, and data mining response times must be close to zero (see Raden, 2003).

To achieve real-time business analysis, real-time data warehouses need to be updated very frequently, not just weekly or monthly. Since 2003, daily updating has become popular; and the time interval has continued to shrink. In addition to real-time queries, BA real-time applications are being deployed. The latter can instantaneously identify, for example, customer buying patterns based on store displays and recommend immediate changes to placement of the display itself. Other applications include call-center support, fraud detection, revenue management, transportation, and many finance-related transactions.

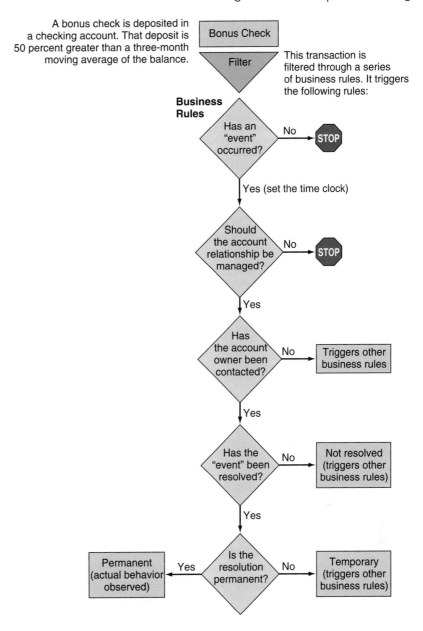

A bonus check is deposited in a checking account. That deposit is 50 percent greater than a three-month moving average of the balance.

Bonus Check

Filter

This transaction is filtered through a series of business rules. It triggers the following rules:

**Business Rules**

Has an "event" occurred? — No → STOP

Yes (set the time clock)

Should the account relationship be managed? — No → STOP

Yes

Has the account owner been contacted? — No → Triggers other business rules

Yes

Has the "event" been resolved? — No → Not resolved (triggers other business rules)

Yes

Is the resolution permanent? — Yes → Permanent (actual behavior observed)    — No → Temporary (triggers other business rules)

**Figure 11.8** Example of real-time BI using business rules to respond to a customer's action. (*Source:* Adapted from Gessner and Volonino, 2005.)

Real-time requirements change the way we view the design of databases, data warehouses, OLAP, and data mining tools, since they are literally updated concurrently while queries are active. On the other hand, the substantial business value in doing so has been demonstrated, so it is crucial that organizations consider adopting these methods in their business processes.

Examples of Web-based, real-time business intelligence software include BusinessObjects' WebIntelligence; Cognos Supply Chain Analytics and BI Series 8; IBM DB2 Intelligent Miner Scoring (IMS); NetIQ Corp.'s WebTrends; and SAS Supply Chain Intelligence Suite.

**Concerns About Real-Time Systems.** An important issue in real-time computing is that not all data should be updated continuously. This may certainly cause problems when reports are generated in real time, because one person's results may not match another person's. For example, a company using BusinessObjects' WebIntelligence noticed a significant problem with real-time intelligence. Real-time reports are all different when produced at slightly different times (see Peterson, 2003). Also, it may not be necessary to update certain data continuously.

**COMPETITIVE INTELLIGENCE**

As in war, information about one's competitors can mean the difference between winning and losing a battle in business. Many companies continuously monitor the activities of their competitors to acquire **competitive intelligence.** Such information gathering drives business performance by increasing market knowledge, improving knowledge management, and raising the quality of strategic planning. For example, consider the following uses of computer-based competitive intelligence, cited by Comcowich (2002):

- Within days of launch, a software firm found dissatisfaction with specific product features, enabling the technicians to write a patch that fixed the problem within days instead of the months normally required to obtain customer feedback and implement software fixes.
- A packaging company was able to determine the location, size, and production capacity for a new plant being built by a competitor. The otherwise well-protected information was found by an automated monitoring service in building permit documents within the Web site of the town where the new plant was being built.
- A telecommunications company uncovered a competitor's legislative strategy, enabling the company to gain an upper hand in a state-by-state lobbying battle. (Remarkably, the strategy was posted on the competitor's own Web site.)

Competitive intelligence can be facilitated with technologies such as optical character recognition, RFID, intelligent agents, and especially the Internet.

The Internet is an important tool to support competitive intelligence. The visibility of information that a competitor places on the Internet and the power of Web-based tools to interrogate Web sites for information about prices, products, services, and marketing approaches have generated increased corporate interest in these intelligence-gathering activities. For example, online niche bookseller Fatbrain.com (now part of *barnesandnoble.com*) uses "e-spionage" firm Rivalwatch.com to keep track of competitors in Fatbrain's specialist professional and educational book market. By tracking prices at rival firms such as Amazon.com, Fatbrain can offer competitive prices without giving away profit margins when it does not need to.

However, it's not enough just to gather information on a competitor. Analyzing and interpreting the information is as important as collecting it. For these tasks, one can use BI tools ranging from *intelligent agents* (software tools that allow the automation of tasks that require intelligence) to *data mining*. For example, J.P. Morgan Chase (New York) uses data mining to track several sources of information. Chase's goal is to determine the possible impact of the information on the bank, the customers, and the industry.

Another, more sinister, aspect of competitive intelligence is *industrial espionage*. Corporate spies, who actually do exist in some industries, look for confidential marketing plans, cost analyses, proposed products/services, and strategic plans. Industrial espionage is considered to be unethical and usually illegal. One type of industrial espionage is the theft of portable computers at airports, hotels, and conferences. Many of the thieves are interested in the information stored in the computers, not the computers themselves. Protecting against such activities is an important part of maintaining competitive advantage.

*Baseline* magazine dedicated its December 15, 2005 issue to security threats including competitor attacks (e.g., Gage, 2005). Does competitive intelligence include espionage? Not according to *scip.org*. Espionage is the use of illegal means to gather information. Competitive intelligence on the other hand uses legal and ethical means to gather and analyze information. Several companies can assist you (for a fee) in conducting competitive intelligence (e.g., *fuld.com*). For comprehensive resources on business intelligence, see *b-eye-network.com/home*.

# 11.6 Business (Corporate) Performance Management, Scorecards, and Dashboards

It is difficult for a business to align its strategies, plans, analytical systems, and actions in such a way that they ensure successful performance. It is this alignment that performance management addresses.

**BUSINESS PERFORMANCE MANAGEMENT (BPM) DEFINED**

In the business and trade literature, performance management has a number of names, including business performance management (BPM), corporate performance management (CPM), enterprise performance management (EPM), and strategic enterprise management (SEM). While different terms are employed, they all mean essentially the same thing. For example, Gartner (*gartner.com*) defines *corporate performance management* as an "umbrella term covering the processes, methodologies, metrics and technologies for enterprises to measure, monitor, and manage business performance." Finally, the BPM Standards Group (*bpmstandards.net*) defines **business performance management (BPM)** as "a framework for organizing, automating, and analyzing business methodologies, metrics, processes, and systems to drive the overall performance of the enterprise. It helps organizations translate a unified set of objectives into plans, monitor execution, and deliver critical insight to improve financial and operational performance." In this chapter, the term *BPM* has been selected over the other terms because it is the term used by the standards group. *Note:* Unfortunately, the acronym BPM also stands for business process management (Chapter 8).

**THE RELATIONSHIP OF BPM AND BI**

In previous sections we treated BPM as a step of the BI process. Some consider it as a complementary technology. Yet others view BPM as an outgrowth of BI that incorporates many of its technologies, applications, and techniques.

BPM is not new. Every organization has processes in place (for example, budgets, detailed plans, execution, and measurement) that feed back to the overall plan and the goals. The concept of BPM adds to what organizations have been doing for years—the *integration* of these processes, methodologies, metrics, and systems. BPM is an enterprisewide strategy that seeks to prevent organizations from suboptimizing local processes at the expense of overall corporate performance.

**THE BPM PROCESSES**

BPM encompasses a closed-loop set of processes linking strategy to execution in order to optimize business performance (Figure 11.9). The loop implies that optimum performance is achieved by setting goals and objectives (strategize), establishing initiatives and plans to achieve those goals (plan), monitoring actual performance against the goals and objectives (monitor), and taking corrective action (act and adjust).

The BPM process involves the following major steps:

**1.** Design a BPM program and define what you want to measure, when and how.

**2.** Establish standards/metrics against which performance is to be measured (e.g., balanced scorecard).

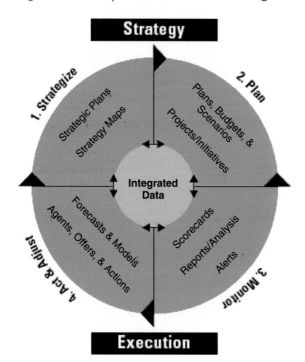

**Figure 11.9** BPM closed-loop processes. (*Source:* W. Eckerson, *Performance Dashboards.* Hoboken, NJ: John Wiley & Sons, 2006.)

**3.** Prepare a system for monitoring performance, including the finding of performance gaps.

**4.** Prepare a system for analyzing performance, its trends, fluctuations, and reasons. This includes comparisons of actual performance against standards.

**5.** Take action if needed. For example, adjust or restructure processes, change staff, introduce incentive programs, reduce defects, optimize processes, and so forth.

BPM has a wide range of applications, as shown in Online File W11.20.

**BALANCED SCORECARD**

Probably the best-known and most widely used performance management system is the *Balanced Scorecard* (BSC). Kaplan and Norton (1996) first described this methodology, which documented how companies were using the BSC to supplement their financial measures with nonfinancial measures and to communicate and implement their strategies. Over the last few years *BSC* has become a generic term (much like Coke) that is used to represent virtually every type of scorecarding application and implementation, regardless of whether it is balanced or strategic. In response to this bastardization of the term, Kaplan and Norton released a new book in 2001—*The Strategic Focused Organization.* This book was designed to reemphasize the strategic nature of the BSC methodology. This was followed a few years later by another *strategy map* (Kaplan and Norton, 2004), which provides a detailed process for linking strategic objectives to operational tactics and initiatives.

**The Meaning of Balance.** From a high-level viewpoint, the **balanced scorecard (BSC)** is both a performance measurement and management methodology that helps translate an organization's financial, customer, internal process, and learning and growth objectives and targets into a set of actionable initiatives. As a measurement methodology, BSC is designed to overcome the limitations of those systems that are financially focused. It does this by translating an organization's vision and

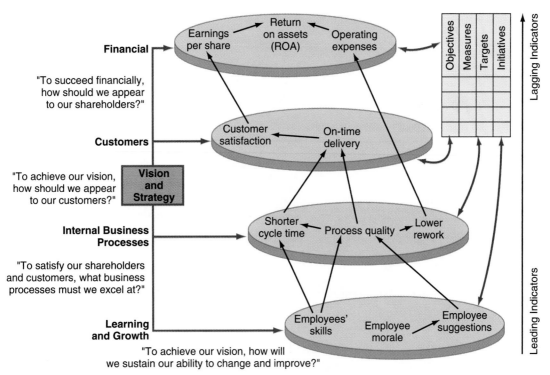

**Figure 11.10** The logic of the balanced scorecard. (*Sources:* Compiled from Dutta and Manzoni, 1999, p. 215; and from The Balanced Scorecard Institute, 2004.)

strategy into a set of interrelated financial and nonfinancial objectives, measures, targets and initiatives. The relations among the financial and nonfinancial objectives are depicted in Figure 11.10. The nonfinancial objectives fall into one of three perspectives:

1. **Customer**: These objectives define how the organization should appear to its customers if it is to accomplish its vision.
2. **Internal business process:** These objectives specify the processes at which the organization must excel to satisfy shareholders and customers.
3. **Learning and growth:** These objectives indicate how an organization can improve its ability to change to achieve its vision.

In BSC the term *balance* arises because the combined set of measures are supposed to encompass indicators that are: financial and nonfinancial, leading and lagging, internal and external, quantitative and qualitative and short-term and long-term.

**Aligning Strategies and Actions.** As a strategic management methodology, BSC helps an organization align its actions with its overall strategies. BSC accomplishes this task through a series of interrelated steps. The specific steps that are involved vary from one methodology to the next. In our case, the process can be captured through five steps including:

1. Identifying strategic objectives for each perspective (about 15 to 25 in all)
2. Associating measures with each strategic objective (a mix of quantitative and qualitative should be used)
3. Assigning targets to the measures

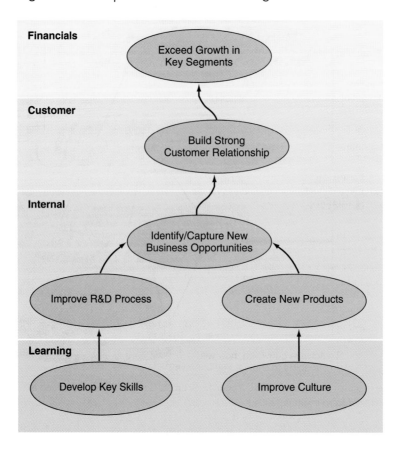

**Financials**

Exceed Growth in
Key Segments

**Customer**

Build Strong
Customer Relationship

**Internal**

Identify/Capture New
Business Opportunities

Improve R&D Process

Create New Products

**Learning**

Develop Key Skills

Improve Culture

**Figure 11.11** Sample strategy map.

**4.** Listing strategic initiatives to accomplish each objective (assigning responsibilities)
**5.** Linking the various strategic objectives through a cause-and-effect diagram called a strategy map

*Strategy Maps.* As an example of the process, consider the strategy map shown in Figure 11.11. A **strategy map** shows the relationships among the key organizational objectives for all four BSC perspectives. In this instance, the map specifies the relationships among seven objectives that cover four different perspectives. Like other strategy maps, this one begins at the top with a financial objective (i.e., exceed growth in key segments). This objective is driven by a customer objective (i.e., build strong customer relationships). In turn, the customer objective is the result of an internal (process) objective (i.e., identify/capture new business opportunities). The map continues down to the bottom of the hierarchy where the learning objectives are found (e.g., develop key skills).

Each objective that appears in a strategy map has an associated measure, target, and initiative. For example, the objective "build strong customer relationships" might be measured by "customer satisfaction." For this measure we might be targeting a 15 percent improvement over last year's figure in our "customer service index." One of the ways of accomplishing this improvement is by "implementing the customer feedback database."

**PERFORMANCE DASHBOARDS**

Scorecards and dashboards are a common component of most, if not all, performance management systems, performance measurement systems, and BPM suites. Dashboards and scorecards both provide visual displays of important information that is consolidated and arranged on a single screen so that information can be digested at a

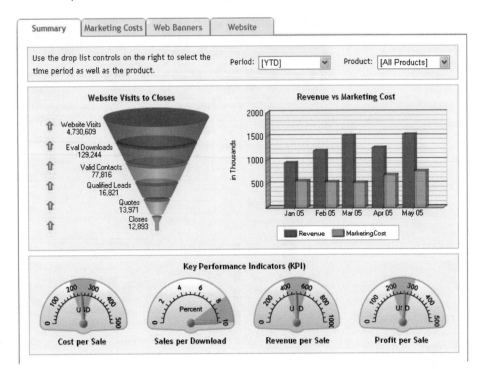

**Figure 11.12** Sample performance dashboard. (*Source:* Dundas Software, *demos1.dundas.com/Dundas Gauge/MarketingDashboard/ Summary.aspx.*)

single glance and easily explored. A typical dashboard is shown in Figure 11.12. This particular dashboard (which can be seen online at Dundas Software's Web site, *dundas.com*) displays a number of key performance indicators (KPIs) and pipeline data for a software company that produces specialized charting and visual displays for software developers and sells them directly on the Web. From the dashboard, it is easy to see, for instance, that the KPIs are all good (i.e., they are all in the green), that for all stages of the pipeline the figures are trending upward (i.e., they are all green arrows pointing upward, although the arrows are green in the figure), and that the growth in revenues is outpacing the increase in marketing costs. This particular dashboard provides end-users with the ability to see whether there are any differences by time period or product (the dropdowns on the upper right) and to further analyze marketing costs and the Web pipeline (by selecting a different tab on the top). Figure 11.13 shows an example of a Hyperion dashboard.

**DASHBOARDS VERSUS SCORECARDS**

While dashboards and scorecards share much in common, there are differences between the two. The key difference is that **performance dashboards** are visual displays used to *monitor operational performance* while **performance scorecards** are visual displays used to *chart progress against strategic and tactical goals and targets.*

Eckerson (2006) distinguishes among three types of performance dashboards:

1. **Operational dashboards.** Used by front-line workers and supervisors to monitor key operational data that are lightly summarized and updated frequently throughout the day.

2. **Tactical dashboards.** Used by managers and analysts to track on a daily or weekly basis detailed and summarized data generated from departmental processes and projects.

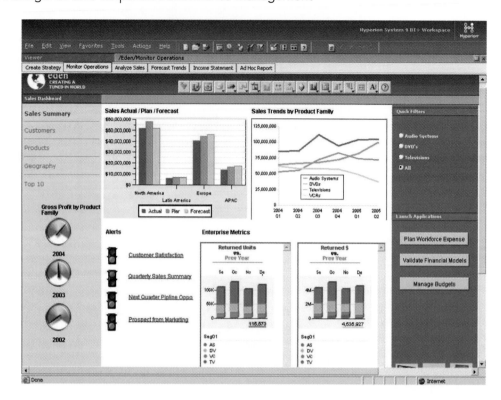

**Figure 11.13** Hyperion dashboard. (*Source:* Dashboard images courtesy of Hyperion®. Used with permission.)

3. **Strategic dashboards.** Used by executives, managers, and staff to monitor on a monthly or quarterly basis detailed and summarized data pertaining to the execution of strategic objectives.

---

**BUSINESS ACTIVITY MONITORING**

*Business activity monitoring* (BAM) is a term coined by Gartner. The term reflects their interest and the interests of others in the strategic concepts of the zero-latency enterprise and straight-through processing. In this context *latency* refers to the gap between when data are collected and when they are available for decision making. A *zero-latency organization* is one in which data are immediately available, enabling an enterprise to be proactive rather than reactive. *Straight-through processing* refers to processing in which inefficient steps (like manual entry) have been eliminated.

**Business activity monitoring (BAM)** systems consist of real-time systems that alert managers to potential opportunities, impending problems, and threats, and then empower them to react through models and collaboration. Information technology can collect data from a variety of internal and external sources in real time, analyze them to detect unexpected patterns that indicate an emerging situation, and then deliver the results to those responsible for reacting. This technically agile aspect of the *real-time enterprise* is often labeled business activity monitoring (see Keating, 2003).

The major users of BAM include line of business (LOB) executives, departmental managers, business operations staff, and CFOs. Typically, BAM is used to monitor the activities of a specific facility, such as a factory or a call center, or a specific business process.

In a 2003 survey conducted by Ventana Research, 1,300 business and IT managers were asked to name the top goals for monitoring their business. The main reasons given were to: manage or reduce costs (29 percent); improve efficiency of organization (29 percent); increase focus on revenue priorities (19 percent); align individual actions to priorities (15 percent); and respond to competitors (5 percent). Not unexpectedly, efficiency won out over effectiveness (see *IT at Work 11.6*).

## IT at Work 11.6

### City of Albuquerque Goes Real-Time

GOV

Efficiency is the main reason that the Albuquerque city government instituted a BAM system. The city government relies on NoticeCast from Cognos (*cognos.com*) to proactively push e-mail notices of important events in "near real time" to city employees, residents, and vendors. NoticeCast has the capability to monitor three basic categories of events:

1. **Notification events**—notifies users whenever a report, OLAP cube, or query is updated.
2. **Performance events**—notifies users whenever an actual or projected threshold is crossed.
3. **Operational events**—notifies users whenever a specific transaction occurs in day-to-day operations.

NoticeCast also allows end-users to create their own events, provides flexible delivery of alerts to wired and wireless devices, and integrates with Cognos' BI and BPM suites.

In the Albuquerque system, NoticeCast sits outside the city's firewall on an extranet and monitors events by periodically querying Oracle database tables that are populated periodically and often automatically by other municipal information systems. The types of events that the system monitors include the following:

- Every morning, NoticeCast sends an e-mail to each vendor that was issued an electronic payment during the night,

directing the vendor to a Web site on the extranet where it can get a remittance report.
- Every evening, NoticeCast sends an e-mail to each Albuquerque resident for whom a water bill was produced. The e-mail contains all the pertinent billing information and directs the resident to a Web site where he may pay his bill online.
- Once a day, the system sends e-mail to certain city employees, letting them know of all online payments made to the city during the past 24 hours.
- Whenever a candidate files a contribution report, NoticeCast sends e-mail to city employees responsible for tracking campaign law compliance.

The BAM system helps the city monitor events faster and more thoroughly than before. It also enables them to perform a number of activities, such as online billing, that were difficult or too expensive in the past. In the future, the city plans to deploy the system inside their firewall on their intranet.

*Sources:* Compiled from Anthes (2003) and from *cognos.com*.

*For Further Exploration:* Why does the city need to monitor events? Why is efficiency more important for the city than effectiveness? How can privacy be protected?

---

**BAM BENEFITS**

BAM helps not just in recognizing and responding to events, but also in enabling managers to resolve event occurrences quickly and review their impacts to make more timely and informed decisions (see McKie, 2003). Essentially the two most important benefits are real-time data access in a usable format, and access to tools to collaborate and model the problem leading to a quick solution; so, faster and presumably better decisions will be made.

A business activity has to be intelligently automated in order to be monitored. The monitoring must be intelligent, and the results must be easy to access, visualize, or act upon to derive value. Activity modeling is the first step in creating a successful BAM system. This involves finding activities worth monitoring, defining their steps and events, and tying those events to performance metrics to be monitored (see McKie, 2003). Analyzing activities leads to improved processes.

## 11.7 Managerial Issues

**1. Why BI/BA projects fail.** Organizations must understand and address many critical challenges for achieving BI success. According to Atre (2003), there are 10 major reasons why business intelligence projects fail. They are:

(1) Failure to recognize BI projects as cross-organizational business initiatives, and to understand that as such they differ from typical standalone solutions

(2) Unengaged or weak business sponsors

**(3)** Unavailable of unwilling business representatives from the functional areas

**(4)** Lack of skilled (or available) staff, or suboptimal staff utilization

**(5)** No software release concept (no iterative development method)

**(6)** No work breakdown structure (no methodology)

**(7)** No business analysis or standardization activities

**(8)** No appreciation of the negative impact of "dirty data" on business profitability

**(9)** No understanding of the necessity for and the use of metadata

**(10)** Too much reliance on disparate methods and tools

**2. System development and the need for integration.** Developing an effective BI application can be fairly complex. For a methodology and a guide see Moss and Atre (2003). Integration, whether of applications, data sources, or even development environment, is a major CSF for BI. For this reason, most BI vendors offer highly integrated collections of applications, including connection to ERP and CRM. Notable are Oracle, BusinessObjects, MircroStrategy, IBM, and Microsoft. An example of integrating OLAP that uses the data warehouse and neural networks is provided by Ho et al. (2004). In the example, the output of OLAP in a logistics workflow system is analyzed by the neural network. Most BI vendors provide for application integration (see Callaghan, 2005), usually Web-enabled (see *businessobjects.com*).

**3. Cost-benefit issues and justification.** Some of the BI solutions discussed in this chapter are very expensive and are justifiable only in large corporations. Smaller organizations can make the solutions cost effective if they leverage existing databases rather than create new ones. A careful cost-benefit analysis must be undertaken before any commitment to the new technologies is made.

**4. Legal issues and privacy.** Data mining may suggest that a company send electronic or printed catalogs or promotions to only one age group or one gender. A man sued Victoria's Secret Corp. because his female neighbor received a mail order catalog with deeply discounted items and he received only the regular catalog (the discount was actually given for volume purchasing). Settling discrimination charges can be very expensive. Conducting data mining may result in the invasion of individual privacy. What will companies do to protect individuals? What can individuals do to protect their privacy? (See Chapter 17.)

**ETHICS**

**5. BI and BPM today and tomorrow.** In today's highly competitive business, the quality and timeliness of business information for an organization is not the choice between profit and loss—it may be a question of survival or bankruptcy. No business organization can deny the inevitable benefits of BI and BPM. Recent industry analyst reports show that in the coming years, millions of people will use BPM dashboards and BI analytics every day (Baum, 2006). Today's organizations are deriving more value from BI by extending actionable information to many types of employees, maximizing the use of existing data assets. Visualization tools including dashboards are used by producers, retailers, government, and special agencies. More and more industry-specific analytical tools will flood the market to do almost any kind of analysis and help to make informed decisions from top level to user level.

BI takes the advantage of already developed and installed components of IT technologies to help companies leverage their current IT investments and use valuable data stored in legacy and transactional systems. For many large-size companies that have already spent millions of dollars building data warehouses and data marts, now is the right time to build BA and BPM as the next step to attain full benefit of their investment, which will directly impact ROI. However, while some components of BI, such as the DW, may change (e.g., data may be stored online), the need for conducting BI is a necessity. For more on the future of BI, see Lal (2005).

# Integrating *IT*

### For the Accounting Major

The prime purpose of BI is to provide quality information in a timely manner. The accounting function is intimately concerned with keeping track of the transactions and internal controls of an organization, many of which are sources of the data in the data warehouse. Modern data warehouses and data mining enable accountants to perform their job more effectively. Data warehouses help accountants manage the flood of data in today's organizations so that they can keep their firms in compliance with the new standards imposed by Sarbanes-Oxley and other government regulations.

Accountants also play a role in cost-justifying the creation of a DW and BI and then auditing their cost-effectiveness. In addition, if you work for a large CPA company that provides management services or sells knowledge, you will most likely use some of your company's best practices that are stored in the data warehouse. Also, CPA companies are involved in many BI and BPM/CPM projects.

### For the Finance Major

Financial managers make extensive use of computerized databases that are external to the organization, such as CompuStat of Dow Jones, to obtain financial data on organizations in their industry. They can use these data in BPM/CPM to determine if their organization meets industry benchmarks in return on investment, cash management, and other financial ratios. A prime finance task is to determine pricing strategies with marketing. Today BA models are used to accomplish this.

Modern data mining techniques are effective in finance, particularly for the automated discovery of relationships in investment and portfolio management. Financial managers, who produce the organization's financial status reports, are also closely involved with Sarbanes-Oxley. Finally, finance people are involved in planning and execution of competitive intelligence.

### For the Human Resources Management Major

Organizations keep extensive data on employees including gender, age, race, current and past job descriptions, and performance evaluations. Human resources personnel access these data to provide reports to government agencies regarding compliance with federal equal opportunity guidelines. HR managers also use these data to evaluate hiring practices, evaluate salary structures, and manage any discrimination grievances or lawsuits brought against the firm. HR people need to analyze vast amounts of data for building employee relationship management. They also need to use DW and BI for employee development and training programs.

### For the IS Major

Installing BI and CPM systems is usually done by vendors collaborating with the ISD. The ISD will probably operate the data warehouse and work with users on BI and CPM applications. This ensures that ISD should understand which data are in the data warehouse. The ISD provides help for installing BI and the data mining tools to help users access and analyze needed data. MIS personnel—and users as well—can now generate ad-hoc reports with query tools much more quickly than was possible using old mainframe systems.

### For the Marketing Major

Marketing personnel need to access data about customers and the organization's marketing transactions. They need to use BA to assess the success of advertising and promotions. They use data mining for both CRM and marketing strategy, as well as to link this information to geographical databases to determine where certain products will sell the best. Data mining helps marketing managers uncover many unanticipated relationships among some aspects of the buyer's "profile," the product, and the marketing and advertising campaigns.

### For the Production/Operations Management Major

The POM people are responsible for fulfilling orders generated by marketing. They need to do it effectively and efficiently; so they need access to organizational data to determine optimum inventory levels for raw materials and parts in a production process. Past production data enable POM personnel to determine the optimum production planning and scheduling using BA technologies. Firms also keep quality data that inform them not only about the quality of finished products but also about quality issues with incoming raw materials, production irregularities, shopping, and logistics, and after-sale use and maintenance of the product. POM controls many segments of the supply chain, and BI reports, queries, and analyses are essential for managing the supply chain.

## Key Terms

Ad-hoc query *440*
Analytics *435*
Balanced scorecard (BSC) *458*
Business activity monitoring (BAM) *462*
Business analytics (BA) *435*
Business intelligence (BI) *429*
Business performance management (BPM) *457*

Competitive intelligence *456*
Data mining (DM) *442*
Data visualization *447*
Geographical information system (GIS) *449*
Geographical positioning system (GPS) *452*
Multidimensionality *440*

Online analytical processing (OLAP) *438*
Performance dashboard *461*
Performance scorecard *461*
Predictive analytics *445*
Strategy map *460*
Text mining *444*
Virtual reality (VR) *453*
Web mining *445*

## Chapter Highlights

(Numbers Refer to Learning Objectives)

❶ Business intelligence is driven by the need to get accurate and timely information in an easy way, and to analyze it, sometimes in minutes, possibly by the end-users.

❶ Business intelligence is moving toward real-time capabilities.

❷ The major components of BI are data warehouse and/or marts, business analytics software (with possibly data mining), data visualization software, and a business performance management system. The analysis is usually done on data in the data warehouse.

❸ Online analytical processing (OLAP) is the umbrella term for the BI tools developed in the 1990s. These include mostly reporting, querying, simple statistical analysis, and visualization.

❸ Reports can be routine or on-demand (ad-hoc). There are dozens of types of reports in all functional areas.

❸ Ad-hoc queries can be made in intelligent ways using intelligent systems. A major query tool is SQL.

❸ Multidimensional presentation enables quick and easy multiple viewing of information in accordance with people's needs.

❹ Business analytics (BA) involve many methods that can be organized in different ways. They can be classified as information discovery, decision support, and business performance management tools. BA is usually conducted on the data in the data warehouse.

❹ Business analytics is an umbrella name for a large number of methods and tools used to conduct data analysis.

❹ Another classification of business analytics is the following: reports, queries, advanced analytics, multidimensionality, and scorecards and dashboards.

❺ Predictive analysis uses different algorithms to forecast results and relationships among variables as well as to identify data patterns. Data mining is one of the tools.

❺ Web intelligence (or Web analytics or Web mining) refers to analysis of Web data (known as clickstream data). Such analyses are useful in market research and competitive intelligence.

❺ Online analytical processing is a data discovery method that uses analytical approaches.

❺ Data mining for knowledge discovery is an attempt to use intelligent systems to scan volumes of data to locate necessary information and knowledge and to discover relationships among data items.

❻ Data visualization is an important business intelligence capability.

❻ Spreadsheet visualization enables instant views of complex data in a single picture.

❻ Geographical information systems (GISs) present geographical reference data as digital maps. They can support decision making in many applications that relate to locations.

❻ Visualization is important for better understanding of data relationships and compression of information. Several computer-based methods exist.

❻ A geographical information system captures, stores, manipulates, and displays data using digitized maps.

❻ Virtual reality is 3-D, interactive, computer-generated graphics that provides users with a feeling that they are inside a certain real environment.

❻ GIS can be integrated with GPS, creating many applications especially related to transportation and location-based e-commerce (l-commerce).

❼ Many business decisions need to be made in real time (or very close to it). To support such decisions with BA, one needs a real-time data warehouse and special BA features.

⑦ Competitive intelligence can be conducted over the Internet using BA tools.

⑦ BI can be designed to support the real-time enterprise environment. This can be done by having certain parts of the data warehouse updated very frequently, or by conducting BA on real-time raw data.

⑧ BPM is an umbrella term covering methodologies, metrics, processes, and systems used to drive performance of the enterprise. It encompasses a closed-loop set of processes such as strategize, plan, monitor, analyze, and act (adjust).

⑧ BPM is based on performance monitoring and comparison to targets (metrics, goals). Also, differences are presented graphically on a dashboard that illustrates the status of performance in colors (e.g., green = ok, red = danger).

⑧ Business activity monitoring (BAM) is a system that measures enterprise performance and alerts, in real time, managers to potential problems and opportunities. It is an integral tool of BPM.

⑧ The major BPM applications include: budgeting, planning, and forecasting; profitability analysis and optimization; scorecarding; financial consolidation; and statutory and financial reporting.

⑧ Probably the best-known and most widely used performance management system is the balanced scorecard (BSC).

⑧ Central to the BSC methodology is a holistic vision of a measurement system tied to the strategic direction of the organization.

⑧ As a measurement methodology, BSC is designed to overcome the limitations of those systems that are financially focused.

⑧ As a strategic management methodology, BSC enables an organization to align its actions with its overall strategies.

⑧ Scorecards and dashboards are a common component of most, if not all, performance management systems, performance measurement systems, and BPM suites.

⑧ The fundamental challenge of dashboard design is to display all the required information on a single screen, clearly and without distraction, in a manner that can be assimilated quickly.

⑧ Business activity monitoring (BAM) is used to monitor the real-time activities and events of a specific facility, such as a factory or a call center, or a specific business process.

## Virtual Company Assignment

### Data Management at The Wireless Café

Go to The Wireless Café's link on the Student Web Site. There you will be asked to think about how to better manage the various types of data that the restaurant uses in its activities.

**Instructions for accessing The Wireless Café on the Student Web Site:**

1. Go to *wiley.com/college/turban*.
2. Select Turban/Leidner/ McLean/Wetherbe's *Information Technology for Management, Sixth Edition*.
3. Click on Student Resources site, in the toolbar on the left.
4. Click on the link for Virtual Company Web site.
5. Click on Wireless Café.

## Online Resources

More resources and study tools are located on the Student Web Site and on WileyPLUS. You'll find additional chapter materials and useful Web links. In addition, self-quizzes that provide individualized feedback are available for each chapter.

## Questions for Review

1. Define business intelligence.
2. List and define the major components of BI.
3. List the major benefits (tangible and intangible) of BI.
4. Describe Teradata's concept of advanced analytics.

5. Describe online analytical processing (OLAP).
6. Describe routine vs. ad-hoc reports and queries.
7. Define business analytics (BA).
8. Define data mining and describe its major characteristics.
9. Define text mining.
10. Define Web mining.
11. Describe data visualization.

12. Describe GIS and its major capabilities.
13. Define virtual reality.
14. Define real-time BI.
15. Define competitive intelligence.
16. Describe business performance management (BPM).
17. Define business activity monitoring (BAM).

## Questions for Discussion

1. Discuss the strategic benefits of business analytics.
2. Will BI replace the business analyst? Discuss. (*Hint:* See McKnight, 2005.)
3. Differentiate predictive analysis from data mining. What do they have in common?
4. Describe the concepts underlying Web mining and Web analytics.
5. Relate competitive analysis to BI.
6. Why is real-time BA becoming critical?
7. Discuss the need for real-time computer support.
8. Relate BI to competitive intelligence. Why do they both include the term *intelligence*?
9. Discuss the relationship between OLAP and multidimensionality.

10. Discuss business analytics and distinguish between decision support and information and knowledge discovery.
11. Discuss the differences between OLAP and OLTP.
12. Why is the combination of GIS and GPS becoming so popular? Examine some applications related to data management.
13. Describe the cycle of activities in BPM.
14. How can data mining support CPM?
15. What are the roles of BAM in BPM?
16. Distinguish text mining from Web mining. In what ways can they be related?

## Exercises and Projects

1. Enter *teradatastudentnetwork.com* (TSN) and find the paper titled "Data Warehousing Supports Corporate Strategy at First American Corporation" (by Watson, Wixom, and Goodhue). Read the paper and answer the following questions:
   a. What were the drivers for the DW/BI project in the company?
   b. What strategic advantages were realized?
   c. What operational and tactical advantages were achieved?
   d. What were the CSFs for the implementation?
2. Enter TSN and find the Web seminar titled: "Enterprise Business Intelligence: Strategies and Technologies for Deploying BI on Large Scale" (by Eckerson and Howson). View the Web seminar and answer the following:
   a. What are the benefits of deploying BI to the many?
   b. Who are the potential users of BI? What does each type of user attempt to achieve?
   c. What implementation lessons did you learn from the seminar?

3. Enter TSN and find the Harrsh's case (by Watson and Volonino). Also read the opening case in Chapter 3. Answer the following:
   a. What were the objectives of the project?
   b. What was the role of the DW?
   c. What kinds of analyses were used?
   d. What strategic advantages does the BI provide?
   e. What is the role and importance of an executive innovator?
4. Visit *teradatastudentnetwork.com*. Search recent developments in the field of BI.
   a. Find the Web seminar on information visualization. View it and answer the following questions.
      i. What are the capabilities of Tableau Software's products?
      ii. Compare the two presentations and cite similarities and differences between them.
   b. Find the assignment "AdVent Technology" and use MicroStrategy's "Sales Analytical Model." Answer the three questions. Ask your instructor for directions.

5. Test drive the demos of business analytics from Computer Associates, Temtec, Hyperion, and Cognos. Prepare a report.

6. Consider the problem faced by the city of London (U.K.), since February 17, 2003, when the city instituted an entrance fee for automobiles and trucks in the central city district. There are about 1,000 cameras digitally photographing the license plate of every vehicle passing by. Computers read the plate numbers and match them against records in a database of cars for which the fee has been paid for that day. If a match is not found, the car owner receives a citation by mail. The citations range from about $128 to $192 depending on when they are paid. Examine the issues pertaining to how this is done, the mistakes that can be made, and the size of the databases involved (assume that 200,000 cars out of 225,000 prepay the fee daily) including that of the images from the license plates. Also examine how well the system is working by investigating press reports (use *google.com*). Finally, relate the exercise to OLTP, business analytics, and OLAP. (This exercise was inspired by Ray Hutton, "London on $8 a Day!" *Car and Driver,* August 2003, pp. 130–131.)

7. Conduct an investigation of clickstream analysis. Compare Google Analytics with Web Trend and other products.

8. Read "Business Analytics" in *Baseline,* May 23, 2005 at *baseline.com.* Examine the success stories. Why do you think BI was one of the top projects of 2005?

9. Enter *computerworld.com* and find QuickLink a4630. Also enter *dmreview.com.* Find the latest developments in business analytics. Prepare a report.

10. Enter *businessintelligence.ittoolbox.com.* Identify all types of BA software. Join a discussion group about topics discussed in this chapter. Prepare a report.

11. Enter *visualmining.com.* Explore the relationship of visualization and BI. See how BI is related to dashboards. Write a report.

12. Read the Toyota opening case and answer the following questions:
    a. In what ways did the old information systems create problems for Toyota?
    b. What information needs of managers are satisfied by the new system? What decisions are satisfied by the BI support?
    c. Relate the problem to the supply chain (from factories, to dealers, to consumers).
    d. List the information technology tools cited here.
    e. What strategic advantage can Toyota derive from this system?
    f. Relate Toyota's decision to make consumer-helping robots to the changing business environment.

## Group Assignments and Projects

1. Enter *temtec.com* and go to the Executive Viewer.
   a. Take the "guided tour." Interact with each feature. Write a report about your experience.
   b. Take the "live test" and create five queries and views. Write a report.
   c. Test the software with your own data.

2. Data visualization is offered by all major BI vendors, as well as by other companies, such as *ilog.com* and Crystal Xcelsius *xcelsius.com*). Students are assigned one to each vendor to find the products and their capabilities. (For a list of vendors, see *tdwi.org* and *dmreview.com*.) Each group summarizes the products and their capabilities.

3. Enter *dmreview.com/resources/demos.cfm.* Go over the list of demos and identify software with analytical capabilities. Each group prepares a report on at least five companies.

4. Enter *sas.com* and look for success stories related to BI. Find five that include SAS video and prepare a summary of each in a class presentation.

5. Prepare a report on vendors in Web analytics. Each group presents the capabilities of two companies such as Digital River, WebSideStory, Omniture, ClickTracks, or NetIQ.

6. Use *google.com* to find combined GIS/GPS applications. Also, look at vendor sites for success stories. (For GPS vendors look at *biz.yahoo.com* [directory] and *google.com*.) Each group will make a presentation of five applications and their benefits.

7. Using data mining, it is possible not only to capture information that has been buried in distant courthouses, but also to manipulate and cross-index it. This can benefit law enforcement but invade privacy. In 1996, Lexis-Nexis, the online information service, was accused of permitting access to sensitive information on individuals. The company argued that the firm was targeted unfairly, since it provided only basic residential data for lawyers and law enforcement personnel. Should Lexis-Nexis be prohibited from allowing access to such information or not? Debate the issue.

8. Each group is assigned to a major BPM vendor such as Hyperion, Business Objectives, Savvion, or Cognos. Identify all major BPM, BAM, and dashboard products. Prepare a list of capabilities. Make a class presentation in which you attempt to convince others that your company has the best product for an auto manufacturing company.

# Internet Exercises

1. America Online, stock brokerages, and many portals (e.g., *money.cnn.com, bloomberg.com*) provide a free personalized service that shows the status of investors' desired or actual list of stocks, including profits (losses) and prices (with a 15-minute delay or even in real time). How is such individualized information retrieved so quickly? Why must such data be updated so quickly?

2. Find three recent cases of successful business analytics applications. Try BI vendors and look for cases or success stories (e.g., *sap.com, businessobjects.com, microstrategy.com*). What do you find in common among the various success stories? How do they differ?

3. Go to BI Web sites (such as those of MicroStrategy, Oracle, Hyperion, Microsoft, SAO, SAS, SPSS, Cognos, Temtec, Business Objects) and look at the business analytics tools offered. Compare the major tools from three vendors and list their capabilities.

4. Enter *ilog.com/products/optimization* and identify the business analytics products (BRMS). Prepare a list of their capabilities.

5. Enter *fairisaac.com* and find products for fraud detection and risk analysis. Prepare a report.

6. Enter *spss.com* and find the demo on predictive analytics. Write a summary of the usability and benefits.

7. Enter *baselinemag.com* and find a list of over 100 BI products. Identify 10 for business analytics.

8. Enter *sas.com* and find their business analytics–related products. Prepare a list of capabilities.

9. Enter *microsoft.com/office/dataanalyzer/evaluation/tour*. Take the four-part tour. Summarize the major capabilities in a report.

10. Enter *ibm.com* and find all their BI products and services (see the BI demo). Prepare a report.

11. Enter *navteq.com*. Review their products and applications. Prepare a report on five applications.

12. Enter *teradatamagazine.com* for 2006/7 issues. Find success stories of BI. Prepare a one-page summary of two of them.

13. Enter *fairisaac.com, egain.com,* and *dmreview.com*. Identify data mining services, products, and service providers. Write a report.

14. Enter *sas.com, spss.com,* and *statsoft.com*. Find three or four customer success stories that use data/text/Web mining. Prepare a summary.

15. Enter *microsoft.com/solutions/BI/customer/biwithinreach_demo.asp* and see how BI is supported by Microsoft's tools. Write a report.

16. Visit the sites of some GIS vendors (such as *mapinfo.com, esri.com, autodesk.com,* or *bently.com*). Join a newsgroup and discuss new applications in marketing, banking, and transportation. Download a demo. What are some of the most important capabilities and new applications?

17. Enter *ibm.com/software* and find their data mining products, such as DB2 Intelligent Miner. Prepare a list of products and their capabilities.

18. Enter *psgroup.com* and find the free report (by M. Kramer, 2004) on customer data mining. Prepare a summary of the applications in your area of interest.

## Minicase 1

### Lexmark International Improves Operations with BI

POM    MKT    IS

Lexmark International (*lexmark.com*) is a global manufacturer of printing products and solutions with about 12,000 employees and over 50 sales offices worldwide. Thousands of retail partners sell Lexmark's products in over 160 countries.

#### The Problem

Being in an extremely competitive business, Lexmark needs detailed, accurate, and timely information for decision support and strategy implementation. This is especially important when it comes to data flow between Lexmark and its retail partners. The most

important information is detailed by item, sales volumes, and inventory levels. The old system was slow, inefficient, and error-ridden. Problems occurred both with flows from the partners and with data delivery. In delivering the data, results were often copied from spreadsheets and pasted into reports, typically taking four days or longer to produce answers to common business questions. Sales representatives out in the field had to dial into the intranet. Once a connection was established, analysts and sales representatives had to write SQL queries and navigate the mainframe to generate reports for management, some of which were based on inaccurate, week-old data.

## The Solution

Lexmark implemented a BI solution from MicroStrategy. The application is a BI adaptation for retailing, known today (June 2006) as Retail BI System. The system enables buyers, financial analysts, marketing analysts, regional managers, merchandisers, and field sales representatives to analyze sales and inventory data from their desktop or moble devices. The system, which is fed by IBM's data warehouse, provides users with the ability to track sales performance and inventory levels of every Lexmark product at each of the thousands of retail stores, worldwide. A large number of reporting and analysis tools are available in the software, including extensive reports, statistical models (over 50), and visualization techniques. Using the system, Lexmark's user community can answer queries like these instantly and easily:

- "What are my weekly sales and inventory levels in each of a specific customer's stores throughout the country?"
- "Who were my top retailers for a given product last week, last month, or this weekend versus last weekend?"
- "Looking at a given store that reports electronic data interchange (EDI) sales and inventory data to Lexmark, what are the inventory levels of a certain top-selling product?"

## The Results

Lexmark reported that decision makers now receive timely, accurate, and detailed information. It helped to identify sales opportunities, increased partner loyalty, eliminated inventory problems, and increased profitability. For example, the company identifies that a specific retail location is about to sell out of a certain printer. An automatic *alert* is then sent to the store manager and, within hours, a replenishment order is placed, avoiding a stockout. Overall, $100,000 of potentially lost sales were recovered. The retail stores appreciate Lexmark for this service, making Lexmark a preferred vendor.

Almost all Lexmark employees are using the systems. Novice workers are able to use the information to improve how they do their job. Management can better understand business trends and make appropriate strategic decisions. They have a better understanding of consumer demand by country and store, so they can better decide, for example, on pricing and promotions. Also, customer and partner services have been greatly improved.

*Sources:* Compiled from *Microstrategy.com* (2006) and Valentine (2004).

## Questions for Minicase 1

1. Identify the challenges faced by Lexmark regarding information flows.
2. How were information flows provided before and after implementation of the BI system?
3. Identify decisions supported by the new system.
4. How can the system improve customer service?
5. Go to MicroStrategy's Web site (*microstrategy.com*) and examine the capabilities of Retail BI System. Prepare a list.
6. Go to the SAS Web site (*sas.com*) and find their Retail Intelligence product (take the interactive tour). Compare it with MircoStrategy's product. Also, compare it with Oracle Retail (*oracle.com/retek*).

# Minicase 2

**GOV    POM    IS**

## State Governments Share Geospatial Information

GeoStor (*geostor.arkansas.gov*) is a public GIS system operated by the state of Arkansas. It includes mapping, charting, surveying land and real estate, as well as other public data about Arkansas. It is an enterprise system with its own data warehouse (Oracle Applications Server 10g) and a special device (Oracle MapViewer) for visualizing geospatial data. A major use of the system is to help businesses make a decision about where to locate (or relocate) a facility in Arkansas. For example, according to the Arkansas Geographical Information System (reported by Wiseth, 2004), an industrial prospect with a strict list of criteria—distance to transportation, including rail and road, and availability of water, electric, and gas utilities—was in the process of evaluating a site in Arkansas as a new location for its business. The data available through GeoStor were used to pull together labor information, education resources, health-care resources, and numerous other details, providing a complete package of information within the 24-hour time limit the prospect required. The result was a new business in Osceola, Arkansas—and 500 new jobs in that community.

GeoStor was developed in Arkansas, but now it is being installed in several other states in the United States (using their own data). It supports many daily activities involved in running a state: everything from improving education to providing critical, up-to-date location information for responding to emergencies and natural disasters. For example, GeoStor is being used to identify the location of all education resources in the state and to map that information against school performance metrics, so that policymakers at the Arkansas Department of Education can visualize how educational resources are performing today and plan the future of education in Arkansas.

## The Benefits of the System

GeoStor supports policy- and decision making, as well as saving money for the state (over $2 million in the first 18 months). The savings resulted from reducing the average search time per document from 23.5 hours to 1.5 hours.

Time was reduced so significantly because working with geospatial data in traditional systems is time- and labor-intensive. For example, the typical GIS is map- or file-based: Users download an entire file of a particular area or section of a map, and then work to extract just what they need; conversely, users might have to knit together a multitude of files that might comprise the area of interest. GeoStor, on the other hand, allows users access the precise area they need. Perhaps more important than cost savings and improved efficiency, however, are quality-of-life issues. Because the system provides a single source of truth to various agencies and supports interoperability of all client applications, the information in the GeoStor data warehouse can be kept absolutely current—a fact that may even translate into saved lives. When there is a disaster, for example, it's important that all state infrastructure entities be up-to-date—for emer-

gency personnel, a life-or-death scenario may rely on whether a bridge exists or not.

Finally, as described earlier, the system provides competitive advantage to the State of Arkansas over other states. It can also provide competitive advantage to firms using the system to make location decisions.

*Sources:* Compiled from Wiseth (2004) and from *geostor. arkansas.gov* (accessed February 2006). For additional information about the topic, see *opengis.org* and *otn.oracle.com/ products/spatial*. Oracle MapViewer 10g Preview can be downloaded for free at *otn.oracle.com/software/htdocs/devlic/html?/ software/products/spatial/htdocs/winsoft.html*.

## Questions for Minicase 2

1. Why is a data warehouse needed in this system?
2. List the major benefits to Arkansas and to private-sector users.
3. Check Oracle's MapViewer and comment about its data visualization capabilities.
4. The State of Arkansas was the first to have such a system, so it has a competitive edge in attracting new business to the state. Explain why. Can it be sustained when other states come to use a similar system in the future?
5. Can any of the GIS data be combined with GPS data? For what uses?

# References

Anthes, G., "Eyes Everywhere: Business Activity Monitoring Offers a Constant Watch on Business Processes" *Computerworld,* November 2003, *computerworld.com/printthis/2003/0,4814,86895,00.html* (accessed March 2006).

Atre, S., "The Top 10 Critical Challenges for BI Success," *Computer World* (special advertising supplement) June 30, 2003.

Baer, T., "Analyzing Data at Real Time," *Application Development Trends,* April 2002.

Barke, J., "Traffic Taming," *Technology Review,* October 3, 2005.

Bates, J., "Business in Real Time—Realizing the Vision, *DM Review,* May 2003.

Baum, D., "The Face of Intelligence," *ORACLE Magazine,* March–April 2006.

Bonde, A., and M. Kuckuk, "Real-World Business Intelligence: The Implementation Perspective," *DM Review,* April 2004.

Briody, D., "Toyota's Business Intelligence: Oh! What a Feeling!" *CIO Insight,* white paper from Hyperion Solutions Corporation, October 2005.

Buss, D., "Danskin Launches Virtual Showroom for Retail Clients," *Stores,* March 2003.

Calderon, T. G., et. al., "How Large Corporations Use Data Mining to Create Value," *Management Accounting Quarterly,* Winter 2003.

Callaghan. D., "BI Vendors Stress Need for Integration," *eWeek,* February 7, 2005.

CIO Insight, "The 2003 CIO Insight Business Intelligence Research Study: Are Your BI Systems Making You Smarter?" *CIO Insight,* No. 26, May 23, 2003.

Coffee, P., "'Active' Warehousing," *eWeek,* June 23, 2003.

Comcowich, W. J., "Integrated Internet Monitoring Solutions for CI," *ScipOnline,* October 22, 2002, *imakenews.com/scip2/e_ article000101312.cfm* (accessed February 2006).

Davenport, T. H., "Competing on Analytics," *Harvard Business Review,* January 2006.

Devlin, B., "Solving the Data Warehouse Puzzle," *DB2 Magazine,* May 14, 2003.

Dragoon, A., "Putting IT on the Map," *CIO,* May 15, 2003.

Dunham, M., *Data Mining: Introductory and Advanced Topics.* Upper Saddle River, NJ: Prentice Hall, 2003.

Eckerson, W., *Performance Dashboards.* Hoboken, NJ: Wiley, 2006.

Eckerson, W., *Smart Companies in the 21 Century.* Seattle, WA: Data Warehousing Institute, 2003.

Essaypage, "Ben & Jerry's Homemade Inc./Information Systems," special report from *essaypage.com* (accessed May 14, 2006).

Etzioni, O., "The WWW: Quagmire or Gold Mine," *Communications of the ACM,* November 1996.

Fagg, S., "Continuity for the People," *Risk Management Magazine,* March 2006.

*Fiber Optics Weekly Update,* "Telstra Uses NetEx Gear," January 13, 2006.

Fogarty, K., "Primer: Predictive Analytics," *Baseline,* December 1, 2004.

Franklin, D., "Any Way You Slice It," *Credit Union Management,* November 2002.

Gage, D., "When Competitors Attack," *Baseline,* December 14, 2005, *baselinemag.com/article2/0,1397,1901400,00.asp* (accessed March 2006).

Gartner Inc., *Using Business Intelligence to Gain a Competitive Edge*, special report. Stamford, CT: Gartner, Inc., *garnter.com*, 2004.

Gessner, G. H., and L. Volonino, "Quick Response Improves Returns on Business Intelligence Investments," *Information Systems Management Journal*, Summer 2005.

Gonzales, M. L., "The New GIS Landscape," *Intelligent Enterprise*, February 1, 2003.

Hallett, P., "Web-Based Visualization," *DM Review*, June 2001.

Ho, G. T. S., H. C. W. Lau, W. H. Ip, and A. Ning, "An Intelligent Information Infrastructure to Support the Streamlining of Integrated Logistics Workflow," *Expert Systems*, July 2004.

Hormozi, A. M., and S. Giles, "Data Mining: A Competitive Weapon for Banking and Retail Industries," *Information Systems Management*, Spring 2004.

Hyperion, "A Hyperion Customer Success Story: Toyota Motor Sales," 2006, *hyperion.com/customers/stories/us_toyota_motor_sales.pdf* (accessed October 2006).

IBM, "Data Mining—An IBM Overview," *IBM.com*, 2006, *direct.boulder.ibm.com/bi/info/overview.html* (accessed April 2006).

Imhoff, C., and R. Pettit, "The Critical Shift to Flexible Business Intelligence," white paper, Intelligent Solutions, Inc., 2004.

Inmon, W. H., *Building Data Warehouses*, 4th ed. New York: Wiley, 2005.

Jonietz, E., "Traffic Avoidance," *Technology Review*, December 2005–January 2006.

Kaplan, R., and D. Norton, *The Balanced Scorecard*. Boston, MA: Harvard University Press, 1996.

Kaplan, R., and D. Norton, *Strategy Maps: Converting Intangible Assets into Tangible Outcomes*. Boston, MA: Harvard Business School Press, 2004.

Keating, W., "Fast Tracking," *Optimize*, March 2003, *optimizemag.com/article/showArticle.jhtml?articledId=17700874* (accessed March 2006).

Kellner, M., "Is This the Year for Wireless Gear?" *GCN*, January 27, 2003, *gcn.com/print/22_2/20950-1.html* (accessed October 2006).

Lal, V., *The Future of Business Intelligence*, white paper. Santa Clara, CA: Hyperion Solutions Corp., 2005.

Lam, W., "Ensuring Business Continuity," *IT Pro*, June 2002.

Langnau, L., "Business Intelligence and Ethics: Can They Work Together? *Controls & Systems* Editorial—Industry Overview," November 2003, *findarticles.com/p/articles/mi_hb4374/is_200311/ai_n15263344* (accessed February 2006).

Ledman, T., "TCF Bank," *What Works: Best Practices in Business Intelligence and Data Warehousing*, Vol. 15. Chatsworth, CA: Data Warehousing Institute, June 2003, p. 10.

Levinson, M., "Jackpot! Harrah's Entertainment," *CIO Magazine*, February 1, 2001.

Linoff, G. S., and J. A. Berry, *Mining the Web: Transforming Customer Data*. New York: Wiley, 2002.

Loschin, D., *Business Intelligence: The Savvy Manager's Guide*. San Francisco, CA: Morgan Kaufmann, 2003.

Loveman, G., "Diamonds in the Data," *Harvard Business Review*, May 2003.

Luftman, J. N., et al., *Managing the Information Technology Resources*. Upper Saddle River, NJ: Pearson Education, 2004.

McConnell, M., "Information Assurance in the Twenty-first Century," *Supplement to Computer*, February 2002.

McKie, S., "The Big BAM." *Intelligent Enterprise*, July 18, 2003, *intelligententerprise.com//030718/612feat3_1.jhtml* (accessed March 2006).

McKinley, E., "We're Not Asking, We Know You Want Fries with that Predictive Technology," *Stores*, November 2004.

McKnight, W., "Building Business Intelligence: Will Business Intelligence Replace the Business Analyst?" *DMReview*, February 2005, *dmreview.com/article_sub.cfm?articleId=1018117* (accessed March 2006).

MicroStrategy, "Applications of Industrial-Strength Business Intelligence," special report, *Microstrategy.com*, 2005.

*Microstrategy.com*, "Success Story: Lexmark," 2006, *microstrategy.com/Customers/Successes/lexmark.asp?* (accessed May 2006).

Miller, T. W., *Data and Text Mining*. Upper Saddle River NJ: Prentice Hall, 2005.

Moss, L. T., and S. Atre, *Business Intelligence Roadmap*. Indianapolis, IN: Addison-Wesley Professional, 2003.

NEC, "Revision of NEC Corporation's Financial Forecast for Fiscal Year Ended March 31, 2006," *nec.co.jp/press/en/0604/2101.html* (accessed October 2006).

Patel, J., "Seven Simple Rules for Successful Real-Time Business Intelligence," *DM Review*, May 2005.

Peterson, T., "Getting Real About Real Time," *ComputerWorld*, April 21, 2003.

Raden, N., "Real Time: Get Real, Part I," *Intelligent Enterprise*, June 17, 2003.

Raisinghani, M., *Business Intelligence in the Digital Economy*. Hershey PA: The Idea Group, 2004.

Ranadive, V., *The Power of Prediction*. New York: McGraw Hill, 2006.

Rosencrance, L., "Railroads Hot for Satellite Monitoring," *Computer World*, April, 2000.

Saarenvirta, G., "The Untapped Value of GIS," *Business Intelligence Journal*, Winter 2004.

Sandia National Laboratories, "Intelligent Agents Challenge Computer Intruders," 2002, *sandia.gov/media/NewsRel/NR2000/agent.htm* (accessed October 2006).

Schlosser, J., "Looking for Intelligence in Ice Cream," *Fortune*, March 17, 2003.

Schwartz, M., "Louisiana Bottles Food Stamp Fraud," *Business Intelligence Journal*, Fall 2005.

Tan, P. N., et al., *Introduction to Data Mining*, 2005.

Telecomworldwire, "NSF to Introduce Virtual Reality Tour of Monticello," April 7, 2003, *findarticles.com/p/articles/mi_m1272/is_2696_131/ai_101497538* (accessed June 2006).

Thompson, O., "Business Intelligence Success, Lessons Learned," *Technology Evaluation.com*, October 9, 2004.

Thompson, O., and P. J. Jakovljeric, "Business Intelligence Status Report" (7-part series), *TechnologyEvaluation.com*, July 16, 2005.

Ursery, S., "GIS More Prevalent in Big Cities," *The American City and County*, February 2004.

*USA Today*, "Virtual Reality Will Change Your Reality, Your Life," May 2003, *findarticles.com/p/articles/mi_m1272/is_2696_131/ai_101497538* (accessed June 2006).

Valentine, L., "Lexmark CIO: Supporting a Changing Business Environment," *CIO Today*, July 21, 2004, *cio-today.com/story.xhtml?story_id=25966* (accessed May 2006).

Wells, J. T., "Occupational Fraud: The Audit as a Deterrent," *Journal of Accountancy*, April 2002.

White, C., "Now Is the Right Time for Real Time BI," *DM Review*, September 2004.

Whiting, R., "Predict the Future—or Try Anyway," *InformationWeek*, May 29, 2006.

Wiseth, K., "The Expanding Role of Location," *Oracle Magazine*, January–February 2004, *oracle.com/technology/oramag/oracle/04-jan/014geostore_feature.html* (accessed February 2006).

Zaman, M., "Predictive Analytics; the Future of Business Intelligence," *Technology Evaluation Centers*, November 8, 2005.

Zdanowicz, J. S., "Detecting Money Laundering and Terrorist Financing via Data Mining," *Communications of the ACM*, May 2004.

Ziama, A., and J. Kasher, *Data Mining Primer for the Data Warehousing Professional*. Dayton, OH: Teradata (division of NCR), 2004.

## Part V | Managerial and Decision Support Systems

10. Knowledge Management
11. Business Intelligence and Corporate Performance Management
▶ 12. Management Decision Support and Intelligent Systems

Chapter

# 12

# Management Decision Support and Intelligent Systems

New Balance Makes Sure That Shoes Fit

**12.1** Managers and Decision Making

**12.2** Decision Support Systems: For Individuals, Groups, and the Enterprise

**12.3** Intelligent Support Systems: The Basics

**12.4** Expert Systems

**12.5** Other Intelligent Systems

**12.6** Automated Decision Support (ADS)

**12.7** Managerial Issues

Minicases:

1. *Netherlands Railway*
2. *Singapore and Malaysia Airlines*

## Learning Objectives

After studying this chapter, you will be able to:

❶ Describe the concepts of managerial decision making and computerized support for decision making.

❷ Justify the role of modeling in decision making.

❸ Describe decision support systems (DSSs) and their benefits, and describe the DSS structure.

❹ Describe the support to group (including virtual) decision making.

❺ Describe organizational DSS and executive support systems, and analyze their role in management support.

❻ Describe artificial intelligence (AI) and list its benefits and characteristics.

❼ List the major commercial AI technologies.

❽ Define an expert system and its components, and describe its benefits and limitations.

❾ Describe natural language processing and compare it to speech understanding.

❿ Describe artificial neural networks (ANNs), their characteristics, and major applications; compare them to fuzzy logic and describe their role in hybrid intelligent systems.

⓫ Describe automated decision support, its advantages, and areas of application.

⓬ Describe special decision support applications including the support of frontline employees.

## Integrating *IT*

 **ACC**
 **FIN**
 **MKT**
 **POM**
 **HRM**
 **IS**
 **SVC**

# NEW BALANCE MAKES SURE THAT SHOES FIT

## The Problem

New Balance (*newbalance.com*) is a $1.5 billion privately held athletic shoe company. As recently as 2001, New Balance executives did not have the tools to deliver accurate forecasts for the number of shoes it would sell through its various outlets.

The company's forecasting process worked like this: The person in charge of the forecasting department was supposed to collect forecast sheets from about half of the company's 160 sales representatives, compile them, and create overall predictions of what shoes the company's factories should turn out and when. However, she was lucky to get 20 forecasts back each month.

The problem for the sales representatives was that filling out the sheets consumed a lot of time—as much as a day for the forecasts for larger accounts. Reps had to pore through reams of printouts to plug answers into the company's spreadsheet. For salespeople paid on commission, the process took money out of their wallets, and they were unhappy.

The problems multiplied for the forecasters. The format of the company's spreadsheet was not properly designed and secured. That meant, first of all, that reps would delete columns, type in the wrong style names, and move information around as they saw fit. It took at least a day for New Balance forecasters to validate the data from each sales rep's forecast, put the data into the correct form, and collate and analyze it.

**POM**

In reality, New Balance forecasters produced their forecasts without much input of sales reps. This seat-of-the-pants approach caused sudden spikes in orders to factories for some products and backlogs of others. There would be deep valleys of production, when inventory that had piled up was sold off. The worst problem was that New Balance could not get orders to customers on time.

**MKT**

Also, the company used these forecasts to push sales quotas down from headquarters. The quota typically was the prior year's number plus some estimate of growth for the coming year. Because the quotas had little basis in reality, the sales force paid little attention to them.

## The Solution

New Balance turned to a decision support system (DSS) to give it the ability to manage its complex production plan-

ning by account, region, salesperson, and other criteria. The DSS helped New Balance forecasters take into account such predictors of demand as general economic indicators, current orders, and historic sales data. The DSS produces forecast numbers for each shoe style. These forecasts help the company's manufacturing managers to plan for production capacity using the DSS tool, namely making capacity and scheduling decisions. The forecasts are done with special mathematical and statistical models.

Also, with the new DSS, information about customers can be gathered for each sales rep from corporate databases. The reps download that information from a secure Web site as each month ends. Using the data and consulting with business customers, each sales rep updates the forecast of each customer's orders, not just for the rest of the current year, but for the following year as well. Also, the company can assign reps to the accounts they do best.

Then, instead of using a malleable spreadsheet, sales reps enter their revisions in a locked-down template created by corporate forecasters. This template makes it easier and quicker for sales reps to fill out required information, and it is easy for forecasters to "roll up" all the sales reps' forecasts. In four hours, corporate forecasters can send out consolidated reports and breakouts by account and product.

## The Results

The DSS has produced several beneficial results for New Balance. For the first time, the company can tell which representatives can best predict orders and which representatives can best resolve problems with key business customers. In addition, the DSS has added accountability to everyone's role.

Second, New Balance now has a much more accurate picture each month of what its production should be. Because New Balance has a six-month lead time for delivery from its factories and overseas suppliers, rapid information and more accurate forecasts enable the company to react more quickly to retailers' needs. Since the implementation of the DSS, the number of shoes left in inventory when the company discontinues a style has dropped on average by 8 percent.

Third, using the DSS, the company discovered that its best-selling shoe sales had shifted from the $120-to-$160 basketball shoes to less-expensive, multipurpose shoes that cost between $60 and $90 per pair. So, the company produced styles in this price range in all widths.

Fourth, company executives now routinely call individual sales reps whose top business customers have fallen behind on purchases. The source of the executives' information is the "Top Accounts" report, an update distributed at noon every Monday that gives company executives a detailed look at sales figures for the past, present, and forecasted future. Executives have a wealth of information: a report for each style of shoe in New Balance's lineup; the to-date sales for the year and the month for each major retailer that New Balance serves; the sales of that shoe (or its predecessor) for the same period last year at that retailer; the orders for that retailer that have not been filled by New Balance's factory or warehouse; and what the sales rep had forecast for the current month. The sales force has access to the same report, meaning that everyone is on the same page and there are far fewer surprises.

The bottom line? Worldwide sales have more than doubled from $560 million in 1997 to $1.3 billion in 2002. New Balance now stands second only to Nike in the sale of running shoes. For all types of athletic shoes, New Balance ranks third, behind Nike and Reebok.

*Sources:* Compiled from Barrett (2003) and Gallagher (2003).

### Lessons Learned from This Case

The opening case illustrates that a solution to complex production and other problems can be enhanced with the use of a decision support system (DSS). In fact, the DSS software supported several important decisions in production/operations, marketing, and HRM. Furthermore, the case illustrates the concepts of modeling and quantitative analysis. Finally, the Web is playing an increasing role in facilitating the use of such systems.

This chapter describes direct computerized and Web support to *managerial decision makers*. This is in contrast with Chapter 11, where the support was primarily indirect (e.g., find information trends, associations, etc.). We begin by reviewing the manager's job and the nature of today's decisions, which help explain why computerized support is needed. Then we present the concepts and methodology of the computerized decision support system for supporting individuals, groups, and whole organizations. Next, we introduce several types of intelligent systems and their role in decision support. After that, we introduce the new topic of automated decision making. Finally, we describe the topic of decision support in the Web environment.

## 12.1 Managers and Decision Making

Decisions are being made by all of us, every day. However, most major organizational decisions are made by managers. We begin with a brief description of the manager's job, of which making decisions is a major activity.

THE MANAGER'S JOB

*Management* is a process by which organizational goals are achieved through the use of resources (people, money, energy, materials, space, time). These resources are considered to be *inputs,* and the attainment of the goals is viewed as the *output* of the process. Managers oversee this process in an attempt to optimize it.

To understand how computers support managers, it is necessary first to describe what managers do. They do many things, depending on their position in the organization, the type and size of the organization, organizational policies and culture, and the personalities of the managers themselves. Mintzberg (1973) divided the manager's roles into three categories: *interpersonal* (figurehead, leader, liaison), *informational* (monitor, disseminator, spokesperson), and *decisional* (entrepreneur, problem solver, resource allocator, and negotiator). Mintzberg and

Westley (2001) also analyzed the role of decision makers in the information age. Finally, Huber (2003) describes the role of top management in today's complex, turbulent environment.

Early information systems mainly supported informational roles. In recent years, however, information systems have grown to support all three roles. In this chapter, we are mainly interested in the support that IT can provide to *decisional* roles. We divide the manager's work, as it relates to decisional roles, into two phases. Phase I is the identification of problems and/or opportunities. Phase II is the decision of what to do about them. Online File W12.1 provides a flowchart of this process and the flow of information in it.

**Decision Making and Problem Solving.** A *decision* refers to a choice made between two or more alternatives. Decisions are diverse in nature and are made continuously by both individuals and groups. The purposes of decision making in organizations can be classified into two broad categories: *problem solving* and *opportunity exploiting*. In either case, managers must make decisions.

The ability to make crisp decisions was rated first in importance in a study conducted by the Harbridge House in Boston, Massachusetts. About 6,500 managers in more than 100 companies, including many large, blue-chip corporations, were asked how important it was that managers employ certain management practices. They also were asked how well, in their estimation, managers performed these practices. From a statistical distillation of these answers, Harbridge ranked "making clear-cut decisions when needed" as the *most important* of 10 management practices. Ranked second in importance was "getting to the heart of the problems rather than dealing with less important issues." Most of the remaining eight management practices were related directly or indirectly to decision making. The researchers also found that only 10 percent of the managers thought management performed "very well" on any given practice, mainly due to the difficult decision-making environment. It seems that the trial-and-error method, which might have been a practical approach to decision making in the past, is too expensive or ineffective today in many instances.

Therefore, managers must learn how to use the new tools and techniques that can help them make better decisions (see Huber, 2003). Many such techniques use a quantitative analysis (see the opening case) approach, and they are supported by computers. Several of the computerized decision aids are described in this chapter.

**COMPUTERIZED DECISION AIDS**

The discussion on computerized decision aids here deals with four basic questions: (1) Why do managers need the support of information technology in making decisions? (2) Can the manager's job be fully automated? (3) What IT aids are available to support managers? (4) How are the information needs of managers determined? We answer the first three here; for answers to the fourth, see Online File W12.2. For further discussion, see Huber (2003).

**Why Managers Need the Support of Information Technology.** It is very difficult to make good decisions without valid and relevant information. Information is needed for each phase and activity in the decision-making process.

Making decisions while processing information manually is growing increasingly difficult due to the following trends:

- The number of alternatives to be considered is ever increasing, due to innovations in technology, improved communication, the development of global markets, and the use of the Internet and e-business. A key to good decision making is to explore and compare many relevant alternatives. The more alternatives there are, the more computer-assisted search and comparisons are needed. Computers can sometimes be used to generate alternative solutions.

- Many decisions must be made under time pressure. Even in real time, frequently it is not possible to manually process the needed information fast enough to be effective.

- Due to increased fluctuations and uncertainty in the decision environment, it is frequently necessary to conduct a sophisticated analysis to make a good decision. Such analysis usually requires the use of mathematical modeling. Processing models manually can take a very long time.

- It is often necessary to rapidly access remote information, consult with experts, or have a group decision-making session, all without large expenses. Decision makers can be in different locations and so is the information. Bringing them all together quickly and inexpensively may be a difficult task.

- Decision making frequently requires an organization to conduct a forecast of prices, market share, and so on. Reliable forecasting requires analytical and statistical tools.

- Making decisions requires data. The amount of data, especially Internet click-stream data, is enormous, and growing rapidly. Data are located in multiple sources and need to be integrated from those sources.

These trends cause difficulties in making decisions, but a computerized analysis can be of enormous help. For example, a DSS can examine numerous alternatives very quickly, can support forecasting, can provide a systematic risk analysis, can be integrated with communication systems and databases, and can be used to support group work. And all this can be done with relatively low cost. *How* all this is accomplished will be shown later.

According to Bonabeau (2003), intuition plays an important role in decision making, but it can be dangerously unreliable. Therefore, one should use analytical tools such as those presented in this chapter and in Chapter 11.

***Complexity of Decisions.*** Decisions range from simple to very complex. Complex decisions are composed of a sequence of interrelated subdecisions. As an example, see the decision process pursued by a pharmaceutical company, Bayer Corp., regarding developing a new drug, as shown by Stonebraker (2002).

**Can the Manager's Job Be Fully Automated?** The generic decision-making process involves specific tasks (such as forecasting consequences and evaluating alternatives). This process can be fairly lengthy, which is bothersome for a busy manager. Automation of certain tasks can save time, increase consistency, and enable better decisions to be made. Thus, the more tasks we can automate in the process, the better. A logical question that follows is this: Is it possible to completely automate the manager's job?

In general, it has been found that the job of middle managers is the most likely job to be automated (Davenport, 2006 and Section 12.6). Mid-level managers make fairly routine decisions, and these can be fully automated. Managers at lower levels do not spend much time on decision making. Instead, they supervise, train, and motivate nonmanagers. Some of their routine decisions, such as scheduling, can be automated; other decisions that involve behavioral aspects cannot. But, even if we completely automate their decisional role, we cannot automate their jobs. *Note:* The Web also provides an opportunity to automate certain tasks done by *frontline* employees. (This topic is discussed in Section 12.6.) The job of top managers is the least routine and therefore the most difficult to automate. For further discussion, see Huber (2003).

**What Information Technologies Are Available to Support Managers?** In addition to discovery, communication, and collaboration tools that provide *indirect support* to decision making, several other information technologies have been successfully used to support managers. The Web can facilitate them all. Collectively, they are referred to as **management support systems (MSSs)** (see Turban et al., 2007). The first of these technologies are *decision support systems,* which have been in use since the mid-1970s. They provide support primarily to analytical, quantitative types of decisions. Second, *executive (enterprise) support systems* represent a technology developed initially in the mid-1980s, mainly to support the informational roles of executives. This technology is the predecessor of BI and BA, topics covered in Chapter 11. A third technology, *group decision support systems,* supports managers and staff working in groups. A fourth technology is *intelligent systems.* These four technologies and their variants can be used independently, or they can be combined, each providing a different capability. They are frequently related to data warehousing. Also, attempts to automate the decision-making process resulted in the ADS approach.

A simplified presentation of such support is shown in Figure 12.1. As Figure 12.1 shows, managers need to find, filter, and interpret information to identify potential problems or opportunities and then decide what to do about them. The figure shows the support of the various MSS tools (in yellow circles) as well as the role of a data warehouse, which was described in Chapter 11.

Several other technologies, either by themselves or when integrated with other management support technologies, can be used to support managers. One example is the **personal information manager (PIM).** A set of tools labeled PIM is intended to help managers be more organized. A PIM can play an extremely important role in supporting several managerial tasks. Lately, the use of mobile PDA tools, such as

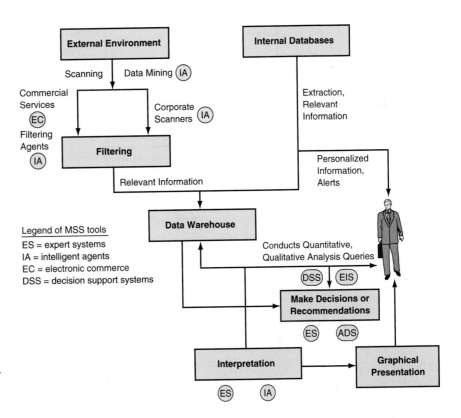

**Figure 12.1** Computerized support for decision making.

personal Palm computers, is greatly facilitating the work of managers. Several other analytical tools are being used. For example, Bonabeau (2003) describes them in complex decision situations.

**THE PROCESS OF COMPUTER-BASED DECISION MAKING**

When making a decision, either organizational or personal, the decision maker goes through a fairly systematic process. Simon (1977) described the process as composed of three major phases: *intelligence, design,* and *choice.* A fourth phase, *implementation,* was added later. Simon claimed that the process is general enough so that it can be supported by *decision aids* and modeling. A conceptual presentation of the four-stage modeling process is shown in Figure 12.2, which illustrates what tasks are included in each phase. Note that there is a continuous flow of information from intelligence to design to choice (bold lines), but at any phase there may be a return to a previous phase (broken lines).

The decision-making process starts with the *intelligence phase,* in which managers examine a situation and identify and define the problem. In the *design phase,* decision makers construct a model that simplifies the problem (opportunity). This is done by making assumptions that simplify reality and by expressing the relationships among all variables. The model is then validated, and decision makers set criteria for the evaluation of alternative potential solutions that are identified. The process is repeated for each subdecision in complex situations. The output of each subdecision is an input for the main decision. The *choice phase* involves selecting a solution, which is tested

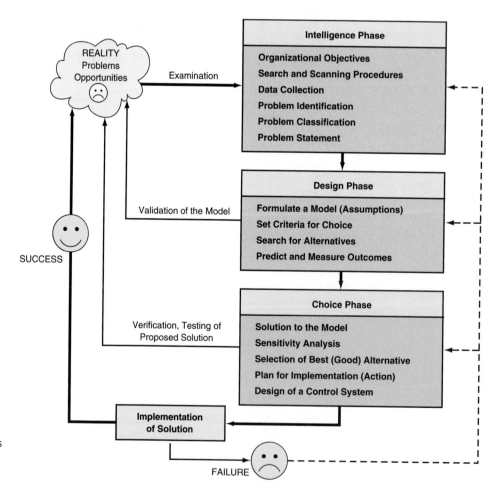

**Figure 12.2** The process and phases in decision making/modeling.

"on paper." Once this proposed solution seems to be feasible, we are ready for the last phase—*implementation.* Successful implementation results in resolving the original problem or opportunity. Failure leads to a return to the previous phases. A computer-based decision support attempts to automate several tasks in this process, in which *modeling* is the core.

**Modeling and Models.** A **model** (in *decision making*) is a *simplified representation,* or abstraction of reality. It is usually simplified because reality is too complex to copy exactly, and because much of its complexity is actually irrelevant to a specific problem. With modeling, one can perform virtual experiments and an analysis on a model of reality, rather than on reality itself. The benefits of modeling in decision making are:

- The cost of virtual experimentation is much lower than the cost of experimentation conducted with a real system.
- Models allow for the simulated compression of time. Years of operation can be simulated in seconds of computer time.
- Manipulating the model (by changing variables) is much easier than manipulating the real system. Experimentation is therefore easier to conduct, and it does not interfere with the daily operation of the organization.
- The cost of making mistakes during a real trial-and-error experiment is much lower than when models are used in virtual experimentation.
- Today's environment holds considerable uncertainty. Modeling allows a manager to better deal with the uncertainty by introducing many "what-ifs" and calculating the risks involved in specific actions.
- Mathematical models allow the analysis and comparison of a very large, sometimes near-infinite number of possible alternative solutions. With today's advanced technology and communications, managers frequently have a large number of alternatives from which to choose.
- Models enhance and reinforce learning, and support training.

Representation by models can be done at various degrees of abstraction. Models are thus classified into four groups according to their degree of abstraction: *iconic, analog, mathematical,* and *mental.* Brief descriptions are presented in Online File W12.3.

**A FRAMEWORK FOR COMPUTERIZED DECISION ANALYSIS**

Gorry and Scott-Morton (1971) proposed a framework for decision support, based on the combined work of Simon (1977) and Anthony (1965). The first half of the framework is based on Simon's idea that decision-making processes fall along a continuum that ranges from highly structured (sometimes referred to as *programmed*) to highly unstructured *(nonprogrammed)* decisions. *Structured* processes refer to routine and repetitive problems for which standard solutions exist. *Unstructured* processes are "fuzzy," complex problems for which there are no cut-and-dried solutions.

In a structured problem, the intelligence, design, and choice are all structured, and the procedures for obtaining the best solution are known. Whether the solution means finding an appropriate inventory level or deciding on an optimal investment strategy, the solution's criteria are clearly defined. They are frequently cost minimization or profit maximization.

In an unstructured problem, *none* of the three phases is structured, and human intuition is frequently the basis for decision making. Typical unstructured problems include planning new services to be offered, hiring an executive, predicting markets (see Berg and Rietz, 2003), or choosing a set of research and development projects for next year.

*Semistructured* problems, in which only some of the phases are structured, require a combination of standard solution procedures and individual judgment. Examples of semistructured problems include trading bonds, setting marketing budgets for consumer products, and performing capital acquisition analysis. Here, a DSS is most suitable. It can improve the quality of the information on which the decision is based (and consequently the quality of the decision) by providing not only a single solution but also a range of *what-if* scenarios.

The second half of the decision support framework is based upon Anthony's taxonomy (1965). It defines three broad categories that encompass managerial activities: (1) *strategic planning*—the long-range goals and policies for resource allocation; (2) *management control*—the acquisition and efficient utilization of resources in the accomplishment of organizational goals; and (3) *operational control*—the efficient and effective execution of specific tasks. Anthony's and Simon's taxonomies can be combined in a nine-cell decision support framework (see Online File W12.4).

**Computer Support for Structured Decisions.** Structured and some semistructured decisions, especially of the operational and managerial control type, have been supported by computers since the 1950s. Decisions of this type are made in all functional areas, especially in finance, marketing, and operations management.

Problems that are encountered fairly often have a high level of structure. It is therefore possible to abstract, analyze, and classify them into standard classes. For example, a "make-or-buy" decision belongs to this category. Other examples are capital budgeting (e.g., replacement of equipment), allocation of resources, distribution of merchandise, and some inventory control decisions. For each standard class, a prescribed solution was developed through the use of mathematical formulas. This approach is called *management science* or *operations research,* and it is also executed with the aid of computers.

*Management Science.* The *management science* approach takes the view that managers can follow a fairly systematic process for solving problems. Therefore, it is possible to use a scientific approach to managerial decision making. Management science frequently attempts to find the best possible solution, an approach known as **optimization.**

## 12.2 Decision Support Systems: For Individuals, Groups, and the Enterprise

**DSS CONCEPTS**

Broadly defined, a **decision support system (DSS)** is a computer-based information system that combines models and data in an attempt to solve semistructured and some unstructured problems with intensive user involvement. But the term decision support system (DSS), like the terms MIS and MSS, means different things to different people. DSSs can be viewed as an *approach* or a *philosophy* rather than a precise methodology. However, a DSS does have certain recognized characteristics, which we will present later. First, let us look at a classical case of a successfully implemented DSS, which though it occurred long ago is a typical scenario, as shown in *IT at Work 12.1.*

The case demonstrates some of the major characteristics of a DSS. The risk analysis performed first was based on the decision maker's initial definition of the situation, using a management science approach. Then, the executive vice president,

# IT at Work 12.1                                                    $

## Using a DSS to Determine Risk                                    FIN

An oil and minerals corporation in Houston, Texas, was evaluating a proposed joint venture with a petrochemicals company to develop a chemical plant. Houston's executive vice president responsible for the decision wanted analysis of the risks involved in areas of supplies, demand, and prices. Bob Sampson, manager of planning and administration, and his staff built a DSS in a few days by means of a specialized planning language. The results strongly suggested that the project should be accepted.

Then came the real test. Although the executive vice president accepted the validity and value of the results, he was worried about the potential downside risk of the project, the chance of a catastrophic outcome. Sampson explains that the executive vice president said something like this: "I realize the amount of work you have already

done, and I am 99 percent confident of it. But I would like to see this in a different light. I know we are short of time and we have to get back to our partners with our yes or no decision."

Sampson replied that the executive could have the risk analysis he needed in less than one hour. As Sampson explained, "Within 20 minutes, there in the executive boardroom, we were reviewing the results of his what-if questions. Those results led to the eventual dismissal of the project, which we otherwise would probably have accepted."

*Source:* Information provided to author by Comshare Corporation (now a subsidiary of Geac Computer Corp., a Goldengate Capital Company).

*For Further Exploration:* What were the benefits of the DSS? Why was the initial decision reversed?

---

using his experience, judgment, and intuition, felt that the model should be modified. The initial model, although mathematically correct, was incomplete. With a regular simulation system, a modification of the computer program would have taken a long time, but the DSS provided a very quick analysis. Furthermore, the DSS was flexible and responsive enough to allow managerial intuition and judgment to be incorporated into the analysis.

Many companies are turning to DSSs to improve decision making (Davenport, 2006). Reasons cited by managers for the increasing use of DSSs include the following: New and accurate information was needed; information was needed fast; and tracking the company's numerous business operations was increasingly difficult. Or, the company was operating in an unstable economy; it faced increasing foreign and domestic competition; the company's existing computer system did not properly support the objectives of increasing efficiency, profitability, and entry into profitable markets. Other reasons include: the IS department was unable to address the diversity of the company's needs or management's ad-hoc inquiries, and business analysis functions were not inherent within the existing systems. For a brief history of DSS, see Power (2002).

In many organizations that have adopted a DSS, the conventional information systems, which were built for the purpose of supporting transaction processing, were *not sufficient* to support several of the company's critical response activities, described in Chapter 1, especially those that require fast and/or complex decision making. A DSS, on the other hand, can do just that. (See Turban et al., 2007.)

Another reason for the development of DSS is the *end-user computing movement.* With the exception of large-scale DSSs, end users can build systems themselves, using DSS development tools such as Excel.

**CHARACTERISTICS AND CAPABILITIES OF DSSs**

Because there is no consensus on exactly what constitutes a DSS, there obviously is no agreement on the characteristics and capabilities of DSSs. However, most DSSs at least have some of the attributes shown in Table 12.1. DSSs also employ mathematical models and have a related, special capability, known as sensitivity analysis.

| TABLE 12.1 | Capabilities of a DSS |
| --- | --- |

A DSS provides support for decision makers at all management levels, whether individuals or groups, mainly in semistructured and unstructured situations, by bringing together human judgment and objective information.

A DSS supports several interdependent and/or sequential decisions.

A DSS supports all phases of the decision-making process—intelligence, design, choice, and implementation—as well as a variety of decision-making processes and styles.

A DSS is adaptable by the user over time to deal with changing conditions.

A DSS is easy to construct and use in many cases.

A DSS promotes learning, which leads to new demands and refinement of the current application, which leads to additional learning, and so forth.

A DSS usually utilizes quantitative models (standard and/or custom made).

Advanced DSSs are equipped with a knowledge management component that allows the efficient and effective solution of very complex problems.

A DSS can be disseminated for use via the Web.

A DSS allows the easy execution of *sensitivity analyses.*

**Sensitivity Analysis: "What-If" and Goal Seeking. Sensitivity analysis** is the study of the impact that changes in one or more parts of a model have on other parts. Usually, we check the impact that changes in input variables have on result variables.

Sensitivity analysis is extremely valuable in DSSs because it makes the system flexible and adaptable to changing conditions and to the varying requirements of different decision-making situations. It allows users to enter their own data, including the most pessimistic data (worst scenario) and to view how systems will behave under varying circumstances. It provides a better understanding of the model and the problem it purports to describe. It may increase the users' confidence in the model, especially when the model is not so sensitive to changes. A *sensitive model* means that small changes in conditions dictate a different solution. In a *nonsensitive model,* changes in conditions do not significantly change the recommended solution. This means that the chances for a solution to succeed are very high. Two popular types of sensitivity analyses are *what-if* and *goal seeking* (see Online File W12.5).

**STRUCTURE AND COMPONENTS OF DSS**

Every DSS consists of at least data management, model management components, user interface, and end users. A few advanced DSSs also contain a knowledge management component. What does each component (subsystem) consist of?

**Data Management Subsystem.** A DSS data management subsystem is similar to any other data management system. It contains all the data that flow from several sources and that usually are *extracted* prior to their entry into a DSS database or a data warehouse. In some DSSs, there is no separate database, and data are entered into the DSS model as needed (e.g., as soon as they are collected by sensors).

**Model Management Subsystem.** A model management subsystem contains completed models, and the building blocks necessary to develop DSSs applications. This includes standard software with financial, statistical, management science, or other quantitative models. An example is Excel, with its many mathematical and statistical functions. A model management subsystem also contains all the custom models written for the specific DSS. These models provide the system's analytical capabilities. Also included is a **model-based management system (MBMS)** whose role is analogous to that of a DBMS. (See Chapter 3.)

# IT at Work 12.2

## Web-Based Decision Support System Helps a Brewery to Compete

MKT    GLOBAL

Guinness Import Co., a U.S. subsidiary of UK's Guinness Ltd. (*guinness.com*), needed a decision support system for (1) executives, (2) salespeople, and (3) analysts. The company did not want three separate systems. Using InfoAdvisor (from Platinum Technology Inc., now part of Computer Associates, *cai.com*), a client/server DSS was constructed. In the past, if manager Diane Goldman wanted to look at sales trends, it was necessary to ask an analyst to download data from the mainframe and then use a spreadsheet to compute the trend. This took up to a day and was error-prone. Now, when Diane Goldman needs such information she queries the DSS herself and gets an answer in a few minutes. Furthermore, she can quickly analyze the data in different ways. Over 100 salespeople keep track of sales and can do similar analyses, from anywhere, using a remote Internet access.

To expedite the implementation of the system, highly skilled users in each department taught others how to use the DSS. The DSS helped to increase productivity of the employees. This improved productivity enables the company to compete against large companies such as Anheuser-Busch, as well as against microbrewers. The system reduced the salespeople's paperwork load by about one day each month. For 100 salespeople, this means 1,200 extra days a year to sell. Corporate financial and marketing analysts are also using the system to make better decisions. As a result, sales increased by 20 percent every year since the system was installed.

*Sources:* Compiled from *Computerworld* (July 7, 1997); *platinum.com* (2000); and *dmreview.com* (2001).

*For Further Exploration:* What can a DSS do that other computer programs cannot do for this company?

---

The model base may contain standard models (such as financial or management science) and/or customized models as illustrated in *IT at Work 12.2.*

**The User Interface.** The term *user interface* covers all aspects of the communications between a user and the DSS. Some DSS experts feel that the user interface is the most important DSS component because much of the power, flexibility, and ease of use of the DSS are derived from this component. For example, the ease of use of the interface in the Guinness DSS (*IT at Work 12.2*) enables, and encourages, managers and salespeople to use the system. Most interfaces today are Web-based and some are supplemented by voice.

The user interface subsystem may be managed by software called *user interface management system* (UIMS), which is functionally analogous to the DBMS.

**The Users.** The person faced with the problem or decision that the DSS is designed to support is referred to as the *user,* the *manager,* or the *decision maker.*

The user is considered to be a part of the system. Researchers assert that some of the unique contributions of DSSs are derived from the extensive interaction between the computer and the decision makers. A DSS has two broad classes of users: managers, and staff specialists (such as financial analysts, production planners, and market researchers).

**DSS Intermediaries.** When managers utilize a DSS, they may use it via an intermediary person who performs the analysis and reports the results. However, with Web-based systems, the use of DSSs becomes easier. Managers can use the Web-based system by themselves, especially when supported by an intelligent knowledge component.

**Knowledge-Based Subsystems.** Many unstructured and semistructured problems are so complex that they require expertise for their solutions. Such expertise can be provided by a knowledge-based system, such as an expert system. Therefore, the more advanced DSSs are equipped with a component called a *knowledge-based* (or *an intelligent*) *subsystem.* Such a component can provide the required expertise for solving some aspects of the problem, or provide knowledge that can enhance the operation of the other DSS components.

The knowledge component consists of one or more expert (or other intelligent) systems, or it draws expertise from the *organizational knowledge base* (or repository) (see Chapter 10).

A DSS that includes such a component is referred to as an *intelligent DSS,* a *DSS/ES,* or a *knowledge-based DSS* (KBDSS). An example of a KBDSS is in the area of estimation and pricing in construction. It is a complex process that requires the use of models as well as judgmental factors. The KBDSS includes a knowledge management subsystem with 200 rules incorporated with the computational models. Knowledge-based subsystems are the key component in ADSs (Section 12.6).

**HOW A DSS WORKS**

The DSS components (see Figure 12.3) are all software, they run on standard hardware, and they can be facilitated by additional software (such as multimedia). Tools like Excel include some of the components and therefore can be used for DSS construction by end users.

The figure also illustrates how the DSS works. As you recall from Chapter 11, the DSS users get their data from the data warehouse, databases, and other data sources. When a user has a problem, it is evaluated by the processes described in Figures 12.1 (page 479) and 12.2 (page 480). A DSS system is then constructed. Data are entered from the sources on the left side and the models from the right side in Figure 12.3. Knowledge can be also tapped from the corporate knowledge base. As more problems are solved, more knowledge is accumulated in the organizational knowledge base.

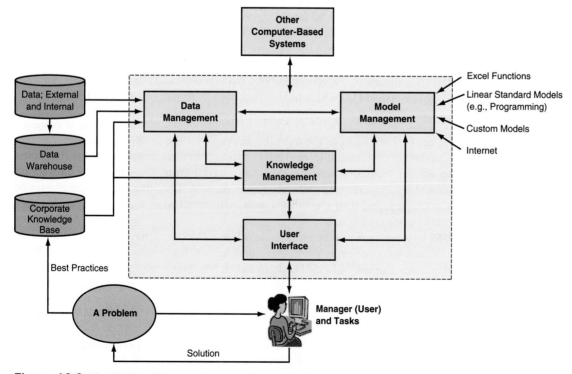

**Figure 12.3** The DSS and its computing environment. Conceptual model of a DSS shows the four main software components and their relationships with other systems.

**FIN**

A large number of DSS applications can be found in almost any industry, including both manufacturing and services, as shown in the following examples.

*Example 1: Wells Fargo Targets Customers.* Wells Fargo (*wellsfargo.com*) has become so good at predicting consumer behavior that it practically knows what customers want before they realize it themselves. The bank developed a decision support system (DSS) in-house. The DSS collects data on every transaction—whether it is over the phone, at an ATM, in a bank branch, or online—and combines that data with personal data that the customer provides. The Wells Fargo DSS program then analyzes the data and models the customer's behavior to automatically come up with prospective offerings, like a low-cost second mortgage, just at the right time for the customer. The result: Compared with the industry average of 2.2 products per customer, Wells Fargo sells four (Hovanesian, 2003).

**FIN**

*Example 2: Schwab Targets the Rich.* In 2000, Charles Schwab (*schwab.com*) changed its strategy to target high-net-worth investors. This meant turning itself from a discount brokerage into a full-service investment firm. To avoid the $20-million-per-year cost of hiring analysts, it made a onetime, $20 million investment in a decision support system. Schwab Equity Ratings, an online intelligent DSS, offers recommendations for buying and selling more than 3,000 stocks. It automatically sends e-mail alerts to Schwab customers and to Schwab analysts. Schwab says the system picks stocks as efficiently as its human counterparts. In addition, the system does away with potential employee conflicts of interest. In the wake of Wall Street scandals, the DSS makes some investors feel safer (Edwards, 2003).

**SVC**

**ACC**

*Example 3: Lowering Costs in Health Care.* For Owens & Minor (*owensminor.com*), one of the largest suppliers for the health-care industry, success means driving down the price of thousands of hospital supplies. The company uses its decision support system to help customers hunt for bargains. The DSS lets hospitals track purchases they make with hundreds of competing medical suppliers. The DSS pinpoints lower pricing on similar items, helping customers take advantage of discounts already negotiated. Hospitals keep better tabs on their bills and cut costs an average of 2 to 3 percent. For Owens & Minor, the DSS attracts new customers, and when existing customers find lower prices, they order more (Ante, 2003).

These examples exhibit the diversity of decisions that DSSs can support. Other examples are provided by Fagerholt (2004), Huber (2003), and McKinley (2003), and Minicase 1 at the end of this chapter. In addition, many examples can be found at *sas.com* or *microtrategy.com,* where hundreds of applications (success stories) are listed by industry.

The DSS methodology just described was designed initially to support individual decision makers. However, most important organizational decisions are made by groups, such as an executive committee. Next we see how IT can support such situations.

Over the last four decades, several specialized tools were developed for decision support. One of the most popular tools is *simulation,* which is described in Online File W12.6. Also, it is possible to improve decision support results (such as those generated by spreadsheets) by using visualization.

**Visualization Spreadsheets.** Spreadsheets are the major end-user tools for end-user programming of decision support applications. Excel offers dozens of mathematical, statistical, report generation, query (including *what-if* and *goal-seeking*), and other decision support tools.

Microsoft Excel has been widely adopted as an easy-to-use and powerful tool for free-form data manipulation. Excel has evolved beyond a simple data calculation tool

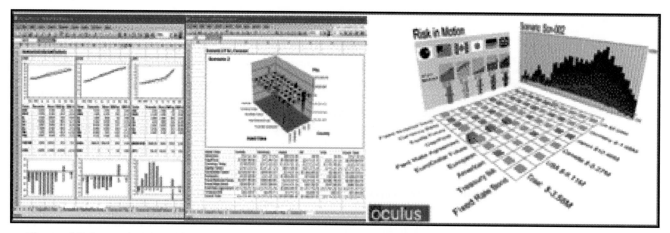

**Figure 12.4** Visual spreadsheet of risk analysis. (*Source:* R. Brath and M. Peters, "Visualizing Spreadsheets: Add Exponential Value to Excel for Monitoring, Analysis and Modeling," *DM Direct Newsletter,* January 6, 2006.)

to the point where it is now used as a sophisticated and flexible tool for collecting, analyzing, and summarizing data from multiple sources. People use Excel, for example, to track travel expenses, devise budgets and forecasts, and create reports. Some users are adept enough to create advanced pivot tables and macros that rival the work of IT programmers. According to Brath and Peters (2006), the power of Excel can be leveraged with visualization in many different ways: enhancing effectiveness, focusing communications, helping make anomalies pop out, facilitating comprehension, and empowering collaboration. Brath and Peters provide the following example:

*Example: Risk Management.* Figure 12.4 shows the power of visualization. The spreadsheets on the left represent two pages out of a risk report with approximately 100 pages of risk scenarios and resultant impacts (center image, generated by standard Excel charts). The same report presented as an animated and interactive visualization (right side of figure) consolidates all 100 pages of the information into a single screen.

Several other examples of visualizing spreadsheets and their benefits are provided by Brath and Peters (2006).

**DECISION SUPPORT/BUSINESS INTELLIGENCE RELATIONSHIP**

In the previous chapter, we covered the topic of BI, which included business analytics, and indeed BI provides extensive support to managers and to decision making. However, the technologies in Chapter 11 provide mostly indirect support to managers. For example, they will provide accurate and timely information, answer queries, illustrate situations graphically, evaluate alternatives, and much more.

In this chapter, we go one step further; we have technologies that are referred to as decision support systems (DSSs). These systems either provide complete solutions to given problems, or help managers solve specific problems.

Let's look at some of the similarities and differences between DSS and BI. First, the architecture is very similar because BI evolved from DSS. However, notice that BI implies the use of a data warehouse while DSS may or may not have such a feature. BI is more appropriate to large organizations (data warehouses are expensive to build and maintain), while DSS can be appropriate to any type of organization.

Second, BI has an executive and strategy orientation, especially in its BPM and dashboard components. DSS has been oriented toward analysts.

Third, most BI systems are constructed with commercially available tools and components that are fitted to the needs of organizations. In building DSSs, the interest may be in constructing solutions to very unstructured problems. This means that more programming (e.g., using tools such as Excel) is used to customize solutions.

Fourth, DSS methodologies and a few tools were developed mostly in the academic world. BI methodologies and tools were developed mostly by software companies (see Zaman, 2005, on how BI was evolved).

Fifth, many of the tools used by BI are also considered DSS tools. For example, data mining and predictive analysis are core tools in both areas.

While some people equate DSS with BI, these systems do not, at the present, seem to be the same. It is interesting to note that some people believe that DSS is a part of BI, being one of its analytical tools. Others think that BI is a special case of DSS that deals mostly with reporting, communication, and collaboration (kind of data-oriented DSS). Another explanation (Watson, 2005) is that BI is a result of a continuous revolution and as such DSS is one of the original BI elements. In this book, we separate DSS from BI.

**GROUP DECISION SUPPORT SYSTEMS**

Decision making is frequently a shared process. For example, meetings among groups of managers from different areas are an essential element for reaching consensus. The group may be involved in making a decision or in a decision-related task, like creating a short list of acceptable alternatives or deciding on criteria for accepting an alternative. When a decision-making group is supported electronically, the support is referred to as *group decision support*. Two types of groups are considered: a same-room group whose members are in one place (e.g., a meeting room), and a virtual group (or team), whose members are in different locations.

A **group decision support system (GDSS)** is an interactive computer-based system that facilitates the solution of semistructured and unstructured problems when made by a group of decision makers by concentrating on the *process* and procedures during meetings. The objective of a GDSS is to support the *process* of arriving at a decision. Important characteristics of a GDSS are shown in Online File W12.7. These characteristics can negate some of the dysfunctions of group processes described in Chapter 4, Table 4.2 (page 144).

The first generation of GDSSs was designed to support face-to-face meetings in what is called a *decision room*.

**SOME APPLICATIONS OF GDSSs**

An increasing number of companies are using GDSSs, especially when virtual groups are involved. One example is the Internal Revenue Service, which used a one-room GDSS to implement its quality-improvement programs based on the participation of a number of its quality teams. The GDSS was helpful in identifying problems, generating and evaluating ideas, and developing and implementing solutions. Another example is the European automobile industry, which used a one-room GDSS to examine the competitive automotive business environment and make ten-year forecasts, needed for strategic planning. Adkins et al. (2002) report on successful application at the U.S. Air Force. A virtual GDSS application is described in *IT at Work 12.3* (page 490). For further discussion of virtual teams and IT support, see Chapter 4 and Powell et al. (2004), and for examples, see Agres et al. (2005).

*GOV*

*MKT*

**ENTERPRISE DECISION SUPPORT SYSTEM**

The term **organizational** (or **institutional**) **decision support system (ODSS)** was first defined by Hackathorn and Keen (1981), who discussed three levels of decision support: individual, group, and organization. They maintained that computer-based systems can be developed to provide decision support for *each* of these levels. They defined an ODSS as one that focuses on an organizational task or activity involving a *sequence* of operations and decision makers, such as developing a divisional marketing plan or doing capital budgeting. Each individual's activities must mesh closely with other people's work. The computer support was primarily seen as a vehicle for improving communication and coordination, in addition to problem solving. Today, such systems are referred to as *enterprisewide DSSs*.

# *IT* at Work 12.3

## *Virtual Meetings at the World Economic Forum*

POM    GLOBAL

The World Economic Forum (WEF, at *weforum.org*) is a consortium of top business, government, academic, and media leaders from virtually every country in the world. WEF's mission is to foster international understanding. Until 1998, the members conferred privately or debated global issues only at the forum's annual meeting in Davos, Switzerland, and at regional summits. Follow-up was difficult because of the members' geographic dispersion and conflicting schedules.

A WEF online strategy and operations task force developed a collaborative computing system to allow secure communication among members, making the nonprofit group more effective in its mission. Now WEF is making faster progress toward solutions for the global problems it studies. Called the World Electronic Community (WELCOM), the GDSS and its complementary videoconferencing system give members a secure channel through which to send e-mail, read reports available in a WEF library, and communicate in point-to-point or multipoint videoconferences. Forum members now hold real-time discussions and briefings on pressing issues and milestones, such as, for example, the global war against terrorism.

The WELCOM system was designed with a graphical user interface (GUI) to make it easily accessible to inexperienced computer users, because many WEF members might not be computer-literate or proficient typists. The forum also set up "concierge services," based in Boston, Singapore, and Geneva, for technical support and to arrange videoconferences and virtual meetings. To handle any time/any place meetings, members can access recorded forum events and discussions that they may have missed, as well as an extensive library, which is one of the most heavily used features of the system. The site also operates a knowledge base ("knowledge navigator") and media center.

As of 2001 the system has been completely on the Web. With *Webcasting*, all sessions of the annual meetings can be viewed in real time. The virtual meetings are done in a secured environment, and private chat rooms are also available.

*Sources:* Compiled from *weforum.org* (accessed June 29, 2003) and *PC Week* (August 17, 1998).

*For Further Exploration:* Check the Netmeeting and Netshow products of Microsoft, and see how their capabilities facilitate the WEF virtual meetings. How does an environment such as *eroom* at *documentum.com* support the process of group decision making, if at all?

---

**EXECUTIVE INFORMATION (SUPPORT) SYSTEMS AND PERFORMANCE MANAGEMENT**

The majority of personal DSSs support the work of professionals and middle-level managers. Organizational DSSs provide support primarily to planners, analysts, researchers, or to some managers. For a DSS to be used by top managers it must meet the executives' needs. An executive information system (EIS), also known as an executive support system (ESS), is a technology designed in response to the specific needs of executives.

The terms *executive information system* and *executive support system* mean different things to different people, though they are sometimes used interchangeably. The following definitions, based on Rockart and DeLong (1988), distinguish between EIS and ESS:

- **Executive information system (EIS).** An EIS is a computer-based system that serves the information needs of top executives. It provides rapid access to timely and relevant information, to aid in monitoring an organization's performance by directly accessing management reports and to improve managerial growth and learning (*Business World*, 2004). An EIS is very user friendly, is supported by graphics, and provides the capabilities of *exception reporting* (reporting of only the results that deviate from a set standard) and *drilldown* (investigating information in increasing detail). It is also easily connected with online information services and electronic mail.

- **Executive support system (ESS).** An ESS is a comprehensive support system that goes beyond EIS to include analysis support, communications, office automation, and intelligence support.

| TABLE 12.2 | Comparison of the Capabilities of Natural vs. Artificial Intelligence | |
|---|---|---|
| **Capabilities** | **Natural Intelligence** | **Artificial Intelligence** |
| Preservation of knowledge | Perishable from an organizational point of view | Permanent |
| Duplication and dissemination of knowledge | Difficult, expensive, takes time | Easy, fast, and inexpensive once knowledge is in a computer |
| Consistency of knowledge | Can be erratic and inconsistent Incomplete at times | Consistent and thorough |
| Documentability of process and knowledge | Difficult | Fairly easy |
| Creativity | Can be very high | Low; uninspired |
| Use of sensory experiences | Direct and rich in possibilities | Must be interpreted first; limited |
| Recognizing patterns and relationships | Fast, easy to explain | Machine learning still not as good as people in most cases, but in some cases can do better than people |
| Reasoning | Making use of wide context of experiences | Good only in narrow, focused, and stable domains |
| Cost of knowledge | Expensive | Inexpensive if shared by many users or with repetitive use |

**CAPABILITIES AND CHARACTERISTICS OF ESSs**

Executive support systems vary in their capabilities and benefits (e.g., see Singh et al., 2002). Capabilities common to many ESSs are summarized in Table 12.2. A sample graphical presentation is provided in Figure 12.4 (page 496). One of these capabilities, the CSF, is measured by key performance indicators (KPIs), as shown in Online File W12.8.

# 12.3  Intelligent Support Systems: The Basics

*Intelligent systems* is a term that describes the various commercial applications of artificial intelligence (AI).

**ARTIFICIAL INTELLIGENCE AND INTELLIGENT BEHAVIOR**

Most experts (see Cawsey, 1998, and Russell and Norvig, 2002) agree that **artificial intelligence (AI)** is concerned with two basic ideas. First, it involves studying the thought processes of humans; second, it deals with representing those processes via machines (computers, robots, and so on). Following 9/11, AI has been getting lots of attention, due to its capability to assist in fighting terrorism (Kahn, 2002). Another development that helps AI to get attention is the large number of intelligent devices in the marketplace (Rivlin, 2002).

One well-publicized definition of AI is "behavior by a machine that, if performed by a human being, would be considered *intelligent.*" Let us explore the meaning of the term *intelligent behavior.* The following capabilities are considered to be signs of intelligence: learning or understanding from experience, making sense of ambiguous or contradictory messages, and responding quickly and successfully to a new situation. Using reasoning to solve problems and direct actions effectively is another indicator of intelligence. Some other indicators include the ability to deal with complex situations, and understanding and inferring in ordinary, rational ways. Applying knowledge to manipulate the environment and recognizing the relative importance of different elements in a situation complete our list.

An interesting test to determine whether a computer exhibits intelligent behavior was designed by Alan Turing, a British AI pioneer. According to the **Turing test,** a computer could be considered "smart" only when a human interviewer, conversing with both an unseen human being and an unseen computer, cannot determine which is which. Also see Von Ahn et al. (2004).

So far we have concentrated on the concept of *intelligence*. According to another definition, artificial intelligence is the branch of computer science that deals with ways of representing *knowledge*. It uses symbols and numbers rather than just numbers, and *heuristics,* or rules of thumb, rather than algorithms for processing information.

**Knowledge and AI.** Although a computer cannot have experiences or study and learn as a human can, it can use knowledge given to it by human experts. Such knowledge consists of facts, concepts, theories, heuristic methods, procedures, and relationships. Knowledge is also information organized and analyzed to make it *understandable* and *applicable* to problem solving or decision making. The collection of knowledge related to a specific problem (or an opportunity) to be used in an intelligent system is organized and stored in a **knowledge base.** As discussed in Chapter 10, the collection of knowledge related to the operation of an organization is called an *organizational knowledge base* to distinguish it from a specific problem knowledge base.

COMPARING
ARTIFICIAL AND
NATURAL
INTELLIGENCE

The potential value of AI can be better understood by contrasting it with natural (human) intelligence. AI has several important commercial advantages over natural intelligence, but also some limitations, as shown in Table 12.2.

**TABLE 12.3** | Commercial AI Techniques

| Name | Short Description |
|---|---|
| Expert system (ES) | Computerized advisory systems usually based on rules. (See Section 12.4.) |
| Natural language processing (NLP) | Enables computers to recognize and even understand human languages. (See Section 12.5.) |
| Speech understanding | Enables computers to recognize words and understand short voice sentences. (See Section 12.5.) |
| Robotic and sensory systems | Programmable combination of mechanical and computer programs. Recognize their environments via sensors (see Patterson, 2005). |
| Computer vision and scene recognition | Enable computers to interpret the content of pictures captured by cameras. |
| Machine learning | Enables computers to interpret the content of data and information captured by sensors (see next three techniques). |
| Handwriting recognition | Enables computers to recognize characters (letters, digits) written by hand. |
| Neural computing (networks) | Using massive parallel processing, able to recognize patterns in large amount of data. (See Section 12.5.) |
| Fuzzy logic | Enables computers to reason with partial information. (See Online File W12.20.) |
| Intelligent agents | Software programs that perform tasks for a human or machine master. (See Online File W12.12.) |
| Semantic Web | An intelligent software program that "understands" content of Web pages. (See Online File W12.20.) |
| Genetic programming | Automatic analysis and synthesis of computer programs. (See Online File W12.20.) |

**BENEFITS OF AI**

Despite their limitations, AI applications can be extremely valuable. They can make computers easier to use and can make knowledge more widely available. One major potential benefit of AI is that it significantly increases the speed and consistency of some problem-solving procedures, including those problems that are difficult to solve by conventional computing and those that have incomplete or unclear data. Another benefit of AI is that it significantly increases the productivity of performing many tasks; it helps in handling information overload by summarizing or interpreting information and by assisting in searching through large amounts of data. Finally, rule-based systems are the key to automated decision making, as shown in Section 12.6.

**CONVENTIONAL VERSUS AI COMPUTING**

Conventional computer programs are based on algorithms. An *algorithm* is a mathematical formula or sequential procedure that leads to a solution. It is converted into a computer program that tells the computer exactly what operations to carry out. The algorithm then uses data such as numbers, letters, or words to solve problems. AI software is using knowledge and heuristics instead of, or along with, algorithms.

In addition, AI software is based on **symbolic processing** of knowledge. In AI, a symbol is a letter, word, or number that represents objects, processes, and their relationships. Objects can be people, things, ideas, concepts, events, or statements of fact. Using symbols, it is possible to create a knowledge base that contains facts, concepts, and the relationships that exist among them. Then various processes can be used to manipulate the symbols in order to generate advice or a recommendation for solving problems.

The major differences between AI computing and conventional computing are shown in Online File W12.9.

**Does a Computer Really Think?** Knowledge bases and search techniques certainly make computers more useful, but can they really make computers more intelligent? The fact that most AI programs are implemented by search and pattern-matching techniques leads to the conclusion that *computers are not really intelligent.* You give the computer a lot of information and some guidelines about how to use this information, and the computer can then come up with a solution. But all it does is test the various alternatives and attempt to find some combination that meets the designated criteria. The computer appears to be "thinking" and often gives a satisfactory solution. For example, chess legend Garry Kasparov had difficulties in winning against computers and even lost to IBM's Deep Blue supercomputer in 1997 and was forced to a draw with Deep Blue and with X3D Fritz in 2003. *Computers certainly cannot think,* but they can be very useful for increasing our productivity. This is done by several commercial AI technologies.

**COMMERCIAL AI TECHNOLOGIES**

The development of machines that exhibit intelligent capabilities draws upon several sciences and technologies, ranging from linguistics to mathematics (see the roots of the tree in Online File W12.10). Artificial intelligence itself is not a commercial field; it is a collection of concepts and ideas that are appropriate for research but cannot be marketed. However, AI provides the scientific foundation for several commercial technologies.

The major intelligent systems are: expert systems, natural language processing, speech understanding, robotics and sensory systems, fuzzy logic, neural computing, computer vision and scene recognition, and intelligent computer-aided instruction. In addition, a combination of two or more of the above is considered a *hybrid* intelligent system. The major commercial intelligent systems are listed in Table 12.3 (p. 492) and are discussed further in Online File W12.11. A discussion of the state of the art of these systems can be found in Iserlis (2004).

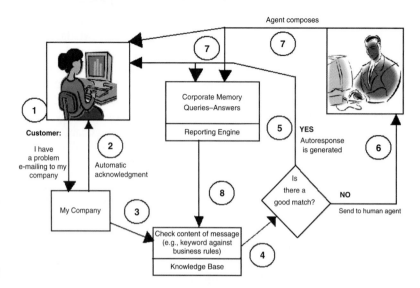

**Figure 12.5** How an autoresponder works. (*Source:* Drawn by E. Turban.)

**Intelligent Agents. Intelligent agents** are small programs that reside on computers to conduct certain tasks automatically. A virus detection program is a good example. It resides on your computer, scans all incoming data, and removes found viruses automatically. An intelligent agent runs in the background, monitors the environment, and reacts to certain trigger conditions. Intelligent agents have applications in personal assistant devices, electronic mail/news filtering and distribution, appointment handling, and Web applets for e-commerce and information gathering.

Intelligent agents include one or more of the intelligent systems listed above, frequently rule-based expert systems, case-base reasoning, and so on. Several names have been used to describe intelligent agents, including *software agents, wizards, software daemons, knowbots, softbots,* and *bots* (intelligent software robots). These terms sometimes refer to different types of agents or agents with different intelligence levels.

An example of an agent application is provided in Figure 12.5. The purpose of this agent is to answer user queries. The intelligence resides in a knowledge base. Notice that the agent basically matches the query against business rules. If no match is found, the agent sends the query to a human. The human's solution is added to the corporate memory, and a new business rule is added for future applications.

For more on intelligent agents, see Online File W12.12 and Martin-Flatin, et al. (2006).

As described in Chapters 4 and 5, intelligent agents play a major role in supporting work on computers (such as search, alerts, monitor Web activities, suggestions to users) and work in general (e.g., configure complex products, diagnose malfunctions in networks).

# 12.4 Expert Systems

When an organization has a complex decision to make or a problem to solve, it often turns to experts for advice. These experts have specific knowledge and experience in the problem area. They are aware of alternative solutions, chances of success, and costs that the organization may incur if the problem is not solved. Companies engage experts for advice on such matters as equipment purchase, mergers and acquisitions, or advertising strategy. The more unstructured the situation, the more

# IT at Work 12.4

## Streamlining Loan and Credit Decisions at China Everbright Bank

FIN

**The Problem.** China Everbright Bank has more than 350 branches in 36 cities. It has assets of $41 billion and outstanding loans totaling $24 billion. Everbright Bank provides commercial loans in a wide range of industries throughout China; however, as the Chinese economy has grown, the bank's diverse client base created a level of process complexity that became difficult to manage effectively. Loan approvals were particularly complex, requiring the evaluation of multiple factors, such as customer preferences, credit history and capacity, regulations, business operations, and industrial risk. Credit risk managers had to collect information from different sources before manually assessing each risk profile to determine eligibility and terms of the loans. This process created a backlog in loan processing, which could take weeks or even months to approve.

**The Solution.** China Everbright Bank has selected ILOG JRules, a key offering in ILOG's business rule management system product line, to create an automated loan and credit decision platform, replacing the cumbersome and inflexible manual process.

**The Results.** The new system allows Everbright Bank to process loan applications in one day instead of several weeks, providing greatly enhanced customer service at significant savings to the bank. The new system automates the prequalification and underwriting, which frees staff from performing this task manually—all while lowering the risk to the bank through better risk assessment. Also, since ILOG JRules ensures loan servicing with timely tracking of repayments, the new system reduces losses from delinquent or delayed payments, which contributes to the overall financial health of the bank.

*Sources:* Compiled from *InfoWorld.com* (2006) and from *ilog.com* (accessed July 2006).

*For Further Exploration:* Why does a rule-based ES work so well in this case? How is customers' privacy protected? How is risk analysis handled?

specialized and expensive is the advice. **Expert systems (ESs)** are an attempt to mimic human experts. Expert systems can either *support* decision makers or completely *replace* them (see Davenport, 2006). Expert systems are the most widely applied and commercially successful AI technology. A recent study by Arnold et al. (2004) suggests that intelligent decision aids may be best viewed as complements to expert decision makers during complex problem analysis and resolution.

Typically, an ES is decision-making software that can reach a level of performance comparable to a human expert in some specialized and usually narrow problem area. The basic idea behind an ES is simple: *Expertise* is transferred from an expert (or other source of expertise) to the computer. This knowledge is then organized and stored in the computer. Users can call on the computer for specific advice as needed. The computer can make inferences and arrive at a conclusion. Then, like a human expert, it advises the nonexperts and explains, if necessary, the logic behind the advice. ESs can sometimes perform better than any single expert can. An example is provided in *IT at Work 12.4.*

**EXPERTISE AND KNOWLEDGE**

*Expertise* is the extensive, task-specific knowledge acquired from training, reading, and experience. It enables experts to make better and faster decisions than nonexperts in solving complex problems. Expertise takes a long time (possibly years) to acquire, and it is distributed in organizations in an uneven manner. A senior expert possesses about 30 times more expertise than a junior (novice) staff member.

The transfer of expertise from an expert to a computer and then to the user involves four activities: *knowledge acquisition* (from experts or other sources), *knowledge representation* (in the computer), *knowledge inferencing,* and *knowledge transfer* to the user.

Knowledge is acquired from experts and/or from documented sources. Through the activity of knowledge representation, acquired knowledge is organized as rules or frames (object-oriented) and stored electronically in a *knowledge base.* Given the necessary expertise stored in the knowledge base, the computer is programmed so that it can make inferences. The inferencing is performed in a component called the **inference engine,** which is the "brain" of the ES, and results in a recommendation for novices. Thus, the expert's knowledge has been *transferred* to users.

A unique feature of an ES is its ability to explain its recommendations. The explanation and justification is done in a subsystem called the *justifier* or the *explanation subsystem* (e.g., presents the sequence of rules used by the inference engine to generate a recommendation).

**THE BENEFITS AND LIMITATIONS OF EXPERT SYSTEMS**

**The Benefits of Expert Systems.** Expert systems have considerable benefits, but their use is constrained. During the past few years, the technology of expert systems has been successfully applied in thousands of organizations worldwide to problems ranging from counterterrorism activities to the analysis of dust in mines. Why have ESs become so popular? It is because of the large number of capabilities and benefits they provide at a reasonable cost. The major ones are listed in Table 12.4. For examples of ES applications, see Online File W12.13.

| TABLE 12.4 | Benefits of Expert Systems | |
|---|---|
| **Benefit** | **Description/Example** |
| Increased output and productivity | At Digital Equipment Corp. (now part of Hewlett-Packard), an ES plans configuration of components for each custom order, increasing preparation production speed fourfold. |
| Increased quality | ESs can provide consistent advice and reduce error rates. |
| Capture and dissemination of scarce expertise | Physicians in Egypt and Algeria use an eye-care ES developed at Rutgers University to diagnose ailments and to recommend treatment. Advice is provided by top physicians. |
| Operation in hazardous environments | ESs that interpret information collected by sensors enable human workers to avoid hot, humid, or toxic environments. |
| Accessibility to knowledge and help desks | ESs can increase the productivity of help-desk employees or even automate this function. |
| Reliability | ESs do not become tired or bored, call in sick, or go on strike. They consistently pay attention to details and do not overlook relevant information. |
| Increased capabilities of other systems | Integration of an ES with other systems makes the other systems more effective. |
| Ability to work with incomplete or uncertain information | Even with a user's input of "don't know" or "not sure," an ES can still produce an answer, though it may not be a certain one. |
| Provision of training | Novices who work with an ES become more experienced thanks to the explanation facility, which serves as a teaching device and knowledge base. They also can play what-if scenarios. |
| Enhancement of decision-making and problem-solving capabilities | ESs allow the integration of expert judgment into analysis. Successful applications are diagnosis of machine malfunction and even medical diagnosis. |
| Decreased decision-making time | ESs can sometimes make times faster decisions than humans working alone. American Express authorizers can make charge authorization decisions in 3 minutes without an ES and in 30 seconds with one. |
| Reduced downtime | ESs can quickly diagnose machine malfunctions and prescribe repairs. An ES called Drilling Advisor detects malfunctions in oil rigs, saving most of the cost of downtime (as much as $250,000/day). |

# IT at Work 12.5

MKT    POM

## Even an Intelligent System Can Fail

Mary Kay (*marykay.com*), the multinational cosmetics company, uses teams of managers and analysts to plan its products. This process attempted to iron out potential weaknesses before production. However, the company still faced costly errors resulting from such problems as product-container incompatibility, interaction of chemical compositions, and marketing requirements with regard to packaging and distribution.

An eclectic group of Mary Kay managers, representing various functional areas, used to meet every six weeks to make product decisions. The group's decision-making process was loosely structured: The marketing team would give its requirements to the product formulator and the package engineer at the same time. Marketing's design requests often proved to be beyond the allocated budget or technical possibilities, and other problems arose as a result of not knowing the ultimate product formulation. The result was more meetings and redesign.

Mary Kay decided to implement an expert system to help. In an effort to keep costs to a minimum, it engaged the services of a research university that developed a system that consisted of a DSS computational tool plus two ES components. The decision support tool was able to select compatible packages for a given cosmetic product and to test product and package suitability. The ES component used this information to guide users through design and to determine associated production costs.

At first the system was a tremendous success. There was a clear match between the abilities of the system technology and the nature of the problem. The director of package design enthusiastically embraced the system solution. The entire decision process could have been accomplished in two weeks with no inherent redesign. By formulating what previously was largely intuitive, the ES improved understanding of the decision process itself, increasing the team's confidence. By reducing the time required for new product development, executives were freed for other tasks, and the team met only rarely to ratify the recommendations of the ES.

However, without support staff to *maintain* the ES, no one knew how to add or modify decision rules. Even the firm's IT unit was unable to help, and so the system fell into disuse. More importantly, when the director of package design left the firm, so did the enthusiasm for the ES. No one else was willing to make the effort necessary to maintain the system or sustain the project. Without managerial direction about the importance of the system to the firm's success, the whole project foundered.

*Sources:* Condensed from Vedder et al. (1999) and (2002).

*For Further Exploration:* What can a company do to prevent such failures? Can you speculate on why this was not done at Mary Kay?

---

**The Limitations of Expert Systems.** Despite their many benefits, available ES methodologies are not always straightforward and effective. Some factors that have slowed the commercial spread of ES are listed in Online File W12.14.

In addition, expert systems may not be able to arrive at any conclusions. For example, even some fully developed complex expert systems are unable to fulfill about 2 percent of the orders presented to them. Finally, expert systems, like human experts, sometimes produce incorrect recommendations.

**Failing Expert Systems.** Various organizational, personal, and economic factors can slow the spread of expert systems, or even cause them to fail, as shown in *IT at Work 12.5.*

The components of ES are described and illustrated in Online File W12.15.

**APPLICATIONS OF EXPERT SYSTEMS**

Expert systems are in use today in all types of organizations. For many examples, by industry, see *exsys.com* (in the case studies). Expert systems are especially useful in ten generic categories, displayed in Table 12.5 (page 498). (For examples, see Minicase 2 and Online File W12.17.) For other examples see Van Fleet et al. (2005) and Pontz and Power (2003).

| TABLE 12.5 | Generic Categories of Expert Systems |
|---|---|
| **Category** | **Problem Addressed** |
| **1.** Interpretation | Inferring situation descriptions from observations. |
| **2.** Prediction | Inferring likely consequences of given situations. |
| **3.** Diagnosis | Inferring system malfunctions from observations. |
| **4.** Design | Configuring objects under constraints. |
| **5.** Planning | Developing plans to achieve goal(s). |
| **6.** Monitoring | Comparing observations to plans, flagging exceptions. |
| **7.** Debugging | Prescribing remedies for malfunctions. |
| **8.** Repair | Executing a plan to administer a prescribed remedy. |
| **9.** Instruction | Diagnosing, debugging, and correcting student performance. |
| **10.** Control | Interpreting, predicting, repairing, and monitoring systems behavior. |

**Embedded Expert Systems.** One of the most useful applications of expert systems is as an embedded component in other systems, including robots. The ES components are so tightly integrated that they have turned into transparent parts of processes or systems. Actually, many software and hardware products include embedded ESs or other intelligent systems, which the users may not be aware of.

# 12.5 Other Intelligent Systems

An expert system's major objective is to provide expert advice. Other intelligent systems can be used to solve problems or provide capabilities on areas in which they excel. Several such technologies are described next.

**NATURAL LANGUAGE PROCESSING AND VOICE TECHNOLOGIES**

Today, when you tell a computer what to do, you usually type commands on the keyboard. In responding to a user, the computer outputs message symbols or other short, cryptic notes of information. Many problems could be minimized or even eliminated if we could communicate with the computer in our own language. We would simply type in directions, instructions, or information. Better yet, we would converse with the computer using voice. The computer would be smart enough to interpret the input, regardless of its format. **Natural language processing (NLP)** refers to communicating with a computer in English or whatever language you may speak.

To understand a natural language inquiry, a computer must have the knowledge to analyze and then interpret the input. This may include linguistic knowledge about words, domain knowledge, common-sense knowledge, and even knowledge about the users and their goals. Once the computer understands the input, it can take the desired action. For details see *wikipedia.org/wiki/The_Natural_Language_Processing.*

In this section we briefly discuss two types of NLP:

1. Natural language *understanding,* which investigates methods of allowing a computer to comprehend instructions given in ordinary English, via the keyboard or by voice (speech understanding), so that computers are able to understand people

2. Natural language *generation,* which strives to allow computers to produce ordinary English language, on the screen or by voice (known as voice synthesis), so people can understand computers more easily

**Applications of Natural Language Processing.** Natural language processing programs have been applied in several areas. The most important are human-to-computer interfaces, which include abstracting and summarizing text, analyzing grammar, understanding speech, and even composing letters by machines. These programs translate one natural language to another, or one computer language to another, and they even translate Web pages (see Chapters 4 and 9).

By far the most dominant use of NLP is "front-ends" for other software packages, especially databases that allow the user to enter queries or operate the applications programs in everyday language.

*Example: Neiman Marcus Uses Natural Language Search to Boost Online Sales.* The online portion of Neiman Marcus (*neiman-marcus.com*), one of the industry leaders in luxury retail, determined that more than 50 percent of its customers had abandoned its Web site because they could not find what they were looking for. The problem was not lack of inventory. In fact, in most cases Neiman Marcus had the product, but the search engine worked so poorly that it was frequently not found. To overcome this problem, Neiman Marcus implemented an iPhrase Technologies One Step natural language search engine. This allows customers to input queries in English-language sentences. The search language improves search capabilities by removing ambiguities and often suggests other products, thereby improving the sales experience and increasing sales. For details see Scheiner (2003).

**Speech (Voice) Recognition and Understanding.** Speech recognition is a process that allows us to communicate with a computer by speaking to it. The term **speech recognition** is sometimes applied only to the first part of the communication process, in which the computer recognizes words of short sentences that have been spoken without necessarily interpreting their meanings. The other part of the process, wherein the meaning of speech is ascertained, is called **speech understanding.** It may be possible to understand the meaning of a spoken sentence without actually recognizing every word. When a speech recognition system is combined with a natural language processing system, the result is an overall system that not only recognizes voice input but also understands it (see Dettmer, 2003). For multiple applications in stores and warehouses, see Amato-McCoy (2003). Speech recognition is deployed today in wireless PDAs and smart cell phones as well.

*Advantages of Speech Recognition and Understanding.* The ultimate goal of speech recognition is to allow a computer to understand the natural speech of any human speaker at least as well as a human listener could understand it. Speech recognition offers several other advantages:

- **Ease of access.** Many more people can speak than can type. As long as communication with a computer depends on typing skills, many people may not be able to use computers effectively.
- **Speed.** Even the most competent typists can speak more quickly than they can type. It is estimated that the average person can speak twice as quickly as a proficient typist can type.
- **Manual freedom.** Obviously, communicating with a computer through typing occupies your hands. There are many situations in which computers might be useful to people whose hands are otherwise engaged, such as product assemblers, pilots of aircraft, and busy executives. Speech recognition also enables people with hand-related physical disabilities to use computers.
- **Remote access.** Many computers can be accessed remotely by telephones. If a remote database includes speech recognition capabilities, you could retrieve information by issuing oral commands into a telephone.
- **Accuracy.** People tend to make mistakes when typing, especially in spelling. These could be reduced with voice input.

- **Security.** An individual's voice has a characteristic voice print, analogous to a thumbprint or written signature, that can be used to authenticate a caller before allowing access to confidential information. Thus a voice user interface is often a preferable, and sometimes necessary, medium for delivering self-service applications to people on the go.
- **Cost-benefit.** According to an Oracle report (2006), call centers with live call agents cost a company between $5 and $25 per call. Handling the same calls with a voice-enabled application costs between $0.25 and $0.50 per call. This same comparison can be made for voice alerts. An automated system can make outbound trigger- or time-based notification calls for little more than the cost of the phone call. Paying a human operator to make outbound calls costs at least ten times as much.

**SVC**

American Express Travel Related Services (AETRS) is using interactive voice recognition (IVR) that allows its customers to check and book domestic flights by talking to a computer over the phone. The system asks customers questions such as: Where do you want to travel? When do you want to go? The system can handle hundreds of city and airport names, and lets callers use more than 10,000 different ways to identify a location. The reservation transaction costs were reduced about 50 percent compared to operator-handled costs. The average transaction time was reduced from 7 to 2 minutes. AETRS offers a similar service on the Web.

*Limitations of Speech Recognition and Understanding.* The major limitation of speech understanding is its inability to recognize long sentences, or the long time needed to accomplish it. The better the system is at speech recognition, the higher is its cost. Also, in voice recognition systems, you cannot manipulate icons and windows, so speech may need to be combined with a keyboard entry, which slows communication. For details see D'Agostino (2005).

**Voice Synthesis.** The technology by which computers convert text to voice is known as **voice synthesis.** It is the artificial production of human speech, and it is also known as *text-to-speech*. The synthesis of voice by a computer differs from the simple playback of a prerecorded voice by either analog or digital means. As the term synthesis implies, sounds that make up words and phrases are electronically constructed from basic sound components and can be made to form any desired voice pattern.

A *text-to-speech system* is composed of two parts: a *front-end* and a *back-end*. Broadly, the front-end takes input in the form of text and outputs a symbolic linguistic representation. The back-end takes the symbolic linguistic representation as input and outputs the synthesized speech waveform (actual sound).

The current quality of synthesized voice is very good, but the technology remains somewhat expensive. Anticipated lower cost and improved performance of synthetic voice should encourage more widespread commercial voice applications, especially those on the Web. Opportunities for its use will encompass almost all applications that can provide an automated response to a user, such as inquiries by employees pertaining to payroll and benefits. A number of banks already offer voice service to their customers, informing them about their balances, which checks were cashed, and so on. Many credit card companies provide similar services, telling customers about current account balances, recent charges, and payments received.

**Application of Voice Technologies.** Voice technologies applications appear under several categories. The major ones are:

- **Call center**—a location where a group of employees answer customer service lines for a business and either provide answers or direct the caller further.
- **Contact or customer care center**—a kind of call center that covers not only telephone calls from customers, but also e-mail, chat, and other Web-based queries.

- **CTI (computer/telephone integration)**—the integration of computers with telephones, often to create sophisticated automated call centers.
- **IVR (interactive voice response)**—a type of automated service that relies on speech recognition or speech concatenation, or both, to create a dialog between a computer and a person.
- **Voice portal**—a Web site with an audio interface that can be accessed through a telephone call for getting information from the Internet, possibly in real time.
- **Voice over IP (VoIP)**—a technology that uses the Internet Protocol, instead of speech recognition, as the conduit for a telephone-like voice conversation. This technology permits cheap overseas calls via the Internet (Chapter 4).

For sample applications of voice technologies, see Table 12.6.

**ARTIFICIAL NEURAL NETWORKS**

**Artificial neural networks (ANNs)** are biologically inspired. Specifically, they borrow ideas from the manner in which the human brain works. The human brain is composed of special cells called *neurons*. Estimates of the number of neurons in a human brain cover a wide range (up to 150 billion), and there are more than a hundred

| TABLE 12.6 | Examples of Voice Technology Applications |
| --- | --- |
| **Company** | **Applications** |
| Scandinavian Airlines, other airlines | Answering inquiries about reservations, schedules, lost baggage, etc.[a] |
| Citibank, many other banks | Informing credit card holders about balances and credits, providing bank account balances and other information to customers[a] |
| Delta Dental Plan (CA) | Verifying coverage information[a] |
| Federal Express | Requesting pickups, ordering supplies[b] |
| Illinois Bell, other telephone companies | Giving information about services,[a] receiving orders[b] |
| Domino's Pizza | Enabling stores to order supplies, providing price information[a,b] |
| General Electric, Rockwell International, Austin Rover, Westpoint Pepperell, Eastman Kodak | Allowing inspectors to report results of quality assurance tests[b] |
| Cara Donna Provisions | Allowing receivers of shipments to report weights and inventory levels of various meats and cheeses[b] |
| Weidner Insurance, AT&T | Conducting market research and telemarketing[b] |
| U.S. Department of Energy, Idaho National Engineering Laboratory, Honeywell | Notifying people of emergencies detected by sensors[a] |
| New Jersey Department of Education | Notifying parents when students are absent and about cancellation of classes[a] |
| Kaiser-Permanente Health Foundation (HMO) | Calling patients to remind them of appointments, summarizing and reporting results[a] |
| Car manufacturers | Activating radios, heaters, and so on, by voice[b] |
| Taxoma Medical Center | Logging in and out by voice to payroll department[b] |
| St. Elizabeth's Hospital | Prompting doctors in the emergency room to conduct all necessary tests, reporting of results by doctors[a,b] |
| Hospital Corporation of America | Sending and receiving patient data by voice, searching for doctors, preparing schedules and medical records[a,b] |

[a]Output device.
[b]Input device.

different kinds of neurons, separated into groups called *networks*. Each network contains several thousand neurons that are highly interconnected. Thus, the brain can be viewed as a collection of neural networks.

Today's ANNs, whose application is referred to as **neural computing,** use a very limited set of concepts from biological neural systems. The goal is to simulate massive parallel processes that involve processing elements interconnected in a network architecture. The artificial neuron receives inputs analogous to the electrochemical impulses biological neurons receive from other neurons. The output of the artificial neuron corresponds to signals sent out from a biological neuron. These artificial signals can be changed, like the signals from the human brain. Neurons in an ANN receive information from other neurons or from external sources, transform or process the information, and pass it on to other neurons or as external outputs.

The manner in which an ANN processes information depends on its structure and on the algorithm used to process the information, as explained in Online File W12.18.

**Benefits and Applications of Neural Networks.** The value of neural network technology includes its usefulness for pattern recognition, learning, and the interpretation of incomplete and "noisy" inputs.

Neural networks have the potential to provide some of the human characteristics of problem solving that are difficult to simulate using the logical, analytical techniques of DSS or even expert systems. One of these characteristics is **pattern recognition.** Neural networks can analyze large quantities of data to establish patterns and characteristics in situations where the logic or rules are not known. An example would be

# *IT* at Work 12.6

## Banks Are Cracking Down on Credit Card Fraud

FIN

Only 0.2 percent of Visa International's turnover in 1995 was lost to fraud, but at $655 million it is a loss well worth addressing. Visa (*visa.com*) is now concentrating its efforts on reversing the number of fraudulent transactions by using neural network technology.

Most people stick to a well-established pattern of credit card use and only rarely splurge on expensive nonessentials. Neural networks are designed to notice when a card that is usually used to buy gasoline once a week in Hawaii is suddenly used to buy a number of tickets to the latest theater premiere on Broadway.

Visa's participating banks believe the neural network technology has been successful in combating fraud. Bank of America uses a cardholder risk identification system (CRIS) and has cut fraudulent card use by up to two-thirds. Toronto Dominion Bank found that losses were reduced, and overall customer service improved, with the introduction of neural computing. Another bank recorded savings of $5.5 million in six months. In its first year of use, Visa member banks lost 16% to counterfeiters; considering such numbers, the $2 million Visa spent to implement CRIS certainly seems worth the investment. In fact, Visa says, CRIS paid for itself in one year.

In 1995, CRIS conducted over 16 billion transactions. By 2003, VisaNet (Visa's data warehouse and e-mail operations) and CRIS were handling more than 8,000 transactions per second or about 320 billion a year. By fall 2003, CRIS was able to notify banks of fraud within a few seconds of a transaction. The only downside to CRIS is that occasionally the system prompts a call to a cardholder's spouse when an out-of-the-ordinary item is charged, such as a surprise vacation trip or a diamond ring. After all, no one wants to spoil surprises for loved ones.

Sumitomo Credit Service Co., a credit card issuer in Japan, is using a neural network-based system from *fairisaac.com*. The product works well reading Japanese characters, protecting 18 million cardholders in Japan. The system is used by many other banks worldwide.

*Sources:* Condensed from "Visa Stamps Out Fraud" (1995), p. viii; "Visa Cracks Down on Fraud" (1996); customer success stories at *fairisaac.com* and *visa.com* (press releases, accessed June 2004).

*For Further Exploration:* What is the advantage of CRIS over an automatic check against the balance in the account? What is the advantage of CRIS against a set of rules such as "Call a human authorizer when the purchase price is more than 200 percent of the average previous bill"?

loan applications. By reviewing many historical cases of applicants' questionnaires and the "yes or no" decisions made by people in the loan request, the ANN can create "patterns" or "profiles" of applications that should be approved or denied. A new application can then be matched by the computer against the pattern. If it comes close enough, the computer classifies it as a "yes" or "no"; otherwise it goes to a human for a decision. Neural networks are especially useful for financial applications such as determining when to buy or sell stock (see Shadbolt, 2002, for examples), predicting bankruptcy (Gentry et al., 2002), predicting exchange rates, and detecting fraud.

Neural networks have several other benefits, which are described in Online File W12.19, together with typical applications. For a comprehensive coverage see Smith and Gupta (2002).

Beyond its role as an alternative computing mechanism, and in data mining, neural computing can be combined with other computer-based information systems to produce powerful hybrid systems, as illustrated in *IT at Work 12.6*.

| | |
|---|---|
| **SPECIAL INTELLIGENT SYSTEMS** | Several other intelligent systems exist, but they are less widespread. Their advantage is that they can be used for especially difficult or unique applications. Several of these are described in Online File W12.20. |

# 12.6  Automated Decision Support (ADS)

**Automated decision support (ADS)** systems are rule-based systems that automatically provide solutions to repetitive managerial problems. ADSs are also known as **enterprise decision management (EDM)** systems. ADSs are closely related to BI and business analytics in the following ways:

- Some business analytical models are used to create and/or operate the business rules.
- The business rules can be used to trigger the automatic decisions that can be a part of BI applications. This is especially true in performance monitoring and analysis systems in which the results of what is monitored are analyzed and some action is triggered by the ADS.

Before we examine how ADSs are implemented, let's look at the concept of business rules.

**BUSINESS RULES**

Automating the decision-making process is usually achieved by capturing a business user expertise in a set of *business rules* that are embedded in a rule-driven workflow (or other action-oriented) engine. These business rules can be part of expert systems or other intelligent systems. As analysis is called for (e.g., by a performance monitoring system), a signal is passed to the rule engine for evaluation against the associated business rules. These rules determine what action needs to be taken, based on the results of the evaluation. An example is provided at *IT at Work 12.7*.

White (2004) describes four types of business rules. These rules usually are found in real-time systems and are associated with business performance management (or BPM) as described in Chapter 11: (1) *Analysis rules* are used to calculate performance metrics from detailed business transaction data. (2) *Context rules* enable performance metrics to be tied to business goals and forecasts. (3) Some basic BPM automation can be achieved by applying *exception rules* to metrics and sending an alert to a business user when a metric exceeds a threshold defined in the exception

# *IT* at Work 12.7

## Cigna Uses Business Rules to Support Treatment Request Approval

**The Problem.** CIGNA is a major health insurance company and its CIGNA Behavioral Health covers 16 million Americans in all 50 states and internationally, and supports a network of more than 50,000 professionals who needed a system that quickly and automatically approved requests submitted by providers, such as therapists, for additional patient care. CIGNA Behavioral Health's business processes for making approval determinations were supported in different locations using several different software applications. Certain rules in use sometimes conflicted with each other and knowledge was lost due to employee turnover. In addition, the rules were hardcoded in inflexible if-then statements. Accessing and changing the rules was a slow, cumbersome, and expensive process.

**The Solution.** To reduce the knowledge loss due to employee turnover and increase consistency and efficiency of rule maintenance, CIGNA Behavioral Health decided to adopt *rule-based intelligent systems* that could automate decision-making situations. CIGNA chose HaleyAuthority knowledge management software and HaleyRules intelligent system to build a Web-based benefit management system named *Provider eCare Online*. With the eCare system, therapists submit requests for authorization of benefits over the Internet and receive, in many cases, an immediate machine-generated approval. HaleyRules is a software tool that allows an expert to describe knowledge in plain English and convert

it into business rules, which can then be incorporated in a rule base for future inferences. CIGNA Behavioral Health compiled the experience and expertise of behavioral health clinicians, then used the software to convert that knowledge into a series of straightforward, easily understood, and modifiable business rules.

**The Results.** An immediate benefit of the project is that over 30 percent of all requests for authorization of benefits are processed (approved or rejected) automatically through eCare, enabling CIGNA Behavioral Health to handle more requests with its existing staff. By expressing business processes in English using HaleyRules, eCare specialists can implement changes to the rules whenever needed, in hours instead of weeks. The adoption of knowledge-based systems has helped CIGNA enhance operational efficiency and reduce costs. The tools of HaleyAuthority and HaleyRules in combination provide a convenient platform for the implementation of such intelligent systems.

*Sources*: Compiled from Haley Case Brief (2006), and *cigna.com* (accessed July 2006).

*For Further Exploration:* Why bother if the system can determine automatically only 30 percent of the cases? Why was a KM component added (visit *haley.com*)? What are the legal applications of machine authorization?

---

rule. (4) Full right-time automated actions can be achieved by defining the manual decision-making processes that business users go through as a series of *action rules* in a workflow. These action workflows can then be implemented in a rules engine to automate the decision-making processes.

**CHARACTERISTICS AND BENEFITS OF ADSs**

ADSs are most suitable for repetitive decisions that must be made frequently and/or rapidly using information that is available electronically. The knowledge and decision criteria, as well as the business rules that express them, must be highly structured and the problem situation must be well understood. High-quality data and/or knowledge about the problem domain must also be available. Approval of a loan or granting a credit line to a customer are typical examples.

Using an ADS system can produce precise, agile decision making due to the following capabilities:

- Rapidly builds rules-based applications to automate or guide decision makers, and deploys them into almost any operating environment (as was shown in *IT at Work 12.7*).
- Injects predictive analytics into rules-based applications, increasing their potency and value.
- Provides decision services to legacy systems, expanding their capabilities while minimizing technical risk.

- Combines business rules, predictive models, and optimization strategies flexibly into state-of-the-art decision management applications.
- Accelerates the uptake of learning from decision criteria into strategy design, execution, and refinement.

**ADS APPLICATIONS**

Davenport and Harris (2005) and Davenport (2006) provide numerous examples of successful ADSs in a variety of industries. Some typical examples are:

- **Product or service configuration and quality.** Customers are allowed to customize a product (or service) such as a PC. The ADS then *configures* the most appropriate final product (service) and its cost (considering profitability to the manufacturer). Dell Computer is using this approach. Quality problems can be minimized through early detection.
- **Yield (price) optimization.** Airlines have extensively used automated decision-making applications to set prices based on seat availability and hour or day of purchase, also known as *revenue management* or *yield management*. A method known as *price optimization* or *smart pricing* (Fleischmann et al., 2004) is being used experimentally with variable-pricing (e.g., rental housing).
- **Routing or segmentation decisions.** Significant productivity improvements have been made by companies that design automated filters for sorting cases and transactions. There are examples in the insurance industry, where clear-cut claims are handled as "priority," and in managing the variety and volume of patients in an emergency room.
- **Corporate and regulatory compliance and fraud detection.** Routine policy decisions are time-consuming and technical; however, rules must be current and need to be applied consistently. For example, in the home mortgage industry, lenders must categorize and process loans that conform to government regulations as well as the requirements of the lenders. If this is completed efficiently, the cost savings is marked. Automated screening is used to identify fraud by the Internal Revenue Service and the U.S. Securities and Exchange Commission. For examples, see Barrett and Carr (2005).
- **Dynamic forecasting and SCM.** Increased automated demand forecasting by manufacturers allows companies to align customer forecasts (i.e., inventory levels) with their own manufacturing and sales plans (see CPFR in Chapter 9). Simulation and optimization of supply chain flows can reduce inventory and stockouts.
- **Operational control.** Some automated decision systems are programmed to sense changes in the physical environment and respond based on rules or algorithms (e.g., temperatures affecting power supply needs; controlling traffic lights at intersections based on real-time traffic volume recorded by cameras). For example, see Navis (2003).
- **Customer selection, loyalty, and service.** Identify customers with the greatest profit potential; increase likelihood that they will want the product or service offering; retain their loyalty. (Examples: Harrah's, Capital One, Barclays.)
- **Human capital.** Select the best employees for particular tasks or jobs, at particular compensation levels. (Examples: New England Patriots, Oakland A's, Boston Red Sox.)

**IMPLEMENTING ADSs**

Software companies provide the following components to ADSs:

- **Rules engines.** Companies such as Exsys, Ilog (see BRMS), FairIsaac (see Blaze Advisor for risk analysis and Falcon for fraud analysis), ARulesXL (*arulesxl.com*), and Pegasystems provide processing of business rules.

- **Mathematical and statistical algorithms.** Companies such as SAS and SPSS provide the formulas for finding optimal solutions (e.g., price or inventory level), conducting trend analyses, etc. See the discussion of advanced analytics earlier in the chapter. For example, SAS provides pricing and product optimization (see *sas.com/success/autozone.html* for an example.)
- **Industry-specific packages.** Dozens of companies provide software packages for specific industries (e.g., LendingTree for consumer financing and mortgages and CSC Continuum for insurance).
- **Enterprise systems.** Companies like SAP and Oracle offer applications that automate, join, and direct information flows and transaction processing in complex organizations using automated decision technology for particular functions (e.g., supply chain management).
- **Workflow applications.** After a rules engine makes a decision, the workflow system moves information-intensive business processes through the required steps. Key vendors of such systems include Documentum and FileNet Corp.

**ADS FOR FRONTLINE EMPLOYEES**

Decisions at all levels in the organization contribute to the success of a business. But decisions that maximize a sales opportunity or minimize the cost of customer service requests are made on the frontlines by those interacting with customers and other business partners during the course of daily business. Whether it is an order exception, an upselling opportunity, resolving a customer complaint, or a contract that hangs on a decision, the decision maker on the frontline must be able to make effective decisions *rapidly,* while interacting with customers, sometimes in seconds, based on context and according to strategies and guidelines set forth by senior management.

**Frontline Systems.** **Frontline decision making** is the process by which companies automate decision processes and push them down to frontline employees. It includes *empowering employees* by letting them devise strategies, evaluate metrics, analyze impacts, and make operational changes, based on information they can access in seconds.

# 12.7 Managerial Issues

1. **Cost justification; intangible benefits.** While some of the benefits of management support systems are tangible, it is difficult to put a dollar value on the intangible benefits of many such systems. While the cost of small systems is fairly low and justification is not a critical issue, the cost of medium-to-large systems can be very high, and the benefits they provide must be economically justified.

2. **Documenting and securing support systems.** Many employees develop their own DSSs to increase their productivity and the quality of their work. It is advisable to have an inventory of these DSSs and make certain that appropriate documentation and security measures exist, so that if the employee is away or leaves the organization, the productivity tool remains. The security is very important since managerial support systems may contain extremely important information for the livelihood of organizations. Taking appropriate security measures is a must. End users who build a DSS are not professional systems builders. For this reason, there could be problems with data integrity and the security of the systems developed.

3. **Specialized ready-made decision support.** Initially, DSSs were custom-built. This resulted in two categories of DSS: The first type was small, end-user DSSs that were built by inexpensive tools such as Excel. The second type was large-scale, expensive DSSs built by IT staff and/or vendors with special tools. For many applications, however, building a custom system was not justified. As a result, vendors started

to offer DSSs in specialized areas such as financial services, banking, hospitals, or profitability measurements (or combinations of these areas). The popularity of these DSSs has increased since 1999 when vendors started to offer them online as ASP services.

Decision support in ready-made expert systems is often provided via the Web.

**4. Intelligent DSS.** Introducing intelligent agents into a DSS application can greatly increase its functionality. The intelligent component of a system can be less than 3 percent of the entire system (the rest is models, a database, and telecommunications), yet the contribution of the intelligent component can be incredible. Intelligent systems are expected to be embedded in at least 20 percent of all IT applications in about 10 years. It is critical for any prudent management to closely examine the technologies and their business applicability.

**ETHICS**

**5. Ethical issues.** Corporations with management support systems may need to address some serious ethical issues such as privacy and accountability. For example, a company developed a DSS to help people compute the financial implications of early retirement. However, the DSS developer did not include the tax implications, which resulted in incorrect retirement decisions.

Another important ethical issue is human judgment, which is frequently used in DSSs. Human judgment is subjective, and therefore, it may lead to unethical decision making. Companies should provide an ethical code for DSS builders. Also, the possibility of automating managers' jobs may lead to massive layoffs.

There are ethical issues related to the implementation of expert systems and other intelligent systems. The actions performed by an expert system can be unethical, or even illegal. For example, the expert system may advise you to do something that will hurt someone or will invade the privacy of certain individuals. An example is the behavior of robots, and the possibility that the robots will not behave the way that they were programmed to. There have been many industrial accidents, caused by robots, that resulted in injuries and even deaths. The issue is, Should an organization employ productivity-saving devices that are not 100 percent safe?

Another ethical issue is the use of knowledge extracted from people. The issue here is, Should a company compensate an employee when knowledge that he or she contributed is used by others? This issue is related to the motivation issue. It is also related to privacy. Should people be informed as to who contributed certain knowledge?

A final ethical issue that needs to be addressed is that of dehumanization and the feeling that a machine can be "smarter" than some people. People may have different attitudes toward smart machines, which may be reflected in the manner in which they will work together.

**6. DSS failures.** Over the years there have been many cases of failures of all types of decision support systems. There are multiple reasons for such failures, ranging from human factors to software glitches. Here are two examples:

**GOV**

**(1)** The ill-fated Challenger Shuttle mission was partially attributed to a flawed GDSS (see *cs.toronto.edu/~sme/papers/1993/csrp227.pdf*). NASA used a mismanaged GDSS session in which anonymity was not allowed and other procedures were violated.

**SVC**

**(2)** In an international congress on airports, failures in Denver, Hong Kong, and Malaysia airports were analyzed. Several DSS applications did not work as intended for reasons such as poor planning and inappropriate models.

Briggs and Arnoff (2002) conducted a comprehensive evaluation of a DSS failure and identified areas that could create system failures. Most DSS failures can be eliminated by using appropriate planning, collaboration, and management procedures. Also, attaching an *intelligent system* can make DSSs more useful and less likely to fail.

**7. Creativity in decision support.** In order to solve problems or assess opportunities it is often necessary to generate alternative solutions and/or ideas. Creativity is an extremely important topic in decision support, but it is outside the scope of this IT book. However, there is one topic that clearly belongs to IT and this is the use of computers to support the process of idea generation (some of which we discussed in Section 12.2) as well as the use of computers to generate ideas and solutions by themselves. Actually, expert systems can be considered contributors to creativity since they can generate proposed solutions that will help people generate new ideas (e.g., via association, a kind of a "brainstorming"). Interested readers are referred to Yiman-Seid and Kobsa (2003) and to Online File W12.2.1.

# Integrating *IT*

### For the Accounting Major

Intelligent systems are used extensively in auditing to uncover irregularities. They are also used to uncover and prevent fraud. Today's CPAs use intelligent systems for many of their duties, ranging from risk analysis and auditing to cost control. Accounting personnel also use intelligent agents for several mundane tasks such as managing accounts and monitoring employees' Internet use. Decision support systems, especially for supporting virtual teams, are useful to collaborators as is the use of ADSs for price optimization, auditing, and cost-benefit analysis.

### For the Finance Major

Financial analysts have been using computers and spreadsheets for decades to solve financial problems. Innovative decision support applications exist for activities such as investment decisions, refinancing bonds, assessing debt risks, analyzing financial health, predicting business failures, forecasting financial trends, and investing in global markets. In many cases, intelligent systems were found to be superior to other computerized methods. Intelligent agents can facilitate the use of spreadsheets and other computerized systems used in finance. Finally, intelligent systems can help reduce fraud in credit cards, stocks, and other financial services.

### For the Human Resources Management Major

Human resources personnel use intelligent systems for many applications. For example, intelligent agents can find resumes of applicants posted on the Web and sort them to match needed skills. Expert systems are used in evaluating candidates (tests, interviews). Intelligent systems are used to facilitate training and support self-service of fringe benefits. Neural computing is used to predict employee performance on the job as well as to predict labor needs. Voice recognition systems provide benefits information to employees using self-service methods.

### For the IS Major

The IS function provides the data and models that managers use in their decision support systems. IS personnel are also responsible for the information presented on each screen of executive support systems. Knowledge engineers are often IS employees, and they have the difficult task of interacting with subject-area experts to develop expert systems. Finally, outsourcing decisions, vendors' control, project management, and other managerial decisions can be facilitated by computerized analysis.

### For the Marketing Major

Analytical models have been used in many marketing and sales applications, ranging from allocating advertising budgets to evaluating alternative routings of salespeople. New marketing approaches such as targeted marketing and database marketing are heavily dependent on IT analytical support in general and on intelligent systems in particular. Intelligent systems are particularly useful in mining customer databases and predicting customer behavior. The new field of ADSs and business rules deals with many marketing decisions ranging from appropriate pricing to sales force optimization. Finally, with the increased importance of customer service, the use of intelligent agents is becoming critical for providing fast and appropriate response.

### For the Production/Operations Management Major

POM decisions of scheduling, production planning, inventory control, and routing have been supported by computerized decision models for over 50 years. Also, intelligent systems and ADSs are being used more as their price declines and functionality increases. For example, intelligent systems were developed in the POM field for tasks ranging from diagnosis of machine failures and prescription of repairs to complex production scheduling and inventory control. Some companies, such as DuPont and Kodak, have deployed hundreds of intelligent systems in the planning, organizing, and control of their operational systems.

## Key Terms

Artificial intelligence (AI) *491*
Artificial neural network (ANN) *501*
Automated decision support (ADS) *503*
Decision support system (DSS) *482*
Enterprise decision management (EDM) *503*
Executive information system (EIS) *490*
Executive support system (ESS) *490*
Expert system (ES) *495*
Frontline decision making *506*

Group decision support system (GDSS) *489*
Inference engine *496*
Intelligent agents *494*
Knowledge base *492*
Management support system (MSS) *479*
Model *481*
Model-based management system (MBMS) *484*
Natural language processing (NLP) *498*
Neural computing *502*

Optimization *482*
Organizational (institutional) decision support system (ODSS) *489*
Pattern recognition *502*
Personal information manager (PIM) *479*
Sensitivity analysis *484*
Speech recognition *499*
Speech understanding *499*
Symbolic processing *493*
Turing test *492*
Voice synthesis *500*

## Chapter Highlights

(Numbers Refer to Learning Objectives)

❶ Managerial decision making is synonymous with management.

❶ In today's business environment it is difficult or impossible to conduct analysis of complex problems without computerized support.

❶ Decision making is becoming more and more difficult due to the trends discussed in Chapter 1. Information technology enables managers to make better and faster decisions.

❶ Decision making involves four major phases: intelligence, design, choice, and implementation; they can be modeled as such.

❷ Models allow fast and inexpensive virtual experimentations with new or modified systems. Models can be iconic, analog, or mathematical.

❸ A DSS is an approach that can improve the effectiveness of decision making, decrease the need for training, improve management control, facilitate communication, reduce costs, and allow for more objective decision making. DSSs deal mostly with unstructured problems. Structured decisions are solved with management science models.

❸ The major components of a DSS are a database and its management, the model base and its management, and the user friendly interface. An intelligent (knowledge) component can be added.

❹ Computer support to groups is designed to improve the process of making decisions in groups, which can meet face-to-face or online. The support increases the effectiveness of decisions and reduces the wasted time and other negative effects of face-to-face meetings.

❺ Organizational DSSs are systems with many users throughout the enterprise. This is in contrast with systems that support one person or one functional area.

❺ Executive support systems are intended to support top executives. Initially these were standalone systems, but today they are part of enterprise systems delivered on intranets.

❻ The primary objective of AI is to build computers that will perform tasks that can be characterized as intelligent.

❻ The major characteristics of AI are symbolic processing, use of heuristics instead of algorithms, and application of inference techniques.

❻ AI has several major advantages: It is permanent; it can be easily duplicated and disseminated; it can be less expensive than human intelligence; it is consistent and thorough; and it can be documented.

❼ The major application areas of AI are expert systems, natural language processing, speech understanding, intelligent robotics, computer vision, neural networks, fuzzy logic, and intelligent computer-aided instruction.

❽ Expert system technology attempts to transfer knowledge from experts and documented sources to the computer, in order to make that knowledge available to nonexperts for the purpose of solving difficult problems.

❽ The major components of an ES are a knowledge base, inference engine, user interface, blackboard, and explanation subsystem.

❽ Expert systems can provide many benefits. The most important are improvement in productivity and/or quality, preservation of scarce expertise, enhancing other systems, coping with incomplete information, and providing training.

❾ Natural language processing (NLP) provides an opportunity for a user to communicate with a computer in day-to-day spoken language.

⑨ Speech understanding enables people to communicate with computers by voice. There are many benefits to this emerging technology, such as speed of data entry and having free hands.

⑩ Neural systems are composed of processing elements called artificial neurons. They are interconnected, and they receive, process, and deliver information. A group of connected neurons forms an artificial neural network (ANN). ANNs are used to discover patterns of relationships among data, make difficult forecasts, and to fight fraud. They can process incomplete input information.

⑩ Fuzzy logic is a technology that helps analyze situations under uncertainty. The technology can also be combined with an ES and an ANN to conduct complex predictions and interpretations. ANNs, fuzzy logic, and ESs complement each other.

⑪ Automated decision support systems are routine, repetitive decisions for situations where business rules can be applied (e.g., approve consumer loans).

⑫ Special applications of decision support include complex simulations, ready-made systems, and empowerment of frontline employees.

## Virtual Company Assignment

### Management Decision Support at The Wireless Café

Go to The Wireless Café's link on the Student Web Site. There you will be asked to think about how automated tools could support better decision making at the restaurant.

***Instructions for accessing The Wireless Café on the Student Web Site:***

1. Go to *wiley.com/college/turban*.
2. Select Turban/Leidner/McLean/Wetherbe's *Information Technology for Management*, Sixth Edition.
3. Click on Student Resources site, in the toolbar on the left.
4. Click on the link for Virtual Company Web Site.
5. Click on Wireless Café.

## Online Resources

More resources and study tools are located on the Student Web Site and on WileyPLUS. You'll find additional chapter materials and useful Web links. In addition, self-quizzes that provide individualized feedback are available for each chapter.

## Questions For Review

1. Describe the manager's major roles.
2. Define models and list the major types used in DSSs.
3. Explain the phases of intelligence, design, and choice.
4. What are structured (programmed) and unstructured problems? Give one example of each in the following three areas: finance, marketing, and personnel administration.
5. Give two definitions of DSSs. Compare DSS to management science.
6. Explain sensitivity analysis.
7. List and briefly describe the major components of a DSS.

8. What is the major purpose of the model-based component in a DSS?
9. Define GDSS. Explain how it supports the group decision-making process.
10. What is an organizational DSS?
11. What is the difference between an EIS and an ESS?
12. Why do executives need specialized support?
13. What causes different decision support systems to fail?
14. Define artificial intelligence and list its major characteristics.
15. What is the Turing test?

16. List the major advantages and disadvantages of artificial intelligence as compared with natural intelligence.

17. List the commercial AI technologies.

18. List three major capabilities and benefits of an ES.

19. Define the major components of an ES.

20. Which component of an ES is mostly responsible for the reasoning capability?

21. List the 10 generic categories of ESs.

22. Describe some of the limitations of ESs.

23. Describe a natural language and natural language processing; list their characteristics.

24. List the major advantages of voice recognition and voice understanding.

25. What is an artificial neural network?

26. What are the major benefits and limitations of neural computing?

27. Define fuzzy logic, and describe its major features and benefits.

28. Define semantic Web and describe its purposes.

29. How can frontline employees be supported for decision making?

## Questions for Discussion

1. What could be the biggest advantages of a mathematical model that supports a major investment decision?

2. Your company is considering opening a branch in China. List several typical activities in each phase of the decision (intelligence, design, choice, and implementation).

3. How is the term *model* used in this chapter? What are the strengths and weaknesses of modeling?

4. American Can Company announced that it was interested in acquiring a company in the health maintenance organization (HMO) field. Two decisions were involved in this act: (1) the decision to acquire an HMO, and (2) the decision of which one to acquire. How can a DSS, ES, or ESS be used in such situation?

5. Relate the concept of a rule-based knowledge subsystem to frontline decision support. What is the role of Web tools in such support?

6. Discuss how GDSSs can negate the dysfunctions of face-to-face meetings (Chapter 4).

7. Read the CIGNA case (*IT at Work 12.7*) and answer the following questions:
   a. Describe the motivation for developing the eCare system.

   b. Explain the role of the intelligent systems and their potential benefits in the case.
   c. What are the major difficulties you can anticipate in the process of developing and using the system?
   d. How are these systems different from traditional analytical systems described earlier in the chapter?
   e. Why was the intelligent system combined with a KM system?

8. A major difference between a conventional decision support system and an ES is that the former can explain a "how" question whereas the latter can also explain a "why" question. Discuss.

9. What is the difference between voice recognition and voice understanding?

10. Compare and contrast neural computing and conventional computing.

11. Fuzzy logic is frequently combined with expert systems and/or neural computing. Explain the logic of such integration.

12. Explain why even an intelligent system can fail.

## Exercises and Projects

1. Sofmic (fictitious name) is a large software vendor. About twice a year, Sofmic acquires a small specialized software company. Recently, a decision was made to look for a software company in the area of data mining. Currently, there are about 15 companies that would gladly cooperate as candidates for such acquisitions.

   Bill Gomez, the corporate CEO, asked that a recommendation for a candidate for acquisition be submitted to him within one week. "Make sure to use some computerized support for justification, preferably from the area of AI," he said. As a manager responsible for

   submitting the recommendation to Gomez, you need to select a computerized tool for conducting the analysis. Respond to the following points:
   a. Prepare a list of all the tools that you would consider.
   b. Prepare a list of the major advantages and disadvantages of each tool, as it relates to this specific case.
   c. Select a computerized tool.
   d. Mr. Gomez does not assign grades to your work. You make a poor recommendation and you are out. Therefore, carefully justify your recommendation.

2. Table 12.5 provides a list of 10 categories of ES. Compile a list of 10 examples from the various functional areas in an organization (accounting, finance, production, marketing, human resources, and so on) that will show functional applications as they are related to the 10 categories.

3. Read Minicase 2 and answer these questions:
   a. Why do airlines need optimization systems for crew scheduling?
   b. What role can experts' knowledge play in this case?

c. What are the similarities between the systems in Singapore and Malaysia?

4. *Debate:* Prepare a table showing all the arguments you can think of that justify the position that computers cannot think. Then, prepare arguments that show the opposite.

5. Enter *sas.com* and find the story of Quaker Chemical. View the video. Write a report about how the Strategic Performance Management tool helped the company. Relate it to the scorecard.

## Group Assignments and Projects

1. Development of an organizational DSS is proposed for your university. As a group, identify the management structure of the university and the major existing information systems. Then, identify and interview several potential users of the system. In the interview, you should check the need for such a system and convince the potential users of the benefits of the system.

2. Prepare a report regarding DSSs and the Web. As a start, go to *dssresources.com.* (Take the DSS tour.) Each group represents one vendor such as *microstrategy.com, sas.com,* and *cai.com.* Each group should prepare a report that aims to convince a company why its DSS Web tools are the best.

3. Find recent application(s) of intelligent systems in an organization. Assign each group member to a major functional area. Then, using a literature search, material from vendors, or industry contacts, each member should find two or three recent applications (within the last six months) of intelligent systems in this area. Try the journals *Expert Systems* and *IEEE Intelligent Systems.*

   a. The group will make a presentation in which it will try to convince the class via examples that intelligent systems are most useful in its assigned functional area.
   b. The entire class will conduct an analysis of the similarities and differences among the applications across the functional areas.
   c. The class will vote on which functional area is benefiting the most from intelligent systems.

4. Each group member composes a list of mundane tasks he or she would like an intelligent system to prepare. The group will then meet and compare and draw some conclusions.

5. Investigate the use of NLP and voice recognition techniques that enable consumers to get information from the Web, conduct transactions, and interact with others, all by voice, through regular and cell telephones. Investigate articles and vendors of voice portals and find the state of the art. Write a report.

## Internet Exercises

1. Enter the site of *microstrategy.com* and identify its major analytics products. Find success stories of customers using these products.

2. Enter *groupsystems.com* and select two customer success stories. Write a summary of each.

3. Find 10 case studies about DSSs. (Try *microstrategy.com, sas.com,* and *google.com.*) Analyze for DSS characteristics.

4. Enter *solver.com, ncr.com, hyperion.com,* and *ptc.com.* Identify their frontline system initiatives.

5. Prepare a report on the use of ESs in help desks. Collect information from *ginesys.com, exsys.com, ilog.com,* and *pcai.com/pcai.*

6. Enter the Web site of Carnegie Mellon University (*cs.cmu.edu*) and identify current activities on the Land Vehicle. Send an e-mail to ascertain when the vehicle will be on the market.

7. Visit *sas.com/pub/neural/FAZ.html/.* Identify links to real-world applications of neural computing in finance, manufacturing, health care, and transportation. Then visit *wolfram.com.* Prepare a report on current applications.

8. Visit *spss.com, informatica.com,* or *accure.com* and identify their Internet analytical solutions. Compare and comment. Relate your findings to business performance measurement.

9. Enter *exsys.com* and identify public systems–oriented advisory systems. Summarize in a report.

10. Enter *fairisaac.com* and find how credit risk scores are calculated. Also find how fraud is treated.

11. Access the Web and e-journals in your library to find at least three reports on the use of integrated intelligent methods for intelligent decision support. Evaluate whether the applications are feasible in the real world.

12. Access *lpa.co.uk/cbr.htm* and find information about LPA's intelligent products. Write a one-page summary. Also, find information at the LPA Web site about products for the other systems described in this chapter. View the demos. Write a short report.

13. Enter *voiceingov.org/blog* and *fluencyvoice.com* and select three applications in each of the voice technologies. Write a summary.

14. Enter *lec.com* and *languageweaver.com* and review all their machine translation products. Write a report.

15. Access *ivoice.com* and describe the capabilities of their products.

16. Enter *xpertrule* and *gensym.com*. Review their business rule products. Write a summary.

# Minicase 1

POM   GLOBAL

## A DSS Reshapes the Railway in the Netherlands

More than 5,000 trains pass through 2,800 railway kilometers and 400 stations each day in the Netherlands. As of the mid-1990s, the railway infrastructure was hardly sufficient to handle the passenger flow. The problem worsened during rush hours, and trains were delayed. Passengers complained and tended to use cars, whose variable cost is lower than that of using the train. This increased the congestion on the roads, adding pollution and traffic accidents. Several other problems plagued the system. The largest railway company, Nederlandse Spoorwegen (NS), was losing money in rural areas and agreed to continue services there only if the government would integrate the railways with bus and taxi systems, so that commuters would have more incentives to use the trains. Government help was needed.

Rail 21 is the name of the government's attempt to bring the system into the twenty-first century. It is a complex, multibillion-dollar project. The government wanted to reduce road traffic among the large cities, stimulate regional economies by providing a better public transportation system, stimulate rail cargo, and reduce the number of short-distance passenger flights in Europe. NS wanted to improve service and profitability. A company called Railned is managing the project, which is scheduled for completion in 2010.

Railned developed several alternative infrastructures (called "cocktails"), and put them to analysis. The analysis involved four steps: (1) Use experts to list possible alternative projects, (2) estimate passenger flows in each, using an econometric model, (3) determine optimization of rail lines, and (4) test feasibility. The last two steps were complex enough that the following computerized DSSs were developed for their execution:

- *PROLOP:* This DSS was designed to do the lines optimization. It involves a database and three quantitative models. It supports several decisions regarding rails, and it can be used to simulate the scenarios of the "cocktails." It incorporates a management science model, called integer linear programming. PROLOP also compares line systems based on different criteria. Once the appropriate line system is completed, an

analysis of the required infrastructure is done, using the second DSS, called DONS.

- *DONS:* This system contains a DSS database, graphical user interface, and two algorithmic modules. The first algorithm computes the arrival and departure times for each train at each station where it stops, based on "hard" constraints (must be met), and "soft" constraints (can be delayed). It represents both safety and customer-service requirements. The objective is to create a feasible timetable for the trains. If a feasible solution is not possible, planners relax some of the "soft" constraints. If this does not help, modifications in the lines system are explored.

- *STATIONS:* Routing the trains through the railway stations is an extremely difficult problem that cannot be solved simultaneously with the timetable. Thus, STATIONS, another DSS, is used. Again, feasible optimal solutions are searched for. If these do not exist, system modifications are made.

This DSS solution is fairly complex due to conflicting objectives of the government and the railway company (NS), so negotiations on the final choices are needed. To do so, Railned developed a special DSS model for conducting cost-benefit evaluations. It is based on a multiple-criteria approach with conflicting objectives. This tool can rank alternative "cocktails" based on certain requirements and assumptions. For example, one set of assumptions emphasizes NS long-term profitability, while the other one tries to meet the government requirements.

The DSSs were found to be extremely useful. They reduced the planning time and the cost of the analysis and increased the quality of the decisions. An example was an overpass that required an investment of $15 million. DONS came up with a timetable that required an investment of only $7.5 million by using an alternative safety arrangement. The DSS solution is used during the operation of the system as well for monitoring and making adjustments and improvements in the system.

*Source:* Compiled from Hooghiemstra et al. (1999) and Zwaneveld et al. (2001).

## Questions for Minicase 1

1. Why were management science optimizations by themselves not sufficient in this case?
2. What kinds of DSSs were used?
3. Enter *NS.nl* and find information about NS's business partners and the system. (English information is available on some pages.)
4. Given the environment described in the case, which of the DSS generic characteristics described in this chapter are likely to be useful, and how?
5. In what steps of the process can simulation be used, and for what?
6. Identify sensitivity analysis in this case.

# Minicase 2

POM GLOBAL

## Singapore and Malaysia Airlines Intelligent Systems

### The Problem

Airlines fly around the globe, mostly with their native crew. Singapore Airlines and Malaysia Airlines are relatively small airlines, but they serve dozens of different countries. If a crewmember is ill on route, there is a problem of quickly finding a replacement. This is just one example why crew scheduling may be complex, especially when it is subject to regulatory constraints, contract agreements, and crew preferences. Disturbances such as weather conditions, maintenance problems, etc. also make crew management difficult.

### The Solution

Singapore airlines uses Web-based intelligent systems including expert systems and neural computing to manage the company's flight crew scheduling and handle disruptions to the crew rosters. The Integrated Crew Management System (ICMS) project, implemented in Singapore since 1997, consists of three modules: one roster assignment module for cockpit crew, one for the cabin crew, and a crew tracking module. The first two modules automate the tracking and scheduling of the flight crew's timetable. The second module tracks the positions of the crew and includes an *intelligent system* that handles crew pattern disruptions.

For example, crews are rearranged if one member falls ill while in a foreign port; the system will find a backup in order to prevent understaffing on the scheduled flight. The intelligent system then determines the best way to reschedule the different crew members' rosters to accommodate the sick person. When a potentially disruptive situation occurs, the intelligent system automatically draws upon the knowledge stored in the database and advises the best course of action. This might mean repositioning the crew or calling in backup staff. The crew tracking system includes a crew disruption handling module that provides decision-support capabilities in real time.

A similar Web-based system is used by Malaysia Airlines, as of summer 2003, to optimize flight crew utilization. Also called ICMS, it leverages optimization software from *ilog.com*. Its Crew Pairing Optimization (CPO) module utilizes Ilog Cplex and Ilog Solver optimization components to ensure compliance with airline regulations, trade union agreements, and company policies, to minimize the costs associated with crew accommodations and transportation and to efficiently plan and optimize staff utilization and activities associated with long-term planning and daily operations. The Crew Duty Assignment (CDA) module provides automatic assignment of duties to all flight crews. The system considers work rules, regulatory requirements, and crew requests to produce an optimal monthly crew roster.

### The Results

Despite the difficult economic times, both airlines are competing successfully in the region, and their balance sheets are better than most other airlines.

*Sources:* Compiled from news item at *Computerworld Singapore* (April 10, 2003), and from *ilog.com* (accessed July 2006).

### Questions for Minicase 2

1. Why do airlines need optimization systems for crew scheduling?
2. What role can experts' knowledge play in this case?
3. What are the similarities between the systems in Singapore and Malaysia?
4. The airlines use ADSs for their pricing strategy (pricing and yield optimization). Can they use an ADS for crew management? Why or why not?

# References

Adkins, M., M. Burgoon, and J. F. Nunamaker, "Using Group Support Systems for Strategic Planning with the United States Air Force," *Decision Support Systems,* Vol. 34, 2002.

Agres, A. B., et al., "A Tale of Two Cities Case Studies of Group Support Systems Transition," *Group Decision and Negotiation,* July 2005.

Amato-McCoy, D. M., "Speech Recognition System Picks Up the Pace in Kwik Trip DC," *Stores,* May 2003.

Ante, S., "Owens & Minor," *BusinessWeek,* November 24, 2003.

Anthony, R. N., *Planning and Control Systems: A Framework for Analytics.* Cambridge, MA: Harvard University Press, 1965.

Arnold, V., et al., "Impact of Intelligent Decision Aids on Expert and Novice Decision-Makers' Judgments," *Accounting and Finance,* 44(1), March 2004.

Barrett, L., "Roadblock: Unequipped Sales Reps," *Baseline,* November 1, 2003.

Barrett, L., and D. F. Carr, "Proud Sponsor of the American Dream," *Baseline,* September 2005.

Berg, J. E., and T. A. Rietz, "Prediction Markets as Decision Support Systems," *Information Systems Frontiers,* January 2003.

Bonabeau, E., "Don't Trust Your Gut," *Harvard Business Review,* May 2003.

Brath, R., and M. Peters, "Visualization Spreadsheets," *DM Direct,* January 2006.

Briggs, D., and D. Arnoff, "DSSs Failures: An Evolutionary Perspective," *Proceedings DSI AGE 2002, Cork, Ireland,* July 2002.

*Business World,* "Executive Information System: The Right Move," May 4, 2004, *itmatters.com.ph/news/news_05042002f.html* (no longer available online).

Cawsey, A., *The Essence of Artificial Intelligence.* Upper Saddle River, NJ: Prentice Hall PTR, 1998.

*Computerworld,* July 7, 1997.

*Computerworld Singapore,* April 10, 2003.

D'Agostino, D., "Lost in the Translation," *CIO Insight,* December 2005.

Davenport, T. H., "Competing on Analytics," *Harvard Business Review,* January 2006.

Davenport, T. H., and J. G. Harris, "Automated Decision Making Comes of Age," *MIT Sloan Management Review,* Summer 2005.

*dmreview.com,* 2001.

Edwards, C., "Charles Schwab," *BusinessWeek,* November 24, 2003.

Fagerholt, K., "A Computer-Based DSS for Vessel Fleet Scheduling," *Decision Support Systems,* April 2004.

Fleischmann, M., J. M. Hall, and D. F Pyke, "Smart Pricing," *MIT Sloan Management Review,* Winter 2004.

Gallager, S., "Following Footwear, Step by Step," *Baseline,* November 2003.

Gentry, J. A., et al., "Using Inductive Learning to Predict Bankruptcy," *Journal of Organizational Computing and Electronic Commerce,* Vol. 12, 2002.

Gorry, G. A., and M. S. Scott-Morton, "A Framework for Management Information Systems," *Sloan Management Review,* 13(1), Fall 1971.

Hackathorn, R. D., and P. G. Keen, "Organizational Strategies for Personal Computing in Decision Support Systems," *MIS Quarterly,* September 1981.

Haley Case Brief, "CIGNA Creates eCare Treatment Request Approval System with Haley Systems' Technology," February 2006.

Hooghiemstra, J. S., et al., "Decision Support Systems Support the Search for Win–Win Solutions in Railway Network," *Interfaces,* March–April 1999.

Hovanesian, M. D., "Wells Fargo," *BusinessWeek,* November 24, 2003.

Huber, G. P., *The Necessary Nature of Future Firms: Attributes of Survivors in a Changing World.* San Francisco: Sage Publications, 2003.

*ilog.com* (accessed July 2006).

*InfoWorld.com,* "China Everbright Bank Selects ILOG JRules to Streamline Its Loan and Credit Decisioning Processes," June 20, 2006, *infoworld.com/ILOG_JRules/product_48127.html?view=8 &curNodeId=7&prId=SFTU09020062006-1* (accessed July 2006).

Iserlis, Y., "Intelligent Programs and Machines: A Snapshot of Where We Are," *PCAI,* March 2004.

Lam, S. S. Y., et al., "Prediction and Optimization of a Ceramic Casting Process Using a Hierarchical Hybrid System of Neural Network and Fuzzy Logic," *IIE Transactions,* January 2000.

Martin-Flatin, J. P., et al., "Self-Managed Systems and Services: Introduction," *Communications of the ACM,* March 2006.

McKinley, E., "Getting a Jump on the Competition," *Stores,* October 2003.

Mintzberg, H., *The Nature of the Managerial Work.* New York: Harper & Row, 1973.

Mintzberg, H., and F. Westley, "Decision Making: It's Not What You Think," *MIT Sloan Management Review,* Spring 2001.

Navis, C., "California DMV Streamlines Fee Processing," case study, *Fair Isaac Corp.,* 2003.

Oracle, "New to Voice Technology," *Oracle.com,* 2006, *oracle.com/ technology/tech/wireless/beginner/voice.html?_template=/ocom/t* (accessed March 2006).

Patterson, D. A., "Robots in the Desert—A Research Parable for our Times," *Communications of the ACM,* December 2005.

*PC Week,* August 17, 1998.

*platinum.com* (now part of Computer Associates, *ca.com*) (accessed July 2006).

Pontz, C., and D. J. Power, "Building an Expert Assistance System for Examiners (EASE) at the Pennsylvania Department of Labor and Industry," 2003, *dssresourses.com/cases/Penndeptlabor.html* (no longer available online).

Powell, A., et al., "Virtual Teams: Review of Current Literature," *Database Journal,* Winter 2004.

Power, D. J., *Decision Support Systems: Concepts and Resources for Managers.* Westport, CT: Quorum Books, 2002.

Rivlin, G., "The Things They Carry," *Fortune,* Winter 2002, *fortune. cnet.com/fortune/0,10000,0-5937473-7-7707001,00.html?tag_txt* (no longer available online).

Rockart, J. F., and D. DeLong, *Executive Support Systems.* Homewood, IL: Dow Jones–Irwin, 1988.

Russell, S. J., and P. Norvig, *Artificial Intelligence,* 2nd ed. Upper Saddle River, NJ: Prentice Hall, 2002.

Scheiner, M., "Neiman Marcus Uses Natural Language Search to Boost Online Sales," *Customer Relationship Management,* July 2003.

Shadbolt, J., et al., *Neural Networks and the Financial Markets: Predicting, Combining, and Portfolio Optimisation (Perspectives in Neural Computing).* New York: Springer-Verlag, 2002.

Simon, H., *The New Science of Management Decisions,* rev. ed. Englewood Cliffs, NJ: Prentice-Hall, 1977.

Singh, S. K., et al., "EIS Support of Strategic Management Process," *Decision Support Systems,* May 2002.

Smith, K., and J. Gupta (eds.), *Neural Networks in Business: Techniques and Applications.* Hershey, PA: The Idea Group, 2002.

Stonebraker, J. S., "How Bayer Makes Decisions to Develop New Drugs," *Interfaces,* November–December 2002.

Turban, E., et al., *Decision Support Systems and Intelligent Systems,* 8th ed. Upper Saddle River, NJ: Prentice Hall, 2007.

Van Fleet, D. D., et al., "Closing the Performance Feedback Gap with Expert Systems," *Academy of Management Executive,* August 2005.

Vedder, R. G., V. Prybutok, and T. VanDyke, "An Expert System That Was," *Proceedings of the Fifth International Decision Sciences Institute Conference,* Athens, Greece, July 4–7, 1999.

Vedder, R. G., et al., "Death of an Expert System: A Case Study of Success and Failure," *Journal of International Technology and Information Management,* 11(1), 2002.

"Visa Cracks Down on Fraud," *Information Week,* August 26, 1996.

*visa.com,* press releases (accessed June 19, 2003).

"Visa Stamps Out Fraud," *International Journal of Retail and Distribution Management,* 23(11), Winter 1995, p. viii.

Von Ahn, L., M. Blum, and J. Langford, "Telling Humans and Computers Apart Automatically," *Communications of the ACM,* February 2004.

Watson, H., "Sorting Out What's New in Decision Support," *Business Intelligent Journal,* Winter 2005.

*weforum.org* (accessed July 2006).

White, C., "Now Is the Right Time for Real-Time BI," *DM Review,* September 2004.

Yiman-Seid, D., and Kobsa, A., "Expert-Finding Systems for Organizations: Problem and Domain Analysis and the DEMOIR Approach," *Journal of Organizational Computing and Electronic Commerce,* Vol. 13, 2003.

Zaman M. "Business Intelligence: Its Ins and Outs," January 2005, *technologyevaluationcenters.com.*

Zwaneveld, P. J., L. G. Kroon, and S. P. M. van Hosel, "Routing Trains through a Railway Station Based on a Node Packing Model," *European Journal of Operations Research,* Vol. 28, 2001.

Part VI | Implementing and Managing IT
▶ 13. IT Strategy and Planning
14. Information Technology Economics
15. Acquiring IT Application and Infrastructure
16. Security
17. Impacts of IT on Individuals, Organizations, and Society

Chapter

# 13

# IT Strategy and Planning

## Learning Objectives

After studying this chapter, you will be able to:

❶ Explain how IT can contribute to strategic objectives and competitive advantage.

❷ Assess potential impacts of IT using several frameworks.

❸ Explain the value and challenges of aligning business and IT strategies.

❹ Describe the importance of IT planning and the methodologies to facilitate it.

❺ Discuss factors to be considered to optimize that allocation of an organization's IT resources.

❻ Identify and describe how to build strong relationships between the information systems department and business units.

## Integrating *IT*

 **ACC**
 **FIN**
 **MKT**
 **POM**
 **HRM**
 **IS**
 **SVC**

# BOEING'S IT STRATEGIC ALIGNMENT: THE *EARLY ENGAGEMENT SYSTEM*

Boeing (*boeing.com*) is the company typically associated with the development and marketing of jet aircraft, a highly technical field. Headquartered in Chicago, the corporation posted 2005 sales of $54.8 billion. Boeing's 153,000 employees are spread throughout 67 countries. Boeing is the United States's number-one net exporter in the global economy. In addition, Boeing is China's largest commercial aviation partner. By 2025, Boeing forecasts that China will need 2,300 jetliners, becoming one of the world's largest airplane markets.

## The Problem/Opportunity

In 1998, Boeing had over 3,800 direct suppliers. Relationships with suppliers were managed strictly through competitive bidding on the basis of price, quality, and delivery. Terms were specified in contracts, which then had to be closely managed. Boeing wanted to move away from this competitive model with its non-value-added processes and form closer business relationships with fewer suppliers. In effect, suppliers would be extensions of Boeing's factories. Information and collaboration systems were needed that would interface with their suppliers to improve the delivery of parts to their factories. Integrated supply chain information systems would improve visibility and flexibility, decrease production time, and increase competitiveness.

## The Solution

Boeing's design and production strategy is to get the 787 built as quickly and economically as possible. That involves an unprecedented degree of collaboration between Boeing and its partners around the world—partners who are participating in the actual design of the plane.

To implement its new strategic plan, Boeing reorganized its supplier operation and collaboration systems. They renamed their supplier management operation Global Partners. In 2006, Boeing had reduced the number of suppliers who supported the manufacture and service

of its commercial aircraft, including the 787 Dreamliner, from 3,800 to 1,200—a 68 percent reduction in the number of suppliers.

**HRM**

**IS**

**POM**

Boeing began development of the 787 by collaborating with those suppliers. Suppliers at over 130 sites around the world are linked to Boeing's development teams through regular face-to-face meetings, known as *partner councils*. Urgent items are dealt with via videoconferencing over secure Internet connections. The videoconferences are, in effect, the modern-day version of engineers gathering around a drawing board to scratch their heads and work out how to make something.

Boeing maintains ten multimedia rooms at its Everett, Washington complex for the use of collaboration teams. The rooms are open 365 days a year, 24 hours a day because *it's always daytime somewhere*. There may be meetings underway between one group of engineers at Boeing and their peers at Mitsubishi Heavy Industries Ltd., in Japan, while another group works with teams at Japan's Kawasaki Heavy Industries Ltd. and Australia's Hawker de Havilland, a Boeing subsidiary. A visualization application developed by Boeing allows the teams to do real-time design reviews of complex geometry without any lag time as the models load. The tone is cordial because it's engineers talking to engineers. Meetings are conducted in English, with sidebar conversations as needed in native languages around the world.

Sharing information between Boeing and suppliers allowed everyone in the supply chain to take a longer-term view of how the market for the new aircraft would develop. Suppliers were able to prepare more effectively for future demand, and Boeing was able to prepare for possible problems. The aim was to smooth out any potential lumps in the supply chain before they materialized. With a price tag of $130 million for each 787, both Boeing and its partners needed to get the logistics right to deliver on time. For airlines struggling with high fuel prices, the 787 offers a large number of seats (about 300 seats), but its lightweight construction gives a 20 percent fuel saving over other aircraft of similar size. The 787 was easy to reconfigure to suit different airlines, thus improving their return on investment.

## The Results

Boeing is making the shift not only for the savings from making the planes faster and cheaper. The company is also spreading the costs of design and development throughout its partner network, and building global relationships that may, in turn, help the company sell its planes overseas.

The previous state of the art in aircraft manufacturing was to have global partners work from a common blueprint to produce parts that were then physically shipped to a Boeing assembly plant near Seattle to see if they fit together. There, successive iterations of the planes were built and refined with onsite teams from around the world. That process and outdated information systems plan is gone.

Now parts are designed concurrently by partners, and *virtually assembled* in a computer model maintained by Boeing outside its corporate firewall. The design is occurring in Japan, Russia, Italy, and the United States. This kind of collaboration has taken a huge amount of time out of the process. Different people build different pieces by creating data that are assembled and checked in real time. Completed sections of the plane are picked up by three specially fitted 747s and carried to a Boeing facility in Everett, Washington. Because of online modeling, Boeing can now trust its global partners with the process of creating entire sections of the plane, from concept through to production.

Global Partners has replaced the company's previous Supply Management and Procurement. The name change reflects Boeing's new strategic approach to its supplier relationships. Global Partners is part of the newly created Airplane Production organization, which consolidates all commercial airplane production operations into a single integrated Boeing production system—from design through production and delivery.

The competitive advantage is critical to Boeing, which is in a global battle for market leadership with Airbus SAS, the Toulouse, France–based aerospace manufacturer that has emerged as its most potent competitor for civil aviation business in the modern era. Boeing has 291 firm orders and 88 commitments from 27 airlines for the new Dreamliner.

Boeing still makes pieces of the planes they sell, but the change in their business model is undeniable. While they still do manufacturing, Boeing is moving up the value stream to become a large-scale systems integrator.

*Sources:* Compiled from Berstein (2006), Cone (2006), and *boeing.com* (accessed October 2006).

## Lessons Learned from This Case

Earlier collaboration with suppliers in the manufacturing process brings Boeing access to crucial technology and ideas. The 787 airplane ends up with much better solutions because the company asks suppliers for ideas and support on solutions. That partnership lets them come back to Boeing with ideas that are more industry-based. The payoff is that suppliers spread their development costs across a larger base while Boeing's aircraft meet their mission requirements.

Through numerous examples, this chapter demonstrates how different kinds of strategic information systems work. We also present some classic models on which strategic information systems have been built and utilized from the 1970s to this very day.

# 13.1 IT Strategic Alignment

The most recent study of chief information officers (CIOs) sponsored by the Society for Information Management found that the number-one issue facing CIOs, from their own perspective, was that of IT and business alignment (Luftman, 2005). Table 13.1 shows the top 10 issues facing CIOs.

Strategic alignment has long been an issue of importance both in information systems (IS) research and to IS practitioners and continues in importance today. Alignment remains an important issue for CIOs in part because failure to align information technology (IT) to business strategy is believed to result in the failure of many IS initiatives. Particularly in the case of organizationwide (or enterprise-wide) information systems initiatives, alignment with the strategic objectives of the organization is an important challenge for organizations. See Figure 13.1 for the relationship among business, IS, and IT strategy.

Aligning IT with the organization has two facets. One facet is aligning the IS function's strategy, structure, technology, and processes with those of the business units so that IS and business units are working toward the same goals. This facet is referred to as *IS alignment* (Chan, 2002). Another type of alignment, referred to as *IS strategic alignment,* involves aligning IS strategy with organizational strategy. The goal of IS strategic alignment is to ensure that IS priorities, decisions, and projects are consistent with the needs of the entire business. Failure to properly align IS with the organizational strategy may result in large investments in systems that have a low payoff, or failure to invest in systems that might potentially have a high payoff.

In order to achieve IT alignment, several preconditions must be achieved. Among these is communication between the line and IS executives and interconnected planning processes, such that IS planning does not occur in isolation. Deloitte Consulting LLP found that 96 percent of IT executives polled indicated that significant or moderate bottom-line impact would result from aligning IT strategy with business strategy. Yet, many still felt that their alignment efforts were unsuccessful (Beal, 2004). Another precondition for successful alignment is a clear definition of IT's role in an organization. A major challenge is that the technology infrastructures built to support one strategy often outlast the strategy that they were intended to support (Beal, 2004).

| TABLE 13.1 | Top Issues Facing CIOs |
|---|---|
| **Rank** | **Issue** |
| 1 | IT and business alignment |
| 2 | Attracting, developing, and retaining IT professionals |
| 3 | Security and privacy |
| 4 | IT strategic planning |
| 5 | Speed and agility |
| 6 | Government regulations |
| 7 | Complexity reduction |
| 8 | Measuring the performance of the IT organization |
| 9 | Creating an information architecture |
| 10 | IT governance |

*Source:* Adapted from Luftman (2005).

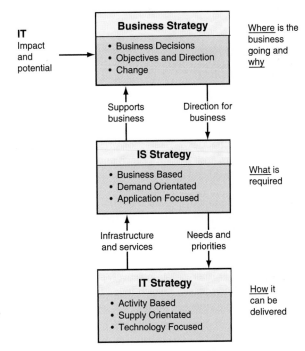

**Figure 13.1** The relationship among business, IS, and IT strategies. (*Source:* Ward and Peppard, 2002, Figure 1.6, p. 41.)

CHALLENGES FOR IT ALIGNMENT

Despite the theoretical importance of IT alignment, organizations continue to demonstrate limited actual alignment. Alignment is a complex management activity, and its complexity increases with the increasing complexity of organizations. *IT at Work 13.1* discusses how Hewlett-Packard addresses alignment.

To align IT with the organization, CIOs need to ensure that the IT department is focused on building those systems that help the organization achieve its major objectives and help business units succeed in achieving their major goals. Rather than being narrow technologists, CIOs must be business and technology savvy. Several frameworks are useful in helping CIOs, and other IT specialists, develop an understanding of the industry and organization in which they operate. These frameworks—the competitive forces model, the value chain model, and the resource-based view of the firm model—can also provide a basis for brainstorming about the potential strategic application of IT to business problems.

# 13.2 Competitive Forces Model

One way to analyze the strategic potential of information systems is to consider their influence on one or more of the five forces presented in Porter's **competitive forces model** (see Appendix 1A). Take, for example, the strategic impact of Internet initiatives. Porter (2001) and Harmon et al. (2001) suggest some ways the Internet influences competition in the five factors:

1. **The threat of new entrants.** For most firms, the Internet *increases* the threat of new competitors. First, the Internet sharply reduces traditional barriers to entry, such as the need for a sales force or a physical storefront to sell goods and services. All a competitor needs to do is set up a Web site. This threat is especially acute in industries that perform an intermediation role as well as industries in which the primary product or service is digital. Second, the geographical reach of the Internet enables distant competitors to bring competition into the local market, or even an indirect competitor to compete more directly with an existing firm.

# IT at Work 13.1

## Hewlett-Packard Aligns Business and IT Strategies

MKT

Hewlett-Packard (*hp.com*) developed a planning methodology in which business process strategies and technologies are defined and aligned concurrently. This methodology was designed to allow the company to make process changes regardless of the limitations of the existing technology, and it gives visibility to the impacts that new technologies and processes have on each other.

In the past, Hewlett-Packard (HP) had used a sequential process. First, it defined the business strategy and the operations and supporting strategies, including technologies. Then, all these functions were aligned and replanned, taking into consideration the technologies available. In the new methodology, the planning is performed for all areas *concurrently*. Furthermore, the entire approach is complemented by a strong focus on teamwork, specialized and objective-driven functional areas and business units, and a commitment to quality and customer satisfaction. The approach links strategy and action. The business alignment framework takes into account the necessary process changes resulting from changes in the business environment, as well as potential technological developments. But, because major changes may result in a change in value systems as well as culture and team structures of the organization, HP includes these factors within the planning methodology.

Target processes, technologies, and standards drive the selection of potential solutions. The participative management approach ensures effective implementation. According to the framework, business processes and information requirements are defined in parallel with technology enablers and models, which are then linked throughout the alignment process.

HP's focus on strategic alignment is evident not only in its planning for internal technology solutions, but also in its quest for technological innovation through a centralized R&D function with an annual budget of $4 billion. The R&D function actively participates in the strategy development process, which helps the R&D department better understand what is driving customers while simultaneously offering a strong technology perspective that influences the business as a whole.

*Sources:* Compiled from Feurer et al. (2000), Collins (2004), and *hp.com* (June 2004).

*For Further Exploration:* Why is concurrent planning superior? What communication and collaboration support is needed?

2. **The bargaining power of suppliers.** The Internet's impact on suppliers is mixed. On the one hand, buyers can find alternative suppliers and compare prices more easily, reducing the supplier's bargaining power. On the other hand, as companies use the Internet to integrate their supply chain and join digital exchanges, participating suppliers will prosper by locking in customers and increasing switching costs.

3. **The bargaining power of customers (buyers).** The Web greatly increases a buyer's access to information about products and suppliers, Internet technologies can reduce customer switching costs, and buyers can more easily buy from downstream suppliers. These factors mean that the Internet greatly increases customers' bargaining power.

4. **The threat of substitute products or services.** Information-based industries are in the greatest danger here. Any industry in which digitalized information can replace material goods (e.g., music, books, software) must view the Internet as a threat.

5. **The rivalry among existing firms in the industry.** The visibility of Internet applications on the Web makes proprietary systems more difficult to keep secret, reducing differences among competitors. In most industries, the tendency for the Internet to lower variable costs relative to fixed costs encourages price discounting at the same time that competition migrates to price. Both are forces that encourage destructive price competition in an industry.

Porter concludes that the *overall* impact of the Internet is to increase competition, which negatively impacts profitability. According to Porter, "The great paradox of the Internet is that its very benefits—making information widely available; reducing the difficulty of purchasing, marketing, and distribution; allowing buyers and sellers to find and transact business with one another more easily—also make it more difficult for companies to capture those benefits as profits" (2001, p. 66).

In many other ways, Web-based systems are changing the nature of competition and even industry structure. Consider the following.

- Bookseller Barnes & Noble, hardware giant The Home Depot, and other companies have created independent online divisions, which are competing against the parent companies. Such companies are termed "click-and-mortar" companies, because they combine both "brick-and-mortar" and e-commerce operations.

- Any company that sells direct to consumers is also a distributor (wholesaler or retailer), competing against its own traditional distributors.

- The variable cost of a digital product is close to zero. Therefore, if large quantities are sold, the product's price can approach zero.

- Competitors are getting together and becoming more willing to share information. Examples are the vertical exchanges owned by industry leaders. The "Big Three" auto manufacturers, for example, operate the auto exchange *covisint.com*. Similar exchanges exist in the paper, chemical, and many other industries. (See Turban et al., 2006.)

Figure 13.2 describes some potential ways in which the use of the Internet by organizations can alter industry structure. For example, buyers may have greater

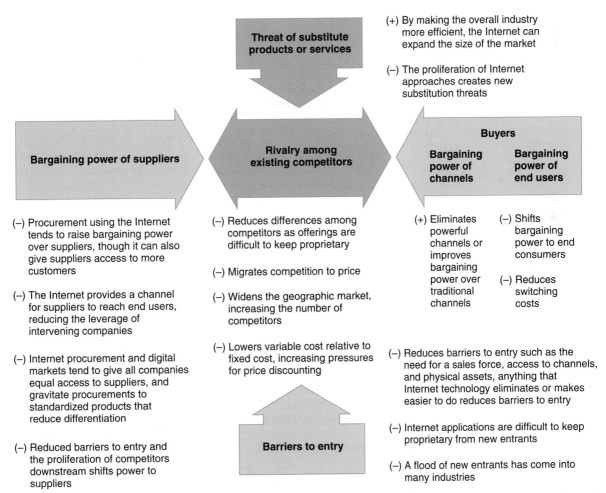

**Figure 13.2** Porter's Competitive Forces Model: How the Internet influences industry structure. (*Source:* Reprinted by permission of *Harvard Business Review*. From "Strategy and the Internet" by Michael E. Porter, *Harvard Business Review*, March 2001. Copyright 2001 by the Harvard Business School Publishing Corporation; all rights reserved.)

## *IT* at Work 13.2

### Britannica Seeks to Compete with Advancing Technology

MKT

The *Encyclopaedia Britannica* was first printed in Scotland in 1768, during the Scottish Enlightenment. It quickly became a world-renowned resource for knowledge and education and remained as such for the next 200 years. However, as technology rapidly advanced in the 1990s, *Britannica* began to suffer at the hands of cheaper, interactive encyclopedias sold on CD-ROMs. In response to this, the company created a media-rich CD-ROM version of their encyclopedia, which was given free with the printed version. Separately, this CD-ROM could be purchased for $1,000, but very few people were willing to pay $1,000 when a competing product was available essentially for free. *Encyclopaedia Britannica*'s next attempt at keeping up with the advancement of technology was to create *Britannica Online* (*britannica.com*), which provides free access to concise articles, but offers added features to paying members. Though this is a noteworthy step for *Britannica*, the ever-competitive online world presents such competition as *encyclopedia.com* and *wikipedia.com*, both of which have free services and vast amounts of information, not to mention catchier Web addresses. *Encyclopaedia Britannica* still markets its annual printed edition, at a cost of $1,659, along with dictionaries, thesauruses, globes, software, DVDs, and more. Though *Britannica* has enjoyed a rich history of success, it is difficult to gauge whether it can stay afloat in this technology-driven age.

*Sources:* Venkatraman (2000), *britannica.com* (accessed June 2006), *encyclopedia.com* (accessed June 2006), and *wikipedia.com* (accessed June 2006).

*For Further Exploration:* What competitive forces eroded *Encyclopaedia Britannica*'s market share? Does the company have any competitive advantages? Why or why not?

bargaining power as a result of the Internet for several reasons, including: Their access to various suppliers increases, their access to price information increases, and their ability to join forces with other buyers to obtain quantity discounts increases.

In some cases it is not a specific strategic information system that changes the nature of competition, but it is the Web technology itself that renders obsolete traditional business processes, brand names, and even superior products. One example is provided in *IT at Work 13.2*.

**STRATEGIES FOR COMPETITIVE ADVANTAGE**

Porter's model identifies the forces that influence competitive advantage in the marketplace. It can provide insight into the potential impact of information systems on an industry. Aside from analyzing the impacts of systems on the industry, of significant importance to managers is the development of a *strategy* aimed at establishing a profitable and sustainable position against these five forces. To establish such a position, a company needs to develop a strategy of performing activities differently from a competitor.

Porter (1985) proposed cost leadership, differentiation, and niche strategies. We discuss seven of these strategies for competitive advantage here.

1. **Cost leadership strategy:** Produce products and/or services at the lowest cost in the industry. A firm achieves cost leadership in its industry by thrifty buying practices, efficient business processes, forcing up the prices paid by competitors, and helping customers or suppliers reduce their costs. A cost leadership example is the Wal-Mart automatic inventory replenishment system. This system enables Wal-Mart to reduce storage requirements so that Wal-Mart stores have one of the highest ratios of sales floor space in the industry. Essentially Wal-Mart is using floor space to sell products, not store them, and it does not have to tie up capital in inventory. Savings from this system and others allows Wal-Mart to provide low-priced products to its customers and still earn high profits.

2. **Differentiation strategy:** Offer different products, services, or product features. By offering different, "better" products, companies can charge higher prices, sell more products, or both. Southwest Airlines has differentiated itself as a low-cost, short-haul, express airline, and that has proven to be a winning strategy for competing in the highly competitive airline industry. Dell has differentiated itself in the personal computer market through its mass-customization strategy.

3. **Niche strategy:** Select a narrow-scope segment (niche market) and be the best in quality, speed, or cost in that market. For example, several computer-chip manufacturers make customized chips for specific industries or companies. Some of the best-selling products on the Internet are niche products. For example, *dogtoys.com* and *cattoys.com* offer a large variety of pet toys that no other pet toy retailer offers.

4. **Growth strategy:** Increase market share, acquire more customers, or sell more products. Such a strategy strengthens a company and increases profitability in the long run. Web-based selling can facilitate growth by creating new marketing channels, such as electronic auctions. An example is Dell Computer (*dellauction.com*), which auctions both new and used computers mainly to individuals and small businesses.

5. **Alliance strategy:** Work with business partners in partnerships, alliances, joint ventures, or virtual companies. This strategy creates synergy, allows companies to concentrate on their core business, and provides opportunities for growth. Alliances are particularly popular in electronic commerce ventures. For example, in August 2000 Amazon.com and Toysrus.com launched a co-branded Web site to sell toys, capitalizing on each others' strengths. In spring 2001 they created a similar baby-products venture. Of special interest are alliances with suppliers, some of whom monitor inventory levels electronically and replenish inventory when it falls below a certain level (e.g., Wal-Mart, Master Builders). Alliances can also be made among competitors in a strategy known as "co-opetition" (cooperation + competition). For example, airlines in global alliances such as OneWorld and the Star Alliance compete for ticket sales on some routes, but once the ticket is sold they may cooperate by flying passengers on competitors' planes to avoid half-full planes.

6. **Innovation strategy:** Introduce new products and services, put new features in existing products and services, or develop new ways to produce them. Innovation is similar to differentiation except that the impact is much more dramatic. Differentiation "tweaks" existing products and services to offer the customer something special and different. Innovation implies something so new and different that it changes the nature of the industry. A classic example is the introduction of automated teller machines (ATMs) by Citibank. The convenience of this innovation gave Citibank a huge advantage over its competitors. Like many innovative products, the ATM changed the nature of competition in the banking industry so that now an ATM network is a competitive necessity for any bank. Eight ways that IT can introduce technological innovation for competitive advantage are shown in Table 13.2.

In the late 1990s innovation became almost synonymous with electronic commerce. The Internet, especially, enabled dot-com entrepreneurs to create innovative Web-based business models, such as Priceline's name-your-own-price model, Auto-by-Tel's infomediary model, and Amazon.com's affiliate program.

When one company introduces a successful innovation, other companies in the industry need to respond to the threat by attempting to duplicate or better

| TABLE 13.2 | Areas of IT Related to Technological Innovations |
|---|---|
| **Innovation** | **Advantage** |
| New business models | Being the first to establish a new model puts one way ahead of possible competitors. The Web enables many innovative new business models, such as Priceline's "name-your-own-price" and Auto-by-Tel's infomediary model. Creating and applying these models can provide strategic advantage. |
| New markets, global reach | Finding new customers in new markets. Using the Web, Amazon.com is selling books in over 200 countries, all by direct mail. Rosenbluth International, backed by its communication systems, expanded to 57 countries. |
| New products | Constantly innovating with new competitive products and services. Electronic Art Inc. was first to introduce CD-ROM-based video games. MP3 Inc. enabled downloading of music from its Web site. |
| Extended products | Leveraging old products with new competitive extensions. When a Korean company was the first to introduce "fuzzy logic" in its washing machines, sales went up 50 percent in a few months. |
| Differentiated products | Gaining advantage through unique products or added value. Compaq Computers at one time became the leading PC seller after providing self-diagnostic disks with its computers. Dell Computer pioneered the concept of home delivery of customized computers. |
| Supersystems | Erecting competitive barriers through major system developments that cannot be easily duplicated. American Airlines' reservation system, SABRE, became so comprehensive that it took years to duplicate; a supersystem always stays ahead of the competition. Caterpillar's multibillion-dollar equipment maintenance system is difficult to duplicate. |
| Interorganizational systems | Linking two organizational information systems together can lock out the competition. In the 1980s, American Hospital Supply installed supply-reordering systems in hospitals, to its competitive advantage. |
| Computer-aided sales | Offering systems that provide computer support to marketing and sales. For example, a company might equip salespeople with wireless handheld computers that allow them to provide price quotations at the customer's location. |

that innovation. Especially in electronic commerce, the visibility of technologies on the Web makes keeping innovations secret more difficult.

7. **Entry-barriers strategy:** Create barriers to entry. By introducing innovative products or using IT to provide exceptional service, companies can create barriers to entry from new entrants. Cisco's Dynamic Configuration Tool (*tools.cisco.com/qtc/config/html/configureHomGuest.htm*) allows prospective buyers to complete an online configuration of a Cisco product and receive intelligent feedback about compatibility and ordering. Service levels such as this make it difficult for new entrants to compete against Cisco. Firms may also create entry barriers by increasing the switching costs of customers or suppliers. A classic example is frequent-flyer and similar buyer-loyalty programs in the airline, hospitality, and retail industries. Companies that have such programs have more customers who are "locked in" by the incentives the loyalty programs offer. A business-to-business example in the car industry is e-procurement system Covisint, which locks in car manufacturers as customers and parts manufacturers as suppliers. By locking in customers, the firm is raising the barriers to entry.

These strategies may be interrelated. For example: Some innovations are achieved through alliances that reduce cost and increase growth; cost leadership improves customer satisfaction and may lead to growth; and alliances are key to locking in customers and increasing switching costs.

A different way to analyze competition and the role of IT is provided in Porter's value chain model, which is the subject we turn to next.

## 13.3 Value Chain Model

**THE MODEL**

The value chain can be diagrammed for both products and services and for any organization, private or public. (See Appendix 1A for the details of the value chain.) The initial purpose of the **value chain model** was to analyze the internal operations of a corporation, in order to increase its efficiency, effectiveness, and competitiveness. The model has since been used as a basis for explaining the support that IT can provide. It is also the basis for the *supply chain management* concept, which was presented in Chapter 7. *IT at Work 13.3* offers a vivid example of a company that occupies a key portion of a supply chain.

The value chain model is useful in conducting a company analysis, by systematically evaluating a company's key processes and core competencies. To do so, we first determine strengths and weaknesses of performing the activities and the values added by each activity. The activities that add more value are those that might provide strategic advantage. Then we investigate whether by adding IT the company can get even greater added value and where in the chain its use is most appropriate. For example, Caterpillar uses EDI to add value to its inbound and outbound activities; it uses its intranet to boost customer service. In Chapters 5 through 12 we

## IT at Work 13.3

### UPS Provides Supply Chain Solutions for High-Tech Companies

GLOBAL  POM  IS

United Parcel Service (UPS, *ups.com*), founded in 1907 as a messenger company in the United States, is a $36 billion corporation that focuses on enabling commerce around the globe. As the world's largest package delivery company and a leading global provider of specialized transportation and logistics services, UPS combines the flows of goods, information, and funds in more than 200 countries and territories worldwide. As an expert in global distribution, UPS recognized a great opportunity in the area of supply chain management. This led to the formation of UPS Supply Chain Solutions (*ups-scs.com*), which provides logistics, global freight, financial services, mail services, and consulting to improve customers' business performance and advance their global supply chains.

One of the sectors that has particularly benefited from this service is high-tech companies. Since the speed of high-tech product obsolescence increases each year, the time to get merchandise to market decreases dramatically. An additional concern for high-tech products is their high value, making inventory levels and security concerns just as important as speed. With experience in computers and peripherals, consumer electronics, telecommunications, semiconductors, and aerospace, UPS Supply Chain Solutions seeks to turn supply chain challenges into competitive advantages. The company

has done just that with such high-tech businesses as Hitachi GST (*hitachigst.com*), Cisco Systems (*cisco.com*), Alcatel (*alcatel.com*), and Silicon Graphics, Inc. (SGI, *sgi.com*). Each of these companies faced supply chain issues that UPS Supply Chain Solutions addressed through use of its global network, IT systems, post-sales support, service parts logistics, field-tech support, returns and repair management, international trade services, and a variety of other valuable resources.

In viewing UPS's history, it is clear that the company has continually been on the cutting edge of advancement. Through the creation of UPS Supply Chain Solutions, the company has once again proven that commitment to progress can lead to success. As high-tech companies face challenges in an intensely competitive market, UPS will undoubtedly be leading the way with new solutions.

*Sources:* Compiled from *ups.com* (accessed June 2006), *ups-scs.com* (accessed June 2006), *hitachigst.com* (accessed June 2006), *cisco.com* (accessed June 2006), *alcatel.com* (accessed June 2006), and *sgi.com* (accessed June 2006).

*For Further Exploration:* How would you describe the industry that UPS is in? What barriers to entry has UPS created?

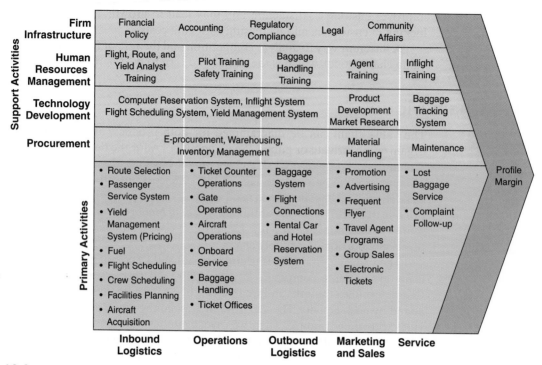

**Figure 13.3** The airline industry value chain superimposed on Porter's value chain. (*Source:* Adapted by Callon, 1996, and reprinted by permission of *Harvard Business Review*. From Michael Porter, "How Competitive Forces Shape Strategy," March–April 1979. © 1979 by Harvard Business School Publishing Corporation; all rights reserved.)

included many examples of how IT supports the activities of the value chain for individual firms. While initially developed with a manufacturing firm in mind, the value chain can also be applied to firms in a service industry, such as the airlines. Figure 13.3 applies the framework to an airline.

## PORTER'S MODELS IN THE DIGITAL AGE

The application of Porter's models is still valid today. But some adjustments may be needed to take into account the realities of business in the digital economy. Consider a company such as Amazon.com. Who are Amazon's competitors? It depends. In books they compete mainly against Barnes & Noble Online, in toys against Wal-Mart, Target, and Sears, and in music against CDNOW.com. Amazon.com could also be seen to compete against television, video games, and the Internet itself, because each of these compete for customers' leisure time. In that view, Amazon.com is not necessarily in the book-selling business, but in the entertainment business. Could we use one diagram such as Figure 1A.1 to describe Amazon.com's competitive environment? Probably not. We might need several figures, one for each of Amazon's major products. Furthermore, due to alliances (such as between Amazon.com and Toysrus.com), the competition and the value chain analysis can be fairly complex and frequently in flux.

For a presentation of strategic information systems frameworks proposed by other researchers, see Online File W13.1 at the book's Web site.

Porter's value chain provides a nice tool with which one can consider the potential impact of IT on an organization's activities. However, it is important to realize that the firm must have the appropriate resources to deploy in order to create value-added applications. We next consider a framework to assess the potential of a firm's IT resources to serve as a basis for strategic advantage.

# 13.4 Strategic Resources and Capabilities

IT can add value to a company in one of two general ways—either *directly* or *indirectly*. IT can add value *directly* by *reducing the costs* associated with a given activity or subset of activities. Cost reduction usually occurs when IT enables the same activity or set of activities to be performed more efficiently. Hence, the firm may reduce its workforce while not reducing its production level. Cost reduction is also possible when IT enables an activity to be redesigned such that it is performed more efficiently. In this case, personnel may also be reduced.

IT can add value *indirectly* by *increasing revenues*. The increase in revenues occurs when IT enables a firm to be more effective. This may occur when a firm is able to either produce more or service more without having to hire more employees. In other words, IT enables the firm to grow in terms of service and revenue without having to grow significantly more in terms of personnel. For example, IT can be used to enable self-service on the part of clients, which enables a firm both to decrease costs and increase revenues. The value chain is useful in visualizing those areas that may benefit from such value-added uses of IT.

However, there is another means by which IT can play a strategic role in a firm, and that is through enabling a temporary or sustained competitive advantage. Both a firm's IT and a firm's deployment of IT may provide a source of strategic advantage.

Three characteristics of resources give firms the potential to create a strategic advantage: value, rarity, and "appropriability." Firm resources can be a source of competitive advantage only when they are *valuable*. A resource has value to the extent that it enables a firm to implement strategies that improve efficiency and effectiveness. But even if valuable, resources that are equitably distributed across organizations are commodities. Resources also must be *rare* in order to confer strategic advantages. Finally, to provide competitive advantage, a resource must be appropriable. *Appropriability* refers to the ability of the firm to create earnings through the resource. Even if a resource is rare and valuable, if the firm expends more effort to obtain the resource than it generates through the resource, then the resource will not create a strategic advantage. Wade and Hulland (2004) give the example of firms attempting to hire ERP-knowledgeable personnel during the 1999–2000 time period, only to discover that they were unable to appropriate a return on their investment because of the higher compensation demanded by these high-in-demand (and hence, rare) and valuable knowledge resources. See Table 13.3.

The three characteristics described above are used to characterize resources that can create an initial competitive advantage. In order for the competitive

| TABLE 13.3 | Key Resource Attributes that Create Competitive Advantage |
|---|---|
| **Resource Attributes** | **Description** |
| Value | The degree to which a resource can help a firm improve efficiency or effectiveness. |
| Rarity | The degree to which a resource is nonheterogeneously distributed across firms in an industry. |
| Appropriability | The degree to which a firm can make use of a resource without incurring an expense that exceeds the value of the resource. |
| Imitability | The degree to which a resource can be readily emulated. |
| Mobility | The degree to which a resource is easy to transport. |
| Substitutability | The degree to which another resource can be used in lieu of the original resource to achieve value. |

advantage to be sustained, however, the resources must be inimitable, imperfectly mobile, and have low substitutability. *Imitability* is the facility with which another firm can copy the resource. Factors that contribute to low imitability include firm history, causal ambiguity, and social complexity (Wade and Hulland, 2004). *Substitutability* refers to the ability of competing firms to substitute an alternative resource in lieu of the resources deployed by the first-moving firm in achieving an advantage. Finally, *mobility* (or *tradability*) refers to the degree to which a firm may easily acquire the resource necessary to imitate a rival's competitive advantage. Some resources, such as hardware and software, are easy to acquire and are thus highly mobile and unlikely to generate sustained competitive advantage. Even if a resource is rare, if it is possible to either purchase the resource (or in the case of a rare expertise, hire the resource), then the resource is mobile and incapable of contributing to a sustained advantage.

Information systems can contribute three types of resources to a firm: technology resources, technical capabilities, and IT managerial resources.

*Technology resources* include the IS infrastructure, proprietary technology, hardware, and software. The IS infrastructure is the foundation of IT capability delivered as reliable services shared throughout the firm. The creation of a successful infrastructure may take several years to achieve and is somewhat different for each organization. Thus, even while competitors might readily purchase the same hardware and software, the combination of these resources to develop a flexible infrastructure is a complex task. It may take firms many years to catch up with the infrastructure capabilities of rivals.

*Technical capabilities* (skills) include IS technical knowledge (programming languages), IS development knowledge (experience with new technologies and experience with different development platforms), and IS operations (cost-effective operations and support). Technical IT skills include the expertise needed to build and use IT applications. IT skills may form the basis of competitive advantage to a firm in an industry where staying abreast of technology is a critical aspect of being competitive.

*Managerial resources* include both those related to IS and those related to IT. IS managerial resources include vendor relationships, outsourcer relationship management, market responsiveness, IS-business partnerships, and IS planning and change management.

Table 13.4 provides definitions for IS resources and capabilities and suggests the degree to which they embody the attributes described in Table 13.3.

**TABLE 13.4** | **IS Resources and Capabilities**

| IS Resource/Capability | Description | Relationship to Resource Attributes |
|---|---|---|
| Technology resources | Includes infrastructure, proprietary technology, hardware, and software. | Not necessarily rare or valuable, but difficult to appropriate and imitate. Low mobility but a fair degree of substitutability. |
| IT skills | Includes technical knowledge, development knowledge, and operational skills. | Highly mobile, but less imitable or substitutable. Not necessarily rare but highly valuable. |
| Managerial IT resources | Includes vendor and outsourcer relationship skills, market responsiveness, IS-business partnerships, IS planning and management skills. | Somewhat more rare than the technology and IT skill resources. Also of higher value. High mobility given the short tenure of CIOs. Nonsubstitutable. |

We have presented three models to help understand the relationship of information systems to strategic advantage. These models can be useful in providing tools for analyzing the current impact that systems are having on a firm and industry. They also may be useful in highlighting potential high-impact areas where systems are not currently used. To achieve strategic advantage through IT, a firm must carefully plan its IT investments. We therefore now turn to the topic of IT planning.

# 13.5 IT Planning

CIOs typically undertake IT strategic planning on a yearly, quarterly, or monthly basis. In the recent survey of the key issues facing CIOs, strategic IT planning was ranked fourth (see Table 13.1). A good IT planning process can help ensure that IT aligns, and stays aligned, with an organization. Because organizational goals change over time, it is not sufficient to develop a long-term IT strategy and not reexamine the strategy on a regular basis. For this reason, IT planning is not a one-shot process.

The IT planning process may result in a formal IT strategy or may result in a reevaluation each year (or each quarter) of the existing portfolio of systems to be developed.

**IT planning** is the organized planning of IT infrastructure and applications portfolios done at various levels of the organization. The topic of IT planning is very important for both planners and end users: End-users often do IT planning for their own units, and they also frequently participate in the corporate IT planning. Therefore, end-users must understand the planning process. Corporate IT planning determines how the IT infrastructure will look. This in turn determines what applications end users can deploy. Thus the future of every unit in the organization could be impacted by the IT infrastructure.

**THE EVOLUTION OF IT PLANNING**

During the early years of information technology, in the late 1950s and 1960s, developing new applications and then revising existing systems were the focal points for the first planning and control systems. Organizations adopted methodologies for developing systems, and they installed project management systems to assist with implementing new applications. These initial mechanisms addressed *operational* planning. As organizations became more sophisticated in their use of information systems, emphasis shifted to *managerial* planning, or resource-allocation control. In the 1990s, the role of IT evolved to helping organizations to reach their business goals and to create competitive advantage. Currently the particular focus of IT strategy is on how IT creates business value.

Typically, annual planning cycles are established to identify potentially beneficial IT services, to perform cost-benefit analyses, and to subject the list of potential projects to resource-allocation analysis. Often the entire process is conducted by an IT *steering committee*. See *A Closer Look 13.1* for the duties of an IT steering committee. The approved projects are then mapped onto a development schedule, usually encompassing a one- to three-year time frame. This schedule becomes the basis for determining IT resources requirements such as long-range hardware, software, personnel, facilities, and financial requirements.

Some organizations extend this planning process by developing additional plans for longer time horizons. They have a *long-range IT plan,* sometimes referred to as the *strategic IT plan*. This plan typically does not refer to specific projects; instead it sets the overall directions in terms of infrastructure and resource requirements for IT activities for five to ten years in the future.

# A Closer Look 13.1

## IT Steering Committees

The corporate *steering committee* is a group of managers and staff representing various organizational units that is set up to establish IT priorities and to ensure that the IS department is meeting the needs of the enterprise. The committee's major tasks are:

- **Direction setting.** In linking the corporate strategy with the IT strategy, planning is the key activity.
- **Rationing.** The committee approves the allocation of resources for and within the information systems organization. This includes outsourcing policy.
- **Structuring.** The committee deals with how the IS department is positioned in the organization. The issue of centralization–decentralization of IT resources is resolved by the committee.

- **Staffing.** Key IT personnel decisions involve a consultation-and-approval process made by the committee. Notable is the selection of the CIO and major IT outsourcing decisions.
- **Communication.** Information regarding IT activities should flow freely.
- **Evaluating.** The committee should establish performance measures for the IS department and see that they are met. This includes the initiation of *service-level agreements* (SLAs).

The success of steering committees largely depends on the establishment of *IT governance,* a formally established set of statements that should direct the policies regarding IT alignment with organizational goals, risk determination, and allocation of resources.

The next level down is a *medium-term IT plan.* It identifies the **applications portfolio,** a list of major, approved IS projects that are consistent with the long-range plan. Since some of these projects will take more than a year to complete, and others will not start in the current year, this plan extends over several years. For more on applications portfolios, see Online File W13.2.

The third level is a *tactical plan,* which has budgets and schedules for current-year projects and activities. In reality, because of the rapid pace of change in technology and the environment, short-term plans may include major items not anticipated in the other plans.

The planning process just described is currently practiced by many organizations. Specifics of the IT planning process, of course, vary among organizations. For example, not all organizations have a high-level IT steering committee. Project priorities may be determined by the IT director, by his or her superior, by company politics, or even on a first-come, first-served basis.

The output from the IT planning process should include the following: a new or revised IT charter and assessment of the state of the information systems department; an accurate evaluation of the strategic goals and directions of the organization; and a statement of the objectives, strategies, and policies for the IT effort.

Ward and Peppard (2002) provided an in-depth analysis of IT strategic planning and proposed a framework for IT strategy formulation and planning. Details are found in Online File W13.3.

**TOOLS AND METHODOLOGIES OF IT PLANNING**

Several tools and methodologies exist to facilitate IT planning. These methods are used to help organizations to align their business IT/IS strategies with the organizational strategies, to identify opportunities to utilize IT for competitive advantage, and to analyze internal processes. Most of these methodologies start with some investigation of strategy that checks the industry, competition, and competitiveness, and relates them to technology (*alignment*). Others help create and justify new uses of IT (*impact*). Ward and Peppard (2002) further categorized these methods with respect to their nature (see Online File W13.4). In the next section, we look briefly at some of these methodologies.

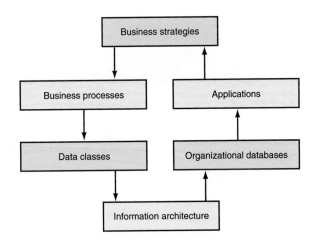

**Figure 13.4** Business systems planning (BSP) approach. (*Source:* Derived from *Business Systems Planning—Information Systems Planning Guide,* Application Manual GE20-0527-3, 3rd ed., IBM Corporation, July 1981. Courtesy of the International Business Machines Corporation.)

**The Business Systems Planning (BSP) Model.** The **business systems planning (BSP) model** was developed by IBM, and it has influenced other planning efforts such as Accenture's *method/1*. BSP is a top-down approach that starts with business strategies. It deals with two main building blocks—*business processes* and *data classes*—which become the basis of an information architecture. From this architecture, planners can define organizational databases and identify applications that support business strategies, as illustrated in Figure 13.4.

BSP relies heavily on the use of metrics in the analysis of processes and data, with the ultimate goal of developing the information architecture.

**The Stages of IT Growth Model.** Nolan (1979) indicated that organizations go through six **stages of IT growth** (called "IS growth" at that time). *A Closer Look 13.2* describes these six stages. In each stage, four processes are active to varying degrees. These are the applications portfolio, users' role and awareness, IT resources, and management planning and control techniques. The *y* axis in the figure in *A Closer Look 13.2* refers to IT expenditures. Note that the growth *rate* of IT expenses is low during data administration, medium during initiation and maturity, and high during expansion (contagion) and integration. In addition to serving as a guide for expenditure, the model helps in determining the seriousness of problems. (For more on Nolan's stages of IT growth, see Online File W13.5.)

The *stages of growth model* was initially intended to explain the growth and maturity of the IT department in an organization. Another way to use the model is to consider that each major system progresses through these growth stages in such a way that an organization might be at the maturity level regarding TPS but at the integration level regarding KM. This underscores an enduring challenge for IS departments in large organizations: One unit of the organization might be predominantly at an initiation stage with its systems (such as a unit in a developing nation), whereas another unit of the same organization in a well-developed region might be mostly at the maturity level. Thus, achieving enterprisewide systems would be particularly challenging in such a situation.

**Critical Success Factors.** **Critical success factors (CSFs)** are those few things that must go right in order to ensure the organization's survival and success. The *CSF approach* to IT planning was developed to help identify the information needs of managers. The fundamental assumption is that in every organization there are three to six key factors that, if done well, will result in the organization's success. Therefore

# A Closer Look 13.2

## Nolan's Six Stages of IT Growth Model

The six stages of IT growth are:

1. **Initiation.** When computers are initially introduced to the organization, batch processing is used to automate clerical operations in order to achieve cost reduction. There is an operational systems focus, general lack of management interest, and a centralized information systems department.

2. **Expansion (contagion).** Centralized rapid growth takes place as users demand more applications based on high expectations of benefits. There is a move to online systems as the IS department tries to satisfy all user demands and little, if any, control. IT expenses increase rapidly.

3. **Control.** In response to management concern about cost versus benefits, systems projects are expected to show a return, plans are produced, and methodologies/standards are enforced. The control stage often produces a backlog of applications and dissatisfied users. Planning and controls are introduced.

4. **Integration.** There is considerable expenditure on integrating (via telecommunications and databases) existing sys-

tems. User accountability for systems is established, and the IS department provides a service to users, not just solutions to problems. At this time there is a transition in computer use and an approach from data processing to information and knowledge processing (transition between the two curves).

5. **Data administration.** Information requirements rather than processing drive the applications portfolio, and information is shared within the organization. Database capability is exploited as users understand the value of the information and are willing to share it.

6. **Maturity.** The planning and development of IT in the organization are closely coordinated with business development. Corporatewide systems are in place. The IS department and the users share accountability regarding the allocation of computing resources. IT has truly become a strategic partner.

*Source:* Compiled from R. L. Nolan, "Managing the Crises in Data Processing," *Harvard Business Review,* March–April 1979. Reprinted

organizations should continuously measure performance in these areas, taking corrective action whenever necessary. CSFs also exist in business units, departments, and other organizational units.

Critical success factors vary by broad industry categories—manufacturing, service, or government—and by specific industries within these categories. For organizations in the same industry, CSFs will vary depending on whether the firms are market leaders or weaker competitors, where they are located, and what competitive strategies they follow. Environmental issues, such as the degree of regulation or amount of technology used, influence CSFs. In addition, CSFs change over time based on temporary conditions, such as high interest rates or long-term trends.

IT planners identify CSFs by interviewing managers in an initial session, and then refine CSFs in one or two additional sessions. Sample questions asked in the CSF approach are:

- What objectives are central to your organization?
- What are the critical factors that are essential to meeting these objectives?
- What decisions or actions are key to these critical factors?
- What variables underlie these decisions, and how are they measured?
- What information systems can supply these measures?

The first step following the interviews is to determine the organizational objectives for which the manager is responsible, and then the factors that are critical to attaining these objectives. The second step is to select a small number of CSFs. Then, one needs to determine the information requirements for those CSFs and measure to see whether the CSFs are met. If they are not met it is necessary to build appropriate applications (see Figure 13.5).

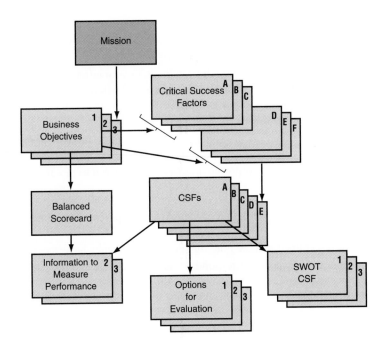

**Figure 13.5** Critical success factors—basic processes. (*Source:* Ward and Peppard, 2002, Figure 4.7, p. 211.)

The critical success factors approach encourages managers to identify what is most important to their performance and then develop good indicators of performance in these areas. Conducting interviews with all key people makes it less likely that key items will be overlooked. On the other hand, the emphasis on critical factors avoids the problem of collecting too much data, or including some data just because they are easy to collect.

**Scenario Planning.** **Scenario planning** is a methodology in which planners first create several scenarios, then a team compiles as many future events as possible that may influence the outcome of each scenario. This approach is used in planning situations that involve much uncertainty, like that of IT in general and e-commerce in particular. With the rapid changes of technologies and business environment, Stauffer (2002) emphasized the need for scenario planning. Five reasons to do scenario planning are: (1) to ensure that you are not focusing on catastrophe to the exclusion of opportunity, (2) to help you allocate resources more prudently, (3) to preserve your options, (4) to ensure that you are not still "fighting the last war," and (5) to give you the opportunity to rehearse testing and training of people to go through the process. Scenario planning follows a rigorous process; the essential steps are summarized in Table 13.5.

Scenario planning has been widely used by major corporations to facilitate IT planning (e.g., *ncri.com* and *gbn.com*). It also has been particularly important to e-commerce planning. For instance, creating customer scenarios helps the company better fit the products and services into the real lives of the customers, resulting in sales expansion and customer loyalty. Seybold (2001) described three cases (National Semiconductor, Tesco, Buzzsaw.com) that used customer scenarios to strengthen customer relationships, to guide business strategy, and to deliver business value.

Although EC proliferation would certainly allow any combination or variation of business scenarios, each company has to select the most appropriate model for its

| TABLE 13.5 | Essential Steps of Scenario Planning |
| --- | --- |

- Determine the scope and time frame of the scenario you are fleshing out.
- Identify the current assumptions and mental models of individuals who influence these decisions.
- Create a manageable number of divergent, yet plausible, scenarios. Spell out the underlying assumptions of how each of these imagined futures might evolve.
- Test the impact of key variables in each scenario.
- Develop action plans based on either (a) the solutions that play most robustly across scenarios, or (b) the most desirable outcome toward which a company can direct its efforts.
- Monitor events as they unfold to test the corporate direction; be prepared to modify it as required.

The educational experience that results from this process includes:

- Stretching your mind beyond the groupthink that can slowly and imperceptibly produce a sameness of minds among top team members in any organization.
- Learning the ways in which seemingly remote potential developments may have repercussions that hit close to home.
- Learning how you and your colleagues might respond under both adverse and favorable circumstances.

*Source:* Compiled from Stauffer (2002).

needs. The use of this model can help EC planners to determine the EC initiatives that best fit their organization.

A major aspect of IT planning is allocating an organization's IT resources to the right set of projects. Organizations simply cannot afford to develop or purchase each application or undertake each application enhancement that business units and end-users might like. The IT steering committee therefore has an important responsibility in deciding how IT resources will be allocated. An example of identifying high-payoff projects is provided in *IT at Work 13.4.*

**RESOURCE ALLOCATION**

**Resource allocation** consists of developing the hardware, software, data communications and networks, facilities, personnel, and financial plans needed to execute the master development plan as defined in the requirements analysis.

Resource allocation is a contentious process in most organizations because opportunities and requests for spending far exceed the available funds. This can lead to intense, highly political competition among organizational units, which makes it difficult to objectively identify the most desirable investments.

Requests for funding approval from the steering committee fall into two categories. Some projects and infrastructure are necessary in order for the organization to stay in business. For example, it may be imperative to purchase or upgrade hardware if the network, or disk drives, or the processor on the main computer are approaching capacity limits. Obtaining approval for this type of spending is largely a matter of communicating the gravity of the problems to decision makers.

On the other hand, the IT planning process identifies an information architecture that usually requires additional funding for less critical items: new projects, maintenance or upgrades of existing systems, and infrastructure to support these systems and future needs. Approval for projects in this category may become more difficult to obtain because the IS department is already receiving funding for mandatory projects.

After setting aside funds for the first category, the organization can use the remainder of the IT budget for projects related mainly to the improved information architecture. The organization can prioritize spending among items in the architecture developed by using information requirements analysis. In addition to formally

# IT at Work 13.4

## Identifying High-Payoff Projects

Wing Fat Foods (WFF) is a wholesaler, delivering perishable and nonperishable foodstuffs, as well as hardware, kitchenware, and household goods, to restaurants, groceries, and similar businesses along the Atlantic Coast of the United States. WFF is famous for its quality and service, which is accomplished with a relatively low level of IT investment. WFF hopes that its additional IT investment will help it to sustain its edge over competitors.

In response to the need of identifying potential new IT projects, Peffers and Gengler (2003) proposed to WFF a new method, the *critical success chain (CSC) method*, for IT planning. The CSC method includes four steps:

*Step 1: Pre-study preparation: Determine scope and participants and collect project idea stimuli.* The analyst invited 25 IT users (6 senior managers, 11 middle managers, 5 journeyman employees, and 3 WFF customers) to participate in an in-depth interview. At the same time, she collected project ideas to serve as stimuli. For example, she asked each participant to describe the functionality of a system that would benefit WFF.

*Step 2: Participant interviews: Elicit personal constructs from organization members.* The analyst then conducted 25–50 minute interviews with each participant, showing the participant three system descriptions and asking them to rank the system attributes and explain their importance to the organization. A line of questions was asked until the participants suggested a concrete feature or attribute that would become part of the project idea. This line of questions was designed to produce specific ideas for features of the system, expected performance, and related organiza-

tional values or objectives. In this study, the analyst collected about 8 chains of suggestions per participant.

*Step 3: Analysis: Aggregate personal constructs into CSC models.* The analyst first clustered the interview statements into constructs and mapped the constructs into a matrix. She then clustered the chains using the Ward and Peppard strategic planning framework (found in Online File W13.3). Mapping each cluster into a CSC map, she represented the constructs as nodes and the links in the chains as lines connecting the nodes. The figure below depicts an organization-specific CSC model consisting of, from left to right, descriptions of desired system attributes, resulting expected performance outcomes (CSS), and associated organizational goals.

*Step 4: Idea workshops: Elicit feasible strategic IT from technical and business experts and customers.* The CSC maps were used by both IT professionals from within WFF and non-IT customers as a starting point for developing a portfolio of IT proposals. Providing the technical and business experts at WFF with the CSC maps, the workshop finally yielded 14 project ideas, including a decision support system for scheduling, routing, and loading trucks for delivery, as well as the support activities for existing systems, including training and updated equipment and maintenance support.

*Source:* Compiled from Peffers and Gengler (2003).

*For Further Exploration:* Why is the method called the CS chain? Why is such a lengthy process, with so many participants, needed?

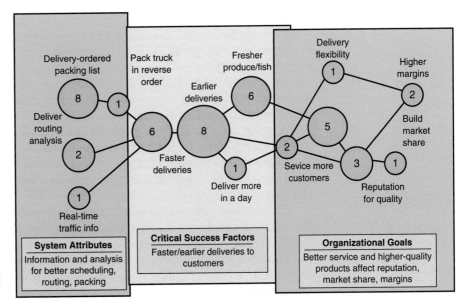

Critical success chain network map. (*Sources:* Peffers and Gengler, 2003 and Peffers and Gengler, 2000.)

allocating resources through budgeting decisions, an organization can use charge-back mechanisms to fund corporate-level projects. In a *chargeback system,* some or all of a system's cost is charged to users. In addition, management may encourage individual units to make their own decisions about IT expenses. Chapter 14 discusses chargeback, cost-benefit analysis, and other, more sophisticated analyses that can also be used to assess investments in individual IT projects as well as infrastructure.

# 13.6 Interorganizational and International IT Planning

IT planning is a complex process. Major planning initiatives are likely to occur following important events such as the merger of organizations, the acquisition of a new company, unexpected poor performance, or the change in upper-level management. *IT at Work 13.5* demonstrates information technology planning that took place after a governmental institution had become private, for example. Even while major planning initiatives may not occur on a yearly basis, because of the pace of technological change, the IT portfolios resulting from an IT plan will be carefully revisited each year to ensure continued alignment with organizational goals.

Of the many special topics in this category, we have elected to focus on IT planning in interorganizational and international systems. Information technology planning may get more complicated when several organizations are involved, as well as when we deal with multinational corporations. In this section, we also address the problems and challenges for IT planning.

**PLANNING FOR INTERORGANIZATIONAL SYSTEMS**

Internal information systems of business partners must "talk" with each other effectively and do it efficiently. In Chapters 4 and 5, we introduced IT technologies such as EDI, e-mail, and extranets that facilitate communication and collaboration between companies. IT planning that involves several organizations may be complex. The problem is that some information systems may involve hundreds or even thousands of business partners. IT planners in such a case could use focus groups of customers, suppliers, and other business partners, especially during the strategic information planning as well as during the information requirements analysis.

Planning for project management of interorganization systems (IOSs) can be fairly complex. IT planners may create virtual planning teams that will work together on projects such as extranets or EDI. Such collaboration is especially important in strategic planning that involves infrastructure. Questions such as who is going to pay for what can become critical factors in cost/benefit analysis and justification of information systems applications.

A comprehensive study of global IT strategic planning was conducted by Curry and Ferguson (2000). In order to increase the success of such planning, they suggest that organizations reduce the planning horizon to two to three years (from three to five years) and that they increase the collaboration between the IT planners and end users.

Examples of joint planning for interorganizational systems can include using an extended supply chain approach and adopting the same enterprise software. If company A will use software from SAP and company B will use Oracle software, there could be additional expenses for connecting these softwares to each other. Web Services (Chapters 2 and 14) may provide the solution for such an integration.

# IT at Work 13.5

## Institute of Technology Turns Its Focus on the Customer

MKT

As noted in this chapter, major IT projects and planning programs are often undertaken following significant events experienced by organizations. Increasingly, an organization's ability to change and adjust to such events depends on its ability to implement new IT solutions. In 1989, the Institute of Technology (TI) in Oslo, Norway, went through a very dramatic change: It was transformed from a public, government-funded institute into a private foundation. The 260 employees of the Institute of Technology served small and medium-sized Norwegian companies by assisting them with technology development and transfer. TI's typical services included technical consulting and practical courses in such disciplines as welding, testing, and calibration, as well as ISO certification.

Following the privatization, government support was gradually reduced to 25 percent and TI was required to generate its income independently, which was a difficult task for an organization that was not accustomed to marketing and selling services.

To expand the organization's focus beyond the technical matters, TI recruited managers from the private sector, who quickly identified a potentially valuable asset: contacts with 8,000 companies and thousands of individuals. TI then developed a strategy of leveraging these contacts and relationships with the goal of transforming itself into a viable market-driven organization. In 1992, the Institute's director launched "The Customer Project." The major objectives of this initiative included better financial control of the consulting projects, more effective and efficient marketing, and development of long-term relationships with the most important customers.

Fostering relationships with the clients requires a variety of customer information and frequent communications with the customers, both of which can be facilitated by the use of information technology. Not surprisingly, TI turned to information technology for a customer relationship management (CRM) solution. The Institute implemented the Customer System, which was based on SalesMaker, a system from a Norwegian company, Software Innovation. The system was extended with a specialized module developed in-house. At the time, the system was very modern: Windows-based and compatible with the financial system and with office productivity applications.

The Customer System was based on information technology tools; however, the entire project was not purely technical. The Institute dedicated considerable effort to ensure user participation and organizational alignment. In fact, the biggest challenge of the initial implementation was not technical: Since the system was not yet integrated in the day-to-day work routines, users failed to verify customer information, creating duplicate records for the same clients. This behavior resulted in serious information quality problems and undermined the users' confidence in the system.

The second CRM initiative was supported by extensive hands-on guidance for the departments and allowed the Institute to segment its market better, reduce direct marketing volume by 50 percent, and improve sales at the same time. Greater effectiveness in direct marketing led to annual savings of at least half a million NOK (Norway kroner) per year, which fully recovered TI's investment in CRM. Nevertheless, this project failed to change the culture from a focus on technical disciplines to a focus on the customer. Furthermore, the partial success that had been achieved was not self-sustaining.

In 1998, the Institute launched the third CRM initiative, in a new version of the Customer System with a new focus on supporting individual consultants with their personal contacts, document management, and calendars. Overall, the organization was able to achieve the first two of the original goals—improve financial control over projects and become more efficient in direct marketing. Unfortunately, the most important goal of establishing strong, lasting relationships with the most important customers had largely failed.

*Source:* Bygstad (2003).

*For Further Exploration:* Why did the outcome of deploying an information system (Customer System) at TI depend so heavily on the Institute's ability to change organizational culture? In addition to CRM, what other IT planning initiatives could have supported the Institute's strategy of becoming a profitable private organization?

**IT PLANNING FOR MULTINATIONAL CORPORATIONS**

Multinational corporations face a complex legal, political, and social environment, which complicates corporate IT planning. Therefore, many multinational companies prefer to decentralize their IT planning and operations, empowering their local IT managers. However, communication, coordination, and collaboration among decentralized business units may require large expenses.

IT planning can be an expensive and time-consuming process. A study of five large-scale planning projects found that such projects may involve ten or more employees, on a half-time or full-time basis, for periods lasting from ten weeks to a year. The estimated costs of these projects ranged from $450,000 to $1.9 million. In addition, a survey reported by King (2000) disclosed that more than 50 percent of the companies surveyed were conducting IS planning using obsolete methodologies.

Teo and Ang (2001) emphasized the importance of understanding IT planning problems. They argued that these problems may result in wasted resources, lost opportunities, duplicated efforts, and incompatiable systems. They studied 138 companies and identified IT planning problems at the three phases of IS planning: the launching phase, the plan development phase, and the implementation phase. In all three phases, failing to get top management support for the IS planning was the most serious problem. Other major IS planning problems included: not having free communication flow and not being able to obtain sufficiently qualified personnel in the planning phase; ignoring business goals and failing to translate goals and strategies into action plans in the plan development phase; neglecting to adjust the IS plan to reflect major environmental changes; and ignoring the IS plan once it has been developed in the implementation phase.

In response to the rapid change of technology and the business environment, IT strategies have to be more flexible and more responsive in order to take advantage of opportunities quickly and in the most cost-effective way. Details in planning for Web-based system and e-commerce are described in the following section.

**E-PLANNING**

IT planning in this chapter refers mostly to corporate planning of IT infrastructure rather than to applications planning. In contrast, **e-planning** is electronically supported IT planning that touches on EC infrastructure and mostly deals with uncovering business opportunities and deciding on an applications portfolio that will exploit those opportunities (see *IT at Work 13.4,* page 537).

Some of the infrastructure needed for e-commerce and Web-based systems may be already in place, as part of the organization's overall IT infrastructure. Nevertheless, e-planning may be conducted as a separate planning exercise. In such a case, ISD people will participate in the steering committee together with end users. Of course, alignment between the two processes is needed. One reason for such separation is that technology is an enabler of e-commerce, but the major objective of e-commerce is to rejuvenate organizations. If the process is controlled by IT people, the success of e-commerce may be constrained. Another reason for the separation is that e-planning is usually less formal, and it must be done quickly. Furthermore, due to rapid changes the e-planning must be more flexible.

Planning for Web-based individual applications is very similar to the planning of any IT application. However, at the macro level of planning, the emphasis is different. The areas where more attention is given in e-planning are the applications portfolio, risk analysis, and strategic planning issues such as the use of metrics. Let's elaborate.

**Applications Portfolio for E-Commerce.** The importance of the applications portfolio in regular IT planning may be declining. Most organizations have their mission-critical systems already in place, and IT activities are fairly distributed. In e-commerce, however, most organizations are starting from scratch. The cost of building systems is high, and so is the risk. Therefore, it is advisable to conduct centralized EC planning and to select appropriate applications and prioritize them. *IT at Work 13.6* offers an example of planning and implementing e-commerce systems at Intel.

Another methodology for planning an applications portfolio was proposed by Tjan (2001).

# IT at Work 13.6

## Market Research Company Benefits from Internet-Based Technologies

MKT

Founded in 1931, Burke Inc. (*burke.com*) is one of the foremost international research and consulting firms in the world. The company provides full-service market research, analysis, and consulting to hundreds of consumer and business-to-business-based clients, helping them to understand and accurately predict marketplace behavior. In 2005, Burke had revenues of $44.1 million and employed 202 full-time and 178 part-time workers.

With increasing client and market demands, Burke has faced the challenge of bringing customers more information in a timely manner. To address this need early, Burke teamed with SPSS (*spss.com*), a leading worldwide provider of predictive analytics software and solutions, over 25 years ago. SPSS has served to keep Burke, which was one of the first market research firms to offer interactive research software, on top of technological advancements and has helped make the company what it is today. Recently, SPSS technology has enabled Burke to implement a Web-based survey platform, which allows clients to customize their own surveys using the software's "Interview Builder" feature. This safe and secure survey technology provides Burke with the ability to offer its survey platform as a Web-based application, with which users can control who has access to projects and their level of interaction. Two-thirds of all surveys Burke collected in 2005 were Web-based, compared with 15 percent in 2000. Additionally, Burke provides some form of Web-based solution for approximately 75 percent of its clients, a figure that was also at 15 percent five years ago.

"We needed a platform that would scale with our clients' business, be capable to run small or large volumes of surveys, and able to easily expand capacity," said Mike Webster, director of technology solutions at Burke. "That is one of the key reasons we moved to SPSS."

Another key factor for Burke was the seamless integration of SPSS software with other technologies and applications. "The open architecture that comes with SPSS allows for better integration with client CRM systems, for example," continued Webster.

As for what lies in Burke's future, the company plans to take advantage of SQL 2005 and incorporate more SPSS survey software with Table Options (TOM), which will create the ability to build sophisticated tables and publish them in a variety of third-party and custom formats. In addition, Burke is working to install more SPSS survey software that will allow clients to build, edit, preview, and test surveys without having to send them to a Web server first. Through use of these advanced Internet-based technologies, Burke seeks to continue doing what they've done for years—give their customers a competitive edge by staying in tune with the most recent technological developments.

*Sources:* Adapted and compiled from Burke (2006), *burke.com* (accessed June 2006), and *spss.com* (accessed June 2006).

*For Further Exploration:* What were the benefits Burke derived by partnering with SPSS? What are Burke's competitive advantages? How sustainable are they?

**Tjan's Portfolio Strategy.** Tjan (2001) adopted a business project portfolio applications approach to create an Internet portfolio planning matrix. However, instead of trading off industry growth and market position, here the strategy is based on *company fit*, which can be either low or high, and the *project's viability*, which can also be low or high. Together these create an *Internet portfolio map (matrix)*.

A project's viability can be assessed by four criteria: market-value potential, time to positive cash flow, personnel requirements, and funding requirements. EC initiatives such as a B2B procurement site, a B2C store, or a portal for kids, for example, can be evaluated on a scale of 1 to 100, for each of the four metrics. Then, an average score (simple average) for each metric is computed. For *fit*, the following criteria are used: alignment with core capabilities, alignment with other company initiatives, fit with organizational structure, fit with company's culture and values, and ease of technical implementation. Again, each EC initiative is assessed on a scale of 1 to 100 (or on a qualitative scale of high, medium, low), and an average is computed.

The various applications initiatives are then mapped on the *Internet portfolio matrix*, based on the average scores for viability and fit. The Internet matrix is

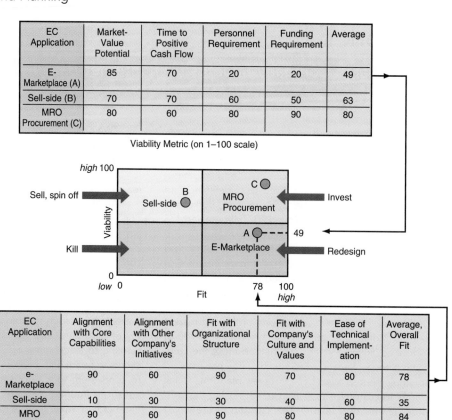

| EC Application | Market-Value Potential | Time to Positive Cash Flow | Personnel Requirement | Funding Requirement | Average |
|---|---|---|---|---|---|
| E-Marketplace (A) | 85 | 70 | 20 | 20 | 49 |
| Sell-side (B) | 70 | 70 | 60 | 50 | 63 |
| MRO Procurement (C) | 80 | 60 | 80 | 90 | 80 |

Viability Metric (on 1–100 scale)

| EC Application | Alignment with Core Capabilities | Alignment with Other Company's Initiatives | Fit with Organizational Structure | Fit with Company's Culture and Values | Ease of Technical Implementation | Average, Overall Fit |
|---|---|---|---|---|---|---|
| e-Marketplace | 90 | 60 | 90 | 70 | 80 | 78 |
| Sell-side | 10 | 30 | 30 | 40 | 60 | 35 |
| MRO Procurement | 90 | 60 | 90 | 80 | 80 | 84 |

Fit Metric (on 1–100 scale)

**Figure 13.6** Application portfolio analysis for a toy distributor. Potential applications: (A) create e-marketplace; (B) direct sale (sell-side); and (C) MRO procurement. The average results determine the location on the grid. Results (at center): invest in project C; redesign project A so it will become viable; and sell the idea (B) to someone else since it does not pay to reengineer the company. (*Source:* Drawn by E. Turban.)

divided into four cells, as shown in Figure 13.6. If both *viability* and *fit* are low, the project is killed. If both are high, then the project is adopted. If *fit* is high, but *viability* is low, the project is sent to redesign. Finally, if the *fit* is low but the *viability* is high, the project may be sold or spun off. The figure shows how several applications were rated for an e-marketplace company for a toy company in Hong Kong.

Tjan's portfolio strategy introduces a systematic approach to EC project selection. The assessment of the points per criterion can be done by several experts to ensure quality. Cases where there is more agreement can be considered with more confidence. Organizations can add their own criteria to the methodology.

**Risk Analysis.** The degree of risk of some Web-based systems is very high, and such risk often leads to failure. For example, Disney Inc. aborted two major EC initiatives in 2000: First, Disney closed its e-toy company (*smartkid.com*), and second, it closed its company (*go.com*) that was managing all of Disney's EC initiatives. The loss was many millions of dollars. Failures of IT applications do not usually cost so much money, especially if they are not enterprisewide in nature. Conducting an appropriate risk analysis could reduce the chance of failures. However, this was difficult to do at that time due to lack of historical data.

# 13.7 Managing the IS Department

A final key element in getting, and keeping, IT aligned with the organization is working to ensure that the IS department has good relationships with end-user departments, and that the CIO has strong relationships with other senior executives. In order to foster such good relationships, the CIO plays a critical role in managing the IS department as a service organization with a view toward treating end-users as "customers."

Managing the IS department is similar to managing any other organizational unit. The unique aspect of the IS department is that it operates as a service department in a rapidly changing environment, thus making the department's projections and planning difficult. The IT resources are scattered all over the enterprise, adding to the complexity of IS department management. Here we will discuss only two issues: (1) the CIO's relationship with other managers and executives and (2) the relationship of the IS department and end-users.

**THE ROLE OF THE CHIEF INFORMATION OFFICER**

The CIO has become an important member of the organization's top management team. Strong CIO–CEO relationships are crucial for effective utilization of IT, especially in organizations that greatly depend on IT, where the CIO joins the top management "chiefs" group.

The CIO in some cases is a member of the corporate *executive committee*, the most important committee in any organization, which has responsibility for strategic business planning. Its members include the chief executive officer and the senior vice presidents. The executive committee provides the top-level oversight for the organization's information resources. It guides the IS steering committee that is usually chaired by the CIO.

CIOs may report to CEOs, COOs, CFOs, or other members of the top executive team. Recent research shows that there is still a roughly 50/50 split in CIOs who report to the CEO and those that don't (Leidner and Mackey, 2006). CIOs who report to the CEO feel that they are in a better position not only to understand the organization's strategy, but to help drive that strategy. These CIOs do not see themselves as simply taking an organizational strategy and creating an IT strategy that helps support it, but rather as working with the other senior executives to craft the organization's strategy. These CIOs combine business and technology savvy to help envision the future of the organization. CIOs in high-growth industries, in large organizations (particularly in global firms), and in technology-dependent environments often find themselves reporting to the CEO. CIOs in lower-growth and or smaller firms may find themselves reporting to a CFO or COO.

**THE CIO IN THE WEB-BASED ERA**

According to Ross and Feeny (2000), Luftman et al. (2004), and Earl (1999–2000), the CIO's role in the Web-based era is influenced by the following three factors:

- **Technology and its management are changing.** Companies are using new Web-based business models. Conventional applications are being transformed to Web-based. There is increasing use of B2B e-commerce, supply chain management, CRM, ERP (see Willcocks and Sykes, 2000), and knowledge management applications.

- **Executives' attitudes are changing.** Greater attention is given to opportunities and risks. At the very least, CIOs are the individuals to whom the more computer literate executives look for guidance, especially as it relates to e-business. Also, executives are more willing to invest in IT, since the cost-benefit ratio of IT is improving with time.

- **Interactions with vendors are increasing.** Suppliers of IT, especially the major ones (HP, Cisco, IBM, Microsoft, Sun, Intel, and Oracle), are influencing the strategic thinking of their corporate customers.

The above factors shape the roles and responsibilities of the CIO in the following eight ways: (1) The CIO is taking increasing responsibility for defining the strategic future. (2) The CIO needs to understand (with others in the organization) that the Web-based era is more about fundamental business change than about technology. (3) The CIO is responsible for protecting the ever-increasing IT assets, including the Web infrastructure, against ever-increasing hazards, including terrorists' attacks. (4) The CIO is becoming a *business visionary* who drives business strategy, develops new business models on the Web, and introduces management processes that leverage the Internet, intranets, and extranets. (5) The CIO needs to argue for a greater measure of central control. For example, placing inappropriate content on the Internet or intranets can be harmful and needs to be monitored and coordinated. (6) The IT asset-acquisition process must be improved. The CIO and end users must work more closely than ever before. (7) The increased networked environment may lead to disillusionment with IT—an undesirable situation that the CIO should help to avoid. (8) The CIO must lead the exploration of new computing environments, such as mobile enterprises and utility computing. These eight challenges place lots of pressure on CIOs, especially in times of economic decline.

As a result of the considerable pressures they face, CIOs may earn very high salaries (up to $1,000,000/year in large corporations), but there is high turnover at this position (see Earl, 1999/2000). As technology becomes increasingly central to business, the CIO becomes a key mover in the ranks of upper management. For example, in a large financial institution's executive committee meeting, attended by one of the authors, modest requests for additional budgets by the senior vice presidents for finance and for marketing were turned down after long debate. But, at the same meeting the CIO's request for a tenfold addition was approved in only a few minutes.

With the growth of utility computing and outsourcing, some question the future of the ISD as an in-house organization. Horner-Reich and Nelson (2003) visualize a major change in the makeup and working of the IS department, and we are in the midst of a transition, as shown in Figure 13.7.

It is interesting to note that CEOs are acquiring IT skills. A company's best investment is a CEO who knows technology. If both the CIO and the CEO have the necessary skills for the information age, their company has the potential to flourish. For this reason some companies promote their CIOs to CEOs.

According to *eMarketer Daily* (May 12, 2003), CEOs see *security* as the second most important area for IT over the next two to three years. We will now turn our attention to that area, where the CIO is expected to lead—the security of data and information systems in the enterprise.

## THE IS DEPARTMENT AND END USERS

It is extremely important to have a good relationship between the IS department and end users. Unfortunately, though, this relationship is not always optimal. The development of end-user computing and outsourcing was motivated in part by the poor service that end users felt they received from the IS department. Conflicts occur for several reasons, ranging from the fact that priorities of the IS department may differ from those of the end users, to lack of communication. Also, there are some fundamental differences between the personalities, cognitive styles, educational backgrounds, and gender proportion of the end users versus the IS department staff (generally more males in the IS department) that could contribute to conflicts. An example of such conflict is illustrated in *IT at Work 13.7*.

The situation described in *IT at Work 13.7* used to be common. One of this book's authors, when acting as a consultant to an aerospace company in Los Angeles, found that end users frequently bought nonstandard equipment by making

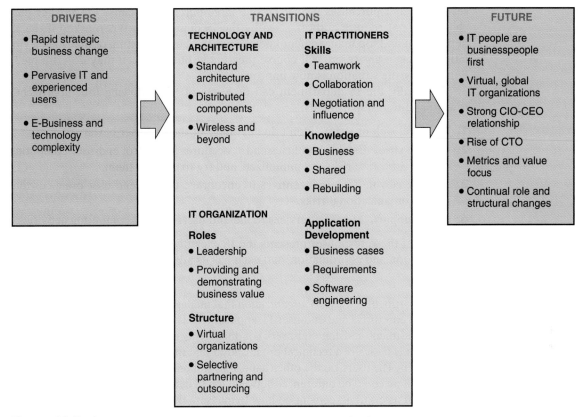

**Figure 13.7** The transition environment. (*Source:* Horner-Reich and Nelson, 2003.)

# *IT* at Work 13.7

## Minnesota's Department of Transportation Violates Procedures

GOV

The Department of Transportation in Minnesota (*dot. state. mn.us*) had come across a hybrid PC system that would allow road surveys to be accomplished with less time and effort, and greater accuracy. The system would require two people to conduct a survey instead of the usual three, and because of the precision of the computer-based system, the survey could be done in half the time.

The department ran into a problem because the ISD for the State of Minnesota had instituted standards for all PCs that could be purchased by any state agency. Specifically, a particular brand of IBM PC was the only PC purchase allowed, without going through a special procedure. The red tape, as well as the unwillingness of the ISD to allow any deviation from the standard, caused a great deal of frustration.

As a last resort, the Department of Transportation procured the hybrid PC and camouflaged the transaction as engineering equipment for conducting surveys. From that point on, its staff decided they would do what they needed to do to get their jobs done, and the less the ISD knew about what they were doing, the better. When asked why they behaved this way, the administrator of the Department of Transportation simply said, "We have to do it this way because the ISD will either try to stop or hold up for a long period of time any decision we want to make, because they just are not familiar enough with the issues that we are facing in our department."

*For Further Exploration:* What are the organizational risks when the Transportation Department takes this attitude? How can the conflict be resolved?

several smaller purchases instead of one large purchase, because the smaller purchases did not require authorization by the IS department. When asked if the IS department and top management knew about this circumventing of the rules, a violating manager answered, "Of course they know, but what can they do—fire me?" Fortunately, the situation is now improving.

Generally, the IS department can take one of the following four approaches toward end-user departments:

1. **Let them sink or swim.** Don't do anything; let the end user beware.
2. **Use the stick.** Establish policies and procedures to control end-user computing so that corporate risks are minimized, and try to enforce them.
3. **Use the carrot.** Create incentives to encourage certain end-user practices that reduce organizational risks.
4. **Offer support.** Develop services to aid end users in their computing activities.

Each of these responses presents the IS executive with different opportunities for facilitation and coordination, and each has its advantages and disadvantages.

## FOSTERING THE IS DEPARTMENT/ END-USER RELATIONSHIPS

The IS department is a *service organization* that manages the IT infrastructure needed to carry on enterprise and end-user IT applications. Therefore, a partnership between the IS department and the end users is a must. This is not an easy task since the IS department is basically a technical organization that may not understand the business and the users. The users, on the other hand, may not understand information technologies. Also, there could be differences between the IS department (the provider) and the end users in terms of agreement on how to measure the IT services provided (quality, quantity). Another major reason for tense relationships in many organizations is the difficulties discussed in Chapter 14 regarding the evaluation of IT investment.

To improve collaboration, end users representing important business units can be members of the steering committee. Other means of improving IS department–end-user relationships include the use of service-level agreements and/or the creation of information centers.

**Service-Level Agreements.** *Service-level agreements* (SLAs) are formal agreements regarding the division of computing responsibility between end users and the IS department and the expected services to be rendered by the IS department. A service-level agreement can be viewed as a *contract* between each end-user unit and the IS department. If a chargeback system exists, it is usually spelled out in the SLA. The process of establishing and implementing SLAs may be applied to each of the *major* computing resources: hardware, software, people, data, networks, and procedures.

The divisions of responsibility in SLAs are based on critical computing decisions that are made by *end-user managers,* who agree to accept certain computing responsibilities and to turn over others to the IS department. Since end-user managers make these decisions, they are free to choose the amount and kind of support they feel they need. This freedom to choose provides a check on the IS department and encourages it to develop and deliver support services to meet end-user needs.

An approach based on SLAs offers several advantages. First, it reduces "finger pointing" by clearly specifying responsibilities. When a PC malfunctions, everyone knows who is responsible for fixing it. Second, it provides a structure for the design and delivery of end-user services by the IS department. Third, it creates incentives for end users to improve their computing practices, thereby reducing computing risks to the firm. SLAs are useful to both the IS department and the user community.

Establishing SLAs requires the following steps: (1) Define service levels. (2) Divide computing responsibility at each level. (3) Design the details of the service levels, including measurement of quality. (4) Implement service levels. (5) Assign SLA owner (the person or department that gets the SLA), (6) monitor SLA compliance, (7) analyze performance, (8) refine SLAs as needed, and (9) improve service to the department or company.

Due to the introduction of Web-based tools for simplifying the task of monitoring enterprise networks, more attention has recently been given to service-level agreement.

**The Information Center.** The concept of *information center (IC)* (also known as the user's service center, technical support center, or IS help center) was conceived by IBM Canada in the 1970s as a response to the increased number of end-user requests for new computer applications. This demand created a huge backlog in the IS department, and users had to wait several *years* to get their systems built. Today, ICs concentrate on end-user support with PCs, client/server applications, and the Internet/intranet, helping with installation, training, problem resolution, and other technical support.

The IC is set up to help users get certain systems built quickly and to provide tools that can be employed by users to build their own systems. The concept of the IC, furthermore, suggests that the people in the center should be especially oriented toward the users in their outlook. This attitude should be shown in the training provided by the staff at the center and in the way the staff helps users with any problems they might have. There can be one or several ICs in an organization, and they report to the IS department and/or the end-user departments.

Information technology, as shown throughout this book, is playing a critical role in the livelihood of many organizations, small and large, private and public, throughout the world. Furthermore, the trend is for even more IT involvement. Effective IS departments will help their firms apply IT to transform themselves to e-businesses, redesign processes, and access needed information on a tight budget.

This chapter has described the alignment of IT within an organization, the means by which CIOs and IT specialists can go about understanding and analyzing the potential impact of IT on their organizations and in their industries, and the process of IT planning. It should be noted that some organizations might decide that the expense of having an in-house IT function outweighs the advantages. For these organizations, outsourcing the entire IT function might be an option. However, *outsourcing* is concerned more with specific aspects—such as outsourcing the IT service function, or outsourcing applications development—than with outsourcing the full IT function (Dibbern et al., 2004).

# 13.8 Managerial Issues

**1. Powerful competitive advantage.** In today's hypercompetitive marketplace, a company must be a powerful competitor to survive. As companies become larger and more sophisticated, they develop resources necessary to more quickly duplicate the successful systems of new and existing competitors.

**2. Importance.** Getting IT ready for the future by successfully planning for or creating that future is one of the most challenging tasks facing management, including IS management. To have a longer lasting competitive advantage, it is important to develop an IT strategy that includes a wide spectrum of techniques. Those techniques can enable a company to compete (or differentiate) on price, time (quick response), service, innovation, quality, or customer service.

**3. Organizing for effective planning.** Many issues are involved in planning: What should be the role of the IS department? How should IT be organized, staffed, and funded? How should human resources issues, such as training, benefits, and career paths for IS personnel, be handled? What about the environment? The competition? Governmental regulations? Emerging technologies? What is the strategic direction of the host organization? What are its key objectives? Are they agreed upon and clearly stated? Finally, with these strategies and objectives and the larger environment, what strategies and objectives should IS pursue? What type of information architecture best supports the business plan—centralized or decentralized? How can and should IT investments be justified? The answer to these questions must fit the particular circumstances of the IS department and the organization of which it is a part.

**4. Fitting the IT architecture to the organization.** Before the IT architecture no longer suits the needs of the organization, that architecture needs to be transformed. That transformation requires that IT technicians determine the future requirements of the organization.

**5. IT architecture planning.** IT architecture planning will not support the business objectives unless IT meets with business users to jointly determine the present and anticipated needs. In some cases, IT should lead (e.g., when business users do not understand the technical implications of a new technology). In other cases, users should lead (e.g., when technology is to be applied to a new business opportunity). Plans should be written and published as part of the organizational strategic plan and as part of the IT strategic plan. Plans should also deal with training, career implications, and other secondary infrastructure issues.

**6. IT policy.** Corporate guidelines and policies need to drive changes in IT architectures. These policies should include the roles and responsibilities of IT personnel and users, security issues, cost-benefit analyses for evaluating IT, and IT architectural goals. Policies should be communicated to all personnel who manage or are affected by IT.

**7. Ethical and legal issues.** Conducting interviews to identify managers' needs and requirements must be done with their full cooperation. Measures to protect privacy must be taken.

**ETHICS**

Implementing organizational transformation by the use of IT may tempt some to take unethical or even illegal actions. Companies may need to use IT to monitor the activities of their employees and customers, and in so doing may invade the privacy of individuals. When using business intelligence to find out what competitors are doing, companies may be engaged in unethical tactics such as pressuring competitors' employees to reveal information, or using software that is the intellectual property of other companies (frequently without the knowledge of these other companies).

**8. IT strategy.** Three basic strategies should be examined when planning IT:

(1) *Be a leader in technology.* Companies such as FedEx, Amazon.com, Dell, and Wal-Mart are known for their leading strategy. The advantages of being a leader are the ability to attract customers, to provide unique services and products, and to be a cost leader. However, there is a high development cost of new technologies and high probability of failures.

(2) *Be a follower.* This is a risky strategy because you may be left behind. However, you do not risk failures, and so you usually are able to implement new technologies at a fraction of the cost.

(3) *Be an experimenter, on a small scale.* This way you minimize your research and development investment and the cost of failure. When new technologies prove to be successful you can move fairly quickly for full implementation.

# Integrating *IT*

### For the Accounting Major

Accountants need to allocate the development and maintenance costs of information systems to cost centers, usually on the basis of usage. For strategic information systems with huge up-front investment requirements, cost allocation methods and budgeting become more complex and those costs may be difficult to justify using purely quantitative methods.

Accountants must understand and be able to balance the need for cost control and containment with the need to invest in IT innovations to remain competitive. They will be involved in the processes of business planning, controlling, cost behavior, cost allocation, budgeting, and performance measurement of IT investments.

### For the Finance Major

With IT budgets and staff trimmed down to the essentials, finance managers need to work closely with IT managers to jointly set priorities for capital investments, negotiate service levels, keep one another up-to-date about how IT is impacting day-to-day business performance, and calculate returns on IT investments. The profitability of the firm depends on the finance function's ability to correctly determine which IT project plans to approve and which to deny. That determination requires understanding the sustainability of competitive advantages provided by various IT architectures and their alignment with the business strategy.

### For the Human Resources Management Major

Not only must new information systems be planned to support strategic objectives, their impacts on personnel must be planned for and controlled. When a company designs new information systems, it redesigns the organization. That is, communication patterns get changed; people who had authority may find that an information system has displaced them; fear and reluctance to change may lead to deliberate or inadvertent sabotage of the information system. Human resources managers need to understand the potential impacts of IT plans on workers to minimize negative consequences on employees and the system itself. Not all employees are comfortable working remotely or in a virtual world. Employee training and other preparations may make the difference between the success and failure of new IT investments.

### For the IS Major

Technical skills are insufficient for information systems managers and professionals. The information systems department must focus on the integration of internal operations with each other and with the environment, the evaluation of business risk and strategy alternatives, and the development of long-range IT plans and programs.

Understanding the strategic potential of information systems is crucial to obtaining significant value from information system investments. Generating value from information systems continues to be one of the most significant challenges facing IS personnel—and of considerable interest to senior executives in other functional areas.

### For the Marketing Major

Without the ability to deliver quality products and services at competitive prices and at the time they are needed (or wanted), the ability to attract new customers and retain existing ones is at risk. Marketers need to be involved in IT planning because they bring to the table the customer's perspective as well as knowledge of what competitors are doing to steal customers away.

Marketers are among the most important end users of information systems. One of the most strategic IT initiatives is customer relationship management (CRM). CMR also has a high failure rate, in part, because the full IT implementation needed for the success of CRM is not completed. Marketers are responsible for insuring that the requirements for successful customer-facing strategic applications are understood by the IT department as well as those in accounting and finance.

### For the Production/Operations Management Major

Flexible production systems and integrated supply chain systems are extremely complex undertakings that require the active involvement of production and operations managers. Suppliers or customers expect, and may even demand, that their business partners provide flexible, integrated systems to be part of their supply chain.

Strategic information systems can quickly become necessary for survival. To eliminate blind spots—and the expensive consequences of finding out about problems belatedly—real-time information systems are needed that alert production managers of delivery delays, production disruptions, product defects, order cancellations, and so on. An efficient production system is one that supports the ability to predict what will happen and when—so that there are no surprises.

## Key Terms

Alliance strategy *525*
Applications portfolio *532*
Business systems planning (BSP) model *533*
Competitive forces model *521*
Cost leadership strategy *524*

Critical success factors (CSFs) *533*
Differentiation strategy *525*
E-planning *540*
Entry-barriers strategy *526*
Growth strategy *525*
Innovation strategy *525*

IT planning *531*
Niche strategy *525*
Resource allocation *536*
Scenario planning *535*
Stages of IT growth *533*
Value chain model *527*

## Chapter Highlights

(Numbers Refer to Learning Objectives)

❶ IT alignment helps organizations do things better by supporting or shaping competitive strategies. An information system is strategic if it is aligned with business goals and strategies, and has an impact on organizational performance.

❶ The Internet continues to change the nature of competition, in part by enabling competitors from outside an industry to enter an industry. The Internet radically alters the traditional relationships between customers, suppliers, and firms within an industry.

❷ The competitive forces model, value chain model, and resource-based view of the firm model are three frameworks for identifying areas in which IT can provide strategic advantage.

❷ Cost leadership, differentiation, and niche were Porter's first strategies for gaining a competitive advantage, but today may other strategies exist. All of the competitive strategies can be supported by IT.

❷ The resource-based view of the firm can help identify those IT-based resources and capabilities that are critical to creating, and sustaining, a competitive advantage.

❸ Acquiring competitive advantage is hard, and sustaining it can be just as difficult because of the innovative nature of technology advances.

❸ IT planning methods have had to evolve as markets have changed. Today, IT planning needs to be much more comprehensive and include consideration of supply chain partners and e-planning.

❹ Aligning IS plans and IT plans with business plans makes it possible to prioritize IS investments on the basis of contribution to organizational strategies and profit performance goals.

❹ IT strategies also need to be aligned with those of business in the company's supply chain. Interorganizational alignment requires a "partnership" IT strategy instead of a competitive one.

❹ Outsourcing the IT service function or outsourcing applications development are IT strategies to free up time for in-house CIOs and IT specialists to go about understanding and analyzing the potential impacts of IT on their organizations.

❺ Information technology architecture can be centralized or distributed. When it is distributed, it often follows the client/server architecture model.

❺ Organizations can use enterprise architecture principles to develop an information technology architecture.

❺ Strategic information systems planning involves methodologies such as business systems planning (BSP), stages of IT growth, and critical success factors (CSFs).

❻ The major information systems planning issues are strategic alignment, architecture, resource allocation, and time and budget considerations, which require the involvement of all business units.

❻ Treating other business units and end users as *customers* of the information systems department is important to the development of good relations with them.

## Virtual Company Assignment

### Strategic Advantage at The Wireless Café

Go to The Wireless Café's link on the Student Web Site. There you will be asked to think about how the competitive forces model and IT planning could contribute to strategic advantage for the restaurant.

*Instructions for accessing The Wireless Café on the Student Web Site:*

1. Go to *wiley.com/college/turban*.
2. Select Turban/Leidner/McLean/Wetherbe's *Information Technology for Management*; Sixth Edition.
3. Click on Student Resources site, in the toolbar on the left.
4. Click on the link for Virtual Company Web site.
5. Click on Wireless Café.

## Online Resources

More resources and study tools are located on the Student Web Site and on WileyPLUS. You'll find additional chapter materials and useful Web links. In addition, self-quizzes that provide individualized feedback are available for each chapter.

## Questions for Review

1. Why would CIOs list *IT and business alignment* as their top-ranking issue?
2. List three examples of information systems that are important to a company's business strategy.
3. Explain the relationship among business strategy, IS strategy, and IT strategy. (Refer to Figure 13.1.)
4. Explain how the Internet has altered the industry structure of: the music industry, the retail industry, and the travel industry.
5. Explain the impacts of the Internet on global competition using Porter's competitive forces model.
6. List three IT strategies for competitive advantage.
7. Why might it be difficult for a business to sustain a competitive advantage for at least one year?
8. Discuss why a company's IT competitive advantage might not be easily duplicated by other companies in the industry sector.
9. What are the characteristics of resources that enable a competitive advantage? Compare and contrast them with the characteristics of resources that enable a sustainable competitive advantage.
10. List one similarity among the three frameworks and one unique feature of each—the competitive forces model, value chain model, and resource-based view of the firm model.
11. What are some of the challenges of IT planning?
12. Explain critical success factors (CSFs). Select three industries and list two CSFs for a company in each of those industries.
13. Explain the role of a steering committee and who should be members of it.
14. Discuss the importance of service-level agreements.
15. List the purpose of portfolio analysis.

## Questions for Discussion

1. Why is it important to align the IT plan with organizational strategies? What could or could not happen if those plans are not aligned?
2. Give two examples showing how IT can help a defending company *reduce* the impact of the five forces in Porter's model.
3. Give two examples of how attacking companies can use IT to *increase* the leverage of the five forces in Porter's model.
4. Can an information system by itself provide a sustainable competitive advantage? Explain.
5. Discuss how strategic planning, as described in this chapter, could help a major league sports team increase the value of its Web site.
6. How might the information architecture limit an organization's ability to implement a new strategic plan? Provide an example.
7. What problems might an organization encounter if it focuses only on resource allocation planning or project planning?
8. Discuss the advantages of using Tjan's approach to an applications portfolio.
9. Some organizations feel that IT planning is a waste of time because the competitive environment and technologies change too rapidly. They argue that their plans will be obsolete before they are completed. Discuss.
10. Service-level agreements (SLAs) are contracts, in effect. Who should be involved in composing and reviewing those agreements? Why?

# Exercises and Projects

For questions 1 through 4, refer to the Boeing case at the beginning of the chapter.

1. Explain why Boeing's commercial airplanes division needed to considerably revamp its supply chain operation.

2. What might be the differences in information and collaboration requirements between the *competitive model* and *early engagement model* for managing supplier relationships?

3. What networks and collaboration technologies did Boeing deploy to improve its competitive position?

4. What are the strategic, social, and ethical issues involved in such a global supply chain?

5. One area of intense competition is online automobile sales. Examine the Web sites of two online automobile sales companies and describe their apparent business strategies. Prepare a report of

their strategies and also compare the IT features of each Web site.

6. Study the Web sites of Amazon.com and Barnes & Noble online (*bn.com*). Also, find some information about the competition between these two companies. Analyze Barnes & Noble's defense strategy using Porter's model. Prepare a report.

7. Visit two major travel-related Web sites and compare their strategies and offerings. Prepare a report.

8. Using the CSF method of strategic planning, identify new strategic initiatives that a video/DVD store might take using information technology.

9. What kind of IT planning is done at your place of work or in a government agency in your area to ensure that the Internet demand in the future will be met?

10. Examine Tjan's applications portfolio method. Discuss the advantages and limitations of that method.

# Group Assignments and Projects

1. Assign group members to each of the major car rental companies. Find out their latest strategies regarding customer service. Visit their Web sites and compare the findings. Have each group prepare a presentation on why its company should get the title of "best customer service provider." Also, each group should use Porter's forces model to convince the class that its company is the best competitor in the car rental industry.

2. The competition in online retailing is growing rapidly, as evidenced in goods such as books, toys, and CDs. Assign groups to study online competition in the above industries and more. Identify successes and failures. Compare the various industries. What generalizations can you make?

3. Assign each group member to a company to which he or she has access, and have each member prepare a value-

chain chart. The objective is to discover how specific IT applications are used to facilitate the various activities. Compare these charts across companies in different industries.

4. Divide the class into groups of six people or less. Each group will be entrepreneurs attempting to start some kind of nationwide company. Each group should describe the IT architecture it would build, as well as the expected benefits from, and potential problems with, the IT architecture it has chosen.

5. Assign groups to the following industries: banking, airlines, health care, insurance, and large retailing. Each group will investigate the use of the mainframe in one industry and prepare a report on the future of the mainframe. Also, include information on how client/server architecture is used in the industry.

# Internet Exercises

1. McKesson Drugs and Pfizer are two of the largest wholesale drug distributors. Visit the companies' Web sites at *mckesson.com* and *pfizer.com*. What can you learn about their strategies toward retailers? Compare their strategies toward their customers. What e-commerce initiatives are evident at their Web sites?

2. Competitive intelligence is offered at EDGAR-related Web sites (e.g., *edgar-online.com*). Prepare a list of the documents that are available, and discuss the benefits of

using this database for conducting competitive intelligence.

3. Visit *www2.cio.com/research*. Review the latest CIO Research Reports pertaining to IT planning and strategic drivers. List five relevant findings.

4. Visit cell phone manufacturer Nokia at *nokia.com* and *nokia.com/A4126176*. What does Nokia offer content developers (e.g., as part of its strategic plan)? Comment on your findings.

# Minicase 1

## Verizon and Rivio Use the Web to Offer Big Benefits for Small Businesses

Verizon Communications (*verizon.com*) is one of the world's leading providers of communications services. With a global presence in 40 countries, approximately 260,000 employees, and more than $65 billion in annual revenues, this Fortune 10 company has access to resources that small businesses could never dream of—until now. Verizon and Rvio, Inc. (*rivio.com*), a company founded in 1999 to develop and deliver Web services to small business, have teamed to provide a suite of Web-based services that will help small businesses streamline and organize daily business operations. Verizon will market the Rivio Business Services suite on its Web site to its more than three million small business customers nationwide.

"Our overall goal is to support the success of our small business customers," said Bob Ingalls, president of Verizon's Business Solutions Group. "Rivio has assembled an impressive suite of services from best-of-class suppliers that can help our customers run their operations more smoothly and efficiently, and allow them to concentrate on their businesses."

Rivio Business Services are designed to make the flow of work, ideas, and information throughout small businesses more streamlined. By providing employees the ability to quickly access, exchange, and integrate information, small businesses are able to run more efficiently and produce superior results. Some of the Rivio Business Services features that small businesses will benefit from include:

- **Employee Communications Management Services.** Organizational charts, announcements, policies and procedures, internal job postings and electronic updates of employees' out of office locations or other contact information are all available in a central online location.
- **Expense Report Management Services.** Expense reports can be efficiently created, tracked, approved, and synchronized with Intuit, Inc.'s QuickBooks accounting software and project-based expense tracking.
- **HR Management Services.** Human resources managers have access to employee records and information from a single workstation. This service also provides flexible reporting for employment status, benefits and compensation information, and payroll integration features, in addition to granting employees access to their respective personnel records, which include compensation history, benefits, and other valuable information.
- **Payroll Management Services.** Through partnering with InterPay, Rivio offers a simplified approach to payroll processing with a seamless user interface. In this approach, human resources records and XML payroll data are integrated and fed to InterPay's payroll engine. Users can view payroll records, make adjustments, and preview the final payroll reports before processing.
- **Time and Attendance Management Services.** Employees can manage time-off requests, timesheet setup, and project-based time tracking from one centralized location.
- **Access to Microsoft bCentral Applications.** Verizon small business customers will have access to Microsoft's bCentral Business Card, bCentral Commerce Manager, bCentral Customer Manager, bCentral Finance Manager, and bCentral Traffic Builder, vastly increasing the small business's resources.

"Offering Rivio Business Services is an excellent opportunity for Verizon to increase its value proposition for small business customers and extend our product offering," Ingalls said. "Verizon selected Rivio because of the power of its Integrated Business Services Network (iBSN), which aggregates an extensive selection of business services from more than 50 best-of-class suppliers."

The Rivio Business Services offered through the Verizon Web site are available at *bizservices.rivio.com*, or by clicking through Verizon's business products and services Web pages at *verizon.com*.

Verizon will provide these Web services for a low monthly subscription fee, with price varying based on number of users and services selection. A variety of promotional and introductory offers and rates also will be available, including "try before you buy" options.

"The alliance with Verizon allows Rivio to significantly increase the availability of our Web services, extending our reach to more than three million new small businesses nationwide," said Navin Chaddha, Rivio chairman and chief executive officer. "By making Rivio's comprehensive services accessible through Verizon—a resource that small business customers already use and trust—Rivio will enable Verizon's small business customers to more efficiently run their businesses, giving owners and employees more time to focus on revenue-generating activities."

*Source:* Verizon Communications (2006), *verizon.com* (accessed June 2006), and *rivio.com* (accessed June 2006).

## Questions for Minicase 1

1. In what ways might IT strategy and alignment differ for small businesses as opposed to that of larger organizations?

2. What are some of the major challenges for aligning IT in a small organization?

3. What are some of the pros and cons of using large providers to meet the IT needs of small business customers?

4. Conduct some research on the Rivio system and make your own assessment as to whether the claim of

Rivio's chairman—that "Rivio will enable Verizon's small business customers to more efficiently run their businesses, giving owners and employees more time to focus on revenue-generating activities"—is hype or reality.

## Minicase 2

# Scenario Planning at National City Bank Aligns IT with Business Planning

**FIN**

The banking industry is very competitive. National City Corp. (national-city.com), one of the largest U.S. bank holding companies, based in Cleveland, Ohio, was confronting three challenges: (1) It needed new ways to generate earnings; (2) it faced increasing competition for market share; and (3) the bank was losing customers who wanted to do banking using the Internet.

National City saw the customer information system it was developing with IBM as a solution to these problems. The bank hoped to use this system to develop new, high-revenue products, tailor programs for customers, and cross-sell products to appropriate customers. But to design it, the bank had to know what kind of information the system would be aggregating. Would it track information about the products the bank offered or the people who bought them? If it was product-focused, it would have to include detailed descriptions of each financial service, whether credit cards or mortgages. If the system was customer-focused, it would track whether they used ATMs, branch offices, or call centers, and would indicate demographics in order to build customer profiles. Furthermore, the bank would need to set up business rules to determine customer profitability.

Management quickly realized that they simply could not answer these questions because the answers were linked to a larger issue: Management didn't have a clear sense of the bank's strategic direction. The required investment in technology was $40 million, so planning to invest it properly was critical.

To clarify the business direction, the bank hired a consulting company, *ncri.com*, to employ scenario planning. The planning process involved six phases used by an implementation team:

## Phase I: Alternative Visions (Scenarios)

In this phase, a few possible visions of the future are selected. In the case of National City, the scenarios were:

- *Utilize a CRM-based strategy.* This was a major industry trend in which everything would be geared to individual customer need. This business model is complex and expensive to pursue.
- *Specialize solely in certain financial services.* This is a low-cost option, but may not bring new customers and may even result in losing existing customers.
- *Create a separate online bank.*

## Phase II: Events Generation

Next, a list of 150 internal and external events that might influence any of the outcomes was generated by the team. Events included new regulations and technological developments (e.g., wireless). These events were simulated as newspaper headlines (e.g., "Demand for real-time banking information via cell phones is skyrocketing"). These events were used later to create scenarios.

## Phase III: The Workshop

A three-day workshop with the 24 top executives was conducted. The participants were divided into three groups. The first task was to rank all 150 events by the *chance that they will occur*. Once done, all participants met to discuss the rankings and, after appropriate discussion, reach a consensus. This process can be lengthy, but it is essential.

Then, each team was assigned one of the bank's three scenarios and was asked to analyze the impact of the most-likely-to-occur events on that scenario, within a five-year planning horizon.

## Phase IV: Presentation

Each group made an oral presentation, in which their goal was to convince the other groups that their vision was the most feasible. This was a difficult task since some team members, who had to play the role of supporters, actually did not like the scenario they were supposed to "sell."

## Phase V: Deliberation and Attempt to Reach a Consensus

The entire group of participants needed to agree on which alternative was the best for the bank. After long deliberation, the group decided to support alternative #1, the CRM-based strategy.

## Phase VI: IT Support

To facilitate the IT planning, an IS plan was devised in which a data warehouse was planned, so that customers' profiles could be built. Data mining was planned for identifying the bank's most profitable customers, and a Web-based call center was designed to provide personalized services.

All in all, the scenario planning process was an exercise in contingency thinking that resulted in prosperity when the system was eventually deployed.

*Sources:* Condensed from Levinson (2000), *ncri.com,* and *national-city.com.*

## Questions for Minicase 2

1. One critique of this approach is that some members who are asked to "sell" a specific scenario may not be enthusiastic to do so. Find information in the scenario planning literature on this issue, or e-mail a scenario consultant (*ncri.com* or *gbn.com*). Write a report on your findings.
2. Can group decision support systems (Chapter 12) be used in this case? Why and what for, or why not?
3. How can the end users learn about technology in scenario planning?
4. What IT tools can be used to facilitate this scenario planning process, which was done manually?
5. How did the scenario planning help the IT people to better understand the business?
6. Why is scenario planning considered a risk-management tool?

# References

Agrawal, V., L. D. Arjona, and R. Lemmens, "E-Performance: The Path to Rational Exuberance," *McKinsey Quarterly,* First Quarter, 2001.

Beal, B., "IT-business Alignment Elusive for Some," *searchCIO.com,* March 24, 2004.

Berstein, M., "Boeing Shrinks Supply Chain to Facilitate Risk Sharing," *World Trade,* April 1, 2006.

Boeing.com, "Major Assembly of First Boeing 787 Dreamliner Starts," June 30, 2006, *boeing.com/news/releases/2006/q2/060630a_nr.html* (accessed October 2006).

Burke, "Digitizing Market Research," *Line56,* June 7, 2006, *line56.com/articles/default.asp?ArticleID=7668.*

Bygstad, B., "The Implementation Puzzle of CRM Systems in Knowledge-Based Organizations," *Information Resources Management Journal* 16(4), October–December 2003.

Callon, J. D., *Competitive Advantage through Information Technology.* New York: McGraw-Hill, 1996.

Carry, J., and J. Ferguson, "Increasing the Success of the IT Strategic Planning Process," *Proceedings, 33rd Hawaiian International Conference on Systems Sciences (HICSS),* Hawaii, January 2000.

Chan, Y. E., "Why Haven't We Mastered Alignment? The Importance of the IT Informal Organization Structure," *MIS Quarterly Executive,* June 2002.

Collins, L., "Efficient and Effective," *IEE Review,* 50(1), January 2004.

Cone, E., "Flying in Formation," *CIO Insight,* March 6, 2006.

Dehning, B., and T. Stratopoulos, "Determinants of a Sustainable Competitive Advantage Due to an IT-enabled Strategy," *Journal of Strategic Information Systems,* Vol. 12, 2003.

Dibbern, J., T. Goles, R. Hirschheim, and B. Jayatilaka, "Information Systems Outsourcing: A Survey and Analysis of the Literature," *The Data Base for Advances in Information Systems,* 35(4), Fall 2004.

Earl, M. J., "Blue Survivors (the CIO's)," *CIO,* December 15, 1999–January 1, 2000.

Feurer, R., K. Chaharbaghi, M. Weber, and J. Wargin, "Aligning Strategies, Processes, and IT: A Case Study," *Information Systems Management,* Winter 2000.

Harmon, P., et al., *Developing E-Business Systems and Architectures: A Manager's Guide.* San Francisco: Morgan Kaufmann, 2001.

Horner-Reich, B., and K. M. Nelson, "In Their Own Words: CIO Visions About the Future of In-house IT Organizations," *Data Base,* Fall 2003.

King, W. R., "Assessing the Efficiency of IS Strategic Planning," *Information Systems Management,* Winter 2000.

Leidner, D. and J. Mackay, "CIO Succession: Approaches and Implications for IT Strategy," working paper, Baylor University, 2006.

Levinson, M., "Don't Stop Thinking about Tomorrow," *CIO Magazine,* January 1, 2000.

Luftman, J. N., et al., *Managing the Information Technology Resources.* Upper Saddle River, NJ: Pearson Education, 2004.

Nolan, R. L., "Managing the Crises in Data Processing," *Harvard Business Review,* March–April 1979.

Peffers K., and C. E. Gengler, "Understanding Internal IS Customer Models of Firm Performance to Identify Potential High-Impact Projects," *Proceedings of the 33rd Annual Hawaiian International Conference on Systems Sciences,* January 4–7, 2000, Maui, Hawaii.

Peffers, K., and C. E. Gengler, "How to Identify New High-Payoff Information Systems for the Organization," *Communications of the ACM,* 46(1), January 2003.

Porter, M. E., "What Is a Strategy?" *Harvard Business Review,* November–December 1996.

Porter, M. E., "Strategy and the Internet," *Harvard Business Review,* March 2001.

Ross J. W., and D. F. Feeny, "The Evolving Role of the CIO," in R. Zmud (ed.), *Framing the Domain of IT Management.* Cincinnati, OH: Pinnaflex Educational Resources, 2000.

Seybold, P. B., "Get Inside the Lives of Your Customers," *Harvard Business Review,* May 2001.

Stauffer, D., "Five Reasons Why You Still Need Scenario Planning," *Harvard Business Review*, June 2002.

Teo, T. S. H., and J. S. K. Ang, "An Examination of Major IS Planning Problems," *International Journal of Information Management*, December 2001.

Tjan, A. K., "Finally, A Way to Put Your Internet Portfolio in Order," *Harvard Business Review*, February 2001.

Turban, E., D. King, and J. K. Lee, *Electronic Commerce 2006*. Upper Saddle River, NJ: Prentice Hall, 2006.

Venkatraman, N., "Five Steps to a Dot-Com Strategy: How to Find Your Footing on the Web," *Sloan Management Review*, Spring 2000.

Verizon Communications, "Verizon Unveils Rivio(TM) Web Services Suite for Small Business Customers; Business Tools Available Through Verizon Web Site," *PRNewswire,* May 29, 2006, *prnewswire.com/cgi-bin/stories.pl?ACCT=104&STORY=/www/story/05-29-2001/0001502754&EDATE=.* (accessed October 2006).

Wade, M., and J. Hulland, "The Resource-based View and Information Systems Research: Review, Extension, and Suggestions for Future Research," *MIS Quarterly*, March 2004.

Ward, J., and J. Peppard, *Strategic Planning for Information Systems*, 3rd ed. New York: Wiley, 2002.

Willcocks, L. P., and R. Sykes, "The Role of the CIO and IT Function in ERP," *Communications of the ACM,* April 2000.

# Chapter 14

# Information Technology Economics

Justifying IT Investment in the State of Iowa

**14.1** Financial and Economic Trends and the Productivity Paradox

**14.2** Evaluating IT Investment: Benefits, Costs, and Issues

**14.3** Methods for Evaluating and Justifying IT Investment

**14.4** IT Economics Strategies: Chargeback and Outsourcing

**14.5** Economic Aspects of IT and Web-Based Systems

**14.6** Managerial Issues

## Minicases:

1. *American Express*
2. *Kone Inc.*

## Learning Objectives

After studying this chapter, you will be able to:

❶ Identify the major aspects of the economics of information technology.

❷ Explain and evaluate the productivity paradox.

❸ Describe approaches for evaluating IT investment and explain why is it difficult to do it.

❹ Explain the nature of intangible benefits and the approaches to deal with such benefits.

❺ List and briefly describe the traditional and modern methods of justifying IT investment.

❻ Identify the advantages and disadvantages of approaches to charging end users for IT services (chargeback).

❼ Identify the advantages and disadvantages of outsourcing.

❽ Describe the economic impact of EC.

❾ Describe economic issues related to Web-based technologies including e-commerce.

❿ Describe causes of systems development failures, the theory of increasing returns, and market transformation through new technologies.

## Integrating *IT*

 **ACC**
 **FIN**
 **MKT**
 **POM**
 **HRM**
 **IS**
 **SVC**

# JUSTIFYING IT INVESTMENT IN THE STATE OF IOWA

## The Problem

For years there was little planning or justification for IT projects developed by agencies of the state of Iowa. State agencies requested many projects, knowing that they would get only a few. Bargaining, political favors, and pressures brought to bear by individuals, groups, and state employees determined who would get what. As a result some important projects were not funded, some unimportant ones were funded, and there was very little incentive to save money.

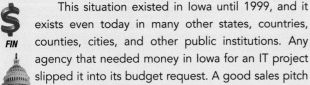 This situation existed in Iowa until 1999, and it exists even today in many other states, countries, counties, cities, and other public institutions. Any agency that needed money in Iowa for an IT project slipped it into its budget request. A good sales pitch would have resulted in approval. But, this situation, which cost taxpayers lots of money, changed in 1999 when a request for $22.5 million to fix the Y2K problem was made. This request triggered work that led Iowans to realize that the state government needed a better approach to planning and justifying IT investments.

## The Solution

The solution that Iowa chose is an *IT value model*. The basic idea was to promote *performance-based government,* an approach that measures the results of government programs. Using the principles deployed to justify the investment in the Y2K fix, a methodology was developed to measure the value any new IT project would create. The system is based on the return on investment (ROI) financial model, and is known as R.O. Iowa (a play on words). Its principles are described below.

First, new IT investments are paid for primarily from a pot of money called the Pooled Technology Account, which is appropriated by the legislature and is controlled by the state's IT department. Pooling the funds makes budget oversight easier and helps avoid duplication of systems. Second, the IT department reimburses agencies for expenses from this fund only after verifying that they are necessary. If an agency's expenditures are not in line with the project schedule, it's a red flag for auditors that the project could be in trouble.

To support spending decisions, agency managers have to document the *expected costs and benefits* according to a standard set of factors. The score for each factor ranges from 5 to 15 points, for a maximum total score of 100 points. In addition they must specify metrics related to those factors to justify requests and later to determine the project's success. The scores are based on ten criteria that are used to determine values. Besides asking for standard financial data, the ROI program also requires agencies to detail their technology requirements and functional needs. This level of detail enforces standards, but it also helps officials identify duplicative expenditures. For example, in 2001 several agencies were proposing to build pieces of an ERP system, such as electronic procurement and human resources management. The IS department suggested that, for less money, the state could deploy a single ERP system that agencies could share. The project, which had an estimated cost of $9.6 million, could easily have cost several times that amount, if agencies were allowed to go it alone.

As noted earlier, once a project is funded, the state scrutinizes agencies' expenses. Agencies have to submit their purchase orders and invoices to the Enterprise Quality Assurance Office for approval before they can be reimbursed.

## The Results

The R.O. Iowa system became, by 2002, a national model for documenting value and prioritizing IT investments in the U.S. public sector. In 2002 the program was named the "Best State IT Management Initiative" by the National Association of State CIOs. It saved Iowa taxpayers more than $5 million in less than 4 years (about 16 percent of the spending on new IT projects).

The process has changed users' behavior as well. For example, during the fiscal-year 2003 budget approval process, agencies asked for 17 IT projects, and were granted only six. For the year 2004 they asked for only four projects, all of which were granted. Also, there is considerable collaboration among agencies and use of cross-functional teams to write applications, so the need to "play games" to get project funding is largely gone. Another improvement is elimination of duplicated systems. Finally, the methodology minimizes politics and political pressures.

The success of R.O. Iowa led to the Iowa Accounting Government Act, which requires establishing similar methodology in all state investments, not just for IT projects.

*Source:* Compiled from Varon (2003) and *CIO* (2003).

## 14.1 Financial and Economic Trends and the Productivity Paradox

**TECHNOLOGICAL AND FINANCIAL TRENDS**

Information technology capabilities are advancing at a rapid rate, and this trend is likely to continue for the foreseeable future. Expanding power and declining costs enable new and more extensive applications of information technology, which makes it possible for organizations to improve their efficiency and effectiveness.

On the hardware side, capabilities are growing at an exponential rate. *Moore's Law,* named for one of the founders of Intel Corp., postulated that the number of transistors, and thus the power, of an integrated circuit (now called computer chip) would double every year, while the cost remained the same. Moore later revised this estimate to a slightly less rapid pace: doubling every 18 months. Figure 14.1 illustrates Moore's Law as it relates to the power of Intel chips, measured in MIPS, or millions of (computer) instructions per second (on the right) and transistors count (on the left). Moore has also applied the law to the Web, electronic commerce, and supply chain management (see Moore, 1997). Others applied it, with slight modifications, to storage capability.

Assuming the current rate of growth in computing power (see Hamilton, 2003), organizations will have the opportunity to buy, for the same price, twice the processing power in 1½ years, four times the power in 3 years, eight times the power in 4½ years, and so forth. Another way of saying this is that the **price-to-performance ratio** will continue to decline exponentially. Limitations associated with current technologies could end this trend for silicon-based chips in 10 or 20 years (or possibly earlier; see Pountain, 1998), but new technologies will probably allow this phenomenal growth to continue. Advances in network technologies and storage, as compared to those in chip technology, are even more profound, as shown in Chapter 2.

What does this growth in computing power mean in economic terms? First, most organizations will perform existing functions at decreasing costs over time and thus become more efficient. Second, creative organizations will find new uses for

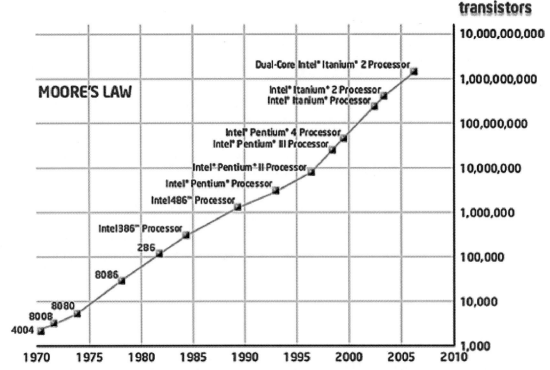

Figure 14.1 Moore's Law as it relates to Intel microprocessors. (*Source:* Modified from Intel Corporation, *intel.com.research/silicon/mooreslaw.htm*. Reprinted by permission of Intel Corporation, ©Intel Corporation.)

information technology—based on the improving price-to-performance ratio—and thus become more effective. They will also apply technology to activities that are technically feasible at current power levels but will not be economically feasible until costs are reduced. Information technology will become an even more significant factor in the production and distribution of almost every product and service. This will increase the attractiveness of automating more manual jobs. Will it also result in more unemployment?

**ETHICS**

These new and enhanced products and services will provide competitive advantage to organizations that have the creativity to exploit the increasing power of information technology. They will also provide major benefits to consumers, who will benefit from the greater product functionality and lower costs (e.g., see Farrell, 2003).

The remainder of this chapter focuses on evaluating the costs, benefits, and other economic aspects of information technology. Productivity is a major focus of economists, and those who studied the payoff from massive IT investments in the 1970s and 1980s observed what has been called the *productivity paradox*. It is that topic we address next.

**WHAT IS THE PRODUCTIVITY PARADOX?**

Over the last 50 years, organizations have invested trillions of dollars in information technology. By the start of the twenty-first century, total worldwide *annual* spending on IT had surpassed two trillion dollars (ITAA, 2000). As this textbook has demonstrated, these expenditures have unquestionably transformed organizations: The technologies have become an integral aspect of almost every business process. The business and technology presses publish many "success stories" about major benefits from information technology projects at individual organizations or even industries (e.g., electronic airline ticketing). It seems self-evident that these investments must have increased productivity, not just in individual organizations, but throughout the economy.

On the other hand, it is very hard to demonstrate, at the level of a national economy, that the IT investments really have increased productivity. Most of the investment went into the service sector of the economy, which, during the 1970s and 1980s, was showing much lower productivity gains than manufacturing. Fisher (2001) reports on a study that showed that only 8 percent of total IT spending actually delivers value. Nobel prize winner in economics Robert Solow quipped, "We see computers everywhere except in the productivity statistics." The discrepancy between measures of investment in information technology and measures of output at the national level has been called the **productivity paradox.**

To understand this paradox, we first need to understand the concept of productivity. Economists define *productivity* as outputs divided by inputs. Outputs are calculated by multiplying units produced (for example, number of automobiles) by their average value. The resulting figure needs to be adjusted for price inflation and also for any changes in quality (such as increased safety or better gas mileage). If inputs are measured simply as hours of work, the resulting ratio of outputs to inputs is *labor productivity*. If other inputs—investments and materials—are included, the ratio is known as *multifactor productivity*.

**EXPLAINING THE PRODUCTIVITY PARADOX**

Economists have studied the productivity issue extensively in recent years and have developed a variety of possible explanations of the apparent paradox (e.g., see Olazabal, 2002). These explanations can be grouped into several categories: (1) Problems with data or analyses hide productivity gains from IT, (2) gains from IT are offset by losses in other areas, and (3) IT productivity gains are offset by IT costs or losses. A summary is provided in Table 14.1. We discuss these explanations in more detail in Online File W14.1.

| TABLE 14.1 | Possible Reasons for the Productivity Paradox |
|---|---|
| **Reason** | **Explanation** |
| Productivity gains are not shown in data or analysis. | Difficulties in defining or measuring benefits and productivity gains. Also, impact may be felt after a long time or in a secondary manner. |
| Productive gains are offset by losses from the same IT in other areas. | Gain in one department or even in one company may result in loss in others (e.g., budget increase in IT may reduce marketing budget); or market share gain in one company may be a loss to others. |
| Productivity gains are offset by high costs. | Some IT projects cost too much (especially when total cost of operations is considered). Secondary impacts may cause losses. |
| Time lag may distort the picture. | IT investment today may be realized in profits years from now. |
| Actual use of IT system is different from what was envisioned. | For legal, labor, or other reasons, systems are used differently than envisioned, yielding less performance than anticipated. |

The productivity-offsetting factors described earlier largely reflect problems with the administration of IT, rather than with the technologies themselves. In many cases these problems in administration are controllable through better planning or more effective management techniques. For organizations, the critical issue is not whether and how IT increases productivity *in the economy as a whole,* but how it improves their own productivity. Lin and Shao (2000) find a robust and consistent relationship between IT investment and efficiency, and they support evaluating IT investments in terms of organizational efficiency rather than productivity. For the results of a comprehensive study on the economic value of IT in Europe see Legrenzi (2003).

Some of the difficulties in finding the relationship between IT investment and organizational performance can be seen in Figure 14.2. The relationships are basically indirect, via IT assets and IT impacts. The figure shows that the relationships between IT investment and organizational performance are not direct; other factors exist in between. This could be the reason why the productivity paradox exists, since these intermediary factors (in the middle of the figure) can moderate and influence the relationship. A similar explanation is provided by Lucas (2005). He divides the IT investment into infrastructure and applications. Then he identifies *direct impact,* such as direct cost savings, revenue generation, major organizational change, and partial success and failures. These may result in *second-order impact,* such as greater market share, strategic advantage, new or improved business processes, and better customer service. The second-order impacts may be very difficult to assess and may occur after a long time period. For further discussion see Thatcher and Pingry (2004).

The inconclusiveness of studies about the value of IT investment and inaccuracies in measurements have prompted many companies to skip formal evaluations (see Seddon et al., 2002, and Sawhney, 2002). However, as became apparent during the dot-com bubble, when many dot-coms were started and almost as many quickly failed, this can be a very risky approach. Therefore, before deciding to skip evaluation, an organization should examine some of the new methods that may result in more accurate evaluation (see Section 14.3).

Many believe that the productivity paradox as it relates to IT is no longer valid, since we are able to explain what caused it. Others believe that the issue is still very relevant, especially on the level of the economy as a whole. They claim that the paradox still matters because IT has failed to lift productivity growth throughout the economy, although it may have improved productivity at the level of firms or of industries. We may not at this point be able to provide a final answer to the question about whether the paradox still matters. The important conclusion that we can draw

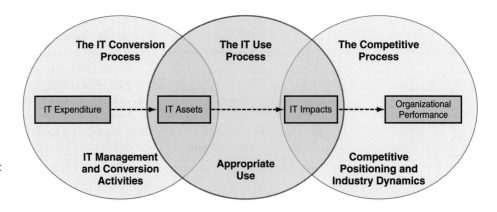

**Figure 14.2** Process approach to IT organizational investment and impact. (*Source:* Soh and Markus, 1995.)

is that we need to be careful in measuring the economic contributions of IT on all three levels—firms, industries, and national economies. Because almost 50 percent of all capital investment in the United States is in IT and it is growing with time, it is even more important to properly assess its benefits and costs, and that is what this chapter is attempting to do.

The next two sections cover ways organizations can evaluate IT benefits and costs and target their IT development and acquisition toward systems that will best contribute to the achievement of organizational goals.

# 14.2 Evaluating IT Investment: Benefits, Costs, and Issues

Evaluating IT investment requires measurement of the value of IT (Tillquist and Rogers, 2005) with a comparison to the cost of IT. Such a study covers many topics. Let's begin by categorizing types of IT investment.

**IT INVESTMENT CATEGORIES**

One basic way to analyze IT investment is to distinguish between investment in infrastructure and investment in specific applications.

*IT infrastructure* provides the foundations for IT applications in the enterprise. Examples are a data center, networks, data warehouse, and a corporate knowledge base. Infrastructure investments are made to exist for a long time, and the infrastructure is shared by many applications throughout the enterprise (see Kumar, 2004). *IT applications* are specific systems and programs for achieving certain objectives—for example, providing a payroll or taking a customer order. The number of IT applications is large and they can be in one functional department, or they can be shared by several departments, which makes evaluation of their costs and benefits more complex (Peppard and Ward, 2005).

Another way to look at IT investment categories is proposed by Ross and Beath (2002). As shown in Online File W14.2, their categories are based on the purpose of the investment (called "drivers" in the table). They also suggest a cost justification (funding approach) as well as the probable owner. Still other investment categories are offered by Devaraj and Kohli (2002), who divide IT investments into operational, managerial, and strategic types, and by Lucas (2005); see Chapter 7. The variety of IT investment categories demonstrates the complex nature of IT investment.

**THE VALUE OF INFORMATION IN DECISION MAKING**

People in organizations use information to help them make decisions that are better than they would have been if they did not have the information. Senior executives make decisions that influence the profitability of an organization for years to come; operational employees make decisions that affect production on a day-to-day basis. In either case, the value of information is the difference between the *net benefits* (benefits adjusted for costs) of decisions made using information and the net benefits of decisions made without information. The value of the net benefits with information obviously needs to reflect the additional costs of obtaining the information. Thus, the value of information can be expressed as follows:

> Value of information = Net benefits with information
>                    − Net benefits without information

<table>
<tr><td>

EVALUATING IT
INVESTMENT
BY TRADITIONAL
COST-BENEFIT
ANALYSIS OR ROI

</td></tr>
</table>

Automation of business processes is a major area where it is necessary to define and measure IT benefits and costs. For example, automation was implemented in the organization's business offices when word processing replaced typing and spreadsheet programs replaced column-ruled accounting pads and 10-key calculators. In the factory, robots weld and paint automobiles on assembly lines. In the warehouse, incoming items are recorded by RFID readers. Another example is replacement of an old information system by a new or improved one. The decision of whether to automate is an example of a *capital investment* decision. Traditional tools used to evaluate investment decisions are net present value, internal rate of return, and payback period, which are known collectively as ROI.

**Return on Investment.** The most common traditional tool for evaluating capital investments is *return on investment* (ROI), which measures the effectiveness of management in generating profits with its available assets (see Anonymous, 2005). The ROI measure is a percentage (and the higher this percentage return, the better). It is calculated essentially by dividing net annual income attributable to a project by the cost of the assets invested in the project. For an overview, see Paton and Troppito (2004) and Pisello (2005). An example of a detailed study of the ROI of a portal, commissioned by Plumtree Software and executed by META group (now partners of Gartner), can be found at *plumtree.com* (also white papers at *metagroup.com*). Davamanirajan et al. (2002) found an average 10 percent annual rate of return on investment in IT projects in the financial services sector. For a comprehensive study see Kudyba and Vitaliano (2003). The following tools, or "financial metrics," are the most commonly used in ROI studies.

**Using NPV. Cost-benefit analysis** compares the total value of the benefits with the associated costs. Organizations often use net present value (NPV) calculations for cost-benefit analyses. In an NPV analysis, analysts convert future values of benefits to their present-value equivalent. They then can compare the present value of the future benefits to the costs required to achieve those benefits, in order to determine whether the benefits exceed the costs. (For more specific guidelines and decision criteria on how NPV analysis works, consult financial management textbooks.)

**Formulas for NPV analysis**

$$PV = \frac{1}{(1-i)^n}$$

where $n$ = number of years and $i$ = interest rate for investment (cost of capital). It is also known as the *discount rate*. The PV factor is then multiplied by the future amounts to figure its value today, and compared with the discounted cost over the same periods, to compute the NPV.

$$NPV = \sum_{t=1}^{T} \frac{A_t}{(1+i)^t} - C$$

where:

$t$ = specific year: 1, 2, etc.

T = project life, e.g., 5 years, 10 years, etc.

$i$ = interest rate (discount rate)

A = income at period $t$

C = initial investment, or PV of all investments over T

See Exercises and Projects #3 for calculations.

The NPV analysis works well in situations where the costs and benefits are well defined or "tangible," so that it is not difficult to convert them into monetary values. For example, if human welders are replaced by robots that produce work of comparable quality, the benefits are the labor cost savings over the usable life of the robots. Costs include the capital investment to purchase and install the robots, plus the operating and maintenance costs.

A project with an estimated NPV greater than zero may be a candidate for acceptance. One with an estimated NPV less than zero would probably be rejected. Of course, one needs to consider the nonfinancial benefits, as will be discussed later.

***Internal Rate of Return (IRR).***  If you have an investment that requires and produces a number of cash flows over time, the internal rate of return (IRR) is defined to be the discount rate that makes the NPV of those cash flows equal to zero. Some companies set a minimum acceptable IRR (or hurdle rate) based on their own cost of capital and the minimum percentage return they'd like to see from their investments.

***Payback Period.***  The payback period is the point at which the yearly benefits of a project equal the costs.

**COSTING IT INVESTMENT**

Placing a dollar value on the cost of IT investments may not be as simple as it may sound. One of the major issues is to allocate fixed costs among different IT projects. *Fixed costs* are those costs that remain the same in total regardless of change in the activity level. For IT, fixed costs include infrastructure cost, cost of IT services (Gerlach et al., 2002), and IT management cost. For example, the salary of the IT director is fixed, and adding one more application will not change it.

Another area of concern is the fact that the cost of a system does not end when the system is installed. Costs for keeping it running, dealing with bugs, and for improving and changing the system may continue for some time. Such costs can accumulate over many years, and sometimes they are not even anticipated when the investment is made. An example is the cost of the Y2K reprogramming projects that cost billions of dollars to organizations worldwide. (For a discussion see Read et al., 2001.)

The fact that organizations use IT for different purposes further complicates the costing process. There are multiple kinds of values (e.g., improved efficiency, improved customer or partner relations); the return on a capital investment measured in numeric terms (e.g., dollar or percentage) is only one of these values. In addition, the probability of obtaining a return from an IT investment also depends on the probability of implementation success. These probabilities reflect the fact that many systems are not implemented on time, within budget, and/or with all the features originally envisioned for them. Finally, the expected value of the return on IT investment in most cases will be less than that originally anticipated. For this reason, Gray and Watson (1998) point out that managers often make substantial investments in projects like data warehousing by relying on intuition when evaluating investment proposals rather than on concrete evaluation.

After the dot-com problems of 2000–2002 it become almost mandatory to justify IT projects with a solid business case, including ROI. However, according to Sawhney (2002), and others, this may have little value due to the difficulties in dealing with intangible benefits. (For further guidelines on cost-benefit analysis, see Clermont, 2002.)

**OPPORTUNITIES AND REVENUE GENERATED BY IT INVESTMENT**

A major difficulty in assessing IT value is measuring possible benefits (tangible and intangible) that drive IT investment (see Peppard and Ward, 2005 and Tillquist and Rogers, 2005). Furthermore, some benefits are opportunities that may or may not materialize, so there is only a certain probability for return on the IT investment. Lucas (2005) refers to these investments as the *opportunity matrix* (see Table 14.2).

| TABLE 14.2 | IT Investment Opportunities Matrix | | | |
|---|---|---|---|---|
| **Type of Investment** | **Example** | **Comments** | **Upside Benefits** | **Probability of Return** |
| Infrastructure | Wide area network | Support current business—may allow for future investments | Little itself, but allows new programs | .2 to 1.0 (.5) |
| Required—(compliance), managerial control | OSHA, SOX reporting system, budgets | Usually a cost of doing business | SOX compliance may generate benefits | 0 to .5 (.2) |
| No other way to do the job | Computerized reservations system, air traffic control | Enable new task or process, provide better customer service, new products | Could gain more than forecast | .5 to 1.0 (.75) |
| Direct return from IT | Merrill Lynch, Chrysler | Structure, cost-benefit, and NPV appropriate | A little if you can build on the investment | .7 to 1.0 (.9) |
| Indirect returns | CRS in travel agencies | Potential for considerable return, but indirect benefits hard to estimate | Could be substantial future benefits | 0 to 1.0 (.5) |
| Competitive necessity | Bank ATMs, much EDI, electronic commerce | Need the system to compete in the business; what is the cost of not investing in technology? | Very little if you are following the industry | 0 to 1.0 (.2) |
| Strategic application | Baxter, Merrill Lynch CMA | High risk–high potential; may be able to estimate return only after implementation | A high potential | 0 to 1.0 (.5) |
| Transformational IT | Virtual organizations, Oticon | Must be combined with changes in management philosophy; good for fast-response organization—risky to change structure, but high potential rewards | A high potential | 0 to 1.0 (.5) |

*Source:* Lucas (2005), Table 6.1, p. 118.

In preparing the business case for IT investment, as will be described later, one should examine potential additional revenues. This is usually referred to as *revenue models*. Listed below are typical revenue models generated by IT and the Web:

- **Sales.** Companies generate additional revenue from selling merchandise or services over their Web sites. An example is when Wal-Mart or Godiva sells a product online.
- **Transaction fees.** A company receives a commission based on the volume of transactions made. IT increases this value. Transaction fees may be a fixed value. Alternatively, transaction fees can be levied *per transaction*. With online stock trades, for example, there is usually a fixed fee per trade, regardless of the volume.
- **Subscription fees.** Customers pay a fixed amount, usually monthly, to get some type of service. An example would be the access fee for AOL. Thus, AOL's primary revenue model is subscription (fixed monthly payments).
- **Advertising fees.** Companies charge others for allowing them to place a banner on their sites.

- **Affiliate fees.** Companies receive commissions for referring customers to others' Web sites.
- **Other revenue sources.** Some companies allow people to play games for a fee or watch a sports competition in real time for a fee (e.g., see *espn.com*).
- **Other ways to increase revenues.** Straub (2004) suggests other ways that IT, and especially EC, can be used to increase revenues:
  - Increased revenues via products or services from a larger global market because of more effective product marketing on the Web
  - Increased margins attained by using processes with lower internal cost (e.g., using lower-cost computers) and from higher prices because of value-added services to the customer (e.g., information attached to product)
  - Increased revenues as a consequence of becoming an online portal
  - Value-added content sold from selling searches, access to data, and electronic documents

    One of the areas of IT impact is the reduction of transaction costs.

**Transaction Costs.** **Transaction costs** cover a wide range of costs that are associated with the distribution (sale) and/or exchange of products and services. Most economists (e.g., Chen, 2005) divide these costs into the following five categories:

1. **Search costs.** Buyers and sellers incur costs in locating each other and locating specific products and services.
2. **Information costs.** For buyers, this includes costs related to learning about the products and services of sellers and the basis for their cost, profit margins, and quality. For sellers, this includes costs related to learning about the legitimacy, financial condition, and needs of the buyer, which may lead to a higher or lower price.
3. **Negotiation costs.** Buyers and sellers need to agree on the terms of the sale (e.g., quantity, quality, shipments, financing, etc.). Negotiation costs result from meetings, communication-related expenses, exchanges of technical data and/or brochures, entertainment, and legal costs.
4. **Decision costs.** For buyers, decision costs result from the evaluation of sellers and their internal processes, such as purchasing approval, to ensure that they meet the buyers' policies. For sellers, decision costs arise in the determination of whether to sell to one buyer instead of another buyer, or not at all.
5. **Monitoring costs.** Buyers and sellers need to ensure that the goods and/or services purchased translate into the goods and services exchanged. In addition, they need to make sure that the exchange proceeds according to the terms under which the sale was made.

Using IT may reduce transactions cost, especially with EC and Web applications. However, it may be difficult to assess these costs.

**Reducing the Impact of Risk.** IT can be used to decrease risk to companies by providing them with timely information. Also, the risk to customers may be reduced. For example, Kambil (2001) suggests that organizations can increase the value of their products or services by using the unique capabilities of IT to reduce risks to consumers, such as those involving psychological relationships, quality concerns, delays, and financial transactions.

Psychological risks can be reduced, for example, by allowing the customers to use an EC-based calculator and avoid potentially embarrassing situations. For example, online tracking tools reduce risk by allowing customers to check the status of a package. By publishing specifications and providing product comparison engines, EC can help reduce a customer's risk of purchasing an unwanted product or one of poor quality. EC also has been instrumental in providing customers with an accurate picture of product availability, helping them avoid the risk of unexpected delays. EC also can mitigate customer concerns over the security of EC transactions. Finally, customer concerns over privacy and security can be addressed by linking the transaction to third-party security providers such as the Better Business Bureau or VeriSign.

| THE PROBLEM OF INTANGIBLE BENEFITS | As indicated above, in many cases IT projects generate **intangible benefits** such as faster time to market, employee and customer satisfaction, easier distribution, greater organizational agility, and improved control. These are very desirable benefits, but it is difficult to place an accurate monetary value on them. For example, many people would agree that e-mail improves communications, but it is not at all clear how to measure the value of this improvement. |

Intangible benefits can be very complex yet substantial. For example, according to Arno Penzias, a Nobel Laureate in physics, the New York Metropolitan Transit Authority (MTA) had not found the need to open another airport for almost two decades, even when traffic had tripled. This, according to his study, was due to productivity gains derived from improved IT systems (quoted by Devaraj and Kohli, 2002). IT systems added by the MTA played critical roles in ticket reservations, passenger and luggage check-in, crew assignment and scheduling, runway maintenance and management, and gate assignments. These improvements enabled MTA to cope with increased traffic without adding new facilities, saving hundreds of millions of dollars. Many similar examples of increased capacity exist. Intangible benefits are especially common in service and government applications (see Steyaert, 2004).

One class of intangible benefits, according to Ryan and Gates (2004), is *social subsystem issues*, such as comfort to employees, impact on the environment, changes to the power distribution in an organization, and invasion of the privacy of employees and customers.

An analyst could ignore intangible benefits, but doing so implies that their value is zero and may lead the organization to reject IT investments that could substantially increase revenues and profitability. Therefore, financial analyses need to consider not just tangible benefits but also intangible benefits in such a way that the decision reflects their potential impact. The question is how to do it.

**Handling Intangible Benefits.** The most straightforward solution to the problem of evaluating intangible benefits in cost-benefit analysis is to make *rough estimates* of monetary values for all intangible benefits, and then conduct an NVP or similar financial analysis. The simplicity of this approach is attractive, but in many cases the assumptions used in these estimates are debatable. If a technology is acquired because decision makers assigned too high a value to intangible benefits, the organization could find that it has wasted some valuable resources. On the other hand, if the valuation of intangible benefits is too low, the organization might reject the investment and then find that it is losing market share to competitors who did implement the technology.

There are many approaches to handling intangibles. Sawhney (2002) suggests the following solutions:

- **Think broadly and softly.** Supplement hard financial metrics with soft ones that may be more strategic in nature and may be important leading indicators of financial outcomes. Measures such as customer and partner satisfaction, customer loyalty, response time to competitive actions, and improved responsiveness are examples of soft measures. Subjective measures can be objective if used consistently over time. For instance, customer satisfaction measured consistently on a five-point scale can be an objective basis for measuring the performance of customer-facing initiatives.

- **Pay your freight first.** Think carefully about short-term benefits that can "pay the freight" for the initial investment in the project. For example, a telecom company found that it could justify its investment in data warehousing based on the cost savings from data mart consolidation, even though the real payoffs from the project would come later from increased cross-selling opportunities.

- **Follow the unanticipated.** Keep an open mind about where the payoff from IT projects may come from, and follow opportunities that present themselves. Eli Lilly & Co. created a Web site called InnoCentive (*innocentive.com*) to attract scientists to solve problems in return for financial rewards ("bounties"). In the process, Lilly established contact with 8,000 exceptional scientists, and Lilly's HR department has used this list of contacts for recruiting.

**THE BUSINESS CASE APPROACH**

One method used to justify investments in projects, or even in entire new companies, is referred to as the *business case approach.*

A **business case** is a written document that is used by managers to garner funding for one or more specific applications or projects. Its major emphasis is the justification for a specific required investment, but it also provides the bridge between the initial plan and its execution. Its purpose is not only to get approval and funding, but also to provide the foundation for tactical decision making and technology risk management. A business case is usually conducted in existing organizations that want to embark on new IT projects (for example, an e-procurement project). The business case helps to clarify how the organization will use its resources in the best way to accomplish the IT strategy. Software for preparing a business case for IT (and for EC in particular) is commercially available (e.g., from *paloalto.com* and from *bplans.com*).

A business case for IT investment can be very complex. Gunasekaran et al. (2001) divided such justification into five parts as shown in Figure 14.3.

Sometimes an IT project is necessary in order for the organization to stay in business, and in those instances, the business case is very simple: "We must do it, we have no choice." Sometimes an organization must invest because its competitors have done so and if it does not follow, it will lose customers. Examples are e-banking and some CRM services. These types of investments do not require firms to do a lot of analysis.

For a description of business cases in e-commerce, see Turban et al. (2008). For a tool for building a business case, see Wang and Shiang (2002) and *sap.com/ solutions/pdf/IDC_Case.pdf*. For a discussion of how to conduct a business case for global expansion, see DePalma (2001). An example of a business case for wireless networks, prepared by Intel Corp. (2002), is presented in Online File W14.3.

**EVALUATING IT INVESTMENT: CONCLUSIONS**

This section has shown that several traditional methods can be used to assess the value of IT information and IT investment.

Traditional methods may not be useful for assessing some of the newest technologies (e.g., see Violino, 1997). (An example of such a case—acquiring expert systems—is shown in Online File W14.4.) Because traditional methods may not be useful for evaluating new technologies, there are special methodologies (some of them incorporated in computerized calculators) for dealing with investment in IT. We will address some of these methods next.

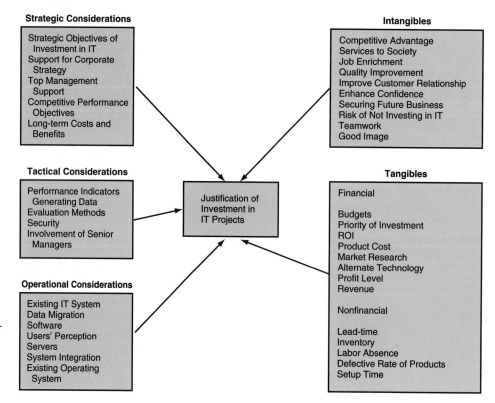

**Figure 14.3** A model for investment justification in IT projects. (*Source:* Gunasekaran et al., 2001, p. 354.)

# 14.3 Methods for Evaluating and Justifying IT Investment

A comprehensive list of over 60 different appraisal methods for IT investments can be found in Renkema (2000). For details of some methods, see McKay and Marshall (2004). The appraisal methods are generally categorized into the following four types.

1. **Financial approach.** These appraisal methods consider only impacts that can be monetary-valued. They focus on incoming and outgoing cash flows as a result of the investment made. Net present value and return on investment are examples of financial-approach methods (described earlier).

2. **Multicriteria approach.** These appraisal methods consider both financial impacts and nonfinancial impacts that cannot be (or cannot easily be) expressed in monetary terms. These methods employ quantitative and qualitative decision-making techniques. *Information economics* and *value analysis* are examples.

3. **Ratio approach.** These methods use several ratios (e.g., IT expenditures vs. total turnover) to assist in IT investment evaluation.

4. **Portfolio approach.** These methods apply portfolios (or grids) to plot several investment proposals against decision-making criteria. The portfolio methods are more informative compared to multicriteria methods and generally use fewer evaluation criteria.

Table 14.3 lists specific evaluation methods that are particularly useful in evaluating IT investment. Discussed in this section are the total cost of ownership and the use of benchmarks. The rest are described in Online File W14.6. Other methods are cited briefly at the end of the section.

| TABLE 14.3 | Methods for Evaluating IT Investments |
|---|---|

- **Value analysis.** With the value analysis method, the organization evaluates intangible benefits using a low-cost, trial EC system before deciding whether to commit to a larger investment in a complete system.
- **Information economics.** Using the idea of critical success factors, this method focuses on key organizational objectives and potential impacts of the proposed EC project on those objectives.
- **Scoring methodology.** This method assigns weights and scores to various aspects of the evaluated project and then calculates a total score. Information economics methods are used to determine the aspects to include in the scoring.
- **Benchmarks.** This method is appropriate for evaluating EC infrastructure. Using industry standards, for example, the organization can determine what the industry is spending on e-CRM. Then the organization can decide how much it should spend. Benchmarks may be industry metrics or best practices recommended by professional associations or consultants.
- **Management by maxim.** An organization may use this method to determine how much it should invest in large EC (and IT) infrastructures. It is basically a combination of brainstorming and consensus-reaching methodologies.
- **Real-options valuation.** This is a fairly complex assessment method, and used only infrequently. It can be fairly accurate in certain situations. The idea behind this method is to look at future opportunities that may result from the EC investment and then place monetary values on them.
- **Balanced scorecard.** This method evaluates the health or performance of the organization by looking at a broad set of factors, not just financial ones. It is becoming a popular tool for assessing EC projects (see Chapter 11).
- **Performance dashboard.** This is a variant of the balanced scorecard that is widely used in e-business situations. A dashboard is a single view that provides the status of multiple metrics (see Chapter 11).
- **Activity-based costing.** This managerial accounting concept was adapted for assessing EC investments in recent years and has been proven to be fairly successful.

Unfortunately, none of these methods is perfect or universal. Therefore, one needs to look at the advantages and disadvantages of each, which vary according to the specific situation.

**TOTAL COST OF OWNERSHIP**

An interesting approach for IT cost evaluation is the **total cost of ownership (TCO)**. TCO is a formula for calculating the cost of owning, operating, and controlling an IT system, even one as simple as a PC. The cost includes *acquisition cost* (hardware and software), *operations cost* (maintenance, training, operations, evaluation, technical support, installation, downtime, auditing, virus damage, and power consumption), and *control cost* (standardization, security, central services). The TCO can be a hundred percent higher than just the cost of the hardware, especially for PCs. By identifying these various costs, organizations can make more accurate cost-benefit analyses. A methodology for calculating TCO is offered by Bothama (2006). Examples of the items to be included in the TCO calculations are provided in Online File W14.5. For a comprehensive study, see Ferrin and Plank (2002).

A concept similar to TCO is **total benefits of ownership (TBO).** These benefits cover both tangible and the intangible benefits. By calculating and comparing both TCO and TBO, one can compute the payoff of an IT investment [Payoff = TBO − TCO]. For details on the calculations, see Devaraj and Kohli (2002) and also Online File W14.5.

**ASSESSING INVESTMENTS IN IT INFRASTRUCTURE**

Information systems projects are usually not standalone applications. In most cases they depend for support on enabling infrastructures already installed in the organization. These infrastructure technologies include mainframe computers, operating systems, networks, database management systems, utility programs, development tools, and more. Since many of the infrastructure benefits are intangible and are spread over many different present and future applications, it is hard to estimate their value or to evaluate the desirability of enhancements or upgrades. In other words, it is much more difficult to evaluate infrastructure investment decisions than investments in specific information systems application projects (see Lewis and Byrd, 2003). Two methods are recommended: use of benchmarks (described here) and management by maxim (see Online File W14.7). For a framework for assessing IT infrastructure, see Kumar (2004).

**Using Benchmarks to Assess Infrastructure Investments.** One approach to evaluating infrastructure is to focus on *objective* measures of performance known as **benchmarks.** These measures are often available from trade associations within an industry or from consulting firms. A comparison of measures of performance or of an organization's expenditures with averages for the industry or with values of the more efficient performers in the industry indicates how well the organization is using its infrastructure. If performance is below standard, corrective action is indicated. The benchmark approach implicitly assumes that IT infrastructure investments are justified if they are managed efficiently.

**IT METRICS**

A **metric** is a specific, measurable standard against which actual performance is compared. Metrics can produce very positive results in organizations by driving behavior in a number of ways. According to Rayport and Jaworski (2001), metrics can:

- Define the value proposition of business models.
- Communicate the strategy to the workforce through performance targets.
- Increase accountability when metrics are linked to performance-appraisal programs.
- Align the objectives of individuals, departments, and divisions to the enterprise's strategic objectives.

An example of IT metrics implementation can be found in a white paper that analyzed the impact of a new online service on the profitability of Axon Computertime, a small computer services business in New Zealand (Green, 2002). Symons (2004) describes the sources of metrics. Axon found the following results were obtained from the implementation of this service as part of their EC strategy:

- **Revenue growth.** Product revenue increased over 40 percent in the first 12 months of operation.
- **Cost reduction.** Selling costs were reduced by 40 percent for each dollar of margin generated.
- **Cost reduction.** Expenditures on brochure design and production were reduced by 45 percent.
- **Cost avoidance.** Obsolete stock write-offs as percentage of revenue were reduced by 93 percent.
- **Customer fulfillment.** Average days to delivery were reduced by 20 percent over 2 years.
- **Customer service.** Customer satisfaction with the delivery process is consistently in excess of 80 percent.
- **Customer communications.** Customer response to e-mail communications is five times the response rate to postal mail.

One important metric is the percentage of IT budget within the total corporate budget (*CIO Insight,* 2006).

The last few metrics in this list highlight the importance of including nonfinancial measures in the measurement of organizational performance.

**OTHER METHODS AND TOOLS**

Several other methods exist for evaluating IT investment. For example, most large vendors provide proprietary *calculators for ROI* and so does *Baseline*. However, according to King (2002), those may be biased (and may lead to a sometimes-unjustified decision to adopt a project). To make the decision less biased, some companies use a third-party evaluator such as IDC (*idc.com*) to conduct ROI studies. An example of such a calculator is SAP Business Case Builder. (For details see *sap.com/solutions/pdf/IDC_Case.pdf*.) Several independent vendors offer ROI calculators (e.g., CIO View Corporation). CIO.com (2004) offers many tools via Nucleus Research Inc. for calculating ROI of different IT systems. Finally, *Baselinemag.com* offers a wide range of calculators for Excel.

According to Rubin (2003a), every IT project *must* be tied to a specific business objective, with its priority indicated, so as to measure the project's success in terms of a specific primary business value. Rubin developed a special "whiteboard" that includes metrics and their stakeholders. For details and examples, see Rubin (2003).

In addition, there are other popular methods (e.g., see Irani and Love, 2000–2001), a few of which we describe briefly next.

**The Exploration, Involvement, Analysis, and Communications (EIAC) Model.** Devaraj and Kohli (2002) propose a methology for implementing IT payoff initiatives. The method is composed of nine phases, divided into four categories: exploration (E), involvement (I), analysis (A), and communication (C). For details see Devaraj and Kohli (2002).

**Activity-Based Costing.** A fairly recent approach for assessing IT investment is proposed by Peacock and Tanniru (2005) and by Roberts (2003), who suggest use of the *activity-based costing (ABC)* approach to assist in IT investment analysis. (For details on how ABC works, see a management or managerial accounting textbook and *wikipedia.com*.) Using a case study, Gerlach et al. showed that the company that utilized ABC derived significant benefits from a better understanding of IT delivery costs and a rationale for explaining IT costs to department managers. Mutual understanding of IT costs is a necessary condition for shared responsibility of IT, which in turn leads to effective economic decision making that optimizes resource utilization and the alignment of IT with business strategy. In addition, the use of ABC helps in reducing operational costs.

**Expected Value Analysis.** It is relatively easy to estimate **expected value (EV)** of possible future benefits by multiplying the size of each benefit by the probability of its occurrence. For example, an organization might consider investing in a corporate portal only if there is a 50 percent probability that this would result in new business worth $10 million in additional profits and the cost will be less than $5 million. The value of this specific benefit would be 50 percent times $10 million, or $5 million. This method is simple but like any EV approach, it can be used only for *repetitive investments*.

Unfortunately, none of the above methods is perfect, and it is not simple for organizations to decide which method to use in which case.

**ROI CALCULATORS**

Vendors and consulting companies have accumulated quite a bit of experience in developing tools for assessing IT investments (called ROI calculators), some of which are in the public domain.

Nucleus Research, Inc. (NRI; *nucleusreasearch.com*), a research and advisory company, uses several ROI calculators in helping businesses evaluate IT investments.

# A Closer Look 14.1

## Calculating the Cost of Sarbanes-Oxley (SOX)

ACC    FIN

To comply with SOX, your company must document every internal process and external effect that will have an impact on its financial health. That's a pretty thin speculation from which to develop a budget. *Baseline* magazine tried to approach the problem by breaking down the process into its smallest components. For example, one procedure is the preparation of a quarterly revenue statement from one division. *Baseline* includes a transition period during which the user can analyze the procedure and add steps to make sure each phase is documented.

To see the details behind this calculator and fill in the user estimates, click on the Tool icon at baselinemag.com/article2/0,1397,1648903,00.asp?kc=BAZD10505TTX1B000 and download the interactive worksheet. (An illustration is provided in Online File W14.9.)

For additional information, see *baselinemag.com/article2/0,1397,1631901,00.asp.*

---

A large number of calculators, mostly using Excel, are offered by *Baseline* magazine for a moderate fee.

ROI calculators for e-services also are available. For instance, Streaming Media, Inc. (*streamingmedia.com*) provides an ROI calculator to measure the costs and benefits of telecommunication bandwidth for videoconferencing, streaming video, and video file servers.

Few organizations have attempted to assess the ROI on e-learning, perhaps because it is so difficult to calculate and justify. However, Learnativity.com (*learnativity.com*) provides resources such as ROI calculators, methodologies, a bibliography, and online communities to support the assessment of e-learning (see *learnativity.com/roi-learning.html*).

ROI calculators also are available from various other companies, such as Phoenix Technologies (*phoenix.com*) and Alinean, Inc. (*alinean.com*). For more examples of ROI calculators, see *roi-calc.com, gantrygroup.com,* and *phormion.com.*

*A Closer Look 14.1* provides a description of a calculator for SOX. An example of calculation of CRM cost-benefit is provided in Online File W14.8.

# 14.4 IT Economics Strategies: Chargeback and Outsourcing

In addition to identifying and evaluating the benefits of IT, organizations also need to account for its costs. Ideally, the organization's accounting systems will effectively deal with two issues: First, they should provide an accurate measure of total IT costs for management control purposes. Second, they should charge users for shared (usually infrastructure) IT investments and services in a manner that contributes to the achievement of organization goals. These are two very challenging goals for any accounting system, and the complexities and rapid pace of change make them even more difficult to achieve in the context of IT.

With the increased use of computing and the diversity of computing services, it becomes very difficult just to identify, let alone effectively control, the total costs of IT as well as departmental costs. As a practical matter, many organizations track costs associated with centralized IS and leave management accounting for desktop IT to the user organizations. However, the trend toward attaching personal computers to networks, and the availability of network management software, make it easier to track and manage costs related to desktop IT. Some organizations indicate "six-digit" savings by using network management software to identify which computers use what software, and then reducing the site licenses to correspond to the actual usage. The same is true, of course, with utility computing.

In this section we look at two strategies for costing of IT services: chargeback and outsourcing.

**CHARGEBACK**

In some organizations, the ISD functions as an unallocated cost center: All expenses go into an overhead account. The problem with this approach is that IT is then a "free good" that has no explicit cost, so there are no incentives to control usage or avoid waste.

A second alternative is called **chargeback** (also known as chargeout or cost recovery). In this approach, all costs of IT are allocated to users as accurately as possible, based on actual costs and usage levels. Accurate allocation sounds desirable in principle, but it can create problems in practice (see Wheatley, 2003). The most accurate measures of use may reflect technological factors that are totally incomprehensible to the user. If fixed costs are allocated on the basis of total usage throughout the organization, which varies from month to month, charges will fluctuate for an individual unit even though its own usage does not change. These considerations can reduce the credibility of the chargeback system.

Nevertheless, organizations can use chargeback systems to influence organizational IT usage in desirable directions. So the way users are charged for these services will influence how much they use them.

**Behavior-Oriented Chargeback.** An interesting approach is to employ a **behavior-oriented chargeback** system. Such a system sets IT service costs in a way that meets organizational objectives, even though the charges may not correspond to actual costs. The primary objective of this type of system is influencing users' behavior. For example, it is possible to encourage (or discourage) usage of certain IT resources by assigning lower (or higher) costs. For example, the organization may wish to encourage use of central processing in off-peak hours, and so it might decide to charge business units less for processing from 1 to 4 A.M. than from 9 A.M. to noon.

Although more difficult to develop, a behavior-oriented chargeback system recognizes the importance of IT—and its effective management—to the success of the organization. It not only avoids the unallocated cost center's problem of overuse of "free" resources; it can also reduce the use of scarce resources where demand exceeds supply, even with fully allocated costs. For more on behavior-oriented chargeback see Online File W14.10.

There are other methods of chargeback. The reason for the variety of methods is that it is very difficult to approximate costs, especially in companies where multiple independent operating units are sharing a centralized system. Therefore, organizations have developed chargeback methods that make sense to their managers and their particular needs.

The difficulties in applying chargeback systems may be one of the drivers of IT outsourcing.

**OUTSOURCING AS AN ECONOMIC STRATEGY**

Although IT is now a vital part of almost every organization and plays an important supporting role in most functions, IT is not the primary business of many organizations. Their core competencies—the things they do best and that represent their competitive strengths—are in manufacturing, retailing, services, or some other function. IT is an *enabler* only, and it is complex, expensive, and constantly changing. IT is difficult to manage, even for organizations with above-average IT management skills. Therefore, for many organizations, the most effective strategy for obtaining the economic benefits of IT and controlling its costs may be **outsourcing,** which is obtaining IT services from outside vendors (see Harmozi, 2003). According to a survey reported by Corbett (2001), the major reasons cited by large U.S. companies for use of outsourcing are: focus on core competency (36%), cost reduction (36%), improved quality (13%), increased speed to market (10%), and faster innovation (4%). For a recent survey, see Fish and Seydel (2006).

Companies typically outsource many of their non-IT activities, from contract manufacturing to physical security. But most of all they outsource IT activities (see Minicase 2 at the end of the chapter, and Online File W14.11). Outsourcing is more than just purchasing hardware and software. It is a long-term result-oriented relationship for whole business activities, over which the provider has a large amount of control and managerial direction. For an overview of the past, present, and future of outsourcing, see Robinson et al. (2005) and Lee et al. (2003).

Outsourcing IT functions, such as payroll services, has been around since the early days of data processing. Contract programmers and computer timesharing services are longstanding examples. What is new is that, since the late 1980s, many organizations are outsourcing the *majority of their IT functions* rather than just incidental parts. The trend became very visible in 1989 when Eastman Kodak announced it was transferring its data centers to IBM under a 10-year, $500 million contract. This example, at a prominent multibillion-dollar company, gave a clear signal that outsourcing was a legitimate approach to managing IT. Since then, many mega outsourcing deals were announced, some for several billion dollars. (For a list of some recent outsourcing deals and the story of a 10-year, $3 billion contract between Procter & Gamble and Hewlett-Packard, see Cushing 2003.)

*Application service provider* (ASP) services are becoming very popular (Chapter 2), but they do have potential pitfalls. Focacci et al. (2003) provided some contingency guidelines for organizations to use to make their specific decision to adopt ASP services. According to Lee et al. (2003), the ASP approach is the future of outsourcing. The authors provide a list of ASPs in different areas and suggest a collaborative strategy with the users. For further discussion see Chapter 15 and Walsh (2003).

**Outsourcing Advantages and Disadvantages.** The use of IT outsourcing is still very controversial (e.g., see Hirschheim and Lacity, 2000). Outsourcing advocates describe IT as a commodity, a generic item like electricity or janitorial services. They note the potential benefits of outsourcing, in general, as listed in Table 14.4.

In contrast, others see many limitations of outsourcing (e.g., see Cramm, 2001). One reason for the contradicting opinions is that many of the benefits of outsourcing are intangible or have long-term payoffs. Clemons (2000) identifies the following risks associated with outsourcing:

- *Shirking* occurs when a vendor deliberately underperforms while claiming full payment (e.g., billing for more hours than were worked, providing excellent staff at first and later replacing them with less qualified ones).

- *Poaching* occurs when a vendor develops a strategic application for a client and then uses it for other clients (e.g., vendor redevelops similar systems for other clients at much lower cost, or vendor enters into client's business, competing against it).

- *Opportunistic repricing ("holdup")* occurs when a client enters into a long-term contract with a vendor and the vendor changes financial terms at some point or overcharges for unanticipated enhancements and contract extensions.

| **TABLE 14.4** | **Potential Outsourcing Benefits** |
| --- | --- |

*Financial*
- Avoidance of heavy capital investment, thereby releasing funds for other uses.
- Improved cash flow and cost accountability.
- Improved cost benefits from economies of scale and from sharing computer housing, hardware, software, and personnel.
- Less need for expensive office space.
- Reduce and control operating costs.

*Technical*
- Access to new information technologies.
- Greater freedom to choose software due to a wider range of hardware.
- Ability to achieve technological improvements more easily.
- Greater access to technical skills not available internally.
- Faster application development and placement of IT applications into service.

*Management*
- Concentration on developing and running core business activity. Improved company focus.
- Delegation of IT development (design, production, and acquisition) and operational responsibility to suppliers.
- Elimination of need to recruit and retain competent IT staff.
- Reduced risk of bad software.

*Human Resources*
- Opportunity to draw on specialist skills, available from a pool of expertise, when needed.
- Enriched career development and opportunities for remaining staff.

*Quality*
- Clearly defined *service levels* (see Chapter 13).
- Improved performance accountability.
- Improved quality accreditation.

*Flexibility*
- Quick response to business demands (agility).
- Ability to handle IT peaks and valleys more effectively (flexibility).

Other risks are: irreversibility of the outsourcing decision, possible breach of contract by the vendor or its inability to deliver, loss of control over IT decisions, loss of critical IT skills, vendor lock-in, loss of control over data, loss of employee morale and productivity, and uncontrollable contract growth.

Another possible risk of outsourcing is failure to consider all the costs. Some costs are hidden. Barthelemy (2001) discusses the following hidden costs: (1) vendor search and contracting, (2) transitioning from in-house IT to a vendor, (3) cost of managing the effort, and (4) transition back to in-house IT after outsourcing. These costs can be controlled to some extent, however.

Despite the risks and limitations, the extent of IT outsourcing is increasing rapidly together with the use of software as a service (SaaS) and ASPs. We will return to these topics in Chapter 15.

The economics of software production suggest that, for relatively standardized systems, purchasing or leasing can result in both cost savings and increased functionality. Purchasing or leasing can also be the safest strategy for very large and complex systems, especially those that involve multiple units within an organization. For example, the SAP AG software firm offers a family of integrated, enterprise-level, large-scale information systems. These systems are available in versions tailored for specific industries, including aerospace, banking, utilities, retail, and so forth, as well as for SMEs. Many organizations feel that buying from a good vendor reduces their risk of failure, even if they have to change their business processes to be compatible with the new system.

**Strategies for Outsourcing.** There are five major risk areas that executives should consider when making the decision to outsource. They are: (1) higher developmental or operational costs than anticipated, (2) inability to provide the expected service levels at implementation, (3) exceeding the time anticipated for development or transition, (4) allowing technical failure to continue, and (5) neglecting to navigate the internal politics of the company (Rubin, 2003b). Therefore, organizations should consider the following strategies in managing the risks associated with outsourcing contracts (For additional information, see Fish and Seydel, 2006).

1. **Understand the project.** Clients must have a high degree of understanding of the project, including its requirements, the method of its implementation, and the source of expected economic benefits. A common characteristic of successful outsourcing contracts is that the client was generally capable of developing the application but chose to outsource simply because of constraints on time or staff availability (Clemons, 2000).

2. **Divide and conquer.** Dividing a large project into smaller and more manageable pieces will greatly reduce outsourcing risk and provides clients with an exit strategy if any part of the project fails (Clemons, 2000).

3. **Align incentives.** Designing contractual incentives based on activities that can be measured accurately can result in achieving desired performance (Clemons, 2000).

4. **Write short-period contracts.** Outsourcing contracts are often written for 5- to 10-year terms. Because IT and the competitive environment change so rapidly, it is very possible that some of the terms will not be in the customer's best interests after 5 years. If a long-term contract is used, it needs to include adequate mechanisms for negotiating revisions where necessary.

5. **Control subcontracting.** Vendors may subcontract some of the services to other vendors. The contract should give the customer some control over the circumstances, including choice of subcontractors, and any subcontract arrangements.

6. **Do selective outsourcing.** This is a strategy used by many corporations who prefer not to outsource the majority of their IT, but rather to outsource certain areas (such as system integration or network security). Cramm (2001) suggests that an organization *insource* important work, such as strategic applications, investments, and HRM.

At this point of time, the phenomenon of large-scale IT outsourcing is approximately 20 years old. The number of organizations that have used it for at least several years is growing. Business and IT-oriented periodicals have published numerous stories about their experiences. Outsourcing is also popular on a global basis, as is demonstrated in Minicase 2 and as described by Robinson et al. (2005). The general consensus of the various sources of anecdotal information is that the cost savings of outsourcing are not large (perhaps around 10 percent) and that not all organizations experience savings. This still leaves the question of whether outsourcing IT can improve organizational performance by making it possible to focus more intensely on core competencies. Further research is necessary to answer this question. One area that can provide cost savings is offshore outsourcing.

**THE OFFSHORE AND GLOBAL OUTSOURCING DEBATE**

**Offshore outsourcing** of software development has become a common practice in recent years. About one-third of Fortune 500 companies have started to outsource software development to software companies in India (Carmel and Agrawal, 2002). This trend of offshore outsourcing is largely due to the emphasis of Indian companies on process quality by adhering to models such as Software Engineering Institute's Software Capability Maturity Model (SW-CMM) and through ISO 9001 certification. India has 15 of the 23 organizations worldwide that have achieved Level 5, the highest in SW-CMM ratings. Davison (2004) highlighted that offshore outsourcing can reduce IT expenditures by 15 to 25 percent within the first year, and in the long term, outsourcing can help reduce cost and improve the quality of IT services delivered. However, organizations must balance the *risks* and *uncertainties* involved in offshore outsourcing, including: (1) cost-reduction expectations, (2) data/security and protection, (3) process discipline, (4) loss of business knowledge, (5) vendor failure to deliver, (6) scope creep, (7) government oversight/regulation, (8) differences in culture, (9) turnover of key personnel, and (10) knowledge transfer. For further details on offshore outsourcing, see Gillin (2003) and Robinson et al. (2005). *IT at Work 14.1* illustrates circumstances under which insourcing becomes preferable to outsourcing.

## *IT* at Work 14.1

### JP Morgan Chase Moves from Outsourcing to Insourcing

In September 2004, JP Morgan Chase, one of the world's largest financial institutions (over $1.2 trillion in assets and the second largest U.S. bank) scrapped a seven-year, $5 billion IT outsourcing contract with IBM, deciding to bring back IT in-house (insourcing). People who oppose outsourcing, especially offshoring, declared the "end of sourcing." As a matter of fact, Adams, the CIO who pushed for the scrapping, said that his move was greatly misunderstood. "I am clearly an advocate of offshoring."

While in the case of such a large bank there was a reason for insourcing, mainly to get a better competitive advantage from IT, Adams believes that in smaller organizations, large-scale outsourcing is logical. Furthermore, Adams presides over 3,000 offshore employees in India, who work in the bank's call center and also do basic operations and accounting functions. This offshoring is expected to grow rapidly.

Here are some observations made by Adams:

- The work ethics, attitudes, and ambitions of the company's employees in India are significantly higher than is true of its U.S. employees.
- Outsourcing of major parts of mission-critical technologies is not a best solution for a large firm. Technology development should be in-house; support services can be outsourced.
- Four criteria were used to determine what and how much to outsource: (1) the size of the company (should be large enough to attract good IS employees), (2) cost of outsourcing vs. cost of insourcing, (3) the interest level of top management to have and properly manage IT assets, and (4) financial arrangements of the outsourcing.
- It may be difficult to align business and technology objectives when large-scale outsourcing exists.
- The insourcing includes data centers, help desks, data processing networks, and systems development.
- Buying technology directly from vendors saved the bank a considerable amount of money (10 to 15 percent).
- Usually less than 5 percent of outsourcing contracts are canceled as in this case.
- The cancellation was driven mainly by the merger with Bank One, which made the combined bank very large.

*Sources:* Compiled from Adams (2006) and from Barrett (2006).

*For Further Exploration:* How can one determine when a company is large enough for insourcing? How important is the financial consideration? How accurate is it?

In addition to the traditionally outsourced services, Brown and Young (2000) identify two more scenarios for future outsourcing: creation of shared environments (e.g., exchanges, portals, e-commerce backbones), and providing access to shared environments (e.g., application service providers, Internet data centers). For example, Flooz.com, an online gift-currency store, outsourced its storage requirements to StorageNetworks, a storage service provider (Wilkinson, 2000). See *outsourcing-center.com* for details on practices in outsourcing of various types of services. Finally, outsourcing of call centers, especially of high-tech companies, mainly to India, has accelerated since 2003.

Today, IT outsourcing can be done in India, China, Russia, South America, and other locations around the globe. It is not only the cost and the technical capabilities that matter. Farrell (2006) suggests looking at the business and political environments in the selected country, the potential risks, the quality of the infrastructure, and other considerations. It is not only the selection of a country, but also the selection of city and business partner. Minevich and Richter (2005) list 20 countries with risks including: geopolitical, IT competency, human capital, economic, legal, cultural, and IT infrastructure.

An example of how to compare the cost of offshore options in different countries is provided in Online File W14.11.

A popular approach is *strategic outsourcing*, whereby you can generate new business, retain skilled employees, and effectively manage emerging technologies. Strategic global outsourcing facilitates the leveraging of knowledge capabilities and investments of others by exploiting intellectual outsourcing in addition to outsourcing of traditional functions and services (Minevich and Richter, 2005 and Robinson and Kalakota, 2004).

# 14.5 Economic Aspects of IT and Web-Based Systems

**THE ECONOMICS OF THE WEB**

In the preceding sections, our focus has been on the economics of *the use of IT* in organizations as an enabler. In this section, we turn to the economics of IT *as a product in itself*, rather than in a supporting role.

In 1916, David Sarnoff attempted to persuade his manager that the American Marconi Company should produce inexpensive radio receivers to sell to the consumer market. Others in the company (which subsequently became RCA) opposed the idea because it depended on the development of a radio broadcasting industry. They did not expect such an industry to develop because they could not see how broadcasters could generate revenues by providing a service without any charges to the listeners. The subsequent commercial development of radio, and the even greater success of television, proved that Sarnoff was right. If it is possible to provide a popular service to a large audience at a low cost per person, there will be ways of generating revenues. The only question is, How?

The World Wide Web on the Internet resembles commercial broadcasting in its early days. Fixed costs—initial investments and production costs—can be high in themselves, but they are low in terms of average cost per potential customer. Let's look at some specifics.

**Cost Reduction and Productivity Increase.** As indicated throughout this text, IT and especially Web-based systems can considerably increase productivity and profitability. In order to understand the economic logic of this, let us first examine the cost curves of digital products versus nondigital products, as shown in Figure 14.4. As the figure shows, for regular physical products (a), the average per-unit cost declines up to a certain quantity, but then, due to increased overhead (e.g., adding a

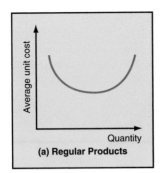
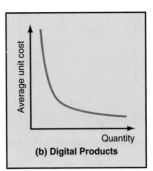

**Figure 14.4** Cost curves of regular and digital products.

manager) and marketing costs, the cost will start to increase. For digital products (b), the cost will continue to decline with increased quantity. The variable cost in the case of digital products is very little, so once the fixed cost is covered, an increase in quantity produces a continuous decrease in average cost.

However, even for nondigital products, IT, and e-commerce can shift economic curves, as shown in Figure 14.5. The *production function* will decline (from L1 to L2 in part a) since you can get the same quantity with less labor and IT cost. Also, the *transaction cost* for the same quantity (size) will be lower due to computerization (part b). And finally, the administrative cost for the same quantity will also be lower (part c).

**Reach versus Richness.**  Another economic impact of EC is the trade-off between the number of customers a company can reach (called *reach*) and the amount of interactions and information services it can provide to them (*richness*). According to Evans and Wurster (2000), for a given level of cost (resources), there is a trade-off between **reach and richness.** The more customers a company wants to reach, the fewer services it can provide to them. This economic relationship is depicted in Figure 14.6. With EC, the curve can be shifted outward.

**Measuring IT Payoffs.**  The justification of EC applications can be difficult. Usually one needs to prepare a business case, as described earlier in the chapter. A proper business case develops the baseline of desired results against which actual performance can and should be measured. The business case should cover both the financial and nonfinancial performance metrics against which to measure the e-business implementation. For further details on use of metrics to justify e-commerce, see Straub et al. (2002a and 2002b), Tjan (2001), and Turban et al. (2008).

The benefits and costs of EC depend on its definitions. If we use the broad definition, there are substantial benefits to buyers, sellers, and society (see Chapter 6). The complexity of the EC payoff can be seen in Online File W14.12. But even when

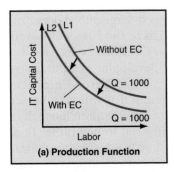
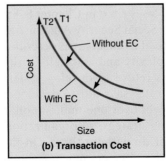
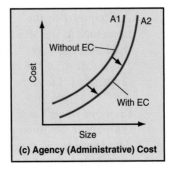

**Figure 14.5** Economic effects of e-commerce.

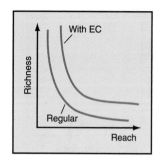

**Figure 14.6** Reach versus richness.

the applications are well defined, we still have measurement complexities. It is difficult even to conduct risk analysis, not to mention cost-benefit analysis. (See insights from Thomas Mesenbourg, of the Economic Programs of the U.S. Bureau of the Census, at *census.gov/epdc/www/ebusins.htm.*)

Web-based systems are being implemented by many organizations. However, hardly any efforts are being made to perform cost-benefit analysis or measure return on investment (ROI) on Web-based systems. Instead, most decisions to invest in Web-based systems are based on the assumption that the investments are needed for strategic reasons and that the expected returns cannot be measured in monetary values. Online File W14.13 illustrates that some organizations calculate ROIs for their intranets and extranets and others do not.

As indicated earlier, many vendors provide ROI examples, proprietary methodologies, and calculators for IT projects, including EC, such as for portals (e.g., *plumtree.com*). Although use of third-party evaluators, such as IDC, is common, the reported high ROIs should be considered with care. As noted earlier, bias is possible. For a comprehensive discussion of the economics of e-commerce, see Vulkan (2003) and Kohli et al. (2003).

**IT FAILURES AND "RUNAWAY" PROJECTS**

Information technology is difficult to manage and can be costly when things do not go as planned. Indeed, a high proportion of IS development projects either fail completely or fail to meet some of the original targets for features, development time, or cost. Many of these are related to economic issues, such as an incorrect cost-benefit analysis or lack of funding.

Many failures occur in smaller systems that handle internal processes within an organization, and they usually remain corporate secrets. The total investment is not large, the failure does not have a major economic impact, and the effects are generally not visible to outsiders so we do not know about them. On the other hand, some IS failures result in losses in excess of 10 million dollars and may severely damage the organization, as well as generate a lot of negative publicity, as in the Nike case in Chapter 1 or the ERP cases cited in Chapter 8. Failures in large public organizations such as the IRS and Social Security Administration have also been well advertised. A large-scale failure at a university is described in *IT at Work 14.2*.

Because of the complexity and associated risks of developing computer systems, some IT managers refuse to develop systems in-house beyond a certain size. The "one, one, ten rule" says not to develop a system if it will take longer than one year, has a budget over one million dollars, and will require more than ten people. Following this strategy, an organization will need to buy rather than develop large systems, or do without them. On the other hand, some organizations believe that if you are large enough you should not outsource your IT (e.g., see Adams, 2006).

# IT at Work 14.2

## A University Accounting System Failed

A large British university (requested to be unnamed) developed a new computer-based accounting system that did not work at all for its first six weeks of operation. Several months later it was evaluated as "failing to do what it was supposed to do" and as "unreliable." This failure led to a major investigation, which concluded that basic project management procedures had not been followed and that it would take at least two years to put things right. A series of smaller oversights and failures led to the catastrophic failure of the system as a whole, because of the interdependent nature of the tasks and responsibilities in the project.

Here are two of the findings of the investigation related to IT justification:

1. **Overspending.** The purchase of new hardware, software, and networks for the accounting system appears to have been planned without any serious attempt to calculate the cost or to identify where the money to pay for it was to come from. This was one reason for the significant overrun of costs for the whole project.

   *Lesson learned:* There was a failure to budget for the cost of these particular project deliverables. An initial costing should have been part of a business case, which was not done. By presenting a full business case before the project is started, a commitment to resources is obtained from stakeholders and senior management. The construction of a business case also ensures that time is allowed to fully assess costs and benefits of any proposed new system before the project gets underway.

2. **Tendering and contracts.** Consultants seem to have been employed without proper tendering practices being done. It appeared that a contract committing the university to an expenditure of millions of pounds was signed with the database software suppliers without the university having taken legal advice about its contents. Also, no attempt was made to justify the purchases.

   *Lesson learned:* A university is expected to demonstrate best value for money in the same way as a commercial organization, and this can be demonstrated only if the organization's procurement procedures are adhered to. The procurement process is itself a project to which basic project management principles should be applied.

*Sources:* Compiled from Laurie (2003).

*For Further Exploration:* Which of the methods of this chapter could be used for the IT justification? Why are the problems related to project management?

---

**MARKET TRANSFORMATION THROUGH NEW TECHNOLOGIES**

In some cases, IT has the potential to completely transform the economics of an industry. For example, until recently the hard-copy encyclopedia business consisted of low-volume sales, primarily to schools and libraries. The physically very bulky product (20–30 volumes) resulted in relatively high manufacturing and shipping costs, which made the price even higher. The high price, the need for periodic updating, and the space required to store the books, reduced potential sales to the home market (see discussion in Chapter 13).

Two things happened to change this situation. First, CD-ROM technology was adapted from storing music to storing other digital data, including text and images. Second, since the mid-1990s use of CD-ROMs has been a standard component of a majority of computers sold for the home market. Encyclopedia producers began selling their products on CD-ROMs, in some cases at reduced prices that reflected the lower production costs. These CD-ROM versions, and now DVDs include new features made possible by the technology, most notably sound, easy search, and hyperlink cross-references to related material in other sections. Lower prices and additional features have the potential to substantially increase the size of the total market, especially when the encyclopedia is placed online, as an electronic book, which is easy to update and requires no shipping cost. The hypothetical example in Online File W14.14 shows how the economics of this business could change.

The encyclopedia industry now includes wikipedia, which is available free online. Its content is provided and maintained by over 30,000 volunteers. While some question the quality of the content, others feel that most of the content is of a good quality. The authors of this textbook examined many entries related to IT and found them to be accurate, but not always complete.

## 14.6 Managerial Issues

Information technology has certain characteristics that differentiate it, and its economics, from other aspects of the organizational world. Therefore IT requires management practices that are more effective than, and in some cases different from, those that are adequate for non-IT activities. For example, organizational resistance on many fronts can turn the most promising system into a failure (Watson and Haley, 1998). Managers need to be aware of and responsive to the following issues.

1. **Constant growth and change.** The power of the microprocessor chip doubles every two years, while the cost remains constant. This ever-increasing power creates both major opportunities and large threats as its impacts ripple across almost every aspect of the organization and its environment. Managers need to continuously monitor developments in this area to identify new technologies relevant to their organizations and to keep themselves up-to-date on their potential impacts.

2. **Shift from tangible to intangible benefits.** Few opportunities remain for automation projects that simply replace manual labor with IT on a one-for-one basis. The economic justification of IT applications will increasingly depend on intangible benefits, such as increased quality or better customer service. In contrast to calculating cost savings, it is much more difficult to accurately estimate the value of intangible benefits prior to the actual implementation. Managers need to understand and use tools that bring intangible benefits into the decision-making processes for IT investments.

3. **Not a sure thing.** Although IT offers opportunities for significant improvements in organizational performance, these benefits are not automatic. Managers need to very actively plan and control implementations to increase the return on their IT investments.

4. **Chargeback.** Users have little incentive to control IT costs if they do not have to pay for them at all. On the other hand, an accounting system may allocate costs fairly accurately to users but discourage exploration of promising new technologies. The solution is to have a chargeback system that has the primary objective of encouraging user behaviors that correspond to organizational objectives.

5. **Risk.** Investments in IT are inherently more risky than investments in other areas. Managers need to evaluate the level of risk before committing to IT projects. The general level of management involvement as well as specific management techniques and tools need to be appropriate for the risk of individual projects.

6. **Outsourcing.** The complexities of managing IT, and the inherent risks, may require more management skills than some organizations possess. If this is the case, the organization may want to outsource some or all of its IT functions. However, if it does outsource, the organization needs to make sure that the terms of the outsourcing contract are in its best interests both immediately and throughout the duration of the agreement.

7. **Increasing returns.** Industries whose primary focus is IT (digital products), or that include large amounts of IT in their products, often operate under a paradigm of increasing returns. In contrast, industries that primarily produce physical outputs are subject to diminishing returns. Managers need to understand which paradigm applies to the products for which they are responsible and apply management strategies that are most appropriate.

## Integrating IT

### For the Accounting Major

The accounting department is heavily involved in most of the issues discussed in this chapter. Most important is the costing of IT activities, chargeback, cost-benefit analysis, and computation of ROI, NPV, and other formulas. While some of the data are already in the accounting/finance system, other data need to be collected, collaborating with IS and other departments. Finally, arranging a chargeback system for IT usage is not simple and certain to occupy the accountant's time.

### For the Finance Major

How much IT to purchase and its costs versus benefits are a major area for finance people to be engaged with. Major economic issues such as buy versus lease and when to replace IT hardware are determined mostly by financial considerations. Most important are the selection of methodologies to assess the investments on various IT projects and infrastructure. Finally, financial considerations are essential in offshore outsourcing decisions. However, finance people must understand the relevant nonfinancial factors.

### For the Human Resources Management Major

Outsourcing IT activities relates to personnel levels and required skills. Furthermore, for some IT projects, short-term recruiting may be required. Finally, training in both new software and procedures related to outsourcing are of great importance to HRM personnel.

### For the IS Major

Buying, leasing, or replacing hardware and software involve not only financial but also technical considerations. And IS people must work together with both end users and various vendors, some of whom may be in other countries. Finally, economic decisions may impact the skills and required training of the IS staff.

### For the Marketing Major

Economic decisions such as pricing, outsourcing, and make or buy may impact on sales and customer relations. Understanding how such decisions are being made with respect to IT is important for marketing and sales strategies. Also, outsourcing may expedite time-to-market, facilitating marketing efforts.

### For the Production/Operations Management Major

The trade-off between labor and automation is a major concern to POM managers, and so is productivity improvement by technology. Many business processes will be impacted by IT and some will need to be changed to fit vendors' software. POM personnel will have to work with vendors, especially in large-scale outsourcing. Finally, managing large-scale projects that involve IT requires the expertise of POM.

## Key Terms

Behavior-oriented chargeback  *575*
Benchmarks  *572*
Business case  *569*
Chargeback  *575*
Cost-benefit analysis  *564*
Expected value (EV)  *573*

Intangible benefits  *568*
Metric  *572*
Offshore outsourcing  *579*
Outsourcing  *576*
Price-to-performance ratio  *559*
Productivity paradox  *561*

Reach and richness  *581*
Total benefits of ownership
  (TBO)  *571*
Total cost of ownership (TCO)  *571*
Transaction costs  *567*

## Chapter Highlights
(Numbers Refer to Learning Objectives)

**❶** The power of computer hardware should continue increasing at an exponential rate for at least 10 years, doubling every 18 months, while costs remain at the same levels as before. Also the performance/cost ratio of storage and networks behaves in a similar way.

**❷** Although organizations have spent tremendous amounts of money on IT, it is difficult to prove that this spending has increased national or industry productivity. The discrepancy between measures of IT investment and measures of output is described as the productivity paradox, and it can be explained.

**❸** Evaluating IT investment requires finding the total costs of ownership and the total benefits of ownership and subtracting the costs from the benefits. The value of information to an organization should be part of that calculation.

❸ The major difficulty in evaluating IT investment is assessing the intangible benefits. Also, some costs are difficult to relate to specific projects.

❸ Traditional financial approaches can be used to evaluate IT investment, but in many cases methods such as value analysis, benchmarking, or real-option analysis fit better, especially for investment in infrastructures.

❹ Intangible benefits cover many areas ranging from customer satisfaction to deferring IT investments. To include intangible benefits in IT justification, one may attempt to quantify them, to list them as arguments for justification, or to ignore them. Specific methodologies may be useful.

❺ The NPV and ROI methods work well with tangible benefits. When intangible benefits are involved, one may try one of the following: value analysis, information economics, benchmarks, management by maxim, real-option valuation, balanced scorecard, and activity-based costing.

❻ Chargeback systems may be used to regulate the use of shared information systems. Behavior-oriented chargeback

systems, if properly designed, encourage efficient and effective usage of IT resources.

❼ Outsourcing may reduce IT costs and can make it possible for organizations to concentrate their management efforts on issues related to their core competencies. However, outsourcing may reduce the company's flexibility to find the best IT fit for the business, and it may also pose a security risk.

❽ EC enables electronic delivery of digital products at very low cost. Also, many nondigital products can be produced and delivered with lower overhead and with less administrative cost.

❾ Web-based technologies may be approached differently for conducting cost-benefit analysis due to their different economic curves, lack of baseline data, frequent changes, etc. Modifying existing concepts, such as is done in portfolio selection, is advisable.

❿ Several topics are related to the economics of IT. IT failures are frequently the result of poor cost-benefit analysis, and IT projects sometimes linger because of poor planning of economic resources.

## Virtual Company Assignment

### IT Economics at The Wireless Café

Go to The Wireless Cafés link on the Student Web Site. There you will be asked to analyze some IT economics issues as you think about how the many useful and innovative technologies that could be implemented at the restaurant will fit into its budget.

***Instructions for accessing The Wireless Café on the Student Web Site:***

1. Go to *wiley.com/college/turban*.
2. Select Turban/Leidner/ McLean/Wetherbe's *Information Technology for Management, Sixth Edition*.
3. Click on Student Resources site, in the toolbar on the left.
4. Click on the link for Virtual Company Web site.
5. Click on Wireless Café.

## Online Resources

More resources and study tools are located on the Student Web Site and on WileyPLUS. You'll find additional chapter materials and useful Web links. In addition, self-quizzes that provide individualized feedback are available for each chapter.

## Questions for Review

1. Describe Moore's Law.
2. Define productivity.
3. Describe the productivity paradox. Why is it important?
4. List three major explanations of the productivity paradox.
5. Define information infrastructure and list some of its costs.

6. Define cost-benefit analysis.

7. What is TCO? What is TBO?

8. List some tangible and intangible benefits of IT.

9. Describe the value analysis method.

10. Define information economics.

11. Define IT benchmarks and metrics.

12. Describe best-practice benchmarks.

13. Describe transaction cost.

14. Describe IT chargeback.

15. Define IT outsourcing.

16. List five benefits of outsourcing.

17. List five drawbacks or limitations of outsourcing.

18. Define reach vs. richness.

## Questions for Discussion

1. What are the general implications for managers, organizations, and consumers of constantly increasing computer capabilities and declining costs?

2. What are the impacts of exponentially increasing computer hardware power and declining price-to-performance ratios on business production activities and new-product development?

3. Discuss what is necessary in order to achieve productivity gains from IT investments.

4. Why is it more difficult to measure productivity in service industries?

5. Compare and contrast metrics and best practices. Give an example of each in an IT in a university.

6. Discuss what may happen when an organization does not charge users for IT services.

7. Identify circumstances that could lead a firm to outsource its IT functions rather than continue with an internal IS unit.

8. Identify arguments for including estimated values for intangible benefits in net present value (NPV) analyses of IT investments, and contrast them with the arguments for excluding such estimates.

9. What is IT infrastructure, and why is it difficult to justify its cost?

10. Discuss the economic advantages of digital products compared to nondigital ones.

11. Discuss the pros and cons of outsourcing IT, including alternatives to outsourcing.

12. Discuss the value of offshore outsourcing. Summarize the benefits and the risks.

## Exercises and Projects

1. Review *A Closer Look 14.1*. Use an Excel program to do a similar calculation using the following data: Number of devices is 350. Per-unit cost of smart phone is $425; laptop cost is $1,430. Software costs are 20 percent lower than in the table, due to discount you receive. However, connectivity costs and support costs are 12 percent higher, due to inflation. All other data are the same as in the *Closer Look* example. Conduct a calculation for one, two, and three years of ownership.

2. Enter *nucleusresearch.com* and view their calculators. Then use a calculator (it is free) and calculate an IT investment of your choice. Explain why this calculator may not be useful for an EC project that has unique intangible cost.

3. A company is considering investing $15 million in a new VoIP project. Operating costs are estimated as $2 million for years 1 and 2, and $1.5 million per year thereafter. The system is expected to increase revenues by $4 million per year for the first year, and $5 million for each year later. For a period of 5 years of operation, calculate the NPV. (Use an interest rate of 10 percent.) Explain how the company can use the NPV to compare this project with a competing one using the same funding.

4. Enter Online File W14.11 and examine the sample calculator. Take two other countries that you may be familiar with and enter data into a spreadsheet for a comparison.

5. If you have access to a large organization, conduct research on the methods it uses to charge users for IT services and how the users feel about these charges.

6. Enter *ibm.com* and find information about how IBM measures the ROI on WebSphere. Then examine ROI from CIOView Corporation (*CIOview.com*). Identify the variables included in the analysis (at both *ibm.com* and *CIOview.com*). Prepare a report about the fairness of such a tool.

7. A small business invests $50,000 in robotic equipment. This amount is shown as a negative value in Year 0. Projected cash flows of $20,000 per year in Year 1 through Year 5 result from labor savings, reduced material costs, and tax benefits. The business plans to replace the robots with more modern ones after 5 years and does not expect them to have any scrap value. The equipment generates a total of $100,000 in savings over 5 years, or $50,000 more than the original investment. However, a dollar saved in the future is worth less than a dollar

invested in the present. If the business estimates its return on investment as 15 percent, then $1.00 should be worth $1.15 in one year, $1.32 after 2 years with compound interest, and so on. Cash flows are divided by these "discount factors" to estimate what they are worth at present. Calculate the total cash flow after this discounting, and discuss whether the investment can be justified.

## Group Assignments and Projects

1. Considerable discussions and disagreements occur among IS professionals regarding outsourcing. Divide the group into two parts: One will defend the strategy of large-scale outsourcing. One will oppose it. Start by collecting recent material at *google.com* and *cio.com*. Consider the issue of offshore outsourcing.

2. Each group is assigned to an ROI calculator (e.g., from *baselinemag.com*, *nucleusresearch.com*, *acecostanalyzer. com*, Oracle, IBM, etc.). Each group should prepare a list of the functionalities included and the variables. Make a report that shows the features and limitations of each tool.

## Internet Exercises

1. Enter *solutionmatrix.com* and find information about ROI, metrics, and cost-benefit tools. Prepare a report.

2. Enter the Web sites of the Gartner Group (*gartnergroup. com*), The Yankee Group (*yankeegroup.com*), and *CIO* (*cio.com*). Search for recent material about outsourcing, and prepare a report on your findings.

3. Enter the Web site of IDC (*idc.com*) and find how they evaluate ROI on intranets, supply chain, and other IT projects.

4. Visit the Web site of Resource Management Systems (*rms.net*) and take the IT investment Management Approach Assessment Self-Test (*rms.net/self_test.htm*)

to compare your organization's IT decision-making process with those of best-practices organizations.

5. Enter *plumtree.com* and see how they conduct ROI on portals. List major elements of the analysis. Is it biased?

6. Enter *sap.com* and use the casebuilder calculator for a hypothetical (or real) IT project. Write a report on your experience.

7. Enter *searchcio.techtarget.com* and find free ROI analysis tools. Download a tool of your choice and identify its major components. Write a report.

8. Enter *roi-calc.com*. View the demo. Prepare a report for your supervisor about the benefits of this service.

## Minicase 1

### How American Express Makes Superb Investment Decisions

American Express (Amex) controls investments with *smart software*. American Express allocates a large amount of money among many projects in its ten divisions every year. In the past, projects were financed based not on how they contribute to the company's overall goals, but on the project's individual merit and who made "the most noise" (politics). At least 35,000 Excel worksheets kept track of the worldwide investments. Each division (unit) used its own system to calculate return on investment using different discount rates. There was little control and no standards. Strategic investments were done in a poor manner.

Introducing the Web-based Investment Optimization System (IOS) enabled the company to automate the process of requesting and allocating investment project money.

With IOS, the spreadsheets were uploaded to the SQL server where they were read and analyzed by business analytics software (Chapter 11). The improved analy-

sis led to the reallocation of tens of millions of dollars for more optimal investments.

With a return on investment of 2,736.1 percent, the first generation of IOS was the grand-prize winner of the *Baseline* 2005 ROI Leadership Awards (see *Baseline*, July 2005, p. 28). The second generation is a Web-based product built in Microsoft.NET by software maker Solver (*solver.com*). By 2006, over 800 employees in four business units entered budget requests, forecasting, and other financial data into an online form. IOS calculates the information and assigns a risk level to each project. The request is passed through a chain of approvers until a final decision is made.

Another generation of IOS was introduced in 2006. Bigger benefits came when Amex's project-tracking system, which consolidates project results and actual return on investments, was integrated with IOS.

*Sources:* Compiled from Dignan (2005) and from *solver.com* (accessed July 2006).

## Questions for Minicase 1

1. Compare this case with the opening case and point to similarities and differences.
2. What are the benefits of IOS?

3. What is the role of the risk analysis?
4. This system optimized both IT investments and other investments. How is this possible?

# Minicase 2

## Outsourcing Its IT, Kone Is Focusing on Its Core Competencies

IS    POM    GLOBAL

### The Problem

Kone Inc. is a multinational corporation, based in Finland. Kone makes over 20,000 new escalators and elevators each year, installing and servicing them in more than 40 countries, with about 30 percent of Kone's business in the United States. The company embarked on a globalization strategy several years ago, and soon discovered that the internal IT processes were insufficient to support the expansion. The same was true with the IT for the company's value-added private communication networks. IT costs were growing rapidly, yet their contribution to reducing the administrative cost of global sales was minimal. Kone was managing different IT platforms around the world with a variety of home-grown and nonstandard applications. None of the regional IT infrastructures was integrated, nor were they connected or compatible. Kone's global strategy was in danger.

### The Solution

Kone Inc. realized that it must implement and manage a global-standard IT environment. But the company also realized that its business is about escalators and elevators, not IT, so it decided to pursue IT outsourcing. Kone had had an experience with IT outsourcing before, when it outsourced its mainframe operations to Computer Science Corp. But this time the scope of outsourcing was much larger, so the company solicited proposals and finally decided to partner with two global IT providers, SAP AG from Germany and Hewlett-Packard (HP) from the United States.

As described in Chapter 8, SAP is the world's largest ERP provider, and almost all of the 72 modules of SAP R/3 software (including a data warehouse) were deployed at Kone. The SAP environment is deployed in 16 countries, with 4,300 users, in all functional areas.

HP was hired to provide and manage the hardware on which SAP is run. The decision to use two vendors was not easy. IBM and Oracle each could have provided both the software and hardware, but using two separate vendors promised the best-of-breed approach.

HP manages 20 Kone Unix Servers in three data centers (one in Atlanta for North America, one in Singapore for Asia, and one in Brussels for Europe). HP uses its latest technology. HP's OpenView network and system management and security software are also deployed with the system to ensure high availability environment. The system is linked with EMC storage and backup. The annual cost of this global outsourcing is $5 million.

The entire global IT infrastructure is connected and integrated, and it supports identical business processes and practices in all countries. The system provides management with real-time data on product sales, profitability, and backlogs—on a country, regional, or global basis.

Kone maintains some IT competencies to allow it to actively manage its outsourcing partners. The internal team meets online regularly, and SAP and HP collaborate and work closely together.

### The Results

The outsourcing arrangement allows Kone to concentrate on its core competencies. The cost is only 0.02 percent of sales. Large fixed costs in infrastructure and people have been eliminated. The company has better cost control, as well as flexible opportunity for business process redesign, thus speeding up restructuring. The outsourcing vendors guarantee to have the system available 99.5 percent of the time. Actual uptime has been very close to 100 percent.

*Sources*: Compiled from "The Elevation of IT Outsourcing Partnership" (2002), and *rsleads.com/208cn-254* (accessed February 13, 2003).

### Questions for Minicase 2

1. What were the major drivers of the outsourcing at Kone?
2. Why did Kone elect to work with several vendors?
3. What are some of the risks of this outsourcing?
4. How can Kone control its vendors?

# References

Adams, A., "Mistaken Identity," *CIO Insight*, March 2006.

Anonymous, "Top Trends 2005: ROI Practices," Special Issue, *CIO Insights*, December 2004.

Barrett, L., "A Retrun Home," *Baseline*, January 2006.

Barthelemy, J., "The Hidden Costs of IT Outsourcing," *MIT Sloan Management Review*, Spring 2001.

Bothama, H., "State of the Art in TCO," *Sap.com* white paper with ASUG, January 2006.

Broadbent, M., and P. Weill, "Management by Maxim: How Business and IT Managers Can Create IT Infrastructures," *Sloan Management Review*, Spring 1997.

Brown, R. H., and A. Young, "Scenarios for the Future of Outsourcing," *GartnerGroup*, December 12, 2000.

Chen, S., *Strategic Management of E-Business*, 2nd ed. West Sussex, England: John Wiley & Sons, Ltd., 2005.

CIO, "How Iowa Scores Investments," *CIO*, June 1, 2003.

CIO Insights, "Is Your IT Budget Stretched Too Thin?" *CIO Insights Research Study*, February 6, 2006.

*CIO.com*, "ROI Analysis Tools," *Nucleus Research Inc.*, searchcio. *techtarget.com/generic/0,295582,sid19_gci1049484,00.html* (accessed July 2006).

Clemons, E. K., "The Build/Buy Battle," *CIO*, December 1, 2000.

Clermont, P., "Cost-Benefit Analysis: IT's Back in Fashion, Now Let's Make It Work," *Information Strategy: The Executive's Journal*, Winter 2002.

Corbett, M. F., "Taking the Pulse of Outsourcing," *Firmbuilder.com* (data and analysis from the 2001 Outsourcing World Summit), December 6, 2001.

Cramm, S. H., "The Dark Side of Outsourcing," *CIO*, November 15, 2001.

Cushing, K., "Procter & Gamble's 3bn HP Deal Shows Mega IT Outsourcing Is Still Tempting Some," *Computer Weekly*, April 22, 2003.

Davamanirajan, P., et al., "Assessing the Business Value of Information Technology in Global Wholesale Banking: Case of Trade Service," *Journal of Organizational Computing and Electronic Commerce*, January–March 2002.

Davison, D., "Top 10 Risks of Offshore Outsourcing," Meta- GroupInc., 2004, *www2.cio.com/analyst/report2224.html* (accessed July 2006).

DePalma, D., "Make the Business Case for Global Expansion," *e-Business Advisor*, April 1, 2001.

Devaraj, S., and R. Kohli, *The IT Payoff*. New York: Financial Times/Prentice Hall, 2002.

Dignan, L., "Triumphs and Trip-ups in 2005," *Baseline*, December 2005.

Dixit, A. K., and Pindyck, R. S., "The Options Approach to Capital Investment," *Harvard Business Review*, May–June 1995.

Evans, P., and T. S. Wurster. *Blown to Bits: How the New Economics of Information Transforms Strategy*. Boston, MA: Harvard Business School Press, 2000.

Farrell, D., "IT Investments that Pay Off," *Special Report of Harvard Business School to Search CIO.com*, November 26, 2003.

Farrell, D., "Smarter Offshoring," *Harvard Business Review*, June 2006.

Ferrin, B. G., and R. E. Plank, "Total Cost of Ownership Models: An Exploratory Study," *Journal of Supply Chain Management*, Summer 2002.

Fish, K.E., and J. Seydel, "Where IT Outsourcing Is and Where It is Going," *Journal of Computer Information Systems*, Spring 2006.

Fisher, A., "A Waste of Money?" *Financial Times*, October 25, 2001.

Focacci, L., et al., "Using Application Service Providers: Yes or No?" *Strategic Change*, 2003.

Gerlach, J., et al., "Determining the Cost of IT Services," *Communications of the ACM*, September 2002.

Gillin, P., "Offshore Outsourcing Becoming 'In' Thing for CIOs," *CIO News & Analysis*, June 24, 2003.

Gray, P., and H. Watson, "Present and Future Directions in Data Warehousing," *Database*, Summer 1998.

Green, S., *Profit on the Web*. Auckland, NZ: Computertime, 2002.

Gunasekaran, et al., "A Model for Investment Justification in Information Technology Projects," *International Journal of Information Management*, March 2001.

Hamilton, S., "Intel Research Expands Moore's Law," *Computer*, January 2003.

Harmozi, A., et al., "Outsourcing Information Technology: Assessing Your Options," *SAM Advanced Management Journal*, Autumn 2003.

Hirschheim, R., and M. Lacity, "Information Technology Insourcing: Myths and Realities," *Communications of the ACM*, February 2000.

ITAA (Information Technology Association of America), "Skills Study 2000 — Bridging the Gap: Information Technology Skills for a New Millennium," April 2000, *uen.org/techday/html/technology.html* (no longer available online).

Kambil, A., "Reduce Customer Risks with eCommerce," *Accenture*, 1999, *accenture.com/Global/Research_and_Insights/Institute_For_High_Performance_Business/By_Subject/Customer_Relationship_Management/ReduceECommerce.htm* (accessed July 2006).

King, J., "User Beware," *Computerworld*, March 18, 2002.

Kohli, R., et al., "IT Investment Payoff in E-Business Environments: Research Issues," *Information Systems Frontiers*, September 2003.

Kudyba, S., and D. Vitaliano, "Information Technology and Corporate Profitability: A Focus on Operating Efficiency," *Information Resources Management Journal*, January–March 2003.

Kumar, R. L., "A Framework for Assessing the Business Value of IT Infrastructures," *JMIS*, Fall 2004.

Laurie, J., "Why Projects Fail," *JISC InfoNet* (*jiscinfonet.ac.uk*), Northumbria University, Newcastle Upon Tyne, UK.

Legrenzi, C., "The 2nd Edition of the European Survey on the Economic Value of IT," *Information Systems Control Journal*, May–June 2003.

Lewis, B. C., and T. A. Byrd, "Development of a Measure for IT Infrastructure Construct," *European Journal of Information Systems*, June 2003.

Lin, W. T., and B. M. Shao, "Relative Sizes of Information Technology Investments and Productivity Efficiency: Their Linkage and Empirical Evidence," *Journal of AIS*, September 2000.

Lucas, H. C., Jr., *Information Technology: Strategic Decision Making for Managers*. Hoboken, NJ: Wiley, 2005.

McKay, J., and P. Marshall, *Strategic Management of e-Business*. Milton, Australia: Wiley, 2004.

Minevich, M., and F. J. Richter, "The Global Outsourcing Report," *CIO Insight*, special whiteboard report, 2005.

Moore, G. E., "Moore's Law," *CIO*, January 1, 1997.

Murphy, R. M., "Tech Doesn't Matter . . . Want to Bet?" *Fortune Small Business*, January 31, 2006.

Olazabal, N. G., "Banking: The IT Paradox," *McKinsey Quarterly*, January–March 2002.

Paton, D., and D. Troppito, "Eye on ROI: ROI Review," *DM Review*, March 2004.

Peacock, E., and M. Tanniru, "Activity-Based Justification of IT Investments," *Information & Management*, March 2005.

Peppard, J., and J. Ward, "Unlocking Sustained Business Value from IT Investments," *California Management Review*, Fall 2005.

Pisello, T., "The Three Rs of RFID: Rewards, Risk, and ROI," *Technology Evaluation*, March 5, 2005.

Pountain, D., "Amending Moore's Law," *Byte,* March 1998.

Rayport, J., and B. J. Jaworski, *E-Commerce.* New York: McGraw-Hill, 2001.

Read, C., et al., *eCFO: Sustaining Value in the New Corporation.* Chichester, England: Wiley, 2001.

Renkema, T. J. W., *The IT Value Quest: How to Capture the Business Value of IT-Based Infrastructure.* Chichester, England: Wiley, 2000.

Roberts, A., "Project Aquarius: Measuring the Impact of Technology," *Management Services,* 2003.

Robinson, M., and R. Kalakota, *Offshore Outsourcing: Business Models, ROI, and Best Practices,* 2nd ed. Alpharetta, GA: Mivar Press, October 2004.

Robinson, M., et al., *Global Outsourcing.* Alpharetta, GA: Mivar Press, 2005.

Ross, J. W., and C. M. Beath, "Beyond the Business Case: New Approaches to IT Investment," *MIT Sloan Management Review,* Winter 2002.

Rubin, H. A., "How to Measure IT Value," *CIO Insight,* May 1, 2003a.

Rubin, R.,"Outsourcing Imperative: Do or Die," *Optimize,* 2003b.

Ryan S. D., and M. S. Gates, "Inclusion of Social Subsystem Issues in IT Investment Decisions: An Empirical Assessment," *Information Resources Management Journal,* January–March 2004, *sap.com/ solutions/pdf/IDC_Case.pdf* (accessed July 2006).

Sawhney, M., "Damn the ROI, Full Speed Ahead," *CIO,* July 15, 2002.

Seddon, P., et al., "Measuring Organizational IS Effectiveness: An Overview and Update of Senior Management Perspectives," *The Data BASE for Advances in Information Systems,* Spring 2002.

Steyaert, J. C., "Measuring the Performance of Electronic Government Services," *Information and Management,* January–February 2004.

Straub, D., *Foundations of Net-Enhanced Organizations.* Hoboken, NJ: Wiley, 2004.

Straub, D. W., et al., "Measuring e-Commerce in Net-Enabled Organizations," *Information Systems Research,* June 2002a.

Straub, D. W., et al., "Toward New Metrics for Net-Enhanced Organizations," *Information Systems Research,* September 2002b.

Swamy, R., "Strategic Performance Measurement in the New Millennium," *CMA Management,* May 2002.

Symons, C., "Where Do Metrics Come From?" *Best Practices,* WhitePaper. Cambridge, MA: Forrester Research, December 28, 2004.

Thatcher, M. E., and D. E. Pingry, "An Economic Model of Product Quality and IT Value," *Informs,* 15(3) September 2004.

"The Elevation of IT Outsourcing Partnership: With HP/SAP Trained Staff, Kone's Global Strategy Is Top Level," *Communication News,* August 2002.

Tillquist, J., and W. Rodgers, "Measuring the Value of IT," *Communications of the ACM,* January 2005.

Tjan, A. K., "Put Your Internet Portfolio in Order," *Harvard Business Review,* February 2001.

Turban, E., et al., *E-Commerce 2008.* Upper Saddle River, NJ: Prentice Hall, 2008.

Varon, E., "R. O. Iowa," *CIO,* June 1, 2003.

Violino, B., "Return on Investment Profiles: The Intangible Benefits of Technology Are Emerging as the Most Important of All," *Information Week,* June 30, 1997.

Vulkan, N., *The Economics of e-Commerce.* Princeton, NJ: Princeton University Press, 2003.

Walsh, K. R., "Analyzing the Application ASP Concept: Technologies, Economics, and Strategies," *Communications of the ACM,* August 2003.

Wang, A. L., and D. Shiang, "SAP Business Case Builder," *An IDC Case Study* (sponsored by SAP), *IDC.com,* May 2002.

Watson, H. J., and B. J. Haley, "Managerial Considerations," *Communications of the ACM,* September 1998.

Wheatley, M., "Chargeback for Good or Evil: Charging Users for IT Costs Can Rein in Budgets and Bring Rigor to Planning, But It Can Also Turn You into an Unpopular Bean Counter," *CIO,* March 1, 2003.

Wilkinson, S., "Phone Bill, Electricity Bill . . . Storage Bill? Storage Utilities Attract New Economy Companies with Pay-as-You-Go Service," *Earthweb.com,* October 24, 2000.

Chapter

# 15

# Acquiring IT Applications and Infrastructure

## Learning Objectives

After studying this chapter, you will be able to:

① Describe the process of IT systems acquisition.

② Describe IT project identification, justification, and planning.

③ List the major IT acquisition options and criteria for option selection.

④ Discuss various IT application outsourcing options, including the use of an application service provider (ASP) and utility computing.

⑤ Describe the criteria for selecting an acquisition approach.

⑥ Describe the process of vendor and software selection.

⑦ Understand some major implementation issues.

⑧ Understand the issue of connecting IT applications to databases, other applications, networks, and business partners.

⑨ Describe the need for business process redesign, the methodologies for doing it, and IT support for process redesign.

## Integrating *IT*

 **ACC**
 **FIN**
 **MKT**
 **POM**
 **HRM**
 **IS**
 **SVC**

# HOW STERNGOLD ACQUIRED AN E-COMMERCE SYSTEM

Sterngold (*sterngold.com*), a century-old manufacturer of dental materials, is a subsidiary of London-based Cookson Group PLC. Sterngold is based in Attleboro, Massachusetts; it has only 90 employees but has offices in Europe and South America.

## The Problem

The company sells more than 4,000 products either directly to 350,000–400,000 dental professionals or through distributors to another 5 million dental professionals. Orders come in small quantities, very frequently from repeat customers, with a frequent demand for same-day shipment. Sterngold realized that moving its sales online might create easy ordering for its customers, reduce its own transaction costs, and enable customers to get its products faster—all of which could provide a competitive advantage. The company had a Web site, but without selling capabilities. Sterngold decided that it had two choices to solve this problem: (1) to develop an e-commerce application in-house, or (2) to find an outsourcer to provide the application.

## The Solution

The company wanted a technology solution that allowed it fast time to market, access to best-of-breed technology and people, high security, superb reliability, and the ability to focus on core competency. Having only one IT person, the company knew that the in-house solution required hiring additional personnel, creating a temporarily large IT department. Therefore, Sterngold decided to use application outsourcing.

The question then became how to select a trusted business partner who understood the need to move quickly, but carefully. After long deliberation and interviews with potential outsourcers, the company selected Surebridge Inc. to develop and then host the e-commerce application. The selection was "blessed" by the parent company, Cookson Group.

## The Process

Surebridge followed its own proprietary eMethodology approach. First, a vendor's implementation team was cre-ated. The team started by evaluating Sterngold's business needs, using interviews to gather the information. Then goals and a timetable were created. A major consideration was to finish the project before the industry's annual trade show, so that Sterngold would be able to demonstrate to its customers how easy it is to order products in the online store.

The next step was to create an architecture. This step included a front-end ordering system (phase I) and its integration with the back-office systems (phase II). This was not an easy task, given that there were over 4,000 products whose information attributes resided in disparate areas of the company. The relevant information was channeled into a large database. A major task was the creation of a search engine that would be useful to diverse groups of customers (e.g., dentists, dental labs). Each group of customers had different knowledge, requirements, and buying habits. Working hand-in-hand, Sterngold and Surebridge completed phase I in less than three months.

To execute phase II there were many challenges to meet. First, expertise was needed on how financial, inventory, and order fulfillment could best be integrated with the ordering system. This required the services of a consultant and resulted in redesign of some business processes. Also, several internal policies were modified to support the Web initiative. For example, a complex pricing policy was simplified by creating clear rules about discounting.

## The Results

The new system offers a number of major capabilities: Because the ordering system was integrated with the back office, the system reduces errors due to manual data entry. Real-time inventory status is given to customers before they place an order, and a tracking feature provides real-time status of orders. Discounts are related to specific customers, so they know what they will pay as soon as they log in. Real-time authorization of customers' credit cards is provided when orders are placed. In addition, the company now can offer promotions to its customers without the need to send letters. The site also offers the ability to track customer clickstream movements, allowing the company to personalize products and to offer cross-sell and up-sell products and services. Also, the site includes capabilities for conducting e-mail marketing campaigns using permission marketing.

By 2006, three years after implementation, Sterngold has recorded the following results:

- By offering free shipping, Sterngold has encouraged more and more customers to order online, thus increasing the customer base (at the expense of the competitors).
- More product promotion (which has been easy to do online) has resulted in more customers and sales.
- Both the company and the customers have experienced increasing efficiencies and savings on administrative costs.

- Much fax and snail mail have been eliminated.
- The online presence has resulted in greater exposure to business partners.
- A strong relationship with the technology partners has been created. (Since Sterngold owns the IT infrastructure and Surebridge just operates it, finger pointing in case of problems is minimized.)

Use of an outside vendor enabled phase I to be finished in less than three months, rather than two to three years if it had been done in-house. This enabled Sterngold to be the *first mover* in its industry. The Web site is now being translated into several languages for the global market.

*Sources:* Compiled from Craig (2003) and from *sterngold.com* (accessed June 2006).

## Lessons Learned from This Case

First the case demonstrates how an IT application starts. Then it describes how a company selects an alternative for acquiring an IT application. In this case, an outsourcer was selected to build a custom-made application. Then, a team is created to implement the application. The implementation requires a study of existing processes and redesign of some. Critical to the project is the need to integrate the ordering system with the back office (order fulfillment, inventory, accounting, payment). Finally, we learn that being first mover can be advantageous. All of these issues and a few related ones are the subject of this chapter.

## 15.1 The Landscape and Framework of IT Application Acquisition

This chapter focuses on IT systems acquisition. We include in "acquisition" all approaches to obtaining systems: buying, leasing, or building. The acquisition issue is complex for various reasons: There is a large variety of IT applications, they keep changing over time, and they may involve several business partners. There is also no single way to acquire IT applications.

The diversity of IT applications requires a variety of acquisition methodologies and approaches. Small applications (e.g., EC storefronts) can be developed with HTML, Java, or another programming language. They can also be quickly implemented by using commercial packages, or those leased from an *application service provider* (ASP). Larger or special applications can be developed in-house or outsourced. Building medium-to-large applications requires extensive integration with existing information systems such as corporate databases, intranets, enterprise resource planning (ERP), and other application programs. Therefore, the process of IT application acquisition may vary. However, in many cases, it follows a fairly standard form.

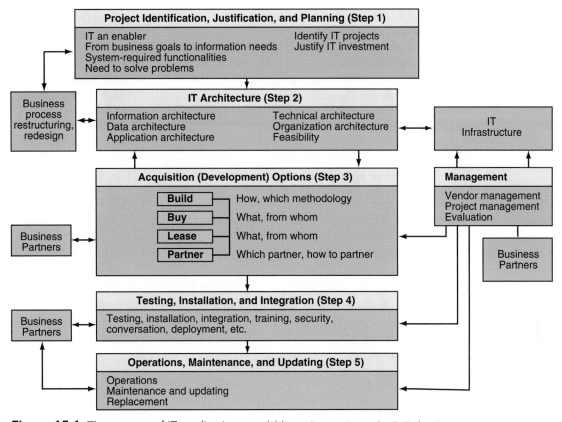

**Figure 15.1** The process of IT application acquisition. (*Source:* Drawn by E. Turban.)

**THE IT ACQUISITION PROCESS**

The acquisition process of an IT application has five major steps, which are shown in Figure 15.1 and discussed below.

**Step 1: Planning, Identifying, and Justifying IT-Based Systems.** IT-based systems are usually built as *enablers* of some business process(es). Therefore, their planning must be aligned with that of the organization's overall business plan and the specific decisions or tasks they intend to support. Such processes may need to be restructured to fully reap the benefits of the supporting IT applications (see Section 15.7). Also, the systems may need to be justified (e.g., by a cost-benefit analysis; see Chapter 14). Both of these activities may be complex, especially for systems that require a significant investment to acquire, operate, and maintain. The output of this step is the decision to invest (or not) in a specific application and a timetable, budget, and assigned responsibility. This step is usually done in-house, with consultants if needed. All other steps can be done in-house or outsourced.

**Step 2: Creating an IT Architecture.** **IT architecture,** as discussed in Chapter 2, is a plan for organizing the underlying infrastructure and applications of the IT project. The architecture plan includes the information and data required to fulfill the business goals and vision; the application modules that will deliver and manage the information and data; the specific hardware and software on which the application modules will run, as well as the security, scalability, and reliability required by the applications; and the human resources and procedures for implementing the IT project.

Various IT tools and methodologies can be used to support the creation of an IT application architecture (e.g., see Kendall and Kendall, 2005). The results obtained from step 2 are routed to the strategic planning level (e.g., to a steering committee). Based on the results of step 2, the application portfolio (mix of applications) or a specific project may be changed. For example, the steering committee may defer or scale down a specific project because it is too risky. Once the architecture is compiled and the project gets final approval, a decision about *how* to acquire the specific IT application must be made.

**Step 3: Selecting an Acquisition Option.** IT applications can be acquired through several alternative approaches that will be discussed in detail in Section 15.3. The major options are:

- Build the system in-house.
- Have a vendor build a custom-made system.
- Buy an existing application and install it, with or without modifications, in-house or through a vendor.
- Lease standard software from an application service provider (ASP), or lease through utility computing or a software-as-a-service arrangement.
- Enter into a partnership or alliance that will enable the company to use someone else's application.
- Use a combination of these approaches.

The consideration criteria for selecting among the various options are presented in Section 15.5. Once an option is chosen, the system can be acquired. At the end of this step, an application is ready to be installed and deployed. No matter what option is chosen, you most likely will have to select vendor(s) and/or software, and then work with and manage these vendors.

**Step 4: Testing, Installing, Integration, and Deploying IT Applications.** Once an acquisition option has been selected, the next step involves getting the application up and running on the selected hardware and network environment. One of the steps in installing an application is connecting it to back-end databases, to other applications, and often to partners' information systems. Details of the connection process are supplied in Section 15.6. This step can be done in-house or outsourced.

During this step, the modules that have been installed need to be tested. A series of tests are required (Sommerville, 2004): *unit testing* (testing the modules one at a time), *integration testing* (testing the combination of modules acting in concert), *usability testing* (testing the quality of the user's experience when interacting with the portal or Web site), and *acceptance testing* (determining whether the application meets the original business objectives and vision).

After the applications pass all of the tests, they can be rolled out to the end-users. Here one may deal with issues such as conversion (from the old to the new system) strategies, training, and resistance to change (see Whitten and Bentley, 2007).

**Step 5: Operations, Maintenance, and Updating.** It usually takes as much time, effort, and money to operate and maintain an application as it does to acquire and install it in the first place. To enjoy continual usage, an application needs to be continually updated. Software maintenance can be a big problem due to rapid changes in the IT field. Operation and maintenance can be done in-house and/or outsourced (Kendall and Kendall, 2005).

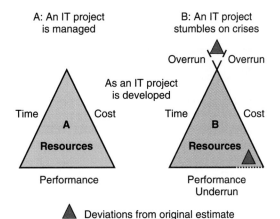

A: An IT project is managed

B: An IT project stumbles on crises

As an IT project is developed

**Figure 15.2** Triple constraints of IT project management. (*Source:* Drawn by L. Lai.)

Deviations from original estimate

**MANAGING THE DEVELOPMENT PROCESS**

The IT acquisition process can be a fairly complex project and must be managed properly (e.g., Xia and Lee, 2004). For medium-to-large applications, a project team is usually created to manage the process and the vendors. Projects can be managed with *project management* software (see examples of various project management software at Online File W15.1, *office.microsoft.com/project*, and *primavera.com*.). Three conditions that are generally used to evaluate the effectiveness of IT project management are performance, time, and cost (Rakos, 2005). Standard project management techniques and tools are used by project managers to manage project resources to keep them on time, on budget, and within performance specifications. (See Figure 15.2).

Finally, implementing an IT project may require restructuring one or more business processes. See Kanter and Walsh (2004) for further discussion of this topic. Let's now look at steps 1, 3, and 4 in more detail.

## 15.2 Identifying, Justifying, and Planning IT Systems Applications (Step 1)

In Chapter 13 we described the process of IT planning from a *macro* point of view — that is, looking at the entire IT resources in the organization. When we look at a specific application or a specific infrastructure, we need to go through an application-by-application planning process as well. Note that the need to acquire an application can be the result of the macro planning, usually due to its inclusion in the proposed new applications in the *application portfolio* (Chapter 13). However, applications can be initiated for other reasons, such as to solve a recurrent problem, as illustrated in the Swedish bank case described in *IT at Work 15.1*.

Other sources of IT project applications can be any of the following: requests from user departments; vendors' recommendations; need to comply with new government regulations; auditors' recommendations; recommendation of the steering committee; recommendation of the IS department; top management requests (orders); or search for high-payoff projects.

**IDENTIFYING HIGH-PAYOFF PROJECTS**

It is natural that organizations will prefer to search for high-payoff applications, especially if they are not difficult to implement. Minicase 2 illustrates how National Commercial Bank Jamaica Limited achieved a 100 percent–plus return on investments by rebuilding its IT infrastructure.

# *IT* at work 15.1

## Web Services Get Swedish Banking Applications Talking to Each Other    *FIN*    *GLOBAL*

Centrala Studie Stodsnamnden (CSN) is the Swedish government's banking authority responsible for providing student loans and grants to Swedes who are pursuing higher education. Each year, CSN loans out SEK$2.5 billion to a half-million people and delivers a host of financial services to thousands more. In January 2002, at the start of the new school semester, when online traffic to the organization is typically four to five times greater than in other months, CNS's Web site went down. Students were forced to phone CSN representatives directly to receive help with new loan and grant applications and payback information. The voice-response system, which was designed to meet a much lower demand, had proved inadequate.

A group of technicians led by the production team worked hard to stabilize the Web site and ease the burden caused by overuse of the voice-response system. "We found the load problem and tried to tame it by adding servers, but the solution was like patchwork—and in the following weeks we could see the same pattern with instability occur," says Orjan Carlsson, Chief Architect of CSN's information technology department. Consistently poor Web site performance coupled with long waits on the telephone was enough to cause a public outcry.

Given CSN's heterogeneous enterprise environment—which comprised everything from IBM mainframes to UNIX-based applications, to systems running Microsoft Windows NT—a solution that could support cross-platform communication was a necessity. Only a flexible, scalable, open-standards-based integration architecture could supply the level of interoperability the organization desired, especially for the high volume during the start of a semester.

A locally based IBM team worked closely with CSN to investigate solution possibilities. Together, the technical teams decided that the best way for the organization to realize cross-platform, program-to-program communication was through Web Services built on IBM WebSphere. This architecture allows CSN's disparate applications to exchange information with each other without human intervention. The team implemented a system that also eliminated the organization's reliance on an outsourced application service provider for its voice-response system. The system leverages Web Services to enable the Windows NT–based voice-response system to execute transactions that are easily recognized by CSN's back-end (back-office) operations.

The new Web Services–enabled system allows CSN to deliver student account status and transaction information to phones (voice response) and to CSN's portal at a significantly reduced cost. "Web Services are essential for us today and in the future," says Carlsson. According to Carlson, Web Services enable a loosely coupled architecture, resulting in a highly integrated solution.

Reuse of code also gives CSN an advantage. One interface can serve several business systems using different channels, making it easy to modify existing channels or add new ones, a feature that significantly reduces total cost of ownership. CSN dramatically saves on developer costs as well as gets new functionality to market faster and with more frequency. The result is a flexible and scalable Web services–enabled architecture that is essentially transparent to end users, giving CSN the cross-platform communication system it needs to operate efficiently, serve its customers, and lower costs.

*Sources:* Compiled from Plummer and McCoy (2006), and IBM (2002).

*For Further Exploration:* How did this application arise? What does the solution provide? What role does the business partner play?

---

**PROJECT JUSTIFICATION**

Once potential projects are identified, they usually need to be justified. To do so, one can use some of the methods described in Chapter 14. Since organizations have limited resources, they cannot embark on all projects at once. Therefore, all proposed projects must be scrutinized.

Information system applications may be expensive. Therefore, an organization must analyze the need for applications and justify it in terms of cost and benefits. Because most organizations operate with tight budgets, this analysis must be carefully done. The investigation is usually divided into two parts. First, it is necessary to explore the need for each system (i.e., find the information needs of the users and how the application will meet those needs). Second, it is necessary to justify it from a cost-benefit point of view. The need for information systems is usually related to organizational planning and to the analysis of its performance vis-à-vis its competitors (see Chapter 11). The cost-benefit justification must look at the wisdom of the specific IT investment vis-à-vis investing in alternative IT or other projects.

Once justification is done, a plan for the application acquisition can be made.

<table>
<tr><td>

**PLANNING FOR THE SPECIFIC APPLICATION**

</td><td>

Before a project is implemented, or even before a company decides how to acquire the software, it is necessary to understand the organization's current way of doing business (the business process) in the area the application is going to be used. For example, if you plan to install an e-procurement application, it makes sense to study the ins and outs of procurement in your business. This can be done in a systematic way as part of *system analysis,* as described in Technology Guide 6.

The planning process includes documenting system requirements, studying data and information flows, and studying the users' community and their specific objectives. Also included is the risk of failure and how to manage that risk. This then leads to the creation of a timetable (schedule) and milestones (which are needed in order to determine how to acquire the application). For example, if you need the system very quickly, you will favor buying or leasing one. The planning process covers resources other than time—specifically, money (budget), labor, and equipment (if needed). Project planning also examines the issue of connectivity to databases and to partners' systems, relevant government regulations, what to do if some employees lose their jobs as a result of the implementation of the application, and so on.

Issues such as connecting to business partners and databases are the foundations for step 2, the creation of the IT architecture. This step is discussed in detail in Technology Guide 6.

</td></tr>
</table>

# 15.3 Acquiring IT Applications: Available Options (Step 3)

There are several options for acquiring IT applications. The major options are: buy, lease, and develop in-house. Each of these is described in this section, along with several minor options.

<table>
<tr><td>

**BUY THE APPLICATIONS (OFF-THE-SHELF APPROACH)**

</td><td>

Standard features required by IT applications can be found in many commercial packages. This option is also known as a *turnkey approach.* Buying an existing package can be a cost-effective and time-saving strategy compared with in-house application development. The "buy" option should be carefully considered and planned for to ensure that all critical features for current and future needs are available in the selected package. Otherwise, such packages will quickly become obsolete. However, organizational needs are rarely fully satisfied by one software package. It is therefore sometimes necessary to acquire multiple packages to support even a single business process. These packages then need to be integrated with each other as well as with existing software (see Section 15.6). The advantages and limitations of the buy option are summarized in Table 15.1.

The buy option is especially attractive if the software vendor allows for modifications. However, the option may not be attractive in cases of high obsolescence rates or high package cost.

</td></tr>
<tr><td>

**LEASE THE APPLICATIONS**

</td><td>

Leasing an IT application can result in substantial cost and time savings. In those cases where extensive maintenance is required or where the cost of buying is very high, leasing is very advantageous, especially for small-to-medium enterprises (SMEs). Leasing is also advantageous when a company wants to experiment with a package before making a heavy up-front buy investment, protect its own internal networks, quickly utilize the application, or rely on experts to establish a major project, usually with a Web site.

</td></tr>
</table>

| TABLE 15.1 | Advantages and Limitations of the "Buy" Option |
| --- | --- |
| **Advantages of the "Buy" Option** | **Disadvantages of the "Buy" Option** |
| • Many different types of off-the-shelf software are available.<br>• Much time can be saved by buying rather than building.<br>• The company can know what it is getting before it invests in the software.<br>• The company is not the first and only user.<br>• Purchased software may avoid the need to hire personnel specifically dedicated to a project.<br>• The vendor updates the software frequently.<br>• The price is usually much lower for a buy option. | • Software may not exactly meet the company's needs.<br>• Software may be difficult or impossible to modify, or it may require huge business process changes to implement.<br>• The company will not have control over software improvements and new versions. (Usually it may only recommend.)<br>• Purchased software can be difficult to integrate with existing systems.<br>• Vendors may drop a product or go out of business. |

Leasing can be done in one of several ways:

- Lease the IT application from an *outsourcer* and then install it on the company's premises. The vendor can help with the installation and frequently will offer to contract the operation and maintenance of the system as well. Many conventional IT applications are leased this way.
- Lease the IT application from an *application service provider (ASP)* that hosts the application at its data center. An ASP is an agent or vendor who assembles the software needed by enterprises and packages them usually with outsourced development, operations, maintenance, and other services. Major ASPs for enterprise IT systems are Oracle, Microsoft, and IBM. Outsourcing and application service providers are explored in Section 15.4. A concept related to the lease option is "software-as-a service."

**Software-as-a-Service.** **Software-as-a-service (SaaS)** refers to software that is rented. Rather than purchase a software product and pay for occasional upgrades, SaaS is subscription based, and all updates are provided during the term of the subscription. When the subscription period expires, the software is no longer valid. Web-based applications lend themselves to the SaaS model because they can be easily controlled at the server level. SaaS usually costs less than store-bought software and requires users to install and boot up nothing more than a browser.

The biggest obstacle to renting software is the inability to integrate different applications. Sharing data between a CRM program and billing software, for example, is a challenge, especially if some of your applications are hosted while others are kept in-house.

The major factors driving the switch to SaaS are (D'Agostino, 2005):

- Reducing the risks involved in acquiring new software
- Influencing product and service quality via an ongoing relationship with vendors
- Changing usage commitments as business circumstances change
- Preparing financially justifiable business cases

- Predicting ongoing expenses more accurately, which is important with IT budgets being tightened and scrutinized for better return on investment and value

**IN-HOUSE DEVELOPMENT: INSOURCING**

A third development strategy is to develop ("build") applications in-house. Although in-house development—*insourcing*—can be time consuming and costly, it may lead to IT applications that better fit an organization's strategy and vision (e.g., the X4ML project of Merrill Lynch discussed in Minicase 1) and differentiate it from the competition. The in-house development of IT applications, however, is a challenging task, as most applications are novel, and may involve multiple organizations. Shurville and Williams (2005) demonstrate how a combination of hard and soft projects and change management methodologies guided successful in-house development of a campuswide information system.

**Development Options for In-House Development.** Three major options exist for in-house development:

- **Build from scratch.** This option should be considered only for specialized IT applications for which components are not available. This option is expensive and slow, but it will provide the best fit to the organization's needs.
- **Build from components.** The required applications are often constructed from standard components (e.g., random number generators or Web servers such as Microsoft's IIS). Commercially packaged and homegrown components must integrate tightly for component-based development to meet its requirements. This is especially critical for real-time applications and for e-business systems. The scope of component integration and code reuse is broadening, too. Component reuse may be the key to integration, especially if the components have been integrated in other applications (Srivastava, 2004). For a methodology of evaluating component-based IT applications, see Ding and Napier (2006).
- **Integrating applications.** The application integration option is similar to the build from components option, but instead of using components, entire applications are employed. This is an especially attractive option when IT applications from several business partners need to be integrated. Integration methods such as using Web Services or Enterprise Application Integration (EAI) can be used (see Bussler et al., 2005).

Insourcing is a challenging task that requires specialized IT procedures and resources. For this reason, most organizations usually rely on packaged applications or outsource the development and maintenance of their IT applications.

**Methods Used in In-House Development.** Several methods can be used when you develop IT applications in-house (see Satzinger et al., 2006). Two major development methods are:

- **Systems development life cycle (SDLC).** Large IT projects, especially ones that involve infrastructure, are developed according to a systematic set of procedures known as the systems development life cycle (SDLC) using several tools, notably CASE tools. Details about this approach are provided in Technology Guide 6.
- **Prototyping methodology.** With a prototyping methodology, an initial list of basic system requirements is defined and used to build a prototype. The prototype is then improved in several iterations based on users' feedback. This approach can be very rapid. The prototype is then tested and improved, tested again, and developed

further based on the users' feedback. The prototyping approach, however, is not without drawbacks. There is a risk of getting into an endless loop of prototype revisions, as users may never be fully satisfied. Such a risk should be planned for because of the rapid changes in IT technology and business models.

**END-USER DEVELOPMENT**

**End-user development** (also known as **end-user computing**) is the development and use of computer-based information systems by people outside the formal information systems area. This includes users in all functional areas at all skill levels and organizational levels: managers, executives, staff, secretaries, and others. For the different types of end-user computing, see Online File W15.2.

**Reasons for End-User Development.** PCs have diffused throughout organizations, communication with data servers (mainframes and others) has improved, and software tools have improved in capability, quality, price, and user-friendliness. Consequently, users now have the necessary tools to develop their own IT applications, including Web-based systems. Web-based tools such as wikis and content management make end-user development more efficient and effective, as illustrated in *IT at Work 15.2.*

# *IT* at Work 15.2

## *End-User Development Using Wikis*

IS

In Hawaiian, *wiki wiki* means "quick." In IT-speak, a wiki is a Web site that lets anyone quickly add or edit content. It is a Web site designed for collaboration (see Chapter 4). The concept began small, as a grassroots way to build online knowledge repositories (such as *Wikipedia.org*). But now startups such as JotSpot (*jot.com*) are out to harness the power of wikis for businesses.

JotSpot's wiki-based software lets companies create wikis for business processes. Here are some end-user developments utilized by JotSpot's customers:

- **Create an intranet.** Publish company information, such as news or employee guidelines (Sundia, *watermelonworks. com*).
- **Project management.** Schedule project deadlines, assign tasks, and define product specifications (Roxor Games, *roxorgames.com*).
- **Document collaboration.** Multiple users author documents with the aid of version history and MS Word integration (Symantec, *symantec.com*; Insider Pages, *insiderpages.com*).
- **Collaborate with virtual teams.** Communicate with remote contractors or clients (Wingate Studios, *wingatestudios.com*; Unimedia, *unimedia.org*).
- **Track software bugs.** Log defects and build custom queries (Al Technology, *a1technology.com*).
- **Call center support.** Access case histories and increase customer support (Your Privacy Info, *yourprivacy.info*).

Opsware (*opsware.com*), a data center automation software vendor, has used JotSpot to create in a few hours applications that might have cost $50,000 to $100,000 to develop in Java. Opsware's technical sales team uses one JotSpot wiki to manage information such as proposals and status reports associated with pilot projects for prospective customers. "It's a very rich document management system," says Jason Rosenthal, vice president of client services at Opsware. "It's so quick and easy that a new user can learn to use it in 10 to 15 minutes." The software also reduced the time it took the company to prepare for a proof of concept from five days to three, Rosenthal claims, adding that wikis will revolutionize how companies share information internally. Says Rosenthal, "it's easier for new users to do what it used to take a Webmaster to do."

*Sources:* Compiled from Dragoon (2005); and from *jot.com* (accessed June 2006).

*For Further Exploration:* One of the extraordinary stories of the Internet age is that of *Wikipedia*, a free online encyclopedia that anyone can edit. The encyclopedia has added 4 million articles in 200 languages since it was founded in 2001. Experts now suggest that the quality and accuracy of Wikipedia is as good as that of *Britannica* (recall *IT at Work 13.2*), a highly prestigious encyclopedia. Use Wikipedia as an example to discuss the power of end-user development.

**Risks of End-User Development.** End-user development, as discussed in *IT at Work 15.2,* is beneficial to both workers and the organization as a whole. It also has some limitations. End users may not be skilled enough in computers, so quality and cost may be jeopardized unless proper controls are installed. Also, many end users do not take time to document their work and may neglect proper security measures.

There are three categories of potential quality risks: (1) substandard or inappropriate tools used in IT application development; (2) risks associated with the development process (e.g., the inability to develop workable systems or the development of systems that generate erroneous results); and (3) data management risks (e.g., loss of data or use of stale, inappropriate, or incorrect data). See Regan and O'Connor (2002) and Sutcliffe and Mehandjiev (2004) for quality-control issues related to end-user development.

<table>
<tr><td>

OTHER
ACQUISITION
OPTIONS

</td><td>

A number of other acquisition options are available to IT developers, and in particular for e-commerce applications.

</td></tr>
</table>

**Join an E-Marketplace or an E-Exchange.** With this option, the company "plugs" itself into an e-marketplace. For example, a company can place its catalogs in Yahoo's marketplace.

**Join a Third-Party Auction or Reverse Auction.** Similar to the previous option, a company can plug into a third-party auction or reverse auction site fairly quickly. Alternatively, a company can join a B2B exchange that offers auctions, as described in Chapter 5.

**Engage in Joint Ventures.** There are several different partnership or joint venture arrangements that may facilitate EC application development. For example, four banks in Hong Kong have developed a joint e-banking system.

**Join a Public Exchange or a Consortium.** Finally, a company can join a public exchange (Chapter 5) or join a consortium (a vertical exchange owned by a group of big players in an industry), which may have applications developed to fit the needs of companies in the industry.

**Hybrid Approach.** A hybrid approach combines the best of what the company does internally with an outsourced strategy. Hybrid models work best when the outsourced partner offers higher security levels, faster time-to-market, and superb service-level agreements.

Criteria for selecting a development strategy are provided in Section 15.5. However, before proceeding to that topic, let's look further at the recent trend of outsourcing and ASPs.

# 15.4 Outsourcing, Application Service Providers, and Utility Computing

In developing IT applications, outsourcing is a viable option because many systems need to be built quickly and special expertise is needed. As illustrated in the opening case, Sterngold, a 100-year-old dental products manufacturer, takes the plunge into EC by trusting an application outsourcer to move its sales initiative online. IT software delivery from ASPs is another popular option.

**OUTSOURCING**

Small or medium-sized companies with few IT staff and smaller budgets are best served by outside contractors. Outside contractors have also proven to be a good choice for large companies in certain circumstances. Use of outside contractors or external organizations to acquire IT services is called **outsourcing** (Chapter 14).

According to Gartner, "the IT service market will grow to $760 billion by 2009, with more IT services purchased as part of an outsourcing arrangement than on a one-off project basis" (Potter and Brown, 2006). Gartner has also projected that nearly half of Fortune 1000 global enterprises will choose not to own their IT assets. Instead, they will derive business benefits from shared IT utility infrastructures that are owned and operated by service provider hybrids (Plummer and McCoy, 2006). Most leading enterprises today adopt outsourcing as a core strategy to achieve agility and manage changes in an ever-changing environment (see Figure 1.6 in Chapter 1).

**Offshoring.** While the trend to outsource is rising, so is the trend to offshore, mainly in India and China. **Offshoring** is the practice of migrating business processes overseas to lower costs without significantly sacrificing quality (Gottschalk and Solli-Saether, 2006). Offshore outsourcing is certainly less expensive, but it includes risks as well (see, for examples, Beulen, et al., 2005). The delivery and process risks of offshore outsourcing include cultural difference, language and communication gaps, knowledge transfer, change management, lack of mutual trust, security, and so forth. See Online File W15.3 for a discussion of the potential risks of offshore outsourcing.

One of the most common types of IT outsourcing is the use of ASPs.

**APPLICATION SERVICE PROVIDERS (ASPs)**

An **application service provider (ASP)** is a vendor who assembles the software needed by enterprises and packages it, usually with outsourced development, operations, maintenance, and other services. The essential difference between an ASP and an outsourcer is that an ASP will manage application servers in a centrally controlled location, rather than on a customer's site. Applications are then accessed via the Internet or networks through a standard Web browser interface. Such an arrangement provides a full range of services for the company using the ASP: Applications can be scaled, upgrades and maintenance can be centralized, physical security over the applications and servers can be guaranteed, and the necessary critical mass of human resources can be efficiently utilized. The determinants of ASP adoption as an innovation are discussed by Daylami et al. (2005).

In this arrangement, the client businesses pay monthly fees to the ASP. In general, the fees include payment for the application software, hardware, service and support, maintenance, and upgrades. The fee can be fixed or based on utilization. Gartner predicts that renting will be the software model of choice by 2008, with more than 50 percent of all software purchases being made on a subscription rather than license basis (reported by D'Agostino, 2005). While software buying is still widespread, leasing is growing rapidly, resulting in the success of new ASP vendors, such as *salesforce.com*.

**Benefits and Limitations of Leasing from ASPs.** Leasing IT applications from an ASP is a particularly desirable option for SME businesses, for which in-house development and operation of IT applications can be too time consuming and expensive. ASPs are particularly effective for IT applications for which timing, flexibility, and agility are crucial.

Leasing from ASPs does have its disadvantages. Many companies are concerned with the adequacy of protection offered by the ASP against hackers, theft of confidential information, and virus attacks. A detailed list of the benefits and risks associated with ASPs is provided in Figure 15.3.

| Type | Benefits | Potential Risks |
|---|---|---|
| Business | Reduces the need to attract and retain skilled IT professionals<br>Enables companies to concentrate on strategic use of IT<br>Enables small-and medium-sized companies to use tier-1 applications (e.g., BI, ERP, SCM, and CRM)<br>Application scalability enables rapid growth of companies | Loss of control and high level of dependence on ASP<br>Inability of ASP to deliver quality of service; lack of skills and experience |
| Technical | Fast and easy application deployment<br>Higher degree of application standardization<br>Access to wide range of applications<br>Application maintenance simplified and performed by ASP<br>Simplified user support and training | Level of customization and legacy application integration offered by ASP is insufficient<br>Low reliability and speed of delivery due to bandwidth limitations<br>Low capability of ASP to deal with security and confidentiality issues |
| Economic | Low total cost of ownership<br>Low up-front investments in hardware and software<br>Improved cost control as result of predictable subscription costs | Pricing changes by ASP unpredictable for application updates and services |
| Maintenance | Maintenance is done by vendor to many customers<br>Can select another application from the ASP to meet changing needs<br>Not to further invest in upgrading the existing one | Modification may not fit your needs exactly<br>Becoming the victim of pass-the-buck syndrome when you call for technical support; ASP may not control all these processes of a system failure |

**Figure 15.3** Benefits and risks of using an ASP. (*Sources:* Kern and Kreijger, 2001, and Schachter, 2002.)

An interesting institution is the ASP Industry Consortium (*aspstreet.com*), whose founding members include AT&T, Cisco, Citrix Systems, Ernst & Young, Verizon, IBM, Marimba, Sharp Electronics, Sun Microsystems, UUNet, and Verio. Information about the general state of the ASP market space can be obtained from Computing Technology Industry Association's (CompTIA) Software Services (*comptia.org/sections/ssg/default.asp*).

An important variation of leasing and ASP is *utility computing.*

**UTILITY (ON-DEMAND) COMPUTING**

Tapping into computing resources with the simplicity equal to plugging an electrical lamp into an outlet has been a goal of many companies for years. The approach is known as **utility computing.** The idea is to provide unlimited computing power and storage capacity that can be used and reallocated for any application—and billed on a pay-per-use basis.

As shown in Figure 15.4, the utility-computing value proposition consists of three layers of tools and two types of value-added services. Each tool must be integrated to create a comprehensive solution, but usually will be implemented separately.

Utility computing faces obstacles. One obstacle is the immaturity of the tools. Another is the fact that each vendor prefers to push its own unique variation on the utility-computing vision and standards, with different names and terminology. However, utility computing will accelerate acceptance of ASPs, which may distribute it as discussed in Online File W15.4. For current information on utility computing, see *utilitycomputing.com.*

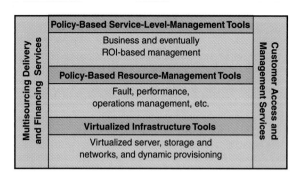

**Figure 15.4** The five elements of a successful utility-computing value proposition. (*Source:* Kucharvy, 2003.)

# 15.5 Selecting an Acquisition Approach and Other Implementation Issues

This section is about selecting an acquisition approach, vendor and software selection, and implementation issues.

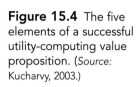

**CRITERIA FOR SELECTING AN IT ACQUISITION APPROACH**

A major issue faced by any company is which method(s) of acquisition to select. To do so, the company must consider many criteria, such as those provided in Table 15.2. Some criteria may conflict with others, so managers must decide which criteria are most important. For a discussion of the criteria in the table, see Online File W15.5.

Using all the previous criteria, an organization can select one or more methods for acquiring IT systems. A comparison of the buy/build/rent options is given in Table 15.3.

For additional information on the selection of an IT acquisition approach, see Satzinger et al. (2006) and Whitten and Bentley (2007).

**VENDOR AND SOFTWARE SELECTION**

Externally acquired IT applications should be evaluated to ensure that they provide the following advantages:

- **On-time.** Completion and implementation of the system by the scheduled target date.
- **On-budget.** System cost is within budget.
- **Full functionality.** System has all features in the original specifications.

| TABLE 15.2 | Criteria for Determining Which Acquisition Approach to Use |
|---|---|
| • The functionality and flexibility of packages | • Ability to measure tangible benefits |
| • Information requirements | • Personnel needed for development |
| • User friendliness of the application | • Forecasting and planning for technological evolution (what will come next) |
| • Hardware and software resources | |
| • Installation difficulties; integration | • Scaling (ease, cost, limits) |
| • Maintenance services requirements | • Sizing requirements |
| • Vendor quality and track record | • Performance requirements |
| • Estimated total costs of ownership | • Reliability requirements |
| | • Security requirements |

| **TABLE 15.3** | The Rent versus Buy versus Build Consideration | | |
|---|---|---|---|
| **Consider software as a service (to rent) if your company . . .** | **Consider a traditional license (to buy) if . . .** | **Consider an in-house development (to build) if . . .** |
| has an expense budget that is larger than its capital budget | the application requires a fair degree of customization or integration | the application or the development platform is unique |
| has limited IT support | you have a team of experienced IT personnel | you need to reward your dedicated internal IT staff |
| has a distributed workforce | you have already invested significantly in internal IT operations | you have very expensive investment in legacy systems |
| has a sales- or service-oriented business model | laws require data to remain behind your firewall | you need absolute control of your data |
| has ever-changing computing needs and requirements | your needs for computing resources are relatively stable | you need a fixed amount of computing resources |
| needs to free IT resources to focus on critical business operations | the application is tied to a major function of your business | the application is critical to your core business |

*Sources:* D'Agostino (2005) and Witner and Krumwiede (2003).

Several independent organizations and magazines conduct software comparisons. For smaller packages, users can use "trialware" (e.g., *trialware.org*) from the Internet before purchase. Most vendors offer demo software for a limited testing time. Also, vendors may demonstrate the software. Six steps in selecting a vendor and software package are:

**1.** Determine the evaluation criteria and weight the importance of each.
**2.** Identify potential vendors.
**3.** Evaluate vendors and packages and interview current users.
**4.** Choose the vendor and package based on criteria, weights, and feedback.
**5.** Negotiate a contract and get legal advice.
**6.** Establish a service-level agreement (SLA).

These six steps are illustrated in Figure 15.5 and explained in Online File W15.6.

**OTHER IMPLEMENTATION ISSUES**

The following implementation issues are related to IT resource acquisition.

- **Insource or outsource Web site?** Many large enterprises are capable of running their own publicly accessible Web sites for advertising purposes. However, Web sites for online selling may involve complex integration, security, and performance issues. For those companies venturing into such Web-based selling, a key issue is whether the site should be built in-house, thus providing more direct control, or outsourced to a more experienced provider. Outsourcing services, which allow companies to start small and evolve to full-featured functions, are available through many ISPs, telecommunications companies, and software vendors.

- **Consider an ASP.** The use of ASPs is recommended for SMEs and should be considered by many large companies as well.

- **Evaluate the alternatives to in-house systems development.** In-house systems development requires highly skilled employees to undertake a complex project. Organizations may sometimes find it preferable to acquire IT resources rather than build in-house. Methods for acquiring IT resources outside the information

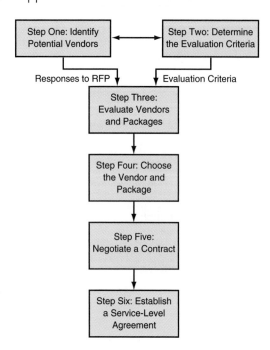

**Figure 15.5** The process of selecting a vendor and software package. (*Source:* Drawn by E. Turban.)

systems department include purchase, lease, outsourcing, use of ASPs, and end-user development.

- **Do a detailed IT architecture study.** Some companies rush this process, which can be a big mistake. If the high-level conceptual planning is wrong, the entire project is at great risk.
- **Security and ethics.** During the IT acquisition process, pay close attention to security risks. It is likely that vendors and business partners will be involved. Protecting customers' privacy is a must, and consideration of how to use clickstream and other data legally is essential.

## 15.6 Connecting to Databases, Enterprise Systems, and Business Partners: Integration (Step 4)

IT applications, especially large ones, need to be connected to other systems (e.g., ERP) and infrastructure (including databases). They also must be connected to such items as partners' systems or public exchanges. Such connections are referred to as integration and are the subject of this section. See also Chapters 7 and 8, and Hodge et al. (2005) and Chang (2005) for related discussion.

**CONNECTING TO DATABASES**

Most IT applications need to be connected to a database. For example, when you receive a customer's order, you must check if the item is in stock. To check availability, the ordering system needs to be connected to the inventory system. Several possibilities exist. Customers with a Web browser can access catalogs in the seller's database, request specific data, and receive an instant response. Here the application server manages the client's requests. The application server also acts as the front end to complex databases.

**CONNECTING TO BACK-END SYSTEMS**

In addition to connecting to back-end databases, many IT applications also require integration with a variety of other systems—ERP, CRM, KM, SCM, EDI, data warehouses, and other applications both inside and outside the company. The integration can also be handled with a class of software called *enterprise application integration* (EAI). These products integrate large systems. TIBCO (*tibco.com*), WebMethods (*Webmethods.com*), and WebSphere InterChange Server from *ibm.com* are examples of companies that have offerings in the EAI arena.

As learned from the opening case, Sterngold needed to integrate the ordering system with the back office (order fulfillment, inventory, accounting and payment). The integration required a study and redesign of existing processes.

**CONNECTING TO BUSINESS PARTNERS**

Connecting to business partners is critical, especially for B2B e-commerce. As described in Chapter 9, such connection is done via EDI, EDI/Internet, XML, and extranets.

Connection to business partners along the supply chain involves connecting a company's front- and back-office e-commerce applications, as shown in Figure 15.6. In addition to the networking problem, one must deal with issues of connectivity, compatibility, security, scalability, and more.

Companies connect to business partners for many reasons (e.g., to better work with vendors' designers, as in the case of Boeing described in Online File W15.7). Another example is content visualization from a partner's Web site; see *IT at Work 15.3*. Both internal and external integration can be improved by using Web Services.

**WEB SERVICES AND SERVICE-ORIENTED ARCHITECTURE (SOA) FOR INTEGRATION**

**Web Services** are self-contained, self-describing business and consumer applications delivered over the Internet that users can select and combine through almost any device, ranging from personal computers to mobile phones. In a *service-oriented style of architecture* (SOA), software components such as Web Services can be invoked by other programs that act as clients or consumers of those services (see also Chapter 2).

With Web Services and SOA, functions within existing programs and within ERP (enterprise resource planning), CRM (customer relationship management), SCM (supply chain management), and other packages can be automatically invoked and executed anywhere in the world based on business rules. As illustrated in the Merrill Lynch case (Minicase 1), Web Services and SOA provide inexpensive and rapid solutions for integration across different hardware, operating systems, new applications, and legacy systems. Furthermore, business processes that are

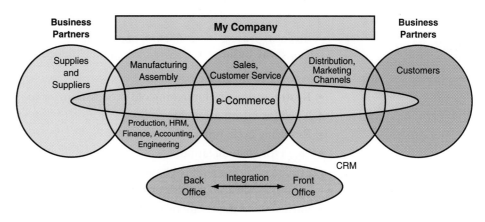

**Figure 15.6** Connecting to business partners. (*Source:* Drawn by E. Turban.)

# IT at Work 15.3

## Lincoln Financial Excels by Using Web Services

**$**

**FIN**

Lincoln Financial is a $5 billion provider of life insurance, retirement products, and wealth management services. It distributes its offerings through financial advisors, banks, and independent brokers. In most of the insurance industry, if consumers want to access their accounts or download a form from a broker site, they click on a link that takes them to the insurance provider's site, where they input a separate password or user ID. To become a "partner of choice" on such sites, Lincoln Financial wanted tighter integration with brokers' Web sites. But Lincoln also wanted to go a step further, providing content and account access within its partners' Web sites, as well as single sign-on for consumers.

This was not simple. Outlining the Lincoln content in an HTML frame would not provide the partner's look and feel. A pure Web Services approach was also out, since most of Lincoln's clients could not support that kind of system, since the partner then had to process the XML/SOAP messages. For a short time, Lincoln maintained subsites for its partners that wanted them, and those sites linked to requested content. However, maintenance of the subsites was burdensome.

The ultimate answer was Service Broker. It took three developers four months to build the pilot of Service Broker, which is a Web Services–based application with a front end that the company calls a *servlet*. When the servlet is installed on a partner's server, it provides a wrapper that can accept Lincoln's content and applications and still maintain the partner's look and feel.

The servlet manages in a Web Services application many of the functions the partner would have to manage, such as authentication, digital signature, passwords, and page rendering. When the partner wants to include Lincoln content or an application, it needs to add just one line of code.

In Spring 2004, Lincoln was the only insurer that did not require customers to leave a partner's Web site to access information. This capability provided Lincoln with competitive advantage.

*Source:* Compiled from Brandel (2004) and *lfg.com* (accessed June 2006).

*For Further Exploration:* What systems were connected between the business partners? Why was it important to maintain the partner's look and feel?

managed via Web Services and SOA adapt faster to changing customer needs and business climates than home-grown or purchased applications (Deitel et al., 2003; Shirky, 2005).

# 15.7 Business Process Redesign

Of the organizational responses to environmental pressures (Chapter 1), business process redesign and its variants have received a lot of management attention (e.g., see Reijers and Mansar, 2005, and Al-Mashari, 2006). A variant and predecessor of business process redesign is business process reengineering. In this section, we will explore business process redesign. Let's begin by looking at some of its drivers.

**THE DRIVERS OF PROCESS REDESIGN**

A **business process** is a collection of activities that convert inputs into outputs. Some reasons why business process redesign may be needed are listed below:

- Adding commercial software
- Restructuring or eliminating old processes prior to automation
- Need for information integration
- Reducing cycle time
- Need for customization
- Streamlining the supply chain
- Improving customer service and implementing CRM
- Participating in private or public e-marketplaces

- Conducting e-procurement
- Enabling direct online marketing
- Transforming to e-business

See Online File W15.8 for a detailed discussion of the BPR drivers.

**METHODOLOGIES FOR RESTRUCTURING**

**Business process reengineering (BPR)** is a methodology in which an organization *fundamentally* and *radically* changes its business processes to achieve *dramatic improvement*. Initially, BPR referred to *complete restructuring* of organizations (Hammer and Champy, 2001). The concept later changed to include only one of a few processes (rather than an entire organization) due to numerous failures of BPR projects (e.g., Sarker and Lee, 1999) and the emergence of Web-based applications that solved many of the problems that BPR was supposed to solve. Today, the concept of BPR has been refined to *business process redesign,* which can focus on anything from the redesign of an individual process to redesign of a group of processes (e.g., processes involved in e-procurement), to redesign of the entire enterprise (see El Sawy, 2001). Another extension of BPR is business process management.

**Business process management (BPM)** is a new method for restructuring that combines workflow systems (Chapter 9) and redesign methods. This emerging methodology covers three process categories: people-to-people, systems-to-systems, and systems-to-people interactions, all from a process-centered perspective. In other words, BPM is a blending of workflow, process management, and applications integration. For further information about BPM software and vendors, see *plmworld.org* and Chapter 9. Business process redesign, or even the redesign of only one process, depends on IT, which we address in the next section.

**THE ROLE OF IT IN BUSINESS PROCESS REDESIGN**

IT has been used to improve productivity and quality by automating existing processes. However, when it comes to restructuring or redesign, the traditional process of looking at problems first and then seeking technology solutions for them may need to be reversed. A new approach is first to recognize powerful solutions that make redesign and BPR possible, and then to seek the processes that can be helped by such solutions.

Process redesign can break old rules that limit the manner in which work is performed. Some typical rules are given in Online File W15.9. IT-supported redesign and BPR examples can be found in any industry, private or public (e.g., MacIntosh, 2003, and Folorunson and Ogunde, 2005). The role of IT in redesigning business processes can be very critical and is increasing due to the Internet and intranets (Salladurai, 2002).

**IT Tools for Business Process Redesign.** A large variety of IT tools can be used to support redesign and BPR. Some of these tools are generic and can be used for other purposes, while others are specifically designed for redesign and BPR.

According to El Sawy (2001), *special BPR software* enables the capture of the key elements of a business process in a visual representation made up of interconnected objects on a timeline. The elements of this visual representation usually include activities, sequencing, resources, times, and rules. BPR software is much more than drawing or flowcharting software in that the objects on the screen are intelligent and have process and organizational data and rules associated with them. The software is also interactive in real time. BPR software may incorporate some aspects of project management in terms of allocating resources and costs to work activities and their time sequencing. BPR software also has what-if capabilities in that it enables process simulation and performance comparison of alternative process designs. The ten major reasons why special BPR software is of value for business process redesign are summarized in Online File W15.10.

However, for many projects there is no need for a comprehensive suite; in those situations, generic tools or special tools designed to be used for only one or two BPR activities are both efficient and effective. Examples of generic and single-activity tools include: simulation and visual simulation tools, flow diagrams, work analysis, workflow software, comprehensive modeling tools, and integrated toolkits.

**BPR AND INFORMATION INTEGRATION**

One objective of redesign is to overcome problems by integrating fragmented information systems. Besides creating inefficient redundancies, information systems developed along departmental or functional boundaries, making it difficult to generate the information required for effective decision making. Integration may cross not only departmental boundaries, but also organizational ones, reaching suppliers and customers. Namely, it should work along the extended supply chain. This is especially important in B2B e-marketplaces and exchanges.

The integration of an organization's information systems can offer new capabilities such as the introduction of a single point of contact for customers (e.g., a case manager or a deal structurer). We can see how this single point of contact works by looking at a credit-approval process at IBM. The old process took seven days and eight steps. It involved creation of a paper folder that was routed sequentially through four departments (sales, credit check, business practices, finance, and back to sales). In the redesigned process, one person, the deal structurer, conducts all the necessary tasks. This one generalist replaces four specialists. An expert system provides the deal structurer with the guidance needed to find information in the databases, plugging numbers into an evaluation model, and pulling standardized clauses (boilerplates) from a file. For difficult situations, the generalist can get help from a specialist. As a result, the turnaround time has been slashed from seven days to four hours.

**BPR FAILURES AND SUCCESSES**

During the 1990s, there were many success stories of BPR (Grant, 2002; El Sawy, 2001) and just as many cases of failures.

- **BPR failures.** The PROSCI organization conducted a survey of several hundred companies to learn the best BPR practices and the reasons for BPR failures, which can be found at the organization's Web site (*prosci.com*). Another summary of research into business process redesign failure is available at *managingchange.com/bpr/bprcult/4bprcult.htm*. The summary indicates a failure rate of 50 to 80 percent. Some of the reasons cited for failure are high risk, inappropriate change management, failure to plan, internal politics, lack of participation and leadership, insufficient stakeholder involvement, poor analyses of business processes, inflexible software, lack of motivation, and lack of top management support.

- **BPR successes.** Despite the high failure rate of business process redesign, there are many cases of success, especially when less than the entire organization is restructured. While BPR failures tend to get more widespread publicity, success stories are published mostly by vendors and in academic and trade journals. For example, there is evidence of the success of BPR in the public sector (MacIntosh, 2003). Khong and Richardson (2003) report on extensive BPR activities and successes in banking and finance companies in Malaysia; Hughes, et al. (2005) describe the critical role of business process redesign in successfully creating e-government in Ireland.

Organizations should consider restructuring their business processes or sometimes the entire business. See Online File W15.11 for a full description of restructuring processes and organizations. When successful, redesign has great potential to improve an organization's competitive position.

# 15.8 Managerial Issues

**GLOBAL**

**1. Global and cultural issues.** Developing systems across organizations and countries could result in problems in any phase of system development. For example, in developing the Nagano Olympics system in 1998, IBM found at the last minute that pro-North-Korea groups in Japan took offense at a reference to the Korean War written on the Web site. Although the material was taken from the *World Book Encyclopedia,* it offended some people. IBM had to delete the reference and provide an apology. IBM commented, "Next time we're going to do a ton of research first versus just do it and find out the hard way." A special difficulty exists with Internet-related projects, where legislation is still evolving.

Offshore outsourcing is increasingly a proper option for IT systems acquisition. Yet many offshore outsourcing relationships get into trouble due to cultural differences where both the client and vendor organizations believe they are fulfilling their obligations, yet both sides end up being disappointed with the results and frustrated with the relationship. The client organization must take the time to understand the vendor's cultural milieu and educate the internal organization on these differences. This may entail developing teambuilding workshops with the vendor organization to help identify and bridge the cultural differences (Power et al., 2004).

**ETHICS**

**2. Ethical and legal issues.** In designing systems, one should consider the people in the system. Redesigning IT systems means that some employees will have to completely reengineer their work. Some may feel too old to do so. Conducting supply chain or business process reorganization may result in the need to lay off, retrain, or transfer employees. Should management notify the employees in advance regarding such possibilities? What about those older employees who may be difficult to retrain?

Other ethical issues may involve sharing computing resources or personal information, which may be part of the new organizational culture. Finally, individuals may have to share computer programs that they designed for their departmental use, and may resist doing so because they consider such programs their intellectual property. Conducting interviews to find managers' needs and requirements must be done with full cooperation. Measures to protect privacy must be taken. Appropriate planning must take these and other issues into consideration.

**IS**

**3. User involvement.** The direct and indirect users of a system are likely to be the most knowledgeable individuals concerning requirements and alternatives that will be the most effective. Users are also the most affected by a new information system. IS analysts and designers, on the other hand, are likely to be the most knowledgeable individuals concerning technical and data-management issues as well as the most experienced in arriving at viable systems solutions. Functional managers must participate in the development process and should understand all the phases. They must also participate in the make-or-buy decisions and software selection decisions. The right mixture of user involvement and information systems expertise is crucial.

**HRM**

**4. Change management.** People use information systems and get used to how existing systems work. They may react to new systems in unexpected ways, making even the best technically designed systems useless. Changes brought about by information systems need to be managed effectively. Of special interest is the issue of motivating programmers to increase their productivity by learning new tools and reusing preprogrammed modules.

Technology transfer is a transfer of knowledge rather than physical devices. It is now increasingly recognized that changes in technology and work processes are fundamentally culture changes, and preparing organizational members for such culture changes is an important undertaking that cannot be ignored.

*FIN*

**5. Risk management.** Building information systems involves risk. Systems may not be completed, completed too late, or require more resources than planned. The risk is large in enterprise systems (Levine, 2004). It is helpful to think of IT system acquisition as a process of embodying technical knowledge and knowledge of customer needs into a coherent solution. Under this view, those who want to understand and manage the risks associated with IT systems acquisition must first focus on the translation of customer needs into project requirements and specifications. See Tiwana and Keil (2004) for a risk assessment tool that can be used to perform intuitive what-if analyses to guide managers in determining how they can proactively reduce IT project risk.

## Integrating *IT*

### For the Accounting Major

Accounting professionals are often required to work closely with those in information technology on the design of IT systems specifications and acquisition of enterprise systems applications such as electronic commerce and data warehouses. Accountants play important managerial, advisory, and evaluative roles in connection with the acquisition of various information technologies by organizations of all types and sizes. To maintain the accountancy profession's credibility and capability in supporting new, strategic information technology initiatives, the competence of accountants in IT resources acquisition must be preserved and enhanced.

### For the Finance Major

Since the bursting of the dot-com bubble, information systems projects require significant financial justification. The strategy to acquire IT resources (to buy or to rent or to build) today is a major managerial as well as financial decision. The choice of systems acquisition is heavily determined by financial considerations such as the total cost of ownership (TCO) and return on investment (ROI). Multiple sets of assumptions and implementation plans look into every facet of an IT project's costs and expected benefits. IT project evaluation thus requires valuable advice and input from financial professionals.

### For the Human Resources Management Major

IT systems acquisition is not an acquisition of hardware and software, but a knowledge acquisition. People do not pay for technology; they pay for what they can get from technology. The importance of training on the use of a new IT-based system cannot be overemphasized. Training includes the transmission of technical expertise to fundamental change of work activities and attitudes. Thus, the role of the human resources professional in providing adequate and proper training to end users is critical in IT systems acquisition.

### For the IS Major

The subject of information systems grew out of computer science to fill a gap created by the failure of computer programmers to understand and solve business problems. An information systems professional, by virtue of background and training, plays a key role in IT acquisition. The processes of systems acquisition—from project planning to the creation of IT architecture, to the acquisition (buying, leasing or building) of technology, testing, integration, and implementation of IT systems—all require extensive skills and knowledge from IS professionals.

### For the Marketing Major

An organization should leverage the power of technology and the strategic vision of marketing during the process of IT systems acquisition. To improve Web traffic and increase orders and revenue, the marketing staff can redevelop the content of the Web site so that it speaks to the audience in clear, action-oriented language. Then the IT staff can explore ways to capture the traffic that comes in and organize it in ways that marketing can use. Marketing professionals should always consider what they can achieve if a particular IT infrastructure and system is acquired.

### For the Production/Operations Management Major

An organization acquires IT capability not just to automate, but also to redesign its existing business processes. The implementation of enterprise systems is a technological change that leads to organizational and cultural changes. Production and operations management (POM) traditionally focuses on managing processes to produce and distribute products and services. A great deal of POM focus is on efficiency and effectiveness of processes. Therefore, the expertise and services from POM professionals are needed to stabilize and fully utilize an acquired IT infrastructure and system.

## Key Terms

Application service provider
(ASP) *600*

Business process *610*

Business process management
(BPM) *611*

Business process reengineering
(BPR) *611*

End-user computing *602*

End-user development *602*

IT architecture *595*

Offshoring *604*

Outsourcing *604*

Software-as-a service (SaaS) *600*

Utility computing *605*

Web Services *609*

## Chapter Highlights

(Numbers Refer to Learning Objectives)

❶ Information systems acquisition includes all approaches to obtaining systems: buying, leasing, or building. The objective of IT application acquisition is to create, buy, or rent applications and implement them.

❶ The process of acquiring IT applications can be divided into five steps: planning and justification; IT architecture creation; selecting development options; testing, installing, and integrating new applications; and conducting operations and maintenance. This process needs to be managed.

❷ There are several sources for identifying new projects (applications) such as the need to solve a business problem. The justification process is basically a comparison of the expected costs versus the benefits of each application. The planning of projects involves schedules, milestones, and resource allocation.

❸ The major options for acquiring applications are buy, lease, or build (develop in-house). Other options are joint ventures and use of e-marketplaces or exchanges (private or public).

❸ Building in-house can be done by using the SDLC, by using prototyping or other methodologies, and it can be done by outsourcers, the IS department employees, or end users (individually or together).

❹ Many enterprises elect to outsource the development and maintenance of their IT applications. The most common type of IT applications outsourcing is the use of application service providers (ASPs). Utility computing is an emerging option.

❹ ASPs lease software applications, usually via the Internet. Fees for the leased applications can be the same each month or can be based on actual usage (like electricity). This is the basic idea of utility computing, which will be provided by ASPs or by software vendors.

❺ In deciding how to acquire applications, companies must consider multiple criteria. These criteria may conflict (e.g., quality and price). Companies need to make sure that all criteria are considered and to evaluate the importance of each criterion for the company.

❻ The process of vendor and software selection is composed of six steps: identify potential vendors, determine evaluation criteria, evaluate vendors and packages, choose the vendor and package, negotiate a contract, and establish service-level agreements.

❼ Most of the implementation issues are related to decisions regarding selection of development options and vendor and software selection. Also, security and ethics need to be considered.

❽ New applications need to be connected to databases, other enterprise systems, and so on inside the organization. They may also be connected to partners' information systems. Web Services and service-oriented architecture (SOA) provide inexpensive and rapid solution for application integration.

❾ Introducing new technology may require restructure or redesign of processes. Also, processes may need to be redesigned to fit standard software. Several methodologies exist for redesigning processes, notably BPR and BPM. IT can help in analyzing, combining, improving, and simplifying business processes.

## Virtual Company Assignment

### Acquiring Information Systems for The Wireless Café

Go to The Wireless Cafés link on the Student Web Site. There you will be asked to plan and recommend how to proceed in upgrading and adding information systems for the restaurant.

*Instructions for accessing The Wireless Café on the Student Web Site:*

1. Go to *wiley.com/college/turban.*
2. Select Turban/Leidner/McLean/Wetherbe's *Information Technology for Management,* Sixth Edition.
3. Click on Student Resources site, in the toolbar on the left.
4. Click on the link for Virtual Company Web site.
5. Click on Wireless Café.

## Online Resources

More resources and study tools are located on the Student Web Site and on WileyPLUS. You'll find additional chapter materials and useful Web links. In addition, self-quizzes that provide individualized feedback are available for each chapter.

## Questions for Review

1. List and briefly discuss the five steps of the information systems acquisition process.
2. List the options of system acquisition.
3. Describe some implementation and management issues.
4. What is involved in identifying IT projects? How is such identification done?
5. What is the basic idea of justifying an application?
6. List the major acquisition and development strategies.
7. Compare the buy option against the lease option.
8. List the in-house development approaches.
9. Describe end-user development and cite its advantages and limitations.
10. List other acquisition options.
11. What are the major factors driving a switch to software-as-a-service?
12. Define outsourcing.
13. Is outsourcing a viable option for IT acquisition?
14. What type of companies provide outsourcing services?
15. Define ASPs and list their advantages to companies using them.
16. List some disadvantages of ASPs.
17. Define utility computing and describe its benefits.
18. List five criteria for selecting a development option.
19. List the major steps of selection of a vendor and a software package.
20. List three major implementation issues.
21. List some internal systems that usually need to be connected to new applications.
22. Why is it especially important to connect to databases?
23. Define Web Services and service-oriented architecture.
24. What is mainly connected between business partners?
25. Why is integration critical to the success of IT systems acquisition?
26. Define business processes and BPR.
27. List the drivers of process redesign.
28. Define BPM.
29. Describe the enabling role of IT in BPR.
30. Why do so many BPR projects fail?

## Questions for Discussion

1. Discuss the advantages of leasing an IT application over purchasing one.
2. Why is it important for all business managers to understand the issues of IT resource acquisition?
3. Review the opening case. What approach was used to develop an information systems plan?
4. Discuss the relationship between IT planning (Chapter 13) and project (application) planning.
5. You have decided to use a third-party application to develop and deploy a Web-based EC system. Create a checklist for determining which third-party EC application products will best meet your application requirements.
6. A firm decides to make its EC system more dynamic by tying its application to a back-end data warehouse. What are some of the ways in which the firm could accomplish this task?

**7.** Discuss the reasons why end-user-developed IT systems can be of poor quality. What can be done to improve the situation?

**8.** End-user systems developers usually work for managers whose IT knowledge is limited. Discuss the types of problems to which this situation could lead, and suggest possible ways of dealing with these problems.

**9.** Discuss the role of ASPs. Why is their attractiveness increasing? (*Hint:* Consider utility computing.)

**10.** Identify the major reasons why utility computing tools may become the next big thing in IT systems acquisition.

**11.** Discuss the relationship between system acquisition and business process restructuring.

**12.** Explain why IT is an important enabler of business process redesign.

**13.** Some people say that BPR is a special case of a strategic information system, whereas others say that the opposite is true. Comment.

## Exercises and Projects

**1.** Enter *ecommerce.internet.com*. Find the product review area. Read reviews of three software payment solutions. Assess them as possible components.

**2.** Prepare a comparison of the following utility computing initiatives: IBM's On Demand, HP's Adaptive Enterprise, and Fujitsu's Triole Utility. What is the focus of each? What are their strategies?

**3.** Examine some business processes in your university or company. Identify two processes that need to be redesigned. Employ some of the discussed BPR drivers to plan the redesign. Be innovative.

**4.** Explore project management software on vendors' Web sites. Select a single project management package, download the demo, and try it. Make a list of the important features of the package. Be sure to investigate its Web, repository, and collaboration features. Report your findings to the class.

## Group Assignments and Projects

**1.** Assessment of the functionality of an application is a part of the planning process (step 1). Select three to five Web sites catering to the same type of buyer (e.g., several sites that offer CDs or computer hardware), and divide the sites among the teams. Each team will assess the functionality of its assigned Web site by preparing an analysis of the different sorts of functions provided by the site. In addition, the team should assess the strong and weak points of its site from the buyer's perspective.

**2.** Divide into groups, with each group visiting a local company (include your university). At each firm, study the systems acquisition process. Find out the methodology or methodologies used by each organization and the types of application to which each methodology applies. Prepare a report and present it to the class.

**3.** As a group, design an information system for a startup business of your choice. Describe your chosen IT resource acquisition strategy, and justify your choices of hardware, software, telecommunications support, and other aspects of a proposed system.

**4.** Have teams from the class visit IT acquisition efforts at local companies. Team members should interview members of the project team to ascertain the following information.

**a.** How does the project contribute to the goals and objectives of the company?

**b.** Is there any information architecture in place? If so, how does this project fit into that architecture?

**c.** How was the project justified?

**d.** What project planning approach, if any, was used?

**e.** How is the project being managed?

## Internet Exercises

**1.** *DMReview.com*'s Software Demo Lab allows visitors to preview the latest software from industry vendors. Try some of the Software Demo on EC applications.

**2.** Enter the Web sites of the GartnerGroup (*gartnergroup.com*), the Yankee Group (*yankeegroup.com*), and *CIO* (*cio.com*). Search for recent material about ASPs and outsourcing, and prepare a report on your findings.

**3.** Enter the Web site of IDC (*idc.com*) and find out how the company evaluates ROI on portals, supply chain, and other IT projects.

**4.** Enter *teradatastudentnetwork.com* and take the Web-based course, "What Do Business & IT Have in Common?" (*teradata.com/t/page/145089/index.html*). Learn how to create a data warehouse that meets your needs and expectations.

**5.** Visit the Web site of Resource Management Systems (*rms.net*) and take the IT Investment Management Approach Assessment Self-Test (*rms.net/self_test.htm*). Compare your organization's IT decision-making process with those of best-practices organizations.

6. StoreFront (*storefront.net*) is the leading vendor of e-business software. At its site, the company provides demonstrations illustrating the types of storefronts that it can create for shoppers. The site also provides demonstrations of how the company's software is used to create a store.

   a. Run the StoreFront 6.0 demonstration to see how this is done.

   b. What sorts of features does StoreFront 6.0 provide?

   c. Does StoreFront 6.0 support larger or smaller stores?

   d. What other products does StoreFront offer for creating online stores? What types of stores do these products support?

7. Surf the Internet to find some recent material on the role IT plays in support of BPR. Search for products and vendors and download an available demo.

8. Identify some newsgroups that are interested in BPM. Initiate a discussion on the role of IT in BPM.

9. Enter *gensym.com* and find their modeling products. Explain how they support BPR and redesign.

---

## Minicase 1

## Web Services Give Merrill's Legacy Systems New Life in the Web World

**FIN**

### The Problem

Merrill Lynch (*ml.com*) is one of the world's leading financial management and advisory companies, with offices in 36 countries and territories. Founded in 1914, Merrill has a huge IBM mainframe installation—one of the largest in the world—with 1,200 programmers supporting some 23,000 mainframe programs that process 80 million transactions per day.

There are limitations to Merrill's mainframe infrastructure. As new Internet-based applications, such as self-help credit card balance checks, were being developed, programmers needed to access data locked in the mainframe vaults. It is difficult to tap directly into those vaults using nonmainframe-based software. Merrill tried copying the data into Oracle, Sybase, or Microsoft SQL databases, which could more easily integrate with server-based applications. But the copying of the data created two problems: Copying tends to be unreliable because of disk errors, read errors, and running-out-of-space errors. Second, the data could be out-of-date as soon as it was copied. For example, a client making several trades would have to wait until the following day to see an accurate balance in his account. As a result, a client might make a trade believing there were adequate funds, but that trade would have to be rejected because, in fact, the funds were not available.

It was estimated that 90 percent of all new development costs would involve the plumbing to integrate mainframe applications with newer platforms.

### The Solution

Web Services seemed the ideal solution to the challenge. In 2001, Merrill Lynch created a service-oriented architecture platform (SOAP) that it named X4ML (ML for Modernizing Legacy) to leverage its heavy investment in mainframe applications and hardware. X4ML enables mainframe legacy programs and the functions contained within them to be exposed as Web Services.

It was possible to open up Merrill's mainframe vault to modern applications. In a simple scenario, a client using an online application to look up his credit card balance submits a request via a Web browser. The mainframe runs the requested operation (obtain credit card balance) and sends the information back to the client via SOAP. X4ML makes it easier for the mainframe to interpret the online application, and in turn assists in allowing the online program to understand the response delivered by the mainframe.

There was a centralized directory for listing Web Services at Merrill so that programmers could reuse and combine services that had been developed. Creating new applications from the Web Services then became a matter of accessing and combining operations in the directory.

The value of Web Services was demonstrated over the last three years when Merrill launched a $1 billion effort to create a new suite of applications for wealth management that are available for use by Merrill's 14,000 desktop financial advisers.

### The Results

Since 2001, the in-house development team of Merrill has generated more than 420 Web Services by reusing existing legacy applications. There was no need to purchase additional hardware or to change application codes on the mainframe systems. The company managed to use Web Services technology to cut as much as (US$42 million) 90 percent of the cost of developing new applications. As a result, the profit margin of Merrill increased from 17 percent in 2001 to 28.5 percent in 2005.

In December 2005, Merrill sold the X4ML technology for an undisclosed sum to SOA Software, a Los Angeles–based vendor of service-oriented architecture systems. X4ML has since been renamed Service-Oriented Legacy Architecture (SOLA).

By building a service-oriented architecture, Merrill easily integrated its decades-old legacy applications with new Web-based software and has preserved the firm's multibillion-dollar investment in mainframe technology.

*Sources*: Compiled from Duvall (2006), Joshi and Namjoshi (2006), and from *ml.com* (accessed June 2006).

## Questions for Minicase 1

1. What are the limitations of Merrill's mainframe infrastructure?

2. What IT acquisition option was selected by Merrill Lynch? Why?

3. Relate the case to the issue of integration.

4. What is the role of Web Services in integrating Merrill's legacy applications with new software?

5. What problems were solved by the use of SOA and Web Services in modernizing Merrill's mainframe technology?

6. It was trendy to talk about migrating off the mainframe in the 1990s. Do you think the mainframe will go away or remain strategic in the twenty-first century? Discuss.

---

# Minicase 2

## NCBJ Achieves a 500 Percent–Plus ROI by Rebuilding Its IT Infrastructure

### The Problem

National Commercial Bank Jamaica Limited (NCBJ) launched a project to consolidate its back-office systems and processes in 2003. By the end of 2004, the bank had trimmed approximately 150 full-time equivalents (FTEs), primarily as a result of centralizing or outsourcing back-office tasks. Nevertheless, "we did not feel we were fully leveraging our US$52 million investment," Courtney Campbell, the company's general manager of retail banking reports. "Many branches were complaining that they did not have enough staff to deliver what they'd delivered before," particularly in the crucial areas of service and sales. This was a serious problem, especially given that a central purpose of the consolidation effort was to free up branch employees to focus more on the customer.

### The Solution

Campbell and his group recognized the need to take a more scientific approach to cutting staff and assigning workloads. They also recognized the need to bring in outside help. After evaluating a number of consulting firms, NCBJ chose Demos Solutions, a Norwell, Massachusetts–based consulting and software company that has done similar projects with other large banks.

Using StaffSmart, Demos's workforce optimization software suite, Demos consultants performed a time study and analysis of current workloads at two of NCBJ's pilot branches. Using handheld devices, they timed daily transactions, such as cashing a check or closing a sale. They used regression models to help determine how much time was taken by nonautomated tasks, such as answering customer queries. Once the baseline was established, Demos used a combination of best practices, benchmarking data, and expertise garnered from past jobs to create a new branch operating model. The model is designed to "improve wait time, reduce costs, and allocate more time for selling," Demos says.

The entire workforce optimization project with Demos, including pilots at two branches, companywide rollout, and software deployment, took about eight months.

### The Results

The Demos project enabled NCBJ to reallocate an additional 175 FTEs. A 500 percent–plus ROI is projected over a two-year period, Campbell says. Less easily quantifiable, but at least as important, are the soft benefits the bank is gaining in customer satisfaction and revenue growth from reallocating FTEs from back-office work to service and sales. At least one dedicated salesperson has been added at each branch. The bank had a record month in loan sales in March, "although we can't attribute that solely" to the workforce optimization effort, Campbell notes.

Another key aspect of the Demos collaboration: Bank personnel gained the knowledge, skills, and software tools they need to analyze and optimize workforce allocations and processes on an ongoing basis. "We want to create sustainable ROI," Demos says. "We have a much more scientific basis and a tool to assess staff levels at each branch, instead of having to rely on intuition," Campbell agrees.

NCBJ learned an important lesson from acquiring its IT infrastructure: To realize the big paybacks from such an IT project, you need to do a thorough, up-front analysis of business processes and workloads. Then you can optimize processes and allocate resources where they'll do the most good.

*Sources:* Compiled from Horwitt (2006) and *jncb.com* (accessed June 2006).

## Questions for Minicase 2

1. What IT acquisition option was selected by National Commercial Bank Jamaica (NCBJ) Limited? Why?
2. Do you think the workforce optimization project at NCBJ is a high-payoff project? Why?
3. Use the Demos project as an example to discuss the relationship between systems acquisition and business process restructuring.
4. What are the wider implications of the Demos project on knowledge management at NCBJ?
5. IT systems developers have to be technical experts as well as management change agents. Discuss the concept of organizational complements to technology changes with reference to the NCBJ case.

# References

Al-Mashari, M., "Innovation through Information Technology (IT) Enabled Business Process Management (BPM): A Review of Key Issues," *International Journal of Innovation and Learning,* 8(4), 2006.

Beulen, E., P. V. Fenema, and W. Currie, "From Application Outsourcing to Infrastructure Management: Extending the Offshore Outsourcing Sever Portfolio," *European Management Journal,* 23(2), 2005.

Brandel, M. "Lincoln Financial Syndicates Content with Web Services," *ComputerWorld,* March 15, 2004.

Bussler. C., D. Fensel, and N. M. Sadeh, "Introduction to the Special Section: The Role of Semantic Web Services in Enterprise Application Integration and E-Commerce," *International Journal of Electronic Commerce,* 9(2), 2005.

Chang, V., "Design of Middleware Platform to Enhance Abilities of Application Systems Integration." *Proceedings of the International Conference on Information Technology: Coding and Computing (ITCC'05).* Washington, DC: IEEE Computer Society, 2005.

Craig, G., "Old Dental Manufacturer Adopts New IT Tricks," *Outsourcing Magazine,* November–December 2003.

D'Agostino, "Rent or Buy," *CIO Insight,* May, 2005.

Deitel, H., et al., *Web Services: A Technical Introduction.* Upper Saddle River, NJ: Prentice Hall, 2003.

Ding, Y., and N. Napier, "Measurement Framework for Assessing Risks in Component-Based Software Development," *Proceedings of the 39th Annual Hawaii International Conference on System Sciences,* Big Island, Hawaii, January 4–7, 2006.

Dragoon, A., "End-User Development: Something Wiki This Way Comes," *CIO Magazine,* April 2005.

Duvall, M., "Supercharged," *Baseline,* October, 2005.

El Sawy, O., *Redesigning Enterprise Processes for E-Business.* New York: McGraw-Hill, 2001.

Folorunso, O., and A. O. Ogunde, "Data Mining As a Technique for Knowledge Management in Business Process Redesign," *Information Management and Computer Security,* 1, September 2005.

Gottschalk, P., and H. Solli-Saether, *Managing Successful IT Outsourcing Relationships.* Hershey, PA: Idea Group, 2006.

Grant, D., "A Wilder View of Business Process Reenginnering," *Association for Computing Machinery,* 45(2) 2002.

Hammer, M., and J. Champy, *Re-engineering the Corporation.* New York: Harper Business, 2001.

Hodge, G. L. Hill, M. L. Zeng, J. Qin, and D. Tudhope, "Next Generation Knowledge Organization Systems: Integration Challenges and Strategies." *Proceedings of the 5th ACM/IEEE-CS Joint Conference on Digital Libraries.* Denver, June 7–11, 2005.

Horwitt, E., "Bank Achieves over 500% RIO in 8 Months," *Techtarget Case Study,* May 3, 2006.

Hughes, M., M. Scott, and W. Golden, "The Role of Business Process Redesign in creating E-Government in Ireland," *Business Process Management Journal,* May 2005.

IBM, "Financial Authority for Education," *IBM Case Study, 2002, www-306.ibm.com/software/success/cssdb.nsf/CS/KHAL-62GL7N? OpenDocument&Site=gicss67educ* (accessed October 2006).

Joshi, M., and J. Namjoshi, "Evolving an Agile Enterprise: A Business Case for SOA Adoption," *Patni white paper.* India: Patni Computer Systems Ltd., February 2006.

Kanter, J., and J. J. Walsh, "Toward More Successful Project Management," *Information Strategy: The Executive Journal,* Summer 2004.

Kendall, K. E., and J. E. Kendall, *Systems Analysis and Design,* 6th ed. Upper Saddle River, NJ: Prentice Hall, 2005.

Kern, T., and J. Kreijger, "An Exploration of the ASP Outsourcing Option," *Proceedings of the 34th Hawaiian International Conference on System Sciences,* Maui, Hawaii, January 3–6, 2001.

Khong, K. W., and S. Richardson, "BPR in Malaysian Banks and Finance Companies," *Managing Service Quality,* January 2003.

Kucharvy, T., *The Five Rules for Jump-Starting the Utility-Computing Market.* Boston, MA: Summit Strategies, Inc., January 2003.

Levine, R., "Risk Management Systems: Understanding the Needs," *Information Strategy—The Executive Journal,* Summer 2004.

MacIntosh, R., "BPR: Alive and Well in the Public Sector," *International Journal of Operations and Production Management,* 23(3/4), 2003.

Plummer, D. C., and D. W. McCoy, "Achieving Agility: The View through a Conceptual Framework," *Gartner Research,* ID Number: G00137820, April 2006.

Potter, K. S., and R. H. Brown, "The Future of Outsourcing: What the Numbers Tell Us," *Gartner Research,* ID Number: G00139007, May 2006.

Power, M., C. Bonifazi, and C. Desouza, "The Ten Outsourcing Traps to Avoid," *Journal of Business Strategy,* 25(2), 2004.

Rakos, J., *Managing Successful Software Development Projects* (Audio CD), ON, Canada: Multi-Media Publications Inc., September 2005.

Regan, E. A., and B. N. O'Connor, *End User-Information Systems,* 2nd Ed. Upper Saddle River, NJ: Prentice Hall, 2002.

Reijers, H. A., and S. L. Mansar, "Best Practices in Business Process Redesign: An Overview and Qualitative Evaluation of Successful Redesign Heuristics," *Omega,* August 2005.

Salladurai, R., "An Organizational Profitability, Productivity, Performance (PPP) Model: Going Beyond TQM and BPR," *Total Quality Management,* 13(5), 2002.

Sarker, S., and A. S. Lee, "IT-Enabled Organizational Transformation: A case Study of BPR Failure at TELECO," *Journal of Strategic Information Systems,* Vol. 8, 1999.

Satzinger, J. W., R. B. Jackson, and S. D. Burd, *Systems Analysis and Design in a Changing World*, 4th ed. Boston: Course Technology, 2006.

Schacter, D., "Using an Application Service Provider Has Benefits, Risks," *Denver Business Journal*, April 2002.

Shirky, C., "Web Services: An Executive Summary," *XML.com*, 2005, *webservices.xml.com/pub/a/ws/2002/04/12/execreport.html* (accessed May 2005).

Shurville, S., and J. Williams, "Managing In-House Development of a Campus-wide Information System," *Campus-Wide Information Systems*, 22(1), January 2005.

Sommerville, I., *Software Engineering*, 7th ed. Boston: Addison-Wesley, 2004.

Srivastava, B., "A Decision-Support Framework for Component Reuse and Maintenance in Software Project Management," *Proceedings of the Eighth Euromicro Working Conference on Software Maintenance and Reengineering*, Tampere, Finland, March 24–26, 2004.

Stucliffe, A., and N. Mehandjiev, "End-User Development," *Communications of the ACM*, 47(9), September 2004.

Tiwana, A., and M. Keil, "The One-Minute Risk Assessment Tool," *Communications of the ACM*, 47(11), November 2004.

Whitten, J. L., and L. D. Bentley, *Systems Analysis and Design Methods*, 7th ed. New York: Irwin/McGraw-Hill, 2005.

Witner, L., and T. Krumwiede, "Purchasing, Leasing, and Developing Software," *Tax Adviser*, 34(7), 2003.

Xia, W., and G. Lee, "Grasping the Complexity of IS Development Projects," *Communications of the ACM*, 47(5), May 2004.

Part VI | Implementing and Managing IT

13. IT Strategy and Planning
14. Information Technology Economics
15. Acquiring IT Applications and Infrastructure
▶ 16. Security
17. Impacts of IT on Individuals, Organizations, and Society

Chapter

# 16

# Security

## Learning Objectives

After studying this chapter, you will be able to:

❶ Recognize the business value of security and control.

❷ Discuss the role of the chief privacy officer and responsibility of senior management.

❸ Recognize IS vulnerabilities, threats, attack methods, and cybercrime symptoms.

❹ Describe the factors that contribute to risk exposure of an asset and methods to mitigate them.

❺ Describe the major methods of defending information systems, networks, and wireless devices.

❻ Describe IT internal control and fraud.

❼ Describe business continuity and disaster recovery planning.

❽ Discuss the role of IT in defending critical infrastructures and supporting counterterrorism.

❾ Describe the role of computer forensics in investigating and deterring security incidents.

## Integrating *IT*

**ACC**

**FIN**

**MKT**

**POM**

**HRM**

**IS**

**SVC**

# SECURITY FAILURE MOVES STOCK PRICE AT CHOICEPOINT

ChoicePoint is a leading data broker with access to 19 billion public records and information on more than 220 million U.S. citizens. The company collects personal information, including names, Social Security numbers, birthdates, employment information, and credit histories, which it then sells to over 50,000 businesses and government agencies. Marketing, human resources, accounting, and finance departments rely on ChoicePoint's data for customer leads, background checks, or verification.

## The Problem

On February 15, 2005, ChoicePoint reported that personal and financial information of 145,000 individuals had been "compromised." All the individuals were at risk of becoming victims of identity theft, but only 800 cases of identity theft actually arose from the data breach. The compromise was not due to hackers or malicious spyware. ChoicePoint had sold the information to Olatunji Oluwatosin, a Nigerian national living in California, who had pretended to represent several legitimate businesses. Ironically, Oluwatosin's credentials had not been verified, which enabled him to set up over 50 bogus business accounts with ChoicePoint. Those accounts gave him access to databases containing personal financial data. Oluwatosin was arrested in February 2005, pleaded guilty to conspiracy and grand theft, and was sentenced to 10 years in prison and fined $6.5 million. The state and federal penalties facing ChoicePoint were considerably larger and set new precedents.

At the state level, ChoicePoint was compelled to disclose what had happened. California's privacy breach legislation required ChoicePoint to inform residents that their personal information had been compromised. Within days, outraged Attorneys General in 38 other states demanded that the company notify every affected U.S. citizen. At the federal level, ChoicePoint was charged with multiple counts of negligence for failing to follow *reasonable* information security practices. The Federal Trade Commission (FTC) charged ChoicePoint with violating:

- The Fair Credit Reporting Act (FCRA), by furnishing credit reports to subscribers who did not have a permissible purpose to obtain them; and by not maintaining reasonable procedures to verify their subscribers' identities and intended use of the information

- The FTC Act, by making false and misleading statements about its privacy policies on its Web site

On March 4, 2005, in what was a first for a publicly held company, ChoicePoint filed an 8-K report with the SEC warning shareholders that revenue would be affected by the security breach. In the report, the company warned of a $20 million decline in income by December 31, 2005, and a $2 million increase in expenses from the incident. In addition, FTC fines were imminent. On January 26, 2006, the FTC announced that ChoicePoint had agreed to pay a $10 million fine, the agency's largest-ever civil penalty, plus $5 million to compensate customers for losses stemming from the data breach. Legal expenses of $800,000 were incurred in the first quarter of 2006 alone. With the announcement of the impending $15 million settlement, ChoicePoint's stock price plunged, as shown in Figure 16.1.

## The Solution

The solutions to ChoicePoint's risk exposure were mandated by the FTC as part of the settlement. The company implemented new procedures to ensure that it provides consumer reports only to legitimate businesses for lawful purposes, established and maintains a comprehensive information security program, and obtains audits by an independent third-party security professional every other year until 2026.

To reassure stakeholders and legitimate customers, ChoicePoint hired Carol DiBattiste, the former Transportation Security Administration (TSA) deputy administrator, as chief privacy officer (CPO). DiBattiste leads an independent office that reports to the board of directors. The stock market and business customers responded favorably to the new security measures and CPO.

## The Results

ChoicePoint reformed its business practices and data security measures, which were too lax relative to the growing seriousness of the threats. Its tightened security practices are costing it revenue because customers not meeting new security standards are refused. This business decision is a necessary and ethical trade-off.

**ETHICS**

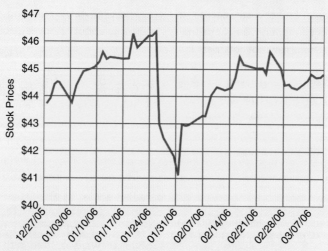

**Figure 16.1** Stock market reacts to ChoicePoint's $15 million settlement for data breach.

ChoicePoint's data breach brought businesses' security policies to national attention. Together with high-profile frauds and malware, data breaches have triggered a new era in corporate governance and accountability. CPOs and chief security officers (CSOs) gained genuine authority—no longer functioning primarily as public relations agents. The security of company assets and operations became one of the top concerns of management.

*Sources:* Compiled from *ftc.gov*, Gross (2005), Mimoso (2006), and Scalet (2005).

## Lessons Learned from This Case

IT security risks are business risks. IT security broadly refers to the protection of information and other digital assets, communication networks, and traditional and e-commerce business operations to assure their integrity, availability, and authorized use and to defend against financial loss and liability. Digital assets that are relied on for a competitive advantage include BI, ERP or CRM implementations, SOX compliance documentation, proprietary HR training material, accounts receivable management systems, and intellectual property. IT security is so integral to business objectives that it can no longer be treated as a standalone function.

IT security failures have a direct impact on business performance, often in large part because they can no longer be hidden from customers, business partners, stakeholders, or regulators. In ChoicePoint's case, there was no hacker, spyware infection, phishing, virus, denial of service (DoS) attack, or sabotage commonly associ-ated with information theft. (See Online File W16.1 for key security terminology.) The vulnerability stemmed from underestimating the risk exposure of its consumer information—and consequently to safeguards that were unreasonably weak. Information is highly attractive to criminals because it is a universal currency.

In this chapter, we begin with an overview of enterprisewide security issues. We discuss the key IT security measures, IT internal controls, and the **COBIT** framework, which help managers and other professionals gain greater value from IT and mitigate IT-related risk exposure. We introduce a **risk exposure model** for assessing reasonable levels of protection for digital assets. We describe major threats and types of fraud—and how spam, bots, and phishing have increased their incidence; business continuity plans to recover from incidents and disruptions; and computer forensics to investigate how and why incidents occurred.

# 16.1 Securing the Enterprise

Until 2002, securing business information and computer systems was considered to be a technical issue assigned to the IT department. Many companies addressed incidents on a case-by-case "cleanup" basis rather than taking a preemptive approach to protect ahead of the threats. IT security was viewed as a *cost*—rather than as a *resource* for preventing business disruptions by preventing incidents that interrupt the availability of information systems or that expose the company to liability. A cost-based view is dangerous given the global reach of cybercrimes, malware, spyware, and electronic fraud, which threaten to disrupt key information systems, steal customer and product data, misdirect money, and shut down e-commerce operations. The cleanup expenses alone of a single incident can be enormous.

**CSI/FBI COMPUTER CRIME AND SECURITY SURVEY FINDINGS**

Each year the Computer Security Institute (CSI) and the FBI conduct the *CSI/FBI Computer Crime and Security Survey.* Visit *gocsi.com* for the most recent CSI/FBI report. Compared with the 2004 survey, the 2005 survey results indicated that the loss per respondent had increased in two key categories—both related to profit-motivated crimes as shown in Table 16.1. Losses for theft of proprietary information averaged $2.7 million per company in 2005. Keep in mind that, by itself, this figure does not help guide IT in a company's security decisions. Later in this chapter, you will learn about factors and methods to determine what defensive measures are necessary for a company from operational, financial, marketing, and legal perspectives.

Not all security breaches are too sophisticated or high-tech to avoid. Some could have been prevented if IT security policies had been implemented and enforced. In May 2006, the mundane theft of a laptop computer during a burglary at the home of a Veterans Affairs employee was estimated to cost taxpayers $100 million to remedy. See *IT at Work 16.1* for a description of the Department of Veterans Affairs (VA) data theft.

**GLOBAL REACH INCREASES IS VULNERABILITY**

Information resources are distributed throughout the organization and beyond as Internet and wireless technologies extend organizational boundaries. The *time-to-exploitation* of today's most sophisticated spyware and worms has shrunk from months to days. **Time-to-exploitation** is the elapsed time between when a vulnerability is discovered and the time it is exploited. For more on spyware, see SpywareGuide, a public reference site, at *spywareguide.com*. As a result, CSOs have an ever-shorter time frame to find and fix flaws before they are compromised by an attack. New vulnerabilities are continuously being found in

| TABLE 16.1 | CSI/FBI Survey Results: Losses in 2004 and 2005 | | |
|---|---|---|---|
| | Loss per Respondent | | Percent Change from 2004 to 2005 |
| Crime Category | 2004 (n = 269) | 2005 (n = 639) | |
| Unauthorized access to information | $51,545 | $303,234 | 488% |
| Theft of proprietary information | $168,529 | $355,552 | 111% |
| Total losses from all crimes | $526,010 ($141,496,560/269) | $203,606 ($130,104,542/639) | (61%) |

# IT at Work 16.1

## VA Policy Violation and Home Burglary Cause Security Breach Estimated to Cost $100 Million

One of the largest single thefts of personal data occurred on May 3, 2006, when a laptop computer and external hard drive were stolen during a home burglary. The U.S. Department of Veterans Affairs reported that information on 26.5 million veterans and their spouses was stored in plaintext on the laptop stolen from the home of a senior-level (GS-14-level) IT specialist in the Office of Policy. He had taken the laptop and data from the office to do after-hours work on his PC. The data included veterans' names, birthdates, and Social Security numbers. The IT specialist immediately reported the theft, but it was not until 13 days later that it was reported to VA Secretary Jim Nicholson. Nicholson testified before Congress that it will cost at least $10 million to inform veterans of the security breach.

**VA Ignored Risks and Failed to Enforce Security Policy.** The VA's policy required encrypting sensitive data and prohibited removal of VA data from the offices. Employees had not been informed of the policy or realized it was not being enforced. The IT specialist, who had authorization to access sensitive information, admitted he had been routinely taking data home to do after-hours work since 2003.

**Response After the Security Breach.** To mitigate its risks, Nicholson promised a relentless investigation of VA policies on information security and implemented plans:

- To have all VA employees take cybersecurity and privacy training courses
- To increase background checks of employees with access to sensitive information
- To review data access controls to minimize employees' access to sensitive data

Despite the enormous cost of the VA's data breach, it may not scare companies into more rigorous security policy monitoring and training. Rick LeVine, a senior manager in Accenture's global security practice, predicted that "It's going to take several high-profile incidents at Fortune 500 companies to cause people to say, 'Oh, my God, one guy's cell phone can lose us a billion dollars'" (Spangler, 2006).

*Sources:* Condensed from Spangler (2006), and several articles from the *Washington Post* and *InformationWeek*, May–June 2006.

*For Further Exploration:* Could such a massive security breach happen at any company? Why or why not? Do you agree with LeVine's prediction? What prediction would you make?

---

operating systems, applications, and networks. Left undetected or unprotected, these vulnerabilities provide an open door for IT attacks—and business interruptions and their financial consequences. See Online File W16.2 for examples of incidents.

With data resources available on demand 24/7, companies clearly benefit from the opportunities for productivity improvement and data sharing with customers, suppliers, and business partners in their supply chain. IT on demand is an operational and competitive necessity for global companies, which creates vulnerabilities and the need for strong IT governance as described in *A Closer Look 16.1*.

**NATIONAL AND INTERNATIONAL REGULATIONS DEMAND TOUGHER IT SECURITY**

Customer and employee data must be protected against ever-new attack schemes and satisfy a growing list of ever-stricter government and international regulations. SOX, HIPAA, GLB, SB 1386, FISMA, and USA Patriot Act in the United States; Japan's Personal Information Protection Act; Canada's Personal Information Protection and Electronic Document Act (PIPEDA); Australia's Federal Privacy Act; the U.K.'s Data Protection Act; and Basel II (global financial services) all mandate the protection of personal data.

**Industry Self-Regulations.** In addition, industry groups are self-regulating to protect their customers' and their members' brand images and revenues. One example is the **Payment Card Industry (PCI) Data Security Standard** created by a coalition

# A Closer Look 16.1

ACC    FIN    HRM    IS    POM

## IT Governance

Managing information resources has become extremely complex. Organizations must understand and manage the risks associated with new technologies. The following are five critical issues:

1. Aligning IT strategy with the business strategy (see Chapter 13)
2. Disseminating strategy, goals, and policies down into the enterprise (Chapter 13)
3. Measuring IT's performance (Chapter 13)
4. Providing organizational structures that facilitate the implementation of strategy, goals, and policies (Chapters 15 and 16)
5. Insisting that an IT control framework be adopted, implemented, and enforced (Chapter 16)

Addressing these issues is at the core of IT governance. To help organizations successfully meet business challenges and regulatory requirements, the IT Governance Institute® (ITGI) (*.itgi.org*) publishes *Control Objectives for Information and Related Technology* (COBIT®). See *isaca.org* to download a copy of COBIT.

One critical element of SOX compliance (see Chapters 1 and 2) is providing evidence that the financial applications and supporting systems and services are adequately secured to ensure that financial reports can be trusted. This requires that IT security managers work with business representatives to do a risk assessment to identify which systems depend on technical controls rather than on business process controls.

All IT projects should have the same objectives, which are based on:

- The higher principle of economic use of resources (effectiveness and efficiency)
- The principle of legality (meets legal requirements)
- Accounting standards regulations, which are integrity, availability, and reliability

---

including Visa, MasterCard, American Express, and Discover. PCI Data Security Standard is required for all members, merchants, or service providers that store, process, or transmit cardholder data.

**Small Business Regulations.** Small companies are not immune. The Council of Better Business Bureaus, Visa USA, Equifax, IBM, Verizon, and eBay launched a program in March 2006 to help small businesses harden their data security procedures. At a press conference for the new program, Lydia Parnes, the director of the FTC's bureau of consumer protection, warned that the agency would bring enforcement action against small businesses lacking adequate policies and procedures to protect consumer data.

**Cyber-Blackmail.** Among the new generation of threats is **cyber-blackmail,** as exemplified by the hacker Krotten. This is where a Trojan encrypts the data on a user's computer, then the attacker offers to decrypt it for $300 or more. The Krotten cracker's location was believed to be the Ukraine or United States, indicating that he could be anywhere. The Krotten password to decrypt was broken, but there are new versions of these Trojans, suggesting it is profitable.

**INFORMATION SYSTEMS BREAKDOWNS**

At a strategic level, the totality of a company's data resources is nearly irreplaceable. Yet data at this macro-level remains largely overlooked by corporate leadership. In 2005, the U.S. Office of Management and Budget (*whitehouse.gov/omb*) designated IT security as the "sixth line of business." For an example of the impact of an enterprisewide network crash on business, read how UBS PaineWebber's business operations were debilitated by malicious code planted by an employee in Online Minicase W16.1.

In its fourth annual study on information security and the workforce released in 2006, the *Computing Technology Industry Association* (CompTIA), a nonprofit trade group, said human error was responsible for nearly 60 percent of information security breaches in organizations in 2005—up from 47 percent the year before. Yet despite the key role of human behavior in information security breaches, only 29 percent of the 574 government, IT, financial, and educational organizations surveyed worldwide said security training was a requirement in their companies. Only 36 percent of organizations offered end-user security awareness training.

Many companies of all sizes fail to implement a number of basic IT security management best practices, business continuity plans, and disaster recovery plans. Consider the strategic and financial impact of the following breakdowns.

*Incident 1.* In April 2006, Idaho Power Co. disclosed that company and personnel information had been released on computer drives that were supposed to be recycled. The drives contained confidential employee information, correspondence with customers, and memos discussing proprietary corporate information. The company recycled 230 such drives through a salvage vendor. About 84 were sold to 12 people over eBay.

*Incident 2.* In 2006, the Web sites of three Florida banks, Premier Bank, Wakulla Bank, and Capital City Bank, were hacked in an attack that security experts described as the "first of its kind." Hackers broke into servers of the ISP hosting the three banks' sites and redirected their traffic to a bogus server to steal credit card numbers, PINs, and other personal information on the banks' customers.

*Incident 3.* In February 2006, Jim Grago, CTO of online payment processing company StormPay.com, thought his mail server had failed. He was wrong. Cybercriminals had launched a DDoS attack to extort money from the company. The traffic generated by the attack reached eight gigabits of data per second—taking out StormPay's two data centers and its business for two days. Because the company could not process any of its 40,000 daily transactions, there were financial losses, stress on the management team, and 3 million upset customers (Thomas, 2006).

The cybercriminals had stealthily infected and taken control of thousands of broadband users' computers, turning them into **bots** (short for robot), creating a network of bots or a **botnet.** Extortion demands for money in return for stopping the attacks were received via e-mail.

*Incident 4.* Lower Manhattan (see Figure 16.2) is the most communications-intensive real estate in the world. Many companies lacked off-site-based business

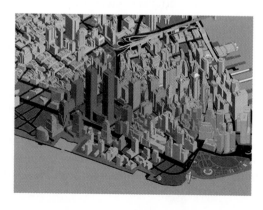

**Figure 16.2** Lower Manhattan, the most communications-intensive real estate in the world. (Photo courtesy of Verizon Communications. Used with permission.)

**Figure 16.3** Verizon's central office (CO) at 140 West St., harpooned by steel girders. (Photo courtesy of Verizon Communications. Used with permission.)

continuity plans and permanently lost critical data about their employees, customers, and operations in the aftermath of the September 11 attacks. Mission-critical systems and networks were brought down. They also lost network and phone connectivity when 7 World trade Center collapsed and Verizon's 140 West St. central office (CO), which was directly across the street, suffered massive structural damage. The Verizon facility at 140 West St. was one of the largest and most complex telecommunications facilities in the world. The CO was "harpooned" by huge steel girders, as shown in Figure 16.3. In all, 300,000 telephone lines and 3.6 million high-capacity data circuits served by that CO were put out of service.

These incidents and the opening case illustrate the vulnerability of information systems, the diversity of causes of computer security problems, and the substantial damage that can be done to organizations anywhere in the world as a result. The fact is that computing is far from secure (e.g., see Online Mini-case W16.2 and *secretservice.gov*). Until recently, many hacker groups did not know how to calculate their demands and asked for absurdly small amounts of money for either returning sensitive data or stopping automated attacks. Now they routinely demand tens of thousands of dollars and many companies would prefer to pay up in order to hush up the security breach.

**DIRECTED AND REFINED THREATS CALL FOR NEW IT SECURITY STRATEGIES**

Driven by egotistic or profit motives, criminals are using the Internet and private networks to hijack large numbers of PCs to spy on users, spam them, shake down businesses, and steal identities.

The Information Security Forum (*securityforum.org*), a self-help organization that includes many Fortune 100 companies, compiled a list of the top information problems that cost companies money in 2005. They discovered that nine of the top ten incidents were the result of one of the following mistakes:

- Human error
- Systems malfunctioning
- Failure to understand the effect of adding a new piece of software to the rest of the system

Compared with the categories of threats to information systems shown in Online File W16.3, the number-one reason — *human error* — has not changed since 2002. The

## A Closer Look 16.2

ACC    FIN    IS    POM

### Money Laundering, Organized Crime, and Terrorist Financing

International organized crime syndicates, al-Qaida groups, and other cybercriminals steal hundreds of billions of dollars every year. Cybercrime is safer and easier than selling drugs, dealing in black market diamonds, or robbing banks. Online gambling offers easy fronts for international money-laundering operations. And hack attacks are a key weapon of global jihad.

For example, the 2002 explosion that killed more than 200 people at a nightclub in Bali, Indonesia was financed through credit card fraud. Imam Samudra, the man behind the attack, wrote a book in jail in which he exhorts followers to "learn to hack." The book continues, "Not just because it makes more money in three to six hours than a policeman makes in six months, because it is how we can bring America and its cronies to its knees."

*Sources:* Compiled from Altman (2006) and Wolfe (2006).

IT security technologies discussed in this chapter, namely spam filtering, VPN, WEP, WPA, server access controls, intrusion detection and prevention, encryption, password management, smart cards, password tokens, and biometrics, can still be defeated by mistakes.

There are specific indicators of the transition to directed and stealth threats. In 2004, the Blaster worm accounted for over half of the worst corporate security incidents. A year later in 2005, no single worm or virus had this kind of impact. Instead, many different variants of malicious code were attacking company networks. There was a huge rise in Trojans and spyware, malicious code designed to remain undetected on computers. The stealth code can collect keystrokes a user enters for passwords or PINs. Spyware was virtually unknown in 2004, but accounted for about one in seven severe security attacks in 2006.

A 2006 security report from the SANS Institute noted that companies were seeing an increasing number of **zero-day incidents,** or attacks through previously unknown weaknesses in their computer networks. This suggests that cybercrime has become so lucrative that hackers are now willing to invest more time and effort in researching new ways of getting in.

Greater dependence on mobile devices, e-commerce, and online operations; stricter privacy and antifraud regulations; and more profit-driven exploits have made IT security a strategic part of business processes and a corporate governance issue. The former CIO of Dresdner Kleinwort Wasserstein, an investment bank, stated, "There is no fundamental difference between information security and knowledge management" (Cane, 2006). CIOs as well as CSOs are worried about proprietary information walking out of the door on people's iPods, PDAs, and USB drives. Rather than banning it altogether, the company has software running on all machines that tracks (and manages) what is being passed across to any USB drive.

As *A Closer Look 16.2* indicates, the intentions and determination of cybercriminals are getting worse.

As you have read throughout this book, business success depends on fast and easy access to accurate information—and keeping it protected against many dangers. For e-commerce to survive, with its potential number and scope of customers, companies must invest in complex and expensive information management, identity management, and security management systems. IT security and internal control of this magnitude requires an enterprisewide model, which is discussed next.

**IT SECURITY AND INTERNAL CONTROL MODEL**

The success of an IT implementation is always dependent on the commitment and involvement of executive management. That is, the "tone at the top." The same is true of IT security. An emphatic and visible tone at the top that IT security is a core business function is needed to convince users that insecure practices and mistakes will not be tolerated. Therefore, an IT security and internal control model for effective enterprisewide IT security begins with senior management commitment and support, as shown in Figure 16.4 The model views IT security as a combination of people, processes, and technology.

**Step 1: Senior Management Commitment and Support.** Basically, the power of senior managers is needed to set and maintain secure and ethical security and

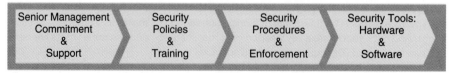

**Figure 16.4** Enterprisewide IT security and internal control model. (*Source:* Adapted from Volonino and Robinson, 2004.)

privacy practices. The decision to commit necessary resources and adjust business operations as needed to control risk exposure, which is discussed later in the chapter, must be made.

Management's duties to maintain effective IT security and internal control have expanded to the point that they are inseparable. The **Committee of Sponsoring Organizations of the Treadway Commission (COSO)** (*coso.org/key.htm*) defines internal control as a *process* designed to provide *reasonable* assurance of effective operations and reliable financial reporting. Federal agencies, most often the FTC, DHS, and SEC, and state Attorneys General are imposing harsh penalties to deter weak security or internal control situations.

**Step 2: Security Policies and Training.** The next step in building an effective IT security program is to develop security policies and provide training to ensure that everyone is aware of and understands them. The greater the understanding of how security issues directly impact production levels, customer and supplier relationships, revenue streams, and management's liability, the more security will be incorporated into business projects and proposals.

Most critical is an **acceptable use policy (AUP)** that informs users of their responsibilities. An AUP serves two main purposes: (1) It helps to prevent misuse of information and computer resources and (2) it reduces exposure to legal liability. To be effective, the AUP needs to define the responsibilities of every user by specifying both acceptable and unacceptable actions—and the consequences of noncompliance. E-mail, Internet, and computer AUPs should be thought of as an extension of other more traditional corporate policies, such as those that address equal opportunity, harassment, and discrimination. The survey results in *IT at Work 16.2* illustrate the importance of AUP training and consent.

**Step 3: Security Procedures and Enforcement.** Without continual monitoring of user activity to verify compliance and consistent enforcement of consequences, the AUP is useless. Therefore, the next step is to implement procedures, training, and enforcement of the AUP.

Security procedures require an evaluation of the digital assets at risk—including cost and operational considerations. Businesses cannot afford to ignore security risks nor can they afford the infinite cost of perfect security. To calculate the proper level of protection, managers responsible for a digital asset need to assess its **risk exposure.** The risk exposure model for digital assets is comprised of the five factors shown in Table 16.2.

# IT at Work 16.2

## Employee-Caused Breaches on the Rise

Employee-caused breaches are on the rise. In the CompTIA fourth annual report (2005), 573 respondents at small and mid-size companies reported on the size, scope, and frequency of security attacks and detailed governance structures for security management. In each of the four annual surveys, internal human error proved the single biggest cause of security breaches (McCarthy, 2006). In 2005, 59.2 percent of respondents attributed their last security breach mainly to human error, up sharply from 47.1 percent in 2004 and 46.8 percent in 2003. Failure of staff to follow internal security policies and procedures was the most common mistake.

*For Further Exploration:* What are some reasons why staff do not follow internal security policies and procedures? How can they be motivated to more diligently follow AUPs and security procedures?

| TABLE 16.2 | Risk Exposure Model for Digital Assets |
|---|---|
| **Factor** | **Cost and Operational Considerations** |
| **1.** Asset's value to the company | What are the costs of replacement, recovery, or restoration? What is the recoverability time? |
| **2.** Attractiveness of the asset to a criminal | What is the asset's value (on a scale of low to high) to identity thieves, industrial spies, terrorists, or fraudsters? |
| **3.** Legal liability attached to the asset's loss or theft | What are the potential legal costs, fines, and restitution expenses? |
| **4.** Operational, marketing, and financial consequences | What are the costs of business disruption, delivery delays, lost customers, negative media attention, inability to process payments or payroll, or a drop in stock prices? |
| **5.** Likelihood of a successful attack against the asset | Given existing and emerging threats, what is the probability the asset will be stolen or compromised? |

FIN   HRM   MKT

Another assessment is the **business impact analysis (BIA)**. BIA is an exercise that determines the impact of losing the support of any resource to an organization and establishes the escalation of that loss over time, identifies the minimum resources needed to recover, and prioritizes the recovery of processes and supporting systems. A BIA needs to be done when conditions change, new threats emerge, or risks get worse. Consider changes in customers' attitudes, for example. According to a 2004 Harris Interactive study, more than 80 percent of consumers said they would stop doing business entirely with companies that misuse information (Ewing et al., 2006). See Online File W16.4. After the risk exposure of digital assets has been estimated, resources can be focused where the risks are the greatest.

**Step 4: Security Tools: Hardware and Software.** Once the "tone at the top" and AUP have been made clear and the risk assessment completed, then the software and hardware needed to support implementation of the policy and enforcement of secure practices can be put in place.

Keep in mind that security is an ongoing, multilayered process and not a problem that can be solved with hardware or software tools. Hardware and software security defenses cannot protect against irresponsible business practices. For more information on the reasons for a multilayered security approach, read Online File W16.5. We outline the basic security hardware and software later in the chapter.

# 16.2 IS Vulnerabilities and Threats

One of the biggest mistakes managers make is that they underestimate vulnerabilities and threats. Most workers use their PCs and laptops for both work and leisure, and in an era of multitasking, they often do both at the same time. Yet off-time or off-site use of personal computers remains risky because, despite years of policies designed to control them, employees continue dangerous surfing and communication habits that can make them the weak link in an organization's otherwise solid security efforts.

The vulnerability of information systems is increasing as we move to a world of networked and especially wireless computing. These threats can be classified as *unintentional* or *intentional*.

**UNINTENTIONAL THREATS**

Unintentional threats can be divided into three major categories: human errors, environmental hazards, and computer system failures.

Many computer problems result from *human errors*. Errors can occur in the design of the hardware and/or information system. They can also occur in the programming, testing, data collection, data entry, authorization, and instructions. Human errors contribute to the *majority* of control- and security-related problems in many organizations.

*Environmental hazards* include earthquakes, severe storms (e.g., hurricanes, snow, sand, lightning, and tornadoes), floods, power failures or strong fluctuations, fires (the most common hazard), defective air conditioning, explosions, radioactive fallout, and water-cooling-system failures. In addition to damage from combustion, computer resources can incur damage from other elements that accompany fire, such as smoke, heat, and water. Such hazards may disrupt normal computer operations and result in long waiting periods and exorbitant costs while computer programs and data files are recreated.

*Computer systems failures* can occur as the result of poor manufacturing or defective materials. Unintentional malfunctions can also happen for other reasons, ranging from lack of experience to inappropriate testing.

**INTENTIONAL THREATS**

As headlines about computer crime indicate, computer systems can be damaged as a result of intentional actions as well. Examples of intentional threats include: theft of data; inappropriate use of data (e.g., manipulating inputs); theft of mainframe computer time; theft of equipment and/or programs; deliberate manipulation in handling, entering, processing, transferring, or programming data; labor strikes, riots, or sabotage; malicious damage to computer resources; destruction from viruses and similar attacks; and miscellaneous computer abuses and Internet fraud. See Online File W16.6. Intentional threats can even be against whole countries. Many fear the possibility of *cyberattacks* by some countries against others (see *A Closer Look 16.3*).

**COMPUTER CRIMES**

Crimes done on the Internet, called cybercrimes (discussed later), can fall into any of these categories. **Hacker** is the term often used to describe an outside person who penetrates a computer system. *White-hat hackers* perform ethical hacking, doing penetrating tests on their clients' systems to find the weak points, so that they can be fixed. *Black-hat hackers*, also referred to as crackers, are the

# A Closer Look 16.3

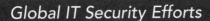

## *Global IT Security Efforts*

GLOBE    IS    POM

Most countries are updating laws and regulations to protect networked information.

- In May 2006, Transport and Communication Minister Christopher Mushowe announced the Zimbabwe government would pass legislation to curb cybercrime in the country in view of its increasing threat to world economies.
- Zhang Changsheng, Vice President of China Netcom, stated that China Netcom would play an active role in a series of countermeasures, including regulation on SMS and mobile services, registration of mobile phone users'

legal names, cleaning up Internet domain names, and elimination of spam.

- In 2006, the U.S. DHS launched **Cyber Storm,** the first wide-scale government-led IT security exercise to examine response, coordination, and recovery mechanisms in simulated cyberattacks against critical infrastructures. One of the exercise scenarios simulated a breach against a utility company's computer systems, causing numerous disruptions to the power grid. The exercise was done to show the interconnectivity between computer and physical infrastructures.

criminals. A **cracker** is a *malicious hacker,* who may represent a serious problem for a corporation.

Hackers and crackers may involve in their crimes unsuspecting insiders. In a strategy called **social engineering,** computer criminals or corporate spies build an inappropriate trust relationship with insiders for the purpose of gaining sensitive information or unauthorized access privileges. For a description of social engineering and some tips for prevention, see Online File W16.7.

In addition to computer crimes against organizations, there is an alarming increase of fraud committed against individuals, on the Internet. These are a part of cybercrimes. For a discussion of what the private sector is doing to fight cybercrime, see Online File W16.8.

**METHODS OF ATTACK ON COMPUTING FACILITIES**

There are many methods of attack, and new ones appear regularly. In this section we look at some of these methods. Two basic approaches are used in deliberate attacks on computer systems: data tampering and programming attack.

**Data tampering,** the most common means of attack, refers to entering false, fabricated, or fraudulent data into the computer or changing or deleting existing data. This is the method often used by insiders.

In 2004, owners of a small Baltimore office furniture company realized that their CFO had embezzled $4.5 million over six years. The CFO had diverted funds from a payroll account and drained money from an account that collected customer payments.

**Programming attacks** are popular with computer criminals who use *programming techniques* to modify a computer program, either directly or indirectly. For this crime, programming skills and knowledge of the targeted systems are essential. Programming attacks appear under many names, as shown in Online File W16.9. Several of the methods were designed for Web-based systems. Viruses and malware merit special discussion here, due to their frequency, as do denial of service attacks, due to the effects they have had on computer networks.

**Viruses.** A highly publicized attack method is the **virus.** It receives its name from the program's ability to attach itself to ("infect") other computer programs, without the owner of the program being aware of the infection (see Figure 16.5). When the software is used, the virus spreads, causing damage to that program and possibly to others.

**OTHER MALWARE**

Unlike a virus, a **worm** can spread itself without any human intervention. Worms use networks to propagate and infect a computer or handheld device (e.g., cell phone) and can even spread via instant messages. Also unlike viruses, which generally are confined within a target computer, worms' ability to self-propagate can degrade network performance.

**ZOMBIES, PHISHING, AND DoS**

Zombied PCs—and the spyware that controls them—can be used to launch DoS attacks or spread adware. Connecting wireless laptops and palmtops to insecure networks in airport Wi-Fi facilities, hotels, and Internet cafés totally exposes data to threats.

Even though most people are aware of phishing scams, phishers still remain a serious threat because they change their tactics.

**BOTNETS**

A botnet is a huge number (e.g., hundreds of thousands) of hijacked Internet computers that have been set up to forward traffic, including spam and viruses, to other computers on the Internet. An infected computer is referred to as a computer robot,

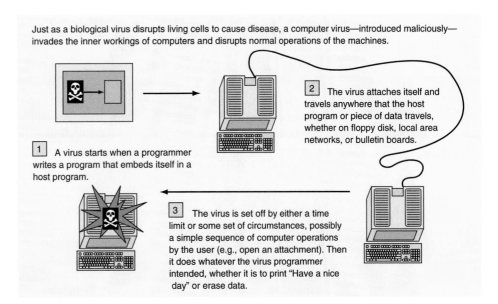

**Figure 16.5** How a computer virus can spread.

Just as a biological virus disrupts living cells to cause disease, a computer virus—introduced maliciously— invades the inner workings of computers and disrupts normal operations of the machines.

1  A virus starts when a programmer writes a program that embeds itself in a host program.

2  The virus attaches itself and travels anywhere that the host program or piece of data travels, whether on floppy disk, local area networks, or bulletin boards.

3  The virus is set off by either a time limit or some set of circumstances, possibly a simple sequence of computer operations by the user (e.g., open an attachment). Then it does whatever the virus programmer intended, whether it is to print "Have a nice day" or erase data.

or bot. Botnets are controlled by botmasters, or bot herders. The combined power of these coordinated networks of computers can scan for and compromise other computers and be used for DoS attacks.

In the next section, we discuss crime—specifically fraud, which is also known as white-collar crime, and computer crime. Companies suffer tremendous loss from occupational fraud. It is a widespread problem that affects every company, regardless of size, location, or industry. The FBI has labeled fraud the fastest growing crime.

# 16.3  Fraud and Computer Crimes

Fraud is a serious financial crime that always involves three elements: deception, confidence, and trickery. Fraudsters carry out their theft by taking advantage of the trust of others (or the trust they have as a result of their position in an organization) to deceive and trick others out of something of value, typically money. For example, see Online File W16.10.

New computer crimes appear frequently and with novel names that quickly become part of our everyday vocabulary. For example, spyware researchers at Webroot Software had uncovered a stash of tens of thousands of stolen identities from 125 countries that they believe were collected by a new variant of a Trojan program the company named **Trojan-Phisher-Rebery** (Roberts, 2006). The Rebery malicious software is an example of a **banking Trojan,** which is programmed to come to life when computer owners visit one of a number of online banking or e-commerce sites. Without strong defenses—including AUP and secure procedures—e-commerce can lose a lot of customers.

Next, we discuss the most common and devastating types of fraud and computer crimes.

**FRAUD**

When a person uses his or her occupation for personal gain through deliberate misuse of the organization's resources or assets, it is called **occupational fraud.** Examples of occupational fraud are listed in Table 16.3.

| TABLE 16.3 | Types of Organizational Fraud | |
| --- | --- | --- |
| **Type of Fraud** | **Financial Statement Fraud?** | **Typical Characteristics** |
| Operating-management corruption | No | Occurs *off the books*. Median loss due to corruption: over 6 times greater than median loss due to misappropriation ($530,000 vs. $80,000). |
| Conflict of interest | No | A breach of confidentiality, such as revealing competitors' bids and often occurs with bribery. |
| Bribery | No | Uses positional-power or money to influence others. |
| Embezzlement or "misappropriation" | | Employee theft. Employees' access to company property creates the opportunity for embezzlement. |
| Senior management financial reporting fraud | Yes | Involves a massive breach of trust and leveraging of positional power. |
| Accounting cycle fraud | Yes | "Earnings management" in violation of GAAP (Generally Accepted Accounting Principles). See *aicpa.org*. |

**Fraud Prevention and Detection.** Internal audits and internal controls (covered later in the chapter) are critical to the prevention and detection of occupation frauds. Fraud deterrence and investigation methods will be covered in Section 16.9 on computer forensics. High-profile examples of occupational fraud that were executed because of the lack of internal audits and controls include:

- **Adelphia.** A year after the public learned of the $600 million Enron scandal, the Rigases made Enron's fraud look like penny-change. The SEC uncovered the misappropriation and theft of tens of billions of dollars. In addition to the $2.3 billion the family stole from the company for their personal use, they caused losses to investors of more than $60 billion.
- **Global Crossing.** Corporate insiders knowingly sold more than $1.5 billion of artificially inflated company stock. In April 2005, the SEC filed a settled action for civil penalties against Global Crossing's former CEO, CFO, and VP of Finance for aiding and abetting the fraud. Each executive agreed to pay a $100,000 civil penalty.
- **Tyco.** In 2003, the SEC charged former CEO Dennis Kozlowski, CFO Swartz, and Chief Corporate Counsel Mark Belnick with many counts of fraud. Kozlowski and Swartz had swindled over $170 million in corporate loans and pocketed $430 million by manipulating the company's stock price. Belnick was indicted for falsifying business records to hide $17 million loans given to him by Tyco.

**Crime by Computer, Flash Drives, and MP3 Players.** Flash drives, MP3 players, and e-mail have created more ways to commit traditional crimes. Networked computers, EFT, poor oversight, and lax accounting controls provide opportunities for employees to misdirect POs (purchase orders), bribe a supplier, manipulate a computer program, or misappropriate company assets. There is an electronic component to almost every fraud. Whether it is electronic fund transfers or e-mailing of intellectual property, there is nearly always a computer in it somewhere. Because physical possession of stolen property is no longer required and it is just as easy to program a computer to misdirect $100,000 as it is $1,000, the size and number of frauds have increased tremendously. (See the *Report to the Nation,* at *cfenet.com/ pdfs/ Report_to_the_Nation.pdf.*)

**COMPUTER CRIMES**

In its April 2006 report, the Anti-Phishing Working Group (APWG) reported that the number of *unique* phishing Web sites it detected was 11,121 in April 2006, a monumental increase in unique phishing sites from March 2006 and the highest ever recorded by the APWG. (See *antiphishing.org/reports/apwg_report_apr_06.pdf.*) The danger is that phishing scams lead to identity theft. Many types and examples of computer crimes have already been discussed throughout the chapter, but identity theft warrants further review.

**Identity Theft.** One of the worst and most prevalent crimes is identity theft. Such thefts where individuals' Social Security and credit card numbers are stolen and used by thieves are not new. Criminals have always obtained information about other people—by stealing wallets or dumpster digging. But widespread electronic sharing and databases have made the crime worse. Because financial institutions, data processing firms, and retail businesses are reluctant to reveal incidents in which their customers' personal financial information may have been stolen, lost, or compromised, laws continue to be passed that force those notifications. Examples in Table 16.4 illustrate different ways in which identity crimes have occurred.

| TABLE 16.4 | Examples of Identity Crimes Requiring Notification | |
|---|---|---|
| **How It Happened** | **Number of Individuals Notified** | **Description** |
| Stolen desktop | 3,623 | Desktop computer was stolen from regional sales office containing data that was password protected, but not encrypted. Thieves stole SSNs and other information from TransUnion LLC, which maintains personal credit histories. |
| Online, by an ex-employee | 465,000 | Former employee downloaded information about participants in Georgia state Health Benefits Plan. |
| Computer tapes lost in transit | 3.9 million | CitiFinancial, the consumer finance division of Citigroup Inc., lost tapes containing information about both active and closed accounts while they were being shipped to a credit bureau. |
| Online "malicious user" used legitimate user's login information | 33,000 | The U.S. Air Force suffered a security breach in the online system containing information on officers and enlisted airmen, and personal information. |
| Missing backup tape | 200,000 | A timeshare unit of Marriott International Inc. lost a backup tape containing SSNs and other confidential data of employees and timeshare owners and customers. |

*Source:* Koster and Scott (2006).

Furthermore, computer criminals do not need IT skills to steal a laptop (recall the VA employee's home robbery) or PDA, or find one that was left behind. Therefore, unencrypted sensitive data on laptops or handheld devices that leave the office increase the risk. For an example of how lax physical security created an opportunity for computer crime, read Online File W16.11.

**Calculating the Cost of Computer Crimes.** It is difficult for companies that have been attacked to assess the damage. Most companies do not do a proper post-mortem, or if they do, they have no idea what to include in the analysis. Cost estimates may include the soft cost of diverting the IT department from a strategic project, lost sales, and customer attrition, or take a minimalist approach that only includes recovery costs. Download Online File W16.12 to calculate the cost of a spam attack.

# 16.4 IT Security Management Practices

The objective of IT security management practices is to defend all of the components of an information system, specifically data, software applications, hardware, and networks. Before any decisions on defenses, the decision makers must understand business requirements and operations. In the next section, we describe the major defense strategies.

**DEFENSE STRATEGY: HOW DO WE PROTECT?**

The selection of a specific defense strategy and controls depends on the objective of the defense and on the perceived cost-benefit. The following are the major objectives of *defense strategies:*

1. **Prevention and deterrence.** Properly designed controls may prevent errors from occurring, deter criminals from attacking the system, and better yet, deny access to unauthorized people. These are the most desirable controls.

2. **Detection.** Like a fire, the earlier an attack is detected, the easier it is to combat, and the less damage is done. Detection can be performed in many cases by using special diagnostic software, at a minimal cost.

3. **Limitation of damage.** This strategy is to minimize (limit) losses once a malfunction has occurred (damage control). This can be accomplished, for example, by including a *fault-tolerant system* that permits operation in a degraded mode until full recovery is made. If a fault-tolerant system does not exist, a quick (and possibly expensive) recovery must take place. Users want their systems back in operation as fast as possible.

4. **Recovery.** A recovery plan explains how to fix a damaged information system as quickly as possible. Replacing rather than repairing components is one route to fast recovery.

5. **Correction.** Correcting the causes of damaged systems can prevent the problem from occurring again.

6. **Awareness and compliance.** All organization members must be educated about the hazards and must comply with the security rules and regulations.

Any defense strategy that aims to attain one or more of these objectives may involve the use of several controls, as shown in Figure 16.6. **General controls** are established to protect the system regardless of the specific application. For example, protecting hardware and controlling access to the data center are independent of

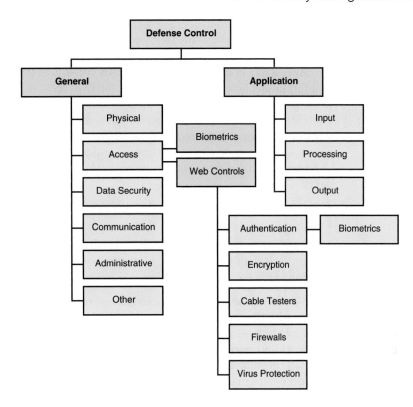

**Figure 16.6** Major defense controls.

the specific application. **Application controls** are safeguards that are intended to protect specific applications. In the next two sections, we discuss the major types of these two groups of information systems controls.

**GENERAL CONTROLS**

The major categories of general controls are physical controls, access controls, data security controls, communications (networks) controls, and administrative controls.

**Physical Controls.** Physical security refers to the protection of computer facilities and resources. This includes protecting physical property such as computers, data centers, software, manuals, and networks. It provides protection against most natural hazards as well as against some human hazards. Appropriate physical security may include several controls such as the following:

- Appropriate design of the data center. For example, the site should be noncombustible and waterproof.
- Shielding against electromagnetic fields.
- Good fire prevention, detection, and extinguishing systems, including sprinkler system, water pumps, and adequate drainage facilities.
- Emergency power shutoff and backup batteries, which must be maintained in operational condition.
- Properly designed, maintained, and operated air-conditioning systems.
- Motion detector alarms that detect physical intrusion.

**Access Control.** Access control is the restriction of unauthorized user access to a portion of a computer system or to the entire system. It is the major defense line against unauthorized insiders as well as outsiders. To gain access, a user must first be *authorized*. Then, when the user attempts to gain access, he or she must be *authenticated*. See Online Files W16.13 and W16.14.

Access to a computer system basically consists of three steps: (1) physical access to a terminal, (2) access to the system, and (3) access to specific commands, transactions, privileges, programs, and data within the system. Access control software is commercially available for large mainframes, personal computers, local area networks, mobile devices, and dial-in communications networks. Access control to *networks* is executed through firewalls and will be discussed later.

User identification can be accomplished when the following identifies each user:

- Something only the user *knows,* such as a password.
- Something only the user *has,* for example, a smart card or a token.
- Something only the user *is,* such as a signature, voice, fingerprint, or retinal (eye) scan. It is implemented via *biometric controls,* which can be physiological or behavioral (see Alga, 2002).

*Biometric Controls.* A **biometric control** is an automated method of verifying the identity of a person, based on physiological or behavioral characteristics. Most biometric systems match some personal characteristic of a person against a prestored profile (in a template). A comparison of the characteristics against the prestored template produces a "matching score," which indicates how closely the actual and prestored data match. The most common biometrics are the following:

- **Faceprint.** The computer takes a picture of your face and matches it with a prestored picture.
- **Thumbprint or fingerprint.** Each time a user wants access, a thumb- or fingerprint (finger scan) is matched against a template containing the authorized person's fingerprint to identify him or her. Note that in 2001 Microsoft introduced a software program, now a part of Windows, that allows users to use Sony's fingerprint recognition device. Computer manufacturers started shipping laptops secured by fingerprint-scanning touchpads in 2004. These devices reject unauthorized access (see *synaptics.com*).
- **Hand geometry.** This biometric is similar to fingerprints except that the verifier uses a television-like camera to take a picture of the user's hand.
- **Retinal scan.** A match is attempted between the pattern of the blood vessels in the back-of-the-eye retina that is being scanned and a prestored picture of the retina.
- **Voice scan.** A match is attempted between the user's voice and the voice pattern stored on templates.
- **Signature.** Signatures are matched against the prestored authentic signature. This method can supplement a photo-card ID system.
- **Keystroke dynamics.** A match of the person's keyboard pressure and speed is made against prestored information.

Biometric controls are now integrated into many e-business hardware and software products. Biometric controls do have some limitations: They are not accurate in certain cases, and some people see them as an invasion of privacy (see Caulfield, 2002).

**Administrative Controls.** While the previously discussed general controls were technical in nature, administrative controls deal with issuing guidelines and monitoring compliance with the guidelines. Representative examples of such controls are shown in Table 16.5.

| **TABLE 16.5** | **Representative Administrative Controls** |
| --- | --- |

- Appropriately selecting, training, and supervising employees, especially in accounting and information systems
- Fostering company loyalty
- Immediately revoking access privileges of dismissed, resigned, or transferred employees
- Requiring periodic modification of access controls (such as passwords)
- Developing programming and documentation standards (to make auditing easier and to use the standards as guides for employees)
- Insisting on security bonds or malfeasance insurance for key employees
- Instituting separation of duties, namely dividing sensitive computer duties among as many employees as economically feasible in order to decrease the chance of intentional or unintentional damage
- Holding periodic random audits of the system

**APPLICATION CONTROLS**

Sophisticated attacks are aimed at the application level, and many applications were not designed to withstand such attacks. For better survivability, information processing methodologies are being replaced with agent technology. **Intelligent agents,** also referred to as softbots or knowbots, are highly intelligent applications. The term generally means applications that have some degree of reactivity, autonomy, and adaptability—as is needed in unpredictable attack situations. An agent is able to adapt itself based on changes occurring in its environment. (See Figure 16.7.)

In the next section, the focus is on the company's digital perimeter—the network. We discuss the security of wireline and wireless networks and their inherent vulnerabilities.

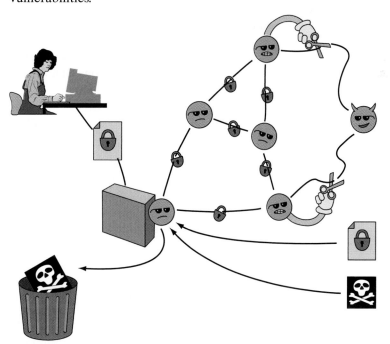

**Figure 16.7** Intelligent agents. (*Source:* Courtesy of Sandia National Laboratories.) Agents in a collective communicate over secured links on the Internet or an intranet. Malicious agents (with horns) are detected and cut off from the collective. Properly authenticated data are allowed into the collective, but bad information is rejected.

# 16.5 Network Security

Companies need to implement an effective approach to protecting networks from damaging security threats from any endpoint device. Unenforced access from end-point devices puts networks at risk.

For a list of techniques attackers can use to compromise Web applications, in addition to what was described in Section 16.1, see Online File W16.15. The table covers the major security measures of the Internet. Security issues regarding e-business are discussed in Chapters 5 and 6.

Internet security measures involve three layers: *perimeter security* (access), *authentication,* and *authorization.* Details of these layers are shown in Figure 16.8. Several of these are discussed in some detail in the remainder of this chapter. For more details and other measures, see Panko (2004). Some commercial products include security measures for all three levels—all in one product (e.g., WebShield from McAfee, and Firewall/VPN Appliance from Symantec).

Many security methods and products are available to protect the Web. We briefly describe the major ones in the following sections.

**PERIMETER SECURITY**

The major objective of perimeter security is access control, as seen in Figure 16.8. Several tools are available. First we consider firewalls.

**Firewalls.** A **firewall** is a system, or group of systems, that enforces an access-control policy between two networks. It is commonly used as a barrier between a secure corporate intranet or other internal networks and the Internet, which is unsecured.

The firewall follows strict guidelines that either permit or block traffic; therefore, a successful firewall is designed with clear and specific rules about what can pass through. Several firewalls may exist in one information system.

Useful as they are, firewalls do not stop viruses that may be lurking in networks. Viruses can pass through the firewalls, usually hidden in an e-mail attachment.

All Internet traffic (i.e., packets) needs to pass through a firewall, but that is rarely the case for instant messaging (IM) and wireless traffic, which as a result "carry" malware into the network and applications on host computers. Firewalls do not control anything that happens after a legitimate user (who may be a disgruntled employee or whose username and password have been compromised) has been authenticated and granted authority to access applications on the network. For these reasons, firewalls are a necessary but insufficient defense.

**Malware Controls.** The most common solution used by over 99 percent of all U.S. companies (Gordon et al., 2004) is to use antivirus software (e.g., from *symantec.com*). However, antivirus software provides protection against viruses only after they have attacked someone and their signatures are known. New viruses are difficult to detect in their first attack, or zero-day attack.

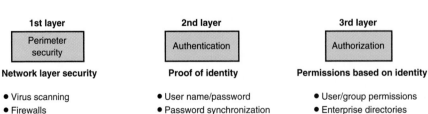

**Figure 16.8** Three layers of Internet security measures. (*Source:* Adapted from McConnell, 2002.)

| 1st layer | 2nd layer | 3rd layer |
|---|---|---|
| Perimeter security | Authentication | Authorization |
| **Network layer security** | **Proof of identity** | **Permissions based on identity** |
| • Virus scanning | • User name/password | • User/group permissions |
| • Firewalls | • Password synchronization | • Enterprise directories |
| • IDS | • PKI | • Enterprise user administration |
| • Virtual private networking | • Tokens | • Rules-based access control |
| • DoS protection | • Biometrics | |
| | • Single-sign-on | |

**Intrusion Detection Systems (IDSs).** Because protection against denial of service is difficult, the sooner one can detect an usual activity, the better. Therefore, it is worthwhile to place an *intrusion detection system* near the entrance point of the Internet to the intranet (close to a firewall). The objective is early detection, and this can be done by several devices (e.g., Caddx from Caddx Controls, and IDS from Cisco). Intrusion detecting is done by different tools, such as statistical analysis or neural networks. For details see *dshield.org*, *sans.org*, and *acm.org*.

**Virtual Private Networking (VPN).** The last major method of perimeter security described here is a virtual private network (VPN). VPNs are based on encryption. Encryption converts a file or message that is in **plaintext** (readable) into unreadable **ciphertext.** To read the contents, the ciphertext must be decrypted. For an explanation of encryption, see *mathworld.wolfram.com/RSAEncryption.html*. All confidential information e-commerce transactions rely on some form of strong encryption.

A VPN creates an encrypted "tunnel" between remote computers to keep data safe while in transit. The encryption also keeps information about the sender shielded from intruders. VPNs are used in combination with firewalls to allow only filtered and anonymous traffic between the private network and the public Internet. VPNs should never be used by computers without active updated firewalls installed.

The advantage of using a VPN is that users communicate over shared Internet connections securely for a fraction of the cost of private networking. That is, VPNs replace traditional private leased lines and/or **remote access servers (RASs)** that provide direct communication to a company's LAN (see Chapter 4 and Technology Guide 4).

*Technology Guides are located at the book's Web site.*

| AUTHENTICATION |

As applied to the Internet, an *authentication* system guards against unauthorized access attempts. Many companies use an access protection strategy that requires authorized users to dial in with a preassigned personal identification number (PIN). This strategy is usually enhanced by a unique and frequently changing password. A communications access control system authenticates the user's PIN and password. Some security systems proceed one step further, accepting calls only from designated telephone numbers. Access controls also include biometrics.

**How Authentication Works.** The major objective of authentication is the proof of identity (see Figure 16.8). The attempt here is to identify the legitimate user and determine the action he or she is allowed to perform, and also to find those posing as others.

Because phishing and identity theft prey on weak authentication, and usernames and passwords do not offer strong authentication, other methods are needed. There are **two-factor authentication** (also called **multifactor authentication**) and **two-tier authentication.** With two-factor authentication, other information is used to verify the user's identity such as biometrics. There are three key questions to ask when setting up an authentication system (Vance, 2006):

1. **Who are you?** Is this person an employee, a partner, or a customer? Different levels of authentication would be set up for different types of people.
2. **Where are you?** For example, an employee who has already used a badge to access the building is less of a risk than an employee or partner logging on remotely. Someone logging on from a known IP address is less of a risk than someone logging on from Nigeria or Kazakhstan.
3. **What do you want?** Is this person accessing sensitive or proprietary information or simply gaining access to benign data?

When dealing with consumer-facing applications, such as online banking and e-commerce, strong authentication must be balanced with convenience. If authentication is too difficult to bank or shop online, users will go back to the brick-and-mortars. There is a trade-off between increased protection and turning customers away from your online channel. In addition, authentication of a Web site to the customer is equally critical. E-commerce customers need to be able to identify if it is a fraudulent site set up by phishers.

## AUTHORIZATION

*Authorization* refers to permission issued to individuals or groups to do certain activities with a computer, usually based on verified identity. The security system, once it authenticates the user, must make sure that the user operates within his or her authorized activities.

## SECURING WIRELESS NETWORKS

Wireless networks are more difficult to protect than wireline ones. All the vulnerabilities that exist in a conventional wireline network apply to wireless technologies. **Wireless access points (APs or WAPs)** behind a firewall and other security protections can be a backdoor into a network. Sensitive data that are not encrypted or that are encrypted with a poor cryptographic technique, such as **wired equivalent privacy (WEP)**, and that are transmitted between two wireless devices may be intercepted and disclosed. Wireless devices are susceptible to DoS attacks because interlopers may be able to gain connectivity to network management controls and then disable or disrupt operations. **Wireless packet analyzers,** such as AirSnort (*airsnort. shmoo.com*) and WEPcrack *wepcrack.sourceforge.net*), are readily available tools putting wireless networks at great risk.

Unauthorized wireless APs could be deployed by malicious users—tricking legitimate users to connect to those **rogue access points (APs).** Malicious users then gain access to sensitive information stored on client machines, including logins, passwords, customer information, and intellectual property.

Through war driving or war chalking, malicious users can connect to an unsecured wireless AP and gain access to the network. See *A Closer Look 16.4* for details on war driving and war chalking. Data can be extracted without detection

# A Closer Look 16.4

## *War Chalking and War Driving*

MKT    IS

Free Wi-Fi Internet hubs are marked in some places by symbols on sidewalks and walls to indicate nearby wireless access. This practice is called *war chalking*. It was inspired by the practice of hobos during the Great Depression who used chalkmarks to indicate which homes were friendly.

A number of people have also made a hobby or sport out of war driving. *War driving* is the act of locating wireless local area networks while driving around a city or elsewhere (see *wardriving.com*). To war drive, you need a vehicle, a computer or PDA, a wireless card, and some kind of an antenna that can be mounted on top of or positioned inside the car. Because a WLAN may have a range that extends beyond the building in

which it is located, an outside user may be able to intrude into the network, obtain a free Internet connection, and possibly gain access to important data and other resources. The term war driving was coined by computer security consultant Peter Shipley. (It derives from the term *war dialing*, a technique in which a hacker programs his or her system to call hundreds of phone numbers in search of poorly protected computer dial-ups. The term war dialing in turn came from the movie *WarGames*, which features Matthew Broderick performing the technique.)

*Source:* Compiled from Kellner (2003) and *wardrive.net* (accessed October 2006).

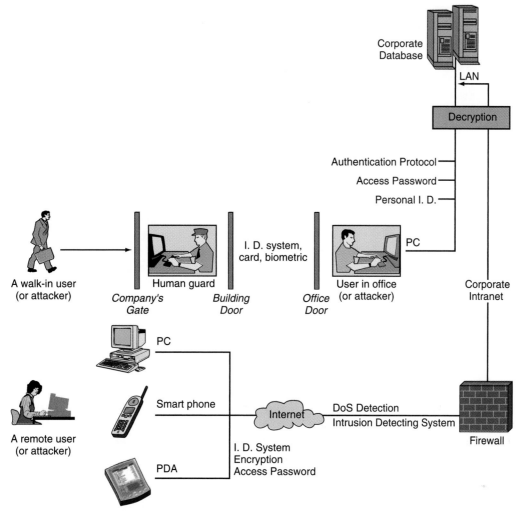

**Figure 16.9** Where the defense mechanisms are located. (*Source:* Drawn by E. Turban.)

from improperly configured devices. See Online File W16.16 for a description of wireless and VoIP security.

A schematic view of all major defense mechanisms, which protect against attackers of all types, is shown in Figure 16.9.

With an understanding of the vulnerabilities, risk exposure, and types of crimes committed with or against IT resources, we examine issues of great importance to executive management and the entire enterprise—internal control and compliance management.

# 16.6 Internal Control and Compliance Management

The **internal control environment** is the work atmosphere that a company sets for its employees. *Internal control (IC)* is a process designed to achieve: (1) reliability of financial reporting, (2) operational efficiency, (3) compliance with laws, (4) regulations and policies, and (5) safeguarding of assets. Figure 16.10 illustrates how the role of IT in internal control has changed.

| Cost | Value | Risk |
|------|-------|------|
| • Increase efficiency.<br>• Improve ROI. | • Generate higher revenues.<br>• Provide business intelligence and decision support.<br>• Improve customer and supplier relationship management.<br>• Increase shareholder value. | • Safeguard assets.<br>• Ensure the integrity of financial reporting.<br>• Disclose security breaches in a timely manner.<br>• Prevent, detect, and investigate fraud and intrusions.<br>• Visibly monitor employee behavior.<br>• Retain electronic business records.<br>• Provide for recovery from devastating disasters.<br>• Provide a defensible basis for investigations and audits. |
| *Operational* | *Strategic* | *Governance* |
| **Pre–1990s** | **1990–2001** | **2002–2010** |

**Figure 16.10** Increasing role of IT in internal control.

## INTERNAL CONTROL IN CORPORATE GOVERNANCE AND RISK MANAGEMENT

One of the most important elements in an IC environment is management's role and example.

According to the Association of Certified Fraud Examiners (*acfe.com*), a rigid IC program plus a strong commitment by management to its continued effectiveness is a strong deterrent to fraud. Properly designed ICs give employees the perception that fraudulent activity will be detected. With U.S. losses from fraud rising to an estimated $638 billion in 2005—up from $600 billion in 2002 and $400 billion in 1996—stronger ICs are still needed. See Minicase 1 for more details on occupational risk.

## EXPOSURE CREATED BY INADEQUATE MONITORING

If controls can be ignored, there is no control. Therefore, fraud prevention and detection requires an effective monitoring system. If the company shows its employees that the company can find out everything that every employee does and use that evidence to prosecute that person to the fullest extent, then the feeling that "I can get away with it" drops drastically. Approximately 85 percent of occupational fraud could have been prevented if proper IT controls had been designed, implemented, and followed. There are two categories of fraud that the internal control system needs to protect against.

**Fraud Committed Against a Company.** Fraud committed against a company tends to take advantage of weaknesses in ICs and is usually committed by those at the operational level. Examples are corruption, conflict of interest, bribery, and embezzlement. One of the most common instances of embezzlement is employee theft.

**Fraud Committed For a Company.** Fraud committed for a company typically involves a breach of trust and leveraging of executive management power to override ICs. These frauds also involve financial benefit for the perpetrators, and often lead to fraud against the company.

| TABLE 16.6 | Symptoms of Fraud that Can Be Detected by Internal Controls |
|---|---|
| Missing documents | A large drop in profits |
| Delayed bank deposits | A major increase in business with one particular customer |
| Holes in accounting records | |
| Numerous outstanding checks or bills | Customers complaining about double billing |
| Disparity between accounts payable and receivable | |
| | Repeated duplicate payments |
| Employees who do not take vacations or go out of their way to work overtime | Employees with the same address or telephone number as a vendor |

Companies that do not (or that try not to) investigate and prosecute fraudsters have unlimited exposure to fraud. Recall the office manager's fraud described in Online File W16.10, showing the risk stemming from inadequate internal control.

**INTERNAL CONTROL PROCEDURES AND ACTIVITIES**

Every fraud is comprised of three elements, which are the *theft* itself, when the assets are taken; *concealment,* which is the attempt to hide the fraud; and *conversion,* in which the perpetrator spends the money or converts the stolen assets to cash and then spends the money. Effective accounting information systems are needed to provide an *audit trail* that allows frauds to be discovered and makes concealment difficult. There are five primary internal control activities:

1. **Segregation of duties and dual custody.** Fraud can be better controlled by dividing responsibility among two or more individuals. See *auditnet.org/docs/CCAP.doc* or *bis.org/publ/bcbs40.pdf.*

2. **Independent checks.** If people know their activities are monitored by others, the tendency to commit and conceal a fraud is reduced.

3. **Proper system of authorizations.** Passwords authorize individuals to use computers and to access certain databases. Spending limits authorize individuals to spend only what is in their budget or approved level.

4. **Physical safeguards.** Physical safeguards protect assets from theft by fraud.

5. **Documents and records.** Documents or records create an audit trail. Without documents or data, no accountability or internal control exists.

**IT for Detecting Fraud Symptoms.** There are a number of symptoms, or red flags, that indicate fraud or embezzlement. Information security systems can be designed to detect for these red flags, shown in Table 16.6, so that these crimes can be detected early.

Because of rampant occupational fraud and the general ease of committing fraud, SOX requires the CEO and CFO to report four times a year on the integrity of the financial reporting, as described in Online File W16.17.

# 16.7  Business Continuity and Disaster Recovery Planning

Disasters may occur without warning. The best defense is to be prepared. Therefore, an important element in any security system is the **business continuity plan,** also known as the **disaster recovery plan.** Such a plan outlines the process by which businesses should recover from a major disaster. Destruction of all (or most) of the computing facilities can cause significant damage. Therefore, it is difficult for many

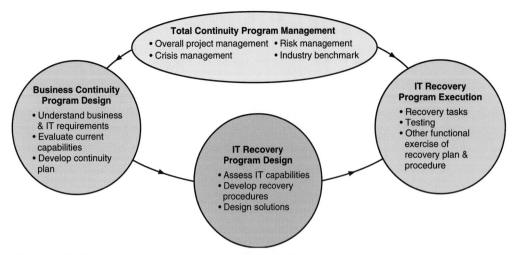

**Figure 16.11** Business continuity services managed by IBM. (*Source:* IBM, Business Continuity and Recovery Services, January 2000, produced in Hong Kong. Courtesy of IBM.)

organizations to obtain insurance for their computers and information systems without showing a satisfactory disaster prevention and recovery plan. The comprehensiveness of a business recovery plan is shown in Figure 16.11.

**BUSINESS CONTINUITY PLANNING**

Disaster recovery is the chain of events linking the business continuity plan to protection and to recovery. The following are some key thoughts about the process:

- The purpose of a business continuity plan is to keep the business running after a disaster occurs. Each function in the business should have a valid recovery capability plan.
- Recovery planning is part of *asset protection.* Every organization should assign responsibility to management to identify and protect assets within their spheres of functional control.
- Planning should focus first on recovery from a total loss of all capabilities.
- Proof of capability usually involves some kind of what-if analysis that shows that the recovery plan is current (see Lam, 2002).
- All critical applications must be identified and their recovery procedures addressed in the plan.
- The plan should be written so that it will be effective in case of disaster, not just in order to satisfy the auditors.
- The plan should be kept in a safe place; copies should be given to all key managers, or it should be available on the intranet. The plan should be audited periodically.

Methodologies can be found in Volonino and Robinson (2004) and Luftman et al. (2004). See *IT at Work 16.3.*

Disaster recovery planning can be very complex, and it may take several months to complete. Using special software, the planning job can be expedited.

**Disaster Avoidance. Disaster avoidance** is an approach oriented toward *prevention.* The idea is to minimize the chance of avoidable disasters (such as fire or other human-caused threats). For example, many companies use a device called *uninterrupted power supply* (UPS), which provides power in case of a power outage.

# *IT* at Work 16.3

## Business Continuity and Disaster Recovery

Ninety-there percent of companies that suffer a significant data loss die within five years, according to Freeman Mendel, the chair of the FBI's 2006 Infragard National Conference. Even though business continuity/disaster recovery (BC/DR) is a business survival issue, many managers have dangerously viewed BC/DR as an IT security issue.

Disasters teach the best lessons for both IT managers and corporate executives who have not implemented BC/DR processes. The success or failure of those processes depends on IT, as the following case indicates.

The city of Houston, Texas, and Harris County swung into action by turning Reliant Park and the Houston Astrodome into a "temporary city" with a medical facility, pharmacy, post office, and town square to house more than 250,000 hurricane Katrina evacuees. Coast Guard Lt. Commander Joseph J. Leonard headed up the operation, drawing on his knowledge of the National Incident Command System. As Leonard explained, ineffective communication between the command staff and those in New Orleans, who could have informed Houston authorities about the number and special needs of the evacuees, caused a serious problem. In addition, agencies and organizations with poor on-scene decision-making authority hampered and slowed efforts to get things done.

Now businesses in hurricane alleys, earthquake corridors, and major cities are deploying BC/DR plans supported with software tools that allow them to replicate, or back up, their mission-critical applications to sites away from their primary data centers. In case of a disaster, companies can transmit vital accounting, project management, or transactional systems and records to their disaster recovery facilities, limiting downtime and data loss despite an outage at the primary location.

Globally, regulators are increasingly paying closer attention to business continuity and recovery times, which are now measured in hours rather than days. The Australian Prudential Regulation Authority (APRA) released its prudential standard on business continuity in April 2005. APRA gave Australian firms only 12 months to fix their compliance gaps.

*Sources:* Compiled from Fagg (2006), *Fiber Optics Weekly* (January 13, 2006), and the Infragard (*infragardconferences.com*).

*For Further Exploration:* Why might a company that had a significant data loss not be able to recover? Why are regulators requiring that companies implement BC/DR plans?

# 16.8 Implementing Security: Auditing and Risk Management

Implementing controls in an organization can be a very complicated task, particularly in large, decentralized companies where administrative controls may be difficult to enforce. Of the many issues involved in implementing controls, three are described here: auditing information systems, risk analysis, and IT security trends, including use of advanced intelligent systems.

Controls are established to ensure that information systems work properly. Controls can be installed in the original system, or they can be added once a system is in operation. Installing controls is necessary but not sufficient. It is also necessary to answer questions such as the following: Are controls installed as intended? Are they effective? Are they working reliably? Did any breach of security occur? If so, what actions are required to prevent reoccurrence? These questions need to be answered by independent and unbiased observers. Such observers perform the information system *auditing* task (e.g., see Stone and Marotta, 2003).

**AUDITING INFORMATION SYSTEMS**

An **audit** is an important part of any control system. In an organizational setting, it is usually referred to as a periodical *examination and check* of financial and accounting records and procedures. In the information system environment, auditing can be viewed as an additional layer of controls or safeguards. Auditing is considered as a deterrent to criminal actions (Wells, 2002), especially for insiders.

Auditors attempt to answer questions such as these:

Are there sufficient controls in the system? Which areas are not covered by controls? Which controls are not necessary?

Are the controls implemented properly?

Are the controls effective? That is, do they check the output of the system?

Is there a clear separation of duties of employees?

Are there procedures to ensure compliance with the controls?

Are there procedures to ensure reporting and corrective actions in case of violations of controls?

**Auditing Web Systems and E-Commerce.**  Auditing a Web site is a good preventive measure to manage the legal risk. Legal risk is important in any IT system, but in Web systems it is even more important due to the content of the site, which may offend people or be in violation of copyright laws or other regulations (e.g., privacy protection). Auditing EC is also more complex since in addition to the Web site one needs to audit order taking, order fulfillment, and all support systems.

**RISK MANAGEMENT AND COST-BENEFIT ANALYSIS**

It is usually not economical to prepare protection against every possible threat. Therefore, an IT security program must provide a process for assessing threats and deciding which ones to prepare for and which ones to ignore or provide reduced protection against.

**Risk-Management Analysis.**  Risk-management analysis can be enhanced by the use of DSS software packages. A simplified computation is shown here:

$$\text{Expected loss} = P_1 \times P_2 \times L$$

where:

$P_1$ = probability of attack (estimate, based on judgment)

$P_2$ = probability of attack being successful (estimate, based on judgment)

$L$ = loss occurring if attack is successful

*Example:*

$$P_1 = .02, P_2 = .10, L = \$1,000,000$$

Then, expected loss from this particular attack is:

$$P_1 \times P_2 \times L = 0.02 \times 0.1 \times \$1,000,000 = \$2,000$$

The amount of loss may depend on the duration of a system being out of operation. Therefore, some add duration to the analysis (e.g., see Volonino and Robinson, 2004).

**ETHICS**

**Ethical Issues.**  Implementing security programs raises many ethical issues. First, some people are against any monitoring of individual activities. Imposing certain controls is seen by some as a violation of freedom of speech or other civil rights. A GartnerGroup study showed that even after the terrorist attacks of 9/11/2001, only 26 percent of Americans approved a national ID database. Using biometrics is considered by many a violation of privacy.

Handling the privacy versus security dilemma is tough. There are other ethical and legal obligations that may require companies to "invade the privacy" of employees and monitor their actions. In particular, IT security measures are needed to protect against loss, liability, and litigation. Losses are not just financial, but also include the loss of information, customers, trading partners, brand image, and ability to conduct business due to the actions of hackers, malware, or employees. Liability stems from two legal doctrines: *respondeat superior* and duty of care. *Respondeat superior* holds employers liable for the misconduct of their employees that occurs within the scope of their employment. With wireless technologies and a mobile workforce, the scope of employment has expanded beyond the perimeters of the company. Under the doctrine of duty of care, senior managers and directors have a fiduciary obligation to use reasonable care to protect the company's business operations (*National Law Journal,* 2002). Litigation, or lawsuits, stems from failure to meet the company's legal and regulatory duties. According to the *2004 Workplace E-Mail and Instant Messaging Survey* of 840 U.S. companies from American Management Association and the ePolicy Institute (*epolicyinstitute.com*), more than one in five employers (21 percent) have had employee e-mail and IM subpoenaed in the course of a lawsuit or regulatory investigation—up from 9 percent in 2001 and 14 percent in 2003 (*epolicyinstitute.com*).

In the next section, we discuss the important role of computer forensics in IT security. Computer forensics is used in the detection or discovery of hack attacks, intrusions, fraud, theft of intellectual property, employment violations (e.g., harassment, discrimination, or noncompete agreement violation), and other criminal activities.

## 16.9 Computer Forensics

Crime has a new digital frontier—wired and wireless communications and devices that record activities with precision. Computers and communication devices create and store huge amounts of "digital details" in their memory, data files, and logs. In addition, as files and messages are saved or sent, software automatically generates detailed records of them. As businesses move steadily in the direction of electronic communication, computer files, and data storage, business records, communication, and other activities are in electronic format. Computers and Internet activities record what has been said and done. Laptop computers, PDAs, iPods, DVDs, digital cameras, and cell phones leave cybertrails of **electronic evidence (e-evidence)** (Volonino et al., 2007). When any of those devices are used to commit a crime, those devices become crime scenes. When law enforcement or regulators demand—with a subpoena or search warrant—that electronic records be turned over as part of an investigation, failure to do so is an **obstruction of justice.** Recall that Arthur Andersen no longer exists and Martha Stewart served time in jail because they had been found guilty of obstruction of justice.

The search, discovery, and recovery of e-evidence is referred to as **computer forensics.** E-mail, whether it has been deleted or not, is the most common form of e-evidence.

**ELECTRONIC FRAUD AND CYBERCRIMES**

Crimes occur in organizations and organizations are victims of crimes. When a computer crime involves money, it is referred to as **computer fraud** or **electronic fraud (e-fraud).** Investigations of fraud or malfeasance almost always require the discovery of e-evidence. Forensic accounting methods may be needed to discover complex financial statement fraud.

Perpetrators may be insiders who embezzle funds, violate another's civil rights by sending objectionable e-mail, or download child pornography (a federal crime) to laptops. E-evidence left by their electronic activities needs to be found. *A Closer Look 16.5* gives an example of the value of computer forensics to a company victimized by a cybercriminal.

# A Closer Look 16.5

## Computer Forensics Used to Discover Weaknesses

In September 2004, hackers dropped a malicious program on the application platform of CardSystems Solutions, a credit card payment processor. The malware was injected via the Web application that customers use to access account information. Every four days, the program would run—extracting data, zipping them, and exporting them to an FTP site. Its function was to search servers for track data (i.e., name, credit card number, expiration date, and CVV code contained on the magnetic strip on the back of a credit card). The only time data were successfully exported was May 22. The exported data—records of failed transactions that were kept for research purposes—were in readable (plaintext) form, a violation of the Payment Card Industry (PCI) security standard.

CardSystems hired AmbironTrustWave, a security auditor, to perform a forensic analysis and consult on compliance. The forensics analysis was needed to understand where card data was kept and how it was accessed, and to ensure that the hack could not be replicated. After another security breach at CardSystems' Tucson service center, Visa USA dropped CardSystems Solutions Inc. from its network of transaction processors. Visa's member banks had until October 31, 2005 to stop using CardSystems to process card transactions.

*Sources:* Compiled from Mimoso (2006) and Wichner (2005).

## ROLE OF COMPUTER FORENSICS

The following two cases illustrate the key role of computer forensics. The FBI learned that a former defense contractor was trying to sell secrets to foreign governments about the B-2 stealth bomber, one of the most powerful weapons in the U.S. defense arsenal. They analyzed deleted documents from the suspect's computer, including electronic correspondence with people the suspect had contacted. On October 26, 2005, Noshir S. Gowadia, who had worked for Northrup for 18 years, was arrested and indicted on three counts of illegally transmitting national defense information and three counts of violating the Arms Export Control Act.

The creator of the Melissa virus, David L. Smith, who was the first person convicted for spreading a computer virus, was tracked down by a combination of e-evidence. A few of those trails included the following: the unique hardware identification number in Office 97 files that made it traceable to the PC on which it was created; the AOL return-address used in the virus's original post and AOL's log files showing the phone line that had been used to send the virus; and the destroyed and disposed of PC used to create and launch the Melissa virus in the trash bin at David L. Smith's apartment complex.

## FORENSIC ACCOUNTING

In cases involving fraudulent financial reporting issues, such as listing phony assets or concealing debts, a forensic accounting investigation is conducted. Forensic accounting investigations are a specific type of fraud investigation used, for example, to distinguish between cases of illegal criminal fraud and legal "creative accounting." Fraud investigators of all types typically include the search for e-evidence of concealing, altering, or destroying documents or financial transactions. See Minicase 2 for a discussion of how accounting fraud was discovered at NEC. The following examples of use of computer forensics to investigate occupational fraud illustrate its importance.

- A fraud investigation was undertaken in response to allegations that revenues of a manufacturer had been deliberately manipulated to significantly inflate profits, which in turn would inflate bonuses to senior staff. Recovered incriminating e-mail messages revealed that senior staff were behind the accounting fraud. Some were dismissed and asked to repay their bonuses (Tait, 2005).

- Two accountants at Cisco Systems received 34-month jail terms for using their access privileges to Cisco's databases to credit themselves with $8 million in company stock (Leibs, 2002).
- A database administrator at Prudential Insurance Co. was charged with money laundering, credit card fraud, and identity theft. He was alleged to have copied the confidential data of 60,000 employees, which he then attempted to sell over the Internet (Leibs, 2002).

Fraud is a crime that is rarely noticed. The purpose of forensic accounting is to detect ongoing fraud and investigate it after it has occurred. More generally, computer forensics is used to discover and compile e-evidence necessary to prosecute illegal acts or violations of AUPs.

# 16.10  Managerial Issues

**1. What is the business value of IT security and internal control?** IT security risks are business risks. IT security is so integral to business objectives that it cannot be treated as a standalone function. Information security has evolved into a core business issue with legal obligations.

**2. Why are there legal obligations?** The legal issues surrounding information security are rooted in the fact that virtually all of a company's daily transactions and confidential records are created, used, communicated, and stored in electronic form and must be protected.

**3. How important is IT security to management?** Management's obligation to insure data security has increased significantly. The financial damages and disruption caused by hackers, phishers, spammers, identity thieves, malware, and terrorists worldwide are tremendous.

**ETHICS**

**4. IT security and internal control must be implemented top-down.** Effective enterprisewide IT security begins with senior management commitment and support. The power of senior managers is needed to enforce secure and ethical security and privacy practices.

**5. Acceptable use policies (AUPs) and security awareness training are important for any organization.** The number-one threat to IT security since 2002 has been human error. IT security depends on people as well as processes and technology.

**6. Digital assets are relied upon for competitive advantage.** At a strategic level, the totality of a company's data resources is nearly irreplaceable. BI, ERP, CRM, and e-commerce business operations depend on the integrity, availability, and authorized use of IT resources.

**7. What does risk management involve?** Risk management includes securing corporate systems, networks, and data, ensuring availability of systems and services, planning for disaster recovery and business continuity, complying with government regulations and license agreements, and protecting the organization against malware, spyware, and profit-motivated hacking.

**8. What are the impacts of IT security breaches?** Privacy breaches and security incidents lead to fines and customer attrition. IT security failures have a direct impact on business performance because they can no longer be hidden.

**9. Federal and state regulations.** Stringent federal and state regulations are having a major impact on data security practices. Record-setting fines are being used to compel management to invest in all reasonable security defenses.

**10. Internal control and computer forensics.** If internal controls can be ignored, there is no control. If the company shows its employees that the company can find out everything that every employee does and use that evidence to prosecute that person to the fullest extent, then the feeling that "I can get away with it" drops drastically.

## Integrating *IT*

Pressure to meet compliance, security, and risk management responsibilities is felt by every business department. Defenses against formidable external and internal threats, business continuity, and quick recovery from control and policy failures are demanded by customers, trading partners, investors, regulators, professional ethics boards, and various laws.

### For the Accounting Major

The information security requirements for public companies, their accountants, and auditors have changed significantly. Accountants are being held professionally responsible for reducing risk, assuring compliance, eliminating fraud, and increasing the transparency of transactions according to GAAP (Generally Accepted Accounting Principles). The SEC and PCAOB (Public Company Accounting Oversight Board), among other regulatory agencies, demand information security, fraud prevention and detection, and internal controls over financial reporting. One of the hottest accounting careers is forensic accounting.

### For the Finance Major

As IT security becomes ever more critical to the success of any organization, it is no longer just the concern of the CTO or CIO. With global regulatory requirements and Sarbanes-Oxley §302, responsibility for information security lies with the CEO and CFO. As a result, all aspects of the audit, including security of information and IT systems, are a key concern for the finance function.

At the same time, CFOs and treasurers are increasingly involved in IT investment decision making. They are realizing that a security breach of any kind can have catastrophic financial effects on a company. Just as it is important to have a good insurance policy in place to protect against unforeseen business circumstances, so, too, is it important to have good security protocols in effect to protect against unforeseen attacks.

### For the Human Resources Management Major

The HR function is responsible for two key legal obligations: (1) the duty to provide reasonable security for their corporate data and information systems; and (2) the duty to disclose security breaches to those who may be affected adversely by them. HR departments have clear obligations to secure confidential employee data and provide a nonhostile work environment. Getting explicit consent from all employees verifying that they understand the acceptable use policy is a critical defense against charges of harassment, discrimination, and wrongful termination.

### For the IS Major

All application development, network deployment, and introduction of new IT have to be guided by IT security considerations. Some of the technologies the information systems department (ISD) must understand are spam filtering, VPN, VoIP, WEP, WPA, server access controls, intrusion detection, encryption, password management, authentication, and biometrics. The ISD must customize the risk exposure security model to help the company identify security risks and prepare responses to incidents or disasters.

Senior executives look to the ISD for help in meeting its SOX mandates, particularly in detecting "significant deficiencies" or "material weaknesses" in internal controls and remediating them. Other departments look to the ISD to help them meet their security responsibilities.

### For the Marketing Major

Customers expect their data to be safe. Profit-motivated hackers want that data. Marketers need to weigh the risk exposure of their operations. Failure to protect corporate and customer data is likely to bring on significant public relations problems and very angry customers. CRM operations and tracking customers' online buying habits can expose data to misuse (if not encrypted) or result in privacy violations. Marketers need to insure customer data security and privacy, which can be used to attract and retain customers.

### For the Production/Operations Management Major

Every process in a company's operations—inventory purchasing, receiving, quality control, production, and shipping—can be disrupted by an IT security failure or the failure of a trading partner. Basically, any weak link in supply chain management or enterprise resource management systems puts everyone at risk. Companies are held liable for IT security failures that impact other companies.

# Key Terms

Acceptable use policy
   (AUP) *631*
Application controls *639*
Audit *649*
Banking Trojan *635*
Biometric control *640*
Bot *628*
Botnet *628*
Business continuity plan *647*
Business impact analysis
   (BIA) *632*
Ciphertext *643*
COBIT *624*
Committee of Sponsoring
   Organizations of the Treadway
   Commission (COSO) *631*
Computer forensics *651*
Computer fraud *651*
Cracker *634*

Cyber-blackmail *627*
Cyber Storm *633*
Data tampering *634*
Disaster recovery plan *647*
Electronic evidence
   (e-evidence) *651*
Electronic fraud (e-fraud) *651*
Firewall *642*
General controls *638*
Hacker *633*
Intelligent agents *641*
Internal control environment *645*
Multifactor authentication *643*
Obstruction of justice *651*
Occupational fraud *635*
Payment Card Industry (PCI) Data
   Security Standard *626*
Plaintext *643*
Programming attack *634*

Remote access servers
   (RASs) *643*
Risk exposure *631*
Risk exposure model *624*
Rogue access point (AP) *644*
Social engineering *634*
Time-to-exploitation *625*
Trojan-Phisher-Rebery *635*
Two-factor authentication *643*
Two-tier authentication *643*
Wired equivalent privacy
   (WEP) *644*
Wireless access points
   (APs or WAPs) *644*
Wireless packet analyzers *644*
Worm *634*
Zero-day incidents *630*

# Chapter Highlights

(Numbers Refer to Learning Objectives)

❶ Businesses that neglect to consider and implement privacy requirements are subject to enforcement actions, huge lawsuits, penalties, and fines that significantly increase expenses.

❶ A company's top line (revenue) suffers when customers discover that their private information has been compromised.

❶ Criminals invest considerable effort planning and preparing tactics to bypass company security measures.

❷ Responsibility for internal control and compliance rests directly on the shoulders of senior management and the board of directors. SOX and other antifraud regulations force better business reporting and disclosure of GAAP violations, thus making it necessary and easier to find and root out fraud.

❷ The chief privacy officer (CPO) and chief security officer (CSO) are corporate-level positions demonstrating the importance and changing role of IT security in organizations.

❸ Data, software, hardware, and networks can be threatened by internal and external hazards.

❸ One of the biggest mistakes managers make is they underestimate vulnerabilities and threats.

❸ Computer criminals are increasingly profit-driven.

❹ The risk exposure model for digital assets has five factors: the asset's value to the company, attractiveness to criminals, legal liability attached to its loss or theft, impact on business performance, and likelihood of a successful attack.

❹ The consequences of wireless attacks include data theft, legal and recovery expenses, tarnished image, lost customers, and disrupted operations due to loss of network service.

❺ With two-factor authentication, two types of information are used to verify the user's identity, such as passwords and biometrics.

❺ Biometric controls are used to identify users by checking physical characteristics such as a fingerprint or voice-print.

❺ Encryption is extremely important for confidential data that are sent or stored.

❻ The Committee of Sponsoring Organizations of the Treadway Commission (COSO) defines internal control as a process designed to provide reasonable assurance of effective operations and reliable financial reporting.

❻ There is no such thing as small fraud, only large fraud that was detected and stopped early.

7 Disaster recovery planning is an integral part of effective internal control and security management.

7 Business continuity planning includes data backup and a plan for what to do when disaster strikes.

8 Protecting critical infrastructures, including energy, IT, telecommunications, and transportation sectors, is a key part of national security.

8 A large range of IT security tools, including intelligent agents and antifraud measures, help defend against counterterrorist activities.

9 Computer forensics is used to detect and investigate computer intrusions, policy violations, and illegal activities.

9 Forensic accounting investigations are a specific type of fraud investigation.

## Virtual Company Assignment

### Managing Information Resources and Security at The Wireless Café

Go to The Wireless Café's link on the Student Web Site. There you will be asked to analyze security vulnerabilities of the restaurant's information resources.

**Instructions for accessing The Wireless Café Web Site on the Student Web Site:**

1. Go to *wiley.com/college/turban*.
2. Select Turban/Leidner/McLean/Wetherbe's *Information Technology for Management*, Sixth Edition.
3. Click on Student Resources site, in the toolbar on the left.
4. Click on the link for Virtual Company Web Site.
5. Click on Wireless Café.

## Online Resources

More resources and study tools are located on the Student Web Site and on WileyPLUS. You'll find additional chapter materials and useful Web links. In addition, self-quizzes that provide individualized feedback are available for each chapter.

## Questions for Review

1. Define IT governance.
2. Explain COBIT's IT governance framework.
3. Explain the PCI Data Security Standard.
4. What is cyber-blackmail?
5. Define bot and botnet.
6. What is the Infragard? What is its purpose?
7. Define zero-day incidents.
8. Why is "tone at the top" important to IT security effectiveness?
9. Define acceptable use policy. Explain its importance.
10. Define risk exposure.
11. List five components of the risk exposure model.
12. Define business impact analysis.
13. What is a banking Trojan?
14. Define occupational fraud. List four examples.
15. What is the general meaning of intelligent agents?

16. Define plaintext and ciphertext.
17. Explain VPNs. What do they replace?
18. What is the difference between two-factor authentication and two-tier authentication?
19. Define biometrics. List five of them.
20. Why are biometric controls popular? What are some of their limitations?
21. Describe voice over IP (VoIP). What technology does it replace?
22. List and describe internal control procedures and activities.
23. Define cyberterrorism. List three IT tools that can help defend against terrorist tactics.
24. Define access control.
25. Explain computer forensics and list two examples of what it can reveal.
26. Define forensic accounting.

## Questions for Discussion

1. Many firms concentrate on the wrong questions and end up throwing a great deal of money and time at minimal security risks while ignoring major vulnerabilities. Why?

2. How can the risk of occupational fraud be decreased?

3. Why should information control and security be of prime concern to management?

4. Compare the computer security situation with that of insuring a house.

5. Explain what firewalls protect and what they do not protect. Why?

6. Describe how IS auditing works and how it is related to traditional accounting and financial auditing.

7. Why are authentication and authorization important in e-commerce?

8. Some insurance companies will not insure a business unless the firm has a computer disaster recovery plan. Explain why.

9. Explain why risk management should involve the following elements: threats, exposure associated with each threat, risk of each threat occurring, cost of controls, and assessment of their effectiveness.

10. Some people have recently suggested using viruses and similar programs in wars between countries. What is the logic of such a proposal? How could it be implemented?

11. Compare a corporatewide security plan to another enterprisewide IT-based plan (such as KM or CRM). What is similar? What is different?

12. Why is cross-border cybercrime expanding rapidly? Discuss some possible solutions.

13. Discuss why the Sarbanes-Oxley Act is having an impact on information security.

## Exercises and Projects

1. A critical problem is assessing how far a company is legally obligated to go. Since there is no such thing as perfect security (i.e., there is always more that you can do), resolving these questions can significantly affect cost.
   a. When are security measures that a company implements sufficient to comply with its obligations? For example, does installing a firewall and using virus detection software satisfy a company's legal obligations?
   b. Is it necessary for an organization to encrypt all of its electronic records?

2. The SANS Institute and the National Infrastructure Protection Center (NIPC) at the FBI published the Top 20 Internet Security Vulnerabilities (*sans.org/top20*).
   a. Which of those vulnerabilities are most dangerous to financial institutions?
   b. Which of those vulnerabilities are most dangerous to marketing firms?
   c. Explain any differences.

3. Read the "Model Letter for the Compromise of Social Security Numbers" (at *ftc.gov/bcp/conline/pubs/buspubs/ idtrespond.htm*) suggested by the FTC for companies to use to notify people whose names and Social Security numbers have been stolen.
   a. Why does the FTC provide such a letter?
   b. What does the letter instruct potential victims to do?

4. Access the Anti-Phishing Working Group Web site (*antiphishing.org*) and download the most recent Phishing Activity Trends Report.
   a. Describe the recent trends in phishing and pharming attacks.
   b. Explain the reasons for these trends.

5. Read Online File W16.6. Answer the "For Further Exploration" questions.

6. Read Online File W16.10. Answer the "For Further Exploration" questions.

7. Read Online File W16.13. Answer the "For Further Exploration" questions.

8. Read Online File W16.14. Answer the "For Further Exploration" questions.

9. Download Online File W16.12, *Exercise-9-Spam-costs. xls*. Complete the spreadsheet to estimate the cost of spam on the organization.

10. Assume that the daily probability of a major earthquake in Los Angeles is .07 percent. The chance of your computer center being damaged during such a quake is 5 percent. If the center is damaged, the average estimated damage will be $1.6 million.
    a. Calculate the expected loss (in dollars).
    b. An insurance agent is willing to insure your facility for an annual fee of $15,000. Analyze the offer, and discuss whether to accept it.

11. The theft of laptop computers at conventions, hotels, and airports is becoming a major problem. These categories of protection exist: physical devices (e.g., *targus.com*), encryption (e.g., *networkassociates.com*), and security policies (e.g., at *ebay.com*). Find more information on the problem and on the solutions. Summarize the advantages and limitations of each method.

12. Expert systems can be used to analyze the profiles of computer users. Such analysis may enable better intrusion detection. Should an employer notify employees

that their usage of computers is being monitored by an expert system? Why or why not?

13. Twenty-five thousand messages arrive at an organization each year. Currently there are no firewalls. On the average there are 1.2 successful hackings each year. Each successful hacking results in loss to the company of about $130,000. A major firewall is proposed at a cost of $66,000 and a maintenance cost of $5,000. The estimated useful life is 3 years. The chance that an

intruder will break through the firewall is 0.0002. In such a case, the damage will be $100,000 (30%), or $200,000 (50%), or no damage. There is an annual maintenance cost of $20,000 for the firewall.

a. Should management buy the firewall?

b. An improved firewall that is 99.9988 percent effective and that costs $84,000, with a life of 3 years and annual maintenance cost of $16,000, is available. Should this one be purchased instead of the first one?

## Group Assignments and Projects

1. Each group is to be divided into two parts. One part will interview students and businesspeople and record the experiences they have had with computer security problems. The other part of each group will visit a computer store (and/or read the literature or use the Internet) to find out what software is available to fight different computer security problems. Then, each group will prepare a presentation in which they describe the problems and identify which of the problems could have been prevented with the use of commercially available software.

2. Create groups to investigate the latest development in IT and e-commerce security. Check journals such as *cio.com* (available free online), vendors, and search engines such as *techdata.com*, and *google.com*.

3. Research the botnet attack in 2006. Explain how the botnet works and what damage it causes. Examine Microsoft's attempts to prevent similar future attacks. Investigate similarities between the 2006 hackers and earlier ones. What preventive methods are offered by security vendors?

4. Read *In the Matter of BJ's Wholesale Club, Inc.,* Agreement containing Consent Order, FTC File No. 042 3160, June 16, 2005 at *ftc.gov/opa/2005/06/bjswholesale.htm.* Describe the security breach at BJ's Wholesale Club. What was the reason for this agreement? Using the enterprisewide IT security and internal control model in Figure 16.4, identify some of the causes of the security breach and how BJ's can better defend itself against hackers and legal liability.

## Internet Exercises

1. Visit *cert.org* (a center of Internet security expertise). Read one of the recent Security Alerts and write a report.

2. Visit *cert.org/csirts/services.html*. Discover the security services a CSIRT can provide in handling vulnerability. Write a summary of those services.

3. Visit *dhs.gov/dhspublic* (Department of Homeland Security). Search the site for "National Strategy to Secure Cyberspace" and write a report on their agenda and accomplishments to date.

4. Visit *first.org* (a global leader in incident response). Find a current article under "Global Security New" and write a summary.

5. Visit *issa.org* (Information Systems Security Association) and choose a Webcast to listen to—one concerned with systems security. Write a short opinion essay.

6. Visit *wi-fi.org* (Wi-Fi Alliance) and discover what their mission is and report on what you think about their relevance in the overall wireless security industry.

7. Visit *securitytracker.com* and select one of the vulnerabilities. Describe the vulnerability, its impacts, its cause, and the affected operating system.

8. Visit *cio.com/security* and select a recent article on security, privacy, or compliance. Write a brief summary of the article.

9. Enter *scambusters.org*. Find out what the organization does. Learn about e-mail and Web site scams. Report your findings.

10. Enter *epic.org/privacy/tools.html*, and examine the following groups of tools: Web encryption, disk encryption, and PC firewalls. Explain how these tools can be used to facilitate the security of your PC.

11. Access the Web sites of the major antivirus vendors (*symantec.com, mcafee.com,* and *antivirus.com*). Find out what the vendors' research centers are doing. Also download VirusScan from McAfee and scan your hard drive with it.

12. You have installed a DSL line in your home and you need a firewall. Enter *securitydogs.com, macafee.com* or *symantec.com*. Find three possible products. Which one do you like best? Why?

13. Access a good search engine (e.g., *google.com* or *findarticles.com*). Find recent articles on disaster planning. Prepare a short report on recent developments in disaster recovery planning.

**14.** The use of smart cards for electronic storage of user identification, user authentication, changing passwords, and so forth is on the rise. Surf the Internet and report on recent developments. (For example, try the Web sites *microsoft.com/windows/smartcards, litronic.com, gemplus.com,* or *scia.org.*)

**15.** Enter *biopay.com* and other vendors of biometrics and find the devices they make that can be used to access control into information systems. Prepare a list of major capabilities.

# Minicase 1

## Preventing and Detecting Operational Risk Caused by Employees

**ACC    FIN    IS    MKT    OM**

One of the most threatening types of risk to an organization, according to risk and compliance managers, is employees—either through deliberate fraud or unintended mistakes. These risks cannot be dealt with from a departmental or business-unit perspective. An enterprisewide approach to operational risk management is required to create a seamless solution.

Brendon Young, chief executive of the Operational Risk Research Forum (ORRF) (*orrf.org*), estimates that most organizations lose 2 to 5 percent of their annual revenues through fraud committed by either staff, customers, or outsiders. Of that, about 80 percent of frauds are committed by staff. Other fraud researchers report similar estimates. See Albrecht and Albrecht (2003).

In addition to financial theft by an employee, a company may be victimized in less obvious ways. An employee taking client or product information with him to a new company may not understand that he is committing a crime or even have a sense of what impact his actions can have on the new or old company. In other cases, employees may consider confidential and proprietary information developed in part or in whole by them to be their own personal property or an entitlement for years of service. Intellectual property theft can hurt a company's competitive advantage and brand image.

Disgruntled employees pose serious risks because of their access to information and networks. An informative example is that of a former employee of clothing retailer American Eagle Outfitters, who was sentenced to prison for password trafficking and computer damage (DOJ, 2003). After being terminated, the disgruntled former employee sought revenge. On a Yahoo! hacker posting board, he posted and maintained the username and password combinations of legitimate American Eagle Outfitters users, together with detailed instructions on how to hack into American Eagle Outfitters' network using those passwords. "The former employee then hacked into the American Eagle Outfitters computer network. These [intrusions] were attempts to deny computer services to American Eagle Outfitters during the beginning of the Christmas shopping season."

Since frauds that have a material impact on financial statements or that involve data theft must be reported, they will be made public and may get media attention. Customers do not ignore those risks even if they are not a victim.

There is also increasing evidence that organized criminal groups are placing people in financial services firms so that they can learn about firms' systems and controls and how to circumvent them. Traditional criminals are getting more interested in cybercrime as evidenced by the kidnapping of a Russian software developer in order to get him to write malicious code.

The World Bank has identified fraud and corruption as the greatest obstacles to economic and social development. Such crimes delay growth and development by stealing away resources and weakening the institutional foundations on which economic growth depends.

### Basel II Guidelines

The Basel II Capital Accord provides guidance for managing operational risk and internal fraud. It defines operational risk as "the risk of loss resulting from inadequate or failed internal processes, people and systems or from external events." It recommends that any internal operational risk measurement system be consistent with this definition and with the loss event types defined in Annex 7. To download the podcast "How to Avoid the Seven Pitfalls of Basel II Operational Risk" (.mp3, 3MB), visit *bearingpoint.com/survey/index.asp?survey_id=287.* Annex 7 defines seven categories of loss:

**1.** Internal fraud
**2.** External fraud
**3.** Employment practices and workplace safety
**4.** Clients, products, and business practices
**5.** Damage to physical assets
**6.** Business disruption and systems failures
**7.** Execution, delivery, and process management

Well-executed internal fraud or money-laundering operations can severely damage or destroy any size company. Preventing internal fraud is high on the political agenda, with the FSA in the U.K. and the SEC in the United States both requiring companies to deal with the issue. Also, the Basel II accord imposes rigorous antifraud requirements for banks.

## IT Helps Detect Internal Fraud

IT has a key role to play in demonstrating good corporate governance and fraud prevention. Regulators will look favorably on companies that can demonstrate good corporate governance and best practice operational risk management. Management and staff of such companies will then spend less time worrying about regulations and more time adding value to their brand and business.

Internal fraud prevention measures are based on controls that reduce the opportunity for unauthorized use of corporate resources, including perimeter defense technologies, such as firewalls, e-mail scanners, and biometric access. They are also based on soft procedures, such as recruitment screening and training.

Much of this detection activity can be handled by intelligent analysis engines using advanced data warehousing and analytics techniques. These systems take in audit trails from key systems and personnel records from the human resources and finance departments. The data are stored in a data warehouse where they are analyzed to detect anomalous patterns, such as excessive hours worked, deviations in patterns of behavior, copying huge amounts of data, attempts to override controls, unusual transactions, and inadequate documentation about a transaction. Information from investigations is fed back into the detection system so that it learns.

Since insiders might work in collusion with organized criminals, insider profiling is important to find wider patterns of criminal networks.

An enterprisewide approach to operational risk management that combines risk, security, compliance, and IT specialists greatly increases the prevention and detection of fraud. Prevention is the most cost-effective approach since detection and prosecution costs are enormous in addition to the direct cost of the loss. It starts with corporate governance culture and ethics at the top levels of the organization.

*Sources:* Compiled from Albrecht and Albrecht (2003), DOJ (2003), and Imeson (2006).

### Questions for Minicase 1

1. Relate the issues in this case to the four components of the IT security model in Figure 16.4.
2. What events triggered the strong measures to prevent and detect internal fraud? Name three laws that have antifraud measures.
3. State one example of each of the seven categories of loss defined by Annex 7. How could they be prevented or, if they had already occurred, how could they be detected?
4. How might expert systems or AI be used to detect fraud in realtime or after it has occurred?
5. Do you think that prevention is the only cost-effective approach to fraud? Explain.

---

## Minicase 2

## Accounting Fraud at NEC Leads to Five-Year Earnings Restatement

In 2006, NEC had to restate its earnings for five prior years after discovering that a 50-year-old manager/engineer had been fabricating business deals. The bogus deals inflated sales by 36.3 billion yen ($311 million). The false transactions enabled the manager to embezzle tens of millions of yen, which he spent on entertainment.

NEC (2006) released the following cautionary note in their April 21, 2006 financial forecast:

> As announced on March 22, 2006, NEC is planning to restate its consolidated financial results for past fiscal years as a result of revisions relating to fictitious transactions carried out at an NEC subsidiary and other revisions based on U.S. generally accepted accounting principles (U.S. GAAP). However, as exact figures have yet to be determined, NEC has not set forth the restated results for the fiscal year ended March 31, 2005, but will disclose such information as soon as possible.

NEC had discovered a series of false transactions that occurred from March 2002 until December 2005 in the semiconductor production department at NEC Engineering (NECE) Ltd., a wholly owned subsidiary. The fraudulent transactions amounted to nearly 10 percent of NECE's sales between 2001 and 2004.

The NECE manager, who in March 2002 anticipated poor performance in his department, convinced a client-company to make up bogus transactions. He went on to make up about 200 orders and payments by forging order and estimation forms. He allowed firms that pretended to have received deliveries to make payments to NECE for items that were never delivered.

NEC filed criminal actions against the manager, reviewed its internal control system, and strengthened the administration of those controls. The company had not been able to detect the fraud because the manager involved had been in a position to prepare all necessary documents that made the fictitious trades look real. There was no separation of duties, oversight, surprise audits, or forced vacation times, which might have caught the fraud. For more information on preventing and detecting fraud, see *ACFE.com* and *AICPA.org*. Despite an internal investigation, it did not become clear how the manager was able to falsify all the data and payments.

*Sources:* Compiled from NEC, *NEC* (2006), Nakamoto (2006), and Yomiuri (2006).

## Questions for Minicase 2

1. What might have been some of the indicators that the NECE manager/engineer was committing fraud? What type of information systems could have helped to detect the fraud?

2. Use an Internet browser to do a search on the term "restatement of earnings." Explain the results.

3. Create a table consisting of five columns. In the columns list (1) the company names, (2) the period over which the restatement was made, (3) the incident or regulatory agency that prompted or required the restatement, (4) the impact of earnings, and (5) the stock price at the start of the period of restatement and the stock price soon after the announcement of the restatement.

4. From your Internet search, select four companies that had announced within the past three years that they were restating their earnings and fill in the first four columns.

5. Use a financial Web site, such as *finance.yahoo.com*, to find the stock prices for the fifth column.

6. What impact did the restatement have on each of the four companies?

# References

2004 Survey, *Workplace E-Mail and Instant Messaging Survey*, American Management Association and The ePolicy Institute, *epolicyinstitute.com/survey/index.html* (accessed June 11, 2006).

2005 *Identity Fraud Survey Report,* January 26, 2005, *javelinstrategy. com/reports/2005IdentityFraudSurveyReport.html* (accessed June 9, 2006).

Alga, N., "Increasing Security Levels," *Information Systems Control Journal,* March–April 2002.

Albrecht, W. S., and C. O. Albrecht, *Fraud Investigation and Prevention.* South-Western, 2003.

Altman, H., "Jihad Web Snares Online Shops, Buyers," *Tampa Tribune,* February 20, 2006.

Cane, A., "Lock It or You'll Lose It," *Financial Times* (London), May 31, 2006.

Caulfield, B., "The Trouble with Biometrics," *Business 2.0,* September 2002.

DOJ, "Former Employee of American Eagle Outfitters Sentenced to Prison for Password Trafficking and Computer Damage," December 2, 2003, *usdoj.gov/criminal/cybercrime/pattersonSent.htm* (accessed June 9, 2006).

Ewing, J., G. Kral, and K. Young, "Protecting Reputational Risk Through Data Privacy Compliance," *Metropolitan Corporate Counsel,* January 2006.

Fagg, S., "Continuity for the People," *Risk Management Magazine,* March 2006.

*Fiber Optics Weekly Update,* "Telstra Uses NetEx Gear," January 13, 2006.

Gage, D., "Bank of America Seeks Anti-Fraud Anodyne," *Baseline,* May 15, 2006.

Gross, G., "ChoicePoint's Error Sparks Talk of ID Theft Law," *IDG News Service,* February 23, 2005, *pcworld.com/news/article/0,aid, 119790,00.asp* (accessed June 9, 2006).

Hearing of the Senate Armed Services Committee on Worldwide Threats to U.S. National Security. Washington, D.C.: *Federal News Service,* February 28, 2006.

Imeson, M., "Foiling The Till Raiders," *The Banker,* January 1, 2006.

Kellner, M., "Is This the Year for Wireless Gear?" GCN, January 27, 2003, *gcn.com/print/22_2/20950-1.html* (accessed October 2006).

Koster, E. S., and A. Scott, "Breach and Tell: Security Breach Notification Laws," *Computer & Internet Lawyer,* March 2006.

Lam, W., "Ensuring Business Continuity," *IT Pro,* June 2002.

Leibs, S., "First, Who's On?" *CFO,* August 2002.

Luftman, J. N., et al., *Managing the Information Technology Resources.* Upper Saddle River, NJ: Pearson Education, 2004.

McCarthy, B., "The Security-Staff Disconnect," *Optimize,* April 1, 2006.

McConnell, M., "Information Assurance in the Twenty-first Century," *Supplement to Computer,* February 2002.

Mimoso, M. S., "Cleaning Up After a Data Attack: CardSystems' Joe Christensen," *Information Security,* April 14, 2006, *searchsecurity. techtarget.com/originalContent/0,289142,sid14_gci1180411,00.html* (accessed June 11, 2006).

Nakamoto, M., "NEC to Restate Earnings After Fraud," *Financial Times,* March 23, 2006.

"Now More Than Ever, Cybersecurity Audits Are Key," *National Law Journal,* 24(27), March 11, 2002.

NEC, "Revision of NEC Corporation's Financial Forecast for Fiscal Year Ended March 31, 2006, *nec.co.jp/press/en/0604/2101.html* (accessed October 2006).

Panko, R. R., *Corporate Computer and Network Security.* Upper Saddle River, NJ: Prentice-Hall, 2004.

Roberts, P. F., "Webroot Uncovers Thousands of Stolen Identities," *InfoWorld,* May 8, 2006, *infoworld.com/article/06/05/09/78139_ HNTrojanrebery_1.html* (accessed June 9, 2006).

Sandia National Laboratories, "Intelligent agents challenge computer intruders," 2002, *sandia.gov/media/NewsRel/NR2000/agent.htm* (accessed October 2006).

Scalet, S. D., "The Five Most Shocking Things About the ChoicePoint Debacle," *CSO,* May 1, 2005.

Spangler, T., "What You Can Learn from the VA's Snafu," *Baseline,* May 24, 2006, *baselinemag.com/article2/0,1540,1966952,00.asp* (accessed June 9, 2006).

Stone, D. L., and D. L. Marotta, "Leveraging Risk Technology," *Internal Auditing,* December 2003.

Tait, N., "Computer Records Provide 80% of Fraud Case Evidence," *Financial Times,* October 18, 2005.

Thomas, D., "StormPay Caught in a Whirlwind," *Financial Times,* May 31, 2006.

Thomas, T. L., "Al Qaeda and the Internet: The Danger of Cyberplanning," *Parameters,* March 22, 2003.

Vance, J., "It's Not Who You Know; It's What You Know Plus What You've Got," *Network World,* June 5, 2006.

Volonino, L., J. Godwin, and R. Anzaldua, *Computer Forensics: Principles and Practices.* Upper Saddle River, NJ: Prentice-Hall, 2007.

Volonino, L., and S. Robinson, *Principles and Practice of Information Security.* Upper Saddle River, NJ: Prentice-Hall, 2004.

Wells, J. T., "Occupational Fraud: The Audit as a Deterrent," *Journal of Accountancy,* April 2002.

Wichner, D., "Visa USA Drops CardSystems," *Arizona Daily Star,* July 19, 2005, *azstarnet.com/sn/related/84710.php* (accessed June 17, 2006).

Wolfe, D., "Security Watch," *American Banker,* June 2, 2006.

Yomiuri, "NEC Eyes Charges Over Fake Deals," *The Daily Yomiuri,* March 23, 2006.

**1G** The first generation of wireless technology, which was analog based.

**2G** The second generation of digital wireless technology; accommodates voice and text.

**2.5G** An interim wireless technology that can accommodate voice, text, and limited graphics.

**3G** The third generation of digital wireless technology; supports rich media such as video.

**3GSM (Third-generation Global System for Mobile Communications Services)** 3GSM enables mobile multimedia services such as music, TV and video, rich entertainment content and Internet access.

**4G** The expected next generation of wireless technology that will provide faster display of multimedia.

**802.11a** This Wi-Fi standard is faster than 802.11b but has a smaller range.

**802.11b** The most popular Wi-Fi standard; it is inexpensive and offers sufficient speed for most devices. However, interference can be a problem.

**802.11g** This fast but expensive Wi-Fi standard is mostly used in businesses.

**Acceptable use policy (AUP) Policy** that informs users of their responsibilities. An AUP serves two main purposes: (1) It helps to prevent misuse of information and computer resources and (2) It reduces exposure to legal liability.

**Adaptability** The ability to adjust the design of the supply chain to meet structural shifts in markets and modify supply network strategies, products, and technologies.

**Adaptive enterprise** An organization that can respond properly and in a timely manner to changes in the business environment.

**Ad-hoc query** Any query that cannot be determined prior to the moment the query is issued.

**Agility** An EC firm's ability to capture, report, and quickly respond to changes happening in the marketplace.

**Alignment** The ability to create shared incentives that align the interests of businesses across the supply chain

**Alliance strategy** The competitive strategy of working with business partners in partnerships, alliances, joint ventures, or virtual companies.

**Analytical processing** Analysis of accumulated data, frequently by end users, through data mining, decision support systems (DSSs), enterprise information systems (EISs), and Web applications; also referred to as *business intelligence*.

**Analytics** The science of analysis.

**Application controls** Security controls designed to protect specific applications.

**Applications portfolio** The collection of major, approved IS projects that are consistent with an organization's long-range plan.

**Application program** A set of computer instructions written in a programming language, the purpose of which is to support a specific task or business process or another application program.

**Application service provider (ASP)** Company that provides business applications (standard or customized) over the Internet for a per-use or fixed monthly fee.

**Artificial intelligence (AI)** A subfield of computer science concerned with symbolic reasoning and problem solving.

**Artificial neural network (ANN)** A computer technology attempting to build computers that will operate like a human brain; ANN programs can work with ambiguous information.

**Attribute** Each characteristic or quality describing a particular entity (corresponds to a field on a record).

**Auction** A competitive process in which either a seller solicits consecutive bids from buyers or a buyer solicits bids from sellers, and prices are determined dynamically by competitive bidding.

**Audit (of ISs)** A regular examination or check of systems, their inputs, outputs, and processing.

**Automated decision support (ADS)** Systems that are rule-based systems that automatically provide solutions to repetitive managerial problems.

**Automatic crash notification (ACN)** Still-experimental device that would automatically notify police of the location of an ACN-equipped car involved in an accident.

**Back-office operations** The activities that support fulfillment of sales, such as accounting and logistics.

**Balanced-scorecard (BSC)** Method that evaluates the overall health of organizations and projects by looking at metrics in finance, customers' view of the organization, internal business processes, and ability to change and expand.

**Banking Trojan** Rebery malicious software which is programmed to come to lifewhen computer owners visit one of a number of online banking or e-commerce sites.

**Batch processing** Processing system that processes inputs at fixed intervals as a file and operates on it all at once; contrasts with *online* (or *interactive*) processing.

**Behavior-oriented chargeback** Accounting system that sets IT service costs in a way that encourages usage consistent with organizational objectives, even though the charges may not correspond to actual costs.

**Benchmarks** Objective measures of performance, often available from industry trade associations.

**Best practices** In an organization, the best methods for solving problems. These are often stored in the knowledge repository of a knowledge-management system.

**Biometric control** An automated method of verifying the identity of a person, based on physiological or behavioral characteristics.

**BitTorrent** A protocol designed for transferring or sharing files. The most distinctive feature of BitTorrents is that they were designed to handle huge files.

**BitTorrent tracker** A server used in the communication between peers using the BitTorrent protocol.

**Blog** A personal Web site, open to the public, in which the owner expresses his or her feelings or opinions.

**Bluetooth** Chip technology that enables voice and data communications between many wireless devices through low power, short-range, digital two-way radio frequency.

**Bot** Computer stealthily infected and controlled by a cyber criminal.

**Botnet** A network of bots.

**Brick-and-mortar organizations** Organizations in which the product, the process, and the delivery agent are all physical.

**Broadband** High-speed networks can be wireline, wireless, or both. Broadband comes from the words *broad bandwidth*.

**Bullwhip effect** Erratic shifts in orders up and down the supply chain.

**Business activity monitoring (BAM) system** A BPM tool that alerts managers in real time to opportunities, threats, or problems and provides collaboration tools to address these issues.

**Business analytics (BA)** The application of models directly to business data. Using MSS tools, especially models, in assisting decision-makers. Essentially it is an OLAP decision support.

**Business architecture** Organizational plans, visions, objectives, and problems, and the information required to support them.

**Business case** A written document that is used by managers to justify funding for a specific investment and also to provide the bridge between the initial plan and its execution.

**Business continuity plan** A comprehensive plan for how a business and IT systems will operate in case a disaster strikes.

**Business impact analysis (BIA)** An exercise that determines the impact of losing the support of any resource to an organization and establishes the escalation of that loss over time, identifies the minimum resources needed to recover, and prioritizes the recovery of processes and supporting systems.

**Business intelligence (BI)** Category of applications for gathering, storing, analyzing, and providing access to data to help enterprise users make better decisions.

**Business model** A method by which a company generates revenue to sustain itself.

**Business performance management (BPM)** A methodology for measuring organizational performance, analyzing it through comparison to standards, and planning how to improve it.

**Business process** A collection of activities performed to accomplish a clearly defined goal.

**Business process management (BPM)** Method for business restructuring that combines workflow systems and redesign methods; covers three process categories—people-to-people, systems-to-systems, and systems-to-people interactions.

**Business process reengineering (BPR)** A methodology for introducing a fundamental and radical change in specific business processes, usually supported by an information system.

**Business systems planning (BSP) model** An IBM top-down planning model that starts with business strategies and uses business processes and data classes to define organizational databases and identify applications that support business strategies.

**Business-to-business EC (B2B)** E-commerce in which both the sellers and the buyers are business organizations.

**Business-to-business-to-consumers (B2B2C) EC** E-commerce in which a business sells to a business but delivers the product or service to an individual consumer.

**Business-to-consumers (B2C) EC** E-commerce in which the sellers are organizations and the buyers are individuals; also known as *e-tailing*.

**Business-to-employees (B2E) EC** A special type of intrabusiness e-commerce in which an organization delivers products or services to its employees.

**Buy-side marketplace** B2B model in which organizations buy needed products or services from other organizations electronically, often through a reverse auction.

**CDMA (Code Division Multiple Access)** Wireless communication protocol, used with most 2.5G and 3G systems, that separates different users by assigning different codes to the segments of each user's communications.

**CASE tools (Computer-aided software engineering)** The use of software tools to assist in the development and maintenance of software.

**Cell-broadcast SMS Messaging service** mode in which messages such as traffic updates or news updates are sent to multiple recipients.

**Channel conflict** The alienation of existing distributors when a company decides to sell to customers directly online.

**Channel systems (in marketing)** A network of the materials and product distribution systems involved in the process of getting a product or service to customers.

**Chargeback** System that treats the IT function as a service bureau or utility, charging organizational subunits for IT services with the objective of recovering IT expenditures.

**Chief information officer (CIO)** The director of the IS department in a large organization, analogous to a CEO, COO, or CFO; also known as *chief technology officer*.

**Chief knowledge officer (CKO)** The director assigned to manage an organization's knowledge management (KM) program.

**Ciphertext** Text that is unreadable because it has been encrypted or disguised in some way.

**Click-and-mortar organizations** Organizations that do business in both the physical and digital dimensions.

**Clickstream data** Data that can be collected automatically using special software from the company's Web site.

**Clickstream data warehouses** Data warehouses capable of showing both e-business activities and the non-Web aspects of a business in an integrated fashion.

**COBIT** Framework that helps managers and other professionals gain greater value from IT and mitigate IT-related risk exposure.

**Collaborative commerce (c-commerce)** E-commerce in which business partners collaborate electronically.

**Commercial portals** Gateways to the Internet that offer content for broad and diverse audiences; these are the most popular portals on the Internet, such as *yahoo.com* and *msn.com*.

**Committee of Sponsoring Organizations of the Treadway Commission (COSO)** An IT security body that defines internal control as a *process* designed to provide *reasonable* assurance of effective operations and reliable financial reporting.

**Communities of practice (COPs)** Groups of people in an organization with a common professional interest.

**Competitive forces model** A business framework devised by Michael Porter, depicting five forces in a market (e.g., bargaining power of customers), used for analyzing competitiveness.

**Competitive intelligence (CI)** Tracking what competitors are doing by gathering sources of materials on their recent and in-process activities.

**Computer-based information system (CBIS)** Information system that includes a computer for some or all of its operation.

**Computer forensics** The search, discovery, and recovery of e-evidence.

**Computer fraud** A computer crime involving money.

**Computer-integrated manufacturing (CIM)** Integrates several computerized systems, such as CAD, CAM, MRP, and JIT into a whole, in a factory.

**Consumer-to-business (C2B) EC** E-commerce in which consumers make known a particular need for a product or service, and suppliers compete to provide the product or service to consumers; an example is Priceline.com.

**Consumer-to-consumer (C2C) EC** E-commerce in which an individual sells products or services to other individuals (not businesses).

**Content management system (CMS)** An electronic document management system that produces dynamic versions of documents, and automatically maintains the current set for use at the enterprise level.

**Context awareness** Capturing a broad range of contextual attributes to better understand what the consumer needs, and what products or services he or she might possibly be interested in.

**Contextual computing** Enhancement of the computational environment for each user, at each point of computing.

**Cooperative processing** Teams two or more geographically dispersed computers to execute a specific task.

**Corporate (enterprise) portal** The gateway for entering a corporate Web site. It is usually a home page, which allows for communication, collaboration, and access to diversified information.

**Cost-benefit analysis** Study that helps in decisions on IT investments by determining if the benefits (possibly including intangible ones) exceed the costs.

**Cost leadership strategy** The competitive strategy of producing products and/or services at the lowest cost in its industry group.

**Cracker** A malicious hacker.

**Critical response activities** The major activities used by organizations to counter *business pressures.*

**Critical success factors (CSFs)** Those few things that must go right in order to ensure the organization's survival and success.

**Customer relationship management (CRM)** The entire process of maximizing the value proposition to the customer through all interactions, both online and traditional. Effective CRM advocates one-to-one relationships and participation of customers in related business decisions.

**Cross-border data transfer** The flow of corporate data across nations' borders.

**Cyberbanking** Various banking activities conducted electronically from home, a business, or on the road instead of at a physical bank location.

**Cyber-blackmail** Occurs when a Trojan encrypts the data on a user's computer, then the attacker offers to decrypt it for $300 or more.

**Cyber Storm** The first widescale government-led IT security exercise to examine response, coordination, and recovery mechanisms in simulated cyberattacks against critical infrastructures launched U.S. DHS in 2006.

**Dashboards** A BPM tool that provides a comprehensive, at-a-glance, view of corporate performance with graphical presentations, resembling a dashboard of a car. These graphical presentations show performance measures, trends, and exceptions, and integrate information from multiple business areas.

**Data definition language (DDL)** The language used by programmers to specify the types of information and structure of the database. It is essentially the link between the logical and physical views of the database.

**Data dictionary** Stores definitions of a data elements and data characteristics such as usage, physical representation, ownership (who in the organization is responsible for maintaining the data), authorization, and security.

**Data inconsistency** The actual values across various copies of the data no longer agree or are not synchronized.

**Data integrity** The accuracy, correctness, and validity of data.

**Data isolation** A problem caused by faulty file organization leading to difficulty in accessing data from different applications.

**Data item** An elementary description of things, events, activities, and transactions that are recorded, classified, and stored, but not organized to convey any specific meaning; can be numeric, alphanumeric, figures, sounds, or images.

**Data manipulation language (DML)** The language used with a third- or fourth-generation language to manipulate the data in the database. This language contains commands that permit end users and programming specialists to extract data from the database to satisfy information requests and develop applications. The DML provides users with the ability to retrieve, sort, display, and delete the contents of a database.

**Data mart** A subset of the data warehouse, usually originated for a specific purpose or major data subject.

**Data mining (DM)** The process of searching for unknown information or relationships in large databases using tools such as neural computing or case-based reasoning.

**Data model** Defines the way data are conceptually structured. Examples of model forms include the hierarchical, network, relational, object-oriented, object relational, hypermedia, and multidimensional models.

**Data quality (DQ)** A measure of the accuracy, accessibility, relevance, timeliness, completeness, and other characteristics that describe useful data.

**Data redundancy** The same data duplicated in several files as applications and their data files are created by different programmers over a period of time.

**Data tables** Tables that represent the physical view of the data.

**Data tampering** Deliberately entering false data, or changing and deleting true data.

**Data visualization** Visual presentation of data and information by graphics, animation, or any other multimedia.

**Data warehouse** A repository of historical data, subject-oriented and organized so as to be easily accessed and manipulated for decision support.

**Data workers** Clerical workers who use, manipulate, or disseminate information, typically using document management, workflow, e-mail, and coordination software to do so.

**Database** A collection of stored data items organized for retrieval.

**Database management system (DBMS)** The program (or group of programs) that provides access to a database. The DBMS permits an organization to centralize data, manage them efficiently, and provide access to the stored data by application programs.

**Decision portal** A portal that provides team members with models they can use to evaluate decision criteria, objectives, and alternatives from their desktops.

**Decision support system (DSS)** A computer-based information system that combines models and data in an attempt to solve semistructured problems with extensive user involvement.

**Delphi Method** A qualitative forecasting methodology using anonymous questionnaires.

**Demand-driven supply networks (DDSNs)** Networks driven from the front by customer demand. Instead of products being pushed to market, they are pulled to market by customers.

**Desktop purchasing** E-procurement method in which suppliers' catalogs are aggregated into an internal master catalog on the buyer's server for use by the company's purchasing agents.

**Differentiation strategy** The competitive strategy of offering different products, services, or product features than those offered by competitors.

**Digital economy** Another name for today's Web-based, or Internet, economy.

**Digital enterprise** A new business model that uses IT in a fundamental way to accomplish one or more of three basic objectives: reach and engage customers more effectively, boost employee productivity, and improve operating efficiency. It uses converged communication and computing technology in a way that improves business processes.

**Direct file access method** Method of keeping records that uses the key field to locate the physical address of a record.

**Disaster avoidance** An approach oriented toward preventing or minimizing a controllable catastrophe.

**Disaster recovery plan** See *Business continuity plan.*

**Disintermediation** The elimination of intermediaries in EC; removing the layers of intermediaries between sellers and buyers. Effective for technological forecasting and for forecasting involving sensitive issues.

**Distributed processing (computing)** Computing architecture that divides processing work between two or more computers that may not be (and usually are not) functionally equal.

**Document management** The automated control of electronic documents, page images, spreadsheets, voice word processing documents, and other complex documents through their entire life cycle within an organization, from initial creation to final archiving.

**Document management systems (DMSs)** Systems that provided decision makers with information in an electronic format and usually include computerized imaging systems that can result in substantial savings.

**E-business** A company that performs most of its business functions electronically; the broadest definition of ecommerce, including intrabusiness, interorganizational business, and e-commerce; many use the term interchangeably with e-commerce.

**EDGE network (Enhanced Data rates for GSM Evolution)** A technology that significantly increased the capacity of GSM networks to enable data speeds of up to 384 kilobits per second (Kbps).

**e-CRM (electronic CRM)** The use of Web browsers and other electronic touch points to manage customer relationships. E-CRM covers a broad range of topics, tools, and methods, ranging from the proper design of digital products and services to pricing and to loyalty programs

**E-government** The use of e-commerce to deliver information and public services to citizens, business partners, and suppliers of government entities, and those working in the public sector.

**E-planning** Electronically supported IT planning that touches on EC infrastructure and mostly deals with uncovering business opportunities and deciding on an applications portfolio that will exploit those opportunities.

**E-procurement** Purchasing by using electronic support.

**E-supply chain** A supply chain that is managed electronically, usually with Web-based software.

**E-wallets (digital wallets)** A software component in which a user stores secured personal and credit card information for one-click reuse.

**Electronic bartering** The electronically supported exchange of goods or services without a monetary transaction.

**Electronic commerce (e-commerce, EC)** The process of buying, selling, transferring, or exchanging products, services, or information via computer networks, including the Internet; business conducted online.

**Electronic evidence (e-evidence)** cybertrails left by laptop computers, PDAs, iPods, DVDs, digital cameras, and cell phones.

**Electronic fraud (e-fraud)** See *computer fraud.*

**Electronic exchanges** Web-based public e-marketplaces, where many business buyers and many sellers interact dynamically.

**Electronic mall** A collection of individual shops under one Internet address.

**Electronic market (e-market)** A network of interactions and relationships over which products, services, information, and payments are exchanged.

**Electronic retailing (e-tailing)** The direct sale of products and services through electronic storefronts or electronic malls, usually designed around an electronic catalog format and/or auctions.

**Electronic storefront** The Web site of a single company, with its own Internet address, at which orders can be placed.

**Employee relationship management (ERM)** The use of Web-based applications to streamline the human resources process and to better manage employees.

**End-user computing** The use or development of information systems by the principal users of the systems' outputs or by their staffs.

**End-user development** See *end-user computing.*

**Enhanced Messaging Service (EMS)** An extension of SMS capable of simple animation, tiny pictures, and short tunes.

**Enterprise decision management (EDM)** See *automated decision support (ADS).*

**Enterprise resource planning (ERP)** Software that integrates the planning, management, and use of all resources in the entire enterprise; also called *enterprise systems.*

**Enterprise search** A technology that offers the potential of cutting much of the complexity accumulated in applications and intranet sites throughout an organization.

**Enterprise (enterprisewide) system**   Information system that encompasses the entire enterprise, implemented on a company-wide network.

**Enterprise Web**   The sum of a company's systems, information, and services that are available on the Web, working together as one entity.

**Enterprisewide computing**   A client/server architecture that connects data that are used throughout the enterprise.

**Entity-relationship diagrams (ERDs)**   Diagrams that represent the logical view of how the data are organized.

**Entry-barriers strategy**   The competitive strategy of creating barriers to entry of new market entrants.

**Ethics**   A branch of philosophy that deals with what is considered to be right and wrong. computers and uses these computers to send a flood of data packets to the target computers.

**EV-DO (Evolution Data Optimized)**   A fast wireless broadband access (3G) that does not need a Wi-Fi hotspot.

**Executive information system (EIS)**   System specifically designed to support information needs of executives.

**Executive support system (ESS)**   A comprehensive executive support system that includes some analytical and communication capabilities.

**Expense management automation (EMA)**   Systems that automate data entry and processing of travel and entertainment expenses.

**Expert location systems**   Interactive computerized systems that help employees find and connect with colleagues who have expertise required for specific problems—whether they are across the country or across the room—in order to solve specific, critical business problems in seconds.

**Expert system (ES)**   A computer system that applies reasoning methodologies or knowledge in a specific domain to render advice or recommendations—much like a human expert.

**Expected value (EV)**   A weighted average, computed by multiplying the size of a possible future benefit by the probability of its occurrence.

**Explicit knowledge**   The knowledge that deals with objective, rational, and technical knowledge (data, policies, procedures, software, documents, etc.).

**Extranet**   A secured network that allows business partners to access portions of each other's intranets. It is usually Internet-based.

**Financial value chain management (FVCM)**   The combination of financial analysis with operations analysis, which analyzes all financial functions in order to provide better financial control.

**Firewall**   A network node consisting of both hardware and software that isolates a private network from a public network.

**Foreign keys**   Keys that provide relationships between two tables.

**Forward auction**   An auction that sellers use as a selling channel to many potential buyers; the highest bidder wins the items.

**Frontline decision making**   The process by which companies automate decision processes and push them down to frontline employees.

**Front-office operations**   The business processes, such as sales and advertising, that are visible to customers.

**General controls**   Security controls aimed at defending a computer system in general rather than protecting specific applications.

**Geographical information system (GIS)**   Computer-based system that integrates GSP data onto digitized map displays.

**Geographical positioning system**   See *global positioning system.*

**Global information systems**   Interorganizational systems that connect companies located in two or more countries.

**Global positioning systems (GPS)**   Wireless devices that use satellites to enable users to detect the position on earth of items (e.g., cars or people) the devices are attached to, with reasonable precision.

**Government-to-business (G2B) EC**   E-commerce in which a government does business with other governments as well as with businesses.

**Government-to-citizens (G2C) EC**   E-commerce in which a government provides services to its citizens via EC technologies.

**Government-to-government (G2G) EC**   E-commerce in which government units do business with other government units.

**Grid computing**   The use of networks to harness the unused processing cycles of all computers in a given network to create powerful computing capabilities.

**Group decision support system (GDSS)**   An interactive, computer-based system that facilitates finding solutions to semistructured problems by using a set of decision makers working together as a group.

**Group purchasing**   The aggregation of purchasing orders from many buyers so that a volume discount can be obtained.

**Group work**   Any work being performed by more than one person.

**Groupthink**   In a meeting, continual reinforcement of an idea by group members.

**Growth strategy**   The competitive strategy of increasing market share, acquiring more customers, or selling more products.

**GSM (Global System for Mobile Communications Services)**   GSM is a digital mobile telephone system that is widely used in Europe and other parts of the world.

**Hackers**   People who illegally or unethically penetrate a computer system.

**Indexed sequential access method (ISAM)**   A method that uses an index of key fields to locate individual records.

**Inference engine**   The component of an expert system that performs a reasoning function.

**Information**   Data that have been organized so they have meaning and value to the recipient.

**Information infrastructure**   The physical arrangement of hardware, software, databases, networks, and information management personnel.

**Information system (IS)**   A physical process that supports an organization by collecting, processing, storing, and analyzing data, and disseminating information to achieve organizational goals.

**Information technology (IT)**   The technology component of an information system (a narrow definition); or the collection of the computing systems in an organization (the broad definition used in this book).

**Information technology architecture**   High-level map or plan of the information assets in an organization; on the Web, it includes the content and architecture of the site.

**Innovation strategy**   The competitive strategy of introducing new products and services, putting new features in existing.

**Intangible benefits**  Benefits that are hard to place a monetary value on (e.g., greater design flexibility).

**Intellectual capital (intellectual assets)**  The valuable knowledge of employees.

**Intelligent agents**  Software agents that exhibit intelligent behavior and learning.

**Internal control environment**  The work atmosphere that a company sets for its employees. *Internal control (IC) is a process* designed to achieve: (1) reliability of financial reporting, (2) operational efficiency, (3) compliance with laws, (4) regulations and policies, and (5) safeguarding of assets.

**Internet Protocol (IP)**  Protocol used to prepare data and documents for transmission, they are converted into digital packets based on the and sent via computer networks or LANs.

**Internet telephony (voice over Internet Protocol)**  Technology that makes it possible to talk long distance on the Internet without paying normal long-distance telephone charges.

**Interoperability**  Connectivity between devices.

**Interorganizational information systems (IOSs)**  Communications system that allows routine transaction processing and information flow between two or more organizations.

**Intrabusiness (intraorganizational) commerce**  E-commerce in which an organization uses EC internally to improve its operations.

**Intranet**  A corporate network that functions with Internet technologies, such as browsers and search engines, using Internet protocols.

**IT architecture**  A plan for organizing the underlying infrastructure and applications of the IT project.

**IT planning**  The organized planning of IT infrastructure and applications portfolios done at various levels of the organization.

**Just-in-time (JIT)**  An inventory scheduling system in which material and parts arrive at a work place when needed, minimizing inventory, waste, and interruptions.

**Knowledge**  Data and/or information that have been organized and processed to convey understanding, experience, accumulated learning, and expertise.

**Knowledge base**  A collection of facts, rules, and procedures, related to a specific problem, organized in one place.

**Knowledge discovery in databases (KDD)**  The process of extracting knowledge from volumes of data in databases (e.g., in data warehouses); includes data mining.

**Knowledge management (KM)**  The process that helps organizations identify, select, organize, disseminate, and transfer important information and expertise that are part of the organization's memory and that may reside in unstructured form within the organization.

**Knowledge management system (KMS)**  A system that organizes, enhances, and expedites intra- and inter-firm knowledge management; centered around a corporate knowledge base or depository.

**Knowledge repository**  The software system that is a collection of both internal and external knowledge in a KMS.

**Knowledge workers**  People who create and use knowledge as a significant part of their work responsibilities.

**Knowware**  A name for knowledge management (KM) software.

**Leaky knowledge**  Another name for explicit knowledge, due to the ease with which it can leave its source after it has been documented.

**Learning organization**  An organization capable of learning from its past experience, implying the existence of an organizational memory and a means to save, represent, and share it through its personnel.

**Location-based commerce (1-commerce)**  M-commerce transactions targeted to individuals in specific locations, at specific times.

**Logical view**  The user's view, of a database program represents data in a format that is meaningful to a user and to the software programs that process those data.

**Logistics**  The operations involved in the efficient and effective flow and storage of goods, services, and related information from point of origin to point of consumption.

**M-wallet (mobile wallet)**  Technology that enables cardholders to make purchases with a single click from their mobile devices; also known as *wireless wallet.*

**Management information systems (MISs)**  Systems designed to provide past, present, and future routine information appropriate for planning, organizing, and controlling the operations of functional areas in an organization.

**Management support system (MSS)**  The application of any type of decision-support technology to decision-making.

**Marketing transaction database (MTD)**  An interactive database oriented toward targeting marketing messages in real time.

**Master data management (MDM)**  A method of managing data with the purpose of integrating all data in an organization at the highest level, both internally and externally.

**Mesh network**  A type of wireless sensor network composed of motes, where each mote "wakes up" or activates for a fraction of a second when it has data to transmit and then relays that data to its nearest neighbor. So, instead of every mote transmitting its information to a remote computer at a base station, an "electronic bucket brigade" moves the data mote by mote until it reaches a central computer where it can be stored and analyzed.

**Metadata**  Data about data, such as indices or summaries.

**Meta-tags**  Information that influences the description of a Web page in crawlers.

**Metric**  A specific, measurable standard against which actual performance is compared.

**Mobile commerce (m-commerce, m-business)**  Any ecommerce done in a wireless environment, especially via the Internet.

**Mobile computing**  Information system applications in a wireless environment.

**Mobile handset**  Hardware in a mobile system that consists of two parts: terminal equipment that hosts the applications (e.g., a PDA) and a mobile terminal (e.g., a cell phone) that connects to the mobile network.

**Mobile portal**  A gateway to the Internet accessible from mobile devices; aggregates content and services for mobile users.

**Model (in decision making)**  A simplified representation or abstraction of reality; can be used to perform virtual experiments and analysis.

**Model-based management system (MBMS)**  A software program to establish, update, and use a model base.

**Multidimensional database**   Specialized data stores that organize facts by dimensions such as geographical region, time, product line, or salesperson.

**Multidimensionality**   Organizing, presenting, and analyzing data by several dimensions, such as sales by region, by product, by salesperson, and by time (four dimensions).

**Multifactor authentication**   See *two-factor authentication.*

**Multimedia messaging service (MMS)**   The next generation of wireless messaging, which will be able to deliver rich media.

**MySpace**   A social network that started as a site for fans of independent rock music.

**Natural language processing (NLP)**   Using a natural language processor to interface with a computer-based system.

**Networked computing**   A corporate information infrastructure that provides the necessary networks for distributed computing. Users can easily contact each other or databases and communicate with external entities.

**Neural computing**   The technology that attempts to achieve knowledge representations and processing based on massive parallel processing, fast retrieval of large amounts of information, and the ability to recognize patterns based on experiences.

**Niche strategy**   The competitive strategy of selecting a narrow-scope segment (niche market) and being the best in quality, speed, or cost in that market.

**Nominal group technique (NGT)**   A simple brainstorming process for nonelectronic meetings.

**Occupational fraud**   Fraud that occurs when a person uses his or her occupation for personal gain through deliberate misuse of the organization's resources or assets.

**Offshore outsourcing**   Use of vendors in other countries, usually where labor is inexpensive, to do programming or other system development tasks.

**Offshoring**   See *offshore outsourcing.*

**Online analytical processing (OLAP)**   An information system that enables the user, while at a PC, to query the system, conduct an analysis, and so on. The result is generated in seconds.

**Online processing**   Processing system that operates on a transaction as soon as it occurs, possibly even in real time.

**Online transaction processing (OLTP)**   A transaction processing system, created on a client/server architecture, that plans needed to execute the master development plan; stage 3 of the four-stage planning model.

**Operational data store**   A database that provides clean data to the operational, mission-critical, short-term-oriented applications.

**Optimization**   An approach used by management science to find the best possible solution.

**Order fulfillment**   All of the activities needed to provide customers with ordered goods and services, including related customer services.

**Organizational (institutional) decision support system (ODSS)**   A network system that provides decision support for organizational, group, and individual tasks or activities.

**Organizational learning**   The process of capturing knowledge and making it available enterprise-wide.

**Organizational memory**   That which an organization "knows."

**Outsourcing**   Acquiring IS services from an external (outside) organization rather than through internal IS units.

**Packet technology**   A technology that converts voice, video, and data into packets that can be transmitted together over a single, high-speed network—eliminating the need for separate networks.

**Pattern recognition**   The ability of a computer to classify an item to a predetermined category by matching the item's characteristics with that of a stored category.

**Partner relationship management (PRM)**   Business strategy that focuses on providing comprehensive quality service to business partners.

**Payment Card Industry (PCI) Data Security Standard**   Standard created by a coalition of self-regulating industry group including Visa, MasterCard, American Express, and Discover. PCI Data Security Standard is required for all members, merchants, or service providers that store, process, or transmit cardholder data.

**Performance dashboards**   Visual displays used to monitor operational performance.

**Performance scorecards**   Visual displays used to chart progress against strategic and tactical goals and targets.

**Permission marketing**   Method of marketing that asks consumers to give their permission to voluntarily accept online advertising and e-mail.

**Personal digital assistant (PDA)**   A small, handheld wireless computer.

**Personal information management (PIM)**   A system that supports the activities performed by individuals in their work or life through the acquisition, organization, maintenance, retrieval, and sharing of information.

**Pervasive computing**   Invisible, everywhere computing that is embedded in the objects around us.

**Physical view**   A view of a database that deals with the actual, physical arrangement and location of data in the *direct access storage devices (DASDs).* Database specialists use the physical view to make efficient use of storage and processing resources.

**Plaintext**   Text that is readable by humans.

**Podcast (pod)**   Audio or video files sent over the Internet.

**Podcaster**   An author of a podcast.

**Podcasting**   A way to distribute or receive audio and, more recently, video files (*pods* or *podcasts*) over the Internet.

**Point-to-point SMS**   A mode of SMS in which a message is sent to another subscriber.

**Portals**   Web-based personalized gateways to information and knowledge in network computing.

**Practice approach**   The practice approach toward knowledge management focuses on building the social environments or communities of practice necessary to facilitate the sharing of tacit understanding. See personalization strategy.

**Predictive analytics**   Tools that help determine the probable future outcome for an event or the likelihood of a situation occurring. They also identify relationships and patterns.

**Presence functionality**   A function that allows users of e-mail or instant messaging to communicate their current availability to associates.

**Price-to-performance ratio**   The relative cost, usually on a per-mips (millions of instructions per second) basis, of the processing power of a computer.

**Primary key** The identifier of a field of a record so that the record can be retrieved, updated, and sorted.

**Primary activities** In Porter's value chain model, those activities in which materials are purchased and processed to products, which are then delivered to customers. Secondary activities, such as accounting, support the primary ones.

**Private branch exchange** A privately-owned telephone network used within an organization.

**Process approach** Knowledge management approach that attempts to codify organizational knowledge through formalized controls, processes, and technologies.

**Process-centric integration** Integration solutions designed, developed, and managed from a business-process perspective, instead of from a technical or middleware perspective.

**Process modeling** A modeling method that includes techniques and activities used as part of the larger business process management discipline. It is an activity similar to drafting a blueprint for a house. The purpose of modeling business processes is to create a blueprint of how the company works.

**Product lifecycle management (PLM)** Business strategy that enables manufacturers to control and share product-related data as part of product design and development efforts.

**Productivity paradox** The seeming discrepancy between extremely large IT investments in the economy and relatively low measures of productivity output.

**Programming attack** Criminal use of programming techniques to modify a computer program, either directly or indirectly; examples are computer worms, viruses, and denial of service attacks.

**Public exchange (exchange)** E-marketplace in which there are many sellers and many buyers, and entry is open to all; frequently owned and operated by a third party.

**Publishing portals** Gateways to the Internet that are intended for communities with specific interests; involve little content customization but provide extensive online search in a specific area.

**Radio frequency identification (RFID)** Generic term for technologies that use radio waves to automatically identify individual items.

**Reach and richness** An economic impact of EC: the trade-off between the number of customers a company can reach (called *reach*) and the amount of interactions and information services it can provide to them (*richness*).

**Real-time system** An information system that provides real-time access to information or data.

**Reengineering** The radical redesign of an organization's business.

**Reintermediation** Occurs where intermediaries such as brokers provide value-added services and expertise that cannot be eliminated when EC is used.

**Remote access servers (RAS)** Servers that provide direct communication to a company's LAN.

**Resource allocation** Developing the hardware, software, data communications, facilities, personnel, and financial plans needed to execute the master development plan; stage three of the four-stage planning model.

**Reverse logistics** A flow of material or finished goods back to the source; for example, the return of defective products by customers.

**Risk exposure** The degree of risk to which a digit asset is exposed.

**Risk exposure model** A model for assessing reasonable levels of protection for digital assets.

**Rogue access points (Aps)** Unauthorized wireless APs deployed by malicious users to gain access to sensitive information stored on client machines, including logins, passwords, customer information, and intellectual property from legitimate users.

**RSS (Really Simple Syndication)** Various standards of Web feed formats that automate the delivery of Internet content. They are an easy way to receive newly released information customized to a person's interests and needs.

**Sales automation software** Productivity software used to automate the work of salespeople.

**SAP R/3** The leading EPR software (from SAP AG Corp.); a highly integrated package containing more than 70 business activities modules.

**Scenario planning** A planning methodology for dealing with an uncertain environment by examining different scenarios; a what-if analysis.

**Schema** The logical description of the entire database and the listing of all the data items and the relationships among them.

**SCM software** Applications programs specifically designed to improve decision making in segments of the supply chain.

**Search engine** Web sites designed to help people find information stored on other sites. They index billions of pages, and respond to tens of millions of queries per day.

**Secondary keys** Fields in a database that have some identifying information, but typically do not identify the file with complete accuracy.

**Sell-side marketplace** B2B model in which organizations sell to other organizations from their own private e-marketplace and/or from a third-party site.

**Sensitivity analysis** Study of the effect of a change in one or more input variables on a proposed solution.

**Sequential file organization** File organization method in which data records must be retrieved in the same physical sequence in which they are stored. In **direct** or **random file organization,** users can retrieve records in any sequence, without regard to actual physical order on the storage medium.

**Service-oriented architecture (SOA)** An architectural concept that defines the use of services to support a variety of business needs. In SOA, existing IT assets (called *services*) are *reused* and *reconnected* rather than the more time consuming and costly reinvention of new systems.

**Short messaging service (SMS)** Technology that allows for sending of short text messages on some cell phones.

**SIP (Session Initiation Protocol)** The protocol and industry standard that provide easy and intuitive access to the network from any device, anywhere, any time, seamlessly.

**Smart phone** Internet-enabled cell phones that can support mobile applications.

**Social engineering** Getting around security systems by tricking computer users into providing information or carrying out actions that seem innocuous but are not.

**Social network** A place where people create their own space, or homepage, on which they write blogs (Web logs), post pictures, videos, or music, share ideas, and link to other Web locations they find interesting.

**Software-as-a Service (SaaS)** Also referred to as *on-demand computing, utility computing,* or *hosted services.* Instead of buying and installing expensive packaged enterprise applications, users access applications over a network, with an Internet browser being the only absolute necessity.

**Speech recognition** The ability of a computer to recognize spoken words.

**Speech understanding** The ability of a computer to understand the meaning of sentences, in contrast with merely *recognizing* individual words.

**Spend management** The way in which companies control and optimize the money they spend. It involves cutting operating and other costs associated with doing business. These costs typically show up as operating costs, but can also be found in other areas and in other members of the supply chain.

**Spiders (crawlers)** Spider-based search engines that use automated software agents that scour the Web every few minutes searching for information on Web pages.

**Stages of IT growth** Six commonly accepted stages, suggested by Nolan, that all organizations seem to experience in implementing and managing an information system from conception to maturity over time.

**Sticky knowledge** Another name for tacit knowledge because it may be relatively difficult to pull away from its source.

**Strategy map** Methodology that delineates the relationships among the key organizational objectives for all four BSC perspectives.

**Structured query language (SQL)** A data definition and management language of relational databases. It front-ends most relational DBMS.

**Supplier relationship management (SRM)** A comprehensive approach to managing an enterprise's interactions with the organizations that supply the goods and services it uses.

**Supply chain** Flow of materials, information, money, and services from raw material suppliers, through factories and warehouses, to the end customers; includes the organizations and processes involved.

**Supply chain management (SCM)** The management of all the activities along the supply chain, from suppliers, to internal logistics within a company, to distribution, to customers. This includes ordering, monitoring, and billing.

**Supply chain team** A group of tightly coordinated employees who work together to serve the customer; each task is done by the member of the team who is best capable of doing the task.

**Support activities** Business activities that do not add value directly to a firm's product or service under consideration but support the primary activities that do add value.

**Symbolic processing** The use of symbols, rather than numbers, combined with rules of thumb (or heuristics) to process information and solve problems.

**Tablet PCs (pen-based computing)** A popular device for professionals. They have a stylus to write handwritten notes on the screen, usually about 12 inches. Tablet PCs typically work with Wi-Fi, Bluetooth, and EDGE.

**Tacit knowledge** The knowledge that is usually in the domain of subjective, cognitive, and experiential learning; it is highly personal and hard to formalize.

**TDMA (Time Division Multiple Access)** A technology for delivering digital wireless service using time-division multiplexing such as the GSM digital cellular system.

**Telematics** The integration of computers and wireless communications to improve information flow using the principles of telemetry.

**Text mining** The application of data mining analysis to nonstructured or less-structured text files and documents.

**Time-to-exploitation** The elapsed time between when a vulnerability is discovered and the time it is exploited.

**Total benefits of ownership (TBO)** An approach for calculating the payoff of an IT investment by calculating both the tangible and intangible benefits and subtracting the costs of ownership: TBO _ TCO _ Payoff.

**Total cost of ownership (TCO)** A formula for calculating the cost of owning and operating an IT system; includes acquisition cost, operations cost, and control cost.

**Transaction costs** Costs that are associated with the distribution (sale) and/or exchange of products and services including the cost of searching for buyers and sellers, gathering information, negotiating, decision making, monitoring the exchange of goods, and legal fees.

**Transaction processing system (TPS)** An information system that processes an organization's basic business transactions such as purchasing, billing, and payroll.

**Transmission Control Protocol (TCP)** A protocol that provides a reliable, connection-oriented method of packet delivery over the Internet.

**Trojan-Phisher-Rebery** The name given to a variant of a Trojan program that was suspected to have been used to steal tens of thousands of identities from people in 125 countries.

**Trust** The psychological status of involved parties who are willing to pursue further interaction to achieve a planned goal.

**Turing test** Named after the English mathematician Alan Turing, a test designed to measure if a computer is intelligent.

**Two-factor authentication** Method of authentication where other information is used to verify the user's identity such as biometrics.

**Two-tier authentication** See *two-factor authentication.*

**Utility computing** Unlimited computing power and storage capacity that, like electricity, water, and telephone services, can be obtained on demand, used and reallocated for any application, and billed on a pay-per-use basis.

**User Datagram Protocol (UDP)** Internet protocol that allow video streams to be compressed and sent as IP packets.

**Value chain model** Model developed by Michael Porter that shows the primary activities that sequentially add value to the profit margin; also shows the support activities.

**Value system** In Porter's value chain model, the stream of activities that includes the producers, suppliers, distributors, and buyers (all with their own value chains).

**Vendor-managed inventory (VMI)** Strategy used by retailers of allowing suppliers to monitor the inventory levels and replenish inventory when needed, eliminating the need for purchasing orders.

**Vertical portals (vortals)** B2B portals that focus on a single industry or industry segment.

**Virtual corporation (VC)** An organization composed of two or more business partners, in different locations, sharing costs and resources for the purpose of producing a product or service; can be temporary or permanent.

**Virtual credit card** A payment mechanism that allows a buyer to shop with an ID number and a password instead of with a credit card number, yet the charges are made to the credit card.

**Virtual factory** Collaborative enterprise application that provides a computerized model of a factory.

**Virtual organizations** Organizations in which the product, the process, and the delivery agent are all digital; also called *pure-play organizations*.

**Virtual reality** A pseudo-3-D interactive technology that provides a user with a feeling that he or she is physically present in a computer-generated world.

**Virtualization** The separation of business applications and data from hardware resources allowing companies to pool hardware resources—rather than to dedicate servers to applications—and assign those resources to applications as needed.

**Virus** Software that attaches itself to other programs and can damage or destroy data or software.

**Voice portal** A Web site with audio interface, accessed by a standard or cell phone call.

**Voice-over-Internet Protocol** Communication systems that transmit voice calls over Internet Protocol–based networks.

**Voice synthesis** The technology that transforms computer output to voice or audio output.

**Wearable devices** Mobile wireless computing devices for employees who work on buildings and other difficult-to-climb places.

**Web-based system** An application delivered on the Internet or intranet using Web tools, such as a search engine.

**Web mining** The application of data mining techniques to discover meaningful and actionable patterns from Web resources.

**Web Services** Modular business and consumer applications, delivered over the Internet, that users can select and combine through almost any device, enabling disparate systems to share data and services.

**Wiki** A piece of server software available in a Web site that allows users to freely create and edit Web page content using any Web browser. 10

**Wikilog** A blog that allows everyone to participate as a peer; any one may add, delete, or change content.

**Wikipedia** An immensely content-rich, multilingual wiki that collects knowledge by consensus.

**WiMax** A wireless standard (IEEE 802.16) for making broadband network connections over a large area.

**Wired equivalent privacy (WEP)** An encryption algorithm that uses a poor or weak cryptographic technique.

**Wireless access points (APs or WAPs)** Backdoors into a networks.

**Wireless Application Protocol (WAP)** A set of communications protocols designed to enable different kinds of wireless devices to talk to a server installed on a mobile network, so users can access the Internet.

**Wireless Encryption Protocol (WEP)** Built-in security system in wireless devices, which encrypts communications between the device and a wireless access point.

**Wireless fidelity (Wi-Fi)** The standard on which most of today's WLANs run, developed by the IEEE (Institute of Electrical and Electronic Engineers). Also known as *802.11b*.

**Wireless LAN (WLAN)** LAN without the cables; used to transmit and receive data over the airwaves, but only from short distances.

**Wireless 911 (e-911)** Calls from cellular phones to providers of emergency services.

**Wireless mobile computing (mobile computing)** Computing that connects a mobile device to a network or another computing device, anytime, anywhere.

**Wireless packet analyzers** Tools that can capture and analyze the contents of packets sent over a network.

**Wireless sensor networks (WSNs)** Networks of interconnected, battery-powered, wireless sensors called *motes* (analogous to nodes) that are placed into specific physical environments. Each mote collects data and contains processing, storage, and radio frequency sensors and antennas. The motes provide information that enables a central computer to integrate reports of the same activity from different angles within the network. Therefore, the network can determine information such as the direction a person is moving, the weight of a vehicle, or the amount of rainfall over a field of crops with great accuracy.

**Wireless wide area networks (WWANs)** Wide area networks for mobile computing.

**Worm** A software program that runs independently, consuming the resources of its host in order to maintain itself, that is capable of propagating a complete working version of itself onto another machine.

**XBRL** A programming language and an international standard for electronic transmission of business and financial information.

**XML (eXtensible Markup Language)** A simplified version of the general data description language, SGML; used to improve compatibility between the disparate systems of business partners by defining the meaning of data in business documents.

**Zero-day incidents** Attacks through previously unknown weaknesses in their computer networks.

# Company Index